Environmental Regulation

Wherever possible, the articles in these volumes have been reproduced as originally published using facsimile reproduction, inclusive of footnotes and pagination to facilitate ease of reference.

For a list of all Edward Elgar published titles visit our website at
www.e-elgar.com

# Environmental Regulation

*Edited by*

John McEldowney

*Professor of Law*
*University of Warwick, UK*

*and*

Sharron McEldowney

*Principal Lecturer*
*Molecular and Applied Biosciences*
*University of Westminster, UK*

**An Elgar Research Collection**
Cheltenham, UK • Northampton, MA, USA

Published by
Edward Elgar Publishing Limited
The Lypiatts
15 Lansdown Road
Cheltenham
Glos GL50 2JA
UK

Edward Elgar Publishing, Inc.
William Pratt House
9 Dewey Court
Northampton
Massachusetts 01060
USA

A catalogue record for this book is available from the British Library

Library of Congress Control Number: 2014932593

MIX
Paper from responsible sources
FSC® C013056

ISBN 978 0 85793 820 6

Printed and bound in Great Britain by T.J. International Ltd, Padstow

# Contents

# Acknowledgements

The editors and publishers wish to thank the authors and the following publishers who have kindly given permission for the use of copyright material.

Annual Reviews, Inc. via the Copyright Clearance Center for article: Maria Carmen Lemos and Arun Agrawal (2006), 'Environmental Governance', *Annual Review of Environment and Resources*, **31**, November, 297–325.

Blackwell Publishing Ltd for articles: Neil Carter and Philip Lowe (1994), 'Environmental Politics and Administrative Reform', *Political Quarterly*, **65** (3), July, 263–74; Veerle Heyvaert (2011), 'Governing Climate Change: Towards a New Paradigm for Risk Regulation', *Modern Law Review*, **74** (6), November, 817–44; Julia Black (2012), 'Paradoxes and Failures: "New Governance" Techniques and the Financial Crisis', *Modern Law Review*, **75** (6), November, 1037–63.

Roger Brownsword for his own excerpt: (2010), 'The Age of Regulatory Governance and Nanotechnologies', in Graeme A. Hodge, Diana M. Bowman and Andrew D. Maynard (eds), *International Handbook on Regulating Nanotechnologies*, Chapter 4, 60–80.

Cambridge University Press for article: Benjamin J. Richardson (2009), 'Climate Finance and its Governance: Moving to a Low Carbon Economy Through Socially Responsible Financing?', *International and Comparative Law Quarterly*, **58** (3), July, 597–626.

Philippe Cullet for his own excerpt: (2010), 'Environment and Development – The Missing Link', in Julio Faundez and Celine Tan (eds), *International Economic Law, Globalization and Developing Countries*, Chapter 16, 354–78.

Jan Hancock for her own excerpt: (2003), 'The Human Right to Natural Resources', in *Environmental Human Rights: Power, Ethics and Law*, Chapter 6, 137–56, references

Hart Publishing Limited for article: Jingchen Zhao (2012), 'The Harmonious Society, Corporate Social Responsibility and Legal Responses to Ethical Norms in Chinese Company Law', *Journal of Corporate Law Studies*, **12** (1), April, 163–200.

Maria Lee for her own excerpt: (2008), 'GMOs in the EU: The Scope of the Debate', in *EU Regulation of GMOs: Law and Decision Making for a New Technology*, Chapter 2, 19–60.

Rohan Mukherjee for his own article: Rohan Mukherjee and David M. Malone (2011), 'Global Responsibilities: India's Approach', *Jindal Journal of International Affairs*, **1** (1), October, 182–203.

National Institute of Ecology for article: V.K. Agarwal (2005), 'Environmental Laws in India: Challenges for Enforcement', *Bulletin of the National Institute of Ecology*, **15**, 227–38.

Oxford University Press for excerpts: Jane Holder (2004), 'Tracking Environmental Assessment', in *Environmental Assessment: The Regulation of Decision Making*, Chapter 2, 32–74, references; Jonathan B. Wiener (2007), 'Precaution', in Daniel Bodansky, Jutta Brunnée and Ellen Hey (eds), *Oxford Handbook of International Environmental Law*, Chapter 25, 597–612; Daniel Barstow Magraw and Lisa D. Hawke (2007), 'Sustainable Development', in Daniel Bodansky, Jutta Brunnée and Ellen Hey (eds), *Oxford Handbook of International Environmental Law*, Chapter 26, 613–38; Joanne Scott (2009), 'REACH: Combining Harmonization and Dynamism in the Regulation of Chemicals', in *Environmental Protection: European Law and Governance*, Chapter 3, 56–91; Tony Prosser (2010), 'The Environment Agency', in *The Regulatory Enterprise: Government, Regulation, and Legitimacy*, Chapter 4, 66–88; Richard Macrory (2011), 'Environmental Regulation as an Instrument of Constitutional Change', in Jeffrey Jowell and Dawn Oliver (eds), *The Changing Constitution (Seventh Edition)*, Chapter 11, 291–311.

Oxford University Press via the Copyright Clearance Center's RightsLink service for articles: Neil Gunningham (2009), 'Environment Law, Regulation and Governance: Shifting Architectures', *Journal of Environmental Law*, **21** (2), 179–212; Elizabeth Fisher, Bettina Lange, Eloise Scotford and Cinnamon Carlarne (2009), 'Maturity and Methodology: Starting a Debate about Environmental Law Scholarship', *Journal of Environmental Law*, **21** (2), 213–50; William Howarth (2009), 'Aspirations and Realities under the Water Framework Directive: Proceduralisation, Participation and Practicalities', *Journal of Environmental Law*, **21** (3), 391–417; Gerd Winter (2010), 'The Climate is No Commodity: Taking Stock of the Emissions Trading System', *Journal of Environmental Law*, **22** (1), 1–25; Elizabeth Fisher, Pasky Pascual and Wendy Wagner (2010), 'Understanding Environmental Models in Their Legal and Regulatory Context', *Journal of Environmental Law*, **22** (2), 251–83; Hans Vedder (2010), 'The Treaty of Lisbon and European Environmental Law and Policy', *Journal of Environmental Law*, **22** (2), 285–99; Elizabeth A. Kirk and Kirsty L. Blackstock (2011), 'Enhanced Decision Making: Balancing Public Participation against "Better Regulation" in British Environmental Permitting Regimes', *Journal of Environmental Law*, **23** (1), March, 97–116; Neil Gunningham (2011), 'Enforcing Environmental Regulation', *Journal of Environmental Law*, **23** (2), July, 169–201; Daniel A. Farber (2011), 'The Challenge of Climate Change Adaptation: Learning from National Planning Efforts in Britain, China, and the USA', *Journal of Environmental Law*, **23** (3), November, 359–82; Michael G. Faure and Katarina Svatikova (2012), 'Criminal or Administrative Law to Protect the Environment? Evidence from Western Europe', *Journal of Environmental Law*, **24** (2), July, 253–86.

Priscilla Schwartz for her own excerpt: (2010), 'The Polluter-Pays Principle', in Malgosia Fitzmaurice, David M. Ong and Panos Merkouris (eds), *Research Handbook on International Environmental Law*, Chapter 12, 243–61.

Colin Scott for his own excerpt: (2007), 'Rethinking Regulatory Governance for the Age of Biotechnology', in Han Somsen (ed.), *The Regulatory Challenge of Biotechnology: Human Genetics, Food and Patents*, Chapter 2, 19–35.

University of Toronto for article: Steven Bernstein (2005), 'Legitimacy in Global Environmental Governance', *Journal of International Law and International Relations*, **1** (1–2), December, 139–66.

Vathek Publishing for article: Ole W. Pedersen (2010), 'Environmental Principles and Environmental Justice', *Environmental Law Review*, **12** (1), 26–49.

David Vogel for his own excerpt: (1986), 'Government Regulation in Great Britain and the United States', in *National Styles of Regulation: Environmental Policy in Great Britain and the United States*, Chapter 5, 193–225, 308–309.

Jill Wakefield for her own article: (2012), 'Common Fisheries Policy Reform and Sustainability', *European Policy Analysis*, June, 1–12.

Every effort has been made to trace all the copyright holders but if any have been inadvertently overlooked the publishers will be pleased to make the necessary arrangement at the first opportunity.

In addition the publishers wish to thank the Library at the University of Warwick, UK, and the Library of Indiana University at Bloomington, USA, for their assistance in obtaining these articles.

# Introduction
# Regulating the Environment: 21st Century Challenges

*John McEldowney and Sharron McEldowney*

Regulating the environment in the UK is conceptually complex, involves a diverse range of institutions, techniques and methodologies, and crosses geographical and national boundaries. Environmental regulation as Neil Carter and Philip Lowe (Chapter 4) have pointed out is conceived not simply as 'a policing function but as an active agent for the promotion of sustainable practices'. Approaches to environmental regulation in both style and content have varied and over recent years changed considerably. David Vogel's study in 1986 (Chapter 3) sets an interesting tone by contrasting the UK with the USA. The former was said to be flexible, pragmatic and discretionary. General rules and standards accompanied voluntary self-regulation that was informally achieved as part of the architecture of social control. Deference was often given to hierarchies. Standard setting was achieved very often through a mixture of policy making and law, with informal rules much in evidence. The USA was comparatively more formalised, juridical, adversarial and formally dependent on legal rules. This is very much a reflection of culture, as well as recognition of legal specialism growing from the dominance of corporate culture.

Despite differences in US and UK regulatory styles, environmental regulation today shares many similarities in approach within both traditions. The UK's administrative law, however, remains distinctive, but influenced by sharing policy making between EU and member states. This, together with legal controls, a mixture of common law, statute, procedures and practices, set the framework for environmental regulation in the UK. Environmental regulation carried out largely administratively has become progressively more legalistic, particularly with the increasing use of administrative sanctions. A priority for regulation is to address the sustainable management of the economy while meeting the challenge of global warming. In contrast to other regulatory areas where the main rationale may be to address market failure to secure public benefits, environmental regulation works within the broader context of the exploitation of the global environment and effective management of scarce resources. Expectations are high based on the principle of sustainable development, and needs are great post the Kyoto Protocol of 1972. Even the most optimistic, however, have to come to terms with doubts about the effectiveness of regulatory responses to environmental protection and management. *The Economist*, at the end of 2012, emphasised that the United Nations Environment Programme estimated greenhouse gas emissions to be 50 gigatons of carbon annually, which is likely to increase to 58 gigatons in 2020. This is 20 per cent more than in 2000 and 14 per cent above the level it should reach if emissions are to meet the 2020 Kyoto target. The most remarkable change, in the recent past, is the shift between the developed and developing worlds in a competition for the most polluting nations' status. The USA and Europe are no longer the most polluting. China and India are the world's largest emitters of greenhouse gases as an effect of rapid economic growth. China contributes to 25 per cent of global emissions and India, in 2000–11, accounted for 83 per cent of the increase in carbon emissions. In contrast to developed countries, developing countries face enormous challenges. The disproportionate effect of global warming on developing countries is clear. It is estimated that a 2.5 per cent rise in global temperature would cut agriculture productivity by 6 per cent in the USA but 38 per cent in India. At the same time as the speed of climate change intensifies, UN international summits, the eighteenth held in Doha, struggle to respond. Promises made have not been met or are unrealistic. The European Union (EU) offered a 30 per cent reduction below 1990 levels and Brazil offered a reduction of 36.1 per cent by 2020. The first period of the Kyoto Protocol ended in December 2012. The second period is less robust and leaves much to be negotiated. Countries such as Japan, Canada and Russia have either withdrawn from the Protocol or are in the process of renegotiation. There is a growing energy need that lies at the heart of the problem. China and India are outstripping the USA in energy demands, most notably in China which has embarked on building new coal fired power stations at an alarming rate. Developing economies pose a major pollution challenge as the abundance of coal and its relative cheapness make it the fuel of choice.

There are also serious questions about the participation of developing countries in international treaties or in engaging with best available techniques to reduce pollution threats. The 2008 financial crisis has severely impacted the resources available from rich nations to provide adequate financial incentives to encourage best practice by poor nations.

This is not to say the only challenge facing the environment comes from climate change. There are many others that range around the protection of scarce resources and collide in the water, food and energy nexus, nuanced or precipitated by climate change. Resource use and waste generation seem an almost inevitable consequence of economic growth, and new developments, the very foundation stone of economies, pose new risks for regulating the environment. Managing and protecting the environment is to confront a multi-headed hydra that is a shape shifter. There is no stasis but fundamental complexity bound up in the merging of economic, social and environmental change. Effective environmental regulation is a formidable task.

The main objective of this volume is to provide an analysis of environmental regulation in the UK, taking account of international law and EU perspectives. The volume brings together papers containing various themes and analysis that allow an assessment and critical understanding of environmental regulation. This is only possible through a consideration of the myriad of regulatory principles, some of which are legal and procedural and others of which are economic, rights based, social and political. Environmental regulation is facilitated by ensuring that there are adequate systems of accountability over the various institutions and processes, and these too must be understood. It is clear that environmental regulation in the UK has undergone considerable changes in recent years. Not least because of the influences of the European Union, but also because of the introduction of the precautionary principle, and techniques to combat global warming and move towards sustainable development such as the polluter pays principle, carbon trading and setting emissions levels. Against this background it is clear that environmental regulation is at a critical stage in an ongoing process of controlling environmental degradation and climate change. To be effective, regulation is very much a collaborative exercise, with a variety of regulatory bodies involved in the active management of scarce resources. While law plays a prominent role alongside regulatory and management functions in regulatory policy making, it has to work within the boundaries of political influences over policy. Environmental regulation faces many difficulties. The economic advantages of growth and development are irresistible for newly advanced developing countries such as China and India, which cause substantial environmental costs locally. The economic downturn in many developed countries brings pressures to place the environment low on the list of priorities. These together bring a whole range of issues for the formulation, effective implementation and enforcement of environmental regulation at international, EU and UK levels.

## Part I Environmental Regulation, Sustainable Development and Climate Change

Economic development and environmental protection are often mutually antagonistic. Environmental regulation may be seen by some as an unnecessary impediment to growth and a financial burden. Alternatively it can be argued that environmental regulation is part of a process to achieve growth while taking account of environmental and human wellbeing. Achieving some form of mutually reinforcing relationship between economic development and environmental protection is an ongoing process. Sustainable development is a complex set of at times conflicting principles that attempt to reconcile environmental protection with development issues. Use and conservation are linked at local and global levels. Ultimately environmental regulation depends on turning sustainable development into a sufficiently robust form of environmental protection. In the first paper, Daniel Barstow Magraw and Lisa Hawke (Chapter 1) raise the significance of sustainable development from an international law perspective. As a paradigm, rather than a legal concept, there is great uncertainty about the legal status and meaning of international environmental law, but four core elements are identified in the paper: intra-generational equity, inter-generational equity, the need to protect the environment and the need to integrate economic, social and environmental policies.

Today climate change sets a key driver for environmental regulation in the policing and management of the environment and often has the greatest implications for the most vulnerable in societies, including the poor and elderly, and for distinct communities, for example on coasts. It appears already to be causing the predicted extreme weather events that are socially and economically costly. As a consequence, setting priorities for climate change has begun to take on a political priority. Daniel Farber (Chapter 2) compares efforts to plan adaptation to climate change in developing and developed countries including the UK.

## Part II Models of Regulation, Precaution and Risk

Defining different approaches and principles relevant to environmental regulation is the main focus of this part of the collection. David Vogel (Chapter 3) makes clear that the British approach to regulation is likely to be flexible and informal, while the USA is likely to be comparatively rigid and rule orientated. Neil Carter and Philip Lowe (Chapter 4) define environmental regulation in terms of two functions: policing pollution and as an active agent for the promotion of sustainable practices. Neil Gunningham (Chapter 5) gives an account of the evolution of environmental regulation into a broader concept of environmental governance. He makes the argument that environmental regulation also concerns the relationship between those who manage the environment and those who regulate through, for example, conservation and pollution control strategies. Pivotal to environmental regulation is precaution as a strategy for addressing risk. Jonathan Wiener (Chapter 6) explains the influence of the precautionary principle both in international law and national legal systems. Precaution is considered to inform policy making, engage with regulatory strategies and provide a variety of techniques such as impact assessment to manage the environment. Priscilla Schwartz (Chapter 7) discusses the polluter pays principle as an influential tool in environmental regulation with important policy-making implications. Elizabeth Fisher, Pasky Pascaul and Wendy Wagner (Chapter 8) examine how different environmental models play an important role in decision-making related to regulatory strategies, policy catalysts and institutional mandates. They argue that lawyers and policy makers need to be more aware of the importance of modelling and the consequences for effective regulation. Jane Holder (Chapter 9) provides an analysis of the operation of environmental assessment in the UK, outlining underlying assumptions and principles. She shows how influential such methods and procedures are when making decisions.

## Part III Environmental Regulation, Policy and Governance

In this part different policy and governance responses are considered as environmental regulation continues to undergo change and adaptation. In the past thirty years it has become more politically salient and often stricter in enforcement strategies. Maria Carmen Lemos and Arun Agrawal (Chapter 10) address questions of environmental governance and Steven Bernstein (Chapter 11) considers connected issues relating to the legitimacy of global environmental governance. Elizabeth Kirk and Kirsty Blackstock (Chapter 12) consider public participation in UK environmental permitting decisions and how enhancing participatory rights may lead to more effective regulation. This is a topical issue, particularly in the context of the objectives of the Better Regulation agenda. Tony Prosser (Chapter 13) considers how UK environmental regulation has been advanced through the Environment Agency, a single agency with substantial regulatory responsibilities. The agency's role encompasses water, river management, flood protection, regulation of industry and administrating the EU Emissions Trading Scheme. Richard Macrory (Chapter 14), the author of an influential report on administrative sanctions, considers the role of environmental regulation in the UK and how constitutional implications are often overlooked. Neil Gunningham (Chapter 15) looks at the way environmental regulation can be enforced and assesses the strengths and weaknesses of different strategies that may lead to a broader concept of environmental governance. Actively engaging in participation strategies with stakeholders is seen as a key feature of success. Smart regulation has this attraction and may lead to substantive compliance with regulatory goals through flexible strategies. Michael Faure and Katarina Svatikova (Chapter 16) consider the role of criminal and administrative sanctions in the broader context of European developments and the cost benefit of each strategy adopted. Benjamin Richardson (Chapter

17) examines the role of climate finance and socially responsible environmental law in climate change mitigation and adaptation and the problems that adopting this strategy may overcome. There is no single model of effective environmental regulation; rather, there are many different approaches that may be made effective through a combination of strategies rather than over reliance on a single method of enforcement.

## Part IV Environmental Regulation across Sectors

Environmental regulation is highly specialised within specific sectors employing different methodologies and techniques. This section is intended to illustrate new techniques and challenges through carefully selected examples.

The EU has a world-wide reputation as one of the most enthusiastic proponents of internationally binding and enforceable climate change commitments. Veerle Heyvaert (Chapter 18) argues that the impact of climate change on the EU regulatory agenda is significant. It alters and recalibrates risk and Heyvaert assesses the impact on regulatory responses. The need for risk regulation scholarship to address past regulatory failures in the pursuit of ambitions to mitigate climate change is highlighted in this analysis. Hans Vedder (Chapter 19) considers the changes brought about by the Treaty of Lisbon and the attempt to develop a European environmental law and policy that is integrated with environmental regulation.

Gerd Winter (Chapter 20) considers how cap and trade operates under the emissions trading system and how this might be improved. He questions whether allowing emissions allocations to be traded through purchase and sale and to be acquirable through overseas investment is the best way to make emissions targets effective. Improving this regulatory model has remained elusive to date.

William Howarth's discussion of the EU's development of a Water Framework Directive is an example of the breadth of national regulatory discretion within an overall framework at EU level (Chapter 21). It is also an excellent illustration of an evolving and pragmatic approach embracing public engagement, even in the face of technical issues and operational methodologies that do not necessarily meld with public opinion.

Joanne Scott's discussion of REACH explains how chemical regulation is an attempt for product market integration with environmental health protection (Chapter 22). This is a complex subject that is intended to create harmonisation but falls short of this aspiration. It is a multi-layered example of how risk is assessed and responded to and brings questions of how best to implement effective regulation. Jill Wakefield (Chapter 23) explains how regulating fisheries policy is difficult to reconcile with sustainability. This is an ongoing policy debate.

## Part V Regulation and Environmental Human Rights

Jan Hancock (Chapter 24) argues that universal environmental human rights are a necessary component for environmental protection. Environmental harm, when linked to rights, provides a compelling set of stipulations that ought to be intrinsic to regulating the environment. Ole Pedersen (Chapter 25) suggests that the emerging concept of environmental justice should inform many of the basic regulatory mechanisms – the polluter pays principle, the precautionary principle and also sustainable development. Finding compatibility between rights and the principles of environmental regulation is not always easy. Despite ambiguities and some vagueness in concepts, the goal of environmental justice is worth aspiring to.

## Part VI Environmental Regulation and New Technologies

New technologies bring new challenges. Roger Brownsword (Chapter 26) argues that emerging nanotechnologies have challenged existing regulatory approaches and are likely to engage with the principles of precaution and proportionality as the technology evolves. Colin Scott (Chapter 27) considers the implications of biotechnology and how this interacts with policy makers especially in the areas of genetically modified organisms (GMOs) and the food industry. Maria Lee (Chapter 28) debates the role of GMOs in the context of the EU, which goes to the centre of the legitimacy of EU regulation and policy making in a multi-layered level of governance. This serves to reinforce the diversity of tasks environmental regulation is called upon to encompass.

## Part VII Environmental Regulation and Economic Development

The necessity for effective environmental regulation is not confined to developed countries. As outlined above, developing countries, under the pressures of rapid economic growth, face important questions about the necessity for regulation. Linkages between international environmental law, economic development and developing countries are discussed by Philippe Cullet (Chapter 29). Reconciling different objectives, such as sustainable development and protecting the environment in the face of economic growth, sets difficult questions for international law and policy makers. Jingchen Zhao (Chapter 30) considers how China is dealing with environmental regulation through company corporate social responsibility. V.K. Agarwal (Chapter 31) shows how India, another country with unprecedented growth, has a prolific number of environmental laws which are far from effective and are poorly enforced and implemented. Agarwal argues that this requires the Indian judiciary to be more proactive in their interpretation of environmental obligations on corporate governance in India. Rohan Mukherjee and David Malone (Chapter 32) examine the impact of globalisation and development on India in terms of international regulation of the environment. It is argued that India must take seriously its political and economic obligations if it is to take its place as a leading global influence. This aspiration has yet to be fulfilled.

## Part VIII 21st Century Challenging Environmental Regulation

How should environmental law scholarship advance to meet the needs of the future? Elizabeth Fisher, Bettina Lange, Eloise Scotford and Cinnamon Carlarne (Chapter 33) consider how maturity and methodology should inform environmental law scholarship. They single out the speed and scale of legal regulatory change, the challenges of governance arrangements and the multi-jurisdictional nature of the subject as particularly problematic for environmental law scholarship. The final two papers query how robust are regulatory strategies and how able to meet current needs. Learning the lessons from risk assessment, Julia Black (Chapter 34) considers the so-called 'new governance' techniques of regulation – principles based regulation, risk based regulation, meta-regulation and enrolment. She concludes that the experience of using regulatory techniques suggests that a greater understanding of the dimensions of regulatory governance is needed to adapt their use and achieve more effective outcomes. Lessons from the financial crisis are worth learning for better environmental regulation to contribute successfully to climate change mitigation and adaptation, and to make sustainable development a reality.

# Part I
# Environmental Regulation, Sustainable Development and Climate Change

# [1]

# SUSTAINABLE DEVELOPMENT

DANIEL BARSTOW MAGRAW

LISA D. HAWKE

# 1 Introduction

The paradigm of sustainable development evolved over many years through attempts to take account of concerns regarding economic development, environmental protection (including human health), and social development (including human rights). Its adoption and core content evidence a profound change in the way society views the relationship between economic activity and the natural environment. Nevertheless, although sustainable development is now viewed by the international community as the overarching framework for improving quality of life throughout the world (and by many as the best approach to maintaining a healthy planet), important disagreements exist about its precise meaning and implications, and resistance to it still surfaces from time to time. This chapter examines the evolution and content of the concept of 'sustainable development', its legal status and function, and its implications for principles and tools of international environmental law.

# 2 Origin and Evolution

In 1971, as a precursor to the Stockholm Conference on the Human Environment, a group of persons experienced in development and environment produced *Development and Environment: The Founex Report*, which addressed the efforts, especially by developed countries, to protect the environment and developing countries' struggle to achieve economic development. The report was one of the earliest documents to identify the specific environmental issues that developed and developing countries face with respect to matters such as agriculture, transport, and human settlements. The purpose of the report was to draw attention to the relationship between economic growth, poverty, and environmental protection and to conceptualize environmental policy with these linkages in mind with an eye to the Stockholm Conference.[1]

The main purpose of the Stockholm Conference was to be a practical means and source of encouragement for governments to work towards protecting and improving the human environment.[2] The Stockholm Declaration on the Human

[1] Preparatory Committee for the United Nations Conference on the Human Environment, *Development and Environment: The Founex Report* (Founex, Switzerland, 4–12 June 1971) at para. 5.1. Five regional meetings on development and environment were also held as well as a meeting of scientists from developing countries (see, for example, International Council of Scientific Unions Special Committee on Problems of the Environment, Environmental Problems in Developing Countries Report, Canberra, Australia (24 August–3 September 1971)).

[2] G.A. Res. 2581(XXIV), UN Doc. A/RES/2581(XXIV) (8 January 1970).

Environment, which emerged from this conference and was endorsed by the United Nations General Assembly (UNGA) in 1972, deals with the integration of economic, environmental, and social justice issues. For example, the preamble mentions human rights, economic development, and developing countries' priorities; Principle 1 relates to human rights; Principle 8 relates to economic and social development; Principle 11 relates to the effects of environmental policies on development and international economies; Principle 21 includes the economic activity of exploiting natural resources; and Principle 23 relates specifically to developing countries. Thus, without using the phrase 'sustainable development', the Stockholm Declaration foreshadowed the holistic approach embodied in this concept and helped give rise to it.

The first publicly visible use of the term 'sustainable development' was most probably in 1980 when it appeared in the World Conservation Strategy (WCS), a document prepared by the International Union for Conservation of Nature and Natural Resources (IUCN). The WCS defined sustainable development as 'the integration of conservation and development to ensure that modifications to the planet do indeed secure the survival and well-being of all people.' [3] The WCS examined the contribution of living resource conservation to human survival and sustainable development, identified the priority conservation issues and the main requirements for dealing with them, and proposed ways for effectively achieving the strategy's aim.

The term 'sustainable development' was given international prominence and refined in 1987 by the World Commission on Environment and Development (WCED or the Brundtland Commission), an independent body created by the UNGA. Its report, *Our Common Future*,[4] brought the term 'sustainable development' to the forefront of international discourse and policy-making. The Brundtland Commission's discussion of sustainable development emphasized that technology and social organization are affecting the natural environment, and its provision of what are now referred to as 'environmental services', in ways that limit societies' ability to meet current and future needs and, thus, that the environment must be protected. Soon thereafter, the 1990 Dublin Declaration by the European Council on the Environmental Imperative identified sustainable development as one of the objectives of the European Community.[5]

The 1992 UN Conference on Environment and Development (UNCED) in Rio de Janeiro, Brazil, was the first time that the world's governments officially adopted sustainable development as the development paradigm. Sustainable development is the underlying theme of the five instruments adopted by the 172 countries

[3] International Union for Conservation of Nature and Natural Resources (currently World Conservation Union) (IUCN), *World Conservation Strategy: Living Resource Conservation for Sustainable Development* (Gland, Switzerland: IUCN, 1980).

[4] World Commission on Environment and Development, *Our Common Future* (Oxford: Oxford University Press, 1987) at 43–6.

[5] Declaration by the European Council on the Environmental Imperative, Bull. Eur. Comm. No. 6 (1990) at 17.

represented by heads of state or other national leaders at UNCED. For example, the Rio Declaration on Environment and Development, which contains 27 key principles to guide the integration of environment and development policies, focuses on sustainable development in Principle 1 ('[h]uman beings are at the centre of concerns for sustainable development. They are entitled to a healthy and productive life in harmony with nature.'). Agenda 21, a comprehensive global plan of action for the implementation of sustainable development, was designed to create a 'global partnership for sustainable development.' The United Nations Framework Convention on Climate Change (UNFCCC), a legally binding international agreement intended to stabilize greenhouse gases in the atmosphere at a level preventing dangerous anthropogenic interference with the climate system, provides, in Article 3, on principles that '[t]he Parties have a right to, and should, promote sustainable development.' The Convention on Biological Diversity (CBD), a legally binding agreement that strives to conserve the world's genetic, species, and ecosystem diversity emphasizes 'sustainable use'. Finally, the Statement of Principles on Forests expressed the global consensus on the management, conservation, and 'sustainable development' of the world's forests.

In 1994, sustainable development was recognized as an objective of the World Trade Organization (WTO) in the first paragraph of the preamble to the Marrakech Agreement Establishing the World Trade Organization (WTO Agreement).[6] The role of sustainable development as the overarching paradigm was also being challenged, however. In 1994, during negotiations related to the International Conference on Population and Development (ICPD), a battle to recognize 'sustained economic growth' as a paradigm ensued. Some developing country delegations expressed the view that 'sustained economic growth' was more important than sustainable development, and that sustainable development was a guise for keeping developing countries in a subservient position. Other countries resisted these arguments, expressing their view that environmental and health protection and social justice cannot be ignored in order to achieve a healthy economy and society over the long term. The final ICPD Programme of Action reaffirmed the primacy of sustainable development while also recognizing the importance of economic growth, through the use of the phrase 'sustained economic growth in the context of sustainable development.'

The debate continued in connection with the 1995 World Summit for Social Development. Developing country negotiators insisted on language stating that 'sustained economic growth and sustainable development are equally important.' Norway and the United States, later joined by the European Union, argued that sustainable development remained the appropriate paradigm. This issue was the final one decided on the brink of the head-of-state summit. The process of negotiating this issue revealed that high-level politicians from developing countries readily acknowledged the need to integrate social, economic, and environmental considerations.

[6] Marrakech Agreement Establishing the World Trade Organization, 15 April 1994, 33 I.L.M. 15 (1994).

The result was a clear reaffirmation of sustainable development as the paradigm, and, for the first time in a United Nations instrument, an explicit linkage was made between economic development, social development, and environmental protection. Paragraph 6 of the Copenhagen Declaration on Social Development makes this clear: 'We are deeply convinced that economic development, social development and environmental protection are interdependent and mutually reinforcing components of sustainable development, which is the framework for our efforts to achieve a higher quality of life for all people.'[7]

The years following the Social Summit showed that developing countries remained suspicious that demands for environmental protection would interfere with their economic development. Many difficult negotiations ensued, including about who will pay the costs that are required to achieve sustainable development. Nevertheless, international discussions continued to utilize sustainable development as the fundamental organizing concept.

In 2000, the UNGA adopted the United Nations Millennium Declaration, which reaffirmed the UNGA's support for principles of sustainable development agreed upon at UNCED. The declaration identified six fundamental values to be essential to international relations, including freedom, equality, solidarity, tolerance, respect for nature, and shared responsibility.[8] The UNGA stated that '[p]rudence must be shown in the management of all living species and natural resources, in accordance with the precepts of sustainable development . . . The current unsustainable patterns of production and consumption must be changed in the interest of our future welfare and that of our descendants.'[9] The Millennium Declaration also identified eight goals, known as the millennium development goals (MDGs), which all 191 United Nations member states have agreed to try to achieve by the year 2015. MDG-7 focuses on environmental sustainability, and the first of three targets under MDG-7 is to '[i]ntegrate the principles of sustainable development into country policies and programmes; reverse loss of environmental resources.'

At the World Summit on Sustainable Development (WSSD) in Johannesburg, South Africa, in 2002, representatives from around the world again reaffirmed their commitment to sustainable development. The WSSD Plan of Implementation recognizes poverty eradication, changing unsustainable consumption and production patterns, and protecting and managing the natural resource base for economic and social development as 'overarching objectives of, and essential requirements for, sustainable development.'[10]

[7] Copenhagen Declaration on Social Development, UN Doc. A/CONF.166/9 (19 April 1995) at para. 6.

[8] United Nations Millennium Declaration, G.A. Res. 55/2, UN Doc. A/RES/55/2 (8 September 2000) at I, para. 6.

[9] *Ibid.*

[10] Johannesburg Plan of Implementation, in *Report of the World Summit on Sustainable Development*, Johannesburg, South Africa, 26 August-4 September 2002, UN Doc. A/CONF.199/20 (2002) at para. 11. Adopted at the seventeenth plenary meeting of the World Summit on Sustainable Development on 4 September 2002.

In May 2005, the United Nations released the *Millennium Development Goals Report*, which detailed the progress, if any, made towards achieving the MDGs. The report states that most countries have committed to the principles of sustainable development by incorporating them into national policies as well as agreeing to relevant international instruments. However, it also states that these good intentions have not resulted in sufficient progress to reverse the loss of environmental resources.[11]

Also in 2005, the UNGA adopted the 2005 World Summit Outcome, as a follow-up to the 2000 Millennium Summit.[12] The World Summit Outcome, which frequently uses the term 'development' as an apparent shorthand for 'sustainable development', reaffirms the Millennium Declaration (para. 3) and recognizes sustainable development as a key element of United Nations activities (para. 10). The environment *per se* is mentioned relatively infrequently (see, for example, para. 10), and uncertainty may have been reintroduced regarding the relationship between sustainable development and sustained economic growth (para. 19, for example, lists both of these concepts as 'commitments'). Taking the 2005 World Summit Outcome as a whole, together with the other instruments mentioned earlier and the fact that day-to-day discourse at the United Nations and elsewhere routinely use the term 'sustainable development', sustainable development as described in this chapter remains the overarching paradigm for both development and environmental protection.

## 3 Meaning

The most often quoted definition of 'sustainable development' is the one contained in the Brundtland Commission's report, *Our Common Future*:

> Sustainable development is development that meets the needs of the present without compromising the ability of future generations to meet their own needs.
>
> It contains within it two key concepts:
>
> - the concept of 'needs,' in particular the essential needs of the world's poor, to which overriding priority should be given; and
> - the idea of limitations imposed by the state of technology and social organization on the environment's ability to meet present and future needs.[13]

While the international community has not agreed to this definition in any legally binding instrument, the definition is so frequently cited that it has acquired a quasi-official status. Considering the Brundtland Commission's definition together with

[11] *Millennium Development Goals Report* (New York: United Nations, 2005) 30, Goal 7: Ensure Environmental Sustainability.

[12] See 2005 World Summit Outcome, G.A. Res. 60/1, UN Doc. A/RES/60/1 (24 October 2005).

[13] World Commission on Environment and Development, see note 5 above at 43.

official intergovernmental statements such as the Copenhagen Declaration on Social Development, the Millennium Declaration, the World Summit on Sustainable Development, and the 2005 World Summit Outcome, referred to earlier, sustainable development may be considered to consist of the following core elements:

- the needs of present and future generations must be taken into account (inter-generational equity);
- the needs of the world's poor must receive priority, and abject poverty must be eliminated (intra-generational equity);
- the environment needs to be preserved at least to a significant degree; and
- economic, social, and environmental policies must be integrated.

The first of these elements, inter-generational equity, is stated very clearly in the Brundtland Commission's definition (see Chapter 27 'Equity'). It finds further support in many other international instruments, for example, in Principle 3 of the Rio Declaration, which states that '[t]he right of development must be fulfilled so as to equitably meet the developmental and environmental needs of present and future generations.' It is also recognized in national jurisprudence, as demonstrated, for example, in the well-known case of *Oposa v. Factoran.*[14] In this case, the petitioners sought to 'prevent the misappropriation or impairment' of Philippine rainforests by deforestation, and asserted that they represented their generation as well as future generations in addressing the present and future harms. The Supreme Court of the Republic of the Philippines allowed the petitioners to sue for cancellation of timber license agreements, and granted them standing to represent their generation and generations yet unborn, based on the constitutional right to a balanced and healthful ecology and the 'twin concepts of "inter-generational responsibility" and "inter-generational justice."' The court stated that this right belongs to a different category of rights, since it is concerned with the self-preservation and self-perpetuation of humanity, therefore, the right to a balanced and healthful ecology need not even have been written in the Constitution as it was assumed to exist from the inception of humankind.[15]

The role of intra-generational equity in achieving sustainable development is indicated by the Brundtland Commission's statement that overriding priority should be given to the needs of the world's poor. Similarly, Principle 5 of the Rio Declaration provides that '[a]ll states and people shall cooperate in the essential task of eradicating poverty as an indispensable requirement for sustainable development, in order to decrease the disparities in standards of living and better meet the needs of the majority of the people of the world.' Intra-generational equity finds further support in many other international instruments, such as the second sentence of paragraph 6 of the Copenhagen Declaration: 'Equitable social development that recognizes empowering the poor to utilize environmental resources sustainably

[14] *Oposa v. Factoran*, G.R. No. 101083 (30 July 1993) (Supreme Court, Republic of the Philippines).

[15] *Ibid.* at 7. See also Constitution of the Republic of the Philippines, Article II at para. 16.

is a necessary foundation for sustainable development.' This concept of intra-generational equity is also found in MDG-1 ('[e]radicate extreme poverty and hunger') as well as in the Millennium Declaration (paras. 6, 11, and 21) and the 2005 World Summit Outcome (paras. 11 and 19).

That the environment must be preserved is clear from the Brundtland Commission's conclusion that human and technological capital are not infinitely substitutable for natural capital, therefore, natural capital itself needs to be preserved. This idea can be traced back to pre-Stockholm UNGA Resolution 2849 (XXVI), which states that 'the rational management of the environment is of fundamental importance for the future of mankind.'[16] The crucial importance of protecting the environment is also clear from a myriad of other international instruments. For example, the first target of MDG-7 includes 'revers[ing] loss of environmental resources'; and the International Law Association's 2002 New Delhi Declaration on Principles of International Law Relating to Sustainable Development (ILA Sustainable Development Principles), states that '[t]he protection, preservation and enhancement of the natural environment, particularly the proper management of climate system, biological diversity and fauna and flora of the Earth, are the common concern of mankind' and that states are under a duty to manage natural resources in a rational, sustainable way.[17] Indeed, the increasing recognition of the critical importance of environmental services and of the fact that nature is the true infrastructure of society implies clearly that the environment must be preserved, at least to some significant extent.

The need to integrate economic, social, and environmental policies is a logical outgrowth of the foregoing three aspects of sustainable development and is explicit in the first sentence of paragraph 6 of the Copenhagen Declaration, quoted earlier, and in the numerous subsequent repetitions of this language in international instruments. It finds further support in paragraph 5 of the 2002 Johannesburg Declaration on Sustainable Development, which states that 'we assume a collective responsibility to advance and strengthen the interdependent and mutually reinforcing pillars of sustainable development—economic development, social development, and environmental protection—at the local, national, regional, and global levels.'[18] Moreover, paragraph 10 of the 2005 World Summit Outcome, referred to earlier, reinforces this responsibility by emphasizing that sustainable development is to be a key element of United Nations activity.

Identification of these core elements, however, does not eliminate significant disagreements about what they imply or require. One important question is what the need to achieve equity—or simply the practical necessities of achieving progress

[16] G.A. Res. 2849 (XXVI), UN Doc. A/RES/2848(XXVI) (20 December 1971).

[17] New Delhi Declaration of Principles of International Law Relating to Sustainable Development, 70th Conference of the International Law Association Resolution 3/2002 (2–6 April 2002).

[18] Johannesburg Declaration on Sustainable Development, 4 September 2002, UN Doc. A/CONF. 199/L.6/Rev.2 (2002).

towards sustainable development—requires developed countries to do in terms of assisting developing countries by providing funding, technology, and capacity building. It is well recognized that developing countries, generally speaking, lack the financial and other resources (for example, scientific, technical, regulatory, legal, and institutional resources) needed to make the desired progress towards sustainable development (see Chapter 41 'Technical and Financial Assistance'). This topic arises in virtually every serious international discussion of sustainable development, including in the context of negotiating or implementing multilateral environmental agreements, and is a source of significant North-South tension.

Another critical question involves how to view inter-generational sustainability. Is this a question of 'utility' (in the neo-classical economic sense) or should one instead view this question in terms of the ongoing ability of nature to provide essential environmental services (biological and physical), such as providing sufficient raw material inputs and sufficient capacity to absorb wastes (an approach that some economists refer to as addressing 'throughputs')? The former approach leads to the goal of enabling each future generation to be at least as well off as the present generation with respect to the future generation's utility or happiness as experienced by that generation. The latter approach leads to the goal of enabling future generations to be at least as well off as the present generation with respect to their access to environmental services. How one approaches the question of inter-generational sustainability thus has profound implications. For example, should developed countries restrict themselves to achieving a level and type of resource use that both ensures a good life for their populations and also is within the carrying capacity of the biosphere if generalized to the whole world? And is the current drive for quantitative economic growth through trade and investment liberalization good policy?[19] Our sense is that many economists are intellectually addicted to growth and that economic theory needs to take into account the crucial roles that environmental services perform and the effects that economic growth can have on the biosphere's ability to continue to provide these services.

The generality of the concept of sustainable development raises yet another issue. One could ask whether the concept is so vague as to be meaningless and not of any practical use. The generality of the concept, however, is both inevitable and appropriate because the concept must provide guidance and inspiration to policy-makers while simultaneously being capable of application in a wide variety of contexts, involving different economic realities, ecological conditions, population characteristics, legal systems, cultures, values, and preferences. Indeed, in practice, sustainable development must be tied closely to local conditions. Because of the simultaneous needs for global generality and local specificity, the tools and approaches used by countries and sub-national units in their efforts to achieve sustainable development

[19] See H.E. Daly, *Beyond Growth, The Economics of Sustainable Development* (Boston, MA: Beacon Press, 1998) at 1–3; see also H.E. Daly, *Sustainable Development: Definitions, Principles, Policies*, invited address (Washington, DC: World Bank, 2002).

are of particular importance. The implications of sustainable development for such tools are addressed in section 6 of this chapter, following a discussion of sustainable development's legal status and function (section 4) and its implications for important principles of international environmental law (section 5).

## 4 Legal Status and Function

Countries, commentators, and courts have taken a variety of positions with respect to the normative status of sustainable development (see Chapter 18 'Different Types of Norms in International Environmental Law: Policies, Principles, and Rules'). Issues relating to the legal status and function of sustainable development can be best assessed by examining its possible status under the three major sources of international law—international agreements, customary international law, and general principles of law (see Chapter 19 'Formation of Customary International Law and General Principles' and Chapter 20 'Treaty Making and Treaty Evolution')—and also by considering its use at the domestic level in municipal law. This chapter addresses each of these in turn.

### 4.1 International Agreements

When the term 'sustainable development' appears in a binding international agreement, its legal implications depend both on where it appears in the instrument and on the precise text in which it is used. Use of 'sustainable development' in the preamble of an instrument is primarily important for determining the object(s) and purpose(s) of the treaty and in interpreting the treaty. It may carry less normative weight than if identical words were to appear in the operative text of the same instrument. An example of preambular use is the first paragraph of the preamble of the WTO Agreement, which recognizes sustainable development as an objective of the agreement. The WTO Appellate Body used this preambular language as a guide to the interpretation of Article XX(g) of the General Agreement on Tariffs and Trade (GATT), in the 1998 *United States—Import Prohibition of Certain Shrimp and Shrimp Products*.[20] Sustainable development plays a similar role in the preamble of the North American Free Trade Agreement (NAFTA), in which the parties resolve to '[p]romote sustainable development.'[21]

[20] *United States—Import Prohibition of Certain Shrimp and Shrimp Products*, adopted WTO Dispute Settlement Body, 6 November 1998, WTO Appellate Body Report, Doc. WT/DS58/AB/R (1998); and General Agreement on Tariffs and Trade, 30 October 1947, 55 U.N.T.S. 194.

[21] North American Free Trade Agreement, 1 January 1994, 32 I.L.M. 612 (1993).

Sustainable development—or 'sustainability'—is sometimes expressly identified as an 'objective' in the operative text of an international agreement. For example, Article 2 of the UNFCCC states that the objective of the agreement is to stabilize greenhouse gas concentrations in a timeframe allowing 'economic development to proceed in a sustainable manner'; and Article 1 of the CBD states that '[t]he objectives of this Convention . . . are . . . the conservation of biological diversity [and] the sustainable use of its components.' In these instances, the term does not directly create obligations but is of use in identifying the object(s) and purpose(s) of the agreement, in interpreting it, and thus in assessing the consistency of parties' and signatories' actions with respect to it. The effect of using the term 'sustainable development' in this context is thus similar to using it in a preamble. However, in this case, it would be beyond cavil that sustainable development indeed is among the objects and purposes of the agreement, and should be given significant weight in interpreting and applying the provisions of the agreement.

When 'sustainable development' is included as a 'principle' in a binding international agreement, the text may create rights or obligations on the part of the parties, depending on the wording of the text. The fourth principle in Article 3 of the UNFCCC, for example, states that '[t]he Parties have a right to, and should, promote sustainable development.' The use of the word 'right' indicates that parties have a legal right to promote sustainable development. In contrast, the use of 'should' is hortatory and, thus, does not, by itself, impose a legal obligation on parties to promote sustainable development. By definition, the term 'principle' implies a higher normative content than 'objective'. Beyond that, any practical difference between including sustainable development as an 'objective' and including it as a 'principle' may depend primarily on the wording of the provision rather than on its title.

## 4.2 Customary International Law

The possible status of sustainable development as customary international law is the subject of considerable disagreement (see Chapter 19 'Formation of Customary International Law and General Principles'). This disagreement is related to the fact that numerous international instruments of varying normative status mention sustainable development, often many times in the same instrument and typically (as described earlier) in an important role. Some of these instruments are legally binding, such as the CBD. Others are non-legally binding international declarations, which have been adopted by large numbers of states and sometimes the UNGA. Examples of non-legally binding instruments include the Copenhagen Declaration on Social Development, the Johannesburg Declaration on Sustainable Development, the ILA Sustainable Development Principles, and the 2005 World Summit Outcome, referred to earlier in this chapter. Unless such an instrument purports to be codifying an existing norm of international law, its legal implications can best be understood by considering its relevance to determining whether sustainable development has become, or is in the process of becoming, a norm of customary international law.

In any event, at one end of the spectrum, sustainable development has been identified as nothing more than a global policy, with no normative value. Somewhat further along the spectrum towards sustainable development being a binding legal norm is the view that sustainable development is 'soft law'—that is, a normative statement supported by a political or other commitment and, thus, something more than policy even though it is not legally binding (though it may become binding in the future). An apparently related position—but one that does not use the term 'soft law'—is that sustainable development is more than just a policy goal and that neither the category of non-normative policy statement nor the category of customary international law accurately characterizes sustainable development.[22]

It is not entirely clear where the International Court of Justice (ICJ) stands in this respect. In its decision in the *Case Concerning the Gabčíkovo-Nagymaros Project (Hungary v. Slovakia)*, the ICJ, after referring to new 'norms and standards' that have been developed to deal with the relationship between economic activities and environmental protection, stated that the concept of sustainable development expresses 'the need to reconcile environmental protection and economic development.'[23] Although recognizing sustainable development only as a 'concept', the majority indicated that the concept has substantial relevance. However, they failed to develop the analysis further. This analysis seems to fall short of stating that sustainable development is one of those new norms or standards to which the majority referred.

In the same case, however, Judge Christopher Weeramantry authored a separate opinion in which he stated: 'I consider [sustainable development] to be more than a mere concept, but as a principle with normative value which is crucial to the determination of this case.'[24] Weeramantry also stated that 'the law necessarily contains within itself the principle of reconciliation. That principle is the principle of sustainable development.' He further stated that he considers sustainable development to be 'a part of modern international law by reason not only of its inescapable logical necessity, but also by reason of its wide and general acceptance by the global

[22] See M.-C. Cordonier Segger and A. Khalfan, *Sustainable Development Law Principles, Practices, and Prospects* (Oxford: Oxford University Press, 2004) at 45–6.

[23] *Ibid.* See also *Case Concerning the Gabčíkovo-Nagymaros Project (Hungary v. Slovakia)*, Judgment of 25 September 1997, [1997] I.C.J. Rep. 92 (25 September) at para. 140 [*Gabčíkovo-Nagymaros*]. The court stated: 'Throughout the ages, mankind has, for economic and other reasons, constantly interfered with nature. In the past this was often done without consideration of the effects upon the environment. Owing to new scientific insights and to a growing awareness of the risks for mankind—for present and future generations—of pursuit of such interventions at an unconsidered and unabated pace, new norms and standards have been developed, [and] set forth in a great number of instruments during the last two decades. Such new norms have to be taken into consideration, and such new standards given proper weight, not only when States contemplate new activities, but also when continuing with activities begun in the past. This need to reconcile economic development with protection of the environment is aptly expressed in the concept of sustainable development.' *Ibid.*

[24] *Gabčíkovo-Nagymaros*, see note 23 above, separate opinion of Vice-President, Judge Weeramantry.

community.'[25] Weeramantry appears to consider sustainable development a legal principle of customary international law with an *erga omnes* character and, thus, is at the other end of the spectrum from those who consider sustainable development to be only a policy, with no normative content.[26]

Vaughn Lowe has stated that sustainable development law describes a group of congruent norms, which can be analysed as a 'metaprinciple, acting upon other legal rules and principles—a legal concept exercising a kind of interstitial normativity, pushing and pulling the boundaries of true primary norms when they threaten to overlap or conflict with each other.'[27] The precise role of this 'metaprinciple' is unclear (as is how it came into existence); but in terms of its function, it may be similar to the customary international law norm to act in good faith, which is relevant in several different contexts (for example, cooperation, negotiation, and dispute settlement) and which is highly fact-dependent in its application.

Although Lowe's reference to 'true primary norms' suggests that the sustainable development metaprinciple is somehow different than other customary international law norms, he does not say that clearly. Thus, unless Lowe is positing an entirely new type of international law (which he does not claim to do), the sustainable development metaprinciple seems to be best understood as a norm of customary international law.

The role of the metaprinciple might be somewhat similar to that of a preamble to an agreement (described earlier). Like preambular language, a metaprinciple helps in clarifying appropriate objectives and in interpreting norms, particularly when they threaten to overlap or conflict with one another. The reference to 'overlap or conflict' also brings to mind the principle of integration, discussed later in this chapter, because the principle of sustainable development surely favours reconciliation over conflict, as in the idea that trade and environmental protection can (and should) be mutually supportive. It does seem clear that Lowe's use of 'interstitial' does not refer simply to filling gaps in the legal structure because of the reference to (gap-less) situations in which existing norms threaten to overlap or conflict. It is possible that Lowe's and Weeramantry's views are quite similar. Weeramantry refers to reconciliation, which could apply in a situation of possible overlap or conflict, and of the desirability of avoiding 'normative anarchy,' which is reminiscent of Lowe's goal of avoiding conflict.

[25] *Ibid.*

[26] Judge Christopher G. Weeramantry, vice-president of the International Court of Justice, *Sustainable Development: An Ancient Concept Recently Revived*, invited address at the United Nations Environment Programme's Global Judges Symposium on Sustainable Development and the Role of Law, Johannesburg, South Africa, 19 August 2002.

[27] Vaughn Lowe, 'Sustainable Development and Unsustainable Arguments,' in A. Boyle and D. Freestone, eds., *International Law and Sustainable Development: Past Achievements and Future Challenges* (Oxford: Oxford University Press, 1999) 19 at 30–1.

## 4.3 General Principles of Law Recognized by Major Legal Systems

General principles of law, as this category is most commonly understood by international lawyers, are principles that are widely shared among states representing major legal systems around the globe (see Article 38 of the ICJ Statute). The key question, therefore, is whether and how the concept of sustainable development has been embraced by states' domestic laws.

Sustainable development has been incorporated into municipal (domestic) law of some states, such as Australia and Canada (see section 4.4 later in this chapter). The number and range of states that incorporate sustainable development in their domestic legislation, however, is not yet sufficient for this concept as such to have reached the level of a general principle of law under Article 38 of the ICJ Statute. It is possible, however, that some of the principles related to sustainable development may have such wide recognition that they have become general principles of law. For example, as discussed in section 5, precaution is an inevitable and essential element of all domestic regulatory regimes aimed at protecting health, safety, and the environment. Although details may vary from country to country as to, for example, the burden of proof, the standard of proof and the technical methodology in assessing new chemicals or foods, it most probably is the case that it is a general principle of law, within the meaning of Article 38 of the ICJ Statute, that a country may regulate in the face of scientific uncertainty where the risk to the environment (or health or safety) is serious.

There is yet no definitive judicial or arbitral ruling on this question or on the status of precaution as customary international law, however. For example, in *EC Measures Concerning Meat and Meat Products (Hormones)*, the Appellate Body declined to take a position: 'The status of the precautionary principle in international law continues to be the subject of debate among academics, law practitioners, regulators and judges . . . We consider . . . that it is unnecessary, and probably imprudent for the Appellate Body in this appeal to take a position on this important, but abstract question.'[28] Alternatively, in *Southern Bluefin Tuna (New Zealand v. Japan; Australia v. Japan)* (Order), the International Tribunal for the Law of the Sea (ITLOS) seems to have based its ruling on the precautionary principle. The tribunal, in light of scientific uncertainty, ruled that the parties 'should act with prudence and caution to ensure that effective conservation measures are taken to prevent serious harm to the stock of southern bluefin tuna (see Chapter 25 'Precaution').[29]

[28] *EC Measures Concerning Meat and Meat Products (Hormones)*, Apellate Body Report, WTO Doc. 98-0099, WTO Doc. WT/DS26/AB/R, and WTO Doc. WT/DS48/AB/R (AB-1997–4). See also *EC Biotechnology (GMOs)*, Interim Panel Report, para. 7.87 (2006).

[29] *Southern Bluefin Tuna cases* (Provisional Measures), 38 I.L.M. 1624 (1999) at para. 77.

## 4.4 Sustainable Development in Municipal (Domestic) Law

On the national level, the concept of sustainable development as the integration of environmental concerns with all other policy areas is usually formulated as a procedural rule to be applied by legislative and administrative bodies. This approach, for example, has been adopted in those states that utilize the tools identified in section 6 of this chapter, such as environmental impact assessments (for example, the United States's practice of conducting environmental assessments of prospective free trade agreements) and natural resource accounts.

Some countries have also expressly included sustainable development as a substantive requirement in their domestic law. In Australia, for example, the term 'sustainable development' has been written into domestic statutory law. The National Environment Protection Council Act states that 'the concept of ecologically sustainable development should be used by all levels of Government in the assessment of natural resources, land use decisions and approval processes.'[30] In addition, Australia's Environment Protection and Biodiversity Conservation Act states that wildlife conservation plans must minimize 'any significant adverse social and economic impacts, consistently with the principles of ecologically sustainable development.'[31] The Canadian Environmental Protection Act also includes sustainable development in several sections. For example, the preamble states: '[T]he Government of Canada seeks to achieve sustainable development that is based on an ecologically efficient use of natural, social and economic resources and acknowledges the need to integrate environmental, economic and social factors in the making of all decisions by government and private entities.'[32]

Sustainable development may also influence domestic law even when it is not explicitly mentioned in a statute. For example, the United States National Environmental Policy Act recognizes 'the critical importance of restoring and maintaining environmental quality to the overall welfare and development of man, [and] declares . . . to use all practicable means and measures, including financial and technical assistance, in a manner calculated to foster and promote the general welfare, to create and maintain conditions under which man and nature can exist in productive harmony, and fulfill the social, economic, and other requirements of present and future generations of Americans.'[33] While this statute, which antedated UNCED by

[30] National Environment Protection Council Act, 1994 (Australia).

[31] Environment Protection and Biodiversity Conservation Act, 1999 (Australia).

[32] Canadian Environmental Protection Act, 1999, ch. 33 (Canada). The statute reads: 'An Act respecting pollution prevention and the protection of the environment and human health in order to contribute to sustainable development.' The declaration also states: 'It is hereby declared that the protection of the environment is essential to the well-being of Canadians and that the primary purpose of this Act is to contribute to sustainable development through pollution prevention' (*ibid*).

[33] National Environmental Policy Act, § 101, 42 U.S.C. § 4331 (1969).

two decades, does not include the term 'sustainable development', it embodies the concepts of inter-generational equity and of integrating social and economic development with protection of the environment.

# 5 Implications for Principles of International Environmental Law

The concept of sustainable development has implications for key concepts in international environmental law, including integration, equity and the duty to cooperate, precaution, good governance, and prior informed consent for local communities. These concepts are considered in the following section.

## 5.1 Integration

Perhaps the most important implication of the concept of sustainable development is its focus on a holistic approach to policies that may affect development and environment. Sustainable development is based, to some degree, on the interdependence of the biosphere (that is, the connective layers of earth, water, and air on which life depends), of human endeavours *inter se*, and of human activities and nature. Taking account of these interdependencies requires integrating a wide variety of factors. Indeed, as described in section 3 earlier in this chapter, integration of economic, social, and environmental policies is one of the core elements of sustainable development. The principle of integration thus highlights the need for policy-makers to take into account the interdependencies and importance of nature, to be inclusive and comprehensive in their analyses, and to consider the impacts and implications of proposed policies. Principle 4 of the Rio Declaration expresses this concern as follows: 'In order to achieve sustainable development, environmental protection shall constitute an integral part of the development process and cannot be considered in isolation from it.' The principle of integration thus emanates from sustainable development.

The principles of good governance and of prior informed consent by communities, described immediately below, are examples of developments that reflect the principle of integration.

Sustainable development requires governance free of official corruption. Corruption often interferes with efforts to achieve all core aspects of sustainable development (both intra- and inter-generational equity, environmental protection, and sound policy integration). For example, public resources may go to a few relatively well-off officials or their families instead of being used for the public good; projects may be selected for their potential to generate bribes rather than for their potential to further the public good; less-efficient contractors may be chosen resulting in waste and inefficiency; and environmental regulations may not be enacted or enforced. Attention to sustainable development and the need to integrate relevant policies were most probably factors leading to the recent flood of anti-corruption treaties (for example, the Inter-American Convention against Corruption, the Convention on the Fight against Corruption Involving Officials of the European Communities or Officials of Member States of the European Union, the Council of Europe Criminal Law Convention on Corruption and the Council of Europe Civil Law Convention on Corruption, the OECD Convention on Combating Bribery of Foreign Public Officials in International Business Transactions, and the United Nations Convention against Corruption) and corresponding municipal legislation (often building on the 1978 US Foreign Corrupt Practices Act). As a result of this spate of activities, the principle of good governance may be an emerging norm of customary international law.

Achieving sustainable development requires that natural resources be used in an equitable and sustainable manner. International human rights norms require that those affected by decisions have a right to express their views during the decision-making process. Consistent with the principle of integration, these have been integrated into a requirement that local communities (including, but not limited to, indigenous communities) have both the right to participate in any decisions that will affect them, including decisions affecting the resources on which they depend, and substantive rights (referred to as community-based property rights) to such resources, the content of which depends both on international human rights norms and local law and custom. Even apart from the issue of equity, the role that these communities play is critically important to achieving sustainable development, *inter alia*, because of the frequent need to involve them in protecting natural resources, and because of the knowledge they possess from traditional practices. This has become a particularly important issue in the context of creating protected areas, the CBD (Article 8(j), regarding access to genetic resources), the World Intellectual Property Organization (regarding genetic resources, traditional knowledge, and folklore), and the International Bank for Reconstruction and Development (World Bank, under the rubric 'broad community support'), and it may be relevant to other activities and institutions as well, including the clean development mechanism under the Kyoto Protocol to the UNFCCC (which requires project proponents and the approval body to invite and consider the comments of stakeholders, including individuals, groups, or communities affected, or likely to be affected, by the proposed project activity). There may be an emerging international norm of prior informed consent (sometimes also referred to as free, prior informed consent) in this context, and, in any event, its effective implementation will be critical to achieving sustainable development in many situations.

## 5.2 Equity and the Duty to Cooperate

The principles of inter-generational and intra-generational equity are core elements of sustainable development and, in fact, have emanated in part from—or in tandem with—this concept (see Chapter 27 'Equity'). Many international instruments refer to inter-generational and intra-generational equity, such as the UNFCCC and the CBD as well as the widely accepted definition of sustainable development in the Brundtland Commission report, quoted earlier. Inter-generational equity, even if its generality makes it difficult to apply in concrete situations, at least requires that some good faith effort be made to consider the interests of future generations. Intra-generational equity likewise requires that the possible impact of policies and decisions on the poor be taken into consideration. Inter- and intra-generational equity thus have implications with respect to the assessment of environmental and other impacts, as discussed in section 6.

A particularly thorny equity issue has to do with equity between developed and developing countries. This issue is not a core element of sustainable development, which is concerned with equity between generations and between individuals, rather than between countries. Nevertheless, the North-South context played an important part in the negotiations leading up to the 1992 Earth Summit and the multilateral environmental treaties (MEAs) adopted at the summit and thereafter. The North-South context, moreover, has important practical implications for sustainable development. Whether sufficient effective assistance is forthcoming from developed countries and whether developing countries make appropriate use of assistance will be very important in determining progress towards sustainable development (see Chapter 41 'Technical and Financial Assistance').

The North-South context has, in particular, given rise to the principle of common but differentiated responsibilities (CBDR), which is now reflected in virtually all multilateral environmental agreements (MEAs). The principle of CBRD can be regarded as a further specification of the duty to cooperate as contained in, among other instruments, the Rio Declaration. Principle 7 of the Rio Declaration states: 'States shall cooperate in a spirit of global partnership to conserve, protect and restore the health and integrity of the Earth's ecosystem. In view of the different contributions to global environmental degradation, States have common but differentiated responsibilities.' This principle—which is directly related to equity between countries and, practically, though not necessarily theoretically, related to intra-generational equity—takes into account each state's contribution to the creation of environmental problems in connection with its ability to prevent, control, and reduce them. The first aspect—the duty to cooperate—is well established in international law (see, for example, Articles 55 and 56 of the Charter of the United Nations), and applies at the global, regional, and bilateral levels. The second aspect—CBDR—as mentioned, is included in most MEAs to achieve equity and encourage universal participation. CBDR takes various forms, including different standards or commitments for developed countries and for developing and economy-in-transition countries, delayed compliance for developing and economy-in-transition countries, and commitments to transfer financial and other resources from developed to developing and economy-in-transition countries (see Chapter 41 'Technical and Financial Assistance').

The implementation of CBDR, thus, is not only crucial to the attainment of sustainable development but also has affected the nature of the obligation to cooperate in international environmental law. For developing countries, sustainable development, through CBDR, has conditioned the duty to cooperate upon the receipt of financial and technological assistance, and, for developed states, it has broadened the duty to cooperate to include the commitment to transfer financial and technological assistance. An example of the former is a provision contained in many MEAs that stipulates: '[T]he extent to which developing country Parties will effectively implement their commitments under the Convention will depend on the effective implementation by developed country Parties of their commitments under the Convention related to financial resources and technology.'[34]

## 5.3 Precaution

All states have the duty to protect the environment and thus prevent harm to the environment, a principle contained in Principle 21 of the Stockholm Declaration and Principle 2 of the Rio Declaration and recognized by the ICJ in its advisory opinion in *Legality of the Use of Nuclear Weapons.*[35] Prevention remains the point of departure in international environmental law. However, in case of scientific uncertainty, states may be faced with the duty to adopt precautionary policies or measures (see Chapter 26 'Precaution'). While the nature of what might be appropriate measures in such a context often is contentious, sustainable development, based on equitable considerations as discussed in the previous section, also has affected what such measures might legitimately entail in a developing or an economy-in-transition state.

Given the prevalence of scientific uncertainty, precaution, which is often also referred to as the 'precautionary principle' or the 'precautionary approach', now is one of the most commonly encountered concepts in international environmental

[34] See UN Framework Convention on Climate Change, Article 4.

[35] *Legality of the Threat or Use of Nuclear Weapons*, Advisory Opinion, 8 July 1996, [1996] I.C.J. Rep. 226.

law. Some countries oppose referring to precaution as a 'principle', however, because of a concern that it could easily disguise trade protectionism. Precaution is thus one of the most controversial concepts of sustainable development. Precaution also is an essential part of all municipal (domestic) systems for protecting health, safety, and the environment. This is because regulators seldom, if ever, possess all the scientific and other information they need and want, but they nevertheless have to make decisions one way or another—they must make decisions in the face of uncertainty. The exercise of precaution is thus critical to protecting the environment in the face of competing demands and is one of the core elements of sustainable development.

The concept of precaution is articulated in many international instruments, including binding international agreements such as the CBD and the Cartagena Protocol on Biosafety, as well as the UNFCCC. The most commonly used definition is found in Principle 15 of the Rio Declaration: '[i]n order to protect the environment, the precautionary approach shall be widely applied by States according to their capabilities. Where there are threats of serious or irreversible damage, lack of full scientific certainty shall not be used as a reason for postponing cost-effective measures to prevent environmental degradation.' By virtue of the term 'according to their capabilities,' Principle 15 links precaution to CBDR and thus, more directly, to sustainable development. If capabilities are limited in terms of scientific knowledge or technical or financial capabilities, which is likely to be the case in developing and economy-in-transition countries, thresholds for precautionary action may be lower. As a result of the need for developed countries to transfer financial and technological resources to developing and economy-in-transition countries, the latter countries are to some extent dependent on the former countries in how they implement precaution. Moreover, if capabilities are strong, as is likely to be the case in developed countries, the definition of precaution implies that stronger measures should be taken. The concept of sustainable development thus implies that implementing precaution may entail different consequences in dissimilar contexts, and it may thus have profound implications for what may be considered appropriate precautionary policies and measures in a given context. The manner in which precaution is defined and applied in these different contexts in the future will be significant both in determining success in achieving sustainable development and in elaborating its substantive content.

## 6 Implications for Tools of International Environmental Law

Various tools and approaches have been used to pursue sustainable development. Generally speaking, these tools help gather needed information, set priorities, understand inter-relationships, build credibility and support, and improve implementation and monitoring of sustainable development policies and laws. As a result, all tools used to pursue the protection of the environment, such as, for example, corporate responsibility mechanisms (see Chapter 21 'Private and Quasi-Private Standard Setting'), transparency, public participation and access to justice (see discussion later in this chapter), impact assessment tools, education, and monitoring and verification (see Chapter 42 'Monitoring and Verification'), can support the attainment of sustainable development. Sustainable development, however, has had significant consequences for how and where these tools are utilized and has made their proper use a matter of international concern.

Education offers a pertinent example. Its importance to attaining sustainable development was emphasized by the Decade of Education for Sustainable Development, which was proposed at the WSSD in 2002 and proclaimed by the UNGA to comprise the period between 2005 and 2014.[36] Education is a primary instrument of change towards sustainable development because it is essential to individual and societal capacity building. Public education, in particular, fosters values, actions, and lifestyles that are required to achieve a sustainable future, which often involves changes in the behaviour of individuals, business, non-governmental organizations (NGOs), intergovernmental institutions, and governments. The UN Educational, Scientific, and Cultural Organization has emphasized that the 'education and full and equal engagement of women and girls is crucial to ensuring balanced and relevant Education of Sustainable Development messages and to providing the best chance for changed behaviors for sustainable development in the next generation.'[37] In the remainder of this section of the chapter, we discuss by way of example two sets of tools (transparency, public participation, and access to justice and impact assessment and accounting techniques) to illustrate how sustainable development has affected the tools associated with environmental law.

## 6.1 Transparency, Public Participation, and Access to Justice

Transparency, public participation, and access to justice have been and will remain crucial instruments at the national level of decision-making for attaining sustainable development. They allow for the active engagement of individuals and civil society organizations in providing information and other input with respect to all aspects of sustainable development. They are particularly critical tools because of the importance of integrating local aspects into decisions regarding sustainable development.

[36] G.A. Res. 57/254, UN Doc. A/RES/57/254 (21 February 2003) at paras. 1–2.

[37] See generally United Nations Educational, Scientific and Cultural Organization (UNESCO), Education for Sustainable Development (United Nations Decade 2005–14), *Gender Equality* (Paris: UNESCO, 2006).

Moreover, as Principle 10 of the Rio Declaration, the Convention on Access to Information, Public Participation in Decision-making and Access to Justice in Environmental Matters (Aarhus Convention), and the 1994 Draft Declaration of Principles on Human Rights and the Environment (see Chapter 28 'Environmental Rights') illustrate, their use at the national level has become a matter of concern at the international level of decision-making (see Chapter 29 'Public Participation').

Sustainable development, however, also has resulted in the enhanced importance of these tools at the international level of decision-making, *per se*. This development is particularly evident in those situations where international institutions, such as development banks, make decisions regarding projects to be executed in developing and economy-in-transition countries (see Chapter 32 'International Institutions'). Since such projects may have considerable impacts on individuals and groups in society, their participation in decision-making regarding relevant projects becomes important both at the national level and at the international level of decision-making. This point can be illustrated with reference to the World Bank, which has adopted Operational Policy/Bank Procedure (OP/BP) 4.01 on Environmental Impact Assessment. OP/BP 4.01 determines, among other things, that project-affected groups and local NGOs are to be involved in the environmental impact assessments that are to be conducted for projects carried out with the assistance of the World Bank. While these assessments are carried out within the state concerned, their outcome directly affects decision-making at the international level—in this case, project-related decisions of the World Bank. Moreover, NGOs and representatives of civil society participate in international meetings as observers and in consultations regarding individual projects (see Chapter 33 'Non-Governmental Organizations and Civil Society').

In addition, the establishment of the World Bank Inspection Panel illustrates a similar development with respect to access to justice, albeit a procedure that involves a quasi-judicial process. In this case, communities or groups of at least two individuals may submit a complaint against the World Bank, alleging that they have suffered or are likely to suffer harm as a result of the World Bank not abiding by its own internal rules, such as OP/BP 4.01.

Sustainable development, due to its focus on integration and the links that it establishes between individuals, states, and international institutions, through, for example, the need for poverty alleviation, good governance, and environment and development, thus has changed the nature of transparency, public participation, and access to justice. The use of these instruments, while originally conceived as of concern to individual states, has become a matter of international concern. Moreover, such tools are now also being employed at the international level of decision-making—that is, to decisions taken by international institutions. The Almaty Guidelines in Promoting the Application of the Principles of the Aarhus Convention in International Forums, which were adopted by the parties to the Aarhus Convention, also illustrate this point[38]—access to information and public participation are a matter of concern at the international level, *per se*.

## 6.2 Impact Assessment and Accounting Techniques

The concept of sustainable development also has crucially affected the nature of impact assessments and the accounting techniques used in such assessments and other valuations. Principle 17 of the Rio Declaration refers to the need to conduct environmental impact assessments (EIA) in the following terms: EIAs 'shall be undertaken for proposed activities that are likely to have a significant adverse impact on the environment and are subject to a decision of a competent national authority.' Principle 17 as well as the Convention on Environmental Impact Assessment in a Transboundary Context illustrate that EIAs and the manner in which they are conducted are a matter of concern to the international community, as are transparency, public participation, and access to justice. As already discussed in the previous section, EIAs are also conducted in those cases where international institutions, such as the World Bank, are involved in decision-making and are thus relevant at the international level of decision-making, *per se*.

The scope of EIAs, however, also has been influenced profoundly by sustainable development, extending their scope to global impacts and international agreements. In the United States, for example, Executive Order 13141 and its Guidelines for Implementation require assessment and consideration of the environmental impacts—including the global impacts in some circumstances—of trade agreements.[39]

Sustainable development also has had far-reaching consequences for the nature of the assessments to be conducted and the methods of accounting to be used in conducting impact assessments and other valuations. In essence, these consequences amount to both a broadening of the issues to be considered in the assessment, to issues other than environmental consequences, and to the introduction of new accounting techniques. A relevant example of the former is the process of sustainability assessment; a relevant example of the latter is natural resources accounting.

Sustainability assessment is a process designed to enable policy-makers to engage in integrated decision-making on projects, plans, policies, and programmes. Sustainability assessments differ from EIAs because they address social and economic as well as environmental outcomes. Ideally, sustainability assessments are

[38] Almaty Guidelines in Promoting the Application of the Principles of the Aarhus Convention in International Forums, Annex to Decision II/4, *Report of the Second Meeting of the Parties*, Doc. ECE/MP.PP/2005/2/Add.5 (20 June 2005).

[39] See Executive Order No. 13141, 64 Fed. Reg. 63, 169 (18 November 1999).

characterized by an integrative approach to improving social, economic, and environmental outcomes and increased information resulting from the identification of relevant social issues. Efforts are currently underway to identify sustainable development criteria, and conduct pilot projects because sustainability assessments remain primarily aspirational due to difficulties in integrating environmental, social, and economic aspects. An interesting example of a framework for conducting sustainability assessments are the CBD's *Akwé: Kon Guidelines*, which outline best practices for conducting environmental, cultural, and social impact assessments.[40]

Sustainable development also has given rise to the recognition that the accounting techniques used, in order to be accurate, need to reflect the use of natural assets in addition to produced capital consumption.[41] Conventional accounting procedures such as gross domestic product, however, focus solely on the measurement of economic performance and growth as reflected in market activity and disregard essential factors such as the depletion of natural resources, thus failing to provide policy-makers and the public with the complete picture.[42] Natural resource accounting does include such factors (often in non-monetized form), and thus provides a more comprehensive assessment of the sustainability of growth and development by displaying both positive and negative changes in the environment over the period in question, including the full impact resulting from the depletion and degradation of natural capital (for example, changes in the extent of forest cover).

Natural resource accounting also avoids some of the problems associated with cost-benefit analysis (also referred to as benefit-cost analysis), a widely used, and sometimes legally mandated, methodology for evaluating the economic feasibility of a proposed policy, programme, or project (hereinafter referred to jointly as a project). In a cost-benefit analysis, the projected benefits and costs of a project over time are calculated and compared. In theory, this comparison indicates whether the project will reap more benefits than it will cost, and which projects among several alternatives will reap the largest gains as well as the relative importance of, and relationship between, relevant variables. In practice, however, cost-benefit analysis encounters serious problems. For example, it is very difficult, if not impossible, to accurately assign economic values to the social and environmental impacts of a project. Many of these impacts are, by their nature, non-monetary or non-quantifiable, at least not in any reasonably accurate way—for example, how much is a human life, an ecosystem, a species, a view of a mountain range, or a national park worth in monetary terms, both now and in the future? Similarly, how should the myriad of environmental services (for example, air and water purification, provision of food, pollination of plants, prevention of erosion, provision of shade and windbreaks, provision of fuel, and

[40] See *Akwé: Kon Guidelines* (Montreal: Secretariat of the Convention on Biological Diversity, 2004).

[41] United Nations Department of Economics and Social Affairs Statistics Division and United Nations Environment Programme Economics and Trade Unit Division of Technology, Industry and Economics, *Integrated Environmental and Economic Accounting: An Operational Manual*, UN Doc. ST/ESA/STAT/SER.F/78 (2000).

[42] *Ibid.*

recreation) be valued? Other difficult questions include how should externalities be taken into account; how should distributional issues be calculated and considered; what discount rate should be used to convert future costs and benefits into present value; and how should the values that future generations will place on specific items or services be calculated. It is expected that sustainability assessment processes and natural resource accounting methodology will address some of these problems.

## 7 Conclusions

Sustainable development, which was adopted by the international community in 1992 as the paradigm, but not a legal norm, for improving the quality of life for people around the world, has had profound effects on international environmental law. While significant differences and uncertainties remain regarding its precise meaning and legal status, its four core elements are clear: inter-generational equity; intra-generational equity; the need to protect the environment; and the need to integrate economic, social, and environmental policies. It is also clear that the concept of sustainable development has not only expressly appeared in many international environmental instruments (both legally binding and non-legally binding) but has also affected both international environmental law principles and the tools used to implement these principles.

With respect to principles, sustainable development has significantly altered the content of the duty to cooperate, for both developing and developed states, through the principle of CBDR. Similarly, sustainable development has affected the duty to protect the environment in the face of scientific uncertainty and thus precaution. In the case of developing countries, for example, the content of precaution is dependent both on their capabilities and on the extent to which developed states transfer financial and technical assistance to developing states in order to enhance those capabilities. Sustainable development thus has further contextualized both the duty to cooperate and the notion of precaution.

At the level of tools, sustainable development has resulted in such tools and their use at the national level now being of concern to the international community *per se* as well as fostered the use of these instruments at the international level. The concept of sustainable development also has had profound effects on the nature of the impact assessments and accounting processes. In particular, it has resulted in broadening their scope both geographically and with respect to the elements assessed, to include social and economic considerations as well as environmental ones, and thus facilitate a more holistic assessment of the projects or activities concerned. How sustainable development has had these effects—whether as a non-normative policy, as soft law, as a reconciling norm of customary international law (as submitted by Judge

Christopher Weeramantry), as a 'metaprinciple' to avoid conflict (as submitted by Vaughn Lowe), or simply through the normative power of the actual—will probably remain the subject of debate among lawyers for many years.

## Recommended Reading

A. Boyle and D. Freestone, eds., *International Law and Sustainable Development: Past Achievements and Future Challenges* (Oxford: Oxford University Press, 1999).

M.-C. Cordonier Segger and A. Khalfan, *Sustainable Development Law: Principles, Practices, and Prospects* (Oxford: Oxford University Press, 2004).

D. Magraw, 'Legal Treatment of Developing Countries: Differential, Contextual and Absolute Norms' (1990) 1 Colo. J. Int'l L. & Pol'y 69.

Millennium Ecosystem Assessment, *Ecosystems and Human Well-Being: Synthesis* (Washington, DC: Island Press, 2005).

H.E. Daly, *Beyond Growth: The Economics of Sustainable Development* (Boston, MA: Beacon Press, 1998).

# [2]

*Journal of Environmental Law* **23**:3 
doi:10.1093/jel/eqr015 Advance Access published on 25 August 2011

# The Challenge of Climate Change Adaptation: Learning from National Planning Efforts in Britain, China, and the USA

Daniel A. Farber*


## Abstract

This article examines projected climate impacts and national planning efforts in three major countries: the USA, UK and China. The three countries are in varying stages of planning for climate adaptation. Planning frameworks in all three countries suffer from a lack of specificity and urgency. To address this situation, the article recommends two measures. The first is the use of scenario planning, including consideration of high-impact scenarios, to address the downside risks of climate change. Planning in the UK has begun to make use of scenario analysis, although in a less comprehensive manner, while the USA had an earlier experiment in the use of the worst-case scenario as a planning tool. The second recommendation is to identify and prioritise impacts on vulnerable populations such as the elderly, the poor and coastal communities. This recommendation has roots in the US planning proposals, but also resonates with international human rights law.


* Sho Sato Professor of Law and Chair of the Energy and Resources Group at the University of California, Berkeley (dfarber@law.berkeley.edu). This Article is based on the Journal of Environmental Law Annual Lecture delivered at the Institute of Advanced Legal Studies in London on 7 December 2010. Caitrin McKiernan provided valuable research assistance, in particular with regard to developments in China. Eric Biber and Christopher Hilson provided helpful comments on an earlier draft.

## 1. Introduction

Mitigation may affect the degree of adaptation that is ultimately required, but whatever mitigation measures are adopted, a significant degree of climate change seems unavoidable.[1] As the IPCC explains, 'warming and sea level rise would continue for centuries due to the time scales associated with climate processes and feedbacks, even if greenhouse gas concentrations were to be stabilized'.[2]

Given the unavoidability of significant climate impacts, adaptation is a necessity. Business as usual (BAU) assumes that past weather patterns will remain characteristic of the future. Adaptation is the response to the almost certain failure of this assumption of stationary climate. Adaptation can be defined to include any deviation from BAU to reduce harm from predicted changes in climate or from uncertainty about future climate, including extreme events as well as average weather. Adaptation encompasses a panoply of programmes such as improvements in the infrastructure for water supply and flood protection; new plant varieties; public health measures to deal with heat waves and changing disease patterns; limiting population and construction in vulnerable areas and assisting relocation where necessary; new forms of insurance for catastrophic events; and programmes to protect forests and wetlands. The goals include making systems more robust, so that they can cope with a broader range of events, and more resilient, so they can respond quickly to events and recover readily from events beyond their capacity to control.

National governments have already begun planning for adaptation, but planning efforts are still at a relatively early stage: it is almost more accurate to say that governments are making plans to engage in adaptation planning exercises. Although much of the actual effort to adapt to climate change will take place at the regional and local levels, national governments have an important role to play as well.[3]

This article will consider adaptation planning in the USA, the UK and China. These countries were chosen because of the central importance of the USA, the European Union (with the UK as a representative member),[4] and China to

1 Indeed, some effects of climate change are already being seen. See IPCC, 'Summary for Policymakers' in Susan Solomon and others (eds), *Climate Change 2007: The Physical Science. Contribution of Working Group I to the Fourth Assessment Report of the Intergovernmental Panel on Climate Change* (CUP 2007) 1, 5.

2 IPCC (n 1) 16. Failure to reach international agreement on binding greenhouse gas limitations makes the need for adaptation all the greater. 'Facing the Consequences: Adapting to Climate Change' *The Economist* (27 November 2010) 85.

3 Daniel A Farber, 'Climate Adaptation and Federalism: Mapping the Issues' (2009) 1 San Diego J of Climate & Energy L 259.

4 For a broader survey of EU efforts, see E Carina H Keskitalo (ed), *Developing Adaptation Policy and Practice in Europe: Multi-level Governance of Climate Change* (Springer 2010).

the world economy and to international climate change policy. Collectively, the USA, EU and China represent over two billion people.

The three countries in the study have made promising beginnings in setting guidelines for future planning. Nevertheless, these planning guidelines may result in business as usual accompanied by boilerplate and platitudes about adaptation needs, unless steps are taken to give the planning process urgency. Planning mandates need some sharp edges if they are to generate a sense of urgency and commitment.

In some respects, adaptation planning resembles environmental assessment, in that it involves forecasting and responding to future environmental changes. The US experience with impact statements under the National Environmental Policy Act (NEPA) provides two useful cautions. First, broad guidelines are not enough to force agencies to confront uncertainties. A clearer mandate is required, such as a directive to consider the worst-case scenario. Second, it is not enough to tell agencies to make decisions based on a spectrum of desirable goals. There need to be genuine constraints. For this reason, although NEPA continues to shape agency processes, the substantive policies articulated in NEPA had little effect and were ultimately held unenforceable by the Supreme Court. In contrast, because the Endangered Species Act has a clearly defined mandate to avoid jeopardising rare organisms, agencies are forced to take biodiversity seriously.

Based partly on this US experience, this article proposes that nations adopt two requirements for adaptation planning. First, adaptation plans should be required to consider multiple scenarios, including at least one based on high climate sensitivity and emission levels. The approach should be precautionary in the sense that plans should be robust in the pessimistic scenario as well as more favourable circumstances. Second, adaptation plans should guarantee protection of the most vulnerable individuals and communities, although that protection could take alternative forms. Governments should assume an obligation to ensure that individuals do not lose their lives or become homeless as a result of climate change, and that displaced individuals be treated appropriately. Adaptation must at a minimum protect core human rights.

The least developed countries will face the most difficult challenges.[5] This article focuses on the somewhat more tractable problems faced by countries of varying wealth but substantial governmental capacity and economic resources. Even these better-situated countries face serious challenges. The two adaptation pillars of precaution and human rights apply with even more force, however, in the case of less favourably situated countries.

5 'The poorest developing countries will be hit earliest and hardest by climate change, even though they have contributed little to causing the problem'. Nicholas Stern, *The Economics of Climate Change: The Stern Review* (CUP 2007) xxvi.

Section 2 of this article contains national case studies of the USA, the UK and China. One purpose of the case studies is to demonstrate the range and potential severity of the climate impacts facing these nations. Another is to help identify best practices—in particular, the UK's use of scenario planning and the US emphasis on vulnerable populations are both promising techniques.

Section 3 makes the case for precautionary adaptation taking into account lower probability, extreme outcomes and for a human rights approach that mandates protection for vulnerable individuals and communities. These proposed practices are action forcing in the sense that uncovering dangerous risks and mandating protection of vulnerable communities help combat the force of inertia toward continuing business as usual.

## 2. National Case Studies

We begin with an examination of the steps that some key nations are already taking toward adaptation planning. This section first examines the need for adaptation globally, and then focuses on the situations in the USA, the UK and China. Although this section sets the stage for the recommendations in Section 3, it should also be useful because up-to-date cross-national information about adaptation is not widely known (and in the case of China is particularly difficult to locate).

### *2.1 Global Impacts and the Need for Adaptation*

With rare exceptions, recent years rank at the top of the list of the warmest global temperatures,[6] and depending on future emissions and climate sensitivity, the world will end up 2–7°C warmer than it is today.[7] Temperature change in the Arctic will be about twice as large.[8] Even warming of 2°C would leave the earth warmer than it has been in millions of years.[9]

Clearly, we need to begin assessing and responding to the foreseeable impacts. Sea level rise is one of the most predictable.[10] Apart from the potential contribution of melting from Greenland and Antarctica,[11] the simple change

6 David Archer and Stefan Rahmstorf, *The Climate Crisis: An Introductory Guide to Climate Change* (CUP 2010) 43.
7 ibid 129.
8 ibid 133.
9 ibid 225.
10 See K Hasselman and others, 'The Challenge of Long-Term Climate Change' (2003) 302 Science 1923, 1924. Figure 2 predicts a two meter increase in sea level under a 'business as usual' scenario by 2100; but only 20 cm under an optimum regulatory strategy.
11 On the potential for catastrophic melting in these areas, see Stern (n 5) 16; IPCC (n 1) 16.

in temperature of the oceans will contribute to thermal expansion, just as increased temperature causes the mercury in a thermometer to rise.[12] This rise in sea level will result in loss of coastal lands,[13] inundation of some estuary systems with salt water, salt-water intrusions into some drinking sources and increased exposure to flood damage.[14]

Other changes are also foreseeable. Snow cover will decrease in most areas,[15] and oceans will become increasingly acidic.[16] Even moderate climate change will trigger significant extinctions,[17] and extreme events such as fires, floods and heat waves will become more widespread.[18]

Adaptation to these impending changes poses serious challenges.[19] *The Stern Review* estimates that the cost of adapting infrastructure 'to a higher-risk future could be $15—150 billion each year (0.05—0.5% of GDP), with one-third of the costs borne by the US and one-fifth in Japan'.[20] Furthermore, '[e]xtreme events such as floods and drought cause extensive damage to many parts of society, and thus a critical issue for adaptation is the degree to which frequency, intensity, and persistence of extreme events change'.[21]

National governments are now beginning to consider how to adjust to these changes. Hopefully, mitigation efforts will limit the extent of future impacts—and it should go without saying that mitigation should be an international priority—but some degree of adaptation will be required in any event.

12 Changes in ocean temperature will also affect fish stocks; see Hans O Pörtner and Rainer Knust, 'Climate Change Affects Marine Fishes Through the Oxygen Limitation of Thermal Toleration' (2007) 315 Science 95.

13 A Barrie Pittock, *Climate Change: Turning Up the Heat* (Earthscan 2005) gives examples, including China, ibid 264, India, Pakistan, Bangladesh, ibid 268, and the USA, ibid 278.

14 See Elizabeth Kolbert, *Field Notes from a Catastrophe: Man, Nature, and Climate Change* (Bloomsbury Pub 2006) 123–24 (British governmental study indicating that what are now 100-year flood events could become routine by late in this century); see also Pittock (n 14) 118 (stating that without adaptive measures, annual financial losses as a result of flooding would increase from 1 to 24 billion in different scenarios).

15 Archer and Rahmstorf (n 6) 147.

16 ibid 148.

17 ibid 162.

18 ibid 174; Heidi Cullen, *The Weather of the Future: Heat Waves, Extreme Storms, and Other Scenes from a Climate-Changed Planet* (Harper 2010); on the flooding issues (in particular, the impact of climate change on catastrophic weather events), see Howard C Kunreuther and others, *At War with the Weather: Managing Large-Scale Risks in a New Era of Catastrophes* (MIT Press 2009) 11–12.

19 These challenges are discussed in Tim Bonyhady, Andrew Macintosh and Jan McDonald, *Adaptation to Climate Change: Law and Policy* (The Federation Press 2010); US Government Accountability Office, 'Climate Change Adaptation: Strategic Federal Planning Could Help Government Officials Make More Informed Decisions' (GAO-10-113 2009).

20 Stern (n 5) 417.

21 William E Easterling III, Brian H Hurd and Joel B Smith, 'Coping with Global Climate Change: The Role of Adaptation in the United States' (Pew Center on Global Climate Change 2004) 17.

### *2.2 US Adaptation Needs and Strategies*

This section will survey some of the most likely impacts of climate change in the USA, the sorts of adaptation that may be required and current adaptation planning efforts. Under the Bush Administration, climate change was nearly a taboo topic for US government officials, given the Administration's determination to avoid any serious engagement with mitigation efforts. That strategy would have been undermined by serious consideration of climate impacts, so planning for adaptation had to await the Obama Administration. Given this late start, the USA has only begun to think seriously about adaptation at the national level.

The USA will be faced with a variety of serious climate impacts. The country is large and geographically diverse, with correspondingly varied climate impacts.[22] Wetter conditions are expected in the Northeast and on the coasts, while drier conditions are expected in the inland west.[23] Temperatures are expected to rise everywhere, but more inland than in coastal or southern areas in the continental USA, with the greatest increases in Northern Alaska.[24] In the southeast, even though absolute changes will be smaller, the baseline is high, resulting in many more very hot days later in this century.[25] Cities in the Midwest will experience increasing heat waves and decreased air quality.[26]

Sea level rise may cause dramatic losses in wetlands in the United States.[27] Two-thirds of all US coastal wetlands would be lost with a one-meter rise in sea level.[28] What used to be a 100-year flood in New York City is now an 80-year flood, and may be a 20-year flood by mid-century.[29]

Meanwhile, in the arid southwestern USA, the future of the water supply is uncertain, with potentially major impacts on agriculture.[30] Scientists have examined the prospect of prolonged drought over the next 100 years.[31] Increased temperature, drought, wildfire and invasive species will change the southwestern landscape, while ironically the droughts may be punctuated by increased flooding.[32]

22 Recent information about nationwide climate impacts in the United States can be found in US Global Change Research Program, *Global Climate Change Impacts in the United States: A State of Knowledge Report* (Thomas R Karl and others eds, CUP 2009) (hereinafter US Impacts).
23 ibid 42.
24 ibid 29.
25 ibid 112.
26 ibid 117.
27 Victor S Kennedy and others, 'Coastal and Marine Ecosystems & Global Climate Change: Potential Effects on US Resources' (Pew Center on Global Climate Change 2002).
28 US Impacts (n 22) 84.
29 Cullen (n 18) 238.
30 Gina M MacDonald, 'Water, Climate Change, and Sustainability in the Southwest' (2010) 107(50) Proceedings of the National Academy of Sciences 21256.
31 Kenneth Strzepek and others, 'Characterizing Changes in Drought Risk for the United States from Climate Change' (2010) 5(4) Environmental Research Letters <http://iopscience.iop.org/1748-9326/5/4/044012> accessed 28 May 2011.
32 US Impacts (n 22) 131–2.

Public health impacts of climate change are also a concern.[33] The number of heat-wave days in Los Angeles is expected to at least double by midcentury and to quadruple by the end of the century.[34] The most vulnerable group (aged over 65) will double as a proportion of the California population over the same time.[35] Higher ozone levels due to the increased temperatures will cause additional deaths.[36] The probability of large wildfires is also expected to increase by 12—53% by the end of the century.[37]

The US government is just beginning to seriously address adaptation issues, following most of a decade in which climate change issues of all kinds were ignored or downplayed. President Obama appointed a task force composed of key federal agencies to investigate adaptation. The Task Force's Report[38] is a solid step forward in preparing the US to deal with the challenges of climate change. There are three key recommendations relating to domestic adaptation measures at the federal level.

First, according to the Report, adaptation needs to become a standard part of agency planning.[39] The plans should focus on ecosystems rather than either individual species or governmental jurisdictions.[40] An important recommendation is that adaptation plans should prioritise the most vulnerable people, places and infrastructure:[41]

> Adaptation plans should prioritize helping people, places, and infrastructure that are most vulnerable to climate impacts. They should also be designed and implemented with meaningful involvement from all parts of society. Issues of inequality and environmental justice associated with climate change impacts and adaptation should be addressed.[42]

Second, the government needs to ensure that scientific information about the impacts of climate change is easily accessible.[43] Without solid scientific information, public and private sector decision-makers cannot plan intelligently.

33 See Louise Bedworth, 'Climate Change and California's Public Health Institutions' (Public Policy Institute of California 2008).
34 ibid 2.
35 ibid 3.
36 ibid 7.
37 ibid 10.
38 The White House Council on Environmental Quality, 'Progress Report of the Interagency Climate Change Adaptation Task Force: Recommended Actions in Support of a National Climate Change Adaptation Strategy' (2010) <http://www.whitehouse.gov/sites/default/files/microsites/ceq/Interagency-Climate-Change-Adaptation-Progress-Report.pdf> accessed 24 May 2011.
39 ibid 10, 25–26.
40 ibid 22.
41 ibid 11.
42 ibid 21.
43 ibid 30–33.

This effort would build on the US Geologic Survey and its National Climate Assessment.[44]

Third, the government needs to address climate impacts that cut across agency jurisdictions and missions.[45] Unfortunately, this is the case for many of the main impacts, such as those that threaten water resources,[46] public health,[47] oceans and coasts[48] and communities.[49] Some important arenas for agency action are to improve water-use efficiency,[50] strengthen public health systems,[51] integrate climate risks into insurance[52] and develop an open-source risk assessment model.[53]

The Task Force's Report is not an adaptation plan. Instead, it is essentially a plan of how to *begin* adaptation planning. Nevertheless, this is an important first step to responding to the impacts of climate change; to the extent those impacts cannot be avoided by reducing emissions.

### *2.3 Adaptation in the UK*

The UK began to address climate adaptation earlier than the USA or China and is correspondingly more advanced in its planning. Since the European Union has been a leader internationally in addressing the problem of climate change in terms of mitigation, it is not surprising that an EU country such as UK is also in the forefront of addressing adaptation issues.

A key distinction between the UK and the other two countries is that climate adaptation is mandated by statute, with primary responsibility given to a single government agency and specific implementation requirements for local authorities.[54] Flooding has long been a key public concern, and some notable television programmes increased public awareness of climate impacts.[55] A 2005 Climate Change Programme report helpfully assembled available information about climate impacts in England.[56] The discussion of coastal flooding

44 ibid 23, 49.
45 ibid 34.
46 ibid 35–36.
47 ibid 37–38.
48 ibid 42–43.
49 ibid 39–40.
50 ibid 36.
51 ibid 38.
52 ibid 41.
53 ibid 21.
54 ibid 103–110.
55 E Carina H Keskitalo, 'Climate Change Adaptation in the United Kingdom: England and Southeast England' in Keskitalo (n 4) 97–147, 102.
56 Chris West and Megan Gawith (eds) *Measuring Progress: preparing for climate change through the UK Climate Impacts Programme. UK Climate Impacts Programme Technical Report.* (UKCIP 2005).

illustrates the report's approach:

> With rising sea levels and increased storminess, coastal areas may be affected by severe flooding. Under the High scenario sea defences designed to withstand a 1 in 100 year event would only withstand events with a 2—8 year return period in East Anglia by the 2050s. Work in Scotland suggests that frequencies for the 1 in 100 year events would increase to 1 in 10 or 20 years by the 2050s under the same scenario . . . Coastal erosion could also increase substantially, with annual damages expected to increase by 3—9 times, costing up to £126 million per year by the 2080s.[57]

Note that the report distinguishes between different scenarios (here referring to a particular 'High' scenario). The use of scenarios is an aspect of UK planning that we will consider again.

In 2008, the British government issued a framework for climate adaptation in England.[58] The report focuses on a series of impacts including hotter, drier summers and more extreme weather events such as heat waves and heavy rain.[59] The report establishes some basic principles, suggesting that adaptation should follow the principles of sustainable development, be proportional to the level of risk, and involve collaboration and transparency.[60] Importantly, the report calls for the use of scenarios, one with a 50% probability and a more extreme one with a 10% probability.[61] Inclusion of the more extreme scenario seems to embody an implicit use of the precautionary principle.

The report also stresses the important role of local and regional authorities.[62] Like the US Task Force report, the British report calls for adaptation metrics[63] and for mainstreaming adaptation within agency and programme planning.[64]

In September 2010, the Adaptation Subcommittee of the Committee on Climate Change issued an assessment of current readiness to deal with climate change.[65] Part 2 of the Climate Change Act 2008 established the Committee on Climate Change and charged it, among other duties, with making recommendations regarding adaptation. The report concluded:

> The UK has started to build capacity for adaptation, with evidence of growing awareness of the risks and appropriate responses, particularly

57 ibid 33.
58 DEFRA, 'Adapting to Climate Change in England: A Framework for Action' (DEFRA 2008).
59 ibid 13.
60 ibid 27.
61 ibid 29.
62 ibid 36.
63 ibid 39.
64 ibid 42–45.
65 Sebastion Catovsky and others, 'How Well Prepared is the UK for Climate Change?' (Committee on Climate Change Adaptation 2010).

> in public sector organisations. This compares favourably with progress in other countries, with some examples of good practice in adaptation decision-making. However, from the evidence reviewed, we conclude that capacity building is not yet systematically translating into tangible action on the ground . . . .[66]

Thus, despite the relatively advanced state of planning in UK compared with the USA and China, a great deal remains to be done.

### *2.4 Adaptation in China*

Officials within the Chinese government have begun to give formal attention to the need for adaptation. This effort is at a relatively early stage but provides grounds for hope about China's long-term adaptation effort.

Like the USA, China is large and geographically diverse; as such, the impacts of climate change vary across the country. For example, the Chinese government reports worsening of heat waves and droughts in northern China, flooding in southern China, and heavy snow in the west.[67]

The Chinese government notes that 'discernible adverse impacts on . . . agriculture and livestock industry' have already emerged.[68] The effects include:

> increased instability in agricultural production, severe damages to crops and livestock caused by drought and hot extremes and heat waves in some parts of the country, aggravated spring freeze injury to early-budding crops due to climate warming, decline in the yield and quality of grasslands, and augmented losses caused by meteorological disasters.

China projects a likely drop in the:

> yield of the three major crops — wheat, rice and corn; changes in the agricultural production layout and structure; accelerated decomposition of organic carbon in the soil; enlarged scope of crop diseases and insect outbreaks; accelerated potential desertification trend of grasslands; increasing frequency of natural fire; decreasing livestock productivity and reproductive ability; and growing risk of livestock disease outbreak.[69]

In the water sector, Chinese officials note that the overall water supply in northern China has decreased significantly, while water supply in southern

66 ibid 6.

67 Information Office of the State Council of the People's Republic of China, 'China's Policies and Actions for Addressing Climate Change' (2008) <http://www.ccchina.gov.cn/WebSite/CCChina/UpFile/File419.pdf> accessed 24 May 2011.

68 ibid 7.

69 ibid 7–8.

China has slightly increased. Chinese officials report increased flooding and droughts.[70] Looking forward, they predict reductions in:

> the area of glaciers and glacier ice reserves, thus having significant impacts on rivers and run-offs with sources in glacier melt water. Climate warming could reinforce the drought trend in northern China, and intensify water scarcity and imbalance between water supply and demand.[71]

Chinese authorities report an 'accelerating trend of sea level rise' over the past three decades, which has caused 'seawater intrusion, soil salinization and coastal erosion', has damaged the ecological systems of coastal wetlands, mangroves and coral reefs, and has 'diminished the service functions and bio-diversity of ecological system in coastal areas'.[72] Continuing sea level rise will 'undermine the capacity of public drainage facilities in coastal cities, and impair the functions of harbours'.[73]

Overall, Chinese government reports are far from sanguine about the potential impacts of climate change. The government's prediction is that 'climate change will also produce far-reaching impacts on society, economy and other fields, and cause huge losses to the national economy'. Finally, China predicts increased 'threats to the safety of life and property, and to the normal order and stability of social life'.[74]

As in the USA and the UK, adaptation efforts in China are in their infancy, according to research and informal conversations with experts working on climate change in China. We know that at least some government attention has been given to the problem, but not whether there is a real resolve to follow up.

This article does not attempt to present an exhaustive look at adaptation in China. Indeed, information on the subject is difficult to come by. Few studies exist assessing the efficacy of China's adaptation efforts. Some information does exist, however. Research into English-language literature, as well as informal discussion with multiple experts, revealed some independent analysis, by sector. Also, in 2007, the year China's first climate plan was released, independent experts produced a National Assessment Report on impacts and adaptation.[75] Release of a revised assessment was planned to take place before the

70 ibid 9.
71 ibid.
72 ibid 9–10.
73 ibid 10.
74 ibid.
75 Lin Erda and others, *Synopsis of China National Assessment Report (II): Climate Change Impacts and Adaptation* (English translation 2007), <http://www.law.berkeley.edu/centers/envirolaw/capandtrade/Lin%20Erda%202-5-07.pdf> accessed 24 May 2011.

end of 2010 and to contain some information about adaptation,[76] but as of March 2011 the report had not yet appeared.

China has at least announced a commitment, at the national policy level, to adaptation. China was the 'first major developing economy to issue an action plan'.[77] In 2007, China released the *China National Climate Change Programme*.[78] The following year, the government released a white paper, *China's Policies and Actions for Addressing Climate Change (Policies and Actions)*[79]; and in 2009, China followed up with a *Progress Report* on those policies and actions.[80] Notably, they devote sections to the 'present and imminent task'[81] of adaptation,[82] as contrasted with the 'long and arduous challenge' of mitigation.[83]

An analysis by the World Resources Institute calls the plan 'impressive,' and generally 'large in scope and scale'.[84] Broadly speaking, the plan stresses the 'need for adaptation of human and natural systems without hindering economic development. There is also a great focus on national level policy/legislative approaches to enhance China's overall adaptive capacity'.[85] However, the plan 'lacks specific targets and action-steps for realizing' goals.[86] This is, as we have seen, an endemic issue with national planning efforts, as illustrated by the US effort to date.

In addition to addressing adaptation in specific reports on climate change, the Chinese Communist Party recently discussed adaptation in the context of broader national governance plans. To understand the significance, some

76 Qian Wang, 'Climate Change Resulting in Wild Weather in China' (*China Daily* 9 September 2010) <http://www.chinadaily.com.cn/china/2010-09/09/content_11276617.htm> accessed 24 May 2011.

77 Taryn Fransen and others, 'National Climate Change Strategies: Comparative Analysis of Developing Countries' (World Resource Institute 2009) 1, <http://pdf.wri.org/working_papers/developing_country_actions_table.pdf> accessed 24 May 2011; the framework for adaptation efforts in China is briefly addressed in Jolene Lin, 'Supporting Adaptation in Developing Countries at the National and Global Levels' in Benjamin J. Richardson and others (eds), *Climate Law and Developing Countries: Legal and Political Challenges for the World Economy* (Edward Elgar 2009) 127–50, 138–9.

78 National Development and Reform Commission, People's Republic of China, 'China's National Climate Change Programme' (2007) <http://www.ccchina.gov.cn/WebSite/CCChina/UpFile/File188.pdf> accessed 24 May 2011.

79 Information Office (n 67).

80 National Development and Reform Commission, People's Republic of China, 'China's Policies and Actions for Addressing Climate Change: The Progress Report' (2009) <http://www.ccchina.gov.cn/WebSite/CCChina/UpFile/File571.pdf> accessed 24 May 2011.

81 Information Office (n 67) 12.

82 This article relies upon the English translations provided by the Chinese government of its plans and reports.

83 Information Office (n 67) 12.

84 Fransen and others (n 77).

85 ibid.

86 ibid 1.

background on Chinese governance may be necessary. Twice a decade, the Chinese government issues a five-year plan for the nation's priorities.[87] In October 2010, the Communist Party issued an 'Opinion' on the country's forthcoming 5-year plan (essentially a 'set of structures and parameters' for the drafters of the plan to follow).[88] Notably, the Opinion is the 'most comprehensive public statement the Chinese Communist Party has made on climate change', according to Deborah Seligsohn at the World Resources Institute.[89] While the majority of the section on climate change is devoted to mitigation, the Opinion explicitly references the need for adaptation.[90]

In China's *Policies and Actions*, the Chinese government notes that climate change 'threats are particularly pressing in the fields of agriculture and animal husbandry, forestry, natural ecological systems and water resources and in coastal and ecological fragile zones'; therefore China outlines broad plans for adaptation in these arenas, as well as 'Impacts on Society, Economy and Other Fields'.[91]

In another promising development, China[92] partnered in June 2009 with the UK and Switzerland to launch 'Adapting to Climate Change in China (ACCC)', a three-year, $6.75 million dollar pilot project to assess how 'climate change will impact China and how China can better plan to adapt to its effects'.[93] The project focuses on three provinces, Guangdong, Inner Mongolia

87 Andrew Batson, 'China Seeks a New Self Through an Old Method' *Wall Street Journal* (New York, 13 October 2010) <http://online.wsj.com/article/SB10001424052748703927504575541030493518168.html> accessed 24 May 2011.

88 Deborah Seligsohn, 'China's Party Plenum Recommends Actions in the 12th Five Year Plan' (*ChinaFAQs: The Network for Climate and Energy Information* 29 October 2010) <http://www.chinafaqs.org/blog-posts/chinas-party-plenum-recommends-climate-actions-12th-five-year-plan> accessed 24 May 2011; see also 授权发布:中共中央关于制定国民经济和社会发展第十二个五年规划的建议 (www.news.cn, 27 October 2010) <http://news.xinhuanet.com/politics/2010-10/27/c.12708501.htm> accessed 24 May 2011.

89 Seligsohn (n 88).

90 See ibid. The Party recently issued an opinion to the drafters of the Five-Year Plan. In Section 6, Item 22, the Opinion notes that: 'As parts of efforts for climate adaptation, China will emphasize capacity building to address extreme weather events', according to the informal translation by the World Resources Institute. ibid. (The original text is 加强适应气候变化特别是应对极端气候事件能力建设 <http://news.xinhuanet.com/politics/2010-10/27/c.12708501.6.htm> accessed 24 May 2011). The draft of the Five-Year Plan places considerable emphasis on climate change mitigation and discusses the need for adaptation measures such as preparation for extreme weather events. See Deborah Seligsohn and Angel Hsu, 'How Does China's 12th Five-Year Plan Address Energy and the Environment?' (*ChinaFAQs: The Network for Climate and Energy Information* 7 March 2011) <http://www.chinafaqs.org/blog-posts/how-does-chinas-12th-five-year-plan-address-energy-and-environment> accessed 24 May 2011.

91 Information Office (n 67) 1.

92 The main Chinese partner is the National Development and Reform Commission, see Ellen Kelly 'Introduction to ACCC' (Powerpoint presentation, ACCC Meeting 3 March 2010, *ACCC Project Workshop Documents*) <http://www.ccchina.gov.cn/en/NewsInfo.asp?NewsId=23050> accessed 24 May 2011.

93 ibid slide 2.

and Ningxia. It seeks to improve the climate change science; conduct comprehensive risk assessments in selected sectors; integrate climate risks into planning and management within the three project provinces, and inform national policymakers.[94] In August 2010, the project launched a bilingual website, 'Adapting to Climate Change in China', with information about the pilot project and adaptation more generally.[95]

In terms of future Chinese adaptation efforts, agriculture is an obvious priority given the need to feed a billion people. Some representative adaptation response measures include improving 'agricultural infrastructure', promoting the 'use of high-yield, stress-resilient crops' and promoting 'large-scale, water-saving irrigation'.[96] According to a 2010 independent study on China's mitigation and adaptation measures in the agricultural sector, the majority of China's adaptation responses are still in the planning phases. China has, however, made 'tangible progress'.[97] The government is also exploring the insurance industry and how to 'provide insurance for household losses, which will be in greater demand in a world that suffers from more severe weather events'.[98]

With respect to water issues, representative response measures include unifying 'water management planning and allocation'; 'speeding up water infrastructure development' including the South to North Water Diversion Project; and sloping and shoring 'protection through engineering and biological measures'.[99] The 2009 *Progress Report* lists accomplishments including flood control projects on all of the major rivers, investments in water and soil conservation projects, and the completion of the east and beginning of the middle line of the South–North Water Diversion Project.[100]

Adaptation measures under discussion include establishing an 'emergency response mechanism for marine disasters', and 'advanc[ing] and strengthen[ing] R&D of technologies for marine ecological system protection and restoration'.[101] According to the 2009 Progress Report, China now has a 'Working Plan for Investigating and Assessing the Impacts of Sea Level Rise', has built eight 'national-level special marine reserves', has 'established 18 areas in the coastal zones for marine ecology monitoring covering a total

94 ibid slide 3.
95 See *Adapting to Climate Change in China* <http://www.ccadaptation.org.cn/en/index.aspx> accessed 24 May 2011.
96 Fransen and others (n 77) 2.
97 Jinxia Wang, Jikun Huang and Scott Rozelle, *Climate Change and China's Agricultural Sector: An Overview of Impacts, Adaptation and Mitigation* (International Centre for Trade and Sustainable Development and International Food & Agricultural Trade Policy Council 2010) 12.
98 ibid.
99 Fransen and others (n 77) 2.
100 National Development and Reform Commission, People's Republic of China, 'China's Policies and Actions for Addressing Climate Change: The Progress Report' (n 80) 32–33.
101 Information Office (n 67) 34.

area of 52,000 square kilometres',[102] and 'enhanced emergency management of marine hazards'.[103]

While it is unclear whether there is yet a strong commitment to adaptation at high levels in the government, the groundwork is being laid for future planning efforts and reports do make some actionable recommendations. Given the climate impacts that will face China, beginning a genuine planning process soon would obviously be prudent.

## 3. Strategies for Sharpening the Focus for Adaptation

The planning efforts discussed in Section 2 are useful beginnings to the process of adaptation. The risk, however, is that actual planning and implementation on the ground will be half hearted. National adaptation guidelines in all three countries suffer from vagueness and a lack of urgency. If planning focuses on averages—the average citizen and the most probable estimate of future impacts—then assessments of planning needs will be mild and action will be modest. Instead, to provide focus and impetus to planning, we need to keep a clear eye on the worse than average: vulnerable portions of the population and scenarios where we are unlucky about climate developments. This section suggests two ways of putting teeth into adaptation planning: requiring the use of specified pessimistic scenarios as part of the planning process and mandating protection for the rights of vulnerable populations.

### *3.1 Scenario Planning*

Unfortunately, climate change is accompanied by great uncertainties.[104] We can be fairly sure of the lower end of the potential temperature increase but not of the higher end; we are even less sure about the scale of impacts on humanity from greater temperature increases. Current models allow for a 'wide range of possible temperature increases . . . including a 5% probability that temperature increases will equal or exceed 6°C and a 2% probability of increases equal to or greater than 8°C within the next 100 to 200 years'.[105]

102 National Development and Reform Commission, People's Republic of China, 'China's Policies and Actions for Addressing Climate Change: The Progress Report' (n 80) 33–34.

103 ibid 34–35.

104 For a good overview of these uncertainties and potential strategies for managing them, see Robert Willows and Richenda Connell (eds) *Climate Adaptation: Risk, Uncertainty and Decision-Making* (UKCIP 2003).

105 Daniel H Cole, 'The *Stern Review* and Its Critics: Implications for the Theory and Practice of Benefit-Cost Analysis' (2008) 48 Nat Resources J 53, 75. Feedback effects, such as methane releases triggered by temperature increases, threaten to accelerate temperature changes. Katey Walter Anthony, 'Methane: A Menace Surfaces' (2009) 301(6) Scientific American 68, 73.

Basically, the 'further we push our Earth outside of its mode of operation of the past millennia, the further we steer it into uncharted waters'.[106] Projecting regional or local impacts, which is necessary for adaptation planning, is even more difficult. As the IPCC explains:

> Most sources of uncertainty at regional scales are similar to those at the global scale, but there are both changes in emphasis and new issues . . . Spatial inhomogeneity of both land use and land cover change and aerosol forcing adds to regional uncertainty. When analysing studies involving models to add local detail, the full cascade of uncertainty through the chain of models has to be considered . . . [M]odels agree more readily on the sign and magnitude of temperature changes than of precipitation changes.[107]

When it is impossible to give confident odds on the outcomes, scenario planning may be the most fruitful approach.[108] Scenario planning can identify unacceptable courses of action and then assist in choosing among appealing remaining alternatives. Robustness rather than optimality is the goal.[109]

The UK Climate Impact Programme advocates scenarios as a 'key tool for climate change risk assessment'.[110] Scenarios are designed to deal with uncertainty by making speculation 'more disciplined, more anchored to scientific knowledge where it is available and more transparent'.[111] Scenario analysis avoids the pitfall of projecting a single probable future when vastly different outcomes are possible, broadens the decision maker's knowledge by requiring more holistic projections, and most importantly 'forces decision-makers to use

106 Archer and Rahmstorf (n 6) 152.

107 Jens Hesselbjerg Christensen and others, 'Regional Climate Projections' in Susan Solomon and others (eds), *Climate Change 2007: The Physical Science. Contribution of Working Group I to the Fourth Assessment Report of the Intergovernmental Panel on Climate Change* (CUP 2007) 847, 921.

108 Scenario planning rests on a realisation that plans need to take into account multiple possible futures. The flip side of this is the realisation that our plans may not work out as we hope. This observation seems too obvious to be worth mentioning, but often the possibility of failure is entirely overlooked in government planning. Dave Owen, 'Probabilities, Planning Failures, and Environmental Law' (2009) 84 Tulane L Rev 265. According to the *Economist*,

> It is tempting to imagine that adaptation decisions might wait for models that can provide greater certainty about what might happen where. This is a forlorn hope . . . Decisions about adaptation will be made in conditions of pervasive uncertainty. So the trick will be to find ways of adapting to many possible future climates, not to tailor expectations to one future in particular.

'Facing the Consequences' (n 2) 86.

109 Robert Verchick, *Facing Catastrophe: Environmental Action for a Post-Katrina World* (Harvard UP 2010) 239–49.

110 Willows and Connell (n 104) 79.

111 E A Parson, 'Useful Global-Change Scenarios: Current Issues and Challenges' (2008) 3(4) Environmental Research Letters 5 <http://iopscience.iop.org/1748-9326/3/4/045016> accessed 24 May 2011.

their imaginations'.[112] In addition, '[t]he very process of constructing scenarios stimulates creativity among planners, helping them to break out of established assumptions and patterns of thinking'.[113]

It may be particularly important to require consideration of extreme outcomes rather than just the most likely scenario. At one time, the White House directed agencies to deal with catastrophic uncertainty by discussing the 'worst-case' scenario in environmental impact statements.[114] This rule mandated 'reasonable projections of the worst possible consequences of a proposed action'.[115] An environmental impact statement does not dictate the substance of regulatory decisions but is at least supposed to force the agency to take a 'hard look' at the relevant factors.[116] The worst-case requirement was criticised as being excessively pessimistic and too intrusive on agency discretion.[117]

In response to these criticisms, the White House issued a new regulation dealing with uncertainty, replacing the worst-case scenario requirement with a requirement that uncertainties be explicitly discussed.[118] The revised regulation applies when an agency completing an environmental impact statement (EIS) has 'incomplete information' that is relevant to 'reasonably foreseeable significant adverse impacts' (including credible low-probability catastrophic impacts).[119] In such cases, the agency must discuss uncertainties and give its evaluation based on the best available information (even though incomplete).[120] The Supreme Court upheld this regulation in *Robertson v Methow Valley Citizens Council* and held that the governing statute does not require a worst-case analysis.[121]

The BP Deepwater Horizon oil blowout has brought a renewed argument for reinstating the worst-case requirement.[122] In the absence of such a requirement, it is all too easy for agencies to pick the scenario that best suits their

112 Verchick (n 109) 242–43.
113 ibid 243. For this reason, it is particularly important to consider 'wild-card scenarios' in which the planner's assumptions are violated; see James A Dewar, 'The Importance of "Wild Card" Scenarios' RAND discussion paper <http://www.au.af.mil/au/awc/awcgate/cia/nic2020/dewar_nov6.pdf> accessed 24 May 2011.
114 40 CFR § 1502.22(b) (1991).
115 Vicki O'Meara Masterman, 'Worst Case Analysis: The Final Chapter?' (1989) 19 Envt L Rep 10026, 10027.
116 See *Robertson v Methow Valley Citizens Council*, 490 US 332 (1989). For an overview, see Edward A Fitzgerald, 'The Rise and Fall of Worst Case Analysis' (1992) 18 U Dayton L Rev 1.
117 See Notes, 'Federal Agency Treatment of Uncertainty in Environmental Impact Statements Under the EPA's Amended NEAP Regulation § 1502.22: Worst Case Analysis or Risk Threshold?' (1987-1988) 86 Mich L Rev. 777, 807–09
118 40 CFR § 1502.22(b).
119 ibid.
120 ibid.
121 *Robertson v Methow Valley Citizens Council*, 490 US 332 (1989).
122 Oliver A Houck, 'Worst Case and the Deepwater Horizon Blowout: There Ought to be a Law' (2010) 40 Envt L Rep 11033; William H Rodgers Jr and Anna T Moritz, 'The Worst Case and the Worst Example: An Agenda for Any Young Lawyer Who Wants to Save the World from Climate Chaos' (2009) 17 Southeastern Environmental LJ 295.

plans, ignoring other risks as speculative and dismissing entirely any risks that they cannot quantify.[123]

One difficulty with requiring consideration of the worst-case scenario is that it is difficult if not impossible to identify a single scenario that stands out as the 'worst' among all credible scenarios. It is important, however, that planning not be limited to relatively benign scenarios or to the most likely outcome. Thus, it would be useful to identify benchmark scenarios that are considered credible, but substantially more extreme than the most likely outcome. Scenario users are entitled to know the uncertainties associated with particular scenarios, to the extent those are understood.[124]

Scenario planning is beginning to find use in the adaptation area. The UK is making a useful start in this direction in reporting rainfall scenarios that represent mid-range and 10% probabilities.[125] The scenario for the natural gas grid used high-level emissions as the base scenario; this was the worst case among the scenarios considered, featuring an 8°C increase in summer temperatures and much higher rainfall and severe weather.[126] In the USA, some local authorities are also beginning to use scenario planning.[127] Other countries would do well to issue scenarios reflecting plausible extreme outcomes, which could be heuristically identified as having a 5 or 10% probability. Planners should be required to take into account such possible extreme events and, if they find it infeasible to respond to such scenarios, make risks clear at the time of their decisions. The important point, however, is not the choice of the extreme scenario but the willingness to consider multiple designs and their vulnerabilities.[128]

### *3.2 Protecting the Most Vulnerable*

Vulnerable individuals, communities and species can provide harbingers of what is to come for all of us. Vulnerability means either a higher degree of

123 Daniel A Farber, 'Confronting Uncertainty under NEPA' (2009) 8(3) Issues in L Scholarship <http://www.bepress.com/ils/vol8/iss3/art3> accessed 24 May 2011.

124 Parson (n 111).

125 See text accompanying (n 61).

126 National Grid Gas plc 'Climate Change Adaptation Report: National Grid Gas - Gas Transmission and Distribution' (September 2010) <http://archive.defra.gov.uk/environment/climate/documents/interim2/national-grid-cca-gas-report-100927.pdf> accessed 26 May 2011.

127 The San Francisco Bay Conservation and Development Commission is using scenario planning to address sea level rise. See <http://www.bcdc.ca.gov/planning/climate_change/climate_change.shtml> accessed 24 May 2011 (staff recommendations can be found under 'Proposed Climate Change Bay Plan Amendment'). The New York Sea Level Rise Task Force is taking a similar approach. See <http://www.dec.ny.gov/energy/45202.html> accessed 24 May 2011.

128 This kind of scenario planning resembles Toyota's set-based concurrent planning which encourages the consideration of large numbers of designs before a decision is made. See Durward K Sobek, Allen C Ward and Jeffrey K Liker, 'Toyota's Principles of Set-Based Concurrent Engineering' (1999) 40 Sloan Management Rev 67.

exposure to climate impacts (such as flood risk to people living in coastal areas), higher levels of damage from a given level of exposure (such as the greater physical vulnerability of the elderly to high temperatures) or a lower ability to adapt without assistance (such as the difficulty of financing infrastructure improvements in poor communities). By attending to impacts on these vulnerable entities, we can not only provide adaptation measures to those most in need but anticipate broader needs that may be soon to come. In addition, as Chinese adaptation planning notes, the effect of climate change on social stability deserves careful consideration, and one major cause of instability may be mass relocations by vulnerable populations if they are unable to manage in their current locations.[129]

According to the IPCC, '[i]n the absence of an improvement to protection, coastal flooding could grow tenfold or more by the 2080s, to affect more than 100 million people/yr, due to sea-level rise alone'.[130] In addition:

> Those densely-populated and low-lying areas where adaptive capacity is relatively low, and which already face other challenges such as tropical storms or local coastal subsidence, are especially at risk. The numbers affected will be largest in the mega-deltas of Asia and Africa while small islands are especially vulnerable.[131]

More developed countries have more adoption options, but there, too, coastal communities will clearly be among the first to be threatened by climate change. For instance, the Louisiana coast is already 'disappearing before our very eyes' despite its importance for buffering storms, nurturing Gulf of Mexico fisheries and maintaining water quality.[132] The coast is also home for fishing communities with unique history and cultures, many of them dating back 200 years.[133] Cajun identity is so distinct that each town often has its own cuisine, musical style and dialect.[134] Rising sea levels increase the stress on these unique communities. Combined with the erosion of the coastal buffer, rising sea levels also threaten New Orleans because of potential increases in storm surges, with scientists predicting 'a vast swath of the coastal

129 Alex de Sherbinin, Koko Warner and Charles Ehrhart, 'Casualties of Climate Change' (2011) 304(1) Scientific American 64. For further discussion, see Kurt W. Campbell and others, 'The Age of Consequences: The Foreign Policy and National Security Implications of Global Climate Change' (Center for Strategic International Studies 2007).

130 Robert J Nicholls and others, 'Coastal Systems and Low-Lying Areas' in M L Parry and others (eds), *Climate Change 2007: Impacts, Adaptation and Vulnerability. Contribution of Working Group II to the Fourth Assessment Report of the Intergovernmental Panel on Climate Change* (CUP 2007) 315, 339.

131 IPCC, 'Summary for Policymakers' in Parry and others (n 130) 1, 12.

132 Verchick (n 109) 16–19.

133 Herbert R Padgett, 'Physical and Cultural Associations on the Louisiana Coast' (1969) 59 Annals of the Association of American Geographers 481.

134 ibid.

lands around New Orleans will be underwater by the dawn of the next century'.[135]

Climate change will disproportionately affect vulnerable individuals[136] and 'poorer regions and countries, that is, those who have generally contributed the least to human-induced climate change'.[137] For example, climate change will make what are now extremely rare heat waves more common in the future.[138] By the end of the century, the number of heat wave days in Los Angeles could double, while the number in Chicago could quadruple.[139] The number of heat wave deaths could rise proportionately.[140] We have already seen the extent of the threat with the death of approximately 35,000 people in the 2003 European heat wave.[141] Elderly people are more vulnerable to heat stress; they are especially at risk when they are socially isolated.[142]

In China, 'poor farming communities will be hit harder by droughts and floods than urban populations' and 'women and men will be affected in different ways according to their roles in the household and at work'.[143] This differential impact on women seems to be a widespread problem in developing countries.[144]

135 Suzanne Goldenberg, 'Rising Sea Level to Submerge Louisiana Coastline by 2100, Study Warns' *The Guardian* (London, 29 June 2009) <http://www.guardian.co.uk/environment/2009/jun/29/rising-sea-level-new-orleans> accessed 24 May 2011.

136 Stephen Humphreys, *Climate Change and Human Rights: A Rough Guide* (International Council on Human Rights Policy 2008) 3. According to Eakin and Pratt:

> Studies on adaptive capacity, in many cases, challenge existing social and economic orders by illustrating that adaptation by the most vulnerable social classes may require redistribution of resources and improved access to finance, land, technology, water, and other assets, as well as enhanced access to decision making and governance.

See Hallie C Eakin and Anthony Pratt, 'Are Adaptation Studies Effective, and What Can Enhance Their Practical Impact?' (2011) 2 Wiley Interdisciplinary Reviews: Climate Change 141. London's adaptation planning explicitly recognises risks to vulnerable groups, see Greater London Authority, *The Draft Climate Change Adaptation Strategy for London: Public Consultation Draft* (Greater London Authority 2010).

137 The Office of the UN High Commissioner for Human Rights also discusses the 'human rights implications of response measures'. See UN Office of the High Commissionerr for Human Rights, 'Report of the Office of the United Nations High Commissioner for Human Rights on the Relationship between Climate Change and Human Rights' UN Doc A/HRC/10/61 (2009).

138 US Impacts (n 22) 90.

139 ibid 91.

140 ibid.

141 Ulisses Confalonieri and others, 'Human Health' in Parry and others (n 130) 391, 397. This is a relatively low estimate.

142 US Impacts (n 22) 90.

143 Kelly (n 92) slide 4.

144 Kate Raworth and others, 'Climate Wrongs and Human Rights: Putting People at the Heart of Climate-Change Policy' (Oxfam International 2008) Briefing Paper 117, 7 <http://www.oxfam.org/sites/www.oxfam.org/files/bp117-climate-wrongs-and-human-rights-0809.pdf> accessed 24 May 2011.

It is not surprising that relatively disempowered groups would be the most vulnerable to climate change, as well as other risks. As in other contexts, we must be ready to address 'the failure of law to provide vulnerable people with the protections and benefits they need to lead safe and productive lives', an issue that has already been recognised in the contexts of environmental harms and natural disasters.[145]

Many humanitarian agencies and international institutions have focused on adaptation measures as a solution to the human rights impacts of climate change.[146] However, adaptation response measures themselves may create unintended consequences.[147] For example, an adaptation policy aimed at saving water by using wastewater in agriculture could also increase the risk of disease or contamination[148] or could impact food security by altering crop irrigation patterns.[149] In another scenario, an adaptation policy to relocate a coastal community affected by sea-level rise may also 'exacerbate existing cultural, economic and political stresses on dislocated individuals'.[150] Relocated individuals may lose livelihoods; their arrival in new communities may create violent tensions over already scarce resources.[151]

At present, no mechanism exists to assist states in evaluating and preventing the unintended consequences of adaptation policies themselves.[152] In response, some have called for the UNFCC to develop a 'new structure and process' for international agencies, institutions and NGOs to assist states to '(1) clarify human rights principles applicable to the development of climate change policies; (2) facilitate information sharing; (3) provide technical

Women produce up to 80 per cent of food grown in sub-Saharan Africa, and 60 per cent in Asia. Yet only five per cent of agricultural services are directed to women farmers, and they own just two per cent of the land and receive one per cent of agricultural credit worldwide. In addition, women and girls spend many more hours fetching fuel and water during floods or droughts in poor countries. Women are also the main [caretakers] for sick children and family members, and will usually be the first in the family to eat less when food is scarce. As a result, climate impacts put women's rights to food, life, security, and health particularly at risk.

145 Verchick (n 109) 128.

146 Zoe Loftus-Farren and Cáitrín McKiernan, 'Protecting People and the Planet: A Proposal to Address the Human Rights Impacts of Climate Change Policy' (International Human Rights Law Clinic, Miller Institute for Global Challenges and the Law, and Center for Law & Global Justice 2009) 4 <http://www.law.berkeley.edu/files/IHRLC/Protecting_People_and_the_Planet.pdf> accessed 26 May 2011.

147 The Office of the High Commissioner for Human Rights also discusses the 'human rights implications of response measures'. See Office of the High Commissioner for Human Rights (n 137).

148 Loftus-Farren and McKiernan (n 146) 6.

149 ibid.

150 ibid 5.

151 ibid 5.

152 ibid 7. For a brief description of the impacts of climate change on the right to life and security, the right to health, the right to food, the right to subsistence, and the right to health, see Kate Raworth and others (n 144) 6, Table 2.

assistance; and (4) operate in these capacities at the international, regional and state levels'.[153]

Merely announcing a variety of worthy goals may be less effective than actually mandating some protection of the most vulnerable entitles. The example of NEPA is again illuminating. NEPA announces a federal policy to 'foster and promote the general welfare, to create and maintain conditions under which man and nature can exist in productive harmony, and fulfil the social, economic and other requirements of present and future generations of Americans'.[154] The federal government is then directed 'to use all practical means, consistent with other essential considerations of national policy, to improve and coordinate' federal actions.[155] The goal is to assure (*inter alia*) 'the widest range of beneficial uses of the environment without degradation, risk to health or safety, or other undesirable and unintended consequences', while also assuring 'for all Americans safe, healthful, productive and aesthetically and culturally pleasing surroundings'.[156] While these are admirable goals, the statute clearly does not provide very concrete direction.

The Supreme Court has found these NEPA policies to be merely advisory. *Strycker's Bay Neighborhood Council, Inc v Karlen*,[157] involved construction of a housing project in a middle-income area. The lower court held that the agency's choice of site was unjustifiable because 'environmental factors, such as crowding low-income housing into a concentrated area, should be given determinative weight'.[158] The Supreme Court summarily reversed the Second Circuit decision, holding that NEPA required nothing more than consideration of environmental consequences by the agency. In a later case, the Court again emphasised that '[o]ther statutes may impose substantive environmental obligations on federal agencies, but NEPA merely prohibits uninformed—rather than unwise—agency action'.[159]

In contrast, biodiversity receives particularly strong protection under US law. The Endangered Species Act (ESA)[160] stems from the formative period of US environmental law in the 1970s. Section 4 requires the government to determine whether any species is endangered and to designate critical habitat, based on the best scientific data available.[161] Section 7, entitled 'Interagency Cooperation', requires consultation to ensure that agency actions do not jeopardise any endangered species—the 'consultation' has turned out to be less

153 Loftus-Farren and McKiernan (n 146) 7.
154 42 USC 4331(a).
155 42 USC 4331(b) (1), (3).
156 ibid.
157 444 US 223 (1980).
158 ibid.
159 *Robertson v Methow Valley Citizens Council*, 490 US 332, 351 (1989).
160 16 USCA § 1531 *et seq.*
161 16 USCA § 1533.

important than the 'do not jeopardize'.[162] Section 9 goes on to forbid 'taking' any endangered species.[163]

Section 7, which prohibits the government from jeopardising any endangered species, has received strong support from the courts. For example, in *National Wildlife Federation v Coleman*,[164] the court enjoined construction of an interstate highway that would cross a critical habitat of the Mississippi Sandhill Crane. The court was also concerned about the effect of the highway in encouraging development in the area, placing the crane at further risk. The court emphasised that § 7 'imposes on federal agencies the mandatory duty to insure that their actions will not either (i) jeopardize the existence of an endangered species, or (ii) destroy or modify critical habitat of an endangered species'.[165] Thus, a strict mandate under the ESA has proved far more efficacious than a multi-factored set of goals under NEPA.

Similarly, a requirement that agencies consider a host of adaptation-relevant factors will empower the best agencies but do little to produce genuine planning by the laggards. It is all too tempting to ignore risks that fall on marginal individuals or communities. The USA has taken a useful step to address this problem with the admonition that agency adaptation plans should prioritise the most vulnerable people, places and infrastructure.[166] But a simple admonition may have little effect if it conflicts with other agency priorities.

Nations can combat the insidious tendency to downplay the needs of vulnerable individuals and communities with a requirement that planners identify marginal or disempowered groups or communities and ensure that their actions do not jeopardise the lives, homes or livelihoods of those people if possible—and where not possible, that every step is taken to respect the rights of the affected individuals. Depending on local legal conditions, enforcement of this duty could take place in various ways: through the courts, legislative oversight, bureaucratic review, or even through international human rights law. Human rights law, whether or not it provides the best legal mechanism for protecting the most vulnerable, will be at least a valuable source of inspiration:

> A human rights focus can redirect attention to people who are otherwise likely to be ignored or unheard. Where communities are already living in precarious circumstances (shanty towns, polluted or otherwise fragile environments), posing human rights questions may help to locate some of the hazards posed by climate change – from desertification, water

162 16 USCA § 1536.
163 16 USCA § 1538.
164 529 F.2d 359 (5th Cir 1976).
165 ibid 371.
166 See text accompanying n 41 to 42.

salination, sea level rise, and so on – as well as those who are most at risk from them.[167]

Domestic adaptation planning could clearly profit from incorporating these principles.

In short, two pillars of adaptation planning should be a precautionary adaptation principle and protection of human rights of vulnerable populations. Given differences in political and legal culture, these pillars may also be expressed in various ways.

Domestic legal systems will differ in the mechanisms that they use to implement these proposals, but serious enforcement should be assured. The precautionary principle has not, as such, been adopted by the USA, and so in the US setting it may be more constructive to stress 'robustness' rather than precaution. The Chinese generally resist the concept of international human rights, so they may be more receptive to a different vocabulary—one that explains protection of the most vulnerable populations in terms of an early warning system for society as a whole and a method of reducing potential social unrest. This article focuses on the basic principles, leaving for later the questions of how to best give these principles concrete legal form domestically or internationally.

## 4. Conclusion

We have seen that the USA, China and the UK have all begun the process of planning for climate adaptation. Given the ubiquity and seriousness of climate impacts, the efforts to date are only a prelude to what is likely to become a pervasive governmental effort. Adaptation will require vigilance to protect against the foreseeable impacts of climate change and action at all levels of government.

To ensure that planning efforts remain focused and on task, this article proposes two action-forcing requirements: first, that planning include at least one pessimistic scenario based on high climate impact projections (embodying a precautionary approach); and second, that planners be required to avoid jeopardising the lives or homes of especially vulnerable societal subgroups (embodying human rights concerns). In the end, as with all governmental actions, leadership is the most critical ingredient, but providing some risk-averse guardrails for planners can help to avoid at least the most egregious mistakes.

167 Humphreys (n 136) 28.

# Part II
# Models of Regulation, Precaution and Risk

# [3]

# *Government Regulation in Great Britain and the United States*

We are now in a position to appraise the significance of the similarities and the differences to be found in the British and American approaches to environmental regulation. This chapter examines the extent to which environmental regulation constitutes a unique case of government regulation in either society. Can we, in fact, use environmental regulation as a vehicle for generalizing about the legitimacy and effectiveness of government regulation of industry in Great Britain and the United States? Or are the differences we have described rooted in the particular characteristics of this issue?

Environmental regulation certainly exhibits anomalies in both nations. The Alkali Inspectorate, for example, does represent a vestige of Victorian public administration. Not only did it keep the same name for more than a century, but its current statutory authority derives from legislation approved by Parliament before World War I. Few dimensions of British regulatory policy are governed by such carefully defined rules of procedure or provide such extensive opportunity for public participation as does the British system of land-use planning, and few aspects of British regulation of industry have been so contentious over the last two decades.

Environmental regulation also exhibits anomalies within the context of American regulatory policy. No aspect of the wave of "new social" regulation enacted over the last two decades has produced so much political conflict. For more than fifteen years, conflicts over environmental policy have occupied a prominent place on the American political agenda. While the focus of public debate has changed since the late 1960s, the salience of the issue itself has not: the controversy over automobile emissions has given way to concern over acid rain, while the urgency of cleaning up the nation's lakes and rivers has been transformed into a concern over the disposal of toxic wastes. In no other area of social regulation have the attempts at "regulatory reform" initiated by the Reagan administration created so much conflict and controversy. And in no other policy area have the changes in the balance of power between industry and nonindustry constituencies been more substantial or proved more durable; the environmental movement entered the 1980s with more political strength than that of any of the public interest groups whose emergence so transformed business–government relations during the late 1960s and early 1970s. Compliance with environmental regulation has been a greater burden on industry than compliance with regulations in any other area; not surprisingly, in no other area of social regulation has the American business community devoted so many resources in an attempt to influence policy outcomes.

These distinctions persist if one turns to the actual dynamics of regulatory policy making. While Congress has come to play a much more important role in the policy process in every area of regulation over the last fifteen years, in no area has it become more involved than that of pollution control. The eight-volume legislative history of the 1977 Clean Air Act Amendments spells out in considerable detail the intent of Congress concerning a wide variety of matters that formerly would have been left to the discretion of agency officials. Similarly, while the federal judiciary has become much more involved in the making of regulatory policy, in no area of government–business relations other than antitrust activities has its role been so important as in environmental regulation. In addition, the EPA's rule-making procedures are more elaborate and legalistic than those of most other regulatory agencies.

The differences between British and American environmental policies may also be due to the unique characteristics of this issue. Thus the greater degree of political conflict over environmental regulation in the United States may simply reflect the greater saliency of amenity issues among the American citizenry. Whether owing to the heritage of citizen activism generated by the civil rights and antiwar movements or the actual magnitude of the nation's environmental problems or a combination of the two, the public certainly became far more preoccupied with government policy in this area in the United States than in Britain. The British public, lacking the experience of 1960s citizen activism and benefiting from the regulations adopted during the 1940s and 1950s, appears to have been less concerned with this particular dimension of business–government relations over the last two decades. The relatively strong performance of the American economy during the second half of the 1960s may have contributed to the raising of public expectations in this policy area, while Britain's persistent balance-of-payment difficulties and slower growth rates may have tempered public expectations and thus made the task of government officials easier. Finally, the greater degree of cooperation between industry and regulatory officials in Britain may in part be due to the fact that a relatively large proportion of the major industrial sources of pollution in Britain are owned by the government. In America, with the notable exception of the Tennessee Valley Authority, they are in the private sector.

In order to evaluate the significance of these factors, this chapter compares British and American regulatory policies and outcomes in three other policy areas: occupational health and safety, consumer protection, and the regulation of financial markets. Its conclusion is that environmental regulation does *not* constitute a unique case of government regulation in either society: the two nations regulate the impact of business decisions on the environment in much the same manner—and with substantially the same results—as they regulate a wide variety of other dimensions of corporate conduct. Moreover, neither the degree of public concern, the nature of ownership, nor the profitability of particular industries appears to be decisive in explaining either nation's regulatory style. It is rooted rather in the broader dynamics of business–government relations—a subject we shall examine in Chapter 6.

Students of comparative public policy disagree over the extent to which public policy processes and outcomes are due to factors unique to a particular policy area—the so-called policy sector hypothesis—or whether they are a function of the political and social characteristics of the nation in which they are developed—the so-called national differences hypothesis. Gary Freeman writes:

> The question can be stated very simply. Which is more important in the study of comparative public policy—the structure of politics in a particular country and the differences in such structures between countries (that is, the nature of the national *apparatus* for making public policy), or the characteristics of the political issues (the policy arena or sector) with which public policy is attempting to deal? Will countries with dissimilar political systems produce significantly different responses to similar political issues, or will the imperatives of particular types of public problems compel more or less similar responses, whatever the shape of the political system involved?[1]

The evidence presented in this chapter supports the conclusion that the characteristics of a political regime are more important than the nature of the particular policy area itself in explaining policy processes. On the other hand, both the policy agenda and policy outcomes appear to be more affected by socioeconomic variables. Accordingly, among advanced industrial societies, the former vary much more than the latter.

## Occupational Health and Safety

The area of regulation that most closely resembles environmental protection is occupational health and safety. As in the case of pollution control, the efforts of the British government to protect the health and safety of workers have a long history. The first factory act was enacted in 1833, and legislation regulating the working conditions of miners was enacted in 1850. Throughout the nineteenth century, a series of amendments to the Factory Regulation Act of 1833 steadily expanded its scope. The original legislation applied only to children, but by the turn of the century, factory legislation had begun to apply to many adults as well. Many factory inspectors, like local public health officials, were not technically trained. The technical qualifications of the Mines Inspectorate, however, did closely resemble those of the Alkali Inspectorate: it consisted—and still consists—of qualified mining engineers with considerable experience in industry.

From the outset the inspectorates responsible for safety at the workplace operated on the assumption that while inspectors might do all they could to see that manufacturers and mine operators complied with the law's technical requirements, the ultimate responsibility for improving the working conditions of employees rested upon the owners and managers themselves. Accordingly, the success of the various inspectorates was to be judged not by their ability to secure compliance with minimum legal requirements but by their success in persuading employers and managers to assume greater responsibility for the physical welfare of their employees. The critical role of industry itself in improving health and safety conditions for employees was repeatedly emphasized in the reports of the Factory Inspectorate. In his 1963 annual report, for example, the chief inspector noted that most industrial accidents were not connected with violations of factory legislation. Rather, they "occur in circumstances which cannot readily be controlled by legislation, for example, lack of attention to good industrial housekeeping and to general tidiness . . . and above all lack of knowledge and application of safe methods of work."[2]

While prosecutions for breaches of factory legislation were somewhat more common than those for violations of pollution-control regulations, they were still relatively infrequent: one study of an inspector's files between 1961 and 1965 revealed that although inspectors had uncovered

3,800 contraventions of the factory acts and their regulations, in nearly 75 percent of the cases "the inspector took action by means of a formal notification of matters requiring attention while in less than 4 percent did he either threaten prosecution directly or actually institute proceedings."[3] Another study reported:

> It is extremely rare for a general inspection *not* to result in a "discovery" and formal notification of a number of breaches of the law for which criminal proceedings could be instituted. But in the vast majority of cases such matters are not regarded as criminal offenses in any ordinary sense either by the Inspectorate or by the employees concerned.[4]

In the case of the Mines Inspectorate, a royal commission noted in 1938 that prosecutions, which had averaged thirty-two a year at the beginning of World War I, had fallen to nine a year by the 1930s. Between 1948 and 1975 they ceased altogether.

As in the United States, criticism of the effectiveness of occupational health and safety regulation increased substantially in Britain during the 1960s. While much of it came from individual workers, in both nations a significant source of pressure derived from trade unions. Unions in Britain wanted not only to increase the representation of workers in the administration of safety procedures at the plant level but also to strengthen the enforcement efforts of the Inspectorate. Because the Inspectorate continued to insist that the primary responsibility for providing a safe workplace rested with management, the unions suspected that too little attention was being paid to the views and needs of employees. Moreover, the activities of the Factory Inspectorate came under increased scrutiny as part of the public's heightened interest in environmental regulation, since the public's interest in its safety and that of a firm's employees in their own were identical.

In Britain, as in the United States, public concern was also heightened by a number of highly publicized instances in which the government's regulatory body appeared to have been negligent in protecting the health and safety of British workers. Her Majesty's Factory Inspectorate was criticized, for example, for failure to protect the workers exposed to asbestos at the Bermondsey Factory of Central Asbestos and to control the lead pollution produced by the RTZ smelter at Avonmouth. Both works were eventually closed—but not before many of their employees had been injured.[5]

Immediately before the general election of 1970, the secretary of state for employment and productivity appointed a committee under the chairmanship of Lord Robens to reexamine the entire question of safety and health in the workplace. Its mandate was extremely broad: it was not only to examine the entire question of safety and health at the workplace but to consider what was needed to protect the public from hazards arising from industrial production. The Robens Committee released its report in 1972. Its main conclusion was that the existing system of regulation relied too much on specific rules and regulations. It urged a more flexible statutory system that would encourage greater "personal responsibility and voluntary self-generating effort."[6] The committee also recommended that a new authority be established with exclusive responsibility for health and safety at work and that the six existing regulatory bodies concerned with this function be merged into a single unified inspectorate.

While explicitly rejecting the argument that what was most needed was a strengthening of the police powers of the Factory Inspectorate and greater willingness to prosecute employers, the Robens report did propose strengthening the administrative sanctions available to inspectors. Its primary recommendation, however, was that strict legal enforcement be deemphasized and that the role of inspectors as advisers to both employees and industry be strengthened. This position more closely reflected the preferences of the Confederation of British Industry than it did that of the Trades Union Congress. The latter recognized the importance of self-regulation but did not regard it as an alternative to stricter enforcement of safety legislation.

After considerable interdepartmental conflict—much of which centered on the extent to which each of the previously independent inspectorates should become part of one organization—the government proposed the Health and Safety at Work Act of 1974. (Some of the strongest objections came from the Royal Commission on Environmental Pollution, which unsuccessfully opposed the removal of the Alkali Inspectorate from the Department of the Environment to this new regulatory body.) A governmental spokesman for the legislation did concede that "there was anxiety and apprehension about the general philosophy of the report," which seemed to call for a retreat from strictly enforced statutory requirements.[7] However, the legislation submitted to and approved by Parliament accepted the report's main recommendations.

The 1974 legislation established two new bodies: a Health and Safety Commission (HSC), to be composed of nine members appointed by the secretary of state for employment after consultation with representatives of employees, employers, local government, and various professional associations, and a Health and Safety Executive (HSE), which was to be responsible for administering the policies made by the commission. The latter's responsibilities included information and advisory services, research, and inspection. The HSE was also responsible for establishing special working bodies, comprised of members drawn from the various bodies represented on the HSE, which would develop guides and codes of practice for particular occupational hazards. The new law also extended protection to the self-employed and provided for the protection of the general public from hazards to their health and safety from industrial activities. The latter provision involved factory inspectors for the first time in environmental regulation.

The contrast between the Health and Safety at Work Act (HSWA) and the Occupational Safety and Health Act (OSHA), signed into law by President Nixon on December 19, 1970, is marked. While both laws were enacted in response to considerable public and union dissatisfaction with existing regulatory arrangements, the American legislation was enacted after an extremely bitter legislative struggle. The unions originally supported a bill that would have given the secretary of labor the power to set and enforce standards as well as the right to shut down plants where an "imminent danger" was found to exist. After considerable opposition from Republican legislators and business lobbyists, a compromise was reached. The final version of the bill placed the power to set standards and review violations in a separate body, the Occupational Safety and Health Administration (also known as OSHA), which was placed under the jurisdiction of the Department of Labor. More important, while the British statute essentially reinforced existing trends in British regulatory practice—its primary innovation was organizational—its American counterpart represented a radical policy departure in two significant respects. Like the National Environmental Policy Act of 1969, the Clean Air Act Amendments of 1970, and the Clean Water Act Amendments of 1972, the Occupational Safety and Health Act transferred the primary responsibility for the making and enforcement of regulations from the states to the federal government: states could continue to administer their own regulations, but only if they were at least as stringent as those promulgated by OSHA. Second, it reflected a shift to a more adversarial and rule-oriented approach to policy making and enforcement.

The two nations' regulatory strategies thus differ substantially. The British have moved in the direction of increasing the responsibility of private parties for designing and maintaining safe conditions at work. Thus the HSWA contains a series of "general duty" clauses that define the respective obligations of employer, self-employed persons, managers, and employees to ensure safety and reduce health risks in the workplace. Consistent with the recommendations of the Robens Committee, over the last decade the Factory Inspectorate has found itself increasingly drawn into "develop[ing] new techniques for monitoring what the employer does, appraising safety organizations rather than simply seeing that employees conform to specific rules."[8] In addition, the 1974 legislation formally institutionalized a tripartite system that enables worker representatives as well as employers to participate in the development of standards and codes of conduct. In fact, the HSC routinely ratifies the standards approved by labor and management negotiators—each of whom has the power of veto.

The American statute, by contrast, placed the authority to promulgate occupational safety and health standards exclusively in the hands of the Department of Labor—though subject to the formal procedures of administrative rule making. By turning over the task of establishing standards to the representatives of the interest groups directly affected by them, the British system reduced the direct role of government in the regulatory process; by establishing a new agency responsible for promulgating workplace health and safety standards, the American approach increased it. While the HSWA "reflects well-known features of British regulatory policy in favoring a decentralized, flexible development of rules, which apply ordinarily to specific employers rather than entire industries," the OSHA "calls for rules to be promulgated by a central government agency to be uniformly applicable to whole classes of employers."[9] And while OSHA has severely restricted the autonomy of its field inspectors, encouraging them to "go by the book," the British system continues to provide inspectors with substantial discretion.

The Occupational Safety and Health Act encouraged penalties both by allowing fines to be imposed through a "civil penalties" procedure that required a relatively low standard of proof and by requiring inspectors to cite employers for every breach of a regulation that they observed (whether or not it actually threatened workers' health or safety). British regulators, now as in the past, rely more on conciliation than on coercion to achieve policy objectives and employ legal action only as a last resort when persuasion proves inadequate. In 1980, 140,000 fines were imposed on coal-mining companies for health and safety violations in the United States, while in Britain there have been no prosecutions for more than two decades. Although the number of prosecutions by the Factory Inspectorate has increased since 1974, British inspectors continue to "prefer advice and persuasion to the big stick of the criminal law." As the 1979–80 Annual Report of the HSE put it: "In raising the level of workplace health and safety awareness, and encouraging a more positive approach to combating hazards, we have proceeded . . . on a basis of agreement."[10] Charles D. Drake and Frank B. Wright add:

> This consensual approach operates at the national level using consultation on regulations and codes of practice and relying on the advice of advisory committees and at the plant level by consulting safety representatives and safety committees. The new summary powers to issue improvement and prohibition notices backed up by the ultimate discretion to prosecute are seen as reserve powers to coerce the recalcitrant.[11]

By contrast, Steven Kelman writes:

> Perhaps the best single word to describe the American enforcement process, in its various aspects, is *formal*. OSHA lays out inspection procedures in great detail. Inspections take the form of searches for violations. They result in formal citations (and penalties) for specific regulatory infractions. These citations are frequently formally contested by employers. If contested, OSHA must formally prove, in a court setting, that the violations did in fact occur. The process of enforcing the rules thus itself goes according to well-defined rules.[12]

The two nations also differ in their approaches to the weighing of costs and benefits in the setting of standards. The British legislation mandates that workers should be protected "so far as is reasonably practicable"—a phrase that represents the rough equivalent to the criterion of "best practicable means" employed by the Alkali Inspectorate in establishing emission requirements. As in the area of pollution control, inspectors, acting within the guidelines established by the working parties established by the HSE, are responsible for balancing what is appropriate on safety grounds against the degree of risk and the cost of prevention. The British system of regulatory decision making obviates the need for a formal system of cost-benefit analysis. Sheila Jasanoff notes:

> Accustomed to negotiating with each other, neither labor nor industry requires the other's demands to be spelled out in monetary terms, and the possibility of bargaining on policy outcomes removes the need for explicit principles of decision. Because government ratifies agreements among the relevant private interests, rather than making choices of its own, there is little reason for regulators to justify policy decisions through economic or other technical arguments. The consultative documents on major regulatory policies often include some discussion of costs and benefits. But the analysis is more qualitative than quantitative, neither pretending to excessive methodological rigor nor serving to justify a particular policy choice.[13]

In the United States, on the other hand, the use of cost-benefit analysis in the making of regulatory decisions has been the subject of considerable controversy. The statute itself is ambiguous: one section appears to encourage the weighing of costs and benefits in formulating specific regulations while another appears to prohibit it. In the one Supreme Court decision that has addressed this issue, the "cotton-dust" case (*American Textile Manufacturers Institute* v. *Donovan*) the Court held that the phrase "the extent feasible" in section 6(b)(5) superseded the "reasonable" requirements of section 3(8). The majority argued that "feasible" meant "capable of being done," and that if Congress had wanted costs to be taken into consideration when standards were formulated, it would have said so in the statute.[14] Whether or not the Court's decision applies solely to those regulations promulgated under rule 6(b)(5) or to all OSHA regulations remains unclear. In the early 1980s, British officials did become more concerned about the cost-effectiveness of particular regulations, and the HSE hired its first economist. But the use of cost-benefit analysis remains far less contentious in Britain than in the United States. Whereas American regulatory officials have come under substantial pressure to establish standards that "guarantee" a safe workplace, the British public appears to accept a certain amount of occupational injury as a necessary concomitant of industrial production.

## VINYL CHLORIDE

The contrasts in the British and American approaches to protecting health and safety in the workplace emerge with particular clarity in the two nations' approaches to the regulation of vinyl chloride (VC), a chemical that is the cornerstone of the plastics industry in both the United States and Western Europe. In January 1974 B. F. Goodrich announced the deaths of three of its workers who had been exposed to vinyl chloride and formally informed the National Institute of Occupational Safety and Health (NIOSHA), OSHA's research arm, that VC appeared to be linked to cancer in humans. Within a relatively short time, Goodrich's finding had become available to government officials, corporate managers, and trade unionists in both Western Europe and Japan. The issue received considerable international media attention and both government and industry throughout the industrialized world found themselves subjected to substantial public pressure to reduce the exposure of workers to what was clearly an extremely hazardous substance.

The first country to act was the United States. On January 30, 1974, OSHA announced in the *Federal Register* a fact-finding hearing on VC to be held the next month. The purpose of the hearing was to determine if OSHA should issue an emergency temporary standard (ETS) immediately to protect workers from "grave danger" or if it should follow its regular rule-making procedures. Industrial spokesmen vigorously argued against an ETS, contending that they had already reduced average exposure to below 50 parts per million (ppm), a level at which no threat to human health had been demonstrated. Union officials, on the other hand, insisted that VC was clearly a human carcinogen and that the government should immediately require companies to eliminate all worker exposure. On April 5 OSHA issued an ETS that specified that no worker could be exposed to more than 50 ppm. A month later OSHA issued its "Proposed Standard for VC," which proposed that VC exposures be set at the "nondetectable level, as determined by a sampling and analytical method capable of detecting VC at concentration levels of one ppm." Companies had to comply "as soon as feasible."

This regulation fell, in the words of one industry official, like a "bombshell." One executive noted: "The standard made a lot of people in the industry furious. I mean mad enough to start fist fights. People said, 'They can't do that to us—we're running a clean operation.' When further OSHA announcements came out, the attitude was, 'Did you see what those bastards did to us today?' " The trade association that represents most major plastics producers in the United States convened a series of special meetings to plan its political and legal strategies. After considerable intra-industry conflict, the producers decided to recommend an average exposure level of 25 ppm, to be effective in October 1974, and a level of 10 ppm to take effect two years later. Industry officials publicly attacked OSHA's proposed standard, calling it "impractical," "unachievable," and "a disaster for industry." Union officials counterattacked: an official of the Oil, Chemical and Atomic Workers Union stated that "workers are tired of being used as guinea pigs." The president of the United Rubber Workers sent a message to President Nixon, urging that the government "stop the cruel and unnecessary killing of our workforce."[15]

In June and July, OSHA held a total of eight days of hearings. The official record exceeded 4,000 pages and included more than 800 oral and written submissions. While industry representatives contended that recent deaths were due to the very high levels of exposure that had prevailed in the industry ten or twenty years earlier, cancer specialists from NIOSHA and the National Cancer Institute testified that no threshold level had been established for human carcinogens. Industry officials claimed that OSHA's standards were not economically feasible, while various union officials and representatives of public interest organizations disputed this claim. In October 1974 OSHA published its final standard: it set "an exposure limit of 1 ppm average over any eight-hour period and a ceiling of 5 ppm average over any period not exceeding five minutes."[16] While labor's response was lukewarm, within two minutes of OSHA's announcement seven firms had filed suits in various federal courts challenging OSHA's ruling. These appeals were unsuccessful and the industry then set about seeking to comply. Within two years most firms were in compliance; the total costs to industry were estimated at between $200 and $280 million. As this cost was substantially less than had been predicted, critics accused the firms of having cried wolf.

The chief inspector of factories in Great Britain was informed of B. F. Goodrich's announcement almost immediately after it was made. Within a week, Imperial Chemical Industries (ICI), the major British chemical firm, had furnished the government, officials of the Trades Union Council (TUC), and its own employees all the information on VC it had available. Following a series of meetings among industry scientists, the TUC's medical adviser, and the senior government officials responsible for occupational health, the two major British chemical producers, British Petroleum Chemicals and ICI, voluntarily agreed on an initial objective of reducing VC levels to below 50 ppm. A few months later the Chemical Industry Association established a special VC Committee to coordinate the technical research efforts of the industry and to work with the VC working group of the HSC. (In fact, the membership of these groups overlapped.)

In the spring of 1974, the Factory Inspectorate, seeking to comply in advance with the provisions of the Health and Safety at Work Act—which was then in its final stages of parliamentary approval—invited industry and labor to form a joint working group to develop an industry code of practice. The group, chaired by the chief inspector of factories, consisted of five labor representatives and an equal number from industry; its staff included a medical statistician, the deputy chief of the Alkali Inspectorate, and representatives of the Department of Health and Social Services. All of its meetings were held in private, and while its members kept their constituencies informed of its work, contacts with the press were extremely limited. In December the committee approved a draft code of practice, which established an "interim hygiene standard," defined as

> a ceiling value of 50 parts per million, that must not be exceeded; the average exposure over the whole shift must not exceed 25 parts per million. These are outside limits and it is further asked that exposure should be brought as near as practicable to zero. This standard, which was to be kept under review by the Working Group, therefore encourages progressive reductions of exposure to the lowest possible levels given present engineering knowledge.[17]

Members of the committee subsequently made a series of visits to VC plants in order to discuss the hazard informally with workers and examine the monitoring and control technology available to industry. These visits served the additional purpose of developing close personal relations among the members of the group. An official of the Transport and General Workers Union noted that while initially both industrialists and labor representatives viewed each other with suspicion, after observing industry efforts to control VC, the participants achieved "a real breakthrough in relations" and got along "famously"; industry members in turn described their trade union counterparts as "level-headed and responsible men."[18]

In May 1976 the group approved a final code of practice. It established a "ceiling value of 30 ppm in a time weighted average of 10 ppm," with the understanding that "whenever practicable exposure should be brought as near as possible to zero concentrations."[19] This code had no legal status: it was simply a voluntary agreement. Even before it was announced, however, average weekly VC levels in British plants had been reduced to somewhere below 5 ppm, and by 1977, plants in Great Britain were maintaining levels between 0.5 and 3.0 ppm. The capital costs of compliance for British industry as a whole were estimated at more than £20 million.

Thus, while the exposure level of workers in the United States may have declined somewhat more rapidly, within three years VC exposure levels were virtually identical in the United States and Great Britain. The ways in which this objective was achieved, however, differed dramatically. The United States established a strict, technology-forcing standard that left no room for variation among producing firms in controlling VC exposure levels; all had to comply with uniform requirements as soon as possible. The British, on the other hand, deliberately set the standard *above* the lowest level possible with available technology, and companies were able to calculate costs and benefits individually. They could decide on a plant-by-plant basis whether further reductions in exposure made good economic sense. As a result, while the effective exposure levels tended to be relatively similar among all plants in the United States, exposure levels in Britain tended to be higher in some plants than in others.

## Evaluating Health and Safety Regulation

As in the case of environmental regulation, Britain's efforts in the area of occupational health and safety have become more controversial over the last decade. The inability of government and industry to provide adequate protection to workers exposed to asbestos, for example, has been persistently criticized. The first British regulations on occupational exposure to asbestos dust were issued in 1933. In 1968, responding to research by the British Occupational Hygiene Society, the maximum occupational exposure was reduced to 2 million fibers per cubic meter. This standard was attacked as "grossly inadequate," however, and in 1982 the Health and Safety Commission acted to reduce it by half. The asbestos industry, which was already operating at the 1-fiber standard level, vigorously opposed the government's efforts to reduce it to 0.5 fiber. It spent £500,000 on a public relations campaign designed to "influence reports, legislation and government regulations on new safety standards."[20] A report issued by the British Society for Social Responsibility in Science countered by predicting that 500,000 workers might die from asbestos-related diseases over the next thirty years.

In the late 1970s the National Union of Agricultural and Allied Workers challenged the government's unwillingness to ban the use of the pesticide 2,4,5-T, "claiming that a terrifying trend of abortions, miscarriages, and infant deformities in the families of agricultural workers can be related to [its] use."[21] The government, however, agreed only to restrict its use. A resolution passed at the 1980 TUC Annual Conference termed the voluntary registration scheme a failure and urged that the control of pesticides be removed from the Advisory Committee on Pesticides and placed in the hands of the HSC.

In 1982 W. G. Carson published *The Other Price of Britain's Oil,* which sharply criticized the safety standards being applied to workers on oil-drilling equipment in the North Sea. While acknowledging that the accident rate from the British sector of the North Sea was lower than that for the Norwegian sector, Carson contended that a significant number of accidents to British workers could easily have been avoided had safety considerations been accorded a higher priority by both the Department of Energy and the oil industry.[22]

In comparison with the turmoil generated by health and safety legislation in the United States, however, the controversy in Britain has been relatively modest. In the United States, dissatisfaction with occupational health and safety regulation has been pervasive in the ranks of both labor and industry; indeed, no other regulatory agency has been so universally unpopular as OSHA. Industry has accused it of being obsessed with enforcing detailed rules that often bear no relationship to actual hazards, overeager to prosecute, indifferent to the costs of compliance, and contemptuous of industry expense and expertise; indeed, critics of OSHA have argued that in spite of its zealousness, it has actually done nothing to improve occupational safety. Trade unions, on the other hand, have accused OSHA of being far too lax in both setting and enforcing standards.

As in the case of pollution controls, measuring the impact of regulation on health and safety at the workplace is extremely difficult. Workers' health and safety are affected much more by their ages, their turnover rates, and the type of production than by government regulation. On balance, the British appear to have been slightly more effective in reducing employee injuries. Between 1974 and 1980 the incidence rate of fatal injuries in Great Britain fell between 4.5 per 100,000 workers at risk to 2.7 (from 16.0 to 13.0 in construction). The incidence rate of reportable accidents per 100,000 workers at risk fell from 3,570 in 1976 to 2,860 in 1980 (from 3,410 to 3,000 in construction). On the other hand, the consensus of those who have analyzed the data is that during OSHA's first decade the agency had a negligible effect on the occupational injury rate in the United States, though since 1980 the rate has fallen.[23] While the Mine Safety Program did bring about a significant decline in coal mine fatalities in the United States, the American fatality rate per mine-worker-hour is currently three times higher than the British.

Regulatory officials in both societies have placed less emphasis on the more difficult challenge of protecting the health of workers, but the efforts they have made have been roughly comparable. While the two nations currently have comparable standards for workplace exposure, British authorities identified asbestos as a hazard thirty years before the danger was recognized in the United States: it was not until 1964 that the American asbestos industry agreed to place labels on its products. The British also adopted a standard of 2 million fibers per cubic meter for workplace exposure four years earlier than did the United States. On the other hand, American officials have placed greater restrictions on the use of pesticides, thus providing more protection to agricultural workers. Because the resources available for scientific research on new workplace hazards are much greater in the United States, American authorities now appear to be in a better position to identify new sources of occupational disease at the workplace, although, as we have seen in regard to vinyl chloride, the results of such research are readily made available to regulatory authorities in Britain. Since, however, fatalities due to exposure to sources of occupational illness may not appear for many years, it may be some time before we can fully access the relative effectiveness of British and American regulatory efforts in this area. (As things now stand, the much more important role played by private lawsuits in the area of occupational illness in the United States may, in the long run, have a greater deterrent effect on corporate conduct than either nation's formal system of regulation.)

As in the case of environmental protection, one reason that the stricter American occupational safety and health standards have not brought about a more rapid reduction in accident and disease rates has been the difficulties the government has faced in implementing them. Largely because of industry opposition, OSHA was able to issue only four major health standards during its first six years. While the number of both health and safety standards issued increased somewhat between 1977 and 1980, so did industry resistance to their enforcement: in 1980, approximately 25 percent of all violations were contested by industry. Graham Wilson argues that OSHA might be able to issue regulations more speedily if it adopted an approach less likely to provoke opposition from industry. He asks:

> Might not a slightly less than perfect regulation which industry might accept be preferable to a perfect regulation which, like OSHA's benzene regulation, was invalidated after five years work, leaving the agency with nothing? As is often the case, a decent argument can be made for accepting compromise rather than defeat.[24]

These comparisons of British and American practices and policies in regard to the protection of workers from disease and injury are particularly significant because the political and organizational contexts of environmental protection and occupational health and safety policy differ so substantially in the two countries. The American public, on the whole, appears to have been more preoccupied with environmental regulation than the British. In addition, in comparison with their counterparts in the United States, British environmental organizations have fewer legal and organizational resources with which to participate in the policy process, particularly in areas that are highly technical.

These contrasts are much less striking in the area of occupational health and safety. Unlike British environmental organizations, the British trade union movement is relatively well staffed and funded. Not only is a far larger proportion of industrial workers unionized in Britain than in the United States, but those workers enjoy considerably more access to the regulatory process. While American trade unions function primarily as litigators and lobbyists, British union officials fully participate in the actual making of the occupational health and safety regulations that fall under the jurisdiction of the HSE. Yet despite these differences, both the contrasts and the similarities we have observed in the environmental regulations of the two countries can also be found in the area of occupational health and safety regulation. And as both the vinyl chloride case and our comparative accident data suggest, the more cooperative British approach to compliance has proved at least as effective as the more adversarial enforcement strategy adopted by officials in the United States, if not more so. It has, however, produced far less political conflict between industry and government.

### Chemical Regulation

These differences in occupational health and safety regulation in Great Britain and the United States extend to the more general area of health and safety regulation. An exhaustive study of chemical regulation and cancer in the United States, Great Britain, France, and the Federal Republic of Germany concludes that in virtually every case, U.S. standards tend to be relatively specific and detailed, while British rules tend to be much more flexible and informal. Thus while the United States makes extensive use of specific tolerance standards, "with equal regularity Britain avoids obligatory, legally enforceable controls of any type, except in the case of food additives and a few other specialized instances" (some of which were designed to conform with EEC directives).[25] And when the British do prescribe exposure limits, they generally take the form of recommendations rather than requirements.

> In the view of British public authorities, their non-statutory approach to the control of pesticides and workplace chemical hazards succeeds because of a high degree of compliance with voluntary standards on the part of industry. In the United States, in contrast, it is traditionally assumed that the behavior of those regulated requires close scrutiny under threat of punitive sanctions.[26]

Not surprisingly, British industry has generally been quite satisfied with its government's approach to the regulation of chemicals. By assessing and controlling chemical hazards substance by substance and by tailoring test requirements to specific chemicals, industry avoids the need for unnecessary and costly testing of new substances—frequently cited as a major bar to innovation in the United States. In contrast to the United States, which has devised highly specific regulations governing substances suspected of causing cancer—the most well known is the Delaney Amendment, which requires the Food and Drug Administration (FDA) to ban any food additive suspected of causing cancer—Britain has tended to subsume the regulation of carcinogens within its existing regulatory framework. And whereas American regulatory officials have on occasion banned particular substances or proposed drastic reductions in their use, the British prefer to cut back production gradually and to introduce restrictions on use. A comprehensive cross-national study of chemical regulation concludes:

> Managers of individual firms and officials at the Chemical Industries Association, the industry's trade association, enjoy close, even cozy relations with civil servants at the . . . Health and Safety Executive and the Department of the Environment. Informality is the way of doing business in Britain, founded on a spirit of trust between industry and government that permits the tackling of tough policy problems without public battles. . . . In sum, as one industry spokesman put it, if British chemicals must abide some form of government intervention for regulatory purposes, they could hardly design something superior to the existing approach.[27]

When the British system for the control of hazardous substances is understood in its broadest terms, the tripartite arrangement for controlling exposure to toxic substances in the workplace established under the auspices of the HSE is seen to be highly unusual. Two British scholars have surveyed the nature of the advisory bodies established to make decisions with respect to the regulation of dangerous chemicals in the workplace and in other policy areas: foods and food additives, medicines, pesticides, tobacco, consumer products. In every case but the first, the governmental body charged with formulating regulatory policy consists exclusively of "technically trained individuals who are selected not as representatives of any particular economic interest or political viewpoint but rather as independent experts who are able to evaluate the scientific evidence." Moreover, none of the bodies publishes transcripts of its deliberations or publicizes its agenda or minutes, and "each advisory body enjoys a high degree of discretion in selecting the form of recommendations which it deems suitable to specific circumstances."[28]

While some bodies, such as the Food Additives and Contaminants Committee, tend to follow relatively rigid guidelines, in general "standards are [not] rigidly enforced but are weighed against economic, industrial, or geographic conditions." Each advisory body tends to make a relatively sharp distinction between "insiders," who are able to participate fully in its deliberations, and "outsiders," members of the general public, whose access to the policy process is virtually nonexistent. Government officials justify this arrangement on the grounds that "it encourages . . . informal co-ordination and flexibility of approach in a manner which a more open and adversarial system (such as that found in the

United States) would not be able to achieve."[29] In this sense, the distinction between the decision-making procedures of these bodies and that of the Health and Safety Executive is roughly analogous to that between the Alkali Inspectorate and the British system of land-use planning.

Do the advantages that industry enjoys because of its close ties to the scientific community and the limited ability of nonindustry interests to challenge regulatory policies publicly expose British workers and consumers to unnecessary hazards? Certainly "the fortunes of the chemical industry are more favorably balanced against the need to protect health and the environment in Britain than elsewhere." Yet at the same time, when one turns from the way in which policy is made and implemented to specific policy outcomes, one finds that British and American regulatory policies are remarkably similar. Thus the use of all fourteen substances identified as carcinogenic by the highly respected International Agency for Research on Cancer has been restricted by regulatory authorities in both countries; in most cases these restrictions are identical. Despite the initiative shown by American regulatory officials and the stricter requirements of American law, the United States "has regulated few suspected carcinogens that do not also appear on the lists of controlled substances in Europe."[30] While the United States has moved somewhat more aggressively to restrict the use of food additives and some pesticides, the British have tended to place tighter controls on occupational carcinogens.

## Drug Regulation

The dimension of British health and safety regulation that has attracted the greatest interest in the United States is that of prescription drugs. The inspection of the quality of medicinal products in England dates from the reign of Henry VIII. In 1858 Parliament established quality-control standards for medicines and in 1875 legislation was enacted fixing penalties for the adulteration of drugs. The Therapeutic Substances Act (1925) provided for the licensing of medicines and established standards for the manufacture or import of substances "the purity or potency of which cannot be adequately tested by chemical means."[31] Following the thalidomide disaster in 1963, a Committee on Safety of Drugs (CSD) was established by the Ministry of Health after consultation with both the medical and pharmaceutical professions and the pharmaceutical industry. The committee established a voluntary regulation system similar to that adopted a few years earlier to regulate the production and use of pesticides. Under this system, approximately six hundred companies, most of which belonged to either the Proprietary Association of Great Britain or the Association of the British Pharmaceutical Industry, agreed to submit their products for scrutiny before conducting clinical trials or marketing; a system was also established to monitor approved drugs for adverse effects.

This scheme of self-regulation was subsequently changed. In 1968, faced with evidence that many British companies were not participating in the voluntary regulation scheme, Parliament enacted the Medicines Act, which established a mandatory licensing system to be administered by the Department of Health and Social Security. A Medicines Commission, composed primarily of professional experts, was formed to advise the minister on its implementation. Of several expert committees that were formed, the two most important were the Committee on Safety of Medicines, which advises the licensing authority on questions of the safety, quality, and efficiency of medicines for human use, and the Committee on the Review of Medicines, which reviews the safety, quality, and efficiency of existing products on the British market. Despite this shift from a voluntary to a statutory system of regulation, the pattern of industry–government cooperation established earlier in the decade has persisted.

> The Committee on Safety of Drugs and the voluntary system did set the pattern of informality of approach and good relationships with the industry that the Committee on Safety of Medicines and the Licensing Authority have striven to maintain. This "approachability" and flexibility of the British licensing system, which is much appreciated both by industry and by the medical profession and is admired throughout the world, is largely due to the attitudes engendered by the Committee on Safety of Drugs during its period of operation from 1964 to September 1971.[32]

Ironically, while the British system of drug regulation has been frequently cited by both academic and industry critics of American regulatory practices as a model for the United States, in fact the British legislation of 1968 has been subject to many of the criticisms leveled at the 1962 amendments to the Food and Drug Act. A survey of the British pharmaceutical industry found that the shift from a voluntary to a legally mandated licensing system

> had *not* resulted in a substantial improvement in patent safety. Firms were ... unanimous that the Act has had *harmful* effects through delays in the introduction of new drugs.... The industry claimed that the 1968 Act has had a major adverse effect on its R and D [research and development]

> activity. The result is longer development, less innovation, less basic research, and more clinical R and D being undertaken abroad.[33]

These criticisms are similar to those made of the FDA's policies since the passage of the Food and Drug Act Amendments of 1962.

Nonetheless, substantial differences remain between the two nations' approaches to drug regulation—differences that parallel those we have observed in other areas of regulation.[34] In 1981 the average approval time for a new drug in Great Britain was thirteen months; in the United States it was twenty-three months. The United States figure actually represented a considerable improvement over 1979, when the average delay was thirty-five months; nonetheless, the average gap (dubbed the "drug lag") between the approval of a drug in Britain and its approval in the United States has remained constant at fourteen months. During the 1970s, nine of the twelve most important new drugs introduced in the United States were available an average of two years earlier to patients in Britain. According to one drug company, Eli Lilly, the seven best-selling drugs it introduced between 1970 and 1979 were approved for use on average twenty-three months earlier in Great Britain. The world's best-selling drug, Tagamet, an anti-ulcer medication developed by Smith-Kline Corporation, was approved by British authorities in two months; the FDA took thirteen months to process the application.

Moreover, the FDA's procedures for approving new drugs are far more burdensome than those of the Committee on Safety of Drugs. Thus while the FDA requires that its permission be obtained before even the first phase of clinical testing begins, British regulatory authorities require only that they be notified. The FDA has far stricter standards as to what constitutes an adequate and well-controlled trial than does the CSD. It also requires considerably more documentation: the application for the approval of Tagamet in the United States consisted of 160 volumes, whereas in Britain only 12 were required. On the other hand, the British have a far more extensive system for monitoring adverse reactions following approval than do the Americans, and have not hesitated to suspend drug licenses when ill effects have become evident.

There is no evidence that the British system of drug regulation provides less protection for the public than the far stricter American system: dangerous drugs, such as Oraflex, continue to be approved for use occasionally in both countries. On balance the American public appears to be worse off, since it also suffers from the FDA's delays in approving the use of beneficial new drugs. According to one study,

> of the 82 drugs that became mutually available, 14 were introduced in the same year in both countries, 43 were introduced in Britain first, and 25

> were introduced in the United States first. Britain enjoyed 120 drug years of prior availability, while the United States only enjoyed 59 drug years of prior availability. Of the other 98 drugs that were not mutually available, 73 were exclusively available in Britain, while 21 were exclusively available in the United States.... Many of the drugs exclusively available in Great Britain had become the drugs of choice in British teaching hospitals.
>
> Significantly, of those drugs exclusively available in Great Britain, only two were eventually withdrawn from use because of toxicity, and these contributed negligibly to total drug toxicity in Great Britain during the study period.[35]

The way the two nations have chosen to address the risks associated with the licensing of ethical drugs closely parallels their approach to regulating potential hazards in other dimensions of health and safety. While the British system, by expediting the approval of new drugs, makes it more likely that its citizens will be harmed by too little regulation, it minimizes the likelihood that restrictions will be imposed that do not contribute to the health and safety of the public. The American strategy produces precisely the opposite result: it makes it less likely that its citizens will be exposed to hazards that could have been avoided through stricter controls but more likely that costs will be imposed on industry that produce no discernible benefits to the public. Much the same could be said of the two nations' approaches to risk assessment in the area of environmental regulation. Thus in all three areas—occupational health and safety, environmental protection, and consumer protection—the approach of American authorities to risk assessment has been more conservative; British officials consistently appear willing to take somewhat greater risks. Yet at the end of the day, as the English say, the American public has received no better protection; indeed, in the case of drug regulation it actually appears to be somewhat worse off.

These comparisons of health and safety regulation in areas other than environmental protection also suggest that the pattern of ownership is *not* a critical factor in accounting for the differing patterns of government intervention in the two societies. For while some major industrial sources of air and water pollution in Great Britain—most notably automobiles, steel, and utilities—are either wholly or predominantly owned by the British government, the industries whose regulation we have reviewed in detail are not. Asbestos, vinyl chloride, pesticides, chemicals, medicines, food and food additives are all exclusively manufactured by privately owned firms in both countries. And yet the differences we have observed in the area of pollution control persist. Moreover, if the pattern of ownership were of political significance, one would expect the dynamics of regulation to have been affected by the significant expansion of the British public sector over the last half-century. But this has not been the case: the British approach to social regulation has remained remarkably stable over the last century. On the other hand, the relationship between publicly owned utilities such as TVA and regulatory authorities in the United States has been no less contentious than that between investor-owned utilities and the EPA.

## Consumer Protection

Like the United States, Britain has, over the last two decades, enacted several new laws designed to increase the amount of protection available to consumers.[36] The Consumer Protection Act (1961), the Weights and Measures Act (1963), the Trade Descriptions Act (1968), the Fair Trading Act (1973), and the Consumer Credit Act (1974) regulate both product description and product quality and are roughly analogous in scope to statutes enacted over a similar time period by the United States government. They differ, however, in two important respects. First, while U.S. consumer protection laws tend to deal with either specific kinds of products (i.e., automobiles) or hazards (i.e., radiation), Britain's laws have been much more general. As a result, Congress has enacted far more consumer legislation than Parliament.

Second, a relatively larger proportion of consumer protection legislation is administered by the national government in the United States than in Britain, although the role of the states in this area remains extremely important. In Britain the enforcement of consumer protection legislation has remained almost exclusively in the hands of local authorities. The two most notable exceptions are drugs, which are regulated by the Department of Health and Social Security, and agricultural products, which are under the jurisdiction of the Ministry of Agriculture, Fisheries, and Food. In 1973 an Office of Fair Trading was established to encourage competition and protect consumers, but in the main the Department of Prices and Consumer Protection was given little direct regulatory authority; its responsibilities lay primarily in supervising and coordinating the efforts of local consumer agencies. (It was subsequently abolished in 1979.) Unlike the United States' new consumer protection laws, then, Britain's have not been administered by newly established regulatory bodies; rather, in most cases the scope of the authority of existing regulatory units has simply been expanded.

During the 1960s and 1970s many American regulatory officials at the federal level came to identify their mission as that of protecting the interests of consumers vis-à-vis business. Indeed, several officials appointed to regulatory agencies during the Carter administration had previously been active as consumer lobbyists. In Britain, however, the officials of consumer agencies continue to define their roles as those not of advocates but of impartial arbiters. One British enforcement official noted:

> We don't see ourselves as the British version of Nader's Raiders. But we do see ourselves as standard bearers—trading standard bearers—committed to the continuing task of ensuring those standards are respected and neither flouted nor eroded. Unlike Mr. Nader we don't see ourselves wholly involved in taking sides in a fight. We know from experience that we are not best employed fighting battles for or with consumers.[37]

On the whole, consumer agencies in Britain enjoy extremely good relationships with the companies whose conduct they are responsible for regulating: "enforcement officials see themselves not as policemen whose sole duty is to detect offences, but as officials who must prevent them before they occur."[38] Moreover, they appear to have a higher opinion of the integrity of the companies with which they interact than at least some of their counterparts in the United States.

As in the case of pollution control, the public portrayal of business as basically law-abiding and well intentioned is critical to the enforcement strategy of British consumer protection agencies.

> If business were publicly labelled as unscrupulous or exploitative, its resistance to regulation would increase. By emphasizing that business is mainly law-abiding, the state and its enforcement agencies can reduce the fear of regulation and maximize the potentiality of obtaining compliance with their designs through persuasion.[39]

In America, by contrast, the enforcement of many consumer protection laws became more adversarial during the 1970s, particularly at the federal level, with government officials frequently publicly chastising companies for their insensitivity to the welfare of consumers and ordering a large number of product recalls. American executives have a long litany of cases of "unreasonable" enforcement on the part of such agencies as the Federal Trade Commission, the National Highway Traffic Safety Administration, the Consumer Products Safety Commission, and the Food and Drug Administration.[40] In Britain, industry and government have experienced far less conflict in this policy area. Unfortunately, we lack any data as to the relative effectiveness of the two nations' regulatory styles.

Economic Regulation

There is little point in comparing the patterns of economic regulation in the United States and Great Britain since their institutional structures vary so enormously: industries that are regulated in the United States, such as airlines, telephone and telegraph companies, railroads, and utilities, have generally been publicly owned in Britain. This is not the case, however, in three important sectors: banking, securities, and insurance. With the exception of the Bank of England, which does not engage in direct commercial lending, all financial institutions are privately owned in both countries. How does each country go about the regulation of these institutions? The two nations' approaches to the regulation of these sectors closely parallel the patterns we have observed in the areas of health and safety regulation and consumer protection. While the British make extensive use of self-regulation and place considerable reliance on informal social controls, the American approach is rule-oriented and legalistic. On balance, the amalgam of British financial institutions that constitute "the City" enjoy less nonstatutory regulation than any other major financial center; American financial institutions and markets are more strictly regulated than those in any other capitalist country.[41]

The American securities industry is formally regulated by the Securities and Exchange Commission (SEC), established in 1934 in response to the scandals associated with the stock market collapse of 1929. While relations between the SEC and the industry it regulates have in general been more cooperative than has been the case with such social regulatory agencies as the EPA, OSHA, and the FDA, its basic approach to regulation is similar: it promulgates a large number of detailed and specific rules, issued after a set of formal hearings, and frequently resorts to prosecution when these rules have been violated. While Congress has tended to place fewer restrictions on the SEC than on many other regulatory agencies, the agency's decisions are subject to judicial scrutiny. Each of the major stock exchanges has its own governing committee that establishes rules for the firms under its jurisdiction, but ultimate authority rests with the SEC.

Britain has enacted a number of statutes establishing regulations for publicly held companies. These regulations are extremely detailed and roughly analogous to those promulgated by the Securities and Exchange Commission. The first British Company Act was enacted in 1948 and the most recent in 1981; the latter implemented the requirements of the European Community's fourth directive on company accounting and reports: its "provisions on the form and content of the accounts and the notes to the accounts represent some of the most detailed and prescriptive requirements in British common law."[42] However, the British government plays virtually no formal role in the regulation of securities markets themselves. Whatever regulation exists takes place primarily under the auspices of two private organizations: the Council for the Securities Industry, established in 1978, and the Panel on Takeovers. The former is composed of a number of powerful bodies within the City, including the Stock Exchange Council, which oversees listed and unlisted companies and their dealings on the exchanges, while the latter is responsible for enforcing a voluntary code on takeovers and for policing the stock market on a deal-by-deal basis. Neither body enjoys any legal authority. There does exist a Prevention of Fraud (Investments) Act and the Department of Trade did issue new regulations following the folding of a major licensed securities dealer in 1981, but their scope is limited.

Banks in the United States operate under a complex set of federal and state regulations, the most important of which originated in the 1930s. Until the late 1970s, however, banks in Britain were free from statutory controls. In 1979, Parliament, partially in response to an EEC directive requiring each member state to establish a uniform system of banking regulation, enacted the 1979 Banking Act. This law, however, established only a deposit protection scheme and a two-tier structure of recognized banks and licensed deposit-taking institutions. All other regulatory functions are still performed by the Bank of England, which continues to be responsible for approving applications for new banks, judging them on such vague criteria as the applicants' reputations and standing in the financial market. The Bank also monitors the activities of banks by examining their quarterly returns and conducting regular interviews with senior managers. Instead of applying fixed rules, it attempts to influence key individuals. One observer notes: "Frequent discussion between senior management of banks and senior officials of the Bank of England are more conducive to the maintenance of good banking practices than the technique adopted in many other countries of sending in teams of inspectors to examine the banks' books." The style of these discussions, which in the Bank's words are "the cornerstone of the . . . system of supervision," is "designed to recreate the intimacy and informality of the old approach to regulation."[43]

The two nations' approaches to insurance regulation follow similar patterns. In the United States, the industry is supervised by regulatory commissions established by the various states. While theoretically the industry in Britain is supervised by the Department of Trade, in practice this extremely important British industry is regulated by a body known as the Council of Lloyd's. Most of its twenty-eight members are drawn from the industry itself. Following scandals in 1979 and 1980, Parliament enacted the Lloyd's Act, which made it considerably easier for the council to exercise disciplinary powers over its member companies. And in 1982, following another series of scandals—the most dramatic of which involved an American company—that "raised doubts about Lloyd's ability to regulate questionable transactions by its brokers and underwriter members," Parliament approved additional controls.[44] Under the terms of the statute enacted in 1982, brokers who do business with Lloyd's are forbidden to own a controlling interest in a Lloyd's underwriter; this separation must be complete by 1987. In addition, the public will now be provided with substantially more information about the financial activities of Lloyd's brokers. Lloyd's itself, however, will continue to enjoy substantial independence from direct government supervision.

As in the case of ethical drugs, the regulation of British financial institutions and markets has become more detailed and legalistic over the last decade. To a significant extent Britain has moved from a system based on self-regulation to one that combines self-regulation with a more formal system of statutory controls. Indeed, no area of British regulation of industry has been in such a state of flux since the late 1970s. While in the past the British sense of "fair play" made a system of regulation essentially based on clubbishness a viable one, its effectiveness has been increasingly called in question, in part as a result of the growing number of non-British firms with offices in London. Yet while the gap between British and American standards and policies has narrowed, substantial differences persist. In general, American regulations are stricter, are more formal, and provide much less scope for self-regulation. Britain places fewer restrictions on insider trading than does the United States, for example, and while the Securities and Exchange Commission closely monitors—and on occasion has overruled—the accounting standards established by the Financial Accounting Standards Board, in Britain the Accounting Standards Committee, composed of Britain's six accounting bodies, both determines standards and is responsible for enforcing them. In the related area of antitrust policy, Britain's Monopolies and Mergers Commission approaches each takeover or merger on an ad hoc basis. In America, in contrast, antitrust policy proceeds through the application of explicit standards whose interpretation is then subject to exhaustive judicial review.

The far stricter legal controls exercised by American regulatory authorities appear to have been no more successful in preventing periodic scandal and frauds; such episodes continue to occur in both societies. On balance, British holders of insurance policies, bank depositors, and investors appear to be no better or worse protected than their counterparts in the United States.

This brief survey of economic regulation also reinforces the argument that state ownership in Great Britain is not a critical factor in accounting for the differences in the regulatory policies pursued in the two countries. In these three sectors, the patterns of ownership in the two societies are identical, yet the differences in the styles of regulation that we have observed in other areas persist. It also suggests the limits of purely economic factors in accounting for the differences in the patterns of regulation in the two societies. For while many British industries, public as well as private, that directly affect public health and safety have certainly been less profitable than their counterparts in the United States, British financial institutions have been, and remain, extremely competitive in the world marketplace. (The same can be said of the British pharmaceutical industry.) And yet the British and American regulatory policies in these sectors show the familiar contrasting patterns.

## Conclusions

In sum, each nation does exhibit a distinctive regulatory style, one that transcends any given policy area. The British government regulates the impact of business decisions on the environment in much the same way it attempts to control a variety of dimensions of corporate conduct. Regulation of industry tends to be more informal in Britain than in the United States, more flexible, and more private. Regulatory officials are able to exercise considerable discretion and tend to make policy on a case-by-case basis rather than through the application of general rules and standards. Little use is made of prosecution and much reliance is placed on securing compliance through informal mechanisms of social control, including, in many instances, self-regulation. Regulatory officials tend to have close working relationships with the members of those industries whose conduct they are responsible for supervising; the latter are closely consulted before rules are issued and regulations enforced. In America, on the other hand, regulation tends to be highly formalized: it proceeds on the basis of the application of broad rules that are made and enforced in accordance with strictly defined procedures. The entire regulatory process is subject to close scrutiny by the courts, the legislature, and the public as a whole. Fines are levied for violations relatively frequently and little reliance is placed on industry self-regulation.

Participation by nonindustry constituencies does vary widely across regulatory areas in both countries. The Alkali Inspectorate and the system of land-use planning, for example, represent virtually polar opposites in terms of the opportunities they extend for participation by nonindustry constituencies. On the other hand, the American system of regulation does not invariably provide more opportunity for nonindustry participation than the British: trade unions are more directly involved in the making and enforcement of occupational health and safety regulation in Britain than in the United States. The critical distinction between the British and American approaches to regulation has to do with the terms in which nonindustry participation takes place.

In America there are numerous points of access to the regulatory process: interest groups can lobby Congress, participate in agency rule-making procedures, attempt to influence the regulatory review process at the White House, and challenge particular regulations in the courts. If state and local governmental units are also affected, the opportunities for intervention are multiplied still further. In Britain the number of forums at which the public can intervene in the regulatory process is more limited; to the extent that public participation takes place at all, it is generally restricted to a handful of arenas. An important reason why government regulation of industry has created so much less overt political conflict in Britain than in the United States is that the relationship among the interest groups involved in particular policy areas tends to be relatively structured. This is clearly true in the case of industry, whose interaction with government officials usually takes place through trade associations, though large companies generally negotiate with the government directly. But to a significant extent it is also true of nonbusiness constituencies: both by controlling access and by using private organizations to implement various regulatory policies, the British government has played an important role in shaping both the number and scope of the political pressures placed upon it. Alternatively, it is in part the relative openness of the American regulatory process that makes it so contentious.

There are exceptions to each of these generalizations. The making of British land-use policies takes place in highly visible forums and the procedures governing the "large public inquiries" are highly legalistic. In addition, over the last decade the regulation of both ethical drugs and the City has come to resemble more closely the more formal approach adopted earlier by the United States. Nor are the politics of British regulation invariably less contentious: the four case studies of British environmental policy described in Chapter 1 demonstrate the extent to which disputes over various policies have spilled over from the forums originally established to contain them and become highly public, involving both Parliament and the cabinet. Yet if one compares policies in any particular area of regulation, significant differences remain. Particularly over the last fifteen years, a significantly larger proportion of regulatory policies have been formulated and implemented through relatively informal and private negotiations between regulatory officials and interest groups in Britain than in the United States. On the whole, the regulatory process has been far more public—and therefore more politicized—in the United States than in Great Britain. It has not, however, been notably more effective.

This conclusion does not, however, unequivocally support the position of political scientists who contend that policy process and outcomes are primarily the result of factors peculiar to the countries where they are developed, that is, that "politics matters." For the agenda of regulatory policy itself does appear to be shaped by socioeconomic factors that transcend any particular political system. It is not merely that the issues of environmental quality and of worker and consumer health and safety in general have become more salient in both Great Britain and the United States over the last two decades. Rather the specific ways in which these issues have been defined are strikingly similar. Consider the following examples of issue convergence: the construction and expansion of airport facilities, highways, and offshore energy facilities (i.e., LNG), the safety of nuclear power (Windscale and Three Mile Island), the health impact of exhaust from the internal combustion engine (i.e., lead), the effects of pesticide use on the health of both birds and agricultural workers (DDT, dieldrin, 2,4,5-T), the environmental impact of energy production (the North Sea and the North Slope), the pollution produced by the burning of coal in power plants (acid rain), offshore oil spills (Santa Barbara and *Torrey Canyon*), the disposal of toxic wastes (Love Canal, Nuneaton), health hazards to workers (asbestos and vinyl chloride), the safety of ethical drugs (thalidomide, Oraflex).

This convergence of regulatory agendas appears to be due to two factors. One is the similar levels of industrial development in the two nations.[45] The economies of both Britain and the United States are dominated by many of the same industries—indeed, in many cases, the very same multinational companies. Obviously these firms—and their products—produce many of the same externalities. Moreover, because significant segments of their populations are both affluent and highly educated, they have similar expectations: they are in a position to demand—and to pay for—less hazardous working conditions, safer products, and a more scenic and healthful physical environment. Industrial growth in a democratic society thus simultaneously creates environmental problems and places pressures on policy makers to ameliorate them. It is certainly not coincidental that public interest in these policy areas increased in both countries in the late 1960s and early 1970s, following two decades of relatively sustained and rapid economic growth.

There is a second explanation for the convergence of the regulatory agendas of Great Britain and the United States in the postwar period: international communication. The media have played an important role in disseminating information about various regulatory issues to interested citizens on both sides of the Atlantic. The London "killer fog" of 1952, the blowout at Santa Barbara in 1966, the wreck of the *Torrey Canyon* in 1965, the publication of *Silent Spring* in 1962, Love Canal in 1977—all received considerable press coverage in both countries. Policy makers and scientists have also communicated extensively: they attend the same conferences, read the same journals, and regularly exchange technical information. While on occasion scientists in Great Britain and the United States disagree about the hazards associated with particular products, chemicals, or technologies, these differences are far outweighed by their areas of agreement. This scientific consensus has played an important role in shaping the regulatory agendas of both nations. As a result, whenever one nation has identified a particular product, chemical, or production process as hazardous, officials on the other side of the Atlantic invariably find themselves under pressure from both activists and scientists in their own country to do likewise.

Since the early 1970s, activists in both countries have developed increasingly close ties: both Greenpeace and Friends of the Earth have British and American chapters, and Ralph Nader provided some of the initial funding for the investigatory journalism of the *Social Audit*. The German Marshall Fund regularly sends American environmentalists to European countries, including Britain. British environmental organizations, with fewer resources and with less access to government documents, have come to rely on their counterparts in the United States for information, and so raise in Britain many of the issues that have recently appeared on the political agenda in the United States.

Why do regulatory outcomes appear relatively similar in the two countries? Why have they been only marginally affected by the substantial differences in the ways in which policies have been made and enforced? One reason is that policy makers in both capitalist democracies operate under a similar set of constraints. For while economic growth both creates externalities and provides the available resources to ameliorate them, it also constrains the amount of resources that can be committed to such efforts. Obviously, national priorities do differ somewhat and there can be legitimate disagreements about what a nation or a particular industry, firm, or plant can "afford." But in the long run, the severity of enforcement is strongly influenced by the interests of policy makers, industrial workers, and the public as a whole in keeping their nation's industries internationally competitive. Again, it is not coincidental that enforcement efforts in both nations slackened somewhat following the increase in oil prices in late 1973. Moreover, as I have previously argued, regulation is only one factor among many that affect either environmental quality or public health and safety. To the extent that the actual quality of the environment varies in Great Britain and the United States, the difference appears to be due less to their systems of regulation than to geographical conditions and industrial and technical factors.

Yet at the same time, the ways in which regulatory decisions are made vary substantially in Great Britain and the United States. In this context, the importance of each nation's political system remains decisive: these are distinctive national styles of regulation. Compared to both the regulatory agenda and regulatory outcomes, the way in which each political system has gone about making and implementing regulatory controls remains highly distinctive. The latter dimension appears to have been much less affected by technological or socioeconomic factors than the former two. The evidence presented in these two chapters does not of course resolve the debate over the relative importance of political and structural factors in shaping public policies across national boundaries. Their conclusion is valid only for the two countries and the limited numbers of issues they have addressed. At the same time, the body of scholarly literature on this subject does suggest that these generalizations can be applied to other industrialized democracies as well.

Lennart Lundquist's *Hare and the Tortoise* compares the regulation of air pollution in the United States and Sweden during the 1960s and 1970s.[46] In two critical respects, Swedish and British public policies in this area are roughly comparable: both nations have placed primary emphasis on the reduction of pollution from stationary sources and both have tailored their regulatory requirements to the capacity of industry to comply with them. When the number of miles traveled is taken into consideration, automobile emissions did decline more rapidly in the United States than in Sweden. Because the Swedes made more progress in reducing pollution from stationary sources, however, the overall levels of air pollution in the two countries declined to a virtually identical degree: approximately 8 percent in Sweden and 10 percent in the United States. This similarity in regulatory outcomes is particularly striking when one reflects that Sweden is one of the most environmentally conscious nations in Europe. Moreover, the control of air pollution produced far less conflict there than in the United States.

In 1982 an exhaustive and comprehensive cross-national study of environmental regulation was completed. Conducted under the auspices of the International Institute for Environment and Society in Berlin, it examined the implementation of controls over the emissions of sulfur dioxide in ten Western European countries. The authors of the study found that there was no systematic relationship between the formal regulatory system adopted by each country and its actual level of sulfur dioxide emissions; in fact, the levels of sulfur dioxide emissions actually varied more *within* each country than among countries. They found no relationship between the amount of public participation in the regulatory process permitted in each country and the stringency of the permits issued by its regulatory authorities. The project's directors conclude:

> The output analysis meticulously carried out in . . . selected [regions] . . . did not reveal any significant differences with regard to the environmental substance of the consents between those countries with a more open enforcement process (e.g., FRG, Belgium, France, and the Netherlands) and those with closed administrative procedures; i.e., those without institutionalized inclusion of members of the affected public (e.g., Italy, Switzerland, and the United Kingdom).[47]

The conclusions of both these studies are similar to those reached by three other cross-national studies of social regulation. The study of chemical regulation in Great Britain, France, the United States, and the Federal Republic of Germany carried out by Ronald Brickman and his colleagues and Joseph Badaracco's analysis of the control of vinyl chloride in the United States, France, Great Britain, and Japan—both of which have been summarized here—make the same argument: regulatory agendas and outcomes vary much less than regulatory processes.[48] While Steven Kelman's book *Regulating America, Regulating Sweden* does not explicitly deal with the issue of effectiveness, it draws a similar conclusion: occupational health and safety regulations are comparable in the two countries but the level of political conflict is substantially greater in the United States.[49]

These studies and my own analysis suggest that at least among the advanced capitalist democracies, the politics and administration of amenity and health and safety regulation vary much more than either actual regulatory outcomes or the political agenda itself. We now need to account for the differences in regulatory style between Great Britain and the United States; that is the subject of Chapter 6.

NOTES

CHAPTER 5. *Government Regulation in Great Britain and the United States*

1. Gary Freeman, "Do Policy Issues Determine Politics? State Pensions Policy in Britain and America," paper presented to the 1984 annual meeting of the American Political Science Association, Washington, D.C., pp. 2–3.
2. Quoted in Gerald Rhodes, *Inspectorates in British Government: Law Enforcement and Standards of Efficiency* (London: Allen & Unwin, 1981), p. 71.
3. Ibid., p. 75.
4. Quoted in ibid., p. 75.
5. See Charles D. Drake and Frank B. Wright, *Health and Safety at Work: The New Approach* (London: Sweet & Maxwell, 1983), p. 15.
6. Sheila Jasanoff, "Deregulation in the Workplace: A Comparative Analysis," unpublished paper, p. 3.
7. Rhodes, *Inspectorates in British Government*, p. 82.
8. Ibid., p. 89.
9. Jasanoff, "Deregulation in the Workplace," p. 9.
10. Quoted in Drake and Wright, *Health and Safety*, p. 14.
11. Ibid., p. 14.
12. Steven Kelman, "Enforcement of Occupational Safety and Health Regulations: A Comparison of Swedish and American Practices," in *Enforcing Regulation*, ed. Keith Hawkins and John M. Thomas (Boston: Kluwer-Nijhoff, 1984), p. 99.
13. Sheila Jasanoff, "Negotiation or Cost-Benefit Analysis: A Middle Road for U.S. Policy," *Environmental Forum*, July 1983, p. 38.
14. American Textile Manufacturers' Institute v. Donovan, 101 S.C. 2478 (1981).
15. Quoted in Joseph L. Badaracco, "Networks and Hierarchies: A Study of Business–Government Cooperation," Ph.D. dissertation, Harvard Business School, 1982, chap. 3, pp. 5, 8.
16. Ibid., p. 13.
17. Ibid., p. 24.
18. Ibid., p. 26.
19. Ibid.
20. Nicholas Hildyard, *Cover Up* (London: New English Library, 1981), pp. 169, 170.
21. "Killing What?" *Economist*, June 21, 1980, p. 71. For more on this controversy, see Hildyard, *Cover Up*, pp. 98–125, and Alan Irwin and Kenneth Green, "The Control of Chemical Carcinogens in Britain," *Policy and Politics* 11 (1983): 439–59.
22. W. G. Carson, *The Other Price of Britain's Oil: Safety and Control in the North Sea* (Oxford: Martin Robertson, 1982).
23. Graham Wilson, "Legislation on Occupational Safety and Health: A Comparison of the British and American Experience," unpublished paper, pp. 13, 12.
24. Graham Wilson, "Social Regulation and Explanations of Regulatory Failure," *Political Studies* 32 (1984): 220.
25. Ronald Brickman, Sheila Jasanoff, and Thomas Ilgen, *Chemical Regulation*

*Notes*

*and Cancer: A Cross-national Study of Policy and Politics* (Ithaca: Cornell University, Program on Science, Technology, and Society, 1982), p. 36.

26. Ibid., p. 39.

27. Ibid., pp. 259, 261.

28. Irwin and Green, "Control of Chemical Carcinogens," p. 443.

29. Ibid., pp. 446, 448.

30. Brickman et al., *Chemical Regulation and Cancer*, pp. 259, 380.

31. M. F. Cuthbert, J. P. Griffin, and W. H. W. Inman, "The United Kingdom," in *Controlling the Use of Therapeutic Drugs: An International Comparison*, ed. William M. Wardell (Washington, D.C.: American Enterprise Institute, 1978), p. 99.

32. Ibid., p. 103.

33. Keith Hartley and Alan Maynard, "The Regulation of the U.K. Pharmaceutical Industry: A Cost-Benefit Analysis," unpublished paper, 1981, p. 27.

34. The data in the following two paragraphs are drawn from "Testing Time for Drugs," *Economist*, August 7, 1980, pp. 69–70.

35. Quoted in David Leo Weimer, "Organizational Incentives: Safe and Available Drugs," in *Reforming Social Regulation*, ed. LeRoy Graymer and Frederick Thompson (Beverly Hills, Calif.: Sage, 1982), p. 44.

36. This section is based on Ross Cranston, *Regulating Business Law and Consumer Agencies* (London: Macmillan, 1979). For more on British consumer regulations see Peter Smith and Dennis Swann, *Protecting the Consumer* (Oxford: Martin Robertson, 1979).

37. Cranston, *Regulating Business Law*, pp. 27–28.

38. Ibid., p. 28.

39. Ibid., p. 33.

40. See "Self-Control in the City," *Economist*, July 2, 1983, p. 8.

41. This section is based on Les Metcalfe, "From Crisis Management to Preventive Medicine: The Evolution of U.K. Bank Supervision" (Berlin: International Institute of Management, 1979); "Self-Control in the City," p. 18; "Who Polices the City?" *Economist*, July 2, 1982, p. 69; "Policing the City of London," *Economist*, July 17, 1984, pp. 70–71; "A Little Cleaner," *Economist*, October 20, 1984, pp. 86–87; Barnaby Feder, "Overseeing Insurance Reform at London's Venerable Mart," *New York Times*, January 8, 1984, sec. III, p. 6.

42. R. I. Tricker, *Corporate Governance* (Aldershot: Gower, 1984), p. 23.

43. Michael Moran, *The Politics of Banking* (New York: St. Martin's, 1984), p. 117.

44. Feder, "Overseeing Insurance Reform."

45. For an extended discussion of this issue, see John Elkington, *The Ecology of Tomorrow's World* (London: Associated British Press, 1983).

46. Lennart Lundqvist, *The Hare and the Tortoise: Clean Air Policies in the United States and Sweden* (Ann Arbor: University of Michigan Press, 1980).

47. Peter Knoepfel and Helmut Weidner, "Implementing Air Quality Control Programs in Europe: Some Results of a Comparative Study," in *International Comparisons in Implementing Pollution Laws*, ed. Paul Downing and Kenneth Hanf (Boston: Kluwer-Nijhoff, 1983), p. 207.

48. Brickman et al., *Chemical Regulation and Cancer*; Badaracco, "Networks and Hierarchies."

49. Steven Kelman, *Regulating America, Regulating Sweden: A Comparative Study of Occupational Safety and Health Policy* (Cambridge: MIT Press, 1981).

[4]



# ENVIRONMENTAL POLITICS AND ADMINISTRATIVE REFORM

NEIL CARTER and PHILIP LOWE*

> We will establish a new Environment Agency which will bring together the functions of the National Rivers Authority, Her Majesty's Inspectorate of Pollution and the waste regulation functions of local authorities [Conservative Party Manifesto 1992].

THE promise to set up a new cross-sectoral environment agency was the centrepiece of the environment policy section of the Conservative Party manifesto for the 1992 general election; to be precise, it was the only domestic environmental policy pledge in the manifesto. The pledge, in part, reflected a remarkable near-consensus across government, opposition parties and the network of pressure groups with an interest in the issue of environmental regulation. This agreement was remarkable on two counts. First, the creation of an agency with cross-media regulatory responsibilities for air, water and land would appear to represent a significant departure from the traditional pattern of British environmental administration. Secondly, rarely is there agreement across such a range of producer, consumer and environmentalist interests from different policy networks. It is therefore not surprising that the political consensus stretches only to the principle of establishing such an agency, and that there has been considerable disagreement both within government and between pressure groups as to the form and functions it should take. This paper examines the thinking behind the proposed agency because it provides a useful insight into the British administrative system and the pressures to which it has been subjected in recent years.

The Prime Minister, John Major, announced the government's intention to create a combined environmental agency on 8 July 1991. Yet just ten months earlier, the White Paper *This Common Inheritance* had rejected institutional reform, preferring to give the recently-formed unified pollution inspectorate (Her Majesty's Inspectorate of Pollution or HMIP), the National Rivers Authority (NRA), and the unified conservation agencies for Scotland and for Wales (Scottish Natural Heritage and

* Neil Carter is Lecturer in Politics at the University of York, at Heslington, and Philip Lowe is Duke of Northumberland Professor of Rural Economy at the Centre for Rural Economy, University of Newcastle-upon-Tyne.

the Countryside Council for Wales respectively) time to establish themselves.

John Major's announcement was undoubtedly motivated by immediate political considerations. It was his first speech on the environment as Prime Minister and he was keen to establish his own 'green' credentials in a way that his predecessor, Margaret Thatcher, had been unable to do. In the run up to the general election, with both opposition parties in favour of the need for institutional reform in the environmental field, he was also intent on minimising the possibility of party competition over this issue.

However, although there was general (if sometimes lukewarm) support for an agency, the details of the proposal generated bitter conflict within Whitehall as the Ministry of Agriculture, represented by John Gummer, Minister of Agriculture, fought to secure control over various river authority functions which would be left over if only water pollution regulation was to be absorbed by the new agency. Fearful of the consequences of dismembering the newly-formed NRA with its growing reputation for 'taking on' producer interests, the environmental lobby mobilised in its defence. This conflict tarnished the Prime Minister's personal initiative. Rather than risk the dispute simmering over in the lead up to the general election, Michael Heseltine, Secretary of State for the Environment, in October 1991, attempted to defuse the controversy by publishing a consultation paper setting out a number of options for the new agency and, consequently, delaying any final decision on the form of the agency well beyond the date of the election.

Since then the omission of an environment bill from the government's legislative plans for the 1992–93 parliamentary session prompted speculation that the proposal would be quietly dropped. Although Michael Howard, Secretary of State for the Environment, reiterated the government's commitment to the agency in July 1992 neither the immediate political origins of the agency proposal—characterised by political symbolism, transitory leadership commitment and the disappearance of the issue during the general election campaign—nor the subsequent decline in the political significance of the environment augured well for the proposed agency. However, the 1993 Queen's Speech included paving bills allowing money to be spent on preparations for two agencies—one for England and Wales, a second for Scotland—with final legislation expected in the 1994–95 session. This would allow the agency to be in operation by the end of 1995.

## The emerging consensus

It was always unlikely that the government would ditch the project. John Major's announcement was not only political opportunism but also the culmination of a process of rethinking government policy that had begun at least two years earlier.

ENVIRONMENTAL POLITICS AND ADMINISTRATIVE REFORM

There was considerable and growing support for an inclusive environmental agency in government circles. William Waldegrave had devoted a speech to the issue as long ago as October 1984. The Conservative-controlled House of Commons Select Committee on the Environment had supported the concept in 1989. Chris Patten had seriously considered it when drawing up the White Paper during 1989–90 although the final version rejected immediate amalgamation of HMIP and the NRA but suggested that in the longer term an umbrella body might be set up to oversee and co-ordinate their activities. David Trippier, Minister for the Environment and Countryside, told the Environment Committee that the government was 'very seriously considering' an agency two months before John Major's announcement. As the Environment Committee put it: 'In just two years, the government's policy had shifted from outright rejection of the notion of such an agency, to enthusiastic acceptance.'

Yet support for an agency sits uneasily alongside the established traditions of environment policy. Britain has the oldest system of environmental protection of any industrialised nation and probably one of the most elaborate. Briefly, five main features characterise the distinctive administrative system and style of policy-making.

First, government structures and legislation have been a fragmented accretion of common law, statutes, agencies, procedures and policies. There has been no overall environmental policy other than the sum of the individual elements, most of which have been pragmatic and incremental responses to specific problems and to the evolution of scientific knowledge.

Secondly, regulation has been highly devolved and decentralised: responsibility for taking action has fallen mostly to local government or to one of a wide range of administrative agencies. The roles allocated to these bodies usually combine policy development and advice with regulation and implementation.

Thirdly, environmental control, like many other aspects of state regulation in Britain, is pervaded by administrative rather than judicial procedures. The approach pursued is informal, accommodative and technocratic, rather than formal, confrontational and legalistic. Legislation tends to be broad and discretionary. Regulatory agencies are usually given wide scope to determine environmental objectives and considerable latitude in their enforcement. When laws are demonstrably broken, prosecutions have traditionally been rare because regulatory officials prefer to exercise the considerable discretion allowed to them by their relative insulation from the scrutiny of both parliament and the judiciary.

Fourthly, the voluntarist approach adopted in dealing with private concerns seeks to foster co-operation and strives to achieve the objectives of environmental policy through negotiation and persuasion. Where other countries have made extensive use of uniform standards of emissions and environmental quality backed up by law, the British government prefers implementation through consent by means of industry self-regulation and informal agreement.

Lastly, environmental policy-making, where it impinges on major economic interests like pollution control, has traditionally taken place in closed policy communities, in which producer interests—industrialists, trade associations, farmers and landowners—are heavily represented. Consequently, the negative view of the voluntarist tradition is the belief—widely held among environmentalists—that government officials have been 'captured' by industrial managers and agricultural interests.

These core characteristics of British environmental policy remain dominant but, by the late 1980s, pressures from a number of different directions had built up to stimulate a major reappraisal of policy and structures. In particular, support grew for a consolidation of regulatory functions. Much of the intellectual case was formulated by the Royal Commission on Environmental Pollution. For many years it has argued for unified control of discharges to air, water and land, to avoid the all too common situation where control over one medium simply displaces the problem to another, without any overall strategy for the most appropriate treatment of disposal routes. This key concept of integrated (or cross-media) pollution control (IPC) was behind the Commission's call for a unified pollution inspectorate which eventually came about with the creation of HMIP amalgamating the air, water and solid waste, and radioactive waste directorates. In itself, it was a modest administrative reform motivated primarily by the desire to improve the technical effectiveness of pollution control within the established traditions of British pollution control practices. But, soon after, the DoE issued a consultation paper making clear its new commitment to IPC: a decision that, in breaking with established traditions, reflected a general international movement away from 'end-of-pipe' approaches. In the light of its acceptance of IPC and with HMIP still lacking a coherent mandate, the government introduced the Environmental Protection Act 1990 (EPA) which created the framework within which HMIP could operate (although, characteristically, it prescribed a gradualist, step-by-step, implementation of the terms of the Act).

There remain, however, many polluting and hazardous processes that HMIP does not regulate, and there are regulations concerning the use of particular media (most notably water) that potentially cross-cut HMIP's powers. Indeed, soon after creating HMIP, the government established, first, the National Rivers Authority under the Water Act 1989 (see below) and, then, local Waste Regulation Authorities under the EPA. None of these bodies was formally within the legal framework of integrated pollution control. With respect to the NRA the matter was resolved by transferring primary responsibility for the majority of discharges from it to HMIP. The NRA was left with the power to set conditions relating to discharges to controlled waters within the authorisation given by the HMIP. As regards Waste Regulation Authorities (which are local authority based), the confusion remained unresolved. The environmental White Paper put forward the possibility of giving HMIP the leading responsibility for the regulation of waste disposal (under the EPA it already has the duty of auditing the performance of local authorities in this field). Significantly, though, when the Opposition moved an amendment in the Lords to the EPA which would have achieved just this resolution, Lord Hesketh, a government minister, rejected it with the comment: 'Local knowledge and the capacity for a fast response which lies with local authorities could be put at risk by a centralised system.'

Clearly, rather than resolving the issue of the consolidation of regulatory functions, the formation of HMIP simply fuelled the debate in environmental circles. Recognition of such divisions has prompted calls for further rationalisation of the structure of regulation. For O'Riordan and Weale, they are examples of 'inappropriate coordination and mismanagement of what should be a total environmental regulatory function'.[1] The White Paper summarises succinctly the arguments for amalgamating regulatory bodies:

> It might make it easier for industry and others to have only one inspectorate to approach; that with separate organizations there is always the risk of some overlap or duplication of effort; and that combining the bodies under one management might lead to greater consistency of approach across all pollution types and environmental media.

Support for this position grew rapidly. Submissions to the consultation paper reveal support for an encompassing regulatory agency from a broad coalition of interests ranging from the CBI to most environmental groups.

The government's response to the call for a consolidated Environmental Protection Commission made by the Select Committee on the Environment indicates one of the potential counter-arguments. The response, published in April 1989, rejected the proposal on the grounds that a multiplicity of agencies, tailor-made to regulate specific issues, was more effective.

But by 1991 things had moved on rapidly and the new Secretary of State, Michael Heseltine, was able to 'look at these matters afresh'. What he observed was a widespread, growing consensus in environmental circles about the need for some kind of cross-sector agency, although the form that the agency should take remained a matter of dispute.

## What form of agency?

The decision to issue a consultation paper in Autumn 1991 reflected the existence of substantial divisions, both inside and outside government, regarding the best form of any future agency. Thus the consultation paper

[1] Tim O'Riordan and Albert Weale, *Greening the Machinery of Government*, Friends of the Earth, London, 1992.

set out four possible options and provoked over 600 responses. Never before had there been such a welter of proposals for new official structures for environmental protection. This spate of institutional blueprints marked a significant departure not only in indicating a gathering consensus over the need for major reform, but also in breaking with the strong tradition of institutional pragmatism in Britain whereby machinery and measures were devised to address the problem to hand rather than by reference to more general principles. Nevertheless, to raise the chances of successful reform of the system of environmental protection, proposals had to recognise the nature and structure of existing agencies and procedures, and work 'with the grain' of the British administrative tradition.

A number of issues have come to the fore in the reform debate: the degree of independence that the regulatory agencies should enjoy; the role of local authorities; the scope for and limits to the consolidation of regulatory functions; and the desirability of and scope for separating operational roles from regulation. The dilemmas involved and their resolution go to the very heart of the British tradition of environmental management.

The arguments for independence from government seem very persuasive. Indeed, some commentators take the case as self-evident. O'Riordan and Weale, for example, simply declare that 'independence of regulation both from those who are licensed and from governments that might interfere' is a fundamental principle on which the greening of the machinery must be founded.[2] The Select Committee on the Environment, following its investigation of toxic waste, proposed the need for an independent regulatory and enforcement agency in the light of the scandalous dilatoriness of the DoE and local authorities in implementing the requirements of the 1974 Control of Pollution Act. Environmental protection, it was felt, should not be so subject to the vagaries of political fortune. To maintain public and scientific confidence demanded objectivity. The case for independence has also been put in terms of avoidance of possible conflict of interest problems where a minister has to settle appeals. The final argument for not putting a regulatory agency under the control of any particular department is that the agency's responsibilities should not be restricted by departmental boundaries.

The counter-argument for retaining regulatory agencies as departmental bodies is that this ensures political accountability—a principle underpinning the Next Steps agency initiative. Ministers argued against various proposals for an Environmental Protection Executive during the passage of the EPA in just these terms. It was claimed that to devolve important responsibilities to an outside statutory body would remove them from the normal system of parliamentary control and scrutiny. However, such an arrangement is not unusual and the so-called Addison Rules, which relate to parliamentary scrutiny in these cases, specify that

[2] O'Riordan and Weale, 1992, *op. cit.*, para. 2.11.

when questions affecting public bodies arise in parliament, the government is alone responsible to parliament. In practice, however, ministers often refer parliamentary questions to the head of the appropriate body to answer by correspondence.

In the event, the government has decided that the agency should be independent of government. Members of its Board will be appointed by government, presumably with a mix of industrialists, agriculturalists, environmentalists and scientists. It will be answerable to parliament either directly or via a minister. This arrangement does not entirely resolve another long-standing accountability issue, relating to local government. There are two extreme models of the local role of the proposed agency: one view envisages it maintaining consistency across a series of locally organised activities; the other sees it as a single national body responsible for regulation as well as strategic planning. Currently it is envisaged that the agency will fall somewhere between the two perspectives, raising the problem of how, for functions remaining with local authorities, the agency can be accountable simultaneously to parliament and to locally elected officials.

Local authorities have attracted criticism for their record in waste management, particularly in planning sufficient disposal capacity and in establishing handling and treatment facilities for specialised wastes. The EPA sought to address the problems by separating the operational and regulatory functions with the intention of opening up waste disposal to competitive tendering and encouraging local authorities to combine in regional waste disposal companies operating at arms length from the regulatory authorities. However, considerable unease remained concerning the effectiveness of this voluntary strategy to overcome the tendency of local authorities to 'free ride' by hoping that neighbouring authorities would accept their waste. Consequently, all options outlined in the consultation paper envisaged removing responsibility for waste management regulation from local authorities and vesting it with the new agency. The central argument for this approach is the possibility of developing a national waste regulation strategy, and making best use of resources and expertise that are currently distributed inefficiently among a multitude of authorities. In addition, a single agency will create the 'one stop shop' organisation so attractive to industry.

This centralisation of powers away from local government follows a pattern that the Conservative government has adopted in other policy areas. Local authority associations employed fashionable concepts in their defence. The principle of subsidiarity was cited to emphasise local expertise, knowledge and speed of response against the putative benefits of greater managerial and technical competence claimed for centralisation. The 'democratic deficit' was deployed to condemn the proposed agency for lacking the accountability of elected local members. They also argued that the new organisations arising out of the EPA had not yet had the opportunity to prove themselves. But the government had, apparently, already made up its mind. After all, subsidiarity had resulted in the very problems that now need solving; other regulatory bodies such as the NRA were not directly accountable to elected representatives; and once the principle of an agency had been accepted, then if the newly-established HMIP and NRA were to be reorganised, why not waste regulation? However, it is unlikely that the new agency will be rid of the local contention that surrounds the siting of waste management facilities.

The issue that has probably caused most controversy concerns the degree of comprehensiveness of possible regroupings, i.e. how inclusive should the new agency be? The more all-embracing the proposed regrouping, the more likely that it produces a large, unwieldly structure and that the upheaval and difficulties involved in the reorganisation will outweigh, at least in the short term, any advantages to be gained. Even in the longer term, it is possible that existing problems of external co-ordination would be reproduced as difficulties of internal coordination. The need, for example, for the sort of memorandum of agreement that the HMIP and NRA have had to negotiate is hardly likely to disappear just because the two organisations have been subsumed into the one agency. On the other hand, although a less comprehensive regrouping might reduce some of these difficulties, other problems would arise, particularly in determining the boundary between what should be included and excluded, and then ensuring effective liaison and co-ordination across that boundary. Significantly, the different proposals for an environmental agency each contained somewhat different groupings of functions. While there was a broad agreement that HMIP should be central to any new agency, it is the fate of the NRA that has divided opinion. Some proposals incorporated it, others excluded it; others would have dismembered it.[3]

The consultation paper presented four options for institutional re-organisation. Under the first option the new agency would have had a remit for emissions to air and land by taking over responsibility for most of HMIP's functions, together with those of waste regulation from local authorities. HMIP's responsibilities for the water environment would be transferred to the NRA. A second option was to have created an umbrella body to coordinate the work of the NRA and HMIP. The third option was to incorporate HMIP, waste regulation and the NRA within a single, all-embracing agency. The final option was for the agency to combine waste regulation, HMIP and the NRA's pollution control functions, thus consolidating responsibilities for emissions to air, land and water, but leaving a rump of NRA activities covering river, water and fisheries management. For each option, the relative merits and drawbacks were rehearsed, but as the consultation paper candidly admitted 'the govern-

[3] Other agencies included or excluded from various blueprints were the Countryside Commission, English Nature, the Health and Safety Executive and the Pesticides Safety Directorate.

ment has not reached a firm view on which of these options might best fulfill its objectives for the environment agency'.

Close examination reveals that two quite different notions of integration were being played off against one another; one being intra-sectoral, the other inter-sectoral. The inter-sectoral notion, which is central to the concept of IPC, is about the pursuit of a coordinated and coherent strategy of environmental protection across different sectors and media.

The NRA, in contrast, is a clear example of a multi-purpose agency based on the integrated management of a single resource. As Lord Crickhowell, the Chairman of the NRA, has commented:

> It is . . . a waste of time talking in grandiloquent, generalised terms about environment protection agencies, without stopping to define objectives or to examine the nature of the organisations which might be incorporated in any such authority. The NRA, for example, is not simply a regulator. It is also manager of a major resource—water. I believe that it would be a profound mistake to dismember that organisation and separate its functions.

The intra-sectoral notion is central to the idea of sustainable development and involves reconciling conflicting demands on particular natural resources. It is this sense of the term that is meant, for example, when the government discloses in the White Paper that one of its objectives is 'to integrate agricultural and environmental policy'.

This raises another area where the principles guiding regulatory reform need to be clarified; namely the separation of operational roles from regulation (an issue central to the debate about reorganising waste regulation). The key aim here is to reduce the potential scope for 'gamekeeper-turned-poacher' conflicts of interest. This argument was used by those in favour of fragmenting the NRA which was accused of both regulating pollution and managing the river basin. So, for example, who would bring the NRA to task when, in seeking to raise revenue, it damages the environment by drawing too heavily on its navigation or abstraction functions? The counter-argument underlined the merits of integrated river basin management and stressed that the NRA's pollution control functions cannot easily be separated from its management functions. In short, it is impossible to control pollution without exercising control over water volume. Indeed, to prevent the gamekeeper-poacher conflict it is not necessary to separate control or enforcement roles from promotional roles, or to strip from regulatory authorities all their other executive functions. That would be to take an unnecessarily narrow view of regulation and diminish the scope for a 'sticks-and-carrots' strategy or for the pursuit of preventative policies.

Quite clearly, divisions over reorganisations go deeper than this debate about abstract principles of form and function: they reflect the view of different interests and the way those interests are responding to the changing arena of environmental policy-making. The various approaches attracted the backing of different powerful interest groups, although the majority preferred either Option 3 or Option 4: i.e. polarised around the question of whether the NRA would be transferred wholesale into a new agency or whether its regulatory and operational functions should be fragmented. Industrial interests, led by the Confederation of British Industry, plus some local authorities, favoured the notion of a unified environmental agency centred on the HMIP. Business leaders won backing from the influential Environmental Select Committee. One of the arguments used was that business needs a one-step agency for all of its licensing needs. Traditionally also, firms have had close links with the pollution inspectorate (dating back to its former life as the Alkali Inspectorate), whose officers usually have a training in process or production engineering and practical experience of the industry they are regulating. The cooperative, non-interventionist relationship with industry attracted accusations that the inspectorate had been captured by those interests that it should be regulating—an image that the HMIP has sought to throw off in demonstrating that it is no pushover.

On the other hand, the NRA drew strong support from fisheries interests, farmers, riparian owners and amenity interests. They argued the need for a single, powerful agency to mediate the various demands on the water within river catchments to ensure the healthy state of the river and its associated fish stocks and aquatic habitats. These interests found particular support amongst backbench members of parliament, particularly on the Conservative side. Adding weight to these arguments has been the growing reputation of the NRA as a more interventionist and pro-environmental agency.

Nevertheless divisions appeared on the issue within the environmental movement. Friends of the Earth has been a keen advocate of a unified environmental agency but traditional nature conservation and countryside interests were initially alarmed at the possibility that the NRA might be dismembered or emasculated within such an arrangement. There was particular concern lest, shorn of its water pollution responsibilities, the rump of the NRA's responsibilities for water and fisheries management and land drainage were to be absorbed by the Ministry of Agriculture (fears which the press suggested were not without foundation). But a common position was reached across the environment lobby to accept a new grouping of regulatory functions as long as this did not involve any dismemberment of the NRA.

In the event, Michael Howard declared the government's preference for option 3: to form an agency which would amalgamate the functions of the NRA, HMIP and the waste regulation work of local authorities. The agency will cover England and Wales and a separate body will be set up for Scotland. However, the debate itself it not foreclosed by the government's decision. In particular, although the 'bigger' option has been chosen, the fears of industry may have been partially allayed by Howard's declaration that the agency will be seeking 'both effective protection to the environment and value for money'. This has prompted concern amongst environmentalists that insufficient funding in a climate of economy and 'market testing' may constrain the agency.

## Discussion

Environmental protection is not a traditional self-contained policy sector like agriculture, energy, transport and industry. Ideally it should cut across all these and act as a guiding principle within each. Even the Royal Commission has recognised, in the past, that 'it would be unrealistic to expect one Department of State to be responsible for all aspects of the pollution and that there are strong arguments for requiring environmental protection to be an integral part of good management in all areas of government activity',[4] Concentration and centralisation of environment regulation is therefore not necessarily desirable, especially if the aim is to integrate environmental considerations into economic decision-making. Indeed, if environmental regulation is conceived not simply as a policing function but as an active agent for the promotion of sustainable practices, it is vital that regulatory bodies establish working relationships with all those who control the management and exploitation of natural resources. This is, indeed, a characteristic feature of the various conservation agencies in Britain (for example, the Countryside Commission, English Nature and the Forestry Commission) which combine regulatory and management functions.

Devolved, cooperative, tailor-made regulation is, in fact, the British tradition. It has manifest weaknesses; but, its supporters contend it is better to tackle these, or at least ponder long and hard before abandoning long established administrative practices completely. Certainly, the more devolved regulation is, the more pressing is the need for detached strategic policy-making and for open and accountable auditing of regulatory practice—to ensure consistency between sectors and to guard against the 'capture' of regulators by the interests being regulated. That calls for a coherent framework for environmental protection, not necessarily a single grand authority.

Modern environmentalist thinking is firmly committed to the view that one of the major problems to be overcome is the sectoral perspective on the environment that permeates governmental policy and administrative structures in all countries. Instead, it is argued that governments need to adopt a more holistic strategy which recognises the interlocking nature of all environmental problems and integrates environmental policy across individual policy sectors. But, for the foreseeable future, the dilemma facing any government is how—in a sectorally-administered world consisting of different policy arenas, departments and disciplines—to control and implement cross-sectoral functions without compromising its

[4] 7th Report, 1979, para. 8.5.

strategic perspective. In Britain, this dilemma has been recognised (implicitly) since the rise of modern environmentalism in the late 1960s/ early 1970s in the way that the government has adopted two separate but parallel strategies.

First, it has tried to improve administrative co-ordination wedded to strong departmental authority; a strategy manifested in the establishment of the DoE in 1970. However, it is important to note that although the DoE was formed as a high level super-department combining a number of responsibilities and possessing Cabinet status, it was very much a ministry *of* the environment (of which the environment was but one [minor] responsibility alongside local government and housing), rather than a ministry *for* the environment. Gradual change in this direction is detectable, particularly with the declining importance of the housing portfolio and the growing political visibility of the environment. Unfortunately, the establishment of an independent agency might impede progress in this direction. For, in the past, where environmental functions have been allocated to various individual quangos (for example, the National Parks, or the Nature Conservancy Council [now English Nature]) these bodies have subsequently been treated in Whitehall like sectional concerns seeking to influence government, rather than central actors within the political process. The integrated agency may suffer a similar fate. Yet it is vitally important that the DoE be encouraged to provide the environment with a powerful, firmly-rooted voice at the heart of central government. Care is needed, however, not to reproduce the situation found in some countries where a small specific ministry of the environment has been formed which possesses a clear sense of purpose but which finds itself isolated from the main policy-making arenas and lacking muscle in interdepartmental power struggles.

The second strategy of the government has been to nurture and protect the holistic vision: manifested in the Royal Commission on Environmental Pollution which possesses no executive functions at all. The Commission has a remit to roam where it pleases through government with the purpose of following a scientific strategy directed by a broad, holistic aim. It is probably only because the Commission lacks regulatory powers that civil servants have been prepared to accept its free-ranging role. It is not surprising that it was the Commission that first proposed IPC in the 1970s: a concept that it failed to locate in any political context.

Thus this parallel strategy reflects a central dilemma in British environmental policy. On the one hand, a scientific strategy unencumbered by political or administrative responsibilities; on the other hand, a strategy of administrative coordination which often lacks a clear sense of environmental purpose. Viewed in this way, the formation of a cross-sector Environment Agency is simply the final (or latest) twist.

# [5]

*Journal of Environmental Law* **21**:2 
doi:10.1093/jel/eqp011 Advance Access published on 30 April 2009

# Environment Law, Regulation and Governance: Shifting Architectures

Neil Gunningham*

## Abstract

Environmental law and policy has come a long way since the birth of the US Environmental Protection Agency in 1970 and the launch of the first European environmental policy in 1972. Today law is no longer centre stage but simply one instrument among others in the environmental regulator's toolkit. And talk of regulation may itself be giving way to the broader concept of environmental governance. This article examines the evolution of environmental law, regulation and governance over almost four decades. It explores the major initiatives of that period and the lessons that can be learned from them, it maps shifting regulatory architectures and explains what has worked and why and it considers the changing nature of the environmental challenge itself. Finally, it seeks to identify which particular architectures are most suited to deal with particular types of environmental problems.

Keywords: environment, law, regulation, governance, enforcement, compliance

## 1. Introduction

How can the substantial shifts that have taken place in environmental law, regulation and governance over the last four decades be explained? Are the sorts of policy mechanisms that are in place today more effective, efficient or politically acceptable than their predecessors? Has the nature of the environmental challenge itself changed and if so, with what implications? Are the

*Fenner School of Environment and Regulatory Institutions Network, Australian National University and BRASS, Cardiff University. This article is based on the annual *Journal of Environmental Law* lecture, presented at the University of Reading on 22 October 2008.

techniques that are necessary to deal with today's challenges radically different from those that served us well in earlier decades? And what is the role of the state in countries substantially shaped by neo-liberal ideology, in which the roles of government have been both changed and weakened? Have we, for example, moved 'from regulation to governance'?

This article explores these and related questions by seeking to examine the basic architectures of environmental law, regulation and governance and how they have changed since the first major environmental legislation was enacted in the 1970s. The metaphor of 'architecture' is invoked because it enables the writer to step back from the detail and to examine the underlying structures, the basic pillars on which environmental law, regulation and governance are built, and to show how those pillars are often connected in such a way that the whole is far more than the sum of the parts. Put differently, the aim of this article is not to describe individual statutory provisions or case law but rather to focus on the broader underpinnings on which the laws, regulations and governance mechanisms of a particular period are based, to examine the ambitions and underlying philosophy of the instruments that have been relied upon to achieve environmental outcomes, and to understand why different actors played different roles under different architectures of control.

Inevitably, such a broad-brush approach runs risks of subjectivity, selectiveness and over generalisation. The writer pleads guilty to all of the above. For example, the article does not engage with planning law or with international environmental law although both are self-evidently important in their own right. Sometimes, for heuristic purposes, developments are described as occurring in distinct 'stages' and sequentially, when in practice there may have been overlap between them (with some 'first generation' initiatives lingering long after 'second generation' developments had reached their zenith). The focus is purely on the environmental sphere and does not purport to generalise about developments under neo-liberalism in other spheres of social regulation.[1] The analysis is mainly confined to the developments in 'Anglo-Saxon' jurisdictions, primarily Australia, Canada, New Zealand, the UK (noting the constraints imposed by EU Directives) and the USA and it does not account for challenges faced by developing countries. Nevertheless, it does attempt to provide a coherent and 'big picture' account of developments in mainstream environmental law, regulation and governance in Anglo-Saxon jurisdictions over a protracted period.

1 For example this article argues that neo-liberalism has at times resulted in a winding back of environmental regulation, a reduction in resources for enforcement and a search for 'light handed' alternatives to direct regulation. But in many other social spheres, it can be argued that after the first few years of Reagan and Thatcher deregulatory zealotry, business regulatory agencies resumed their long-term growth, the numbers of regulations grew unabated and enforcement budgets continued to expand. See J Braithwaite, *Regulatory Capitalism: How It Works, Ideas For Making It Work Better* (Edward Elgar, Cheltenham 2008) ch 1.

For present purposes, environmental law, regulation and governance are treated as three points on a continuum. At one end is highly specific state-based law, being that which is promulgated by parliament and interpreted by the courts. Regulation is a rather broader category and includes much more flexible, imaginative and innovative forms of social control which seek to harness not just governments but also markets (as with economic instruments), business and third parties. For example, it may involve persuasion, self-regulation and co-regulation, it may utilise both commercial interests and non-government organisations (NGOs) and it may invoke surrogates for direct government regulation—mechanisms that are only partially or indirectly related to state law. But it still involves the state as a central player because even mechanisms that are not reliant on legislation for their authority are negotiated directly with the state and operate 'in the shadow of the state'. For example, tradeable permits, an economic instrument that relies heavily on market forces, nevertheless must operate according to rules set and enforced by the state. And New Zealand's approach to ozone-depleting substances, based on voluntary agreements, nevertheless involved an explicit understanding that if certain targets were not achieved, then these arrangements would be replaced by statutory intervention. In contrast, at the other end of the continuum, governance does not privilege the state and state law is simply one node amongst many in a world of diffused power and responsibility. Governance, so defined involves:

> an inchoate post-modern world where there is 'no longer a single sovereign authority' and in which regulatory mechanisms do not need to be endowed with formal authority to function effectively. The consequence is a 'centreless society' or 'polycentric state' characterised by multiple centers in which the amorphous tasks of government are described in unaccustomed fashion as being 'to enable socio-political interactions, to encourage many and various arrangements for coping with problems and to distribute services among the several actors'.[2]

As a means of martialling the material and structuring the article, the three main 'actors'—the state, civil society and business—and their contributions to environmental law, regulation and governance are initially examined separately. However, in practice, the actions of any one actor can rarely be understood in isolation from that of others, and later sections explore the interactions between them. This enables the development of a more sophisticated and nuanced account of how and why environmental architectures have shifted in particular directions, the consequences of those shifts, and the

2 Rhodes cited in C Harlow, 'Deconstructing Government?' in T Ginsburg and R Rabin (eds), *Institutions and Public Law, Comparative Approaches* (P Lang, New York 2005) 59.

virtues of using complementary combinations of policy instruments harnessing a variety of stakeholders as surrogate regulators.

## 2. *Roles of the State*

According to most accounts, modern environmental law dates back to 1970, the year in which the first major federal United States' legislation was enacted, the first Earth Day celebrated and the US Environmental Protection Agency (EPA) created. These developments were preceded by the considerable environmental activism of the late-1960s, by Rachel Carson's *Silent Spring*,[3] by Paul Ehrlich's *The Population Bomb*[4] and by a series of environmental disasters, all of which played a role in galvanising legislators to act, not just in America but also in other advanced western nations. The first Australian legislation of note, the Victorian Environment Protection Act, was also enacted in 1970 as was the Canadian Waters Pollution Prevention Act and the Water Act. Although British pollution control legislation can claim a longer lineage,[5] there too, the 1970s was the first decade of substantial legislative action.

The environmental legislation that the Anglo-Saxon countries enacted in the 1970s was distinctive in its architecture. The dominant approach was to promulgate legislation designed to prohibit or restrict environmentally harmful activities, (particularly pollution) by using 'direct' or 'command and control' (to use the unfairly but widely adopted pejorative label applied by free-market economists) mechanisms. The preferred technique was to identify an environmental target such as a limit on emissions of a pollutant to water or the air (the 'command'), with penalties that would be imposed if this target is not met (the 'control').

Direct regulation of this nature took a variety of forms, the most common of which involved environmental standards imposing uniform requirements (maximum emission concentrations or introduction of a prescribed technology) relating to broad categories of activities (eg all chemical plants of a certain type or all 'scheduled' industries). The aim was to reduce environmental harm (primarily pollution to air and water) to a socially acceptable level. Heavy reliance was placed on design (Best Available Technology) or specification standards (which tell duty holders precisely what measures to take) rather

3 R Carson, *Silent Spring* (Houghton Mifflin, Boston 1962).

4 P Ehrlich, *The Population Bomb* (Ballantine Books, New York 1968).

5 In the UK, pollution legislation at least, substantially preceded the 1970s legislative activism. Not least, the Clean Air Act 1956—a direct response to the London smog of 1952 that killed an estimated 4,000 people—was a particularly important legislative landmark. And of course the Alkali Inspectorate, the principal regulator at that time, had a substantially longer history. Nevertheless, it is fair to say that until the 1970s, environmental law did not have much 'bite'. See generally N Gunningham, *Pollution, Social Interest and the Law* (Martin Robertson, UK 1974).

than on performance standards (which specify outcomes or the desired level of performance). Permits and licences were (and largely still are) the favoured instrument through which such standards were to be achieved—an approach which enables firms to continue to emit pollutants, but only at levels that do not breach the relevant standards. Of course there were some differences between the approaches of different jurisdictions, most notably with regard to enforcement (where the adversarial approach of the US EPA can be contrasted with the 'softly softly' approach of the other Anglo-Saxon jurisdictions).[6] Nevertheless, the regulation of all the Anglo-Saxon countries had the same basic architecture.

This architecture, at least in the way it dealt with point-source pollution from large business enterprises, achieved some significant victories in halting, or at least slowing, some forms of environmental degradation.[7] Indeed, direct regulation, in imposing technology-based standards on large industries, has sometimes achieved quite dramatic improvements in environmental performance. For example, Gunningham, Kagan and Thornton[8] in their study of pulp and paper mills in the USA, Canada, Australia and New Zealand, found that all the mills they visited were generally in compliance with their regulatory permits and that those permits had compelled pulp mills to install secondary treatment plants for wastewater, sharply reducing biological oxygen demand, and to substantially reduce use of elemental chlorine as a bleaching agent, greatly reducing dioxin emission. Their findings—consistent with international surveys of environmental and corporate managers that suggest that regulation is the single most important driver of improved environmental performance[9]—suggest that pollution reduction technologies induced by regulatory demands have largely been responsible for dramatic reductions in pulp mill pollution.

Nevertheless, by the 1980s direct/'command and control' regulation was widely criticised, both within the USA and elsewhere, for being inflexible and excessively costly for business. Centralised, bureaucratic standard-setting—the centre-piece of traditional forms of direct regulation—was routinely castigated by its critics for being 'inherently inefficient and cumbersome'.[10] This critique of direct regulation can be seriously overstated. Criticism is often

6 E Bardach and R Kagan, *Going by the Book: The Problem of Regulatory Unreasonableness* (Philadelphia, Temple University Press 2002); K Hawkins, *Environment and Enforcement* (OUP, Oxford 1984).
7 S Cohen, 'EPA: A Qualified Success' in S Kamieniecki, R O'Brien and M Clarke (eds), *Controversies in Environmental Policy* (State University of New York Press, Albany, 1986) 174.
8 N Gunningham, R Kagan and D Thornton, *Shades of Green: Business, Regulation and Environment* (Stanford University Press, California 2003) ch 3.
9 KPMG, *Canadian Environmental Management Survey* (KPMG, Toronto 1996).
10 E Elliott, 'Environmental TQM: Anatomy of a Pollution Control Program that Works!' (1994) 92 Michigan Law Review 1840.

directed at the relatively unrepresentative adversarial approach adopted in the USA, and fails to acknowledge a significant movement towards more flexible and cost-effective forms of regulation that avoid the worst excesses of highly prescriptive versions. Some businesses, moreover, continued to support command and control as providing them with predictability, a clear set of rules by which to operate and a level playing field. Moreover some critics conveniently overlook the fact that regulatory agencies are often constrained or prevented from performing their mandate by lack of resources or other factors entirely beyond their control.

But the fundamental critique—that direct regulation, whatever its effectiveness, scores poorly in terms of efficiency—was becoming increasingly pertinent as regulators sought to expand their reach. As they did so, it became apparent that the relative strengths and weaknesses of direct regulation vary substantially with the context. In broad terms, the more complex the environmental problem, the more obvious become the limitations (and the inefficiencies) of direct regulation in addressing it. For example, it is one thing to regulate point-source pollution caused by large, homogeneous industrial facilities operating within a single jurisdiction—and as indicated above, command and control has done this reasonably well. But it is quite another to apply the same approach to pollution caused by heterogeneous enterprises, where it may prove to be an extremely costly and inefficient approach, as neo-classical economists have been quick to point out.[11] Equally, direct regulation is a crude and often inappropriate tool for engaging with such complex problems as diffuse source pollution from agriculture,[12] or biodiversity loss on private land.[13]

In any event, direct regulation was falling into disfavour as a consequence of broader shifts in the political and ideological landscape. By the 1980s there had been, particularly in the USA and the UK, a considerable turn towards neo-liberalism—essentially the enterprise of embedding market values and structures within economic 'and' social and political life. This project took a particularly strident form under Ronald Reagan and Margaret Thatcher. During their reign, assisted by the economic and political collapse of the former Soviet Union, neo-liberalism triumphed almost unchallenged and environmental policy received a sharp injection of free-market ideology. Although public opposition precluded the sort of wholesale de-regulation, which occurred in some other areas, environmental regulatory budgets were

11 R Stavins, *Economics of the Environment: Selected Readings* (W.W. Norton & Company, New York 2005); C Sunstein, 'The Paradoxes of Regulation' (1990) 67 University of Chicago Law Review 408.

12 N Gunningham and D Sinclair, 'Policy Instrument Choice and Diffuse Source Pollution' (2005) 17 JEL 51.

13 C Perrings and others (eds), *Biodiversity Conservation: Problems and Policies* (Dordrecht, Kluwer Academic Press 1994).

substantially cut in almost all jurisdictions. As Richard Lazarus, writing of the USA, points out:

> . . . limited budgets, appropriation riders, interpretive agency rulings, massive delays in rulemaking and simple non enforcement are more than capable of converting a seemingly uncompromising legal mandate into nothing more than a symbolic aspirational statement.[14]

During the same period, governments also experienced considerable pressure from industry to reduce the economic burden of complying with environmental regulation. Although on most calculations the costs of compliance are relatively modest,[15] nevertheless, industrial lobby groups have argued strongly, and often successfully, that the imposition of such regulation would put industry at a competitive disadvantage. In an era of globalisation in which capital flight to low tax, low regulation regimes is increasingly plausible (though far less often demonstrated), governments listened particularly closely to industry concerns and frequently responded sympathetically. Thus the confluence of economic pressures and political ideology sometimes constrained the introduction of further direct regulation (though many earlier forms of direct regulation remained on the statute book).

Nevertheless, since environmental problems appeared to be increasing rather than going away, and since the public still appeared to value environment protection, the question for neo-liberal politicians became: what was to replace direct regulation (or rather, operate along side it, though the question was rarely put in these terms)? This question was a considerable focus of attention for policy-makers from the early-1980s onwards. Antagonistic to direct government intervention but largely unable to deregulate, policy-makers during this era sought to devise a range of less intrusive regulatory interventions, which were rolled out during the late-1980s and early-1990s.

One important change was the shift towards economic instruments, which, by 'mimicking the market', were perceived to be far more efficient than command and control regulation, and capable of providing industry with the flexibility and autonomy to make least cost decisions. Thus there was an increasing focus on the use of price signals in the shape of taxes or charges, property rights in the form of tradable permits, and supply side instruments in terms of subsidies. Perhaps, the best-known economic instrument of this period was the Acid Rain Program, which was established in the USA by the

14 R Lazarus, 'Super Wicked Problems and Climate Change: Restraining the Present to Liberate the Future', (2009) 94 Cornell Law Review, forthcoming.

15 On most calculations, these are between 1% and 2% of GDP. H Hodges, 'Falling Prices: Cost of Complying with Environmentla Regulations Almost Always Less Than Advertised' (1997) Economic Policy Institute, Briefing Paper 69 <http://www.epi.org/publications/entry/bp69/> accessed 2 April 2009.

Clean Air Act Amendments of 1990. This legislation introduced two innovative features that represented dramatic departures from conventional environmental regulation. First, an overall industry-wide cap on emissions of sulphur dioxide was set at approximately 'one half of historic levels'. Second, the programme allowed operators of affected facilities (including existing facilities) to trade emissions allowances between their own facilities or with other utilities in order to save costs in achieving the national emissions cap.

However, notwithstanding their theoretical attraction, in practice economic instruments were only used to a limited extent either during this period or beyond.[16] Despite their criticisms of command and control, regulated businesses consistently opposed the introduction of taxes and charges, preferring the certainty of regulation to the uncertainty of novel approaches. More fundamentally, they worried that pollution taxes would be used by politicians as an underhand way of raising the overall tax burden upon them, rather than as a genuine environmental tool. To accept even a modest tax, they feared, would be the 'thin end of the wedge' because over time politicians would succumb to the temptation to ratchet such taxes upwards, even where this could not be justified in environmental policy terms. There were also concerns about competitiveness arising from the imposition of unilateral taxes, for example the proposed EU carbon tax, which failed for this reason.

More popular with business were a variety of voluntary initiatives which came of age during the same period. Such approaches included self-regulation, voluntary codes, environmental charters, co-regulation, covenants and negotiated environmental agreements. Three types of voluntary arrangement, in particular, became prevalent in the domain of environmental policy:

- 'unilateral commitments', which are set by the industry acting independently without any involvement of a public authority (eg the chemical industry's definitive Responsible Care programme, was developed in 1985);
- 'public voluntary programmes', which involve commitments devised by the environmental agency and in which individual firms are invited to participate (eg the US EPA's 33/50 Programme invited firms to commit to reducing 17 priority chemicals and set as its goal a 33% reduction in releases and transfers of these chemicals by 1992 and a 50% reduction by 1995, measured against a 1988 baseline) and
- 'negotiated agreements', which involve commitments for environmental protection developed through bargaining between a public authority and industry (eg the Federated Association of German Industry in 1995 agreed to propose a reduction of carbon dioxide emissions by up to 20% by 2005, in exchange for which the federal government announced the withdrawal

16 A Jordan, R Wurzel and A Zito, '"New" Instruments of Environmental Governance: Patterns and Pathways of Change' (2003) 12 Environmental Politics 1.

of plans to introduce a waste heat ordinance and promised an exemption from a possible energy tax).

For more than a decade such approaches proved to be increasingly popular, and, in one form or another, their use permeated internationally. Negotiated agreements were particularly widespread in the EU, where by the mid-1990s there were over 300 such agreements, almost all focused on large enterprises. Similar trends also characterised environmental policy in other Anglo-Saxon countries, and especially in Canada and Australia.[17]

The reasons for this interest in voluntarism are many but include the limits of command and control regulation and the interest of industry itself in seeking (at best) a flexible, cost-effective and more autonomous alternative to direct regulation, or (at worst) a means of avoiding the imposition of binding standards altogether.[18]

Unfortunately, by the late-1990s a number of systematic reviews of the various voluntary initiatives had concluded that either there were few demonstrated benefits or those benefits were confined to 'soft' issues (such as information diffusion and consciousness raising). Harrison,[19] for example, argues that first reports of environmental benefits of many voluntary programmes relative to reference years almost certainly exaggerate programme effectiveness. Another general survey has also concluded that many negotiated agreements had not been markedly successful.[20] Even the claim that negotiated agreements tend to reduce administrative burdens is not confirmed by existing empirical evidence or analysis.[21] There may be a variety of reasons for the limited success of many voluntary approaches more generally, including the central role of industry in the target-setting process, the scope for free riding, the uncertainty over regulatory threats, non-enforceable commitments, poor monitoring and lack of transparency.

By the mid- to late-1990s, in part because of the manifest failings of many of the alternatives to direct regulation, and in part because of a change in the political flavour of government, a further shift in the architecture of

17 See for example in the 1990s, Environment Canada and its predecessors developed programmes such as the Accelerated Reduction/Elimination of Toxics (ARET) programme (1995–2000) and Memoranda of Understanding (MOUs) with companies and industry associations as a means to achieve beyond-compliance reductions in the release of substances of concern. See also, K Webb, *Voluntary Codes: Private Governance, the Public Interest and Innovation* (Carlton University Press, Montreal 2004). For Australia see for example, C Parker, 'The Greenhouse Challenge: Trivial Pursuit?' (2001) 16 Environment & Planning Journal 63.

18 J Moffet and F Bregha, 'An Overview of the Issues with Respect to Voluntary Environmental Agreements' (1999) 8 Journal of Environmental Law and Practice 63.

19 K Harrison, 'Voluntarism and Environmental Governance' in EA Parson (ed), *Governing the Environment* (University of Toronto Press, Toronto 2001).

20 R Gibson, *Voluntary Approaches: The New Politics of Corporate Greening* (Broadview Press, Ontario 2000).

21 OECD (Organisation for Economic Cooperation and Development), *Voluntary Approaches for Environmental Policy: An Assessment* (OECD, Paris 1999) 131. See also OECD, *Voluntary Approaches to Environmental Policy* (OECD, Paris 2003).

environmental regulation could be identified. Whereas in the Thatcher and Reagan years, the emphasis had been on voluntarism and (where this was manifestly impracticable) on economic instruments, their successors placed greater emphasis on a return to regulation. However, even under Blair Labour Government in the UK and Clinton Democratic Administration in the USA (and under State and Federal Labour Governments in Australia), neo-liberalism still held sway (albeit in a gentler form). 'New regulation' (rather like 'New Labour') proved to be very different from 'old regulation' and especially from the command and control regulation that characterised the 1970s. In these and other Anglo-Saxon jurisdictions, concerted efforts were made to avoid measures that might intrude on business flexibility or competitiveness and regulation, to the extent that it was back in fashion, was to be very 'light handed' both in its design and its application.

The Clinton–Gore administration played an influential role in rethinking what neo-liberal regulation might look like. Its 'reinventing environmental regulation' agenda, unveiled in President Clinton's State of the Union address in January 1995, outlined the future programme as follows:

> It is time to draw upon the lessons we have learned over the last 25 years to reinvent environmental protection for the 21st century. We have learned that the American people are deeply committed to a healthy environment for their children and communities. We have learned that pollution is often a sign of economic inefficiency and business can improve profits by preventing it. We have learned that better decisions result from a collaborative process with people working together, than from an adversarial one that pits them against each other. And we have learned that regulations that provide flexibility—but require accountability—can provide greater protection at a lower cost.[22]

Under this agenda, the Clinton–Gore administration sought to nurture a co-operative relationship with business based on trust and reciprocity. Accordingly, there was less concern with imposing sanctions to persuade laggards to come up to a minimum legal standard, and more with encouraging enterprises to find new ways of both saving money and improving their environmental performance. Firms were encouraged to develop environmental strategies which incorporate pollution prevention, internal compliance auditing and compliance assurance and to seek out win-win outcomes which combine environmental and economic goals.[23] The new policy challenge was to design environmental policies which reward, facilitate and encourage environmental leaders to go 'beyond compliance' with regulation and to shift the

22 Bill Clinton, 'Reinventing Environmental Regulation' (State of the Union Address, Washington, January 1995) <http://govinfo.library.unt.edu/npr/library/rsreport/251a.html#overview> accessed 19 December 2008.

23 S Hart, 'Strategies for a Sustainable World' (1997) 75 Harvard Business Review 66.

entire regulatory compliance curve (embracing laggards at one end and leaders at the other) in the direction of improved environmental performance. But in contrast to the voluntary approaches described above, the new regulatory flexibility initiatives sought to integrate with other policy instruments rather than to use such instruments as substitutes for regulation.

Early efforts at regulatory flexibility focused on a shift away from specification or technology-based environmental regulations (which tell duty holders precisely what measures to take) towards performance standards (which specify outcomes or the desired level of performance). The logic was that performance standards could foster innovation because they free up an enterprise to respond to a regulator's requirement in the way it best thinks fit.[24] However, performance standards still have a substantial limitation, namely they only require enterprises to achieve minimum standards and provide no incentives or encouragement to go beyond those minima or to engage in continuous improvement.

Accordingly, the Clinton–Gore administration, along with a number of other Anglo-Saxon governments (most notably in Canada and some Australian States) began experimenting with an innovative approach to standard setting variously termed 'process-based', 'systems-based' or 'management based' regulation.[25] This approach involves firms developing their own process and management system standards, and developing internal planning and management practices designed to achieve regulatory goals. Such standards have the considerable attractions of providing flexibility to enterprises to devise their own least-cost solutions to social challenges, of facilitating their going beyond compliance with minimum legal standards, and (in contrast to direct regulation) of being applicable to a broad range of circumstances and to heterogeneous enterprises. For present purposes, such initiatives will be termed 'management-based regulation'.

In part, this approach was made possible by the development of management tools designed to assist firms to focus on systemic problems rather than individual deficiencies. Such tools involve the assessment and control of risks and the creation of an in-built system of maintenance and review. For example, an environmental management system focuses on organisational structure,

24 M Porter and C van der Linde, 'Green and Competitive: Ending the Stalemate' (1995) 73 Harvard Business Review.

25 C Coglianese and D Lazar, 'Management-Based Regulation: Prescribing Private Management to Achieve Public Goals' (2003) 37 Law and Society Review 691. Process based or 'management based' standards identify a particular series of steps (or processes), to be followed in the pursuit of environmental protection. The most important example is the approach to managing hazards by incorporating the steps of hazard identification, risk assessment and risk control. Other examples include: the requirements for employers to provide information, instruction, training and supervision; to monitor environmental matters, and to keep information and records relating to them. In their more advanced forms, process based standards involve a holistic and systematic approach to managing the environment across the organisation as a whole—usually through a formal environmental management system.

responsibilities, practices, procedures and on resources for implementing and maintaining environmental management. As such management tools were formalised (eg through the International Organization for Standardization's ISO 14001 environmental management systems standard), many regulators saw an opportunity to harness such standards in the development of a new form of regulation—requiring regulated entities to achieve public goals through planning, systems of work or other process-based management techniques rather than through remedying individual deficiencies or by achieving particular outcomes.

Management-based regulation is now to be found in a diversity of policy domains.[26] Many of these initiatives are mandatory (Risk Management Planning required under the US Clean Air Act and Major Hazard Management Plans under Queensland mine legislation). However, a substantial number of others are incentives based. These have included regulatory flexibility programmes in the USA such as the National Environmental Performance Track[27] and its state equivalents,[28] Environmental Improvement Plans in a number of Australian jurisdictions[29] and a multiplicity of Canadian initiatives.[30] In broad terms, these programmes offer regulatory rewards and incentives in return for a commitment to adopt and implement an environmental management system, sometimes coupled with a process of dialogue with the local community, or even some more formal means of direct community participation in the decision-making process.[31]

Taken one step further, management-based regulation can become a form of 'meta-regulation' or 'meta-risk management' in which government (or corporations seeking to regulate their multiple facilities), rather than regulating directly, risk-manage the risk management of individual enterprises or facilities. Under such an approach (epitomised by the UK 'safety case' regime for North Sea oil and Major Hazards Facilities)[32] the role of regulation ceases to be primarily about inspectors or auditors checking compliance with rules,

26 Coglianese and Lazar (n 25); C Coglianese and J Nash (eds), *Leveraging the Private Sector: Management-based Strategies for Improving Environmental Performance* (Resources for the Future, Washington, DC 2006).

27 US EPA, 'National Environmental Performance Track' <http://www.epa.gov/perftrac/> accessed 1 July 2008.

28 Wisconsin Department of Natural Resources, 'Green Tier' <http://dnr.wi.gov/org/caer/cea/environmental/> accessed 19 December 2008.

29 C Holley and N Gunningham, 'Environment Improvement Plans: Facilitative Regulation in Practice' (2006) 23 Environmental and Planning Law Journal 448.

30 K Webb, *Voluntary codes: Private Governance, the Public Interest and Innovation* (Carleton Research Unit for Innovation, Science and Environment, Carleton University, Ottawa 2004). To a much lesser degree some elements of this approach can also be found in the UK Environment Agency's approach to risk management initiatives, particularly in terms of Operator and Pollution Risk Appraisal (OPRA) as a tool for assessing environmental risk.

31 See for example, N Gunningham 'The New Collaborative Environmental Governance: The Localization of Regulation' (2009) 36 Journal of Law and Society 145.

32 This was first instituted in the UK and later adopted in the European Union with regard to Major Hazard Facilities under the Seveso II Directive. What is distinctive about this approach

and becomes more about encouraging the industry or facility to put in place processes and management systems which are then scrutinised by regulators or corporate auditors. Rather than regulating prescriptively, meta-regulation seeks to stimulate modes of self-organisation within the firm in such a way as to encourage internal self-critical reflection about its performance. Distinctive to meta-regulation is the onus it places on the duty holder to develop their own self-regulatory initiatives and to put in their own systems and oversight mechanisms.[33] Thus under meta-regulation, the primary role of the inspectorate becomes that of 'regulating at a distance', relying upon the organisation itself to put in place appropriate systems and oversight mechanisms, but taking the necessary action to ensure that these mechanisms are working effectively.

The ultimate test of the success or otherwise of regulatory flexibility initiatives or meta-regulation as described above is an empirical one. The early evidence was not particularly positive. Regulatory flexibility initiatives seemed to 'operate more or less at the margins of the existing regulatory system, tinkering with incremental changes'.[34] Project XL (the Clinton–Gore flagship regulatory flexibility initiative), in particular, met with sustained criticism from a variety of quarters as experience mounted of serious problems. The programme attracted far fewer applications than had been anticipated, applicants proposed fewer innovations than EPA had hoped, the approval process took longer than expected, and the administrative law implications of what is essentially 'contract based regulation' were not worked through.[35] Too high transactions costs, a failure to overcome mutual mistrust, the lack of a statutory base and a vague definition of 'better' results, have also been identified as particular weaknesses.[36]

But it would be dangerous to generalise from the particular limitations of the American initiatives. In contrast, a rather different approach to regulatory flexibility in the Australian state of Victoria, the Environmental Improvement

is that responsibility is placed on the operator of a Major Hazard Facility to submit their plans to the regulator (or conceivably a third party) for approval (eg to 'make their case' that they have addressed all hazards and ensured that the facility is as safe and capable of minimising its environmental impact, as practicable). Those plans are then audited and, if satisfactory, form the basis for accreditation. The regulator's role is not to prescribe what action should be taken by the operator but to accredit the Safety Case and oversee its implementation.

33 C Parker, *The Open Corporation: Effective Self-Regulation and Democracy* (CUP, Cambridge 2002).

34 M Crow, 'Beyond Experiments' (2000) May/June Environmental Forum 19.

35 The best account of the administrative law dimension of this evolving saga, is J Freeman, 'The Contracting State' (2000) 28 Florida State University Law Review 155.

36 For a general critique of Project XL see R Steinzor, 'Regulating Reinvention: Does the Emperor Have any Clothes?' (1996) 26 Environmental Law Reporter. For a broader critique of environmental flexibility initiatives see T Davies and J Mazurek *Industry Incentives for Environmental Improvement: Evaluation of US Federal Initiatives* (Global Environment Management Initiative, Washington, DC 2000).

Plan, has been a considerable success,[37] particularly in engaging with industry leaders and in integrating a management-based approach in conjunction with community participation and regulatory oversight. Not only have these plans empowered local communities directly but they also have increased pressure on companies to improve their environmental performance and, through structured dialogue, have greatly improved relationships between communities, enterprises and the EPA. In doing so, they have improved environmental outcomes on issues of community concern, increased the level of trust between communities and companies and created a more predictable investment environment. While the success of this approach in dealing with environmental laggards has been more qualified than in dealing with leaders, even here the evidence indicates a substantial improvement on the status quo.[38]

Nevertheless, the jury is still out on the ultimate success of regulatory flexibility initiatives and on whether or to what extent, the benefits of the various initiatives outweigh the costs.[39] It remains an open question whether the skeptics are correct in questioning why so many resources are being devoted to making the top 20% (or perhaps only the top 5%) even better, rather than concentrating on the most serious problems or on underperformers. And the efficacy of environmental management systems (particularly those which are mandated) remains hotly contested, with only limited evidence currently available as to how they work in practice.[40]

In the case of meta-regulation, the evidence is more positive. The conventional wisdom is that the safety case model has achieved considerable success. This is not only the view of senior and experienced regulators closely associated with this approach,[41] but also of a number of independent studies.[42]

37 Holley and Gunningham (n 29).

38 N Gunningham and D Sinclair, *Leaders and Laggards: Next Generation Environmental Regulation* (Greenleaf, Sheffield 2002) ch 8.

39 For a summary of empirical evidence see the National Database on Environmental Management Systems, <http://www.eli.org/isopilots> accessed 17 December 2008. See also J Borck, C Coglianese and J Nash, 'Environmental Leadership Programs: Toward an Empirical Assessment of Their Performance' Ecology Law Quarterly, forthcoming.

40 Coglianese and Nash (n 26) 20; National Database on Environmental Management Systems, 'Study Concludes Environmental Management Systems Can Boost Performance, Compliance' <http://www.eurekalert.org/pub.releases/2003-03/uonc-sce030603.php> accessed 23 February 2007; R Andrews, A Hutson and D Edwards, 'Environmental Management Under Pressure: How Do Mandates Affect Performance?' in C Coglianese and J Nash (eds), *Leveraging the Private Sector: Management-based Strategies for Improving Environmental Performance* (Resources for the Future, Washington, DC 2006); M Potoski and A Prakash, 'Covenants with Weak Swords: ISO 14001 and Firms' Environmental Performance' (2005) 24 Journal of Policy Analysis and Management 745.

41 P Wilkinson, 'Safety Case: Success of Failure', National Research Centre for OHS Regulation' (2002) <http://www.ohs.anu.edu.au/publications/pdf/seminar.paper_2.pdf> accessed 23 February 2007.

42 See for example: P Øystein Saksvik and K Nytro, 'Implementation of Internal Control of Health, Environment and Safety in Norwegian Enterprises' (Paper presented to Seventh European Congress on Work and Organisational Psychology, Gyor, Hungary, 2005); P Øystein

However, not all the evidence is in one direction.[43] Heiler, in an important review, concludes that:

> objective evidence about the effectiveness of a [Safety Case Regime] is difficult to locate . . . there are more assertions about the effectiveness of a SCR than hard evidence. This may not detract from the *actual* effectiveness of a SRC . . . but it is clear that claims about demonstrable effects must be treated carefully.[44]

A meta-analysis commissioned by the Health and Safety Executive in 2003, is particularly illuminating. This pointed out that there have been 'disappointingly few attempts at objective research'.[45] It does, however, suggest that, on some indicators at least, the safety case approach has been beneficial, including its capacity to improve overall hazard identification and control. However, it was not clear whether a safety case improves overall safety culture and safety communications.[46]

## 3. The Roles of Business

For many years business's approach to environmental issues was an essentially reactive one. Business regarded environmental regulation as imposing a largely unjustified economic burden that threatened its profitability, and competitiveness and business lobby groups devoted considerable energy to resisting the enactment of environmental regulation.[47] They regarded such legislation as unnecessary, the problems it was intended to address as of little significance, and the costs of compliance as unconscionable. Even those who came to regard it as a necessary evil were hardly enthusiastic participants in the regulatory enterprise.

But over the last 15 years or so, a transformation has taken place in the attitude of some parts of business. Today, a growing number of corporations have been convinced that there is a 'business case' for going beyond compliance. This case can take a number of forms. In the mining industry,

Saksvik and K Nytro, *Implementation of Internal Control of Health, Environment and Safety: An Evaluation and a Model for Implementation* (Institute for Social Research in Industry, Trondheim, Norway 1995).

43 C Woolfson, J Foster and M Beck, *'Paying for the Piper': Capital & Labour in Britain's Offshore Oil Industry* (Mansell Publishing Ltd, UK 1997) 385.

44 K Heiler, 'Is the Australian Mining Industry Ready for a Safety Case Regime?' (2006) National Research Centre for Occupational Health and Safety Regulation, Working Paper 45 at 9 <http://www.ohs.anu.edu.au/> accessed 23 January 2007.

45 Vectra Group Ltd, *Literature Review on the Perceived Benefits and Disadvantages of UK Safety Case Regimes* (HSE, UK 2003) <http://www.hse.gov.uk/RESEARCH/misc/sc402083.pdf> accessed 23 February 2007.

46 Ibid 3.

47 See generally A Hoffman, *From Heresy to Dogma: An Institutional History of Corporate Environmentalism*, (Stanford Business Books, Stanford 2001).

it is based on cost-reduction, competitive advantage and reputational enhancement,[48] while large chemical companies usually go beyond compliance for reasons related primarily to the perceived need to protect their reputation and maintain the trust of local communities.[49] In these and a variety of other industries, an increasing number of corporations are seeking to combine the objectives of environmental protection and economic growth, whether by preventing pollution and, thereby, cutting costs and avoiding waste directly, by more effective risk management (including minimising the risk of accidents, costly cleanups and environmental liability) or by gaining an increasing share of expanding 'green markets'. Thus a common refrain is that going beyond compliance is both good for business and good for the environment, whether this was couched in terms of harnessing the benefits of natural capitalism, a shift to clean production and product stewardship, taking advantage of the incentives for innovation and competitive advantage provided by environmental regulation or risk management (the principal driver being the fear that without taking measures to protect one's reputation, communities, NGOs, regulators or others may take action which will adversely affect the corporate bottom line).[50]

Those who view the environment in these terms do not have a problem with environmental regulation per se since they believe there are good reasons for achieving levels of environmental performance at least as high as that required by law. However, they do have problems with 'forms' of regulation that impose unnecessary costs upon them and that constrain their environmental initiatives. And they are particularly dissatisfied with the cost and inflexibility of command and control regulation, and for these reasons have sought less confrontational alternatives. In this regard the Yorktown experiment in the USA, where an Amoco refinery found that they were able to achieve the same level of emissions reduction as required by regulation at a quarter of the cost, if they were 'freed up' from the regulatory requirements, is salutary.[51]

Nevertheless, it is only a limited proportion of businesses that take this view and the empirical evidence that is available suggests that certain firms and

48 J Walker and S Howard, *Finding the Way Forward: How Could Voluntary Action Move Mining Towards Sustainable Development?* (International Institute for Environment and Development and WBCSD, London 2002). See also N Yakovleva, *Corporate Social Responsibility in the Mining Industries* (Ashgate, Aldershot 2005).

49 N Gunningham, D Thornton and R Kagan, 'Motivating Management: Corporate Compliance in Environmental Protection' (2005) 27 Law and Policy 289–316, 301.

50 F Reinhardt, *Down to Earth: Applying Business Principles to Environmental Management* (Harvard Business School Press, USA 2000) ch 6. Note that Vogel argues that 'there *is* a business case for CSR, but it is . . . best understood as a niche rather than as a generic category: it makes business sense for some firms in some areas under some circumstances', D Vogel, *The Market for Virtue The Potential and Limits of Corporate Social Responsibility* (Brookings Institution Press, Washington DC 2005) 3.

51 Amoco/EPA Yorktown Project, *Lessons Learned and Future Steps* (undated) <http://www.fischer-tropsch.org/DOE/.conf.proc/MISC/CONF-94013319/CONF-94013319.%20Tabs%2012%20-%2018%20(pgs.%201-35).pdf> accessed 10 January 2009.

certain sectors are much more likely to go beyond compliance than others. Gunningham, Kagan and Thornton have suggested that the business risks that going beyond compliance may circumvent and the opportunities that it provides can best be thought about in terms of a socially constructed 'licence to operate'.[52] This licence includes economic and social demands as well as the demands of government regulators, what they termed the economic, social and regulatory licences, respectively. What a company decides to do in terms of going beyond compliance, it was suggested, can be explained largely by how it interprets and responds to the various licence terms. For example large, reputation sensitive companies, which are regularly scrutinised by environmental groups and local communities, will be particularly driven to go beyond compliance by the conditions of their 'social licence'. Other firms or industries, which are not subjected to such external pressures (including most small- and medium-sized business), are far less likely to do so.

Importantly, the various licence terms are interconnected. For example, corporations fear that not meeting the requirements of the 'social licence' will ultimately result in increased regulation or greater economic costs to the company. One consequence is that the interaction of the different types of licence often exceeds the effect of each type of licence in isolation.

This analysis has important normative implications, because understanding the connections between the different strands of the licence to operate enables policy-makers to understand more clearly how various licence terms might be invoked to better shape and design environmental regulation. For example, procedural empowerment through law (the regulatory licence) was found to be a particularly potent means of expanding the terms of the social licence and thereby the scope of corporate environmental initiatives, as was the use of the regulatory licence to expand the social licence through requirements to disclose comparative information (such as by the Toxic Release Inventory (TRI) described below.

Moreover, as Christmann and Taylor argue, to the extent that there is a business case for corporate environmental responsibility, it may be appropriate for public policy itself to shift from a corporate accountability model (as through environmental regulation) to a corporate responsibility model.[53] The latter implies a lesser role for legal compliance and a much wider role for voluntarism and self-regulation and/or regulatory flexibility, driven by the enlightened self-interest of business in regulating itself. It is beyond the scope of this article to explore this argument in detail. Suffice it to say that much depends on the industry sector in question and upon its economic circumstances.

52 Gunningham, Kagan and Thornton (n 8).

53 P Christmann and G Taylor, 'Globalization and the Environment: Strategies for International Voluntary Environmental Initiatives (2002) 16 Academy of Management Executive 121.

## 4. Roles of Civil Society

While government regulators have been losing both their power and resources, others, including communities and NGOs have begun to fill the regulatory space they previously occupied.

Community-based environmental protection has gained increasing attention as either a complement or a substitute for traditional direct regulation. At least in principle it can deliver both procedural and outcome benefits.[54] Such an approach also fosters environmental awareness in the community, which in turn can lead the community to mobilise in ways that result in improvements in environmental performance at a local level.[55]

At a regional, national or global level, probably the biggest gains have been achieved by Environmental NGOs. These organisations, aided by advanced techniques for information gathering (from digital cameras to satellite imaging) have become increasingly sophisticated at communicating their message (via global television, international newspapers and the internet) and in using the media (and sometimes the courts) to amplify the impact of their campaigns. They have not only sought to shape public opinion, to lobby governments and to pressure them to enact and enforce tougher environmental laws and regulations but also to influence consumers and markets through strategies such as orchestrating consumer boycotts or preferences for green products. And some NGOs, frustrated with their limited impact on governments, or at the ineffectiveness of government in protecting the environment, have redirected their attention towards corporations through strategies ranging from confrontation and direct action to partnership and co-operation.

In terms of the former, perhaps the definitive incident was the confrontation between Shell and Greenpeace UK concerning the proposed dismantling and disposal at sea of a disused oil rig, the Brent Spar. The company, with the endorsement of the British government, proposed disposal of the oil rig in the deep sea. There was considerable scientific support for this option but Greenpeace organised a worldwide, high-profile media campaign against the plan. This included direct action and the occupation of the oil rig. Public support for Greenpeace actions was international and there was a widespread boycott of Shell service stations in Northern Europe. Ultimately Shell abandoned its disposal plans for the Brent Spar. The incident had a searing effect not just on Shell itself but also on other major reputation sensitive companies which realised, perhaps for the first time, the economic and social damage that could be unleashed upon them by NGOs.

54 S Meyer and D Konisky, 'Community-based Environmental Protection: A Status Report and Some New Evidence' (Massachusetts Institute of Technology, 2005) <http://web.mit.edu/polisci/research/meyer/Outcomes.April05.pdf> accessed 17 December 2008.

55 Holley and Gunningham (n 29).

In terms of co-operative strategies, perhaps the most popular have involved environmental partnerships which came of age in the 1990s when parts of industry and NGOs recognised that conflict and confrontation were not necessarily the best means of achieving either the best economic or environmental results.[56] According to their proponents, environmental partnerships provide opportunities to replace adversarialism with co-operation, and in doing so, may provide benefits for all sides. For example, through 'green alliances' business may obtain the political goodwill and credibility which NGOs bring to the partnership, while in return, environmental groups gain commitments to improved environmental practices on the part of their business partner.

Over time, the diverse actions of NGOs and communities to protect the environment became seen as a form of surrogate or indirect regulation, sometimes termed 'civil regulation'. As defined by Murphy and Bendall 'civil regulation is where organisations of civil society such as NGOs, set the standards for business behaviour. Enterprises then choose to adopt or not to adopt those standards'.[57] Those who advocate this approach argue that the regulatory state is starved of resources, lacking in political will, and incapable of reaching the many businesses, which can now operate outside national territorial boundaries. The goal of civil regulation is to fill the vacuum left by the retreating state and to compensate for 'the deficit of democratic governance that we face as a result of economic globalisation'.[58]

Under civil regulation, the various manifestations of civil society act in a variety of ways to influence corporations, consumers and markets, often bypassing the state and rejecting political lobbying in favour of what they believe to be far more effective strategies. Sometimes NGOs take direct action, usually targeted at large reputation-sensitive companies, as in the Brent Spar example. Sometimes, they boycott products or producers deemed to be environmentally harmful, as with the effective boycott of Norwegian fish products organised by the Greenpeace in protest against that nation's resumption of whaling. Market campaigning, focusing on highly visible branded retailers, is a particularly favoured strategy. Less so, are campaigns, which seek to provide a market premium for 'environmentally preferred' produce, due largely to the unwillingness of consumers to support such a strategy. More recently, certification programmes such as the Forest Stewardship Council are 'transforming traditional power relationships in the global arena. Linking together diverse and often antagonistic actors from the local, national

56 D Murphy and J Bendell, *In the Company of Partners: Business, Environmental Groups and Sustainable Development Post-Rio* (Policy Press, Bristol 1997).

57 D Murphy and J Bendell, 'Editorial' (1998) Winter Greener Management International 8.

58 J Bendell, 'Civil Regulation: A New Form of Democratic Governance for the Global Economy' in J Bendall (ed), *Terms of Endearment: Business, NGOs and Sustainable Development* (Greenleaf, London 2000) 239 at 241.

and international levels . . . to govern firm behaviour in a global space that has eluded the control of states and international organisations'.[59]

However, the evolving role of civil regulation has not been entirely divorced from state intervention. On the contrary, either in response to pressure from the institutions of civil society or in recognition of the limits of state regulation, governments are gradually providing greater roles for communities, environmental NGOs and the public more generally. Thus a number of 'next generation' policy instruments are geared to empower various institutions of civil society to play a more effective role in shaping business behaviour. In effect, they facilitate civil regulation.

Chief amongst these initiatives is 'information based regulation'[60] which has been defined as 'regulation which provides to affected stakeholders information on the operations of regulated entities, usually with the expectation that such stakeholders will then exert pressure on those entities to comply with regulations in a manner which serves the interests of stakeholders'.[61] This is epitomised by Community Right to Know (CRTK) legislation, the most powerful manifestation of which is the US TRI (a response to the Bhopal chemical disaster of 1984). The TRI, by requiring facilities to track and report their emissions, not only empowers community groups and enables markets to make more informed judgments but also leads to a degree of corporate self-reflection on how things might be done differently. Thus a strategy which involves no requirement to do anything other than estimate discharges and disclose them may have a variety of broader consequences, including generating internal organisational change (and corporate shaming) which may in turn result in substantially improved environmental performance for many companies. Following the success of this initiative, a number of European, Canadian and Australian initiatives were also introduced, broadly modelled on the same principles of transparency and accountability[62]—the Global Reporting Initiative being the most recent and arguably the most important international initiative of this type.[63]

59 G Gereffi, R Garcia-Johnson and E Sass, 'The NGO-Industry Complex' (2001) July/August Foreign Policy <http://www.foreignpolicy.Council of Ministers/issue julyaug.2001/gereffi.html> accessed 19 December 2008.

60 C Sabel, A Fung and B Karkkainen, *Beyond Backyard Environmentalism* (Beacon Press, Boston 2000).

61 P Kleindorfer and E Orts, 'Informational Regulation of Information Risks' (1996) Wharton School, University of Pennsylvania Working Paper at 6.

62 See generally B Karkkainen, 'Information as Environmental Regulation: TRI Performance Benchmarking, Precursor to a New Paradigm?' (2001) 89 Georgetown Law Journal 257.

63 H Brown, 'Turning the Lens on Corporate Transparency: Is the Global Reporting Initiative becoming a Global Institution for Civil-Private Regulation?' (Paper presented at the annual meeting of the ISA's 49th Annual Convention, Bridging Multiple Divides, San Francisco 2008) <http://www.allacademic.com/meta/p250770.index.html> accessed 11 December 2008.

## 5. State, Business and Civil Society: Bringing It All Together

By the 1990s, regulatory agencies were becoming acutely aware of their limited knowledge, capacities and resources to regulate directly, particularly with regard to increasingly complex environmental problems. Although they had survived a deregulatory assault during the era of Ronald Reagan and Margaret Thatcher, they rarely found their new political masters supportive of stronger regulatory intervention, or willing to provide the resources necessary to extend their ambit.

In this context it is important to point out that it was not just politically conservative administrations such as those of George W Bush in the USA, Stephen Harper in Canada or John Howard in Australia, that opposed tougher regulation but also the Blair Government in the UK and a range of state and provincial labour governments in Australia and Canada. The approach of the Blair government is illustrative of the attitudes of even purportedly 'reformist' neo-liberal governments towards regulation. The titles of the various official inquires into regulation initiated by the Blair government tells its own story. The influential Hampton Review in 2005 was entitled 'Reducing Administrative Burdens',[64] while the Better Regulation Task Force Report in the same year was entitled 'Regulation—Less is More: Reducing Burdens, Improving Outcomes'.[65] The bureaucracies that such governments set up also betrayed their misgivings about regulation and their sympathy with 'overregulated' business—as in the fact that the various 'Better Regulation' initiatives in the UK are located in the Department for Business, Enterprise and Regulatory Reform, or that the Australian Office of Regulatory Reform was for a long time located within the Productivity Commission.

In such a political environment, environmental regulators have had to explore alternatives to traditional regulation that would meet with the approval of governments and their constituencies. It was far more acceptable for regulators to talk about encouraging, facilitating, and shaping environmental partnerships with business than it was to talk about the need for more resources, greater sanctioning powers and tougher penalties. Increasingly, regulators talked of 'regulating at a distance', 'light handed regulation' and 'steering not rowing' in policy design. This last approach[66] was particularly attractive in an era of diminishing resources where the regulatory space once

64 P Hampton, 'Reducing Administrative Burdens: Effective Inspection and Enforcement' (HM Treasury, London 2005).

65 Better Regulation Task Force, 'Regulation—Less is More: Reducing Burdens, Improving Outcomes' (A BRTF report to the Prime Minister, 2005) <http://archive.cabinetoffice.gov.uk/brc/upload/assets/www.brc.gov.uk/lessismore.exec.summary.pdf> accessed 17 December 2008.

66 D Osborne and T Gaebler, *Reinventing Government: How the Entrepreneurial Spirit is Transforming the Public Sector* (Addison-Wesley, Reading 1992).

occupied almost exclusively by the state was now being filled by NGOs, business self regulation and by a variety of third parties who might conceivably act as surrogate regulators. In the terminology of the Blair administration, was there a 'third way' that would enable agencies to better avoid the pitfalls of both direct regulation and markets in such a way as to achieve their environmental objectives, but without threatening legitimate business or damaging business competitiveness?

In this new political environment, there were a number of attempts to design more business friendly and less demanding alternatives to traditional regulation but without leaving business with an entirely free rein. Some of these have already been mentioned, including environmental partnerships with industry, regulatory flexibility in conjunction with greater industry self-regulation, the expanded use of meta-regulation and the encouragement of voluntary initiatives. But two other initiatives—regulatory pluralism and the new environmental governance—merit more detailed treatment: because they recognise the extent to which it is no longer practicable, or even desirable, for government regulators to 'go it alone' and because they recognise and harness the reality that business and civil society cannot be treated as bit players or (in the case of business) passive recipients of government regulation, but can and should play increasingly important roles in the regulatory enterprise.

### A. *Towards Regulatory Pluralism?*

One concept that resonated with what practitioners were seeking or in some cases already designing (but in the absence of a broader theoretical framework) was that of regulatory pluralism or 'Smart Regulation'. This latter term has been used to refer to an emerging form of wide-angled regulation that seeks to harness not just governments but also business and third parties to provide policy alternatives that include, but often go beyond, direct regulation.

The central normative argument of Smart Regulation is that, in the majority of circumstances, the use of multiple rather than single policy instruments, and a broader range of regulatory actors can and should be used to produce better regulation than single instrument or single party approaches. This will allow the implementation of complementary combinations of instruments and participants tailored to meet the imperatives of specific environmental issues, and will result in a more flexible, efficient and effective approach to environmental regulation than has so far been adopted in most circumstances.[67]

67 N Gunningham, P Grabosky with D Sinclair, *Smart Regulation: Designing Environmental Policy* (OUP, New York 1998).

To put this concept in context, it is important to remember that regulation was traditionally thought of as a bi-partite process involving government and business, with the former acting in the role of regulator and the latter as regulatee. However, a substantial body of empirical research reveals that there is a plurality of regulatory forms, that numerous actors influence the behaviour of regulated groups in a variety of complex and subtle ways,[68] and that mechanisms of informal social control often prove more important than formal ones. In the case of the environment, Smart Regulation suggests that we should focus our attention on how behaviour can be shaped by a diversity of unconventional but (in a broad sense) regulatory mechanisms such as the influence of: international standards; trading partners and the supply chain; commercial institutions and financial markets; peer pressure and self-regulation through industry associations; internal environmental management systems and culture and civil society in a myriad of different forms.

In particular, Smart Regulation invites policy-makers to investigate how legislative structures and public agencies may harness institutions and resources residing 'outside' the public sector to further policy objectives in specific concrete situations. This approach can be seen as part of the broader transition in the role of governments internationally: from 'rowing the boat to steering it'[69] or choosing to 'regulate at a distance' by acting as facilitators of self- and co-regulation rather than regulating directly. Thus for Smart Regulation, environmental policy-making involves government harnessing the capacities of markets, civil society and other institutions to accomplish its policy goals more effectively, with greater social acceptance and at less cost to the state.[70] And since parties and instruments interact with each other and with state regulation in variety of ways, careful regulatory design will be necessary to ensure that pluralistic policy instruments are mutually reinforcing, rather than being duplicative, or worse, conflicting.[71]

In short, Smart Regulation argues that policy-makers should take advantage of a number of largely unrecognised opportunities, strategies and techniques for achieving efficient and effective environmental policy, including: by designing complementary instrument mixes rather than relying on single instrument approaches; by preferring less interventionist measures to the extent that this is practicable; by escalating response up an instrument

68 J Rees, *Reforming the Workplace: A Study of Self-Regulation in Occupational Safety* (University of Pennsylvania Press, Philadelphia 1988).

69 Osborne and Gaebler (n 66).

70 N Gunningham, M Phillipson and P Grabosky, 'Harnessing Third Parties as Surrogate Regulators: Achieving Environmental Outcomes by Alternative Means' (1999) 8 Business Strategy and the Environment 211–224.

71 Gunningham, Grabosky with Darren Sinclair (n 67) ch 6.

pyramid (utilising not only government but also business and third parties) so as to build in regulatory responsiveness and dependability of outcomes; by empowering third parties (both commercial and non-commercial) to act as surrogate regulators and by maximising opportunities for win-win outcomes (expanding the boundaries within which such opportunities are available and encouraging business to go 'beyond compliance' with existing legal requirements).[72]

A substantial number of policy instruments of the last decade are consistent with the precepts of Smart Regulation,[73] which has also been a driver of ecological modernisation (that emphasises how it is possible to simultaneously increase efficiency and minimise pollution and waste). Others, such as the regulatory flexibility initiatives established under the Clinton–Gore 'Reinventing Environmental Regulation' initiative, were directly inspired by Osborne and Gaebler's concept of 'steering not rowing'.[74] Under both approaches (as indeed under meta-regulation), attempts have been made to embed environmental values and processes within the corporate culture in such a way that it becomes self-regulating, relying upon oversight from local communities and perhaps third-party auditors, to supplement or even replace direct regulation. This is the case with the more advanced regulatory flexibility initiatives in the USA, with the 'safety case' and Major Hazard Facilities regulation in the UK and EU, and with a number of initiatives in some Australian states, most notably the development of Environment Improvement Plans in Victoria. More recently the European Community Regulation on chemicals and their safe use,[75] which deals with the Registration, Evaluation, Authorisation and Restriction of Chemical substances (REACH) is also built on very similar principles.[76] While some of these initiatives, such as REACH, are of such recent origin that evaluation would be premature, others (most notably EIPs, safety case and MHF regulation) are widely regarded as amongst the most successful of regulatory initiatives, as discussed above.

72 Ibid.

73 See in particular the Canadian government's regulatory reform programme under this banner. Government of Canada, 'Implementation Plan for Smart Regulation' (2005) <http://www.tbs-sct.gc.ca/media/ps-dp/2005/0324-eng.asp> accessed 17 December 2008; and W Leese, 'Smart Regulation and Risk Management' (A paper prepared at the request of the Bureau du Conseil Privé/Privy Council Office Comité Consultatif Externe sur la Réglementation Intelligente (CCERI) External Advisory Committee on Smart Regulation (EACSR) 2005) <http://www.smartregulation.gc.ca> accessed 17 December 2008. See also M Janicke, 'Ecological Modernization: New Perspectives (2008) 16 Journal of Cleaner Production 557, at 559.

74 Osborne and Gaebler (n 66).

75 European Community, 'Reach' (2007) <http://ec.europa.eu/environment/chemicals/reach/reach_intro.htm> accessed 11 Jan 2009.

76 D Farber, 'Five Regulatory Lessons from REACH' UC Berkeley Public Law Research Paper No. 1301306/2008 <http://papers.ssrn.com/sol3/papers.cfm?abstract_id=1301306> accessed 17 December 2008.

### B. From Regulation to Governance?

A more recent and far-reaching environmental initiative that also directly involves the state, business and civil society is commonly referred to as the 'new environmental governance'. This enterprise involves collaboration between a diversity of private, public and non-government stakeholders who, acting together towards commonly agreed (or mutually negotiated) goals, hope to achieve far more collectively, than individually. It relies heavily upon participatory dialogue and deliberation, devolved decision-making, flexibility rather than uniformity, inclusiveness, transparency and institutionalised consensus-building practices.[77]

The framing of this initiative as one of 'governance' rather than 'regulation' is deliberate and suggests an approach based on 'societal steering' in its broadest sense[78] with decision-making involving the totality of interactions between public and private actors, and the state no longer playing a central role in decision-making. For example a variety of non-state actors may assume administrative, regulatory, managerial and mediating functions previously undertaken by the state.

Since the 'new environmental governance' is still evolving, its precise architecture remains open to debate and numerous versions of 'democratic experimentalism' arguably fall under this heading.[79] In the USA they can be found in Habitat Conservation Plans under the Endangered Species Act and in the Chesapeake Bay and San Francisco Bay Delta Programmes.[80] Within the EU, new collaborative environmental governance is expressed in increased flexibility in the setting of Community norms, accompanied by a 'proceduralisation' of Community law, increasingly open-ended environmental standards and an increased role of a range of stakeholders in decision-making processes.[81] The Water Framework Directive, an example of the Open Method of Coordination, is sometimes held up as an exemplar of this approach.[82]

77 See generally D Trubek and L Trubek, 'New Governance & Legal Regulation' (2007) 13 Columbia Journal of European Law 540, 542.

78 By this they mean the management of the course of events in a social system and the use of institutions and structures of authority (including collaboration) to allocate resources and coordinate or control societal activity. For a fuller and widely quoted definition see J Kooiman, *Governing as Governance* (Sage, London 2003) 4.

79 M Dorf and C Sabel, 'A Constitution of Democratic Experimentalism' (1998) 98 Columbia Law Review 267.

80 B Karkkainen, 'Collaborative Ecosystem Governance: Scale, Complexity, and Dynamism' (2001/2002) 21 Virginia Environmental Law Journal 189; J Freeman and D Farber, 'Modular Environmental Regulation' (2005) 54 Duke Law Journal 795.

81 J Scott and D Trubek, 'Mind the Gap: Law and New Approaches to Governance in the European Union' (2002) 8 European Law Journal 1.

82 J Scott and J Holder, 'Law and Environmental Governance in the European Union' in G De Burca and J Scott (eds), *Law and New Governance in the EU and the US* (Hart Publishing, Portland 2006).

In New Zealand, this approach can be found in the Resource Management Act 1991, which locates decision-making within regional organisations.

An illustration of how at least one version of 'new governance' may play out, is provided in Box 1 below, which describes an ambitious experiment that is currently taking place in the sphere of Natural Resource Management (NRM) in Australia.

**Box 1** Regional NRM in Australia

In an attempt to overcome the shortcomings of previous NRM policy initiatives, NRM decision-making power in Australia is being devolved to the regional level. Fifty-six regional NRM bodies have been created across Australia at the initiative of the Federal Government. These bodies generally comprise a mix of community, rural and other stakeholders; have formal office holders; and responsibility for undertaking NRM consultation, planning and priority setting. They must each develop a regional plan and regional investment strategy and implement these under a collaborative partnership-based decision-making process. These plans and strategies are subject to performance indicators and other controls imposed by the Federal Government.

This collaborative regional approach involves a style of governance that seeks wide-ranging 'partnerships' between landholders (including indigenous Australians), regional communities, industry, local, State and Territory and Commonwealth governments, and the wider community in which power (in terms of priority setting and how to achieve those priorities, and programme delivery) is exercised through multi-stakeholder participation in decision making (including local land-managers, local communities, NGOs and other ground-level stakeholders), coupled with monitoring, evaluation and oversight by the regional bodies by themselves, by State–Commonwealth Steering Committees, the NRM Ministerial Council, and (through the relevant Ministers themselves) the State and Federal Government itself. There is an emphasis on 'joined-up' institutional arrangements, networks and knowledge exchange. Crucially, the Federal Government, which is providing the money without which these initiatives could not operate, maintains tight control over the purse strings, and regional bodies are well aware that they should depart substantially from the parameters laid down by the Commonwealth, they risk losing their funding, dissolution and replacement by a new entity.

Central to the architecture of the new regional NRM is recognition that different regions/ecosystems raise very different environmental challenges that NRM in each of these regions involves multiple stakeholders and that the resources, capacities and institutions necessary to address the NRM challenges can themselves vary significantly. Accordingly, provision is made to enable each region to develop their own mechanisms for addressing NRM challenges within parameters set nationally, thereby combining 'the advantages of decentralised local experimentation with those of centralised coordination'.[83] Like the Open Method of Coordination (OMC) in the EU, it is a means of reconciling the pursuit of common objectives while respecting the need for diversity at lower levels, and of fostering collective learning 'on the ground' in a manner that is arguably a prerequisite for the advancement of sustainable policies.[84]

An evaluation of the new regional governance is difficult since these initiatives are still in their early stages and have not yet been subject to detailed evaluation. In any event, since they are designed to facilitate considerable experimentation at regional level, different approaches are likely to yield different outcomes. Evaluation of the various initiatives being rolled out in the EU under the Open Method of Coordination is somewhat more advanced but still tentative. Nevertheless, critics are building up an increasing head of steam on the basis of preliminary evidence. Some suggest, for example, that the OMC has failed as a means of pursuing common policies at EU level, while others argue that the OMC has only limited direct effects in the short-term and indirect effects in the medium to long term.[85] In terms of 'a new democratisation', it is said that 'only big corporations, well-organised interest groups, trade-unions, NGOs and some journalists and scholars show an active interest in the decision-making process'.[86] The result may be that 'under the guise of consultation, regulatory powers are virtually delegated to private actors'.[87] And these private actors, in any event, may themselves be vulnerable to co-optation.[88]

With regard to the new regional NRM in Australia, questions yet to be answered include: to what extent this new networked and decentralised approach will bring about a genuine new diffusion of labour between governments, industry, NGOs and others or whether the limits of voluntarism, the burn out of volunteers, and the disparity of resources and power of different interest groups will substantially undermine these aspirations. Certainly the

83 C Sabel and J Zeitlin, 'Learning from Difference: The New Architecture of Experimentalist Governance in the EU' (2008) 14 European Law Journal 271.
84 J Dryzek, *The Politics of the Earth: Environmental Discourses* (OUP, New York 1997).
85 V Hatzopoulos, 'Why the Open Method of Coordination Is Bad For You: A Letter to the EU' (2007) 13 European Law Journal.
86 Ibid 326.
87 Harlow (n 2) 72.
88 D Obradovic and J Vizcaino, 'Good Governance Requirements Concerning the Participation of Interest Groups in EU Consultations' (2006) 43 CML Rev 1049.

new regional NRM is much more pluralistic and deliberative than previous forms of NRM governance, but given the extent to which regional bodies lack autonomy and ultimately power, one might argue that they are primarily a means of incorporating a broader range of stockholders into the existing political establishment without threatening the status quo,[89] which can be maintained through the Commonwealth Government's control of financial resources. And it may even be that rather than identifying, mobilising and co-ordinating local, diverse and dispersed knowledges and capacities, the regional bodies (or at least some of them) will simply become delivery vehicles for government initiatives. For example, some of the new regional bodies have contracted out the consultation, planning and prioritisation phase to independent consultants, which is hardly in keeping with the spirit of deliberative governance. Furthermore, if participation is premised on an increasing level of accountability to central governments, then regional bodies may 'evolve into bureaucracies, undermining both their potential and their original purpose'.[90]

### C. *Law, Regulation and Governance?*

The questions raised immediately above suggest the need to address the fundamental question of the relationship between the new environmental governance and earlier forms of environmental law and regulation. In particular, to what extent is it essential for the state to fulfil certain functions or can the state be effectively 'decentred', becoming simply one of a number of actors involved in governance but no longer privileged in terms of power and influence?[91] And can the environmental policy initiatives of the last four decades be characterised as involving a gradual shift from law, to regulation and now, towards governance?

While law (involving statutory commands and the imposition of sanctions for breach) was dominant in the 1970s and the early-1980s, it gradually had to share the 'regulatory space' with other forms of social control. The interventions of the 1980s and early-1990s involved a much gentler approach on the part of government, with persuasion, informal influence, negotiated agreements, environmental partnerships, and self and co-regulation to the fore. 'Regulation' in its broadest sense (and a particularly 'light-handed form of

89 M Ottaway, 'Corporatism Goes Global: International Organisations, Nongovernmental Organization Networks and Transnational Business' (2001) 7 Global Governance 265–292.

90 T Wallington and G Lawrence, 'Making Democracy Matter: Responsibility and Effective Environmental Governance in Regional Australia' (2008) Journal of Rural Studies, forthcoming.

91 See generally A Mol, 'Bringing the Environmental State Back In: Partnerships in Perspective' in P Glasbergen, F Biermann and A Mol (eds), *Partnerships, Governance and Sustainable Development* (Edward Elgar, Cheltenham 2007).

regulation at that) took centre stage, although the laws of an earlier era were (as a result of public resistance or regulatory gridlock) only exceptionally repealed, and particularly following environmental crises, were gradually expanded. Indeed, if one looks at either the Anglo-Saxon jurisdictions or the Directives of the EU, there is evidence that substantial pockets of command and control regulation are alive and well, and that that even neo-liberal governments continue to favour this approach in some areas[92] and Sabel and Zeitlin argue that even 'new governance' approaches are sometimes to be found in 'old style' instruments (eg the Water Framework Directive).[93]

But during the late-1990s and the early years of the new millennium, some would argue that a further development took place, one that involved a shift from 'regulation to governance' and roles for economic actors and civil society in self-managing what had previously been exclusive state responsibilities. In the writer's view, this is to overstate the significance of what has taken place during that period. While a number of policy initiatives have engaged with non-state agents and agencies, it is only collaborative governance that can credibly claim to have 'decentred the state' and to involve 'governance' rather than 'regulation'. The other major initiatives of this period (regulatory flexibility, meta-regulation and regulatory pluralism) have sought to 'regulate at a distance' with the state acting as facilitator of self and co-regulation and playing important oversight roles rather than regulating directly. While these initiatives evidence an important shift in regulatory architecture and in the roles of the state, they have certainly not resulted in its 'decentering'.

But even under the new environmental governance, although much of the 'rowing' is to be done locally by a variety of stakeholders acting collaboratively, nevertheless, certain central 'steering' functions remain with the state. What is involved is 'collaboration in the shadow of hierarchy' with the state underpinning community-based initiatives in a variety of ways (eg providing the ground rules, resources and enforcement mechanisms in the event of default) without which they are unlikely to succeed. In this combination collaboration provides local knowledge, ownership and legitimacy while the state provides essential steering functions and resources. Indeed, research on three very different new environmental governance initiatives in Australia suggests that the state must continue to play three particular roles: definitional guidance, participatory incentives and enforcement capability.[94] Definitional guidance refers to the state defining the nature of the collaborative governance arrangement in terms of its scope and anticipated outcomes, extent of participation, geographical boundaries and funding arrangements. Participatory incentives

92 Jordan and others (n 16). The Bush administration for example, adopted a series of command and control regulations to address carbon emissions in areas such as lighting and electricity and corporate average fuel economy.

93 Sabel and Zeitlin (n 83).

94 Gunningham (n 31).

refer to the state providing positive or negative incentives for participation (including resources). Enforcement capability refers to mechanisms through which the state ensures that collaborative governance participants fulfil their obligations. Thus it is argued that in many contexts, there is an essential policy coordination role for government in encouraging, facilitating, rewarding and shaping such outcomes, at least unless some other actor/s are ready, willing and able to take on this role. Usually they are not.[95]

The broader point is that many, less interventionist strategies are far less likely to succeed if they are not underpinned by direct regulation. For example, under regulatory flexibility, some enterprises may be tempted to develop 'paper' management systems and tokenistic responses, which 'independent' third-party auditors may fail to detect.[96] However, the threat of sanctions if they fail to deliver on performance targets set by the state will substantially reduce the risk of free riding. Similarly there is evidence that information-based strategies cannot necessarily replace traditional regulation and enforcement practices but rather that the two instruments work best when they are used in a complementary combination.[97] So too in the case of small business, the fear of regulation or its enforcement can be used to good effect to complement other more innovative approaches.[98] Even some market-based instruments, such as tradable emission rights, on closer examination involve a combination of markets and direct regulation (since although trading is a market mechanism, governments design the trading scheme, impose caps on emissions and police compliance).

And lest it be forgotten, according to various surveys, the single most important motivator of improved environmental performance is regulation.[99] The more general conclusion, as the USA EPA has recognised, is that 'in some cases, nationwide laws and regulations will continue to be the best way to reduce risk. But in others, tailored strategies that involve market-based approaches, partnerships or performance incentives may offer better results at lower costs'. However, even the latter, it must be emphasised, are likely to work best 'in the shadow of regulation'.[100]

95 While E Ostrom, *Governing the Commons* (CUP, Cambridge 1990) and others have documented a range of cases where communities, through self-organisation, have evolved solutions to such problems without government intervention, in the case of the sort of complex environmental challenges confronting developed countries, such an approach is exceptional.

96 D O'Rourke, Monitoring the Monitors: A Critique of PricewaterhouseCoopers (PWC) Labor Monitoring (Department of Urban Studies and Planning, MIT, Massachusetts 2000).

97 J Foulon, P Lanouie and B Lapante, *Incentives for Pollution Control: Regulation and (?) or (?) Information* (1999) Policy Research Working Paper, World Bank, Washington DC.

98 N Gunningham, R Kagan and D Thornton, 'Motivating Management: Corporate Compliance in Environmental Protection' (2005) 27 Law and Policy 89.

99 I Henriques and P Sadorsky *The Determinants of an Environmentally Responsive Firm: An Empirical Approach* (Faculty of Admin Studies, York University, Ontario 1995).

100 US EPA, 'A Decade of Progress: Innovation at the Environmental Protection Agency' (EPA Innovation Annual Report, Washington DC 2000) 4.

All this suggests that environmental policy has strayed a substantial way from the classic precepts of neo-liberalism—the hollowing out of the state, privatisation and deregulation—and that a more accurate term to describe governments' behaviour (as distinct from their rhetoric) may be 'regulatory capitalism'. This implies using markets as regulatory mechanisms (rather than seeing them as the antithesis of regulation), the growth of a plethora of non-state regulators and of networks of governance, the expansion rather than the retreat of regulation (albeit in new forms) and 'hybridity between the privatisation of the public and the publicisation of the private'.[101]

## 6. Conclusion

This article has analysed some four decades of environmental law, regulation and governance in various Anglo-Saxon jurisdictions (and to a more limited extent, the EU). It has shown how, after the heydays of command and control regulation and the swing to markets, property rights and voluntarism, a new phase evolved—its most important manifestations being regulatory flexibility and meta-regulation, pluralistic regulation and collaborative governance. Stepping back from the detail of these developments and the particular successes and failures of individual instruments, the broader question remains: what sorts of architectures are likely to work best in terms of effectiveness, efficiency and political acceptability? Unfortunately, the general answer to such questions is it all depends.

Each of the architectures examined in this article proposes its own solutions: the internalisation of externalities by mandating standards in the case of direct regulation, freeing up markets in tandem with establishing clear property rights in the case of market-based instruments, enrolling firms as more active participants in their own governance in negotiated agreements, establishing regulatory structures that provide for business flexibility while also strengthening the capability of individual institutions or enterprises for internal reflection and self-control in the case of regulatory flexibility and meta-regulation. For Smart Regulation, it is a plethora of instruments that enable the state to steer not row, and to harness the capacities of second and third parties to fill the space vacated by the contracting regulatory state. From a civil regulation perspective, the state's principal role is to provide mechanisms that will empower the institutions of civil society to make corporations more accountable. And for the new collaborative governance it is to empower local communities and other stakeholders to engage in 'on the ground' decision-making subject to central government oversight.

101 J Braithwaite, *Regulatory Capitalism: How It Works, Ideas for Making it Work Better* (Edward Elgar, Cheltenham, UK 2008). See also D Levi-Faur 'The Global Diffusion of Regulatory Capitalism' (2005) 598 Annals of the American Academy of Political and Social Science 12.

The point is that each of the above frameworks has something valuable to offer (albeit some have more to offer than others) and that none of them is 'right' or 'wrong' in the abstract. Rather, they make differing contributions depending upon the nature and context of the environmental policy issue to be addressed. For example, free-market approaches and voluntarism have value where self-interest and the public interest largely coincide.[102] Direct regulation has worked well in dealing with large point sources, particularly where 'one size fits all' technologies can be mandated. Economic instruments such as tradeable permits work best when dealing with pollutants that can be readily measured, monitored and verified and where there are good trading prospects. Regulation has considerable power when it comes to changing the behaviour of large reputation-sensitive companies, which are vulnerable not only to shaming but also to market forces and consumer pressure. Meta-regulation appears to be effective in dealing with complex and sophisticated environmental issues such as regulating major hazardous facilities but may be redundant when it comes to more traditional challenges. Regulatory flexibility has potential in engaging with 'good apples'—large corporations who have reason to contemplate going 'beyond regulation' in return for greater flexibility and less 'green tape'—but it may do so at the cost of downplaying the resources necessary to drag 'bad apples' into compliance with minimum legal standards. And the new environmental governance, though sometimes touted as a 'best' solution to multiple problems, may be most suited to dealing with 'wicked' problems of such complexity that few if any other options seem viable.[103]

The limitations of each of the major policy innovations, and of the architectures that underpin them, lead to a plea for pragmatism and pluralism. None of the policy instruments or perspectives examined above work well in relation to all sectors, contexts or enterprise types. Each has weaknesses as well as strengths, and none can be applied as an effective stand-alone approach across the environmental spectrum. Such a conclusion suggests the value of designing complementary combinations of instruments, compensating for the weaknesses of each, with the strengths of others, while avoiding combinations deemed to be counterproductive or at least duplicative. This indeed was the central message of Smart Regulation. From this perspective, no particular instrument or approach is privileged. Rather, the goal is to accomplish substantive compliance with regulatory goals by any viable means using whatever regulatory or quasi-regulatory tools that might be available.

102 Market solutions may also be credible where the environmental challenge involves a small number of players all of whose self interest could be harnessed by the provision of property rights. The tragedy of the commons is the classic example. See G Hardin, 'The Tragedy of the Commons' (1968) 162 Science 1243. However, the larger the number of players, the greater the transactions costs and the greater the potential for free riding, the less credible a property rights approach becomes.

103 Gunningham (n 31).

Nevertheless, this is not to suggest a static situation, in which there is simply a 'menu' of options from which to select. On the contrary, the environmental challenges that policy-makers confront has changed considerably over the last four decades, as different architectures have emerged over that period—partly not only as a result of the need to find solutions to different challenges but also—and perhaps more so—as a result of shifting ideologies and the increasing influence of neo-liberalism in all the Anglo-Saxon jurisdictions. Thus too, the balance between efficiency, effectiveness and political acceptability has also shifted. These three criteria are often in conflict[104] and trade offs between them are sometimes inevitable. In the 'first generation' of environmental law, effectiveness trumped efficiency but neo-liberalism, with its emphasis on market values and criteria, reversed this. And at times political acceptability—or under neo-liberalism, some would say ideological purity—became more important than either efficiency or effectiveness.

Thus the main 'reforms' introduced by the neo-liberal governments of the late-1980s and early-1990s, with their focus on voluntarism and negotiated agreements were by and large, markedly unsuccessful, but this did not seem to detract from their popularity with governments. And it was never clear that the regulatory flexibility initiatives of the late-1990s and beyond, were capable of delivering a 'big bang for the regulatory buck' given their focus on encouraging the top 5–10% to become even better rather than on bringing laggards up to a minimum legal standard. Certainly meta-regulation (introduced usually after large scale disasters that demanded immediate political attention) placed a higher premium on effectiveness but even the new environmental governance has sometimes been seen in terms of political expediency (enabling the passing of intractable problems to community level thereby avoiding central government blame).

If political acceptability was closely tied to evidence-based decision-making, then the gap between such acceptability and effectiveness, in particular, would often be a relatively narrow one. But unfortunately this is not the case. Governments, of whatever variety, seem far more concerned with political and economic dogma, than with rational and evidence-based decision-making. For example, in Australia the Rudd Labour Government has gone one better than the Blair Government's various 'Reducing Regulatory Burdens' initiatives by establishing a Department of Finance and Deregulation. No longer is it necessary to debate the complexity of public policy, options involving varying degrees of government intervention or how to achieve an efficient and effective policy mix, the answer in each case will be clear—regulation bad, deregulation good.

104 N Gunningham and D Sinclair, 'Curbing Non-Point Source Pollution: Lessons from the Swan-Canning' (2004) 21 Environmental and Planning Law Journal 181.

Whether the market failures that precipitated the current global financial crisis, or the ongoing revelations concerning billion dollar frauds for which unregulated or weakly regulated markets were equally culpable, will cause any major rethinking among governments about the roles of regulation only time will tell. Certainly, there are some early signs of a 'change in the wind' with Australian Prime Minister Rudd, for example, calling for a new era of 'social capitalism' involving substantial government intervention and regulation to replace the freshly discovered evils of neo-liberalism and free-market fundamentalism.[105]

But if any such reassessment does not go beyond the realm of political rhetoric then the prognosis for efficient or effective regulation, may be dire. One is reminded of the comment of the UK Financial Services Authority Chairman Lord Turner, as the global financial crisis unfolded in the late-2008.

> If a year and a half ago the FSA had wanted higher capital adequacy, more information on liquidity – had said that it was worried about the business models of Northern Rock – and had wanted to ask questions about remuneration, it would have been strongly criticised for harming the competitiveness of the City of London, for red tape, and for over-regulation . . . over-regulation and red tape has been used as a polemical bludgeon. We have probably been over-deferential to that rhetoric.[106]

If there is one lesson to be derived from the history of environmental law, regulation and governance (or indeed other areas of regulation) over the last four decades, it is this: matters are almost always more complex than politicians and policy-makers would prefer them to be.[107] Unless they act on this realisation and take advantage of the wealth of empirical evidence that has been accumulated in that period, we are destined to repeat the mistakes of the past.

105 P Coorey 'It's Time For a New World Order: Rudd', *Sydney Morning Herald* (Sydney, 31 January 2009) 1.
106 'We'll Get Tough with City, Says Watchdog' *The Guardian* (London, 17 October 2008) 1.
107 See further K Hawkins, 'Regulatory Encounters of the Green Kind: An Appreciation of Robert Kagan's Recent Work' forthcoming.

[6]

# PRECAUTION

JONATHAN B. WIENER

# 1 Introduction

Precaution is a strategy for addressing risk. Risk of future harm is always uncertain. At its essence, precaution entails thinking ahead and taking anticipatory action to avoid uncertain future risks. Doing so necessitates the capacities to identify hazards and opportunities, to forecast scenarios and their associated outcomes, and to take anticipatory measures to manage causes before adverse outcomes occur. This idea is not new—success at risk assessment and management, including the astute exercise of precaution, has been central to the survival of the human species over millennia as well as to its continuing health and prosperity.[1] Early hominids had to forecast and avoid risks such as predators, poisons, and adverse weather. Modern humans use risk analysis to invest, insure, and protect, including precaution against uncertain future risks.

Precaution finds expression in timeless commonsense adages such as 'better safe than sorry'. Yet precaution is far easier said than done. On one hand, advances over time in scientific methods of risk identification and prediction have uncovered more subtly related causes and effects that unfold over longer latency periods, thereby calling for ever-earlier actions to anticipate uncertain future effects and to manage the suspected present causes. On the other hand, recognition that in the real world we confront multiple interconnected risks means that simple adages are insufficient or incoherent. Of course, one prefers 'safe' to 'sorry', but the real questions are 'better safe against this or against that?' and 'what are the consequences of seeking safety?' The serious issue is safe versus safe, not safe versus sorry. And because every human institution is imperfect—including both markets and government, both private and public—precautionary regulations of technological risks can also create new 'countervailing' risks.[2] 'Better safe than sorry' may be an old adage, but 'the cure is worse than the disease' has at least as old a pedigree. Advocates of precaution advise innovators of new technologies to 'look before you leap' and invoke Hippocrates's adage 'first, do no harm', but innovators say the same to government regulators.

At a deeper level than simplistic maxims, applying precaution as a legal concept involves several more complex issues, including the optimal balance between benefits and costs, safety and innovation, and risk-aversion and risk-taking; assumptions (often unstated) about vulnerability or thresholds and resilience or assimilative capacity (and the evidentiary requirements for demonstrating each); the tradeoff between false negative errors (neglecting a significant risk) and false positive errors

[1] For a popular account, see P.L. Bernstein, *Against the Gods: The Remarkable Story of Risk* (New York: John Wiley and Sons, 1996).

[2] See J.D. Graham and J.B. Wiener, eds., *Risk vs. Risk: Tradeoffs in Protecting Health and the Environment* (Cambridge, MA: Harvard University Press, 1995); and J.B. Wiener, 'Precaution in a Multi-Risk World,' in D. Paustenbach, ed., *Human and Ecological Risk Assessment: Theory and Practice* (New York: John Wiley and Sons, 2002) 1509.

(overreacting to an insignificant risk); the optimal response to uncertainty and irreversibility; the plural consequences of precaution in an interconnected multi-risk world, including effects on target risks, countervailing risks, and ancillary benefits; the role of law in constraining or empowering government; and the societal selection of which risks to regulate. These complex considerations mean that the astute exercise of precaution requires far more than an earnest commitment to protecting health, safety, and the environment. Intelligent precaution requires careful consideration of facts, values, consequences, and tradeoffs.

## 2 Precautionary Principle (PP)

The PP is an attempt to codify the concept of precaution in law. The PP is the most prominent—and perhaps the most controversial—development in international environmental law in the last two decades. Fifteen years ago, advocates forecast that the PP 'could become *the* fundamental principle of environmental protection policy and law.'[3] Even then, '[t]he speed with which the precautionary principle has been brought on to the international agenda, and the range and variety of international forums which have explicitly accepted it within the recent past, are quite staggering.'[4] Today, the forecast is partly confirmed: 'If international environmental law were to develop Ten Commandments, the precautionary principle would be near the top of the list.'[5] Yet the controversy continues: 'The precautionary principle may well be the most innovative, pervasive, and significant new concept in environmental policy over the past quarter century. It may also be the most reckless, arbitrary, and ill-advised.'[6]

States have adopted versions of the PP in their domestic law since at least the 1970s. The concept of '*Vorsorgeprinzip*' in German law dates at least to the early 1970s, which is about the same time that similar doctrines were introduced in Swedish law and Swiss law. In the 1992 Maastricht Treaty, the European Union (EU) expressly provided that EU policy on the environment 'shall be based on the precautionary principle' (Article 130R, now renumbered Article 174). In February 2000, the European Commission elaborated its interpretation of the PP in an important statement.[7] In

[3] J. Cameron and J. Abouchar, 'The Precautionary Principle: A Fundamental Principle of Law and Policy for the Protection of the Global Environment' (1991) 14 B.C. Int'l & Comp. L. Rev. 1 at 2.

[4] D. Freestone, 'The Precautionary Principle,' in R. Churchill and D. Freestone, eds., *International Law and Global Climate Change* (London: Graham and Trotman, 1991) 21 at 36.

[5] D. Bodansky, 'Deconstructing the Precautionary Principle,' in D.D. Caron and H.N. Scheiber, eds., *Bringing New Law to Ocean Waters* (Leiden: Koninklijke Brill NV, 2004) 381.

[6] G.E. Marchant and K.L. Mossman, *Arbitrary and Capricious: The Precautionary Principle in the EU Courts* (Washington, DC: AEI Press, 2004) at 1.

[7] Communication from the Commission on the Precautionary Principle, Brussels, Doc. COM(2000)1 (2 February 2000).

1999, Canada incorporated the precautionary principle in its revised Canadian Environmental Protection Act. In February 2005, France adopted the PP as part of its environmental charter and constitution.[8]

In the United States, precautionary pre-market safety review of new drugs under the US Federal Food, Drug and Cosmetic Act began before World War Two, and the precautionary prohibition of carcinogens in food dates to the Delaney Clause in 1958, although neither of these laws used the term 'precaution.' Landmark court decisions in *Ethyl Corp v. EPA* and *TVA v. Hill* expressly endorsed the notion of 'precautionary' regulation under the Clean Air Act and the Endangered Species Act, respectively.[9] However, the ruling in *Industrial Union Department, AFL-CIO v. American Petroleum Institute et al.* (the *Benzene* case),[10] which required a risk assessment prior to regulating workplace hazards, and the 1983 guidebook on risk assessment from the National Academy of Sciences, cast doubt on whether anticipatory precaution is required or even allowed in US federal regulation, at least if precaution means adopting regulatory policies before conducting a scientific risk assessment. Still, precaution is often invoked; for example, the US Food and Drug Administration adopted 'precautionary measures' to shield the blood supply from mad cow disease (BSE and vCJD) in 1999, and the city of San Francisco adopted a modest version of the PP in 2003. Thus, precaution has been adopted in numerous specific US laws, but the United States has not officially adopted the PP as a general basis for regulation.[11]

Given this history, one view is that the United States was more precautionary than Europe in the 1970s, but that since 1990 the positions have reversed so that now Europe endorses the PP and seeks proactively to regulate risks, while the United States opposes the PP and waits more circumspectly for evidence of actual harm before regulating.[12] Others argue that the pattern is more complex, with precaution adopted (or not) by different states for different risks, depending more on the specific context and societal processes of risk selection than on a uniform approach to regulation—a pattern of precautionary particularity, not principle.[13] For example, viewed very generally, Europe appears to have been more precautionary than the United States regarding such risks as marine pollution, genetically modified foods, climate change, toxic substances, phthalates, and antibiotics in animal feed, whereas the United States appears to have been more precautionary than Europe regarding such risks as chlorofluorocarbons (CFCs) and stratospheric ozone protection,

[8] Environment Charter of 2004, Article 5, adopted as part of the French Constitution (attached to the Preamble) on 28 February 2005.

[9] *Ethyl Corp. v. EPA*, 541 F.2d 1 (D.C. Cir. 1976); and *TVA v. Hill*, 437 U.S. 153 (1978).

[10] *Industrial Union Department, AFL-CIO v. American Petroleum Institute et al.*, 448 U.S. 607 (1980).

[11] J.S. Applegate, 'The Precautionary Preference: An American Perspective on the Precautionary Principle' (2000) 6 Human & Ecological Risk Assessment 413.

[12] See D. Vogel, 'The Hare and the Tortoise Revisited: The New Politics of Consumer and Environmental Regulation in Europe' (2003) 33 Br. J. Pol. Sci. 557.

[13] See J.B. Wiener, 'Whose Precaution after All ? A Comment on the Comparison and Evolution of Risk Regulatory Systems' (2003) 13 Duke J. Comp. Int'l L. 207.

nuclear power, mad cow disease (especially in blood donations), fine particulate matter air pollution, cigarette smoking, youth violence, and terrorism and weapons of mass destruction (see section 5 below). Yet there is also variation within the United States and Europe. And, in any case, these are selective examples. A quantitative analysis of a much larger sample of almost 3,000 risks over the last three decades found no significant pattern of shifting relative transatlantic precaution.[14]

In international environmental law, versions of the PP have been adopted in over 50 multilateral instruments, including several treaties on marine pollution adopted in the 1980s, the Montreal Protocol on Substances That Deplete the Ozone Layer (1987), the Rio Declaration on Environment and Development (1992, paragraph 15), the UN Framework Convention on Climate Change (UNFCCC) (1992), the Convention on Biological Diversity (1992), the Cartagena Protocol on Biosafety (2000), and the Stockholm Convention on Persistent Organic Pollutants (2002).[15] Some scholars point to even earlier international environmental treaties that employed the logic, if not the terminology, of precaution, such as the Convention on the Prevention of Marine Pollution by Dumping of Wastes and Other Matter (London Convention) (1972), the Convention on International Trade in Endangered Species of Wild Fauna and Flora (CITES) (1973), and the Organisation for Economic Co-operation and Development Declaration of Anticipatory Environmental Policies (1979).

Yet not all states have consented to the PP in international law. For example, although the United States has ratified most of the treaties just mentioned, it has repeatedly urged use of the term 'precautionary approach' rather than 'principle', and it has stayed out of the 1997 Kyoto Protocol to the UNFCCC and the 2000 Cartagena Protocol. And disputes in the World Trade Organization (WTO) over precautionary restrictions on beef hormones, asbestos, and genetically modified foods have raised the question whether international trade law, particularly the Agreement on the Application of Sanitary and Phytosanitary (SPS) Measures, precludes the precautionary principle by requiring regulation to be based on risk assessment. In response, some have asserted that the PP may now be so widely adopted that it is ripening into an enforceable norm of customary international law,[16] potentially binding states even if they have not consented to it explicitly (see Chapter 19 'Formation of Customary International Law and General Principles'). Others have argued that state practice on precaution is so diverse and inconsistent, and the formulations of the PP so varied (see next section), that no clear and binding norm can be discerned.[17]

[14] J.K. Hammitt, J.B. Wiener, B. Swedlow, D. Kall, and Z. Zhou, 'Precautionary Regulation in Europe and the United States: A Quantitative Comparison' (2005) 25 Risk Analysis 1215.

[15] A. Trouwborst, *Evolution and Status of the Precautionary Principle in International Law* (The Hague: Kluwer Law International, 2002) at 63.

[16] See J. Cameron and J. Abouchar, 'The Status of the Precautionary Principle in International Law,' in D. Freestone and E. Hey, eds., *The Precautionary Principle and International Law* (The Hague: Kluwer Law International, 1996) 29; and O. McIntyre and T. Mosedale, 'The Precautionary Principle as a Norm of Customary International Law' (1997) 9 J. Envt'l L. 221.

[17] See J.B. Wiener and M.D. Rogers, 'Comparing Precaution in the US and Europe' (2002) 5 J. of Risk Res. 317 at 343 (observing that divergent state practice regarding the PP undermines its claimed status as

# 3 Versions of the Precautionary Principle

In the face of risks, government has two basic strategies: *ex ante* precautions, *ex post* remedies, or a combination. *Ex post* remedies include cleanup projects and tort litigation in the courts. *Ex ante* precautions include scientific research and regulation administered by agencies. Some regulations are more *ex ante* than others, intervening earlier to anticipate the time path over which the risk is forecast to become manifest. On these sliding scale dimensions, regulation can be said to be 'more precautionary' when it intervenes earlier and/or more stringently to prevent uncertain future adverse consequences.

Despite widespread endorsement of precaution as a *strategy* in many (but not all) cases, there is no single agreed statement or understanding of the PP as a *principle*.[18] Nor is it clear whether the PP is meant to be an aspirational principle or a binding rule. If it is an aspirational principle, then it can more easily be vague and ambiguous but will be of little help in making difficult policy choices. If it is a binding regulatory rule, then it must be more concrete but will more often be arbitrary. Two experts sympathetic to the PP observe: 'Paradoxically, we conclude that the application of precaution will remain politically potent so long as it continues to be tantalizingly ill-defined and imperfectly translatable into codes of conduct, while capturing the emotions of misgiving and guilt... [I]t is neither a well-defined nor a stable concept. Rather, it is has become the repository for a jumble of adventurous beliefs that challenge the status quo of political power, ideology, and environmental rights.'[19]

Versions of the PP diverge on several key issues. These include:

- Is the PP part of the mainstream process of risk assessment and risk management or is it an alternative? The view that the PP is inconsistent with, and an alternative to, the traditional risk assessment/risk management framework is held by

customary international law). US courts have so far rejected claims that the PP or related environmental norms constitute enforceable customary international law. See *Beanal v. Freeport-McMoran, Inc.*, 197 F.3d 161, 167 (5th Cir. 1999); and *Flores v. Southern Peru Copper Co.*, 343 F.3d 140, 158–61 (2d Cir. 2003).

[18] See P. Sandin, 'Dimensions of the Precautionary Principle' (1999) 5 Human & Ecological Risk Assessment 889 (finding 19 versions, with significant differences regarding threat, uncertainty, action, and command); D. VanderZwaag, 'The Precautionary Principle in Environmental Law and Policy: Elusive Rhetoric and First Embraces' (1999) 8 J. Envt'l L. & Practice 355 (identifying 14 formulations); C.D. Stone, 'Is There a Precautionary Principle?' (2001) 31 Envtl. L. Rep. 10790 at 10799 (finding no coherent statement, 'disarray'); and Bodansky, see note 5 above at 383–6 and 391 (finding key differences on multiple dimensions, including legal instruction (reason not to postpone action, licence to act, duty to act), trigger of application, and what action should be taken, hence the PP has 'not moved . . . towards consensus' and 'the only point of overlap is a truism').

[19] A. Jordan and T.O'Riordan, 'The Precautionary Principle in Contemporary Environmental Policy and Politics,' in C. Raffensperger and J. Tickner, eds., *Protecting Public Health and the Environment: Implementing the Precautionary Principle* (Washington, DC: Island Press, 1999) 15.

both advocates (who dislike the risk-based approach and see the PP as a desirable alternative) and critics (who favour the risk-based approach and see the PP as undesirable). In contrast, the European Commission takes the view that the PP is part of risk management.[20] Similarly, the San Francisco version of the PP calls for an analysis of alternatives and their consequences. And many see the PP already at work in traditional risk assessment through the adoption of conservative default assumptions and methods for calculating risks.

- Does the PP apply only to the environment or more broadly to all health and environmental risks? The Rio Declaration (paragraph 15) and the Maastricht Treaty (Article 130r, now Article 174) address the environment, but the European Commission, the Court of Justice of the European Communities, the WTO, and other bodies have considered the PP to be equally relevant to health, food, and consumer safety risks.
- What degree of risk triggers the PP? Some versions refer to uncertain, serious, or irreversible risks (for example, the Rio Declaration), but some versions omit these trigger criteria.
- What action should be taken under the PP? Most versions give no real guidance, simply stating that uncertainty is no excuse for inaction, or warrants action, without saying what that action should be. Other versions call for a ban on the proposed product or activity until uncertainty is reduced to some degree, usually by shifting the burden of proof onto the proponent of the product or activity. Some versions call for adoption of best available control technology, but others do not.
- May costs be considered? Some versions exclude cost and many analysts pose the PP in opposition to cost-benefit analysis. But the Rio Declaration (paragraph 15) refers to 'cost-effective' measures, and the European Commission maintains that precautionary regulation must be based on an analysis of costs and benefits.
- Does the PP require zero risk? Most versions do not, and the European Commission explicitly states that the PP 'must not aim at zero risk', but some versions lean toward banning activities posing any uncertain risk. For example, 'where potential adverse effects are not fully understood, the activities should not proceed'.[21] Risks are never 'fully understood', so this version would amount to a ban.
- Is there a difference between 'precaution' and 'prevention'? Early versions used the terms interchangeably. For example, the Bergen Declaration (1990, paragraph 7) provided that the PP requires states to 'anticipate, prevent and attack' risks. By contrast, the European Environment Agency has argued that precaution applies to 'uncertain' risks whereas prevention applies to 'known' risks.[22] It is not clear, however, what is meant by a 'known' risk. Either there is no such thing (because all risks are uncertain), in which case prevention is an empty set and the PP applies to all

[20] See Communication from the Commission, note 7 above.

[21] United Nations General Assembly, *World Charter for Nature*, UNGA Resolution 37/7 (1982).

[22] European Environment Agency (EEA), *Late Lessons from Early Warnings: The Precautionary Principle 1896–2000*, Environmental Issue Report no. 22 (Luxembourg: Office for Official Publications of the European Communities, 2001 and Copenhagen: Earthscan, 2001).

risks, or there are many 'known' risks (in the sense of well-understood cause and effect relationships), in which case the PP is only about risks for which there is fundamental ('true' or 'deep') uncertainty about the cause-and-effect or hazard-and-harm relationship, and the PP applies only to those few rare and temporary cases of utter mystery that later become understood as scientific advances.

From all of these variations, it is useful to consider three archetypal versions of the PP.

## 3.1 Version 1: 'Uncertainty Does Not Justify Inaction'

In its most basic form, the PP permits precautionary regulation in the absence of complete evidence about the particular risk scenario. A common phrasing is: 'Where there are threats of serious or irreversible damage, lack of full scientific certainty shall not be used as a reason for postponing measures to prevent environmental degradation' (Bergen Declaration (1990) and the Rio Declaration (1992), paragraph 15, which adds 'cost-effective' before 'measures'). In short, uncertainty does not justify inaction: 'The precautionary principle is formulated in many ways, and differences between them may be significant. However, all formulations have an essential element in common: rational decisions may and should be taken on the basis of uncertain science, despite a "lack of full scientific certainty" or of "conclusive evidence to prove a causal relation between inputs and their effects." '[23]

This version of the PP does not go very far. Its salient merit is that it rebuts the frequently heard claim that 'uncertainty warrants inaction' (or, stated another way, that regulation should not occur unless regulatory authorities 'prove' that a risk is 'real') or, similarly, that regulation is unwarranted because the 'assimilative capacity' of the environment can be assumed to absorb residuals without adverse effect until the contrary is shown. If these claims were valid, *ex ante* regulation would never be warranted. Only *ex post* tort liability could constrain risks. If we are ever to act before harms occur, then we must act in the face of uncertainty. Responding to these claims that uncertainty warrants waiting, as just noted, and to the particular challenge of finding a basis for anticipatory action to assess and prevent transboundary harms under international law (which until the 1970s had emphasized *ex post* state liability for transboundary harm, as under *Trail Smelter Arbitration (United States v. Canada)*),[24] this version of the PP states that we may act in advance of actual harm. But it does not say what we should do. It only permits action, rather than compelling it. It responds only to the situation of 'lack of full scientific certainty', but there is *never* 'full scientific certainty' or 'conclusive evidence'. We always face uncertainty, and we

[23] C. Henry, 'The Essence of the Precautionary Principle,' in K. von Moltke and C. Weill, eds., *European Precautionary Practice*, Les actes de l'IDDRI no. 1, Proceedings of the International Workshop, Paris, 3–4 December 2002 (Paris: Institut du Développement Durable et Relations Internationales, 2004) 29.

[24] *Trail Smelter Case (United States v. Canada)*, Award, 1941, 3 U.N.R.I.A.A. 1905.

must *always* make decisions under uncertainty. This version of the PP does not answer the real question, which is *what* action to take in the face of (inevitable) uncertainty.

## 3.2 Version 2: 'Uncertainty Justifies Action'

A second version of the PP is somewhat more aggressive. It says that uncertain risk justifies action. For example, the 1998 Wingspread Conference concluded: 'When an activity raises threats of harm to human health or the environment, precautionary measures should be taken even if some cause and effect relationships are not fully established.'[25] Similarly, the German Federal Interior Ministry wrote: 'The principle of precaution commands that the damages done to the natural world (which surrounds us all) should be avoided *in advance* and in accordance with opportunity and possibility... it also means acting when conclusively ascertained understanding by science is not yet available.'[26] Or, '[a]ccording to the precautionary principle, the more uncertain the risk, the more justified is some form of regulatory intervention.'[27] Article 5 of the 2004 French Environment Charter provides: 'When the environment is at risk from serious and irreversible harm, even if this cannot be scientifically proven, public authorities must, through the application of the precautionary principle and according to their competences, implement procedures to assess the risks and adopt temporary and appropriate measures to prevent the damage occurring.'

Like the first version of the PP, this version is based on a truism. Since cause and effect relationships are never 'proven' or 'fully' or 'conclusively' established (even in retrospect), we are always dealing with uncertain and probabilistic relationships. This version, while calling for proactive precautionary measures, still does not address the real question of *what* measures should be taken. Still, version 2 is more precautionary than version 1, insofar as version 2 affirmatively impels regulatory intervention rather than just permitting it. Yet if precaution itself would have adverse consequences, this affirmative principle would be too strong (hence, the French qualification to adopt 'temporary and appropriate' measures). And if greater uncertainty itself warranted more regulatory action, it would perversely skew social investments away from more certain risks.

[25] Quoted in Raffensperger and Tickner, see note 19 above at 343.

[26] S. Boehmer-Christiansen, 'The Precautionary Principle in Germany—Enabling Government,' in T. O'Riordan and J. Cameron, eds., *Interpreting the Precautionary Principle* (London: Cameron May, 1994) 31 at 37.

[27] W.E. Wagner, 'The Precautionary Principle and Chemical Regulation in the U.S.' (2000) 6 Human and Ecological Risk Assessment 459 at 461.

## 3.3 Version 3: Shifting the Burden of Proof

A third version of the PP requires forbidding the potentially risky activity until the proponent of the activity demonstrates that it poses no (or acceptable) risk: 'As described in the Wingspread Statement on the Precautionary Principle, the applicant or proponent of an activity or process or chemical needs to demonstrate to the satisfaction of the public and the regulatory community that the environment and public health will be safe. The proof must shift to the party or entity that will benefit from the activity and that is most likely to have the information.'[28] This version of the PP is more precautionary than the first or second version. Unlike the first two versions, version 3 specifies a particular action to take in the face of uncertain risk: forbid the activity unless the standard of proof is met by the proponent. Version 3 has two key components: shifting the *burden* of proof to the proponent of the activity or product and setting a *standard* of proof (what must be demonstrated—no risk, *de minimus* risk, 'safety', acceptable risk, or something else).

Depending on the standard of proof, version 3 could invite overregulation. What counts as 'safe' is unclear. Some interpretations of version 3—for example, the World Charter for Nature quoted earlier—would impose a standard of proof of no risk. Such a measure would often yield overregulation where the risk of the substance or activity is small relative to its benefits. For example, many medicines are toxic at some dose, as are vitamins and oxygen, and no drug company could offer proof that they were not toxic or posed no risk of harm at all doses. More generally, because, as Paracelsus taught, 'the dose makes the poison,' potentially every substance would have to be banned if proof of no toxicity or no harm were the universal principle. As a result, real world applications of version 3 tend to employ a more balanced standard of proof. In the *Benzene* case (cited above), the US Supreme Court held that 'safe' does not mean 'no risk' but rather means 'no significant risk', and then left it up to the federal Occupational Safety and Health Administration (OSHA) to determine which workplace health risks are 'significant'. Laws requiring pre-market approval of new products typically require that product proponents demonstrate 'acceptable risk' or 'no unreasonable risk' or 'net benefits'.

Meanwhile, version 3 does contain the useful idea of putting the *burden* of proof on the party best able to generate the information needed to make the decision. This idea is analogous to the notion of putting the burden of accident avoidance on the 'least cost avoider'.[29] California's Proposition 65 and the 1996 protocol to the London Convention take this approach: substances initially listed may be removed from the list if producers demonstrate that the substance falls below a threshold of risk.

The stringency of version 3 can also be seen by analogy to criminal law. Violence is a problem of public risk and public health. Version 3 would shift the burden of proof

[28] P.L. deFur, 'The Precautionary Principle: Application to Policies Regarding Endocrine-Disrupting Chemicals,' in Raffensperger and Tickner, see note 19 above at 345–6.

[29] G. Calabresi, *The Costs of Accidents* (New Haven, CT: Yale University Press, 1970).

from 'innocent until proven guilty' to 'guilty until proven innocent'. Yet such a shift in criminal law would be opposed by many who favour version 3 for environmental risks. Talbot Page argued that version 3 should apply to environmental law but not to criminal law on the ground that, although both protect public health, the cost of mistaken precaution in criminal law is foregone liberty, but in environmental law it is only money.[30] Page's analysis, however, neglects the possibility that environmental precaution could create countervailing risks that harm health and impair liberty.

## 4 Normative Analysis of the Precautionary Principle

As noted at the outset, despite the common sense of precaution as a strategy in many (but not all) cases, the PP as a legal principle remains controversial. The crux of the controversy is precisely the fact that, judged on its consequences, precaution is desirable in some but not all cases, whereas the PP seems to insist on precaution in all cases of uncertain risk. Efforts to connect the PP to consequentialist decision-making, such as the European Commission's 2000 communication, are efforts to enable precaution where warranted based on the expected consequences, but to avoid mandating precaution in all cases.[31] This section examines the variables relevant to such a consequentialist normative framework for precaution.

As noted earlier, uncertainty is the primary focus of the PP. Health and environmental problems are regularly characterized by uncertainty about probability, severity, timing, and cause-effect relationship. Moreover, latency between cause and effect means that waiting for better evidence may mean missing the opportunity to address the cause. Thus, if uncertainty is cited as a reason not to act, the result may be incurring the harm. Hence, version 1 of the PP offers a sensible rebuttal to the generic claim that uncertainty justifies inaction or that the environment can assimilate all residuals absent proof to the contrary.

Uncertainty, however, can also be handled in standard decision analyses, without invocation of the PP. Uncertainty can be quantified in calculations of expected value. Risk premia for uncertainty can be added to expected benefits and costs. Moreover, uncertainty does not justify inaction, but neither does uncertainty itself justify action. The choice depends on the relative expected consequences of each action compared to alternatives. Uncertainty affects all risks, including the countervailing

[30] T. Page, 'A Generic View of Toxic Chemicals and Similar Risks' (1978) 7 Ecology L.Q. 207.

[31] For approaches to melding the PP with consequentialist decision analysis, see, for example, the symposium in volume 4 of the *Journal of Risk Research* (2001); R.B. Stewart, 'Environmental Regulatory Decisionmaking under Uncertainty' (2002) 20 Res. L. & Econ. 71; and C. Gollier and N. Treich, 'Decision Making under Uncertainty: The Economics of the Precautionary Principle' (2003) 27 J. Risk & Uncertainty 77.

risks induced by precaution. We never decide under certainty—the hard question is not whether uncertainty justifies action or waiting, but rather what action to take given the degree of uncertainty.

A distinct basis for precaution is irreversibility. As noted earlier, many versions of the PP cite the threat of irreversible damage. It has long been observed that irreversible impacts warrant precautions as a way to preserve the option value of greater flexibility—that is, to defer the irreversibility while more can be learned.[32] However, irreversibility cannot simply mean impossible to reverse, because in a world with a one-way flow of time, all choices are irreversible in that sense, even trivial ones. Risks neglected may prove irreversible, but, likewise, the costs and countervailing risks of precautionary regulation are also irreversible opportunities foregone. To evaluate precaution, one must compare the seriousness of 'irreversible' impacts, including the options lost and the cost and time needed to reverse or heal the results.[33]

A third factor favouring precaution is the possibility of catastrophe. Worst-case or catastrophic scenarios may warrant special efforts to avoid them even if they are very unlikely because their harms would be so great, and because people tend to put more value on preventing a single devastating incident than they do on preventing an equal number of deaths spread out over multiple smaller incidents.[34] As with uncertainty, the problem of catastrophic risk can also be handled with standard decision analysis. A very low probability multiplied by a very large harm can yield a significant expected value, and risk premia can be added for the greater value of avoiding devastating incidents. Advocates of precaution argue that the PP is needed to counter the heuristic error that people may make in neglecting or ignoring very low-probability risks,[35] but critics counter that people also sometimes exaggerate the risk of low-probability catastrophic and dreaded events, and, indeed, invocation of the PP may be selectively spurred by such errors of exaggeration.[36] Meanwhile, some suggest that the probabilities of risks may follow a 'power law' distribution such that worst-case scenarios are not so unlikely.[37]

All of these factors, however, also characterize the risks that precaution may *induce*. In a world of multiple contending risks, the factors just noted (uncertainty, irreversibility, catastrophe, and skewed probability distributions) can attach to *both*

[32] See K.J. Arrow and A.C. Fisher, 'Environmental Preservation, Uncertainty, and Irreversibility' (1974) 88 Q. J. Econ. 312; and C. Henry, 'Investment Decisions under Uncertainty: The "Irreversibility Effect" ' (1974) 64 Am. Econ. Rev. 1006.

[33] See C.R. Sunstein, 'Irreversible and Catastrophic' (2006) 91 Cornell L. Rev., 841.

[34] See R.A. Posner, *Catastrophe: Risk and Response* (New York: Oxford University Press, 2004).

[35] D. Dana, 'A Behavioral Economic Defense of the Precautionary Principle' (2003) 97 Nw. U. L. Rev. 1315.

[36] See P. Slovic and E.U. Weber, *Perception of Risk Posed by Extreme Events* (Columbia University Center for Hazards and Risk Research, 2003).

[37] See D.A. Farber, 'Probabilities Behaving Badly: Complexity Theory and Environmental Uncertainty' (2003) 37 U.C. Davis L. Rev. 145.

the target risk being reduced by precaution *and* the countervailing risks that are created by precautionary actions. Measures to reduce one uncertain irreversible catastrophic risk might induce another.[38] For example, banning nuclear power might induce global warming, while preventing global warming by shifting to a new energy technology such as nuclear fusion or space-based solar power might introduce uncertain new risks of irreversible catastrophic impacts. Or banning genetically modified foods might perpetuate hunger in poor countries and hasten the irreversible conversion of tropical forests to farmland. Banning a product might induce the risks of substitute products. Historically, introducing the seemingly benign CFCs in order to replace highly toxic refrigerants turned out to yield a new and unintended countervailing risk of stratospheric ozone depletion.

Thus understood, the PP should not call for precautionary regulation of uncertain irreversible risks if such regulation would itself yield the very dangers the PP seeks to avoid. At the extreme, the PP could swallow itself, prohibiting both the risky activity and the risky regulation of this activity. Of course, the countervailing risks might be small or worth running in some cases, and there might also be ancillary benefits of regulation. The central point is that invoking the PP cannot escape the need to weigh the full portfolio of consequences.

Greater precaution reduces the risk of false negatives (inattention to significant risks) but increases the risk of false positives (attention to insignificant risks—false alarms). Avoiding false negatives is often cited as the primary benefit of the PP.[39] Yet overreaction to false positives (or even to true positives) also entails harms: opportunities foregone, innovations rejected (including those that would improve human and environmental health), public cynicism about future warnings (the 'crying wolf' syndrome), and new countervailing risks. As noted earlier, Talbot Page argued in 1978 that false positives are worth tolerating in the environmental context because their cost is only money, but this argument assumes that money is lexically less important than environmental protection regardless of its magnitude, and, more importantly, it neglects the countervailing adverse health and environmental impacts of precautionary measures.

The real world does not come one risk at a time. It is an interconnected web of multiple interdependent risks. In a multi-risk world, prudent precaution requires analysis of the full portfolio of expected consequences. Such analysis is needed for both new technologies and new public policies. The portfolio of consequences includes reduction of the target risk, costs, ancillary benefits such as other risks reduced, and countervailing risks increased.

[38] See, e.g., Graham and Wiener, note 2 above; F.B. Cross, 'Paradoxical Perils of the Precautionary Principle' (1996) 53 Wash. & Lee L. Rev. 851; and C.R. Sunstein, *The Laws of Fear: Beyond the Precautionary Principle* (Cambridge: Cambridge University Press, 2004).

[39] European Environment Agency, *Late Lessons from Early Warnings: The Precautionary Principle. 1896–2000*, note 22 above.

In addition, a dynamic approach recognizes that knowledge improves over time. Both 'wait and learn' and 'act and learn' are plausible strategies—the choice between them depending on the relative expected consequences. Precaution is 'act and learn', to preserve the option value of avoiding irreversibility. As such, precaution must be accompanied by further research and adaptive management towards the updating of the initial policy over time. Thus, the French version of the PP calls precaution 'temporary', and the European Commission requires precaution to be 'provisional' as new science is gathered. The challenge is to design institutions and incentives to generate this new science and to apply it to update policies. The concern is that once policies are adopted, institutions become reluctant to review and revise them.

In sum, version 1 of the PP is helpful to decision-makers as a rebuttal to the mistaken claim that uncertainty warrants inaction. Latent risks mean that inaction under uncertainty may invite future harms. Irreversibility and catastrophe offer additional warrants for precaution. Version 1 of the PP, however, like any permissive principle of law, authorizes the exercise of government power while leaving unaddressed the serious question, namely, what action government should take in the face of such risks. On the other hand, versions 2 and 3 of the PP could be counterproductive. They incur the costs of false positives and neglect the countervailing risks of regulation. In the real world of multiple risks and imperfect government, precaution itself may be a risky activity. Amidst multiple risks, we need to exercise precaution against excessive precaution. Or, to put it differently, given the reality of multiple interrelated risks, we need a principle of optimal precaution rather than of maximum precaution. Precautionary regulation should be based on full portfolio impacts analysis and followed by continuing research to foster learning and adaptive revisions. Ultimately, we need to seek 'risk-superior' options that reduce multiple risks in concert.

## 5 Future of the Precautionary Principle

The reality of precautionary regulation has been more moderate than the extreme versions of the PP sometimes advocated. When the EU and domestic legal systems have adopted precaution, they have included qualifications and exceptions to account for costs, countervailing risks, and provisionality. Extreme forms of the PP are unlikely to be implemented (though examples such as the Delaney Clause do arise). Rather, the trend in Europe appears to be towards a reconciliation of the PP with the principle of proportionality and with methods of regulatory impact analysis (RIA) under the Better Regulation initiative. The new Barroso Commission (stimulated by the Lisbon Agenda for economic growth and by UK Prime Minister

Tony Blair's emphasis on regulatory reform) has issued new RIA guidelines[40] and may construct a centralized process of regulatory review.[41]

Moderation may also be inspired to address the concerns of developing countries. Poorer countries face pressing needs to develop, eradicate poverty, and attract investment. For them, the costs of highly precautionary policies may loom much larger than do those costs in wealthier countries. Further, poorer countries may sensibly choose different tradeoffs among risks, such as favouring reduction of large near-term risks even if this requires tolerating some small long-term risks that the PP would address. For example, developing countries may resist the application of the PP by Europe or other trading partners as a means to impose restrictions on developing countries' use of genetically modified foods to combat hunger and of pesticides such as DDT to combat malaria. As the conversation about precaution broadens to become less a transatlantic dispute and more a global dialogue, the greater variety of interests may foster a more moderate approach to the PP than some of the articulations to date.

Meanwhile, the US government, while criticizing the PP in the environmental sphere, has adopted the logic and language of the PP as the centerpiece of its new National Security Strategy, pledging to anticipate and prevent terrorist attacks despite uncertainty.[42] In essence, the US approach is the converse of the EU's, which endorses the PP in the environmental arena and criticizes it in the national security arena (at least insofar as it authorizes *unilateral* precautionary use of force), although some European states, such as the United Kingdom, appear to favour the PP in both arenas. This turn of events may invite further diplomatic friction, but it also offers a fresh opportunity for governments to reassess the advantages and disadvantages of precaution in each context.[43]

The future thus offers two contrasting paths. On the one hand, there could be a continuation of precautionary particularity: the selective use of precaution by different states against different risks, often driven by heuristic reactions to recently visible or dreaded risks. On this path, no shared understanding on optimal precaution would emerge. Precautionary particularity would serve domestic interests and would

[40] European Commission, *Impact Assessment Guidelines*, Doc. SEC(2005) 791 (15 June 2005), with 15 March 2006 update.

[41] See, J.B. Wiener, 'Better Regulation in Europe' forthcoming in (2006) 59, Current Legal Problems.

[42] The National Security Strategy of the United States of America, 17 September 2002, Introduction and Part V ('We cannot let our enemies strike first . . . [but must take] anticipatory action to defend ourselves, even if uncertainty remains as to the time and place of the enemy's attack. To forestall or prevent such hostile acts by our adversaries, the United States, will, if necessary, act preemptively . . . America will act against such emerging threats before they are fully formed . . . The greater the threat, the greater is the risk of inaction and the more compelling the case for taking anticipatory action to defend ourselves, even if uncertainty remains as to the time and place of the enemy's attack'). On the similar UK position, see D. Runciman, 'The Precautionary Principle' (April 2004) 26(7) London Review of Books.

[43] See J. Stern and J.B. Wiener, 'Precaution against Terrorism,' (2006) 9 J. Risk Research 393.

offer some avenues for hybridization (legal borrowing) across states, but it would also give rise to repeated disputes among states over mismatches in the selection of specific risks and precautionary measures, especially in cases of international trade in products regulated differently in different countries.

Alternatively, if these developments stimulate mutual understanding of both the merits and demerits of the PP and a forthright conversation about a sensible middle ground, they could lead to a new transatlantic and even global consensus on the criteria for optimal precaution based on analyses of consequences. This consensus could be embodied in international accords on environment, development, and security. It could also play a role in the emergence of a new body of global administrative law (see Chapter 4 'Global Environmental Governance as Administration'), including shared rules and norms for international regulatory policy. This consensus could support the creation of a network of national and international institutions to conduct full portfolio impact analyses of national and international precautionary measures in diverse domains (including health, safety, environment, and security), both restraining unwarranted precaution and prompting desirable precaution.

## Recommended Reading

D. Bodansky, 'Scientific Uncertainty and the Precautionary Principle' (September 1991) 33 Env't 4.

J. Cameron and T. O'Riordan, eds., *Interpreting the Precautionary Principle* (London: Cameron May, 1994).

D. Freestone and E. Hey, eds., *The Precautionary Principle and International Law* (The Hague: Kluwer Law International, 1996).

J.D. Graham and J.B. Wiener, eds., *Risk vs. Risk: Tradeoffs in Protecting Health and the Environment* (Cambridge, MA: Harvard University Press, 1995).

J. Morris, ed., *Rethinking Risk and the Precautionary Principle* (Woburn, MA: Butterworth-Heinemann, 2000).

C. Raffensperger and J. Tickner, eds., *Protecting Public Health and the Environment: Implementing the Precautionary Principle* (Washington, DC: Island Press, 1999).

P.H. Sand, 'The Precautionary Principle: A European Perspective' (2000) 6 Human and Ecological Risk Assessment 445.

A. Trouwborst, *Evolution and Status of the Precautionary Principle in International Law* (The Hague: Kluwer Law International, 2002).

J.B. Wiener, 'Precaution in a Multi-Risk World,' in D. Paustenbach, ed., *Human and Ecological Risk Assessment: Theory and Practice* (New York: John Wiley and Sons, 2002) 1509.

——, 'Whose Precaution after All ? A Comment on the Comparison and Evolution of Risk Regulatory Systems' (2003) 13 Duke J. Int'l & Comp. L. 207.

# [7]

## The polluter-pays principle

*Priscilla Schwartz*

### Introduction

Despite the lack of a universally accepted definition of what pollution entails, aand the special problems in addressing it, regulating pollution has been a consistent endeavour in international law, policy and relations. Controlling pollution has been addressed with a focus on specific media (land, air, or water) in the context of its detrimental effects, its interference with other uses of the environment or in terms of allowable quality standards of discharge of substances in relation to the assimilative capacity of the environment (Ando 1981: 350–1; Springer, 1983: 13–15). Generally, international regulatory trends have emphasised prohibition of pollution (*Trail Smelter Arbitration,* 1938/1941), state responsibility or liability upon proof of damage (*Case Concerning Factory at Chorzów (Claim for Indemnity),* 1928: No. 17), complicity with broad standards, use of specified technology, emergency plans, preparedness and cooperation and in some cases sector-specific institutional controls.

This regime became insufficient to deal with the wave of environmental pollution, resource depletion and damage engendered by contemporary economic activities, especially since there is still no global treaty on civil liability for transboundary pollution or damage and the availability of civil law remedies for transboundary damage cannot be assumed (Boyle, 2005: 4). The international system therefore needed to develop a consistent global strategy for allocating responsibility for the cause and effects of pollution, including a mechanism by which the *costs* of pollution can be integrated into resource use planning and decision-making. Such a system would minimise the pollution regulatory burden on states. As an initial effort, the Stockholm Declaration calls for all countries to support taking measures against environmental pollution, including steps to prevent pollution of the seas, and cooperation in reviewing and developing environmental liability regimes (Principles 6, 7, 12 and 24). States later expressed their support by propounding a set of principles in the Rio Declaration that defines the way resources are exploited in development activities. The polluter-pays principle (PPP) is formally identified amongst them, generally canvassing an 'approach' that the polluter should in principle bear the cost of pollution (Rio Declaration, 1992: Principle 16).[1]

An earlier version of the PPP is however credited to a 1972 Recommendation of the Organisation of Economic Co-operation and Development, which identifies it as the principle to be used in allocating the costs of pollution prevention and control. The PPP is thus assured of a place in international and domestic law and policy, judicial determination and scholastic literature. In all cases, its scope is generally directed at pollution regulation, though the emphasis on furthering environmental, trade, competition or social policy goals respectively will vary according to the specific context.

This chapter seeks to explore the role of the PPP as a legal or policy implement for regulating polluting economic activities, production processes and consumption patterns for the protection of the environment, human health and safety, resource management and generally in ensuring environmentally sustainable activities. It will identify the origin of the principle as espoused by the OECD, and highlight the extent to which it is applied in international law in order to determine the level of international acceptance. Next, an analysis is made of the content of the principle based on legal and theoretical scrutiny. This will reveal the contexts in which the PPP imputes responsibility or liability on polluters to pay or bear the costs of pollution, and the obligation or responsibilities they are likely to assume as implied in the term 'costs'. The chapter will further articulate the implications of the principle for domestic environments, including the relevant methods of its implementation. Various models are canvassed here indicating the procedural dimension of the principle in its objective of ensuring enforcement and compliance. A critical appraisal is then made of the economic efficency of the principle and its adequacy as a legal and policy tool for regulating international and domestic pollution.

**PPP: origin and international application**

In its most general formulation, the PPP is a reflection of what it entails – that persons who pollute, engage in polluting or hazardous activities or cause damage to the environment (and individuals) in the conduct of economic activities must be held responsible for the consequences of their action. In other words, they must bear the costs arising from such pollution or damage, or associated with employing pollution prevention or control measures. The origin of the principle in relation to pollution regulation is credited to the OECD, distinguishing its role in environmental matters from its origin as an economic rule of externalities.

Recommending its application to its members in 1972, the OECD Guiding Principles[2] primarily envisaged the PPP as 'the principle to be used for allocating costs of pollution prevention and control measures [so as] to encourage rational use of scarce environmental resources and to avoid distortions in international trade and investment'.

A further recommendation (OECD, suggesting methods of implementing the principle, explains that '... the polluter should *bear the expenses* of carrying out the pollution prevention and control measures introduced by public authorities in member countries, to ensure that the environment is in an acceptable state (emphasis added).

This rationale includes measures which reflect the cost of goods and services that cause pollution in production and/or consumption. The aim here was to set a general rule that member countries should not assist the polluters in bearing the costs of pollution control whether by means of subsidies, tax advantages or other measures, unless some specified exceptions apply (OECD, 1974: 17).[3]

The application of the principle was later extended to matters involving accidental pollution risks from hazardous installations (OECD, 1989)[4] and a final recommendation urged member countries to specifically use 'economic instruments' to implement the principle as a means of improving the allocation and efficient use of natural and environmental resources and a way to better reflect the social cost of using these resources (OECD, 1991).[5] A more prominent adoption of the PPP was eventually pioneered by the European Community (1973).[6] Both the OECD and EC are considered to have transformed a mere economic rule into a true legal principle that has transcended its mandate from one of recommendations, to binding treaties and EC secondary legislation (de Sadeleer, 2002: 26), with the status of regional custom in most OECD and EC countries.

*1. Application in international law*

The PPP has diverse applications or reference in several international, regional and global instruments. In particular contexts, it is represented as cost-bearing for pollution control, prevention and reduction measures which are set by national authorities or required by the polluting activity.[7] Other instruments require that the principle be used as an 'approach' that forms the basis for fulfilling their mandate; or urge members to be 'guided' by the principle, 'take it into account' or 'apply' it in their respective contexts.[8]

A further set of instruments recognises the PPP as a general principle of international environmental law.[9] For others, it applies as an indication of acceptance of responsibility for polluting activities or their likely effects. For example, the Kyoto Protocol to the 1992 Climate Change Convention applies the principle through responsibility and commitments by states to take measures through schemes of emissions trading, joint implementation and clean development mechanisms, all aimed at reducing specific greenhouse gases and so leadinng to slower climate change. Also, under the Waste Packaging Directive, those involved in the production, use, import and distribution of packaging and packaged products should in accordance with the polluter-pays principle, accept responsibility for such waste (Kyoto Protocol, 1997; Council Directive 94/62/EC on Packaging and Packaging Waste).[10]

The principle is expressed in other instances, especially in liability regimes, through an approach that imputes responsibility directly or indirectly to persons dealing with hazardous or dangerous substances, requiring them to take preventive or remedial action. International civil liability regimes that apply the principle, including those incorporated in MEAs, have been notable in the context of oil pollution, sea transfer of hazardous substances, waste exports, carriage of dangerous goods, industrial accidents on transboundary watercourses, nuclear pollution and a general system of liability for damage resulting from activities dangerous to the environment.[11]

The EC has also applied the principle of pollution regulation in policy areas of environmental cost allocation generally, disposal of waste oils, waste landfills, packaging of wastes, water policy and quite recently to nuclear liabilities respectively.[12] In a judicial context, the principle has been held by the WTO dispute settlement body to be compatible with GATT rules on tax adjustment (*United States – Taxes on Petroleum and Certain Imported Substances*, 1987: para 5:2:5),[13] and by the ECJ, as applicable in financing indemnities for undertakings relating to collecting and/or disposing of waste oils (Case 172/82, *Inter-Huiles and Others,* 1983: 507). Conventional forms of the principle have been interpreted as requiring regulated entities to pay the costs of meeting national environmental standards (Gaines, 2002: 265). However, under certain treaties, polluters may incur primary liability or direct accountability for environmental harm at the national level.[14]

In addition to the conventional references, the principle is also incorporated in Principle 16 of the Rio Declaration. In that context, the polluter-pays principle is made a national endeavour to be directly promoted or implemented by national authorities, based on an economic rationale. The authorities should ensure that both environmental and social costs resulting from development activities are met by the polluter either through the internalisation of such costs, or by use of economic instruments. The general approach of polluter cost-bearing or responsibility was also advocated at the World Summit for Sustainable Development (WSSD) through the concept of 'Corporate Accountability', to be ensured through transparent regulations, international initiatives and public-private partnerships (Johannesburg Declaration on Sustainable Development, 2002: para. 49; Plan of

Implementation of the WSSD, 2002: para. 18). In other words, 'corporations also have responsibilities pursuant to the PPP' (ILA, 2002: Principle 3 (3:1)).

The scope of application of the PPP elaborated above would reveal it both as a principle for pollution regulation generally in international law,[15] and as a component of the concept of sustainable development for environmental protection.[16] Taken together in its entirety and interpreted within the discipline of international environmental law, it represents a 'principle' or an 'approach' that embodies peculiar elements and varying approaches directed at pollution regulation for environmental protection and sustainable development. The elements of the principle relating to the definition of who is a 'polluter' and the costs he or she is to pay or bear is discussed *infra*. The different approaches to the principle are formulated as an implementation strategy for national and international pollution regulatory controls. The main strands of this strategy are identified in the economic rationale of internalisation of pollution costs (such as through investment or trade programmes), use of economic instruments like environmental taxes, charges and permits, and polluter responsibility and liability schemes. These approaches are illustrated *infra*. The PPP thus represents a significant development in the evolution of international environmental law as a discrete sub-discipline of public international law (Sunkin et al., 2002: 73).

**Functions of the PPP**

In the absence of clear substantive obligations, the principle is deemed to serve a variety of functions. For instance, it may impose political obligations on governments when they set the framework for the exploitation or use of components of the environment. The PPP also serves a purpose in reiterating and rendering more precise existing customary law and as a solution to technically complex regional and global problems for which customary international law is limited (Wolfrum, 2000: 23; Rest, 1995: 313; Gündling, 1991: 93). Its internalising, redistributive, preventive and curative functions (de Sadeleer, 2002 : 34–7) combine different objectives – economic, social and environmental – thereby making it an invaluable tool for directing sustainable activities.

The PPP is also designed to encourage rational use of scarce resources in order to ensure that the environment is in an acceptable state and aims to avoid distortion in international trade by encouraging fair competition and investment location (OECD, 1972; Rio Declaration, 1992: Principle 16). Its 'efficiency' and 'equity' functions aim to allocate pollution cost through effective instruments with some consistency and manageability of enforcement (OECD, 1974: 25 and 26).

The principle also functions to encourage attitudinal change in polluters towards environmental values and provides clear incentives to alter behaviour, such as in the granting of aid to developing countries to combat pollution and the influencing of production and consumption patterns where prices of goods and services are made to reflect true production and user costs (Agenda 21, 1992: UN Doc A/CONF.151/26: Ch: 8, s. 4:4; 8:31; 8:37; Commission on Global Governance, 1995: 211; Gillespie, 1997: 210; Coffey and Newcombe, 2001). In context of liability regimes which employ the principle, it functions to establish a framework for environmental liability to prevent and remedy environmental damage or serve as an alternative or complement to state responsibility in international law (Environmental Liability Directive, 2004: Art. 1).

Thus, while the general dimension of the PPP is orientated towards addressing pollution, its consequential environmental protection biases cannot be overlooked, nor can its broad array of policy implications for trade, investment, competition, development, economic and social issues. These functions become very important in analysing the PPP because they represent the basis upon which polluters assume the responsibility to bear the cost in respect of pollution regulation for environmental protection. The following section will analyse the principle to expose the contexts in which it imputes responsibility or liability on polluters to pay or bear the costs of pollution and the scope of undertaking that is implied in the term costs.

**Content of the principle**

The analysis of the content of the PPP will revolve around three concepts that I consider to form the bedrock of the principle. First is the issue of the polluter. Next is the determination of costs that he/she is obligated to bear and the third, how he/she should be made to pay for such costs. Together, these together should illustrate the substantive and procedural aspects identified as forming the legal status of the principle. The procedural aspects will be discussed under methods of implementing the principle in the next section. The analysis here will rely on legal instruments and scholarly interactive, to reveal the signposts for understanding the nature and character of the principle for sound legal and policy direction in pollution regulation for sustainability.

*1. The polluter*

When the principle was first conceived by the OECD, 'polluter' was defined as persons engaged in activities that contaminate the environment whether through industrial emissions in excess of legally binding stipulated thresholds; or whether damage resulted from polluting activities regardless of whether the conduct was lawful (OECD, 1974). But the meaning of the concept has diverged considerably under international treaties and declarations, some reflecting flexibility while others restrict its application (Smets, 1994: 134).

The concept of polluter has evolved first in respect of personality category to include states, corporations, industries and individuals (EURATOM, 1975). The second development is in relation to the nature and effects of conduct or activity, extending these to include natural resource use for economic or social purposes and attaching liability to direct or indirect environmental consequences (EURATOM, 1975; Agenda 21, 1992: chapter 8, 8:28). Here a 'polluter' is used not necessarily in reference to polluting activities per se, but to any activity that contributes to the deterioration of the environment, such as the handling or disposal of waste, the use and management of water resources, or an enjoyment of environmental quality as in use of recreational facilities. A third category of polluter is discerned by extending the scope of responsibility, such as the giving of aid or technology transfer or emission reduction programmes by developed countries to developing countries as an incentive to preserve or improve their environmental quality through the principle of common but differentiated responsibilities (Rio Declaration, 1992: Principle 7). But it will also include the provision of an incentive to polluters to emulate best practice. To give effect to the varying polluter capacity, polluter responsibility can be individual, collective, partial or total, actual or potential so as to avoid charging only the physical polluter (OECD, 1972: 26).

These various categorisations of 'polluter' have engendered certain descriptive terminologies of the principle in both legal instruments and scholarly articulations, in tandem with several objectives. For instance the 'polluter-pays pprinciple' has been deemed to suggest making polluters pay the cost of preventing or minimising pollution; or as assigning environmental rights to those who benefit from environmental improvement. The 'beneficiary- pays principle' indicates that whoever benefits from a cleaner environment should bear the costs of pollution control. 'Polluter responsibility principle' assumes that industrial polluters should compensate their victims. The 'user pay principle' has been defined by the United Nations as a variation of the polluter pays principle that calls upon the user of a natural resource to bear the cost of running down natural capital while the 'user pay cousin' has been used to suggest that polluters and resource users should internalise all the environmental externalities of their activities (Horesh, 2004; Gaines, 2002: 265; Coffey and Newcombe, 2001).[17]

Then there is the concept of 'Producer responsibility' which places responsibility for the environmental impact associated with a product onto the producers of that product.[18] The EU has applied producer responsibility through directives on packaging and packaging waste, waste electronic and electrical equipment, and end of life vehicles (OECD Accidental Pollution, 1989: Art. 12).[19] Also, 'extended polluter responsibility' (EPR) is used to describe 'a policy in which the producer's financial and or physical responsibility for a product is extended to the post-consumer state of the product's life cycle'.[20] EPR internalises the cost of waste disposal into the cost of the product, shifting the responsibility for reducing the environmental impacts of waste upstream to consumers.

Theoretically, EPR assumes that polluters will improve the waste profile of their products, thus decreasing waste and increasing the possibility of reuse and recycling. This interrelationship between producers of products and users of products has been severally expressed as 'apportionment of liability' (Environmental Liability Directive, 2004: Art. 22), 'appropriation of burden' and 'burden sharing' (Restriction of Hazardous Substances (ROHs) Directive 2002/95/ EC, 2002; Waste Electrical and Electronic Equipment (WEEE) Directive 2002/96/EC, 2002). A further distinction has been made between burden of responsibility and burden of cost.

These various meanings of who is a polluter – actual, extended, inverted or converted – in the articulation of the PPP has no doubt been the result of an effort to address the complexities inherent in pollution regulation, given the fact that the effects of pollution are not always the immediate result of human activity created or displaced by the source per se, and warranting the need for different regulatory regimes (Springer, 1983). Since the objective of the principle aims at allocating environmental responsibility for pollution costs generally and specifically, varying the meaning of polluter serves as a logical capacity basis for applying different regulatory regimes to achieve its purpose and the ultimate goal of ensuring sustainable development. It is this effect that de Sadeleer essentially contemplates in describing the PPP amongst directing principles as embodying types of reasoning (as opposed to rigid rules) which seek to balance interest with a flexibility that makes it possible for divergent values and interests or contradictory policies to coexist (de Sadeler, 2002).

### 2. *Cost bearing and paying*

Like the 'polluter', the content of the costs to be borne or paid as an effect of the PPP has also diverged considerably and continues to expand to meet the environmental challenges of modern economic activities. Initially, OECD polluter cost related to measures needed to prevent, control and reduce pollution, or other costs of administrative measures taken by the authorities in response to pollution, including the cost of implementing anti-pollution policies, developing anti-pollution technologies and grants for modernising out-of-date plants (OECD, 1972; OECD, 1974: 26).

Beyond the preventive strategy of the OECD, Rio Principle 16 provides for the polluter to bear the cost of pollution and 'environmental costs', thereby allowing for the inclusion of other costs that might be connected with pollution regulation, environmental protection and management generally (Smets, 1994: 134; WECD, 1987; Agenda 21, 1992: chapter 8, 8:28). Some indications of the likely cost to be borne by polluters include the cost of achieving prescribed environmental quality, preventing or remedying environmental damage, preventing accidental pollution and the clean-up or reinstatement of the environment after an accident, the 'cost of exceptional measures' needed to protect human health and the environment (EURATOM, 1975; OECD, 1974: 68; Environmental Liability Directive, 2004; OECD, 1989: Arts 10 and 16; OECD, 1991). Social costs, remaining external cost of investment on technology, the cost incurred when a ban is placed on polluting activity, indemnity cost, operational costs, including the cost of present and future expenditure and loss of profit, even if not accessible in monetary terms, have all been identified (Waste Oils Directive, 1975; Landfill Directive, 1999: Art 10; see also Göransson, 1999: 352–3).

In the context of liability under international law, the incidence of the burden of cost will include the cost of abatement, compensation and reparation, while as applied to international environmental law generally, it will relate to the cost of promoting best environmental practices, best available technology and the cost of a prompt and effective response to environmental emergencies (Stoll, 2000: 182; Wolfrum et al., 2000: 255; Antarctic Treaty Secretariat, 2005). However polluters may not have to bear costs arising under these categories in certain exceptional circumstances (EURATOM, 1975).

**Implementing the PPP**

The true substantive content of the PPP cannot be completely captured without the procedural and institutional framework within which the law and policies operate, and which could be either global, regional, domestic or local. The procedural aspects aim at mechanisms for making polluters pay and are translated through specific commitments and techniques for cost internalisation and pollution reduction (Coffey and Newcombe, 2001; Wolfrum, 2000). The implications of the PPP specifically for the domestic environment cannot be overstated. Reliance is placed on the national authorities to implement the principle through various techniques and mechanisms, in some cases requiring conformity with national laws (OECD, 1989: Arts 10 and 11). Many law-makers have so far expressly recognised the PPP as a guiding norm of environmental policy (de Sadeleer, 2002: 32).

For purposes of clarity, four categories of implementation methods advocated under the PPP have been identified. These are headed respectively, the regulatory regime, economic strategies, liability and cooperative regimes. The reasonableness of any measure will depend on the circumstances under which it is implemented, the nature and extent of the measures, the threats and hazards existing when the decision is taken, the laws and regulations in force and the interests which must be protected (OECD, 1989: Art. 12). The overall choice of measures must be reasonable, economically efficient and provide adequate protection of human health and the environment.

*1. Regulatory regime: command and control, self-regulation and voluntary initiatives*

The regulatory regime relates to direct controls which impose an absolute obligation to comply with process and product standards and charges fixed by law at regional, national or local level, with which polluting activities must comply. These must also be directly enforceable. Commonly described as 'command and control' systems, the regulatory function limits directly or indirectly the quantity of residuals that each actor must generate or that must be generated from each source. This regulatory limitation will be based on the level of control that can be achieved – either in reliance on a particular technology, setting environmental quality targets, or setting aggregate limits on pollution loading (Stewart, 2000: 175). It is recommended that such measures be linked with the pre-existing body of regulation on environmental quality (OECD, 1974: 26; EURATOM, 1975: Annex, para. 2, Art. 4). It is in aid of this regulatory function that the Rio Declaration requires states to institute environmental regulation and directs national authorities to endeavour to promote the internalisation of environment costs (Rio Declaration, 1992: Principles 11, 13, 16).

Another approach under the regulatory regime deals with 'environmental contracting', under which the government or source contractually agrees on an aggregative, multi-media umbrella of residuals limitations for the facilities in lieu of the uniform technology-based requirements imposed by regulation on a specific residual stream into particular media (Stewart, 2000: 175). Then there is what are known as 'information-based strategies' (Stewart, 2000: 175). Here, governments take measures to provide consumers and investors with information regarding the environmental performance of products and firms in the hope that the market will penalise firms with an inferior performance through diminished sales.

### 2. *Economic strategies: internalisation, incentives, initiatives, innovations*

The principal economic strategy of the PPP advocated under Principle 16 of Rio Declaration is 'internalisation'. Cost internalisation facilitates the inclusion of external effects in economic calculation and corrects misallocations, while assuring the rational management of resources (OECD, 1974: 23). In other words, all economic activity which impinges upon the environment should be fully accounted for in the economic pricing system of the goods and services produced by such activity (Sunkin et al., 2002: 53). It starts with incorporation of cost of prevention, reduction and control in planning, processing and production and is complete when the polluter takes responsibility for all the costs arising from pollution (Stewart, 2000; de Sadeleer, 2002: 22). Internalisation can be enhanced by the consistent use of market mechanisms as a complement to or substitute for other policy instruments (OECD, 1991).

A major economic instrument for effectuating the principle is through pollution charges and taxes and burden-sharing between polluters and beneficiaries (OECD, 1991; OECD, 1974: 26; Pearce and Turner, 1992).[21] If the charge is linked to the damage function, the polluter pays for the exact amount of damage he caused. Another strategy is the 'economic incentive system' (EIS), which establishes directly or indirectly a price that must be paid for each unit of residual generated – whether in processing, production disposal or emission as an ongoing process – but which leaves each actor free to decide on the level that it generates (Stewart, 2000: 175–6). This is achieved through fees and taxes, a tradable quota system, or via variable emissions reduction credits, and transferable market permit systems. Imposing a price on residuals under EIS provides continuing incentives for sources to reduce their existing residual levels (Stewart, 2000: 175–6; see also OECD, 1991; De Bieg, 2005: 125). Other incentive and aid measures include payments – a bargaining instrument for buying from the polluter his or her right not to pollute (inverted PPP), auction of polluting rights, tax benefits, subsidies, financial assistance and other payments made to reinforce other measures designed to achieve appropriate natural resource use and pricing (OECD, 1991).

The Kyoto Protocol to the Climate Change Convention represents an example of use of economic instruments and incentive systems in implementing the PPP. The Protocol seeks to regulate the reduction of carbon dioxide and other specified greenhouse gas emissions (GHG) in the atmosphere to certain prescribed levels using flexible economic strategies. The parties can meet their commitments to reducing GHG emissions either by transferring or purchasing GHG emission reductions from other parties through emissions trading schemes, or increasing their removal by sinks through emissions reduction units between developed countries (joint implementation), or as certified emissions reduction obtained through investments in clean development projects in developing economies (clean development mechanism), or a combination of these. The European Union Emissions Trading Scheme (Directive 2003/87/Ec 2003: 275) is the largest multinational GHG emissions trading scheme, allowing regulated entities to use carbon credits and carbon projects to meet obligations under the protocol.

The imposition of carbon taxes – that is, excise taxes based on the carbon content of fuel – is another component of broader national strategies to reduce greenhouse gas emissions, pursuant to the PPP, to meet Kyoto Protocol commitments. Carbon taxes provide a market-based incentive for firms to shift away from carbon-intensive production by internalising the negative externalities of fossil fuels into prices and decision-making. Fuels with higher carbon contents are made relatively more expensive than cleaner-burning fuels, in order to reduce demand for carbon-based fuels (coal and petroleum) and encourage a substitution toward cleaner fuels (natural gas or renewable energy), shifts that will result in decreased emissions of carbon dioxide and ultimately to slower climate change. Several countries that are parties to the Kyoto Protocol have implemented taxes on carbon in an effort to reduce emissions of carbon dioxide (Rich, 2004).

Initiative and innovative strategies find application generally under the concept of corporate responsibility. Here firms are pressured or encouraged to self-regulate or take voluntary initiatives or employ best available techniques to meet their quality targets and liabilities. Companies could cover themselves against any costs by taking out insurance or using other forms of financial assurances and guarantees (Environmental Liability Directive, 2004: Arts 8:2 and 14).[22] Innovative strategies advocate investments to be made in adapting new measures, technology designs or environmentally friendly products.

### *3. Liability regime*

Liability for loss or damage remains an important part of most systems of environmental law even when supplemented or in part superseded by regulatory regime, risk avoidance procedures and criminal penalties (Boyle, 2005: 3). A liability regime does have a purpose in the implementation of the PPP, especially to ensure polluter responsibility and accountability to victims – the curative dimension of the PPP. Governments are required under Principle 22 of the Stockholm Declaration and Principle 13 of the Rio Declaration to develop international and national law regarding liability and compensation for the victims of pollution and other environmental damage. And relying on Principles 13 and 16 of the Rio Declaration, the ILC has drafted environmental liability principles which aim at ensuring prompt and adequate compensation for natural or legal persons, including states that are victims of transboundary damage, including damage to the environment (International Law Commission Draft Principles on Environmental Liability, 2005: 155–7, Principle 3).[23]

Thus, at the international level thus, the effect of the PPP as a liability and compensation regime is explained in the application of various principles, mechanisms and institutional practices. Traditionally, it is expressed through principles of state responsibility or liability for breach of general environmental obligations, under the rule prohibiting transboundary harm, including the duty to take preventive measures; and the principle according to which an illegal act (or omission) requires reparation by compensation or restitution corresponding to the value of the damage or loss sustained (*Trail Smelter,* 1938/41; *Chorzów Factory* case, 1928; *Corfu Channel* case, 1949: 39–40; ILC Articles on Responsibility of States for Internationally Wrongful Acts, 2001: Art. 34; Fitzmaurice, 2007: 1011). Under this fault-based liability regime, the state is made responsible and liable for pollution caused by industry, a consequence that is believed to undermine the principle unless state responsibility and the liability of states could be made no more than residual sources of redress (Boyle, 2005: 8–9). But it should be remembered that the concepts of deterrence, redress, reparation and restitution that define state responsibility and liability form the core of the PPP.

Beyond the fault-based liability of states, the PPP is also reflected in international civil liability regimes for high risk activities which are likely to create some environmentally harmful consequences no matter the amount of precaution taken. Such regimes tend to employ strict and limited liability. International civil liability regimes, including those incorporated in multilateral enviromental agreements (MEAs), have been notable in the context of oil pollution,[24] the sea transfer of hazardous substances (HNS Convention, 1996), waste exports, carriage of dangerous goods (Basel Liability Protocol, 1999; ECE Convention on Civil Liability for Damage Caused during Carriage of Dangerous Goods by Road, Rail and Inland Navigational Vessels, 1989), industrial accidents on transboundary watercourses (the Kiev Protocol, 2003),[25] nuclear pollution[26] and a general system of liability for damage resulting from activities dangerous to the environment (Lugano Convention, 1993). These regimes channel liability from state to persons in control of dangerous activities or operators, with polluter cost implications in the case of oil-transporting shipowners, carriers of dangerous goods, waste transporters, recipient waste disposers and operators of nuclear plants, respectively.[27] The latest application of the principle in the context of liability is the Antarctic Treaty regime, which adopts a new Annex VI to the Protocol on Liability Arising from Environmental Emergencies. This annex seeks to hold operators active in the Antarctica *inter alia* liable for the cost of prompt and effective actions to environmental emergencies or the costs of response actions taken by another party (Antarctic Treaty Secretariat, 2005).

Furthermore, in what has been described as an application of the 'broader version' of the PPP, the international system of liability implicates society by making it accountable for the collective choices it makes to undertake dangerous activities and thus the benefits and costs emanating form such activities (Louka, 2006). Under this rationale, such regimes provide for additional compensatory mechanisms supported by entities which cannot have control over specific incidents that give rise to liability but are responsible in a broader sense as receivers of benefits from dangerous activities. Drawing heavily on state practices, Boyle has been able to identify in this approach some 'common principles of diverse solution' which include strict liability, attaching liability to several 'operators', spreading of the burden of loss through additional compensation schemes, an ultimate burden on states of residual compensation funding or residual liability in the case of operator insolvency and industry burden (Boyle, 2005: 8 *et seq.*; see also Churchill, 2001; Brunnée, 2004: 351).

This system is best illustrated by the Fund Conventions regime for oil pollution in which oil-receiving industries (as customers who initiate the transfer of oil) contribute money to supplement the compensation provided by the shipowner for the externalities generated by oil transport (the Fund Convention, 1971). This regime translates liability through increasing the financial limits of contributions for compensating victims and establishing a mechanism for simplified future updating of the amounts. It also allows for more heads under which to claim such compensation and introduces a regime of compulsory liability insurance or other financial security (Sunkin et al., 2002: 76–9; Göransson, 1999: 346 *et seq.*). The nuclear liability regime also allows all other states that have subscribed to the nuclear regime to contribute to supplementing the compensation provided by the liable nuclear operator (Convention on Supplementary Compensation for Nuclear Damage, 1997).

These institutional practices of international liability and compensation schemes for victims of pollution under a system of operator non-fault liability, including the apportionment of responsibility between states, industry and private parties, is now widely recognised as the basis for emerging general principles on environmental liability, including for pollution (ILC, 2005: 155–7). At the substantive level, the objective of PPP is addressed through implementation methods which require states to impose non-fault liability on operators, establish and maintain financial security and guarantees to cover compensation claims, establish industry-wide funds at the national level and allocate additional financial resources. The efficiency of the PPP is also to be enhanced by procedural requirements (ILC, 2005: Principles 4, 5 and 7).

In respect of national implementation, a traditional liability regime for environmental damage, including for pollution, is commonly assumed under tort law or statutory schemes. Liability could either be strict, such as imposing a price on conduct that causes harm or loss, or negligence or fault-based, which exacts damages payment for harm caused where an actor fails to observe a relevant standard of care analogous to a regulatory standard. Liability in compensatory cost and compensatory measures also define the effect of the principle (Report on the joint text approved by the Conciliation Committee for the Environmental Liability Directive (PE-CONS 3622/2004 – C5-0079/2004 – 2002/0021(COD)) Doc.: A5-0139/2004; Stewart, 2000: 177). It must be stated, however, that the application of the principle under national law is generally regarded as an alternative to state responsibility under international law.

The question of compensation to victims as an aspect of the PPP can be tenuous, especially if the liability of the operator cannot be established or is limited (Boyle, 1991). Therefore new methods of regulation under the PPP have evolved. First, there is what has been described as 'negotiated rule-making', by which the main interest groups are diverted from the public regulatory process to negotiations, through an agency-directed process with an emphasis on the creation of trusts (funds) for adversarial relations (Morris et al., 2005: 181). An instant example is the United States Comprehensive Environmental Response, Compensation and Liability Act of 1980[28] – 'Superfund' Law – which provides a strong liability scheme and remedial relief for hazardous waste problems through the imposition of a fee on the oil and chemical industries to finance a trust fund.

Then there is what has been dubbed 'regulation by litigation'. Here, agencies use enforcement actions against regulated entities and interest groups to create new substantive obligation for the regulated (Morris et al., 2005: 181). This approach is best illustrated by two US cases, one reported to involve the major producers of heavy-duty diesel engines signing a $1 billion settlement with the US Environmental Protection Agency which imposed new controls for nitrogen oxide emissions (Morris et al., 2004); the other pertains to a 1998 settlement between the attorneys general of 46 US states and several major cigarette manufacturers requiring $246 billion in payments by the latter (National Association of Attorneys General, Tobacco Master Settlement Agreement).[29] In both cases, regulators obtained substantive provisions through the settlement that they could not have imposed directly on the regulated as legislation barred further imposition of standards (Morris et al., 2005).

What can be gleaned from the forgoing analysis of liability regimes at international and national level is their effectiveness as essential principles and mechanisms for turning the PPP into practice. But mention must be made of the importance of enforcement mechanism for making the polluter pay. The ILC has recommended the provision of international and domestic remedies *inter alia* through expeditious and less expensive international claims settlement procedures and competent and effective domestic administrative and judicial mechanisms (ILC, 2005: Principles 6(2) and (3)). Most civil liability regimes recognise the competence of national courts, either in a state where the damage was caused or in the state of nationality of the polluter, to decide the liability of the actual parties causing damage outside the state in which they are based. Such decisions become enforceable in other states parties to the agreement (Fitzmaurice, 2007: 1124).

Others have advocated judicial implementation of the PPP through 'ingenious gap-filling' techniques and by allowing its application over weak and inconsistent laws and underdeveloped administrative systems (Lord Justice Carnwarth, 2004: 317–18). The Indian judiciary represents an impressive example of adopting this gap-filling technique. The Indian Supreme Court has relied on the PPP to impose liability on the polluter for injury to private persons, financial costs of preventing or remedying damage and costs for reinstatement of the environment (*Vellore Citizens Welfare Forum v. Union of India*, 1996; *Council for Environment Legal Action v. Union India*, 1996). Also the High Court in Ireland lifted the veil of incorporation in order to fix directors of a company with personal liability (in addition to company) for unauthorised dumping in order to give full effect to the 'polluter pays' principle.[30]

### *4. From liability to cooperation*

Liability is not considered a sufficient means of implementing the PPP, especially in solving transboundary pollution and protecting the global commons. International cooperation is important in this respect. It is based on the conviction that unilateral actions by states to control transfrontier pollution are not adequate. Therefore, liability regimes in MEAs shift from the compensatory approach of responsibility or liability regimes towards more proactive systems set up in MEAs aimed at encouraging or assisting states to fulfil their obligations in relation to the environment (Fitzmaurice, 2007: 1011).

Speaking of environmental effects generally, Rio Principle 19 reflects the polluter responsibility of states for early notification and consultation in good faith. The cooperation principle has been applied by bilateral, regional and global treaty regimes to the management of transboundary risks posed by hazardous or potentially harmful activities, including nuclear installations near borders, continental shelf operations, long-range transboundary air pollution and marine pollution from land-based sources or dumping (Stoll, 2000: 187). Through regional cooperation in protecting the Baltic Sea for instance, HELCOM proceeds to joint pollution reduction by identifying pollution hot-spots through special action plans for the most severely polluted areas and joint comprehensive action programmes (Wolfrum et al., 2000: 255).

An access to justice approach through principle of non-discrimination, transboundary civil litigation, supranational application of laws and transnational enforcements all represent the cooperative dimension of polluter cost-bearing responsibility. Accordingly, cooperation to make the polluter pay can be deduced from measures which allow foreign states, foreign public entities, and individuals to participate in domestic proceedings, especially at municipal level (Recommendation of the Council on Principles concerning Transfrontier Pollution – C(74) 224, 1974: Art. 7; Protocol on Liability Arising from Environmental Emergencies: Annex VI, Arts 5(2) and 6(1); see also Boyle, 2005: 9–16; Stoll, 2000: 191). Other cooperative measures worth mentioning include aid given for the purpose of stimulating experimentation with new pollution-control technologies, and 'common action' to encourage states to absorb the cost of prevention of pollution damage to the *res communis* by switching to more costly land-based dumping sites or to forgo the production of polluting chemicals altogether; and cooperation to take enforcement action (OECD, 1974; Springer, 1983: 14; Antarctic Treaty, 2005: Arts 2; 6(2)(b) and 13(2); OECD, 1989: Art. 13).

The cooperative model of responsibility for implementing the PPP dismisses concerns that the effect of state responsibility or inter-state compensation and pollution control arrangements is to undermine the PPP.

**Critical appraisal of the PPP**

The mechanisms advocated by the principle for pollution prevention and control, whether in its regulatory context, liability and cooperative aspects, has met criticisms on various fronts in all its implementation dimensions. First, it attaches a price to the right to pollute, thereby accepting environmental degradation as inevitable provided the agent pays (de Sadeleer, 2002: 35). This has been described '... as implicitly endorsing immoral behaviour by selling indulgences to pollute'. The flexibility which they afford is a disadvantage in dealing with localised pollution impacts that threaten serious damage if health or ecological thresholds are exceeded (Bugge, 2006; Stewart, 2000: 173–4). It is further argued that the principle does not itself imply a strict pollution control policy as it leaves room for substantial discretion to the public authorities who are to decide on implementation measures.

Further, it is argued that allowances made for mitigation through the techniques of the PPP will not result in the perfect information social optimum, but will bias the outcome towards one favouring the property right, and that the global incentive mechanisms dictated by the principle, including out-of-court settlements, indicate large benefits from pollution, which somehow contradict the polluter-pays principle (Huber and Wirl, 1998: 69–87). Similarly, technology-based command requirements, which take into account the ability of an industry to absorb the cost of technology in determining whether it is available, also tend to impose disproportionately costly regulatory burdens on more productive and profitable industries because they can 'afford' more stringent controls. Such a strategy penalises innovation and investment and perpetuates older, more polluting products and processes (Stewart, 2000: 185).

Above all, 'non-use values' are believed to be frequently underestimated or ignored in determinations of how much polluters should pay for damages inflicted upon natural resources (Czarnezki and Zahner, 2005: 197). It must be mentioned that to achieve the objectives of the polluter-pays principle necessitates the institution of methods that could value the environment correctly in an economic setting (see Schwartz, 2007: 89). The goal of environmental valuation is intended to assist the decision-maker not to make decisions that are wrong from both an economic and an environmental point of view. This 'environmental valuation' aspect of the principle and concerns with financial reparations has its sceptics. Valuing the environment in monetary terms has been considered 'an environmentally dangerous and intellectually deceptive exercise' (Jacobs, 1991: 202).

Notwithstanding the varied criticisms levied at the theoretical objectives and practical application of the PPP, its importance for sound policy direction in dealing with contemporary pollution problems cannot be overstated. The principle stresses the close relationship between development and environmental protection through its emphasis on achieving environmental and social objectives by using an economic rationale. Its 'internalising', 'redistributive', 'preventive' and 'curative' functions (de Sadeleer, 2000: 34–7) combine different objectives – economic, social and environmental – thereby making it an invaluable tool for directing economic activities towards sustainability. Also, by combining efficiency requirements (internalisation of external effects) with equity (charging costs to responsible parties), the PPP represents 'a rule of economic, juridical and politically good sense' (OECD, 1974: 25). It is not surprising therefore that the principle has been regarded as the essential conceptual basis for a range of legal instruments at the core of environmental legislation (de Sadeleer, 2002: 22).

The mechanisms dictated by the principle are more cost effective, allowing the worst offenders to be targeted. They provide for proper cost allocation, encouraging polluters to avoid or reduce pollution. The mechanism can promote sustainable development by providing increased flexibility and incentives for business innovation in less polluting, more resource-efficient technologies and methods (Stewart, 2000: 173). They also provide a valuable source of finance for local and national governments through pollution taxes, product taxes, effluent charges or emissions trading. These can minimise the total cost of pollution control to society, including the easing of the administrative burden of regulatory costs and strains on investment in other sectors (Swiss Session on Water Pollution: New Approaches to Face Risks to the Environment and Human Health, 2003).[31]

Finally, another advantage of the principle is the centrality of it concern for responsibility and liability. Its relationship with the development of rules of civil and state liability for environmental damage from pollution as a social ill is said to have received broad support (Sands, 1995: 66). The way it combines compensatory and preventive functions has been commended as surpassing conventional civil liability regimes (de Sadeleer, 2002: 21). The effect of the PPP through liability regimes places external controls on corporate decision-making processes and allows for direct application at the international level, thus by-passing the usual systemic requirement for national or domestic ratification of internationally agreed rules. While the principle does not wholly contribute to reducing pollution, it has the tendency to speed up the process by which those responsible for pollution accept responsibility for ecological damage (Sunkin et al., 2002: 77; de Sadeleer, 2002: 35). Its regime of responsibility through the evolution of compensation funds, environmental trust funds, development funds and even insurance schemes attests to this. The question of liability is totally absent from the ideology of these measures, as they usually derive from a show of support, solidarity or some sort of general concern, and these funds can be accessed even where the polluter is unavailable or unknown.

**Conclusion**

In spite of the variances in dimension, the PPP, originally devised to allocate the cost of pollution prevention and control measures, has matured into a formidable strategy for the protection of the environment, human health and safety, resource management and generally ensuring environmentally sustainable activities. These goals are made attainable under the PPP through implementation, mechanisms and liability systems designed to make polluters bear various costs in relation to the effects – direct, indirect or potential – on environmental components, and in proportion, where applicable, to their responsibility. Though the practical application of the principle will depend on the particular economic activity to be pursued, yet its values and objectives hold far-reaching implications, not only for environmental management, regulation and liability, but also for the ideology of environmental protection in general.

## Notes

1. Note that 'polluter' in this chapter includes those engaging in, sponsoring or benefiting from polluting activities, or dealing with hazardous substances or otherwise having responsibility to regulate or render assistance in combating pollution.
2. OECD Guiding Principles, accessible at: http://www.oecd.org/ (last visited on 10 April 2008).
3. Exceptions include government assistance and aid payments given to polluters in transition periods with regard to efforts to reduce their emissions; where steps to protect the environment would jeopardise the specific social and economic policy objectives of a country or region; and aids to promote the research and development of new pollution-control or abatement technologies.
4. Accessible at: http://www.oecd.org/ (last visited on 10 April 2008).
5. http://webdomino1.oecd.org/horizontal/oecdacts.nsf/ (OECD Economic Instruments, 1991) (last visited on 10 April 2008).
6. See also Art. 130(r)(2) (Art. 174(2)) Single European Act.
7. See, for instance, EC, 1973; Barcelona Convention for the Protection of the Mediterranean Sea against Pollution, 1976 (as amended in 1995): Art. 4(3)(a); Agreement concerning the Protection of the Scheldt and Meuse Rivers, 1994: Art. 3:2(d); Council Recommendation 75/436/EURATOM, ECSC, EEC, 1975: Annex para. 2 (hereinafter EURATOM, 1975).
8. See, for instance, Directive of the European Parliament and of the Council on Environmental Liability with Regard to the Prevention and Remedying of Environmental Damage PE-CONS 3622/04, 2004 (hereinafter, Environmental Liability Directive, 2004); Rotterdam Convention on the Protection of the Rhine, 1998: Art. 4; London Protocol to the Convention on the Prevention of Marine Pollution by Dumping of Waste and other Matters, 1996: Art. 3(2); European Union Council Directive 96/61/EC Concerning Integrated Pollution Prevention and Control; Convention on Co-operation for the Protection and Sustainable Use of the Danube River, 1994: Art. 4:4; Helsinki Convention on the Protection of the Marine Environment of the Baltic Sea Area, 1992: Art. 2(5); Helsinki Convention on the Protection and Use of Transboundary Watercourses and International Lakes, 1992: Art. 2:5(b); Convention on the Protection of the Marine Environment of the North East Atlantic, 1992: Art. 2:2(b) (hereinafter, OSPAR Convention, 1992); Convention on the Protection of the Alps, 1991: Art 2(1).
9. Such as: the London Protocol on Preparedness, Response, and Co-operation to Pollution Incidents by Hazardous and Noxious Substances, 2000: Preamble; UNECE Convention on the Transboundary Effects of Industrial Accidents, 1992: Preamble; OPRC Convention, 1990: Preamble.
10. See also: Convention on the Ban of Import into Africa and the Control of Transboundary Movement of Hazardous Wastes within Africa, 1991 (Bamako Convention); Convention on the Control of Transboundary Movement of Hazardous Wastes and their Disposal, 1989 (Basel Convention).
11. International Convention on Civil Liability for Oil Pollution Damage 1969 (replaced by Protocol of 1992); Convention on the Establishment of an International Fund for Compensation for Oil Pollution Damage, 1971 (replaced by Protocol of 1992) (The Fund Convention); International Convention on Liability and Compensation for Damage in Connection with the Carriage of Hazardous and Noxious Substances by Sea, 1996 (HNS Convention); Protocol on Liability and Compensation for Damage Resulting from Transboundary Movement of Hazardous Wastes and their Disposal, 1999 (Basel Liability Protocol); The 2003 UNECE Protocol on Civil Liability and Compensation for Damage Caused by the Transboundary Effects of Industrial Accidents on Transboundary Waters, 2003 ('Kiev Protocol'); Paris Convention on Third Party Liability in the Field of Nuclear Energy, 1960 (as amended by the 2004 Protocol); Convention on Civil Liability for Damage Resulting from Activities Dangerous to the Environment, 1993 (Lugano Convention) respectively.
12. See, for instance, EC Recommendation Regarding Cost Allocation and Action by Public Authorities on Environmental Matters, 1975: 1; Directive 75/439/EEC on the Disposal of Waste Oils, 1975: Arts 13 and 14;

Directive 1999/31/EC on Waste Landfill, 1999: Art. 10; Directive 94/62/EC on Packaging and Packaging of Wastes, 1994; Directive 2000/60/EC on Water Policy, 2000: Art. 9. See also State Aids: Commission Opens Formal Investigation into UK Nuclear Decommissioning Authority IP/04/1430, accessible at: http://uk.ihs.com/news-06Q2/eu-en-nuclear-energy.jsp (last visited on 10 April 2008).

13. Hereinafter *US Chemical* case, 1987.
14. See Convention on Civil Liability for Oil Pollution Damage Resulting from Exploration for the Exploitation of Seabed Mineral Resources, 1977: Annex III, Art. 22; Wellington Convention on the Regulation of Antarctic Mineral Resource Activities, 1988: Art. 8.
15. This envisages a wider scope for pollution regulation under international environmental law, and applies in the context of *inter alia* protecting the environment from pollution from wars, hazardous substances, technologies and wastes, transboundary pollution and protection of global atmospheric components.
16. This dimension is more narrowly defined in connection with natural resource management (see Munro and Lammers, 1987: ix).
17. The article by Horesh is accessible at: http://socialgoals.com/blog/2004/12/polluter-pays-principle.html (last visited on 10 April 2008).
18. 'Principles: Make the Polluter Pay' accessible at http://www.actionforsustainability.org/principles/introduction.php?id=8 (last visited on 10 April 2008). Producer responsibility is intended to address the whole life-cycle environmental problems of the production process, from initial minimisation of resource use, through extended product life span, to recovery and recycling of products once they have been disposed of as waste.
19. Ibid. See also Hristev (2006: 62–2).
20. The concept was first defined by the Swedish government in 1975: http://en.wikipedia.org/wiki/polluter (last visited on 10 April 2008).
21. The article by Pearce and Turner is accessible at http://www.uea.ac.uk/env/cserge/pub/wp/wm/wm_1992_01.pdf (last visited on 10 April 2008).
22. On financial guarantees, see Hubert (2006: 13).
23. Hereinafter ILC, 2005.
24. See, for instance, International Convention on Civil Liability for Oil Pollution Damage, 1969 (replaced by Protocol of 1992); International Convention on Civil Liability for Bunker Oil Pollution Damage, 2001; Convention on Civil Liability for Oil Pollution Damage Resulting from Exploration for and Exploitation of Seabed Mineral Resources, 1977.
25. It provides a legal claim to compensation for individuals affected by industrial accidents on transboundary watercourses. See also Swiss Session on Water Pollution: New Approaches to Face Risks to the Environment and Human Health, 2003, accessible at: http://www.unep.org/ (last visited on 10 April 2008).
26. See among others: Paris Convention on Third Party Liability in the Field of Nuclear Energy, 1960 (as amended by 2004 Protocol); Brussels Convention Supplementary to the 1960 Convention on Third Party Liability in the field of Nuclear Energy, 1963 (as amended by the 2004 Protocol); Vienna Convention on Civil Liability for Nuclear Damage, 1963 (as amended by 1997 Protocol); Brussels Convention on the Liability of the Operators of Nuclear Ships, 1962; Brussels Convention Related to Civil Liability in the Field of Maritime Carriage of Nuclear Material, 1971.
27. For overviews on the operation of these regimes see Louka (2006: 448 *et seq.*); Fitzmaurice (2007: 1024 *et seq*); Göransson (1999: 346 *et seq.*).
28. See also Driesen (2002–2003: 48).
29. Accessible at: http://www.naag.org/backpages/naag/tobacco/msa/msa-pdf/1109185724_1032468605_cigmsa.pdf (last visited on 15 May 2007).
30. This can be found in an article by Fry accessible at: www.williamfry.ie/article.asp?categoryID=29&articleID=631) (last visited on 10 March 2008).
31 Accessible at: http://www.unep.org/ (last visited on 20 March 2008). See also the arguments of the US in the *US Chemicals Case*, 1987: 23).

## References

Ando, N. (1981), 'The Law of Pollution Prevention in the International Rivers and Lakes', in R. Zacklin and L Caflisch (eds) (1981), *The Legal Regime of International Rivers and Lakes,* The Hague: Martinus Nijhoff Publishers, 331–70.

Boyle, A. (1991), 'Making the Polluter Pay? Alternatives to State Responsibility in the Allocation of Transboundary Environmental Cost', in F. Francioni and T. Scovazzi (eds), *International Responsibility for Environmental Harm*, London: Graham and Trotman, 363 *et seq.*

Boyle, A.E. (2005), 'Globalising Environmental Liability: The Interplay of National and International Law', *JEL* **17**(1), 3–26.

Brunnée, J. (2004), 'Of Sense and Sensibility: Reflections on International Liability Regimes as Tools for Environmental Protection', *ICLQ* **53**, 351–67.

Bugge, H.C. (2006), 'Environmental Justice and the Polluter Pays Principle', in *Stockholm Conference on Environmental Law and Justice*, accessible at: http://www.juridicum.su.se/smc/envjusticeconf/abstracts/HansChristianBugge.htm.
Churchill, R. (2001), 'Civil Liability Litigation for Environmental Damage by Means of Treaties: Progress, Problems and Prospects', *YBIEL* **12**, 3–41.
Coffey, C. and Newcombe, J. (2001), 'The Polluter Pays Principle and Fisheries: The Role of Taxes and Charges', London: Institute for European Environmental Policy, accessible at: http://www.jncc.gov.uk/pdf/ thepolluted2.pdf.
Commission on Global Governance (1995), *Our Global Neighbourhood,* Oxford: OUP.
Czarnezki, J.J. and Zahner A.K. (2005), 'Utility of Non-use Values in Natural Resource Damage Assessments', *Boston College Environmental Affairs Law Review* **32**, 509–26.
De Bie, G.H. (2005), 'Transboundary Air Pollution: Developments During 2004', *Colorado Journal of International Environmental Law and Policy* **19**, 123–32.
de Sadeleer, N. (2002), *Environmental Principles – From Political Slogans to Legal Rules*, Oxford: OUP.
Driesen, D.M. (2002–2003), 'Sustainable Development and Air Quality: The Need to Replace Basic Technologies with Cleaner Alternatives', *Buffalo Environmental Law Journal* **10**, 25 *et seq.*
Fitzmaurice, M. (2007), 'International Responsibility and Liability' in Bodansky, D. *et al., The Oxford Handbook of International Environmental Law*, Oxford: OUP, 1010–35.
Gaines, S.E. (2002), 'International Trade, Environmental Protection and Development as a Sustainable Development Triangle', *RECIEL* **11**(3), 259–74.
Gillespie, A. (1997), *International Environmental Law Policy and Ethics,* Oxford: OUP.
Göransson, M. (1999), 'Liability for Damage to the Marine Environment', in A. Boyle and D. Freestone (eds), *International Law and Sustainable Development*, Oxford: OUP, 345–58.
Gündling, L. (1991), 'Protection of the Environment by International Law: Air Pollution' in W. Lang and H. Neuhold (eds), *Environmental Protection and International Law,* London: Graham and Trotman, 91–100.
Horesh, R. (2004), 'Polluter Pays Principle', accessible at http://socialgoals.com/blog/2004/12/polluter-pays-principle.html.
Hristev, I. (2006), 'ROHS and WEEE: The New European Directives: Do They Work and Why', *European Environmental Law Review* **15**, 62–74.
Huber, C. and Wirl, F. (1998), 'The Polluter Pays Versus the Pollutee Pays Principle under Asymmetric Information', *Journal of Environmental Economics and Management*, **35**, 69–87.
Hubert, B. (2006), 'Financial Guarantees in the Environmental Liability Directive: Next Time Better', *European Environmental Law Review* **15**, 13–32.
Jacobs, M. (1991), *The Green Economy,* London: Pluto Press.
Lord Justice Carnwarth (2004), 'Judicial Protection of the Environment at Home and Abroad', *JEL* **16**(3), 315–27.
Louka, E. (2006), *International Environmental Law*, Cambridge: CUP.
Morriss, A., Yandle, B. and Dorchak, A. (2004), 'Regulation by Litigation: EPA's Regulation of Heavy-Duty Diesel Engines', *Administrative Law Review* **56**, 403–518.
Morriss, A., Yandle, B. and Dorchak, A. (2005), 'Choosing How to Regulate', *Harvard Environmental Law Review* **29**, 179–250.
Munro, R.D. and Lammers J.G. (eds) (1987), *Environmental Protection and Sustainable Development: Legal Principles and Recommendations/Adopted by the Experts Group on Environmental Law of the WCED*, London: Graham and Trotman/Martinus Nijhoff.
Pearce, D. and Turner, K. (1992), 'Packaging Waste and the Polluter Pays Principle: A Taxation Solution', accessible at: http://www.uea.ac.uk/env/cserge/pub/wp/wm/wm_1992_01.pdf.
Quarrie, J. (ed.) (1992), *Earth Summit '92*, London: The Regency Press Corporation.
Rest, A. (1995), 'Implementation of Rio Targets – Preliminary Efforts in State Practice', *Environmental Policy and Law* **25**(6), 312–21.
Rich, D. (2004), 'Climate Change, Carbon Taxes, and International Trade', accessible at: http://are.berkeley.edu/courses/EEP131/fall2006/NotableStudent04/ClimateChangeRich.pdf.
Robb, C.A.R (ed.) (2001), *International Environmental Law Reports Volume 2: Trade and Environment*, Cambridge: CUP.
Sands, P. (1995), 'International Law in the Field of Sustainable Development – Emerging Legal Principles', in W. Lang (ed.), *Sustainable Development and International law,* London: Graham and Trotman/Martinus Nijhoff, 53–66.
Schwartz, P. (2007), *Sustainable Development and Mining in Sierra Leone*, Kent: Pneuma Springs.
Smets, H. (1994), 'The Polluter Pays Principle in the Early 1990s', in L. Campiglio (ed.), *The Environment After Rio*, London: Graham and Trotman/Martinus Nijhoff, 131–47.
Springer, A.L. (1983), *The International Law of Pollution*, Westport, CT: Greenwood Press.
Stewart, R.B. (2000), 'Economic Incentives for Environmental Protection: Opportunities and Obstacles', in E. Revesz *et al.*, (eds), *Environmental Law, The Economy and Sustainable Development*, Cambridge: CUP, 171–244.

Stoll, P.T. (2000), 'Tranboundary Pollution', in F. Morrison and R. Wolfrum (eds), *International, Regional and National Environmental Law,* The Hague: Kluwer Law International, 169–200.
Sunkin, M. *et al.* (2002), *Sourcebook on Environmental Law,* London: Cavendish Publishers.
WCED (1987), *Our Common Future,* Oxford: OUP.
Wolfrum, R. (2000), 'International Environmental Law: Purposes, Principles and Means of Ensuring Compliance', in F. Morrison and R. Wolfrum (eds), *International, Regional and National Environmental Law,* The Hague: Kluwer Law International, 3–70.
Wolfrum, R. *et al.* (2000), 'Preservation of the Marine Environment', in F. Morrison and R. Wolfrum (eds), *International, Regional and National Environmental Law,* The Hague: Kluwer Law International, 225–83.

## *Cases*

Case 172/82, *Syndicat National des Fabricants Raffineurs d'Huile de Graissage et al. v. Groupement d' Intérêt Economique 'Inter-Huiles'* (*Inter-Huiles* case) (1983), *ECR* 555.
*Case Concerning Factory at Chorzów (Claim for Indemnity),* 1928 *PCIJ,* Ser. A No. 17, 4.
*Corfu Channel* case *(United Kingdom v. Albania)*, 1949, *ICJ Rep.*, 4.
*Council for Environment Legal Action v. Union India* (1996), *AIR SCW* 1069; *SCC* **3,** 212.
*Trail Smelter Case (United States of America v. Canada)* (1941), *RIAA* **III**, 1905.
*United States – Taxes on Petroleum and Certain Imported Substances* (BISD/34S/136), report of the panel adopted on 17 June 1987.
*Vellore Citizens Welfare Forum v. Union of India* (1996), *AIR SC* 2715.

## *Treaties and documents*

Agenda 21, Report of the UNCED, I (1992) UN Doc. A/CONF.151/26/Rev.l, *ILM* **31**, 874.
Agreements on the Protection of the Rivers Meuse and Scheldt (1994), *ILM* **34**, 851.
Antarctic Treaty Secretariat (2005), 'A Liability Annex for the Environmental Protocol', *Antarctic Treaty Secretariat Newsletter*, **1**(3), 3.
Bamako Convention on the Ban of the Import into Africa and the Control of Transboundary Movement and Management of Hazardous Wastes within Africa (1991), *ILM* **30**, 773.
Barcelona Convention for the Protection of the Mediterranean Sea against Pollution (1976), *UNTS* **1102**, 27.
Barcelona Convention for the Protection of the Mediterranean Sea against Pollution (amended and renamed in 1995 as Convention for the Protection of the Marine Environment and the Coastal Region of the Mediterranean) (1995), accessible at: http://www.unep.ch/regionalseas/regions/med/t_barcel.htm.
Basel Convention on the Control of Transboundary Movement of Hazardous Substances (1989), *ILM* **28**, 657.
Basel Protocol on Liability and Compensation for Damage Resulting from Transboundary Movements of Hazardous Wastes and their Disposal (1999), accessible at: http://www.basel.int/meetings/cop/cop5/docs/prot e.pdf.
Brussels Convention Relating to Civil Liability in the Field of Maritime Carriage of Nuclear Material (1971), *UNTS* **974**, 255.
Brussels Convention Supplementary to the 1960 Convention on Third Party Liability in the field of Nuclear Energy (1963) (as amended by the 2004 Protocol), accessible at: http://www.nea.fr/html/law/ brussels_supplementary_convention.pdf.
Commission opens formal investigation into UK Nuclear Decommissioning Authority (2004), Doc. IP/04/1430, accessible at: http://uk.ihs.com/news-06Q2/eu-en-nuclear-energy.jsp.
Convention for the Protection of the Marine Environment of the Baltic Sea Area (1992), reprinted in R. Wallace (1994), *The Marine Mammal Commission Compendium*, Washington, DC: United States Government Printing Office, 1493.
Convention for the Protection of the Marine Environment of the North-East Atlantic (OSPAR Convention) (1992), *ILM* **32**, 1072.
Convention on Civil Liability for Damage Resulting from Activities Dangerous to the Environment (1993), *ILM* **32**, 1228.
Convention on Civil Liability for Oil Pollution Damage Resulting from Exploration for the Exploitation of Seabed Mineral Resources (1977), *ILM* **16**, 1450.
Convention on Supplementary Compensation for Nuclear Damage (1997), *ILM* **36**, 1473.
Convention on the Liability of Operators of Nuclear Ships (1962), reprinted in *AJIL* **57**, 268.
Convention on the Protection and Use of Transboundary Watercourses and International Lakes (1992), *ILM* **31**, 1312.
Convention on the Protection of the Alps (Alpine Convention) (1991), *ILM* **31**, 767.
Convention on the Regulation of Antarctic Mineral Resource Activities (CRAMRA) (1988), *ILM* **27**, 868.
EC (1973), *First Programme of Action on the Environment*, *OJ* **CI 12/1**.
EC (1975), 'Recommendation of 3 March 1975 Regarding Cost Allocation and Action by Public Authorities on Environmental Matters', *OJEC* **L 194**, 1.

ECE Convention on Civil Liability for damage caused during Carriage of Dangerous Goods by Road, Rail and Inland Navigational Vessels (1989), UN Doc. ECE/TRANS/79.
ECE Convention on the Transboundary Effects of Industrial Accidents (1992), *ILM* **31**, 1330.
European Parliament (2004), 'Report on the Joint Text Approved by the Conciliation Committee for the Environmental Liability Directive (PE-CONS 3622/2004 – C5-0079/2004 – 2002/0021(COD)', Doc. A5-0139/2004, accessible at: http://www.europarl.europa.eu/sides/getDoc.do;jsessionid=2D9A8F8194F689FE5EB8386597230681.node1?objRefId=71980&language=EN.
ILA (2002), 'New Delhi Declaration of Principles of International Law relating to Sustainable Development', in ILA, *Report of the Seventieth Conference, New Delhi*, London: ILA, 25–9; UN Doc. A/57/329.
ILC (2001), 'Report of the International Law Commission on Articles on Responsibility of States for Internationally Wrongful Acts', UNGAOR **56,** Supp. (No. 10) at 43, UN Doc. A/56/10.
ILC (2005), 'International Law Commission Draft Principles on Environmental Liability', *Journal of Environmental Law* **17**(1), 155–7.
International Convention on Civil Liability for Bunker Oil Pollution Damage (Bunkers Convention) (2001), *ILM* **40**, 1493.
International Convention on Civil Liability for Oil Pollution Damage (1969, amended in 1984, and 1992), *ILM* **9**, 45; **23**, 177; *UNTS* **1956**, 255.
International Convention on Liability and Compensation for Damage in Connection with the Carriage of Hazardous and Noxious Substances by Sea (HNS Convention) (1996), *ILM* **35**, 1406.
International Convention on Oil Pollution Preparedness, Response and Co-operation (1990), *ILM* **30**, 733.
International Convention on the Establishment of an International Fund for Compensation for Oil Pollution Damage (FUND) (1971), *ILM* **11**, 284.
Johannesburg Declaration on Sustainable Development (2002), UN Doc. A/CONF.199/20, Resolution 1.
London Convention on the Prevention of Marine Pollution by Dumping of Wastes and Other Matter (1972), *UNTS* **1046**, 120.
London Protocol on Preparedness, Response and Co-operation to Pollution Incidents by Hazardous and Noxious Substances (2000), accessible at: www.ecolex.org/server2.php/libcat/docs/multilateral/en/TRE002482.doc.
OECD (1972), 'Recommendation of the Council Concerning International Economic Aspects of Environmental Policies, C(72)128, OECD Guiding Principles', accessible at: http://www.oecd.org.
OECD (1974), 'The Implementation of the Polluter-pays Principle Recommendation, C(74)223/Final' in OECD, *Polluter Pays Principle: Definition, Analysis, Implementation*, Paris: OECD.
OECD (1989), 'Council Recommendation on the Application of the Polluter-Pays Principle to Accidental Pollution, C(89) 88/Final', accessible at: http://www.oecd.org/.
OECD (1991), 'Recommendation of the Council on the Use of Economic Instruments in Environmental Policy, C(90)177/Final', accessible at: http://webdomino1.oecd.org/horizontal/oecdacts.nsf/.
Paris Convention on Third Party Liability in the Field of Nuclear Energy (1960), *AJIL* **55**, 1082.
Paris Convention on Third Party Liability in the Field of Nuclear Energy (1960) (as amended by the 2004 Protocol), accessible at: www.nea.fr/html/law/nlparis_conv.html.
Plan of Implementation of the WSSD (2002), UN Doc. A/CONF.199/20 Resolution 2.
Protocol of 1992 to Amend the International Convention on the Establishment of an International Fund for Compensation for Oil Pollution Damage (1971), *UNTS* **1110**, 57.
Protocol to the Convention on the Prevention of Marine Pollution by Dumping of Wastes and Other Matter of 1972 (1996), *ILM* **36**, 1.
Rio Declaration on Environment and Development (1992), *ILM* **31**, 874.
Rotterdam Convention on the Protection of the Rhine (1998), *UNTS* **1404**, 59.
Single European Act (1987), *ILM* **25**, 506.
Sofia Convention on Cooperation for the Protection and Sustainable Use of the Danube (1994), accessible at: http://www.icpdr.org/icpdr-pages/drpc.htm.
Stockholm Declaration of the United Nations Conference on the Human Environment (1972), UN Doc. A/Conf.48/14, reprinted in *ILM* **11**, 1416.
Tobacco Master Settlement Agreement (1998), accessible at: http://www.naag.org/backpages/naag/tobacco/msa/msa-pdf/1109185724_1032468605_cigmsa.pdf.
UNECE Protocol on Civil Liability for Damage and Compensation for Damage Caused by Transboundary Effects of Industrial Accidents on Transboundary Waters (2003), *ILM* **44**, 258.
UNEP (2003), 'Swiss Session on Water Pollution: New Approaches to Face Risks to the Environment and Human Health', accessible at: http://www.unep.org/.
United Nations Framework Convention on Climate Change (1992), *ILM* **31**, 849.
Vienna Convention on Civil Liability for Nuclear Damage (1962) ( as amended by 1997 Protocol), accessible at: http://www.iaea.org/Publications/Documents/Conventions/protamend.html.

*Journal of Environmental Law* **22**:2 
doi:10.1093/jel/eqq012

# Understanding Environmental Models in Their Legal and Regulatory Context

Elizabeth Fisher,* Pasky Pascual** and Wendy Wagner***

## Abstract

Environmental models are playing an increasingly important role in most jurisdictions and giving rise to disputes. Despite this fact, lawyers and policy-makers have overlooked models and not engaged critically with them. This is a problematic state of affairs. Modelling is a semi-autonomous, interdisciplinary activity concerned with developing representations of systems and is used to evaluate regulatory behaviour to ensure it is legitimate. Models are thus relevant to lawyers and policy-makers but need to be engaged with critically due to technical, institutional, interdisciplinary and evaluative complexities in their operation. Lawyers and policy-makers must thus think more carefully about models and in doing so reflect on the nature of their own disciplines and fields.

Keywords: Models, environmental regulation, science and law, administrative decision-making

This article is about the important and complex role that models play in environmental regulation. While models tend to be perceived as inanimate, technical inputs for environmental decision-making, in truth models are contingent on numerous policy-relevant assumptions and framing decisions

*Corpus Christi College and Faculty of Law, University of Oxford (liz.fisher@law.ox.ac.uk)
**US Environmental Protection Agency. The author's views do not necessarily reflect US Environmental Protection Agency policy.
***Faculty of Law, University of Texas, Austin; This article was completed as part of a larger project that examines the interface between models and decision-making—TransAtlantic Uncertainty Colloqium (TAUC). TAUC was funded by a generous US National Science Foundation Grant 0533024. We would like to thank reviewers for comments on previous drafts of this article. All errors and omissions remain our own.

for which policy-makers should be centrally involved. In this piece, we discuss not only the key role that lawyers and policy-makers should play in the development and use of models, but highlight for these non-scientific groups the inner workings of models so that they can better appreciate their contributions. Despite our focus on the inner working of models, however, no specialist expertise in modelling is required of our readers. Nor will we dazzle you with numbers, bamboozle you with language, or overwhelm you with diagrams. Our purpose is simultaneously more modest and more challenging. It is more modest because our aim is to provide an overarching conceptual explanation of why environmental models are relevant to lawyers and policy-makers, and why, because they are relevant, lawyers and policy-makers must critically engage with models. Achieving this objective is more challenging, because neither the relevance nor the need for critical engagement is self-evident to lawyers and policy-makers.

The structure of this article is as follows. First, we briefly review the increasing role that models play in environmental decision-making. Models are playing three different roles: as policy catalysts; as devices for fleshing out institutional mandates; and as regulatory strategies. Moreover, models are increasingly the focus of policy and legal disputes. Despite the prevalence of models and disputes over them, lawyers and policy-makers have not understood them to be in their domain due to their technical and administrative nature. In the second section, we show that while models may not be within the conventional expertise of lawyers and policy-makers, they are relevant to what they do. This is because modelling is a semi-autonomous, interdisciplinary activity concerned with developing representations of systems which provide the rationale and basis of much regulatory behaviour. Or to put the matter another way, models govern what is understood as legitimate regulatory action.

In the third section, we show how lawyers and policy-makers must not only appreciate the relevance of models to what they do, but also the complexity of models. We examine four particular types of complexity: technical, institutional, interdisciplinary and evaluative. In the final section, we argue there are three important conclusions that can be drawn from our analysis. Models cannot be ignored by lawyers and policy-makers. Models need to be treated with care by these groups and in thinking about models there is also a need to reflect on what is understood to be the scope of law and policy.

Five important points should be made before starting our analysis. First, this article is not an article arguing for or against the validity of models. Our starting point is that models are an inherent feature of environmental regulation. Second, the focus of this article is upon identifying the generic features of models which make them relevant and challenging for lawyers and policy-makers to think about. Third, and related to this point, while the importance of regulatory and legal culture is central to our argument,[1] in this article we deliberately discuss a number of different jurisdictions in passing as we want to highlight that models are an omnipresent feature of nearly all environmental regulation regimes. Fourth, in referring to lawyers and policy-makers we define these two groups broadly to include all those involved in environmental regulation decision-making and its review including those who wish to support or challenge regulatory decisions. Finally, we do not see our critical agenda as an exhaustive analysis of the role of models in environmental regulation. Much more could and should be said about models.[2]

## 1. The Prevalence of Models in Environmental Regulation

An obvious starting point in an article about models is to define what a model is. The National Research Council (NRC), a prestigious science policy-making body in the United States, organized a panel that has defined a model as:

> a simplification of reality that is constructed to gain insights into select attributes of a particular physical, biological, economic, or social system. They can be of many different forms.[3]

This definition is bland but it is a good starting point for the simple fact that most readers will recognise something familiar in such a definition. This is because, most environmental lawyers and policy-makers will have stumbled across such 'simplifications of reality' in their work and found themselves needing to think about a particular model whether it be a model concerning climate change, groundwater contamination, air quality, economic impact or something else. These models may be large scale and very complex or small and relatively simple. Likewise, lawyers and policy-makers may interact with them directly or may find themselves interacting with decisions based on a model or based on particular interpretations of a model.

Our focus in this article is upon why lawyers and policy-makers find themselves engaging with models, and what they should keep in mind when they do. Yet before we can discuss these two issues, we must provide a brief sketch of the current regulatory landscape—a landscape in which models and disputes over them are increasingly prevalent but despite that fact, lawyers and policy-makers do not see models as relevant to what they do.

1 E Fisher, *Risk Regulation and Administrative Constitutionalism* (Hart Publishing, Oxford 2007).
2 W Wagner and others, 'Misunderstanding Models in Environmental and Public Health Regulation' (2010) 18 New York University Environmental Law Journal 101.
3 National Research Council (NRC), *Models in Environmental Regulatory Decision Making* (National Academies Press, Washington DC 2007) 31.

### 1.1 The Prevalence of Models in Environmental Regulation

Models are now omnipresent in environmental regulation and they are playing many diverse roles in both law and policy in different legal cultures.[4] It is thus impossible in one article to either collate or even summarise the use of models in environmental law and we do not begin to attempt this. What is useful to do, is to highlight the different functional roles that models are performing in environmental regulation. Three large grouping of functions can be identified.

First, there are *policy-catalyst* models which play a role in informing policy in circumstances where no well established regime for regulatory action exists. The use of models in early climate change policy is the most obvious example here.[5] Thus, for example, the Intergovernmental Panel on Climate Change First Report was the foundation for the United Nations Framework Convention on Climate Change.[6] These models are thus establishing the premises for future state action where no such premises existed before. With that said, by acting as a foundation for new regimes they are then invariably incorporated into those regimes.[7] Moreover, these models are often relied upon in decision-making, the formulation of new laws[8] and legal disputes.[9]

Second, there are those models that have as their purpose the fleshing out of a discretionary legislative mandate by establishing the premises and rationale for particular action within a regulatory regime.[10] This very large group of models are our primary focus and are best described as *institutional mandate* models in that their primary function is to apply the institutional mandate of a regulatory institution to the issues that that institution is dealing with.

4 For examples in US environmental law, see <http://www.epa.gov/epahome/models.htm> accessed 16 June 2010 and NRC, ibid 47–8.

5 S Jasanoff and B Wynne, 'Science and Decision Making' in S Rayner and E Malone (eds), *Human Choice and Climate Change – Volume One* (Pacific Northwest National Laboratory, Battelle Press 1998); D Farber, 'Modeling Climate Change and Its Impacts: Law, Policy, and Science' (2008) 86 Texas Law Review 1655.

6 Intergovernmental Panel on Climate Change, *Intergovernmental Panel on Climate Change – First Assessment Report* (World Meteorological Organization/UNEP, Geneva 1990).

7 Intergovernmental Panel on Climate Change, *Climate Change 2007: Synthesis Report* (IPCC, Geneva 2007).

8 Council Directive (EC) 2008/101 of the European Parliament and of the Council of 19 November 2008 amending Council Directive (EC) 2003/87 so as to include aviation activities in the scheme for greenhouse gas emission allowance trading within the Community [2009] OJ L8/3.

9 The IPCC reports have been touched upon in numerous legal cases see *Walker v Minister for Planning* [2007] NSWLEC 741, [122]–[128]; *Xstrata Coal Queensland Pty Ltd v Queensland Conservation Council Inc* [2007] QLRT 33; Case C-440/05 *Commission v Council* [2008] 1 CMLR 22, [93] per AG Mazak; *Massachusetts v Environmental Protection Agency* (2007) 549 US 497, 508; *Small Hydro Power Developers' Association, v Transmission Corporation of AP Ltd* Appellate Tribunal for Electricity for New Delhi, MANU/ET/0033/2008. See also very indirectly *Dimmock v Secretary of State for Education & Skills* [2007] EWHC 2288 (Admin).

10 K J Holmes and others, 'Regulatory Models and the Environment: Practice, Pitfalls and Prospects' (2009) 29 Risk Analysis 159, 162. For a list of US examples see <http://cfpub.epa.gov/crem/knowledge.base/knowbase.cfm> accessed 14 June 2010.

The basis of that mandate is usually outlined in legislation but how that mandate is interpreted will depend on the prevailing legal and institutional culture.[11]

An important point to appreciate here is that the institution operating and utilising a model is nearly always administrative. That is, it is a non-elected institution that has been delegated its mandate by a primary lawmaker.[12] This occurs because modelling is part of assessment—an information, expert and communication-intensive process that can only be carried out by the administrative arm of government.[13] As we shall see, the fact that modelling is primarily occurring within the administrative realm has significant consequences for not only how models are understood, but also how lawyers and policy-makers interact with them.

Institutional mandate models include models which play a background policy-making role and those which directly inform particular decisions. Examples can be seen in air quality,[14] land contamination,[15] hazardous substances,[16] water quality,[17] flooding risk,[18] environmental assessment,[19] genetically modified organisms[20] and nature conservation.[21] Moreover, it also includes models deployed both formally and informally by private actors as

11 Fisher (n 1).
12 Ibid 19–22.
13 Ibid.
14 US Clean Air Act 42 USC §7409 (b)(1); Council Directive (EC) 96/62 of 27 September 1996 on ambient air quality assessment and management [1996] OJ L296/55 arts 4 and 6; Council Directive (EC) 2004/107 of the European Parliament and of the Council of 15 December 2004 relating to arsenic, cadmium, mercury, nickel and polycyclic aromatic hydrocarbons in ambient air [2005] OJ L23/3, Annex IV.
15 Department for the Environment Food and Rural Affairs, *Guidance on the Legal Definition of Contaminated Land* (DEFRA, London 2008).
16 Toxic Substances Control Act 15 USC §2605(a); Council Directive (EC) 98/8 of the European Parliament and of the Council of 16 February 1998 concerning the placing of biocidal products on the market [1998] OJ L123/1 Annex VI, para 79; Commission Directive (EC) 95/36 of 14 July 1995 amending Council Directive 91/414/EEC concerning the placing of plant protection products on the market [1995] OJ L172/8, Annex II; Council Directive (EC) 2005/25 of 14 March 2005 amending Annex VI to Directive 91/414/EEC as regards plant protection products containing micro-organisms [2005] OJ L90/1, B.1.7.
17 Schedule 1, Water Act 2007 (Australia) and 33 USC §1313(d). See O Houck, *The Clean Water Act TMDL Program: Law, Policy and Implementation* (Environmental Law Institute, Washington, DC 1999).
18 Environment Agency, *Flooding in England: A National Assessment of Flood Risk* (Environment Agency, Bristol 2009).
19 42 USC §4332(2)(C) (1982) and 40 CFR §1502.22 (1987). See also R Smith, 'Lands Council v. Powell and the Ninth Circuit's Refusal to Blindly Refer to Unreliable Forest Service Science' (2007) 28 Public Land and Resources Law Review 65.
20 Commission Regulation (EC) 641/2004 of 6 April 2004 on detailed rules for the implementation of Regulation 1829/2003/EC of the European Parliament and of the Council as regards the application for the authorisation of new genetically modified food and feed, the notification of existing products and adventitious or technically unavoidable presence of genetically modified material which has benefited from a favourable risk evaluation [2002] OJ L265/1, Annex I, 2.E.5.
21 R Glicksman, 'Bridging Data Gaps Through Modelling and Evaluation of Surrogates: Use of Best Available Science to Protect Biological Diversity under the National Forest Management Act' (2008) 83 Indiana Law Journal 465.

part of the regulatory process so as to establish that a particular course of action that a private actor wishes to take is valid under a regulatory regime.[22] Examples here include the use of models in environmental impact assessment[23] and food and chemical licensing.[24] The fact that all these models are established with the primary purpose of fulfilling a legal mandate means that these models are deeply embedded within the legal and institutional cultures in which they are operating.

The final category of models is the emerging category of *regulatory strategy* models.[25] These models are tools for networking public and private actors into collaborative decision-making. Regulatory strategy models are not just a catalyst for action and/or an assessment tool but are also understood as a vehicle for collaborative deliberation between a diverse set of parties.[26] These models are thus explicitly crossing the science/policy divide. Moreover, regulatory strategy models are expected to be dynamic and those involved in decision-making are expected to be engaged with model development, interpretation and utilisation. In some cases these models will be part of a formal legal regime such as the EU Water Framework Directive,[27] but in other cases these models will be the focus of more informal forms of public/private negotiated governance.[28] The popularity of regulatory strategy models can particularly be seen in the context of integrated assessment where models are playing a significant role in reframing how historically sector-specific issues are understood.[29]

In each of the uses described above, models are not simply plugged into the regulatory machinery but are deeply intertwined into the structure and logic of environmental regulation. At its most obvious, the role of models is now being explicitly recognised in some legislative frameworks as part of the

22 Commission Regulation (EC) 641/2004 (n 20).

23 *R (on the application of Edwards) v Environment Agency* [2008] UKHL 22, [2008] 1 WLR 1587.

24 *Gulf South Insulation v CPSC* 701 F 2d 1137 (5th Cir 1983); Case T-13/99 *Pfizer Animal Health SA v Council* [2002] ECR II-3305.

25 M Van Asselt and N Rijkens-Klomp, 'A Look in the Mirror: Reflection on Participation in Integrated Assessment from a Methodological Perspective' (2002) 12 Global Environmental Change 167; O Renn and P-J Schweizer, 'Inclusive Risk Governance: Concepts and Application to Environmental Policy Making' (2009) 19 Environmental Policy and Governance 174.

26 C Prell and others, 'If You Have a Hammer Everything Looks Like a Nail: Traditional Versus Partcipatory Model Building' (2007) 32 Interdisciplinary Science Reviews 263.

27 Council Directive (EC) 2000/60 of the European Parliament and of the Council of 23 October 2000 establishing a framework for Community action in the field of water policy [2000] OJ L327/1. B Page and M Kaika, 'The EU Water Framework Directive: Part 2. Policy Innovation and the Shifting Choreography of Governance' (2003) 13 European Environment 328.

28 Directorate Generals for Economic and Financial Affairs – Enterprise – Transport and Energy – Environment – Research and Taxation and Customs Union, *The Auto Oil II Programme: A Report from the Services of the European Commission* (2000) <http://ec.europa.eu/environment/archives/autooil/pdf/auto-oil.en.pdf> accessed 14 June 2010.

29 SEAMLESS and SEAMFRAME models integrating agricultural and environmental issues in the European Community. See <http://www.seamless-ip.org/> accessed 14 June 2010.

policy-making process[30] and there are also examples where regulatory institutions are producing substantial policy guidance concerning the use of models by private and public actors in order to provide some oversight over their use.[31] Regulatory institutions such as the US Environmental Protection Agency (EPA), moreover, have bodies that oversee modelling practice.[32] Most regulatory institutions in advanced democracies have modelling departments and dedicate considerable resources to modelling exercises.[33] These modellers are not isolated within the agency organisation, but instead are in regular communication with the agency's legal department, policy-making staffs and enforcement units. This process of institutionalisation means that modelling is part of the waft and weave of the regulatory fabric of a regime.[34] Modelling is not just fashion, easily shed with the new season, but rather is now a permanent feature in the institutional structure and logic of regulation.

### 1.2 *Models and Disputes*

It is not just that models are prevalent in environmental regulation, however. Disputes over them are also increasingly prevalent. Those disputes can be seen across all jurisdictions in both policy and legal contexts including political debate, policy discourse, media discussion and specific legal disputes.[35]

In the policy sphere many of these disputes have been in relation to policy-catalyst models. This is not surprising. As such models are establishing the premises for potential state action, it is obvious they will be controversial

30 Council Directive (EC) 2008/50 of the European Parliament and of the Council of 21 May 2008 on ambient air quality and cleaner air for Europe [2008] OJ L152/1; Water Act 2007 (Australia) Schedule One; US S Rep No 106-410 (2001), 90, reporting that the 'Committee is concerned that EPA has not peer-reviewed the 3MRA risk assessment model,' <http://frwebgate.access.gpo.gov/cgi-bin/getdoc.cgi?dbname=106.cong.reports&docid=f:sr410.106> accessed 14 June 2010.

31 US EPA, *Guidance on the Development, Evaluation and Application of Environmental Models* (EPA, Washington DC 2009) <http://www.epa.gov/crem/library/cred.guidance.0309.pdf> accessed 16 June 2010; New South Wales Department of Environment and Conservation, *Approved Methods for the Modelling and Assessment of Air Pollutants in New South Wales* (New South Wales Government Gazette, Sydney 2005).

32 Council for Regulatory Environmental Modelling (CREM). See <http://www.epa.gov/crem/index.html> accessed 14 June 2010.

33 The Environment Agency of England and Wales has an Air Quality Modelling and Assessment Unit (AQMAU) and see the European Topic Centre on Air and Climate Change which is contracted to the European Environment Agency.

34 US Government Accountability Office, *Human Health Risk Assessment: EPA Has Taken Steps to Strengthen Its Process, but Improvements Needed in Planning, Data Development, and Training* (Publication No GAO-06-595), 41. <http://www.gao.gov/new.items/d06595.pdf> accessed 16 June 2010.

35 D Michaels, *Doubt Is Their Product: How Industry's Assault on Science Threatens Your Health* (OUP, New York 2008); case studies in P Harremoës and others (eds), The *Precautionary Principle in the Twentieth Century: Late Lessons From Early Warnings* (Earthscan Publications, London 2002).

with different actors arguing for and against such action.[36] Moreover, these disputes will also involve a range of public and private institutions as the models in question are derived from a range of sources.[37]

Disagreements over climate change models are again the most high profile examples of these types of disputes. Thus, for example, within popular science literature there has been a critique of some of the climate temperature models which have contributed to the understanding of climate change.[38] Likewise, the disclosure of emails derived from the hacking of the computer servers at the Climate Research Unit at the University of East Anglia gave rise to a debate over the validity of data related to particular modelling practices.[39]

Yet, policy disputes have also arisen in relation to institutional mandate models. There has been ongoing political discussion and commentary concerning the validity of models used in regulatory impact assessment and cost/benefit analysis.[40] Likewise, reports have focused on the validity of models used in different regulatory areas.[41] Particular controversies such as the banning of flights in European air space due to volcanic disruption in Iceland also led the models on which the ban was based to be discussed in the media.[42]

Disputes about models however, are not limited to the policy realm and there have been a growing number of legal challenges to regulatory action where models have been the focus. These disputes primarily concern judicial and merits review of administrative decision-making. This development has occurred in all jurisdictions, although most obviously in the United States due to both a tradition of intensive judicial review and a legal culture of adversarial legalism.[43] The legal arguments concerning models have been striking in

36 For examples see the two papers making up 'The Stern Review: A Dual Critique' (2006) 7 World Economics 165; the issues raised in *Downs v Secretary of State for Environment Food and Rural Affairs* [2009] Env LR 19; and A Macintosh, 'The Garnut Review's Targets and Trajectories: A Critique' (2009) 26 Environmental Planning And Law Journal 88. See the case studies in Michaels (n 35), and B Lomborg, *The Skeptical Environmentalist: Measuring the Real State of the World* (CUP, Cambridge 2001).

37 A W Montford, *The Hockey Stick Illusion: Climategate and the Corruption of Science* (Stacey International, London 2010).

38 R Pielke and T Wigley, 'Dangerous Assumptions' (2008) 452 Nature 531.

39 E Kintisch, 'Stolen E-mails Turn Up Heat on Climate Change Rhetoric' (2009) 326 Science 1329.

40 B Ackerman and L Heinzerling, *Priceless: On Knowing the Price of Everything and the Value of Nothing* (The New Press, New York 2004); S Shapiro, 'OMB and the Politicization of Risk Assessment' (2007) 37 Environmental Law 1083.

41 Royal Commission on Environmental Pollution, 'Crop Spraying and the Health of Residents and Bystanders' (The Stationery Office, London 2005) [6.10]; Royal Commission on Environmental Pollution, 'Novel Materials in the Environment: The Case of Nanotechnology' (Cm 7468, 2008) [3.115].

42 C Gammell, D Millward and B Waterfield, 'Volcanic Ash Cloud: Met Office Blamed For Unnecessary Six-day Closure' *Telegraph.co.uk* (London 19 April 2010) <http://www.telegraph.co.uk/news/7608722/Volcanic-ash-cloud-Met-Office-blamed-for-unnecessary-six-day-closure.html> accessed 5 May 2010; P Marks, 'Can we Fly Safely Through Volcanic Ash?' *New Scientist* (London 20 April 2010) <http://www.newscientist.com/article/dn18797-can-we-fly-safely-through-volcanic-ash.html> accessed 5 May 2010.

43 R Kagan, *Adversarial Legalism: The American Way of Law* (Harvard UP, Cambridge 2003).

their diversity. Thus, for example, legal arguments directly relevant to models have included:[44] that the procedures for considering a model were procedurally improper;[45] that a model was oversimplified;[46] that a model did not apply to a specific factual situation;[47] that the assumptions embedded in a model were incorrect;[48] that the data and statistics used in a model were flawed;[49] that the model was not subject to adequate peer review;[50] and that there was a better model or source of information which could be used.[51] There have also been some striking examples of where courts and tribunals have ruled that a specific model was incorrect.[52]

What is particularly interesting about these arguments is that nearly all of them require judges and lawyers to engage with the inner workings of models and the technical aspects of modelling practice. Moreover, while judges have tended to stress their lack of competence[53] and the importance of deference to expert discretion,[54] they have tended to consider arguments about models and modelling at length.

A good example of the type of legal issues raises by models can be seen in the recent English litigation concerning a challenge by a pesticides campaigner to the Department of Environment, Food and Rural Affair's (DEFRA's) decision not to implement no-spray buffer zones around agricultural land to protect rural residents.[55] The dispute was legally complex involving as it did a mixture of EU law, English principles of judicial review, and an intricate regulatory scheme. The claimant, Downs, argued (among other things) that there

44 Also see T McGarity and W Wagner, 'Legal Aspects of the Regulatory Use of Environmental Modeling' (2003) 33 Environmental Law Reporter 10751.

45 *R (on the application of Edwards)* (n 23); *McLouth Steel Products Corp v Thomas* 838 F2d 1317 (DC Cir 1988); and *Chemical Manufacturers Association v EPA* 28 F 3d 1259 (DC Cir 1994) (the *MDI* case).

46 *Small Refiner Lead Phase Down Taskforce v EPA* 705 F 2d 506 (DC Cir 1983); *Leather Industries Of America v EPA* 40 F 3d 392 (DC Cir 1994); and *Flue-Cured Tobacco Co-op v EPA* 4 F Supp 2d 435 (MD NC, 1998).

47 *Small Refiner* (n 46); *MDI* (n 45); *Edison Electric Institute v EPA* 2 F 3d 438 (DC Cir 1993).

48 *Gulf South Insulation* (n 24); *American Iron & Steel Institute v EPA* 115 F 3d 979 (DC Cir 1997); *Leather Industries of America* (n 46); *Downs* (n 36).

49 *American Iron & Steel Institute* (n 48); *Central Arizona Water Conservation District v EPA* 990 F 2d 1531 (9th Cir 1993); *Flue-Cured Tobacco Co-op* (n 46).

50 *Flue-Cured Tobacco Co-op* (n 46).

51 Case T-229/04 *Sweden v Commission* [2007] ECR I-2437; *Downs* (n 36); *Ulan Coal Mines Ltd v Minister for Planning* [2008] NSWLEC 185.

52 *Chlorine Chemistry Council v EPA* 206 F3d 1286 (DC Cir 2000); *Xstrata Coal Queensland Pty Ltd* (n 9)

53 *Downs* (n 36) [38].

54 *Small Refiner* (n 46) 535; Case C-280/02 *Commission v France* [2004] ECR I-8573 and *Australian Pork Ltd v Director of Animal and Plant Quarantine* [2005] FCA 671.

55 *Downs* (n 36); *Secretary of State for Environment, Food and Rural Affairs v Downs* [2009] EWCA Civ 664, [2009] 3 CMLR 46. For a discussion of the case see L Warren, 'Healthy Crops or Healthy People? Balancing the Needs for Pest Control Against the Effect of Pesticides on Bystanders' (2009) 21 JEL 483.

was a failure to properly implement the relevant EU directive concerning pesticides.[56] The information on which the decision had been made involved a range of different studies and a risk assessment which included a model for bystander exposure. One of the claimant's arguments was that this model was in breach of the directive. The model had already been criticised by the Royal Commission on Environmental Pollution (RCEP) and that criticism has been subject to a response by DEFRA's Advisory Committee on Pesticides (ACP).[57]

In the Divisional Court, Collins J sketched in outline the different views of the parties on the adequacy of the bystander model but noted that 'I am not qualified to decide between those views nor is it an appropriate exercise for a judge to undertake on judicial review' unless there was evidence that the approach was 'tainted by irrationality in the *Wednesbury* sense'[58]—*Wednesbury* unreasonableness being the traditional and very high threshold test for substantive review in England and Wales.[59] Collins J also concluded that 'the alleged inadequacies of the model and the approach to authorisation and conditions of use have been scientifically justified'.[60] Later on, in relation to a different point he additionally noted:

> that a judge must be astute not to substitute his own view for that of the decision maker unless the decision maker has failed to have regard to a material factor, has had regard to an immaterial factor or has reached a truly perverse decision. The defendant in this case was bound to act on the advice given to him by experts. The advice conflicted and so he was entitled to choose between them.[61]

Yet he also found that the claimant had produced 'solid evidence . . . that residents have suffered harm to their health . . . or, at the very least, doubts have reasonably been raised as to the safety of pesticides under the regime which presently exists . . . It is clear that the precautionary principle must apply'.[62] The failure to consider this evidence as 'solid and that the conditions come within the scope of the Directive' was 'a failure to have regard to material considerations and a failure to apply the Directive properly'.[63] The requirement of 'solid evidence' was derived from a European Court of Justice (ECJ) judgment ruling on the same Directive where that Court found that

> It follows from that provision [Article 5(1) of Directive 91/441], interpreted in combination with the precautionary principle, that, in the

56 Council Directive 91/414/EC of 15 July 1991 concerning the placing of plant protection products on the market [1991] OJ L230/1. For her arguments see *Downs* (n 36) [6].
57 For a discussion of this see *Downs* (n 36) [4–5] and Warren (n 55) 492–4.
58 *Downs* (n 36) [38].
59 *Associated Provincial Picture Houses Ltd v Wednesbury Corporation* [1948] 1 KB 223.
60 *Downs* (n 36) [39]
61 Ibid [64].
62 Ibid [40].
63 Ibid [47].

> domain of human health, the existence of solid evidence which, while not resolving scientific uncertainty, may reasonably raise doubts as to the safety of a substance, justifies, in principle, the refusal to include that substance in Annex I to Directive 91/414.[64]

We will return to this judgment in a moment but it is also useful to note that Collins J also concluded that the failure to consider skin and eye irritancy was a failure to comply with the Directive.[65]

What this meant was that Collins J, through a different legal route, was effectively ruling on the adequacy of the model and in particular the types of information and exposure DEFRA had considered. This becomes particularly obvious when the ECJ's reference to 'solid evidence' is viewed in the context of its judgment where it made clear that the phrase must be seen in light of the principles of evaluation laid down in Annex VI of the Directive.[66] Those principles including references to modelling.[67] 'Solid evidence' was thus evidence which complied with principles of evaluation as set out in the Directive.

The case was appealed to the Court of Appeal. Downs argued that the bystander exposure model was not a 'suitable calculation model for residents', the language of 'suitable calculation model'[68] coming from the Directive.[69] Sullivan LJ concluded that:

> The Appellant was entitled to have regard to the ACP's views when considering what should be the Government's response to the RCEP's criticisms of the current model. Given that eminent scientists could not reach agreement as to whether there were significant shortcomings in the existing model, but were agreed that an improved model should be devised, even though they were not agreed as to whether it should be a probabilistic model, it is impossible to conclude that there is any error, much less a 'manifest error' in the Government's conclusions which are, in effect, that while the current approvals system is 'suitable' [for the purposes of the Directive] . . . . . . because it is 'at the forefront of international standards and provides adequate protection for both spray operators and members of the public' (paragraph 44, Defra's Response), it should be reviewed against a 'more transparent model' which is not currently available, but which should be developed (paragraphs 45–6, Defra's Response).[70]

64 *Sweden* (n 51) [161].
65 *Downs* (n 36) [52].
66 *Sweden* (n 51) [167].
67 See B.1.5 of Annex VI of Directive 91/414/EEC (n 56).
68 *Secretary of State for Environment, Food and Rural Affairs* (n 55) [42].
69 Para 7.2.2. of Annex III of Council Directive 91/441/EEC (n 67).
70 *Secretary of State for Environment, Food and Rural Affairs* (n 55) [53].

In regard to the argument that DEFRA had ignored 'solid evidence' he concluded that:

> The Report, the Commentary and the RCEP's Response all make it clear that there is no consensus in the scientific community that there is 'solid evidence' as found by Collins J. In Defra's response the Appellant did not accept that there was such evidence (paragraph 81 above). Collins J. was not entitled to substitute his own view for that of the Appellant, and in the absence of such a scientific consensus, had Collins J. applied the 'manifest error' test, he would have been bound to conclude that there was no manifest error in the Appellant's approach to the issue of causality.[71]

Our analysis of the above does not do justice to what was a very complex piece of litigation but these cases are paradigm examples of how models become the focus in legal disputes. Moreover, it highlights three things. First, despite statements that scientific issues were not within the competence of judges, the judgments by the Divisional Court and the Court of Appeal were both lengthy and detailed. This is even when, as with the Court of Appeal, they ultimately upheld the decision. Second, the legal arguments concerning the bystander exposure model were not just 'Is this right or wrong?' but involved a series of complex and overlapping legal arguments derived from different sources—was the model a 'suitable calculation model', was there 'solid evidence', was there a 'manifest error of assessment?' These are all arguments with a very real legal dimension. Third, the courts in these cases were not only engaging with the details of the bystander exposure model but also the administrative process in which it was embedded.

### *1.3 The Lack of Sustained Engagement with Models by Lawyers and Policy-Makers*

At this stage in our analysis two points need to be made. First, there is nothing novel in us identifying the important role models are playing in environmental regulation. In recent years many academic commentators,[72]

71 Ibid [61].

72 Holmes and others (n 10); S Yearley, 'Sociology and Climate Change After Kyoto: What Roles for Social Science in Understanding Climate Change?' (2009) 57 Current Sociology 389; A Petersen, 'Models as Technological Artefacts' (2000) 30 Social Studies of Science 793; S Rayner and E Malone (eds) *Human Choice and Climate Change, Volume One: The Societal Framework* (Pacific Northwest National Laboratory, Battelle Press, Columbus 1998); and M Lahsen, 'Seductive Simulations? Uncertainty Distribution Around Climate Models' (2005) 35 Social Studies of Science 895.

decision-makers[73] and even novelists[74] have pointed to the significance of models. The most high profile has been the highly respected US NRC which published *Models in Environmental Regulatory Decision-Making* in late 2007.[75] Moreover, most of these publications have highlighted the complexity of models.

Second, despite all of the above and the types of disputes seen in *Downs*, most policy-makers and lawyers have shown little sustained interest in the substance of models or the nature of modelling practice. These publications have been met mainly with silence and there has been no ongoing policy or legal dialogue concerning the nature of models, beyond the work of a few specialists. More significantly, on being faced with a model, many lawyers and policy-makers are only interested in asking the 'plain man's question', namely does the model amount to a 'real prediction?',[76] but they are not interested in probing further.

As seen in the previous section, specific cases or disputes may force a policy-maker or lawyer to engage with the inner workings of a particular model but this engagement is invariably in the time-pressured context of that case or dispute. In this context there is often a heavy reliance on different forms of deference whether it be to particular experts, administrative institutions, or decision-making processes.[77] The discussion of any particular model is in isolation and there is no precedent concerning models and just as a case is distinguishable on its facts, it is understood to be distinguishable in regards to the model.

We explicitly highlight this lack of sustained engagement with models by lawyers and policy-makers because it has been ignored in much of the literature. Indeed, many articles on models proceed on the assumption that the relevance of the substance of models to lawyers and policy-makers is self-evident. Yet we would argue that is not the case. Moreover, we would argue that this lack of substantive engagement is largely due to two different reasons.

First, models are perceived by lawyers and policy-makers to be 'scientific' and thus not within their expertise. Thus, while the outcomes of models are understood as relevant to law and policy, the inner workings of models—fat tails, uncertainty analysis, model coding, stochasticity, parameter variation, methods of corroboration and so on—are all understood to belong to the province of science. This view is of course not unfounded—models present a 'thicket of

73 P Pascual, 'Wresting Environmental Decisions From an Uncertain World' (2005) 35 Environmental Law Reporter 10539.

74 M Crichton, *State of Fear* (HarperCollins, New York 2004).

75 NRC (n 3).

76 J Ravetz, 'Models as Metaphors', in B Kasemir and others (eds) *Public Participation in Sustainability Science: A Handbook* (CUP, Cambridge 2003) 75.

77 *Secretary of State for Environment, Food and Rural Affairs* (n 55) [91] (assessing the view in the scientific community); WTO Panel Report, *Japan—Measures Affecting Agricultural Products (Varietals)*, AB-1998-8, 22 February 1999, [8.32] (deference to expert panel).

formulae and computer codes',[78] which require specialist knowledge to navigate—a thicket which is a barrier to understanding.

Second, for lawyers in particular, whose focus is upon law and its application, models are seemingly too much part of what occurs in the back office of administrative practice—they are not where the legal focus has traditionally been. To engage with an environmental model is thus also to engage with large expanses of the administrative landscape and its organisation and operation. Thus, cases in which models are subject to legal dispute often contain lengthy examinations of the role of different decision-making bodies and their relationship to each other. For example, in *Downs* both the Divisional Court and the Court of Appeal spent much time explaining the relationship and interactions between RCEP and ACP.[79]

The lack of engagement with models can thus be seen as due to a perception that models are neither within the *expertise or traditional domain* of what lawyers and policy-makers do. Yet what the disputes highlight in the last section is that, despite this, models are clearly *relevant* in some way to what lawyers and policy-makers do. What can be seen in cases like *Downs* is that the issues to do with modelling cannot be untangled from legal questions. Models are not just facts, but raise issues for the application of the law. This point was well made by the Australian Federal Court in relation to another modelling case where it noted:

> There is an added level of complexity in cases such as the present where the exercise of a statutory discretion is preceded by fact finding and it is sought to allege that irrationality and capriciousness have tainted both parts of the process and where the exercise of power is informed, in part, by scientific predictions.[80]

Thus, in *Downs* the 'bystander exposure model' sparked arguments about whether DEFRA had understood its legal obligations properly. Likewise, in other cases, the use and interpretation of models has raised issues to do with procedural fairness and legislative interpretation.[81] These cases thus highlight that models are relevant to what lawyers and policy-makers do—the question now raised is why that is the case?

78 Ravetz (n 76) 70.

79 See eg the discussions of the administrative frameworks in *Downs* and as re-described in *Secretary of State for Environment, Food and Rural Affairs* (n 55). Other examples include Case T-13/99 *Pfizer* (n 24) and *Australian Pork Ltd* (n 54).

80 *Lawyers for Forests Inc v Minister for the Environment Heritage and the Arts* [2009] FCA 330, [86].

81 Case T-13/99 *Pfizer* (n 24); *R (on the application of Eisai Ltd) v National Institute for Health and Clinical Excellence* [2008] EWCA Civ 438, (2008) 11 CCL Rep 385.

## 2. Why Models are Relevant to Lawyers and Policy-Makers

To answer that question our approach is conceptual and returns back to two more basic questions. What are the key features of models in environmental regulation and what role are they playing in that context? In answering this question it needs to be acknowledged that models have made a long, varied and important contribution to the sciences and social sciences,[82] but our focus is only on their use within the regulatory context.

### *2.1 Five Key Things to Know About Models*

If we return to our bland definition of a model that we quoted in Section 1 it can be seen that models are 'a simplification of reality that are constructed to gain insights into select attributes of a particular . . . .system'.[83] Using this definition as a springboard there are five key things to note about models in environmental regulation.

First, models are simplifications of reality.[84] Or to put the matter another way—a model is not reality. A model of a river basin will only capture some elements of that ecosystem just as a model of the solar system only captures some elements of the planets and their relationship to the sun. In relation to environmental regulations, models are particularly useful because the systems they represent are so complex and open ended that they can be difficult to conceptualise.[85] As Oreskes notes:

> Complex earth systems – such as the climate response to increased carbon dioxide, the transport of contaminants through groundwater, or the workings of a forest ecosystem – are difficult to address by traditional scientific methods. An ecosystem cannot be brought into the laboratory; the Earth's climate cannot be the site of controlled experiments. If you had proposed adding carbon dioxide to the Earth's atmosphere to test its effects, the experiment would have been rejected on ethical grounds. Numerical simulation models provide an ethical and pragmatic means to grapple with complex natural systems. [86]

82 M Hesse, *Models and Analogies in Science* (University of Notre Dame Press, Notre Dame 1966) and A Creager and others (eds) *Science Without Laws: Model Systems, Cases, Exemplary Narratives* (Duke University Press, Durham 2007).
83 NRC (n 3) 31.
84 Ibid 31.
85 N Oreskes, 'Why Believe a Computer? Models, Measures, and Meaning in the Natural World' in J Schneiderman (ed), *The Earth Around Us: Maintaining a Livable Planet* (WH Freeman and Co, San Francisco 2000) 73.
86 Ibid 73.

Moreover, models are frames that enable 'better questioning, exploration, handling and manipulation of the topic'.[87] As frames, models will draw (among other things) on both scientific theories about how a system works and available data about that system.[88] Models may draw on a single scientific discipline or many,[89] and they may be adapted as information and disciplinary understandings change.[90]

One of the most common types of model used in environmental regulation are computational models developed by selecting different elements of a system and formalising relationships among these elements through mathematical equations that are then codified in a computer program.[91] That computer program is not reality however. Nor is it a 'truth telling machine'[92] or a 'fact'.[93]

Second, for a model to be able to provide insight it must be a *rigorous* representation of reality. It must have a level of rigour that is defensible as fit for the purpose in hand. A model of ocean currents which is based on no data and a presumption that the world is flat is clearly inferior to one incorporating ocean current data and grounded in the theory that the world is round. A good model will be a coherent representation of a system that is based on well-established scientific theories and relevant, quality data. To say this is not to say that models are facts or that a model's truth can be validated. Rather it is saying that despite this, distinctions can be made in the quality of models. Moreover, the quality of a model will determine the quality of the insight which can be gained from it. Of course that raises the difficult question of how quality is judged and who is to judge it—this is an issue raised in many of the disputes above.

Third, as a simplification of reality a model is constructed for a purpose or set of purposes. That purpose is defined by the NRC as 'gaining insight'[94] but this should be understood in context. In the environmental regulatory context the main role of models is not so much to gain disinterested insight into a particular system but rather models are developed to assist decision-makers in discharging their regulatory responsibilities. Those responsibilities can vary dramatically but generally speaking models are concerned with assessing the existing state of the environment, human health and the economy, and predicting impacts on these different things. This will be considered in detail in the next section.

87 M Meyer, 'Increasing the Frame: Interdisciplinarity, Transdisciplinarity, and Representativity' (2007) 32 Interdisciplinary Science Reviews 203, 209.
88 M Morrison and M Morgan, 'Models as Mediating Instruments', in M Morgan and M Morrison (eds), *Models as Mediators* (CUP, Cambridge 1999).
89 Lahsen (n 72) 898.
90 I Grosse and others, 'Ontologies for Supporting Engineering Analysis Models' (2005) 19 Artificial Intelligence for Engineering Design, Analysis and Manufacturing 1.
91 NRC (n 3) 32.
92 Holmes and others (n 10) 161; NRC (n 3) 21.
93 NRC (n 3) 3.
94 NRC (n 3) 31.

Fourth, the purpose or purposes for which a model is developed will directly influence how reality is simplified. Thus, for example, if a model is being developed to assess water quality in a river then a model may represent water flow, oxygen concentration and contaminants but is unlikely to represent how many rocks are in the river or how many bridges cross it. In other words, the regulatory purposes of a model will influence what it represents. Moreover, the purposes of a model will directly influence how simplified the representation of a model is. Thus, for example, a model may be oversimplified to increase transparency of a system or the use of a system by non-scientists.[95] Models, then are not just products of theory and data but are also shaped by the priorities of the decision-makers who are deploying them.

Fifth, a logical consequence of all of the above is that modelling is an interdisciplinary activity. This is in two different ways—internally and externally. *Internally*, the process of modelling itself requires the integration of many different forms of information and assumptions from a variety of different disciplines.[96] Thus, while modelling is a distinct activity, it is only semi-autonomous in nature as it is drawing on a range of different disciplines.[97] Modelling also has an *external* interdisciplinary aspect because it is being carried out for a set of regulatory and policy-making purposes. Modelling is not just a scientific activity which is of relevance to policy-makers, but a scientific activity developed *for* policy-makers with the purposes of policy-making in mind.[98] Indeed, a model can be understood as a 'boundary object' in that it is a technical 'object' that inhabits 'several intersecting social worlds . . . and satisf[ies] the informational requirements of each of them'.[99]

### 2.2 *The Role of Models in Environmental Regulation*

The discussion so far has established that modelling is a semi-autonomous and interdisciplinary activity concerned with developing representations of reality for a purpose or purposes where that purpose or those purposes will influence how reality is represented. It is thus important to focus on the role of models in environmental regulation. What such a focus makes very obvious is that models are not just playing a back office and/or scientific role but rather are making a major contribution to regulating administrative behaviour and thus to establishing the legitimacy of administrative decision-making.

95 Holmes and others (n 10) 159.
96 P Pascual, 'Avoiding Tragedies of the Intellectual Commons through Integrated Impact Assessments' (2007) 21 Water Resources and Management 2005.
97 Morrison and Morgan (n 88).
98 In this regard it can be thought of as part of 'regulatory science'. See S Jasanoff, *The Fifth Branch: Science Advisers as Policy Makers* (Harvard UP, Cambridge 1990) 81.
99 S Leigh Star and J Greisemer, 'Institutional Ecology, 'Translations' and Boundary Objects: Amateurs and Professionals in Berkeley's Museum of Vertebrate Zoology, 1907-39' (1989) 19 Social Studies of Science 387, 393. Also see Pascual (n 96).

As seen above, it can be generally said that models are an activity of assessment. Assessment is the means by which regulators determine the existing states of, and predict future impacts of particular activities on, the environment, human health, the economy and society. Most of the time, they will be doing this in pursuance of their regulatory responsibilities. This is why institutional mandate models make up the vast bulk of models in environmental regulation. There are many examples of different assessment tools developed by regulators for specific purposes such as risk assessment, regulatory impact assessment and environmental impact assessment.[100] Models can be integrated into these tools but also can operate independently from them.

As part of assessment, models as workable representations of complex systems have three particular purposes. First, models are 'succinctly encoded' archives of existing knowledge about a particular system.[101] The knowledge that is being archived is often from disparate disciplinary sources including monitoring data, epidemiology studies, toxicology studies and expert opinion. Such information may also be of erratic quality and can range from raw observational data to theoretical assumptions. The way in which models can collate knowledge makes their utility to the regulatory process obvious—they increase the potential that the weight of available information about a system will inform regulatory decision-making.

The second purpose of models in the assessment context is to organise and integrate this information by placing it into a formalised construct that relates different pieces of information to each other. That construct is the simplified representation of reality and as we saw above a model is a powerful frame which aids focus.[102] As such models will dictate what is relevant and irrelevant to consider. Models are thus not just tools for collating information but also interpreting and making sense of that information. The rigor and quality with which a model does this can vary dramatically. Moreover, different models will frame issues differently and thus result in divergent understandings and interpretations of issues.[103]

The third purpose of a model is to serve as a tool of prediction. One aspect of environmental regulation is that it is an *ex ante* activity which seeks to regulate future human activity.[104] To do that, assessment tools are required to determine what the potential impacts of that human activity are. Prediction is an inherently uncertain process but models, by collating available information, may potentially reduce those uncertainties. At the same time however, because

100 NRC, *Risk Assessment in the Federal Government: Managing the Process* (National Academy Press, Washington, DC 1983); C Sunstein, *The Cost Benefit State: The Future of Regulatory Protection* (American Bar Association, Washington, DC 2002); J Holder, *Environmental Assessment: The Regulation of Decision-Making* (OUP, Oxford 2005).

101 NRC (n 3) 25.

102 Meyer (n 87).

103 E Tufte, *The Visual Display of Quatntitative Information* (Graphics Press, Cheshire 2001).

104 C Sunstein, *The Partial Constitution* (Harvard UP, Cambridge 1993).

models are shaped by their purposes and uncertainty still exists, modelling is neither a perfect nor a solely factual tool of prediction.

A single model may be developed for all three purposes or only one. Likewise, a model may be developed for one purpose and used for another. In all cases however, models are playing a role in ascertaining the relationship between the activity being regulated and the regulatory aim to be achieved. The significance of this is that models are ascertaining the premises and rationale of regulatory action. They are ascertaining the premises of regulation because models, through the collation and interpretation of knowledge, are a tool for identifying problems that need regulatory responses. They are establishing the rationale because through interpretation and prediction a model can direct what form that regulatory response should take.

In other words models, when relied on in regulatory decision-making, are regulating the power of a regulator in that a model is intended to 'govern behaviour',[105] particularly in relation to defining what is reasonable action on the part of a decision-maker. Models are laying down a blueprint for identifying which decisions are 'worthy' to be recognised as authoritative—or in other words as legitimate.[106] Models are thus playing a normative role in that they are part of a decision-making framework telling decision-makers what they ought to do.

Our analysis above has been very basic, but this stark analysis helps in aiding an understanding of why models, and in particular the inner workings of models, are of relevance to lawyers and policy-makers. Models are clearly setting the limits of legitimate action and therefore directly relevant to legal and policy questions concerning what is it reasonable for a decision-maker to do. If the model is understood to be legitimate, and it is followed by a decision-maker, then the decision-maker's decision is understood to be legitimate. However, if the decision-maker, does not follow a model they are expected to follow then the legitimacy of the final decision is open to question. Models thus limit and direct regulatory power.

Yet the relevance of models does not stop there. If models are regulating power then it becomes very important that the models themselves are legitimate. As such, the substance and detail of models become relevant to lawyers and policy-makers. If a model is understood as a rigorous representation of reality then it can be understood as a legitimate basis for action. If a model is understood to be of poor quality then it is not. That is why in cases such as *Downs* the Divisional Court and Court of Appeal were faced with many arguments about the legitimacy of the bystander exposure model and the other types of assessment undertaken by DEFRA. If these exercises in modelling and assessment were found to be problematic then so too would be the exercise

105 H Collins, *Regulating Contracts* (OUP, Oxford 1999) 7.

106 On worthiness and legitimacy see J Habermas, *Communication and the Evolution of Society* (The Polity Press, Cambridge 1984) 178.

of discretion based on that assessment. To put it bluntly—the quality of models directly affects the quality of law and policy.

## 3. Models and Complexities

At this stage, the reaction of readers to our analysis of why models are relevant to policy and law may be to conclude that the appropriate response is to rush out to read a modelling textbook. But that is not our argument—our argument is that, on appreciating that models are relevant to what lawyers and policy-makers, there is also a need to appreciate the intellectual challenges in dealing with models. These intellectual challenges arise from the nature and role of models in environmental regulation

Those intellectual challenges are many but here we begin to identify some of them by discussing four different sets of complexities created by models in environmental regulation. First, there is a set of technical complexities due to the fact that models are representations of reality where data is imperfect, systems are not always well understood, and theories are capable of revision. Second, there is institutional complexity because there is an ongoing interrelationship between how models are developed and the institutional context in which they are operating. The third complexity is interdisciplinary complexity due to models straddling the science/policy divide. The fourth and final form of complexity is that there is a need to evaluate the quality of models. This however is not a straightforward task.

### *3.1 Technical Complexity*

The first type of complexity is technical complexity. By this we mean that modelling is complex due to the fact that it operates in conditions of uncertainty and the structure and nature of models is open to variation. The technical complexity of models has been well discussed by commentators arguing the need for them to be treated with care and there is a voluminous literature on the topic.[107] That literature, while very valuable, can also be overwhelming to the novice particularly because in identifying many different forms of uncertainty it quickly becomes enmeshed in the technical detail. Moreover, at times the literature can veer into Rumsfeldian farce with its discussion of different

107 K Beven, *Environmental Modelling: An Uncertain Future?* (Routledge, London 2009); N Oreskes, 'Evaluation (Not Validation) of Quantitative Models' (1998) 106 Environmental Health Perspectives 1453; Jasanoff and Wynne (n 5); D Frame and others 'Probabilistic Climate Forecasts and Inductive Problems' (2007) 365 Philosophical Transactions of the Royal Society A 1971.

types of uncertainty.[108] Indeed, while those who write about uncertainty hope to 'de-mystify' objectivity, their discussion of the concept can often do the opposite.[109] For these reasons, in this section, we take a simpler route by highlighting the different sources of uncertainty and the different reasons why models are variable.

The most important point to appreciate is that scientific uncertainty is inherent in all parts of the process of environmental modelling. As a first step, the modeller must decide which elements of a system she should focus on; uncertainty already pervades this choice, as the modeller exercises some expert judgment in determining whether she has properly identified the components driving the system she wishes to model. Secondly, the modeller collects data about the system, a process replete with uncertainties about whether she has chosen and properly applied the correct method to gather representative data that characterise how the system operates. Even when the modeller has properly executed these first two steps, it is often the case that multiple mathematical equations can describe the same data set. It is therefore the case that uncertainty inevitably permeates the *development* of environmental models.

When a model is *used* for a specific regulatory application—such as to establish discharge limits for nitrogen in an estuary—another source of uncertainty arises. It is usually the case that the features of the system being modelled vary over time and space. Because a model may have been developed based on an initial set of conditions, the model developer and user must determine whether a model is sufficiently robust to use even when these conditions have changed. This determination, too, is subject to uncertainty.

In relation to each source of uncertainty, the nature of uncertainty will vary depending on the available data and the rigour with which the features of a particular system are understood. The natural environment is a holistic system made up of numerous complex and little understood interrelationships. Likewise social phenomena are not easily subject to predictive analysis and as Rayner and Malone note we 'have inaccurate and conflicting theories about how and why people make choices, for themselves and in societies'.[110] Thus, for each source of uncertainty there is a range of methodological, epistemological and even ontological issues which manifest themselves as a tangled web of complex uncertainties. Uncertainty is not always reducible through additional data. Furthermore, irreducible ignorance about a complex system

108 D Logan, 'Known Knowns, Known Unknowns, Unknown Unknowns and the Propagation of Scientific Enquiry' (2009) 60 Journal of Experimental Botany 712 and S Dovers and J Handmer, 'Ignorance, Sustainability and the Precautionary Principle' in R Harding and E Fisher (eds), *Perspectives on the Precautionary Principle* (Federation Press, Sydney 1999).

109 G Bammer and M Smithson (eds), *Uncertainty and Risk: Multidisciplinary Perspectives* (Earthscan, London 2008) xiv.

110 S Rayner and E Malone (eds), *Human Choice and Climate Change – Volume Four* (Pacific Northwest National Laboratory, Battelle Press, Columbus, OH 1998) 120.

will always be an inherent feature of modelling. It is for these reasons that the literature on uncertainty in modelling can appear so impenetrable.

The fact that modelling is shrouded in uncertainty has three important implications for policy-makers and lawyers. First, models cannot be expected to deliver certainty. They cannot generate facts and they cannot generate definitive answers. Any argument based on such an assumption is wrong. Likewise, to criticise models for not generating certainty is also wrong. Second, it is important for policy-makers and lawyers to have some understanding about uncertainty in modelling. Such an understanding significantly increases the effective and proper utilisation of models as policy-makers and lawyers would have a better appreciation of what it is valid to expect, and not to expect, from models. Third, uncertainties (and the fact that models are developed for a purpose) mean that embodied in models are also professional judgements, values and assumptions about the world. These are often described as forms of undesirable subjectivity but the reality is that these features of models are necessary to make models operate. The issue is thus not removing these unavoidable features of models, but being able to evaluate the quality of these assumptions. To do that, some transparency is required but the technical complexity of models makes such transparency difficult to achieve.

Uncertainty also creates another form of technical complexity. In light of uncertainty, a single physical system can be validly modelled in a number of different ways. As Beven notes:

> .... [A]chieving '*the*' model of an environmental system may be fraught with difficulty. Instead, there may be different model structures, and parameter sets within model structures, that are consistent in some sense with the uncertainties in the available data, and many different ways of estimating uncertainty in the predictions.[111]

In other words, models are not innately objective scientific constructs that—if done correctly—yield a single, verifiable depiction of reality. Rather, even when developed according to the best principles of science, models may yield multiple versions of reality, each of which may be perfectly valid on its own terms in a way that is logically consistent with the assumptions and framework used to develop the model. This is a technical complexity in itself because rigorous modelling is not an inflexible formula yielding strict results but something far more creative (albeit still highly disciplined).

Modelling is about fashioning and moulding data, assumptions, uncertainties and theories. In this sense it is akin to sculpting[112]—it is inherently a transformative enterprise in that as a semi-autonomous activity it is creating

111 Beven (n 107) 251.

112 Michaels (n 35) 68; J Smith and P Smith, *Environmental Modelling: An Introduction* (OUP, Oxford 2007) 2.

a representation. Recognising that fact is not to recognise that models are simply fictions, but rather that modelling is working with highly malleable matter. The consequences of this malleability is not just that a model can take a variety of forms but also that there are real challenges in determining what is a valid model. In light of the malleability, the determination of what is a valid model cannot simply be on the basis of it conforming to a single construct or a single process—other criteria need to be developed.

Again, all of this has major implications for policy-makers and lawyers. First, there cannot be an assumption that modelling is about developing a single perfect representation of a system. Any arguments based on this belief are wrong. Second, it is increasingly clear that the characterisation of models as being purely 'scientific' and 'objective' is naive. Indeed, a study of the technical complexity of models makes increasingly obvious the problematic nature of understanding regulatory decision-making in terms of the science/policy division. Third, and following on from above, a more sophisticated understanding is needed of how to evaluate models. This is discussed in Section 3.4.

### *3.2 Institutional Complexity of Models*

Models are not only technically complex however. They are also institutionally complex.[113] This is due to the fact that models interact with the institutional context in which they operate. Moreover, the interactions between a model and its institutional context are multi-dimensional and subtle and can seem overwhelming to the uninitiated.[114] Models are developed for regulatory purposes and those regulatory purposes will influence how models are developed. Models regulate power and thus their use relates to the legitimacy of regulatory decision-making. Models are increasingly institutionalised and the subject of policy and legal disputes. Models are thus part of the administrative and legal landscape. As with technical complexity, we do not aim to survey the whole of institutional complexity but rather seek to highlight one aspect of this complexity—the way in which models are conceptualised in policy and legal discussions is heavily dependent on what is understood to be legitimate public administration.

As we saw above, models are playing a normative role in establishing the authority of decisions. They are doing so against a background in which the authority of regulatory decision-makers is more generally contested.[115]

113 Yearley (n 72).

114 This can particularly be seen in the related area of financial models. See G Tett, *Fool's Gold: How Unrestrained Greed Corrupted a Dream, Shattered Global Markets and Unleashed a Catastrophe* (Little Brown, London 2009).

115 B Cook, *Bureaucracy and Self Government: Reconsidering the Role of Public Administration in American Government* (Johns Hopkins UP, Baltimore, MD 1996); Fisher (n 1).

The reason for this is not just that environmental issues themselves are controversial[116] but also, more significantly, because decision-makers are administrative.[117] Not only is it the fact that unelected administrative power has a paradoxical position in liberal democracy, but the wide and opaque discretion required in environmental regulation only exacerbates that paradox and makes administrative power even more difficult to justify.[118] Indeed, the history of environmental regulation in most jurisdictions has been a history of an ongoing legal and policy debate about what is, and should be, the role of public administration.[119] A feature of this history has been how assumptions about what a regulator *should do* influences what is understood a regulator *is* doing.[120] Legal and policy disputes are invariably about which assumptions about good public administration should dominate.[121]

The issue in regard to models is thus what assumptions are made about them by policy-makers and lawyers about what it is they contribute to the administrative process to ensure that process is legitimate. In policy and legal debates we can see two broad characterisations of modelling—as an analytical-deliberative process *or* as a method for generating truth. It is important to remember that these characterisations are based on assumptions about what it is an environmental regulator is *expected to do*. They reflect the institutional complexity of models because they highlight the fact that models are understood and conceptualised in their institutional context—a context which is contested.

The first characterisation of modelling is that seen in this article—where modelling is understood as an 'analytical-deliberative process'. That is models are understood as a process for helping frame issues so as to allow sharper and more rigorous focus on them. This aids analysis, deliberation and problem solving. Thus, as the NRC notes:

> Models provide a framework that defines the relationships that are valuable to study and specify how measured quantities are to be interpreted in the real world.[122]

By doing this a model allows for the development of more rigorous approaches to examining a problem and allows for actors to discuss issues in a more sophisticated way. At the same time, however, modelling is understood to be a

116 J Dryzek, *The Politics of the Earth: Environmental Discourses* (2nd edn OUP, Oxford 2005).

117 Fisher (n 1) 19–22.

118 Ibid.

119 S Shapiro and R Glicksman, *Risk Regulation At Risk: Restoring A Pragmatic Approach* (Stanford UP, Stanford 2003); C Sunstein, *Risk and Reason: Safety, Law and the Environment* (CUP, Cambridge 2002); T McGarity, 'A Cost Benefit State' (1998) 50 Administrative Law Review 7.

120 J Mashaw, *Greed, Chaos and Governance: Using Public Choice to Improve Public Law* (Yale UP, New Haven 1997) 1–29.

121 Fisher (n 1) 53–241.

122 NRC, *Understanding Risk: Informing Decisions in a Democratic Society* (National Academy Press, Washington DC 1996) 100.

limited method due to uncertainty, the fact that a model is always a representation, and that the systems being modelled are holistic, open ended and dynamic. Models don't generate final answers but they do generate useful 'insights' that aid both deliberation and analysis.

This characterisation of modelling does not exist in isolation however. If models and environmental problems are understood as complex then it is also understood that the role of public administration must be about solving complex problems shrouded in uncertainties. Indeed, understandings of modelling as an analytic-deliberative method coexist with a more general understanding of public administration as a deliberative-constitutive (DC) institution. By this we mean that public administration is understood to be constituted as a substantive institution which is engaging in on-going problem solving through the exercise of flexible discretion based on deliberation and analysis.[123]

While the characterisation of modelling as an 'analytic-deliberative' process is common among those who are either engaged in modelling or work closely with models,[124] it is not the characterisation that has predominated among lawyers and policy-makers. This is not because these groups have formed any strong views about the nature of models. Rather, their views of models have been shaped by their views about the desired role of public administration which they understand as needing to be as restrained and controlled as much as possible.[125] For this group, the DC paradigm with its emphasis on flexible deliberation and analysis is problematic because it grants too much discretion to the decision-maker. Rather, those concerned with control of public administration have tended to promote the rational-instrumental (RI) paradigm of public administration. On this basis, public administration is understood as akin to a robot or a 'transmission belt'[126] that applies the 'facts' to specific legislative commands. Facts include information rigorously policed by scientific and social scientific methodology and preferences voiced through a fair, pluralist participatory process.[127] Reasonable RI administrative action is to carry out this process of application in the most efficient and effective manner possible and RI administration is understood as legitimate because the problems that RI administration is dealing with are understood to be inherently manageable.

If the role of public administration is understood in RI terms then it becomes inevitable that models are understood as 'truth generators' producing the truth which then can be applied to a legislative mandate. In other words,

123 Fisher (n 1) 30–2.

124 M B Beck (ed), *Environmental Foresight and Models: A Manifesto* (Elsevier, Amsterdam 2002); E Fisher, 'Drowning by Numbers: Standard Setting in Risk Regulation and the Pursuit of Accountable Public Administration' (2000) 20 OJLS 109.

125 Ibid.

126 R Stewart, 'The Reformation of American Administrative Law' (1975) 88 Harvard Law Review 1661.

127 Fisher (n 1) 29.

**Table 1.** Two paradigms of models and their relationship to ideals of good public administration and understandings of environmental problems

| | Analytic-deliberative method | Fact generating |
|---|---|---|
| Conceptualisation of modelling | Models as constructs to assist in problem solving, deliberation and analysis | Models as scientific constructs that produce truth. |
| Nature of environmental problems and scientific uncertainty | Complex and dynamic. Uncertainty as inevitable and irreducible | Manageable and easily assessed. Uncertainty as undesirable and needing to be avoided. |
| Public administration[a] | Deliberative-constitutive: constituted to engage in ongoing, flexible problem solving grounded in analysis and deliberation | Rational-instrumental: limited agent of the legislature that applies the facts (including public preferences) to legislative mandates. |

[a]Fisher (n 1) ch 1.

models are not understood as representations produced for particular purposes but rather as scientific reality. On this basis, modelling is presumed to be able to capture reality accurately and uncertainty is an avoidable nuisance. For models to be able to do this then reality needs to be presumed to be easily captured by the process of modelling. The problems created by open ended, holistic ecosystems thus need to be downplayed. As is clear from our analysis so far, this characterisation of models is simply wrong.[128] Thus, while the accountability impulse behind the RI paradigm is understandable, the conceptualisation of models that it promotes is deeply misleading.

There are three implications of all of this. First, models are not understood in isolation. The way in which models are conceptualised is highly dependent on broader understandings of legitimate public administration and environmental problems. Those broader relationships are summarised in Table 1.

Second, an implication of these relationships is that lawyers and policy-makers will always be characterising models even when they are not explicitly engaging with them. Thus in the disputes seen above, lawyers and policy-makers are making assumptions about models. For example, Collins J understood the existence of what he understood as 'solid evidence' as a need to rethink the model to make it a more accurate factual construct.[129] The fact it was not, meant, that for him, DEFRA was not in compliance with the Directive. In contrast, the Court of Appeal understood the model as a heuristic tool that captured general scientific consensus but which would change over time.[130] The point about these assumptions is that they are not based on explicit engagement with models but rather are dependent on broader

128 Wagner and others (n 2).
129 *Downs* (n 36) [46]–[47].
130 *Secretary of State for Environment, Food and Rural Affairs* (n 55) [76]–[91].

understanding of public administration. Thus, Collins J analysis was resting on a RI understanding of public administration and the Court of Appeal's analysis was resting on a DC understanding.

Third, what this means is that in thinking about models, lawyers and policy-makers must also reflect on their understandings of good public administration and environmental problems. Indeed, the analysis above forces lawyers and policy-makers to reflect upon the logic behind a RI model of public administration in particular. While such a model is appealing because of the control of public administration it seems to offer up, it is deeply problematic in how it characterises the role a model can play.[131]

In highlighting these implications it should be remembered that the relationship between models and paradigms of good public administration is only one aspect of institutional complexity. There are also many others. For lawyers and policy-makers, the major implication of this form of complexity is that models cannot be viewed in scientific and technical isolation but rather must be analysed as part of the institutional context in which they operate. That may require lawyers and policy-makers to broaden their intellectual field of vision.

### *3.3 Interdisciplinary Complexity*

The third form of complexity that needs to be engaged with in relation to policy-makers and lawyers engaging with models is interdisciplinary complexity. Interdisciplinary complexity has three main aspects.

The first type of interdisciplinary complexity is that models themselves are often interdisciplinary constructs, particularly those models developed by integrated assessment which incorporate knowledge and data from a range of scientific and social scientific disciplines.[132] How that integration occurs presents a series of intellectual and practical challenges. Not only may theory and data differ from discipline to discipline, but the activity of modelling has an iterative feedback to the different disciplines upon which it draws.[133] Focusing on modelling thus highlights that the physical and social sciences are not monolithic domains and the knowledge drawn on for regulatory decision-making comes from a range of different disciplinary sources.[134] Likewise, different models will be grounded in different disciplines. There is

131 Wagner and others (n 2).

132 J Rotmans and H Dowlatabadi, 'Integrated Assessment Modelling' in S Rayner and E Malone (eds), *Human Choice and Climate Change: Volume Three Tools for Policy Analysis* (Battelle Press, Columbus, OH 1998); H Nowotny and others *Re-thinking Science: Knowledge and the Public in an Age of Uncertainty* (Polity Press, Cambridge 2001) 106; Pascual (n 99).

133 Rotmans and Dowlatabadi (n 132) 294.

134 J Kagan, *The Three Cultures: Natural Sciences, Social Sciences, and the Humanities in the 21st Century* (CUP, Cambridge 2009).

no single modelling textbook or university course which will equip someone with the ability to understand all models.

The second aspect of interdisciplinary complexity concerns the fact that modelling is a distinct and highly technical discipline which must interact with other disciplines and contexts. The problem is that policy-makers and decision-makers need to engage with models, but it cannot be pretended that in doing so they are modelling experts who have in-depth knowledge of modelling as a discipline. Modelling is a highly specialised practice distinct from law and policy. The reluctance on the part of lawyers and policy-makers to engage with models is thus entirely understandable. Models may span the science/policy divide but it does not mean that it is easy for lawyers and policy-makers to become modelling experts. Models are a product of particular specialist bodies of knowledge and modelling is a discipline in its own right with its own vocabulary, concepts and internal debates. Thus, while it is common (and correct) to argue for modelling to be transparent,[135] the challenge in doing so should not be underestimated. It is not the case that modelling is a hidden practice, but instead that the language and techniques of modelling are opaque to non-modellers who lack the necessary background to understand modelling arcana.

The third type of interdisciplinary complexity which arises from this is one about accountability. There are some who have argued that interdisciplinary discourses lead to greater accountability,[136] but the reality is that holding decision-makers to account becomes far more difficult when they are drawing on a highly technical model. This is because it becomes far harder for a decision-maker or lawyer to evaluate the quality of the arguments when they are based on something that a lawyer and policy-maker finds difficult to understand. Models thus may regulate administrative power but their role in accountability processes is fraught. Indeed, when models do become the subject of legal and policy disputes, the ability of lawyers and policy-makers to assess the accountability of decisions based on a model becomes questionable.[137]

There are two important implications of recognising interdisciplinary complexity. The first is that while models are of relevance to lawyers and policy-makers it is not the case that they are easily understandable by those groups. Care and thought should be taken with how lawyers and policy-makers engage with these models. Indeed, the policy and legal landscape are littered with instances of where lawyers and policy-makers have engaged with models in completely inappropriate ways.[138]

135 NRC (n 3) 100–11.

136 M Strathern, *Commons and Borderlands: Working Papers on Interdisciplinarity, Accountability and the Flow of Knowledge* (Sean Kingston Publishing, Wantage 2004) 68–86.

137 *Downs* (n 36) [38].

138 For a discussion of this point see Shapiro (n 40); McGarity and Wagner (n 44).

Following on from this, it needs to be appreciated that lawyers and policy-makers need to develop some form of expertise in dealing with models. Clearly, it is not the same expertise as a modeller who is expected to directly contribute to modelling as a discipline. Rather, the expertise that lawyers and policy-makers need to develop is an expertise in interacting with modelling.[139] This is a form on interactional expertise which is '[e]xpertise in the *language* of a specialism in the absences of expertise in its *practice*'.[140]

The distinction between these two forms of expertise is difficult to draw and care should be taken with that distinction.[141] With that said, it is a useful distinction to draw because it clarifies the scope of interaction.[142] Clarifying that scope of interaction does not necessarily provide any simple answers—interactional expertise is not a straightforward concept and developing even linguistic expertise is difficult.[143]

By engaging with interdisciplinary complexity it is again seen that the science/policy divide looks increasingly problematic, albeit in a different way than discussed above. Interdisciplinary complexity arises from the fact that distinctions between policy and science do exist and thus there is effectively a divide. At the same time, however that divide does need to be bridged and crossed.

### 3.4 *Evaluative Complexity*

The final form of complexity that lawyers and policy-makers must consider is the most significant – evaluative complexity. This is the most significant because the primary concern of lawyers and policy-makers in dealing with a model is whether that model serves as a legitimate basis for a decision and, to evaluate that, there needs to be a focus on the quality of the model. Indeed, this was the fundamental focus of the NRC report *Models in Environmental Regulatory Decision-Making* and it dedicated significant consideration to the issue.[144] As with above, we do not attempt to solve the problems created by

139 The distinction between contributory and interactional expertise is taken from H Collins and R Evans, *Rethinking Expertise* (University of Chicago Press, Chicago 2007). See also H Collins and others, 'Trading Zones and Interactional Expertise' (2007) 38 Studies in History and Philosophy of Science 657.

140 Collins and Evans (n 139) 28.

141 S Jasanoff, 'Breaking the Waves in Science Studies: Comment on H.M. Collins and Robert Evans, "The Third Wave of Science Studies"' (2003) 33 Social Studies of Science 389; B Wynne, 'Seasick on the Third Wave? Subverting the Hegemony of Propositionalism: Response to Collins & Evans (2002)' (2003) 33 Social Studies of Science 401.

142 For a broader discussion of its use in environmental law see E Fisher and others 'Maturity and Methodology: Starting a Debate about Environmental Law Scholarship' (2009) 21 JEL 213 at 231–5.

143 And often problematic because the same word can mean different things in different disciplines. See Kagan (n 134) 5–11.

144 NRC (n 3) 104–69.

this form of complexity but cannot overstress the importance of recognising this as a complexity in its own right. Indeed, nearly all the policy and legal disputes seen above are disputes that raise issues to do with evaluative complexity because in them lawyers and policy-makers need to evaluate the quality of models which regulate decision-making.

Evaluative complexity largely arises due to the confluence of technical, institutional and interdisciplinary complexity. Technical complexity means that uncertainty is inherent in modelling and that modelling is malleable. In terms of evaluating models this means 'that while the rigor of a model can be established it is impossible to verify the truth of a model'.[145] Models can be evaluated for rigour but cannot be validated as true (although they can be invalidated for being false).[146] It is for this reason that the term 'model evaluation' is favoured over 'model validation'.[147] Yet, in focusing on the rigour of modelling it needs to be recognised that modelling is an inherently malleable exercise. Therefore, model evaluation cannot be about assessing whether a model adheres to a strict formula—at the same time, it is not the case that 'anything goes'.[148]

Again, one response to this problem has been to argue that a way of evaluating models is to determine their fitness for purpose.[149] As Morrison and Morgan note, a model is not assessed 'on its ability to accurately mirror a system, rather the legitimacy of each representation is a function of the model's performance in specific contexts.'[150] This would seem to offer a possible way of developing a framework for evaluating models but it needs to be understood this is not a purely functional and straightforward exercise but rather one that encounters institutional complexity. Whether a model is understood to be fit for purpose is not an objective or isolated question but will depend on what is understood to be legitimate public administration. Moreover, as seen above, the way in which models are conceptualised under the RI paradigm of public administration is wrong. Therefore there exists a danger that models will be judged against inappropriate yardsticks.

This problem is exacerbated by interdisciplinary complexity. Models do need to be evaluated by lawyers and policy-makers but they are not modelling experts. Thus, while models do enable decision-makers to base their decisions on information, the technical nature of such models can prevent the

145 Oreskes (n 107).
146 NRC (n 3) 104.
147 Oreskes (n 107); B Beck, 'Model Evaluation and Performance' in A El-Shaarawi and W Piegorsch (eds), *Encyclopedia of Environmetrics* (John Wiley & Sons, Chichester 2002).
148 P Feyerabend, *Against Method: Outline of an Anarchistic Theory of Knowledge* (3rd edn Verso, London 1993).
149 NRC (n 3) 3.
150 Morrison and Morgan (n 88) 28.

evaluation of both models and the information on which they are being based.[151] With that said, what is clear from above is that while the technical nature of models must be acknowledged, models are not simply scientific structures—they are interdisciplinary 'boundary objects' and 'infrastructures'[152]—and thus must be engaged with.[153]

Evaluative complexity does not end with the conflation of the forms of complexity already discussed however. Another aspect of it is the fact that regulatory actors will engage with models and utilise them to their own ends. The different forms of complexity described above can thus be manipulated for particular ideological or instrumental purposes.[154] This form of manipulation has been described by different commentators as 'manufacturing uncertainty'[155] and 'analytical opportunism'.[156] The typical practice that these labels refer to is where a regulatory actor, wishing to achieve a certain regulatory outcome, will argue that the scientific uncertainty inherent in models is a fundamental flaw which means that a model is not reliable.[157] This type of manipulation is complicated by interdisciplinary complexity in that it can be difficult to know whether such arguments have some merit. The important point to appreciate is that the issue of evaluating models also has a profoundly ideological and regulatory-outcome-driven dimension.[158] Again that is the reason why modelling has become the focus for legal and policy disputes.

We do not offer up any easy solutions to how lawyers and policy-makers should evaluate models – we do not pretend that the process of evaluation will be easy. This is particularly because lurking close to the issue of evaluative complexity are broader problems stemming from an overly simplistic understanding of science and policy.[159] What we do think is that it is essential that the issue of evaluative complexity is on the agenda for lawyers and policy-makers and that an important starting point is an appreciation of just

151 S Leigh Star and K Ruhleder, 'Steps Towards An Ecology of Infrastructure Design and Access for Large Information Spaces' (1996) 7 Information Systems Research 111, 111.
152 Pascual (n 93).
153 G Bowker and S Leigh Star, *Sorting Things Out: Classification and Its Consequences* (MIT Press, Cambridge 2000) 24, 34.
154 T McGarity and W Wagner, *Bending Science: How Special Interests Corrupt Public Health Research* (Harvard UP, Cambridge 2008); W Wagner, 'The Science Charade in Toxic Risk Regulation' (1995) 95 Columbia Law Review 1613.
155 D Michaels and C Monforton, 'Scientific Evidence in the Regulatory System: Manufacturing Uncertainty and the Demise of the Formal Regulatory System' (2005) 13 Journal of Law and Policy 17.
156 Fisher (n 1) 121–2.
157 W Freudenburg and others 'Scientific Uncertainty Argumentation Methods (SCAMs): Science and the Politics of Doubt' (2008) 78 Sociological Inquiry 2.
158 Wagner and others (n 2).
159 Fisher (n 1); Michaels (n 35).

how difficult an issue evaluation is. Thus, statements ensuring that models are 'transparent', and 'fit for purpose' should be treated less as solutions and more as the serious intellectual and practical challenges they are.[160]

## 4. Conclusions

Our argument in this article has been that models are not just a prevalent feature of environmental regulation but they are also relevant to what lawyers and policy-makers do and need to be engaged with critically. There are three important conclusions that we draw from our analysis.

First, models cannot be ignored or overlooked by lawyers or policy-makers. Models are not just the province of the scientific boffins and the techno-heads. Models frame how environmental issues are understood, they provide the basis and rationale for regulatory action, and they play a significant role in establishing the legitimacy of regulatory regimes. Indeed the increasing prevalence and institutionalisation of models in environmental regulation, as well as the fact that they are subject to disputes, points to their importance. Lawyers and policy-makers have no choice but to engage with them.

Second, that engagement must take a critical and sophisticated form. We have not set out in this article how that process of engagement should occur. In light of the complexities discussed above, such prescriptions would be unhelpful and counter-productive. One thing is clear however—the real issue for lawyers and policy-makers is how to properly evaluate the quality of models and that requires not only engagement with evaluative complexity but also technical, institutional and interdisciplinary complexity.

Third, the critical engagement with models cannot be seen in isolation but also requires lawyers and policy-makers to reflect more generally on the boundaries of their discipline. Much of the analysis in this article has argued for lawyers and policy-makers to broaden their field of intellectual vision. Models cannot be ignored just because they lie on the other side of a disciplinary divide. Likewise, lawyers in particular, need to engage with parts of the administrative process which they have not traditionally understood as within their domain. A critical engagement with models is not then just about learning a lot about models and their role in environmental regulation but also thinking more carefully about what lawyers and policy-makers do.

Thus, while in this article we have not dazzled, bamboozled or overwhelmed you with technical jargon or data, we have laid down a serious intellectual

160 Pascual (n 96) 2011; Beck (n 147). On the abuse of transparency see Michaels (n 35) 176–91.

challenge for lawyers and policy-makers. We have shown that models are prevalent and relevant and require the development of a broad critical agenda. What we have not done is provide any easy formulae or techniques for how policy-makers and lawyers should engage with models and we know that will frustrate many readers. As our analysis makes clear however, no such formulae or techniques exist.

# [9]

# Tracking Environmental Assessment

Integration, precaution, participation, prevention, proceduralization, sustainability: these are the bywords of environmental law which have recently been attributed to environmental assessment. In this chapter I give an account of the evolution of environmental assessment within the overall development of environmental law, particularly as a means of giving effect to the concept of sustainable development. The focus is upon the development of environmental impact assessment in the United Kingdom, which has been strongly influenced by the EC model of assessment contained in the EIA Directive. Tracing this development allows me to pinpoint the origin of information theories of environmental assessment in the idea that environmental assessment was inherent in the town and country planning system because planning authorities could avail themselves of a power to request 'additional information' from developers. Adopting a broader scope, I then relate the development of environmental assessment to the ascendancy of the sustainable development concept. In particular, the enlargement of environmental assessment to encourage the integration of different policy areas in strategic environmental assessment may be seen as an expression of this concept. This brings me to critically view attempts to further develop environmental assessment as a form of sustainability analysis.

From this development of different levels of environmental assessment (project- and policy-based) the analysis shifts to *sites* of decision making engaging environmental assessment. I survey some of the legal variations of environmental assessment that have evolved in different jurisdictional and functional contexts—land use planning and control, conservation for biodiversity, pollution controls, and development assistance. This analysis suggests that environmental assessment has contributed to the standardization of decision making with respect to environmental concerns. These key aspects (the practical implementation of sustainable development via environmental assessment, and the pervasiveness and adaptability of environmental assessment in various contexts) are linked by an essential characteristic of environmental assessment, that as a highly procedural mechanism it contains no absolute standards, suggesting that it is capable of adjusting to the conceptual and legal frames in operation. Environmental assessment incorporates environmental concerns or criteria into different contexts, but in a flexible and accommodating way and without the 'hard edges' of substantive standards, or the conferral of enforceable rights relating to environmental quality.[1] This has implications for the roles performed by law in environmental assessment—as a framework for interdisciplinary inquiry, as a means of incorporating environmental values or principles in a standardized way into decision making and planning, or, more critically, permitting 'lip service' to be paid to environmental ideals. In summary, considering a broad range of applications of environmental assessment helps to pinpoint its legal core. First, though, I broadly define the environmental assessment process, building upon the identification of its main characteristics in Chapter 1.[2]

## Defining Environmental Assessment

Environmental assessment practice and literature has developed apace, but there is no general and universally accepted definition of the procedure. A traditional starting point is the United States' National Environmental Policy Act (NEPA) 1969 which defines environmental assessment as 'a systematic interdisciplinary approach which will insure the integrated use of the natural and social sciences and the environmental design arts in planning and in decision making which may have an impact on man's environment'.[3] More specifically, policy guidance for England and Wales currently defines environmental impact assessment as:

> . . . a means of drawing together, in a systematic way, an assessment of projects likely to have significant environmental effects. This helps to ensure that the importance of the predicted effects, and the scope for reducing them, are properly understood by the public and the relevant competent authority before it makes its decision.[4]

A more rounded definition, also applicable to strategic environmental assessment (of plans and programmes), explains environmental assessment as a process for identifying the likely consequences for the biological, geological, and physical environment and human health and welfare of implementing particular activities, policy, and plans, particularly arising from the participation of those likely to be affected, and for conveying this information to those responsible for sanctioning the

[1] However, the right to participate in decision making governed by environmental assessment is now recognized and enforceable. On human rights approaches and environmental assessment, see Ch. 8, pp. 291–4.

[2] See pp. 12–22.

[3] S.102(a) 42 USC 4321–4361. See Appendix I.

[4] Department of Environment, Transport and the Regions, Circular 02/99, *Environmental Impact Assessment* (London: HMSO, 1999), para. 9. See the change in emphasis from Department of the Environment, Circular 15/88 (Welsh Office 23/88), *Environmental Assessment* (London: HMSO, 1988), para. 7: 'essentially a technique for drawing together in a systematic way expert quantitative analysis and qualitative assessment of a project's environmental effects, and presenting the results in a way which enables the importance of the predicted effects, and the scope for modifying or mitigating them, to be properly evaluated by the relevant decision making body before a decision is given'.

proposal at a stage when it can materially affect their decision, or their ongoing regulation.[5] This concentrates not so much on a final decision, but rather recognizes environmental assessment to be a process with several stages—negotiation, participation, and monitoring. The description of the social effects of environmental assessment also recognizes that qualitative as well as quantitative data may be used to assess the likely significance of impacts and that value judgments are (and should be) engaged in identifying and predicting impacts.[6]

Questions remain about the exact subject matter of environmental assessment procedures, particularly what is meant by 'environment' and 'impact'. There is, for example, some debate about whether 'the environment' refers to the human (or 'man's')[7] environment in cases such as *Hanly* v *Kleindienst*[8] (concerning the building of a jail in Lower Manhattan) or whether this is restricted to the natural environment. In the United Kingdom, the purpose of the 1999 Regulations[9] (as well as that of the EC EIA Directive[10] implemented by the 1999 Regulations) has been interpreted as the protection of the environment in the public interest. Whilst the Regulations may have the effect of avoiding harm to residential amenity, they may not be applied specifically to protect the amenity of individual buildings.[11] The likelihood of severe shadowing from the development of a football stadium was therefore considered not to have a potential effect upon the environment.[12] Such an interpretation suggests some narrowing of the meaning of 'environment' in the law relating to environmental assessment, particularly when compared to a definition of 'environment' as surroundings, whether these be urban, rural, 'man-made', or 'natural'.

'Impact' has been taken to mean the environmental consequences of a particular activity compared with what might otherwise have occurred. An impact may be both spatial and temporal, as well as positive or negative in environmental terms. The possibly positive nature of impacts was at issue in the *BT* case[13] in which the High Court decided that a local authority should have considered whether there were likely to be any significant effects, adverse or otherwise, by requiring an environmental assessment of a proposed project. This interpretation was based upon a textual reading of the EC EIA Directive as well as an argument that individuals should form their own judgments about the nature of a potential impact through their participation in the environmental assessment process. It is also clear that the term 'impact' may include indirect impacts. For example, building a dam may

[5] Based on a definition given by R. E. Munn (ed.) *Environmental Impact Assessment: Principles and Procedures* (New York: John Wiley, 1979).

[6] See P. McAuslan's argument about the importance of value judgments in planning decisions more broadly, in *Ideologies of Planning Law* (Oxford: Pergamon Press, 1980).

[7] S. 102(a) NEPA.

[8] 471 F2d 823, 4 ERC 1785, 2 *Envtl L Rep* 20, 717 (1972). For discussion of this case, see Ch. 4, p. 105.

[9] Town and Country Planning (Environmental Impact Assessment) (England and Wales) Regulations 1999 (SI 1999, No. 293).

[10] Directive 85/337/EEC, OJ 1985 L 175, p. 40, as amended by Directive 97/11/EC, OJ L 73, p. 5.

[11] *R (Malster)* v *Ipswich Borough Council* [2001] EWHC 711 (Sullivan J).

[12] ibid.

[13] [2001] EWHC Admin 1001 (Elias J). See further Ch. 4, pp. 136–7.

have direct implications for migratory fish movement up a river for spawning, but its indirect effects—on recreational fishing or coastal commercial fisheries—due to the possible decline in fish stocks, should also be appreciated.[14] Arguably, such indirect impacts (or 'flow-on' effects) should be made as obvious as direct effects by the environmental assessment process. After all the failure of more traditional methods of pollution control to deal with the indirect effects of activities was a major trigger for the initial development of environmental assessment.[15]

Legal interpretations of 'environment' and 'impact' (and related terms such as 'significance' and 'likelihood') tend to be limited in scope. On the contrary, the varying and contingent meanings of these terms suggest that they are socially defined and interpreted rather than physically or technically determined. The broader legal and social meanings attributed to terms such as these are discussed in the following chapters.[16] The more practical meanings of terms used in environmental assessment are considered below.

## The Procedure in Outline

The environmental impact assessment process is the main subject of this book and also provides its structure since in each of the following chapters I critically and thematically analyse an important stage in the process—predicting impacts,[17] evaluating the significance of these,[18] considering alternatives,[19] engaging in consultation and deliberation,[20] and making a final and informed decision.[21] Because of the centrality of environmental assessment as a *process* I here outline the key stages (mainly using the example of the EC EIA Directive)[22] and explain the terminology used to describe these. A summary is provided in Figure 2.1 which matches each stage of the process with its rationale and leading actor. The assessment of plans and programmes by strategic environmental assessment (governed by the EC SEA Directive)[23] broadly follows the procedural pattern of environmental impact assessment (of proposed projects). Whilst focusing on environmental impact assessment, I explain how and where strategic environmental assessment departs from the EIA model later in this chapter.[24]

### Screening and Scoping

Screening is generally the first stage of the environmental assessment process.[25] This involves differentiating between projects and policy proposals that should

[14] R. K. Morgan, *Environmental Impact Assessment: A Methodological Perspective* (Dordrecht: Kluwer, 1998), 40.
[15] ibid. See further Ch. 4, pp. 130–6.
[16] See Ch. 3, pp. 76–80 and Ch. 4, pp. 102–8.
[17] Ch. 3.
[18] Ch. 4.
[19] Ch. 5.
[20] Ch. 6.
[21] Ch. 7.
[22] Directive 85/337/EEC, as amended.
[23] Directive 2001/42/EC on the assessment of the effects of certain plans and programmes on the environment, OJ 2001 L 197, p. 30. See Appendix III.
[24] See pp. 60–5.
[25] As required by Arts. 2 and 4 of the EC EIA Directive.

36 *Tracking Environmental Assessment*

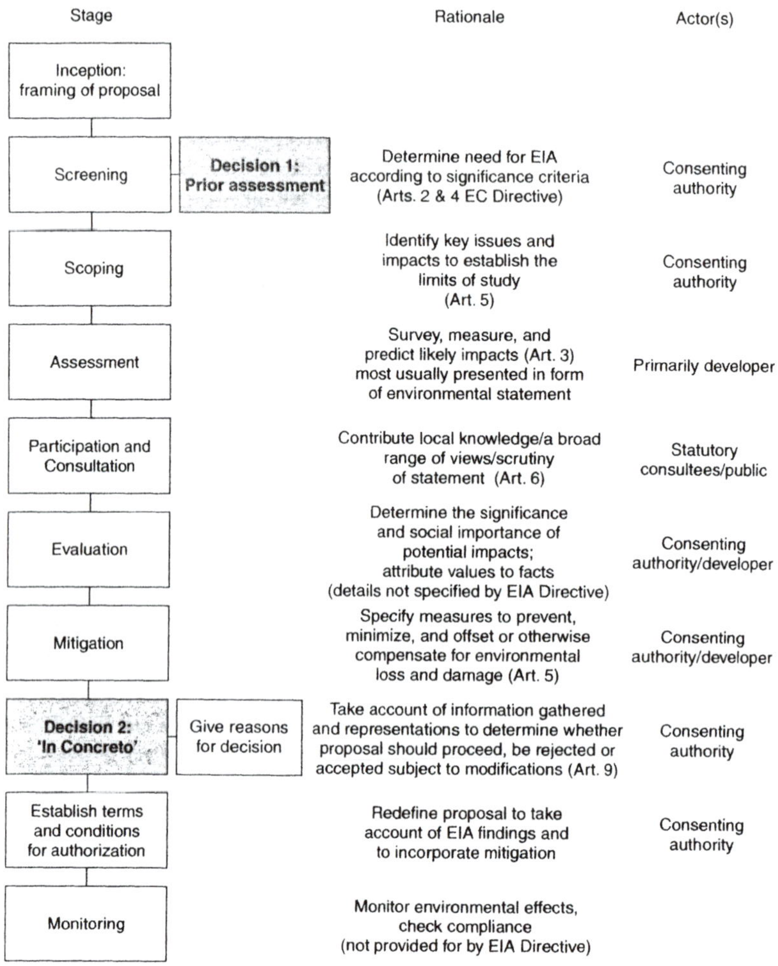


**Figure 2.1** The environmental impact assessement process

Based upon the structure of the EC EIA Directive, with departures marked.

be made subject to the full environmental assessment process on the basis of the likelihood of significant harm. The screening of proposals is therefore defined by the potential for actual harm (although potential environmental benefits may also be assessed) which creates a trigger for the entire process. This creates a circular inquiry because it is only by carrying out a preliminary screening assessment that the decision maker can decide whether it is necessary formally to go through the process, in compliance with the rules relating to the environmental assessment process.

Looking more specifically at the trigger for the process, the harm-based assessment of *significant* environmental impacts is a highly subjective and difficult evaluation.[26] As Hertz states '[V]erbal descriptions of "significance" are not very illuminating and mathematical ones are generally impossible. Moreover it is no mean feat to evaluate the significance of an impact that has not occurred or been studied'.[27] Notwithstanding the inherently subjective nature of determining whether impacts are likely to be significant, environmental assessment procedures are designed to manage the discretionary nature of this judgment, in the case of the EIA Directive by listing projects which must be subject to assessment,[28] combined with thresholds and indicative criteria. Following research which found that the number of environmental assessments being conducted varied widely (a dozen or fewer in Denmark and Portugal, a couple of hundred in the United Kingdom, 1,000 in Germany, 5,500 in France),[29] the EIA Directive was amended more carefully to structure judgment of significance, in accordance with a list of selection criteria.[30] Since these amendments, local planning authorities in the United Kingdom no longer appear to be avoiding the need for environmental impact assessment wherever possible and there is some evidence of a more considered and transparent approach to screening.[31]

In the case of the United Kingdom procedures designed to implement the EIA Directive, the decision whether or not an environmental impact assessment is required can take place at a number of stages, including when the developer submits an environmental statement for the purposes of the 1999 Regulations.[32] Where there is uncertainty about whether a full environmental assessment is required, a developer may request a 'screening opinion' from the local planning authority before submitting an application for planning permission.[33] A planning authority may request an environmental statement where one has not previously been provided, even though a negative screening opinion has already been given. In contrast, a screening opinion provides a determinative judgment where a planning authority decides that an environmental impact assessment is required.[34]

[26] On the nature of this prediction, see Ch. 3, pp. 76–80, 94–7.

[27] M. Hertz, 'Parallel Universes: NEPA Lessons for the New Property' (1993) *Columbia L Rev* 1668, at 1712.

[28] See Annexes I and II of Directive 85/337/EEC, to be read in conjunction with Arts. 2 and 4 (see Appendix I). See further Ch. 4, pp. 108–16.

[29] European Commission, *Report from the Commission on the Implementation of Directive 85/337/EEC on the Assessment of the Effects of Certain Public and Private Projects on the Environment*, COM(93)28, 2.4.1993 (Brussels: CEC, 1993), 37–8. On the national disparities in initial implementation of the Directive, see discussion of varying application of thresholds at the screening stage, Ch. 4, pp. 116–23.

[30] Annex III of Directive 85/337/EEC (amended by Directive 97/11/EC OJ 1997 L 73, p. 73) to be read in conjunction with Art. 4(3). See Appendix II. On this judgment, see further Ch. 4, pp. 106–8.

[31] G. Wood and J. Becker, *Screening Decision-Making under the Town and Country Planning (Environmental Impact Assessment) (England and Wales) Regulations 1999* (Oxford: Oxford Brookes University, 2003).

[32] Reg. 4(2)(a) Town and Country Planning (Environmental Impact Assessment) (England and Wales) Regulations 1999.

[33] Reg. 5(1). This opinion is subject to a direction from the Secretary of State (reg. 4(3)).

[34] *R (Fernback)* v *Harrow London Borough Council* [2002] Env LR 10 (Richards J).

Once a decision has been taken to embark upon a formal environmental assessment procedure, the extent of the study to be made, and therefore the onus upon the developer (or policy maker in the case of strategic environmental assessment) must be evaluated. This is referred to as the exercise of 'scoping'.[35] In the case of environmental impact assessment, scoping includes identifying potential receptors, impacts, alternatives, and mitigation measures (as well as relationships between these), and deciding what methodologies to use and who to consult. It may also involve determining the geographical and temporal boundaries of the assessment. This is particularly the case with potential indirect and cumulative impacts which may well extend beyond the given site boundaries of a project, and may only be discerned over a period of time.

At the stage of scoping, characterizing the baseline condition of a receiving environment is necessary to predict the likely state of the environment in the absence of the proposed activity or development, and thus in predicting the main impacts which are likely to flow from these. Taking an ecological approach to impact assessment shows up the inadequacy of one-off surveys to establish baselines, since these provide only a snapshot of current conditions.[36] However, even extending the 'lead times' for such surveys may not fully overcome the difficulty that the variability of biological phenomena makes it difficult to confidently establish baseline conditions.[37]

Under the 1999 Regulations,[38] a developer may request a 'scoping opinion' from the local planning authority (or 'scoping direction' from the Secretary of State)[39] which outlines what are considered to be the main likely effects of the development and therefore the topics on which the environmental statement should focus. This is often drawn up after consulting other authorities with environmental responsibilities, thus compelling an exchange between the authorities and developer and other groups. The identification of potential impacts forms the principal focus of scoping (with landscape and visual impact considered to be by far the most important impact). In comparison, the role of alternatives tends to be given relatively less attention at this stage.[40] Most importantly, decisions about scoping (as well as screening) are typically made by experts, with little input from the public or interest groups.[41] This has led to the suggestion that parallel scoping exercises might be

[35] As required by Art. 5(2) EC EIA Directive. This provision was added by Directive 97/11/EC, following research which found that the content of environmental statements, submitted by developers, varied greatly; see *Report from the Commission on the Implementation of Directive 85/337/EEC*. See Reg. 10 of the 1999 Regulations. See generally, P. Morris and R. Therivel (eds.) *Methods of Environmental Impact Assessment* (London: Spon, 2001).

[36] See further Ch. 3, pp. 92–4.

[37] See J. Treweek, *Ecological Impact Assessment* (Oxford: Blackwell, 1999), 131–2.

[38] See n. 9.

[39] Regs. 10 and 11 of the 1999 Regulations.

[40] J. Becker and G. Wood, *Scoping Decision-Making under the Town and Country Planning (Environmental Impact Assessment) (England and Wales) Regulations 1999* (Oxford: Oxford Brookes University, 2003).

[41] See further Ch. 4, pp. 145–6 on judgments of significance.

carried out which employ conventional methods (public meetings, displays, advertisements) as well as more focused small group consultation.[42]

## Information Provision, Consultation, and Decision Making

Following the screening and scoping stages, responsibility falls to the developer to provide information about the likely environmental effects of the proposed development in the form of an environmental statement.[43] At the very least this statement should include descriptions of the project, the measures envisaged to mitigate (avoid, reduce, and, if possible, remedy) adverse effects, the data used to ascertain this information, and an outline of the main alternatives considered,[44] all of which should be accompanied by a non-technical summary of these descriptions. This obligation is subject to the qualification that the developer 'may reasonably be required to compile this information having regard *inter alia* to current knowledge and methods of assessment'.[45] This gathering of information also relies upon a freedom of information requirement of sorts, since any authorities holding relevant information must make this available to the developer, subject to some exceptions.[46] Policy guidance makes clear that there is no obligation on public bodies to undertake research or otherwise to take steps to obtain information which they do not already have.[47] This reasonably low standard of obligation on the part of authorities means that there is frequently a lack of baseline information for the purpose of measuring potential impacts.[48]

The developer (in practice the environmental consultant) may use several methods to identify and predict the severity or otherwise of impacts, each of which is underpinned by differing assumptions about the measurability of the environment and the predictability and nature of impacts. At their simplest, these methods may consist of checklists to ensure that key impacts are not overlooked and statutory thresholds are taken into account. Looking to the future, sustainability checklists, involving a broader range of criteria than environmental protection, are likely to be used more frequently.[49] Matrices are similarly used to identify potential impacts which may be weighted or ranked to encourage evaluation of their significance,

[42] Becker and Wood, *Scoping Decision-Making*, para. 2.5.8.

[43] Art. 5(1) of the EIA Directive, implemented by Reg. 2(1) and Sch. 4 of the 1999 Regulations (see Appendix VII).

[44] On alternatives, see further Ch. 5, pp. 149–50.

[45] Art. 5(1)(b) EIA Directive.

[46] Art. 5(4) EIA Directive. Exceptions include defence projects (Art. 10). In the United Kingdom, the general regime of freedom of information is governed by the Environmental Information Regulations (SI 1992, No. 1447).

[47] Department of the Environment, Transport and the Regions, Circular 02/99, *Environmental Impact Assessment*, para. 99.

[48] Although, in the case of the Lewes Flood Defence Strategy, English Nature commissioned extensive baseline surveys in order to ascertain the existence of sites with similar ecological conditions to those threatened by flood defence works. See further Ch. 3, pp. 89–92.

[49] For a critique of this methodological and conceptual development see below, pp. 57–9, and for a practical example, see Ch. 5, pp. 164–76.

and may additionally show cause-effect links between impacts and their sources when plotted on axes.[50] The most common method for predicting impacts is the use of models based upon mathematical or statistical functions which are applied to calculate the probability of quantitative values from data. Modelling may be carried out on computer spreadsheets, but more complex models are capable of incorporating many variables.[51] This method relies primarily upon the availability of baseline data which, as mentioned above, may simply be unavailable or may be questioned in terms of accuracy and representativeness. A further method, network and systems analysis, is used particularly to determine the nature of cumulative and indirect impacts. This is based on the concept that there are links and interaction pathways between individual elements of the environment and that when one element is specifically affected this will have an effect on those elements which interact with it. The results of this method are often portrayed in flow diagrams which are liable to become complex.[52] More simply, maps are frequently used to indicate the features of areas subject to the likely impacts and the location of receptors. Overlay maps or picture imaging can integrate several layers, often to represent the effect of different impacts. Increasingly, geographical information systems (GIS) are used to analyse a number of layers, and to manipulate quantitative information derived from modelling. GIS may also allow for a project's effects to be superimposed on selected receptors to establish areas where impacts would be most significant. Furthermore, carrying capacity analysis, based on the recognition that thresholds exist in the environment, addresses the accumulation of impacts against thresholds and identified trends.

Most of the methods described so far elicit quantitative information. More qualitative categories of information may instead be articulated in public opinion surveys, consultation exercises, public inquiries and, more recently, by focus groups, citizens' juries, and consensus conferences[53] in order to ascertain what values may be held by those affected or interested in the project. These exercises in consultation and participation are more often carried out by public authorities than private entities.

Taking a further look at these specifications, detailing mitigation methods is an important part of compiling an environmental statement. Mitigation includes any deliberate action taken to alleviate adverse effects, either by controlling the sources of impacts or the exposure of species and habitats. The description of mitigating measures is important because without this the decision maker cannot properly evaluate the severity, or significance, of the potential effects.[54] However,

[50] See generally the descriptions of techniques in Morris and Therivel, *Methods* 7–8.

[51] ibid.

[52] European Commission, *Indirect and Cumulative Impacts and Impact Interactions* (CEC, Brussels, 2002).

[53] See further Royal Commission on Environmental Pollution, *Setting Environmental Standards*, ch. 7.

[54] The correspondence between judgments of significance and the offer, or acceptance, of mitigation measures is discussed in Ch. 4, pp. 136–40. This interrelationship is also considered in the context of the Cairngorm funicular railway project: Ch. 7, pp. 272–83.

as a matter of law, developers need only *recommend* suitable mitigating measures. There is no formal obligation to demonstrate that they can and will be undertaken, or to conduct post-assessment monitoring, aside from controls imposed under planning legislation, for example by conditions.[55]

Mitigation comes in many forms, ranging from avoidance (for example, avoiding areas during sensitive periods such as breeding seasons), moderation (emission controls, noise barriers), rescue (translocation of animals), repair (reinstatement of plants or animals), and compensation (donating or creating substitute habitat areas or 'shadow projects').[56] These forms of mitigation are commonly seen as technical exercises, about which there is some optimism that the adverse effects of development may be reduced and beneficial effects increased, thus rendering the project or policy more acceptable in environmental terms. Along these lines, Morgan states:

> In its extreme form, the use of environmental impact assessment can be seen as fine-tuning proposals to a particular environment, to avoid the worst excesses of development. There may not be any doubt about the project going ahead, nor any need to consider alternative sites or project designs. Consequently, in that sense, environmental impact assessment becomes a technical tool for designing mitigation measures.[57]

The suggestion is that the mitigation of adverse effects defines and explains the entire environmental assessment process. However, the adequacy of mitigation by the replication of habitats and translocation of species, and even the appropriateness of trying to 'compensate' for environmental loss should be questioned.[58]

The next stage of the environmental assessment process is the consultation of 'a larger audience' which recognizes the public interest nature of activities with environmental effects.[59] Comments on the developer's environmental statement and any other information arising from the assessment process may be provided by statutory consultees (an extensive list of consultees is contained in the 1999 Regulations)[60] and sought from members of the public, particularly those living near to a proposed project.[61] As indicated by Figure 2.1 the opportunity for statutory consultees and members of the public to contribute to the assessment process is a relatively narrow window when compared to the more significant roles of the consenting authority and developer.

[55] Treweek, *Ecological Impact Assessment*, 239. A different approach is taken in the Netherlands in which consenting authorities must carry out post-assessment monitoring of projects, and report the findings to the independent EIA Commission and statutory consultees; remedial action may be taken, for example by tightening up licence conditions.

[56] As listed by Treweek, *Ecological Impact Assessment*.

[57] Morgan, *Environmental Impact Assessment*, 13. [58] See discussion in Ch. 1, pp. 25–6.

[59] Art. 6 of the EIA Directive. See further Ch. 6, pp. 189–94.

[60] Statutory consultees according to the 1999 Regulations (various provisions) include any principal council for the area where the development is situated, other than the consenting planning authority, the Countryside Commission and English Nature, the Environment Agency, and the Countryside Commission for Wales and the Secretary of State for Wales.

[61] See Regs 13–18 of the 1999 Regulations.

When deciding whether or not to grant development consent, or grant this subject to conditions, the planning authority must take into account information provided by the developer as well as representations about the proposed project made by statutory consultees and members of the public. Making this decision involves a final evaluation of environmental effects on the part of the authority. The exact form of this evaluation is not prescribed, except that it must be capable of forming the basis of reasons for the decision.[62] Although not yet a feature of the EIA Directive, post-assessment monitoring offers an opportunity to analyse the realization of predicted impacts and possibly adjust conditions in the light of these.

## Roots and Evolution

Environmental assessment of sorts has existed for centuries. The *ad quod damnum* writ, first documented in the seventeenth century, was an early form of assessment in which those who might 'be damned' by certain works were identified and possibly compensated.[63] The aim of the writ was to protect the Crown's interest in land development, which later developed as representative of the public interest. That the writ was inevitably concerned with the effects of works *beyond* the location in which they were taking place has provided an important legacy for the development of environmental assessment.

The modern forms of the EIA and SEA procedures evolved as a response to the increasing recognition of the harmful environmental impacts of post-war development schemes such as dams and motorways, and an upsurge in public environmental activism.[64] Sheate, for example, considers that the development of environmental impact assessment was 'a natural consequence of the politicisation of the environment'.[65] Whatever the exact nature of the initial impulse, this development has been analysed according to discrete and broadly chronological stages. First, procedures were established to formally assess a project's viability on the basis of engineering and economic factors. The second stage saw the employment of conventional cost-benefit analysis in which an emphasis was placed upon efficiency within a broad context of economic development, but which effectively ignored environmental and social costs. At the next stage of innovative cost-benefit analysis, pricing mechanisms were used in which economic development became just one of a number of objectives. Finally, at the (current) stage of environmental assessment, the concern is with describing the impact of policy or project proposals on the biological and physical systems which make up the environment.[66] The

[62] On the duty to give reasons, see Ch. 7, pp. 269–72. [63] See Ch. 1, pp. 3–5.

[64] B. D. Clark, 'Environmental Impact Assessment: Scope and Objectives', in B. D. Clark, R. Bissett, and A. Gilad (eds.) *Perspectives on Environmental Impact Assessment* (New York: Reidel, 1984), 3–13.

[65] W. Sheate, 'From Environmental Impact Assessment to Strategic Environmental Assessment: Sustainability and Decision-Making', in J. Holder (ed.) *The Impact of EC Environmental Law in the United Kingdom* (Chichester: Wiley, 1997), 268.

[66] J. Garner and T. O'Riordan, 'Environmental Impact Assessment in the Context of Economic Recession' (1982) 148 *Geog J* 343.

appropriate relationship between environmental assessment and these other forms of project and policy evaluation is still a matter of concern.[67]

In legal terms, modern environmental assessment originated in the United States' NEPA 1969,[68] which has since provided a template for environmental assessment regimes the world over. NEPA required federal agencies to formally document how they considered the environment when making decisions to authorize works and pursue policies. These agencies are still required to include a detailed environmental impact statement in every recommendation or report on proposals for legislation and other major public developments and actions *significantly* affecting the quality of the human environment. When planning an action or policy, an agency must first determine whether an EIS (Environmental Impact Statement) is required. It does this by applying regulations which identify actions which almost always require an EIA and those which the agency has determined never have significant environmental impacts. If the action falls into neither category the agency must prepare an Environmental Assessment (EA). If on the basis of this assessment the agency finds that the action will not have a significant environmental impact, the process is completed. Otherwise, an EIS must be prepared which considers the likely environmental impacts of the proposal. This begins with 'scoping' to determine what issues the EIS will address, in part through public meetings. The agency then prepares the EIS itself, first as a draft for circulation to the public and all interested agencies and then in a final form which reflects and responds to the specific comments received. The statement must describe the state of the present environment and detail changes that the proposed action is likely to cause, both direct and indirect. There is also an obligation to discuss alternatives to the proposal, including a 'do-nothing' alternative, and to evaluate the variability and likely environmental harm of other options. Finally, once the agency has decided to proceed with a particular action, it must prepare a record of decision. This states the agency's final decision, explains how it reached this, and identifies the main alternatives and reasons for rejecting these.[69] The entire procedure is overseen by a Council of Environmental Quality which establishes guidelines for good practice. Although views differ, it has been argued that the process has significantly altered federal decision making because agencies are exposed to criticism from 'outsiders' based on the content of environmental statements, and must respond to these.[70]

[67] For example, Petts now calls for greater integration between cost-benefit analysis and environmental assessment, in 'EIA: Overview of Purpose and Process', in J. Petts (ed.) *Handbook of Environmental Impact Assessment: Vol. 1 Process, Methods and Potential* (Oxford: Blackwell, 1999). See also I. J. Bateman, 'Environmental Impact Assessment, Cost-Benefit Analysis and the Valuation of Environmental Impacts', in Petts, *Handbook*, 93.

[68] S. 102(2)(c) NEPA 1969, 42 USC 4321–4361. See Appendix I.

[69] Described by M. Hertz, 'Parallel Universes: NEPA Lessons for the New Property' (1993) *Columbia L Rev* 1668, at 1678.

[70] Taylor, *Making Bureaucracies Think*, 80–1. See also L. K. Caldwell, *Science and the National Environmental Policy Act: Redirecting Policy through Procedural Reform* (Alabama: Alabama University Press, 1982). See further Ch. 7, pp. 251–6 on the nature of decision making governed by environmental assessment procedures in the United States.

The United States' legislation influenced a number of international organizations to adopt similar forms of environmental assessment. In the mid-1970s the Organization for Economic Cooperation and Development recommended that member countries establish procedures for assessing environmental impacts of significant public and private projects and exchanging information on forecasting environmental effects.[71] Similarly, the United Nations Environment Programme produced guidelines on conducting environmental assessment which stressed also the evaluation of possible social and economic effects.[72] As a body specifically concerned with environmental change giving rise to health hazards, the World Health Organization recommended that environmental and health impact assessment studies be carried out prior to the implementation of all major economic development projects, particularly dams, and offered guidance to member countries to encourage them to undertake environmental health assessments at national level.[73] In line with these initiatives, environmental appraisal was also developed in various development assistance programmes,[74] for example, the OECD issued guidelines for assessing assistance projects[75] and the World Bank began to categorize development assistance projects which required full-scale environmental assessment.[76] These few examples suggest the initial adoption of environmental assessment procedures by organizations hitherto primarily concerned with economic, development, and human health agendas. It also suggests the beginning of a process of standardizing environmental assessment procedures.

The operation of environmental assessment procedures in the United States, and the recommended use of the technique by international organizations stimulated interest in environmental assessment in Europe. Environmental impact assessment had become a frequently litigated area in the United States and this acted as a warning to European countries engaged in introducing similar legislation,

[71] *Environmental Consequences of Significant Public and Private Projects* C(74)216 (Paris: OECD, 1974); *Coordinated Methods of Assessing the Potential Environmental Effects of Chemical Compounds* C(74)215, 14.11.74 (Paris: OECD, 1974); *Coordination Guidelines in Respect of Procedures and Requirements for Anticipating the Effects of Chemicals on Man and the Environment* C(77)97 final, 7.6.77 (Paris: OECD, 1977); *The Assessment of Projects with Significant Impact on the Environment* C(79)116 (Paris: OECD, 1979).

[72] United Nations Environment Programme, *Guidelines for Assessing Industrial Environmental Impact and Criteria for the Siting of Industry* (Paris: UNEP, 1980); see M. N. Htun, 'Development of United Nations Environment Programme Guidelines for Assessing Industrial Criteria for the Siting of Industry', in Clark *et al., Perspectives on Environmental Impact Assessment*, 253–63.

[73] World Health Organization, *Rapid Assessment of Sources of Air, Water and Land Pollution Resolution* WHO/35.17 (Geneva: World Health Organization, 1982); see also E. Giroult, 'World Health Organisation Interest in Environmental Health Impact Assessment', in Wathern, *Environmental Impact Assessment*, 258–71, at 258.

[74] W. V. Kennedy, 'Environmental Impact Assessment and Bilateral Development Aid: An Overview', in Wathern, *Environmental Impact Assessment*, 272–85, at 272.

[75] Organization for Economic Cooperation and Development, *Recommendation of the Council on Measures Required to Facilitate the Environmental Assessment of Development Assistance Projects and Programmes*, C(86)26 (Paris: OECD, 1986).

[76] World Bank, *The World Bank and the Environment: First Annual Report* (Washington: World Bank, 1990). See further below, pp. 71–2.

even though the American and European contexts were essentially different. NEPA was imposed upon a land use planning system in which there were few existing procedures for predicting a proposed development's environmental impacts.[77] In contrast, when the (then) EEC adopted the EIA Directive in 1985 most Member States had established land use laws, including in some cases procedures for predicting environmental effects of development proposals. One of the most comprehensive of these was the French regime, introduced by the Protection de la Nature 1978 which mandated the preparation of environmental assessments for all major public or private development projects requiring authorization. The role of environmental assessment in other European countries varied considerably.[78] Initially, the United Kingdom, the Federal Republic of Germany, and the Nordic countries adapted their already well-developed land use planning systems to take account of the effects of development on the environment. The United Kingdom was later obliged to introduce specific legislation on environmental assessment in order to comply with Community law. Over a period of about ten years, this has involved wide-ranging amendments of planning and environmental law to fill the gaps in legislation which have allowed for opportunistic as well as well-founded legal action by groups wishing to oppose development.[79]

## Developing Environmental Impact Assessment in the United Kingdom

In addition to the influences already mentioned, the introduction of environmental impact assessment in the UK took place against a background of growing disillusionment with the public planning inquiry system. This was because its adversarial approach tended to inhibit agreement on matters of fact prior to the inquiry and discouraged witnesses from making evidence known in advance. The additional practical difficulties of combining national policy and local issues in the single inquiry procedure (with political resistance to analysing national policy in this forum), and the limited scope for effective public participation that the inquiry system appeared to offer[80] were shown up by the Windscale (later to become Sellafield) inquiry.[81] Idealistically, some writers considered that inquiry

[77] K. Von Moltke, 'Environmental Impact Assessment in the United States and Europe', in Clarke *et al.*, *Perspectives on Environmental Impact Assessment*, at 28.

[78] See the review of European responses to environmental assessment in A. Gilpin, *Environmental Impact Assessment: Cutting Edge for the Twenty-First Century* (Cambridge: Cambridge University Press, 1995) which surveys these countries in chs. 6, 8, and 9; P. Wathern, 'The EIA Directive of the European Community' in Wathern, *Environmental Impact Assessment*, 194–200 also describes the position in France and other Member States prior to the adoption of the EIA Directive.

[79] See further Ch. 6, pp. 206–18.

[80] N. Hutton, *Lay Participation in a Public Inquiry: A Sociological Case Study* (London: Gower, 1986); see also J. Herington, 'Environmental Values in a Changing Planning System', in M. Clark and J. Herington (eds.) *The Role of Environmental Impact Assessment in the Planning Process* (London: Mansell, 1988), 145.

[81] R. Kemp, 'Planning, Legitimation and the Development of Nuclear Power: A Critical Theoretic Analysis of the Windscale Inquiry' (1986) 14 *Policy and Politics* 350, at 351. Some of these

procedures would be greatly improved by the onset of an environmental impact assessment regime:

> . . . a fully informed inquiry process could only be achieved if preceded by some form of environmental impact assessment which would consider all the diverse effects of a particular proposal upon the natural environment. Such an examination could be interpreted as the optimum stage of instrumental or purposive rationality and therefore of fundamental value to practical decision making on major planning proposals.[82]

Particular faith was placed in the ability of environmental assessment procedures to strengthen the hand of environmental and conservationist groups:

> [Environmental impact assessment] will ensure that inquiry participants are fully prepared and that common ground and areas of dispute have been identified in advance. It will help all the parties with information and allow the public to be well informed and it should add a further element of objectivity to hearings.[83]

However, empirical evidence suggests poor integration of environmental impact assessment and planning inquiry procedures in practice, mainly because little consideration was given as to how environmental impact assessment would be integrated into planning inquiry procedures.[84] The consequence was an uneasy relationship between the European model of environmental assessment and the British inquiry procedure, which may still be discerned, particularly in relation to major projects.[85]

This concern with the planning inquiry system was combined with private initiatives to develop environmental assessment. For example, during the 1970s environmental impact assessment methodologies were developed by companies operating in the newly discovered oil fields of the North Sea.[86] This form of environmental assessment was not particularly transparent, but the financial risks involved in oil exploration meant that environmental assessment acted as a genuine search for the best option amongst alternative sites (but on economic as well as environmental grounds).

criticisms were addressed in the House of Commons Environment Committee, Fifth Report, *Planning Appeals and Call-in and Major Public Inquiries*, Session 1985–1986 HC 181, Cm 43.

[82] Kemp, 'Planning, Legitimation and the Development of Nuclear Power', at 364.

[83] M. Clark, 'Environmental Impact Assessment: An Ideology for Europe' (1978) *TCP* 395, at 388.

[84] See J. Holder, 'An Analysis of Council Directive 85/337/EEC on the Assessment of the Effects of Certain Public and Private Projects on the Environment and the Development of Environmental Law in the United Kingdom' (Ph.D., University of Warwick, 1995), ch. 7.

[85] On which, see J. Popham and M. Purdue, 'The Future of the Major Inquiry' [2002] *JPL* 137, at 144, which describes as particularly problematic the environmental assessment of projects subject to Hybrid Bills since there are no legal requirements as to the content of the environmental statement provided to Parliament. See further on the relationship between environmental assessment and the planning inquiry, Ch. 6. pp. 229–32.

[86] See also R. Smith, 'The Implementation of EIA in Britain', in H. Heinelt, T. Malek, R. Smith and A. E. Toller, *European Union Environment Policy and New Forms of Governance* (Aldershot: Ashgate, 2001).

Literature in this early period of development gave guidance on methods of assessment,[87] although there were also theoretical appraisals of assessment as a regulatory technique.[88] The scope of application of environmental impact assessment then expanded beyond its use as a management tool for investment, but instead became closely identified with the planning system as a technique for controlling the harmful effects of pollution by influencing the siting of industrial activities. Miller and Wood,[89] for example, concluded that environmental impact assessment could help identify and possibly remedy environmental harm which ensued after planning permission was granted for industrial projects, and that this would additionally reduce unjust social distribution of pollution. Their work influenced the European Commission's proposals for a Community-wide environmental impact assessment regime, and the authors helped to draft a directive.[90]

Following the implementation of the EC EIA Directive in the town and country planning system in England and Wales, environmental assessment became a central part of development consent requirements in the planning system.[91] Environmental assessment procedures have since been applied to a wide range of policy issues and operate in a number of contexts—nature conservation, pollution control, development assistance[92]—but they have been developed most fully in the planning system. This is because environmental impact assessment was initially project-based and the need to obtain development consent for projects provided a trigger for the application of assessment rules. This compares to procedures in the United States in which agency *policies* were also subject to environmental assessment from the outset.

The adoption of the EIA Directive by the European Economic Community in 1985 represented the first incursion of European Community law into the planning systems of the Member States. In England and Wales this formalized existing methods of taking environmental effects into account in decision making.[93] Prior to the implementation of the Directive, information about the environmental effects of a proposed development was obtained in a number of ways. A type of environmental

[87] Munn, *Environmental Impact Assessment*; B. D. Clark *et al.*, 'Methods of Environmental Analysis' (1978) 4 *Built Env* 111. More recently, see Morris and Therivel *Methods of Environmental Impact Assessment.*

[88] O'Riordan and Hey, *Environmental Impact Assessment.*

[89] C. Miller and C. Wood, *Planning and Pollution: An Examination of the Role of Land Use Planning in the Protection of the Environmental Quality* (Oxford: Oxford University Press, 1983), 216–22.; see also M. J. Ledger, 'An Assessment of the Effectiveness of Land Use Planning Powers to Control Pollution' (Ph.D., University of Manchester, 1982); and C. Wood, *Planning Pollution Prevention: A Comparison of the Siting Controls over Air Pollution in Great Britain and the USA* (Oxford: Heineman Newnes, 1989).

[90] Commission of the European Communities, *Draft Directive 7972/80 on Environmental Assessment* COM(80) 313 final.

[91] For example, see Herington, 'Environmental Values,' at 159, on the role of environmental assessment in the town and country planning system.

[92] Discussed below, pp. 65–72.

[93] N. Haigh, 'The EEC Directive on Environmental Assessment of Development Projects' (1983) JPL 585; R. Macrory, 'Environmental Assessment: Critical Legal Issues in Implementation', in D. Vaughan (ed.) *EC Environmental and Planning Law* (London: Butterworths, 1986); M. Grant, 'Implementation of the EC Directive on Environmental Impact Assessment' (1989) 4 *Conn J of Int L* 463; J. Salter, 'EIA: The Question of Implementation' [1992] JPL 313.

assessment was first required by the Town and Country Planning Act 1971. This stipulated that the written statement of a structure plan should include measures for the improvement of the physical environment, reinforced by Department of Environment guidance that the local planning authority should set out in the development plan how environmental considerations had been taken into account, including measures for reducing water, air, and noise pollution.[94] Environmental information could also be obtained under the procedure set out in the General Development Order 1977.[95] This gave planners powers to request further information from a prospective developer beyond that contained in their planning application 'to enable them to determine the application'. However, this national precursor to environmental impact assessment did not entitle the local authority to insist upon the submission of environmental information and analysis as a formal assessment.[96] The effect of this procedure was that environmental impacts were assessed according to information provided solely by the developer (although the usual forms of consultation in the planning system also applied). An assessment of sorts was also to be conducted in the case of special categories of development.[97] At the same time, environmental assessments were conducted outside the town and country development consent system when a proposed project fell outside the statutory definition of 'development',[98] or became the subject of a public planning inquiry.[99]

These various procedures ensured that environmental appraisal was clearly a feature of the land use planning system prior to the adoption of the EIA Directive. Use of the 'further information' power by local authorities meant that assessments could be made beyond those which formed the subject of specific policy guidance. But planning legislation and policy guidance still imposed few constraints upon the internal procedures for judging the weight to be given to environmental information derived from the various procedures. Studies of pre-statutory environmental assessment in the planning system found an absence of any rigorous

[94] Department of the Environment, Circular 4/79 *Memorandum on Structure and Local Plans* (London: HMSO, 1979).

[95] Reg. 5 Town and Country Planning General Development Order 1977 (SI 1977, No. 289) (enacted under s. 25 Town and Country Planning Act 1971 as amended).

[96] For example, supplementary written analysis of the House of Lords report on the proposed Directive, Eleventh Report, *Environmental Assessment of Projects*, Session 1980–81, at p. 149: 'there is doubt whether local authorities can require all the information now specified in the proposed directive, but in any event, this provision (Reg. 5 General Development Order 1977) is discretionary'.

[97] According to Department of Environment guidance, an assessment of harm was to take place if the proposed project involved the storage of hazardous materials (Circular 1/72 *Development Involving the Use of Storage in Bulk of Hazardous Material*), was likely to be a noisy development (Circular 10/73 *Planning and Noise*) or was a small business sited in a residential area (Circular 61/72 *Small Firms*).

[98] e.g. a *de facto* environmental assessment arose from the statutory requirement that official notices about a road building project 'shall state the general effect of the proposed scheme', Highways Act 1959, Sch. 1, para. 7.

[99] T. O'Riordan, 'Beyond Environmental Impact Assessment' in O'Riordan and Hey (eds.) *Environmental Impact Assessment*, 207: 'The present method of assessing environmental impacts is the planning inquiry'. On the relationship between the planning inquiry and environmental assessment, see further Ch. 6, pp. 229–32.

environmental appraisal on the part of local planning authorities and considerable variation in the structure, content, and role of environmental assessments.[100] While not denying that the informal assessment procedures conducted as part of the development consent system generally permitted the impact of a proposed development on the surrounding area, this assessment was generally carried out in relation to a specific site. In contrast, the EIA Directive was designed explicitly to require an assessment with respect to the wider environment, including in terms of the cumulative, indirect, and integrated effects of development.

The existence of these various non-statutory and loosely prescribed forms of environmental assessment meant that the initial attempt to implement the Directive proved a tricky affair. Faced with a draft Directive on environmental assessment,[101] the government's view was that environmental assessment was 'implicit in the United Kingdom's town and country planning system'[102] and thus mandatory assessment should be avoided. From this perspective, the consequence of statutory environmental assessment was the removal of discretion and in its place an arbitrary classification system. In line with its policy of 'lifting the burden' on developers, the government considered that the EIA Directive would also impose unreasonable costs on developers. The Commons concurred.[103] The government's view that environmental assessment was already to be found in the planning system led it to attempt to achieve the Directive's results by absorbing its requirements into existing legislation and administrative arrangements for applying for development consent. Tellingly, the working party set up by the Department of the Environment to explore the means of implementation concluded principally: '[T]he requirements of the Directive can be met within the context of the existing planning system without imposing significant new burdens on either developers or planning authorities'.[104] This view expresses information theories of environmental assessment, since the power to request 'additional information' from developers on the part of local authorities was considered to adequately reflect the purpose and content of the EIA Directive, although this interpretation effectively ignored the advances made in the Directive to encourage participation and consultation in decision making.

A minimalist approach to implementation was therefore pursued by absorbing the Directive's requirements into existing planning procedures by means of secondary legislation,[105] primarily the Town and Country Planning (Assessment of

[100] P. H. Selman, 'The Use of Ecological Evaluations by Local Planning Authorities' (1982) 15 *J of Env Plg and Management* 1; Royal Commission on Environmental Pollution, *Air Pollution Control: An Integrated Approach* Cmnd 6371 (London: HMSO, 1976).

[101] Draft Directive 7972/80 Com(80) 313 final.

[102] House of Commons Select Committee on the European Communities, Eleventh Report, *Environmental Assessment of Projects*, Session 1980–81 (London: HMSO, 1981), para. 31.

[103] Department of the Environment, *Implementation of the European Directive on Environmental Assessment* (London: HMSO, 1986), para. 6.

[104] House of Lords Select Committee on European Legislation, Twelfth Report, Session 1980–81. This Report warmly welcomed the Directive.

[105] By powers contained in s. 2 European Communities Act 1972.

Environmental Effects) Regulations 1988 ('the 1988 Regulations')[106] in the case of applications for development consent in the town and country planning system. This was incongruent with the breadth of purpose of the principle that 'projects which are likely to have significant effects should be granted only after prior assessment of the likely significant effects has been carried out'.[107] This discrepancy is illustrated by the environmental impact assessment of projects designed to intensively farm semi-natural or uncultivated land. Though listed in Annex II of the Directive, this category of project fell outside the scope of the implementing 1988 Regulations because these were based upon the existing categories of 'development' requiring planning permission,[108] which excludes certain agriculture and forestry projects.[109] This, and other gaps, led the European Commission to question the adequacy of the implementing provisions. Lengthy negotiations between the Commission and the Secretary of State took place against a political background of the United Kingdom opting out of the Social Chapter of the Treaty on European Union, and invoking the subsidiarity principle in respect of individual projects which also formed the basis of the Commission's enforcement action. The United Kingdom government eventually conceded in 1992 (in exchange for the Commission terminating legal proceedings on five specific projects)[110] that environmental impact assessment procedures should apply to cases involving the use of semi-natural and uncultivated areas for intensive agriculture.[111] Separate sets of Regulations requiring the environmental impact assessment of such projects likely to have significant effects on the environment were not issued until 2001 (2002 in the case of Scotland).[112] This and other examples suggest that the initial implementation effort had the effect of narrowing the scope of the

[106] (SI 1988, No. 1199). J. Salter, 'EIA: The Challenge from Brussels' [1992] JPL 14, at 14 recounts that the Directive was also implemented by contract in those cases in which the assessment of projects relates to land lying below the low water mark—within the scope of Community law, but outside the jurisdiction of the local planning authority.

[107] Ninth recital, preamble to the EIA Directive, to be read in conjunction with Arts. 5 and 8 of the Directive.

[108] S. 55(1)(e) Town and Country Planning Act 1990. On this regulatory gap and the regime introduced to remedy this, see further Royal Commission on Environmental Pollution, Twenty-third Report, *Environmental Planning* Cm 5459 (London: HMSO, 2002), paras. 9.48–9.53.

[109] Other notable gaps included those projects which do not constitute 'development', such as those permitted under a development order. The filling of such gaps was completed in stages, for example by the Town and Country Planning (Assessment of Environmental Effects) (Amendment) Regulations 1990 (SI 1990, No. 367), the Town and Country Planning (Assessment of Environmental Effects) (Amendment) Regulations 1992 (SI 1992, No. 1494) and the Town and Country Planning (Assessment of Environmental Effects) (Amendment) Regulations 1994 (SI 1994, No. 677).

[110] These included the extension of the M3 motorway through Twyford Down, on which see further Ch. 6, p. 223, and Ch. 7, pp. 257–8.

[111] HC Written answers, 16.12.1992, Cols. 319–20.

[112] Environmental Impact Assessment (Uncultivated Land and Semi-natural Areas) (England) Regulations 2001 (SI 2001, No. 3966); Environmental Impact Assessment (Uncultivated Land and Semi-natural Areas) (Northern Ireland) Regulations 2001 (SI 2001, No. 435) and Environmental Impact Assessment (Uncultivated Land and Semi-natural Areas) (Scotland) Regulations 2002 (SI 2002, No. 6).

environmental assessment process as set out in the Directive, and that this has taken a long time to rectify.[113]

In summary, the implementation of the EIA Directive was influenced in an immediate sense by political events, but more fundamentally by the existence in the United Kingdom of a long-standing, informal, and discretionary approach to environmental assessment. Several conclusions can be drawn from the process of implementation. Primarily, 'indigenous' procedures for predicting the effects of development on the environment were formalized and codified as a result of the EIA Directive's implementation. The Directive provided for the formal introduction of expert and public opinion on the effects of development on the environment into essentially political planning procedures. Notwithstanding the formal nature of assessment, fragmentation in the administration of assessment procedures still exists because of the piecemeal absorption of the Directive's provisions into existing planning procedures by means of many different sets of regulations.[114] It was therefore perhaps inevitable that the legal and administrative features of the ad hoc and largely informal pre-statutory environmental assessment procedures came to be combined with those designed to give legal effect to the EIA Directive, in particular that an onus was placed upon the developer to provide information about the effects of development on the environment and that, in eliciting and presenting this information, the developer should enjoy discretion. For this reason also, the planning system's existing lacunae, notably the exclusion of all but a handful of agricultural and forestry projects from the need for development consent, similarly prevailed in law designed to implement the Directive.

In terms of the exercise of discretion, the 1988 Regulations and other implementing Regulations have continued to confer considerable discretion on planners to determine the application of environmental assessment rules, the adequacy of environmental statements submitted by developers with an application for planning permission (despite overall responsibility for the implementation of a statutory and uniform assessment system lying with central government), and, of course, the final decision. Unlike the procedures existing prior to the implementation of the EIA Directive, this discretion is now subject to the requirement that a project likely to have significant effects upon the environment must be subjected to an environmental assessment,[115] which has involved the establishment of statutory and judicial boundaries on judgments of significance.[116] However, similarly to pre-statutory assessment, the implementing Regulations grant discretion to the

[113] Although the enactment of s. 15 of the Planning and Compensation Act 1991, which inserted s. 71 into the Town and Country Planning Act 1990 enabled the Secretary of State to require environmental impact assessment of planning projects other than those listed in the European Directive, for example motorway service stations and golf courses.

[114] There are currently 37 sets of regulations in force for this purpose (with more planned). See Appendix X.

[115] As confirmed by *Berkeley* v *Secretary of State for the Environment and Fulham Football Club* (*Berkeley No. 1*) [2000] WLR 420, [2001] AC 603, (2001) 13 *JEL* 89. HL.

[116] See Ch. 4, pp. 108–30.

developer with respect to the selection and presentation of information. Such control over information on the effects of development on the environment entering the decision-making procedures of the planning system is particularly important in cases in which the developer's environmental statement is mistakenly treated as though it were an account of the full assessment process.

The initial attempts to implement the Directive led to research being conducted on its legal implications, as well as more practical concerns about its administration by various professional and interest groups, not least the European Commission.[117] The relative neglect of legal aspects of environmental assessment at the time of the adoption of the Directive on environmental assessment was partially remedied by works which highlighted the inadequacies of English law in accommodating its aims and methods, something which came to light through analysis of judicial review cases on environmental assessment.[118] Since the bulk of this research was conducted, there has been an explosion of governance literature which has considerably advanced theories on participation, deliberation, and the regulation of decision making. The existing literature on environmental assessment fails almost entirely to recognize this. This is striking when the general characteristics of environmental assessment, outlined in Chapter 1,[119] are considered. In particular, environmental assessment contributes to the sharing of responsibility for providing environmental information on which decisions may be based and, in formal terms at least, provides opportunities for the consultation of a broad range of participants. These features suggest that environmental assessment is capable of relating the style and premises of modern forms of environmental governance to the regulation of decision making,[120] and in so doing expressing aspects of the concept of sustainable development. The interpretation of environmental assessment as a means of putting into operation the concept of sustainable development can be explained to a large extent by its development as an instrument of international environmental law and custom.

[117] E. Gouge, 'The UK Implementation of Environmental Assessment: Organisational and Political Implications' (1989) *Local Government Policy Making* 55; W. Sheate, *The Environmental Assessment Directive: Five Years On* (London: Council for the Protection of Rural England, 1991); Institute of Environmental Assessment, *Practical Experience of Environmental Assessment in the United Kingdom* (East Kirkby: Institute of Environmental Assessment, 1993), Royal Institute of Chartered Surveyors, *Environmental Assessments* (London: RICS, 1989); C. Wood and C. Jones, *Monitoring Environmental Assessment and Planning* (London, HMSO, 1990); C. Wood and C. Jones, 'The Impact of Environmental Assessment on Local Planning Authorities' (1992) 35 *JEPM* 115–27; C. Wood, 'Five Years of British Environmental Assessment', in D. Cross and C. Whitehead (eds.) *Development and Planning* (Cambridge: Cambridge University Press, 1994); Wathern, *Environmental Impact Assessment*; European Commission, *Report from the Commission on the Implementation of Directive 85/337/EEC on the Assessment of the Effects of Certain Public and Private Projects on the Environment* COM(93) 28, 2.4.1993 (Brussels: CEC, 1993).

[118] J. Alder, 'Environmental Impact Assessment: The Inadequacies of English Law', (1993) 5 *JEL* 203; A. Ward, 'The Right to an Effective Remedy in European Community Law: A Case Study of United Kingdom Decisions Concerning the Environmental Assessment Directive' (1993) 5 *JEL* 221 also examines this case law, but from a different perspective—the effectiveness of remedies in Community law.

[119] See pp. 12–22.

[120] See particularly Chs. 6 and 7.

## International Law and Custom

The position of environmental assessment in international law has been slowly enhanced to the extent that it has reached the status of a general principle of international law, and possibly even a requirement of customary international law. This progression has been reflected in the gaining in significance of environmental assessment in national legal systems, and in the European Community. It begins, though, with statements about the desirability of environmental assessment governing decision making in several non-binding instruments.[121] One such early formulation was contained in the 1982 World Charter for Nature which called for an exhaustive examination and assessment of activities likely to pose a significant risk to nature and required that activities should either not proceed (if likely to cause irreversible damage to nature based on an assessment's findings) or proceed with minimal potential effects.[122] This also (unusually at this time) detailed that such assessments were to be disclosed to the public to allow for effective consultation and participation and that all persons, in accordance with national legislation, were to be given an opportunity to participate in the formulation of decisions of direct concern to their environment.[123] In this respect, the Charter was prophetic in its reinforcement of participatory democracy by environmental assessment. For example, this idea formed the core of Agenda 21 in 1992 in which references to environmental assessment abound,[124] but in particular requires the signatory states to ensure that relevant decisions are preceded by environmental impact assessments and take into consideration the costs of development in terms of its ecological consequences.[125] The most influential of non-binding references (in terms of initiating national measures on environmental assessment) is Principle 17 of the Rio Declaration which states that: 'Environmental impact assessment, as a national instrument, shall be undertaken for proposed activities that are likely to have a significant adverse impact on the environment and are subject to a decision of a competent national authority'.[126] Arguably the mandatory language of Principle 17 is consistent with the view that environmental impact

[121] Described in detail by P. Sands, *Principles of International Environmental Law* (Cambridge: Cambridge University Press, 2nd edn., 2003), ch. 16. Notably, an early draft of the Stockholm Declaration contained a reference to environmental impact assessment (Principle 20) but this was withdrawn, only to be revived as Principle 5 of the 1978 UNEP Draft Principles of Conduct, on which see Sands, *Principles*, 801. Gray's interpretation of the withdrawal of Principle 20 was because this was perceived by developing countries to offer a means by which developed countries could impede projects; see K. Gray, 'International Environmental Impact Assessment: Potential for a Multilateral Environmental Agreement' (2000) *Col J of Int Env L and Policy* 83, at 105–6. The opposite appears to be true; see below, pp. 71–2.

[122] World Charter for Nature, (1982) 23 ILM 455, p. 11 (a)–(c).

[123] At pp. 16–23.

[124] See specifically Sands, *Principles*, 802–3.

[125] UNCED, Agenda 21: Programme of Action for Sustainable Development (1992), Ch. 8 of which is devoted to integrating environmental protection and development in decision making.

[126] UNCED (1992) 31 ILM 874.

assessments are now required as a general principle of international law, particularly in respect of environmentally harmful activities which may have transboundary consequences.[127]

Unsurprisingly, binding instruments tend to be less prescriptive,[128] for example the United Nations Convention on the Law of the Sea (1982)[129] sets out requirements for environmental assessment as follows:

> When states have reasonable grounds for believing that planned activities under their jurisdiction or control may cause substantial pollution of or significant and harmful changes to the marine environment, they shall, as far as practicable, assess the potential effects of such activities on the marine environment and shall communicate reports of the results of such assessments at appropriate intervals to the competent international organisations, which should make them available to all states.[130]

Whilst conferring an obligation to carry out an assessment of activities that have potential effects on the marine environment, this is clearly restricted to what is practicable. In addition, there is no binding requirement on states to take the results of an environmental impact assessment procedure into account when authorizing an activity.[131]

In contrast, instruments negotiated by United Nations Economic Commission of Europe on transboundary environmental assessment[132] and strategic environmental assessment,[133] and on participation, public access to environmental information, and access to justice in environmental matters[134] have provided an important impetus in the European Community's development of enforceable environmental assessment legislation. In particular, the Espoo Convention creates obligations to take appropriate and effective measures to prevent, reduce, and control significant adverse transboundary environmental impacts from proposed development and other activities, and to provide for public participation in such cases.[135] This required the EIA Directive to be strengthened in several respects.[136]

With varying degrees of precision, these declarations and instruments forge a potential alliance between the principle of sustainable development and the use of

[127] Sands, *Principles*, 800.

[128] On the nature of these instruments, see generally, Gray, 'International Environmental Impact Assessment'.

[129] United Nations Convention on the Law of the Sea (1982) 21 ILM 1261.

[130] Arts. 205 and 206. See further comment by Gray, 'International Environmental Impact Assessment', at 92.

[131] See further comment by Gray, op. cit. at 92. See also reliance on UNCLOS in *Ireland* v *United Kingdom (the MOX case)* ITLOS Order, 41 ILM 405 (2002), discussed below, p. 56.

[132] Convention on environmental impact assessment in a transboundary context (Espoo Convention) 30 ILM 802 (1991).

[133] Protocol on strategic environmental assessment (Kiev) 21 May 2003 (not yet in force).

[134] Aarhus Convention, 38 ILM 517 (1999). For the set of EC measures designed to implement Aarhus, see Ch. 6, pp. 192–4.

[135] See further Ch. 6, pp. 186–7 and 191. See also Gray, 'International Environmental Impact Assessment', 100 ff. and J. Beggs, 'Combating Biospheric Degradation: International Environmental Impact Assessment and the Transboundary Pollution Dilemma' (1995) *Fordham Env L J* 379.

[136] By its amendment in 1997 by Directive 97/11/EC OJ 1997 L 73, p. 5.

environmental assessment.[137] The accomplishment of environmental assessment as a general principle of international law, as foreseen by the Legal Experts Group on Environmental Law of the WCED,[138] has been realized in the course of several judgments of the International Court of Justice. In *New Zealand* v *France*[139] New Zealand challenged France's decision to resume underground nuclear tests in the Pacific Atolls on the ground that France was under an obligation in customary international law to conduct an environmental impact assessment of the potential effects of this before carrying out the tests.[140] Amongst the *dissenting* judgments, Judge Palmer advocated the recognition of environmental limits via such mechanisms as environmental assessment, 'otherwise the paradigm of sustainable development enhanced by the world at the Rio Conference cannot be achieved'.[141] Judge Weeramantry also expressed a dissenting opinion that the principle of environmental impact assessment, being ancillary to the precautionary principle, 'was gathering strength and international acceptance and had reached a level of general recognition such that the Court should take notice of it'.[142]

The International Court of Justice revisited the status of environmental impact assessment *vis-à-vis* sustainable development in the *Gabčíkovo-Nagymaros Project* case[143] which concerned a dispute between Hungary and Slovakia over the breakdown of agreement between the states to cooperate in the building of the barrages on the River Danube contained in a 1977 Treaty between the parties. Hungary had unilaterally suspended construction of a barrage at Nagymaros (ostensibly due to evidence of environmental harm), but the Slovak government had continued to build a new dam at Gabčíkovo within their territory but with effects upon the flow of the river. The majority view of the Court in this case was that there was imposed on the states a duty of continuous environmental impact assessment in the light of developments in knowledge, and that this duty influenced the provisions of the Treaty governing their cooperation in this field. Judge Weeramantry (now in the majority) stated:

> . . . Environmental law in its current state of development would read into treaties which may reasonably be considered to have a significant impact upon the environment, a duty of environmental impact assessment and this means also, whether the treaty expressly so provides or not, a duty of monitoring the environmental impacts of any substantial project during the operation of the scheme.[144]

Judge Weeramantry additionally argued that sustainable development is not merely a concept but a recognized principle of customary international law, albeit

[137] Discussed below, pp. 56–60.

[138] Environmental assessment was identified as a legal principle of sustainable development and international law by the World Commission on Environment and Development's Experts Group on Environmental Law, *Legal Principles for Environmental Protection and Sustainable Development* (Dordrecht: Martinus Nijhoff, 1987), 58.

[139] (1995) ICJ Reports, 288.

[140] New Zealand also based its case on Art. 16 of the Convention for the Protection of the Natural Resources and Environment of the South Pacific Region (Noumea Convention) 26 ILM (1987).

[141] At para. 68.

[142] (1995) ICJ Reports, 344.

[143] (1997) ICJ Reports, 7.

[144] (1997) ICJ Reports, 7, at 11.

one which suggests procedural rather than substantive obligations. The case suggests a stringent obligation of continuous monitoring of the environmental impacts of a project, which has not been as fully accepted on the domestic front.[145]

The third significant case heard before the International Court of Justice is ongoing. *Ireland* v *United Kingdom* was brought on the basis that the United Kingdom had violated its obligations under the United Nations Convention on the Law of the Sea[146] by authorizing a new nuclear plant in 2001 (on the existing Sellafield site) to manufacture mixed oxide (MOX) fuel on the basis of an environmental impact assessment from 1993. This statement failed to take into account the potential effects of the manufacturing process on the marine environment of the Irish Sea,[147] suggesting also that the customary principle of 'continuous environmental impact assessment' established by the International Court had been infringed. In the preliminary stages of the case on provisional measures before the International Tribunal, Ireland failed to have the works suspended, but secured a minority view that the inadequate environmental impact assessment would have warranted this on the grounds that this 'is a central tool of the international law of prevention'.[148]

## Relating Environmental Assessment and Sustainable Development

The profound shift in environmental discourse and environmental law by which sustainable development became an organizing theme and objective of international environmental law (and environmental law more generally) has been reflected in the functions ascribed to environmental assessment. As mentioned above, environmental impact assessment was originally considered to assist mainly with pollution control (though also habitat and landscape concerns) through informing decisions about siting industrial development, thus performing a technicist function in environmental law. It has since been acknowledged to have a far broader role in implementing the principle of sustainable development by influencing decision makers to take account of the quality of development and its effects upon the conservation of natural resources, as well as still influencing locational issues. This parallel shift in the perceived function of environmental impact assessment reflects the rejection of purely technocratic practices in favour of a more general reformist environmental strategy (although more extreme interpretations

[145] Instead a pragmatic approach to continuous monitoring, and the application of environmental assessment throughout the lifetime of a project has been taken by British courts, with the effect that a narrower version of environmental assessment prevails. See e.g. *R (Prokopp)* v *LUL* [2003] EWCA 960 (Admin), cf. Ch. 6, p. 209.

[146] Art. 206.

[147] See further, Sands, *Principles*, 806–7.

[148] ITLOS Order, 3 December 2001, 41 ILM 405 (2002). Opinion of Judge Szekely, paras. 12–17.

of sustainable development have advanced economic methodologies which are similarly technicist).[149] Encouraging popular participation in environmental decision making formed an important part of this strategy. In this vein, the World Commission on Environment and Development specifically identified environmental assessment of projects and policies as offering a means to achieve sustainable industrial development, alongside the use of economic instruments,[150] a role similarly identified for environmental assessment in the Rio Declaration (1992)[151] and Agenda 21[152] which followed the WCED's report. The potential contribution of environmental assessment to sustainable development has since been described by, amongst others,[153] Pearce in his blueprint for 'implementing' sustainable development,[154] and Jacobs who welcomed environmental assessment as 'a reasonably considered and open approach to mediating conflict within the sustainability framework by allowing those most likely to be affected by a project's environmental effects to communicate their views to decision makers'.[155]

Environmental assessment is clearly thought capable of being further developed to include the assessment of environmental impacts on communities,[156] human health,[157] and habitats.[158] Moving further beyond environmental protection, the prediction of impacts prior to decision making may be used to reflect a range of concerns, for example human rights,[159] and the burden of regulation on administration.[160] This expansion may ultimately lead to an all-embracing sustainability assessment, a development which reflects the adoption of the sustainable development agenda in environmental law. Relating the evolution of environmental assessment to the ascendancy of the concept of sustainable development in law and policy offers an explanation for this. For example in the context of the European Union, the sustainable development principle has undergone a process

[149] For an excellent review of this shift, see M. A. Hajer, *The Politics of Environmental Discourse: Ecological Modernisation and the Policy Process* (Oxford: Oxford University Press, 1997), ch. 3.

[150] World Commission on Environment and Development, *Our Common Future* (Oxford: Oxford University Press, 1987), 221–4.

[151] UNCED (1992) 31 ILM 874.

[152] UNCED, 1992.

[153] For example. A. Blowers, *Planning for a Sustainable Future* (London: Earthscan, 1993), 23; Council for the Protection of Rural England, *Sense and Sustainability: Land Use Planning and Environmental Sustainable Development* (London: CPRE, 1993), 15; and T. Clarke, 'Environmental Assessment and Sustainable Development' (1991) 6 *EIA* at 2–3.

[154] D. W. Pearce, *Blueprint for a Green Economy* (London: Earthscan, 1989), 120–30.

[155] M. Jacobs, *The Green Economy* (London: Pluto Press, 1993), 220–1.

[156] On the evaluation of social impacts of development, see N. Lichfield, *Community Impact Evaluation: Principles and Practice* (London: University College Press, 1996).

[157] See e.g. the Royal Commission on Environmental Pollution's recommendation that human health issues be incorporated explicitly in the environmental impact assessment process. *Environmental Planning*, paras. 7.36–7.38.

[158] For example, M. Montini, 'Habitats Impact Assessment: An Effective Instrument for Biodiversity Conservation?' (2001) 9 *Env Liab* 182.

[159] As discussed by S. I. Skegly, *The Human Rights Obligations of the World Bank and Monetary Fund* (London: Cavendish, 2001).

[160] B. Morgan, 'The Economisation of Politics' (2003) 12 *SLS* 489.

of 'mainstreaming' which describes its adoption as a guiding principle, informing the formation and fulfilment of all policies pursued by the Union,[161] not just those with an environmental purview. Since sustainable development is predicated upon the integration of environmental considerations in decision making in exactly the manner achieved by environmental assessment instruments, this suggests some inevitability about the remit of environmental assessment being extended (as impact assessment or sustainability analysis) and being placed at the centre of policy making.

Sadler[162] offers an evangelical view of the expansion of the remit of environmental assessment as a means to take fuller account of social and economic (as well as environmental) factors in decision making. He predicts a transition from environmental impact assessment ('a first-generation' process typically concerned with mitigating the impacts of major developments rather than maintaining the capacity and integrity of natural systems')[163] and strategic environmental assessment ('a second generation process that addresses both the sources and symptoms (or effects) of environmental damage')[164] towards a third generation form of ESA (Environmental Sustainability Assessment) involving a 'full cost analysis' of social, economic, and environmental impacts. Sadler considers that, where critical and 'high value' environmental functions and areas may be affected by development, the acceptability of potential environmental effects should be evaluated against the composition and value of natural capital stock.[165] He considers that the current focus on mitigation in traditional forms of environmental assessment (EIA and SEA) is misplaced in cases of 'medium and low environmental value' and instead that compensation, whether to offset impacts or provide 'like for like' compensation for the residual impacts that cannot be mitigated or avoided, should be pursued in such cases.[166] In elaborating the importance of compensation, and approving the making of 'trade-offs' in this manner, Sadler tends to skirt over the diversity of human values by simplistically categorizing environmental 'value' as high, medium, and low. His following analysis of 'compensation packages' inevitably raises questions about the valuation of 'naturalness', discussed previously,[167] raised here in the context of sustainable development.

Based on an impact damage assessment, different compensation-packages can be identified, e.g. *in full (no trade-off)* to identically offset high-value loss incurred, e.g. for key species or wetland functions; *equal replacement* to generally offset the high-medium-value

[161] Art. 2 EC Treaty, as amended, states: 'The Community shall have as its task, by establishing a common market and an economic and monetary union and by implementing common policies or activities . . . to promote throughout the Community a harmonious and balanced sustainable development of economic activities . . . a high level of protection and improvement of the quality of the environment'. Art. 2 Treaty on European Union similarly states that the Union shall 'promote economic and social progress to achieve balanced and sustainable development'.

[162] B. Sadler, 'Environmental Sustainability and Assurance', in J. Petts (ed.) *Handbook of EIA: Vol. 1 Process, Methods and Potential* (Oxford: Blackwell, 1999).

[163] At p. 27.

[164] ibid.

[165] At p. 30. On the nature of 'in-kind' compensation, see Ch. 1, p. 25.

[166] Sadler, 'Environmental Sustainability and Assurance', 31.

[167] See Ch. 1, p. 26.

loss, e.g. so that habitat units can be traded across important species; *relative replacement* for medium-value loss to ensure other types of habitat or wetland functions are improved or rehabilitated in areas of concern; *flexible trading* to compensate for low-value loss of abundant resources or where there is no equivalency, e.g. carbon sequestering for carbon dioxide emissions. Undoubtedly, this type of asset-trading and replacement will be crude and imprecise. As such, impact compensation will need to be promoted and implemented pragmatically.[168]

The enthusiasm for environmental assessment as a means to secure a weak form of sustainable development (even without its development into 'environmental sustainability assessment') demonstrates a key characteristic of the procedure—an ability to absorb other concerns, be they environmental, economic, or social—and thus encourage recognition of diverse concerns, and the connections between them.[169] From a more critical standpoint, environmental assessment facilitates the balancing of competing interests, or rather contributes to an impression of balance, or mediation (rather than absolute environmental protection) which similarly underlies the concept of sustainable development. Of course, this also facilitates the identification of 'trade-offs' that may be made. A key point, however, is that having secured the integration of environmental concerns in land use systems, and policy making, the further inclusion within the scope of environmental assessment of other indicators or indices may lead to the marginalization of environmental impacts as against a broader spectrum of concern.[170]

In conceptual terms, the development of environmental assessment is in accordance with aspects of the efficiency-oriented ecological modernization agenda[171] of which sustainable development is an important part. This is particularly the case with moves to integrate environmental concerns into broader social and political issues (and to facilitate the identification of trade-offs) and correspondingly encourage shared responsibility for environmental *management*, as opposed to protection. The mainstreaming of 'alternative' regulatory forms, such as environmental agreements and taxes, stems from this development. The underlying self-regulatory mode of control of these mechanisms has also come to be identified with environmental assessment.[172]

[168] Sadler, 'Environmental Sustainability and Assurance', 30.

[169] For example, the Royal Commission on Environmental Pollution discusses the prospects for sustainability appraisal which would extend appraisal to include social and economic criteria as being of equal concern to environmental criteria, See Twenty-Third Report, paras. 7.43–7.45. See, already, Department of the Environment, Transport and the Regions, *Proposals for a Good Practice Guide on Sustainability Appraisal of Regional Planning Guidance* (London: DETR, 2000).

[170] See e.g. case study on the European Commission's development of a form of sustainability assessment to review policy choices, Ch. 5, pp. 164–81.

[171] Hajer, *The Politics of Environmental Discourse*. On the ecological modernization justification for EU environmental policy, see also Weale *et al.*, *Environmental Governance in Europe*, ch. 1.

[172] As identified by E. Bregman and A. Jacobsen, 'Environmental Performance Review: Self-Regulation in Environmental Law' in G. Teubner , L. Farmer, and D. Murphy (eds.) *Environmental Law and Ecological Responsibility: The Concept and Practice of Ecological Self-Organisation* (Chichester: Wiley, 1994) and more generally, Heinelt *et al.*, *European Union Environmental Policy*.

The association of environmental assessment with the ideas of ecological modernization and sustainable development may be further explained by the influence of ecological science, and the changing paradigms within the discipline.[173] Early environmental assessment was held up as an example of 'ecological science in action', synthesized with law in the United States' NEPA 1969.[174] The conception of ecology at the time of this enactment was one based upon the dominant paradigm of homeostasis or equilibrium between organisms and the environment—a 'balance of nature'—which could be maintained only by resistance to change.[175] Although not prescribing a particular environmental standard, environmental assessment was a culturally significant evocation of the importance of such ecological concerns in decision making, so that the fairly strict environmental assessment requirements contained within the 1969 Act (alongside the development of nature reserves, biodiversity preservation strategies, and the setting of emission standards) suggest the absorption of some of this thinking into environmental law. In the meantime, the equilibrium paradigm underwent a revolution, with the result that ecological science now stresses change and instability of ecosystems, and no longer upholds as ideal the withdrawal of humankind from nature. This 'New Ecology' recognizes instead the inevitability of interactions between humans and the natural environment,[176] and thus the management of ecosystems, rather than their preservation, or restoration. The reformed perspective of ecology inevitably informed the evolution of the political concept of sustainable development by providing a scientific basis for it, and the associated drive for the integration of environmental factors in all decision making. Bosselman and Tarlock sum this up: 'Environmentalism's initial objective was to make environmental quality a relative quality to be considered. This battle has now largely been won and the movement's focus has shifted to the assured comprehensive and long-term integration, if not dominance, of this perspective in all resource decision making'.[177] A triumvirate of law, ecology, and politics therefore acted to reconceive environmental assessment as a legal expression of sustainable development, particularly giving practical effect to the more integrative aspects of this concept, so that environmental concerns are taken into account in decision making, but do not (by design) necessarily predominate.

## Expanding Environmental Impact Assessment: Strategic Environmental Assessment

To recap, with the rapid evolution and expansion in the function and form of environmental assessment, law has attempted to keep pace with, and control, its development. Taking the United Kingdom as an example, relatively weak statutory

[173] F. P. Bosselman and A. D. Tarlock, 'The Influence of Ecological Science on American Law' (1994) 69 *Chicago-Kent L Rev* 847.

[174] See Appendix I.

[175] Bosselman and Tarlock, 'The influence of Ecological Science', at 866.

[176] This paradigm shift is attributed to several ecologists: B. T. McKibben, *The End of Nature* (New York: Random House, 1989); D. B. Botkin, *Discordant Harmonies: A New Ecology for the Twenty-First Century* (Oxford: Oxford University Press Inc, 1990).

[177] 'The Influence of Ecological Science', at 872.

provisions, codes of practice, and guidelines on taking account of environmental considerations have been replaced with a formal legislative requirement to conduct environmental assessment in certain cases, accompanied by indicative and prescriptive thresholds which narrow discretion on the part of the decision maker. This is largely the consequence of European Community legislation, although procedures conceptually similar to environmental assessment were also given a legislative base without a European impetus.[178] Law has also provided a basis for the expansion of the remit of environmental assessment—from project-based procedures to the broader scope of strategic level of assessment. This is because, although the environmental impact assessment of projects was initially considered a way of giving effect to the concept of sustainable development, fairly soon it became clear that this level of assessment was too limited in scope to achieve this because decision making at the project level was often superseded by higher-level policy decisions. The development of strategic environmental assessment is a response to the need for multiple levels of assessment (to reflect different levels and scales of environmental decision making) and suggests a deeper level of integration and policy coordination than is the case with project-based assessment.[179]

An early form of strategic environmental assessment was developed in the United States under NEPA which required agencies to make a detailed assessment of the environmental implications of any action (be it a development project or policy) significantly affecting the quality of the human environment.[180] This influenced the European Commission's proposal for a similar model of assessment (though additionally applying to the private sector) in 1980.[181] Strong resistance by some Member States to the proposed element of policy appraisal in the instrument led to the exclusion of this element from the final Directive, even though it had been strongly favoured by the European Parliament. This meant that the scope of the resulting EIA Directive was severely restricted,[182] in keeping with its portrayal as an instrument for fostering competitive conditions,[183] rather than aiding forward planning.[184] Shaving off the policy element inevitably resulted in a strong focus on

178 For example, best practicable environmental option assessments (s. 7(4) Environmental Protection Act 1990), on which see further below, p. 70.

179 For example, see arguments made for strategic environmental assessment in European Commission, *SEA and the Integration of the Environment into Strategic Decision Making* (Brussels: CEC, 2001).

180 See above, p. 43.

181 Draft directive on environmental assessment, 7972/80 COM(80) 313 final.

182 The final draft directive (there were several versions) also included provisions on post-assessment monitoring and the supervision of conditions made following environmental assessment.

183 This rationale for the draft directive was given in its preamble: 'beyond environmental protection . . . significant divergence in the principles and criteria of assessment at present in the Community may well produce disparities in investment conditions between one region of the Community and another and thus create distortion of competition with negative effects on the functioning of the Common Market'. Such a rationale was needed because of the lack of a specific legal base in the EEC Treaty for environmental measures.

184 Although a policy commitment to policy appraisal was made in the Fourth Environmental Action Programme, COM(86) 485 final (Brussels: CEC, 1987) which stated that EIA 'will also be extended, as rapidly as possible, to cover policies and policy statements, plans and their implementation, procedures,

'the project', with an accordingly weaker emphasis placed upon cumulative and indirect effects, and alternative options. To some extent this focus has been retained in the current SEA Directive[185] (which is due to be fully implemented in the Member States in 2004) since this requires the environmental assessment of certain plans and programmes *in order* to provide a framework for the future development consent of projects. The omission of 'policies' from the scope of this Directive reflects the concerns of Member States that its inclusion would severely restrict their discretion in policy making. These concerns had resulted in a legislative stalemate on this proposal for several years. So, although the SEA Directive is admittedly broader in scope than previous versions (one of which, controversially, limited environmental assessment requirements to plans and programmes for town and country planning purposes)[186] it nevertheless remains a European apology for a more complete, strategic, assessment regime. The further development of environmental assessment by the UNECE Kiev Protocol to the Espoo Convention to include (fairly weak) strategic elements is unlikely to detract fundamentally from this criticism.[187]

Although strategic environmental assessment has been presented as an advance on project-based appraisal, particularly in terms of encouraging the consideration of alternatives, in practice it is sometimes difficult to pinpoint exactly where environmental impact assessment ends and strategic environmental assessment begins.[188] For example, strategic environmental assessment has been advocated as a means to assess the overall impact of licensing regimes (e.g. oil and gas development) in which individual consents are made subject to environmental impact assessment, but the full, cumulative effects of many such licences are not examined. However, the gradual strengthening of the requirements to consider alternatives,[189] and cumulative effects[190] in project-based environmental assessment detract from this argument in favour of SEA. Similarly, a strategic assessment of the ecological impacts of transport networks may use geographical information systems to identify areas designated for conservation of birds which would be within several kilometres of proposed routes. Such an assessment is remote from a particular site, but remains tied to the physical condition of a specified area so that it appears more like a 'bundle of environmental impact assessments'.[191] This

programmes . . . as well as individual projects'. This was reiterated in the Fifth Environmental Action Programme, *Towards Sustainability: A European Programme of Policy and Action in Relation to the Environment and Sustainable Development*, COM(92) 23 final (Brussels: CEC, 1992) in the context of achieving sustainable development.

[185] Directive 2001/42/EC on the assessment of the effects of certain plans and programmes on the environment, OJ 2001 L 197, p. 30.

[186] Art. 2(a) Commission proposal for a Council Directive on the assessment of the effects of certain plans and programmes on the environment, COM(96) 511 final, OJ C 129, p. 14. On which see critical commentary, S. Tromans and C. Roger-Machart, 'Strategic Environmental Assessment: Early Evaluation Equals Efficiency?' [1997] JPL 993.

[187] UNECE Draft Protocol on Strategic Environmental Assessment (Kiev Protocol). See Appendix V.

[188] This was the case with the Lewes Flood Defence Strategy case study; see Ch. 3, pp. 86–9.

[189] See Ch. 5, pp. 149–50. [190] See Ch. 4, pp. 130–6.

[191] J. Treweek, *Ecological Impact Assessment* (Oxford: Blackwell, 1999), 26.

is particularly the case when compared to an assessment of alternatives to road transport—air, rail, or local production programmes—which is spatially unlimited by the condition of a particular site, or sites, and may span policy on local, regional, and national scales. The latter example of strategic environmental assessment genuinely represents a sea-change in decision making. Whereas most environmental impact assessments are triggered by a proposed development, and are most often underpinned by a private (usually property) interest, strategic environmental assessment is by its very nature conducted by public bodies or agencies of government with the aim of better administration or governance. A further genuine difference between the forms of assessment is that environmental impact assessment is a reactive device, responding to a developer's application for development consent concerning an individual site whereas strategic environmental assessment may be used as a mechanism for forward planning.

To summarize, environmental impact assessment and strategic environmental assessment have different rationales, and operate on different levels, but they remain closely related and may overlap in subject matter and methodologies, because an important aim of strategic environmental assessment is to provide a framework for decisions about development consent on individual sites. This is borne out by the EC SEA Directive[192] which explicitly states:

> . . . an environmental assessment shall be carried out for all plans and programmes for agriculture, forestry, fisheries, energy, industry, transport, waste management, water management, telecommunications, tourism, town and country planning, or land use and which set the framework for future development consent of projects listed in Annex I and II to the EIA Directive, or which, in view of the likely effect on sites, require an assessment under the Habitats Directive.[193]

The potentially fruitful (but also possibly problematic) relationship between environmental impact assessment and strategic environmental assessment has been acknowledged by the Environment Directorate of the European Commission:

> It is very likely that the strong link of Directive 2001/42/EC, referred to as 'the SEA Directive' with the EIA Directive . . . will strengthen the administrative capacities of the respective authorities in the Member States in their assessment procedures and will complement in many cases the application and better implementation of the EIA Directive. Implementation is also likely to reveal some difficulties (e.g. the boundary with the EIA Directive and the definition of project).[194]

The relationship with other forms of environmental assessment is also addressed:

> Looking ahead, the 2006 review of the operation of the SEA Directive ought to address the relationship between it and the EIA Directive and the other directives which require

[192] Art. 3(2) SEA Directive 2001/42/EC OJ 2001 L 197, p. 30 on the assessment of the effects of certain plans and programmes on the environment.

[193] Arts. 6 and 7 Habitats Directive 92/43/EC OJ 1992 L 206, p. 7.

[194] Internal note to the Policy Group, DG Environment, on the *Five Years Report to the European Parliament and the Council on the Effectiveness of the EIA Directive* (Brussels: CEC, 2002), 12.

environmental assessments of some kind (for example, IPPC and Habitats). It may be that by then the time will be ripe for clarification of these relationships.[195]

The future convergence of forms of environmental assessment,[196] envisaged by the Commission and the subject of research,[197] is to some extent already provided for by the SEA Directive, which allows Member States to provide for coordinated or joint procedures fulfilling the requirements of other pieces of Community legislation in order to avoid the duplication of assessment procedures.[198] Further in terms of scope, the SEA Directive also applies to plans and programmes concerned with the use of small areas at local level and modifications to plans and programmes where Member States consider that they are likely to have significant environmental effects, and to those plans and programmes not listed in the EIA and Habitats Directives but which set the framework for future development consent concerning projects likely to have significant effects upon the environment.[199] The Directive does not apply to plans and programmes financed under the structural funds (until 2007).[200] The official reason for this is that such plans and programmes have already been put in place. In practice this provides scope for disintegrated policy making, at least until that date. However, even a broad-ranging model of strategic environmental assessment is not a panacea for the limitations of project-based assessment. Methodological problems experienced with environmental impact assessment are compounded when applied to higher level considerations. For example, it has proved difficult to separate out different stages in the formulation of a policy as discrete steps in a hierarchical or even chronological sequence and to identify boundaries to complex and often open-ended policy-making processes. Moreover, even where boundaries are set and discrete stages are identified, the dynamic nature of the policy process means that the implementation stage may well be critical in interpreting and thereby formulating policy. These amount to important conceptual problems in undertaking policy appraisal.[201] These are general observations. There are also more specific problems difficulties associated with strategic environmental assessment, such as securing meaningful participation.[202]

In summary, environmental assessment is now applied in many different contexts, but in the United Kingdom at least, it has been developed most fully in the planning system and remains closely tied to planning procedures and objectives. Within planning, environmental assessment has survived a substantial expansion of its remit: in early literature it was identified almost exclusively as a means of

[195] Internal note to the Policy Group, DG Environment, on the *Five Years Report to the European Parliament and the Council on the Effectiveness of the EIA Directive* (Brussels: CEC, 2002), 12.

[196] Discussed below pp. 73–4.

[197] IMPEL, *Report on the Interrelationship between the IPPC, EIA and SEVESO Directives and EMAS Regulation* (Brussels: CEC, 1998).

[198] Art. 11.

[199] Arts. 3(3) and 3(4).

[200] Art. 3(9).

[201] E. Wilson, 'Progress towards Strategic Environmental Assessment of Policies, Plans and Programmes', paper delivered at the IRNES conference on Perspectives on the Environment, September 1992.

[202] See particularly Ch. 6, p. 191.

controlling the harmful effects of pollution by influencing the siting of industry; in recent years it has been acknowledged as a means by which the principle of sustainable development may be 'implemented'. The development of environmental assessment may therefore be seen in light of its use as a mechanism for integrating environmental concerns into policy making in response to growing pressure from international organizations and the public that such concerns be given greater prominence. This development reflects many of the broader developments taking place simultaneously in the evolution of environmental law more generally.

## Sites of Environmental Assessment

Above I traced the development of different levels of environmental assessment (project- and policy-based) by focusing upon the expansion of environmental impact assessment into strategic environmental assessment in the context of Community law (the EIA and SEA Directives). Here the analysis shifts to multiple *sites* of decision making engaging environmental assessment by surveying some of the legal variations of environmental assessment that have evolved in different jurisdictional and functional contexts—land use control and planning, bio-diversity conservation, pollution control regimes, and development assistance.[203] In Chapter 1, I outlined the general characteristics of environmental assessment by reference to the EC EIA Directive. This was necessarily a simplified account of the form of environmental assessment, but other types of assessment follow a similar pattern, suggesting some convergence of the form of assessment and the adoption of common methodologies, at least with regard to these core requirements. Further sites of decision making not considered below include procedures concerning climate change[204] and activities in Antarctica.[205] Other relevant Conventions include the 1986 Noumea Convention[206] and the 1982 United Nations Convention on the Law of the Sea,[207] discussed in the context of the development of environmental assessment in international law.[208] On the domestic front, environmental assessment is becoming a feature of decision making in the utilities sector, for example a duty may be imposed on the Gas and Electricity Markets Authority to carry out impact assessments when 'proposing to do anything for the purposes of, or in connection with, the carrying out of any function exercisable by it . . . '.[209] This is a prime example of statutory backing for environmental assessments through primary legislation.

203 I discuss the development of environmental assessment by the European Commission separately, as an example of the ecologization of governance; Ch. 5, pp. 164–81.

204 Under the Climate Change Convention 31 ILM 849 (1992).

205 Antarctic Environment Protocol 30 ILM 1461 (1991).

206 Noumea Convention for the Protection of the Natural Resources and Environment of the South Pacific Region 26 ILM 38 (1986).

207 21 ILM 1261 (1982).

208 See above, pp. 53–6.

209 Sustainable Energy Bill, Clause 6, which would insert a new s. 5A into the Utilities Act 2000.

## Land Use

As discussed earlier in this chapter, land use control is the main and traditional site of decision making using environmental assessment instruments, within which environmental assessment methodologies and guidance have been developed because of the clear repercussions for environmental protection of decisions about the nature and location of development. In addition the inherently anticipatory nature of the planning system (due to the need to obtain development consent prior to development taking place—the licence) is reinforced by the predictive nature of environmental assessment. This compatibility is borne out by the Royal Commission on Environmental Pollution's presentation of environmental assessment as part of a suite of techniques of environmental planning, including also state of the environment reports, and auditing.[210]

Under the development control regimes of the United Kingdom, 363 environmental statements were prepared in 2002, divided between the main categories of project controlled by the town and country planning system.[211] In the case of England and Wales, these Regulations prohibit the grant of planning permission without consideration of environmental information for projects defined as 'EIA development'.[212] As Table 2.1 shows, this category makes up over half of all statements submitted. However, there has also been an increase in the number of statements submitted outside this system, particularly offshore oil and gas projects which were brought under the EIA regime in 1999.[213] The progression of proposals for which development consent is sought and which are subject to environmental assessment is considered in later chapters, including the determination of the proposed development's likely significance,[214] the requirement to consider alternatives, and to consult statutory consultees and public,[215] so that this is a necessarily truncated account of environmental assessment within decision making on land use.

Related to the specific application of environmental assessment rules in development-consent procedures is the environmental appraisal of development plans used to guide decision making at local and county levels.[216] This has been 'good practice' for several years,[217] reflecting that to some extent the process of

[210] Royal Commission on Environmental Pollution, Twenty-third Report, *Environmental Planning*, Cm 5459 (London: HMSO, 2002).

[211] Town and Country Planning (Environmental Impact Assessment) (England and Wales) Regulations 1999 (SI 1999, No. 293) (the 1999 Regulations), the Environmental Impact Assessment (Scotland) Regulations 1999 (SI 1999, No. 1), the Planning (Environmental Impact Assessment) Regulations (Northern Ireland) 1999 (SR 1999, No. 73). See further Appendix X.

[212] Reg. 3.

[213] Offshore Petroleum Production and Pipelines (Assessment of Environmental Effects) Regulations 1999 (SI 1999, No. 360).

[214] Ch. 4

[215] Ch. 6

[216] S. 54A Town and Country Planning Act 1990, as amended. The Planning and Compulsory Purchase Bill will overhaul the system of development planning in England and Wales by replacing the existing local and structure plans with local development documents and regional spatial strategies (see Parts I and II of the Bill).

[217] DETR, *Proposals for a Good Practice Guide on Sustainability Appraisal of Regional Planning Guidance* (GPG 25) (London: DETR, 2000). See generally, B. Dalal-Clayton, *Getting to Grips with Green Plans: National Level Experience in Industrial Countries* (London: Earthscan, 1996).

**Table 2.1** Environmental statements under different authorization regimes, 2002

| | Number | % of total | % change over 2000 |
|---|---|---|---|
| Planning, England | 363 | 52 | −1 |
| Planning, Scotland | 69 | 10 | +15 |
| Planning, Wales | 53 | 8 | +66 |
| Land drainage | 34 | 5 | +100 |
| Fish farms | 32 | 5 | +146 |
| Offshore oil and gas | 23 | 3 | +15 |
| Highways | 21 | 3 | +600 |
| Power stations/overhead lines | 16 | 2 | +14 |
| Forestry | 8 | 1 | +14 |
| Transport | 7 | 1 | −13 |
| Offshore wind/water generating | 7 | 1 | N/A[1] |
| Pipelines (gas) | 5 | 1 | −38 |
| Harbour works | 4 | 0.5 | −67 |
| Nuclear reactors | 2 | 0.5 | N/A[1] |
| Northern Ireland, all | 50 | 7 | +28 |

[1]N/A = not applicable (0 in 2000).

environmental appraisal of plans at the policy level is conceptually and practically similar to 'high level' environmental impact assessment, particulary in terms of making opportunities for public participation.[218] As discussed above, the EC SEA Directive now makes the process of environmental appraisal of development plans mandatory.[219] A related development is that the review of proposals in plans according to sustainability criteria looks set to move from 'good practice' to a statutory requirement,[220] the implications of which are discussed in Chapter 5.[221] With the broader 'sustainability' appraisal of development plans now likely, it is important that existing practice in appraising plans is patchy, with innovative approaches being taken by a number of local authorities, but also omissions in terms of procedures (for example, consideration of alternative policies) and content, such as a failure to describe the baseline condition of the environment, or to describe environmental objectives.[222] Predictably, environmental

218 An examination in public for structure plans roughly corresponded to requirements in environmental assessment regimes. This mode of participation is retained by the Planning and Compulsory Purchase Bill in the case of regional spatial strategies. The Bill will additionally require a statement of community involvement in the formation of local development documents (s. 17).

219 See above, pp. 60–5. On the relationship between the EIA Directive and development planning, see Case C-81/96 *B en W Haarlemmerliede en Spaarnwoude and Others* v *GS van Noord-Holland* [1998] ECR I-3923.

220 S. 5(4) Planning and Compulsory Purchase Bill.

221 Pp. 60–5.

222 J. M. Curran, C. Wood, and M. Hilton, 'Environmental Appraisal of UK (Local) Plans: Current Practice and Future Directions' (1998) *25 Environment and Planning B: Planning and Design* 411.

appraisal of plans at the local level has been instrumental in shaping the proposed strategy and policies rather than in recommending radical changes.[223]

## Conservation of Biological Diversity

The above account of the development of environmental impact assessment points to the fact that this was designed primarily as an instrument for environmental planning rather than for the conservation of biodiversity.[224] Nevertheless, the UN Convention on Biological Diversity[225] requires impact assessment studies to be conducted on 'proposed projects that are likely to have significant adverse effects on biological diversity in order to minimise their effects'.[226] Furthermore it requires parties to promote the exchange of information and consultation on activities under their jurisdiction or control which are likely to significantly affect the biological diversity of other states or areas beyond their jurisdiction and to provide immediate notification in the event of any imminent danger or damage to biodiversity.[227] This marks the utility of environmental assessment in identifying potential risks to biodiversity from development projects.[228] However, difficulties exist in this process of identification, for example the paucity of criteria for assessing the significance of impacts on biodiversity, particularly when compared with the employment of quality and emission standards in pollution control,[229] means that what constitutes a critical level for biodiversity loss is uncertain. A further difficulty is that in practice the onus of assessment tends to be on threatened species, whereas non-listed or endangered species also need to be taken into account to arrest any early decline.[230] Overall, though, it may be that the development of an information base through the assessment process may strengthen action taken to secure biodiversity in the long run.[231]

Within the European Union, the Habitats Directive[232] has impinged directly upon land use and development controls in the Member States. In order to fulfil Article 6 of this Directive,[233] in the United Kingdom a competent authority must make an 'appropriate assessment' in order to predict the implications of a project or plan for the conservation status of a 'European' site,[234] before deciding whether to grant planning permission for a project which is likely to have a significant

223 J. M. Curran, C. Wood, and M. Hilton, 'Environmental Appraisal of UK (Local) Plans: Current Practice and Future Directions' (1998) *25 Environment and Planning B: Planning and Design* 429.

224 On the ecological and biodiversity premises of environmental impact assessment, see Treweek, *Ecological Impact Assessment*.

225 31 ILM 822 (1992).

226 Art. 14(1)(a).

227 Art. 14(1)(c) and (d).

228 As recognized, for example by G. Wynne (ed.) *Biodiversity Challenge: An Agenda for Conservation Action in the UK* (Sandy: RSPB, 1993) which advocates that environmental appraisal should be widely carried out as a guiding principle of biodiversity.

229 Treweek, *Ecological Impact Assessment*, 36.

230 ibid.

231 For example by providing baseline information for biodiversity action plans, as discussed by Treweek, *Ecological Impact Assessment*.

232 Council Directive 92/43/EC on the conservation of natural habitats and of wild fauna and flora (OJ L 206, 21.5.1992).

233 See Appendix IX.

234 The term 'European site' includes both Special Protection Areas, as defined by Directive 79/409/EEC on the conservation of wild birds, OJ L 103, 25.12.1979, and Special Areas of Conservation designated for the purposes of the Habitats Directive.

effect.[235] In the absence of alternative solutions and notwithstanding a negative assessment of the implications of the plan or project for the site's conservation objectives, a local planning authority may grant planning permission for a project if they are satisfied that it must be carried out for imperative reasons of overriding public interest, which may be of a social or economic nature, and if compensatory measures are taken. However, where the site concerned hosts a so-called priority, or particularly endangered, natural habitat type or species, then the planning authority may only grant planning permission for reasons relating 'to human health or public safety, to beneficial consequences of primary importance for the environment, or further to an Opinion from the Commission, to other imperative reasons of overriding public interest'.[236] A two-tier system of protection therefore operates with the effect that greater weight in decision making is given to information relating to a priority European habitat site or species, thus making development consent more difficult to obtain. The main point to take from this is that species and habitats of European conservation importance should be accorded substantive respect and protection in the national legal systems of the European Union.

The trigger for an assessment under the Habitats Regulations is almost identical to that for the purposes of the 1999 Regulations (for environmental impact assessment for the purposes of the town and country planning system)[237]—the likely significant effects of the proposed plan or project on the environment—except that these effects are more closely prescribed in the Habitats Regulations as affecting a site's 'conservation objectives'. The obligations contained in the Habitats Directive do not replicate exactly the provisions of the EIA Directive, the procedural details of which are more extensively described, particularly with regard to participation requirements. The European Commission has provided guidance that where an 'appropriate assessment' takes the form of an assessment under national legislation on EIA (in line with the EC EIA Directive), this will 'provide obvious assurances in terms of records and transparency'.[238] However, this raises the question as to what may be considered an 'appropriate assessment' where an assessment for the purposes of the Habitats Regulations does not take the form of assessment under the EIA regime. The Commission's answer is that an 'appropriate assessment' should be capable of being recorded, that it should be reasoned (in the light of particular information relating to the environment) and timely, taking place before the decision to approve or refuse the plan or project.[239] The relationship between appropriate assessments under the Habitats Regulations 1994 and the 1999 (EIA) Regulations

[235] Reg 48 Conservation (Natural Habitats &c.) Regulations 1994 (SI 1994, No. 2716) ('the Habitat Regulations 1994').

[236] Reg. 49 of the Habitats Regulations 1994, implementing Art. 6(4) of the Habitats Directive. On the Commission's Opinions on imperative reasons, see Ch. 5, pp. 158–62.

[237] Reg. 48 (1)(a) requires that 'a competent authority, before deciding to undertake, or give any consent, permission or other authorisation for, a plan or project which is likely to have a significant effect on a European site in Great Britain . . . shall make an appropriate assessment of the implications for the site in view of that site's conservation objectives'.

[238] European Commission, *Managing Natura 2000 Sites* (Brussels: CEC, 2000), para. 4.5.1.

[239] ibid.

is further complicated by guidance issued by the Environment Agency.[240] This advises that in carrying out an 'appropriate assessment', the applicant may be required to carry out a full environmental impact assessment under the 1999 Regulations (to 'aid the appropriate assessment process').[241] This variance in guidance strongly suggests the practicality of conducting a single assessment for the fulfilment of biodiversity and environmental planning objectives.

## Pollution Controls and Water Resources

A similar conclusion is reached when considering the potential for overlaps in carrying out environmental assessments for pollution control and water resource purposes. Under the system of pollution prevention and control established by the 1999 Act,[242] an application for a permit to operate an industrial (or in certain circumstances, agricultural) activity, must be accompanied by a wide variety of information, including information on the condition of the site and any associated pollution risks, the raw materials and energy used in carrying out the activity, waste minimization and prevention measures, the foreseeable emissions and environmental effects of the activity, information on the technology and other techniques used for reducing emissions and other environmental impacts and arrangements for monitoring impacts. This body of information must be accompanied by a non-technical summary. These requirements echo those under the 1999 (EIA) Regulations. This was perhaps more clearly the case with the previous integrated pollution control regime in which an explicit reference to the 'best practicable environmental option'[243] required an assessment of the various pathways and environmental effects of different operating options, thus bringing the concept into line with environmental assessment. Although the Pollution Prevention and Control regime under the 1999 Act does not have any corresponding requirement to undertake an assessment of the best practicable environmental option for an activity, an operator has to consider all of the environmental impacts of an activity (including a wide-ranging obligation to return a site to a satisfactory state after an installation has closed). It has recently been confirmed that a planning authority (but equally the Environment Agency) must base its decision about an application for waste disposal facilities (whether for a waste management licence, a pollution prevention and control permit, or planning permission) on the outcome of a properly structured process which identifies the best practicable environmental option for the waste stream involved.[244]

[240] Environment Agency, Habitats Directive: Executive Summary (providing guidance for English Nature and the Countryside Council for Wales, both of which constitute a 'competent authority' for the 1994 Regulations).

[241] At p. 4.

[242] Pollution Prevention and Control Act 1999, augmented by the Pollution Prevention and Control (England and Wales) Regulations 2000 (SI 2000, No. 1973).

[243] S. 7(7) Environmental Protection Act 1990.

[244] *Blewett* v *Derbyshire County Council* [2003] EWHC 2775 (Admin), Sullivan J. On the implications of this, see D. Wolfe, 'A Duty to Find the Least Worst Option?' (2004) 17e-law(u.k. environmental law association e-journal).

More specific environmental assessment requirements exist with regard to water resources, as a result of the need to implement the provisions of the amended EIA Directive, which extended the range of projects to which the Directive applies to include groundwater abstraction, artificial recharge of groundwater, or the transfer of water resources between river basins. In terms of overlap with existing environmental assessment requirements, where planning permission is required for a project involving water resources, the need for an assessment is linked to the planning process, but where no planning permission is required, the need for an environmental assessment will be linked to the need to obtain a licence from the Environment Agency.[245] The similarities in the relative duties of the planning authorities and Environment Agency suggest that a unified approach to environmental assessment within the two systems of environmental control appears likely.

## Development Assistance

Instruments such as the Espoo Convention, and other environmental impact assessment regimes have been considered to be the product of developed countries, reflecting a common outlook that projects having significant environmental impacts in another country must be reviewed.[246] This observation is difficult to sustain when the nature of disputes heard before the International Court of Justice (particularly the *MOX* case)[247] is considered. It is even more difficult to support when the application of environmental assessment is addressed in the context of development assistance in which the environmental consequences of projects (particularly large-scale infrastructure development) are more easily obscured by donor countries and lending institutions. However, as mentioned above in the context of the development of environmental assessment regimes,[248] it is now commonplace for multilateral development banks to incorporate environmental assessment into their approval procedures. Notwithstanding a slow process of standardization, such procedures vary greatly between institutions. There is, for example, no international set of guidelines for use by all such banks (and development assistance agencies) in conducting an environmental assessment. This means that when lending or development assistance is at stake 'EIA requirements are often eased if not exempted'.[249] Perez, for example, highlights in this context the advent of the 'Pseudo-EIA' which is carried out with the single objective of securing a project, irrespective of its true environmental costs.[250]

245 By virtue of the Water Resources (Environmental Impact Assessment) (England and Wales) Regulations 2003 (SI 2003, No. 164).

246 Gray, 'International Environmental Impact Assessment', at 104.

247 See above, p. 56.

248 See pp. 44–5 on the accommodation of environmental impact assessment procedures in international organizations and multinational banks.

249 Gray, 'International Environmental Impact Assessment', at 196.

250 O. Perez, 'Using Private-Public Linkages to Regulate Environmental Conflicts: The Case of International Construction Contracts' (2002) 29 *JLS* 77, at 94, which further examines the content of construction contracts for enforceable environmental obligations.

In the case of the World Bank, environmental assessment procedures have been applied since 1989.[251] These now include an Operation Policy which requires an environmental assessment of projects to be financed by the Bank. The extent and type of environmental impact assessment to be conducted in each case depends upon a judgment of a project's likely significance. The scope of assessment is broad, in keeping with the 'mainstreaming' of environmental considerations; an environmental impact assessment should cover 'the natural environment (air, water and land), human health and safety; social aspects (involuntary resettlement, indigenous people and cultural property); and transnational and global environmental aspects'.[252] A sticking point in the procedures for assessment is public participation, with World Bank project personnel often failing to solicit a variety of cultural perspectives and adjusting the process in a way that is amenable to the values of the community likely to be affected by a project.[253] A necessary review procedure was introduced in 1993 by the establishment of an Inspection Panel with the authority to make recommendations to the Board of the Bank, and ensure compliance with the Operational Policy. An inescapable conclusion, however, is that approval of projects, even those subject to the Bank's internal environmental assessment rules, will result in funds being allocated to private construction corporations often operating on a global scale, and governed by contractual obligations which rarely feature environmental considerations.[254]

The WCED Experts Group[255] suggested that an international assessment body be created to help developing countries assess the environmental impact of planned development projects, but no such body was established. This suggestion has recently been revived in the form of an international Commission for Environmental Impact Assessment, proposed by the Dutch EIA Commission. The Commission envisages a membership organization, by which experts are called upon to judge the completeness and quality of environmental information supporting decision making (but with no say upon the social and environmental acceptability of an intended project or policy).[256] Attempts such as this suggest not just the widespread use of environmental assessment, but also the need to implement generally agreed minimum standards for environmental assessment.

## Conclusions

The evolution of environmental assessment has spanned several decades and has taken place in greatly varying contexts. One aim of this chapter was to give a sense

[251] For a critique of the early form of assessment, including the failure of the assessment regime to mandate public participation of those affected by the Bank's decisions, see Sands, *Principles of International Environmental Law*, 821.

[252] Operational Policy 4.01 (1991) 5P3. See World Bank, *Mainstreaming the Environment: The World Bank Group and the Environment since the Rio Earth Summit* (Washington: World Bank, 1995).

[253] Gray, 'International Environmental Impact Assessment', at 112.

[254] Perez, 'Using Private-Public Linkages'.

[255] *Legal Principles*.

[256] This proposal is still at the formative stages, see http://www.geocities.com/iciaos/Mission1.html.

of the panorama of environmental assessment—informal assessment, statutory assessment, public and private forms, wide-ranging assessment, and assessment applied to specific concerns—from which three trends can be identified. First, is the convergence of the form of environmental assessment. Notwithstanding the many different applications and sites of environmental assessment, the process[257] is remarkably consistent, as seen by the similarity of various forms of assessment (contained in national, European Union, and international law).[258] This means that in practice a single project, or policy area, may be subject to several similar forms of environmental assessment operating at different levels. For this reason there are indications of the development of a unitary environmental assessment procedure, at least for obtaining development and pollution control consents.[259] For example, the preamble to the SEA Directive permits that where the obligation to carry out assessments of the effects on the environment arises simultaneously from the SEA Directive and other Community legislation such as the Wild Birds Directive, Habitats Directive, or Water Framework Directive, in order to avoid duplication of the assessment, Member States may provide for coordinated or joint procedures fulfilling the requirements of the relevant Community legislation.[260] This raises an issue of the responsiveness of environmental assessment, when engaging common assessment methodologies, to different legal and political contexts. Second, there has been a clear expansion of the remit of environmental assessment, so that the environmental assessment process is increasingly being used to take account of social and economic impacts, in recognition of the indivisible and interrelated nature of environmental problems, popularized by the concept of sustainable development. Ultimately, a form of 'sustainability assessment' may override the more specific forms of environmental impact assessment and strategic environmental assessment.[261] A less amenable consequence of this expansion is the identification of potential trade-offs between social, economic, and environmental 'resources' which may be acted upon in decision making. This absorption of the concept of sustainable development in environmental assessment clearly reflects the more general evolution and mainstreaming of environmental law. The third trend, related to the expansion of subject matter in environmental assessment, is the accommodation of multiple levels of decision making, seen most clearly in the development of strategic environmental assessment at European Union and international levels.

I continue to track the parallel development of environmental assessment and environmental law in the following chapters by considering environmental assessment as a gauge for the arrival and fulfilment of new forms of environmental

[257] Outlined in Figure 2.1, p. 36.

[258] Several of which are reproduced in the Appendices to this book.

[259] For example, in EC law, the assessment of effects upon the environment required by Directive 96/61/EC OJ L 275, also suffices for the purposes of the EC Directive on EIA, as urged by UKELA, *Overlaps in the Requirements for Environmental Assessment* (London: UKELA, 1993).

[260] See also Art. 2a of the EIA Directive with regard to a joint procedure for the purpose of fulfilling EIA and IPPC procedural requirements.

[261] I consider this process in greater detail in Ch. 5, pp. 164–82.

regulation. In particular, I highlight aspects of environmental assessment which serve to demonstrate the broader development of environmental law—recognition of the need for interdisciplinary inquiry,[262] expansion of environmental concern to take into account social and economic conditions,[263] and enhancing opportunities for participation.[264] I explain how the environmental assessment process gives rise to these issues by analysing its main constituent parts, the first of which is the central requirement that the effects of development be predicted prior to consent being granted, or a policy or programme being adopted.

262 Ch. 3. 263 Ch. 5.
264 Ch. 6.

## References


Alder, J. 'Environmental Impact Assessment: The Inadequacies of English Law' (1993) 5 *JEL* 203.

Bateman, I. J. 'Environmental Impact Assessment, Cost-Benefit Analysis and the Valuation of Environmental Impacts', in Petts, J. (ed.) *Handbook of Environmental Impact Assessment: Vol. I Process, Methods and Potential* (Oxford: Blackwell, 1999).

Becker, J. and Wood, G. *Scoping Decision Making under the Town and Country Planning (Environmental Impact Assessment) (England and Wales) Regulations 1999* (Oxford: Oxford Brookes University, 2003).

Beggs, J. 'Combating Biospheric Degradation: International Environmental Impact Assessment and the Transboundary Pollution Dilemma' (1995) *Fordham Env L J* 379.

Blowers, A. (ed.) *Planning for a Sustainable Future* (London: Earthscan, 1993).

Bosselman, F. P. and Tarlock, A. D. 'The Influence of Ecological Science on American Law' (1994) 69 *Chicago-Kent L Rev* 847.

Botkin, D. B. *Discordant Harmonies: A New Ecology for the Twenty-First Century* (Oxford: Oxford University Press, 1990).

Bregman, E. and Jacobsen, A. 'Environmental Performance Review: Self-Regulation in Environmental Law', in Teubner, G. Farmer, L. and Murphy, D. (eds.) *Environmental Law and Ecological Responsibility: The Concept and Practice of Ecological Self-Organisation* (Chichester: Wiley, 1994).

Caldwell, L. K. *Science and the National Environmental Policy Act: Redirecting Policy through Procedural Reform* (Alabama: Alabama University Press, 1982).

Clark, B. D. 'Environmental Impact Assessment: Scope and Objectives', in Clark, B. D. Bissett, R., and Gilad, A. (eds.) *Perspectives on Environmental Impact Assessment* (New York: Reidel, 1984).

Clark, M. 'Environmental Impact Assessment: An Ideology for Europe' (1978) *TCP* 395.

Clarke, T. 'Environmental Assessment and Sustainable Development' (1991) 6 *EIA* 2.

Council for the Protection of Rural England, *Sense and Sustainability: Land Use Planning and Environmental Sustainable Development* (London: CPRE, 1993).

Curran, J. M., Wood, C., and Hilton, M. 'Environmental Appraisal of UK (Local) Plans: Current Practice and Future Directions' (1998) 25 *Environment and Planning B: Planning and Design* 411.

Dalal-Clayton, B. *Getting to Grips with Green Plans: National Level Experience in Industrial Countries* (London: Earthscan, 1996).

Department of the Environment, Circular 4/79 *Memorandum on Structure and Local Plans* (London: HMSO, 1979).

——— *Implementation of the European Directive on Environmental Assessment* (London: HMSO, 1986.

——— Circular 15/88 (Welsh Office 23/88) *Environmental Assessment* (London: HMSO, 1988).

——— *Monitoring Environmental Assessment and Planning* (London: HMSO, 1990).

Department of the Environment, Transport and the Regions, Circular 02/99, *Environmental Impact Assessment* (London: HMSO, 1999).

——— *Proposals for a Good Practice Guide on Sustainability Appraisal of Regional Planning Guidance* (GPG 25) (London: DETR, 2000).

European Commission, Fourth Environmental Action Programme, COM(86) 485 final (Brussels: CEC, 1987).
——— Fifth Environmental Action Programme, *Towards Sustainability: A European Community Programme of Policy and Action in Relation to the Environment and Sustainable Development*, COM(92) 23 final (Brussels: CEC, 1992).
——— *Report from the Commission on the Implementation of Directive 85/337/EEC on the Assessment of the Effects of Certain Public and Private Projects on the Environment*, COM(93) 28, 2.4.1993 (Brussels: CEC, 1993).
——— *Managing Natura 2000 Sites* (Brussels: CEC, 2000).
——— *SEA and the Integration of the Environment into Strategic Decision Making* (Brussels: CEC, 2001).
——— *Five Years Report to the European Parliament and the Council on the Effectiveness of the EIA Directive* (Brussels: CEC, 2002).
——— *Indirect and Cumulative Impacts and Impact Interactions* (Brussels: CEC, 2002).
Garner, J. and O'Riordan, T. 'Environmental Impact Assessment in the Context of Economic Recession' (1982) 148 *Geog J* 343.
Gilpin, A. *Environmental Impact Assessment: Cutting Edge for the Twenty-First Century* (Cambridge: Cambridge University Press, 1995).
Giroult, E. 'World Health Organisation Interest in Environmental Health Impact Assessment', in Wathern, P. (ed.) *Environmental Impact Assessment: Theory and Practice* (London: Routledge, 1988).
Gouge, E. 'The UK Implementation of Environmental Assessment: Organisational and Political Implications' [1989] *Local Government Policy Making* 55.
Grant, M. 'Implementation of the EC Directive on Environmental Impact Assessment', (1989) 4 *Conn J of Int L* 463.
Gray, K. 'International Environmental Impact Assessment: Potential for a Multilateral Environmental Agreement' [2000] *Col J of Int Env L and Policy* 83.
Haigh, N. 'The EEC Directive on Environmental Assessment of Development Projects' [1983] *J of Plg and Env Law* 585.
Hajer, M. A. *The Politics of Environmental Discourse: Ecological Modernisation and the Policy Process* (Oxford: Oxford University Press, 1997).
Heinelt, H., Malek, T., Smith, R., and Toller, A. E. (eds.) *European Union Environmental Policy and New Forms of Governance* (Aldershot: Ashgate, 2001).
Herington, J. 'Environmental Values in a Changing Planning System', in Clark, M. and Herington, J. (eds.) *The Role of Environmental Impact Assessment in the Planning Process* (London: Mansell, 1998).
Hertz, M. 'Parallel Universes: NEPA Lessons for the New Property' (1993) 93 *Columbia L Rev* 1668.
Holder, J. *'An Analysis of Council Directive 85/337/EEC on the Assessment of the Effects of Certain Public and Private Projects on the Environment and the Development of Environmental Law in the United Kingdom'* (Ph.D., University of Warwick, 1995).
House of Commons Environment Committee, Fifth Report, *Planning Appeals and Call-in and Major Public Inquiries*, Session 1985–86 HC 181, Cm 43.
House of Lords Select Committee on the European Communities, Eleventh Report, *Environmental Assessment of Projects*, Session 1980–81 (London: HMSO, 1981).
Htun, M. N. 'Development of United Nations Environment Programme Guidelines for Assessing Industrial Criteria for the Siting of Industry', in Clark, B. D., Bissett, R. and

Gilad, A. (eds.) *Perspectives on Environmental Impact Assessment* (New York: Reidel, 1984).
Hutton, N. *Lay Participation in a Public Inquiry: A Sociological Case Study* (London: Gower, 1986).
IMPEL, *Report on the Interrelationship between IPPC, EIA* and *SEVESO Directives and EMAS Regulation* (Brussels: CEC, 1998).
Institute of Environmental Assessment, *Practical Experience of Environmental Assessment in the United Kingdom* (East Kirkby: Institute of Environmental Assessment, 1993).
Jacobs, M. *The Green Economy* (London: Pluto Press, 1993).
Kemp, R. 'Planning, Legitimation and the Development of Nuclear Power: A Critical Theoretic Analysis of the Windscale Inquiry' (1986) 14 *Policy and Politics* 350.
Kennedy, W. V. 'Environmental Impact Assessment and Bilateral Development Aid: An Overview', in Wathern, P. (ed.) *Environmental Impact Assessment: Theory and Practice* (London: Routledge, 1988).
Ledger, M. J. 'An Assessment of the Effectiveness of Land Use Planning Powers to Control Pollition', Unpublished Ph.D. thesis (University of Manchester, 1982).
Lichfield, N. *Community Impact Ealuation: Principles and Practice* (London: University College Press, 1996).
McAuslan, P. *Ideologies of Planning Law* (Oxford: Permagon Press, 1980).
McKibben, W. T. *The End of Nature* (Random House, 1989).
Macrory, R. 'Environmental Assessment: Critical Legal Issues in Implementation', in Vaughan, D. (ed.) *EC Environmental and Planning Law* (London: Butterworths, 1986).
Miller, C. and Wood, C. *Planning and Pollution: An Examination of the Role of Land Use Planning in the Protection of Environmental Quality* (Oxford: Oxford University Press, 1983.
Montini, M. 'Habitats Impact Assessment: An Effective Instrument for Biodiversity Conservation' (2001) 9 *Env Liab* 182.
Morgan, B. 'The Economisation of Politics' (2003) 12 *SLS* 489.
Morgan, R. K. *Environmental Impact Assessment: A Methodological Perspective* (Dordrecht: Kluwer, 1999).
Morris, P. and Therivel, R. (eds.) *Methods of Environmental Impact Assessment* (London: Spon, 2nd edn., 2001).
Munn, R. E. (ed.) *Environmental Impact Assessment: Principles and Procedures* (New York: John Wiley, 1979).
Organization for Economic Cooperation and Development, *Coordinated Methods of Assessing the Potential Environmental Effects of Chemical Compounds*, C(74)215 (Paris: OECD, 1974).
——— *Environmental Consequences of Significant Public and Private Projects*, C(74)216 (Paris: OECD, 1974).
——— *Coordination Guidelines in Respect of Procedures and Requirements for Anticipating the Effects of Chemicals on Man and the Environment*, C(77)97 final (Paris: OECD, 1977).
——— *The Assessment of Projects with Significant Impact on the Environment*, C(79)116 (Paris: OECD, 1979).
——— *Recommendation of the Council on Measures Required to Facilitate the Environmental Assessment of Development Assistance Projects and Programmes*, C(86)26 (Paris: OECD, 1986).

O'Riordan, T. and Hey, R. D. (eds.) *Environmental Impact Assessment* (Farnborough: Saxon House, 1976).

Pearce, D. W., Markandya, A. and Barbier, E. *Blueprint for a Green Economy* (London: Earthscan, 1989).

Perez, O. 'Using Private-Public Linkages to Regulate Environmental Conflicts: The Case of International Construction' (2002) 29 *JLS* 77.

Petts, J. (ed.) 'EIA: Overview of Purpose and Process', in Petts, J. (ed.) *Handbook of Environmental Impact Assessment: Vol. I Process, Methods and Potential* (Oxford: Blackwell, 1999).

Popham, J. and Purdue, M. 'The Future of the Major Inquiry' [2002] *JPL* 137.

Royal Commission on Environmental Pollution, *Air Pollution Control: An Integrated Approach* Cmnd 6371 (London: HMSO, 1976).

——— *Setting Environmental Standards*, Twenty-First Report, Cm 4053 (London: HMSO, 1998).

——— *Environmental Planning*, Twenty-Third Report, Cm 5459 (London: HMSO, 2002).

Royal Institute of Chartered Surveyors, *Environmental Assessments* (London: RICS, 1989).

Sadler, B. 'Environmental Sustainability Assessment and Assurance', in Petts, J. (ed.) *Handbook of EIA: Vol. I Process, Methods and Potential* (Oxford: Blackwell, 1999).

Salter, J. 'EIA: The Question of Implementation' [1992] *JPL* 313.

——— 'EIA: The Challenge from Brussels' [1992] *JPL* 14.

Sands, P. *Principles of International Environmental Law* (Cambridge: Cambridge University Press, 2nd edn., 2003.

Selman, P. H. 'The Use of Ecological Evaluations by Local Planning Authorities' (1982) 15 *J of Env Plg and Management* 1.

Sheate, W. *The Environmental Assessment Directive: Five Years On* (London: Council for the Protection of Rural England, 1991).

——— 'From Environmental Impact Assessment to Strategic Environmental Assessment: Sustainability and Decision-Making', in Holder, J. (ed.) *The Impact of EC Environmental Law in the United Kingdom* (Chichester: Wiley, 1997).

Skegley, S. I. *The Human Rights Obligations of the World Bank and Monetary Fund* (London: Cavendish, 2001).

Smith, R. 'The Implementation of EIA in Britain', in Heinelt, H., Malek, T., Smith, R. and Toller, A. E. (eds.) *European Union Environment Policy and new Forms of Governance* (Aldershot: Ashgate, 2001).

Taylor, S. *Making Bureaucracies Think: The Environmental Impact Statement Strategy of Administrative Reform* (Stanford: Calif.: Stanford University Press, 1984).

Treweek, J. *Ecological Impact Assessment* (Oxford: Blackwell, 1999).

Tromans, S. and Roger-Machart, C. 'Strategic Environmental Assessment: Early Evaluation Equals Efficiency?' [1997] *JPL* 993.

UKELA (United Kingdom Environmental Law Association), *Overlaps in the Requirements for Environmental Assessment* (London: UKELA, 1993).

United Nations Environment Programme, *Guidelines for Assessing Industrial Environmental Impact and Criteria for the Siting of Industry* (Paris: UNEP, 1980).

Von Moltke, K. 'Environmental Impact Assessment in the United States and Europe', in Clarke, B. D., Bissett, R. and Gilad, A. (eds.) *Perspectives on Environmental Impact Assessments* (New York: Reidel, 1984).

Ward, A. 'The Right to an Effective Remedy in European Community Law and Environmental Protection: A Case Study of United Kingdom Jucicial Decisions concerning the Environmental Assessment Directive' (1993) 5 *JEL* 221.

Wathern, P. (ed.) *Environmental Impact Assessement: Theory and Practice* (London: Routledge, 1988).

——— 'The EIA Directive of the European Community', in Wathern, P. (ed.) *Environmental Impact Assessment: Theory and Practice* |(London: Routledge, 1988).

Weale, A., Pridham, G. *et al.* (eds.) *Environmental Governance in Europe: An Ever Closer Ecological Union* (Oxford: Oxford University Press, 2000).

Wilson, E. 'Progress towards Strategic Environmental Assessment of Policies, Plans and Programmes', paper delivered at the IRNES conference on Perspectives on the Environment, September 1992.

Wood, C. *Planning Pollution Prevention: A Comparison of the Siting Controls over Air Pollution in Great Britain and the USA* (Oxford: Heinemann Newnes, 1989).

——— 'Five Years of British Environmental Assessment', in Cross, D. and Whitehead, C. (eds.) *Development and Planning* (Cambridge: Cambridge University Press, 1994).

——— and Jones, C. 'The Impact of Environmental Assessment on Local Planning Authorities' (1992) 35 *JEPM* 115.

Wood, G. and Becker, J. *Screening Decision Making under the Town and Country Planning (Environmental Impact Assessment) Regulations 1999* (Oxford: Oxford Brookes University, 2003).

World Bank, *The World Bank and the Environment: First Annual Report* (Washington: World Bank, 1990).

——— *Maintaining the Environment: The World Bank Group and the Environment since the Rio Earth Summit* (Washington: World Bank, 1995).

World Commission on Environment and Development, *Our Common Future* (Oxford: Oxford University Press, 1987).

——— WCED Experts Group on Environmental Law, *Legal Principles for Environmental Protection and Sustainable Development* (Dordrecht: Martinus Nijhoff, 1987).

World Health Organization, *Rapid Assessment of Sources of Air, Water and Land Pollution Resolution* WHO/35.17 (Geneva: WHO, 1982).

# Part III
# Environmental Regulation, Policy and Governance

# [10]

Annu. Rev. Environ. Resour. 2006. 31:297–325
doi: 10.1146/annurev.energy.31.042605.135621

First published online as a Review in Advance on July 5, 2006

# ENVIRONMENTAL GOVERNANCE

Maria Carmen Lemos and Arun Agrawal
*School of Natural Resources and Environment, University of Michigan, Ann Arbor, Michigan 48109; email: lemos@umich.edu, arunagra@umich.edu*

**Key Words** climate change, cogovernance, decentralization, ecosystem degradation, globalization, market

■ **Abstract** This chapter reviews the literature relevant to environmental governance in four domains of scholarship: globalization, decentralization, market and individual incentives-based governance, and cross-scale governance. It argues that in view of the complexity and multiscalar character of many of the most pressing environmental problems, conventional debates focused on pure modes of governance–where state or market actors play the leading role–fall short of the capacity needed to address them. The review highlights emerging hybrid modes of governance across the state-market-community divisions: comanagement, public-private partnerships and social-private partnerships. It examines the significant promise they hold for coupled social and natural systems to recover from environmental degradation and change and explores some of the critical problems to which hybrid forms of environmental governance are also subject.

CONTENTS



## INTRODUCTION

The Millennium Ecosystem Assessment, perhaps the most ambitious and extensive examination of the state of Earth's ecosystems, outlines what might reasonably be expected to happen to them under different future scenarios (1). Its conclusions are pessimistic; the changes required to address the declining resilience of ecosystems are large and currently not under way. It ends with a discussion of the types of responses that can lead to sustainable management of ecosystems. Ostensibly, only the first of these responses focuses directly on institutions and governance—the subject of this review. Others concern economics and incentives, social and behavioral factors, technology, knowledge and cognition, and decision-making processes. Although some of these other responses may seem unrelated to environmental governance, in reality, the effectiveness of every single one of them depends on significant changes in existing strategies of environmental governance.

Our chapter reviews the literature on environmental governance to examine how different approaches have attempted to address some of the most pressing environmental challenges of our time: global climate change, ecosystem degradation, and the like. We find that a significant proportion of this literature has tended to emphasize a particular agent of environmental governance as being the most effective—typically market actors, state actors and, more recently, civil society-based actors such as nongovernmental organizations (NGOs) and local communities.

Today, a broad array of hybrid environmental governance strategies are being practiced, and it has become clear that seemingly purely market-, state-, or civil society-based governance strategies depend for their efficacy on support from other domains of social interactions. Our discussion examines the importance of spatial and institutional scales to environmental governance, focusing especially on emerging hybrid forms. Of significant interest to our review are (*a*) soft governance strategies that try to align market and individual incentives with self-regulatory processes and (*b*) cogovernance, which is predicated on partnerships and notions of embedded autonomy across state-market-society divisions (2, 3). These innovations in environmental governance can potentially be extended to engage multiple types of environmental problems and conflicts.

## DEFINING ENVIRONMENTAL GOVERNANCE

For the purposes of this review, environmental governance is synonymous with interventions aiming at changes in environment-related incentives, knowledge, institutions, decision making, and behaviors. More specifically, we use "environmental governance" to refer to the set of regulatory processes, mechanisms and organizations through which political actors influence environmental actions and outcomes. Governance is not the same as government. It includes the actions of the state and, in addition, encompasses actors such as communities, businesses, and NGOs. Key to different forms of environmental governance are the political-economic relationships that institutions embody and how these relationships shape identities, actions, and outcomes (4–6). International accords, national policies and legislation, local decision-making structures, transnational institutions, and environmental NGOs are all examples of the forms through which environmental governance takes place. Because governance can be shaped through nonorganizational institutional mechanisms as well (for example, when it is based on market incentives and self-regulatory processes), there is no escaping it for anyone concerned about environmental outcomes. Environmental governance is varied in form, critical in importance, and near ubiquitous in spread.

To investigate emerging trends in environmental governance in a way that is both sufficiently general for a review and reflects ongoing changes in the world of governance, we focus on four themes around which some of the most interesting writings on environmental governance cluster. The ensuing discussion first reviews the scholarship on globalization, decentralized environmental governance, market- and individual-focused instruments (MAFIs), and governance across scales to uncover how the conventional roles and capacities of important actors and institutions are getting reconfigured. This discussion leads us to a framework through which approaches to environmental governance and the terrain of environmental governance can usefully be explored. We apply insights from this framework to two sets of consequential environmental problems: global climate change and ecosystem degradation. We identify important limitations of hybrid forms of environmental governance and conclude with a discussion of some of the implications of ongoing developments related to environmental governance.

## THEMES IN ENVIRONMENTAL GOVERNANCE

The four themes upon which we focus below—globalization, decentralized environmental governance, market- and individual-focused instruments, and governance across scales—are among the most important emerging trends that are shaping environmental governance. They are generating pressures for innovative ways to address environmental and natural resource crises and challenging existing forms of governance. They are emblematic of the possibilities present in efforts to engage seriously with environmental problems, and their shortcomings are a reason to be concerned about the extent to which environmental actors have the capacity to deal with worsening environmental dilemmas. Although we treat each of these themes distinctly below, it goes without saying that there are close, perhaps even causal, connections among them, even if a review permits only speculation about how they may be related.

### Globalization and Environmental Governance

Globalization describes an interconnected world across environments, societies, and economies. Multiplicity, diversity, interdependence, and flows of influence and materials are common themes associated with globalization even if there is significant disagreement about its definition, implications, impacts, and usefulness as a concept (7–10). (See References 11–13 for definitions and implications of globalization.)

From an environmental perspective, globalization produces both negative and positive pressures on governance. Economic globalization produces tremendous impacts on environmental processes at the local, regional, national, and global levels. By integrating far-flung markets and increasing demand, globalization may intensify the use and depletion of natural resources, increase waste production, and lead to a "race to the bottom" as capital moves globally to countries and locations that have less stringent environmental standards (14–17). Most free trade regimes—facilitated by and assisting globalization—provide limited or inadequate environmental provisions and insufficient safeguards for their enforcement (18–20). Analogously, despite evidence of the negative effect of international trade on carbon-dioxide emissions, it remains uncertain how economic provisions of trade agreements such as those of the World Trade Organization (WTO) intersect with the goals of climate regimes such as the Kyoto Protocol (15). Additionally, the global flow of energy, materials, and organisms through the environment, which Clark labels "environmental stuff," "couples the actions of people in one place with the threats and opportunities faced by people long distances away" (21, p. 86).

By broadening the range of problems national governments are called upon to address, globalization strains the resources of nation states at the same time as it may contribute to socioeconomic inequalities. These pressures can ultimately enhance levels of vulnerability to climate change and other environmental threats (22). Finally, neoliberal policy reforms associated with globalization may complicate the efficacy of state action by shifting power to alternative actors and levels of decision making through decentralization and privatization as well as through the use of MAFIs (see below).

Observers of globalization also argue in favor of its potentially positive impacts on economic equity and environmental standards through a virtuous circle and the diffusion of positive environmental policy initiatives. Clearly, the globalization of environmental problems has contributed to the creation and development of new global regimes, institutions, and organizations dedicated to environmental governance. More efficient use and transfer of technology, freer flow of information, and novel institutional arrangements based on public-private partnerships have the potential to contribute positively to environmental governance (23, 24).

Globalization can also enhance the depth of participation and the diversity of actors shaping environmental governance. For instance, the globalization of social action through international environmental groups expands the role of social movements, so that they can produce deep social changes across national boundaries instead of being limited to negotiations with governments within a nation state (25). By introducing new ways of organizing, interacting, and influencing governmental processes, globalization can help increase the social and political relevance of non-state actors such as NGOs, transnational environmental networks, and epistemic communities—defined as networks of knowledge-based expertise (26). Finally, more accessible and cheaper forms of communication improve access to knowledge and technology and enhance the rate of information exchange, speeding up the dissemination of both technological and policy innovations (21–24).

The analytical argument for global environmental governance lies in the "public bads" implications of processes and outcomes related to environmental problems. Ozone depletion, carbon emissions, and climate change cannot be addressed by any single nation. Global cooperation and institutional arrangements are therefore necessary to address them. Historically, this conceptualization of environmental problems and their solutions meant that nation states were viewed as the appropriate agents of environmental action (27, 28), and international regimes as the appropriate governance mechanism.

Writings about international regimes have tended to cluster around two significant foci: understanding, measuring, and comparing the effectiveness of regime performance (29, 30) and exposing their inherent democratic deficit (31). There are three main aspects to the democratic deficit of international environmental regimes. First, countries participating in the negotiating process may not be democracies. Second, limited participation from nonstate actors (with the exception of large NGOs and at times epistemic communities); the unequal distribution of power, knowledge, and resources among the participant countries; and the ability of some powerful countries to impose their preferences may undermine the capacity of certain participants to make much of an impact on final outcomes. Additionally, the opaque character of the negotiation process itself strengthens the perception that international regimes and negotiations within the scope of multilateral organizations are driven by the more powerful actors (9, 30, 32). Finally, most international environmental agreements lack effective enforcement, especially when the more binding provisions in an agreement are at stake (33, 34).

The failure of state-centered international regimes to address many of the most pressing global problems successfully prompted a search for new institutions, partnerships, and governance mechanisms. A more inclusive global environmental governance paradigm holds the promise not only of innovative governance strategies, but also of expanded cooperation among social actors that may have been previously outside the policy process: corporate interests, social movements, and nongovernmental organizations (21, 35). The fragmentary nature of the sources of complex environmental problems, such as global climate change, and the reluctance or inability of nation states to regulate the sources of these problems, means that nonstate actors and organizations may be able to play an essential role in mobilizing public opinion and generating innovative solutions (36). It is for this reason that scholars of environmental governance such as Haas have proposed multilevel, nonhierarchical, information-rich, loose networks of institutions and actors as an alternative to ineffective state-centric international regimes (37–39).

These new international environmental governance mechanisms are viewed as being superior along a number of dimensions: (*a*) integrating scientific, technological, and lay knowledge and at quickly relaying information; (*b*) providing sufficient redundancy and flexibility in functional performance; (*c*) gaining the involvement of multiple actors; (*d*) recognizing that the relationship between international regimes and nonstate actors is fundamental to address economic and environmental changes; (*e*) identifying modalities of cooperation that go beyond legal arrangements; (*f*) working across scales to develop cooperation and synergy to solve common problems; and (*g*) promoting social learning and compromise seeking. However, these mechanisms may also fail to limit the negative externalities emerging from lack of implementation capacity. Their characteristic reliance on decentralized action and interdependent coordination and their lack of instruments to deal with system disruption and unanticipated systemic effects mean that major environmental problems may be difficult to address directly and efficaciously through them (40, 41).

## Decentralized Environmental Governance

Climate change, globalization, recent sociopolitical transformations, and the challenges they pose for environmental processes have been the major concerns occupying many of the scholars who have written and talked about environmental governance. Indeed, for many interested in environmental governance, it is synonymous with what happens on the international or the global stage (42). However, it is at least equally correct that some of the most important contemporary changes in environmental governance are occurring at the subnational level and relate to efforts to incorporate lower-level administrative units and social groups better into formal processes of environmental governance. It is perhaps only a matter of historical record today, but the landscape of natural resource management has undergone a breathtaking shift since the colonial period and its immediate aftermath. Until as recently as the late 1970s and early 1980s, those concerned about loss of biodiversity, soil erosion, desertification, deforestation, decline of fisheries, and other such environmental phenomena used to call for more elaborate and thoroughgoing centralized control. Indeed, the elaborate forms of coercive control that marked governance arrangements for most natural resources continued with little change between the colonial and the postcolonial period. State bureaucratic authority appeared to many policy makers and academic observers as the appropriate means to address the externalities associated with the use of environmental resources. Centralized interventions were therefore essential to redress resulting market failures (43, 44) (for a review of relevant claims, see References 45 and 46).

A loss of faith in the state as a reliable custodian of nature has accompanied the analogous loss of faith in states as effective managers of the economy (47, 48). The reasons for the shift away from centralized forms of governance also have to do, however, with very real forces of change, among them the fall of economies relying on centralized control. Economic pressures on states, resulting both from greater integration of economic activities across national boundaries and a decline in aid flows, have been supplemented by fiscal crises in many developing countries (49). Many nation states no longer have the resources to manage their environments. At the same time, as emerging economic forces have challenged the political and economic capacities of nation states, a shift toward more democratic political processes throughout much of the developing world has facilitated the move toward alternative forms of governance whose effectiveness depends on higher levels of participation and greater involvement of citizens in processes of governance.

In addition, extensive research by scholars of common property and political ecology, emphasizing the capacity of communities and other small-scale social formations to manage resources, has provided the intellectual grounds for a shift toward comanagement, community-based natural resource management, and environmental policy decentralizations (50–54). It has done so by demonstrating that forms of effective environmental governance are not exhausted by terms such as "state" and "free market institutions" and that users of resources are often able to self-organize and govern them. By identifying literally thousands of independent instances of enduring governance of resources and at the same time highlighting arenas in which external support can improve local governance processes, scholars of common property and political ecology have helped prepare the ground for decentralized environmental governance.

Since the mid-1980s, decentralization of authority to govern renewable resources such as forests, irrigation systems, and inland fisheries has gathered steam. Indeed, it has become a characteristic feature of late twentieth and early twenty-first century governance of renewable resources, even if nonrenewable resources continue to be held by state authorities in a tightfisted grip (55–58). As Hutchcroft (59) suggests, "The decentralization of government functions is 'the latest fashion (60),' or at least 'a fashion of our time (61).' " Three distinct justifications for decentralization of environmental governance are available. It can produce greater efficiencies because of competition among subnational units; it can bring decision making closer to those affected by governance, thereby promoting higher participation and accountability; and finally, it can help decision makers take advantage of more precise time- and place-specific knowledge about natural resources.

National governments across the developing world have advanced strong claims about the imperative to establish and strengthen partnerships in which local administrative and organizational arrangements complement or substitute for more central efforts to govern environmental resources (62–64). In many cases, they have backed these claims with changes in renewable resource policies. Whether these changes have occurred because of the alleged advantages of decentralized governance or because of the significant flows of aid funds tied to decentralized governance is difficult to judge. But the shift in favor of decentralization has brought alternative means and new political claimants to the fore in the process of governance as nation states attempt to reclaim governance through partnerships with local organizations.

Indeed, the vast literature on decentralized environmental governance contains many different conclusions regarding the nature and depth of the changes that have occurred since the 1980s. Positions adopted by the participants range from those for whom nothing much has changed (65, 66) to those who see the world of governance to have undergone a major transformation with decentralization (67–69). Much of the debate's heat is explained by the variations in the regional focus and the organizational affiliations of those involved. Because there is enormous patchiness in the reforms different countries have undertaken, indeed even within countries in the case of federal polities, the geographical focus of analysis often leads to different conclusions about the meaningfulness and effectiveness of institutional reforms (70). Similarly, those belonging to organizations involved actively in reforms tend to assess them more positively in comparison to outside observers and academic analysts.

When successful, decentralized governance of natural resources can be seen as effecting at least three sets of changes in the political relationships through which human beings relate to resources (71). The first set of changes concerns how decision makers in lower-level units in a territorial-administrative hierarchy relate to those at higher levels (72). Indeed, much of the existing literature on decentralized governance focuses precisely on this aspect of ongoing changes. A second set of issues is linked with the ways local decision makers relate to their constituents. This aspect of the decentralization of environmental governance has been researched extensively in writings on local resource management, especially by scholars of the commons. However, a third aspect of decentralized governance—alterations of the subjective relationships of people with each other and with the environment as part of changing relationships of power and governance—is also crucial to understand outcomes, an issue that has received far less attention than the preceding two aspects of environmental governance (6).

Contemporary efforts at decentralized environmental governance, like those in earlier periods, aim to make the exercise of control both more thorough and more economical. Decentralization disperses multiple points of political leverage throughout an administrative structure and makes them available to central decision makers (73, 74). It does so by encouraging the systematic creation of legal codes and performance standards that are specified through the exercise of legislative or executive authority. Adherence to these codes and standards is the price of inclusion in decision-making processes. Paradoxically perhaps, decentralization appears to be perfectly compatible with the existence of centralized authority when formal inclusion in decision-making processes occurs together with a clear delineation of spheres of authority within which local actors are supposed to operate. In addition to helping effect fiscal economies, decentralization also serves political and strategic considerations to the extent that dissatisfaction with governance can find local points of authority against which to protest instead of engaging centralized authority.

Contemporary decentralized environmental governance is different from earlier attempts at decentralization of authority in two critical ways. For the most part, earlier efforts in the form of indirect rule in colonial south Asia and Africa and community development programs in the postcolonial developing world relied on existing authority structures and incorporated them into the formal process of the exercise of authority. In contrast, decentralized environmental governance, especially at the local level, has been built upon new organizational entities such as community-based user groups and has established new lines of institutionalized authority. An even more striking difference that characterizes contemporary environmental governance is the way it conceptualizes individual citizens and their responsibilities. By focusing on the incentives that prompt individuals to participate in new institutional arrangements to govern the environment, present day decentralization processes help produce the very individual subjects they require for their effective functioning. The rhetoric of capacity building, local knowledge, and individual rationality is a lynchpin of decentralized environmental governance (6). Ongoing changes in subnational environmental governance hold intriguing possibilities for reshaping the future landscape of political decision making related to the environment. Therefore, further research on environmental policy decentralization holds great promise both for furthering the insights that work on common property institutions has produced and for enhancing the involvement of local decision makers in new forms of environmental governance.

At the same time, it is worth highlighting that ongoing changes are not just an occasion for optimism that less powerful human agents may come to exercise greater voice in how they and their resources are governed. There is also room for cynicism that decentralization policies have typically been motivated by powerful state actors to enhance their own political positions. Without effective safeguards against arbitrary exercise of localized power and clear relations of accountability, decentralization may lead to forms of regulation even more suffocating than those encouraged by more centralized control. The contingent outcomes of contemporary shifts in governance, therefore, depend crucially on the ways local actors mobilize and establish alliances across sociopolitical and administrative scales of governance (64, 75).

## Market- and Agent-Focused Instruments

The decline of the state since the 1970s as the prime agent of environmental governance has also propelled market and voluntary incentives-based mechanisms to the fore. Instead of relying on hierarchically organized, regulatory control or even purely participatory structures, MAFIs aim to mobilize individual incentives in favor of environmentally positive outcomes through a careful calculation and modulation of costs and benefits associated with particular environmental strategies. They differ from more conventional regulatory mechanisms along a number of dimensions, including the source of their legitimacy and authority. Cashore (76) suggests that the strength of these instruments lies in their utilization of market exchanges and incentives to encourage environmental compliance.

MAFIs encompass a broad range: ecotaxes and subsidies based on a mix of regulation and market incentives, voluntary agreements, certification, ecolabeling, and informational systems are some of the major examples. At the national level, the popularity of these instruments and frameworks has increased quickly, even if their adoption and implementation can be differentiated by sector and geography rather than being uniform (23, 77). Their popularity seems to relate to a general dissatisfaction with old policy instruments; the influence, transfer, and diffusion of emerging governance paradigms based in neoliberal institutionalism and free trade agreements; and the need for market innovations that keep national economies competitive in a globalizing world (23).

Energy taxes, tradable permits, voluntary agreements, ecolabeling, and certification were introduced as early as the 1960s in a number of western countries (23, 78). However, their adoption has gathered steam especially since the 1990s (24). These instruments are founded upon the bedrock of individual preferences and assumptions about self-interested behavior by economic agents. A strong claim advanced in their favor is their superiority in terms of economic efficiency related to implementation. Although an emerging literature focuses on the extent to which process-oriented evaluative criteria such as popularity, responsiveness, legitimacy, transparency, and accountability may also be associated with market incentive-focused instruments, the extent to which they meet these criteria needs much greater exploration (39, 76).

Environmental taxes of different kinds are among the more common market-based instruments aimed to alter environmental actions of agents (by changing the costs and benefits of environmental choices). Over time, a number of countries have adopted a sophisticated mix of different kinds of ecotaxes as well as distinct policy positions about allocation of revenues generated from such taxes (23). Taxes on commodities and services, such as energy, nutrients used in agriculture, or tourism, are enacted in the belief that existing markets do not fully incorporate the externalities associated with the production and use of these commodities and services and that taxes are an effective mechanism to raise revenues to offset damages associated with the overexploitation of underpriced resources. Similarly, tradable permits are based on the idea that some ecosystem services, such as clean water and air, are not priced fully by existing markets. In such situations, incentives for conservation and economic efficiency of allocation can be improved through economic exchange only if appropriate legal and institutional arrangements are in place and polluters pay a tax on their polluting activities. The resulting markets for some kinds of emissions can reach significant proportions: the total value of trading in carbon markets, according to some recent estimates, may reach 10 to 40 billion dollars by 2010 (1).

Voluntary agreements are negotiated to meet environmental targets regarding, for example, lower waste generation and emissions or higher energy efficiency. Industry and corporate actors often pursue such voluntarily imposed targets as a strategy to preempt legal regulation. It can therefore be argued that the shadow of law is crucial to their emergence and effectiveness (79). Indeed, some researchers of voluntary environmental compliance have argued that without leadership by state agencies, voluntary agreements will produce anemic results at best (80). Others such as Ruggie (35) suggest that the irony of the current reliance on corporate actors to implement environmental sustainability lies in the fact that "the corporate sector, which has done more than any other to create the growing gaps between global economy and national communities, is being pulled into playing a key bridging role between them. In the process, a global public domain is emerging, which cannot substitute for effective action by states but may help to produce it" (35, p. 95).

Primary sector commodities such as coffee, timber, and energy provide familiar examples of ecolabeling and certification schemes (81–83). Both ecolabeling and certification schemes are forms of voluntary agreements wherein producers agree to meet environmental standards related to production and marketing activities. Such standards may be the result of work by third party actors, an industry association, or even the government. The operation of these schemes hinges upon the idea that consumers are willing to express their preferences related to cleaner energy or greener products through their choices in markets and through a willingness to pay higher prices. Perceptions about environment-friendly preferences among consumers have led many corporations to adopt certification mechanisms and advertising campaigns that represent both real and cosmetic shifts in how corporate actors govern their environmental actions.

Some of the drivers of market-based policy instruments in the developed world are analogous to those motivating decentralized environmental governance in much of the developing world (84). Dissatisfaction with regulatory control by state agencies and the bureaucratization associated with their growth play an important role in the expansion of market incentives-based instruments and in their adoption across sectors and national boundaries (85). Difficulties in implementation of traditional regulatory instruments provide a partial explanation of the willingness of governments to experiment with market-oriented efforts. High costs of compliance with environmental regulations and increasing awareness of environmental issues among consumers are other parts of the explanation. Although many economists had argued for the economic superiority of market-based instruments as early as the mid-1960s and 1970s (86, 87), it is only recently that their application to environmental governance is becoming more widespread.

The schematic review of a range of different instruments of environmental governance based on market incentives and exchanges suggests that their success depends significantly on the internalization of positive environment preferences among relevant stakeholders, most importantly citizens and consumers (88), and effective leadership by governments. For example, in their comparative study across eight European Union countries, Jordan et al. (23) found that among the constraints to the implementation of MAFIs was the opposition of environmental policy actors (especially environmental movements) and other vested interests (such as energy-intensive industries). Other constraints to successful implementation are lack of expertise across policy systems, fear among corporate sectors about loss of economic competitiveness, and unequal distributional impacts because of ecotaxing schemes (e.g., fuel taxes). Not surprisingly, corporate and industry actors are less likely to adhere voluntarily to new environmental standards to the extent that they prove more costly in comparison to when such standards are absent or weak (89). Indeed, efforts to induce voluntary compliance by economically motivated actors have been found to be vulnerable to free-riding behavior when effective mechanisms to deter free riding are not in place. For example, in a study of the U.S. Environmental Protection Agency's WasteWise program, Delmas & Keller (90) found that organizations joining the program were likely not to report their creation of waste unless there were private benefits to such reporting.

Other research, especially that focusing on corporate social responsibility, examines the extent to which environmentally oriented actions of market actors are tied to their expectations about consumer preferences—both those specific to their products and to "green preferences" more generally (91, 92). Citizen preferences expressed in the form of a greater willingness to purchase green products and policy environments in which superior environmental outcomes are prized are important drivers of the success of new MAFIs of environmental governance. These considerations suggest that the growing popularity of market incentives-based instruments should not lead to the conclusion that governance is replacing governments. A conclusion more broadly supported by existing evidence would be that there is a complex relationship between governments and governance: governments are the source of credible threats of regulatory action that would require costly compliance and such threats encourage the adoption of voluntary agreements on environmental standards. Government agencies also remain the monitoring authorities to which appeals regarding violations of environmental standards can be made.

## Cross-Scale Environmental Governance

The multiscalar character of environmental problems—spatially, sociopolitically, and temporally—adds significant complexity to their governance (93–95). The implications of spatial scales for environmental governance are twofold. First, the decoupling across scales of the causes and consequences of environmental problems introduces major concerns about the unequal distribution of costs and benefits of environmental issues. For example, a problem such as global climate change may have been caused primarily by the major producers of greenhouse gases in the developed world, but many of their more dramatic effects will negatively affect low-emitting countries in the global south. The spatial distribution of environmental problems, such as acid rain, ozone depletion, and transboundary water pollution, transcends national borders and adds to the challenge of designing and implementing solutions (26). As mentioned above, the main strategy to address these issues has been international environmental regimes. Although more than 1700 multilateral and bilateral environmental agreements have hitherto been signed, their effectiveness is at best mixed (30).

Sociopolitically, cross-scale environmental problems affect and are affected by institutionalized decision making at local, subnational, national, and transnational levels. A common prescription to address the multilevel character of environmental problems is to design governance mechanisms across levels of social and institutional aggregation. Multilevel governance is intended to counteract the fragmentation that is characteristic of sectorally based decision making or, indeed, of decision making that is organized by territorial, social, and political divisions. The involvement of public-private networks in multilevel governance can enhance the representation of the diversity of interests that are affected by environmental problems (39, 96). At the same time, the configuration of cross-scale governance strategies is also conducive to compromise seeking and social learning, often enabling less formal modes of decision making, greater transparency, and higher levels of representativeness (39).

Increasingly, cross-scale governance mechanisms are being shaped by nonstate actors including NGOs, transnational environmental organizations, intergovernmental and multilateral organizations, market-oriented actors (e.g., transnational and multinational companies), and epistemic communities (26, 97–101). These new actors both introduce innovative tools and mechanisms and positively shape power relations within the policy arena (31, 102), even if their transformative potential is contested (103).

The cross-temporal implications of environmental problems are especially severe because of two major obstacles to action: contempocentrism and uncertainty regarding cause and effect relationships involving long-term environmental changes. Contempocentrism, in part a consequence of high market discount rates, is the tendency to disregard the welfare of future generations and believe in the power of technology and technological change to take care of environmental degradation and scarcities. It means humans are likely to "spend" the environment now and discount the future heavily (33, 104). Coupled with the seeming high costs of action that will shift existing trajectories of economic development, the uncertainty surrounding the science of causes and effects of environmental degradation often leads to a "do nothing until we know more" attitude–strongly reflected in the contemporary policy positions of some nations that are the largest emitters of greenhouse gases. Many of the impacts of global climate change on humans and ecosystems are still undetermined, and the design and implementation of policies necessary to reduce emissions are both economically and politically quite costly.

## THE TERRAIN OF ENVIRONMENTAL GOVERNANCE

The elaboration above of environmental governance-related changes and challenges involving four different themes shows that there are intriguing parallels across them despite the many (and expected) differences in how governance is becoming reconfigured as a result of globalization and decentralization. It also shows the increasing importance of cross-scale governance, market instruments, and individual incentives. Perhaps the most obvious of these parallels relates to the emergence of alternative institutional forms of governance. Some of the new forms of governance are innovative hybrids between the conventionally recognized social roles that markets, states, and, more recently, communities play. Others are the result of a clearer appreciation that the effectiveness of what was conventionally understood as a pure form of governance based in the market or the state may be the result of existing relationships among market, state, and civil society actors. Figure 1 presents a schematic structure to classify strategies of environmental governance as they are founded upon the actions of three different social mechanisms.

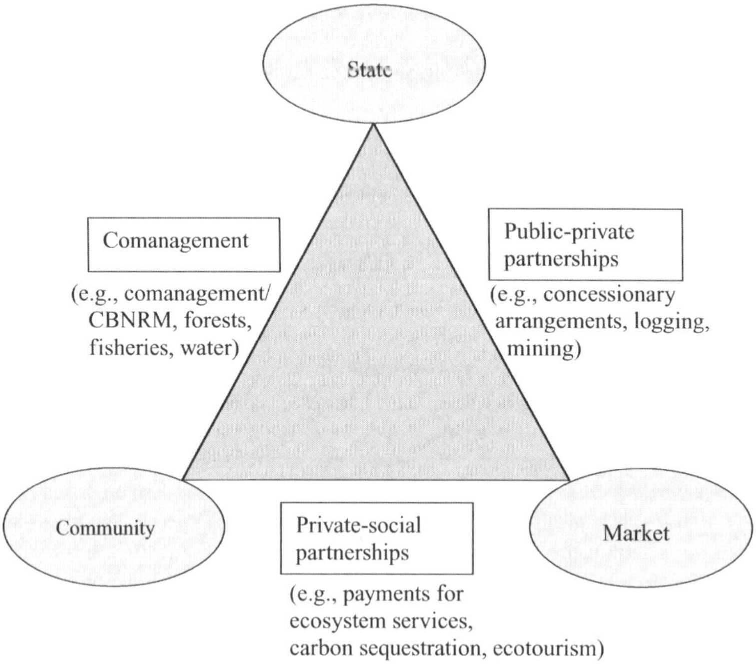


**Figure 1** Mechanisms and strategies of environmental governance. Abbreviation: CBNRM, community-based natural resource management.

The triangle connecting state, market, and community constitutes the core of the figure. The emphasis in the figure on these social mechanisms is a reflection of early conversations related to the environment that viewed environmental governance strategies as being especially necessary to address the externalities stemming from the public goods nature of environmental resources and processes. To overcome these externalities, some writers saw state action as necessary; others, surmising that externalities could lead to market failure, advocated clearer definition of property rights to allow functioning markets to emerge (43, 105). Arguments advanced by scholars of the commons engaged these policy prescriptions and identified communities as a third potential locus of environmental governance (51). These efforts, championing state-, market-, and community-based governance strategies, were built around perceived strengths of the particular social arena or mechanism being considered: the capacity for action across jurisdictions backed by state authority; the mobilization of basic human incentives through market exchanges; and the deployment of solidaristic relationships and time- and place-specific knowledge embodied in communities (107).

In the past decade and a half, however, an exciting array of research has identified opportunities for more nuanced arguments regarding hybrid forms of collaborations across the dividing lines represented by markets, states, and communities. The three major forms we identify in Figure 1—comanagement (between state agencies and communities), public-private partnerships (between state agencies and market actors), and private-social partnerships (between market actors and communities)—each incorporate joint action across at least two of the social mechanisms/arenas in the core triangle and correspond to scores if not hundreds of specific experiments in which constituent social actors find differing levels of emphasis. They simultaneously illustrate the dynamic and fast-changing nature of contemporary environmental governance. The emergence of these hybrid forms of environmental governance is based upon the recognition that no single agent possesses the capabilities to address the multiple facets, interdependencies, and scales of environmental problems that may appear at first blush to be quite simple.

The hope embodied in hybrid forms of environmental governance is evident in each case. They seek simultaneously to address the weaknesses of a particular social agent and to build upon the strength of the other partner. Thus, the involvement of market actors in environmental collaboration is typically aimed at addressing the inefficiencies of state action, often by injecting competitive pressures in the provision of environmental services. In the same vein, market actors are also viewed as enabling greater profitability in the utilization of environmental resources. The addition of community and local voices to environmental governance is seen as providing the benefit of time- and place-specific information that may help solve complex environmental problems and, at the same time, allow a more equitable allocation of benefits from environmental assets. Higher levels of participation by different stakeholders and the blessings of state authorities can help overcome the democratic deficit and lack of legitimacy often associated with market-focused instruments. Moreover, state actors, ostensibly, create the possibility that fragmented social action by decentralized communities and market actors can be made more coherent and simultaneously more authoritative.

A second obvious parallel across the discussion of the different themes related to environmental governance is that within hybrid strategies one can discern a mobilization of individual incentives that had initially been the core of market-oriented instruments and is now becoming increasingly common. Thus, contemporary co-governance strategies, in contrast to their historic counterparts, focus on how the individual subject will respond to efforts at governance. Through such a calculation of individual responses, decentralized environmental governance aims to elicit the willing cooperation of those subject to the goals of governance (6, 108). The emphasis on willing cooperation has even prompted some scholars of incentive-based governance strategies to term them "governance without government" (109, p. 652).

In view of the extent to which an appeal to individual self-interest is a part of new environmental governance strategies, it is reasonable to conclude that a pervasive attempt to restructure agent-level incentives and attitudes toward the environment underpins governance instruments related to civil society-based solidarities, market-based policies, and voluntary compliance mechanisms (110, 111).

The same is true for public-private and social-private partnerships, each of which is enabled by a level of valorization of corporate entities and market actors that would have been quite unimaginable in the 1970s (112–114). Here, the logic of efficiency, which is the hallmark of capitalist organization of production, is also coming to colonize the goal of environmental conservation and sustainable development.

## LIMITATIONS OF HYBRID GOVERNANCE STRATEGIES

The reconfiguration of environmental governance so that the state is no longer the only actor viewed as capable of addressing environmental externalities has many implications, but not all of them have found an easy acceptance among those concerned about environmental outcomes. The focus on individual incentives, the creation of new property rights and markets in relation to water or carbon, and the encouragement to the corporate sector (insofar as the policy environment enables more extensive public-private and social-private partnerships) have been construed by some scholars as moves toward increasing democratic deficit and higher levels of inequality in the allocation of environmental resources. Those who are able to exercise greater access and expertise in relation to these new mechanisms are more likely to derive greater benefits from them (66). Other scholars have expressed significant concerns about the likely results of market actors being incorporated in a more thoroughgoing manner into environmental governance, which Liverman (115), among others, has called the "commodification of nature." Greater efficiency in the utilization of natural resources, for many, is equivalent to higher rates of extraction and, thereby, brings up issues of intergenerational equity.

For scholars coming from a radical political economy perspective, there is no new approach to global environmental governance; rather, the supposed new mechanisms of governance are little more than a natural evolution of traditional regime politics because outsiders and disempowered groups continue to have little opportunity to participate in contemporary efforts at governance despite the greater incorporation of civil society actors (31). Here, the key differences between models of new global environmental governance and older conceptions of regime theory concern the role of and the importance accorded to members of global civil society, which is understood as a sphere of voluntary societal associations located above the individual and below the state as well as across state boundaries (31, 98). Ford (31) argues, for example, that the rhetoric of societal participation introduced by the Brundtland Report did little to change regime politics because it failed to democratize the negotiation process itself. New forms of global environmental governance, and their newly incorporated players, can be viewed simply as reflecting existing distributions of power rather than having changed anything fundamental. Indeed, global environmental governance is seen as being embedded in a neoliberal political economy, which is hegemonic in the neo-Gramscian sense that dominant power relations are maintained by consent as well as by coercion (31). In this sense, global environmental governance is part of a broader agenda of corporate interests developed to promote economic globalization and to regulate what both NGOs and nation states do (116). In a world of weak states, deterritorialized action, and concentrated power, corporate interests and multilateral organizations can control and reframe environmental action as a means to legitimize their model of development (117). These dominant interests place greater weight on the problem-solving aspect of new instruments rather than on ameliorating the unequal power relations that the new system also continues to preserve. Indeed, actors who are mostly responsible for nature's degradation are defining the terms of environmental protection. "Governance from below," represented by the role of social movements and protests against organizations such as transnational corporations, the WTO, and the International Monetary Fund, is currently the only recognizable challenge, despite the risk that it too may be coopted (117).

In contrast, the inclusion of a wider array of social actors such as private and corporate interests is justified by the need to guarantee that veto players, whose "voice" or "exit" can jeopardize public action, agree with policy choices. The rationale is that if these elite actors are provided with a privileged space for participation, they will have no incentive to exert their veto power or obstruct the decision-making process. Moreover, the belief in the efficiency of market-led forms of governance to produce positive outcomes justifies compromising for the "greater good." Radical political economists, however, argue that this is hardly a justification for legitimacy (39) and that the mere inclusion of more social actors does not necessarily make governance systems more democratic (118). Although advocates of new forms of governance argue that their democratic deficit is no worse than that of traditional representative democracy (39), critics point out that they fail to meet normative models of deliberative democracy whose fairness is grounded in the equal participation of all stakeholders. The opacity of governance networks may prevent the mass public from identifying and evaluating the role of specific agents, such as experts who play prominent roles in the building of relevant issues and action agendas. For example, in cases of environmental issues with potentially catastrophic impacts (e.g., global climate change), the predominance of "less than democratic" expert politics is justified in the name of the urgency and severity of the problem.

MAFIs and multilevel governance frameworks may also have negative effects on policy capacity, specifically in relation to environmental problems. In multilevel governance systems, the "denationalization" of statehood, reflected empirically in the "hollowing out" of the national state apparatus, reorganizes old and new capacities territorially and functionally—but not always for the better (119). Indeed, globalization and subnational challenges have led to the emergence of a rescaled state that simultaneously transfers power upward to supranational agencies and downward toward regional and local levels (120), changing the way policy-making capacity is distributed. This transfer of power to different levels of decision making may have already negatively affected policy capacity of the modern state (121). Hybrid modes of environmental governance and emerging partnerships across conventional divisions suggest that the state is not the only, and perhaps not even the most important, actor in governance (119). Yet, advocates of a bigger role for the state contend that, especially in cases where redistributive policy making becomes necessary (e.g., adaptation), it is unlikely that either the market or hybrid forms of governance will be able to accomplish much (122).

## APPLICATIONS: CLIMATE CHANGE AND ECOSYSTEM DEGRADATION

The four themes we highlighted above and the framework for viewing emerging hybrid mechanisms of environmental governance are visible in the major problem areas related to the environment. Two significant arenas in which these themes and hybrid governance strategies are especially evident are global climate change and ecosystem degradation. An examination of these areas of environmental concern and crisis provides useful indications about the extent to which contemporary and emerging environmental governance approaches have the capacity to help address major problems.

### Climate Change

Among the factors that challenge environmental governance structures, global climate change promises to be one of the most critical. As the need to design policies to respond to the negative impacts of climate change increases, more attention has been paid to emerging modes of environmental governance and to how they can increase the capacity of economic, social, and cultural systems to help humans mitigate and adapt to climatic change. Considering that climate is one of many stressors, the resilience of already overextended economic, political, and administrative institutions may decrease rapidly, especially in the more impoverished regions of the globe (22). Some signs of how environmental stresses may exacerbate governance challenges related to poverty, violence, and authoritarianism are already visible (1). Among the expected casualties of governance breakdown as a result of climate change may be economic growth, democratic institutions, and livelihood possibilities.

Responses to global climate change fall broadly into two main categories: those seeking to curb or stabilize the level of emissions of greenhouse gases into the atmosphere (mitigation) and those seeking to boost natural and human systems' resilience to prevent, respond, and recover from potential impacts of a changing climate (adaptation). Although at this point adaptation may be inevitable, its magnitude and range depends on how much mitigation is successfully implemented to prevent and avoid the most dangerous interference in the climate regime.

Many of the factors that make global climate change unique also make it complex. Global climate change is the quintessential multiscalar environmental problem; because greenhouse gases mix equally in the atmosphere, the costs of the negative effects of climate change are socialized at the global level, but the effects are likely to be felt at the local level. The fragmented and highly politicized nature of the causes of climate change means that it is extremely difficult to assign blame and target offenders. Effective responses to climate change are likely to require a diversity of actors and organizations across the state-society divide. The high level of uncertainty still involving the definition of the magnitude and character of the impacts of climate change in different human and natural systems and the fact they might not be felt for years also make it a politically and financially costly problem (33). Finally, the differences among those causing climate change (large producers of greenhouse gases) and those likely to be more negatively affected by it, including the global poor and natural and biological systems, make it unique in terms of the distribution of costs and benefits and bring up a whole host of equity and environmental justice questions (123). For example, although mitigation actions are likely to fall upon countries and sectors mostly responsible for the production of greenhouse gases, such as polluting corporations and developed countries, adaptation will be realized mostly by affected groups such as the poor, living in less-developed countries, or agencies entrusted with the task of building generic adaptive capacity to climate change such as local governments, NGOs, and aid organizations. In the literature on adaptation, most efforts to compare differential vulnerability identify already stressed countries and regions in Africa and South Asia and small island states as the most vulnerable (124, 125), but the primary burden of mitigation falls on developed countries under international regimes to curb greenhouse gas emissions, such as the Kyoto protocol (127).

MITIGATION The Intergovernmental Panel on Climate Change (IPCC) defines mitigation of global climate change as "an anthropogenic intervention to reduce the sources or enhance the sinks of greenhouse gases" (128). Mitigation of greenhouse gas emissions has been organized at the international level primarily through the entering into force of the Kyoto Protocol and has been realized at the national level through regulation and implementation of new governance mechanisms across the public-private divide. Mechanisms to mitigate global climate change range from technological fixes to the design of institutions that curb carbon emission practices. Five categories of strategies to mitigate carbon emissions are available: energy conservation, renewable energy, enhanced natural sinks, nuclear energy, and fossil carbon management. Yet the magnitude, complexity, and urgency of the climate change problem suggest that the implementation of any or of a combination of these strategies would require tremendous amounts of financial, human, and political capital (129).

Not surprisingly, the lack of capacity of nation states to implement such strategies (exemplified by the lackluster accomplishments of Kyoto to date) (130), and the general lack of confidence that this capacity will improve dramatically in the near future, suggests that a broader array of hybrid modes of governance is necessary to address global climate change. Comanagement and public-private partnerships in the implementation of Kyoto's Clean Development Mechanism and social-private partnerships to develop community-based carbon sequestration projects are a promising start (131, 132). Carbon taxes and joint development of fuel-efficient technology (e.g., FredomCAR, California Fuel Cell Partnership) are also examples of initiatives involving both public and private actors. Yet, despite the promise of effectiveness, many question the ability of hybrid modes of governance to address mitigation as fast and as broadly as necessary to defuse many of the most negative impacts of global climate change.

Already, in the implementation of mitigation policy, NGOs and businesses have played a particularly important role both in influencing the design and implementation of climate governance mechanisms. Although business interests have focused mostly on flexible mechanisms for carbon trading (see section on market-based mechanisms) and the pursue of fuel efficiency (in addition to playing an oppositional role to the implementation of emission-curbing strategies), NGOs have played a broader role in monitoring implementation and compliance of regulation, lobbying, raising equity issues, and providing scientific and technical knowledge (34, 127, 133, 134). One of the most effective ways NGOs have influenced the global climate change policy process has been through their role as knowledge producers and as members of information networks and epistemic communities seeking to affect the response process.

ADAPTATION The IPCC defines adaptation as an "adjustment in natural or human systems in response to actual or expected climatic stimuli or their effects, which moderates harm or exploits beneficial opportunities." Vulnerability in turn is "a function of the character, magnitude, and rate of climate variation to which a system is exposed, its sensitivity, and its adaptive capacity" (128). Adaptive capacity, the third concept important to understand vulnerability to global climate change, is the "potential and capability to change to a more desirable state in the face of the impacts or risks of climate change" (135). It is the ability of a system to moderate and to adjust to global climate change-related damages. Adaptation policy considers the entitlements, assets, and resources that improve the capacity of this system to resist, cope, and recover from a given hazard.

To date, adaptive capacity indicators have been defined mostly at the national scale both because it is an appropriate level to make adaptation decisions and because it allows for comparison of vulnerability across countries (124). Although the reality of building adaptive capacity involves cascading decisions across scales and a diversity of private and public agents and organizations (136), because of the redistributive character of adaptive capacity building, the bulk of action is expected to fall over nation states (22).

At lower scales of government, global climate change critically intersects with decentralization not only in the assessment of different levels of vulnerability within countries but also in the design of policy to enhance adaptive capacity. For example, at the local level, vulnerability assessment (e.g., participatory vulnerability mapping) holds the promise of a more accurate understanding of the "character" of the vulnerability of specific social and human systems (137). At the global level, adaptation policy is influenced by the role that institutions such as the United Nations Framework Climate Change Convention play in coordinating international action, advancing rationales for compensation, and preparing for future impacts (123, 138).

In sum, the panoply of governance strategies related to global climate change are clearly difficult to view as being centered on any single category of social agent as depicted in Figure 1. Although it might have been argued a decade ago that nation states are the only actors who can generate effective measures to address climate change, it is evident that, although their involvement is necessary, they are not adequate to perform the task by themselves. The willing cooperation of civil society and market actors and changes in individual level actions are critically important to the successful implementation of the set of governance strategies that might have some prospect of being effective.

## Ecosystem Degradation

Like climate change, ongoing and fundamental alterations of the relationship between humans and ecosystems pose a complex set of multiscalar challenges for environmental governance. Ecosystems and their services are the basis upon which human lives and all human actions are founded; thus it is not surprising that when examining human impacts on the environment, the Millennium Ecosystem Assessment (MEA) focused on ecosystem services. In this section, we draw upon this comprehensive assessment of ecosystems to pursue our arguments about changing forms of environmental governance. The MEA (1) categorized the range of benefits available to humans from ecosystems into "*provisioning services* such as food, water, timber, and fiber; *regulating services* that affect climate, floods, disease, wastes, and water quality; *cultural services* that provide recreational, aesthetic, and spiritual benefits; and *supporting services* such as soil formation, photosynthesis, and nutrient cycling." This assessment concludes that humans have altered ecosystem services more comprehensively in the past half century than in any previous comparable period. Although these alterations in the relationships between humans and ecosystems have led to substantial net gains in economic development and well-being, 60% of ecosystem services are being degraded or used unsustainably. Not only are current use and management patterns unsustainable, they are increasing the likelihood of nonlinear and irreversible changes, such as disease emergence, fisheries collapse, alterations in water quality, and regional climate shifts. Finally, the costs of ongoing changes are being borne disproportionately by the poor, thereby contributing to growing disparities (1).

To address these changes, the MEA evaluates a range of potential responses and focuses especially on those that would (*a*) lead to institutional changes and governance patterns that can manage ecosystems effectively, (*b*) align market incentives better with the real costs of environmental services, (*c*) focus on particular social behavioral obstacles to better utilization of ecosystems, (*d*) promote more efficient technologies, (*e*) provide better knowledge about what is happening to ecosystems, and (*f*) improve the efficacy of environment-related decision making.

Throughout the discussion of these responses, it is evident that the authors of the MEA simultaneously define the terrain of environmental governance quite narrowly and extremely broadly. They identify a specific set of responses, those having to do with institutional and governance-related changes, as properly the domain of environmental governance. Such responses include the integration of ecosystem goals into existing sectoral strategies, for example, in the poverty reduction strategies encouraged by the World Bank, increased emphasis on international environmental agreements and target setting, and greater accountability of environmental decision making.

But they treat environmental governance too narrowly in restricting its scope to specifically institutional responses. In fact, the entire set of responses they identify in relation to markets, social behaviors, technological innovation, and monitoring capacity is contingent on changes in governance. Indeed, without comprehensive changes in contemporary national policies, the basis on which market exchanges are organized, and the incentives on which individuals act, there is little reason to think that the real costs of negative environmental outcomes will be incorporated into economic decision making. Similar arguments are not difficult to advance in relation to desired technological changes, social behaviors, or cultural processes. Although we may, in part as a result of a particular division of social-scientific labors, view the world as being divided into economic, social, political, and cultural domains, shifts in human actions in all of these domains require a reconfiguration of the costs and benefits of given actions. In the absence of changes introduced through shifts in governance patterns, there is little likelihood that humans will change their economic, political, social, or cultural behaviors.

Precisely because of the social interconnections across what we view as local, regional, national, and global levels and what we categorize as the economic, political, social, and cultural domains, successful environmental governance strategies will require heightened cooperation of many different actors across these levels and domains. Thus, not only is it the case that human beings will be able to introduce manageable changes in ecosystems only through significant transformations in environmental governance strategies, it is also very likely that successful outcomes will hinge on environmental governance approaches that are founded upon heightened cooperation involving all actors in all three social locations identified in Figure 1: market, state, and community.

## CONCLUSION

Our review of the changing terrain of environmental governance has emphasized four elements. One, we suggest that environmental governance signifies a wide set of regulatory processes, not just international governance mechanisms and their impacts at the international level or just the state and its agencies at the national and subnational levels. Two, we highlight the hybrid, multilevel, and cross-sectoral nature of emerging forms of governance. Our review examines in particular how environmental governance has changed since the 1960s. From a focus on specific agents of change such as state and market actors, advocates of effective environmental management came to view communities and local institutions as important actors to involve in governance. Especially in the past decade and a half, new sets of instruments of environmental governance have emerged. We identify three broad terms that denote these partnerships: comanagement as the form of collaboration between state agencies and communities, public-private partnerships between market actors and state agencies, and social-private partnerships between market actors and communities.

Three, we analyze how emerging forms of environmental governance that have become increasingly popular since the mid-1990s rely, on the one hand, on partnerships and, on the other hand, on the mobilization of individual incentives characteristic of market-based instruments of environmental regulation. Because they seek to gain the willing participation of a range of actors who would be subject to their regulatory effects, they are viewed by many observers as being amenable to more efficient implementation.

Greater efficiency in design and implementation of environmental governance instruments is undoubtedly a major concern of state authorities who may be under fiscal pressures and who may therefore find partnerships with market actors highly desirable. A partnership with private actors may also appear attractive to civil society actors and communities historically strapped for funding. However, a number of observers of changing environmental governance have raised concerns about the degree to which increasing recourse to market actors and processes undermines social goals related to higher levels of democratic participation, creates problems of unequal access to resources, and raises the specter of lack of accountability.

Finally, our review explores valid concerns about the unanticipated consequences of emerging forms of environmental governance. An ethical concern for democratic participation and more equitable outcomes in environmental governance is a welcome development when environmental governance mechanisms emphasize collaboration for greater efficiency. An exclusive focus on greater efficiency in emerging efforts at environmental governance, especially where natural resources are concerned, may yield the unanticipated outcome of increasing commodification of nature. The fact that human interventions in ecosystem processes are already leading to unsustainable use of more than 60% of ecosystems suggests that, together with greater efficiency, it is equally necessary to work toward restraint in human use of major ecosystems. The mobilization of individual incentives and their incorporation into innovative strategies of environmental governance is critical for efficient governance. However, effective environmental governance also requires the incorporation of knowledge about limits on aggregate levels of human activities that rely on high intensities of resource exploitation or lead to high levels of pollutant emissions. In designing and assessing strategies of environmental governance, it is critical therefore to focus not just on efficiency and equity, but also on criteria related to long-term sustainability and a concern for nature.

ACKNOWLEDGMENTS

In writing this review, we are indebted to many conversations and insights that proved instrumental in the development of our arguments. Jon Anderson, Charles Benjamin, Edwin Connorley, Benjamin Cousins, Aaron de Grassi, David Kaimowitz, James McCarthy, James Murombedzi, Ebrima Sall, Gill Shepherd, and Ann Thomas gave their time and ideas at short notice. Long-standing conversations with Jesse Ribot and Elinor Ostrom have shaped our arguments and views considerably, especially in relation to subnational forms of environmental governance. Comments from two anonymous reviewers and extensive responses from Duncan Macqueen on an earlier draft of the chapter are also gratefully acknowledged. Finally, we would like to thank Nate Engle for his careful reading of earlier versions of the chapter.

**The *Annual Review of Environment and Resources* is online at http://environ.annualreviews.org**

LITERATURE CITED

1. Millenn. Ecosyst. Assess. 2005. *Ecosystems and Human Well Being: Synthesis*. Washington, DC: Island
2. Sonnenfeld DA, Mol APJ. 2002. Ecological modernization, governance, and globalization. *Am. Behav. Sci.* 45:1456–61
3. Evans P. 1996. Government action, social capital and development: reviewing the evidence on synergy. *World Dev.* 24:1119–32
4. Ostrom E. 2001. Vulnerability and polycentric governance systems. *Update: Newsl. Int. Hum. Dimens. Program. Glob. Environ. Chang.* 3 http://www.ihdp.uni-bonn.de/html/publications/update/IHDP Update01_03.html
5. Jagers SC, Stripple J. 2003. Climate governance beyond the state. *Glob. Gov.* 9:385–99
6. Agrawal A. 2005. *Environmentality: Technologies of Government and the Making of Subjects*. Durham, NC: Duke Univ. Press
7. Hirst P, Thompson G. 2002. The future of globalization. *Coop. Confl.* 37:247–65
8. Newell P. 2002. *Globalization and the Future State*. Brighton, UK: Inst. Dev. Stud.
9. Nye JS. 2001. Globalization's democratic deficit: how to make international institutions more accountable. *Foreign Aff.* 80:2–6
10. Staeger MB. 2002. *Globalism*. Lanham, MD: Rowman & Littlefield
11. Appadurai A. 1996. *Modernity at Large: Cultural Dimensions of Globalization*. Minneapolis: Univ. Minn. Press
12. Berger P, Huntington S. 2003. *Many Globalizations: Cultural Diversity in the Contemporary World*. New York: Oxford Univ. Press
13. Held D, McGrew A. 2002. *Globalization/Anti-Globalization*. London: Polity
14. Barkin JS. 2003. The counterintuitive relationship between globalization and climate change. *Glob. Environ. Polit.* 3:8–13
15. Frankel J. 2005. Climate and trade: links between the Kyoto Protocol and WTO. *Environment* 47:8–19
16. Santilli M, Moutinho P, Schwartzman S, Nepstad D, Curran L, Nobre C. 2005. Tropical deforestation and the Kyoto Protocol. *Clim. Chang.* 71:267–76

17. Roe E, Eeten MJG. 2004. Three—not two—major environmental counternarratives to globalization. *Glob. Environ. Polit.* 4:36–53
18. Liverman DM, Varady RG, Chavez O, Sanchez R. 1999. Environmental issues along the United States-Mexico border: drivers of change and responses of citizens and institutions. *Annu. Rev. Energy Environ.* 24:607–43
19. Harbine J. 2002. NAFTA chapter II arbitration: deciding on the price of free trade. *Ecol. Law Q.* 29:371–94
20. Sanchez RA. 2002. Governance, trade, and the environment in the context of NAFTA. *Am. Behav. Sci.* 45:1369–93
21. Clark W. 2000. Environmental Globalization. In *Governance in a Globalizing World*, ed. JS Nye, JD Donahue, pp. 86–108. Washington, DC: Brookings Inst.
22. Eakin H, Lemos MC. 2006. Adaptation and the state: Latin America and the challenge of capacity-building under globalization. *Glob. Environ. Chang.* 16:7–18
23. Jordan A, Wurtzel R, Zito AR. 2003. "New" environmental policy instruments: an evolution or a revolution in environmental policy? *Environ. Polit.* 12:201–24
24. Busch PO, Jorgens H, Tews K. 2005. The global diffusion of regulatory instruments: the making of a new international environmental regime. *Ann. Am. Polit. Soc. Sci.* 598:146–67
25. Heijden HA. 2006. Globalization, environmental movements, and international political opportunity structures. *Organ. Environ.* 19:28–45
26. Haas PM. 1989. Do regimes matter? Epistemic communities and Mediterranean pollution control. *Int. Organ.* 43:377–403
27. Krasner SD, ed. 1983. *International Regimes*. Ithaca, NY: Cornell Univ. Press
28. Young OR. 1989. *International Cooperation: Building Regimes for Natural Resources and the Environment*. Ithaca, NY: Cornell Univ. Press
29. Young OR. 2001. Inferences and indices: evaluating the effectiveness of international environmental regimes. *Glob. Environ. Polit.* 1:99–121
30. Mitchell RB. 2003. International environmental agreements: a survey of their features, formation, and effects. *Annu. Rev. Environ. Resour.* 28:429–61
31. Ford LH. 2003. Challenging global environmental governance: social movement agency and global civil society. *Glob. Environ. Polit.* 3:120–34
32. Stiglitz JE. 1999. The World Bank at the millennium. *Econ. J.* 109:F577–97
33. Hempel LC. 1996. *Environmental Governance: The Global Challenge*. Washington: Island
34. Gulbrandsen LH, Andresen S. 2004. NGO infuence in the implementation of the Kyoto Protocol: compliance, flexibility mechanisms, and sinks. *Glob. Environ. Polit.* 4:54–75
35. Ruggie JG. 2003. Taking embedded liberalism global: the corporate connection. In *Taming Globalization*, ed. D Held, M Koenig-Archibugi, pp. 93–129. Cambridge, UK: Polity
36. Brunner R, Klein R. 1999. Harvesting experience: a reappraisal of the U.S. climate change action plan. *Polit. Sci.* 32:133–61
37. Haas P. 2004. Addressing the global governance deficit. *Glob. Environ. Polit.* 4:1–15
38. Sanwal M. 2004. Trends in global environmental governance: the emergence of a mutual supportiveness approach to achieve sustainable development. *Glob. Environ. Polit.* 4:16–22
39. Papadopoulos Y. 2003. Cooperative forms of governance: problems of democratic accountability in complex environments. *Eur. J. Polit. Res.* 42:473–501
40. Schofer E, Hironaka A. 2005. The effects of world society on environmental protection outcomes. *Soc. Forces* 84:25–47
41. Buhrs T. 2003. From diffusion to diffusion: the roots and effects of environmental innovation in New Zealand. *Environ. Polit.* 12:83–101
42. Claussen E. 2001. Global environmental

governance: issues for the new US administration. *Environment* 43:29–34
43. Hardin G. 1978. Political requirements for preserving our common heritage. In *Wildlife and America*, ed. HP Brokaw, pp. 310–17. Washington, DC: Counc. Environ. Qual.
44. Ophuls W. 1977. *Ecology and the Politics of Scarcity: Prologue to a Political Theory of the Steady State*. San Francisco: Freeman
45. Anderson D, Grove R, ed. 1984. *Conservation in Africa: People, Policies and Practice*. Cambridge, UK: Cambridge Univ. Press
46. Peluso NL, Vandergeest P. 2001. Genealogies of the political forest and customary rights in Indonesia. *J. Asia. Stud.* 60:761–812
47. Wunsch JS, Olowu D. 1997. Regime transformation from below: decentralization, local governance, and democratic reform in Nigeria. *Stud. Comp. Int. Dev.* 31:66–82
48. Corbridge S. 1991. Third world development. *Prog. Hum. Geogr.* 15:311–21
49. Silver C. 2003. Do the donors have it right? Decentralization and changing local governance in Indonesia. *Ann. Reg. Sci.* 37:421–34
50. Peluso NL. 1992. *Rich Forests, Poor People: Resource Control and Resistance in Java*. Berkeley: Univ. Calif. Press
51. Ostrom E. 1990. *Governing the Commons: The Evolution of Institutions for Collective Action*. New York: Cambridge Univ. Press
52. Wade R. 1994. *Village Republics: Economic Conditions for Collective Action in South India*. Oakland: ICS Press
53. Blaikie P, Brookfield H. 1987. *Land Degradation and Society*. London: Methuen. 296 pp
54. Bryant RL, Bailey S. 1997. *Third World Political Ecology*. London: Routledge
55. Wantchekon L. 2004. Resource wealth and political regimes in Africa. *Comp. Polit. Stud.* 37:816–41
56. Hardin RD. 2002. *Concessionary politics in the Western Congo Basin: History and Culture in Forest Use*. Washington, DC: World Resour. Inst./Gov. Inst.
57. Watts MJ. 2005. Righteous oil: human rights, the oil complex, and corporate social responsibility. *Annu. Rev. Environ. Resour.* 30:373–407
58. Luong PJ, Weinthal E. 2001. Prelude to the resource curse: explaining oil and gas development strategies in the Soviet successor states and beyond. *Comp. Polit. Stud.* 34:367–99
59. Hutchcroft PD. 2001. Centralization and decentralization in administration and politics: assessing territorial dimensions of authority and power. *Governance* 14:23–53
60. Conyers D. 1983. Decentralization: the latest fashion in development administration. *Public Adm. Dev.* 3:97–109
61. Manor J. 1999. *The Political Economy of Democratic Decentralization*. Washington, DC: World Bank
62. Weber EP. 2000. A new vanguard for the environment: grassroots ecosystem management as a new environmental management. *Soc. Nat. Resour.* 13:237–59
63. Johnson C, Forsyth T. 2002. In the eyes of the state: negotiating a "rights-based approach" to forest conservation in Thailand. *World Dev.* 30:1591–605
64. Lemos MC, Oliveira JLF. 2004. Can water reform survive politics? Institutional change and river basin management in Ceará Northeast Brazil. *World Dev.* 32:2121–37
65. Wunsch JS. 2001. Decentralization, local governance and 'recentralization' in Africa. *Public Adm. Dev.* 21:277–88
66. Ribot JC, Peluso NL. 2003. A theory of access. *Rural Sociol.* 68:153–81
67. Noel E. 1999. Power, politics and place: Who holds the reins of environmental regulation? *Ecol. Law Q.* 25:559–63
68. Campbell T. 2003. *The Quiet Revolution: Decentralization and the Rise of Political*

*Participation in Latin American Cities*. Pittsburgh: Univ. Pittsburgh Press
69. Bardhan P. 2002. Decentralization of governance and development. *J. Econ. Perspect.* 16:185–205
70. Boone C. 2003. Decentralization as political strategy in West Africa. *Comp. Polit. Stud.* 36:355–80
71. Agrawal A. 2001. The regulatory community: decentralization and the environment in the Van Panchayats (forest councils) of Kumaon. *Mt. Res. Dev.* 21:208–11
72. Andersson KP. 2004. Who talks with whom? The role of repeated interactions in decentralized forest governance. *World Dev.* 32:233–49
73. Bagchi A. 2003. Rethinking federalism: changing power relations between the center and the states. *Publius* 33:21–42
74. Ribot J. 1999. Decentralisation, participation, and accountability in Sahelian forestry: legal instruments of political administrative control. *Africa* 69(1):23–65
75. Prud'homme R. 1995. The dangers of decentralization. *World Bank Res. Obs.* 10:201–20
76. Cashore B. 2002. Legitimacy and the privatization of environmental governance: How nonstate market driven (NSMD) governance systems gain rule-making authority. *Governance* 15:503–29
77. Tews K, Busch PO, Jorgens H. 2003. The diffusion of new environmental policy instruments. *Eur. J. Polit. Res.* 42:569–600
78. Lafferty W, Meadowcroft J, eds. 2000. *Implementing Sustainable Development*. Oxford: Oxford Univ. Press
79. Segerson K, Miceli TJ. 1998. Voluntary environmental agreements: Good or bad news for environmental protection? *J. Environ. Econ. Manag.* 36:109–30
80. MacKendrick NM. 2005. The role of the state in voluntary environmental reform: a case study of public land. *Policy Sci.* 38:21–44
81. Bray DB, Sanchez JLP, Murphy EC. 2002. Social dimensions of organic coffee production in Mexico: lessons for eco-labeling initiatives. *Soc. Nat. Resour.* 15:426–46
82. Cashore B, Auld G, Newsom D. 2003. Forest certification (eco-labeling) programs and their policy-making authority: explaining divergence among North American and European case studies. *Forest Policy Econ* 5:225–47
83. Cashore B, Auld G, Newsom D. 2004. *Governing through Markets: Forest Certification and the Emergence of Non-State Authority*. New Haven: Yale Univ. Press
84. Engel S, Lopez R, Palmer C. 2006. Community-industry contracting over natural resource use in a context of weak property rights: the case of Indonesia. *Environ. Resour. Econ.* 33:73–93
85. Durant RF, Chun YP, Kim B, Lee S. 2004. Toward a new governance paradigm for environmental and natural resource management in the 21st century? *Adm. Soc.* 35:643–82
86. Coase R. 1960. The problem of social cost. *J. Law Econ.* 3:1–44
87. Cheung SNS. 1970. The structure of a contract and the theory of a Non-Exclusive Resource. *J. Law Econ.* 13:49–70
88. Brammer S, Millington A. 2003. The effect of stakeholder preferences, organizational structure and industry type on corporate community involvement. *J. Bus. Ethics* 45:213–26
89. Bartley T. 2003. Certifying forests and factories: states, social movements, and the rise of private regulation in the apparel and forest products fields. *Polit. Soc.* 31:433–64
90. Delmas M, Keller A. 2005. Free riding in voluntary environmental programs: the case of the U.S. E.P.A. WasteWise Program. *Policy Sci.* 38:91–106
91. Auperle KE, Carroll AB, Hatfield JD. 1985. An empirical examination of the relationship between corporate social responsibility and profitability. *Acad. Manag. J.* 28:446–63
92. Cochran PL, Wood RA. 1984. Corporate

social responsibility and financial performance. *Acad. Manag. J.* 27:42–56
93. Wilbanks TJ. 2002. Geographic scaling issues in integrated assessments of climate change. *Integr. Assess.* 3:100–14
94. Adger N, Brown K, Tompkins EL. 2006. The political economy of cross-scale networks in resource co-management. *Ecol. Soc.* 10:18
95. Lebel L, Garden P, Imamura M. 2005. The politics of scale, position, and place in the governance of water resources in the Mekong Region. *Ecol. Soc.* 10:9
96. Rival L. 2003. The meaning of forest governance in Esmeraldas, Ecuador. *Oxford Dev. Stud.* 31:479–501
97. Keck ME, Sikkink K. 1998. *Activists Beyond Borders: Advocacy Networks in International Politics*. Ithaca, NY: Cornell Univ. Press
98. Lipschutz RD. 1996. *Global Civil Society and Global Environmental Governance: The Politics of Nature from Place to Planet*. Albany: State Univ. NY Press
99. Wapner P. 1995. Politics beyond the state: environmental activism and world civic politics. *World Polit.* 47:311–40
100. Biermann F. 2002. Institutions for scientific advice: global environmental assessments and their influence in developing countries. *Glob. Gov.* 8:195–219
101. Coate R, Alger C, Lipschutz R. 1996. The United Nations and civil society: creative partnerships for sustainable development. *Alternatives* 21(1):93–122
102. Ford LH. 1999. Social movements and the globalisation of environmental governance. *IDS Bull.* 30:68–74
103. Toke D. 1999. Epstemic communities and environmental groups. *Politics* 19:97–102
104. Speth JG. 2004. *Red Sky at Morning: America and the Crisis of the Global Environment*. New Haven: Yale Univ. Press
105. Alchian A, Demsetz H. 1972. Production, information costs, and economic organization. *Am. Econ. Rev.* 62:777–95
106. Ophuls W. 1977. *Ecology and the Politics of Scarcity: Prologue to a Political Theory of the Steady State*. San Francisco: Freeman
107. Ostrom E, Schroeder L, Wynne S. 1993. *Institutional Incentives and Sustainable Development: Infrastructure Policies in Perspective*. Boulder, CO: Westview
108. McCarthy JJ. 2004. Privatizing conditions of production: trade agreements as neoliberal environmental governance. *Geoforum* 35:327–41
109. Rhodes RAW. 1996. The new governance: governing without government. *Polit. Stud.* 44:652–67
110. Bennett PI. 2000. Environmental governance and private actors: enrolling insurers and international maritime regulation. *Polit. Geogr.* 9:875–99
111. Robertson M. 2004. The neoliberalization of ecosystem services: wetland mitigation banking and problems in environmental governance. *Geoforum* 35:361–73
112. Ashford NA. 2002. Government and environmental innovation in Europe and North America. *Am. Behav. Sci.* 45:1417–34
113. Hardin RD. 2006. *Concessionary Politics*. Berkeley: Univ. Calif. Press. In press
114. Sanderson S. 2002. The future of conservation. *Foreign Aff.* 81:162–82
115. Liverman D. 2004. Who governs, at what scale, and at what price? Geography, environmental governance, and the commodification of nature. *Ann. Assoc. Am. Geogr.* 94:734–38
116. Falkner R. 2003. Private environmental governance and international relations: exploring the links. *Glob. Environ. Polit.* 3:72–87
117. Paterson M, Humphreys D, Pettiford L. 2003. Conceptualizing global environmental governance: from interstate regimes to counter-hegemonic struggles. *Glob. Environ. Polit.* 3:1–10
118. Manor J. 2005. User committees: a potentiality damaging second wave of decentralization? In *Democratic Decentralization through a Natural Resources Lens*,

ed. JC Ribot, AM Larson, pp. 193–13. New York: Routledge
119. Jessop B. 2002. Globalization and the national state. In *Paradigm Lost: State Theory Reconsidered*, ed. S Aronowitz, P Bratsis, pp. 185–220. Minneapolis: Univ. Minn. Press
120. Pelkonen A. 2005. State restructuring, urban competitiveness policies and technopole building in Finland: a critical view on the glocal state thesis. *Eur. Plan. Stud.* 13:687–705
121. Painter M, Pierre J. 2005. Unpacking policy capacity: issues and themes. In *Challenges to State Policy Capacity*, ed. M Painter, J Pierre, pp. 1–18. New York: Palgrave MacMillan
122. Lowi T. 2002. Progress and poverty revisited: toward construction of a statist third way. In *Democratic Governance & Social Inequality*, ed. JS Tulchin, A Brown, pp. 41–74. Boulder, CO: Rienner
123. Adger WN. 2001. Scales of governance and environmental justice for adaptation and mitigation of climate change. *J. Int. Dev.* 13:921–31
124. Brooks N, Adger WN, Kelly M. 2005. The determinants of vulnerability and adaptive capacity at the national level and the implications for adaptation. *Glob. Environ. Chang.* 15:151–63
125. O'Brien KL, Leichenko R, Kelkarc U, Venemad H, Aandahl G. et al. 2004. Mapping vulnerability to multiple stressors: climate change and globalization in India. *Glob. Environ. Chang.* 14:303–13
126. Deleted in proof
127. Streck C. 2004. New partnerships in global environmental policy: the clean development mechanism. *J. Environ. Dev.* 13:295–322
128. Intergov. Panel Clim. Chang. (IPCC). 2001. *Climate Change 2001: Impacts, Adaptation and Vulnerability*. IPCC, Geneva.
129. Socolow R, Hotinsky R, Greenblatt J, Pacala S. 2004. Solving the climate change problem. *Environment* 46:8–19
130. Kates RW. 2004. Beyond Kyoto. *Environment* 46:2
131. Nelson K, Jong BJH. 2003. Making global initiatives local realities: carbon mitigation projects in Chiapas, Mexico. *Glob. Environ. Chang.* 13:19–30
132. Klooster D, Masera O. 2000. Community forest management in Mexico: carbon mitigation and biodiversity conservation through rural development. *Glob. Environ. Chang.* 10:259–72
133. Gough C, Shackley S. 2001. The respectable politics of climate change: the epistemic communities and NGOs. *Int. Aff.* 77:329–45
134. Corell E, Betsill MM. 2001. A comparative look at NGO influence in international environmental negotiations: desertification and climate change. *Glob. Environ. Polit.* 1:86–107
135. Brooks N, Adger WN. 2004. Assessing and enhancing adaptive capacity. In *Adaptation Policy Framework*, ed. B Lim, pp. 165–81. New York: UN Dev. Programme
136. Adger WN, Arnell NW, Tompkins EL. 2005. Successful adaptation to climate change across scales. *Glob. Environ. Chang.* 15:77–86
137. Brooks N. 2003. *Vulnerability, Risk and Adaptation: A Conceptual Framework*. Norwich: Tyndall Cent. Clim. Chang. Res./Cent. Soc. Econ. Res. Glob. Environ.
138. Liverman DM. 2005. *Equity, Justice and Climate Change*. London: Cent. Reform

# [11]



## Legitimacy in Global Environmental Governance

STEVEN BERNSTEIN*

Writing in 1999, Daniel Bodansky predicted that the question of legitimacy would 'emerge from the shadows and become a central issue in international environmental law.'[1] Specifically, Bodansky worried that as authority over environmental policy moved increasingly from domestic to international settings, perceptions that decision-making processes are 'insufficiently democratic' would increase. Such concerns were already simmering in other arenas of global governance. Jürgen Habermas, for example, used similar language nearly ten years earlier in anticipating a legitimacy problem in Europe, commenting that, 'the democratic processes constituted at the level of the nation-state lag hopelessly behind the economic integration taking place at a supranational level.'[2] Both authors, in different ways, worried that the reconfiguration of political authority might not keep pace or adapt appropriately to globalizing pressures. Few topics could be more appropriate for the inaugural issue of a journal devoted to the intersection of International Relations (IR) and International Law (IL).

Whereas Bodansky in 1999 could cite only a handful of works that addressed legitimacy in global governance, as one author recently put it, 'currently there is hardly an essay on international or global governance that does not at least mention the issue of legitimacy.'[3] Still,

---

* Associate Professor, Department of Political Science, University of Toronto.

The author gratefully acknowledges research assistance and comments from Elizabeth Acorn and Sarah Kim, helpful comments and criticisms from Lars Gulbrandsen and an anonymous reviewer, and financial support from a Social Sciences and Humanities Research Council of Canada grant. An earlier version of this paper was presented at the International Studies Association meeting, Honolulu, Hawaii, 1-5 March 2005.

1 Daniel Bodansky, 'The Legitimacy of International Governance: A Coming Challenge for International Environmental Law?' (1999) 93 Am. J. Int'l L. 596 at 596

2 Jürgen Habermas, 'Citizenship and National Identity', reprinted as Appendix II in Habermas, *Between Facts and Norms: Contributions to a Discourse Theory of Law and Democracy*, trans. by W. Rehg. (Cambridge, Mass.: MIT Press, 1996) 491 at 491.

3 Jens Steffek, 'Why IR Needs Legitimacy: A Rejoinder' (2004) 10 European Journal of International Relations 485 at 485. Examples of recent works include Jean-Marc Coicaud & Veijo Heiskanen, eds., *The Legitimacy of International Organizations* (Tokyo: The United Nations University Press, 2001); Roger B. Porter *et al.*, eds., *Efficiency, Equity and Legitimacy: The Multilateral Trading System at the Millennium* (Washington: Brookings Institution Press, 2001); Jens Steffek, 'The Legitimation of International Governance: A Discourse Approach' (2003) 9 European Journal of International Relations 249; Ian Hurd, 'Legitimacy and Authority in

passing references far outnumber systematic treatments. Empirical applications are even more rare. Moreover, existing scholarship on legitimacy draws on diverse disciplinary literatures in political science and philosophy, law, and sociology, which has produced confusion over its meaning and dynamics. This article attempts to sort through different conceptions of legitimacy and evaluate how contemporary environmental governance stacks up to these notions. Ultimately, it proposes that the overall legitimacy of global environmental governance is a consequence of the joint appearance of components emphasized in these different conceptions, but inadequately identified in any alone.

It might seem ironic to focus on environmental governance as a site of legitimacy problems. No equivalent to the 'Battle of Seattle'—the massive public protests at the 1999 World Trade Organization (WTO) Ministerial that became a watershed for public challenges to the legitimacy of international economic institutions—has ever confronted global environmental institutions. They seem largely immune from the protests dogging not only the WTO, but virtually every significant organization or initiative identified with the economic globalization agenda. Moreover, while environmental governance by no means achieves a democratic or deliberative ideal, it is among the most transparent, participatory, and accessible realms of global governance to state and non-state actors alike. It has also generally been responsive to justice and equity concerns—values sometimes linked to notions of legitimacy—especially when compared to other domains of global governance. Global environmental norms, institutions and agreements, especially in the post-Rio Summit (1992) era, often entrench differential obligations and recognize differential capacities of developed and developing countries. They also frequently attempt to combine global concerns with local decision-making and accountability, where activities are focused.

Part of the reason legitimacy concerns have increased despite these conditions is a widespread belief that global environmental governance remains weak, lacks authority, and is unable to make

---

International Politics' (1999) 53 Int'l Org. 379; Benjamin Cashore, 'Legitimacy and the Privatization of Environmental Governance: How Non-State Market-Driven (NSMD) Governance Systems Gain Rule-Making Authority' (2002) 14 Governance 502. Older treatments are rare, although a broad survey of work that directly discusses legitimacy would include Henry Kissinger, *A World Restored* (New York: Gosset Dunlap, 1964); Inis Claude, Jr., 'Collective Legitimization as a Political Function of the United Nations' (1966) 20 Int'l Org. 367; Thomas M. Franck, *The Power of Legitimacy Among Nations* (New York: Oxford University Press, 1990); Abram Chayes & Antonia H. Chayes, *The New Sovereignty: Compliance with International Regulatory Agreements* (Cambridge, Mass.: Harvard University Press, 1995).

significant inroads into solving many of the problems for which institutions and agreements have been established.[4] This suggests greater legitimacy is needed to establish more extensive, enforceable, and effective environmental action at the global level. At the same time, many scholars and activists argue that ostensibly non-environmental institutions such as the WTO or World Bank, which nonetheless play a significant role in international environmental governance, pay insufficient attention to environmental concerns or subordinate them to the goals of open markets, corporate freedom, efficiency and economic growth. Environmental protection and sustainable development thus join human rights, labour rights, and poverty reduction, as unmet goals driving the broader legitimacy challenge to international liberalism and the global governance institutions established to promote and maintain it.[5]

I will argue that a focus on legitimacy can help to understand and address these dilemmas. However, legitimacy must be examined not only from the common perspective of democratic theory, but also from legal and sociological perspectives that may diverge from the democratic normative ideal. Whereas these different conceptions of legitimacy can sometimes push in contradictory directions, the key to legitimate governance is in their convergence. After defining legitimacy, I identify principled, legal, and sociological notions of legitimacy and evaluate environmental governance in light of these notions.[6] I conclude with some observations on what integration of these conceptions of legitimacy might entail and implications for the legitimacy challenge ahead.

---

4 One could cite dozens of works on the inadequacies of efforts to address global environmental problems, failures of global environmental governance, and the need for reform. For an overview of these arguments focused specifically on governance, see James Gustave Speth, 'The Global Environmental Agenda: Origins and Prospects' in Daniel C. Esty & Maria H. Ivanova, eds., *Global Environmental Governance: Options & Opportunities* (New Haven: Yale School of Forestry & Environmental Studies, 2002) 11 and other contributions to that volume; Frank Biermann & Steffen Bauer, eds., *A World Environment Organization: Solution or Threat for Effective International Environmental Governance* (Aldershot, UK: Ashgate, 2005).

5 John G. Ruggie, 'International Regimes, Transactions and Change: Embedded Liberalism in the Postwar Economic Order' (1982) 36 Int'l Org. 357; Steven Bernstein & Louis W. Pauly, eds., *Global Governance: Towards a New Grand Compromise?* (Albany: SUNY Press) [forthcoming].

6 For a detailed discussion and defence of these conceptions of legitimacy, see Steven Bernstein, 'The Elusive Basis of Legitimacy in Global Governance: Three Conceptions' (Globalization and Autonomy working paper series, Institute for Globalization and the Human Condition, McMaster University, 2004).

## I LEGITIMACY AND WHY IT MATTERS

Legitimacy can be defined as the acceptance and justification of shared rule by a community. This definition self-consciously combines an empirical measure of legitimacy (acceptance of a rule or institution as authoritative) and a normative argument concerning whether the authority possesses legitimacy (providing reasons that justify it). It therefore eschews the traditional dividing line in political science writing on the topic between a Weberian social scientific approach and a Habermasean position that a belief in legitimacy is assumed to have an 'immanent relation to truth.'[7] As a practical matter in global governance, this conceptual distinction is untenable. Arguments about why actors *should* accept a decision or rule as authoritative (as opposed to because they are coerced) necessarily include possible reasons why the decision *is* accepted, and vice-versa. That being said, particular conceptions of legitimacy invoked by global governance scholars entail trade-offs in the leverage they provide for normative or positive projects, as will be seen below.

Beyond definitions, the new legitimacy concerns need to be placed in the context of the ongoing debate over the reconfiguration of global authority.[8] The question of authority beyond the state is not especially new. Since the emergence of the 'regimes' literature in the 1980s, IR scholars have asked how, given formal anarchy, institutions gain 'authority' to create obligations on community members to adhere to their rules or norms. Legitimacy is one logical answer, whether the community consists only of states, or includes firms, civil society groups, local populations or sub-state actors who may be involved in rule-making or who might be affected by decisions. Yet, IR scholars until very recently largely ignored legitimacy, assuming instead that states—the nearly exclusive focus of regime theory although not of the newer global governance scholarship—largely obeyed commands out of self-interest, fear, or incentives from more powerful actors.

Whether or not legitimacy was always necessary for international stability and patterned behaviour,[9] the extended scope and reach of contemporary 'global governance' has made that need much

---

7 Jürgen Habermas, *Legitimation Crisis*, trans. Thomas McCarthey (Boston, Mass.: Beacon Press, 1973) at 97. Bodansky, *supra* note 1, and Steffek (2003), *supra* note 3, make much more of this distinction.

8 Miles Kahler & David Lake, eds., *Governance in a Global Economy: Political Authority in Transition* (Princeton, NJ: Princeton University Press, 2003); Edgar Grande & Louis W. Pauly, *Complex Sovereignty and the Foundations of Global Governance* (Toronto: University of Toronto Press, 2005).

9 For arguments that it was, see especially Kissinger, *supra* note 3; Claude, *supra* note 3.

more visible. This need is apparent not only within international organizations (such as the UN, IMF, WTO, or World Bank), but also within hybrid, private, and networked forms of governance that include varying mixes of non-state actors. Many of these governance nodes until recently existed on the fringes of consciousness, except among a few select elites. Others, especially of the hybrid and non-state variety, are only now emerging. These developments create a situation not unlike the legitimacy problems described by Habermas following the expansion of post-war welfare states into more and more areas of economic and social life, in order to maintain economic performance. That expansion, 'enhance[d] the visibility of the conventional and political dimension of social life and encourage[d] citizens to ask the state to legitimize the particular conventions supported by its action.'[10] Similarly, legitimacy demands on international institutions increase to the degree they appear authoritative to ordinary citizens who view them as the institutional embodiment of globalization. Hence, civil society looks to these institutions to provide social justice, equity, or other broad societal values, including ecological integrity, not just functional goals such as financial stability.[11]

Even since the events of 11 September 2001, when the 'anti-globalization' movement appears in retreat, legitimacy pressures in global governance have not abated, nor are governance institutions less 'visible'. For instance, developing countries, which are now better integrated into the world economy than ever before, are demanding with renewed vigor changes in the structure of international institutions to more equitably represent their needs and concerns. Pressure also continues to mount, especially from non-state actors, to make institutions more accountable to domestic populations and transnational civil societies, as well as to increase transparency and access to participatory mechanisms for all affected actors.

Under these conditions, the question of legitimacy concerns who is entitled to make rules and how authority itself is generated—a significant departure from an earlier and much narrower emphasis in IR and IL on legitimacy as a mode of compliance.[12] That earlier literature tended to juxtapose legitimacy to interests or fear of 'punishment' as sources of compliance.[13] The new focus on governance, in contrast,

---

10 William Connolly, 'Introduction: Legitimacy and Modernity' in W. Connolly, ed., *Legitimacy and the State* (Oxford: Basil Blackwell, 1984) 1 at 13, commenting on Habermas's, *Legitimation Crisis*, *supra* note 7.

11 Richard Devetak & Richard Higgott, 'Justice Unbound: Globalization, States, and the Transfer of the Social Bond' (1999) 75 International Affairs 483.

12 Franck, *supra* note 3; Hurd, *supra* note 3.

13 Hurd, *ibid.* at 379.

highlights that legitimacy is intimately connected to power and political community. Max Weber, in his seminal writings on the topic, focused especially on how legitimacy justifies authority and domination,[14] a point not lost on an earlier generation of IR scholars who viewed legitimacy as making rulers 'more secure in the possession of power and more successful in its exercise.'[15] Legitimacy can also be a source of power, enabling some policies or practices while proscribing others.[16] In terms of community, legitimacy always rests on shared acceptance of rules and rule by affected communities and on justificatory norms recognized by the relevant community. However, defining who is a member of a relevant community, on what basis community identification must rest, and to what degree shared norms of appropriateness must be present to achieve legitimacy are all subjects of debate.

Perhaps the most important reason the newer legitimacy agenda applies to environmental governance is that it throws traditional notions of the international community into question by increasingly targeting or affecting non-state actors, whether firms whose production is affected by chemical bans, emission limits or campaigns for corporate responsibility; fishers whose catch is monitored or limited by fisheries regimes; or local communities affected by decisions of an international financing institution such a the Global Environmental Facility (GEF). Under these conditions, traditional sovereign state diplomacy and consent may be an inadequate source of legitimacy. Moreover, international legitimacy may no longer be easily divorced from justice, as some legal scholars have argued it should be.[17] If '[t]here are no settled social bonds [community] in an age of globalization' and therefore 'the Westphalian "givens" of justice [as a concern within states

---

14 Guenther Roth & Claus Wittich, eds., *Max Weber: Economy and Society* (Berkeley: University of California Press, 1978) at 953.

15 Claude, *supra* note 3 at 368.

16 A more radical position is that legitimating discourses are a form of productive power, producing subjectivity by defining identities and practices. Michel Foucault's notion of governmentality comes closest to capturing this process. See M. Foucault, 'Governmentality' in Graham Burchell, Colin Gordon & Peter Miller, eds., *The Foucault Effect: Studies in Governmentality* (London: Harvester Wheatsheaf, 1991) 87. On productive power compared to other conceptions of power in global governance, see Michael Barnett & Raymond Duvall, eds., *Power and Global Governance* (Cambridge: Cambridge University Press, 2004).

17 Franck, *supra* note 3 at 208-9; Bodansky, *supra* note 1. Interestingly, Franck subsequently acknowledged that an emerging global community means the value of fairness applies in international law and institutions (*Fairness in International Law and Institutions* (Oxford: Clarendon Press, 1995)).

but not beyond] no longer pertain,'[18] meeting conditions of democratic legitimacy beyond the state is at least hypothetically possible.

## II A PRINCIPLED CONCEPTION: LEGITIMACY AS DEMOCRACY

A focus on democratic legitimacy tends to dominate the new literature on legitimacy in global governance. As alluded to already, concerns over globalization are now commonly expressed in terms of justice and democracy by utilizing the rationale that institutions of global governance are usurping domestic democratic institutions. Two conclusions follow. Either international institutions should become more democratic—a view expressed most commonly by cosmopolitans[19]—or state governments must be protected from usurpation—a position most strongly expressed by conservative nationalists such as the 'new sovereigntists' in the United States.[20] The latter position rests on a philosophical claim that global governance can only be of peoples, i.e. governance of a community of states whose representatives can engage in rule making, but the legitimacy of those rules ultimately must rest on domestic constitutional order.[21]

In both cases, legitimacy requires democracy because it is the central principle in contemporary politics that justifies authority.[22] However, there is little indication on the horizon of truly democratic institutions at regional, let alone global scales when even the highly institutionalized European Union continues to struggle with a 'democratic deficit.' Cosmopolitan proposals for participatory mechanisms, including referendums and elected representative institutions such as People's Assemblies or a Global Parliament that can hold global regulatory institutions accountable or ensure the protection of local autonomy and individual rights,[23] appear even less likely outside the European context in the short to medium term, even when

---

18 Devetak & Higgott, *supra* note 11 at 484.

19 Most notably, David Held, *Democracy and the Global Order: From the Modern State to Cosmopolitan Governance* (Stanford: Stanford University Press, 1995).

20 For example, Jeremy Rabkin, *Why Sovereignty Matters* (Washington: AEI Press, 1998). For a summary of their views, see John G. Ruggie, 'American Exceptionalism, Exemptionalism and Global Governance', in Michael Ignatieff, ed., *American Exceptionalism and Human Rights* (Princeton: Princeton University Press, 2005) 304.

21 John Rawls, *The Law of Peoples* (Cambridge, Mass.: Harvard University Press, 1999).

22 Held, *supra* note 19 at 1.

23 E.g. Held, *supra* note 19 at 267-286; Iris Marion Young, *Inclusion and Democracy* (Oxford: Oxford University Press, 2001) at 265-75; Esref Aksu & Joseph A. Camilleri, eds., *Democratizing Global Governance* (New York: Palgrave, 2002).

they include principles such as 'subsidiarity'.[24]

Given these practical limitations, actual proposals in environmental governance for institutional reform have not generally included a democratic assembly. For example, discussions around a 2003 French proposal to the United Nations (UN) General Assembly for a new UN Environment Organization (UNEO)—the only initiative for a global environmental organization actually tabled—have so far focused instead on coordinating and strengthening existing agreements, compliance systems, and organizations with an environmental mandate, or improving responsiveness to developing countries. The thrust of the proposal is toward turning the United Nations Environment Programme (UNEP) into a UN specialized agency rather than radical democratic reform, centralization or legal reform along the lines of the WTO. Even this modest proposal has generated limited political momentum, is strongly opposed by the United States, and received no mention in the High-level Panel report on UN reform released in December 2004.[25] Although supporters argue a universal membership UNEO is needed precisely for legitimacy reasons—as put by German Environment Minister Jürgen Tritten, 'the legitimacy of decision-making processes is a key point and therefore all UN Member States should effectively be given the same rights'[26]—any move in that direction has been resisted. States could not even agree at the 2005 UNEP Governing Council meeting whether the Council should be expanded to include universal membership, with the EU strongly in favor and the United States' and developing country governments opposed.[27]

---

[24] The principle, most notably institutionalized in the European Union, envisions central authority being subsidiary to local authority in the absence of a compelling case for the contrary. Cosmopolitan proposals thus usually argue for multiple, non-hierarchical, and overlapping authorities at various scalar levels, with decision-making following democratic norms at all levels.

[25] International Institute for Sustainable Development, 'Summary of the Eighth Special Session of the UNEP Governing Council/Global Ministerial Environment Forum: 29-31 March 2004' 16:35 *Earth Negotiations Bulletin*; United Nations, *A More Secure World: Our Shared Responsibility: Report of the Secretary-General's High-level Panel on Threats, Challenges and Change*, UN Doc. A/59/565 (2004), online: United Nations <http://www.un.org/secureworld/>.

[26] German Federal Ministry for the Environment, Nature Conservation and Nuclear Safety, Press Statement, 'Trittin Calls for a UN Environment Organization' (15 March 2004), online: Bundesministerium für Umwelt <http://www.bmu.de/english/press/pm/5669.php>.

[27] International Institute for Sustainable Development, 'Summary of the 23rd Session of the UNEP Governing Council/Global Ministerial Environment Forum: 21-25 February 2005' 16:47 *Earth Negotiations Bulletin*.

In the absence of radical cosmopolitan reform, many scholars argue that democratic legitimacy can nonetheless be improved with relaxed requirements for full-fledged deliberative and democratic mechanisms. Thus, they focus on the elements of legitimacy in democratic theory, such as accountability, transparency, access to participation, deliberation and, sometimes, fairness. As opposed to direct accountability to publics through elections, proposals are increasingly rooted in deliberative models of legitimation based on Habermas' theory of communicative action, where legitimacy ideally requires that decisions rest on 'good arguments' made under conditions in which free and equal autonomous actors can challenge validity claims, seek a reasoned communicative consensus about their understandings of the situation and justifications for norms guiding their action, and are open to being persuaded.[28] IR scholars generally recognize that such 'ideal speech' situations are unlikely to obtain in international negotiations or forums, but nonetheless suggest that when argumentation occurs in situations approximating these conditions, such as when participants of different capabilities refrain from coercion or pulling rank, it can serve as a source of legitimacy.[29] Whether arguments and justifications occur between state representatives, members of transnational organizations or individual citizens, legitimacy requires a situation where persuasion is possible and common understanding is the goal.[30] Another variant of particular relevance to emerging forms of environmental governance, is 'stakeholder' democracy, 'centered … on new participatory deliberative practices' among stakeholders that include not only governments, but civil society groups, local communities and businesses.[31]

---

28 Jürgen Habermas, *Theory of Communicative Action*, vol. 1 and 2, trans. by Thomas McCarthy (Boston: Beacon Press, 1981 and 1987). On deliberative democracy generally, including formulations critical of Habermas, see Seyla Benhabib, ed., *Democracy and Difference: Contesting the Boundaries of the Political* (Princeton: Princeton University Press, 1996).

29 Thomas Risse, '"Let's Argue!": Communicative Action in World Politics' (2000) 54 Int'l Org. 1.

30 Interpretations of Habermas and deliberative democracy more generally disagree whether consensus is required for legitimacy, or whether there is scope for difference or 'agreeing to disagree'. However, adjudicating that debate is beyond the scope here. For a good discussion, see Simone Chambers, *Reasonable Democracy: Jürgen Habermas and the Politics of Discourse* (Ithaca, NY: Cornell University Press, 1996) at 155-72; Benhabib, *supra* note 28.

31 Karin Bäckstrand & Michael Saward, 'Democratizing Global Environmental Governance? Stakeholder Democracy at the World Summit for Sustainable Development' (Paper presented to the Fifth Pan-European Conference on International Relations, The Hague, 9–11 September 2004); Nancy Vallejo & Pierre Hauselmann, Governance and Multi-stakeholder

Given wide disagreement in this literature on precise criteria of legitimacy, the evaluation below assesses environmental governance across the full range of criteria identified above. By most measures, although varied across institutions and agreements and generally stronger in participation and transparency than deliberation, environmental governance fares relatively well.

Peter Haas, for example, citing the increasing role of scientists in national decision-making and in treaty advisory bodies as well as the proliferation of environmental non-governmental organizations (NGOs), has argued that states, though still the primary locus of authority, 'are increasingly accountable to domestic and transnational constituencies.'[32] Moreover, delegations to multilateral negotiations frequently include members of civil society and the business community. Moreover, these non-state actors sometimes serve as important sources of expertise, especially for developing countries with limited diplomatic and technical resources. NGOs also play formal and informal roles in monitoring and implementation. Transnational corporations have also significantly increased their participation and political organization in a variety of environmental governance forums.[33]

More broadly, international environmental institutions have frequently been leaders in providing non-state actors access to information and participation. Both the 1972 UN Conference on the Human Environment in Stockholm and the 1992 UN Conference on Environment and Development in Rio de Janeiro were breakthrough events for NGO participation in their times. The Stockholm conference originated the idea of a parallel NGO forum, which attracted some 400 groups, and has since become a regular feature of such events.[34] At Rio, 1420 accredited NGOs, about one-third from the South, participated in the official proceedings as a result of the Secretariat's unprecedented decision to relax accreditation rules to allow non-ECOSOC NGOs to

---

Processes (Winnipeg: International Institute for Sustainable Development, 2004).

32 Peter M. Haas, 'Social Constructivism and the Evolution of Multilateral Environmental Governance' in Aseem Prakash & Jeffrey A. Hart, eds., *Globalization and Governance* (London: Routledge, 1999) 103.

33 Mikoto Usui, 'The Private Business Sector in Global Environmental Diplomacy' in Norichika Kanie & Peter M. Haas, eds., *Emerging Forces in Global Environmental Governance* (Tokyo: United Nations University Press, 2004) 216.

34 *Report of the United Nations Conference on the Human Environment*, UN Doc. A/CONF.48/14/REV.1 (1972); Satoko Mori, 'Institutionalization of NGO Involvement in Policy Functions for Global Environmental Governance' in Kanie & Haas, *supra* note 33 at 159.

participate (another 11,000 participated in the parallel Global Forum).[35] Again, the relaxed rules became the norm for subsequent world conferences.

The 2002 World Summit on Sustainable Development (WSSD) in Johannesburg marked a further innovation, multi-stakeholder deliberation and public-private partnership agreements. While it did not invent these concepts, it did much to promote the idea then emerging that environmental governance should not be limited to inter-state agreements. Stakeholders ought to be engaged, not only by informing inter-governmental decisions, but also through collaborative ventures, especially focusing on the implementation of sustainable development.[36] While innovations outside of WSSD also included voluntary measures in the corporate sector and non-state governance,[37] WSSD particularly promoted public-private partnerships or what became known as type II agreements. Some 300 of these partnerships were identified before or at the Johannesburg Summit.[38] WSSD also included 'multi-stakeholder' dialogues as an integral part of the preparatory process and the summit itself. The dialogues promoted deliberations among the nine 'major groups' identified by Agenda 21, reflecting various segments of society, and government officials. Although states never relinquished their sole authority to make decisions, these innovations can be read as an opportunity for 'stakeholder democracy' that moves beyond mere participation to 'collaboration' and truer 'deliberation' among states, business, and civil society.[39]

Multi-stakeholder dialogues had already been part of the Commission on Sustainable Development's regular sessions since 1998, and in 2002 UNEP's Governing Council (GC) institutionalized a Global Civil Society Forum (endorsing an initiative started two years earlier) in conjunction with meetings of the GC and Global Ministerial Environment Forum (GMEF).[40] In 2004, 206 civil society

---

35 *Ibid.* at 159, 173, n. 3; Peter M. Haas, Marc A. Levy & Edward A Parson, 'Appraising the Earth Summit: How Should We Judge UNCED's Success?' (1992) 34:8 Environment 6 at 32.

36 Bäckstrand & Saward, *supra* note 31.

37 See Steven Bernstein & Benjamin Cashore, 'The Two-Level Logic of Non-State Global Governance' [under review] for distinctions among these types of governance.

38 Peter Doran, Briefing Paper, 'World Summit on Sustainable Development: An Assessment for IISD' (Winnipeg: International Institute for Sustainable Development, 2002).

39 Bäckstrand & Saward, *supra* note 31 at 5, 13.

40 The GMEF is a ministerial level meeting of Governing Council members. UNEP, 'Engaging Civil Society in the Governing Council/Global Ministerial Environment Forum' (background document for the regional meetings in preparation of the sixth Global Civil Society Forum, 14

representatives from forty countries attended the Forum, while 126 representatives from about sixty countries attended in 2005. Whereas representatives of civil society elected in regional meetings drafted the civil society statement forwarded to the GC/GMEF, any accredited organization can submit written inputs into working documents in the lead-up to the GC/GMEF meetings, receive working documents at the same time as government representatives, comment on these drafts, and have the comments circulated to governments before they meet to finalize the documents. They can also comment on the final documents.

Environmental governance seems even to make a difference for democratic reform in development finance institutions, where change has otherwise been more difficult. The most notable example is the Global Environmental Facility (GEF), a cooperative venture between UNEP, United Nations Development Program (UNDP), and the World Bank, established in 1991 to be the primary channel for multilateral aid for environmental protection in developing countries. A comparative study that assessed democratization in global governance according to a model of deliberative democracy identified the GEF as 'perhaps the most inclusive and open international organization.'[41] The study's authors note that Southern states' suspicions over environmental 'conditionality' gave way to stronger support after a series of reforms, including a balance of donor and recipient countries in its governing council (although there is still a slight bias towards wealthier countries and affirmative votes require a majority of members and contributors), increased transparency, and direct participation by NGOs through formal consultations. As evidence of its increased legitimacy, membership grew from twenty-nine states in the pilot phase (1991–4) to over 173 members by 2002. Where critics still maintain that actual practices have not lived up to the deliberative ideal, the GEF 'has adopted and implemented democratic procedures virtually unmatched in global politics.'[42]

In addition to these organizational reforms, global environmental norms and treaties support ongoing improvements in public participation and transparency. For example, Rio Declaration Principle 10 asserts that 'environmental issues are best handled with the participation of all concerned citizens, at the relevant level' and promotes access to information, participation in decision-making, and access to judicial and administrative proceedings at the national level. While only soft law, many states have adopted its spirit. The 1998

---

October 2004). See also UNEP's 'Resources for Civil Society', online: <http://www.unep.org/DPDL/ civil_society/GCSF/index.asp>.

41 Roger A. Payne & Nayef H. Samhat, *Democratizing Global Politics* (Albany, NY: SUNY Press, 2004) at 7.

42 *Ibid*. at 98.

*Aarhus Convention on Access to Information, Public Participation in Decision-making and Access to Justice in Environmental Matters,* which came into force in 2001, takes up its provisions formally. Negotiated under the auspices of the UN Economic Commission for Europe, it includes provisions for transparency and participation at the international as well as national levels. Subsequently, the EU adopted implementing directives on access to environmental information and public participation (directive 2003/4/EC), with a 2005 deadline for national implementation. In 2003, parties to the convention adopted a *Protocol on Pollutant Release and Transfer Registers* to create publicly available national inventories of pollution releases from industrial and other sources.

In line with these norms, multilateral environmental negotiations are already remarkably open and transparent. Although practices vary across environmental agreements, detailed information about most negotiations and side meetings is readily available to broader publics, most notably through a non-governmental reporting service run by the International Institute for Sustainable Development, the *Earth Negotiations Bulletin.* Owing to its access and the quality of its reporting, official delegates rely on it as much as NGOs and academics.

These examples suggest that environmental governance stacks up extremely well by most criteria of democratic legitimacy, especially in comparison with economic and security institutions, many of which have weighted voting and much less access for non-state actors. Yet, a sense that legitimacy problems remain in environmental governance reveals limitations of a conception of legitimacy based solely on a democratic or deliberative justificatory discourse.

One problem concerns a possible legitimacy-effectiveness trade-off. Greater participation, whether of larger groups of states or NGOs, can slow down decision-making, make consensus more difficult, and generally increase the challenge of collective action. The assumption that participation leads to influence or meaningful deliberation can also be questioned. If innovations such as stakeholder dialogues provide little influence on government-to-government negotiations, do they really increase legitimacy? Many participants at WSSD, for example, saw their limited impact as a 'disappointment', and as 'more monologues than dialogues' because of limited participation by high-level officials.[43] However, the legitimacy-effectiveness trade-off may be overblown if 'efficient' decision-making lacks support from relevant groups of actors.

Problems of political community and the difficulty in establishing a *demos* (a popular unit that exercises political rights) beyond the state, pose a potentially more significant limitation on

---

43 Bäckstrand & Saward, *supra* note 31 at 17.

democratic legitimacy.[44] Who or what constitutes a political community is a major point of contention in political philosophy, although most literature agrees that communities exist by virtue of a shared identity and communication. The debate is most advanced in Europe, where political institutions with significant authority appear to be moving ahead of a *demos*. One response is that for limited and functional authority, such as that currently demanded in environmental governance, simple recognition of a shared fate may generate sufficient trust and willingness to sacrifice to support the requisite authority for governance.[45] To demand some notion of peoplehood or strong emotional bond is too high a standard for the type of authority being sought.

The problem is exacerbated, however, by unresolved tensions between the community of states and broader transnational society. Global environmental governance is well advanced in recognizing that its legitimacy increasingly rests on authority being granted by the broader communities it addresses beyond state governments. Still, the direction of reform to address these demands has provoked the ire of 'new sovereigntists'. Whatever the merits of the charges,[46] their concerns are best understood from the perspective of legal legitimacy.

## III LEGAL LEGITIMACY

Legitimacy gets surprisingly short-shrift in the IL scholarship, which perhaps accounts for the caricature of international lawyers as tending 'simply to translate legitimacy as *legality*.'[47] It does not help that recent attempts to create dialogue among IR and IL scholars have focused on analyzing and explaining 'legalization' in world politics,[48] a discussion almost completely devoid of whether the trend toward institutionalization of legal constraints is legitimate.[49]

---

44 For example, see Lars-Erik Cederman, 'Nationalism and Bounded Integration. What it Would Take to Construct a European Demos' (2001) 7 European Journal of International Relations 139 at 144.

45 E.g. Melissa S. Williams, 'On Peoples and Constitutions, Sovereignty and Citizenship' (Paper presented to the American Political Science Association annual meeting, Chicago, 2–4 September 2004)[unpublished].

46 There is good reason to be suspicious of their agenda, which targets environmental and human rights NGOs and treaties such as the *Kyoto Protocol*, but has no problem with international rules that protect multinational corporations. Ruggie, *supra* note 20 at 30.

47 Claude, *supra* note 3 at 368.

48 Judith Goldstein *et al.*, 'Introduction: Legalization and World Politics' (2000) 54 Int'l Org. 385.

49 Martha Finnemore & Stephen Toope, 'Alternatives to "Legalization": Richer Views of Law and Politics' (2001) 55 Int'l Org. 743.

This relative neglect started to change in response to the same real world legitimacy challenges that motivated political scientists, leading some IL scholars back to the question of on what basis law can be justified as legitimate. The dominant answer to the question of 'legal legitimacy' is some variant of legal process. Unlike most principled conceptions, which appeal to notions of truth or justice, 'legal legitimacy' supports a sharp dividing line between what is just and what is legitimate. As Bodansky explains, legal legitimacy does not concern whether a decision is unjust, misguided or 'correct'; rather, it 'reflects more general support for a regime, which makes subjects willing to substitute the regime's decisions for their own evaluation of a situation.'[50]

International legal scholars identify state consent as the basis of obligation. Analyses of legitimacy thus focus on the nature of consent and its distance or removal from the particular rule in question. Bodansky, for example, differentiates 'specific consent' such as ratifying a treaty from 'general consent' such as ratifying the *Charter of the United Nations*, which 'creates institutions with quasi-legislative and adjudicatory authority.'[51] The move toward general consent and constitutionalism[52] is one potential source of legitimacy problems if the connection between consent and the rule or institution becomes distanced or obscured, an argument made most vociferously today in regard to the WTO's dispute resolution process.[53] The problem of consent is also linked to notions of 'legality'. Legality is potentially violated when a treaty body, group of experts such as scientists

---

50 Bodansky, *supra* note 1 at 602.

51 *Ibid.* at 604.

52 Legalization blends into constitutionalism when rules define obligation 'as an attribute that incorporates general rules, procedures, and discourse of international law', which invokes what H.L.A Hart identified as secondary rules of a legal system (Kenneth Abbott *et al.*, 'The Concept of Legalization' (2000) 54 Int'l Org. 401 at 403). Whereas primary rules are regulative, obligating to do or refrain from certain actions, secondary rules are 'about rules;' they 'confer powers' to create or change primary rules (H.L.A. Hart, *The Concept of Law* (Oxford: Clarendon Press, 1961) at 79). As constitutionalization progresses, those rules appear further removed from their original source of legitimacy in state consent and more deeply institutionalized.

53 Robert Howse & Kalypso Nicolaïdis, 'Legitimacy and Global Governance: Why Constitutionalizing the WTO is a Step Too Far' in Roger B. Porter *et al.*, eds., *Efficiency, Equity and Legitimacy: The Multilateral Trading System at the Millennium* (Washington: Brookings Institution Press, 2001) 227. For an argument that the WTO is not constitutionalizing, see Jeffrey L. Dunoff, 'Constitutionalism's Conceits' (Paper presented to a conference on Changing Patterns of Authority in the Global Political Economy, Tubingen, Germany, 16 October 2004).

empowered by a treaty (as is the case in the whaling and Antarctic regimes), or even a representative body of state delegates, makes a decision that appears to go beyond the mandate given them by the statute to which states consented.[54] Thus, whereas expertise and rational science (as defined by the rules of the institution in question) have been recognized as possible sources of legitimacy rooted in a Weberian conception of legal-rational authority—a source of legitimacy also emphasized in a newer literature on international administrative law owing to science's presumed ability to 'deliver good results'[55]—legality poses a limit on its legitimating power.

At the same time, there is pressure to move away from specific consent *for* legitimacy reasons, because the pressures of globalization raise questions about whether states can *legitimately* consent to policies that increasingly affect not simply their behaviour vis-à-vis other states, but also directly affect domestic policies, local communities or corporate activities. While some forms of participatory reform, including some already noted, may help shorten or thicken the long 'chains of delegation' that threaten legitimacy under such conditions,[56] it seems unlikely that any reforms that leave even general state consent as a centerpiece of legitimacy can overcome the more fundamental problem of international authority: there is no legitimate basis for states to actually transfer (as opposed to delegate) authority in any tradition of liberal democratic thought.[57] The very notion of state consent engages domestic political processes such as ratification, which is the case in virtually all multilateral environmental agreements (MEAs).

Part of the difficulty in resolving these dilemmas may be rooted in dominant understandings of the normative foundations of international law. While a detailed discussion of competing schools of thought in international legal philosophy is beyond the scope here, one intriguing alternative has been applied to address the problem of

---

54 Bodansky, *supra* note 1 at 605.

55 Daniel C. Esty, 'Towards Good Global Governance: The Role of Administrative Law' (draft, 19 May 2005) [forthcoming] at 35-6; see also Steffek, The Legitimation of International Governance, *supra* note 3.

56 Robert O. Keohane & Joseph S. Nye, Jr,. 'The Club Model of Multilateral Cooperation and Problems of Democratic Legitimacy' in Porter, *supra* note 53 at 276.

57 Unlike social contract theory as it developed to legitimize government authority in the state, no political philosophy recognizes the legitimacy of a process where states give over their authority comparable to individuals entering a contract to give up (authorize) sovereignty to a ruler (Thomas Hobbes, *Leviathan*, ed. by C.B. McPherson (London: Penguin, 1968) at 187), or to self-legislation, following Rousseau and Kant. Thus cosmopolitan democracy proposals must always appeal back to individuals, which creates a conundrum for IL rooted in state consent.

legitimacy in international environmental law. Drawing on the legal theory of Lon Fuller, Jutta Brunnée and Stephen Toope have proposed an 'interactional' theory of international law that emphasizes law's 'internal morality' based on criteria such as avoidance of contradiction, generality, and congruence with underlying rules. Legitimacy also depends on 'cooperation between the governing and the governed' rooted in social practices and conventions among actors.[58] Such cooperation and interaction between actors, within the context of norms and institutions they have created, makes rules understandable, creates stable expectations, and 'thick' acceptance of norms. Thus, instead of holding legitimacy as a yardstick to measure or critique international law, this approach in effect redefines law as legitimacy: 'the stronger the adherence to the criteria, the more legitimate and, thus, the more persuasive and influential—the more legal—are rules likely to be.'[59]

In international environmental law, Brunnée argues that Conferences of the Parties (COPs), which are regular negotiations of the parties to MEAs, offer a possible forum for resolving legitimacy dilemmas around consent by embodying conditions conducive to the 'interactional' processes; that is, parties are engaged in a process both guided by the norms of the MEA and that reproduce and possibly modify the MEA.[60] In some respects, COPs may take on characteristics of legislatures. For example, their decisions may be binding on states, as is the case with 'adjustments' of ozone depleting potential on substances already subject to the Montreal Protocol. Other COPs have been charged with elaborating rules and provisions of an agreement, such as the Framework Convention on Climate Change COP in regard to mechanisms under the Kyoto Protocol.[61] A key point is that they do not operate strictly under general *or* specific consent. Arguably, formal consent will be less necessary under conditions where 'procedural and substantive expectations can develop, and factual as well as normative understandings can grow' leading to shared understandings. To the degree COP processes mirror those identified by interactional scholars, rules gain legitimacy with or without formal consent, and take on characteristics of bindingness.[62] Some of these procedural requirements link back to deliberative conditions noted earlier (for example, treatment of parties as equals, transparency to affected actors), but this perspective

58 Jutta Brunnée & Stephen Toope, 'International Law and Constructivism: Elements of an Interactional Theory of International Law' (2000) 39 Colum. J. Transnat'l L. 19 at 49-53, 66.

59 Jutta Brunnée, 'COPing with Consent: Law-making Under Multilateral Environmental Agreements' (2002) 15 Leiden J. Int'l L. 1 at 46.

60 *Ibid.*

61 *Ibid.* at 23.

62 *Ibid.* at 39.

also stresses interactions with the broader community, both explicitly in terms of transparency but also more implicitly in terms of linking to shared norms. Thus, interactional legal theory takes on a sociological flavour.

This understanding of legitimacy has the advantage of overcoming the tendency of traditional notions of legal legitimacy to strictly focus on the rule or principle in question and deviations from it, not on underlying social purposes or the substance of rules that link those rules to other institutions or norms in society. Strict legal legitimacy ignores the possibility that the substance of rules frequently reflects what John Ruggie has called legitimate social purposes, or the purposes which institutions legitimately may pursue.[63] Sociological conceptions similarly root legitimacy in shared understandings and goals of a community. Still, critics may argue that an interactionist characterization obscures structural power in the creation and effectiveness of international legal rules. A sociological conception allows more explicit attention to this possibility, although it is open to the opposite criticism, that it still lacks a link to 'internal morality' or 'truth,' and thus may not provide a sufficient justification for authority.

## IV A Sociological Conception of Legitimacy

From a sociological perspective, legitimacy is rooted in a collective audience's shared belief, independent of particular observers, that 'the actions of an entity are desirable, proper, or appropriate within some socially constructed system of norms, values, beliefs, and definitions.'[64] Legitimization involves institutionalization of formal and informal rules or practices that become authoritative or understood to obligate by members addressed, whether or not they choose to comply. A sociological conception turns attention to the substance of rules, or the values and goals promoted. To be legitimate, rules and institutions must be compatible or institutionally adaptable to existing institutionalized rules and norms already accepted by a society. This understanding of legitimacy derives primarily from the literature in organizational sociology, the new institutionalism, and its uptake in the constructivist IR literature.[65] It should therefore not be confused with a simple empirical measure of a community's support for, acceptance of, or belief in an institution or rule, although that might be one indicator of legitimacy according to this view.

---

63 Ruggie, *supra* note 5 at 382.

64 Marck C. Suchman, 'Managing Legitimacy: Strategic and Institutional Approaches' (1995) 20 Academy of Management Review 571 at 574.

65 *Ibid.*; Martha Finnemore, 'Norms, Culture, and World Politics: Insights from Sociology's Institutionalism' (1996) 50 Int'l Org. 325.

Extrapolating these insights to the problem of governance, the rules in question define authority relationships and empower actors and institutions that participate in those relationships and construct governing institutions through their interactions. These practices in turn become institutionalized (or accepted) as 'appropriate' by the community in an ongoing process of legitimization and de-legitimization. Thus, there is a constant interaction of rules with the social purposes and goals of relevant audiences. Legitimacy therefore depends on the historically contingent values, goals, and practices of the relevant society. In terms of global governance, different audiences of state, global civil society, or marketplace actors may share different criteria or weightings of 'input' (procedural), 'output' (performance, efficiency), or more traditional notions of 'substantive' (values of justice and fairness) legitimacy.[66]

By putting a spotlight on the problem of community or relevant audiences, a sociological conception of legitimacy highlights the cosmopolitan argument that the boundaries of states and political communities may no longer coincide. An appropriate research strategy, then, is to identify political communities wherever they form, whether in professional or technical networks, relevant marketplaces, or the traditionally demarcated 'international society' of diplomats and state officials, and ask on what bases legitimacy within those communities rests.

From this perspective, legitimacy problems in global environmental governance arise not owing necessarily to a lack of democracy or the distance between state consent and new rules, but owing to tensions within the normative environment that environmental governance insufficiently navigates. For example, emerging norms and soft law around the creation of a 'global public domain'—or realm of social policies at the global level to moderate global liberalism—have focused attention on the need to moderate or 'embed' liberalism in broader societal values at the global level.[67] Such values may include environmental concerns, human rights, labour rights, and the social and material needs of the 'losers' or marginalized under globalization. In this context, what I have elsewhere labelled the 'compromise of liberal environmentalism' institutionalized since the 1992 Rio conference, which has premised environmental governance on embedding the

---

66 The input/output distinction comes from Fritz Scharpf, but it tends to ignore other substantive values that may produce legitimacy. Fritz W. Scharpf, 'Economic Integration, Democracy and the Welfare State' (1997) 4 Journal of European Public Policy 18.

67 John G. Ruggie, 'Reconstituting the Global Public Domain: Issues, Actors, and Practices' (2004) 10 European Journal of International Relations 499.

environment in liberal markets, now faces legitimacy problems.[68]

This compromise originally fit very well with underlying shifts in the international economy and associated neoliberal normative environment reflected in economic and social policies, especially in the late 1980s and 1990s. That institutional environment has gradually started to shift, ironically owing in part to a sense that the environmental side of the equation of sustainable development had been buried under the shift to liberal environmentalism. The original framers of sustainable development were sensitive to the need to combine ecological sustainability with Southern concerns over economic growth, and saw multilateralism as a way to cushion the effects of liberalism and guide global policy. But, they failed to anticipate how forces of global economic integration, the hegemony of neoliberal economic orthodoxy, and the failures of aid-driven development policy would militate against global multilateral management and interventionist policies. Their failure is understandable in light of underlying structural changes associated with globalization, wherein the strength of norms that reinforce the global market have become a powerful legitimating force in their own right, even if their sustainability is questionable.

The immediate effects on environmental governance were to promote market mechanisms, policies on privatizing global commons and the creation of private property rights over resources rather than to attempt centralized management, and to promote the idea, most notably stated in Principle 12 of the Rio Declaration, that free trade and environmental protection were perfectly compatible. That principle states in part that, 'States should cooperate to promote a supportive and open international economic system that would lead to economic growth and sustainable development in all countries, to better address the problems of environmental degradation.'[69]

The 2002 WSSD further reinforced global liberalism, the importance of the private sector, and the declining emphasis on multilateral management, reflecting underlying structural conditions of freer and accelerated transaction flows, globalizing markets and the fragmentation of political authority. Rio provided the normative foundations for environmental governance to adapt to such conditions. Thus, environmentalists should not have been surprised that a number of Northern delegations went to great lengths to ensure that the Johannesburg Declaration and Plan of Implementation, the two

---

68 Steven Bernstein, *The Compromise of Liberal Environmentalism* (New York: Columbia University Press, 2001).

69 *Rio Declaration on Environment and Development*, 12 August 1992, in *Report of the United Nations Conference on Environment and Development*, UN Doc. A/CONF.151/26 (Vol. 1) at Annex 1.

negotiated texts produced by the conference, did not contradict or undermine existing trade agreements.[70] Such arguments simply reinforced Rio Principle 12 which, following the Earth Summit, began to serve a legitimating function for major trade agreements, including the WTO.[71]

The WSSD endorsement and promotion of public-private partnerships for sustainable development is also perfectly consistent with these underlying normative shifts. Partnerships work under the assumption that combining the resources, skills, and commitment of non-state actors with the authority of states will succeed where state action has not. While such projects appear to be the pinnacle of sustainable development—combining economic, environmental and social goals and usually involving community stakeholders and NGO input— skeptics worry that their success depends on the goodwill and voluntary participation of the private sector. Notably, partnerships were not only opposed by many NGOs critical of the 'privatization' of environmental governance and fearful that it let states off the hook in imposing binding regulation, but also by a coalition of Southern states who worried that partnerships would lead to less aid and technology transfer for sustainable development.[72]

Arguably, the ultimate aim of partnerships is to embed the marketplace in broader social and environmental goals. Thus, the engagement of the corporate sector at WSSD should be read as part of the larger response to globalization within the UN system, especially in development policy. The Global Compact, in which the corporate sector is directly enlisted to sign onto an abridged version of environmental principles derived from the Rio Declaration (along with labour, human rights, and anti-corruption principles) is yet another example of this trend. Ideally, partnerships and the Global Compact also aim to respond to demands for greater corporate responsibility and accountability. Yet,

---

70 Paul Wapner, 'World Summit on Sustainable Development: Toward a Post-Jo'burg Environmentalism' (2003) 3 Global Environmental Politics 1; James Gustave Speth, 'Perspectives on the Johannesburg Summit' (2003) 45 Environment 24.

71 For example, see World Trade Organization, *Decision on Trade and the Environment* (15 April 1994), adopted by ministers at the meeting of the Uruguay Round Trade Negotiations Committee in Marrakech, online: WTO <http://www.wto.org/english/tratop_e/envir_e/issu5_e.htm ref>.

72 Melanie Steiner, 'NGO Reflections on the World Summit: Rio + 10 or Rio – 10?' (2003) 12 RECEIL 33; Jan Martin Witte, Charloote Streck & Thorsten Benner, 'The Road From Johannesburg: What Future for Partnerships in Global Environmental Governance?' in Witte, Streck & Benner, eds., *Progress or Peril? Partnerships and Networks in Global Environmental Governance* (Washington, DC: Global Public Policy Institute, 2003) 59 at 60.

the WSSD made much less progress in these areas, which lends some support to the skeptics' view.

Not content with leaving corporate engagement to governments or international institutions, some nongovernmental groups have opted to directly target firms in the global marketplace through the creation of non-state governance schemes. The most common are 'certification' governance systems, where products, processes, or services get 'certified' as meeting specific standards of sustainability established by the scheme, and sometimes get a label so buyers can identify products or services that meet those standards. Such systems arose partly in response to the lack of progress in multilateral negotiations, but also because NGOs worried about the limitations of voluntary codes of conduct, self-regulation, or learning networks, even when backed by the United Nations. Their most unique feature is that their authority derives from their manipulation of global markets independently of states, leading Benjamin Cashore to label them 'non-state, market-driven (NSMD) governance.'[73] A small but accelerating number of such schemes have started to operate at the transnational level over the last ten to fifteen years as demands for governance of the global marketplace increase. They currently cover aspects of forestry, food security and production, labour standards, tourism, fisheries, and human rights. Others are in development in the energy/electricity and mining sectors. Most include specific performance criteria and employ systems of third-party verification and regular auditing and monitoring of compliance in which firms must participate to maintain 'certified' status. They also frequently have governance structures that include representation from corporations, broader civil society, and affected local communities. To the degree they exhibit the above characteristics, they can be considered 'governance' systems with significant authority as opposed to strictly voluntary or self-regulatory schemes.[74]

Such schemes take advantage not only of globalizing markets, but also the spread and influence of global consciousness and civil society organizations to create pressures on companies to participate. In practice, they attempt to combine elements of stakeholder democracy and accountability legitimated by such shifts with the power of the marketplace to create legitimate authority independent of international agreements among states. They thus offer a good example of an innovative form of governance that arose in large part owing to legitimacy and performance limitations in traditional forms of inter-state governance.

While by no means a panacea (NSMD is unlikely to become

---

73 Cashore, *supra* note 3.

74 Bernstein & Cashore, *supra* note 37.

the dominant form of environmental governance), these governance systems show promise in responding to legitimacy concerns from both a principled and sociological perspective. First, NSMD is well positioned to achieve a high standard of stakeholder democracy relative to other governance experiments. For example, the Forest Stewardship Council, which certifies forest products, created environmental, social and economic decision-making chambers, each with equal voting weight, to ensure business interests would not dominate decision-making. The dominance of business interests is a potentially serious drawback to public-private partnerships, voluntary codes including on corporate social responsibility, and even to traditional inter-state governance. In NSMD systems, decision-making is frequently designed to force different stakeholder groups to engage and deliberate, and many develop specific standards at the local level with community involvement rather than through top-down processes.

As Karin Bäckstrand and Michael Saward argue, in the absence of electoral and representative legislative processes, processes that systematically involve stakeholders' range of voices and perspectives create 'ownership' of outcomes, and can 'draw upon principles protecting the vulnerable.'[75] Whereas other forms of standard-setting tend to favour expert-driven decision-making as a source of legitimacy (a move towards international administrative law), both legal and principled conceptions of legitimacy suggest that absent transparency and accountability, such processes risk legitimacy problems. Thus NSMD may have a legitimacy advantage among the full range of relevant communities over the business-dominated International Organization for Standardization (ISO), for example, unless it reforms to be more inclusive and responsive to stakeholders.

From a sociological perspective, NSMD governance systems are clearly enabled by the existing normative environment, both in terms of the shift to liberal environmentalism and the elevation of the global marketplace as an arena for governance, as well as in terms of emerging norms of a global public domain that favour some form of deliberative democracy. Under such circumstances, such systems may even succeed where states could not, as has arguably been the case in attempts to promote global sustainable forest management.[76]

Nonetheless, non-state governance networks are never

[75] Bäckstrand & Saward, *supra* note 31 at 6.

[76] Steven Bernstein & Benjamin Cashore, 'Non-State Global Governance: Is Forest Certification a Legitimate Alternative to a Global Forest Convention?' in John Kirton & Michael Trebilcock, eds., *Hard Choices, Soft Law: Combining Trade, Environment, and Social Cohesion in Global Governance* (London: Ashgate Press, 2004) 33.

completely dis-embedded from wider economic, social and political systems. For example, an attempt to build legitimate governance of sustainable forestry through a transnational network of producers (forest companies) and consumers (retailers and consumers of forest products) must not only generate legitimacy among those parties, but also must navigate existing rules of international trade legitimated through inter-state processes as well as regulatory and social environments of nation-states in which companies operate. In this regard, the tension generated by liberal environmentalism becomes apparent when the Committee on Trade and the Environment of the WTO, for example, is unable to make progress on issues such as labeling and certification, let alone on how to reconcile in practice environmental measures with trade norms based on non-discrimination.

Neither are NSMD systems dis-embedded from wider publics that any governance scheme may affect, which means they must either be included in the network or some other mechanism of accountability must be developed. Ultimately, a sociological perspective suggests various notions of legitimacy may be at least somewhat interdependent when applied to the practice of global governance, since there is an ongoing dynamic of legitimation and delegitimation as norms and institutions vie for legitimacy within the wider institutional contexts in which global politics and authority relations play out.

## CONCLUSION: PROSPECTS FOR CONVERGENCE?

Despite the analytic distinctions made above, the conceptual traditions of legitimacy identified are not mutually exclusive. Indeed, considerable borrowing across fields occurs in the literature, with each conception offering some insight into what legitimacy in global governance requires. Still, I conclude on a cautionary note that it is unlikely that a universal formula to satisfy all legitimacy concerns will emerge. This conclusion is contrary to the tendency to develop abstract criteria of legitimacy for global governance, usually derived exclusively from the democratic legitimacy literature. Rather, insights from the sociological perspective suggest that criteria of legitimacy ultimately are contingent on historical understandings at play and the shared norms of the particular community or communities granting authority. In practice in global governance, these reflect components identified in each conception, but appropriate responses to contemporary legitimacy challenges are conditioned by a variety of contextual factors, discussed below. I highlight four points in this regard.

First, the best way to view the relevance and importance of principled conceptions of legitimacy is through a sociological lens. Whatever the merits of normative arguments on democratic legitimacy, there is an indisputable general normative trend to democratize global governance. Examples range from demands for democratic reform and greater public accountability (whether to states and/or broader affected publics) of international institutions, to calls for 'stakeholder democracy' and 'deliberation'. The relevant point here, which also resonates with the interactionist legal literature, is that these values stem from the communities directly involved and/or affected by global governance, as well as emerging norms of a 'global public domain.' The rationale is also linked to the argument that transparency, participation, accountability in rule-making, and adequate resources to enable participation produce a sense of 'ownership', which links decision-making and outcomes of a governance scheme to the communities that authorize it, and over which it is granted authority.[77] For example, a study of perceptions of legitimacy of the ISO 14000 environmental standards found a strong direct correlation among developing country delegates between involvement in the creation of the standards and their legitimacy.[78] As long as the institutionalization of such norms persists, legitimacy, as a practical matter, will depend on responding to democratic pressures.

Second, the nature and location of political community conditions democratic pressures. The legal legitimacy literature best highlights the general tension created when globalizing pressures create demands that governing authority and decision-making be opened up to wider groups of actors, because its starting point is the existing 'constitutional' order where states have legal status and international law is rooted in state consent. Thus, the tension regarding who participates reflects not only a possible trade-off between effectiveness and participation, as is sometimes portrayed, but also an evaluation of the conditions in which legitimacy would demand that decisions be opened up to wider groups of actors. The simple response is that when decisions directly address or affect actors other than states, which is increasingly the case as the reach and scope of global governance expands, affected communities ought to have access. The practical dilemma remains, however, of whether states can adequately and legitimately represent such groups or who else could, and whether involvement in policy processes or deliberation should translate into actual decision-making authority. This is one question where different conceptions of legitimacy show little sign of convergence. What is clear is that to the degree inter-state processes appear not to reflect the values of relevant communities, alternative forms of governance that are more

77 Ngaire Woods, 'Good Governance in International Organizations' (1999) 5 Global Governance 39; Susan Summers Raines, 'Perceptions of Legitimacy in International Environmental Management Standards: The Participation Gap' (2003) 3 Global Environmental Politics 47; Bäckstrand & Saward, *supra* note 31.

78 Raines, *supra* note 77.

inclusive are emerging.

Still, even innovative forms of governance such as NSMD systems face significant challenges of political community.[79] Unlike self-regulatory networks where businesses, technical experts, and governments likely share common norms and goals such as efficiency and profitability, relevant audiences of NSMD systems differ significantly in terms of identities (producers, consumers, environmentalists), geographic location, and interests. Consensus may even be lacking on what constitutes either procedural or substantive legitimacy. If they are to succeed, institutionalized learning processes and community building are necessary within the governing institutions. Thus, the problem of community may be as daunting, if not more so, than in traditional international governance. The one advantage is potentially greater access of those directly affected to interact with the governance system.

A third point concerns the need for greater attention to the substance of governance in understanding legitimacy problems. In the case of the environment, evaluations of legitimacy historically have been based not only environmental performance, but also the linking of environment with other goals that are highly valued, especially development goals. Presumably, increased participation and influence of developing countries in international environmental negotiations reinforced the legitimacy of institutions that reflected these developments. When these dynamics combined with the broader normative shifts toward neoliberalism, it created legitimacy for what I labelled 'liberal environmentalism.' The contemporary legitimacy challenge, however, stems in part from the very success of liberal environmentalism, if governing arrangements have gone too far towards elevating the normative status of markets, in effect subordinating environmental purposes to economic goals, even within ostensibly environmental institutions. Moreover, if there is indeed some resilience to the idea that global liberal markets need to be embedded in societal purposes, which my cursory application of a sociological conception of legitimacy to the current context of global governance suggests, then the legitimating normative foundation of environmental governance is fragile unless more substantial inroads can be made in economic institutions, not only through voluntary initiatives such as the Global Compact. The discussion of the global challenge to international liberalism also aimed to highlight that societal norms and values inform what 'outputs'—environmental, economic performance, and so on—or combination thereof are deemed as legitimate. This finding clearly has

---

[79] See Bernstein & Cashore, *supra* note 37, for a fuller discussion of challenges that face NSMD governance.

implications for the broader legitimacy problems facing the WTO and other international economic institutions.

Fourth, power cannot be absent in any governance equation. This turns attention back to the balance between states and markets, and whether newer forms of private or hybrid authority can manage that balance absent the public authority of states. For example, many NGOs remain highly suspicious of ever truly reconciling ecological goals with the marketplace. Thus, while the new initiatives promise to be responsive to principled conceptions of legitimacy in terms of inclusiveness, a critical assessment is required of whether the shift towards public-private partnerships and market-based governance systems in practice privileges the market over alternative bases of governance, biases (without good reasons) governance towards market mechanisms and voluntary initiatives over regulatory instruments, or gives corporate voices a disproportionate say in policy development and implementation at the expense of state representatives and public participation.[80] If WSSD is any indication, there is reason for concern. Private sector interests reportedly had 'very strong behind-the-scenes influence' and managed to prevent any strong language on corporate accountability in the Plan of Implementation.[81] Similarly, scholars have noted the largely superficial impact of UNEP's participatory reforms, though laudatory in terms of principled legitimacy, in moving it from an intergovernmental to a more supranational organization and, moreover, its relative inefficacy and failure to become the primary forum for international environmental policymaking.[82] Ultimately, as Erika Sasser found in a recent study on non-state governance (and there is no reason to believe these findings would not extend to state-led governance), most NGOs will not be ready to grant full legitimacy to a governance system until the on-the-ground effects are shown to improve environmental or social integrity.[83]

The question of power highlights that legitimacy ultimately concerns political authority. It, in turn, results from the meshing of power, legitimacy, and community. Deliberation may be fine as a normative goal, but if deliberative processes cannot produce authoritative outcomes owing to a lack of buy-in from relevant actors

---

80 Harris Gleckman, 'Balancing TNCs, the States, and the International System in Global Environmental Governance: A Critical Perspective' in Kanie & Haas, *supra* note 33 at 203.

81 Steiner, *supra* note 67 at 36.

82 Esty, *supra* note 55 at 99.

83 Erika Sasser, 'The Certification Solution: NGO Promotion of Private, Voluntary Self-Regulation' (Paper prepared for presentation to the 74th Annual Meeting of the Canadian Political Science Association, Toronto, Ontario, 29–31 May 2002).

with power resources, the exercise may be empty. Compromises are thus likely necessary between a deliberative ideal and forms of governance acceptable to major states from North and South for legitimate *governance* to emerge.

# [12]

*Journal of Environmental Law* **23**:1 © The Author 2011. Published by Oxford University Press.

doi:10.1093/jel/eqq024 Advance Access published on 7 January 2011

# Enhanced Decision Making: Balancing Public Participation against 'Better Regulation' in British Environmental Permitting Regimes

Elizabeth A. Kirk* and Kirsty L. Blackstock**

## Abstract

An increase in the rights of the public to participate in environmental permitting decisions has paralleled developments in other areas of administrative decision making in Britain. It is generally accepted that one of the key objectives underlying the enhancement of participatory rights was to improve the quality of decision making through improving the quality or range of values and information upon which decisions were based. This objective now has a counterweight in the Better Regulation agenda. The result is a balancing of objectives in which the emphasis increasingly appears to be falling on ensuring speed and consistency in decision making. It is argued here that too much emphasis has now been placed on ensuring the objectives of the Better Regulation agenda and greater emphasis should be placed on the benefits that arise from public participation.

Keywords: Public participation, Better Regulation, permitting, England, Scotland.

## 1. Introduction

Participation in environmental permitting decisions is not a new phenomenon in Britain. Industry in particular has long been able to provide input to,

*Senior Lecturer, School of Law University of Dundee, Dundee, DD1 4HN. (e.a.kirk@dundee.ac.uk)
**Socio-Economics Research Group, Macaulay Land Use Research Institute, Aberdeen, AB15 8QH.

comment on and appeal such decisions. Following adoption of the Aarhus Convention and the EU Public Participation Directive,[1] there has been a general increase in rights to participate across the spectrum of environmental decision making, including in environmental permitting decisions.[2] It is generally accepted that the key driver behind this change was the need to improve the quality of decision making.[3] And while there are a number of ways in which this objective could be interpreted and implemented,[4] the accepted approach in the UK focused on improving the quality or range of information and values upon which decisions were based.[5] Current practice appears, however, to point to a change in approach. Emphasis is increasingly being placed on speed and consistency in decision making as a result of implementation of the Better Regulation agenda.[6] Put simply, this agenda is aimed at the

1 Following adoption of the UNECE Convention on Access to Information, Public Participation in Decision-Making and Access to Justice in Environmental Matters at Aarhus, Denmark, on 25 June 1998, Preamble, art 1, art 6 and Annex 1, and EU Directives such as Council Directive (EC) 35/2003 Providing for Public Participation in Respect of the Drawing up of Certain Plans and Programmes Relating to the Environment and Amending With Regard to Public Participation and Access to Justice Council Directives 85/337/EEC and 96/61/EC OJ L 156/17 (Public Participation Directive).

2 For example, the Pollution Prevention and Control (Public Participation etc) (Scotland) Regulations 2005 SSI 2005/510 and the Water Environment (Controlled Activities) (Scotland) Regulations 2005 SSI 2005/348. See eg P Stookes 'Getting To The Real EIA' (2003) 15 JEL 141. See also J Similä, A Inkinen and J Tritter 'Public Participation by Appeal–Insights from Empirical Evaluation in Finland' (2008) 20 JEL 391.

3 Royal Commission on Environmental Pollution (RCEP), 'Twenty-first Report: Setting Environmental Standards' (Cm 4053, 1998). See also para 6 of the Preamble to the Public Participation Directive 2003 (n 1), which notes that the purpose of participation is 'to contribute to the protection of the right to live in an environment which is adequate for personal health and wellbeing' and art 1 of the Aarhus Convention which contains similar objectives. See also *Hardy No 2* [2002] EWHC 1056 (Admin). For more general discussion on the reasons participatory processes may be used see J Steele, 'Participation and Deliberation in Environmental Law: Exploring a Problem-solving Approach' (2001) OJLS 415; M Lee and C Abbot, 'The Usual Suspects? Public Participation under the Aarhus Convention' (2003) MLR 80; E Gauna, 'The Environmental Justice Misfit: Public Participation and the Paradigm Paradox' (1998) 17 Stan Envtl L J 3; M Appelstrand, 'Participation and Societal Values: The Challenge for Lawmakers and Policy Practitioners' (2002) 4 For Poly Econ 281; K Getliffe, 'Proceduralisation and the Aarhus Convention: Does Increased Participation in the Decision-making Process Lead to More Effective EU Environmental Law?' (2002) 4 ELR 101; J Dryzek, *The Politics of the Earth: Environmental Discourses* (2nd edn Oxford University Press, Oxford 2005); D Fiorino, 'Citizen Participation and Environmental Risk - A Survey of Institutional Mechanisms' (1990) 15 Sci Technol Hum Val 226.

4 See eg the debate on the meaning of 'better': W Howarth, 'Aspirations and Realities Under the Water Framework Directive: Proceduralisation, Participation and Practicalities' (2009) JEL 391; T Le Quesne and C Green, *Can We Afford Not To? The Costs and Benefits of a Partnership Approach to the Water Framework Directive* (WWF 2005) 4.

5 RCEP (n 3) at 8.16–18; Steele (n 3).

6 See generally <http://www.bis.gov.uk/bre> accessed 8 November 2010 and also, <http://www.defra.gov.uk/environment/policy/permits/about.htm> accessed 22 August 2010.

reduction of the costs and administrative burden on business and on regulators associated with regulation, without an associated diminution in regulation's effectiveness.[7] The ultimate objective is to increase Gross Domestic Product by reducing the costs of regulation to business.[8] The objectives are to be achieved by, for example, simplifying the administrative process attached to the granting of permits, by making the outcomes of such processes more predictable and by ensuring that the decision making process is not unduly lengthy. Although the Better Regulation agenda nowhere specifies that public participation is to be reduced, this is likely to be a consequence of implementation of the agenda. Despite this, and while there is a considerable body of literature on the theory of public participation and its use in relation to planning,[9] there has been little debate about the relationship between the objectives of Better Regulation and the objectives underpinning participation in permitting decisions.[10] Instead, the need to balance speed and consistency of decision making against the opportunities for public participation appear to be generally accepted without consideration being given to where the balance between elements ought to lie. This acceptance also masks the fact that there is a divergence in the ways in which the balance is struck in England and Scotland despite the fact that Better Regulation has an equally high profile in both. In England greater emphasis is placed on ensuring speed and consistency in decision making. In Scotland the regulatory system appears torn between enhancing participation in some areas and ensuring speed and consistency in decision making in others. It seems that the question of where the balance should lie does not have a settled answer and it is this question that is addressed here.

7 See N Gunningham, 'Environmental Law Regulation and Governance: Shifting Architectures' (2009) 21 JEL 179; Better Regulation Task Force, 'Executive Summary' in *Regulation – Less is More: Reducing Burdens, Improving Outcomes* (March 2005) BRTF Report; P Hampton, *Reducing Administrative Burdens: Effective Inspection and Enforcement* (HM Treasury, 2005) 3; P Kellet 'Better Regulation: What the Modernising Agenda Might Mean for UK Environmental Laws' (2006) 18 ELM 169.

8 S Anderson, *The Anderson Review. The Good Guidance Guide: Taking the Uncertainty Out of Regulation* (Better Regulation Executive, London 2009); Hampton (n 7).

9 See eg Steele (n 3); Lee and Abbot (n 3); Gauna (n 3); Appelstrand (n 3); Getliffe (n 3); Dryzek (n 3); Fiorino (n 3); S Arnstein, 'A Ladder of Citizenship Participation' (1969) 26 J Am Inst Plann 216; See also, eg Organisation for Economic Co-operation and Development, *Stakeholder Involvement Techniques: Short Guide and Annotated Bibliography, A Report from Nuclear Energy Agency Forum for Stakeholder Confidence* <http://www.nea.fr/html/rwm/reports/2004/nea5418-stakeholder.pdf> accessed 3 November 2010; J D Hamilton and C Wills-Toker, 'Reconceptualizing Dialogue in Environmental Public Participation' (2006) 34 Poly Stud J 755; M Reed, 'Stakeholder participation for environmental management: a literature review' (2008) 141 Biological Conservation 2417; G Cowie and L O'Toole, 'Linking Stakeholder Participation and Environmental Decision-Making: Assessing Decision Quality for Interstate River Basin Management' in F Coenen, D Huitema and L O'Toole (eds), *Participation and the Quality of Environmental Decision Making* (Kluwer, Dordrecht, 1998).

10 See eg RCEP (n 3).

The article begins by giving an overview of participatory rights in the permitting regimes overseen by the Environment Agency (EA) and Scottish Environment Protection Agency (SEPA) before returning to consider their fit with the objective of enhancing the quality of decisions. Throughout, the focus is on *ex ante* decision making and so some opportunities for participation, such as by way of appeal,[11] are not considered.

## 2. Participatory Rights: an Overview

Most environmental regulatory regimes provide some rights to participate, and the processes by which they arise generally fall into a similar pattern. An application for a permit or licence, or the variation or surrender of one, is made by an interested party. The application may fall under a standard permitting process[12] in which case there is no need for public participation. If not caught by this procedure then the application,[13] and sometimes a proposed decision, is advertised and the advertisement contains details of when and how individuals may participate in decision making. The regulations tend to provide only for consultation processes, though at times the regulators may be able to adopt fuller, participatory processes. Normally, however, participation is by way of written (sometimes oral) submissions (to be submitted by a certain date) and the final decision is usually taken by the regulatory body alone, taking account of the submissions received.

In England, environmental and permitting decisions are largely addressed by the Environmental Permitting (England and Wales) Regulations 2010.[14] These regulations update the 2007 regulations of the same name, bringing more areas under the one regime. The 2007 regulations were introduced to bring together the pollution prevention and control regime and the waste management licensing regime in a simpler and more straightforward regulatory system.[15] The objective underpinning their introduction was not directly related to participatory decision making. They were instead introduced under

11 On participation by appeal see Similä and others (n 2).

12 For example, certain installations for the manufacture of biodiesel may be subject to the standard permitting regime. The rules such installations must be able to comply with are set out in the EA's Standard rules SR2009No3—Low Impact Part A Installation for the production of Biodiesel <http://www.environment-agency.gov.uk/static/documents/Business/SR2009No3v2.0.pdf> accessed 3 November 2010.

13 For example, most installations producing cement will require a bespoke permit. See 2010 Regulations sch 1 and sch 7.

14 SI 2010/675 (although these regulations cover both England and Wales the focus of this article is on their application in England as this provides for a clearer comparison with the system operating in Scotland).

15 Forty-one statutory instruments were then replaced by this one regulatory instrument.

the Better Regulation agenda and designed to make the then rather complex regulatory system[16] easier for business to navigate.[17] One of the ways in which this was achieved was by providing operators with the right to apply for one permit to cover all issues raised by an activity where previously they would have required separate permits under the Pollution Prevention and Control (PPC) regime and the waste management regime if their activity was caught by both. The 2010 Regulations revised the 2007 Regulations and extended the system to include discharge consenting, groundwater authorisations and radioactive substances regulation. The regulations provide a uniform process for decision making across the areas they cover.[18] Despite the fact that the Better Regulation Agenda has also been implemented in Scotland, the same streamlining process has not take place there. Instead a conscious decision has been taken to maintain a range of (hopefully complementary) regimes because of the industry's familiarity with them[19]—not because this variety is necessarily deemed more appropriate. This divergence in approaches to permitting regimes creates space for a divergence in approach to participation too.

Under the 2010 Regulations, the right to public participation is determined by whether the applicant applies for a standard or bespoke permit, the difference between which is explained below. In Scotland the right of public participation is determined by the regime by which the activity is covered. There are two areas where no right to participate is provided under the Scottish regulations: waste management licensing[20] and radioactive substances.[21] Both provide only for consultation with a very narrow range of stakeholders,[22] with no general right for participation by the general public. In relation to waste, given that planning permission is required for the activities falling under these regulations and that participation is possible when that is being considered, the omission of an opportunity to participate here is perhaps not

16 Better Regulation Executive, Department for Business, Enterprise and Regulatory Reform and National Audit Office, *Effective Inspection and Enforcement: Implementing the Hampton Vision in the Environment Agency* (London 2008) 5.

17 Their introduction has been welcomed in this respect: Defra, *Environmental Permitting Booklet* <http://www.defra.gov.uk/environment/policy/permits/documents/ep2010booklet.pdf> accessed 4 November 2010; See also <http://www.defra.gov.uk/environment/policy/permits/about.htm> accessed 4 November 2010; the Department of Business, Innovation and Skills (BIS), *Better Regulation, Better Benefits: Getting the Balance Right - Case Studies* (2009).

18 Better Regulation Executive and others (n 16); BIS (n 17).

19 See eg Scottish Government, 'Consultation Paper on the Consolidation of the Waste Management Licensing Regulations and Amendments arising from the Better Waste Regulation Exercise' (February 2010) pt 4.

20 Environmental Protection Act (EPA) 1990 and Waste Management Licensing Regulations 1994 SSI 1994/1056.

21 Radioactive Substances Act 1993, s 16; see also Radioactive Substances (Appeals) Regulations 1990 SI 1990/2504; the High-activity Sealed Radioactive Sources and Orphan Sources Regulations 2005 SI 2005/2686.

22 See eg EPA 1990 s 36A.

so significant (although it does mean that some issues may not be subject to public debate).[23] That aside, these provisions suggest then that in some areas there are more limited rights for participation within Scotland than in England, though as will be seen below, practice departs from the regulations.

In England, suitability for issuing a standard permit under the 2010 Regulations[24] depends on the type of operation and whether it meets particular criteria. The criteria are set out in rules drawn up by the EA under regulation 26 of the 2010 Regulations. To date it has produced four sets of rules and revisions to rules detailing the types of activity that may be eligible to be addressed by the standard rules and the content of those rules.[25] Certain processes, such as those likely to cause controversy, or significant pollution, are excluded from this permitting regime. For example, most incinerators are not covered by this procedure; the only ones that are covered are the relatively uncontroversial 'pet crematoriums', which accept less than 438 tonnes of waste per annum. Other incinerators are obliged to go through the more complex bespoke permitting regime (explained more fully below). At present, standard permits may be applied for in relation to a wide range of waste operations, some activities leading to discharges into water and a limited range of installations subject to the PPC regime: low impact part A installations. The criteria that apply to activities vary according to the type of activity. For example, installations covered by the PPC regime are subject to location and discharge requirements. They cannot be 'on or immediately adjacent to a European Site, Ramsar Site, Site of Special Scientific Interest (SSSI), National Nature Reserve, Local Nature Reserve or Ancient Woodland'; and there cannot be 'direct discharge of aqueous waste within 10km upstream of a European Site, Ramsar Site or a SSSI, within 100 metres upstream of a National Nature Reserve, Local Nature Reserve or Ancient Woodland, or within a National Park.'[26]

The decision making provided for under the standard permit procedure[27] does not, as a rule, allow for public participation in respect of each individual decision.[28] Although the regulations do not make clear whether or not the

23 For example, the public may wish to address questions of flaring and venting that would arise in relation to a waste permitting application for a landfill site, but not in relation to a planning application.

24 2010 Regulations (n 14).

25 See <http://www.environment-agency.gov.uk/business/topics/permitting/32334.aspx> accessed 5 November 2010.

26 <http://www.environment-agency.gov.uk/business/topics/permitting/106530.aspx> accessed 5 November 2010.

27 See eg the Pollution Prevention and Control (England and Wales) Regulations 2000 SI 2000/1973. While there was provision for the application of general rules issued by the Secretary of State under reg 14 in some cases, the same application and decision making process was followed regardless of the scale or nature of activity. A simplified application and decision making process akin to that used for standard permits found in the 2010 Regulations did not exist.

28 2010 Regulations (n 14) sch 5, para 5(1). Part A installations under the PPC regime may still be subject to public participation despite some of them falling within this simplified regime.

grant of permit is automatic, it appears that, so long as the applicant has provided sufficient information, it will be granted. The decision then on whether the activity meets these criteria is left to the applicant and in this sense the process is much simpler than that which previously existed and than that which applies to bespoke permits. (If the applicant makes the wrong choice and is found at a subsequent inspection not to meet the criteria they will be deemed to be 'operating without a valid permit'[29] and so it is not a decision they should take lightly.) If the permit is granted, the applicant is subject to a set of standard rules rather than having conditions generated for their individual situation. There is then no room for debate at the point of issue and this is quite different to the situation prior to the adoption of the 2007 (and 2010) Regulations. In particular, the PPC regime previously provided an opportunity for the public to comment on any application and required the regulator to consider all such representations received by it.[30] There is, however, still some opportunity for the public to participate in decision making related to standard permits. The public may participate in the development of and in revisions to the rules that will apply to standard permits. Under regulation 26, the EA must consult those it considers to be representative of the interests of communities that are likely to be affected by facilities covered by a standard permit, operators of such facilities and anyone else it considers likely to be affected by or to have an interest in the standard rules. How this has operated in practice will be discussed below.[31]

A similar regime applies for some activities in Scotland under the Water Environment (Controlled Activities) Regulations.[32] These provide for permits that look very similar to the standard and bespoke permits issued under the English 2010 Regulations. Those permits equating to standard permits are provided for in regulation 7. It provides for general rules that are applicable to particular types of activity. There is, however, a departure from the procedure adopted under the 2010 Regulations. Whereas, under the 2010 Regulations an operator must still apply for a standard permit, under the Water Environment Regulations, if the activity complies with the appropriate rules, then it is deemed to be authorised. There is then no need for the operator to apply for a permit in relation to these activities. And, unlike the 2010 Regulations, there is no real opportunity for the public to participate in the development of the

29 <http://www.environment-agency.gov.uk/business/topics/permitting/32330.aspx> accessed 5 November 2010.

30 PPC Regulations 2000 (n 21) sch 4, paras 6 and 12.

31 It is, however, worth noting here that the content of standard rules may also be dictated by other processes. For example, they may reflect guidance from the European Commission on the current understanding of best available techniques under the Integrated Pollution Prevention and Control regime. See Council Directive (EC) 1/2008 concerning Integrated Pollution Prevention and Control (Codified version) [2008] OJ L24/8 discussed more fully in the text at n 39.

32 Water Enviroment Regulations (n 2).

standard rules. These are already detailed in Schedule 3 of the Regulations, which also details the activities covered by them.

Up to this point then, the regimes operating north and south of the border seem very similar, though if anything there appear to be greater rights for the public to participate in decision making in England than in Scotland. This changes when we consider participation in decisions on other types of applications.

Under the 2010 Regulations, those operators whose activities do not fall under the standard permitting regime may apply for a bespoke permit. In general, the public does have rights to participate in decision making relating to these applications, though even here, certain processes are excluded from the public participation requirements.[33] Under the proceedings relating to bespoke permits, the EA is under an obligation to 'take the steps it considers appropriate to inform the public consultees of the application' and invite them to make representations giving details of the time frame in which representations are to be made.[34] It is then left to the EA to decide where or how to advertise consultations and whether in fact to contact consultees directly. In practice, the EA has chosen to advertise applications on its website.[35] Although the 2010 Regulations do not specifically say so, it appears that the obligation is to provide for written representations to be made, as paragraph 6 provides that the EA must specify 'the address to which' representations are to be made. Similar provisions exist in relation to the variation of a permit[36] and there is provision for consultation with other States where it is thought that their environment may be harmed by an activity.[37] The EA's obligation then is to consider any representations it receives under either of these routes before granting or refusing the permit.[38] Under the 2010 Regulations, the EA also consults on draft permits for those installations that must meet the requirements relating to integrated pollution protection and control, or where substantial changes to an existing installation covered by those provisions are proposed.[39] It can also consult on other cases at its discretion.

33 2010 Regulations (n 14) sch 5, para 5(1) excludes permits relating to mobile plant, certain radioactive substances activities described in para 5(5) of pt 2 of sch 23, and mining waste operations not involving a facility to which art 7 of Council Directive (EC) 21/2006 On the management of waste from extractive industries and amending Directive 2004/35/EC OJ L 102/15 applies.

34 2010 Regulations (n 14) sch 5, para 6. Details of how the time periods are calculated is given in sch 5, para 16. A public consultee is defined in sch 5, para 1 as any 'person whom the regulator considers is affected by, is likely to be affected by, or has an interest in, an application'.

35 <http://www.environment-agency.gov.uk/research/library/consultations/65546.aspx> accessed 23 August 2010.

36 2010 Regulations (n 14) sch 5, para 7.

37 Ibid sch 5, para 10.

38 Ibid sch 5, para 11.

39 Ibid sch 7, para 6 and Art 15, IPPC Directive (n 31).

In Scotland, participatory rights arise under the PPC regime[40] and in relation to those activities covered by the Water Environment etc Regulations 2005[41] which are not covered by the standard rules. Both invite 'any person' to submit written or electronic comments on applications and variations of permits for consideration by the regulator within certain time limits.[42] Both regimes also provide an opportunity for 'any person' to comment on certain draft permits[43] or object to draft determinations. The Scottish PPC Regulations 2000 provide that where public comment on a draft determination is permitted, the existence of the draft, the reasons underpinning the determination and details of how and when the public may comment on the draft are to be advertised. In other words, it is open to any member of the public on seeing the advertisement to comment on the draft permit. By contrast, the Controlled Activities regime provides for notice of the draft determination and opportunity to object to its terms to be given to those who have made representations in relation to an application.[44]

This difference aside, both of these Scottish regimes provide for more extensive public participation than is possible under the English 2010 Regulations. This is primarily by virtue of the fact that, under the Scottish regulations, comments are welcomed from 'any person' not just those identified as having an interest or as likely to be affected by the activity, as is the case in England. In addition, under the Controlled Activities regime, objections are sent to the Scottish Ministers[45] who then decide whether SEPA may proceed to grant the permit or whether the application should be referred to the Ministers to determine.[46] A more significant difference in the provisions is that the Controlled Activities process opens the way for a local inquiry to be held at which further evidence to be used in determining the application can be gathered. The holding of a local inquiry provides a mechanism by which to check whether comments received by the public have been taken into account by SEPA in arriving at its decisions. It also provides an opportunity for controversial applications to be discussed more fully. Similarly, under the PPC regime, the Scottish Ministers may require decisions on certain types of applications to be referred to them for decision.[47] In these instances, any representations made to SEPA are to be passed to the Scottish Ministers for consideration, but there

40 See the Pollution, Prevention and Control (Scotland) Regulations 2000 SSI 2000/323.
41 Water Environment etc Regulations 2005 (n 2).
42 PPC (Scotland) Regulations 2000 (n 40) sch 4 and 7; the Water Environment etc Regulations 2005 (n 2) regs 13 and 15A.
43 PPC (Scotland) Regulations 2000 (n 40) sch 4, para 15.
44 The Water Environment etc Regulations 2005 (n 2) reg 15 A.
45 Ibid reg 15 A.
46 Ibid reg 17.
47 PPC (Scotland) Regulations 2000 (n 40) sch 4, para 14.

is also provision for a hearing before the Scottish Ministers at which the applicant, SEPA, statutory consultees and anyone who has made written representations may make oral representations. While these provisions suggest the opening up of decision making—at least in these controversial areas—the move is rather limited. In both instances, whether an inquiry or a hearing is held, the decision rests in the hands of the person appointed to hold the hearing[48] and in that sense decision making is not fully opened up to the public.

A review of SEPA's *practices* in implementing the regulations showed, however, that the regulators believed they exceeded the participatory requirements on some occasions in *all* their areas of activity[49] and that they have used a range of mechanisms that may take processes beyond the norm of consultation. The prompt to exceeding the minimum requirements seems to be the need to minimise opposition to potentially controversial permit applications.[50] For example, stakeholders and the general public have been engaged in decision making on radioactive substances through, for example, focus groups and stakeholder panels (which include local residents) despite the fact that there is no obligation even to consult the public in this area, only to make information available.[51] The EA has by contrast taken a decision to focus only on its formally obligated consultation procedures. While it has noted that it may be appropriate to have 'additional participation arrangements' where there is or is likely to be an increased level of public interest,[52] it has limited this to extending the duration of the consultation processes, the range of persons made aware of the opportunity to participate in it, or to including an opportunity to comment on the draft permit and decision document.[53] These differences may indicate a more confusing permitting landscape for applicants and the public to negotiate in Scotland than in England, but they also indicate that there is a stronger culture of participation within SEPA than within the EA. It may also signify that decision making is tailored more accurately to the particular problem in hand rather than aimed at ensuring a uniform, one size fits all approach to permitting decisions. These differences appear likely to lead to variations in the quality of decision making in the two jurisdictions.

48 Ibid sch 8, para 4.

49 K Blackstock and others, *Public Participation and Consultation in SEPA Regulatory Regimes Report to SEPA* (Macaulay Institute, Aberdeen 2006) ch 5.

50 Ibid.

51 Radioactive Substances Act 1993 s 16; see also Radioactive Substances (Appeals) Regulations 1990 (n 21); the High-activity Sealed Radioactive Sources and Orphan Sources Regulations 2005 (n 21).

52 EA, *Working Together: Your Role in our Environmental Permitting: Our Public Participation Statement* (Bristol 2010) [2.2] and [4.8].

53 EA (n 52) [4.9]. It also has a set of corporate principles to guide interaction with the public: Blackstock and others (n 49).

## 3. Improving the Quality of Decision Making?

In both jurisdictions a value judgement has been made as to when the benefits that public participation brings to decision making ought to be preserved and when priority should be given to ensure speed and consistency in decision making. The two sets of permitting regimes indicate quite different approaches being taken to this question. In England, the introduction of standard permits and their use across a broad array of activities severely curtails the opportunities for public participation in decisions on individual applications. Participation is provided for only in relation to non-standard activities—the controversial activities, such as waste incineration, or hazardous activities, such as storing of certain radioactive waste[54]—or activities for which it is not or has not been possible to draw up a set of standard rules, or in relation to the development of standard rules. Elsewhere the public's involvement in decision making appears to diminish the quality of decision making by making it too slow or cumbersome.[55] This approach to public participation may, however, be insufficient to ensure real engagement, as the public tend only to become involved in decision making when they understand the impact of the issue on their lives,[56] which tend to be at the operational stage rather than at strategic planning stages.[57] Indeed this concern appears to be borne out in practice. The EA has published details of the four consultations it has held on standard rules on its website.[58] Details of the EA's third consultation are not available;[59] in relation to the others, however, the statistics indicate that the overwhelming response has been silence, with only small numbers of stakeholders responding. Most of the responses received have come from government agencies or

54 The standard rules procedure applies in essence to the disposal of low level radioactive waste. See EA, 'How to Apply for an Environmental Permit Part RSR-B1 – Standard Facility Guidance Notes' <http://publications.environment-agency.gov.uk/pdf/GEHO0410BSFQ-e-e.pdf> accessed 5 November 2010.

55 It may also be viewed as inappropriate in some circumstances because the EA is obliged to follow standards laid out, eg in the European Commission's BREF guidance notes on BAT under the IPPC regime.

56 J Hathaway, 'The Clean Air Act and the Intermodal Surface Transportation and Efficient Act' in (1994) ABA/Public Participation 28 (ABA Public Service Division Standing Committee on Environmental Law), referred to in N Spyke, 'Public Participation in Environmental Decision Making at the New Millennium: Structuring New Spheres of Public Influence' (1999) 26 Boston Coll Envtl Aff L Rev 263, 281.

57 As discussed in J Tippett and others, 'Social Learning in Public Participation in River Basin Management—Early Findings from HarmoniCOP European Case Studies' (2005) 8 Environ Sci Pol 287. See also Y Rees and others, 'Good European Practices for Stakeholder Involvement – Lessons from Real Planning Processes Case-studies and Experiments: WorkPackage 5 report of the HarmoniCOP project – Harmonising COllaborative Planning' (HarmoniCOP, 2005) 23 <http://www.harmonicop.uos.de/download.php> accessed 5 November 2010.

58 <http://www.environment-agency.gov.uk/research/library/consultations/consultations.aspx> accessed 5 November 2010.

59 See <http://www.environment-agency.gov.uk/research/library/consultations/107784.aspx> accessed 5 November 2010.

industrial stakeholders or business associations, with only one response recorded from a public interest group.[60] If public views are required to improve the quality of decision making, then this process of engagement appears to be flawed.

In Scotland, the more varied approach taken to regulation has left space for greater public participation. SEPA has, as indicated earlier, been proactive in both utilising this space and in going beyond minimal regulatory requirements. Here too, however, the level of engagement by the public in the process appears to have been rather limited. Of 26 consultations in relation to PPC applications held by SEPA and made available online between 5 December 2008 and 17 August 2010, only three had responses from the general public (two do not provide details of whether or not responses were received).[61]

While the differences evident in the Scottish and English regulations may reflect a general difference in the approach taken to regulation rather than philosophical differences in the way participatory rights operate, the result appears to be different approaches to participatory rights in the two jurisdictions. In England, the emphasis appears to be largely upon ensuring speed and consistency in decision making; in Scotland, greater emphasis appears to be placed on the benefits that may follow from public participation in decision making. The fact that neither approach appears, from the limited recent evidence available,[62] to be making a significant difference in engaging the public may be due to the form that participation generally takes. In the following section, the fit between the processes used and the objectives

60 The first and second consultations were each emailed directly to 800 stakeholders and published on the internet. The first received 35 responses all but one of which came from industry, industrial associations or government agencies. The second received 24 responses, all from industry stakeholders or government agencies. For its fourth consultation on rules the EA emailed its consultation directly to 1400 stakeholders as well as making the information available on the internet. It received responses from 32 stakeholders, of which only two were public interest groups, 16 were either industry stakeholders or industry interest groups and the remainder were government agencies. There were no responses from individual members of the public. See EA, 'Summary of Responses to our Consultation on Standard Rules Consultation No 1, "Standard Rules and Guidance for the Introduction of the Environmental Permitting Regulations"' (March 2008) <http://www.environment-agency.gov.uk/static/documents/Business/summary_of_responses_2008889.pdf> accessed 5 November 2010; EA, 'Summary of Responses to our Second Consultation, "Standard Rules for the Environmental Permitting Regulations"' (March 2009) <http://www.environment-agency.gov.uk/static/documents/Research/SR_Cons_No_2_Response_document_final.pdf> accessed 5 November 2010 and EA, 'Summary of Responses to our Fourth Consultation, "Standard Rules for the Environmental Permitting Regulations"' (March 2010) <http://www.environment-agency.gov.uk/static/documents/Research/SR_Cons_No_4_Response_document_v1_0.pdf> accessed 5 November 2010. Unfortunately similar figures are not provided for consultations on bespoke permit applications.

61 See <http://www.sepa.org.uk/air/process_industry_regulation/pollution_prevention_control/public_participation_directive/ppd_consultations.aspx> accessed 5 November 2010. Similar statistics are, unfortunately, not readily available in England.

62 The difficulty of drawing sound conclusions from the limited and rather patchy statistics available is acknowledged.

underpinning the use of public participation in decision making are considered more fully.

### 3.1 Forms of Participation

The considerable body of literature on participatory decision making will not be repeated here. Suffice it to say that there are a variety of ways in which participatory decision making can be implemented. Arnstein, for example, famously categorises processes according to the degree to which decision making involves the public.[63] Broadly, processes range from simply informing the public that the decision has been made, through consultation (where the public respond to questions or information given by the regulator, but decision making remains with the regulator), to co-decision making and finally, to fully delegated decision making. Within this range there is a number of different forms that participation may take.[64] Key, for present purposes, is that those processes near the bottom of Arnstein's ladder of participation, such as informing or consulting, are likely to see the greatest consistency between decisions and to see the fastest decision making. Those nearer the top such as co-decision making are likely to take longer to reach a conclusion and may be more likely to lead to inconsistencies between decisions as variations in local values, expertise or preferences influence the types of decisions that are made. The advantages they bring include a better fit with the objective of improving the range of information and values upon which decisions are based.[65] There is, however, no disguising the fact that the participatory processes described earlier in the paper fall squarely within the approach Arnstein refers to as consultation and which she describes as tokenism.[66] They do not really involve shared decision making and can at best be regarded as a way of improving the quality of information the regulator has before it, which may not be quite the same thing as improving the range of information and values upon which the decision is actually based. With the best will in the world the regulator may fail to understand the significance of information or values presented to it through these processes and better understandings may only truly develop through processes involving dialogue between interested parties.

63 Arnstein (n 9) See also, eg OECD (n 9).

64 See eg S Bell and L Etherington, 'The Role of Consultation in Making Environmental Policy and Law' (1999) 8 Nott LJ 48. O Renn and P Schweizer, 'Inclusive Risk Governance: Concepts and Application to Environmental Policy Making' (2009) 19 Env Pol Gov 174; see also OECD (n 9) (where the OECD outlines the purposes of different forms of public engagement).

65 See text (n 5).

66 Arnstein (n 9) 217.

That consultation is so heavily relied upon is neither controversial nor surprising. The philosophical root of this approach can be found in descriptions of the decision making processes. For example, permitting has been described by the Department of Environment, Food and Rural Affairs (Defra) as 'how'-type decisions in contrast to the 'if'-type decisions seen in planning.[67] That is, decision making with regard to the regulation of activities has been broken into two stages: one stage where the appropriateness of allowing an activity to take place in a particular location is considered and another stage where consideration is given to the constraints that should be placed on how the activity is carried out. (As Defra acknowledges these two stages could and perhaps should take place at the same time.) This division in decision making highlights why permitting decisions were once regarded as falling solely within the purview of technocrats. It was (and perhaps still is)[68] assumed that these decisions rested on technical issues with which the public would have little familiarity.[69]

Reliance on consultation is also justified by the fact that regulators (in common with other government agencies)[70] operate within certain legislative constraints. These constraints may in effect require them to keep control of the agenda and not permit real sharing of decision making powers.[71] These include constraints that place an absolute block on decision making power, such as where planning permission is required in relation to an activity such as waste disposal, but has yet to be granted (in such cases the permit cannot be granted).[72] There may also be requirements to examine or address other

67 Defra, 'Planning and Pollution Control: Improving the Way the Regimes Work Together in Delivering New Development' (2007) 4 <http://www.defra.gov.uk/environment/waste/controls/documents/planning-pollution-control.pdf> accessed 5 November 2010.

68 EA (n 52) [2.2].

69 This could be contrasted with planning decisions which have been regarded as more political decisions and thus more open to public debate. See RCEP (n 3) [8.15] and onwards; and Scottish Executive, 'The Interaction Between Land Use Planning and Environmental Regulation, Scottish Executive Social Research' (Edinburgh 2004). See also J Rowan-Robinson and others, 'Public Access to Environmental Information: A Means to What End?' (1996) 8 JEL 19, 29.

70 See eg planning processes such as under the Town and Country Planning (Scotland) Act 1997, s 25 where there is also a need for the regulatory body to keep some control over the final decision. See also M Poustie, 'Planning Reforms in Scotland' (2007) JPL 489; D Brock, 'Is Nature Taking Over?' (2003) JPL Supp (Occasional Papers No 31) 50–76. See also J Holder, *Environmental Assessment: The Regulation of Decision Making* (Oxford University Press, Oxford 2004) ch 6.

71 See Blackstock and others (n 49) 11. See also H Govan and others, 'Best Practice in Community Participation for National Parks' (1998) SNH Review, Report 107.

72 See eg 2010 Regulations (n 14) sch 9, para 3 and sch 20, para 13. Similarly, there are requirements to exclude information from registers which may relate to national security and confidential business information under the 2010 Regulations, regs 47 and 48. This is not an absolute requirement; rather the regulator must determine whether or not material should be excluded from the register where a request is made on these grounds under reg 50.

factors before granting a permit. For example, the regulations on pollution prevention and control oblige the regulator to require additional measures to be taken where the use of best available techniques are not sufficient to meet an environmental quality standard.[73] The regulator may also be required to consider certain other factors such as the ability of soil to purify pollutants and the risk to groundwater from polluting activities[74] or to assess the risk to the water environment and have regard to the requirements of various pieces of legislation.[75] Or they may be required to ensure that members of the public are not exposed to levels of radiation that are too high.[76] Similarly SEPA is required to take account of COMAH[77] safety reports and determinations under Articles 5–7 of Directive 85/337/EEC[78] in deciding whether or not to grant a permit under the PPC regime.[79] In addition, the conditions they set within permits may, in effect, be dictated elsewhere, for example in European Commission BREF notes.

While these restrictions cannot be ignored, nor can the fact that this reliance on consultation-type processes may not be sufficient to improve the quality of decision making. Consultation provides no guarantee that information made available by the public will be taken into account by the regulator. A right to submit oral or written comments is not quite the same as a right to influence decisions,[80] which requires participation on one of the higher rungs of Arnstein's ladder. While provisions requiring publication of the reasons underpinning decisions and of representations received may go some way to meeting this requirement,[81] they do not go far enough. Nor is it possible to draw firm conclusions from practice on whether information provided by the public will be taken into account. In some areas, regulators have been shown to focus (consciously or unconsciously) on information provided by scientific or professional experts that fit more closely with the types of information that they, the regulators, are used to working with.[82] In others, such as planning,

73 Ibid sch 7, para 5.
74 Ibid sch 22, para 7.
75 See reg 15 and sch 4 of the Water Environment etc Regulations 2005 (n 2).
76 2010 Regulations (n 14) sch 23, pt 3, s 1, para 1.
77 Control of Major Accident Hazards.
78 Council Directive (EC) 1985/337 on the Assessment of the Effects of Certain Public and Private Projects on the Environment [1985] OJ L175.
79 The PPC (Scotland) Regulations 2000 (n 40) sch 4, pt 2, para 13.
80 Holder (n 70) ch 8, 205.
81 See eg the PPC (Scotland) Regulations 2000 (n 40) sch 4, paras 15 and 15C.
82 See H Valve and J Kauppila, 'Enacting Closure in the Environmental Control of Genetically Modified Organisms' (2008) 20 JEL 339; M Kritikos, 'Traditional Risk Analysis and Releases of GMOs into the European Union: Space for Non-Scientific Factors?' (2009) 34 EL Rev 405. See also B Hedelin and M Lindh, 'Implementing the EU Water Framework Directive – Prospects for Sustainable Water Planning in Sweden' (2008) 18 Eur Env 327, noting the preferential treatment accorded to certain disciplines over others by regulators.

more emphasis has been placed in the past on responses to consultations than on the outcome of environmental assessments by decision makers.[83] The limited responses to consultations on environmental permitting from members of the public referred to earlier make it hard to draw sustainable conclusions on how SEPA and the EA address different types of information.[84] Nevertheless, it seems likely that better quality decision making will require greater communication than is possible through consultation alone. This appears to be acknowledged in the Scottish provisions allowing objections to draft permits to trigger local inquiries.[85] And in general the legislation reviewed here provides only minimum requirements with regards to consultations. This means that there is little within the legislation to prevent the EA or SEPA extending consultations, or adopting mechanisms that provide for fuller participation in actual decision making by the public, though legislative requirements to give precedence to certain factors[86] may on occasions limit the degree to which decision making powers can truly be shared. Indeed, as indicated earlier, SEPA has exceeded regulatory requirements on occasion and both are encouraged to do so by the general obligations they operate under,[87] which encourage increased public participation in decision making.

Nevertheless the low response rate to consultations in both jurisdictions raises a further issue about the quality of decision making. If decision making is to be improved in general then there is a need for a culture of participation to develop. The low response rates suggest that this has not developed and may suggest a degree of apathy on the part of the public. But findings in relation to the use of environmental information indicate that the public are not so much apathetic as passive in their approach to the environment.[88] As Rowan-Robinson and his co-authors noted, the public did have a view they were willing to express when directly asked. The lack of participation may be due to individuals self-excluding where they believe they do not possess the knowledge or understanding necessary to make an informed decision.[89]

83 C Wood and C Jones, 'The Effect of Environmental Assessment on UK Local Planning Authority Decisions' (1997) 34 Urb Stud 1237. See also C Jones and others, 'Environmental Assessment: Dominant or Dormant?' in J Holder and D McGillivray (eds), *Taking Stock of Environmental Assessment: Law Policy and Practice* (Routledge Cavendish, Abingdon 2007) 17.

84 See discussion in and at nn 60 and 61.

85 See discussion at n 46, above.

86 See text at n 71.

87 See eg 'Management Statement' issued to the Environment Agency by the Secretary of State for Environment, Food and Rural Affairs and the Welsh Assembly Government, the Scottish Environment Protection Agency 'Management Statement' (2005), 'Policy Priorities Relevant to the Scottish Environment Protection Agency' (2004); and the Scottish Executive, 'The Scottish Environment Protection Agency (SEPA) and Sustainable Development: Statutory Guidance to SEPA made under s 31 of the Environment Act 1995' (2005).

88 Rowan-Robinson and others (n 69) 38.

89 G Marchand and A Askland, 'GM Foods: Potential Public Consultation and Participation Mechanisms' (2003–04) 44 Jurimetrics 99. Or, as noted by Jasanoff, may self exclude because they do not understand the processes by which they could become involved; S Jasanoff, 'Technologies of Humility: Citizen Participation in Governing Science' (2003) 41 Minerva 223.

These tendencies may be exacerbated where there are only limited obligations on regulators to inform the public that participatory processes exist[90] and where it largely falls to the public to find out what opportunities to participate there are by watching for advertisements in newspapers or online and to gather information about decisions by accessing environmental or permitting registers—something only the most diligent of activists are likely to do.[91] If one of the purposes of public participation in regulatory decision making is to improve the quality of decisions by bringing more information, views and expertise to the table, then a more proactive approach may be required.[92] Lessons may be drawn from areas such as planning. It too was once seen as an area where decisions were a matter of interest for planners and the applicant alone, but here decision making has generally been broadened to include members of the public. While the norm in planning may be to hold consultations rather than to have full co-decision making, more innovative practices are also used on occasion.[93] The use of such measures may help explain the apparently greater success in engaging the public in planning type decisions than in permitting decisions. For example, the Ribble Basin Pilot Process used comprehensive mapping techniques to identify appropriate stakeholders to involve.[94]

At present, the choice of whether to use such processes rests largely with the regulators. As Hedelin and Lindh have shown, however, they are likely to use methods with which they are already familiar.[95] It is also possible that regulators could have a negative view of previous involvement of the public in participatory decision making. If, for example, the uptake of opportunities to participate has tended to be low, it is unlikely that the regulator would employ more expensive processes in future particularly if they have limited

90 In this area the obligation to inform the public falls on the EA in England and on the applicant and SEPA (in relation to different activities) in Scotland. The 2010 Regulations (n 14) sch 5, para 6 place the EA under an obligation to 'take the steps it considers appropriate to inform the public consultees of the application' and invite them to make representations, giving details of the time frame in which representations are to be made. It is then left to the EA to decide where or how to advertise consultations and whether in fact to contact consultees directly. Faced with this choice, the EA has chosen to advertise applications on its website. The PPC (Scotland) Regulations 2000 (n 40) sch 4, pt 1 paras 5, 6, 9 and 15 B and C and para 17 detail the different obligations to inform the public placed on SEPA and applicants for permits under these regulations. Certain activities are excluded from the requirement to inform the public under para 8 of sch 4 and there is provision for exclusions in the interests of national security in sch 4, pt 3. Advertisements in relation to variations of permits are addressed under sch 7, para 4. Similar provisions are found in the Water Environment etc Regulations 2005 (n 2), regs 13, 15A and 20.

91 Marchand and Askland (n 89); Rowan-Robinson and others (n 69).

92 See J O'Neill, 'Representing People, Representing Nature, Representing the World' (2001) 19 Environment and Planning C 483.

93 Rowan-Robinson and others (n 69).

94 C Riley, 'Stakeholder Mapping for the Ribble Pilot. "You've been framed" Sustainability and the Water Framework Directive' (WFD 2004) as cited in Tippett and others (n 57).

95 Hedelin and Lindh (n 82) 342.

time and finances available to support such action.[96] Of course, if financial and human resources were available, then that could encourage regulators to use innovative methods to try to improve participation. Their willingness to do so will, however, depend on whether or not they have yet to fully embrace the culture of participation themselves.

It may also be that the format of processes needs to be reconsidered. Primmer and Kyllönen found, for example, that formal processes tend to stifle public participation.[97] One might anticipate that the consultation processes provided for in the regulations would be regarded as formal by the public. It may be appropriate then to ensure that the decision making processes are rather less formal and to draw on a range of approaches in decision making.

## 4. Conclusions

In the last few years different approaches have been taken to securing the balance between the Better Regulation agenda and public participation in environmental permitting decisions. In England, participation is largely limited to decisions where policy type questions are to be answered and is by way of contribution to consultations. In Scotland there is scope for participation in a wider range of decisions and there appear to be opportunities to participate in different forms of decision making. The key development, however, is the streamlining[98] of decision making evident in the standard permit process in the English 2010 Regulations and the Water Environment (Controlled Activities) (Scotland) Regulations. In addition, the emphasis remains on decision making by the regulator. This leads to the conclusion that greater emphasis is now being placed on ensuring speed and consistency in decision making in certain contexts than on improving the quality of information before individual regulators tasked with making certain decisions. These regulations, designed to meet the Better Regulation agenda, have thus altered the meaning of 'better quality decisions' in this context. Rather than the idea of improving the range of information and values on which decisions are based by drawing on public knowledge and expertise, better quality decisions in the context of standard permits appears to mean quicker, more consistent

96 These types of factors have previously been shown to impact on the way in which regulators implement their obligations: E Kirk, A Reeves and K Blackstock, 'Path Dependency and Environmental Regulation' (2007) 25 Environ Plan C 250.

97 E Primmer and T Kyllönen, 'Goals for Public Participation Implied by Sustainable Development, and the Preparatory Process of the Finnish National Forest Programme' (2006) 8 For Poly Econ 838. See also K Soma and A Vatn, 'Is There Anything Like a Citizen? A Descriptive Analysis of Instituting a Citizen's Role to Represent Social Values at The Municipal Level' (2010) 20 Envtl Poly Gov 30.

98 Defra, Welsh Assembly, Department of Energy and Climate Change, 'Environmental Permitting' (2010) 2.

decisions. They appear also to have reversed the move away from government by technocracy and the efforts to restore public faith in decision making[99] that the enhancement of public participation was meant to engender. Instead, decision making has been returned to the regulators once more in respect of many decisions, particularly in England. (In Scotland standard rules apply to a more limited range of permitting applications and the regulators have exceeded the regulatory provisions on participation on a number of occasions.)

This change in emphasis does not detract from compliance with the Aarhus Convention and the EU Public Participation Directive,[100] as the provisions are still sufficient to comply with the UK's obligations under these regimes. It does, however, represent a change in the philosophy of public participation. If there is a desire to see a return to the approach first taken to improving decision making: broadening the range of values and information underpin environmental permitting decisions, and in the authors' view there should be, then the relationship between Better Regulation and participatory decision making must be reconsidered. Greater emphasis should be placed on participatory rights once more, particularly in the regimes overseen by the EA. It would be appropriate for the EA to adopt an approach more akin to SEPA's that enables decisions to be tailored to a specific context, though this could be achieved within the existing English regime by, for example, reducing the range of activities eligible to apply for a standard permit. This would allow for the variations in location caused by geography, weather and economic circumstances to be more fully incorporated into decisions as appropriate. That, it is argued, is what better quality decision making ought to be about.

Rights in legislation may not, however, be sufficient to ensure that a culture of participation does emerge. Despite the divergence in approaches taken both in the legislative regimes in Scotland and England and by the EA and SEPA in practice, there is little difference in the levels of participation by the public in England and Scotland. In both jurisdictions participation remain steadfastly low. Mechanisms then need to be found to help build a stronger culture of participation within the public. One part of addressing this task may be to adopt different forms of participatory process and lessons may be drawn from other areas such as planning in how to address this question. It may not be

99 F Fischer, *Citizens, Experts and the Environment: the Politics of Local Knowledge* (Duke University Press, Durham 2000); Steele (n 3).

100 For example, art 6 of the Aarhus Convention (n 1) only requires the public concerned to be given a right to make submissions or comments in writing and leaves it to States to choose if and when public hearings should be held at which *inter alia* members of the public would have a right to make oral submissions or comments. See also the Public Participation Directive 2003 (n 1). Although para 24 of the preamble to the IPPC Directive 2008 (n 31) suggests that something more may be required in referring to the fact that participation must be sufficient to 'enable the public to express, and the decision maker to take account of, opinions and concerns which may be relevant to those decisions', the procedures laid out in that Directive refer again largely to consultation providing only an additional reference to the right to ask questions of regulators—see Annex V.

necessary to amend the legislation to enable such processes to be adopted as in general, the legislation currently in place sets only the minimum levels of participation that may take place. On the whole, these could be exceeded save for the occasional requirements to give precedence to certain factors in decision making.[101] If, however, the legislative provisions do remain unaltered, current practice indicates a greater likelihood of a range of processes being adopted north of the border than south. The result may be the emergence of a greater culture of participation in regulatory decision making in Scotland than in England and ever more divergence in the meaning of 'better quality decisions' between the two jurisdictions.

101 See text at n 74.

# [13]
# The Environment Agency

Like the Food Standards Agency, the Environment Agency (EA) was the product of controversy, though in this case it was not so much the result of serious scandals but of controversy over the degree to which there should be an umbrella agency for all environmental regulation rather than separate bodies covering, for example, waste disposal and river management. The creation of a single agency also had one unusual consequence; as well as being a regulator, the EA has substantial management responsibilities in relation to water, including river management, and flood protection. It also has a complex relationship with government. These concerns will be central to this chapter, as will the extent to which the creation of the agency has resulted in a major change to the distinctive British regulatory style in environmental matters.

## The origins of the Environment Agency

The immediate genesis of the Environment Agency can be found in an announcement by John Major, the Conservative Prime Minister, in July 1991 that his government intended to create a new agency bringing together the functions of the National Rivers Authority, Her Majesty's Inspectorate of Pollution, and the waste regulation functions of local authorities; this was included in the Conservative Party manifesto for the 1992 general election.[1] Underlying this apparently simple proposal there was considerable earlier conflict as to the merits of such an agency, and this conflict was to continue over exactly what its responsibilities would be.

The background is one of a distinct regulatory style in environmental policy and regulation in the UK. This was identified by Vogel in a celebrated 1986 study as

> more informal in Britain than in the United States, more flexible and more private. Regulatory officials are able to exercise considerable discretion and tend to make policy on a case-by-case basis rather than through the application of general rules and

[1] For more information on the politics behind the creation of the EA, see Carter, N. and Lowe, P., 'Environmental Politics and Administrative Reform' (1994) 65 *The Political Quarterly*, 263–74. I draw heavily on this excellent account here.

> standards. Little use is made of prosecution and much reliance is placed on securing compliance through informal mechanisms of social control, including, in many instances, self-regulation.[2]

This he contrasted with the more formalized, rule-based and adversary approach adopted in the United States. Similarly, Carter and Lowe identified five main features of the distinctive UK administrative system and style of policy-making in this context: government structures and laws were a fragmented accretion of common law, statutes, agencies, procedures, and policies with no overall environmental policy; regulation was highly devolved and decentralized; environmental control was pervaded by administrative rather than judicial procedures; a voluntarist approach was used based on negotiation and persuasion; and policy making took place in closed communities with a heavy representation of producer interests.[3] The idea of a new agency did not fit easily into this model. Indeed, only 10 months before the establishment of the new agency was announced, the government had rejected a proposal for just such an agency made by the House of Commons Select Committee on the Environment.[4] The subsequent government about-turn may partly be attributed to political considerations and establishing the government's 'green' credentials, but also built on support for an inclusive agency by environmentalists and, in particular, by the Royal Commission on Environmental Pollution.[5]

Controversy continued after the announcement, and the 1992 election, as to which responsibilities should be acquired by the new Agency. In particular, it concerned the questions of whether the Agency should take on waste regulation duties of local authorities and the management duties of the National Rivers Authority. The latter (which had only been established as recently as 1989) was responsible not just for regulation but also for managing water resources on the basis of integrated catchment management which could lead to pollution, as well as for leisure traffic and land drainage. The government issued a consultation paper on various options, eventually deciding on one which included both waste regulation previously carried out by local authorities and all the responsibilities of the National Rivers Authority. This was despite opposition from the Environment Select Committee which had strongly supported separating the Authority's regulatory and managerial responsibilities to prevent the new Agency acting both as 'poacher and gamekeeper'.[6] On the other hand, both environmentalists and the Authority itself had strongly opposed such a separation, pointing to the importance of integrated management in its work

[2] Vogel, D., *National Styles of Regulation: Environmental Policy in Great Britain and the United States* (Ithaca: Cornell University Press, 1986), 220.

[3] 'Environmental Politics and Administrative Reform', 265–6.

[4] See the White Paper, *This Common Inheritance* (Cm 1200, 1990); 'Toxic Waste', HC 22, 1988–9, para 12.

[5] Carter and Lowe, 'Environmental Politics and Administrative Reform', 264–7.

[6] 'The Government's Proposals for an Environment Agency', HC 55, 1991–2, paras 98–102, 111.

and opposing the alternative of giving the management functions to the then Ministry of Agriculture. As in the case of food standards, an independent agency was perceived as less open to capture by producer interests than was the government department. The new Agency took up its powers in April 1996 under the Environment Act 1995.

This raises a key issue of regulatory design. The recent tendency, notably in EU regulatory requirements for the liberalized utility sectors such as electronic communications and energy, is to emphasize the importance of a complete separation of regulatory and management or operational functions. As the Select Committee emphasized, this is based on the principle that no authority is placed in the situation of having to regulate its own activities.[7] However, there is also another approach:

> [t]he counter-argument underlined the merits of integrated river basin management and stressed that the NRA's pollution control functions cannot easily be separated from its management functions.... Indeed, to prevent the gamekeeper-poacher conflict it is not necessary to separate control or enforcement roles from promotional roles, or to strip from regulatory authorities all their other executive functions. That would be to take an unnecessarily narrow view of regulation and diminish the scope for a 'sticks-and-carrots' strategy or for the pursuit of preventative policies.[8]

This latter view chimes well with a central theme of this book—that there is no single model for good regulation, and sometimes a collaborative approach may work better than attempts to secure complete regulatory independence at all levels of operation.

Finally, in another respect the establishment of the EA shares the emphasis of that of the other regulatory bodies considered so far; there was a major stress on the importance of openness and deliberation in its procedures. Thus the Environment Select Committee recommended strongly that the Agency make public as much information as possible, including grounds on which applications for permits and consents are objected to and the process by which each is considered.[9] This also applied beyond individual decisions, thus

> 'if environmental regulation is conceived not simply as a policing function but as an active agent for the promotion of sustainable practices, it is vital that regulatory bodies establish working relationships with all those who control the management and exploitation of natural resources. This is, indeed, a characteristic feature of the various conservation agencies in Britain... which combine regulatory and management functions.'[10]

Once more the stress is on the necessity of regulation as a collaborative exercise.

[7] Ibid, para 99.

[8] Carter and Lowe, 'Environmental Politics and Administrative Reform', 271.

[9] 'The Government's Proposals for an Environment Agency', para 59.

[10] Carter and Lowe, 'Environmental Politics and Administrative Reform', 273.

## Functions of the Environment Agency

The remit of the EA has been summarized as follows:

- preventing flooding and pollution incidents—flood protection requires by far the largest proportion of its budget;[11]
- reducing industry's impact on the environment;
- ensuring waste produced is correctly disposed of;
- advising on land use planning, including regional planning, development plans, and planning applications;
- cleaning up rivers, coastal waters, and managing water resources;
- improvement of contaminated land;
- improving wildlife habitats;
- improving and enhancing inland waterways and ensuring sustainable inland fisheries.[12]

As with the case of the Food Standards Agency, the EA also emphasizes its role in working with others, including government and local authorities. It is thus clear that the mix of functions is very different from that of, for example, the public utility regulators. However, the EA does have regulatory functions of licensing in the form of operating permitting schemes, and inspection and enforcement. Currently, the permitting regimes take the form of its Environmental Permitting Programme which will eventually provide a common permitting regime for operators; Pollution Prevention and Control covering the discharge of damaging substances into the environment by businesses; Waste Management Licensing; and Water Abstraction and Water Discharge Licensing.[13] Permitting also gives the EA a role in setting standards through imposing conditions, however, general standards are mainly set by the EU in the form of directives and the Secretary of State through regulations. The pattern of different regulatory institutions and functions is thus once more extremely complex in this area.

A number of functions were transferred to the Agency on its establishment. These included all functions of Her Majesty's Inspectorate of Pollution under the Environmental Protection Act 1990, for example that of enforcement authority in relation to a large number of processes prescribed by regulation and radioactive substances. The new Agency also acquired local authority waste regulation functions under the Control of Pollution Act 1974, and the

[11] The Flood and Water Management Bill announced in the 2009 Queen's Speech will give the EA a strategic overview role in relation to flooding.

[12] Environment, Food and Rural Affairs Committee, 'The Environment Agency', HC 780, 2005–6, para 1.

[13] Better Regulation Executive and National Audit Office, *Effective Inspection and Enforcement: Implementing the Hampton Vision in the Environment Agency* (2008), para 13.

responsibilities of the National Rivers Authority relating to water resources management, control of pollution of water resources, flood defence, fisheries, and navigation.[14] The EA was also later to acquire further responsibilities through the implementation of EU law by the Pollution Prevention and Control Act 1999 ('skeleton legislation' giving broad regulation-making powers to the Secretary of State) and regulations made under it, aiming to integrate more fully the approach to pollution control over a wider range of processes. Most importantly, a new system of pollution control was introduced in 2000 using regulations made under the Act to implement the European Directive on integrated pollution prevention and control.[15] The regime for water resources management was also changed by the Water Act 2003. As a result, both the law and the precise definition of pollution control functions are now highly complex, with 227 pieces of legislation and 16 EU Directives.[16] Indeed, in 2003 the Department undertook a review of legislation which impeded integration within the Agency. Although it did not recommend further legislative change, it noted that the inheritance of a variety of mechanisms for environmental protection licensing unrelated to risk constituted a central barrier to more efficient regulation, and recommended a more graduated and risk-based approach to improve targeting of resources.[17]

## The Environment Agency in regulatory space: the institutions

The Agency itself is a statutory body corporate without Crown status.[18] It is required have between eight and fifteen members appointed by the relevant minister and Secretary of State.[19] The Board is currently comprised of 12 non-executive members and the chairman and Chief Executive; members represent 'a broad cross-section of bodies and individuals with an interest in the environment'.[20] Members may be removed by the minister for failure to attend meetings for three months, for bankruptcy, or if they are unable or unfit to carry out their functions.[21]

[14] Environment Act 1995, s 2.

[15] Pollution Prevention and Control (England and Wales) Regulations 2000, SI 2000/1973, implementing the Directive EC 96/61 concerning integrated pollution prevention and control [1996] OJ L257/26; these are now replaced by Directive 2008/1/EC concerning integrated pollution prevention and control [2008] OJ L24/8, and the Environmental Permitting (England and Wales) Regulations 2007, SI 2007/3538.

[16] Better Regulation Executive and National Audit Office, *Effective Inspection and Enforcement*, para 24.

[17] Department for Environment, Food and Rural Affairs, *Review of Legislation Affecting Integration Within the Environment Agency – Final Report* (2003).

[18] Environment Act 1995, s 1(1), (5).

[19] Section 1(2).

[20] 'Environment Agency Annual Report and Accounts 2007–8', HC 843, 2007–08, 10.

[21] Environment Act 1995, sch 1, para 1(3).

Accounts are audited by the Comptroller and Auditor-General, who was made the EA's auditor in 2003.[22]

It should be remembered that the Agency was designed to introduce a new system of integrated pollution control, taking over from no less than 86 predecessor bodies. In 2000 the Environment Select Committee found strong support for this integrated approach but that the Agency did not yet have a coherent vision of its over-arching role; there were continuing internal divisions and the legislation did not provide for a coherent regime.[23] As we shall see later, steps were taken to correct this by developing a clearer unified vision for the Agency. However, the legislative position has if anything become even more complex with the incorporation of EU requirements. In a further report in 2006, the Committee did not criticize internal integration between the different sections and found that there was now greater consistency in the Agency's regulatory and enforcement functions, but pointed to tensions between the Agency's roles as a regulator and as a 'champion of the environment'.[24] This is, of course, different from the relationship between regulatory and operational responsibilities. Predictably, and perhaps reflecting the different economic and rights/social solidarity approaches to regulation, industry witnesses emphasized the former role and environmental witnesses the latter. The Committee concluded that *'[g]iven the range of cross-cutting environmental issues faced by Government, we strongly support the Agency's role as a "Champion of the Environment". However, it is important that there should be clarity between all the Agency's different functions, particularly between its regulatory and environmental champion roles'*.[25] In its response to the Committee's report, the government stated that it saw no contradiction between the roles of champion of the environment and regulator, although in terms of resources and prioritization the two needed to be appropriately balanced.[26]

Ministerial powers in relation to the EA are extensive. Thus the Act gives the Secretary of State powers to issue directions of a general or specific character with respect to the carrying out of any of its functions, including implementing EU obligations and obligations under other international agreements. The directions must be published.[27] Directions may also be given under other statutes, such as the Environmental Protection Act 1990. Importantly, it is for the minister to define in more detail through guidance the contribution the EA is to make to achieving sustainable development, its principal aim, and to give guidance on

[22] Environment Act 1995, s 46; Government Resources and Accounts Act 2000 (Audit of Public Bodies) Order 2003, SI 2003/1326.

[23] 'The Environment Agency', HC 34, 1999–2000, paras 10–11, 13–18, 25–31.

[24] 'The Environment Agency', HC 780, 2005–6, para 38.

[25] Ibid, para 17 (emphasis retained).

[26] Environment, Food and Rural Affairs Committee, 'The Environment Agency: Government and Environment Agency Responses to the Committee's Seventh Report', HC 1519, 2005–6, 3.

[27] Environment Act 1995, ss 40(1)–(3), 122.

other appropriate objectives.[28] As mentioned above, the Pollution Prevention and Control Act 1999 gives the Secretary of State sweeping powers both to implement EU requirements by regulation, and for 'regulating, otherwise than in pursuance of that Directive, activities which are capable of causing any environmental pollution'.[29] A further role linked to government is that of the delivery of goals set out in Public Service Agreements agreed through the Public Spending Review.[30]

When it is recalled that the Secretary of State has the major role in negotiating EU environmental law and standards, it is clear that relations with government are particularly close in this regulatory context. Indeed, these extend over several departments, including the Departments for Business, Innovation and Skills and for Energy and Climate Change, as well as the Department for Food, Environment and Rural Affairs (Defra). Criticisms of the EA's relationships with government were made by the House of Commons Environment Select Committee in 2006, which noted that evidence it had received had pointed to a lack of distinction between the Department and the Agency in policy making, and that the Agency was too closely involved in the latter (it will be recalled that similar criticisms were made of the Human Fertilisation and Embryology Authority). The EA pointed to the incoherence and inconsistencies in the legislation which had created a policy void it had to fill, especially in the case of EU legislation, and the Committee stressed the need for greater legislative consistency and a common regulatory framework. A different criticism was that the Agency was not properly consulted by government in the development of policy; the Committee recommended earlier consultation.[31] On another occasion, the Public Accounts Committee was critical of the constraint imposed on the Agency by ministerial guidance in relation to waste matters, for example the targeting of inspections of waste operators.[32] The problem seems essentially to be one of a structure lacking coherence; the law is piecemeal and this had made effective cooperation difficult. The 2006 Environment Committee Report recommended the establishment of a common regulatory framework at both European and domestic level, but at the former level the proposal was rejected by the government and at the latter there has not been legislative change. However, a review by the Better Regulation Executive and the National Audit Office in 2008 found an 'increasingly positive' working relationship with Defra, whilst more work had to be done to improve joint working with the Department for Business.[33] Thus collaborative policy development with joint governance by the Department and EA takes place, as does joint consultation.

[28] Section 4(2)–(3). See Department for Environment, Food and Rural Affairs, *The Environment Agency's Objectives and Contributions to Sustainable Development: Statutory Guidance* (2002).

[29] Section 1(1).

[30] Environment Agency, *Corporate Plan 2008–11* (nd), 1–2.

[31] Environment, Food and Rural Affairs Committee, 'The Environment Agency', HC 780, 2005–6, paras 62–77.

[32] 'Protecting the Public from Waste', HC 352, 2002–3, para 3.

[33] *Effective Inspection and Enforcement*, paras 31–9.

Relations with Defra are structured through a *Management Statement* which is more detailed and comprehensive than the Food Standards Agency's Concordat.[34] The Statement emphasizes the partnership role of the EA with central government and other bodies. It also notes that the Agency has a contribution to make to the development of policy, although this is ultimately a matter for central government and the Welsh Assembly. It also sets out the respective roles of the Secretary of State and the EA's chair and Chief Executive, together with requirements for strategic and corporate planning and reporting.

Local government retains responsibilities in the environmental field as well as central government. Here a Local Government Performance Framework has been developed to assist collaboration and deliver shared targets; another example of informal structuring of collaboration familiar from the previous chapter. There were, however, problems of reaching targets for such collaboration and now both the EA and local authorities are made subject to new duties of cooperation in drafting local area agreements and local improvement targets.[35]

It is already evident that EU law has had a major role to play in the work of the Agency; indeed it is now EU law which is responsible for providing the basic framework of standards in this area, in particular through the system of pollution control introduced in 2000 using regulations to implement the European Directive on integrated pollution prevention and control.[36] The law has been seriously criticized as inconsistent and incoherent; the European legislation was drafted in a piecemeal fashion (including different definitions of 'pollution' in different instruments) and national transposition of the law was similarly piecemeal. This prompted the Environment Select Committee to support the EA's proposal for a common EU regulatory code for the environment covering issues such as definitions, permitting, consultation periods, and monitoring arrangements.[37] The recommendation was, however, rejected by the government as potentially infringing subsidiarity, although the EA maintained its support for the principle.[38]

Apart from the central role of EU law, there are special European institutions which are relevant to the work of the Agency. Chief amongst these is the European Environment Agency, established in 1990, which has a central role in establishing the information necessary for the setting of standards. It also coordinates the European environment and information network (Eionet), comprising national regulators and experts. The EA also participates in the EU Network for the Implementation and Enforcement of Environmental Law (IMPEL). Finally,

[34] Department for Environment, Food and Rural Affairs, *Management Statement Issued to the Environment Agency* (2002).

[35] *Corporate Plan 2008–11*, 2; Annual Report 2006/07, HC 834, 2006–7, 5; Local Government and Public Involvement in Health Act 2007, s 106.

[36] See n 15 above.

[37] 'The Environment Agency', 2005–6, paras 68–70.

[38] Environment, Food and Rural Affairs Committee, 'The Environment Agency: Government and Environment Agency Responses', HC 1519, 2005–6, 10, 27.

EU law is also extremely important in providing rights of access to environmental information, as will be discussed briefly below.

## Setting water prices

One striking example of an inter-institutional conflict involving different types of regulation is that of the setting of water price controls by the economic regulator for water, then the Director General of Water Services and Ofwat (see Chapter 9 below) through the periodic review process. This is worth examining in more detail as it illustrates very clearly a major conflict between agencies with predominantly environmental and economic remits.[39] The debate concerned the costs of environmental improvements which had to be included in the Director General's decision on permissible price increases; the environmental standards were specified by ministers after consulting the EA and by EU law requirements, and the conflict was between environmental regulation setting standards and economic regulation protecting consumer interests.

In the 1999 periodic review there was a 'highly charged' debate on the balance to be struck between price cuts and environmental investment with 'an open exchange of claims and counter claims by Ofwat, the DETR, the EA, water companies and non-governmental organisations'.[40] The EA saw its role in the debate as identifying the environmental problems caused by water companies and advising ministers on the relative priority of solving them.[41] Surveys of customers' needs were undertaken by the various parties, but each of the '*confusing plethora of customer surveys*' came up with slightly different rankings of customer preferences.[42]

Further problems arose from the process of deciding the scope of the environmental programme, a decision for the government based on EA advice; the ministerial guidance suggested that there was scope for price cuts as a result of the review. The Director General of Water Services made initial statements indicating that he was considering price reductions; the EA then issued an open letter to a wide range of organizations indicating its concern that the outcome had been pre-judged on the assumption that consumer benefits could only be in the form of a price reduction and that consumers gained no benefit at all from a cleaner environment. The Environmental Audit Committee recommended that ministers should not try to influence decisions of the independent water regulator by announcing price expectations, and that Ofwat should seek to ensure '*that its*

[39] For general background, see Weale, A., 'Environmental Regulation' in Centre for the Study of Regulated Industries, *Regulatory Review 1997* (Bath: CRI, 1998), 201–16, and for more detail Byatt, I., 'The Impact of EC Directives on Water Customers in England and Wales' (1996) 3 *Journal of European Public Policy*, 665–74.

[40] Environmental Audit Committee, 'Water Prices and the Environment', HC 597, 1999–2000, para 3.

[41] Ibid, para 31.

[42] Ibid, para 52 (emphasis retained).

*own statements do not "demonise" environmental and quality investment by portraying it as the key upward pressure on prices without equally emphasising the customer and public benefits which it delivers*'.[43] The position was made worse by criticism of the EA by the Director General of Water Services; he suggested that it had given little attention to establishing that proposed quality improvements offered value for money for the environment or for customers, and that its methodology was inadequate and did not use proper cost-benefit analysis.[44] Yet a further problem was the lack of involvement of stakeholders in the process.[45] Finally, the Environmental Audit Committee noted that the water regulator did not have a specific duty to promote sustainability, and the attitude that sustainability was not a direct matter for Ofwat was evident in much of the latter's work; it recommended that a duty to have regard to sustainable development be added to the Director General's remit.[46]

Thus in the 1999 periodic review there was conflict between different regulators with environmental and economic remits; this could have been resolved by government but in practice government contributed to the confusion. In the case of the next Periodic Review in 2004 the Environment Committee considered that in its earlier stages the Review had been conducted in a more transparent way than previously, however later the process had become more clouded and differences had continued between the environmental and economic regulators, with the former arguing that too much emphasis had been placed on the cost of environmental improvement, partly because of the way in which Ofwat presented the bases for price increases.[47] The EA also claimed that Ofwat had assumed the role more properly for the Secretary of State in taking environmental decisions.[48] The Environmental Audit Committee similarly noted considerable improvements in the process, including in the EA's cost-benefit analysis. The Water Act 2003 added a duty to take into account sustainable development to those applying to the new water regulatory authority, though this was not yet in effect and would only be a secondary, not a primary, duty. However, there had been informational problems in the process and in the review Ofwat's proposals did not rest on the principles of sustainable development which the Director General already professed to be upholding.[49] In conclusion,

> [t]he Economic Regulator's Role has come to impinge on the Environmental Regulator's role. This has been highlighted to us in memoranda received by the Committee and has become obvious to us over the last few months. We are not convinced that the Ofwat has sufficient expertise in determining what should or should not be included in the environmental programme, yet in advice to ministers and evidence to us it would appear that this is part of what the Regulator now sees as his duties.... *We do not believe it is the*

[43] Ibid, para 69 (emphasis retained). [44] Ibid, para 86. [45] Ibid, paras 103–4.
[46] Ibid, paras 215–20. [47] 'Water Pricing: Follow-up', HC 1186, 2003–4, paras 8–16.
[48] Ibid, paras 19–20.
[49] 'Water: The Periodic Review and the Environmental Programme', HC 416, 2003–4, paras 11–16, 21, 33–6.

*role of the Regulator to decide what should or should not be included in the environmental programme.*[50]

As regards the outcome, the EA welcomed the approval of a programme of £3.5 billion investment as part of the review, whilst pointing out that it had argued that more investment was called for and that this figure represented the bare minimum required to comply with European law.[51]

The sources of the difficulties here are obvious; overlapping responsibilities of different regulators with very different duties and remits. This was always likely to cause problems, and indeed it has been suggested that the separation of environmental regulation and price regulation did have the virtue that disputes were brought into the open, and we have seen some improvements in the transparency of the process which have reinforced this.[52] A problem has been, however, that the role of government has not been particularly helpful. In the 1999 Periodic Review the Department was criticized for pre-empting the decision of the water regulator by announcing its price expectations in advance, and in 2004 the (delayed) ministerial guidance was '*the focus of department wrangling, simply because it is the only way the Government can exert any direct influence over water prices*'.[53] The only way in which the difficulties can be resolved will be through a combination of more uniform statutory remits for the different regulators (already partly achieved with the changes in the Water Act 2003), an emphasis on transparent debate, and a more decisive role for government. This does appear to have succeeded in the 2009 review where, as we shall see in Chapter 9 below, there has been an early and clearer statement of objectives by the government and the drafting of a National Environment Programme by the EA setting out the schemes necessary for meeting European and national requirements. Thus procedural improvements do seem to have provided a better framework for resolving disputes between different approaches to regulation. Indeed, in an examination of the 2009 review by the Environment Committee, criticism of institutional conflict was remarkable by its absence.[54]

## The Environment Agency in regulatory space: the duties

The most striking feature of the duties applicable to the EA is that there is one primary duty in the form of a principal aim; this is to discharge its functions 'so to protect or enhance the environment, taken as a whole, as to make the

[50] Ibid, para 37 (emphasis retained, footnote omitted).

[51] 'Annual Report and Accounts 2004/05', HC 201, 2004–5. For discussion of the final outcome of the Review, see Fletcher, P., 'Water Regulation', in Centre for the Study of Regulated Industries, *Regulatory Review 2004–5* (Bath: CRI, 2005), 119–41.

[52] Wheale, 'Environmental Regulation', 212–13.

[53] Environmental Audit Committee, 'Water: The Periodic Review 2004', para 23 (emphasis retained).

[54] Environment, Food and Rural Affairs Committee, 'Ofwat Price Review 2009', HC 554, 2008–9, paras 16–22, 26–34.

contribution towards attaining the objective of achieving sustainable development. . . .'[55] The second important characteristic is that there is a considerable role for ministerial guidance in defining that objective and determining other objectives; indeed, the sustainable development duty only comes into play when such guidance is issued.[56] The original Bill had only included provision for the Secretary of State to issue guidance without reference to sustainable development, the latter was introduced at the report stage in the House of Lords. The Secretary of State has issued guidance on the Agency's objectives and contributions to sustainable development.[57] The guidance emphasizes that it applies to the formulation of approaches by the EA, decisions about its priorities and the allocation of resources, and is not directly applicable to individual decisions. It notes that the EA is required to take account of costs and benefits in achieving its principal aim and in exercising its powers. The Agency is to support the government's Sustainable Development Strategy and its key objectives will be social progress which reflects the needs of everyone, effective protection of the environment, prudent use of natural resources, and maintenance of high and stable levels of economic growth and employment.[58] As well as protecting and enhancing the environment itself, the Agency is to act as an independent adviser on environmental matters affecting policy-making, both within government and more widely. It should develop approaches which do not impose excessive costs.

The guidance also sets more specific objectives for the Agency.[59] These include adopting an integrated approach to environmental protection, discharging its functions in an economical, efficient and effective manner, conducting its affairs in an open and transparent manner, and developing in conjunction with government a 'risk-based, proportionate, consistent, efficient and cost-effective approach to the regulatory process' following better regulation principles. Draft guidance has also been issued in relation to the Agency's exercise of its functions in relation to waste management licensing.[60]

It should thus be apparent that the principal aim is not a simple obligation to promote sustainable development; it is wholly dependent on ministerial guidance, and in that sense ties the EA more closely to government than is the case for most other regulators examined in this book (although the guidance does not directly determine individual decisions by the Agency, for example on enforcement). It is also clear from the guidance that a risk-based approach is to be taken to regulation, and in particular that some form of cost-benefit analysis must

55 Environment Act 1995, s 4(1). 56 Section 4(2)–(3).

57 Department for Environment, Food and Rural Affairs, *The Environment Agency's Objectives and Contributions to Sustainable Development: Statutory Guidance* (2002).

58 Ibid, para 3.2. 59 Ibid, para 4.1.

60 Department for Environment, Food and Rural Affairs, *Statutory Guidance to the Environment Agency on the Exercise of its Functions with Regard to the Waste Management Licensing (England and Wales) (Amendment and Related Provisions) Regulations 2005* (2005).

be used in the exercise of the Agency powers. This reflects the important section 39 of the Act, which imposes a controversial duty on the Agency, in deciding whether and how to exercise its powers, to 'take into account the likely costs and benefits of the exercise or non-exercise of the power or its exercise in the manner in question'.[61] Although 'benefits' are not further defined, 'costs' include costs to the environment as well as costs to any person.[62] The requirement is qualified as not applying 'to the extent that it is unreasonable for it to do so in view of the nature or purpose of the power or in the circumstances of the particular case'.[63] It also does not apply to mandatory obligations, such as complying with standards set by the minister or from the EU. Thus the scope of the duty is relatively restricted; it does, however, require some form of environmental and economic appraisal to take place before taking discretionary decisions.[64]

The 1995 Act also imposes a number of other duties on the EA. Thus it is required to exercise its pollution control powers to prevent or minimize the effects of pollution, and to compile information and (on ministerial request) undertake assessments relating to such pollution.[65] It also has duties in relation to inland and coastal waters to promote their natural beauty and amenity, conservation and the conservation of water resources, and has similar general environmental and recreational duties.[66] Guidance may be issued by the minister relating to these duties, and this has been done in the form of a code of practice.[67] Of course, there are other duties applying to the EA under different statutes and under EU law.

How are these duties translated into practice by the EA? At the highest level, after criticism by a Parliamentary Committee for lack of a clear vision, the Agency issued an *Environmental Vision*, setting as its fundamental goals 'a better quality of life' and 'an enhanced environment for wildlife'.[68] It also set outcomes and changes to be sought. The vision was translated into a Corporate Strategy for the five years 2006–11, which also stressed as the first main objective a better quality of life, with everyone having the opportunity to enjoy a high-quality environment, and with a particular emphasis on improving the environment in disadvantaged areas.[69] The second objective was an enhanced environment for wildlife in both urban and rural areas. Thus in these main objectives there were strong elements of social solidarity. The goals were further translated into a corporate plan

[61] Environment Act 1995, s 39(1). [62] Section 56(1). [63] Section 39(1)(b).

[64] For a summary of the position, see Bell, S. and McGillivray, D., *Environmental Law*, (7th edn, Oxford: Oxford University Press, 2008), 119. [65] Section 5.

[66] Sections 6–7.

[67] Section 9, and see the Water and Sewerage (Conservation, Access and Recreation) (Code of Practice) Order 2000, SI 2000/477 approving the *Code of Practice on Conservation, Access and Recreation* issued by the minister.

[68] *An Environmental Vision* (2000), 5. See also Select Committee on Environment, Transport and Regional Affairs, 'The Environment Agency', 1999–2000, paras 13–18.

[69] Environment Agency, *Creating a Better Place: Corporate Strategy 2006–11.*

covering three years setting out detailed actions and key performance targets.[70] The Annual Reports of the EA also contain detailed analyses of performance against individual targets. In the case of the 2008/9 report, there is detailed analysis of the extent to which 49 targets have been achieved.[71] The EA has now published a new strategy for 2010–15 after consultation; this places a particularly strong emphasis on reducing climate change and its consequences and this now forms the Agency's first objective. The others are to protect and improve water, land, and air; to work with people and communities to create better places; to work with businesses and other organizations to use resources wisely; and to 'be the best we can' as a regulator.[72] Overall, the various documents are an excellent example of the translation of very high-level objectives into more specific targets and of tracking performance in relation to them. The Hampton Implementation Review concluded that the documents were well written and accessible and that the EA is generally a transparent and accountable regulator.[73]

## The Environment Agency and the regulatory models

### Regulation for efficiency and consumer choice

Clearly the EA has important regulatory roles in relation to industry, and economic considerations must play a role here, although it is not concerned directly with promoting consumer choice as is the Food Standards Agency. This is reinforced by the controversial section 39 of the 1995 Act mentioned above, which requires the Agency to take into account the likely costs and benefits of the exercise or non-exercise of its powers. The duty was opposed by environmentalists on the ground that it would open up the Agency to legal challenge whenever it could not be proved that the costs of its action were outweighed by their benefits. However, in practice the effect seems to be more limited. According to the House of Commons Environmental Audit Committee, examining issues relating to water quality, the requirement does not require cost-benefit analysis for every environmental improvement which the Agency puts forward, and only applies to 10 per cent of its National Environment Programme approved by ministers, the rest being based on EU requirements or government policy decisions.[74] In these

[70] Environment Agency, *Corporate Plan 2008–11: Creating a Better Place – Translating Strategy into Action*.

[71] Environment Agency, 'Annual Report and Accounts 2008/09', HC 782, 2008–9, 56–70.

[72] Environment Agency, *Creating a Better Place 2000–2015 -- Our Corporate Strategy 2010–2015* (2009).

[73] Better Regulation Executive and National Audit Office, *Effective Inspection and Enforcement*, paras 20, 23.

[74] Select Committee on Environmental Audit, 'Water Prices and the Environment', paras 78–9.

cases, cost-benefit analysis may have been carried out before the EA is required to apply the rules.

The EA is also fully committed to the better regulation initiatives, to risk assessment and the use of market-based tools. These were described in detail in its publication *Delivering for the Environment – A 21st Century Approach to Regulation*, which emphasized its commitment to the principles laid down by the then Better Regulation Taskforce and to a 'smart regulation' approach, using systems such as cap and trade of emissions, environmental taxes, trading schemes, and negotiated or voluntary agreements and a more risk-based approach to enforcement.[75] Similar commitments have been repeated in each of the Agency's annual reports (eg in 2008–9 it claimed to have exceeded its target for reducing burdens on business with a total reduction of over £17 million), and the Environment Select Committee strongly supported its commitment to a risk-based approach, whilst noting that the full benefits are yet to be realized.[76] Similarly, the Hampton Implementation Review noted the EA's commitment to better regulation and a risk-based approach, whilst also noting scope for improvements in risk appraisal.[77] Provision for trading schemes was made as early as 1990 by the Environmental Protection Act which gives the Secretary of State power to establish total emissions and to allocate quotas.[78] Some such schemes have been established and are administered by the EA, for example the National Emissions Reduction Plan and the Landfill Allowances and Trading Scheme.[79]

Despite this commitment to a more risk-based and market-friendly approach to regulation, a note of caution should be sounded. In evidence to the House of Commons Regulatory Reform Committee the EA, whilst emphasizing its commitment to better regulation, was highly critical of the current regulatory reform agenda and the role of the Better Regulation Executive (BRE). Thus the latter had failed to strike the right balance between better regulation and reducing the burdens on business: '[w]ith an emphasis on cutting red tape there is a risk that the agenda loses sight of the reason for regulation – the very real benefits that regulation delivers to the environment, business and wider society. It is essential that initiatives are seen to be about driving better regulation and that in communicating this agenda the BRE does not undermine the credibility of regulation'. Moreover, the clarity of accountability of the EA 'is weakened when the role of the BRE begins to encroach on regulatory policy or even oversight of the

75 (2003). For a more discursive overview, see also Gray, J., Howes, C., and Clark, R., 'Promoting Compliance in the 21st Century', in Centre for the Study of Regulated Industries, *Regulatory Review 2004/5* (Bath: CRI, 2005), 171–93.

76 Environment, Food and Rural Affairs Committee, 'The Environment Agency', 2005–6, paras 27–31.

77 Better Regulation Executive and National Audit Office, *Effective Inspection and Enforcement*, para 17.

78 Section 3(5).

79 See Large Combustion Plants (National Emission Reduction Plan) Regulations 2007, SI 2007/2325; Environment Agency, *Report on the Landfill Allowances and Trading Scheme (LATS) 2005/6* (2007).

regulator'. These concerns were also emphasized strongly in oral evidence by the then Chief Executive of the EA; for example, its Board 'is very clear that it is not prepared to have the BRE seen as an alternative accountability mechanism'.[80] This is important as an expression of concerns about the effects of the regulatory reform initiatives on regulatory independence, a matter to be considered in more detail in Chapter 10 below.

The EA thus does show a commitment to risk-based regulation and market-based regulatory tools, such as trading schemes, whilst acknowledging their limitations. However, these are primarily concerned with methods and tools of regulation; when we come to the basic regulatory rationales other approaches are more important.

## Regulation and human rights

The notion of environmental human rights is a controversial one which cannot be analyzed in detail here.[81] In brief, there are common goals between human rights activists and environmentalists, but also major tensions including problems of definition of appropriate environmental rights, their status in international law, their perceived anthropocentrism, and conflicts with other rights.[82] Rights may also be difficult to apply in relation to polycentric problems, where an issue involves a complex set of interacting relationships and any one adjustment may affect a large number of other parts of the network.[83] In view of these complexities, it is thus not surprising that direct statements of support for environmental rights are rare in major international instruments.[84]

This is not to say, of course, that other human rights which are fully protected in international instruments are not relevant to the work of the EA. An interesting example was found in an important challenge brought against a sewage provider in nuisance and under the Human Rights Act, claiming repeated foul flooding of the claimant's property breached both Art 8 of the European Convention on Human Rights providing the right to respect for one's home, and Art 1 of the First Protocol to the Convention, providing for the peaceful enjoyment of possessions.[85] The claim succeeded in the Court of Appeal but was rejected in the House

[80] 'Getting Results: The Better Regulation Executive and the Impact of the Regulatory Reform Agenda', HC 474, 2007–8, evid 120–1 and qs 224, 231.

[81] For fuller accounts, see Hancock, J., *Environmental Human Rights – Power, Ethics, Law* (Aldershot: Ashgate, 2003); Boyle, A. and Anderson, M., (eds), *Human Rights Approaches to Environmental Protection* (Oxford: Clarendon Press, 1996).

[82] Anderson, M., 'Human Rights Approaches to Environmental Protection: An Overview', in Boyle and Anderson, *Human Rights Approaches to Environmental Protection*, 1–23.

[83] See Stallworthy, M., *Sustainability, Land Use and Environment – A Legal Analysis* (London: Cavendish, 2002), 258.

[84] For a survey, see Churchill, R., 'Environmental Rights in Existing Human Rights Treaties', in Boyle and Anderson, *Human Rights Approaches to Environmental Protection*, 89–108.

[85] *Marcic v Thames Water Utilities Ltd* [2003] UKHL 66; [2004] 2 AC 42. For background, see Stallworthy, M., 'Whither Environmental Human Rights?' (2005) 7 *Environmental Law Review*, 12–33.

of Lords on the ground that there was a statutory scheme of regulation (in this case in the form of the then Director General of Water Services) which was the appropriate vehicle for prioritizing work taking account of the balance between the rights in question and the acceptable qualifications to them, in particular the interests of the community as a whole. Thus the claim based on breaches of Convention rights 'does not give sufficient weight to the fact that Parliament has decided that the most appropriate method of achieving a fair balance between the competing interests of the individual and the community is by means of a statutory scheme administered by an independent expert regulator'.[86] The statutory scheme set an appropriate balance between Convention rights and interests limiting them; moreover the regulator 'is a public authority within the meaning of the 1998 Act and has a duty to act in accordance with convention rights'.[87] Although this case did not concern the EA directly, the implication is clearly that an environmental regulator has a central role in deciding on the application of Convention rights and in balancing qualified rights in the environmental field against competing public interests. This should open up considerable scope for rights-based arguments addressed to the regulatory body itself.

As in the case of other regulators, procedural rights will also be important in the regulatory context. These include not just the right to a hearing under Art 6 of the European Convention, but extensive rights of access to environmental information under various instruments which will be considered below.[88]

Despite the relative paucity of substantive environmental rights in international instruments, other rights are thus of considerable relevance to the work of an environmental regulator, and moreover may come into conflict with approaches based on economic efficiency and consumer choice.[89] Some of the distrust of rights and some of their limitations in the environmental field may also be explained by the role of other considerations related to social solidarity.

## Regulation and social solidarity

Once more, there is no space here to discuss major debates within the environmentalist movement.[90] Nevertheless, some mention should be made of a concern with 'solidarity rights' which are associated with groups rather than individuals, and 'deep environmentalism' which 'requires a conceptual shift from the

[86] Lord Hope at para 77. [87] Lord Hoffman at para 71.

[88] For the implications of Art 6, see Stallworthy, *Sustainability, Land Use and Environment*, 268–70.

[89] For theoretical development of this theme, see Hancock, *Environmental Human Rights*, 4–5, 17–18, 24.

[90] For further discussion, see generally Hancock, ibid, and Redgwell, C., 'Life, The Universe and Everything: A Critique of Anthropocentric Rights', in Boyle and Anderson, *Human Rights Approaches to Environmental Protection*, 71–87.

individualist atomist approach of rights to holistic processes and systems'.[91] This is reflected in less radical form through the language of sustainability, and we have already seen that this is the principle statutory aim of the EA, as specified more precisely through ministerial guidance.[92] This statutory duty thus places sustainability right at the heart of the EA's work, and it is clear from the corporate planning documents that issues of sustainability and social solidarity are central in setting the context for its operation. For example in its draft Corporate Strategy for 2010–15, the first theme is to act to reduce climate change and its consequences, and the third 'to put people and communities at the heart of what we do'.[93] Sustainability is central to the EA's vision document. It has also adopted a focus on working with excluded communities who are likely to suffer from poor environmental standards, for example in water quality, and is developing more sophisticated means of engaging with such groups.

Thus the EA is not primarily an economic regulator, it does have a role in protecting individual rights but major objectives concern sustainability and inclusion. As a Parliamentary committee put it, '[o]ur quality of life can no longer be measured solely in crude economic terms. It depends crucially on the protection and enhancement of the environment'.[94]

## Deliberation

It may be recalled from my introduction that one of the traditional characteristics of UK environmental regulation was its closed nature. In Vogel's classic account, although there were close links between regulatory bodies and producer interests, the number of institutions through which participation in regulatory decisions could take place was limited, apart from through the land use planning system.[95] Is this still true in the case of the Environment Agency?

It is useful to begin by pointing out that at the highest level of policy-making, an important presence is that of the Royal Commission on Environmental Pollution, an unique standing body to advise government, Parliament, and the public on environmental issues.[96] Indeed, it was largely as a result of the Commission's reports that the integrated EA was established at all. The Commission is free to choose its own topics for study, and invites written evidence from organizations, individuals, and the general public, with some oral presentations by witnesses. The Commission's reports are submitted to the Queen; a government response is prepared. There is also a framework document setting out relations with the

[91] Redgwell, ibid, 79 (footnote omitted). [92] Environment Act 1995, s 4(1), (3).

[93] *Creating a Better Place – Environment Agency Corporate Strategy 2010–2015*, 6–7, 10–11.

[94] Select Committee on Environment, Transport and Regional Affairs, 'The Environment Agency', 1999–2000, para 1. [95] Vogel, *National Styles of Regulation*, 220–2.

[96] For details of the Commissions work see <http://www.rcep.org.uk> (consulted 8 December 2009).

Department. Recent reports have included *Adapting Institutions to Climate Change*, *The Urban Environment*, and *Chemicals in Products*; it also publishes shorter special reports on issues such as *Crop Spraying and the Health of Residents and Bystanders*. The presence of the Commission as a permanent body offers a unique opportunity for independently organized debate on the issue of environmental policy. It should also be recalled that policy-making largely takes place at EU and governmental level so 'Departments, rather than the EA, are responsible for consultation, impact assessment and review at the policy-making stage, with the EA... responsible for implementation'.[97]

Turning to the Environment Agency itself, matters got off to an unpromising start when ministers rejected pressure for its meetings to be held in public, despite the fact that some of its responsibilities were taken on from local authorities which of course met publicly. The minister claimed that to require public meetings would inhibit the development of strategic thinking ahead of publication, and that anyway the Agency would be accountable to Parliament through ministers.[98] In the event, however, the Board has adopted a policy of meeting in public and publishes its agenda, supporting papers and minutes on the internet. Parts of meetings concerned with confidential information are closed. The Agency has also made the strong commitments to openness characteristic of more recently established regulatory bodies. Thus in its *Vision* it commits itself to increased consultation, and in its Corporate Strategy to improving communications.[99] Despite this commitment, there have been criticisms of the degree of openness of the Authority by Select Committees. Thus the Environment Committee in 2000 stated that it would like to see the Agency engaging more vigorously in public debate and raising its profile on matters of importance affecting the environment and sustainable development, though in doing so it must conduct itself in accordance with government policy.[100] It also noted problems of communications with local communities concerned with environmental issues (an issue on which the EA is now working to improve engagement).[101] The examination of the Agency by the Committee in 2006 was also highly critical about a lack of transparency in relation to regulatory charges and how they were spent.[102] However, the Hampton Implementation Review concluded overall that the EA is generally a transparent and accountable regulator.[103]

The role of advisory committees is central to the work of the EA. Thus the 1995 Act requires the establishment of an advisory committee for Wales, regional environmental protection advisory committees, regional and local fisheries advisory

[97] Better Regulation Executive and National Audit Office, *Effective Inspection and Enforcement*, para 31.

[98] Sir Paul Beresford, Parliamentary Under-Secretary of State for the Environment, Standing Committee B, May 2 1995, cols 62–3.

[99] *An Environmental Vision*, 14, 17 and 49, 55–6.

[100] 'The Environment Agency', 1999–2000, para 22.

[101] Ibid, paras 120–3.

[102] 'The Environment Agency', 2005–6, paras 47–51.

[103] Better Regulation Executive and National Audit Office, *Effective Inspection and Enforcement*, para 23.

committees, and regional and local flood defence committees.[104] The committees are seen as an important link with stakeholders and the general public; all committee meetings are open to the public and the press. Initially there were some problems with the committees, thus the House of Commons Environment Committee in its report in 2000 noted that the Regional Environmental Protection Advisory Committees (REPACs) had had a 'shaky' start, had been bombarded with papers, issues, and information and at one stage were close to open revolt. Relations had, however, improved since and they were playing a useful role. The REPACs were now reporting annually on the EA's performance, and the Agency responds to feedback from the Committees to show how it has taken account of their comments. In addition to the statutory committees, the EA had also established 26 Area Advisory Groups drawn from a wide range of different interests. The resulting structure was criticized by the Select Committee as too complex, and the non-statutory committees were replaced by advisory panels for consultation on a more local basis than the regional committees.[105] The Agency has stressed that its arrangements for consultation and participation are intended to operate well beyond the formal advisory committee structure, and include, for example, organizing public consultations.

One further important point needs to be made in relation to deliberation; this is that international law, in particular EU law, has a particularly important role in the environmental context.[106] This can be seen in requirements for participation in decision-making and for access to environmental information. Thus the UN Aarhus Convention on Access to Information, Public Participation in Decision-Making, and Access to Justice in Environmental Matters of 1998 provides for extensive rights of access to environmental information, and also requires public participation in plans, programmes, and policies relating to the environment.[107] A number of pieces of European legislation also require public participation in the drawing up of certain plans and programmes relating to the environment, notably the 2003 Directive implementing the Aarhus Convention in this regard.[108] Similarly, the EU requirement of environmental impact assessment includes public participation and the provision of information.[109] European law and UK implementing regulations also provide rights of access to environmental information. These were introduced in the form of a Directive in 1990 with domestic

104 Environment Act 1995, ss 11–18.

105 'The Environment Agency', 1999–2000, paras 109–16.

106 For a comprehensive overview of arrangements for public participation in environmental decisions, see Bell and McGillivray, *Enviromental Law*, ch 10.

107 See in particular Arts 7–8 of the Convention.

108 Directive 2003/35/EC providing for public participation in respect of the drawing up of certain plans and programmes relating to the environment [2003] OJ L156/17.

109 Directive 85/337/EEC on the assessment of the effects of certain public and private projects on the environment [1985] OJ L175/40; Town and Country Planning (Assessment of Environmental Effects) Regulations 1988, SI 1988/1199. See also *Berkeley v Secretary of State for the Environment* [2000] 3 WLR 420 (HL).

regulations following in 1992 and later replaced by a further Directive on Public Access to Environmental Information and implementing regulations.[110]

EU-based regulatory instruments in specific areas may also require access to information and participation. For example, the system of pollution control originally introduced by the Integrated Pollution Prevention and Control Directive of 1996 and implemented by UK regulations, requires public access to certain information before decisions relating to applications for permits are determined, and this is developed further in the implementing regulations.[111] The regulations provided the basis for a judicial review application against the EA's failure to publish in-house reports on likely emissions should a permit be granted. The application, though ultimately unsuccessful, did illustrate the importance of European law in requiring access to environmental information, although the majority of the House of Lords held that it did not prevent the EA relying on additional, unpublished, information. Common law requirements of fairness were also relevant and were held to have been breached though no remedy was granted as new information had now become available.[112] The regulations also provide a right of appeal to the Secretary of State against decisions relating to environmental permits.[113]

Overall, then, the approach to deliberation taken by the EA is one which has much in common with other regulators discussed in this book, involving open meetings and the extensive use of advisory committees. An important difference is, however, a much more developed legal scheme for access to information and, to a lesser degree, public participation in decisions, which is a result of the requirements of European law and which provides major opportunities both for public access and for enforcement of the requirements by the courts.

## Conclusions

It is possible to draw four tentative conclusions from this analysis of the work of the Environment Agency. The first is that, perhaps surprisingly, the combination of regulatory and operational responsibilities in a single body does not appear to have caused any problems; it is dealt with through the creation of 'Chinese walls' within the EA, through external audit, and indeed much of the operational work is contracted out to other organizations. In recent criticisms

[110] Directive 2003/4/EC on public access to environmental information [2004] OJ L41/26; Environmental Information Regulations 2004, SI 2004/3391.

[111] See now Directive 2008/1/EC concerning integrated pollution prevention and control [2008] OJ L24/8, and the Environmental Permitting (England and Wales) Regulations 2007, SI 2007/3538, reg 46 and Sch 19.

[112] *R (on the application of Edwards) v Environment Agency* [2008] UKHL 22; [2008] 1 WLR 1587.

[113] Regulation 31.

made of the EA by Parliamentary committees and others, this one is remarkable by its absence. There was some criticism of the tensions created by the quite different combination of regulator and environmental champion, but this is a point common to other regulators described in this book and anyway appeared inevitable and did not give rise to serious problems. In this sense the EA's success would seem to contradict the emphasis in much regulatory work on the importance of a complete separation of regulation from operational or management responsibilities.

Secondly, the EA is a further striking example of a collaborative approach to regulation. This is true not only in its relations with stakeholders and its use of advisory committees, but also in its positioning within government structures. The Secretary of State has unusually extensive powers, including the issue of guidance to the Agency, and this goes so far as to define the content of its principal aim. Recent years have seen a huge growth in the importance of the EU, in terms of shaping the design of the regulatory system, determining standards, and not least in setting out participatory requirements and requests for access to information. Environmental law is unusually complex and draws on a wide range of different institutional sources; nothing could be further from the image of an isolated and unaccountable regulator than this rich network of levels of decision-making and accountability.

Thirdly, the EA is a social regulator. The role of human rights arguments, and their relationship with those of sustainability, may be controversial but it is clear that sustainability provides the key objective for regulation here, as economic efficiency and consumer choice do not. Of course the EA uses economic techniques; in some contexts use of cost-benefit analysis is required by statute, and it has been a pioneer in the use of trading schemes for emissions and landfill, but these are methods for attaining social goals, not objectives in themselves. One approach to analyzing the social functions of the regulator may be to see them as correcting economic externalities, but such an approach does not fully appreciate the richness and complexity of the social goals involved.

Finally, it is clear that the conclusions about the UK regulatory style drawn by Vogel in 1986 now need considerable qualification. As a leading environmental law text puts it: '[t]he informal and flexible basis remains, but the approach has undoubtedly become more open, more centralized, more legalistic and more contentious, especially in the last ten years or so'.[114] This is true of his characterization of the UK system as based on discretion and case-by-case decision-making rather than on rules, and also as permitting only limited public participation. In both cases the change has been largely due to the growing role of EU law, which has increased the role of binding national and international standards, created

[114] Bell and McGillivray, *Environmental Law*, 238.

an increasingly rule-based system, and greatly increased opportunities for public participation through requirements of access to information, the environmental impact assessment system, and other more specific regulatory requirements. Of course much discretion remains, and there is still some scope for self-regulation, but the underlying design of the system is now radically different from that of 20 years ago. The creation of the EA as a more integrated regulator may have contributed to this, but the major reason is to be found outside the regulatory system itself in the development of EU law and policy.

# [14]

# ENVIRONMENTAL REGULATION AS AN INSTRUMENT OF CONSTITUTIONAL CHANGE

*Richard Macrory*

## SUMMARY

Less than a generation ago the Chief Scientist of the then Department of the Environment and Transport could argue, with some justification, that one of the defining characteristics of the British approach to environmental policy was a preference for voluntary arrangements between government and industry rather than legal compulsion.[1] Even in areas where there were explicit legal frameworks, the substantive legislation was often expressed in extremely broad terms, allowing regulators and the regulated to negotiate solutions without the intervention of legal process and the courts. To take one example, long familiar to British environmental lawyers, the core legal requirement concerning atmospheric emissions from major industrial processes was to use the 'best practicable means' to prevent or minimize emissions, a statutory expression that remained in force 100 years from 1875 until 1990 – despite the heavily open-textured language of that central duty, there is not a single reported case in the higher courts concerning its interpretation throughout that period. The translation of the legal obligation into practical reality was largely the result of a dialogue and negotiation between chemical engineers and other technically qualified staff working within the regulated industry and the national regulatory body, the Alkali Inspectorate and its successor, the Industrial Air Pollution Inspectorate. These distinctive characteristics of environmental regulation in this country no longer hold true. The last 40 years has seen an extraordinary expansion in the depth and scale of substantive legislation bringing about a fundamental change in the prevailing legal culture operating in this field.

This chapter, though, deals with environmental law not in order to analyze the reasons behind the massive expansion of the law in this area,[2] still less to consider in any detail the substance

[1] M. Holdgate, 'Environmental Policies in Britain and Mainland Europe', in R. Macrory (ed.), *Britain, Europe and the Environment* (1983) 6–18.

[2] See R. Macrory, 'Environmental Law: Shifting Discretions and the New Formalism', reproduced in R. Macrory *Regulation, Enforcement and Governance in Environmental Law* (2010).

of contemporary environmental regulation – rather, the subject serves as a useful illustration of two aspects of constitutional change. First, the environment provides a clear example of the web of complex constitutional connections between different branches of government and different levels of government (local, central, and the European Union) and between other regulatory and non-governmental bodies. Secondly, the environment serves as an illustration of how one area of law, policy and public administration can engage practice and principle that themselves bring about changes to the overall constitutional structure. This chapter should therefore be seen a case study of constitutional interaction and change. Indeed, I will argue that the real significance of the developments over the 30 years, and in hindsight the one with the most long-lasting impact, is the extent to which environmental law and regulation has proved to be at the forefront in articulating principles and precedents that are central to a contemporary constitutional settlement. Legal rights to public information and participation in decision making, access to justice, the accountability of regulatory authorities are issues that have a universality and help define the relationship between citizen and state. In all of these areas environmental law has played a key role in pioneering concepts and practice and continues to do so.

## INTRODUCTION

Why should environmental law have proved a fruitful area for driving legal innovation concerning fundamental principles? The roots of contemporary environmental regulation can still be traced back to the 19th century, and the policy response to unacceptable side effects of the industrial revolution. The first non-governmental organizations concerned with environmental issues were formed in the latter half of that century, with specialized laws and regulatory agencies well developed by the post-War period. Yet it was the growth of modern environmental groups from the 1970s onwards that posed profound challenges to familiar ways of handling issues. Rather than dealing with environmental issues on a topic by topic basis typically reflected in the legislation of the time (air pollution, water, and so on), the new wave of organizations demanded a more holistic approach that looked at environmental impacts as a whole and pressed for more preventative solutions beyond the more immediate amelioration of pollution impacts. Concern at the urgency and enormity of the environmental challenges implied a rejection of the cautious gradualism which appeared to characterize policy development. More recently the concept of sustainable development became a familiar part of language of the policy debate but is equally subject to differing interpretations and competing visions.[3] A simple balancing of environmental, economic and social agendas is pitched against a vision that would argue that without a secure environmental basis, economic and social progress will prove unattainable. Others have promoted a more politically challenging vision of sustainable development incorporating ideas of greater economic and social justice both within and between generations,

[3] R. Macrory, 'The Environment and Constitutional Change', in R. Hazell (ed.), *Constitutional Futures: A History of the Next Ten Years* (1999) 178, 179.

and a revitalization of local and community identities.[4] It took some years before the environmental dimensions of the UK legal structure were seriously addressed in this debate – the UK Environmental Law Association, for example, was not formed until 1987. But the restless challenge to long established ways of thinking about and handling policy issues that have been such an integral part of the modern environmental movement provided a potent basis for treating environmental law as a significant engine for constitutional change. Regulatory practices and styles of policy making were subject to sustained scrutiny and critiques in a way not experienced before. Fundamental re-evaluations provide a powerful engine for innovation.

## PUBLIC ACCESS TO INFORMATION AND PARTICIPATION

General rights of public access to information in the UK as enshrined in the Freedom of Information Act 2000 are now a familiar part of the constitutional landscape. But such broad rights were first enshrined in British law in the environmental field some eight years before, and these in turn found precedent in individual areas of environmental law from the 1970s, deriving from a lengthy period of intellectual and policy argument conducted in the environmental policy community. Registers of regulatory consents in fields such as water pollution had existed since the 1950s but they were open only to persons 'interested' in the register, interpreted narrowly to mean someone with a legal interest such as an owner of fishing rights in the waters concerned rather than a member of the general public. Industry in particular fought hard to restrict wider access on the grounds of confidentiality. The Royal Commission on Environmental Pollution, established in 1970, was the first official body to seriously raise the issue, which it did in its Second Report,[5] urging the Government 'to devise measures which will increase the availability and flow of information on the production and disposal of industrial effluents and wastes'.[6] Largely as a consequence, one of the first major environmental statutes of the time, the Control of Pollution Act 1974, mainly dealing with the regulation of waste, water pollution and noise, contained provisions concerning registers of applications for consents, consents, and monitoring results which were to be open to any member of the public. The Royal Commission demonstrated the value of being a standing commission by constantly returning to the subject of openness over the next 12 years in a number of different reports, and arguing consistently that a presumption of public access would lead to improved environmental protection. In its Tenth Report, published in 1984,[7] the Commission carried out an extensive analysis of the arguments

[4] T. O'Riordan and H. Voisey, *Sustainable Development in Western Europe: Coming to Terms with Agenda 21* (1988).

[5] Royal Commission on Environmental Pollution, *Three Issues in Industrial Pollution*, Cmnd 4894 (1972).

[6] Ibid., para. 9.

[7] Royal Commission on Environmental Pollution, *Tackling Pollution – Experience and Prospects*, Cmnd 9149 (1984).

for and against greater access to environmental information, and concluded that while some progress was being made in more recent individual laws, insufficient priority was being given to the principle. It concluded with a statement that could have formed the rallying-call for general freedom of information legislation:

> A guiding principle behind all legislative and administrative controls relating to environmental pollution should be a presumption in favour of unrestricted access for the public to information which the pollution control authorities obtain or receive by virtue of their statutory powers, with provision for secrecy only in those circumstances where a genuine case for it can be substantiated.[8]

The underlying principle of open access to environmental information was also beginning to gain momentum with the European Community and in 1990 the Community adopted a Directive on the subject, the first sector of Community policy where such a general right was granted.[9] The Directive was framed in the language of a human right, and gave broad rights to anyone, including non-governmental associations, to acquire environmental information held by public authorities and other bodies performing public functions. There was no precondition of holding a legal or other special interest in the matter concerned, a challenge to the administrative practice in many member states.[10]

Transposition of the Directive required the UK to move beyond its then practice of incorporating public registers in specific environmental laws to promoting legislation giving much broader rights in the form of the Environmental Information Regulations 1992.[11] Though containing various exemptions in line with the Directive, the regulations created a precedent in the concept of general access to information held by public authorities.[12] The Freedom of Information 2000 Act acknowledges the distinctive and independent nature of the environmental rights, essentially by providing that any information falling with the terms of the Directive and implementing regulations is treated as not covered by the Act as 'exempt' information.[13] Indeed, it is arguable that the scope of exemptions is narrower under the environmental information regulations than the Freedom of Information Act 2000,[14] and the EU dimension means that the European Court of Justice has jurisdiction in the area, and has already given a strongly progressive, liberal interpretation of the Directive.[15]

[8] Ibid., para. 2.77.

[9] Council Directive (EEC) 90/313 on Freedom of Access to Information on the Environment [1990] OJ L156/58, replaced by Council Directive (EC) 2003/4 on Public Access on Environmental Information [2003] OJ L41/26.

[10] L. Kramer, *EC Environmental Law* (6th edn, 2007) 150, and see generally R. Hallo (ed.), *Access to Environmental Information in Europe* (1997).

[11] SI 2000/227. Replaced by Environmental Information Regulations 2004 (SI 2004/3391).

[12] The first law granting general rights to information was in fact the Local Government (Access to Information) Act 1985 giving rights of access to agendas and background papers for meetings of local authorities.

[13] Freedom of Information Act 2000, s. 39.

[14] D. Hughes, *Environmental Law* (4th edn, 2002) 163.

[15] C-321/96, *Mecklenburg* v. *Kreis Pinneberg-Der Landrat* [1998] ECR I-3809.

The environmental field can also be seen to have developed important legal principles concerning rights of public participation in decision making though its contribution is perhaps somewhat more subtle. The UK had long established opportunities for public participation in certain fields, particularly in town and country planning where public inquiries were regularly held into planning appeals, and formed a familiar part of the administrative landscape.[16] Indeed, in the 1970s and 1980s it was the planning inquiry that was seen by many in the modern environmental movement as a unique forum where new ideas and ways of looking at development proposals could be articulated and raised, leading to a number of major inquiries involving the exploration of complex issues of public policy well beyond the narrow confines of land-use planning.[17] More specialized environmental legislation such as the Control of Pollution Act 1974 reflected a growing demand for participation rights by including provisions for rights of participation in various pollution consent procedures.[18] But as with rights of information, it was at European level that such rights were expressed in law with a more general application. The 1985 Directive on environmental assessment,[19] applying to consent procedures for numerous types of development proposals from transport and energy projects to waste disposal and deforestation, incorporated consultation with the general public as part of the assessment process. It was the first piece of EC environmental legislation to have incorporated such public participation rights, and indeed probably the first EC law in any field to have done so. It took some years before the British courts fully appreciated the significance of these participation rights as an integral and obligatory element of European style environmental assessment,[20] with Lord Hoffmann eventually declaring in *Berkeley* v. *Secretary of State for Environment, Transport and Regions*:[21]

> The directly enforceable right of the citizen which is accorded by the Directive is not merely a right to a fully informed decision on the substantive issue. It must have been adopted on an appropriate basis and that requires the inclusive and democratic procedure prescribed

[16] *Report of the Committee on Administrative Tribunals and Inquiries* (Franks Report) Cmnd 218 (1957). *The Report of the Committee on Public Participation in Planning: People and Planning* (The Skeffington Report) (1969) was a significant endorsement of the public policy value in engaging with the public in land use plan development.

[17] D. Pearce, L. Edwards and C. Bennet, *Decision-making for Energy Futures: A Case Study of the Windscale Inquiry* (1979); T. O'Riordan, R. Kemp and M. Purdue, *Sizewell B: An Anatomy of an Inquiry* (1988); J. Jowell, 'Policy, Inquiries, and the Courts', in R. Macrory (ed.), *Commercial Nuclear Power – Legal and Constitutional Issues* (1982).

[18] R. Macrory and B. Zaba, *Polluters Pay – The Control of Pollution Act Explained* (1978), an example of a citizen's guide to the new legal rights contained in the 1974 Act.

[19] Council Directive (EC) 85/337 on the Assessment of the Effects of Certain Public and Private Projects on the Environment [1985] OJ L175/40.

[20] The EC legislation had been inspired by the US legislation on environmental impact statements under National Environmental Policy Act 1970, s. 102, but while the US law focused on the production of a written assessment by public officials, the EC law was deliberately focused on procedural requirements, including participation.

[21] [2001] 2 AC 603.

by the Directive in which the public, however misguided or wrongheaded its views may be, is given an opportunity to express its opinion on the environmental issues.

The 1998 United Nations Economic Commission for Europe (UNECE) Aarhus Convention (the Convention)[22] developed the participation principle even further by containing a second pillar wholly devoted to participation, and requiring parties to the Convention to ensure that the general public had opportunities to participate in consent procedures for individual projects, plans and programmes relating to the environment, and environmental rule-making and legislative drafting.[23] Considerable discretion is left to the parties as to the precise form of participation that is offered, but the underlying principles are clear. The provisions in the Convention concerning access to justice, considered in the next section, are posing the most immediate challenge to current UK practice, but it would be rash for government to ignore the implications of the Convention's participation provisions, especially those concerning plans and rule making. *R. on the application of Greenpeace* v. *Secretary of State for Trade and Industry*[24] concerned a challenge to the government's consultation procedures on nuclear energy policy. The court found the government's own procedures to have been flawed, but it is significant that Sullivan J noted that even if the government had not committed itself to the widest possible consultation should the nuclear option be re-opened, it might have been obliged to do so because of its obligations under the Convention.

## ACCESS TO JUSTICE

Disputes before the courts involving environmental issues have a long history, and Victorian law reports are littered with cases mainly involving conflicts between private rights such as the use of water or intrusive pollution, or testing the ambit of new public health legislation. It was not, however, until the 1980s that environmental organizations and affected individuals began to use the courts more regularly to explore issues of public law. Those bringing a claim for judicial review must demonstrate that they have 'sufficient interest' in the issue at hand,[25] a phrase that was once interpreted very restrictively by the courts, largely confining it to those with a defined legal interest at stake. Contemporary practice shows a far more liberal approach, and a number of the leading cases involving public interest groups involved questions of environmental law[26] reaching a sort of apotheosis in *R. (Edwards)* v. *Environment Agency*[27] where a

[22] Convention on Access to Information, Public Participation in Decision-Making and Access to Justice in Environmental Matters (the Convention) (25 June 1998).

[23] Convention, Arts 6–8.

[24] [2007] EWHC 311 (Admin).

[25] Supreme Court Act 1981, s. 31(3).

[26] E.g. *R* v. *HM Inspectorate of Pollution ex parte Greenpeace Ltd (No. 2)* [1994] 4 All ER 329 doubting the more restrictive earlier decision of *R* v. *Secretary of State for the Environment ex parte Rose Theatre Trust* [1990] 1 All ER 754, and *R* v. *Secretary of State for Trade and Industry ex parte Greenpeace* [1998] Env LR 415 where Laws J noted that this type of public interest litigation was now an 'accepted and greatly valued dimension of the judicial review jurisdiction'.

[27] [2004] Env LR 43.

homeless individual was still granted standing to challenge the legality of a permit for a local cement works because he breathed the potentially polluted air. Standing in the environmental field will rarely prove a hurdle in the contemporary judicial climate, and the debate has moved on to the question of the exposure to costs in public law cases where the general costs in the cause rule, developed in the context of disputes between private parties, is applied by the courts. Legal aid is increasingly constrained, and in any event is not available to a non-governmental organization.

In recent years the courts themselves have acknowledged that the loser pays principle developed in the context of private law disputes may not always be appropriate in the context of public law where it may be important in the general public interest that the law is tested. In a non-environmental case, the Court of Appeal in 2005[28] revived the more general use of protective costs orders (PCOs) under which a claimant in judicial review would in the early stages of litigation be limited as to the amount of costs they could be exposed to even if the case were lost. The *Corner House* principles were, however, only to be applied if five factors were present: '(i) the issues raised are of general importance; (ii) the public interest requires that those issues should be resolved; (iii) the claimant has no private interest in the outcome of the case; (iv) having regard to the financial resources of the claimant and the respondent(s) and to the amount of costs that are likely to be made it is fair and just to make the order (v) if the order is not made the claimant will probably discontinue the proceedings and will be acting reasonably in so doing'. Expressed as such, the principles were clearly seen as an exception to the general rule concerning costs, and PCOs were expected to be made in only a small number of cases each year.[29] Nevertheless, the general approach might have made a limited but valuable contribution towards reducing the freezing effect of costs exposure in public litigation, and one that would have been legally sound had it not been for developments in the environmental field, both internationally and at European level.

The origins of the Aarhus Convention can be traced back to the 1992 Rio Declaration on Environment and Development which was produced after the major UN Conference known as the Earth Summit. Principle 10 of the Declaration emphasized the importance of citizen participation in environmental issues, both in terms of access to information and active participation in decision making, but also included a tentative reference to access to judicial remedies and redress.[30] Three years later,

[28] *R (Corner House Research)* v. *Secretary of State for Trade and Industry* [2005] 1 WLR 2600.

[29] *R. (on the application of Bullmore)* v. *West Herts Hospital NHS Trust* [2007] LTL, 27 June 2007, and *River Thames Society* v. *First Secretary of State* [2006] EWHC 2829 (Admin).

[30] 'Environmental issues are best handled with the participation of all concerned citizens, at the relevant level. At the national level, each individual shall have appropriate access to information concerning the environment that is held by public authorities, including information on hazardous materials and activities in their communities, and the opportunity to participate in decision-making processes. States shall facilitate and encourage public awareness and participation by making information widely available. Effective access to judicial and administrative proceedings, including redress and remedy, shall be provided', available at www.unep.org/Documents.Multilingual/Default.asp?documentid=78&articleid=1163.

a Pan-European conference adopted the Sofia Guidelines which fleshed out some of the principles particularly in relation to access to information and participation, and this in turn led to the UNECE preparing a Convention on the subject, involving more than 40 countries though with the notable exceptions of the USA and Canada.[31] The proposed Convention was initially confined to provisions concerning access to information and public participation, and had this continued to be the case the provisions would probably have posed little in the way of challenge for the UK where generally such principles in the environmental field were by now well developed. Early on in the negotiations, however, it was agreed to include a so-called 'third pillar' relating to questions of access to justice, and Art. 9 of the Convention gives rights to members of the public and environmental non-governmental organization to challenge the legality of decisions by public authorities granting consent for a wide range of projects as well as other acts or omissions 'which are contrary to the provisions of national laws relating to the environment'. Again, the liberal approach to standing expressed in the Convention would pose little problem for a jurisdiction such as the UK, but Art. 9(4) requires that parties ensure that procedures for rights of access must 'provide adequate and effective remedies, including injunctive relief as appropriate and be fair, equitable, timely, and not prohibitively expensive'. The UK along with all other member states with the exception of Ireland duly signed and ratified the Convention, as did the European Community.

The legal commitment to ensure access to judicial procedures that are not 'prohibitively expensive' has subsequently come to drive the debate in the UK and prove a potent source of change which will spread well beyond the field of environmental law. It is still somewhat unclear why the UK found itself agreeing to a commitment containing such potentially unsettling implications. Given that nearly all the obligations in other parts of the Convention could be readily met and that in many ways the Convention was politically viewed at the time as a means of raising the standards of Eastern European countries to those of the West, it may have just been conveniently ignored. At the same time there was a view that the reference in Art. 9(4) referred only to court fees rather than any exposure or risk of exposure to litigation costs, and the official government line was that UK procedures met the obligations.[32] The restrictive interpretation of Art. 9(4) was given some support by the Irish High Court in 2007,[33] but it is increasingly a view that appears untenable. In 2004 the Court of Appeal had already noted the difficulties of the conventional costs principles in judicial reviews meeting up to the aspirations of the Convention, and clearly felt that Art. 9(4) was not confined to the court fees:

[31] J. Jendroska, 'Public Information and Participation in EC Environmental Law – Origins, Milestones and Trends', in R. Macrory (ed.), *Reflections on 30 Years of EU Environmental Law* (2006) 63, 69–71.

[32] 'Our administrative and judicial systems are fully compliant with the requirements for access to review'. Summary of Implementing Measures to achieve Aarhus Compliance with the UNECE Aarhus Convention, available at www.defra.gov.uk/environment/policy/international/aarhus.

[33] *Sweetman v. An Bord Pleanala and the Attorney General* [2007] IEHC 153.

> If the figures revealed in this case were in any sense typical of the costs reasonably incurred in litigating such cases up the highest level, very serious questions would be raised as to the possibility of ever living up to the Aarhus ideals within our present system[34]

If the Convention had retained the characteristics of a more conventional public law Convention, it may well have been the case that a national government could have resisted pressures for change even where breaches occurred. But this was not the case for a number of reasons.

First, a number of senior members of the judiciary made it increasingly clear that they were sensitive to the implications of the Convention, and expressed concerns both judicially and extra judicially that the UK might not be in compliance. The Court of Appeal, for example, doubted that the principles concerning PCOs developed in *Corner House* which excluded PCOs where a private interest was involved were applicable to environmental cases.[35] The Court reached a clear conclusion that it disagreed with the government's view that the Art. 9(4) obligation was confined to court fees.[36] Pressure continued to mount with a judicial-led initiative to establish a committee to suggest how the Convention principles could be implemented within current procedures. Chaired by a High Court judge and including representatives from environmental practitioners and non-governmental organizations, the resulting report[37] made a powerful case for improving procedures in judicial review cases, and extending the use of PCOs.

The second source of pressure was the enforcement procedures developed under the Convention itself. The Convention was, as with many international conventions, rather vague about compliance mechanisms but required parties to establish compliance arrangements that were of a 'non-confrontational, non-judicial, and consultative nature'.[38] The First Meeting of the Parties went on to establish a Compliance Committee with powers to hear complaints both from parties to the Convention and members of the public, described by one of the leading architects of the Convention as 'strong and unprecedented'.[39] In 2010 the Compliance Committee published draft findings in two cases from the UK which directly raised the compatibility of costs principles in judicial reviews with Art. 9(4) of the Convention, and in both found

[34] *R. (on the applications of Sonia Burkett)* v. *London Borough of Hammersmith and Fulham* [2004] EWCA Civ 1342 at [76], *per* Brooke LJ.

[35] *R. (on the application of England)* v. *Tower Hamlets* [2006] EWCA Civ 1742.

[36] *Morgan and another* v. *Hinton Organics (Wessex) Ltd. and others* [2009] EWCA Civ 107, 'The requirement of the Convention that costs should not be "prohibitively expensive" should be taken as applying to the total potential liability of claimants, including the threat of adverse costs orders', at [47], *per* Carnwath LJ.

[37] Working Party Group on Access to Environmental Justice (Chair Mr Justice Sullivan), *Ensuring Access to Environmental Justice in England and Wales* (2008). The Group issued a follow up report in 2010.

[38] Convention, Art. 15.

[39] J. Jendroska, 'Public Information and Participation in EC Environmental Law – Origins, Milestones and Trends', in R. Macrory (ed.), *Reflections on 30 Years of EU Environmental Law* (2006) 63, 72; V. Koester, 'Review of Compliance under the Aarhus Convention: a rather unique compliance mechanism' (2005) 2 *JEEPL* 31; V. Koester, 'The Compliance Committee of the Aarhus Convention – An Overview of Procedures and Jurisprudence' (2007) 37(2) *EPL* 83.

that British practice did not meet the requirements of costs not being prohibitively expensive.[40]

A finding by the Compliance Committee of a breach might well be politically embarrassing, but at the end of the day there are no formal sanctions available under the Convention. However, the final distinctive nature of the Art. 9 provisions was the fact that the European Community was party to the Convention and had implemented the provisions on access to justice by including the wording under amendments to two core environmental directives, the Directive on Environmental Assessment and the Directive on Integrated Pollution and Prevention Control.[41] Within the context of those Directives, the obligation that access to justice procedures are not prohibitively expensive is now one of EU law, bringing with it the implications of the distinctive enforcement procedures available to the European Commission, leading to potential action before the European Court of Justice and a financial sanction for failure to comply with its judgments. Already in relation to the Assessment Directive the European Commission commenced infringement procedures against the UK following a complaint from a coalition of environmental non-governmental organizations, and in 2010 issued a Reasoned Opinion, the last stage before action before the European Court of Justice.[42] In April 2011 the case was referred to the Court of Justice.[43]

It is difficult to see how this three-way pressure from the judiciary, the international convention, and the European Union will not lead to significant change, even at a time of restrictions on public expenditure. In its most recent decision on Aarhus,[44] the Court of Justice of the European Union has held that the Aarhus Convention now forms 'an integral part of the legal order of the European Union. As such it applies to all areas of environmental protection covered by EU environmental law, and in relation to access to justice, there was a duty on national courts 'to interpret, to the fullest extent possible, the procedural rules relating to the conditions to be met in order to bring

[40] Aarhus Compliance Committee Draft Findings ACCC/C/2008/27, and in particular ACCC/C/2008/33, para. 133: 'The Committee concludes that despite the various measures available to address prohibitive costs, taken together they do not ensure that the costs remain at a level which meets the requirements under the Convention. At this stage, the Committee considers that the considerable discretion of the courts of E&W in deciding the costs, without any clear legally binding direction from the legislature or judiciary to ensure costs are not prohibitively expensive, leads to considerable uncertainty regarding the costs to be faced where claimants are legitimately pursuing environmental concerns that involve the public interest'.

[41] Council Directive (EEC) 85/337 on the assessment of the effects of certain public and private projects on the environment [1985] OJ L175/40, and Council Directive (EC) 96/61/EC concerning integrated pollution prevention and control [1996] OJ L257/26 (now codified under Council Directive (EC) 2008/1 on integrated pollution prevention and control [2008] OJ L24/8.

[42] http://europa.eu/rapid/pressReleasesAction.do?reference=IP/10/312&type=en. European Environment Commissioner Janez Potonik said, 'When important decisions affecting the environment are taken, the public must be allowed to challenge them. This important principle is established in European law. But the law also requires that these challenges must be affordable. I urge the UK to address this problem quickly as ultimately the health and wellbeing of the public as a whole depends on these rights', Press Release, March 2010.

[43] European Commission press release 18/11/439, Brussels, 6 April 2011.

[44] *Lesoochranarske zoskupenie VLK v. Ministerstvo zivotneho prostredia Slovenskej republiky* (Case C-240/09 Court of Justice of the European Union, 8 March 2011).

administrative or judicial proceedings' in light with the objectives of the Convention. In the arguments concerning a specialist environmental court considered below one ground for resisting change was that it was inappropriate to make a special case for the environment compared with other fields of law. In the context of the Convention, the same argument has been made, but, because the legal obligation to implement within the environmental field is a reality, far from providing a ground for maintaining the *status quo*, it has had the reverse effect of creating pressure for change in all areas of judicial review. Both the difficulties of defining the boundaries of the Convention and the unfairness of confining its principles to one area of law have been acknowledged by the courts.[45] Jackson LJ's major review of Civil Litigation Costs published in 2010[46] recognized the significance of the Convention but similarly argued that any change in the costs principles should apply to all judicial reviews. He recommended a solution of 'qualified one way costs shifting' where essentially the defendant pays the claimant's costs if the claim is successful, but the claimant does not pay the defendant's costs if the claim is unsuccessful. Jackson was prepared to allow for exceptions giving considerable judicial discretion and taking in account financial resources of the parties and their conduct in connection with the proceedings. A follow up report of the Sullivan Working Party[47] welcomed the general thrust of the Jackson proposals but recommended a rule that involved less judicial discretion and uncertainty, 'An unsuccessful Claimant in a claim for judicial review shall not be ordered to pay the costs of any other party other than where the Claimant has acted unreasonably in bringing or conducting the proceedings'. The implication of the proposed shifts in approach is that the permission stage of judicial review will become more significant in weeding out unmeritorious claims rather than the potential exposure to costs acting as a surrogate filter to frivolous action. The fundamental reappraisal of costs principles in judicial review, initiated rather cautiously by the judiciary in *Corner House*, is now largely been driven by obligations and perspectives created within environmental law.

## REFORMING REGULATORY SANCTIONS

Despite a long history of regulatory controls in the environmental field, the way in which they were actually enforced remained somewhat obscure until the early 1970s. Discretion and secrecy permeated the enforcement role of regulators, and specialized government agencies such as the Alkali Inspectorate regulating air emissions from key sectors of industry preferred a policy of gentle persuasion rather than aggressive legal

[45] *Compton* v. *Wiltshire Primary Care Trust* [2008] EWCA Civ 749 at [20]; *R. (Buglife – The Invertebrate Conservation Trust)* v. *Thurrock Thames Gateway Development Corporation* [2008] EWCA Civ 1209 at [17]; *Morgan* v. *Hinton Organics (Wessex) Ltd* [2009] EWCA Civ 107 at [33].

[46] www.judiciary.gov.uk/publications-and-reports/reports/civil/review-of-civil-litigation-costs.

[47] Working Group on Access to Justice (Chair Lord Justice Sullivan), *Ensuring Access to Environmental Justice in England and Wales – Follow Up Report* (2010).

action. Pressure from the new wave of non-governmental organizations in the 1970s began to shed light on how these bodies actually operated, and this was followed by a series of sophisticated socio legal research studies designed to analyze how individual enforcement officers exercised their enforcement discretion in dealing with regulatory breaches.[48] Criminal law with offences mainly drafted in strict liability terms dominated the structure of environmental laws, but it was clear that whatever the strict letter of the law officers often exercised their own sense of judgement as to what constituted or did not constitute criminal behaviour before deciding whether to prosecute or not.

The creation of new national regulatory bodies in the 1990s such as the Environment Agency was motivated in part by the desire of industry in particular to see a more consistent approach to the implementation and enforcement of controls across the country. This desire for consistency was not confined to the setting of consents and licences but affected the strategy for enforcement as well, with the result that the Environment Agency became the first national regulatory body to publish a detailed Enforcement Policy setting out the core principles as to how it would respond to regulatory breaches and the circumstances in which it was likely to prosecute or not.

Nevertheless, the range of sanctions available to environmental regulators still remained fairly narrow – warning letters, a formal caution, or an actual prosecution. Many regulators possessed powers under different environmental laws to serve notices requiring the industry concerned to take the necessary steps to come back into compliance, but sanctions for breach of such notices remained equally narrow and in the last step were based on the criminal law. There was criticism both of the apparently small sentences, mostly fines, imposed by the lower criminal courts in dealing with environmental offences, and the opportunity that strict liability offences allowed lawyers to persuade lay magistrates to down-play the seriousness of offences[49] – a somewhat ironic development given that the strict liability offence had originally been developed in the nineteenth century expressly to make prosecution of industry and businesses simpler. This was coupled with critiques of the limited range of sanctions available and the heavy reliance on criminal law, especially compared with the practice in the field of environmental law in other jurisdictions such as Germany and Australia.[50]

In 2004 a report commissioned by the Department for Environment, Food and Rural Affairs[51] called for environmental regulators to be given the power to impose civil financial penalties as an additional form of sanction to criminal prosecution, and

[48] Examples include K. Hawkins, *Environment and Enforcement: Regulation and the Social Definition of Pollution* (1984); G. Richardson, A. Ogus and P. Burrows, *Policing Pollution: A Study of Regulation and Enforcement* (1982); B. M. Hutter, *The Reasonable Arm of the Law? The Law Enforcement Procedures of Environmental Health Officers* (1988).

[49] P. de Prez, 'Excuses, excuses: the ritual trivilization of environmental prosecutions' (2000) 12(1) *JEL* 65.

[50] J. Abbott, 'The Regulatory Enforcement of Pollution Control Laws: The Australian Experience' (2005) 17(2) *JEL* 161.

[51] M. Woods and R. Macrory, *Environmental Civil Penalties – A More Proportionate Response to Regulatory Breach* (2004).

most likely to be appropriate to the normally responsible operator who through carelessness or an oversight had caused a serious regulatory breach. Civil penalties of this sort were not unknown in British law and were extensively used in fields such a financial regulation and competition law, but would have been an innovation in more traditional areas ofbusiness regulation. Although well received, the report did not attract sufficient political support to justify change. Industry in particular was alarmed at the prospect of suddenly shifting from a familiar system of regulatory prosecution with criminal burdens of proof resting on the regulator to one where the regulator could impose large financial penalties on a civil standard of proof and by-pass the courts, leaving the burden on industry to raise any defence by appeal. Given that it was the more responsible end of industry which would most likely be at the receiving end of civil penalties with the criminal law reserved for the more egregious offenders, this seemed potentially doubly unfair. The report laid important groundwork but failed to address in sufficient detail these wider issues of regulatory governance which would be necessary to secure political purchase. More fundamentally, a convincing case had to made out for singling out the environment for special treatment compared to many other areas of regulation such as health and safety and trading standards that would appear to be susceptible to the same analysis.

The debate concerning environmental sanctions appeared to have ground to a halt, and the impetus for what would eventually prove the decisive shift came from a quite unexpected and unconnected government initiative. In 2004 the Treasury commissioned a wide-ranging review of the administrative burdens imposed on business by regulatory enforcement. The Hampton Review published in 2005[52] argued that too many regulators, especially at local government level, had adopted an excessively 'tick-box' mentality to enforcement, losing sight of the overall aims of regulation. Hampton called for a greater emphasis on a risk-based approach to regulatory enforcement, focusing resources on the clearly non-compliant, and adopting a more enlightened and cost-effective approach towards legitimate business. The Review acknowledged that that excessive reliance on the criminal law appeared inimical to a philosophy of a more nuanced relationship between regulators and the regulated, and recommended the government to initiate a special review of regulatory sanctions.

The subsequent Macrory Review on regulatory sanctions reported in 2006.[53] As with Hampton, the Review encompassed an enormous spectrum – some 61 national regulators as well as all local authorities, and covering areas such as health and safety, planning, trading standards, environment, and food standards. Despite very different sets of laws in such a disperse range of regulation, common patterns emerged, with the core formal sanction under nearly all areas being a criminal offence, usually drafted in strict or semi-strict terms. It was equally clear that there were very similar patterns of the range of non-compliant actors, whatever the field of regulation. At one end of the

[52] P. Hampton, *Reducing Administrative Burdens – Effective Inspection and Enforcement* (2005).

[53] R. Macrory, *Regulatory Justice: Making Sanctions Effective*, Final Report, Cabinet Office (2006).

spectrum, there were the truly egregious, individuals or companies who knew exactly what they were doing and were often making large sums of money out of breaking the law. At the other end were responsible businesses who through no intention committed a breach – an unexpected equipment breakdown, for example. The middle ground covered a range of different circumstances, involving carelessness or a failure to give sufficient priority to regulatory compliance but lacking direct intention or recklessness. British enforcement practice has never required the police or regulators to prosecute for every offence, and in many instances warnings or a more formal caution might be an effective response at least where responsible businesses were concerned. But even unintentional breaches might give rise to significant harm or the risk of such harm and in such circumstances a formal sanction would be appropriate and indeed expected by the public. But it was questionable whether the criminal law was appropriate and Macrory argued that the criminal law was in effect being made to do too much work within the regulatory system – indeed there was a danger that the criminal law itself was being devalued in the process.

The Macrory Review advocated six core penalty principles that should underline the design of any effective regulatory sanctions system. A sanction should: (i) aim to change the behaviour of the offender; (ii) aim to eliminate any financial gain or benefit from non-compliance; (iii) be responsive and consider what is appropriate for the particular offender and regulatory issue; (iv) be proportionate to the nature of the offence and the harm caused; (v) aim to reverse harm caused by regulatory compliance; and (vi) aim to deter future non-compliance.

The current system dominated by the criminal law was found wanting against these principles. The Review argued that regulators should have access to a much wider range of non-criminal sanctions including civil penalties, familiar in areas such as competition and economic regulation but far less common in other areas. Civil penalties allow a regulator to calculate and impose a financial sanction without the intervention of a court unless the offender decides to appeal.

For many these proposals could represent an unacceptable shift of discretionary powers to regulators and the Review addressed these issues in a rather more sophisticated way than in previous studies. First, regulators were to be given power to offer enforcement undertakings as an alternative to the imposition of a civil penalty. Here the business itself would in effect design its own self-imposed sanction which could then be accepted by the regulator. The Review was insistent that such undertakings were made available to the public to avoid the impression of secret deals between regulated and the regulated, but they offered an attractive form of sanction for the legitimate business that had made a one-off serious regulatory breach. Perhaps rather surprisingly there was very little evidence presented to the review that the criminal standard of proof presented a significant hurdle in detection and enforcement – the problem with the criminal law was more its inappropriateness for certain types of breaches, the slowness of procedures, and the frequent lack of knowledge amongst lay magistrates. The Review therefore recommended no change to the existing regulatory offences and that the same standard of proof – the criminal standard of beyond all reasonable doubt – should apply whether or nor a criminal or civil penalty was imposed. In practice regulators would continue to investigate to criminal standards and with all the procedural protections of the criminal law, and only then, assuming that a case could be proved and that a formal sanction necessary, determine whether a criminal or civil response was appropriate. This approach was intended to avoid problems that have plagued many other regulatory systems where there can be lack of coordination between different bodies responsible for criminal and civil investigation, or where a civil response may be considered to be reserved for weaker cases. In pure legal terms, this aspect of the proposed design was probably the most innovative element of the Review and offers the prospect of a truly integrated sanctions system not found in other jurisdictions. Finally, the Review contained recommendations designed to diminish the opportunities of abuse by regulators. These principles – termed 'characteristics' in the Review – provide something of a constitutional bedrock in the design of regulatory systems. Regulators who acquired the powers would be legally obliged to publish enforcement policies spelling out the circumstances in which they were likely to impose different sorts of sanction,[54] as well as guidance on how they proposed to calculate civil penalties. Regulators should regularly make public reports on both outputs (the number of enforcement actions taken and so on) and outcomes (the extent to which key policy goals are being secured). Internal practices and procedures that might inadvertently distort the choice of sanction route should be avoided, and in particular the regulator should never receive directly any income from civil penalties – the Review was well aware that the perception whether justified or not that regulators were financially interested in the enforcement of regulatory requirements had undermined public credibility in areas of regulation such as traffic parking or speeding.

Many of the arguments concerning the limitations of wholesale reliance on the criminal law as a regulatory sanction had already been rehearsed in the environmental field, but by looking at regulatory sanctions across such a wide spectrum, the Review did not have to make any special pleading for any particular field of law. Instead, it was able to articulate common principles that should be adopted in all areas, and largely as a result, all the recommendations in the Review were accepted by the government. Regulatory Enforcement and Sanctions Act 2008, Pt III provided the framework for the core powers concerning civil sanctions as well as the recommendations on regulatory governance. The Review did not advocate that all regulators should be obliged to acquire the new powers – it would be up to ministers to draw them down by regulations – and in 2010 two national regulators, the Environment Agency and Natural England were the first to acquire the new powers.[55] Since then the Environment Agency has published its proposed guidance on how to calculate civil penalties, and a revised enforcement policy incorporating the new powers with the first civil penalties are likely to be imposed in 2011.

[54] At the time of the Review, some regulator bodies including the Environment Agency, already published an enforcement policy, but only 17 out of 60 national regulators had a policy that was publicly available: Macrory, ibid., paras 5.7–5.17.

[55] The Environmental Civil Sanctions (England) Order 2010 (SI 2010/1157), and the Environmental Sanctions (Misc. Amendments) (England) Regulations 2010 (SI 2010/1159). Similar regulations have been made for Wales.

Other regulators have expressed interest but it is clear that it is in the environmental field that the first serious experience of the new regime will be tested and evaluated. It is too early to predict the real impact of these reforms but a significant shift in thinking about the design of regulatory sanctions in the UK has begun to take place. Regulators and their departmental sponsors are more than ever conscious of financial pressures on public resources, and a critical element in the eventual success of the reforms in likely to be their impact on cost-savings. The new system deliberately does not lighten the costs of investigation by regulatory bodies, but where a civil penalty is proposed it should make it simpler or faster to resolve the issue without the need for the involvement of a court or tribunal. But it is possible to envisage in practice regulators becoming over confident or ambitious in applying proposed civil sanctions, followed by protracted negotiations and arguments between regulators and the regulated, coupled with an extensive number of appeals. If that were to happen, regulators and their ministers might conclude that in pure economic terms the traditional criminal enforcement system was preferable, and the system would revert back to its familiar pattern of relying on the criminal law.[56]

This scenario is possible but unlikely, not least because the sanctions review has now set in train a substantial review of the use of criminal law in the regulatory system. The Review itself did not advocate the abandonment of criminal law, and made important recommendations concerning the improvement of the current system, including giving criminal judges a wider range of sanctions where a case had been proved. These include publicity orders, corporate rehabilitation orders, and orders that could speedily remove a financial gain made from non-compliance with regulatory requirements. Yet the Review also questioned the continued reliance on offences drafted in strict liability terms allowing companies to be held vicariously liable for acts they knew nothing of or had even prohibited.[57] It fell shy of making blanket recommendations concerning the future structure of the criminal law but recommended that the government initiated a review of the drafting and formulation of criminal offences relating the regulatory non-compliance. As a result, the Law Commission launched a study on the subject, and published an initial consultation paper in 2010.[58]

[56] There are also concerns within the Coalition Government as to whether regulators rather than the courts should have the power to impose financial sanctions: *Civil sanctions regime is 'intolerable' says Minister*, ENDS Report 7 April 2011.

[57] The combination of strict and vicarious liability was described by Glanville Williams as a 'tyrannous combination' and quoted by Simon Brown LJ in *National Rivers Authority* v. *Alfred McAlpine Homes East Ltd* [1994] 4 All ER 286.

[58] The Law Commission, *Criminal Liability in Regulatory Contexts*, Consultation Paper No. 195 (2010).

## AN ENVIRONMENTAL COURT

Legal cases involving environmental issues have in the UK long been heard in the ordinary courts appropriate for the type of action brought. Environmental judicial reviews are handled by the Administrative Court, though clearly with some degree of specialization developing amongst the judges who are assigned particular cases. Similarly, the prosecution for criminal offences concerning the environment has taken place before the ordinary criminal courts, with private civil actions such as nuisance or negligence arising from pollution handled by the civil courts. But for over 20 years in the UK there has been intense debate on a possible role of a specialized environmental court or tribunal, though often the arguments have been dogged by very different visions of what the concept might entail in practice.

The first official recommendation for an environmental court appears to have been contained in a report by Sir Robert Carnwath, then a leading planning barrister and now a judge in the Court of Appeal and the Senior President of the new Tribunal System. The report was largely concerned with strengthening the enforcement mechanisms within the existing town and country planning system[59] but he made a cautious case for combining the jurisdictions of various courts and tribunals dealing with planning and environmental protection into a single judicial forum. Three years later, the then Lord Chief Justice, Lord Woolf, provided a broader vision.[60] He argued that a distinctive feature of environmental law was the possibility of a single pollution incident giving rise to many different types of legal action heard in different legal fora – a coroner's inquest (if deaths involved), criminal prosecution where regulatory offences had been committed, civil actions for compensation, and judicial review if public authorities are involved. He felt there was a strong case for a single environmental court which would handle all the legal consequences that arose from an environmental incident or problem. Lord Woolf's vision was for a body which was not just a court or existing tribunal under another name, but something quite radically different:

> It is a multi-faceted, multi-skilled body which would combine the services provided by the existing courts, tribunals, and inspectors in the environmental field. It would be a 'one-stop shop' which should lead to faster, cheaper, and more effective resolution of disputes in the environmental area.[61]

Largely as a result of Lord Woolf's lecture, the then Department of Environment and Transport and the Regions commissioned a major study examining the experience of specialized environmental courts in other jurisdictions, and considering possible models that could be adopted in the UK. The Grant report[62] considered six different

[59] R. Carnwath, *Enforcing Planning Control* (1989).

[60] H. Woolf, 'Are the Judiciary Environmental Myopic?' (1992) 4(1) *JEL* 1.

[61] Ibid., p. 14.

[62] M. Grant, *Environmental Court Project: Final Report* (2000). S. Tromans, 'Environmental Court Project' (2001) 13(3) *JEL* 423.

forms of court or tribunal that might be adopted, but in essence there were two main routes that could be followed – the so-called 'big bang' approach involving the creation of a major new environmental court probably as a division of the High Court, or strengthening existing judicial and quasi-judicial institutions from the bottom up to develop greater expertise in environmental law. The political appetite for institutional change was, however, not present at the time.[63]

Two years later, following a recommendation of the Royal Commission on Environmental Pollution,[64] the Department for Environment, Food and Rural Affairs commissioned a further study on the subject but one with a narrower focus. The Report[65] examined over 50 sets of environmental regulations to determine the extent to which they contained statutory rights of appeal and where these appeals were heard. The town and country planning system contained a well-established appeal system for developers with appeals heard by an executive agency of government, the Planning Inspectorate. Compared to this, the system for environmental appeals was far more muddled with a wide range of different bodies involved – the Secretary of State, the High Court, magistrates' courts and the Planning Inspectorate amongst others. The lack of coherence appeared to simply a matter of historical accident rather than a conscious decision by policy makers, and the Report recommended that an environmental tribunal be established to act as a single statutory appeals body.

But there were two particular challenges to the proposal. As with the initial debates on the use of civil penalties in environmental enforcement, the question that had to be addressed was whether the environment deserved special treatment. The report argued that there were a number of features that did indeed distinguish environmental law from many other legal fields – the extent to which technical and scientific questions were frequently intertwined with legal issues, the prevalence of EU environmental legislation, the emergence of core underlying legal principles such as the precautionary principle, the heavy involvement of public bodies exercising considerable discretion, the growing significance of international environmental treaties, and the developing concept of sustainable development as an underlying policy goal. Many of these features are to found individually in other areas of law such as workplace safety but it was the combination of all which appeared to place environmental law in a distinctive position and required a more specialized judicial approach. But not all found this argument convincing. The Scottish government, for example, rejected the argument:

> We acknowledge the special characteristics listed by Macrory and Woods and accept that they are features of environmental law. However, we are not persuaded that these features, or indeed this combination of features is unique to environmental law and it could be argued that similar

[63] Lord Brennan initiated a debate on the subject in the House of Lords. According to Lord Bach, the Minister, 'The Government welcome the opportunity to debate this issue. We are not persuaded of the need for an environmental court, certainly not on its possible shape', *Hansard*, HL, col. 100 (9 October 2000).

[64] Royal Commission on Environmental Pollution, *Environmental Planning*, Cm. 5459 (2002) para. 5.37.

[65] R. Macrory and M. Woods, *Modernizing Environmental Justice – Regulation and the Role of an Environmental Tribunal* (2003).

statements could be made equally about other areas of law such as health, health & safety and employment none of which have specialist courts/jurisdiction.[66]

The second challenge related to the proposal's rather modest vision of an environmental tribunal. This may have been workable but at the time did not align with the approach being promoted by environmental non-governmental organizations and lawyers in a study also funded by the Department for Environment, Food and Rural Affairs. The Environmental Justice report[67] was particularly concerned with the costs and risk of exposure to costs involved in environmental litigation, and argued that a far more radical approach was needed in the form of a new division of the High Court with the power to hear all civil law claims with a significant environmental component. Faced with the environmental law community itself advocating very different models of a specialist environmental court or tribunal, it was a hardly surprisingly that the government felt unable to act, and the debate appeared to have ground to a halt.

This proved to be an over-pessimistic presumption. Two years later the Review of Regulatory Sanctions[68] had to consider the question of appeals against the imposition of the civil sanctions it was recommending. Under European Convention on Human Rights, Art. 6, there would in any event have to be a right of appeal to an independent court or tribunal, and even if this had not been the case, the Review would have recommended such a right as a matter of fairness and a check against regulatory abuse. Appeals could have gone back to the ordinary courts, but the Review took advantage of the fact that a new, more flexible tribunal system was being created,[69] and recommended that appeals against civil sanctions should go to a new regulatory tribunal. Once the regulator had decided that a civil sanction was the appropriate route, then all procedures should remain within the administrative system rather than become possibly confused by being heard within criminal courts. The government accepted the recommendation and the Regulatory Enforcement and Sanctions Act 2008 provided that appeals should go to the First-tier Tribunal, the first level of tribunals established under the new system,[70] unless a more specialized and appropriate tribunal already existed.

As discussed above, it is the national environmental regulators who in practice have been the first bodies to acquire the new civil sanction powers, and the Order provided for appeals to go to a Tribunal. The new tribunal system had divided the First-tier level into a number of chambers, grouping together jurisdictions dealing with similar work or requiring similar skills, and was decided that sanctions appeals best fell within the

[66] Environment and Rural Affairs Department, Scottish Government, *Strengthening and Streamlining: The Way Forward for the Enforcement of Environmental Law in Scotland* (2006) para. 2.99.

[67] Environmental Law Foundation, World Wildlife Fund and Leigh Day and Co *Environmental Justice* (2004).

[68] Macrory, above, n. 53.

[69] The system of tribunals was reformed under Tribunals, Court and Enforcement Act 2007 following the major review by Sir Andrew Leggatt, *Report of the Review of Tribunals: Tribunals for Users – One System One Service* (2001), available at www.tribunals-review.org.uk.

[70] Appeals go to the Upper Tribunal.

General Regulatory Chamber. Since the first appeals would fall within the field of environmental regulation, in April 2010 an internal administrative decision was taken to establish an environmental tribunal within the Regulatory Chamber. With remarkably little fanfare or fuss, England and Wales gained a specialist environmental judicial body after almost 20 years of debate. Admittedly, its jurisdiction is extremely limited compared to earlier visions of an environmental court or tribunal but the important institutional step had been taken, and in future its remit may well be extended to encompass a wider environmental remit.[71] From one perspective the creation of the environmental tribunal at this point was purely a matter of chance – if regulators in other fields had been the first movers to acquire civil sanctions the story might have been very different. Yet the initial focus on the environment was not wholly surprising. It was in the environmental field that the most substantial intellectual case for civil sanctions had been made for a number of years prior to the Regulatory Enforcement and Sanctions Act 2008, and it was in the same field of law that the arguments for a new specialist form of court or tribunal had already been extensively rehearsed. It remains to be seen what longer-term impact the presence of a specialist tribunal will make to the development of environmental law in this country but it is likely to be considerable.

## THE FUTURE

Disputes involving environmental law issues often display inherent characteristics that in any event do not lend themselves to easy resolution by conventional legal institutional arrangements, and this has provided some of the impetus for innovation. Lord Woolf has noted how environmental litigation tends to display an unusual combination of technical and scientific complexities, challenging policy issues, and issues that cut across traditional divides between criminal and civil law, and public and private interests.[72] In addition, the fusion of environmental obligations developed under European Union environmental law and international public environmental law has now added a distinctive and powerful pressure to the national discourse, making it difficult for government to stone-wall legal and policy change. But perhaps more significantly the search for new legal ways of doing things reflects an unease with the capability of more traditional legal and regulatory techniques in contemporary environmental challenges. The British environmentalist Tom Burke has spoken of an 'old' and a 'new' environmental agenda.[73] The older agenda encompassed such subjects as water pollution and waste disposal where the problem was generally well understood, the science of cause and effect reasonably settled, and the policy maker is usually faced with situations where nearly all those affected by

[71] In 2010 Lord Justice Carnwath in his capacity as Senior President of Tribunals commissioned a study to re-examine the issue of consolidating administrative appeal, under enviromental regulations. The final report, R. Macrory, *Consistency and Effectiveness – Strengthening the New Environmental Tribunal* (2011) argued that most environmental appeals should now go to the First-tier Tribunal (Environment).

[72] Lord Woolf, 'Environmental Law and Sustainable Development', in H. Woolf, *The Pursuit of Justice* (2008) 391.

[73] R. Macrory, 'Maturity and Methodology – A Personal Reflection' (2009) 21(2) *JEL* 251, 254.

policy change will gain – the public will generally welcome tighter environmental controls, but equally legitimate industry will often support regulation in that it drives out the sub-standard. Legal techniques that are likely to be effective are often well established, and while there will always be problems in enforcement and implementation, the basic legal tool-kit is not called into question. The newer environmental agenda concerns issues such as transport, climate change, resource use and biodiversity, where the underlying knowledge and science may be far less certain, and the policy solutions by no means bring about immediate win–win situations. It is far less clear what sort of legal techniques are appropriate, or indeed what role law may play in their resolution. In this light it is hardly surprising that in recent years much of environmental legal development has shifted from prescribing clearly defined solutions to providing more open-ended approaches where the law provides a combination of legal rights and opportunities for more extensive citizen engagement and obligations and procedures designed to make the state more accountable for what it does. One test of an effective constitutional and legal system is its ability to handle and accommodate competing visions, and to adapt to new perceptions and understandings. From this perspective, environmental law has proved remarkably creative over the past quarter of a century and provided a laboratory and impetus for deeper changes in our legal and constitutional system.

## FURTHER READING

Macrory, R. and Maurici, J., 'Rethinking regulatory sanctions – Regulatory Enforcement and Sanctions Act 2008 – an exchange of letters' (2009) 21(4) *Environmental Law and Management* 183–6.

Macrory, R. and Wood, M., *Modernizing Environmental Justice: Regulation and the Role of an Environmental Tribunal* (2003), reprinted in Macrory, R., *Regulation, Enforcement and Governance in Environmental Law* (2010).

*Regulatory Justice: Making Sanctions Effective* (Final Report of the Macrory Review on Regulatory Sanctions), reprinted in Macrory, R., *Regulation, Enforcement and Governance in Environmental Law* (2010).

Woolf, H, 'Are the Judiciary Environmentally Myopic?' (1992) 4 *Journal of Environmental Law* 1–14.

### USEFUL WEBSITES

Department for Business, Innvoation and Skills: **www.bis.gov.uk/policies/better-regulation/reviewing-regulation/improving-compliance-among-businesses**

Environment Agency: **www.environment-agency.gov.uk/business/regulation/default.aspx, especially under 'Business and industry'**

European Commission, Environment Directorate-General: **http://ec.europa.eu/environment/index_en.htm**

Tribunals Service, First-tier Tribunal (Environment): **www.tribunals.gov.uk/environment**

United Nations Economic Commission for Europe, Aarhus Convention on Access to Information, Public Participation in Decision-making and Access to Justice in Environmental Matters: **www.unece.org/env/pp**

[15]

*Journal of Environmental Law* **23**:2 
doi:10.1093/jel/eqr006 Advance Access published on 26 May 2011

# Enforcing Environmental Regulation

Neil Gunningham*

## Abstract

For environmental legislation to 'work' it must not only be well designed but also efficiently and effectively enforced. Strategies must be developed as to how inspectors should go about the task of intervening in the affairs of regulated organisations to ensure compliance and enforcement—a question regarding which there is little consensus. This article examines this question from a number of angles: descriptive; analytical; and normative. It explores the practices of a representative sample of environmental regulators, identifying a number of distinctive intervention strategies (which are only limitedly shaped by existing theoretical models). It goes on to examine the strengths and weaknesses of each strategy and to consider how best to balance the sometimes competing criteria of effectiveness, efficiency and legitimacy. Finally, it considers how resource allocation and intervention strategies can best be integrated, whether there is a single 'best practice' strategy, and if not, what sorts of hybrids might be developed.

Keywords: compliance, best practice, enforcement, environment, inspection, regulation

*Director of National Research Centre for OHS Regulation, Regulatory Institutions Network, Research School of Pacific and Asian Studies, The Australian National University, Canberra ACT 0200, Australia (neil.gunningham@anu.edu.au). I am grateful to Jacqueline Menager for her excellent research assistance and to two anonymous referees for their insightful comments. The argument developed in Section 4.2 benefited considerably from a series of discussions with Christine Parker while we were conducting an overlapping project for the Victorian Environment Protection Authority.

## 1. Introduction

For legislation to 'work' it must not only be well designed but also effectively implemented and enforced.[1] For the regulator, the latter involves two main tasks. First there is the question of *where* it is best to allocate resources and which sectors and organisations to target for inspection—often viewed in terms of 'how to get the biggest bang for the regulatory buck'. Second, strategies must be developed as to how inspectors should go about the task of intervening in the affairs of regulated organisations. Should they for example, seek stringent enforcement or negotiate outcomes through advice and persuasion? In short, the two main challenges for regulators are determining *where* to intervene and *how* to intervene in the affairs of regulated organisations.

As regards the first of these challenges there is now something approaching consensus that the best way to allocate scarce regulatory resources is through risk-based regulation. This involves 'the development of decision-making frameworks and procedures to prioritise regulatory activities and deploy resources, principally relating to inspection and enforcement, based on an assessment of the risks that regulated organisations pose to the regulator's objectives'.[2] In the UK, risk-based regulation was endorsed by the Hampton Review[3] and subsequently encapsulated in a statutory code of practice.[4] However, this approach is by no means confined to the UK and an increasing number of OECD countries are seeking to develop coherent frameworks for the governance of risk in regulatory policy.[5] Risk-based regulation has limitations as well as strengths, including the sophistication of the risk assessment process and the quality of information available on which to base it.[6] Nonetheless, most regulators and policy makers, at least in the Anglo-Saxon

1 This is a theme that has been pursued on a number of occasions within the pages of the JEL. See for example, R Mushal, 'Reflections upon American Environmental Enforcement Experience as it may relate to Post –Hampton Developments in England and Wales' (2007) 19 JEL 201; C Abbot, 'The Regulatory Enforcement of Pollution Control Laws: The Australian Experience' (2005) 17 JEL 161.

2 J Black, 'Risk-Based Regulation: Choices, Practices and Lessons Being Learned' in *Risk and Regulatory Policy: Improving the Governance of Risk* (OECD Paris 2010) 187.

3 P Hampton, *Reducing Administrative Burdens: Effective Inspection and Enforcement* ('The Hampton Review' 2005).

4 *Statutory Code of Practice for Regulators* (Department of Business Enterprise and Regulatory Reform 2007) <http://www.berr.gov.uk/files/file45019.pdf> accessed 20 March 2011.

5 See generally, *Risk and Regulatory Policy: Improving the Governance of Risk* (OECD 2010).

6 See J Black and R Baldwin, 'Really Responsive Risk-Based Regulation' (2010) 32 Law & Pol'y 181; J Black, 'Managing Regulatory Risks and Defining the Parameters of Blame: The Case of the Australian Prudential Regulation Authority' (2006) 28 Law & Pol'y 1; J Black, 'The Emergence of Risk-Based Regulation and the New Public Risk Management in the United Kingdom' [2005] PL 512.

world, would regard it as approximating best practice in terms of *where* to allocate most of their resources.[7]

In contrast, the second task, determining *how* to intervene in the affairs of regulated organisations to ensure compliance and facilitate enforcement (hereafter *intervention strategy*) has been given far less attention, at least by regulators themselves.[8] Furthermore, there is nothing remotely approaching consensus in terms of how it should best be determined. At first sight this might be surprising, since intervention strategy will have a crucial bearing on regulatory outcomes. This relative neglect by regulators (manifest in the lack of sophistication or coherence of such strategies in many jurisdictions[9]) is perhaps even more surprising, given that there is a rich academic literature that has engaged with this question for over two decades.[10]

Of course individual inspectors 'on the ground' may not actually adhere to their agency's stated intervention strategy, and thus, a related question concerns how inspectors behave in practice (and why) and how to confine inspectoral discretion. How, for example, can discretion be contained without imposing mechanistic rules and driving inspectors to 'go by the book'? This question has been the subject of substantial research, although this has not, to date, generated anything approaching consensus.[11] While this issue will be touched upon in Section 4.3 below, it is not the main focus of the article, which is agency intervention strategy (usually clearly stated in agency documentation) rather than how inspectors exercise their discretion in interpreting that strategy.

The intended contribution of this article is to examine intervention strategy from a number of angles: descriptive, analytical and normative. Section 2 explores the strategies of a representative sample of environmental regulators. Based on their formal published policies, it identifies five distinctive strategies adopted by one or more of these agencies (together with a hybrid approach which combines different strategies with varying degrees of success). Contrasting theory and practice, this section also shows how these intervention strategies are only limitedly shaped by existing theoretical models. Section 3 examines the strengths and weaknesses of each of the above

7 See generally, Black and Baldwin (n 6).
8 See eg *Ensuring Environmental Compliance: Trends and Good Practices* (OECD Paris 2009) 13.
9 See Section 2 below.
10 For overviews, see M Cave, R Baldwin and M Lodge (eds) *The Oxford Handbook of Regulation*, (OUP 2010); C Parker and V Nielsen, (eds), *Explaining Compliance* (Edward Elgar 2011).
11 Compare eg J Black 'Talking About Regulation' [1998] PL 77; P May and S Winter 'Reconsidering Styles of Regulatory Enforcement: Patterns in Danish Agro-Environmental Inspection' (2000) 22 Law & Pol'y 143; M Pautz, 'Trust Between Regulators and the Regulated: A Case Study of Environmental Inspectors and Facility Personnel in Virginia' (2009) 37 Pol'y & Pol 1047.

strategies (and of two additional strategies identified in the academic literature). Against this backdrop, Section 4 turns to normative questions. How can resource allocation strategies and intervention strategies best be integrated? Is there a single 'best practice' strategy or does the most appropriate strategy depend on the context? What should be the role of hybrid intervention strategies? And how should discretion be constrained? Section 5 concludes.

In terms of methodology, intervention strategy is necessarily developed at regulator level and usually set out in a formal policy which is addressed to field officers and often also to regulated organisations and other stakeholders. As such, any relevant strategy is usually to be found in publicly available documentation provided by environmental agencies themselves. Accordingly, the first port of call in investigating intervention strategy is official documentation, via websites, press releases, annual reports and other publications, supplemented, where available, by public expositions of agency policy by senior staff. However, while in the case of most agencies such documentation clearly articulates a particular intervention strategy, this is not always the case. Where no strategy is clearly articulated then external sources, including academic research, commentary by former agency officials and by regulated entities or their associations, were also used to gain a better understanding of intervention strategy.

The jurisdictions chosen for inclusion in this study were the US Federal Environment Protection Agency (US EPA), the Florida Department of Environment Protection (DEP), The Netherlands Ministry of Housing, Spatial Planning and the Environment (VROM), the United Kingdom Environment Agency and the environment protection authorities or similarly named agencies of the Australian states and territories (environment being primarily a state responsibility within the Australian federal system). Initially it was intended to include (in addition to the US EPA) three leading US state agencies: California, Pennsylvania and Florida. These states have multiple agencies (local as well as state) dealing with multiple environmental statutes, so that developing a unitary compliance and enforcement strategy is not practicable. In any event, given the paucity of information available from either internal or external sources, they were dropped from the study. The jurisdictions selected for inclusion are disproportionately Anglo-Saxon and were chosen primarily because their regulatory traditions are distinctive but not so disparate as to make comparisons inappropriate.

## 2. Types of Intervention Strategies

In principle, numerous intervention strategies might be adopted. At least seven such strategies can be identified in the academic literature: Rules and

Deterrence; Advice and Persuasion; Criteria Based Regulation; Responsive Regulation; Smart Regulation; Risk-Based Regulation; and Meta-Regulation[12] (see Box 1 below). Such strategies are 'ideal types', unlikely to be found in the real world in this precise form, but nevertheless helpful as models to be used for heuristic purposes.[13]

As will become apparent from the discussion below, not all of these theoretical models have been applied in practice. Overall, from the analysis of the sample jurisdictions, five distinctive regulatory strategies were identified. Most agencies used one or other of these strategies exclusively but a minority used a combination of strategies. The following sections describe the strategies and how different agencies applied them.

### *2.1 Rules and Deterrence*

The US EPA is arguably the quintessential (and indeed in this sample, the only) example of an agency applying a 'Rules and Deterrence' strategy. Such a strategy relies heavily on a system of rules prescribing uniform standards applicable to diverse circumstances and assumes that 'a ruthless and efficient investigation and enforcement capability will produce compliance through the mechanism of deterrence'.[14] The EPA's traditional focus has been on compliance monitoring to identify violations and the collection of evidence to support enforcement actions coupled with targeted enforcement activity.[15] It has assumed that once violations are detected then some form of enforcement action may be appropriate 'because, in any society, many people will not comply with the law unless there are clear consequences for non-compliance'.[16] Finally, in contrast to many European and Australian agencies, the US EPA is distinctively adversarial, readily resorting to litigation and confrontation

12 Three other strategies; Just Deserts, Restorative Justice and 'Really Responsive Regulation' might arguably have also been included. However, 'Just Deserts' (whose main aim is to punish non-compliance in a way that is proportional and just) is by definition not appropriate as a 'core' intervention strategy because changing behaviour to achieve compliance is not the main aim of this strategy. Restorative Justice (the aim of which in the environmental context is to give the offender a chance to proactively put things right) by its nature can only be used in conjunction with other regulatory approaches, not in isolation, since it only becomes relevant at a stage subsequent to a regulatory breach. Finally, 'Really Responsive Regulation' seeks to theorise *beyond* intervention strategy to matters such as the operating and cognitive environment of organisations, the institutional environment, the different logics of regulatory tools and to changes in these elements.

13 See generally, P May and S Winter, ch 10: Regulatory Enforcement Styles and Compliance, in Parker and Nielsen (n 10) for a review of different enforcement strategies and styles.

14 MK Sparrow, *Imposing Duties: Government's Changing Approach to Compliance* (Praeger Publishers 1994) ix.

15 C Rechtschaffen and D Markell, 'Reinventing Environmental Enforcement and the State/Federal Relationship' in D Zaelke, D Kaniaru and E Kruzikova (eds), *Making Law Work: Environmental Compliance and Sustainable Development* (Vol 1, Cameron May 2005) 158.

16 Office of Enforcement, 'Principles of Environmental Enforcement' (US EPA 1992) 7.1.

**Box 1.** Regulatory strategies: models identified in the regulatory literature

From a review of the regulatory literature seven distinctive (but often mutually compatible) regulatory enforcement and compliance strategies can be identified.

***Advice and Persuasion:*** emphasises cooperation rather than confrontation, and conciliation rather than coercion. The aim is to prevent harm—achieved by bargaining, persuasion and negotiation rather than sanctioning. Recourse to the legal process here is rare, the assumption being that the majority of regulatees are willing to comply voluntarily.

***Rules and Deterrence:*** emphasises a coercive, formal and adversarial style of enforcement and the sanctioning of rule-breaking behaviour. It assumes that regulatees are rational actors capable of responding to incentives, and that if offenders are detected with sufficient frequency and punished with sufficient severity, then they, and others, will be deterred from future violations.

***Criteria Strategies:*** provide inspectors and other decision-makers with a list of criteria which they should consider in arriving at a decision in any given case. There is no prescriptive formula and which mechanism(s) will be used in any particular case will depend on the circumstances.

***Responsive Regulation:*** suggests that best outcomes will be achieved if inspectors employ a blend of persuasion and coercion, the actual mix being adjusted to the particular circumstances and motivations of the regulatee. Regulators should begin by assuming virtue (to which they should respond by offering cooperation and information), but when their expectations are disappointed, they respond with progressively punitive and deterrence oriented strategies until the regulated group conforms (a form of 'tit for tat').

***Smart Regulation***: expands on some of the insights of Responsive Regulation and the enforcement pyramid, by suggesting how markets, civil society and other institutions can sometimes act as surrogate regulators and accomplish public policy goals more effectively, with greater social acceptance and at less cost to the state. It also argues that complementary mixes of enforcement strategies and tools will be more effective than 'stand alone' strategies.

***Risk-Based Regulation:*** argues that the kind of intervention in the event of non-compliance should depend upon an evaluation of degree of risk to the environment posed by the infraction and calculations regarding the impact that the noncompliance will have on the regulatory body's ability to achieve its objectives.

***Meta-Regulation:*** involves placing responsibility on the regulated organisations themselves (usually large organisations) to submit their plans to the regulator for approval, with the regulator's role being to 'risk-manage' the risk management of those individual organisations. The goal is to induce companies themselves to acquire the specialised skills and knowledge to self-regulate, subject to external scrutiny. Accordingly the regulator's main intervention role is to oversee and audit the plans put in place by the regulated organisation. Where it finds inadequacies it may invoke a responsive approach as described above.

where it identifies a breach of rules, notwithstanding the evidence that this can often be counterproductive.[17]

The Rules and Deterrence theme emerges clearly from the US EPA's formal documentation,[18] which emphasises that 'enforcement is a vital part of encouraging governments, companies and others who are regulated to meet their environmental obligations'. The EPA also states that 'enforcement deters those who might otherwise profit from violating the law, and levels the playing field with environmentally compliant companies'.[19] Emphasis is placed upon:

> [S]tringent sanctions, including jail sentences, to promote deterrence and help ensure compliance in order to protect human health and the environment. Criminal enforcement is often used against the most serious environmental violations as well as those which involve egregious negligence or conduct involving intentional or knowing disregard of the law.[20]

Not coincidentally, given the American history of adversarial legalism, 'deterrence' and 'enforcement' are raised far more frequently in US EPA documentation than in comparable documents of its European or Australian counterparts.

Increasingly, the EPA has had to go beyond an exclusive reliance on Rules and Deterrence, as a result of the magnitude of the environmental challenges it is mandated to deal with, and its limited resources. As a matter of necessity, the EPA has had to explore more cooperative methods such as outreach,[21] compliance assistance, mediation and other alternative dispute resolution techniques. Of particular note not only in the Clinton–Gore years, but also

17 R Kagan, *Adversarial Legalism: The American Way of Law* (Harvard University Press 2003).
18 See generally, US Environment Protection Agency, 'Enforcement' <http://www.epa.gov/compliance/index-e.html> accessed 30 July 2010.
19 Kagan (n 17).
20 US Environmental Protection Agency, 'Criminal Enforcement' <http://www.epa.gov/compliance/criminal/index.html> accessed 15 August 2010.
21 Outreach for present purposes includes education and information dissemination, usually targeted at small and medium sized enterprises.

continuing today, is a range of initiatives designed to encourage, reward and facilitate 'good apples' to go 'beyond compliance'.[22]

However, as Dan Fiorino, a past senior administrator of the US EPA, pointed out in 2006, these initiatives have not resulted in a fundamental rethink within the EPA itself. On the contrary, they have often been perceived by EPA regulators as a threat to their autonomy and traditional functions.[23] They have, in short, been less about designing a new regulatory approach and more about fine tuning the old one. Indeed, 'much of what was touted as re-invention in the 1990s may fairly be described as marginal'.[24] Thus, it is no surprise that in its 2005 review of US environmental regulation, the OECD concluded that, '[c]ommand-and-control regulation is still the cornerstone of US environmental protection, accompanied by considerable litigation, which is often costly and time consuming'.[25]

### *2.2 Advice and Persuasion*

An 'Advice and Persuasion' strategy (also widely referred to as a 'compliance' strategy), with its emphasis on cooperation, conciliation and manifest reluctance to use enforcement and prosecution except as a last resort, was hard to identify in its pure form in the agencies studied. However, the Australian Government's Department of Environment, Water, Heritage and Arts is certainly heavily Advice and Persuasion (rather than enforcement) oriented. It emphasises the promotion of self-regulation and the importance of encouraging the community to act in accordance with legislation,[26] and seeks to act primarily 'through measures such as targeted communication and education activities, timely provision of information and advice, persuasion, cooperative assistance and collaboration'.[27] The Department aims to raise awareness of the benefits of complying, remove barriers to compliance and overcome factors that encourage non-compliance, while also encouraging industry-wide codes that promote compliance. However, where these compliance approaches fail, the department does make it clear that enforcement mechanisms will be used. Quite where the Department positions itself on the advice and persuasion—enforcement continuum is difficult to determine from its published documentation but there is some evidence to suggest that the considerable emphasis

22 See generally, N Gunningham and D Sinclair, *Leaders and Laggards* (Greenleaf Publishing Limited 2002) ch 6.
23 See generally, D Fiorino, *The New Environmental Regulation* (MIT Press 2006) ch 1.
24 Fiorino (n 23) 9.
25 'OECD Environmental Performance Reviews: United States 2005' (OECD, Paris) 16.
26 Department of the Environment, Water, Heritage and the Arts, 'Compliance and Enforcement Policy' (December 2009) 5.
27 Department of the Environment, Water, Heritage and the Arts (n 26).

on compliance in its documentation (to the substantial exclusion of enforcement), is replicated in practice.[28]

In Victoria also, the approach of the Environment Protection Authority (EPA Victoria) is, at least in part, oriented to 'Advice and Persuasion'. This agency's *Compliance Framework* suggests for example that 'the majority of people want to comply'[29] and that the goal is 'to identify compliance risks to support and manage those at risk of non-compliance'.[30] There is an overall language of 'clients' and 'service' in this document, with regulation sometimes described as 'mandatory services' and enforcement as 'non-compliance management'. This language suggests that EPA Victoria is trying to frame its compliance and enforcement activities in 'service' terms, consistent with a compliance-oriented approach that downplays enforcement.

The characterisation of the practices of the Commonwealth and Victorian environment agencies as 'Advice and Persuasion oriented' is consistent with Carolyn Abbot's review of the practices of these agencies. She concluded that 'a compliance based strategy is indeed still at the core of their respective environmental enforcement policies'.[31] The Victorian agency's approach is however a hybrid strategy, as discussed further at Section 2.6 below.

### *2.3 Criteria Strategies*

These strategies do not involve a commitment to Advice and Persuasion or to deterrence through enforcement. Rather, a wide range of options are contemplated (and usually listed in an agency's compliance and enforcement policy or similarly named document). Which mechanism(s) to be used in any particular case will depend on the circumstances. There is no prescriptive formula and instead, inspectors and other decision-makers are provided with a list of criteria which they should consider in arriving at a decision in any given case. While no two jurisdictions apply precisely the same criteria, there is considerable commonality in terms of a general approach.[32]

The Florida Department of Environment Protection (DEP) provides a good example of this strategy. Before exploring particular decision-making criteria,

28 Z Lipman, 'An Evaluation of Compliance and Enforcement Mechanisms in the Environment Protection and Biodiversity Conservation Act 1999 (Cth) and their Application by the Commonwealth' (2010) 27 EPLJ 98.

29 EPA, 'Compliance Framework' (EPA Victoria 2009) 3.

30 EPA (n 29) 6.

31 Abbot (n 1) 165.

32 These are similar to (but not identical to) what Yeung elaborates as the constitutional principles which she argues should underpin enforcement, based on the constitutional values of liberal, democratic legal systems. See K Yeung, *Securing Compliance. A Principled Approach* (Hart Publishing 2004).

the DEP makes clear that its primary goal is 'to resolve violations of Florida's environmental requirements effectively and return violators to compliance as quickly as possible'.[33] Accordingly it emphasises that many violations may be dealt with, 'with the cooperation of the responsible party and without the need for formal enforcement'.[34] Nevertheless, the DEP states that deterrence—delivering a potent message to the violator, and to others, that violations are not tolerated—will also be important.[35] Thus, rather than adopting a strategy of either Advice and Persuasion, or Rules and Deterrence, the DEP opts for a mixed or balanced approach. This still begs the question of which tools will be applied under different circumstances.

Here, the DEP's documentation advises that 'determining the right response to any violation requires considering many factors'. These include:

- How serious was the violation?
- Is it a first-time violator or a chronic offender?
- Was the violation inadvertent, was it due to negligence, was it wilful?
- Can the site or facility be brought back into compliance without formal enforcement?
- Can any damage to the environment be undone or remediated quickly?
- Is the violator responding in good faith?[36]

The Dutch VROM has adopted a broadly similar approach in terms of 'doing things right'. Here the inspectorate uses the 'Table of 11' as a framework for determining what intervention to take. This table is a list of factors relevant to non-compliance, based on a combination of social, psychological and criminal theories on compliance behaviour and on practical experience.[37] The factors are divided into three categories: 'aspects of spontaneous compliance' (knowledge of the regulation, cost/benefit ratio, degree of acceptance of the regulation, loyalty and obedience of the regulatee, informal monitoring); 'aspects of monitoring' (informal report probability, monitoring probability, detection probability, selectivity of the inspector); and 'aspects of sanctions' (chance of sanctions, severity of sanctions).

33 Florida Department of Environmental Protection, 'Compliance and Enforcement' (2009) <http://www.dep.state.fl.us/mainpage/ce/default.htm> accessed 2 August 2010.

34 Florida Department of Environmental Protection 'Enforcement in Action' (2009) <http://www.dep.state.fl.us/mainpage/ce/highlights.htm> accessed 9 August 2010.

35 This message 'may be in the form of penalties that hit the pocketbook, compensation required for damages, or implementation of "in-kind" projects that prevent pollution or otherwise enhance the environment. In all cases, ensuring that the violator fixes the problem and comes back into compliance is the first objective' Florida Department of Environment Protection (n 33).

36 See 'Compliance and Enforcement' Florida Department of Environment Protection (n 33).

37 See A Van Der Schraaf, 'Incentive Framework to Comply with Regulations' (Paper for the OECD Conference on Economic Aspects of Environmental Compliance Assurance, Paris, December 2004).

For example, questions asked by inspectors would include:

- What type of organisation is it?
- What is the financial status of the organisation?
- What investments are already made in order to comply?
- What is the history of the organisation: does it have a large history of regulatory non-compliance or is this the first time of non-compliance?
- Is there a compliance pattern detectable within the whole [industry sector]?[38]

Once these factors have been determined, then an appropriate 'intervention mix' is generated.

A number of Australian jurisdictions also adopt Criteria Strategies. The Western Australian Department's *Enforcement and Prosecution Policy* refers to fostering 'consistent, integrated and coordinated enforcement action across all sections of the [Department]'[39] and this is to be achieved via the 'Principles of Enforcement'. According to these principles, 'enforcement action will be taken in proportion to the magnitude of the alleged offence and/or the environmental impact, taking into account the conduct of the parties and implications for the administration of the legislation'.[40] The document goes on to list a number of specific criteria that the Department will consider in choosing the appropriate enforcement action.[41] Three other Australian jurisdictions (South Australia,[42] Tasmania[43] and the Commonwealth[44]) also adopt a Criteria Strategy although the last of these is combined with an Advice and Persuasion strategy that orients the application of the criteria towards less interventionist compliance options such as a preference for informal exhortation over formal administrative notices.

As will be apparent, the application of a Criteria Strategy leaves individual inspectors and other decision-makers with extremely wide discretion as to what action they decide is appropriate. Just in case this is not obvious, the Western Australian policy explicitly states that 'the Department has discretion in considering what is the appropriate enforcement action to be applied'. The agencies studied do not appear to have recognised the need to

38 See Van Der Schraaf (n 37) 5. The Table of 11 is applied mainly to deciding in advance what sort of interventions to take in relation to particular obligations and groups of companies. But it may also be applied to individual cases.

39 Department of Environment and Conservation, 'Enforcement and Prosecution Policy' (Western Australia 2008) 2.

40 ibid 3.

41 ibid 5.

42 Environment Protection Authority, 'Compliance and Enforcement Statement' (South Australia 2009) <http://www.epa.sa.gov.au/what_we_do/compliance_and_enforcement_statement> accessed 30 August 2010.

43 See Department of Primary Industries, Water and Environment, 'Enforcement Policy' (Tasmania 2004) 2.

44 See Department of Environment, Water, Heritage and the Arts, 'Compliance and Enforcement Policy' (2009) 8.

constrain discretion under a criteria approach, notwithstanding that this conflicts with the 'consistent, integrated and coordinated approach' referred to above.

While it could be argued that a Criteria Strategy is a composite approach incorporating some elements of other strategies, it is nevertheless quite distinctive. For example, while an agency adopting a Rules and Deterrence strategy is predisposed towards tough enforcement action and one applying Advice and Persuasion is equally inclined to the opposite approach, an agency with a Criteria-Based Strategy will simply weigh up the various factors before exercising its considerable discretion to use advice, persuasion or more deterrent mechanisms in particular circumstances.

### 2.4 *Risk-Based Strategy*

Under the banner of 'Better Regulation' the England and Wales Environment Agency's approach to resource allocation and targeting is quintessentially risk-based. So too is its approach to other aspects of its operations, including intervention strategy. Thus, the Agency is concerned not only to provide advice and guidance but also to enforce the law where it finds evidence of non-compliance.[45] In each case, *it is the level of environmental risk that is the primary determinant of what action it will take* and this approach is implicit in the Environment Agency's *Compliance and Enforcement Policy*. In particular, the principle of proportionality includes a statement that 'enforcement action . . . will be proportionate to the risks posed to the environment and to the seriousness of any breach of law'.[46] Confirmation that this is indeed the Environment Agency's approach is apparent from a number of other sources. Perhaps the clearest articulation of this strategy is to be found in the following statement from the Agency's Chief Prosecutor:

> Essentially, when dealing either with a pollution incident or with a breach of the terms of a permit or authorisation, the Agency does a form of risk assessment: it endeavours to categorise the effect or potential effect of what has occurred in environmental damage terms.

45 UK Environment Agency, 'Compliance and Enforcement Policy Guidance' <http://www.environment-agency.gov.uk/business/regulation/31851.aspx> accessed 11 July 2010.

46 UK Environment Agency, 'Enforcement and Prosecution Policy' (7 August 2008) oc No EAS/8001/1/1, 3. Note, shortly before going to press, the Environment Agency announced that from 2011, it will use a new enforcement and sanctions policy to guide it in its enforcement and prosecution decisions. The new policy documents consist of: An Enforcement and Sanctions Statement, which sets out a high-level view of the EA's approach to enforcement; Enforcement and Sanctions Guidance, which explains how the EA will make decisions about enforcement; Enforcement and Sanctions Offence Response Options, which lists the sanctions (including civil sanctions where appropriate) and responses available for offences regulated by the EA.

The categorisation is simple and the incident is classified as either being *major, significant, minor* or *having no environmental impact* at all. Although the categorisation is simplistic, it is important as it leads to a suggested enforcement response. For instance, occurrences categorised as being of *major* effect will normally lead to a prosecution, whilst those falling into the lower two categories are more likely to be resolved by way of a formal caution or warning. An incident classified as *significant* is serious enough to recommend a prosecution or caution response rather than just a warning.[47]

The UK Environment Agency uses a number of tools to assist its approach to risk assessment (both in terms of resource allocation, and compliance and enforcement). Principal among these is OPRA (operator risk appraisal), a tool that enables the agency to objectively assess the risks from an activity. In particular, application of OPRA provides a risk-rating which is then used as part of the compliance assessment process. The compliance and enforcement process is also facilitated by Compliance Assessment Plans (CAPs) and the Compliance Classification Scheme (CCS), which provides consistency across different regulatory regimes in the reporting of non-compliance with permit conditions and the action the Agency takes.

In Australia, the New South Wales Department of Environment, Climate Change and Water (DECCW) has also adopted a risk-based strategy (and two other agencies, South Australia and Victoria, have elements of this approach). In New South Wales, regulation in all social spheres has been strongly influenced by the UK Better Regulation initiative and also by the (complementary) views of Malcolm Sparrow.[48] The New South Wales Government's *Guide to Better Regulation* refers to both these sources and endorses the risk-based approach.[49] The document, *Risk-based Compliance* states:

> A risk-based compliance approach enables resources to be targeted to the areas where they are most needed and will prove most effective. It involves a series of steps to identify and assess non-compliance risks and then apply appropriate compliance measures to control these risks.[50]

In turn, the New South Wales DECCW has embraced the general principles set out in the above documents. For example the *Native Vegetation: Compliance*

47 D Stott, 'Environmental Enforcement in the UK' (2009) 11 J Env Mon 470 (emphasis added).

48 M Sparrow, *The Regulatory Craft* (Brookings Institute 2000).

49 The Better Regulation Office, 'Guide to Better Regulation' (Department of Premier and Cabinet, New South Wales Government 2008) see particularly Principle 3, <www.betterregulation.nsw.gov.au> accessed 30 August 2010.

50 The Better Regulation Office, 'Risk-based Compliance' (Department of Premier and Cabinet, New South Wales Government 2008) <www.betterregulation.nsw.gov.au> accessed 3 Sept 2010.

*and Enforcement Policy*, states that:

> A risk-based compliance approach targets the problems that pose the highest environmental and compliance risks. Therefore the regulatory approach will be balanced by a combination of education and information, and for significant breaches the necessary enforcement measures will be taken.[51]

This policy goes on to state that DECCW's response to non-compliance escalates in accordance with the risk that non-compliance poses to the environment and to conservation.[52] The department's intervention strategy is however a hybrid strategy (see Section 2.6 below) as it combines the risk-based approach with Responsive Regulation, the strategy discussed next.

### 2.5 *Responsive Regulation*

In broad terms, Responsive Regulation involves an approach to regulation in which the inspectorate employs a blend of persuasion and coercion, the actual mix being adjusted to the particular circumstances and motivations of the entity with whom they are dealing. The approach is based on a 'tit for tat' response whereby the regulatory agency approaches each organisation in a cooperative, flexible manner, but turns to deterrence if and when the organisation clearly defects from cooperation. Once the organisation begins to cooperate again, the agency does so too.[53]

Although there is widespread endorsement of responsive approaches within academic writings, only two Australian jurisdictions, the Australian Capital Territory (ACT) and the Northern Territory appear to give priority to a strategy of Responsive Regulation, (notwithstanding the widespread endorsement of this approach in academic writing).[54] The ACT Environment Protection Authority's *General Environment Protection Policy* states that this agency's approach to enforcement will be:

- first, to seek to work in partnership with business and the community as 'co-regulators' and educators;
- second, to warn;

51 Department of Environment, Climate Change and Water, 'Native Vegetation: Compliance and Enforcement Strategy' (New South Wales Government 2009) 5.

52 Department of Environment, Climate Change and Water, 'Native Vegetation: Compliance and Enforcement Strategy' (New South Wales Government 2009) 7.

53 I Ayres and J Braithwaite, *Responsive Regulation: Transcending the Deregulation Debate* (OUP 1992).

54 The Environment Protection Authority, 'General Environment Protection Policy' (Department of Territory and Municipal Services, Canberra 2007) 3; Department of Natural Resources, Environment and the Arts, 'Compliance Guidelines' (Northern Territory Government, undated).

- third, to take non-criminal statutory action such as authorisation variations and issuing environment protection orders, together with on-the-spot fines as appropriate and requiring compulsory environmental audits; and
- finally, to consider suspension or cancellation of an agreement or authorisation, or referral to the Director of Public Prosecutions (DPP) for a decision on prosecution, or both, as appropriate.[55]

This approach reflects Responsive Regulation's central operational tool, the 'enforcement pyramid'. This pyramid, which involves advisory and persuasive measures at the bottom, mild administrative sanctions in the middle, and punitive sanctions at the top, is intended to assist in determining what enforcement tools to use in any given case. According to its proponents, regulators should begin by assuming virtue (to which they should respond with cooperation and information), but when their expectations are disappointed, they should respond with progressively punitive and deterrent oriented strategies until the regulated entity conforms.[56]

The Northern Territory agency's *Compliance Guidelines* also suggest a Responsive Regulation strategy. The guidelines state:

> Consistent with the Principles of Compliance, the Office will therefore give priority to cooperative actions that promote compliance such as education and the provision of information and advice. Where this fails or is not appropriate, priority will be given to the use of legislative action such as compliance plans, formal directions, suspension or cancellation of licences, and pollution abatement notices. Consistent with Guidelines issued by the Director of Public Prosecutions, prosecution proceedings may be instituted where there is sufficient evidence and it is in the public interest.[57]

Elements of both Florida's DEP and Victoria's EPA intervention strategies are also suggestive of Responsive Regulation (see Section 2.6 below), as is the New South Wales' DECCW's strategy (see Section 2.4 above). However, Responsive Regulation is not the dominant approach in the policy documents in these jurisdictions.

55 The Environment Protection Authority, 'General Environment Protection Policy' (Department of Territory and Municipal Services, Canberra 2007) 3. Note, however, that this approach is adopted for guidance only and serious cases may justify immediate application of a strict approach to enforcement.

56 Ayres and Braithwaite (n 53).

57 Department of Natural Resources, Environment and the Arts (n 54) 2.

While Responsive Regulation has some superficial resemblance to the Criteria Strategy, the former involves the regulator negotiating an ongoing relationship with a regulatee so as to escalate up or down an enforcement pyramid, in response to the actions and intentions of the regulate.[58] The latter involves an inspector determining what action to take at a particular point in time based on weighing up the relevant criteria. Equally, while Responsive Regulation embraces elements of two other strategies—Advice and Persuasion and Rules and Deterrence (and so might arguably be regarded as a hybrid)—it does so in different circumstances and as part of a single, coherent tit-for-tat strategy.

### 2.6 *Hybrid Strategies*

A number of jurisdictions appear to rely upon more than one of the above strategies, but quite how they do so varies from case to case. What is important about hybrid strategies is the precise mix that is contemplated, for while some mixes are complementary, others are not. This will become apparent from the discussion in Section 4 below.

The South Australian Environment Agency has what in part seems to be a Criteria Strategy but it applies this approach in conjunction with risk-based regulation. Thus, its formal documentation refers to a risk-based approach which is embodied by the Compliance and Enforcement Management Based System (CEMS) which is intended to ensure effective and efficient use of resources, consistency, a comprehensive governance system, continuous improvement and the management of business environment and reputation risk.[59] This involves a six step process which (after categorising a potential non-compliance and validating the original categorisation) focuses on assessment. The assessment prioritises non-compliance by 'generally using a risk-assessment approach, considering a number of categories of risk including environmental and human health and risk to the regulatory regime'.[60] A decision-action plan is then made to address the non-compliance followed by implementation and follow-up.

Another hybrid is the New South Wales' DECCW's combined risk-based and responsive approach to compliance and enforcement. As described earlier, this agency's approach is quintessentially risk-based, with the *Risk-Based*

58 The enforcement pyramid (Ayres and Braithwaite n 53) that involves advisory and persuasive measures at the bottom, mild administrative sanctions in the middle, and punitive sanctions at the top, is intended to assist in determining what enforcement tools to use in any given case. According to its proponents, regulators should begin by assuming virtue (to which they should respond by offering cooperation and information), but when their expectations are disappointed, they respond with progressively punitive and deterrent oriented strategies until the regulated group conforms.

59 Environmental Protection Authority (n 42) s 3.3.

60 ibid s 3.4.

*Compliance* document setting out how such an approach should be applied and describing the series of risk assessment steps.[61] Yet curiously, the following statement (which might easily have come out of a text on Responsive Regulation) is made in the midst of the document:

> Having a combination of measures allows agencies to be responsive to the actions of the regulated party as the agency is able to escalate to harsher measures if a non-complier continues to do the wrong thing after they are given warnings or penalty notices. The availability of severe measures can make persuasive measures more effective. Individuals and businesses are often more likely to respond to persuasive measures knowing that they may be penalised if they do not comply.[62]

This statement is not elaborated in any way in the document, which in all other respects is exclusively risk-based. Nor is any attempt made to explain how Risk-Based and Responsive Regulation can be integrated by inspectors. This question of whether Risk-Based and Responsive Regulation can be effectively integrated in practice is revisited in Section 4 below.

Probably, the most complex hybrid strategy in the sample is EPA Victoria's, as contained in its *Enforcement Policy* and the *Compliance Framework.*[63] The *Enforcement Policy* is primarily descriptive and the *Compliance Framework* does not set out a strategic approach to enforcement. As indicated above, the language used in the *Compliance Framework* suggests that the EPA's approach is oriented to Advice and Persuasion. However, elsewhere in the *Compliance Framework* there are also elements of Responsive Regulation. For example, there is a commitment to 'a clear escalation approach in incidences of non-compliance'.[64] In addition, later parts of the document suggest that EPA Victoria is taking an overarching risk-based approach which extends to the verification and compliance support activities that are to be used to identify and manage compliance risks.[65] While such hybrid strategies are not inherently incoherent or counterproductive, they can only produce efficient and effective policy outcomes if there is considerable thought to ensure that their various components operate in a complementary fashion. There is no indication that these challenges have been given attention in the Victorian approach.

61 The Better Regulation Office (n 50).
62 ibid 12.
63 EPA Victoria, 'Enforcement Policy' (Publication 384.3, July 2006); EPA Victoria, 'Compliance Framework' (Dec 2009).
64 ibid 6.
65 ibid s 6.2.

### *2.7 Intervention Strategies in the Literature and in Practice*

To summarise, many but not all of the strategies that have been advocated in the academic literature can also be found in the implementation strategies of sample agencies. These are: Rules and Deterrence; Advice and Persuasion; the Criteria Strategy; Risk-Based Regulation and Responsive Regulation. Two other strategies—'Smart Regulation' and 'Meta-Regulation'—could be found in the theoretical literature but not in practice in the agencies studied.

As indicated at the outset, the preliminary question of where to allocate resources and which sectors and organisations to target for inspection (*where* to intervene as distinct from *how* to intervene subsequent to resource deployment issues being resolved) is beyond the scope of the article, except insofar as there is an interaction between the two questions (on which see Section 4.1 below).

## 3. Evaluating Different Intervention Strategies

The previous section described five distinctive intervention strategies currently applied by the agencies studied, and several hybrid strategies. This section considers what is known (and particularly what is known empirically) about the strengths and weaknesses of these strategies and also examines the *other* intervention strategies discussed in the academic literature. This examination is a necessary precursor to asking 'what works best?' (Section 4).

Neither Rules-and Deterrence nor Advice and Persuasion have proved to be effective or efficient intervention strategies in isolation. In principle, Rules and Deterrence can play a positive role, especially in reminding organisations to review their compliance efforts and in reassuring them that if they comply, others will not be allowed to 'get away with non-compliance'. Nevertheless, in practice, the impact of 'Rules and Deterrence' approaches is very uneven. Deterrence is, for example, better at influencing rational actors, who consciously balance costs and benefits, than the merely incompetent.[66] However, unless it is carefully targeted, it can actually prove counterproductive—for example, when it prompts organisations and individuals to develop a 'culture of regulatory resistance' or to take a defensive stand, suppressing information

66 R Kagan and J Scholz, 'The Criminology of the Corporation and Regulatory Enforcement Styles' in K Hawkins and J Thomas (eds), *Enforcing Regulation* (Kluwer-Nijhoff 1984); J Braithwaite and T Makkai, 'Testing An Expected Utility Model of Corporate Deviance' (1991) 25 L & Soc'y Rev 7.

and failing to explore the underlying cause of accidents for fear that this information will be used against them in a court of law.[67] Finally, in terms of general deterrence, the evidence shows that regulated business organisations' *perceptions* of legal risk (primarily of prosecution) play a more important role in shaping organisation behaviour than the objective likelihood of legal sanctions.[68] However, even when perceptions of legal risk are high (as distinct from actual risk) this is not necessarily an important motivator of behaviour.[69]

The evidence suggests that Advice and Persuasion, while valuable in encouraging and facilitating those willing to comply with the law to do so, may prove disastrous against those who are not disposed to voluntary compliance.[70] More broadly, Advice and Persuasion may actually *discourage* improved regulatory performance amongst better actors if agencies permit lawbreakers to go unpunished. This is because even those who are predisposed to be 'good apples' may feel at a competitive disadvantage if they invest money in compliance at a time when others are seen to be getting away with non-compliance.[71] In short, a strategy of Advice and Persuasion will have different impacts on organisations according to their motivations. It may be appropriate for environmental leaders but it will not be effective for engaging with reluctant compliers or the recalcitrant, and only effective for the incompetent if it is coupled with education and advice.[72]

Responsive Regulation seeks to overcome the limitations of both Rules and Deterrence, and Advice and Persuasion strategies by taking advantage of the strengths of both, while compensating for their weaknesses. Responsive Regulation has the attraction of being sufficiently flexible to accommodate the various motivations of different organisations, which can drive them to respond on a continuum from leaders who aspire to go substantially beyond compliance with existing regulation, to laggards who are reluctant even to achieve compliance with minimum legal standards, or are simply incompetent in how they go about it.

However, in practice, a responsive approach (which in itself can take a number of different forms[73]) and the related application of an 'enforcement pyramid' involving gradually escalating intervention against regulatees who

67 E Bardach and R Kagan, *Going by the Book: The Problem of Regulatory Unreasonableness* (Temple University Press 1992); N Gunningham, 'Prosecution for OHS Offences: Deterrent or Disincentive?' (2007) 29 Syd LR 359.

68 S Simpson, *Corporate Crime and Social Control* (Cambridge University Press 2002) ch 2.

69 Braithwaite and Makkai (n 66) 35.

70 See for example, N Gunningham, 'Negotiated Non-Compliance: A Case Study of Regulatory Failure' (1987) 9 Law & Pol'y 69.

71 S Shapiro and R Rabinowitz, 'Punishment Versus Cooperation in Regulatory Enforcement: A Case Study of OSHA' (1997) 14 Admin L Rev 713.

72 May and Winter (n 13).

73 See V Nielsen and V Lehmann, 'Are Regulators Responsive?' (2006) 28 Law and Pol'y 395.

do not cooperate, is best suited to the regulation of large organisations with which the regulator has frequent interactions (enabling a strategy of 'tit for tat' to play out). As Johnstone point out:

> . . . for the pyramid to work in the interactive, 'tit for tat' sense envisaged by its proponents, the regulator needs to be able to identify the kind of firm it is dealing with, and the firm needs to know how to interpret the regulator's use of regulatory tools, and how to respond to them.[74] This requires regulators not only to know what is entailed in effective compliance programs and systematic [preventative] approaches, but also to have a sophisticated understanding of the contexts within which organisations operate, and the nature of an organisation's responses to the various enforcement measures.[75]

All this is a tall order. The result is likely to be that the less intense and the less frequent the inspection, and the less knowledge the regulator is able to glean as to the circumstances and motivations of regulated organisations, the less practicable it becomes to apply Responsive Regulation. Where responsiveness *is* applied in practice there is qualified evidence of its virtues[76] although the most recent empirical analysis suggests that Responsive Regulation in its 'tit for tat' form has some effect on behaviour but not on attitudes.[77] There is also evidence to suggest that regulatory inspectors often do not manage to behave responsively (or at least to be fully responsive) when interacting with regulated companies.[78]

Like Responsive Regulation, Risk-Based Regulation provides a strategy for regulators to determine their response to particular regulated entities, it does so primarily on the basis of risk to the environment (though the regulatee's degree of cooperation or responsiveness to the regulator is also a relevant consideration). Risk-Based Regulation has the attraction of enabling regulators to prioritise their regulatory efforts and to maximise cost effectiveness. Nevertheless, a number of serious challenges confront the risk-based strategy—above and beyond the degree of sophistication of the risk assessment and quality of information available on which the assessment and

74 J Black, 'Managing Discretion' paper presented at the Australian Law Reform Commission Conference on *Penalties: Policy and Practice in Government Regulation*, (Sydney, June 2001) 20.

75 R Johnstone, 'From Fiction to Fact- Rethinking OHS Enforcement', National Research Centre for Occupational Health and Safety Regulation, Working Paper 11 (2003) 11: <www.ohs.anu .edu.au> accessed 20 July 2010.

76 For reviews, see R Baldwin and J Black, 'Really Responsive Regulation' (2008) 71 MLR 59.

77 N Lehman and C Parker, 'Testing Responsive Regulation in Regulatory Enforcement' (2009) 3 Reg & Gov'ce 376; see also, P Mascini and EV Wijk, 'Responsive Regulation at the Dutch Food and Consumer Product Safety Authority: An Empirical Assessment of Assumptions Underlying the Theory' (2009) 3 Reg & Gov'ce 27.

78 See Nielsen and Lehmann (n 73).

management of risk can be based. In terms of the contribution of a risk-based approach to intervention strategy, Black and Baldwin point out that while:

> ...risk scoring may provide a very ready basis for detecting high-risk actors...it may offer far less assistance in identifying the modes of intervention that are best attuned to securing compliance...the firm's high risk score does not indicate, in itself, whether the best way to reduce the risks posed by the firm is to use a command-and-control regime applied in, say, a deterrence fashion, or whether an incentive-based, educative, escalating sanctions, or disclosure strategy would prove more effective. The *kind* of intervention required may at best be loosely linked to the level of risk the firm presents.[79]

While this last insight is an important one, there is very little available empirical evidence as to how Risk-Based Regulation (as an intervention strategy distinct from a mechanism for allocating resources) operates in practice. One of the few insights that can be gleaned on this question flows from Julia Black's research on the Australian Prudential Regulation Authority (APRA). She shows how APRA deliberately created a more effective interventionist approach to regulation which involved requiring different inspectoral stances—normal, oversight, mandated improvement and so on—depending upon the organisation's risk profile.[80] The broader questions of how, and how effectively, Meta-Regulation is applied have not been the subject of extensive study, although there is general agreement that much depends on the specialist skills and capabilities of the regulator.

Although the Criteria Strategy (or something closely approximating it) was identified in some of the early writings on regulation[81] it has not subsequently found any notable academic advocates. This is likely because it is essentially a list of different criteria that a field officer can take into account in decision making. As such it is not a coherent intervention strategy in its own right, capable of being developed theoretically or (given the vast discretion it provides to field officers) tested empirically.

The two strategies in the academic literature that were not found in the intervention strategies of any of the sample agencies, are concerned with

79 Black and Baldwin (n 6) 189–190 (emphasis added).

80 Black, 2006 (n 6) 16; J Black, 'The Development of Risk-Based Regulation in Financial Services: Just "Modelling Through"?' in J Black, M Lodge and M Thatcher (eds), *Regulatory Innovation: A Comparative Analysis* (Edward Elgar 2005) 156.

81 See in particular, two early and classic studies: K Hawkins, *Environment and Enforcement* (Oxford University Press 1984) and B Hutter, *Compliance, Regulation and the Environment* (Clarendon Press 1997).

extending the reach of the regulator, rather than choice of intervention mechanisms.[82] Smart Regulation seeks to overcome limitations where interactions between regulators and regulatees are infrequent, by harnessing third parties as surrogate regulators.[83] Those who might fulfil this role include local communities and NGOs bringing complaints or acting to shame recalcitrant businesses into compliance or even business associations acting to police their members. To date, the empirical research on Smart Regulation is supportive but not conclusive.[84] Although 'many governments have adopted the term to provide intellectual justification for a wide range of public-sector regulatory reform initiatives'[85] the success of these initiatives is less studied. Research has focused on occasions where regulators have failed to follow the precepts of Smart Regulation,[86] or on areas where this approach could prove particularly fruitful,[87] rather than on whether existing Smart Regulation initiatives have been demonstrably successful.[88] Perhaps the greatest challenge is coordinating government and third party pressure. While Smart Regulation's three sided enforcement pyramid, which contemplates escalation of pressure by government, business or third parties, seeks to show ways that this might be achieved, its proponents concede that this will not always be possible.[89]

Meta-Regulation also seeks to extend the reach of the regulator and, like Risk-Based Regulation, is both a resource allocation and an intervention strategy. In terms of the latter, the role of the regulator is to oversee the effective development, implementation and monitoring of environmental management and related risk management plans by the regulated organisation itself.

82 Although space precludes further examination, as my colleague Liz Bluff has pointed out to me, intervention strategies themselves are of three broad types. Advice and Persuasion, and Rules and Deterrence are *mechanisms* in themselves and they also define the type of mechanisms the regulator will use in most, if not all, circumstances. Responsive Regulation, the risk-based strategy and the Criteria Strategy are different *ways to determine* which mechanisms the regulator will use in responding to a particular regulatee (from a range of mechanisms from Advice and Persuasion to more deterrent measures (which may be set out in a pyramid)). Smart Regulation and Meta-Regulation are *ways to extend the capacity of the regulator* to enforce by harnessing third parties and/or the regulated entity themselves. But the regulator may still use its range of enforcement mechanisms within the framework of Smart Regulation or Meta-Regulation.

83 See N Gunningham, P Grabosky and D Sinclair, *Smart Regulation: Designing Environmental Policy*, (Oxford University Press 1998).

84 See for example, W Huisman and J Van Erp, 'Smart Regulation and Enforcement of Illegal Disposal of Electric Waste' (2010) 9 Criminology & Pub Pol'y 579.

85 C Tollefson, F Gale and D Haley, *Setting the Standard* (University of British Columbia Press 2008) 257.

86 M Howlett and J Rayner, '(Not so) "Smart Regulation"? Canadian Shellfish Aquaculture Policy and The Evolution of Instrument Choice for Industrial Development' (2004) 28 Marine Pol'y 171.

87 See eg Huisman and Van Erp (n 84); see also the various case studies in N Gunningham and D Sinclair (n 22).

88 For an example of the latter, see Gunningham and Sinclair (n 22).

89 Gunningham, Grabosky and Sinclair (n 83) ch 6.

Meta-Regulation has tended to be used in limited areas to which its application is particularly suited. Most notably, in the guise of a 'safety case' regime, it has been used to ensure health, safety and environment protection in the operations of major hazard facilities such as offshore oil rigs.[90] The highly targeted use of Meta-Regulation is in large part a consequence of limited circumstances in which it is likely to be effective. It requires specialist, high quality regulators to oversee the risk management strategies of the regulated organisation, and highly sophisticated and motivated regulated organisations to develop and implement such strategies successfully and to regulate themselves effectively. At the very least, a receptive corporate culture is a necessary, albeit not a sufficient condition, for its success.[91] Overall there is evidence[92] that Meta-Regulation has a positive impact on corporate behaviour in targeted organisations, although relatively little is known about how this comes about.[93]

Finally, with regard to both Smart Regulation and Meta-Regulation, critics might suggest that these *strategies are not enforcement strategies per se* and for this reason should not have been included in the present analysis.[94] Certainly, as indicated earlier, both these strategies are concerned with extending the reach of the regulator, rather than just with the choice of intervention mechanisms and Meta-Regulation, like Risk-Based Regulation, is both a resource allocation and an intervention strategy. However, there is merit in including them because, notwithstanding that both are ways to extend the capacity of the regulator to enforce (by harnessing third parties and/or the regulated entity themselves) they are intimately connected with 'pure' intervention strategies and the regulator may still use its range of enforcement mechanisms within the framework of Smart Regulation or Meta-Regulation. The reason that such strategies were not identified among sample agencies was not a 'category error', but, rather, because they had not seen reason to invoke them. Had the sample included major hazard facilities (with whom Meta-Regulation is a popular intervention strategy) it would certainly have been identified, as would Smart Regulation had the sample been,

90 On Meta-Regulation generally, see in particular C Parker, *The Open Corporation: Effective Self-Regulation and Democracy* (CUP 2002). For a review of the 'safety case' literature see N Gunningham, 'Designing OHS Standards: Process, Safety Case and Best Practice' (2007) 2 Pol'y and Prac in H'lth and Saf'y 3.

91 N Gunningham and D Sinclair, 'Organizational Trust and the Limits of Management-Based Regulation' (2009) 43 L & Soc'y Rev 865.

92 For a review see N Gunningham, *Mine Safety: Law, Regulation and Policy* (Federation Press 2007) ch 3.

93 Meta-Regulation's image has been tarnished by its failure (as applied in the UK by the Financial Services Authority) to address the failings that led to the Global Financial Crisis. This, however, may be more a lesson about how to handle systemic risk and the dangers of 'light handed' regulation than about inherent defects in Meta-Regulation. See generally Black and Baldwin (n 6).

94 I am grateful to an anonymous referee for making precisely this point.

for example, of occupational health and safety agencies (many of whom actively seek to harness third parties such as trade unions, as surrogate regulators).

## 4. Where Next?

Against a backdrop of multiple intervention strategies, with differing strengths and weaknesses, this section turns to normative questions in terms of designing policy. Is there a need to integrate resource allocation and intervention strategy, and if so how? What should be the role of hybrid intervention strategies? Is there a single 'best practice' strategy, or does the most appropriate approach depend on the context? How should discretion be constrained? Is it possible to balance effectiveness and legitimacy and, if not, how should the tension between them be resolved?

### *4.1 Achieving Integration: Resource Allocation, Intervention and Hybrid Strategies*

While the focus of this article is on intervention strategy rather than resource allocation strategy (in other words how to intervene rather than where to intervene), in the case of some intervention strategies it is important to consider the nexus between the two strategies. In some cases a link is assumed where none exists, while in others there is a relationship but one more complex than is often appreciated.

The assumption of a connection between resource allocation and intervention strategies, where none actually exists, is most apparent in the practices of the UK Environment Agency. This agency (reinforced by the Hampton Report[95]) takes the view that risk-based regulation approximates 'best practice' in terms of both resource allocation *and* intervention strategy.[96] However, almost all the attention (and all the available evidence) concerns the former (for example, risk as a criteria for targeting inspections and allocating resources between different industries or types of firms), and it is either simply asserted or tacitly assumed that a risk-based approach will also be the most efficient and effective intervention strategy. This is not necessarily the case. Indeed, a number of other regulators rely on risk-based targeting while adopting a very different intervention strategy. As the OECD has pointed out:

> How closely the regulators' risk assessments are linked into a particular enforcement approach is a significant point of variation between the

95 Hampton (n 3).
96 See UK Environment Agency (n 45).

> different risk-based frameworks. Many regulators have enforcement policies or compliance strategies. These may categorise firms on the basis of their attitude to compliance . . . The enforcement strategies may themselves be risk-based in that they incorporate an assessment of the likelihood of success of formal enforcement action . . . *Often, however, there is no direct link between the risk category of a firm and the enforcement strategy that the regulator will adopt.*[97]

In other cases, there *is* a link between allocation and intervention strategy but its precise nature is strategy specific. For example, Meta-Regulation relies heavily on an organisation's internal management controls which the regulators will then oversee. This is in effect a resource allocation strategy, which pragmatically takes account of the fact that regulators do not have the resources to do anything else.[98] But what happens when an organisation fails to self-regulate effectively? As discussed, in a rare case study Black has shown how one agency deliberately created a more effective interventionist approach to regulation which involved requiring different inspectoral stances depending upon the organisation's risk profile.[99] This case suggests the capacity for a Meta-Regulatory intervention strategy (relying on risk profiles) to be effectively connected to a strategy of Responsive Regulation applying a pyramid of enforcement mechanisms.[100] Specifically, the combination of Meta- and Responsive Regulation enables more and escalating enforcement responses to be invoked depending on the degree of cooperation of the regulated organisation, with cooperation resulting in de-escalation down the enforcement pyramid and the converse response to resistance.[101]

This example raises more directly the role of hybrid intervention strategies. As we mentioned in Section 2, a number of jurisdictions have adopted a combination of two or more different strategies. They have done so, for the most part, with little apparent attention as to whether such hybrids are complementary or counterproductive.

In South Australia, for example, the policy question is whether or to what extent a Criteria and a Risk-Based Strategy can be successfully integrated. It would appear that the answer is: it all depends. If risk trumps other criteria to the extent of any inconsistency between them, then those criteria are rendered

97 *Risk and Regulatory Policy: Improving the Governance of Risk* (OECD 2009) 215 <http://www.oecd.org/document/60/0,3746,en_21571361_38695295_44840828_1_1_1_1,00.html> accessed 22 March 2011 (emphasis added).

98 Black and Baldwin (n 6).

99 ibid 16; Black 2005 (n 80).

100 See also J Braithwaite 'Meta Risk Management and Responsive: Regulation for Tax System Integrity' (2003) 25 Law & Pol'y 1.

101 Braithwaite (n 100).

meaningless by the introduction of risk. This seems unlikely to have been the intent of policy makers. If, on the other hand, risk is simply one more factor to be taken into account (with no indication as to how conflict between different factors will be resolved) then the indeterminacy of the criteria approach is not addressed and the role of risk may be a modest one, perhaps at most tipping the balance in cases that otherwise are finely weighed between different factors.

Another combination (most readily identified in New South Wales) is to combine Risk-Based with Responsive Regulation. It is understandable that regulators should be tempted to try and integrate these two strategies, given that they have been so influential both in theory and in shaping the behaviour of regulatory agencies.[102] Nevertheless, combining them can give rise to serious problems. A risk-based strategy implies that the higher the risk to the environment, the tougher the enforcement action that should be taken, with past experience of the individual operator being taken into account as one indicator of future risk. In contrast, under Responsive Regulation the regulator should approach the regulated entity assuming virtue and certainly without an evaluation of risk shaping its decision as to the appropriate form of intervention. Its normative basis is also quite different from that of Risk-Based Regulation. Not least, Responsive Regulation appeals to the better nature of the regulatee and appears (and is) just, in a way that Risk-Based Regulation, based as it is on utilitarian assumptions, is not.

### *4.2 'One size fits all' Intervention Strategies May be Inappropriate*[103]

One striking feature of the intervention strategies described above is that they assume that a single strategy is appropriate to all.[104] Certainly, some of these strategies are flexible enough to take account of different motivations. For example, a Criteria Strategy usually includes culpability as one of its criteria but, as we will see, provides no coherent means for choosing between different criteria. In a far more coherent way, Responsive Regulation also take account of different motivations as part of the 'tit for tat' interaction, and Risk-Based

102 Hampton (n 3) and H Van de Bunt, J Van Erp and K Van Wingerde, 'Hoe Stefig is de Pyramid van Braithwaite? (How Strong is Braithwaite's Pyramid?)' (2009) 49 Tijdschrift voor Criminologies 225 (arguing that almost every department in the Netherlands has implemented Responsive Regulation in their strategy).

103 I am grateful to Christine Parker for her insights in writing this section.

104 Although a Criteria Strategy might claim that its listed criteria for decision making could address different circumstances and motivations (though they do not provide any mechanism for doing so), Responsive Regulation that its enforcement pyramid takes account of different motivations (they do, but still as part of a single escalatory strategy) and Smart Regulation that different instruments and actors need to be harnessed in different situations (a more credible claim, but none of the sample agencies had embraced Smart Regulation).

Regulation regards motivation as one important risk factor. Even so, each of these strategies prescribes a single approach—whether it is the application of criteria, escalating up an enforcement pyramid, or taking action on the basis of risk—for all regulatees in all circumstances. In short, none of the strategies described recognises that different intervention strategies might be appropriate in different circumstances.

This is unfortunate, because there is unlikely to be a single identifiable 'best practice' approach that should be applied to all duty holders 'across the board'. Rather, because different duty holders confront different external pressures, and have different skills, capabilities and motivations, a best practice intervention strategy needs to invoke different mechanisms in different contexts. Recent academic work (for example that of Valerie Braithwaite on regulatory postures[105] and John Braithwaite's on the 'new' enforcement pyramid[106]) is increasingly seeking to come to terms with the importance of different motivations and what this means for regulation.

However, only very rarely have regulatory agencies sought to address these issues. In one exceptional case, Black has shown how the Australian Prudential Regulation Authority has deliberately created a more pre-emptive and effective interventionist approach to regulation which involves requiring different inspectoral stances—normal, oversight, mandated improvement and so on—depending upon the organisation's risk profile.[107]

Environmental agencies, like the vast majority of regulatory agencies generally, seem not to have considered these issues at all, yet they deal with a wide range of different individuals and businesses, and have quite diverse relationships with them. Accordingly, the nature of the relationship between the regulator and regulatee can and should depend substantially on the characteristics of the latter and the resources available to the former.

For example, in the case of reluctant compliers and the recalcitrant, it is only if the self-regulation and risk management of the industry is closely scrutinised by government with the threat of more direct intervention if it fails, that an enterprise is likely to take effective action. And in the case of industry leaders, Meta-Regulation will only work if the inspectorate shifts its emphasis from conventional inspection to audit and oversight of the management system and risk assessment and management.

To illustrate, an environmental regulator could usefully think about its intervention strategy in different terms depending on: (i) whether the obligation-holder has self-interest in good environmental performance that

105 V Braithwaite, *Defiance in Taxation and Governance: Resisting and Dismissing Authority in a Democracy* (Edward Elgar 2009).

106 J Braithwaite, T Makkai and V Braithwaite, *Regulating Aged Care: Ritualism and the New Pyramid* (Edward Elgar 2007). See also, the typology set out in N Gunningham, R Kagan and D Thornton, *Shades of Green: Business, Regulation and Environment* (Stanford UP 2003).

107 See Black 2006 (n 6).

goes beyond regulatory requirements; and (ii) the degree of environmental risk posed by the organisation's operations. This might result in four main categories reflecting whether the regulator will have an ongoing relationship with the obligation-bearer and the type of engagement:

(i) *High Performers:* Organisations and perhaps some individuals who are highly motivated to innovate to go beyond compliance to develop continuous improvement in environmental stewardship and sustainability. Organisations and individuals in this group might have licences and other obligations as well, but their 'beyond compliance' activities should be treated differently by the regulator.
(ii) *Environmental Strategists:* Large, sophisticated organisations with self-interest in good environmental performance which require a licence, but which can also be motivated to go beyond compliance to some extent—for example, large reputation-sensitive companies which need to protect their 'social licence to operate'. This is the underpinning for 'two track' regulation designed to provide rewards and incentives for improved compliance and high environmental performance. Under this approach, enterprises with certain environmental credentials are offered a choice between a continuation of traditional forms of regulation on the one hand, and a more flexible approach (the central pillars of which are usually the adoption of an environmental management system, periodic internal environmental audits, and community participation) on the other.[108]
(iii) *Reactive Licensees*: Other organisations with the capacity to cause major environmental harm—put broadly, other licensed premises.
(iv) *Low Risk Enterprises:* Non-licensed premises which do not have the potential to cause major environmental harm, including many small and medium sized organisations, and individuals.

Having made this distinction, a different intervention strategy, or combination of strategies, might be applied for each of the four groups. High Performers, for example, might lend themselves to Meta-Regulation, as these organisations would be motivated to ensure the specialised skills, knowledge and risk management systems to self-regulate. Indeed this group might help the regulator to identify gaps and potential improvements in its own environmental policies and tools.

Environmental Strategists would also be a candidate for Meta-Regulation coupled with Responsive Regulation and Smart Regulation. This approach would enable the regulator to engage with these large organisations with complex environmental problems by inducing them to acquire the specialised

108 See eg the Wisconsin Green Tier Model (Wisconsin Department of Natural Resources 2000).

skills and knowledge to self-regulate, while also ensuring external scrutiny. Underpinning Meta-Regulation with a form of Responsive Regulation would provide a mechanism to manage the risk of backsliding. Meta-Regulation and Responsive Regulation are a complementary combination for reasons argued above. Smart Regulation's insights about the capacity to harness third parties as surrogate regulators might also be taken into account. Significantly, large reputation-sensitive companies confront powerful pressures from concerned local communities (and sometimes from broader-based environmental NGOs) and must protect their 'social licence'.[109] Empowering third parties to bring pressure to bear has sometimes proved a highly effective strategy in these circumstances.[110]

Reactive Licensees are a candidate for Responsive Regulation coupled with risk-based resource allocation and targeting by the regulator to determine the extent of performance verification, reporting and monitoring activity required. Enforcement would be escalated, in accordance with the principles of Responsive Regulation, in the case of failure to comply. The responsive approach would be preferred to a risk-based approach because it provides considerably greater guidance as to the appropriate regulatory response. To the extent that regulatees in this group are reputation sensitive, Responsive Regulation might be strengthened by invoking Smart Regulation's strategy of harnessing surrogate regulators.

In contrast, the regulator is unlikely to need to have regular contact with Low Risk Enterprises because of the lower potential for environmental harm and smaller scale of these organisations' operations. Responsive Regulation is unlikely to be appropriate because the regulator's infrequent contact with such organisations means there is little history on which to base a responsive interaction. Likewise, a risk-based intervention strategy is inappropriate, as risk assessment by the regulator is impractical in these circumstances, the regulator having too little contact and too little information on which to base such an assessment (although of course risk assessment has been used at an earlier stage in terms of determining *where* to intervene). In terms of regulating Small and Medium Sized Enterprises (SMEs) in particular, a different approach might include: facilitating self-inspection and self-audit; harnessing surrogate regulators, such as local Councils or community groups, to report any environmental concerns that do arise; and innovative enforcement, such as publicity campaigns preceding enforcement blitzes targeted to specific industry sectors, and sanctioning and review of the group (iv) status of laggards.[111]

109 See Gunningham, Kagan and Thornton (n 106).
110 See Gunningham and Sinclair (n 22) chs 6–9.
111 For a more developed argument as to how best to regulate SMEs, see Gunningham and Sinclair (n 22) ch 2.

### *4.3 Constraining Discretion*

A further policy issue of considerable practical importance is how to ensure that inspectors exercise their considerable discretion[112] in a manner consistent with agency strategy. How, for example, can discretion be constrained without imposing mechanistic rules and driving inspectors to 'go by the book'? This question has been the subject of substantial research, although this has not generated anything approaching consensus.[113] At the very least, there is broad agreement that channelling field officers' behaviour in accordance with agency strategy is a major challenge.[114]

There are particular problems constraining discretion under a Criteria Strategy. While most sample jurisdictions applying a Criteria Strategy do not appear to have recognised the need to constrain discretion as a particular problem, there are a number of mechanisms that might be invoked to do so. Different regulators have approached the challenge of inspector discretion by different means. In the USA, some regulators have taken a narrow and legalistic approach, insisting that inspectors follow highly detailed formal rules.[115] Elsewhere, regulators have variously required that enforcement decisions be taken (or overseen) by senior rather than field officers, made subject to processes of internal and external review, or that field officers follow a formal model which ensures that they take into consideration a range of issues before making a decision.[116] None of these approaches is without its problems.

One approach with more promise is to develop a decision-making framework to facilitate the balancing or resolution of conflicting factors. For example, the UK Health and Safety Executive's *Enforcement Management Model* (EMM) provides a practical, step-by-step decision-making process for individual inspectors and increases the consistency of enforcement policy and practice. An alternative approach is the United States Sentencing Guidelines[117] which seeks to structure but not eliminate discretion by allocating a numerical value

112 As to variation in the actions of inspectors see R Kagan, 'Regulatory Enforcement' in DH Rosenbloom and RD Schwartz (eds), *Handbook of Regulation and Administrative Law* (Marcel Decker 1994) 383; Mascini and Wijk (n 77); and May and Winter (n 13).

113 Compare eg Black (n 11); May and Winter (n 13); Pautz (n 11).

114 May and Winter (n 13).

115 E Bardach and R Kagan, *Going by the Book: The Problem of Regulatory Unreasonableness* (Temple University Press 1992).

116 For example, the UK Health and Safety Executive, *Enforcement Management Model* <www.hse.gov.uk/enforce/emm.pdf> accessed 5 Oct 2010.

117 The Guidelines determine sentences based primarily on two factors: the conduct associated with the offence (the offence conduct, which produces the offence level); and the defendant's criminal history (the criminal history category). The Sentencing Table in the Guidelines Manual shows the relationship between these two factors; for each pairing of offence level and criminal history category, the Table specifies a sentencing range, in months, within which the court may sentence a defendant. See United States Sentencing Committee, *2010 Federal Sentencing Guidelines Manual and Supplement* (2010) <http://www.ussc.gov/Guidelines/2010.guidelines/ManualPDF/Chapter.5.pdf> accessed 5 April 2011, Ch 5.

to individual criteria. The approach has been relied on to structure prosecutorial discretion in that jurisdiction.

### 4.4 *Maintaining Legitimacy*

Maintaining legitimacy is of particular importance for regulatory agencies even where this conflicts with what might otherwise be judged to be the most appropriate strategy. This is for the simple reason that proposals that cannot gain political acceptance are unlikely to be adopted no matter how effective they may be. As Haines points out, drawing from her own empirical work, the value of regulatory innovations 'can be understood in light of not only their success at reducing risk . . . but also their capacity to develop and retain legitimacy within the broader political arena'.[118] Put differently, 'political needs and community expectations together shape both what is seen as harmful and what is an adequate response'.[119] Elsewhere she refers to this in terms of the importance of dealing with not merely actuarial or technical risk (for example of an environmental incident) but also with sociocultural or political risk.[120]

The point for present purposes is that legitimacy trumps effectiveness and that implementation strategies must take account of this reality. Unsurprisingly, there is evidence that they already do so, though not necessarily in an overt way. For example, when the Chief Prosecutor of the UK Environment Agency states that 'occurrences categorised as being of *major* effect will normally lead to a prosecution'[121] it is arguable that the agency is classifying the effect in terms of what has already happened and determining their response in that way. If so, then what is being assessed is not future risk but the seriousness of past harm. This is not the purported aim of a risk-based strategy but it does enable the agency to assess its political or reputational risk, prosecuting in circumstances where it is deemed necessary to address this risk.[122]

Similarly, it may well be that legitimacy-sensitive regulators that report to Ministers who are themselves sensitive to industry pressure, are better able to justify their actions if they are proportionate to the seriousness of the violation and culpability of the regulatee, reflect the history of offending, and degree of

118 F Haines, 'Regulatory Failures and Regulatory Solutions: A Characteristic Analysis of the Aftermath of a Disaster' (2009) 34 Law and Soc Inq 34.
119 ibid 36.
120 F Haines, A Sutton and C Platania-Phung, 'It's All About Risk Isn't It? Science, Politics, Public Opinion and Regulatory Reform' (2008) 10 FJLR 435.
121 Stott (n 47) (emphasis added).
122 Similarly, see what Fels refers to the constraints imposed by 'the authorizing environment: what may be done'; A Fels, 'A Model of Antitrust Regulatory Strategy' (2010) 41 Loy U Chi L J 519.

environmental damage – core ingredients of the Criteria Strategy described earlier.

The broader point is an important one and has implications for many of the intervention strategies described above, and not just for Risk-Based Regulation. Consider Responsive Regulation, under which the regulator is expected to intervene initially at the bottom of an enforcement pyramid (assuming virtue on the part of the regulatee) and only escalate to enforcement action if this assumption proves incorrect. There may well be circumstances where the regulator cannot credibly maintain this strategy in the face of threats to its legitimacy (in terms of political risk and/or community pressure). For example, suppose there has been a major incident or 'near miss' involving an industrial facility situated close to a residential area. Here there will be considerable pressure to take decisive and immediate action, and to do so in ways which are visible to external audiences—the most obvious being the initiation of a prosecution—with the consequence that the matter will be publicly adjudicated. Even if there is evidence that the regulatee had very limited culpability (their past record being exemplary, the causes of the incident not being reasonably anticipated) then the need to preserve legitimacy will be paramount.

For the regulator who wishes to maintain the trust of a regulatee who is a 'good apple', the situation is a challenging one. Their difficulties may be lessened if the relevant compliance and enforcement policy directs them to take advice, persuasion or enforcement action in specified circumstances[123] (in which case they can legitimately plead that the decision is out of their hands). They may also seek to preserve their relationship with the regulatee by exercising discretion as to what enforcement action they take (for example, prosecuting for a less serious offence or agreeing on a 'reasonable' penalty). By whatever means they try to maintain their relationship with the regulatee, their need to maintain legitimacy in the eyes of the broader community and to minimise political risk will almost certainly prove more compelling.

## 5. Conclusion

Implementation is 'the nitty-gritty of environmental regulation'[124] and every bit as important as its design. For this reason, it should be given considerable emphasis by environmental agencies. Yet in some respects this is not the case. Sophisticated strategies are now available for targeting enforcement activities and the allocation of scarce resources (the 'where' question), but when it

123 See eg UK Environment Agency (n 46) 2. However, in judicial review terms, while public authorities will be expected to follow their policies, they normally are also expected not to follow them blindly.

124 A Hayes, 'Making Things Stick: Enforcement and Compliance' (1998) 14 Ox Rev Econ Pol'y 61.

comes to *how* best to intervene in the affairs of regulated entities, current practice leaves much to be desired.

An analysis of the compliance and enforcement policies of a sample of regulatory agencies reveals a considerable diversity of approaches. Some of them (as in the case of Criteria Strategies) are incoherent and provide almost unconstrained discretion to field officers. Others (particularly some hybrids) are internally inconsistent and/or underdeveloped in that they do not fully embrace a particular strategy. Nor do regulatory agencies appear to have given much attention to empirical findings regarding what sorts of strategies work and why, and even less to the available academic literature on the subject. To say the least, this is unfortunate in terms of its implications for environmental outcomes.

This article has sought to advance the debate as to *how* to intervene by arguing, contrary to conventional wisdom, that rather than seeking to identify a single intervention strategy, what is needed is to consciously apply different intervention strategies according to their suitability to particular regulatory contexts. Different types of regulatees confront different external pressures and have different skills, capabilities and motivations. The environmental risks posed by different operations are also intrinsically different. Accordingly, best practice may mean applying different intervention strategies in different circumstances.

This also embraces (as illustrated in Section 4.2) the development of hybrid approaches incorporating two or more strategies, to invoke the strengths of one strategy while compensating for its weaknesses by integrating it with another complementary strategy. However, not all combinations are complementary. Some lead to incoherence and inconsistency, and a number of hybrids adopted by sample agencies fall into precisely this category. Hybrids can only represent best practice where their structure ensures the complementarity of their different components and the coherence of the overall design.

Finally, it is important to recognise the practical constraints in terms of developing best practice intervention strategies. In particular, there is often a tension between effectiveness and legitimacy. In the necessary trade-off between these criteria, it was argued that the need for the regulator to maintain its legitimacy is paramount. Accordingly, there will be occasions where the rigorous application of a particular strategy, such as Risk-Based or Responsive Regulation, must be compromised to accommodate political risk and the expectations of communities. Even, so, there is an opportunity to advance beyond the status quo in most jurisdictions and to markedly improve environmental outcomes by developing and implementing more nuanced and context specific intervention strategies.

# [16]

*Journal of Environmental Law* **24**:2 © The Author 2012. Published by Oxford University Press.

doi:10.1093/jel/eqs005 Advance Access published on 2 May 2012

# Criminal or Administrative Law to Protect the Environment? Evidence from Western Europe

Michael G. Faure and Katarina Svatikova*

## Abstract

This article studies the scope of criminal and administrative law enforcement of environmental violations in four Western European jurisdictions. The Flemish Region and the United Kingdom have, until mid-2009, largely relied only on criminal sanctioning while administrative sanctions, which have also been in use since mid-2009, have already been widely used in the Netherlands and Germany. This article considers whether, given a fixed budget for the relevant national environment agency, single (criminal) or multiple (criminal and administrative) enforcement instruments are adequate to induce compliance. The fact that administrative proceedings are less strict and more informal than criminal proceedings suggests that the imposition of administrative sanctions is a relatively cheaper alternative. Therefore, in case of environmental violations, it is cost-effective to complement criminal law enforcement by administrative law rather than to allow for a single (criminal) sanctioning instrument. Complementary use of these two instruments might lead to additional deterrence. Data is presented to illustrate this argument.

* Michael Faure, Rotterdam Institute of Law & Economics (RILE), Erasmus University Rotterdam, Postbus 1738, 3000 DR Rotterdam, The Netherlands (michael.faure@maastrichtuniversity.nl); METRO Institute, Faculty of Law, University of Maastricht (www.personeel.unimaas.nl/michael.faure), The Netherlands. Katarina Svatikova, Rotterdam Institute of Law & Economics (RILE), Erasmus University Rotterdam, currently working for ECORYS B.V., Watermanweg 44, 3067 GG, Rotterdam, The Netherlands (katarina.svatikova@ecorys.com).
The authors would like to thank the participants of the workshop 'Beyond the Economics of Crime' in Heidelberg, March 2009, particularly John List and Daan van Soest. We are equally grateful to the participants at the meeting of the European Association of Law and Economics (September 2009). Special thanks to Sandra Rousseau and Carole Billiet for their useful comments, as well as to John Klick, Vincent Buskens and to two anonymous referees of this journal. The usual disclaimers apply.

Keywords: administrative sanctions, administrative fines, criminal sanctions, enforcement

## 1. Introduction

Recent Law and Economics scholarship has paid attention to the question of why criminal law is used at all for certain harmful activities.[1] On the basis of this literature, criteria have been developed indicating when, from an economic perspective, criminalisation would be warranted. These criteria point to the use of the criminal law only under limited circumstances because this instrument is costly for society (in terms of relatively high enforcement costs) as well as for the offender (in terms of relatively severe, legal and non-legal, sanctions). Thus, it could be implied that only for certain, usually serious violations, should criminal sanctions be applied. These insights have been applied to environmental law as well.[2]

Even though Law and Economics recommends a relatively modest role for criminal law to protect the environment, in practice (until recently), in some European jurisdictions, such as the Flemish Region and the UK, one could still observe a large reliance on the criminal law, at least in written legislation. However, Law and Economics scholarship has pointed to the fact that this leads *de facto* to many cases where the criminal law is effectively not applied at all as a result of which no sanctions follow. This results in underdeterrence.[3] Despite this drawback of criminal law enforcement, the European trend remains intent on its use as the primary enforcement instrument. After various unsuccessful attempts, Europe promulgated Directive 2008/99/EC of 19 November 2008 on the protection of the environment through criminal law.[4] This Directive harmonises and strengthens the role of criminal law in environmental protection, obliging the Member States to enforce a large number of environmental directives through criminal law. The type and the level of sanctions are at the discretion of the Member States with one condition: the

1 Roger Bowles, Michael G Faure and Nuno Garoupa, 'The Scope of Criminal Law and Criminal Sanctions: An Economic View and Policy Implications' (2008) 35 Journal of Law and Society 389; Anthony Ogus, 'Enforcing Regulation: Do We Need the Criminal Law?' in Hans Sjogren and Goran Skogh (eds), *New Perspectives on Economic Crime* (Edward Elgar 2004) 42.

2 Anthony Ogus and Carolyn Abbot, 'Sanctions for Pollution: Do We Have the Right Regime?' (2002) 14 Journal of Environmental Law 283.

3 ibid.

4 Directive 2008/99/EC of the European Parliament and of the Council of 19 November 2008 on the protection of the environment through criminal law (Criminal Law Directive) [2008] OJ L328/28.

sanctions implemented into national laws have to be effective, dissuasive and proportional.[5] This is in sharp contrast to the trend in several European countries, where the use of administrative fines is gaining more and more importance. This opens up the interesting question of whether relying so strongly on criminal law (as the EU Directive does) is effective and proportional.

Therefore, this article studies the enforcement of environmental violations in the Flemish Region, the Netherlands, Germany and England and Wales, particularly in so far as the divide between administrative and criminal law enforcement is concerned. The degree to which criminal sanctioning is used will be investigated and whether this is adequate to enforce environmental violations considered. Further consideration is given to whether an additional instrument, such as administrative fines, is necessary for a range of violations that do not merit criminal prosecution but merit enforcement. The reason for choosing these jurisdictions is that the Flemish Region and the UK, until mid-2009, largely relied on criminal sanctions, whereas Germany and the Netherlands used (and continue to use) administrative sanctions as the main enforcement tool for environmental regulations. Since each system is different, we derive more insights by looking at four jurisdictions rather than only two. As we have data for England and Wales only, we will be disregarding Scotland in this article. In 2008–09, administrative fines were introduced both in the Flemish Region and the UK. By administrative law enforcement, we mean that the environmental agency itself has the power to impose an administrative fine (Germany) or an administrative order which results in penalisation through a fine if it is not complied with (the Netherlands). The latter could be seen as a quasi-administrative fine, even though the primary purpose is to stop the harmful activity. Neither in the Flemish Region nor in the UK until recently, did the environmental agency possess the power to impose an administrative fine (with a few exceptions).[6]

The main difference between an administrative and criminal sanctioning system is that administrative fines are easier to administer and impose (and are therefore presumed less costly) than criminal sanctions because of the more complicated criminal procedure.[7] We want to examine whether, given a fixed budget for environmental agencies, a single (criminal) or multiple (criminal and administrative) enforcement instruments are more effective to induce

5 There is still significant discussion at EU and Member State level about what exactly this means. For details see Michael G Faure, 'Effective, Proportional and Dissuasive Penalties in the Implementation of the Environmental Crime and Ship Source Pollution Directives: Questions and Challenges' (2010) 19 European Energy and Environmental Law Review 256.

6 Our main focus in the article is on administrative monetary penalties (fines) since these are similar to criminal fines in the sense that they are punitive and monetary. However, we also have some data on other (non-monetary) administrative penalties (such as notices). We also discuss these so as to cover administrative sanctioning as a whole.

7 Michael G Faure, Anthony Ogus and Niels Philipsen, 'Curbing Consumer Financial Losses: The Economics of Regulatory Enforcement' (2009) 31 Law & Policy 161.

compliance. The fact that administrative proceedings tend to be less strict and more informal than criminal proceedings, and the environmental agency itself imposes the administrative sanction (no further step to the public prosecutor) suggests that the imposition of administrative sanctions, including an administrative fine, is relatively cheaper. Therefore, the working hypothesis is that, in case of environmental violations, it is cost-effective to complement criminal law enforcement with administrative law enforcement that would allow for the imposition of administrative fines, rather than only allowing for a single (criminal) sanctioning instrument.

Complementary use of these two instruments might lead to additional deterrence. Available empirical data will illustrate our argument. Since the data derives from different sources and is rather limited, it does not allow us to engage in a thorough comparative empirical study of enforcement practices in the four jurisdictions. Nonetheless, despite the limitations of the data, it is still important to work with what we currently have rather than wait until more robust statistics become available. For policy relevant research, timely analysis with indicative conclusions, even if based on less precise data is important, since policies might become outdated by the time complete enforcement statistics become available, if at all. The stylised facts indicate that the number of criminal cases dismissed by the prosecutor is, on average, relatively high vis-à-vis the number of environmental violations. Administrative sanctioning might be able to deal with a part of these dismissals at a relatively low cost.

The article is structured as follows: first we briefly sketch the theoretical framework on enforcement of environmental law, mainly paying attention to the choice between enforcement through administrative or criminal law (Section 2); next we sketch experiences with both enforcement systems in four countries (Section 3) and we engage in a critical comparative analysis (Section 4). Our concluding remarks focus on some of the consequences of our findings for enforcement theory and current EU policy.

## 2. Theoretical Framework

### 2.1 *Optimal Enforcement: Inducing Compliance*

The economic approach to law enforcement goes back to the seminal paper by Becker who, using a cost–benefit model, argues that a violation can be deterred when the expected costs of a violation are higher than the expected benefits.[8]

8 Even though this Becker model is still often used as a starting point for the economic analysis of crime policy, there are of course also other approaches (see eg John Braithwaite, *Crime, Shame and Reintegration* (CUP 1989)) holding that non-compliance may not be an intentional decision but for example the result of ignorance. We address the importance of those alternative explanations below in Section 4.

Traditionally, the Becker hypothesis has been applied mainly to the incentives created by the criminal justice system. For the purposes of this article, we presume that the Becker model can be applied to incentives provided by the administrative sanctioning system. The expected costs of a violation refer to the expected sanction (ES) a violator might face when caught. The ES is determined by multiplying the probability of detection and sanctioning (*p*) with the severity of the actual sanction (*S*).[9]

$$ES = p \times S$$

Based on this deterrence hypothesis, the rich and abundant literature on economics of crime and law enforcement suggests that potential offenders respond to the incentives created by the criminal justice system and crime rates hence *inter alia* depend on risks and benefits of crime.[10] The goal of policy making according to the economic framework is to induce compliance at lowest cost. Assuming that potential criminals are rational utility maximisers who base their decisions to commit or not to commit a crime on an expected utility calculation, they will comply with the law as long as the benefits of compliance outweigh the costs of compliance. As such, polluters are expected to comply with environmental regulations if the probability of being apprehended and sanctioned coupled with the penalty imposed will be sufficiently high. Even though the reality shows that enforcement tends to be rather low in terms of the number of sanctions imposed,[11] large numbers of companies nevertheless comply. This phenomenon is in the literature referred to as the 'Harrington paradox'.[12] Many violations are also settled out of court, or there is an agreement made not to impose a sanction for return to compliance.[13] In addition, in some cases no sanction is imposed because the violation took place out of ignorance. In those cases, education may prove more effective than sanctioning.[14] However, this does not render the question of the need for adequate enforcement policies irrelevant.

9 Gary S Becker, 'Crime and Punishment: An Economic Approach' (1968) 76 Journal of Political Economy 169.

10 Nuno Garoupa, 'The Theory of Optimal Law Enforcement' (1997) 11 Journal of Economic Surveys 267.

11 Ogus and Abbot (n 2); Carole M Billiet and Sandra Rousseau, 'Zachte rechtshandhaving in het bestuurlijke handhavingsspoor: de inspectiebeslissing en het voortraject van bestuurlijke sancties. Een rechtseconomische analyse' (Soft law enforcement in the administrative enforcement track: the inspection decision and the preliminary process of administrative sanctions. A law and economics analysis) (2005) 1 Tijdschrift voor Milieurecht (Journal of Environmental Law) 2; Michael G Faure and Katarina Svatikova, 'Enforcement of Environmental Law in the Flemish Region' (2010) 19 European Energy and Environmental Law Review 60.

12 Winston Harrington, 'Enforcement Leverage when Penalties are Restricted' (1988) 37 Journal of Public Economics 29; Anthony Heyes and Neil Rickman, 'Regulatory Dealing – Revisiting the Harrington Paradox' (1999) 72 Journal of Public Economics 361; Robert Innes and Abdoul G Sam, 'Voluntary Pollution Reductions and the Enforcement of Environmental Law: An Empirical Study of the 33/50 Program' (2008) 51 Journal of Law and Economics 271.

13 OECD, *Ensuring Environmental Compliance: Trends and Good Practices* (OECD Publishing 2009).

14 Bowles, Faure and Garoupa (n 1).

Policymakers will still have to look at the efficiency and/or cost-effectiveness of the enforcement instruments to protect the environment. Different legal instruments, such as criminal or administrative sanctions, have different enforcement costs as well as a different impact on the behaviour of potential offenders. There are several trade-offs to be made when using these instruments, which will be presented in the following subsection.

### 2.2 *Administrative versus Criminal Law: General*

Law and Economics scholarship has discussed the trade-offs of using criminal as opposed to administrative law in general, as well as how this applies to the enforcement of environmental law specifically.[15] Based on this literature, enforcement through criminal law is preferred when the harm to society, or benefit to the offender is significant, the probability of detection is low, and when criminal law can provide additional stigma and/or an educative role (expressive function). In these circumstances, administrative law might not suffice. In addition, enforcement through administrative law could give rise to problems of capture (collusion between the regulator and the regulated) and error costs that are too high (as the standard of proof is much lower than under criminal law). Most importantly, administrative sanctions might be too low to provide sufficient deterrence.

On the other hand, the literature points to the fact that due to the high enforcement costs of the criminal system, administrative sanctioning might be preferred in some instances. These are for example, when the harm is low (hence insolvency is less of a problem), prevention (through licensing and monitoring) is more effective than ex post deterrence (through sanctioning), or if a violation is a matter of inadequate information, which could be solved by providing sufficient information to the offenders.[16] Due to the lower standard of proof in administrative law, it is likely that more violations will be sanctioned (enforcement is higher), and hence the *ex ante* probability of sanctioning also increases. Thus, based on this general framework, should environmental law be enforced through administrative or criminal law?

### 2.3 *Criminal Law to Enforce Environmental Regulations?*

There are only a limited number of empirical studies that have tested the question of which enforcement instruments are adequate to protect the environment. In general, these studies point to a similar conclusion: enforcement of environmental offences through criminal law is relatively low in terms of the

15 ibid; Ogus (n 1); Ogus and Abbot (n 2).
16 Ogus (n 1).

number of prosecutions relative to the number of established violations.[17] The main reasons might be the high administrative costs of the criminal justice system (high standard of proof), heavy workload of courts, judges giving priority to 'real crimes' and lacking adequate knowledge to assess environmental harm. As the probability of detection is rather low, coupled with a low sanction and high benefit from undertaking activities that risk environmental harm, according to the Becker model there will be low deterrence. Thus, compliance will follow only if the potential offender is highly risk averse, his subjective perception of the formal sanction is very high, he significantly overestimates the probability of conviction, and he attaches significance to non-legal sanctions coming from a criminal conviction (stigma, loss of reputation).[18] All these factors increase the ES a violator might be facing.

As an alternative to criminal enforcement, sanctioning through administrative law has been proposed. We support this argument for the following reason: given the high costs of criminal law enforcement, legal systems that only have criminal law enforcement systems and no or limited possibilities to enforce via administrative law may be less effective. The assumption is that given the high costs of the criminal procedure, public prosecutors allocate their scarce resources to the 'most important' cases. As a consequence, the majority of environmental offences might not be prosecuted, while there is a range of cases, which deserve sanctions. By also enforcing via administrative penalties, the probability of imposition of a sanction will be increased, as will the deterrent impact of enforcement.

To the extent that no alternative punitive mechanism (like administrative penalties or fines) exists,[19] this could lead to under-deterrence since rational Becker-type polluters are facing low expected (formal) sanctions. Administrative fines might be relatively cheaper to impose than criminal sanctions, as the administrative proceedings are less strict and more informal in terms of money, time and personnel. In addition, as an administrative sanction is imposed by the environmental agency itself, there is no need to forward the case to the public prosecutor. Hence if there are enough cases where the gain from enforcement is greater than the administrative enforcement costs (where the cost of pollution is higher than the cost of imposing an administrative sanction), then there is a role for administrative law.

In addition, suspension or revocation of licences could be seen as having incapacitating or preventative effects, and hence, provide a significant deterrent.[20] Therefore, next to having only a criminal law system in place to enforce

17 Ogus and Abbot (n 2); Billiet and Rousseau (n 11); Faure and Svatikova (n 11).

18 Ogus and Abbot (n 2).

19 The goal of administrative sanctions in general is to stop the harmful activity and repair the damage done. 'Reparatory' sanctions, such as stop notices and orders or suspension or revocation of licences are different from punitive administrative sanctions, such as administrative fines.

20 Ogus and Abbot (n 2).

environmental regulations, allowing environmental agencies to impose administrative sanctions might be more effective in reducing environmental harm and at a lower cost. By letting environmental agencies handle the less serious cases, which are not worth criminal prosecution, the number of dismissed criminal cases decreases and the overall level of enforcement increases (*ex ante*). In the following part of the article, four examples of legal systems will be examined and analysed, where two rely on using a single instrument (criminal law) to enforce environmental violations, and the other two rely on the use of a complementary system of criminal and administrative enforcement. Some implications will be drawn as to their ability to induce compliance with environmental regulations.

## 3. Experiences in Four Legal Systems

This section discusses the enforcement instruments in four jurisdictions, where the UK and the Flemish region rely (at that time) primarily on criminal law to enforce environmental regulations, while Germany and the Netherlands rely on both, administrative and criminal law sanctions. The legal systems are briefly sketched and stylised facts based on the available empirical data are formulated.

### *3.1 Flemish Region*

The enforcement of environmental law in Belgium has been allocated to regions, and in this article we will be focusing on the Flemish region.[21] The most important environmental Acts in the Flemish region are the Flemish Decree concerning environmental permits 1985[22] and the Waste Decree concerning the prevention and the management of waste (*Afvalstoffendecreet*) 1981 (amended by a subsequent Decree of 20 April 1994). The Environmental Inspectorate (*Milieu-inspectie* or MI) of the Flemish Environmental Ministry has the most important competences to control compliance with environmental regulations. Environmental law in the Flemish region was, until 2009, mainly enforced through criminal law. Only for particular offences (related to manure), could an administrative fine be imposed. Since May 2009, the

21 Sabien Lust, 'Administrative Law in Belgium' in René Seerden and FAM Stroink (eds), *Administrative Law of the European Union, its Member States and the United States: A Comparative Analysis* (2nd edn, Intersentia 2007) 5–60.

22 Michael G Faure and Gunter Heine, *Environmental Criminal Law in the European Union. Documentation of the Main Provisions with Introductions* (Max Planck Institute for Foreign and International Criminal Law 2000); K Deketelaere, 'Public Environmental Law in Belgium in General and in the Flemish Region in Particular' in René Seerden, MA Heldeweg and KR Deketelaere (eds), *Public Environmental Law in the European Union and the United States: A Comparative Analysis* (Kluwer Law International 2002) 33.

Flemish Environmental Enforcement Decree (*Milieuhandhavingsdecreet*) 2008 has been in force and gives the regional agency (*gewestelijke entiteit*) the power to impose administrative fines. Some of the crimes have been declassified as administrative offences (*milieuinbreuken*), which are no longer subject to criminal law. In that case the (exclusive) administrative sanction is the only sanction available. For crimes, which are still forwarded to the public prosecutor, there is a possibility for the regional agency to impose an (alternative) administrative fine, but only in cases where the prosecutor decides not to prosecute. Together with the administrative fine, another non-criminal sanction can be imposed, which is equal to the benefit obtained from the illegal activity (in Dutch, *voordeelontneming* or confiscation of illegal gain).

For all crimes, once a violation has been observed, the Environmental Inspectorate (MI) is legally obliged to issue a Notice of Violation (NOV) (in Dutch, *process-verbaal (PV)*) to the public prosecutor. The MI then follows up by formulating a warning, which is submitted to the offender. Once the public prosecutor receives the NOV, he could ask the MI for more information, dismiss the case from any formal consequences, offer a 'transaction' (payment of a sum which will extinguish the criminal prosecution—a 'settlement'), or proceed to prosecute the violator in court. If convicted, a criminal fine or imprisonment could be imposed. All offences are in theory subject to possible imprisonment.

The only source available, and providing at least some 'hard' data, is the yearly enforcement reports of the Environmental Inspectorate (MI).[23] Data on the enforcement of environmental law in the Flemish Region has been collected by the MI at the level of five Flemish provinces over the period of 16 consecutive years, 1993–2008. The sample used consists of several enforcement variables, all of which can be found in the yearly reports. This study has obtained and used yearly data on the number of inspections, violations, the number of firms inspected and some data on the number of administrative reparatory sanctions and administrative fines. Furthermore, there is quite extensive reporting on what the public prosecutor in each province has done with the violations in each given year (1993–2004), giving us the number of dismissed cases from criminal prosecution, 'transactions', acquittals and convictions (see Tables 1 and 2).

Notwithstanding the limitations of this data (incompleteness, inconsistency), some facts can be formulated. First, with regard to the *ex ante* (pre-enforcement) inspecting activity of the Environmental Inspectorate (MI), there are on average 12,125.3 inspections performed and on average 4,786.9 firms inspected per year. As the number of inspections is more than twice the number of firms inspected, at least some firms get inspected more than once.

23 Department of the Environmental Inspectorate, the Flemish Region (*Afdeling Milieu-inspectie*), *Environmental Enforcement Reports* (*Milieuhandhavingsrapporten*) (1993–2008).

**Table 1.** The Flemish Region: inspections activity and calculated probabilities

| Year | Number of inspections | Number of firms inspected | Number of observed violations | Number of Notices of Violations (NOVs) | (1) *p* firm inspected | (2) *p* inspected | (3) *p* prosecuted | (4) *p* convicted | (5) *p* apprehended and prosecuted |
|---|---|---|---|---|---|---|---|---|---|
| 1993 | | | 1,910 | 449 | | | 0.15 | 0.13 | |
| 1994 | | | 1,517 | 938 | | | 0.16 | 0.14 | |
| 1995 | 15,007 | | 1,301 | 1,665 | | 0.60 | 0.19 | 0.18 | |
| 1996 | 12,751 | | 1,233 | 2,217 | | 0.51 | 0.21 | 0.20 | |
| 1997 | 12,469 | | 1,166 | 2,760 | | 0.50 | 0.22 | 0.17 | |
| 1998 | 12,061 | | 1,099 | 356 | | 0.48 | 0.14 | 0.13 | |
| 1999 | 11,595 | | 785 | 419 | | 0.46 | 0.07 | 0.06 | |
| 2000 | 10,584 | 4,380 | 794 | 359 | 0.18 | 0.42 | 0.07 | 0.06 | 0.01 |
| 2001 | 11,351 | 4,505 | 805 | 386 | 0.18 | 0.45 | 0.05 | 0.04 | 0.01 |
| 2002 | 12,060 | 5,280 | 741 | 423 | 0.21 | 0.48 | 0.06 | 0.05 | 0.01 |
| 2003 | 11,605 | 4,612 | 751 | 326 | 0.18 | 0.46 | 0.03 | 0.02 | 0.01 |
| 2004 | 12,156 | 5,082 | 608 | 288 | 0.20 | 0.49 | 0.09 | 0.04 | 0.02 |
| 2005 | 11,150 | 4,721 | 497 | | 0.19 | 0.45 | | | |
| 2006 | 12,518 | 5,481 | 516 | | 0.22 | 0.50 | | | |
| 2007 | 12,017 | 4,422 | 587 | | 0.18 | 0.48 | | | |
| 2008 | 12,430 | 4,599 | 605 | | 0.20 | 0.50 | | | |
| **Mean** | **12,125.3** | **4,786.9** | **932.2** | **882.17** | **0.2** | **0.5** | **0.1** | **0.1** | **0.01** |
| **Mean 1998–2008** | **11,775.18** | **4,786.89** | **708.00** | **365.29** | **0.2** | **0.47** | **0.07** | **0.06** | **0.01** |

*Source:* Environmental Inspectorate (MI), the Flemish Region, probabilities are authors' own calculations. Column (1) is calculated as *p* firm-inspected = the share of the number of firms inspected to the total number of companies; column (2) *p* inspected = the share of the number of inspections to the number of companies; column (3) *p* prosecuted = the share of the number of prosecutions to the number of NOVs; column (4) *p* convicted = the share of the number of convictions to the number of NOVs and column (5) *p* apprehended and prosecuted = *p* firm inspected × *p* prosecuted. For columns (1) and (2), the total number of companies that fall within the investigation powers of the MI is approximately 25,000 (source: MI).

**Table 2.** The Flemish Region: follow up on violations (percentage of total number of NOVs in a given year)

| Year | Dismissal, *n* (%) | Transaction, *n* (%) | Acquittal, *n* (%) | Conviction, *n* (%) | Total NOVs |
|---|---|---|---|---|---|
| 1993 | 265 (59) | 115 (26) | 11 (2.45) | 58 (12.92) | 449 |
| 1994 | 589 (63) | 201 (21) | 13 (1.39) | 135 (14.39) | 938 |
| 1995 | 1,007 (60) | 336 (20) | 19 (1.14) | 303 (18.20) | 1,665 |
| 1996 | 1,255 (57) | 486 (22) | 40 (1.80) | 436 (19.67) | 2,217 |
| 1997 | 1,505 (54) | 659 (24) | 120 (4.35) | 476 (17.25) | 2,760 |
| 1998 | 162 (45) | 144 (40) | 4 (1.12) | 46 (12.92) | 356 |
| 1999 | 263 (63) | 126 (30) | 3 (0.72) | 27 (6.44) | 419 |
| 2000 | 241 (67) | 94 (26) | 3 (0.84) | 21 (5.85) | 359 |
| 2001 | 284 (73) | 84 (22) | 1 (0.26) | 17 (4.40) | 386 |
| 2002 | 282 (67) | 117 (28) | 3 (0.71) | 21 (4.96) | 423 |
| 2003 | 225 (69) | 90 (28) | 5 (1.53) | 6 (1.84) | 326 |
| 2004 | 179 (62) | 83 (29) | 14 (4.86) | 12 (4.17) | 288 |
| **Mean** | **521.42 (62)** | **211.25 (26)** | **19.67 (1.76)** | **129.83 (10.25)** | **882.17 (100%)** |
| **Mean 1998–2004** | **233.71 (64)** | **105.43 (29)** | **4.71 (1.43)** | **21.43 (5.8)** | **365.29 (100%)** |

*Source:* Environmental Inspectorate (MI), the Flemish Region. The table gives the absolute values of the number of dismissals, transactions, acquittals and convictions. The share of each out of total number of violations in % is presented in brackets. These percentages are authors' calculations. The number of prosecutions has been calculated as the sum of acquittals and convictions.

This might be related to the targeting approach used by MI where firms that are more likely to be offenders are more likely to be inspected than compliant firms.[24] In addition, sometimes several inspections are needed to determine one violation. On average of these 12,125.3 inspections per year (on average) there are 932.2 violations detected (per year), meaning in around 8% of the performed inspections a violation is observed (in this article referred to as the 'observed violations ratio').[25] From Table 1 it can be seen that the number of observed violations dropped considerably (from 1,910 in 1993 to 605 in 2008), while the number of inspections and the number of firms inspected remained relatively constant. To suggest that the enforcement is working would be too strong an inference for two reasons: (1) we do not know the 'hidden' number of violations—ie those that go undetected; and (2) the calculation of violations before 1998 differed across the provinces, which might have resulted in an overstatement of the number of observed violations (some provinces counted a violation and its subsequent 'follow-up' violations as a single violation, while other provinces classified these as separate). Once a violation is observed, the MI is legally obliged to issue a NOV. There are on average 882 NOVs per year

24 Sandra Rousseau, 'Timing of Environmental Inspections: Survival of the Compliant' (2007) 32 Journal of Regulatory Economics 17.

25 It should be noted that the calculation of violations has been unified only since 1998, and hence the numbers for years before 1998 might overstate the average number of violations. In other words, there would be less than 8% of inspections resulting in a violation.

dealt with by the public prosecutor's office in the entire Flemish Region.[26] To correct for the non-unified classification of violations of pre-1998, average values have also been calculated for the period 1998–2008. In doing so, we have decreased the number of observations; however, the consistency of data is strengthened. It now shows that there are on average only 708 observed violations per year, which leads to around 6% of inspections where a violation has been observed, and only 365 NOVs on average per year reported by the public prosecutor.[27] It should be noted that a NOV could also arrive at the public prosecutor from the police forces and from other administrations. However, the statistics reported here are only from the MI.

It is more interesting, however, to look at the probabilities that a violation will be detected and prosecuted.[28] As explained in Section 2, a 'rational' company will value the costs and benefits of compliance when making a decision whether to comply or not. The probability of being apprehended and prosecuted ($p$) is one of the two factors determining the level of the ES (ES $= p \times S$). From our collected data, we computed the probability that a firm will be inspected, defined as the ratio of the number of firms inspected to the total number of companies. There are approximately 25,000 companies that fall within the investigation powers of the MI[29] and as mentioned above, on average 47,869 companies are inspected per year. This leads to a probability of 0.2 that a company will be inspected, on average, which could be considered as low.[30]

Furthermore, the (conditional) probability of being prosecuted has been computed based on the number of prosecutions out of the number of NOVs dealt with by the public prosecutor ($p$ prosecuted) (data on the number of prosecutions in Table 2). On average, this probability is 0.1. For the period 1998–2008, this probability of prosecution is only 0.07 (7%). This suggests that even if a company is detected committing a violation and a NOV is issued, 9 out of 10 times it will not be brought to court—ie prosecuted. This implies that to see the real probability that a company will actually be penalised for a

26 The number of NOVs presented in the tables corresponds to the number of NOVs dealt with in a given year by the prosecution office. However, some of these NOVs are not necessarily issued in that given year but could have been issued in a previous year.

27 This is less than half if we disregard the pre-1998 period, which might be due to the differences in reporting pre- and after 1998, or because over years the prosecutor's offices report less and less.

28 It should be noted here that the probabilities of detection relate only to the observed violations and thus it is a conditional probability upon a violation being found. We cannot put a number on the amount of unobserved violations, which implies that the resulting probabilities of being detected are systematically lower than what we report.

29 Environmental Inspectorate, the Flemish Region, personal interview.

30 Calculating the probability of being inspected disregarding the number of companies inspected (defined as the ratio of the number of inspections to the total number of companies) would greatly overestimate this parameter. According to our computations this would result in a probability of 0.5, which would mean every second company is inspected, which is not true.

violation, we must account not only for the probability of being inspected (and hence incur a high chance of being found in violation, assuming a violation was committed), but also for the probability of being prosecuted once a violation has been established. It is a fact that not all violations are found and those that are found are not all prosecuted. Thus, the probability of being apprehended and prosecuted for a violation is defined as the product of the probability that a firm will be inspected (assuming if a firm is in violation and an inspection takes place, the violation will be detected) and the probability it will be prosecuted. On average this probability is less than 0.01—ie less than 1%, meaning only one in a hundred firms that are in violation will be detected and prosecuted (based on this data). The probability of being convicted, which is also important as not all prosecutions lead to convictions, is according to our data on average the same as the probability of being prosecuted. This indicates that once a case is prosecuted, there is a very high chance that the wrongdoer will be convicted. Thus, the public prosecutor seems to select cases according to their chances of winning against the wrongdoer.

When looking at the post-detection enforcement once the MI observes a violation, in addition to sending a NOV to the public prosecutor, the MI could use a soft approach and issue a recommendation or a warning, or impose administrative sanctions and measures, and in case of violations of the regulations concerning manure, administrative fines. Once a NOV is sent to the public prosecutor, he can dismiss the case, issue a transaction or prosecute. The use of these options in absolute numbers as well as in relative terms is shown in Table 2.[31]

Taking into consideration only the period 1998–2004, since from 1998 the system was unified across provinces, as mentioned earlier, there are on average 365 NOVs in total per year (1998–2004). Furthermore, it shows that on average there are 64% of criminal cases dismissed from prosecution, 29% transactions, 5.8% convictions and 1.43% acquittals per year. Thus on average, around 7% of NOVs are prosecuted, which might not provide sufficient incentive *ex ante* to comply with the environmental regulations in the first place.

With regard to the level of fines imposed, although MI does not provide data on the size of penalties imposed, some estimates can be found in the literature. Billiet and Rousseau find an average criminal fine of €5,000 imposed both in

31 The absolute numbers are comparable only from 1998 when the reporting system for violations was unified, and there seem to be three outliers, namely years 1995–97. Therefore, the values are also reported in relative terms (in brackets) as a percentage of the total number of official reports issued in a given year, and hence made more comparable assuming that in a given year the ratios of dismissals and convictions were not affected by the differences in classifying violations across provinces. Average values are also calculated only for the period 1998–2004 to give more reliable estimates. In addition, the data on the follow up might be biased due to the fact that it is based on the voluntary reporting of the public prosecutors' offices. There is a variation in this reporting across offices.

the court of first instance as well as in appeal for Gent region in the period 1990–2000.[32] In case of transactions (settlement with the public prosecutor), the average payment sum was only €260.[33] These average fines have recently been slightly increased.[34] In the period 2003/2004–07 in Gent (in the criminal procedure) and in Brussels (in the administrative procedure),[35] the average criminal fine for legal persons was €14,569 at First Instance and €10,733 on Appeal. For natural persons, the average criminal fine was €3,787 at First Instance and € 7,061 on Appeal. With regard to the length of imprisonment, the majority of prison terms (circa 90%) does not last longer than 6 months. The problem is that usually very short prison sentences are not executed. As a result of this, effectively no sanction is executed. In the administrative track, the average administrative fine for legal persons is €4,477 at First Instance (€672 for natural persons) and €11,276 on Appeal (€1,121 for natural persons). What can be implied from these results is that on average fines are rather low in comparison to the benefits these violators might gain by violating the law, notwithstanding the rather low probability of detection and sanctioning. Unfortunately, we do not have data on the number of prison sentences.

### *3.2 England and Wales*

The Environmental Permitting (England and Wales) Regulations 2010[36] are one of the key pieces of environmental legislation in England and Wales. These, *inter alia*, streamline permitting provisions for waste and pollution prevention and control. The enforcement lies in the hands of the Environment Agency (EA). In the UK in the 1980s, environmental agencies used mainly 'informal' compliance strategies, such as persuasion and verbal warnings to achieve compliance.[37] Until the end of 2008, environmental law was primarily underpinned through more 'formal' criminal law, where the EA could prosecute before a criminal court for criminal sanctions, including fines and imprisonment for violations, as well as a formal caution or issue of a warning.[38]

32 Carole M Billiet and Sandra Rousseau, 'De hoogte van strafrechtelijke boetes. Een rechtseconomische analyse van de milieurechtspraak (1990–2000) van het Hof van Beroep te Gent' (The size of criminal fines. A law and economics analysis of the environmental criminal justice (1990–2000) of the Court of Appeal in Gent) (2003) 2 Tijdschrift voor Milieurecht 120.

33 Billiet and Rousseau (n 11).

34 Carole M Billiet and others, 'Milieucriminaliteit: feiten omtrent bestraffing' (Environmental crime: facts about punishment) (2009) 3 Panopticon 69; Carole M Billiet and others, 'Milieucriminaliteit in handen van strafrechters en beboetingsambtenaren: feiten uit Vlaanderen en Brussel' (2009) 36 Milieu & Recht 342.

35 In the Brussels region, administrative fines already existed before 2009, unlike in the Flemish Region. This allows for the comparison of the criminal track with the administrative track in the former.

36 Environmental Permitting (England and Wales) Regulations 2010, SI 2010/675 (EPR 2010).

37 Carolyn Abbot, *Enforcing Pollution Control Regulation: Strengthening Sanctions and Improving Deterrence* (Hart Publishing 2009).

38 ibid; Environment Agency, *Enforcement and Prosecution Policy* (2008), s 8 (EA EPP 2008).

In England and Wales, the environmental agency can take on the role of prosecutors, unlike in some other legal systems, where the prosecution is separate from administrative agencies.[39] In addition, the enforcing authority can use administrative tools such as powers of suspension and revocation of environmental licences, issue enforcement or prohibition notice or carry out remedial works.[40] However, in the UK the system of administrative fines to enforce environmental regulations was limited.

This changed with the introduction of the Regulatory Enforcement and Sanctions Act 2008,[41] which entered into force on 1 October 2008. This Act gave some regulatory bodies, including the EA, the power to impose a greater repertoire of civil (administrative) sanctions. These administrative sanctions are introduced by the Environmental Civil Sanctions Order 2010[42] and the Environmental Civil Sanctions (Miscellaneous Amendments) Regulations 2010.[43] The EA Enforcement and Prosecution Policy 2008[44] is replaced by the Enforcement and Sanctions Statement 2011[45] and by the Enforcement and Sanctions Guidance 2011.[46] Besides other administrative powers, the EA is enabled with two types of administrative fines—the fixed monetary penalty (FMP), and the variable monetary penalty (VMP). In both cases, a criminal standard of proof ('proof beyond a reasonable doubt') must be applied if the fine is appealed. Hence administrative fines might still be easier to implement (at least if not appealed), but in these cases not because of a lesser standard of proof, as discussed in the introduction. The FMP is similar to the Flemish exclusive administrative fine, as it is a rather low level fine imposed for minor offences, such as the failure to monitor. The VMP bears similarities with the Flemish alternative administrative fine, as it is applied to moderate to serious offences.[47] However, the main difference is that these sanctions do not aim to replace a criminal sanction (as in Flanders), but to fill the gap in enforcement where prosecution does not seem to be in the public interest. This might be the case because in England and Wales, the EA acts also as a prosecutor rather than merely as an administrative body in the strict sense. That is also why the imposition of the VMP is decided by the EA, and does not depend first on the decision of the public prosecutor to prosecute or not, as is the

39 In Scotland and Northern Ireland the relevant environment agencies cannot undertake their own prosecutions but must also refer to public prosecutors.
40 EPR 2010 (n 36); EA EPP 2008 (n 38) s 7.
41 Regulatory Enforcement and Sanctions Act 2008 (Commencement No 2) Order 2009, SI 2009/550.
42 Environmental Civil Sanctions (England) Order 2010, SI 2010/1157.
43 Environmental Sanctions (Misc. Amendments) (England) Regulations 2010, SI 2010/1151.
44 EA EPP 2008 (n 38).
45 Environment Agency, *Enforcement and Sanctions Statement* (2011).
46 Environment Agency, *Enforcement and Sanctions Guidance* (2011).
47 Offence is defined as a breach of legislation. There is no particular classification into criminal or administrative offence.

case in Flanders. Thus, administrative fines in England and Wales were introduced to provide flexibility and proportionality (intermediate sanctions) to the regulator, in this case to the EA.[48] As in Flanders, the aim of these fines can be seen as one of deterring and removing the financial benefit from the violator. Guidance to regulators on how to apply these administrative sanctions is provided by the Department for Environment, Food and Rural Affairs (DEFRA).[49]

Stigma and reputation is likely to be a concern for the businesses, as the EA publishes in their Spotlight reports which companies perform well in terms of environmental protection, and which have been prosecuted for environmental offences.[50]

Published environmental enforcement data in England and Wales is somewhat scarce and inconsistent. The EA provides some data in their Annual Report and Accounts. However, only the latest report is available on their website.[51] Nevertheless, it is possible to get limited data going back 5 years from the EA's Spotlight Reports.[52] These 'Spotlight' reports, published by the EA, report on the performance (good or bad) of business and create a so-called 'naming and shaming' effect. In addition, the House of Lords Written Answers[53] provides some enforcement statistics, as do the Environmental Data Services (ENDS) report[54] and the reports of DEFRA.[55]

Data for the period 2000–07 is available from various sources (see Tables 3 and 4). It shows that on average there were approximately 27,925 pollution incidents per year in total (Categories 1–4),[56] out of which 1,216 on average were serious (Categories 1 and 2 incidents). According to Bell and McGillivray, there are around 25,000 plus pollution incidents (Categories 1–4) per year, resulting in less than 5% prosecution rate.[57] Thus, our data points to a similar estimate, with a prosecution rate of around 3%. However, as the EA states in its Enforcement and Prosecution Policy, only serious incidents with sufficient evidence and public interest will be pursued. As can be seen from Table 4,

48 For example, a review that led to the new system showed that regulators felt that magistrates did not fully understand the gravity of breaches and that a criminal response was not always appropriate—eg if a respectable company had made a mistake for which it had to bear serious consequences. Introduction of alternative sanctions was designed to provide the system with more flexibility and proportionality with regard to sanctioning.

49 DEFRA, *Civil Sanctions For Environmental Offences: Guidance To Regulators In England On How The Civil Sanctions Should Be Applied, And Draft Guidance For Wales* (2010).

50 Environment Agency, *Spotlight Reports* (2004–2008).

51 Environment Agency, *Annual Report and Accounts* (2007–2008).

52 EA (n 50).

53 HL Deb 6 February 2008, vol 698, col WA193.

54 ENDS, 'Agency to Target 'Big, Bad and Nasty' Crime' (May 2005) 364 ENDS Report 14–15.

55 DEFRA, *Effectiveness of Enforcement of Environmental Legislation* (2006); DEFRA, *Trends in Environmental Sentencing in England and Wales* (2003).

56 Category 1 incidents (persistent and extensive effects), Category 2 incidents (significant effect), Category 3 (minimal effect) and Category 4 (no effect).

57 Stuart Bell and Donald McGillivray, *Environmental Law* (6th edn, OUP 2005).

**Table 3.** England and Wales enforcement data

| Year | Pollution incidents[a] | Category 1[b] | Category 2[c] | Prosecutions[d] | Convictions[e] | Cautions[f] | Notices[g] | Average fine business (£)[h] | No. firms fined[i] | Prison[j] |
|---|---|---|---|---|---|---|---|---|---|---|
| 2000 | | | | 733 | | 353 | 389 | 8,532 | | |
| 2001 | 33,723 | 147 | 1,707 | 786 | | 334 | 434 | ~4,600 | | |
| 2002 | ~30,000 | 111 | 1,357 | 820 | | 406 | 371 | 9,243 | | |
| 2003 | ~30,000 | 111 | 1,139 | 693 | | 338 | 396 | 9,070 | 215 | |
| 2004 | 25,196 | 131 | 1,068 | 740 | | 345 | 563 | 8,524 | 233 | 12 |
| 2005 | | ~140 | ~860 | 887 | 876 | 335 | 446 | 8,600 | ~317 | 4 |
| 2006 | | 92 | 818 | 744 | 723 | | | 11,800 | 255 | 10 |
| 2007 | 20,708 | 79 | 748 | 724 | 702 | | | 10,503 | 284 | 6 |
| **Mean** | **27,925** | **116** | **1,100** | **766** | **767** | **352** | **433** | **8,860** | **261** | **8** |

[a]Pollution incidents is the total number of all substantiated pollution incidents, ie category 1–4 incidents (source: DEFRA 2006).
[b]The number of Category 1 incidents (Category 1 means incidents with persistent and extensive effects).
[c]Number of Category 2 incidents (incidents with significant effect) (source: EA Spotlight reports, EA website). Category 3 incidents are those with minimal effects and Category 4 with no effect. The majority are Category 3 incidents.
[d–g]The numbers for each enforcement instrument (Source: ENDS Report and Hansard). The number of cautions and notices for 2005 are only for 1 January to 31 October 2005 (source DEFRA 2006). Notices mean here administrative measures.
[h]Average fine per business in £(source: Spotlight reports and DEFRA 2006 report).
[i]The number of firms fined (source: Spotlight reports and EA website).
[j]The number of all defendants sentenced to custodial sentence (source: Spotlight reports and EA website). This number does not contain other types of sentences, such as community order or probation.

**Table 4.** England and Wales: prosecution rates, cautions rate and notices rate

| Year | Prosecution rate (all incidents) (%) | Prosecution rate category 1+2 (%) | Cautions rate (all incidents) (%) | Notices rate (all incidents) (%) |
|---|---|---|---|---|
| 2000 | | | | |
| 2001 | 2 | 42 | 1.0 | 1.3 |
| 2002 | 3 | 56 | 1.4 | 1.2 |
| 2003 | 2 | 55 | 1.1 | 1.3 |
| 2004 | 3 | 62 | 1.4 | 2.2 |
| 2005 | | 89 | | |
| 2006 | | 82 | | |
| 2007 | 3 | 88 | | |
| **Mean** | **3** | **63** | **1.3** | **1.6** |

*Source*: Authors' calculations based on the available data.

Categories 1 and 2 have a relatively high prosecution rate (increasing over time).

Our data indicates that serious incidents (Categories 1 and 2) have on average a 63% prosecution rate. This implies that the EA uses targeting.[58] Cautions have been given only in 1.3% of all pollution incidents, and administrative tools, such as notices in 1.6% of all pollution incidents, on average. It should be noted that enforcement notices are more widely used by local authorities for environmental enforcement than by the EA,[59] hence the notices rate that we calculated might be underestimated. As to the number of suspended or revoked licences, we do not have supporting data; however, this number is expected to be very low.[60] The percentages of any formal action by the EA seem to be very low, which in turn indicates a very high rate of non-prosecution. This might also have to do with the fact that due to the type of harm specific to environmental offences (diffuse, remote), it is not always easy to identify the offender.[61] This poses serious problems for the Agency to collect sufficient evidence in order to initiate a prosecution. Similar problems related to prosecution are present in all jurisdictions but could be to a certain extent mitigated if the jurisdiction provides for administrative fines.

As to criminal fines and prison sentences, the average fine per business imposed by the courts is £8,860. This still seems to be relatively low compared to the benefits of violation, which might amount to tens or hundreds of

58 Heyes and Rickman (n 12).

59 DEFRA, *Review of Enforcement in Environmental Regulation: Report of Conclusions* (2006).

60 Ogus and Abbot (n 2) show that between 1996 and February 2001, there have been only six waste management licences revoked, and that the EA is using this tool as a last resort.

61 The ENDS Report (n 54) states that in 2004 offenders were identified only in 61% of major incidents.

thousands of pounds.[62] The reason for this has been suggested to be the fact that judges do not know how to evaluate environmental harm properly, and hence underestimate the level of sanctions needed to deter.[63] This might also change with the new regulations, as a part of the administrative fine will involve the removal of the financial benefit. The limited data on the number of defendants sentenced to imprisonment indicates on average eight defendants sentenced in this way, which is extremely low given the number of pollution incidents and the number of prosecutions. Factors that may go some way towards explaining this include the fact that custodial sentences are extremely expensive, require strict procedural safeguards, cannot be imposed upon legal entities (firms) and that it is difficult to identify senior management personnel within companies who could be held liable. Unfortunately we do not have data on the length of imprisonment.

### *3.3 The Netherlands*

In the Netherlands, environmental law is enforced through a mix of administrative and criminal law.[64] The main environmental act in the Netherlands is the Environmental Management Act ('Wet milieubeheer') 1993.[65] This Act integrates a number of previously existing laws in order to increase the transparency of the licensing system.[66] Chapter 18 of this Act deals with enforcement. Administrative enforcement as a whole is regulated via the General Administrative Law Act 1994 ('Algemene Wet Bestuursrecht' or AWB). Criminal law enforcement is regulated via the Dutch Criminal Code ('Wetboek van Strafrecht') 1881 and via the Economic Offences Act ('Wet Economische Delicten' or Wed) 1997.

As a result, there is a wide variety of sanctions available in the Netherlands: the AWB offers the possibility of imposing administrative sanctions—more particularly an administrative order under penalty or an order stating that an illegal activity has to be rectified; administrative fines are not available in the Netherlands for violations of environmental laws. In general criminal law (the Dutch Criminal Code), the most common sanctions are the criminal fine and imprisonment (and an increasing use is also made of the removal of illegal gains). Finally, the Wed still offers additional sanctions such as the publication of the judgment or the closure of a company. This therefore leads to quite a

62 For some examples of inadequate sentencing, see EA Spotlight Reports (n 50) and DEFRA 2006 (n 59).

63 R Navarro and D Stott, 'A Brief Comment: Sanctions for Pollution' (2002) 14 Journal of Environmental Law 283; Michael Watson, 'The Use of Criminal and Civil Penalties to Protect the Environment: A Comparative Study' (2006) 15 European Environmental Law Review 111.

64 Civil law plays a role as well, but we do not discuss that within the scope of our article.

65 René Seerden and MA Heldeweg, 'Public Environmental Law in the Netherlands' in Seerden and others (n 22) 382.

66 Faure and Heine (n 22).

diversified picture. Of course, we have merely addressed the distinction between administrative sanctions (mostly fines) and criminal sanctions from the perspective of operational efficiency. Other, perhaps equally important, aspects could also be included, such as the fact that criminal law has a stigmatic, punitive quality that can be diminished by overuse. Moreover, industries often breach rules unintentionally; this may require a sanction but not necessarily a criminal one.

In practice, when criminal law is used, most of the environmental laws in the Netherlands are enforced through the Wed. In principle, the environmental offences falling under the Wed have a feature of 'abstract' endangerment offence. This means that criminal liability occurs for violations of administrative duties specified in the laws falling under Article 1 of the Wed. An emission or environmental pollution is not required; the abstract danger to the environment (for example operating a plant without a licence) suffices for criminal liability. Article 2 of the Wed specifies, whether the offences under Article 1 are crimes ('misdrijven') or violations ('overtredingen'). Based on this, a corresponding sanction or a measure is applied (Articles 6–8 of the Wed).

On the other hand, the two articles of the Dutch Criminal Code, which are directly related to environmental pollution, Articles 173a and 173b, are an example of a 'concrete' endangerment offence. They read that criminal liability is invoked when a discharge occurs into the water, the soil or the air, and which has been done intentionally (or negligently), and unlawfully. This unlawful discharge is considered to create a concrete endangerment of the environment. However, criminal sanctions are applied only if this discharge threatens public health or someone's life; hence this provision is directed more towards the protection of humans rather than of the environment, and when this has been done unlawfully.[67] The unlawfulness criterion constitutes a problem since most discharges take place lawfully within the scope of the different regulations.[68] As a result, these two articles are not widely applied in practice.

The difference between the three 'enforcement' instruments lies also in the type of sanctions available. The AWB offers a wide variety of sanctioning possibilities. A first possibility for the competent administrative body is to issue an administrative order under penalty.[69] The idea of this competence is to force a perpetrator to comply: the offender has to pay the sum only if he remains unwilling to end the violation in accordance with the administrative order issued by the authorities.[70] This administrative order should not be confused with the sanction of issuing an administrative fine (in Dutch referred to as

67 ibid 237; GA Biezeveld, 'Rol van het Strafrecht bij de Bescherming van het Milieu' (2009) 3 ELSA Leiden Magazine 19.

68 Faure and Heine (n 22).

69 In Dutch referred to as a *dwangsom*. The formal competence can be found in art 5:32 of the General Administrative Law Act (*Algemene Wet Bestuursrecht*).

70 Seerden and Heldeweg (n 65) 382.

*bestuurlijke boete*). The aim of an administrative fine is not primarily to end the offence, but to punish the offender. Thus far, the imposition of an administrative fine in environmental law is not possible in the Netherlands (though it is used, for example, in social security legislation) but, like in the Flemish Region and in England and Wales, proposals have been formulated to introduce such fines in the Netherlands as well.[71] Yet another possibility for the administrative authority is to issue an administrative act stating that the illegal activity has to be rectified (referred to as *bestuursdwang*). This can lead (for example) to a shutting down of an establishment.[72] In the majority of cases (80%), it is reported that no formal action (in the sense of the imposition of a deterrent sanction) is taken, as many companies are forced into compliance via other measures, such as administrative orders under penalty.[73] Serious violations are usually prosecuted in parallel with administrative actions, and the prosecutor may also suggest a 'transaction' (settlement).[74]

The Wed offers a larger choice of sanctions than the Dutch Criminal Code, including reparatory sanctions for environmental offences, publication of the judgment imposing sanctions for environmental violations or the closure of the company (available only under the Wed, Articles 7 and 8). The size of the penalty depends on whether the offence is considered a crime or only an infringement of law, and whether it was committed by a legal or natural person. Under the Wed, a fine can be imposed in addition to a prison sentence. Under the Criminal Code, all offences are regarded as crimes and therefore the available sanctions are usually fines and imprisonment. Under Dutch law, the confiscation of an illegal gain is also possible. This increases the total size of the sanction even further.

In the Netherlands, the legal status of the Wed and the AWB is equal and they are used side-by-side. Hence, the argument that criminal law is used as *ultimum remedium* does not hold in the Netherlands.[75] Once a violation is observed, the criminal and administrative enforcement bodies negotiate together the allocation of tasks. Generally speaking, violations can be divided according to three categories.[76] First, environmental violations without criminally relevant circumstances (simple or minor violations) are addressed by the administrative body by imposing an administrative warning, measure or an administrative fine. Second, environmental violations, which the circumstances show to be relevant for criminal enforcement, and are priority enforcement problems, require an action by the administrative body and/or by the public prosecutor. In this case, criminal sanctions, as articulated in Articles

71 Seerden and Stroink (n 21).
72 Seerden and Heldeweg (n 65) 382; Seerden and Stroink (n 21).
73 OECD (n 13).
74 ibid.
75 Biezeveld (n 67) 19.
76 ibid 23.

6–8 of the Wed, can also apply. Lastly, for serious violations, criminal enforcement is used, with the possibility of being complemented by administrative sanctions, such as the revocation or suspension of permits and possibly shutting down of the company.

A problem with the Netherlands is that there is no systematic data for a longer time period that would register the number of violations and the legal consequences (administrative, criminal), nor on the specific sanctions imposed. One source of data is the inspection reports from the Ministry of the Environment (VROM). However, this data is only available for a limited period of time and comes from the yearly reports of the environmental inspectorate in the Netherlands. The data is available only for a period of 8 years (1999–2007, with the exception of 2001). The data set provides detailed data on the number of inspections of companies, of vehicles and the number of violations observed. It then also provides information on the number of administrative actions taken and the number of times a criminal action was taken (Table 5).

On average 22.8% of inspections result in a violation being observed. On average in 39.8% of these observed violations, an administrative action is taken, whereas in only 23.5% is a NOV issued and hence a criminal prosecutor is involved. However, any conclusions implied from these results should be drawn carefully as the data is available only for 8 years and the results vary greatly across years. Furthermore, 2005 seems to be an outlier as there were 42,321 inspections performed in that year, which is more than 10 times greater in any other year. What can be concluded is the fact that administrative actions are on average used much more than criminal actions (it should be noted that out of the total number of NOVs sent to the criminal prosecutor, only a portion of violations is prosecuted).

### 3.4 *Germany*

As far as the enforcement of environmental law is concerned a variety of legal instruments is available in Germany.[77] They can be found either in administrative law (administrative sanctions), in administrative penal law (*Ordnungswidrigkeitenrecht*) or in 'true' criminal law.[78] First, administrative agencies in Germany have at their disposal a variety of administrative instruments to force an offender to comply with administrative provisions, such as licence conditions.[79] A second possibility is the use of the so-called *Ordnungswidrigkeitenrecht*.[80] This is a system of administrative penal law,

77 Faure and Heine (n 22).

78 Administrative sanctions have as a goal either to repair harm done (restoration) or to prevent further harm in the future. They usually impose specific behaviour upon the perpetrator and their main goal is restoration or prevention. Administrative penal law on the other hand is of a punitive character and imposes fines on the perpetrator to deter violations.

79 Seerden and Stroink (n 21).

80 Administrative Offences Act (*Ordnungswidrigkeitengesetz*) 1987, BGBl. I S. 602.

**Table 5.** The Netherlands: enforcement data of the Ministry of Environment (VROM)

| Year | Number of inspections (in companies) | Number of vehicles inspected | Number of violations observed | Action under administrative law | | Criminal enforcement (number of NOVs) | Observed violations ratio (%) | % Administrative measures | % NOVs |
|---|---|---|---|---|---|---|---|---|---|
| | | | | Warnings | Administrative measures | | | | |
| 1999 | 3,583 | | 632 | 144 | | 323 | 17.6 | 22.8 | 51.1 |
| 2000 | 3,509 | | 1,214 | 277 | | 463 | 34.6 | 22.8 | 38.1 |
| 2002 | 3,541 | 3,097 | 1,119 | 406 | 402 | 223 | 16.9 | 72.2 | 19.9 |
| 2003 | 3,329 | 1,723 | 1,095 | 483 | 239 | 330 | 21.7 | 65.9 | 30.1 |
| 2004 | 2,678 | 3,855 | 1,193 | 249 | 194 | 209 | 18.3 | 37.1 | 17.5 |
| 2005 | 42,321 | 8,730 | 1,025 | 133 | | 144 | 2.0 | 13.0 | 14.0 |
| 2006 | 2,459 | 2,242 | 2,040 | 906 | | 203 | 43.4 | 44.4 | 10.0 |
| 2007 | 6,178 | 2,082 | 2,286 | 921 | | 155 | 27.7 | 40.3 | 6.8 |
| **Mean** | | | **1,325.5** | | | **256.25** | **22.8** | **39.8** | **23.5** |
| **Mean excl. 2005** | | | **1,368.43** | | | **272.29** | **25.74** | **43.64** | **24.79** |

*Source*: Ministry of the Environment (VROM). From 2005 onwards there is no separation made between the different administrative measures. Observed violations ratio indicates the percentage of inspections (of companies and vehicles) which result in an observed violation. % Administrative measures variable shows the percentage of observed violations for which an administrative action was imposed (warnings + administrative measures). % NOV indicates the percentage of observed violations for which a NOV was issued and sent to the public prosecutor (criminal enforcement).

which allows for the imposition of administrative fines (in German referred to as a *Geldbuße*). The *Geldbuße* can, on the basis of paragraph 30 of the *Ordnungswidrigkeitengesetz*, also be imposed against legal persons.[81] These administrative measures or fines are imposed by administrative agencies and hence without any intervention of the public prosecutor. The third means of enforcement involves criminal offences, which have been incorporated into the German Criminal Code (*Strafgesetzbuch*) in 1980.[82] The Criminal Code contains *inter alia* provisions against water pollution, pollution of the soil and air pollution.[83] The enforcement of environmental crime in Germany thus principally takes place via these provisions in the Criminal Code. For less serious offences (usually when no emission took place, but only administrative provisions were violated), the administrative penal law will be applied and this can lead to the imposition of an administrative fine.

In the 1980s and 1990s, a group of criminal lawyers and criminologists from the Max Planck Institute for Foreign and International Criminal Law was engaged in a project on the protection of the environment through the use of criminal law. Günter Heine and Volker Meinberg have some relevant data on enforcement of environmental law for the period 1975–86.[84] It is striking according to these scholars that in 1985 more than 40% of all criminal cases were not prosecuted.[85] The numbers presented by Heine and Meinberg were based on a more detailed study carried out by Meinberg published in 1988.[86]

In German criminal procedure (Strafprozeßordnung[87] or StPO), prosecution of all violations is (formally) the rule.[88] Hence the StPO contains numerous specific rules and conditions under which it can be decided not to prosecute a case. According to Meinberg's study of 1988, 47.5% of the cases end with a decision not to prosecute by the public prosecutor when there is no reason for

81 Code of Criminal Procedure the German Court of Criminal Procedure (*Strafprozessordnung*) 1987, BGBl. I S 1074, ber, S 1.319. This is important since the real criminal law in Germany cannot be applied against legal persons. Since the *Geldbuße* is, however, not considered a criminal sanction, the application of the *Geldbuße* against firms is accepted.

82 German Criminal Code (*Strafgesetzbuch*) 1872.

83 M Rodi, 'Public Environmental Law in Germany' in Seerden and others (n 21) 242–243.

84 Gunter Heine and Volker Meinberg, *Empfehlen sich Änderungen im strafrechtlichen Umweltschutz, insbesondere mit dem Verwaltungsrecht?* (Are changes in environmental criminal law necessary, especially in its relation to administrative law?) (Beck 1988).

85 Although one has to be somewhat careful with interpreting this result: the German term *Einstellung* (dismissal) does not necessarily imply that nothing took place; in some cases a dismissal is conditional upon the payment of a sum of money.

86 Volker Meinberg, 'Empirische Erkenntnisse zum Vollzug des Umweltstrafrechts' (Empirical observations on the enforcement of environmental law) (1988) 100 Zeitschrift fur die gesamte Strafrechtwissenschaft 112.

87 Code of Criminal Procedure the German Court of Criminal Procedure (*Strafprozessordnung*) 1987, BGBl. I S. 1074, ber, S. 1.319.

88 This follows from paragraph § 152 II of the German Court of Criminal Procedure (*Strafprozessordnung* (StPO)).

public prosecution (hence for policy reasons) on the basis of section 170 II StPO.[89] Non-prosecution in case of minor offences amounted to 14.6% of the cases (section 153 I StPO) and 13.1% were not prosecuted provided that specific conditions were met (section 153a I StPO). Altogether, the result was that 75% of cases were not prosecuted by the public prosecutor.[90] With regard to decisions by the courts, Meinberg finds these results remarkable: already a very small number of environmental cases are brought before the criminal court and yet more than 50% of all cases will be dismissed by the court on the basis of section 153 II (dismiss the case after approval of the public prosecutor) or 153a II (conditional dismissal) of the Code of Criminal Procedure (16.4% + 37.2%). This basically means that they are not considered as worthy of a penalty and will thus be excluded from the formal sanctioning procedure.[91] However, this does not mean that there are no consequences for these acts.

Meinberg also discusses the enforcement through administrative fines (*Geldbußen*). He notices that it is mostly the less important violations that are handled through administrative fines. It would be exceptional for cases where a significant emission (and thus a concrete danger for the environment) took place to be handled through administrative penal law.[92] He equally concludes that the procedural costs in this administrative penal law are usually extremely low since this is mostly limited to interviewing the perpetrator.[93] Meinberg found that most of the procedures in administrative penal law with respect to environmental violations end with a decision to impose an administrative fine (a so-called *Bußgeldbescheid*). The amount of the sanction is, however, on average lower than what would be imposed through the criminal law.[94]

Wolfram Lutterer and Hans J Hoch undertook some highly interesting empirical research, which resulted in a representative data set for environmental violations in Germany.[95] They analysed in detail how these violations were dealt with both in criminal law and in administrative law. This research dates from approximately 10 years later than the earlier studies by Heine and Meinberg and was published in 1997. They report on the decisions of the public prosecutor in 1014 cases, which they specifically analysed with respect to environmental crime (Table 6).

89 Meinberg (n 86) 139–143.
90 Here again, the 75% non-prosecution rate means that very few cases are brought before the court, but not that nothing happens. There can be a conditional dismissal made upon the fulfilment of particular obligations by the perpetrator.
91 Meinberg (n 86) 147. Note, however, as mentioned above, if paragraph § 153 a StPO is applied, the dismissal is conditional upon the offender fulfilling specific duties which can amount to paying a sum of money to the state.
92 Meinberg (n 86) 153.
93 ibid.
94 ibid.
95 Wolfram Lutterer and Hans J Hoch, *Rechtliche Steuerung im Umweltbereich* (Legal governance in environmental policy) (Max Planck Institute for Foreign and International Criminal Law 1997).

**Table 6.** Germany: decisions of the public prosecutor, the courts and administrative authorities

| **Public prosecutor** | | **Courts** | | **Administrative authorities** | |
|---|---|---|---|---|---|
| Dismissal for lack of evidence (companies) | 24.9% | Acquittal | 6.6% | Dismissal section 46 | 24.0% |
| Dismissal for lack of evidence (individuals) | 23.2% | Dismissal because of little interest (section 153 II StPO) | 16.1% | Dismissal according to section 47 | 9.0% |
| Dismissal because of small interest of the case (section 153 I StPO) | 14.7% | Dismissal with conditions (section 153a II StPO) | 37.2% | A warning | 8% |
| Dismissal with conditions (section 153a I StPO) | 13.2% | Conviction | 30.1% | Imposition of fine | 53.0% |
| Imposition of a fine | 16.1% | Other | 9.9% | Other | 6% |
| Prosecution | 7.9% | | | | |

*Source*: Lutterer and Hoch (n 95). Dismissal section 46 are cases when there are some uncertainties with respect to the case. Dismissal according to section 47 are cases where the administrative authority does not hold it necessary to impose a sanction.

What is of course striking from the decisions of the public prosecutor is that in almost 60% of the cases a dismissal took place, whereas in only 7.9% of the cases did a prosecution take place. Lutterer and Hoch also analysed data on the procedural decisions within the administrative penal law. It should be noted that warnings were used only in 8% of the cases. Moreover, a warning can, within administrative penal law in Germany, also take place alongside the imposition of a fine (a so-called *Verwarnungsgeld*). A fine was imposed in 53% of the cases by the administrative authorities. This is in sharp contrast with the fine imposed by the public prosecutor, which happened only in 16.1%.

When further comparing administrative penal law and criminal law, the authors conclude that in the case of administrative penal law, in 57% of all cases some noticeable reaction (which one could equate with a sanction) took place. In the criminal procedure (by which we mean in this case the public prosecutor) this was only in 48.9% of the cases. In that respect the authors concluded that the administrative penal law has a higher probability of a sanction being imposed than the criminal procedure.[96] However, the average fines imposed through the criminal system were higher than the average fines imposed through administrative penal law. However, for both cases it is clear that the formal statutory possibilities to impose (much higher) sanctions are rarely used. Lutterer and Hoch therefore conclude that in administrative penal law, sanctions are imposed more often, but that on average they are more severe in the criminal procedure.[97]

96 ibid.
97 ibid.

More recent data is provided by Almer and Goeschl.[98] Their data set comprises the period 1995–2005 for 16 individual states in Germany, leading to 152 observations (some states have incomplete reporting). Their analysis suggests that once a potential violation has been detected (and there are many violations that go undetected and unrecorded), in only 59% of cases is the offender identified, and hence a violation formally established. From this 59% of identified offenders, only 26.3% are tried. Thus the probability that an offender is apprehended and prosecuted is even lower (maximum 15.5%).[99] However, as we indicated above, even in cases where an identified offender is not prosecuted, this does not mean that no reaction takes place at all. With regard to the type of sanctions imposed, only 3.5% of convicted offenders are sentenced to imprisonment and 6.4% have to pay a severe fine, which establishes officially a criminal record. In the remaining 90.1% of convicted offenders, a less stringent criminal sanction is imposed.

## 4. Critical Comparative Analysis and Implications

The theoretical argument we developed in Section 2 has been that allowing for administrative enforcement of environmental violations in addition to relying only on criminal enforcement could be a cost-effective way to decrease the number of criminal cases dismissed by the prosecutor. Assuming there exists a range of offences, which merit sanctions but not necessarily being prosecuted in criminal law, administrative law might play a bigger role. Hence, criminal and administrative sanctions could serve as complementary instruments especially if the budget is constrained.

The previous section analysed the enforcement systems in two countries (Germany and the Netherlands), which rely on both administrative and criminal enforcement, and two jurisdictions (the UK and the Flemish Region) which (at that time) relied primarily (if not exclusively) on criminal law enforcement.

First, it is clear from the data provided that it is not possible to carry out a direct comparative analysis, examining the relative effectiveness of the enforcement systems in the four legal systems. This is not only the case because of data incompatibility, but also because the four legal systems differ in their administrative and criminal systems. As such, the data is not presented as decisive evidence, but used to support the general line of reasoning as discussed

98 Christian Almer and Timo Goeschl, 'Environmental Crime and Punishment: Empirical Evidence from the German Penal Code' (2010) 86 Land Economics 707.

99 The probability that an offender is apprehended and prosecuted equals the probability that an offender is identified multiplied by the probability he will be tried (prosecuted). Moreover, we do not know the number of undetected violations, which decreases the probability of apprehension even further.

**Table 7.** Comparison of enforcement data

| Country | Number of pollution incidents/ observed violations | Observed violations ratio | Criminal enforcement | | | | Administrative enforcement |
|---|---|---|---|---|---|---|---|
| | | | % NOVs | Prosecution rate (%) | Dismissals (%) | Transaction (%) | % Administrative measures |
| Flemish region (1998–2008) | 708 | 6% | 92 | 7 | 64 | 29 | |
| UK (2000–07) | 27,925 (serious 1,216) | | | 3 (63) | | | 1.6% notices rate |
| The Netherlands (1999–2007) | 1,325.5 | 22.80% | 23.50 | | | | 39.80 |
| Germany | | | | | | | |
| (1980s) | | | | 7.90 | 60–75 | | >60% (fine or a warning) |
| (1995–2005) | | | | 26.3 | | | |

above. We believe that the comparison of the legal systems discussed in our article provides some initial indications to support the hypothesis that administrative sanctions, in the form of fines, could be a valuable additional instrument in the enforcement of environmental violations.

### 4.1 A Brief Comparison

The presentation of the four legal systems made clear that at least on paper, until 2008 the institutional arrangements used were quite divergent. Table 7 presents some comparison between several enforcement variables.

The Flemish Region based the enforcement of environmental law mainly on criminal law. Even though the Environmental Inspectorate issued a NOV for all violations (which was legally obliged), only around 7% on average were prosecuted. In England and Wales the prosecution rate is even lower—on average 3% of all pollution incidents. This indicates a very high rate of violations that are not prosecuted. It also indicates a high degree of discretion for the prosecutor in England and Wales. It can be seen that, on average, 63% of serious violations are prosecuted. This shows that there is a range of offences, which merit enforcement action but do not fulfil the requirements for prosecution. The Flemish Region developed an alternative—a so-called 'transaction' within the criminal law system, and used it for 26–29% of the NOVs.[100] In general, what can be observed is a high rate of violations which are not prosecuted and for which no alternative sanctioning mechanism was developed (with the exception of recommendations and warnings, and the 'transaction model' in the Flemish Region), and a rather low level of criminal sanctions compared to the benefits of violations. However, the introduction of administrative fines in both, England and Wales and the Flemish Region indicates that relying only on criminal sanctions also poses a problem for enforcement in practice.

On the other hand, the Netherlands shows a more mixed picture: even though, the Netherlands has no deterring administrative fines for environmental offences, alternatives (like an order under penalty) are often used, as a result of which the perpetrator can be forced to pay a monetary sum. Even though the goal is not deterrence, but to ensure the perpetrator's compliance, in economic terms these administrative orders strongly resemble administrative fines in terms of their deterrent effect. According to the recent estimates of the Ministry of the Environment (VROM), an administrative measure has been imposed on average for around 40% of violations (approximately half are warnings), while a NOV is issued only on average for 23.5% of violations. Germany even has a different formal system to deal with administrative offences—the *Ordnungswidrigkeitenrecht*—which allows the imposition of

100 In the Netherlands, transaction also exists; unfortunately we do not have any data on it.

administrative fines. According to our data, warnings (8%) and administrative fines (53%) were imposed in more than 60% of violations (Table 6). Even though we cannot evaluate properly what happens with the criminal cases that are not brought to court by the public prosecutor in these two countries, the fact that the offender might face, besides criminal, an administrative sanction, increases the level of the ES (under the conditions of sufficiently high probability of being sanctioned and sufficiently high level of the actual administrative sanction imposed) and hence increases the deterrence from an *ex ante* perspective.

### 4.2 *Sufficiently High Probability of Sanctions?*

As mentioned above, for all countries examined only a fraction of NOVs are prosecuted criminally, with the tendency of prosecutors towards a focus on the more serious cases, so-called 'targeting' (for example in England and Wales this is evident as 63% of serious cases are prosecuted). One of the reasons given is the strict evidentiary requirements of criminal proceedings and the costly criminal procedure. Administrative proceedings do not require such stringent requirements, and even if they do (as required under the new regulations in the UK, for example, on appeal), the fact that the violation does not have to proceed to the public prosecutor makes the imposition of administrative sanctions faster and cheaper (disregarding the possibility of appeal). This could imply that the probability of being sanctioned with an administrative penalty strictly outweighs the probability of a criminal sanction. This can also be observed in the Netherlands and Germany.

However, the probability of sanctions being levied also depends on the probability of being detected. This also varies across countries; for example in the Flemish Region the probability of a firm being inspected is 0.2. Hence, the question is not only what is done once a violation is observed, but also how to minimise the 'hidden' number of undetected violations.

In addition, the question arises as to whether one can always interpret the high number of criminal cases that are not brought to court by public prosecutors as cases where 'nothing happened'. First, there could be regulatory dealings[101] whereby the prosecutor, in cooperation with the environmental agency, leads the violator towards compliance. The dismissal may then fit into an approach of negotiation and persuasion, leading the prosecutor to dismiss only when there is evidence of compliance by the perpetrator. However, the problem remains that even if this soft approach were to lead to compliance *ex post*, *ex ante* the average expected (legal) sanction remains low. An interesting alternative for the administrative fine has been developed in the Flemish

101 Paul Fenn and Cento Veljanovski, 'A Positive Economic Theory of Regulatory Enforcement' (1988) 98 The Economic Journal 1055.

Region (and the Netherlands) in the shape of the proposal of a transaction by the public prosecutor (in 26–29% of the NOVs). It is a low-cost alternative that avoids the prosecutor having to choose the costly criminal procedure. However, according to the estimates from the literature (with an average payment of about €300), the deterrent effect seems to be very low. Allowing for the imposition of administrative fines seems to be another plausible alternative for dealing with the cases deserving enforcement.

### 4.3 *Implications for the Actual and ESs*

In a Beckerian world, the ES is a product of the probability of being detected and sanctioned and the actual sanction imposed ($ES = p \times S$). The probability of detection and being sanctioned has been discussed above, and it has been implied that administrative sanctioning might increase the probability of being sanctioned as the administrative procedure seems simpler, hence less costly, and the environmental authority is able to impose the administrative sanction by itself. As to the other variable in the equation, the level of the actual sanction, what can be observed from the four countries analysed is the fact that average criminal fines tend to be relatively low. This is the case when compared with both the harm done and the level of the private benefits of violation. In the Flemish Region, earlier research examined average fines imposed by courts and indicated average fines of between €5,000 and €6,165.[102] If these were the only costs of the criminal procedure, multiplied with the 0.01 probability of detection and sanctioning, this would lead to ESs varying between €50 and €61.[103] Data from England and Wales also leads to low estimates of ESs. We indicated above that average prosecution rates vary between 3 and 5%. An average fine per business imposed by courts is £8.860, whereas prison sanctions are rarely imposed (Table 3). In Germany, the availability of administrative fines can take away some burden from courts, and as mentioned already, the severity of administrative sanctions might in some cases even outweigh that of criminal sanctions, as courts are not always capable of assessing environmental harm correctly.

It is hence not difficult to argue that, given a fixed budget for enforcement of environmental violations, it might be useful to divide the resources between criminal and administrative law systems, as these may prove to be complementary. Obviously, criminal law offers an incapacitation effect by using imprisonment, which is not available under administrative law. However, there is the

102 Billiet and Rousseau (n 34); Sandra Rousseau, 'Empirical Analysis of Sanctions for Environmental Offenses' (2009) 3 International Review of Environmental and Resource Economics 161.

103 As we will indicate below, there may, however, be other costs involved with the criminal prosecution that could increase the (subjective) ES for the perpetrator. Moreover, to this should also be added the probability that a perpetrator has a transaction imposed by the prosecutor.

possibility of suspension or revocation of licences, which has been considered to be a strong deterrent with an incapacitation effect, but has rarely been used (for example in England and Wales). Moreover, stigmatic and negative reputational effects might be missing too from administrative law enforcement. Unfortunately, available data does not allow us to further explore non-legal sanctions stemming from a potential criminal conviction. Prosecution before the criminal courts and criminal sanctioning could impose a 'stigma' on firms and thus create reputational loss, which may lead firms towards compliance.[104] However, environmental agencies can and do (for example in England and Wales) publish a list of companies and their performance, including whether prosecution followed. In addition, even if criminal law does have this additional advantage of creating a stigma or contributing to the creation of social norms, it can barely perform these tasks if it is rarely applied in practice. Moreover, firms might lack information on the actual ES. This has been confirmed in earlier research concerning the Flemish Region, which showed that when firms had to pay a monetary sanction in a first period, the firm was more likely to be in violation in a second period.[105] Firms that did not have to pay a fine hence overestimated the ES. Sanctioning a violator with too low a fine thus had a perverse learning effect: it informed firms about the low ESs and thus reduced compliance.

## 5. Conclusion

To conclude, it has been argued that administrative sanctioning might be able to deal with a range of violations that do not merit going through the high cost criminal procedure but still merit enforcement at a relatively low cost. Hence, for a range of violations, enforcement through criminal and administrative law would work as substitutes. This would hold under the assumption that enforcement through administrative law is cheaper than through criminal law. Unfortunately, to our knowledge there is no empirical evidence on enforcement costs, and hence we can only reason based upon the difference in costs between the administrative and criminal procedures. Especially for minor violations, administrative fines may be more efficient. If that option does not exist, there is a likelihood that as a result of discretion by the public prosecutor, enforcement agencies would focus the criminal law efforts only on the main cases, not prosecuting many others (such as in England and Wales). But if an alternative through administrative law can be offered, one can

104 J Van Erp, 'Reputational Sanctions in Private and Public Regulation' (2008) 1 Erasmus Law Review 145.

105 Billiet and Rousseau (n 11); Sandra Rousseau, *The Impact of Sanctions and Inspections on Firms' Environmental Compliance Decisions* (Katholieke Universiteit Leuven, Centrum voor Economische Studiën, Energy, Transport and Environment 2007) 19.

expect that this takes care of the moderately serious cases deserving enforcement. We looked into four legal systems and examined enforcement practices in two countries with a mainly administrative law enforcement system and two where the criminal law enforcement was the main system. Even though the data is not comparable, our findings as well as the recent legal developments in England and Wales and the Flemish Region seem to confirm this hypothesis. This seems contrary to the current trend in the EU towards the mandatory use of the criminal law to enforce environmental directives.

Our findings basically confirm a statement in earlier literature that whilst criminal prosecution may well be appropriate for the most serious of cases (and therefore must be retained) its deterrent value may be limited due to the fact that the probability of detection, prosecution and conviction can be low. Given a higher probability of imposition, the ES in case of an administrative fine can be higher. This at least calls for a combination of criminal law and administrative fines.

However, one has to be careful with generalising the conclusion that systems that allow for a more balanced use of the criminal law (by combining it with administrative law for minor or moderately serious violations) are more efficient than systems, which merely rely on the criminal law. After all, our data did not allow us to test the overall effectiveness of the differing approaches as far as the effect on environmental quality is concerned, nor on compliance with environmental regulation by firms. Moreover, economic literature has equally indicated that administrative law systems may have the disadvantage that enforcing agencies could enter into a collusive relationship with the regulated firms as a result of which also administrative agencies could not always impose efficient sanctions.[106] Thus, whenever administrative systems are introduced to deal with environmental crime, some control mechanism to verify the decision-making by administrative authorities (for example by an independent judge or public prosecutor) should be put in place.

Interestingly, it was also noted that in practice there is not always a clear dividing line between administrative and criminal law. Some legal systems using criminal law also levy fines of a more administrative nature since these are payments, which can be imposed by the prosecutor as a low cost alternative to the court system. An example of this approach would be the transaction model used within the Flemish and Dutch systems. They have in fact a more administrative character but are imposed by the public prosecutor. Further research is undoubtedly merited to examine the comparative benefits of these transactions versus fines imposed via administrative law.

Important changes have taken place both in England and Wales as well as in the Flemish Region where enforcement seems to be moving away from

106 This danger may also exist with criminal sanctions where the agency itself is able to bring prosecutions, like in England and Wales.

criminal law towards administrative sanctions. The data presented in this article merely reflected the situation until 2009 when these changes had not yet come into force. It will be an interesting issue for further research to examine the effects of these recent changes and more particularly whether this led to an increased use of the administrative sanctioning system.

A striking finding during this analysis was that in none of the four legal systems was reliable data available on the number of violations, the consequences attached to those (transaction, administrative penalty, criminal sanction, other), or on the sanction finally imposed. It seems that the trend is to report less and less over time, as the information reported has decreased in more recent years. Even within the countries, the information is only available to a limited extent and for particular time periods and there is no comparability whatsoever between the systems examined. Hence, it is advisable that a harmonised system of data collection on inspections, violations, measures taken and sanctions be established.

# [17]

# CLIMATE FINANCE AND ITS GOVERNANCE: MOVING TO A LOW CARBON ECONOMY THROUGH SOCIALLY RESPONSIBLE FINANCING?

Benjamin J Richardson*

**Abstract** 'Climate finance' is becoming an important feature of the emerging legal and policy regimes to address global warming. However, the current approach largely confines the financial sector to a transactional agent to mobilise capital for clean energy and to broker emission allowance trading. The sector's potential to leverage more sweeping positive changes in the economy as sought historically through the movement for socially responsible investment (SRI) has been insufficiently acknowledged. Indirectly, by regulating greenhouse gases the legal system is helping to create a business case for investors to respond to climate change threats. However, the potential contribution of SRI to address climate change problems more comprehensively is presently limited owing to inadequate governance frameworks, as well the sector's increasing abandonment of its traditional ethical agenda.

## I. INTRODUCTION

To what extent, and how, can financial markets contribute to climate policy goals? Amidst the mounting international urgency to combat global warming, the financial sector has become an increasingly prominent stakeholder. The Kyoto Protocol's inclusion of various economic mechanisms to achieve cost effective reductions of greenhouse gas (GHG) emissions, created a framework for financial institutions such as banks and pension funds to play a seminal role in the transition to a low carbon economy.[1] They would be able to act as brokers for carbon trading, and as financiers for clean development and climate adaptation. Until recently, however, another role of financial markets has been somewhat overlooked in the climate policy debates. It is the movement for socially responsible investment (SRI).

Rather than limiting financial institutions to mere transactional agents in climate finance, SRI envisions a much more active and enlightened role for

* Osgoode Hall Law School, York University, Canada. brichardson@osgoode.yorku.cg

[1] Kyoto Protocol to the Framework Convention on Climate Change (1998) 37 ILM 22.

[*ICLQ* vol 58, July 2009 pp 597–626] doi:10.1017/S0020589309001213

them. Traditionally, SRI has expected financiers to act as *ethical* investors, who prioritise socially just and ecologically sustainable development over the maximisation of financial returns.[2] In other words, the financial sector should act in the public interest rather than merely for its own economic self-interest. By this approach, SRI promises a radical path to a low carbon world, whereby the financial sector may exploit its economically strategic position to leverage positive changes in corporate behaviour. If successful, SRI can overcome the limitations and gaps in official climate regulation by pushing for early corporate action to reduce GHG emissions.

However, SRI is not a textbook manual for social responsibility, but rather a fluid discourse open to diverse interpretations and practices. In recent years, particularly since 2000, that discourse has changed profoundly.[3] Many SRI actors have jettisoned pretensions to invest solely on 'ethical' grounds; instead, they are motivated primarily by a 'business case' whereby social and environmental problems, including global warming, are addressed on the basis of the relative financial risks and opportunities to the investor. A second important transformation in SRI is the propagation of an array of codes of conduct and other governance standards for responsible finance. Several of these regimes specifically target climate change issues, such as the Carbon Disclosure Project. In general, this trend in SRI governance has tended to reinforce the drift to the business case approach.

This article assesses the contribution of SRI to climate finance and the transition to a low carbon economy. Taking a comparative and international perspective of the subject, it examines in particular the relationship between SRI and the mechanisms for governance of climate finance. This article argues that international financial markets are presently unlikely to be the vanguard of change to a low carbon world. This is for primarily two reasons. First, the shift to a business case approach to SRI has blunted its pretences to be a vehicle for radical reform. Secondly, although SRI arose to provide a form of surrogate market regulation, compensating for the lacunae and weaknesses of official regulation, its dependence on the state to create legal standards conducive to responsible conduct in the area of climate finance is increasingly evident. While the article does not seek to explain in detail how SRI could be legally reformed to enable the financial sector to play a more effective role in responding to climate change—a topic of great length requiring a further essay—it provides insights into future directions.

[2] See S Meeker-Lowry, *Economics as if the Earth Really Mattered: A Catalyst Guide to Socially Conscious Investing* (New Society Publishers, Gabriola Island, Canada, 1988); S Bruyn, *The Field of Social Investment* (Cambridge University Press, Cambridge, 1987).

[3] On recent changes to SRI, see C Krosinsky and N Robins (eds), *Sustainable Investing: The Art of Long Term Performance* (Earthscan, London 2008).

## II. CLIMATE CHANGE CONCERNS FOR THE FINANCIAL SECTOR

### A. An Emerging Issue

Climate change will be the most complex and expensive environmental problem humanity has ever had to address. According to the Stern Review commissioned by the British Government, the cost of business-as-usual, of not taking immediate action to mitigate climate change, will in years to come likely amount to between 5 to 10 per cent of world gross domestic product (GDP) each year, but only 1 to 2 per cent of GDP if we act now.[4] The Stern report, however, sanguinely assumes that climate change can be managed without any fundamental change to our economy, the market system, and the concomitant priority given to economic growth. Other commentators such as Monbiot, Flannery, and Homer-Dixon predict much severer challenges and costs in kicking the carbon economy.[5] Credible government policy measures to reduce emissions rapidly have yet to be advanced, and the political will in many countries to force change is muted.[6]

In the present era of finance capitalism—an economic system dominated by the financial sector and involving the propagation of a complex system of banking services, securities markets, and other financial instruments[7]—the finance sector will likely play a central role in climate policy. It can help to price climate risks and facilitate investment in renewable energy and efficient technologies.[8] The investment community increasingly perceives some action on climate change as in its self-interest, for it poses risks to the value of their investment portfolios or their borrowers' solvency through tightening regulations, impairment of physical assets, and reduced income.[9] A report by the International Finance Corporation assessed climate change as 'a particularly powerful catalyst' for the incorporation of environmental factors into

[4] N Stern, *Stern Review on the Economics of Climate Change* (HM Treasury, 2007).

[5] G Monbiot, *Heat: How to Stop the Planet Burning* (HarperCollins, London, 2005); T Flannery, *The Weather Makers* (Atlantic Monthly Press, New York, 2006); T Homer-Dixon, *The Upside of Down: Catastrophe and Renewal and the Renewal of Civilisation* (Alfred A Knopf, New York, 2006).

[6] F Yamin and J Depledge, *The International Climate Change Regime: A Guide to Rules, Institutions and Procedures* (Cambridge University Press, 2005); M Peeters and K Deketelaere (eds), *EU Climate Change Policy: The Challenge of New Regulatory Initiatives* (Edward Elgar, Cheltenham, 2006), D Zillman et al (eds), *Beyond the Carbon Economy* (Oxford University Press, Oxford, 2008).

[7] See G Edwards, *The Evolution of Finance Capitalism* (Longmans, Green, and Company, 1938); J Froud, A Leaver and K Williams 'New Actors in a Financialised Economy and the Remaking of Capitalism' 12 New Political Economy 339 (2007).

[8] S Labatt and R White, *Carbon Finance: The Financial Implications of Climate Change* (John Wiley, 2007).

[9] A Shell and M Krantz, 'Global Warming a Hot Spot for Investors' *USA Today Online* (27 February 2007); J Leggett, 'Climate Change and the Banking Industry: A Question of Both Risk and Opportunity' (1996) 179 Bankers Magazine 25.

investment decision-making.[10] Some analysts predict 'climate change due diligence . . . will soon become an indispensable facet of inquiry in any transaction'.[11]

Although the financial sector is publishing numerous studies that warn of the impact of global warming on its self-interest,[12] so far tangible changes in investment practices are hard to discern. Financial markets continue to capitalize the fossil fuel industry heavily. The surging investment in Alberta's oil sands is one of the most controversial examples. Even many so-called SRI funds continue to hold stakes in GHG emitting firms.[13] The business case for investment in fossil fuels often remains far more potent than the business case for divestment. Most fundamentally, the turmoil that swept global financial markets in late 2008 and early 2009 epitomized the deep structural failure of the financial sector to manage risks and invest with a view to the long term.[14] The speculative, myopic and avaricious culture embedded in this sector, which precipitated the market turmoil, hardly provides the appropriate milieu to nurture an environmentally responsible financial community that invests for sustainable development.

Presently, the financial sector acts mainly as a transactional mechanism to allocate capital for climate mitigation and adaptation efforts. In other words, it is an intermediary, helping to facilitate investment in renewable energies, Clean Development Mechanism projects, and carbon emission trading. One such player, for instance, is the British-based Carbon Capital Markets, which buys and sells carbon allowances for companies.[15] The financial sector has also pioneered voluntary trading schemes, the most successful example being the Chicago Climate Exchange (CCX). Established in 2003, the CCX is a GHG emission allowance trading hub for emission sources and offset projects in the United States (US) and a growing number of other countries including Canada, Brazil, and Mexico.[16] The CCX members, who include corporate behemoths such as Ford and IBM, make voluntary commitments to reduce their GHG emissions in 2010 by 6 per cent below a baseline period of

[10] International Finance Corporation (IFC), *'Who Cares Who Wins'. One Year On* (IFC, 2005) 8.

[11] J Smith, 'The Implications of the Kyoto Protocol and the Global Warming Debate for Business Transactions' (2005) New York University Journal of Law and Business 511.

[12] J Llewellyn, *The Business of Climate Change: Challenges and Opportunities* (Lehman Brothers, New York, 2007); World Resources Institute (WRI) and Merrill Lynch, *Energy Security and Climate Change: Investing in the Clean Car Revolution* (WRI and Merrill Lynch, 2005); Worldwide Fund for Nature (WWF) and Allianz, *Climate Change and the Financial Sector: An Agenda for Action* (WWF and Allianz, Gland, Switzerland, 2005).

[13] N Lansbury, *Socially Responsible Climate Change? Fossil Fuel Investments of the Socially Responsible Investment Industry in Australia* (Mineral Policy Institute, 2002) 30.

[14] On the crisis, see G Soros, *The New Paradigm for Financial Markets: The Credit Crisis of 2008 and What It Means* (Public Affairs, New York, 2008); R Shiller, *The Subprime Solution: How Today's Global Financial Crisis Happened, and What to Do About It* (Princeton University Press, Princeton, 2008).

[15] See <http://www.carboncapitalmarkets.com>.

[16] See <http://www.chicagoclimatex.com>.

1998–2001.[17] In the retail finance markets, catering mainly to individuals, mutual funds are selling climate-friendly investment portfolios, and banks are offering 'green' home loans that take into account the energy efficiency of mortgaged properties.[18]

In theory, however, the long-standing movement for SRI suggests that the financial sector could play a more ambitious role on climate issues. It evolved from church-based, single-issue activism, where ethical investors eschewed ties to companies and activities deemed immoral, such as gambling, alcohol, and vulgar entertainment. From the late 1960s, the SRI movement began to embrace a wider agenda of concern for human rights, taking up cause against the Vietnam War and, later, South Africa's apartheid regime.[19] Since the 1980s, and especially since the late 1990s, SRI has also championed environmental causes including climate change.[20] The massive growth of international financial markets, fuelled in part by surging household wealth and the participation of mass society in investment schemes such as pension plans and mutual funds, has provided an opportunity for ordinary people to use their investments to promote positive social and environmental changes including stopping global warming.[21] As it has matured, SRI has sought to influence financial markets through several techniques, including ethical screens (excluding assets in problematic firms), 'best-in-class' portfolios (selecting the firms that act the most responsibly relative to their peers), shareholder advocacy (using shareholder rights to advocate change within companies) and, in the banking sector, financing on preferential terms to socially or environmentally beneficial projects. Through such techniques and engagement with a widening agenda of issues, SRI seeks improvements in corporate social and environmental behaviour beyond the letter of the law. However, as this article will discuss shortly, that potential has not yet been generally reached.

### *B. The Market and Legal Context of Climate Finance*

The threat of climate change, which should raise profound questions about the sustainability of our economic system, is hardly debated in the mainstream financial community.[22] Taylor and Brown contend that we need to debate the

[17] Remarks, Richard Sandor. CEO, Chicago Climate Exchange (18th Annual SRI in the Rockies Conference, Santa Ana Pueblo, New Mexico, 3–6 November 2007).

[18] United Nations Environment Program Finance Initiative (UNEPFI), *Green Financial Products and Services: Current Developments and Future Opportunities in North America* (UNEPFI, Geneva, 2007) 17–19.

[19] R Sparkes, 'A Historical Perspective on the Growth of Socially Responsible Investment' in Rory Sullivan and Craig Mackenzie (eds) *Responsible Investment* (Greenleaf Publishing, Sheffield, 2006), 39.

[20] See M Jeucken, *Sustainable Finance and Banking: The Financial Sector and the Future of the Planet* (Earthscan, London, 2001); Labatt and White, above (n 1).

[21] S Davis, J Lukomnik and D Pitt-Watson, *The New Capitalists. How Citizen Investors are Reshaping the Corporate Agenda* (Harvard Business Press, Cambridge, 2006).

[22] See the online climate ethics network at <http://www.climateethics.org>.

ethical issues raised by climate change to reach an urgently needed international consensus for action.[23] They also see ethical deliberation as crucial to leading the world toward an equitable sharing of the burdens and benefits of protecting the planet, as called for in the UN Framework Convention on Climate Change (UNFCCC).[24] Yet, for most investors, global warming is (at most) mainly a matter of financial risk or investment opportunity. With decision-making in financial institutions dominated by fund managers and other investment professionals focused on the 'bottom line', any notion that such institutions are a forum of enlightened ethical deliberation among climate-conscious investors would be naive.

The legal system influences the construction of these risks and investment opportunities. On the upside, the Kyoto Protocol's 'flexible' mechanisms create several market opportunities for financiers.[25] They expand opportunities for lending to companies acquiring emission abatement technologies. Also, the Clean Development Mechanism and Joint Implementation sectors provide opportunities for project finance. Further, carbon emission trading creates a demand for brokerage services. Finally, climate risk assessment in equity and debt financing provides additional work for financial analysts.

On the downside, polluting industries in the oil and gas, heavy manufacturing, and transport sectors should be competitively disadvantaged by climate regulation, thereby hurting their investors.[26] While such losses would concern any rational investor, they would particularly concern institutional investors having fiduciary duties to their fund beneficiaries to promote optimal financial returns.[27] A guide for British pension fund trustees suggests that:

> Climate risk can have a real impact on portfolio holdings. There is a growing case for trustees to attain some level of knowledge around these issues, and to take steps to mitigate any negative consequences of not taking action.

[23] D Brown, *American Heat: Ethical Problems with the United States Responses to Global Warming* (Rowman and Littlefield, Lanham, Massachusetts, 2002); P Taylor, *An Ecological Approach to International Law: Responding to Challenges of Climate Change* (Routledge, London and New York, 1998).

[24] Article 3.1 (1992) 31 ILM 849.

[25] J Janssen, 'Implementing the Kyoto Mechanisms: Potential Contributions by Banks and Insurance Companies' (2000) 25 Geneva Papers on Risk and Insurance 602; J Mandt, 'Managing Risk in Kyoto Projects' (1999) 1(2) Environmental Finance 23; H Hugenschmidt and J Janssen, 'Kyoto Protocol: New Market Opportunities or New Risks?' (1999) 11 Swiss Derivatives Review 22.

[26] World Resources Institute (WRI), *Changing Oil: Emerging Environmental Risks and Shareholder Value in the Oil and Gas Industry* (WRI, Washington DC, 2002).

[27] Fiduciary duties arise where the exercise of some discretionary power in the interests of another person gives rise to a relationship of trust. The fiduciary duties of loyalty and prudence require the trustee to manage assets wisely only on behalf the beneficiaries. On fiduciary duties and SRI, see B J Richardson, 'Do the Fiduciary Duties of Pension Funds Hinder Socially Responsible Investment?' (2007) 22(2) Banking and Finance Law Review 145. While fiduciary duties are a concept of common law systems, functionally equivalent concepts exist in some financial legislation in civil law jurisdictions.

> In line with these definitions of fiduciary responsibility, we suggest that it is consistent with fiduciary responsibility to address climate change risk.[28]

Regulatory risk is thus one of the most material concerns to investors, as some governments have begun to tighten controls on GHG emissions. The growing reliance on market-based policy instruments, such as carbon taxes and subsidies for clean energy investments, will affect the competitive advantage of polluters.[29] Several studies also forecast that participants in emission cap-and-trade schemes will incur cash flow risks from the increased expenditure on GHG reduction measures or the purchase of emission allowances.[30]

This partiality to economic instruments reflects a broader evolution in environmental law worldwide, which is moving away from bureaucratic, command-and-control regulation toward 'reflexive' legal instruments perceived as more congruent with the workings of the market.[31] Thus, the United Kingdom (UK), once a staunch opponent of carbon taxation, in 2001 introduced a climate change levy on non-renewable energy consumed by industry and public sector agencies.[32] The UK's Climate Change and Sustainable Energy Act 2006, Canada's Clean Air and Climate Change Act 2007 and New Zealand's Climate Change (Emissions Trading and Renewable Preference) Act 2008, are among the new climate laws creating a framework for further such initiatives. Even in the US, where federal policy was largely indifferent to global warming until the election of President Barack Obama, several states have acted unilaterally.[33] For instance, California's Global Warming Solutions Act 2006 caps the state's GHG emissions at 1990 levels by 2020, and mandates a cap-and-trade system to help achieve this goal.

Litigation risks may also concern some investors. Several lawsuits initiated in North America against major GHG emitters may ignite fears of a litigation onslaught reminiscent of the anti-tobacco campaign.[34] Big polluters could be

[28] Mercer Investment Consulting (MIC), *A Climate for Change: A Trustee's Guide to Understanding and Addressing Climate Risk* (MIC, Carbon Trust, London, 2005) 18–19.

[29] R Stavins, 'Policy Instruments for Climate Change: How Can National Governments Address a Global Problem?' (1997) University of Chicago Legal Forum 293.

[30] UNEPFI Climate Change Working Group, *CEO Briefing. Emissions Trading* (UNEPFI, Geneva, January 2004), 4; Standard and Poor's (S&P's), *Emissions Trading: Carbon Will Become a Taxing Issue for European Utilities* (S&P's, New York, 2003).

[31] D Driesen, 'Economic Instruments for Sustainable Development' in B J Richardson and S Wood (eds), *Environmental Law for Sustainability* (Hart Publishing, Oxford, 2006) 277. On reflexive law, see G Teubner, L Farmer and D Murphy (eds), *Environmental Law and Ecological Responsibility: The Concept and Practice of Ecological Self-Organisation* (John Wiley and Sons, Hoboken, 1994).

[32] B J Richardson and K Chanwai, 'The UK's Climate Change Levy: Is It Working?' (2003)15(1) Journal of Environmental Law 39.

[33] C Carlarne, 'Climate Change Policies an Ocean Apart: EU and US Climate Change Policies Compared' (2006) 14 Penn State Environmental Law Review 435.

[34] K Healy and J Tapick, 'Climate Change: It's Not Just a Policy Issue for Corporate Counsel—It's a Legal Problem' (2004) 29 Columbia Journal of Environmental Law 89; J Gupta, 'Legal Steps Outside the Climate Convention: Litigation as a Tool to Address Climate Change' (2007) 16 Review of European Community and International Environmental Law 76.

liable for damages associated with the physical effects of climate change, such as flooding, severe storm damage or droughts. In 2004, eight US states and New York City sued five of the country's largest power companies for creating a public nuisance.[35] In the 2006 case of *Lockyer v General Motors*,[36] California commenced a similar tort action against six automobile manufacturers. While some legal commentators believe that 'the probability of legal victories against global warming is low',[37] they also concede that such litigation may generate substantial legal fees and costly delays to new projects.[38] Climate litigation is emerging in other countries, including actions against governments in Australia[39] and Canada.[40]

Climate change also poses both physical risks and intangible reputational risks to investments. Economic sectors dependent on stable climate conditions, such as agriculture, forestry and tourism, face physical threats.[41] The oil industry itself is vulnerable, as illustrated by how Hurricane Katrina in 2005 shut down many refineries in Louisiana. The real estate finance sector is also exposed to damages from extreme weather events.[42] The insurance industry, which covers many of these risks, is thus acutely exposed.[43] High profile companies that disregard climate change also face reputational risks. Fossil fuel dependent corporations like ExxonMobil are often targets of consumer boycotts and shareholder pressure.[44] Civil society groups increasingly target financial institutions associated with such firms; a coalition of mostly US environmental groups in 2006 started a campaign that demanded major banks cease lending to coal power plants.[45] In December 2008, the Bank of America agreed to one of their demands to stop financing environmentally destructive open-cut coal mining.[46]

[35] See eg *State of Connecticut, et al v American Electric Power Company, et al* (2005) 406 F Supp 2d. 265 (SDNY) (under appeal).

[36] No 3:06. Civ 05755 (ND California, filed 20 September, 2006).

[37] M Levinson, *Liability for Climate Change* (JPMorgan Chase, New York November 2006).

[38] ibid 1.

[39] *Australian Conservation Foundation v. Minister for Planning*, [2004] VCAT 2029, 23.

[40] *Friends of the Earth v The Governor in Council and the Minister of the Environment*, [2008] FC 1183.

[41] See UBS, *Climate Change: Beyond Whether* (UBS, Zürich, 2007).

[42] ISIS Asset Management, *A Benchmarking Study: Environmental Credit-Risk Factors in the Pan European Banking Sector* (ISIS Asset Management, 2002), 14.

[43] M Northrop, 'Leading by Example: Profitable Corporate Strategies and Successful Public Policies for Reducing Greenhouse Gas Emissions' (2004) 14 Widener Law Journal 21, 32.

[44] F Barringer, 'Environmental Groups Planning to Urge Boycott of ExxonMobil' *New York Times* (12 July 2005) A14.

[45] J Donnelly, 'Banks are Urged not to Finance Coal Power' *Boston Globe Online* (16 January 2007).

[46] T Zeller, 'Bank of America to Stop Financing Mountaintop Mining' *New York Times* (4 December 2008).

Conversely, companies that pioneer low carbon and energy efficient technologies stand to gain financially.[47] Many investors, at least before the global financial crisis of late 2008, were favouring renewable energies, ethanol production, environmentally efficient technologies, and carbon offset projects.[48] Citigroup's 2007 list of 'climatic consequences companies' identified 74 companies (across 21 industries) 'that seem well positioned to benefit from these trends'.[49] The creation of the Photon Photovoltaic Stock Index, ABN AMRO Biofuel Commodity Index, and the KLD Global Climate 100 Index, among various examples, enable investors to buy into a portfolio of companies in these sectors. The propagation of carbon emissions trading systems promises further lucrative spoils for financial brokers. The World Bank estimated that the value of the global carbon market reached US$64 billion in 2007 (up from US$31 billion in 2006), mostly associated with the European Union's GHG trading scheme.[50]

Yet, incongruously, the fossil fuel sector still thrives. The effusive rhetoric in the financial industry about the threat of global warming does not reflect the wider picture. The spree of investment in the world's new oil frontier, Alberta's oil sands, is just one example.[51] A 2007 study by Ethical Funds of the booming oil sands industry documented that only four of the 50 companies assessed were cutting emissions.[52] Only a handful were taking appropriate measures, such as factoring carbon costs into capital allocation decisions and conducting GHG emission inventories. And few had invested in renewable energy production.

Clearly, so long as fossil fuels remain a relatively cheap alternative and vested interests thwart change, SRI in the energy sector has constrained prospects. Plausibly, new policy instruments are required to create a level playing-field. A report by the World Wide Fund for Nature and the Allianz Group in 2005 advised that 'banks and investors in particular need a clear regulatory framework on climate policy which they can adapt and base their investment and lending decisions'.[53] Yet, the SRI movement arose precisely as an answer to the lacunae and weaknesses of governmental regulation. When governments fail to act, as they did against South Africa's apartheid regime,

[47] World Resources Institute (WRI) and the Coalition for Environmentally Responsible Economics (CERES), *Questions and Answers for Investors on Climate Risk* (WRI, Washington DC, 2004) 23.

[48] D Berman, 'Hot for Green Investing' *Financial Post* (19 February 2007).

[49] Citigroup, *Climatic Consequences* (Citigroup Research, New York 19 January 2007) 1.

[50] K Capoor and P Ambrosi, *State and Trends of the Carbon Market 2008* (World Bank, 2008) 59.

[51] R Walker, Ethical Funds Company (presentation at the Canadian Responsible Investment Conference, Montreal, 27–29 May 2007).

[52] Ethical Funds Company (EFC), *Head in the Sands? Climate Change Risks in Canada's Oil and Gas Sector* (EFC, Vancourer, 2007) 2–4.

[53] World Wide Fund for Nature and Allianz, above (n 12) 9.

ethical investors seek reform through market pressure. Can the same occur for climate change?

### III. SRI AS A MEANS OF CLIMATE GOVERNANCE?

#### *A. SRI Governance on Climate Change*

To what extent can SRI provide an effective means of governance, beyond official regulation, to facilitate action on climate change? Although once led by the churches and charitable foundations, could SRI become a means to articulate the climate concerns of a wider community of interests in a mass investor society?

The following discussion will examine several areas where the financial sector has pushed for action. These are: climate-related financial risk management, corporate reporting on GHG emissions and other climate-relevant information, and shareholder activism to exert change inside companies. However, before canvassing action in these domains, it is necessary to situate that analysis in the broader context of whether SRI can provide a surrogate form of regulation on social and environmental issues generally.

For several reasons, it is doubtful that SRI presently can significantly improve corporate behaviour on climate issues. First, the SRI movement has increasingly disavowed ethical arguments in favour of a business case for social investment. By tying social and environmental activism to furthering the 'bottom line', SRI has diminished its pretences to stand for change; there often remains a countervailing business case for financing socially irresponsible activities, or social and environmental values often cannot be factored into the cost-benefit calculations. Second, the niche SRI market hardly influences the financing costs of firms, and thereby cannot give climate-conscious companies a significant market advantage over their polluting rivals. Third, the SRI movement's own international codes of conduct, such as the UN Principles for Responsible Investment, offer relatively facile and discretionary standards that enable financial institutions merely to tinker with reform. The following sections of this article examine these three issues.

#### *B. The Triumph of Economic over Ethical Values*

SRI was once more commonly known as 'ethical investment'. It referred to investors who, for strictly ethical reasons, either sought to avoid profit from 'sinful' activities (a stance associated with deontological ethics) or who wished to use their financial resources to leverage positive change in the world (a teleological ethical position).[54] Its apotheosis was the divestment movement,

[54] N Carter and M Huby, 'Ecological Citizenship and Ethical Investment' (2005) 14 Environmental Politics 255; P Dembinski et al 'The Ethical Foundations of Responsible Investment' (2003) 48 Journal of Business Ethics 203.

led by religious investors, against the apartheid regime in South Africa during the 1970s and 1980s.[55] From about the late 1990s, SRI began to change its motivations and practices, as mainstream institutional investors such as large pension plans came under pressure to be more mindful of the social and environmental impacts associated with their financing. This pressure arose partly from non-governmental organisations (NGOs) which started to target not merely the front-line polluters, but also their financial backers.[56] The shift in SRI was also influenced by precedent reforms to public development finance, such as the greening World Bank project financing during the 1980s.[57]

Yet, the mainstream financial community is generally not comfortable with SRI's traditional ethical agenda.[58] Primarily, it believes that SRI may hurt financial returns, which could have adverse legal repercussions given that institutional investors owe fiduciary duties to their beneficiaries. There is some truth to this belief, although fiduciary duties give some latitude to invest responsibly, particularly where fund members demand ethical choices.[59] Regardless, financial institutions have marshalled other arguments to avoid ethical investment. Investing on behalf of thousands or millions of investors, financial institutions fear immersion in acrimonious and irresolvable debates about the correct ethical course. On the assumption that their fund members hold diverse ethical views on social and environmental issues, they conclude that it would be impossible to reach a consensus to guide investment policy.[60] Alternatively, the maximization of financial returns is considered by fund managers as a clear and easily measurable benchmark to which they should be held to account.

Another factor undoubtedly shaping this shift in SRI philosophy is the 'ecological modernization' discourse, which became prevalent in Western environmental policy-making during the 1990s. It posits that economic development can be reconciled with environmental protection through technological innovation, managerial know-how, and the entrepreneurial spirit.[61]

[55] Sparkes, above (n 19) 39.

[56] S Waygood, *Capital Market Campaigning. The Impact of NGOs on Companies, Shareholder Value and Reputational Risk* (Risk Books, London, 2006).

[57] The Bank had incurred trenchant criticism for facilitating environmental degradation through project financing. O Perez 'The New Universe of Green Finance: From Self-Regulation to Multi-Polar Governance' in O Dilling, M Herberg, and G Winter (eds) *Responsible Business: Self-Governance in Transnational Economic Transactions* (Hart Publishing, Oxford, 2007) 151, 153.

[58] B J Richardson, 'Putting Ethics into Environmental Law: Fiduciary Duties for Ethical Investment' (2008) 46 Osgoode Hall Law Journal 243, 253.

[59] As outlined in Freshfields Bruckhaus Deringer, *A Legal Framework for the Integration of Environmental, Social and Governance Issues into Institutional Investment* (UNEPFI, Geneva 2005).

[60] J Entine (ed), *Pension Fund Politics: The Dangers of Social Investing* (American Enterprise Institute, 2005).

[61] S Young, *The Emergence of Ecological Modernisation: Integrating the Environment and the Economy?* (Routledge, New York, 2001); M Andersen and I Massa, 'Ecological

It optimistically projects that what is good for the environment is also good for business, based on the notion that cutting waste and using clean technologies improves market competitiveness and profitability.[62] It thus discretely reframes the ethical and political dilemmas of industrialization as mere technical and managerial challenges. Such thinking has spilled into the SRI discourse, where corporate environmental performance is likewise increasingly evaluated in cost–benefit terms and improvements in such performance are seen as strengthening rather than diminishing investment returns.[63]

As a result of these beliefs and arguments, the SRI movement is now driven primarily by a business case. Corporate environmental performance is no longer commonly evaluated against uncompromising ethical standards such as the value of maintaining the integrity of the global climate. Rather, environmental problems such as rising sea level, increasing hurricanes, and other climate impacts are conceptualized as challenges of financial risk management. But only those risks that are deemed to be 'financially material'—ie posing tangible risks to investment assets or lucrative investment opportunities—receive attention.[64] For example, the International Investors Group on Climate Change (IIGCC) proclaims its goal as to:

- Promote better understanding of the implications of climate change amongst our members and other institutional investors.
- Encourage companies and markets in which IIGCC members invest to address any material risks and opportunities to their businesses associated with climate change and a shift to a lower carbon economy.[65]

The SRI community downplays moral arguments. The United Nations Environment Program's Finance Initiative (UNEPFI), which is an industry partnership coordinated by the UN to promote SRI, explains in its report, *Show Me the Money*, that: '[t]he first—and arguably for investors the most important—reason to integrate [SRI] issues is, simply, to make more money'.[66]

Modernisation—Origins, Dilemmas and Future Directions' (2000) 2 Journal of Environmental Policy and Planning 337.

[62] E Cohen-Rosenthal and J Musnikow (eds), *Eco-Industrial Strategies: Unleashing Synergy between Economic Development and the Environment* (Greenleaf Publishing, Sheffield, 2003).

[63] See research on this relationship: M Orlitzky, F Schmidt and S Rynes, 'Corporate Social and Financial Performance: A Meta-Analysis' (2003) 24 Organization Studies 403; M Yamashita, S Sen and M Roberts, 'The Rewards for Environmental Conscientiousness in the US Capital Markets' (1999) 12 Journal of Financial and Strategic Decisions 73; N Lorraine, D Collison and D Power, 'An Analysis of the Stock Market Impact of Environmental Performance Information' (2004) 28 Accounting Forum 7.

[64] UNEPFI, *The Materiality of Social, Environmental and Corporate Governance Issues in Equity Pricing* (UNEPFI, Geneva, 2004).

[65] See <http://www.iigcc.org>.

[66] UNEPFI, *Show Me the Money: Linking Environmental, Social and Governance Issues to Company Value* (UNEPFI, Geneva, 2006), 4.

These attitudes can be contrasted with the ethical investor's position on climate change. The policy of the Interfaith Center for Corporate Responsibility's (ICCR) Global Warming Working Group is to:

- Encourage companies to report on their global warming emissions 'footprints', as well as disclose global warming related risks and opportunities to shareholders; and
- In recognition of future limits on global warming pollutants, encourage companies to behave proactively by reducing greenhouse gas emissions to sustainable levels.[67]

The ICCR, which coordinates SRI among religious investors, goes further than the IIGCC by stressing the priority of reducing carbon emissions. Its aim is to prevent or mitigate global warming for its own sake, rather than as a concern just tied to shareholder value.

The notion that environmental care and business success can be compatible is, of course, not inconceivable. The objection is that any such optimism can be a pretext for the perpetuation of business-as-usual. A huge gap between SRI based on the yardstick of financial materiality and an ecologically sustainable economy persists. Investment analysts often perceive social or environmental values as too nebulous for workable financial quantification.[68] Values such as biodiversity or climate integrity cannot be captured by conventional financial accounting systems unless they give rise to specific expenses and income attributable to an individual organization.[69] Further, a countervailing business case for environmentally problematic activities often exists. The continuing investment in Canada's oil sands is one controversial example.[70] Without additional ethical motivations, financiers may lack the incentive to take actions beyond those prescribed by a business case.

### *C. SRI's Stunted Market Influence*

The SRI sector remains small and appears unable to influence significantly the environmental behaviour of companies. SRI is essentially a boutique niche, likely holding less than ten per cent of the capital markets of the major Western economies.[71] Much of the industry-generated research appears to exaggerate

[67] See <http://www.iccr.org/issues/globalwarm/goalsobjectives.php>.

[68] S McGeachie, M Kiernan and E Kirzner, *Finance and the Environment in North America: The State of Play of the Integration of Environmental Issues into Financial Research* (Canadian Department of the Environment, Ottawa 2005) 57.

[69] S Goodman and T Little, *The Gap in GAAP: An Examination of Environmental Accounting Loopholes* (2003).

[70] K Makin, 'High-stakes Battle Looms over Oil-Sands Pollution' *Globe and Mail* (15 August 2007) A1.

[71] Social Investment Forum (SIF), *2007 Report on Socially Responsible Investing Trends in the United States* (SIF, 2008); European Social Investment Forum (Eurosif), *Socially Responsible Investment among European Institutional Investors* (Eurosif, Paris, 2006).

the extent of the SRI market, because the peak SRI associations are reluctant to define clearly what should qualify as 'socially responsible'. A fund for example that merely screens against tobacco stocks, but otherwise holds a conventional investment portfolio, is sometimes counted as SRI.[72] Despite its increasing pragmatic business stance, the SRI market remains small because many mainstream financial institutions have yet to appreciate the business risks of environmentally irresponsible behaviour, or they even see financial advantages in funding such behaviour. Even if the SRI market were significantly larger, it is doubtful whether that alone would commensurately boost its influence without other reforms.

Advocates of SRI believe that it financially rewards ethical firms through additional investment and punishes unethical ones by divestment. It thereby should both enhance returns for social investors while give firms incentives to improve their environmental and social behaviour.[73] Certainly, 'SRI is more likely to be relevant whenever companies are heavily dependent on the stock market as a financing instrument'.[74] Corporate financing data suggests that most companies, especially mature firms, can self-finance their operations and growth through surplus revenue.[75] Yet, even they do not remain entirely insulated from the demands of investors.[76] A declining stock price can affect a firm's market capitalization and thus its stock market listing. Further, the remuneration of corporate management is often tied to stock options, giving managers incentives to adopt measures to keep stock prices artificially high.

However, theories of corporate finance doubt that stock market trading can achieve the effects predicted by proponents of SRI.[77] Conventional finance theory suggests that investors can trade any quantity of a firm's shares without affecting its price. This is because in an efficient equity market where demand for a company's stock is almost perfectly elastic,[78] the price of a stock simply reflects the expected future cash flows, and all informed investors supposedly

[72] Social Investment Forum (SIF), *2005 Report on Socially Responsible Investing Trends in the United States: A 10-Year* Review (SIF, Washington DC, 2006) 9.

[73] P Camejo, *The SRI Advantage: Why Socially Responsible Investing has Outperformed Financially* (New Society Publishers, Gabriola Island, 2002); R Sparkes and C Cowton, 'The Maturing of Socially Responsible Investment: A Review of the Developing Link with Corporate Social Responsibility' (2004) 52 Journal of Business Ethics 45.

[74] A Beltratti, *Socially Responsible Investment in General Equilibrium* (Università Bocconi, Milan, 2003) 21.

[75] J Corbett and T Jenkinson, 'The Financing of Industry, 1970–1989: An International Comparison' (1996) 10 Journal of the Japanese and International Economies 71; but compare to A Hackethal and R Schmidt, *Financing Patterns: Measurement Concepts and Empirical Results*, Working Paper (University of Frankfurt, 2003).

[76] M Jensen and K Murphy, 'CEO Incentives—It's Not How Much You Pay, But How' (1990) 68(3) Harvard Business Review 138.

[77] J Langbein and R Posner, 'Social Investing and the Law of Trusts' (1980) 79 Michigan Law Review 72 M Knoll, 'Ethical Screening in Modern Financial Markets: The Conflicting Claims Underlying Socially Responsible Investment' (2002) 57 Business Lawyer 681.

[78] C Loderer et al, 'The Price Elasticity of Demand for Common Stock' (1991) 46 Journal of Finance 621.

value the company's stock identically.[79] Any SRI-motivated divestment should not per se change the expected cash flow from the targeted firm's activities, and therefore its stock prices should not change.[80] Of course, the stock price should vary if potential traders believe pressure on the stock reflects a downward or upward view of the company's underlying financial prospects. Business case SRI that educates the market to the financial consequences of firms' environmental behaviour may have such an effect. It is when social investors view unethical behaviour differently from the market as a whole that they may be marginalized. Other theoretical research, which assumes that markets do not always behave according to textbook theory, suggests that SRI can alter the cost of capital when the stock of a firm is risky, unique, or the stock trades in small, restrictive markets.[81] Otherwise, some theoretical models predict that social investors would need to hold at least 20 per cent of the market, but likely much more, to affect stock prices.[82]

Actual evidence of SRI's influence generally supports the foregoing assessments. The most comprehensive studied action is the South African boycott, which appears to have had modest effect on the targeted companies.[83] The widespread divestment from the tobacco industry appears to have had minimal impact on their stock prices.[84] Some research suggests a short-term impact on the stock prices of companies tainted by an environmental scandal or pollution fines, but this is because such news is perceived by the market to have implications for the profitability of the affected firm.[85]

[79] G Arnold, *Handbook of Corporate Finance* (Financial Times and Prentice Hall, 2005) 314, 330.

[80] W Davidson, D Worell and A El-Jelly, 'Influencing Managers to Change Unpopular Corporate Behavior through Boycotts and Divestitures' (1995) 34 Business and Society 171.

[81] P Rivoli, 'Making a Difference or Making a Statement? Finance Research and Socially Responsible Investment' (2003) 13 Business Ethics Quarterly 271.

[82] R Heinkel, A Kraus and J Zechner, 'The Effect of Green Investment on Corporate Behavior' (2001)36 Journal of Financial and Quantitative Analysis 431; J Angel and P Rivoli, 'Does Ethical Investing Impose a Cost Upon the Firm? A Theoretical Perspective' (1997) 6(4) Journal of Investing 57. This discussion, concerning equity investment, is not necessarily applicable to bank lending. Banks can have relatively more influence over borrowers, especially small enterprises with few financing options, and firms in large project financing deals seeking huge loans: Jeucken, above; P Thompson, 'Bank Lending and the Environment: Policies and Opportunities' (1998) 16(6) International Journal of Bank Marketing 243.

[83] S Teoh, I Welch and P Wazzan, 'The Effect of Socially Activist Investment Policies on the Financial Markets: Evidence from the South African Boycott' (1999) 72 Journal of Business 35; but compare to R Kumar, W Lamb and R Wokutch, 'The End of South African Sanctions, Institutional Ownership, and the Stock Price of Boycotted Firms' (2002) 41 Business and Society 133.

[84] T Burroughes, 'Ethical Investors Losing Out as Tobacco Stocks Burn Up Britain's Equity Markets' *The Business* (24 February 2007).

[85] Lorraine, Collison and Power, above (n 63); D Cormier, M Magnan and B Morard 'The Impact of Corporate Pollution on Market Valuation: Some Empirical Evidence' (1993) 8 Ecological Economics 135; J Hamilton 'Pollution as News: Media and Stock Market Reactions to the Toxics Release Inventory Data' (1995) 28 Journal of Environmental Economics and Management 98.

SRI may also achieve some influence when undertaken through shareholder advocacy and engagement with corporate management. Institutional investors have traditionally been passive investors, lacking incentives to monitor companies because of the costs involved and difficulties of coordinating action.[86] While some commentators believe they increasingly are more active,[87] the impact of such activism appears episodic and fleeting. SRI-inspired shareholder resolutions rarely garner more than ten per cent of the votes at a meeting.[88] However, sometimes defeated shareholder resolutions may induce management to work cooperatively, as they may interpret even modest dissent as reflective of broader unease about company policies.

In sum, SRI has yet to transform financial markets and the companies they finance. It has generally not yet had the strength of a surrogate regulator, able to influence companies through reward or divestment to improve their behaviour. Indeed, SRI appears to rely on the underlying system of environmental regulation to alter the financial advantages between polluters and socially responsible firms. Regulatory and public policy reforms are therefore probably essential if SRI is to be a means of advancing action on climate change and other environmental problems. But rather than continue to target only the 'front-line' companies, legal reform should also directly challenge the behaviour of their financial sponsors. Such reforms could include redefining the fiduciary duties of investment institutions to strengthen the mandate for SRI, improving the reporting by companies and their financiers on their social and environmental performance, integrating social accounting standards, and in some cases imposing environmental liability on financial sponsors.[89] The SRI movement, however, has not greatly clamoured for such reforms; it has preferred to draft its own codes of conduct for financiers to adopt voluntarily, as the following section canvasses.

## *D. SRI Codes and Standards*

### *1. Codes related to climate finance*

The SRI sector is more than a just a certain style of financing. It has also fashioned its own codes of conduct to help coordinate, standardize, and facilitate responsible financing. These voluntary mechanisms, developed by market and civil society institutions, have proliferated since 2000.[90]

This web of SRI governance relies on a diversity of methods, structures and objectives, broadly classifiable into four types (although any individual

[86] J Parkinson, *Corporate Power and Responsibility: Issues in the Theory of Company Law* (Clarendon Press, Oxford, 1995) 168–69.

[87] Davis, Lukomnik and Pitt-Watson, above (n 21) 15–16.

[88] ibid 16–18.

[89] B J Richardson, 'Diffusing Environmental Regulation through the Financial Services Sector: Reforms in the EU and other Jurisdictions' (2003) 10(3) Maastricht Journal of European and Comparative Law 1.

[90] Perez, above (n 57).

instrument may contain several of these features). First, there are normative frameworks that set substantive performance standards for social and environmental conduct. An example is the Collevecchio Declaration on Financial Institutions.[91] Process standards, enabling the assessment, verification, and communication of performance, constitute another form of governance. They include the Equator Principles[92] and the Global Reporting Initiative.[93] Third, management systems, such as the International Organization for Standardization's ISO 14001 regime, create a structure to guide the management of environmental and social activities and impacts.[94] Finally, comparative evaluation mechanisms have been developed by the SRI industry to evaluate and rank corporate performance for the purpose of selecting investments. These rating mechanisms include SRI stock market indexes such as the Dow Jones Sustainability Indexes[95] and the FTSE4 Good Index Series.[96]

In these respects, the SRI industry mirrors the general drift to corporate self-regulation in most Western economies. The trend has been extensively analysed in the literature, which need not be repeated here.[97] Many commentators and policy-makers are sceptical of corporate intentions, and doubt that voluntary mechanisms provide a credible means of environmental regulation.[98] Many of the SRI codes are too ambiguous and open-ended in their expectations. The most demanding standards are contained in the Collevecchio Declaration, a product of civil society institutions, which has been largely ignored by mainstream investors. They favour more discretionary and procedural-based standards, dealing with disclosure, reporting, and auditing of investment activities. While some reflexive law scholarship is confident that such measures can induce positive changes in affected organizations' behaviour,[99] by encouraging reflection and learning, the empirical evidence is inconclusive.[100] Voluntary mechanisms also typically lack

[91] See <http://www.foe.org/camps/intl/declaration.html>.

[92] See <http://www.equator-principles.com/index.shtml>.

[93] See <http://www.globalreporting.org>.

[94] See generally Ruth Hillary (ed), *ISO 14001: Case Studies and Practical Experience* (Greenleaf Publishing, Sheffield, 2000).

[95] See <http://www.sustainability-index.com>.

[96] See <http://www.ftse.com/Indices/FTSE4Good_Index_Series/index.jsp>.

[97] See eg S Wood, 'Voluntary Environmental Codes and Sustainability' in B J Richardson and S Wood (eds), *Environmental Law for Sustainability* (Hart Publishing, Oxford, 2006) 229; R Gibson (ed), *Voluntary Initiatives: The New Politics of Corporate Greening* (Broadview Press, Peterborough, 1999); J Moon, 'The Firm as Citizen? Social Responsibility of Business in Australia' (1995) 30(1) Australian Journal of Political Science 1.

[98] eg Ian Maitland, 'The Limits of Business Self-Regulation' (1995) California Management Review (1995) 27(3) 132; Wood, above (n 97).

[99] See Teubner, Farmer and Murphy, above (n 31).

[100] eg M Vidovic and N Khanna, 'Can Voluntary Pollution Prevention Programs Fulfill Their Promises? Further Evidence from the EPA's 33/50 Program' (2007) 53 Journal of Environmental Economics and Management 180; US Government Accountability Office (GAO), *Climate Change: EPA and DOE Should Do More to Encourage Progress Under Two Voluntary Programs* (GAO, Washington DC, 2006); C Woolfson and M Beck (eds), *Corporate Social Responsibility Failures in the Oil Industry* (Baywood Publishing, Amityville, 2005).

credible sanctions or enforcement mechanisms, so that compliance has come to depend on peer pressure, the discipline of the market, or sustained NGO demands. The corporate stone-walling of the draft UN Norms on the Responsibilities of Transnational Corporations illustrates corporate attitudes to regulatory standards with teeth.[101]

A few voluntary codes have been drafted to address climate finance specifically. The Climate Principles is one example of a voluntary initiative that purports to provide a 'common global standard of best practice not only to assist the finance sector in managing its own climate impact but also to assist the sector in supporting its clients and stakeholders in managing their own impacts'.[102] The Principles were finalized in December 2008 by the Climate Group, an NGO, in dialogue with some 20 financial institutions. The Climate Principles address most aspects of the financial industry including investment management, retail banking, insurance, and project finance. For example, in relation to the financing of projects that involve the release of at least 100,000 tons of carbon dioxide equivalent annually, signatories to the Principles are expected to request that their clients 'quantify and disclose' GHG emissions associated with the project, to 'monitor and report GHG emissions annually in accordance with internationally-recognized methodologies' and to 'evaluate technically and financially feasible options to reduce or offset project-related GHG emissions'.[103] The Climate Principles build on the 'Carbon Principles', adopted in February 2008 by six US banks, 'to provide a consistent approach for banks and their US power clients to evaluate and address carbon risks in the financing of electric power projects'.[104] Like the Climate Principles, the Carbon Principles emphasize procedural standards rather than absolute prohibitions on the financing of fossil fuel-intensive developments or companies, thereby providing latitude for business-as-usual. But far more influential and widely endorsed than either of these two codes is the UNPRI, as the next section explains.

### 2. *UN Principles for Responsible Investment (UNPRI)*

Designed primarily for institutional investors, the UNPRI is a voluntary code of conduct that combines process and substantive performance standards. It was developed under the auspices of UNEPFI, which established a working group comprised of invited investment professionals, who were supported by

[101] UN Economic and Social Council (ECOSOC), Sub-Commission on Promotion and Protection of Human Rights, *Norms on the Responsibilities of Transnational Corporations and Other Business Enterprises with Regard to Human Rights* (UN ECOSOC, New York, 2003).

[102] Climate Group: <http://www.theclimategroup.org/about/corporate_leadership/climate_principles>.

[103] Article 2.7, at <http://www.theclimategroup.org/assets/resources/TCP_English.pdf>.

[104] See <http://carbonprinciples.org/>.

a multi-stakeholder collection of some 70 experts including representatives from some major environmental NGOs.

The UNPRI is a succinct code of six core principles, each of which is illustrated by several 'possible actions'. The principles state:

1. We will incorporate environmental, social and corporate governance (ESG) issues into investment analysis and decision-making processes.
2. We will be active owners and incorporate ESG issues into our ownership policies and practices.
3. We will seek appropriate disclosure on ESG issues by the entities in which we invest.
4. We will promote acceptance and implementation of the Principles within the investment industry.
5. We will work together to enhance our effectiveness in implementing the Principles.
6. We will each report on our activities and progress towards implementing the Principles.[105]

The accompanying list of possible actions provides a best practice guide. Concerning the second principle, for instance, the suggested actions to achieve active ownership include to 'exercise voting rights', 'develop an engagement capability', and 'file shareholder resolutions consistent with long-term ESG considerations'. Through such actions, the UNPRI secretariat sees several benefits:

> Implementing the Principles will lead to a more complete understanding of a range of material issues, and this should ultimately result in increased returns and lower risk. There is increasing evidence that ESG issues can be material to performance of portfolios, particularly over the long term.
>
> PRI signatories are also part of a network, with opportunities to pool resources and influence, lowering the costs and increasing the effectiveness of research and active ownership practices. The Initiative also supports investors in working together to address systemic problems that, if remedied, may then lead to more stable, accountable and profitable market conditions overall.[106]

In addition to the narrowness of this business case orientation, the UNPRI has some specific limitations. Among the list of conceivable actions for the first principle, there is no stated expectation that investors actually incorporate social or environmental factors into their ultimate portfolio choices. The Principles do not require a signatory to demonstrate any particular performance standards with regard to human rights or environmental protection. The second principle on active ownership focuses on participation in investee companies, while curiously ignoring the equally pressing need to democratise

[105] See <http://www.unpri.org/principles>.
[106] UNPRI, 'Frequently Asked Questions': <http://www.unpri.org/faqs>.

decision-making within financial institutions. Nor do the UNPRI insist on any independent audit or verification mechanism to assess the quality of signatories' implementation. To reassure investors, the UNPRI explains:

> There are no legal or regulatory sanctions associated with the Principles. They are designed to be voluntary and aspirational. There may be reputational risks associated with signing up and then failing to take any action at all, but the commitments are, for most signatories, a work in progress and a direction to head in rather than a prescriptive checklist with which to comply.[107]

Such an insouciant attitude contrasts with the rigour of the Collevecchio Declaration, developed by NGOs. Its ambitious 'commitment to sustainability' principle obliges investors to:

> expand their missions from ones that prioritize profit maximization to a vision of social and environmental sustainability. A commitment to sustainability would require financial institutions to fully integrate the consideration of ecological limits, social equity and economic justice into corporate strategies and core business areas (including credit, investing, underwriting, advising), to put sustainability objectives on an equal footing to shareholder maximization and client satisfaction, and to actively strive to finance transactions that promote sustainability.

Such a standard, if adopted widely by financial institutions, would provide a strong platform to address climate change as a valuable goal in its own right.

Nonetheless, accommodating rather than radically challenging the financial sector, the UNPRI will likely remain one of the main benchmarks for SRI. As of June 2008, over 350 institutions had signed the Principles, holding more than US$14 trillion in assets.[108] The UNPRI has been generally well received by the finance sector, it being attracted to the Principles for the eminence of their sponsorship by the UN while still maintaining considerable latitude in the open-ended standards.

While the UNPRI does not explicitly refer to climate change, conceivably it is the type of environmental issue that signatories to the Principles should address. Unlike the UNEPFI, the UNPRI secretariat has not established any dedicated working groups or major projects that focus on global warming and SRI.[109] Some individual signatories mention how they use the UNPRI to inform their policies. AMP Capital states that it 'is progressively applying the UNPRI to our investment activities across all asset classes . . . on the potential risks and issues around policy response to climate change'.[110] However, most financiers ostensibly interested in SRI typically are signatories to several

[107] ibid.

[108] UNPRI Secretariat, *PRI Report on Progress 2008* (UNPRI, London, June 2008), 2.

[109] UNEPFI has a Climate Change Work Stream: <http:www.unepfi.org/work_streams/climate_change/index.html>.

[110] AMP Capital, 'AMP Capital a signatory to the United Nations Principles of Responsible Investment', <http://www.ampcapital.com.au/corporatecentre/unpri.asp>.

codes and regimes, and do not purport to attribute actions on climate change or other environmental issues to any one standard such as the UNPRI.

The following section reviews some of the specific ways that institutional investors are addressing climate change issues pursuant to the UNPRI and other evolving SRI standards.

## IV. INVESTOR RESPONSES TO CLIMATE CHANGE

### *A. Risk Management*

Improved understanding and management of the financial risks posed by climate change has been the primary concern of the SRI community. With their diverse portfolios and long-term financial liabilities, all institutional investors have good reasons to be attentive to climate-related risks. They have established some collaborative forums to share ideas and best practices. One example is the Investor Network on Climate Risk (INCR), which was created out of the UN-convened Investor Summit on Climate Risk in 2003.[111] As of January 2009, the INCR claimed a membership of approximately 75 institutional investors. It organizes conferences to educate fund managers about climate risks, and publishes various reports. Another association performing a similar collaborative role is the UK-based Institutional Investors' Group on Climate Change (IIGCC), with some 50 members as of January 2009.[112] The UN is also partnering with institutional investors through the UNEPFI's Climate Change Work Stream. It seeks to raise awareness of climate issues in the financial sector and has been a rare advocate for public policy reform.[113]

Some individual financial institutions are also voicing concerns and taking action. In 2001, the UK's Universities Superannuation Scheme published a working paper examining climate change as a financial risk.[114] In the US, public sector pension funds have also taken the lead in identifying climate change as a long-term risk to portfolio companies.[115] The 'Green Wave Initiative', launched in 2004 by the California State Treasurer with the state's two largest public sector funds,[116] commits the participants to invest millions in climate-friendly technologies and clean energy companies.[117]

For banks, climate change can pose project specific risks, such as to investments located in low-lying coastal areas or projects dependent on

[111] See <http://www.incr.com>.

[112] See <http://www.iigcc.org>.

[113] See <http://unepfi.net/cc>.

[114] M Mansley and A Dlugoleck, *Climate Change—A Risk Management Challenge for Institutional Investors* (Universities Superannuation Scheme, London 2001).

[115] C Williams and J Conley, 'An Emerging Third Way? The Erosion of the Anglo-American Shareholder Value Construct' (2005) 18 Cornell International Law Journal 555.

[116] California Public Employees' Retirement System (CalPERS) and the California State Teachers' Retirement System (CalSTRS).

[117] J Sandred, 'Catching the Green Wave: Investment in Environmental Technology Gaining Momentum', *San Francisco Chronicle* (31 May 2004).

predictable weather patterns.[118] As Philpott explains, 'there is not, at present, a standard approach within the international banking industry for transparency and accountability for the global warming performance of project finance'.[119] A few banks are committing themselves to absolute reductions in GHG emissions in their lending portfolio. In its energy-lending portfolio, the Bank of America promises to reduce the emissions of projects it finances by seven per cent.[120] The HSBC unveiled its carbon management plan in December 2004, committing the bank to 'carbon neutrality' from its operations globally.[121] Both the Bank of America and HSBC are signatories of the Carbon Principles and Climate Principles respectively.

Climate risks have become an even greater concern in the property and casualty insurance industry.[122] Costly weather catastrophes that spiked during the 1980s and 1990s—seen as a harbinger of global warming—pushed the insurance industry into the climate policy debates.[123] Some insurance companies responded by withdrawing coverage for certain risks, hiking premiums, imposing greater deductibles, and adopting physical risk management and other protective measures as a precondition to insurance.[124] Some also exerted pressure on policy-makers, lobbying for regulatory action, and collaborating with public authorities on research and preventative measures.[125] Yet, curiously, some insurance companies appear to have often disregarded the climate risks in their own investment portfolios.[126]

Insurance cannot eliminate the risks of global warming occurring, although it may indirectly help to reduce the ensuing damage by encouraging adoption of mitigation measures, and by channelling compensation to victims of the effects of climate change. Insurers have also pioneered new catastrophe risk mechanisms, such as catastrophe future and weather derivatives, to tap into

[118] J Philpott, 'Keeping it Private, Going Public: Assessing, Monitoring, and Disclosing the Global Warming Performance of Project Finance' (2005) 5 Sustainable Development Law and Policy 45.

[119] ibid 47.

[120] Bank of America, 'Bank of America Climate Change Position', at <http://www.bankofamerica.com/environment>. Yet, as recently as June 2007, the Bank of America was the target of protest actions for its continuing investments in the coal industry: 'Activists Drape 50ft Banner Across From B of A Headquarters, Call on Bank to Stop Funding Dirty Coal' *Asheville Indymedia* (23 October 2007).

[121] 'HSBC Earns Credit for Being First 'Carbon Neutral' Bank' *GreenBiz.com* (7 December 2004).

[122] Innovest, *Climate Change and the Financial Services Industry. Module 1—Threats and Opportunities* (UNEPFI Climate Change Working Group, Geneva, 2002) 16–17.

[123] C Flavin, 'Storm Warnings: Climate Change Hits the Insurance Industry' (1994) 7 World Watch 10.

[124] A Dlugolecki, 'An Insurer's Perspective' in Jeremy Leggett (ed) *Climate Change and the Financial Sector* (Gerling Akademie-Verlag, Munich, 1996) 64, 75.

[125] D Kirk, 'Insurers Voice Need to Combat Climate Risks' (1999) 33(45) Business Insurance 45; F Nutter, 'Global Climate Change: Why US Insurers Care' (1999) 42(1) Climatic Change 45.

[126] FM Research, *Capital Punishment: UK Insurance Companies and the Global Environment* (Friends of the Earth, London, 2000) 47–49.

the deep resources of the capital markets.[127] The market for weather derivatives contracts allows climate-related risks to be hedged.[128] To illustrate, if a disaster occurs, the insurer that issued the catastrophe bond would pay claims with the funds that would otherwise have gone to the bondholders. If good weather prevails during the bond period (typically a year), investors gain by the return of their principal plus interest payments.[129]

### B. Disclosing Investment-Related Climate Impacts

Socially responsible investors need to know about companies' GHG emissions if they are to construct environmentally responsible and less risky investment portfolios. The lack of well established legal obligations to report such information, coupled with the lack of comprehensive, standardised methods for reporting such emissions on a voluntary basis, has hindered SRI on climate issues.[130] Further, companies facing material climate-related financial risks are disinclined to disclose fully such information.[131] In some jurisdictions such as Canada, the UK, and the US, general corporate financial reporting laws require companies to disclose any costs or benefits associated with their environmental performance that may materially affect the firm's financial health.[132] Generally poor implementation of such standards has encouraged the SRI industry to develop its own reporting protocols.

In addition to petitioning securities regulators to improve their enforcement of disclosure rules,[133] financial institutions have designed their own informational tools to enable action on global warming. Among these tools are the Carbon Disclosure Project (CDP) and the Greenhouse Gas Protocol Initiative (GHGPI). They generate data that help facilitate dialogue between financial institutions and firms on climate change.

[127] See further D Jaffee and T Russell, 'Catastrophe Insurance: Capital Markets and Uninsurable Risks' (1997) 64 Journal of Risk and Insurance 205; S D'Arcy and V France 'Catastrophe Futures: A Better Hedge for Insurers' (1992) 59 Journal of Risk and Insurance 575.

[128] See G Chichilnisky and G Heal, 'Managing Unknown Risks' (1998) 24(4) Journal of Portfolio Management 85.

[129] See J Tynes, 'Catastrophe Risk Securitization' (2000) 19(1) Journal of Insurance Regulation 3.

[130] PricewaterhouseCoopers (PWC) and International Emissions Trading Association (IETA), *Uncertainty in Accounting for the EU Emissions Trading Scheme and Certified Emission Reductions* (PWC and IETA, London, 2007) 15–16.

[131] Economist Intelligence Unit, *A Change in the Climate. Is Business Going Green?* (UK Trade and Investment, London, 2007) 8.

[132] eg Canadian Institute of Chartered Accounts (CICA), *MD&A Disclosure about the Financial Impact of Climate Change and Other Environmental Issues: Discussion Brief* (CICA, 2005); J Smith, 'The Implications of the Kyoto Protocol and the Global Warming Debate for Business Transactions' (2005) 1 New York University Journal of Law and Business 511, 529; M Chan-Fishel, *Fifth Survey of Climate Change Disclosure in SEC Filings of Automobile, Insurance, Oil and Gas, Petrochemical, and Utilities Companies* (Friends of the Earth, San Francisco, 2006).

[133] S Mufson, 'SEC Pressed to Require Climate-Risk Disclosures' *Washington Post* (18 September 2007) D01.

The CDP is a mechanism that coordinates requests from institutional investors for information on companies' climate change-related activities.[134] Begun in December 2000, the CDP allows investors to collectively endorse a single global request for disclosure of information regarding companies' GHG emissions, vulnerability to climate change impacts, emission trading activities and their policies on climate change. These requests are made annually to an ever-larger pool of major companies. By mid-2008, over 3,000 corporations were asked to report to the CDP, on behalf of nearly 400 investment institutions.[135] About half responded. Since 2007, the CDP has also asked for information about companies' emissions connected to their supply chains, thereby helping to provide a more comprehensive picture of GHG pollution.[136] The CDP is now probably the largest registry of corporate GHG emissions data in the world, for the benefit of hundreds of climate-conscious institutional investors.

Whereas the CDP focuses on reporting data, the GHGPI aims to improve the underlying methods of accounting behind such data.[137] Developed by the World Business Council for Sustainable Development and the World Resources Institute, the GHGPI consists of two modules. The Corporate Accounting and Reporting Standard Module can assist companies and other organisations to identify, calculate, and report GHG emissions. This module is limited in that it does not adequately address the position of financial institutions, which do not have to account for the GHG emissions of companies they fund (the latter are deemed the responsible entities). The second module is the Project Accounting Protocol and Guidelines, designed for calculating reductions in GHG emissions from specific projects and land use changes. The GHGPI provides the accounting framework for the European Union's Emissions Trading Scheme and other initiatives.

Both the CDP and GHGPI inform some other disclosure regimes. One is the World Economic Forum's Global Greenhouse Gas Register (GHG Register), established in 2004, to provide a global inventory of corporate emissions inventories and reduction targets, based on the GHGPI.[138] The Global Reporting Initiative, to some the gold standard for sustainability reporting, contains directions on reporting relevant information regarding climate change.[139] The Global Reporting Initiative's G3 Reporting Framework of October 2006 introduced a specific reporting indicator on the 'financial implications due to climate change'.[140] Another initiative also informed by the GHGPI is the ISO

[134] See <http://www.cdproject.net>.
[135] See <http://www.cdproject.net/faqs.asp>.
[136] Remarks by Paul Dickinson, Chief Executive Officer, CDP (UNEPFI Global Roundtable, Melbourne, Australia, 24–25 October 2007).
[137] See <http://www.ghgprotocol.org>.
[138] See <http://www.weforum.org/en/initiatives/ghg/GreenhouseGasRegister>.
[139] See <http://www.globalreporting.org>.
[140] See <http://www.globalreporting.org/ReportingFramework/G3Online>.

14064 standard, released in March 2006. It aims to promote consistency, transparency, and credibility in GHG emission quantification, reporting, and verification, to thereby facilitate trade in GHG allowances and credits.[141] The ISO 14064 is complemented by ISO 14065, with requirements to accredit or recognise bodies that undertake GHG validation or verification.[142]

Overall, these reporting mechanisms are perhaps the most promising achievement of the financial sector on climate change issues. They provide a rare example of where SRI can provide leadership on governance of climate issues, setting an example for governments to follow. These successes probably owe to the fact that they do not actually require any changes in the behaviour of financial institutions themselves—only of the companies they fund.

### *C. Shareholder Activism*

Another way that the financial sector may voice its concerns about climate change is through shareholder activism. Financiers sometimes use shareholder resolutions and dialogue to spur corporate management to meet their demands on matters ranging from corporate governance to environmental practices. Shareholder resolutions on climate issues typically ask management to report on climate change risks that may affect the firm, rather than ask the firm to adopt specific actions to mitigate their emissions, which, in some jurisdictions, could be construed as an impermissible attempt to dictate managerial action. While many corporations strenuously resist such 'interferences', some react positively; they may agree to disclose their GHG emissions, to set emission reduction goals, make energy efficiency investments, and integrate climate risks into core business plans.

Nonetheless, shareholder resolutions on climate issues are rare and have garnered little open support until recently.[143] Most such resolutions have been filed in the US. A study of such proposals filed in 81 US companies during the period 2000–2003 found that they only attracted on average support from 13 per cent of the shareholders.[144] A survey by the Social Investment Forum documented 25 shareholder resolutions on climate issues in 2003, rising to

[141] It comprises three specific standards: ISO 14064-1: 2006, *Greenhouse Gases*—Part 1: *Specification with Guidance at the Organization Level for the Quantification and Reporting of Greenhouse Gas Emissions and Removals*; ISO 14064-2: 2006, *Greenhouse Gases*—Part 2: *Specification with Guidance at the Project Level for the Quantification, Monitoring And Reporting of Greenhouse Gas Emission Reductions and Removal Enhancements*; ISO 14064-3: 2006, *Greenhouse Gases*—Part 3: *Specification with Guidance for the Validation and Verification of Greenhouse Gas Assertions*.

[142] ISO 14065: 2007, *Greenhouse Gases—Requirements for Greenhouse Gas Validation and Verification Bodies for Use in Accreditation or Other Forms of Recognition*.

[143] R Monks et al, 'Shareholder Activism on Environmental Issues: A Study of Proposals at Large US Corporations (2000–2003)' (2004) 28 Natural Resources Forum 317, 319.

[144] ibid 321.

35 in 2005. The resolutions attracted an average of 16.7 per cent support in 2003, which declined to 10.8 per cent in 2005.[145] One resolution asking the ExxonMobil board of directors comprehensively to review how it would meet GHG reduction targets in countries subject to the Kyoto Protocol received a relatively high 28.3 per cent of the votes.[146] The 2008 proxy season in the US saw a further spike in climate change-related resolutions, with 57 proposals filed in American companies.[147] Shareholder resolutions that went to a vote garnered a record high average voting support of 21.6 per cent, including nearly 40 per cent backing for a resolution filed with Allegheny Energy, the most ever for a global warming resolution in the US.[148] However, such resolutions remain rare in other jurisdictions, such as in the UK where investors often prefer informal dialogue with corporate management.[149]

Shareholder activism on climate change is usually sponsored by a limited range of financial institutions. Public sector pension funds and faith-based investors are the most climate-conscious shareholders.[150] Mutual funds have been the most taciturn, although some commentators believe this will change in the US and Canada in the wake of securities regulation reforms in 2003 and 2005 respectively requiring such funds in these jurisdictions to disclose their proxy voting records.[151] Until now, the US mutual fund industry has tended to routinely side with management on shareholder resolutions. One report analyzed how the US's 100 largest mutual funds voted their shareholder proxies on climate change resolutions filed in 2005.[152] During that period, only three investment companies (Columbia, Franklin Templeton, and Neuberger Berman) had proxy voting guidelines allowing fund manages to support proposals for corporate disclosure on environmental issues such as climate change. Moreover, of votes actually cast, no mutual funds surveyed supported any climate change proposals filed. For example, Excelsior Funds' *Voting Guidelines on Social and Environmental Issues* (adopted in October 2004) state:

> We do not believe that social and political restrictions should be placed on a company's business operations, unless determined as appropriate by

[145] Social Investment Forum (SIF), *2005 Socially Responsible Investing Trends in the United States: 10-Year Review* (SIF, Washington DC, 2006) 19 (in each year, some of the resolutions were withdrawn before the vote, usually because management agreed in advance to respond positively to the requests made). [146] ibid 10.

[147] Investor Network on Climate Risk, 'Investors Achieve Major Company Commitments on Climate Change' (20 August 2008), at <http://www.incr.com/Page.aspx?pid=227>.

[148] ibid.

[149] As evident in the work of the UK-based IIGCC, at <http://www.iigcc.org>.

[150] SIF, above (n 145) 22.

[151] C Williams and J Conley 'Corporate Social Responsibility in the International Context: Is there an Emerging Fiduciary Duty to Consider Human Rights?' (2005) 74 University of Cincinnati Law Review 75, 96.

[152] D Cogan, *Unexamined Risk: How Mutual Funds Vote on Climate Change Shareholder Risk* (CERES, Boston, 2006) 299.

management. While from an investment perspective we may consider how a company's social and political practices may affect present and prospective valuations and returns, we believe that proposals which prohibit companies from lines of business for social or political reasons are often motivated by narrow interest groups and not in the best interest of the broad base of shareholders of a company. We believe that management is in the best position to determine these fundamental business questions. We will typically vote against such proposals.[153]

While the proxy voting record reforms in the US now require mutual funds to disclose publicly their voting policies and actual voting records, some preliminary research suggests it has not generated significant changes in the industry.[154]

The US Securities Exchange Commission (SEC) has arbitrated over many shareholder resolutions on climate change disputed by the targeted companies.[155] The SEC has tended to rule against resolutions if they raise 'ordinary business' issues deemed a prerogative of management.[156] The SEC, however, has sometimes appeared to view such issues differently. In April 2003, the SEC allowed Xcel Energy to exclude a shareholder request for an evaluation of climate change risks to the market competitiveness of the company.[157] Yet, in March 2005, the SEC allowed a shareholder demand on ExxonMobil to 'undertake a comprehensive review and publish a report on how it will meet the greenhouse gas reduction targets of those countries in which it operates which have adopted the Kyoto Protocol'.[158] The SEC rejected the claim of ExxonMobil's management that the shareholders' request amounted to an attempt to micro-manage the business.

To date, although shareholder resolutions on climate change issues are relatively scarce compared to traditional subjects of shareholder proposals (such as executive pay), climate change as a subject garners more shareholder proposals than virtually any other environmental cause on the SRI agenda.[159] Further, targeted companies may concede to shareholder demands even if a proposal is defeated in a vote. Thus, Ford Motor Company agreed to implement a defeated resolution that asked it to report on the business implications of reducing GHG emissions from its vehicles and manufacturing

[153] Cited in Cogan, ibid 28.

[154] M Cremers and R Romano, 'Institutional Investors and Proxy Voting: The Impact of the 2003 Mutual Fund Voting Disclosure Regulation', ECGI-Law Working Paper No 083/2007 (Social Science Research Network, 24 April 2007) 2–3.

[155] For a more detailed discussion, see S Choi, 'It's Getting Hot in Here: The SEC's Regulation of Climate Change Shareholder Proposals Under the Ordinary Business Exception' (2006) 17 Duke Environmental Law and Policy Forum 165.

[156] ibid 178–79.

[157] Xcel Energy, 'SEC No-Action Letter, 2003', *Lexis* 500 (April 1, 2003) 1.

[158] ExxonMobil Corporation, 'SEC No-Action Letter, 2005', *Lexis* 466 (March 23, 2005) 1.

[159] SIF, above (n 145) 19 (only shareholder proposals on political contributions were more numerous among US investors in 2005).

facilities.[160] In all respects, however, the focus of shareholder activism on climate change and any corporate response is strictly the business implications of climate change.

## V. REFLECTIONS AND FUTURE DIRECTIONS

Climate finance is an essential part of the solution to global warming. So far, most policy-makers and commentators have focused on the transactional side of the financial sector, viewing investment institutions as mere brokers or passive financiers of measures to mitigate or adapt to climate change. The potential role of the financial sector as a means to stimulate far-reaching changes in corporate behaviour through the example set by the long-standing movement for SRI is only just starting to be seriously explored.

Certainly, in the financial sector there is growing awareness of climate change as a threat to investment portfolios or as an opportunity to enhance returns. Yet, even from this pragmatic business case approach to SRI, in various ways investors remain hampered in dealing with global warming.[161] They may believe that climate change is too remote to affect a company's bottom line, or that there are seemingly more pressing issues affecting investment values. Another hindrance is the difficulties of determining the implications of climate change, and government policy responses to it, for financial markets. For instance, there is insufficient research demonstrating the relationship between GHG emission regulations and investment returns. Basic data may also be too imprecise for practical decisions. The present lack of intergovernmental agreement on GHG emission targets beyond 2012, when the Current Kyoto Protocol commitment period expires, also obstructs setting a durable value on carbon reduction and climate adaptation measures.

We can discern two important insights from this exploration of climate finance. First, in an acknowledgement of the limits of current approaches, the World Business Council for Sustainable Development concedes that the transition to a low carbon economy requires government policy instruments to send the correct economic signals.[162] The market has struggled to capture and reflect climate risks efficiently. These failures mean that financing renewable energy supplies and energy efficiency technologies 'generally entail higher risks and initial costs than conventional projects'.[163] Government policies

[160] Ford published its report on 2005, and claimed to have reduced carbon emissions from its manufacturing facilities by 15 per cent, with further reductions planned, and was adopting measures to improve the fuel efficiency of its cars: Ford Motor Company, *Ford Report on the Business Impact of Climate Change* (Ford, Dearborn, Michigan, 2005) 3.

[161] Innovest, *Climate Change and the Financial Services Industry. Module 2—A Blueprint for Action* (UNEPFI, Geneva, 2002) 31–34.

[162] World Business Council for Sustainable Development (WBCSD), *Energy and Climate Change: Sharpening the Focus for Action—A Business Perspective* (WBCSD, Geneva, 2005).

[163] See Z Zhang and A Maruyama, 'Towards a Private-Public Synergy in Financing Climate Change Mitigation Projects' (2001) 29 Energy Policy 1363.

must therefore set a long-term value for carbon if the SRI market driven solely by the business case is to be a force for change. Already, regulation and litigation risks are major drivers for financiers to factor climate change into their investment choices. The prospect of carbon emission caps, carbon taxes, renewable energy subsidies, and mandatory corporate disclosures on climate impacts—imposed by governments—are becoming crucial for the SRI market on climate finance. This fact should remind us of how heavily SRI often depends on market regulation. In this sense, SRI presents a paradox, having emerged as a form of surrogate market regulation to compensate for the lacunae of official regulation, yet often heavily dependent on the state to set environmental standards necessary to stimulate the SRI market.

A second key insight is that the ethical issues posed by climate change have been poorly acknowledged in the SRI movement (let alone by financial markets generally). The business case approach to SRI, even at its most efficient, will probably never be a satisfactory solution because it rests on perpetuating the same economic system premised on infinite growth that has wrought so much ecological damage. There must surely also be an ethical envelope to climate finance, providing a normative framework for restraint to safeguard ecological integrity and ensure social justice in entitlements to use limited environmental resources.

Climate change is very much an ethical issue, as humankind's ability to tamper with the earth's climate should raise profound questions about our relationship with nature.[164] Indeed, the UNFCCC proclaims as one of its core principles that: '[t]he Parties should protect the climate system for the benefit of present and future generations of humankind, on the basis of equity and in accordance with their common but differentiated responsibilities and respective capabilities'.[165] Further, the question of who should shoulder the primary burden of addressing climate change raises significant ethical questions of ensuring social and economic justice between developing and developed countries.[166] But the financial sector has been able to bypass such uncomfortable questions that would raise doubts about the sustainability and justice of our economic system. Instead, the climate finance discourse has been carefully framed around business risks and investment opportunities. There is nothing objectionable to investors financially benefiting from reducing their carbon footprint. The problem is that the business case will not always provide sufficient motivation for change.

Such conclusions, of course, raise questions regarding what policy-makers could do to make ethically-driven SRI on climate change more widespread in financial markets. While the answer requires another article of much longer

[164] P Taylor, 'The Business of Climate Change: What's Ethics Got to Do With It?' (2007), 20 Global Business and Development Law Journal 161.

[165] Article 3.1 (1992) 31 ILM 849.

[166] See L Rajamani, *Differential Treatment in International Environmental Law* (Oxford University Press, 2006).

length, a few concluding comments can be briefly made. As a priority, reformers should target the fiduciary duties of investment institutions, for these provide the very core legal standards that determine their basic economic goals. One option would be to mandate the goal of sustainable development, as the overall benchmark to hold financial investment to account. Thereby, the fiduciary obligation to promote private returns must take into account their public costs. But such a fiduciary standard must be underpinned by concrete performance standards if it is to be workable. Vague stipulations to 'promote sustainability' would not suffice. They would likely be undermined by discretionary interpretations on which financiers could not be legally challenged. The advances in designing sustainable performance indicators in environmental policy-making should be extended to financial investments.[167] One such indicator is the carbon footprint of an investment portfolio—one of the most powerful indicators of environmental performance.[168] It would surely also be necessary to democratize decision-making in financial institutions, giving more voice to ordinary fund members as well as to outside third parties affected by their investments. This should enable other social values to be considered in investment policies. Given the global scale of modern financial markets, parallel reforms to fiduciary duties and investment decision-making must be etched into new international legal rules governing cross-border finance. The existing range of voluntary international standards such as the UNPRI and the Climate Principles fall short of meeting the exacting standards required. The current intergovernmental climate change negotiations could provide a suitable forum to introduce some climate finance standards into international climate law.

In sum, while SRI suggests a more ambitious and enlightened role for financial institutions on climate change issues, so far the SRI sector has made a fairly limited and largely uninspiring contribution. SRI can not yet provide a credible alternative to official regulation, but it could make a more useful contribution with appropriate enabling legal reforms.

[167] J Keeble, S Topiol and S Berkeley, 'Using Indicators to Measure Sustainability Performance at a Corporate and Project Level' (2003) 44 Journal of Business Ethics 149; O Schmid-Schönbein and A Braunschweig, *EPI-Finance 2000; Environmental Performance Indicators for the Financial Industry* (E2 Management Consulting AG, Zürich, 2000).

[168] Carbon footprints of investment portfolios are already been measures: Trucost, *Carbon Counts 2007: The Carbon Footprint Ranking of UK Investment* (Trucost, London, 2007).

# Part IV
# Environmental Regulation Across Sectors

# [18]

THE MODERN LAW REVIEW

THE
MODERN LAW REVIEW

Volume 74 November 2011 No 6

# Governing Climate Change: Towards a New Paradigm for Risk Regulation

Veerle Heyvaert*

This article argues that the ascent of climate change on the EU regulatory agenda signals a new era of risk regulation and calls for the establishment of a new paradigm for risk regulation. Climate change is altering the EU's conception of environmental risks and its design of regulatory responses. In contrast to conventional risk regulation, climate change regulation must prioritise the risks of business-as-usual over the risks of change, must target systemic change instead of stability, and must favour the virtues of integration and orchestration over those of individualisation and compartmentalisation. There is an important role for risk regulation scholarship to analyse this shift and its consequences for regulation, such as the relocation of legitimacy needs and the emergence of new risks of regulatory failure. Such an enterprise would both reinvigorate risk regulation scholarship and offer a vital contribution to the European Union as it tackles the momentous challenge of climate change governance.

## INTRODUCTION

The European Union has a well-established reputation as the world's most forceful advocate for the adoption of internationally binding climate change commitments. The EU has moreover chosen to lead by example and has adopted an impressively diverse arsenal of regulatory measures that together aim to reduce its own carbon footprint by at least 20 per cent by 2020.

This article analyses the core features of the regulatory approach as it emerges out of the sprawling body of climate change legislation and argues that they constitute a significant, in many ways radical, departure from the EU's conventional approach to environmental regulation. Until now, the EU's legal response to environmental and health problems, from biodiversity loss to chemical toxicity, has been heavily dominated by the risk regulation paradigm. The risk regulation paradigm sets the tone for how the EU as a regulatory authority conceptualises the environmental impacts of human activity, for the articulation of its regulatory mandate and for the design and implementation of regulatory strategies in fulfilment of this mandate. The analysis will show that, while climate change is unequivocally recognised as a major environmental risk, it is a risk that is differently understood from those that form the traditional subject of EU risk

*London School of Economics. I thank Rob Baldwin, Jonathan Golub and two anonymous referees for comments on earlier drafts. Any mistakes are mine.

 (2011) 74(6) MLR 817–844

Published by Blackwell Publishing, 9600 Garsington Road, Oxford OX4 2DQ, UK and 350 Main Street, Malden, MA 02148, USA

regulation. Consequently, climate change as a regulatory challenge makes different demands of the EU as a regulator: climate change regulation must target systemic change rather than stabilisation, and regulatory strategies must facilitate integration and orchestration over itemisation and compartmentalisation. The climate change regulatory regime will also display different vulnerabilities from those that characterise EU risk regulation, calling for a rethink of the function and variety of EU legitimation strategies.

The outcomes of the analysis have fundamental implications for the study and practice of risk regulation. Scholars in the area are confronted with the reality that the established risk regulation paradigm is of limited use to understand and guide regulatory efforts to control the most important environmental risk of our time. If scholarship is to play a constructive role in supporting the EU regulatory enterprise, it needs to develop a new paradigm for a new era of risk regulation. Enhanced awareness within EU regulatory circles of the particular nature and needs of climate change regulation can be a pivotal asset towards the further development and implementation of a regulatory regime that offers the best chance of effectiveness and minimises the risks of regulatory failure.

The first section of this contribution sets out the general features of the established risk regulation paradigm. We then move into the analytical heart of the article by examining, firstly, how risk regulation operates in practice in the European Union and, secondly, by comparing and contrasting the discourse, agenda, and strategies of EU risk regulation to those that characterise EU climate change regulation. The final section assesses the outcomes of the preceding analysis. It draws attention to regulatory blind spots that are likely to develop as a consequence of insufficient awareness of the particular context of EU climate change regulation, and discusses the risk that the EU might revert to tried and tested risk regulatory strategies, which have functioned reasonably well in the past but would be ineffective in the battle against climate change. On a positive note, the assessment identifies scope for synergy and mutual learning between conventional risk regulation and climate change regulation, arguing that experiences gained in one area could be productively deployed in the other. The article concludes with a plea for the further articulation of a new risk regulation paradigm that adequately reflects the character and scale of the environmental risks that society faces today.

## THE RISK REGULATION PARADIGM

Risk regulation has become such a staple of contemporary law and policy that it barely needs an introduction. In order to discern the distinctive features of EU risk regulation, however, as well as the particularities of risk within the climate change field, it is useful first to contemplate, in general terms, what we mean when we talk about 'risk' as a catalyst for regulation, what the agenda is of risk regulation, and how regulation seeks to achieve its targets.

We qualify a particular situation or activity as a risk when we are aware of the possibility of undesirable consequences. To gauge the seriousness of the risk, we in the first place take into account the likelihood of negative impacts and the

 
(2011) 74(6) MLR 817–844

anticipated magnitude of impacts.[1] Risk regulation is the exercise of public authority (however broadly construed) with intent to affect the likelihood and/or magnitude of socially undesirable events ('social bads').[2]

As an expression of likelihood, or probability, risk is inherently future-oriented.[3] In German jurisprudence of the 1980s to early 1990s, risk was often defined by reference to the concept of 'danger'.[4] Following a 'danger-based' approach, we acquire experience about the negative impacts of certain goods or activities and modulate our behaviour on the basis of that experience.[5] A risk-based approach, in contrast, seeks to anticipate negative consequences, bypass experience, and modulate behaviour on the basis of predictions.

Presenting future negative occurrences as potential adverse *effects*, or impacts, implies a premise of causation – an assumption that the negative consequence, whatever it may be, happens *because* we engage or omit to engage in a certain activity.[6] I risk getting wet because I go for a walk under a threatening sky; polar bears are at risk of extinction because we are not doing enough to mitigate climate change. The theoretical possibility of a solution is what separates a problem from a calamity. Similarly, the theoretical possibility of choice distinguishes risk from the fickleness of fate. Risk, therefore, implies some degree of free will and ability to act; if harm is absolutely certain and inevitable, whatever we do or wherever we go, the risk evaporates. By extension, risk regulation assumes the possibility of exercising at least some degree of influence, with at least some degree of authority and persistence, on the likelihood and scale of undesirable events occurring.

Of equal relevance is that risk does not have a wholly negative connotation; it is perceived against a backdrop of opportunity.[7] There are, firstly, the benefits to be enjoyed if potential adverse effects do not materialise, such as the joys of a brisk walk in dry weather, or the professed value added of a more abundant and reliable

1 H. Rothstein, M. Huber and G. Gaskell, 'A Theory of Risk Colonization: the Spiralling Regulatory Logics of Societal and Institutional Risk' (2006) 35 *Economy and Society* 91, 92.

2 cf C. Hood, H. Rothstein, and R. Baldwin, *The Government of Risk. Understanding Risk Regulation Regimes* (Oxford: OUP, 2004) 3. It should be noted that the definition of regulation generally, and risk regulation in particular, is both evolving and contested. For a critical discussion of both, see J. Black, 'Decentring Regulation: Understanding the Role of Regulation and Self-regulation in a "Post-regulatory" World' (2001) 54 *Current Legal Problems* 103; and 'The Role of Risk in the Regulatory Process' in R. Baldwin and M. Lodge, *Oxford Handbook on Regulation* (Oxford: OUP, 2010) 302.

3 T. Giddens, 'Risk and Responsibility' (1999) 62 MLR 1, 3.

4 D. Cansier, 'Gefahrenabwehr und Risikoforsorge im Umweltschutz und der Spielraum für Ökonomische Instrumente' (1994) 7 *Neue Zeitschrift für Verwaltungsrecht* 643; K.-H. Ladeur, 'Von der Gefahrenabwehr zum Risikomanagement im Stoffbezogenen Umweltrecht' in G. Winter (ed), *Risikoanalyse und Risikoabwehr im Chemikalienrecht* (Germany: Umweltrechtliche Studien, 1994) 241–263.

5 C. Joerges, 'Law, Science and the Management of Risks to Health at the National, European and International Level – Stories on Baby Dummies, Mad Cows and Hormones in Beef' (2001) 7 Colum J Eur L 2; K.-H. Ladeur, 'Deregulating Environmental Law in a Perspective of Stimulating Knowledge Generation' in U. Collier (ed), *Deregulation in the European Union. Environmental Perspectives* (London: Routledge, 1998) 43.

6 M. Douglas, *Purity and Danger: An Analysis of the Concepts of Pollution and Taboo* (London: Routledge, 1990).

7 Giddens, n 3 above, 3–4.

food supply after switching to genetically modified crops.[8] Secondly, responding to risk creates opportunity costs: we forego the option of exploiting the resources put towards risk mitigation in an alternative way.[9]

Consequently, within this conceptual framework, any quest to 'eliminate risk', whether through regulation or other means, becomes illusory. Not only does society willingly tolerate and even encourage a certain amount of risk-taking,[10] but any attempt to cut out risk altogether is doomed to failure, as risk responses themselves create countervailing risks.[11] By not going for a walk, I might put my health and fitness levels at risk, whatever the weather. Evidently, risks differ in likelihood and magnitude, but the complete absence of risk remains a theoretical impossibility.

### Risk regulation goals and strategy

Our understanding of risk as future-oriented, impressionable, and double-edged informs the agenda and strategies of risk regulation. Risk regulation does not aspire to eliminate risk but to substitute acceptable for unacceptable risk. To accomplish this, risk regulation carves up the amorphous totality of risks we are exposed to into discrete, manageable segments, and it engages with these segments to the exclusion of others.[12] If not, the task of weighing risks against opportunities, which enables the determinations of acceptable/unacceptable risk that drive risk regulatory decision-making, would become unending and futile. Risk regulation, therefore, is as much about risk construction as it is about risk control.

The construction of risk within the regulatory process requires considerable efforts in information production, selection, and collection, in order both to delineate the categories of risk that the regulation recognises, and to weigh and ultimately determine the acceptability of identified risks. To this end, risk regulation deploys techniques of information gathering, classification, and risk assessment, and maps out decision-making procedures that link assessments to control options.[13] The atomisation of risk into an extensive but discrete range of selected harms, caused by specific forms of action or omission, fosters the individualisation of risk governance responsibility: it enables the identification of causal agents that become the target audience of risk regulation, and furthers the establishment of risk regulatory authorities working with a circumscribed mandate and interacting primarily with well-defined social groups (hazardous waste transporters, hedge fund managers, dangerous dog owners, consumers, nuclear facilities, etc).

8 M. Quaim and D. Zilberman, 'Yield Effects of Genetically Modified Crops in Developing Countries' (2003) 299 *Science* 900.

9 See, eg, C. Sunstein, *Free Markets and Social Justice* (Oxford: OUP, 1997) 298–317.

10 N. Baird, 'Tolerance for Environmental Risks: the Influence of Knowledge, Benefits, Voluntariness, and Environmental Attitudes' (1986) 6 *Risk Analysis* 425.

11 J. Graham and J. Wiener, 'Confronting Risk Tradeoffs' in J. Graham and J. Wiener (eds), *Risk vs. Risk* (Cambridge, Mass: Harvard UP, 1995).

12 N. Pidgeon and C. Butler, 'Risk Analysis and Climate Change' (2009) 18 *Environmental Politics* 670, 673.

13 Hood et al, n 2 above.

The communication tools vary, ranging from commands to incentives to ethics-based encouragements. Control options, in turn, run the gamut from decisions to 'wait and see', requests for further data production and/or advanced assessment, to information disclosure requirements, monitoring provisions, standard-setting, and mandatory restrictions.

In the context of information production and processing, it is important to contemplate the relation between risk and uncertainty. Often, and particularly since the ascent of the precautionary principle, risk and uncertainty are treated as qualitatively different, even juxtaposed, notions. Risk, it is said, qualifies situations where sufficient information exists to make a probabilistic assessment of likelihood and magnitude of harm.[14] Uncertainty, in contrast, occurs where indications of harm exist, but there is insufficient data to conduct a 'proper' risk assessment.[15] This distinction may serve as a rough and ready delineator of the remit of certain regulatory regimes, but it is essentially flawed. For one, it ignores that the information required to conduct a risk assessment does not exist 'out there', but is at least partially generated within the context of regulation. Secondly, as defined above, the distinction is entirely subservient to the mode of conceiving of risk assessment.[16] However, it is extremely valuable as a reminder that risk regulation involves the creation of fictional certainty; unknown future events are translated into known probabilities and thereby become actionable.[17] The regulatory response, too, implies the acceptance of a fictional or at the very least unexamined certainty, namely that rules can have a pre-determined impact on risk. Risk regulation does, however, tend to recognise the fragility of its belief system, and correspondingly creates opportunities for the integration of new information, for review and adaptation within regulation.[18]

Before moving on to a discussion of risk regulation as it is practiced within the EU, it should be acknowledged that this rather bloodless portrayal of the key features and dynamics of risk regulation masks a reality riddled by controversy. Longstanding disagreements over the quality of the information on which risk assessment and management should be based, over the dividing line between acceptable versus unacceptable risks, and over the choice of regulatory control techniques, have turned the field of risk regulation into an ideological battleground. Risk, as apparent from the preceding discussion, is a product of perception. Whose perception matters, or matters most, therefore becomes a crucial issue for regulators to wrestle with. Countries with advanced risk regulatory regimes tend heavily to favour expert-based identifications and assessments of risk, giving rise to critiques that alternative, 'lay' perceptions are overlooked to the

14 Commission Communication on the Precautionary Principle COM(2000)1 final, 2 February 2000; V. Heyvaert, 'Facing the Consequences of the Precautionary Principle in European Community Law' (2006) *European Law Review* 185; Black, 'The Role of Risk in the Regulatory Process' n 2 above, 310.

15 cf P. O'Malley, 'Uncertain Subjects: Risk, Liberalism and Contract' (2001) 29 *Economy and Society* 462.

16 cf E. Stokes, 'The EC Courts' Contribution to Refining the Parameters of Precaution' (2008) 11 *Journal of Risk Research* 491, 494.

17 cf N. Luhmann, *Risk: A Sociological Theory* (Berlin: De Gruyter, 1993).

18 cf T. L. McDaniels And R. Gregory, 'Learning as an Objective within a Structured Risk Management Decision Process' (2004) 38 *Environmental Science and Technology* 1921.

detriment of regulatory quality and legitimacy.[19] The tensions caused by the construction and integration of risk information into regulation run deeper and wider, however, than the familiar 'science v public' dilemma. Wider, because risks never affect all segments of the population and the natural world alike. The process of risk identification is therefore simultaneously one of selection, involving controversial normative judgement. Deeper, for even if full agreement existed about what kind of information should inform risk assessment and, consequently, management, this does not preclude debates about how this information should be generated, or about the regulator's role in gathering, processing, and acting upon this information.[20]

## RISK REGULATION IN ACTION: THE EU EXAMPLE

The European Union has developed a rich expertise in the practice of health and environmental risk regulation. The heartland of the EU risk regulation enterprise undoubtedly resides within the realm of market regulation, more specifically product and technology regulation. A quick survey of the study of EU risk regulation as an academic enterprise offers a robust confirmation: scholarly contributions overwhelmingly draw on case studies from areas such as GMO, pharmaceuticals, food safety, and chemicals regulation.[21]

The close connection between EU risk regulation and market regulation is hardly surprising, as the EU was first confronted with the question of health and environmental risks in its efforts to harmonise market conditions to foster the free circulation of goods across national borders. As early as 1967, the EU promulgated harmonised standards for the classification, packaging, and labelling of dangerous substances.[22] This was a thoroughly market-facilitating endeavour, but one that nonetheless set the frame within which chemical risk discourses would later

19 M. Everson and E. Vos, 'European Risk Governance in a Global Context' in E. Vos (ed), *European Risk Governance. Its Science, its Inclusiveness and its Effectiveness* (Connex Report Series Nr 6, 2008) 10–15; S. Rayner, 'Democracy in the Age of Assessment: Reflections on the Roles of Expertise and Democracy in Public Sector Decision-Making' (2003) 30 *Science and Public Policy* 163; J. Applegate, 'A Beginning Not an End In Itself: The Role of Risk Assessment in Environmental Decision-Making' (1995) *University of Cincinnati Law Review* 1643; S. Jasanoff, *Designs on Nature: Science and Democracy in Europe and the United States* (Princeton: Princeton University Press, 2005).

20 See E. Fisher, *Risk Regulation and Administrative Constitutionalism* (Oxford: Hart Publishing, 2007).

21 See, for instance, writings on EU risk regulation by David Vogel (eg, D. Vogel, 'The New Politics of Risk Regulation in Europe' LSE Centre for Analysis of Risk and Regulation Working Paper (2001) 5–7 at http://www2.lse.ac.uk/researchAndExpertise/units/CARR/pdf/DPs/Disspaper3.pdf (last visited 1 August 2011)), Elizabeth Fisher, *ibid*, Ellen Vos, n 19 above and n 41 below, Ragnar Lofstedt, n 40 below, Bill Durodié, 'Plastic Panics: European Risk Regulation in the Aftermath of BSE' in J. Morris, *Rethinking Risk and the Precautionary Principle* (Oxford: Butterworth-Heinemann, 2000) 141, Christian Joerges, n 5 above, Veerle Heyvaert, notes 23 and 35 below and Alberto Alemanno, n 24 below. The European Journal of Risk Regulation identifies European law and policy on chemicals, nanomaterials, pharmaceuticals, pesticides, food and feed, cosmetics, industrial accidents and public health as the central focus of its research. See http://www.lexxion.de/en/zeitschriften/fachzeitschriften-englisch/ejrr/about-ejrr.html (last visited 1 August 2011).

22 Directive 67/548/EEC on the approximation of laws, regulations and administrative provisions of the Member States relating to the classification, packaging and labelling of dangerous substances [1967] OJ Nr 196/1.

unfold.[23] Trade conflicts over the compatibility of national risk regulation with the dictates of Articles 34 and 36 of the Treaty on the Functioning of the European Union also supplied the backdrop for the European Court of Justice's first musings on the nature of risk and its role in regulation.[24] Conflict is in many ways disruptive, but it is grist to the mill of academic scholarship. Trade and marketing disputes, revolving around goods ranging from beef to beer to slimming pills, have fuelled academic, regulatory, and even civil society's interest in risk regulation in no small measure.[25] Thus, the EU's understanding of risk regulation, and of its role as a regulator, matured in a context of trade and economic competitiveness, which imbued the EU regulatory agenda, strategies, and instrumental choices with some pronounced idiosyncrasies.

Over the years, the EU acquired a broader environmental agenda, venturing into areas that are less emphatically defined by their connection to the single market project, such as environmental impact assessment, waste regulation, and nature conservation. These areas typically are not thought of as EU risk regulation '*pur sang*', but they are nonetheless influenced by the risk-orientation that shapes EU product and technology regulations. They also display a comparable understanding of what EU regulation should aspire to achieve in terms of environmental protection, and of the strategies and techniques to be pressed into service towards this aim.[26]

What, then, are the key features of the EU approach to risk regulation? A first point of note is that EU regulation is intensely engaged in the aforementioned practice of carving up risk into discrete, manageable segments. The concept of risk in EU risk regulation is narrowly construed. As a rule, risks are understood as the physical negative side-effects of entrepreneurship. This approach is tellingly exemplified in regulation of trade in genetically modified food and feed, which interprets risk as the likelihood of adverse health or environmental effects, and staunchly abstains from engaging with broader debates on, for instance, the likely cultural impact of GMO farming, the consequences of a permissive or restrictive GMO policy on the global political economy, or the morality of genetic engineering.[27] For the purposes of EU regulation, risk is inconceivable outside the European

23 cf V. Heyvaert, *Coping With Uncertainty. The Regulation of Chemicals in the European Union* (PhD dissertation, European University Institute, Florence, Italy, 1999).

24 A. Alemanno, 'EU Risk Regulation and Science: The Role of Experts in Decision-Making and Judicial Review' in Vos, n 19 above 38–39.

25 Case C-180/96 *UK* v *Commission* [1999] ECR I-2265; Case 178/84 *Comission* v *Germany* [1987] ECR 1227; Joined cases T-74/00, T-76/00, T-83/00, T-84/00, T-85/00, T-132/00, T-137/00 and T-141/00, *Artegodan* v *Commission* [2002] ECR II-4945. We witness a similar phenomenon at the international level, see, inter alia, G. Shaffer and M. Pollack, *When Cooperation Fails. The International Law and Politics of Genetically Modified Food* (Oxford: OUP, 2009); A. Lang and R. Cooney, 'Taking Uncertainty Seriously: Adaptive Governance, Alien Invasive Species and the WTO' (2007) 18 *European Journal of International Law* 523; J. Scott, 'The European Regulation of GMOs and the WTO' (2003) *Columbia Journal of European Law* 213; I. Cheyne, 'Risk and Precaution in World Trade Organization Law' (2006) 40 *Journal of World Trade* 837.

26 cf Black, who observes a similar influence of risk on environmental regulation at the UK level, in Black, 'The Role of Risk in the Regulatory Process' n 2 above, 305.

27 See Regulation (EC) No 1829/2003 on genetically modified food and feed [2003] OJL 268/1. See also Lee on the construction of nanotechnological risk within EU regulation, M. Lee, 'Risk and Beyond: EU Regulation of Nanotechnology' (2010) 35 *European Law Review* 799.

economic context. Differently put, risk becomes the concern of EU regulation as a consequence of there being economic activity with a cross-boundary impact. This is most apparent in the case of EU product regulation, which lays down health, safety, and environmental standards in a context of intra-EU trade facilitation. But it equally resonates in many landmark pieces of EU environmental regulation, which govern the environmentally adverse consequences of economic and industrial activity *if* they are potentially transboundary.[28]

A connected point relates to the concept of foregone opportunities in EU risk regulation. These too are the subject of a distinctly economic interpretation, referring to both the costs of bearing higher regulatory burdens, and foregone economic growth. The acceptability of risk, therefore, not only is a function of the likelihood and magnitude of narrowly interpreted adverse effects, but is also co-determined by economic considerations.[29] This feature, again, characterises both the core of EU (technological) risk regulation and the broader domain of environmental regulation.[30]

The confined discursive space goes some way towards explaining the EU's behaviour as a risk regulator, as well as its choice of regulatory techniques. It would be a serious stretch to portray the EU as an expansive, confident risk manager, secure in the knowledge that its perception and values accord with those of the European public, and happy to cut any Gordian knots on the way. The prerequisite of an inter-State economic impact creates a perennial need for justification of EU risk control strategies. This is compounded by the insistence built into EU law, *inter alia* by way of the subsidiarity principle, that EU risk regulation should be qualitatively superior to what the national level can offer.[31] The agenda of EU risk regulation is, therefore, as preoccupied with the task of justifying decision-making, as it is with substituting acceptable for unacceptable risk.

The narrowness of EU risks, the inter-State context, and the pronounced need for self-justification crystallise into a distinct EU risk regulation pathology, characterised, firstly, by a rigorously itemised approach to risk management.[32]

28 M. Lee, *EU Environmental Law: Challenges, Change and Decision-Making* (Oxford: Hart Publishing, 2005); J. Jans and H. Vedder, *European Environmental Law* (The Netherlands: Europa Law Publishing, 2008). See, eg, preamble 29 of Directive 2008/01/EC concerning integrated pollution prevention and control [2008] OJL 24/8; preambles 17 and 23 of Directive 2000/60/EC establishing a framework for Community action in the field of water policy [2000] OJL 327/1; and para 5 of the preamble to Council Directive 92/43/EEC on the conservation of natural habitats and of wild fauna and flora [1992] OJL 2006/7.

29 See European Commission Impact Assessment Guidelines 2009, SEC[2009]92, 15 January 2009, 27.

30 See, for instance, the references to technical feasibility, economic viability, social and economic impacts as factors for Member States to consider when deciding on the application of or deviation from the waste hierarchy in Art 4(2) of Directive 2008/98/EC on waste [2008] OJL312/3, and the exception of 'overriding public interest, including those of a social or economic nature' to the prohibition on plans or projects posing an environmental risk to special conservation areas (Article 6(4) of Directive 92/43/EEC, n 28 above).

31 D. Chalmers, 'Gauging the Cumbersomeness of EU Law' (2009) 62 *Current Legal Problems* 405.

32 On the link between oversight, accountability, and risk regulation, see Huber, Rothstein, and Gaskell, n 1 above, 96.

Not only does EU regulation painstakingly circumscribe the remit of risk through a strict focus on physical and monetisable adverse impacts, it also reviews identified risks substance-by-substance, technological application-by-application, product-by-product and, within the wider field of EU environmental regulation, installation-by-installation and/or project-by-project. The REACH Regulation on chemicals, for instance, displays a pronounced degree of itemisation. It sets up an institutional framework and procedures for substance evaluation that zero in on the risk particularities of singular chemicals, but are not equipped to generate or even fully integrate information on synergistic effects caused by exposure to chemical compounds.[33] Within EU risk regulation, itemisation fosters the representation of risk as containable and therefore non-threatening to aspirations of economic growth through free enterprise.[34]

Moreover, itemisation facilitates the involvement of regulatory addressees. Under the auspices of EU risk regulation, processes of risk identification and, increasingly, assessment, management, and even communication are characterised by an advanced degree of privatisation.[35] Besides alleviating the public financial burden of risk regulation – a key consideration for a regulator as cash-strapped as the EU – privatisation fulfils vital legitimising functions towards the regulatory addressees, who are co-opted within the regulatory process and regain some degree of self-determination, albeit within tightly drawn parameters, over risk control.

The pressing demand for justification makes the EU deeply beholden to the fiction of certainty in risk decision-making. Regulatory outcomes must appear as the necessary consequences of decision-making, taken in accordance with the dictates of good governance. The 'necessity need' explains the enormous effort EU regulation expends on the organisation and normalisation of information-gathering.[36] Inescapably, risk assessments are based on estimations and predictions, but EU regulation seeks to boost the credibility of its inputs by insisting on their production, in prodigious amounts, through rigorously standardised and

33 Regulation (EC) No 1907/2006 concerning the registration, evaluation, authorisation and restriction of chemicals (REACH), establishing a European Chemicals Agency, amending Directive 1999/45/EC and repealing Council Regulation (EEC) No 793/93 and Commission Regulation (EC) No 1488/94 as well as Council Directive 76/769/EEC and Commission Directives 91/155/EEC, 93/67/EEC, 93/105/EC and 2000/21/EC [2006] OJL 396/1.

34 cf Pidgeon and Butler, n 12 above, 673; M. Granger Morgan, M. Kandlikar, J. Risbey, and H. Dowlatabadi, 'Why Conventional Tools for Policy Analysis are often Inadequate for Problems of Global Change' (1999) 41 *Climatic Change* 270, 273–274.

35 See, eg, the extensive risk assessment management operator responsibilities under the Seveso II Directive (Council Directive 96/82/EC on the control of major accident hazards involving dangerous substances [1997] OJL 10/13), and the chemicals manufacturer, importer and user responsibilities under REACH as discussed in V. Heyvaert, 'Regulating Chemical Risk: REACH in a Global Governance Perspective' in J. Eriksson, M. Gilek, and C. Ruden (eds), *Regulating Chemical Risk: Multidisciplinary Perspectives on European and Global Challenges* (New York: Springer, 2010); and E. Fisher, 'The "Perfect Storm" of REACH: Charting Regulatory Controversy in the Age of Information, Sustainable Development, and Globalization' (2008) 9 *Journal of Risk Research* 541, 548.

36 cf C. Boswell, 'The Political Functions of Expert Knowledge: Knowledge and Legitimation in European Union Immigration Policy' (2008) 15 *Journal of European Public Policy* 471.

independently verified processes.[37] EU legislation, case-law and policy documents are studded with repeated assurances that, even in areas of pronounced uncertainty, risk decision-making must and will happen on the basis of the 'best available information.'[38] The European Courts have moreover been at pains to confirm, in cases from *Pfizer* to *Gowan*, that the precautionary principle should not be understood to absolve decision-makers from the duty to identify and assess risks on the basis of the most reliable scientific data available.[39]

Adherence to good governance, in turn, is secured through the formal incorporation of governance standards, such as openness and participation, into risk regulatory regimes.[40] Thus, EU risk decision-making procedures direct attention towards the regimented and away from the discretionary aspects of decision-making.[41] They present regulatory measures as the logical and rational conclusion of information-gathering and assessment processes conducted beyond the EU decision-maker's (particularly the Commission's) influence.

The wedge between the stages of risk assessment and risk management, as well as the artificiality of this particular divide, are familiar features of EU risk regulation.[42] However artificial, the separation performs a vital function in amplifying the effect of necessity of regulatory outcomes, and allowing the Commission as decision-maker to project the image of a dispassionate, neutral arbiter of exogenously generated information, rather than an unconstrained regulatory force.[43] The quest for apparent neutrality might also go some way towards explaining the EU's well-documented tendency to 'proceduralise' over time the interpretation of decision-making principles, such as the proportionality principle and the precautionary principle.[44]

The EU's understanding of risk as a regulatory trigger is, therefore, narrow, highly compartmentalised, and perceived against a backdrop of economic activity with inter-State ramifications. EU risk regulation aims both to reconcile its understanding of health, environmental, and economic objectives within decision-making on acceptable risk, and to legitimise this decision-making. The pursuit of these objectives dictates reliance on a regulatory methodology that is

37 cf C. Hood and H. Rothstein, 'Risk Regulation under Pressure: Problem Solving or Blame Shifting?' (2001) 33 *Administration and Society* 21, 40.

38 Commission Communication on the Precautionary Principle, n 14 above; Case C-236/01 *Monsanto Agricoltura Italia SpA* v *Council* [2003] ECR I-8105; Heyvaert, n 14 above.

39 Case C-77/09 *Gowan Comércio Internacional e Serviços Lda* v *Ministero della Salute* judgement of 22 December 2010, not yet reported, at pt 75. See also Case T-13/99 *Pfizer Animal Health SA* v *Council* [2002] ECR II-3305; and E. Stokes, n 16 above, 497–501.

40 R. Lofstedt, F. Bouder, J. Wardman and S. Chakraborty, 'The Changing Nature of Communication and Regulation of Risk in Europe' (2011) 14 *Journal of Risk Research* 409.

41 cf E. Vos, 'EU Food Safety Regulation in the Aftermath of the BSE Crisis' (2000) 23 *Journal of Consumer Policy* 227, 234.

42 Everson and Vos, n 19 above, 11.

43 Lofstedt, n 40 above, 412.

44 J. Corkin. 'Science, Legitimacy and the Law: Regulating Risk Regulation Judiciously in the European Community' (2008) 33 *European Law Review* 359; Heyvaert, n 14 above, 196; V. Heyvaert, 'Trade and the Environment: Proportionality Substituted?' (2001) 13 *Journal of Environmental Law* 392; Case C-473/98 *Chemikalieninspektionen* v *Toolex Alpha AB* [2000] ECR I-5681; Case C-309/02 *Radlberger* [2004] ECR I-11763; Case C-320/03, *Commission* v *Austria* [2005] ECR I-9871.

geared towards the creation of actionable 'facts', that maintains a strict functional and institutional separation between fact-finding and decision-making, and that displays a highly formalised approach to good governance.

## EU RISK REGULATION AND CLIMATE CHANGE REGULATION CONSIDERED

Having confronted environmental risks from biodiversity depletion to nanoparticle exposure, the EU now faces up to the risks of climate change. This section inquires whether and to what extent EU climate change regulation is similar to or differs from conventional EU risk regulation, both in terms of the risk discourse that anchors the regulatory enterprise, the formulation of regulatory objectives and the regulatory strategies deployed.

### The climate change regulation package

The EU approach to climate change aims to respond to the need for both mitigation and adaptation, and emphasises the importance of integrating climate change considerations into other EU law and policy areas. Under the Kyoto Protocol,[45] the EU committed to an overall reduction of eight per cent of greenhouse gases (GHG) compared to emission levels in 1990.[46] For the period of 2012 to 2020, the EU has set a target of a 20 per cent reduction compared to 1990, with an option to increase to 30 per cent if its efforts are matched by comparable emissions reduction commitments from other developed nations, and by adequate contributions from economically more advanced developing nations, 'according to their responsibilities and respective capabilities'.[47]

In terms of regulatory instruments, the jewel in the EU crown is undoubtedly the emissions trading regime,[48] as laid down in the 2003 Emissions Trading

45 Kyoto (Japan), 10 December 1997 (entered into force 16 February 2005) (1998) *International Legal Materials* 22.

46 Council Decision 2002/358/EC concerning the approval, on behalf of the European Community, of the Kyoto Protocol to the United Nations Framework Convention on Climate Change and the joint fulfilment of commitments thereunder [2002] OJL130/1.

47 European Parliament and Council Decision 406/2009/EC on the effort of Member States to reduce their greenhouse gas emissions to meet the Community's greenhouse gas reduction commitments up to 2020 [2009] OJL140/136. See also Commission Communication on 20 20 by 2020. Europe's Climate Change Opportunity COM(2008)30 final, 23 January 2008. At the point of writing, the prospects for the 30 per cent option being taken up are slim: the 2010 Cancun negotiations produced modest results on issues such as climate funding, forest protection and technology sharing, but stopped short of a renewed agreement on binding emission reduction targets. See Decisions adopted by COP 16 and CMP 6 at http://unfccc.int/2860.php (last visited 1 August 2011). The recent republican party win in the US congressional elections further dampens the prospects of the US government signing up to an ambitious Kyoto II in the coming year. See D. Keating, 'US Election Leaves EU Isolated on Climate Policy' *ENDS Europe* 5 November 2010.

48 Whether we are talking about diamonds or rhinestones is disputed. A full discussion of the legitimacy and effectiveness of emissions trading as a climate change mitigation instrument exceeds the ambitions of this article, but see, eg, G. Winter, 'The Climate is no Commodity: Taking Stock

Directive (ETD) and ensuing amendments.[49] The ETD, which requires Member States to determine and allocate allowances for the emission of specified greenhouse gases[50] to industrial operators active in energy-intensive sectors such as oil refinery, iron and steel production, pulp and paper,[51] as well as to develop and maintain an infrastructure to enable trade in emission allowances, has been the subject of intense academic scrutiny. I refer to the existing body of literature for detail,[52] confining the present discussion to some observations that are pertinent to the ensuing analysis. It is important to remember that the ETD is, first and foremost, an efficiency tool in pursuit of environmental targets that were set outside the confines of the Directive itself, namely, the aforementioned eight and 20 (respectively 30) per cent emission reduction goals, which were adopted in a European Parliament and Council Decision.[53] It is equally important to recall that the emission allowances allocation and trading regime operates in pursuit but not in fulfilment of said reduction targets. In its current format, the ETD covers about 40 per cent of $CO_2$ emissions, which means that, even if every single unit of emission is duly accounted for and fully covered by a legitimately issued allowance, the regime gives no guarantee that the overall reduction target will be hit. Towards this greater goal, the EU relies instead on an entire portfolio of regulatory measures: the climate change 'package'.[54]

The EU climate change package contains an extensive set of recently adopted measures addressing, *inter alia*, tighter $CO_2$ emission limits for vehicles,[55]

of the Emissions Trading System' (2010) 22 *Journal of Environmental Law* 1; R. Baldwin 'Regulation Lite: the Rise of Emissions Trading' (2008) 2 *Regulation and Governance* 193; R. Stewart, 'Economic Incentives for Environmental Protection: Opportunities and Obstacles' in R. Stewart, P. Sands, and R. Revesz (eds), *Environmental Law, the Economy and Sustainable Development* (Cambridge: CUP, 2000); D. Ellerman and B. Buchner, 'The European Union Emissions Trading Scheme: Origins, Allocation and Early Results' (2007) 1 *Review of Environmental Economics and Policy* 66; A. D. Ellerman, F. Convery, and C. de Perthuis, *Pricing Carbon* (Cambridge: CUP, 2010).

49 Directive 2003/87/EC establishing a scheme for greenhouse gas emission allowance trading within the Community and amending Council Directive 96/61/EC [2003] OJ L275/32, as amended by Directive 2009/29/EC [2009] OJ L140/63.

50 To date, emission allowances overwhelmingly cover $CO_2$ emissions and, to a much lesser extent, nitrous oxide. See Annex I in combination with Annex II of the ETD.

51 For a full listing, see annex II of the ETD.

52 See literature referenced under n 48 above. See also European Commission, *EU Action against Climate Change. The EU Emissions Trading Scheme* (Luxembourg: Office for Official Publications of the European Communities, 2008); M. Wråke, 'Emissions Trading. The Ugly Duckling of European Climate Policy?' Swedish Environmental Research Institute, July 2009 at: http://www3.ivl.se/rapporter/pdf/B1856.pdf (last visited 1 August 2011); S. Weishaar, *Towards Auctioning: The Transformation of the European Greenhouse Gas Emissions Trading System* (Alphen aan den Rijn: Kluwer Law International, 2009); J. Skjaerseth, 'EU Emissions Trading: Legitimacy and Stringency' (2010) 20 *Environmental Policy and Governance* 295; S. Bogojevic, 'Ending the Honeymoon: Deconstructing Emissons Trading Discourses' (2009) 21 *Journal of Environmental Law* 443.

53 n 47 above.

54 K. Kulovesi, E. Morgera, M. Munoz, 'Environmental Integration and Multi-faceted International Dimensions of EU law: Unpacking the EU's 2009 Climate and Energy Package' (2011) 48 *Common Market Law Review* 829.

55 Regulation (EC) 443/2009 setting emission performance standards for new passenger cars as part of the Community's integrated approach to reduce $CO_2$ emissions from light-duty vehicles [2009] OJL 140/1 (the Passenger Car Regulation).

promotion of renewable energy,[56] increased energy efficiency for industrial and domestic buildings, appliances and services,[57] eco-design and labelling,[58] and carbon capture and storage (CCS).[59] Moreover, in observance of the integration principle, the climate change regulatory agenda is partly one of amendment to existing legislation, as areas such as EU waste management, air pollution control, water management, and industrial regulation must be made responsive to climate change concerns.

The EU climate change strategy aims to curb temperature rises, not to stop global warming in its tracks altogether. This is partly because an even more ambitious emissions reduction programme is considered beyond the realm of the politically, economically, and technologically feasible, but also because, strictly speaking, the horse has bolted: the existing build-up of GHG in the atmosphere will cause global temperatures to rise in the coming decades, regardless of our present and future actions.[60] Hence, the climate change challenge is one of adaptation as well as mitigation. The EU's climate change adaptation strategy is at a relatively early stage of development,[61] and poses a number of particular challenges. The efforts of forecasting overall rises in temperature under business-as-usual scenarios are enormous, but they pale in comparison to the challenges of predicting actual localised impacts of climate change (which must take into account a range of different global, European, and domestic mitigation scenarios) and formulating reasonable adaptation responses.[62] Moreover, the predominantly local impacts of adaptation policies raise difficult questions of both EU competency and of shared responsibility. EU environment ministers have therefore agreed that initial EU adaptation action should in the first instance concentrate on the colossal task of data production, gathering, and exchange, on climate-proofing existing EU policies, and coordinating cross-border responses.[63] However, if the history of EU environmental law serves as any indication, it is to be expected that over time the EU's involvement in adaptation policies, and the corresponding development of implementing regulatory strategies, will deepen.

56 Directive 2009/28/EC on the promotion of the use of energy from renewable sources [2009] OJL 140/16.

57 Directive 2002/91/EC on the energy performance of buildings [2003] OJL 1/65 and Proposal for a Directive of the European Parliament and of the Council on the energy performance of buildings COM(2008)780 final, 13 November 2008 Directive 2005/32/EC establishing a framework for the setting of ecodesign requirements for energy-using products [2005] OJL 191/29; Directive 2006/32/EC on energy end-use efficiency and energy services [2006] OJL 114/64.

58 Directive 2009/125/EC establishing a framework for the setting of ecodesign requirements for energy-related products [2009] OJL 285/10; Regulation 66/2010 on the EU ecolabel [2010] OJL 27/1.

59 Directive 2009/31/EC on the geological storage of carbon dioxide [2009] OJL 140/114.

60 'Facing the consequences. Global action is not going to stop climate change. The world needs to look harder at how to live with it' *The Economist* 25 November 2010; M. Stallworthy, 'Legislating against Climate Change: A UK Perspective on a Sisyphean Challenge' (2009) 72 MLR 412, 414.

61 Commission White Paper, Adapting to climate change: Towards a European framework for action COM(2009)147 final, 1 April 2009.

62 See I. Bartle, 'A Strategy for Better Climate Change Regulation: Towards a Public Interest Orientated Regulatory Regime' (2009) 18 *European Politics* 689.

63 'Leaders Focus on How to Share Climate Aid Burden' *ENDS Europe Daily* 29 Oct 2009.

**The risks of climate change: comparing risk discourses and their impact on regulation**

Climate change has lodged itself in our consciousness as a (arguably the) major threat to the future wellbeing of humanity. Stripped to its essentials, the European discourse on climate change undeniably bears the marks of a risk discourse: concerns about climate change relate to the likelihood of adverse impacts of global warming, some of which are already materialising today but most of which will emerge in the decades to come. The EU operates on a widely held assumption that the unprecedented acceleration in climate change is caused by human activity and this assumption comes paired with a belief that the risks of climate change are impressionable; that positive actions can be undertaken to ward off the most destructive manifestations of predicted changes and to adapt to the degree of change that is already deemed inevitable.

The message of climate change as a serious but still actionable risk resonates loudly in authoritative documents such as the Intergovernmental Panel on Climate Change Fourth Assessment Report, the Stern Review,[64] and a plethora of EU climate change policy documents.[65] But a closer look at how the climate change risk is understood and contextualised in EU policy reveals significant differences in the discourse surrounding the risks of climate change when compared to the conceptualisation of risks that drives conventional EU risk regulation.

Risks are double-edged, evoking a potential for gains as well as losses. Regulatory interventions in risk-taking, too, create their own sets of potential benefits and disadvantages. Within conventional EU environmental policy, the ambivalent nature of risk and regulation finds a particularly prominent expression in the 'trade versus environment' dilemma, which presents regulatory decision-making as an ongoing balancing exercise between the Scylla of health and environmental harm and the Charybdis of foregoing innovation and triggering economic stagnation.[66] In theory, climate change risks follow the same pattern: rising temperatures might jeopardise the survival of certain regions but could potentially benefit others. Climate change regulation, in turn, might control global warming-related risks but at the same time could hurt the EU's economic competitiveness.

Trade-off concerns are still part of the global climate change debate, most visibly in the fraught attempts to reconcile a number of developed countries' desires for a broad uptake of binding emission reduction targets with rapidly

64 N. Stern, *The Economics of Climate Change, the Stern Review* (Cambridge: CUP, 2007).

65 Commission Recommendation of 28 April 2010 on the research joint programming initiative on agriculture, food security and climate change [2010] OJL 111/27; European Parliament Resolution of 4 February 2009 on 2050: The future begins today [2010] OJC 67E/44; Commission Green Paper on forest protection and information in the EU: Preparing forests for climate change COM(2010)66 final, 1 March 2010; Commission White Paper on adapting to climate change, n 61 above; 20 20 by 2020, n 47 above; European Parliament Resolution on Climate change [2007] OJC 287E/344.

66 J. Lefevere, 'A Climate of Change: an Analysis of Progress in EU and International Climate Change Policy' in J. Scott (ed), *Environmental Protection. European Law and Governance* (Oxford: OUP, 2009) 171, 183–184.

developing countries' concerns over the impact of mitigation strategies on their economic growth.[67] Within the European Union, however, allusions to conceivably positive consequences of climate change or to the potentially adverse economic impact of intervention are gradually being excised from the debate. The advantages of global warming may be the stuff of private jokes on cold and blustery days, but in the public sphere climate change has become singularly and exceptionally divorced from the positive connotations of risk-taking; it is considered morally suspect even to contemplate foregone opportunities in the wake of climate change mitigation.[68] At most, EU policy documents will concede that rising temperatures might have some beneficial impacts, such as a decline in cold-related deaths during winter, but these are rarely quantified, in marked contrast to predicted negative impacts.[69] Nor is it suggested that any such localised positive impacts should affect determinations on the need for mitigation.[70] The resounding message emanating from EU climate change policy is that global warming is an unambiguous social bad, and that no amount of accidental positive side-effects could ever tilt the scales in favour of regulatory relaxation, let alone inaction.

There is no single, exclusive explanation for the shift of climate change from ambivalent risk to unqualified bad within the EU policy discourse, but the global yet deeply uneven impacts of climate change are certainly a factor. Having acknowledged its role in contributing to the climate change threat, as well as its commensurate responsibility *vis-à-vis* third countries in mitigating and furthering adaptation to climate change, the EU now finds itself in a position where economic competitiveness is a much trickier card to play. Countervailing considerations about potential benefits of temperature rises and the costs of climate change regulation stand to offend global moral sensibilities, particularly when we consider that climate change is predicted to wreak the most havoc in some of the world's most vulnerable regions.[71] Moreover, the EU was the driving force behind the global adoption and entry into effect of the United Nations Framework Convention on Climate Change and the Kyoto Protocol,[72] and remains the most committed promoter of renewing international binding obligations post-2012. The EU has staked its reputation as a global political leader in no small amount on its ability to promote climate change mitigation and adaptation on

67 Z. X. Zhang, *Reconstructing Climate Policy: How Best To Engage China and Other Developing Countries?* East-West Centre Research Program 2003 at http://papers.ssrn.com/sol3/papers.cfm?abstract_id=955044 (last visited 1 August 2011).

68 cf Ellen Goodman's article in the Boston Globe in February 2007, comparing climate change deniers with Holocaust deniers: E. Goodman, 'No Change in Political Climate' *The Boston Globe* 9 February 2007.

69 See Commission Communication on 'Winning the Battle Against Climate Change' COM(2005)35 final 9 February 2005, Annex.

70 *ibid*, pt 7 'Doing nothing is not a sensible option'.

71 Commission Communication on 'Building a Global Climate Change Alliance between the European Union and poor developing countries most vulnerable to climate change' COM(2007)540 final, 18 September 2007. cf M. Paterson and M. Grubb, 'The International Politics of Climate Change' (1992) 68 *International Affairs* 296.

72 Commission White Paper on Adapting to Climate Change, n 61 above.

the international agenda.[73] Thus, it has politically invested in the reality of the climate change risk to an extent that does not characterise other EU risk policies.[74] In this context, any strictly 'EU welfare-oriented' consideration of the pros and cons of regulatory intervention becomes both a moral hazard and a cause for political embarrassment.[75]

The representation of climate change as an unmitigated bad – and correspondingly of regulatory intervention as an unqualified good – is facilitated by a growing reliance on win-win assumptions. EU environmental policy has long been sympathetic to the thesis that economic growth and environmental protection can and should be pursued symbiotically instead of competitively, but climate change policy has embraced the prospect of win-win outcomes with an unprecedented ferocity.[76] The adoption of a win-win rather than a trade-off perspective enables the EU to reintegrate economic opportunities into climate change. However, these opportunities are no longer the foregone opportunities of unfettered economic progress that must be weighed up against the benefits of regulatory control; they are the opportunities created by regulation itself. Thus, when '20 20 by 2020' talks of the climate change opportunity, it resolutely refers to the scope for economic growth and competitiveness in the wake of climate change mitigation and adaptation measures, and most decidedly not to what Europe stands to gain in the absence of climate change control.[77]

The decline of trade-off oriented thinking and ascent of win-win expectations have resulted in a new interpretation of 'risk taking' within EU climate change policy. Whereas, before, 'risk taking' was routinely associated with an active engagement with the new (such as the commercialisation of a new technology or the establishment of a new industrial facility, which activity must be assessed, controlled and, if necessary, curtailed),[78] the European climate risk discourse emphasises the connection between risk and *inaction*.[79] In other areas of health

73 The opening lines of '20 20 by 2020' are: '2007 marked a turning point for the European Union's climate and energy policy. Europe showed itself ready to give global leadership: to tackle climate change, to face up to the challenge of secure, sustainable and competitive energy, and to make the European economy a model for sustainable development in the 21st century' (n 47 above). cf K. Christer and C. Parker, 'Climate Change and the European Union's Leadership Moment: An Inconvenient Truth?' (2010) 48 *Journal of Common Market Studies* 923.

74 See M. Scheurs and Y. Thibergien, 'Multi-Level Reinforcement: Explaining European Union Leadership in Climate Change Mitigation' (2007) 7 *Global Environmental Politics* 19; F. Yamin, 'The Role of the EU in Climate Negotiations' in J. Gupta and M. Grubb (eds), *Climate Change and European Leadership: A Sustainable Role for Europe?* (USA: Kluwer Academic Publishing, 2000).

75 cf S. Oberthur and C. Roche Kelly, 'EU Leadership in International Climate Change Policy: Achievement and Challenges' (2008) 43 *The International Spectator* 35, 39.

76 See the EU's sustainable growth policy at: http://ec.europa.eu/europe2020/priorities/sustainable-growth/index_en.htm (last visited 1 August 2011) and Commission Communication on the 'Analysis of Options to Move beyond 20% Emission Reduction and Assessing the Risk of Carbon Leakage' COM(2010)265 final, 25 May 2010. cf M. Grubb, 'Climate Change Impacts, Energy and Development' in F. Bourguignon and B. Pleskovic, *Rethinking Infrastructure for Development* (Washington DC: The World Bank, 2008) 89, 109.

77 n 47 above.

78 cf O'Malley on the 'enterprising subject', n 15 above, 465; and R. Brockhaus, 'Risk-Taking Propensity of Entrepreneurs' (1980) 23 *Academy of Management Journal* 509.

79 Commission Communication on Winning the Battle, n 69 above; European Environment Agency, *Climate Change: The Cost of Inaction and the Cost of Adaptation* (EEA Technical Report Nr 13/2007).

and environmental risk regulation, business-as-usual tends to function as a relatively stable benchmark, referring to a set of practices and techniques that are usually susceptible to incremental tweaking and upgrading, but that rarely, if ever, need a complete overhaul. In the context of climate change, the relationship between stability and change is inverted, with business-as-usual becoming the path that leads to epic, unpredictable, and possibly catastrophic change.

Uncertainty, too, acquires different connotations in the context of climate change. In EU risk regulation, uncertainty is the antechamber of risk; situations characterised by uncertainty are those where insufficient, or insufficiently consistent, information is available to make conventional risk assessments.[80] What we are uncertain about are the actual health and environmental *impacts* of regulated activities. A pivotal function of the regulatory process is to translate such 'impact uncertainty' into a fictional but actionable form of certainty through highly formalised processes of information gathering and risk assessment. We recall the effort expended on the transformation of discretionary decisions into necessary outcomes of thoroughly documented and rigidly organised procedures. In contrast, far less effort goes into legitimising the effectiveness of risk control techniques.[81] Differently put, the legitimacy-enhancing features built into EU risk regulation overwhelmingly aim to buttress EU decisions on whether and to what extent to intervene; not to justify the choice of risk control instruments *per se*.

Climate change policy is set to confront uncertainty in a markedly different way. Climate change scepticism may be alive and well in some parts of the world, but the EU has accepted and promotes the reality of man-made global warming as a political fact.[82] The overall target of a maximum 2° C rise, and the determination of maximum emission levels cutting back eight, 20, or 30 per cent respectively from 1990 emissions levels, were forged in a political process culminating in the ratification of the Kyoto Protocol and the adoption of the 2002

80 Commission Communication on the Precautionary Principle, n 14 above.

81 EU regulatory regimes display a surprisingly high degree of stability in their choice of risk control techniques. Effectiveness deficits are typically explained as deficiencies in the reach or speed of regulatory decision-making, or as failures in implementation and enforcement. Hence, they are remedied by tightening up standards, streamlining and centralising decision-making and implementation, and stepping up enforcement. For example, for all its claims to innovation, the risk control strategies laid down in REACH regime show a high degree of continuity with those of the preceding regulatory framework. See V. Heyvaert, 'Guidance Without Constraint: Assessing the Impact of the Precautionary Principle on the European Community's Chemicals Policy' (2006) 6 *Yearbook of European Environmental Law* 27, 52. Recent reforms of the EU pesticide control regime betray a similar degree of instrumental continuity ('New Pesticide Approval Regime Begins in Earnest' *ENDS Europe Daily* 14 June 2011). On the judicial front, the Greenpeace case offers an interesting illustration of the European Court's effectiveness assumptions regarding EU risk regulation. The Court denied that it might be appropriate for a Member State to halt an EU decision-making process once it had been set in motion, reasoning that the EU regime was fully equipped to cope with risks, including risks that came to light after the process had started. The fact that the regulatory regime in question was contained in the 1990 Directive on Deliberate Release of GMOs, which had failed to deliver acceptable GMO authorisation outcomes and had been effectively defunct for several years by the time of the ECJ's ruling in the Greenpeace case, underscores the extent to which the ECJ's belief in risk regulatory effectiveness is a matter of principle rather than experience. Case C-6/99, *Association Greenpeace France* v *Ministere de l'Agriculture et de la Peche* [2000] ECR I-1651.

82 See, eg, Commission Communication on Winning the Battle, n 69 above.

and 2009 Council Decisions;[83] not in a regulatory process orchestrated by the European Commission, a European Agency, Member States Committees, regulatory addressees, and public and private interest groups. From a regulatory perspective, the burning question is not whether global warming presents an unacceptable risk and, hence, whether the EU is justified in adopting risk reduction measures, but whether the arsenal of regulatory instruments designed to control climate change can make a dent in the problem. The interdependency of control techniques pushes uncertainty surrounding their effectiveness to yet higher levels, as the success of one regulatory instrument is co-determined by the effectiveness, or lack thereof, of others.[84] For instance, the pressures for energy efficiency regulation to deliver will be far greater if the EU's measures to promote renewable energy production and uptake fall flat. This does not even engage with the far greater imponderable of how the rest of the world is going to respond to the challenge of climate change in the medium term, and how third country policies will affect the effectiveness of the EU regulatory package. In sum, because the question of climate change impacts is treated as a political instead of regulatory question, climate change regulation is likely to be spared some of the controversy triggered by impact uncertainty. However, it is saddled with a looming mass of 'control uncertainty', which affects both the tasks of regulatory goal-setting and strategic design.

### Regulatory goals: micro-management versus systemic change

The risk regulation paradigm is quintessentially managerial. Risk regulation reacts to the economic and social conditions that characterise its field of application and is geared towards optimising the circumstances under which manufacturers develop their products, retailers offer their wares, financial advisers lend their services, and so on, by structuring decision-making processes intended to result in the substitution of acceptable for unacceptable risks. For instance, EU regulation on novel foods does not aspire to reach a wholesale verdict on the desirability of engineering new food products, but seeks to ensure that those new offerings that are released within the EU do not pose unacceptable health or environmental threats.[85] Risk regulation, therefore, exerts an essentially stabilising influence on economic and social development, policing and facilitating enterprise in equal measure.

Moreover, the future-oriented nature of risk tends to direct regulatory attention towards emerging threats, often associated with new practices or products, and de-emphasises the negative externalities of the familiar and well-established, thereby amplifying risk regulation's stabilising function.[86] This is not to say that

83 Decision 2002/358/EC, n 46 above; Decision 406/2009/EC, n 47 above.

84 cf H. Bulkeley, 'Governing Climate Change: the Politics of Risk Society?' (2001) 26 *Transactions of the Institute of British Geographers* 430, 431 (regarding climate change on the Australian political and regulatory agenda).

85 Regulation (EC) No 258/97 concerning Novel Foods and Novel Food Ingredients [1997] OJL 43/1.

86 P. Huber, 'The Old-New Division in Risk Regulation' (1983) 69 *Virginia Law Review* 1025, 1028.

risk regulation is wilfully blind to the burden of the past, but the difference is one of degree. Compare, for instance, the relative tolerance of residual risks posed by the entrenched practice of pesticide use to the much more stringent controls that accompany the introduction of genetically modified crops.

Climate change regulation, too, essentially aims to manage the risks flowing from our high GHG-emitting lifestyle, but the realisation of that goal demands the adoption of a regulatory agenda that is far more ambitious and radical than anything risk regulation has needed to contemplate up to now. In the area of climate change, stabilisation does not equate to effective management but negates it; systemic change is what is needed.[87] Risk regulation's stabilising propensities, therefore, could hinder instead of further climate change control initiatives. Bearing in mind the inverted relationship between stability and change, the objective of the climate change regulatory agenda is as much about fostering as it is about managing change. Hence, within climate change regulation, risk control cannot solely be achieved through 'better' management of existing practices, but must also be accomplished through the active regulatory promotion of new practices and technologies, which will then in turn necessitate the adoption of new technological risk control strategies.[88] The EU's mandate as a regulator is therefore to pursue change through the articulation of a regulatory agenda that encompasses both global warming abatement through a combination of restrictive and facilitating measures, and risk regulation of climate change abatement and adaptation strategies. This results in the formation of a multi-faceted agenda the objectives of which may not always be synchronised, and at times even at odds with one another.

**Regulatory strategies: compartmentalisation versus orchestration**

Risk regulation strategies inevitably entail a degree of compartmentalisation, since the identification of discrete activities with a finite set of impacts is a precondition for their manageability. EU risk regulation, particularly, thrives on the compartmentalisation and even individualisation of risks, both in the sense that risks are narrowly constructed and that they are typically assessed on a case-by-case, substance-by-substance, or installation-by-installation basis, with limited regard for cumulative or synergistic impacts. The pronounced compartmentalisation in EU risk regulation is partly functional, but also partly a response to the limited regulatory mandate that transnational regulatory authorities tend to have, which in the case of the EU moreover finds legal fortification in the subsidiarity principle.[89]

Turning to climate change, the field is certainly undergoing a degree of compartmentalisation, as law and policy makers seek to divide the intellectually

87 H.J. Schnellhuber, M. Molina, N. Stern, V. Huber and S. Kadner (eds), *Global Sustainability. A Nobel Cause* (Cambridge: CUP, 2010).

88 Commission Communication on Winning the Battle, n 69 above. cf D. Farber, 'Confronting Uncertainty under NEPA' (2009) 8 *Issues in Legal Scholarship*: Iss 3 (Balancing the Risks: Managing Technology and Dangerous Climate Change) Article 3 at http://www.bepress.com/ils/vol8/iss3/art3 (last visited 1 August 2011).

89 G. de Burca, 'The Quest for Legitimacy in the European Union' (1996) 59 MLR 349, 366–368.

overwhelming prospect of global warming into discrete economic, health, environmental, social, and security threats.[90] However, this process has not yet reached either the maturity or thoroughness of compartmentalisation that characterises EU risk regulation. Moreover, qualifying climate change as a risk to forestry or food security compartmentalises the risk according to its impacts, not its causes, and it is precisely the identification of separate *causes* of risk that enables their representation as attributable and manageable. It is possible to compartmentalise climate change causes and review climate change risks on a product-by-product or activity-by activity basis,[91] but the attraction of this approach is much reduced in an area where accumulation is everything. It can certainly not hold itself out as a sufficient tool to maintain overall levels of climate risk within the margins of acceptability. The familiar 'divide and conquer' tactics of EU risk regulation are, therefore, at odds with the nature of the problem of climate change, which instead requires the EU to summon its much less practiced powers of orchestration and integrated decision-making.

The more diffuse and interdependent nature of the climate change risk affects the design and instrumentalisation of EU climate change regulation. EU risk regulation frameworks typically operate as self-contained units, largely identifying and fulfilling their own information needs and constructing both regulatory problems and solutions within the confines of singular regulatory frameworks. Climate change regulation, in contrast, enjoys a lesser degree of informational autonomy, as the range of data to be fed into decision-making is much more diverse,[92] and the sources much more dispersed. This implies that climate change regulatory frameworks cannot be self-sufficient in meeting their information needs to the extent that, for instance, pharmaceuticals regulation can, but depend on a combination of inputs sourced from different regulatory instruments, which creates new interdependencies and vulnerabilities within the regulatory design.

In terms of instrumentalisation, the need for orchestration and integrated decision-making calls for a greater reliance on 'packages' of measures which combine a considerable array of controlling, facilitating, incentivising and technology-forcing techniques.[93] The effectiveness of the measures within the package, and the corresponding need for reform, no longer solely hinges on how a measure performs on its own terms, but is just as much affected by the performance of other parts of the package. The flexibility and adaptability needs of climate change regulation are therefore greater than those of traditional risk regulation.

In sum, the instrumental parsimony that typifies the EU risk regulation paradigm, where individualised safety objectives are pursued through a single or narrow set of control techniques (eg, pharmaceutical safety through product authorisation; chemical substance safety through registration, evaluation, and use

90 See the separate studies and communications on climate change and forestry (n 65 above), agriculture and food security (n 65 above), and biodiversity (Commission Communication on 'Our life insurance, our natural capital: an EU Biodiversity Strategy to 2020' COM(2011)244 final, 3 May 2011.

91 See eg, the Passenger Car Regulation, n 55 above.

92 See Art 13 of the Passenger Car Regulation, *ibid* (listing review data).

93 See Kulovesi et al, n 54 above.

authorisation) is lost within the realm of climate risk regulation, which must summon a dazzling variety of regulatory instruments and control techniques to pursue its stated objectives of climate change mitigation and adaptation.

## TOWARDS A NEW RISK REGULATION PARADIGM

The analysis above leaves risk regulation scholars with the unsettling impression that life is elsewhere. The most pressing environmental risk of our time challenges conventional assumptions about the nature of costs and benefits, about the relationship between risk and change, and about the meaning of uncertainty. It calls for regulatory responses that look very different from conventional risk regulation both in terms of goal-setting and instrumentalisation. But this observation constitutes an invitation more than a rejection. Ultimately, climate change throws down the gauntlet for risk regulation scholarship to re-appraise and re-define itself. The discipline has produced a wonderfully rich literature on complex issues such as the impact of probabilistic reasoning on notions of causation, the growing use of regulation as a forum for contestation between different risk perceptions, the phenomenon of proceduralisation and the development of principles such as the precautionary principle to cope with regulatory uncertainty (to name but a few).[94] Yet there is an urgent need for further engagement with the rising prominence on the regulatory agenda of risks, such as the climate change risk, that are more appropriately understood as endemic to our life-style than as the by-product of a particular scientific or technological development. As our conceptualisation of risks evolves, so should our understanding of risk regulation.

Beyond re-energising the discipline, the development of a new paradigm for risk regulation will prove vitally useful to the European Union as it forges on with the development and implementation of its climate change package. The EU has shown considerable mettle in launching itself into the great unknown that is climate change regulation and evidently does not shy away from innovative regulatory approaches, including the establishment of the world's largest market in emission allowances, the imposition of mandatory renewables targets coupled with the adoption of regulatory standards to facilitate conversion to renewable energy sources, and the introduction of regulatory frameworks enabling the controlled development of new and controversial technologies, such as carbon capture and storage (CCS). But there are risks to flying blind, and a stronger theoretical underpinning for the EU regulatory enterprise could improve its chances of identifying potential problem areas and regulatory vulnerabilities, thus creating opportunities for effective anticipatory responses. Moreover, the availability of a fleshed-out climate change risk regulation paradigm might ward off the temptation for the EU to fall back upon old and familiar but unproductive regulatory tactics to tackle new and unfamiliar challenges. Finally, the evolution of climate change regulation into a developed regulatory discipline, characterised by its own narrative, purpose and praxis, would create a host of new learning opportunities that could positively inform the European Union as a risk

94 See citations between notes 1 and 44 above.

regulator, whether operating within the heartland of product and technology regulation, in the realm of environmental regulation more broadly, or in the sphere of climate change regulation itself.

**The risks of flying blind**

Assuming that we accept the basic premise that social science scholarship can make a contribution to the practice of regulation, we readily see how a better understanding of the risk discourse and the regulatory dynamics of climate change could instruct the European Union as it tackles this momentous challenge. We recall that the EU's heavy dependence on justification techniques, both for the adoption of regulatory frameworks[95] and for regulatory decision-making, owes a lot to the representation of environmental risk regulation as a brake on trade and competitiveness. By contrast, the representation of climate change as an unqualified bad places the issue outside of the continuum between health or environmental harm and economic opportunity that demarcates the decision-making zone for conventional risk regulation. Liberating though this may be, the ascent of symbiotic perspectives on environmental regulation and competitiveness entails a new set of legitimacy challenges and raises a host of new questions surrounding the interpretation of regulatory effectiveness. The role of regulatory impact assessments, for instance, needs to be rethought to fit a context where regulation is expected to deliver on both protection and growth. By the same token, regulatory performance assessments and corresponding reform strategies must reflect a broader range of economic and environmental benchmarks. A full understanding of the consequences of embracing a dominant win-win perspective will therefore be invaluable in assisting the EU in its design of assessment and review strategies and in confronting new legitimacy concerns.

A related point concerns the political nature of overall mitigation target-setting within the EU, which lifts impact uncertainty out of the regulatory sphere. Instead of taking the EU regulator to task for the reliability of its impact predictions, the European public is more likely to stumble over the appropriate selection of control techniques. Thus, climate change regulation will have vulnerabilities different from those that beset traditional risk regulation. Consequently, efforts to boost the credibility and resilience of regulation should be re-directed. The insulating mechanisms of EU risk regulation (namely the rigorous data production standards, the tightly maintained separation between assessment and management, the public access provisions in risk evaluation procedures) are all designed to either respond to or deflect concerns about the EU's treatment of impact uncertainty. Climate change regulation could presumably get away with less robust defence mechanisms for its assessment procedures, but it needs to build in opportunities to cope with control uncertainty. In other words, it needs to respond to demands for both the scrutiny and the justification of its selection of regulatory control instruments, and of the relative weight it

95 cf G. Rowe, 'Tools for the Control of Political and Administrative Agents: Impact Assessment and Administrative Governance in the European Union' in H. Hoffmann and A. Türk, *EU Administrative Governance* (Cheltenham: Edward Elgar, 2006) 448–511.

attributes to different climate change instruments within its regulatory package. At the moment, such opportunities are lacking, arguably because the phenomenon of control uncertainty has been insufficiently explored and has not yet percolated down to the level of regulatory practice.

### The risks of reverting to risk regulation

A solid theoretical foundation for EU climate change regulation could also minimise the risk that, in expanding its regulatory framework, the EU reverts to familiar but counterproductive risk regulatory strategies. This is by no means a speculative concern. Within the field of risk research, commentators have long been aware of the powerful draw of 'risk' as an organising principle, pulling complex phenomena into its orbit and converting them into management and communication problems through the application of risk identification and assessment routines.[96] As a mode of governance, risk exerts a particularly, some claim excessively strong influence on regulation.[97] In the field of climate change, too, authors such as Pidgeon and Bulkeley have observed the ascent of risk-based analysis, while simultaneously expressing concern about the suitability of risk-based strategies to govern climate change.[98] Considering the attractions of risk for regulation, combined with the EU's extensive experience as a risk regulator, the prospect of risk-oriented strategies gradually colonising the domain of climate change regulation is anything but farfetched.[99] The EU therefore needs to be armed with a clear understanding of the distinctiveness of its climate change risk discourse, and of the different programmatic and strategic needs of climate change regulation, to avoid mapping new problems onto old formats and to design and select risk control strategies commensurate to the task of climate change mitigation and adaptation.

To illustrate the point, let us consider two distinguishing features of risk regulation: its tendency towards compartmentalisation and its stabilising propensity. Both are prominent in EU risk regulation, but neither is appropriate for the design of an effective framework for climate change regulation, which calls for a fast pace of innovation through regulation,[100] as well as a much higher degree of

96 See more generally J. Adams, *Risk* (London: UCL Press, 1995); U. Beck, *Risk Society: Towards a New Modernity* (London: Sage Publications, 1992).

97 B. Hutter, *The Attractions of Risk-based Regulation: Accounting for the Emergence of Risk Ideas in Regulation* (CARR Discussion Paper 33, LSE) 3–4; and H. Rothstein, P. Irving, T. Walden, and R. Yearsley, 'The Risks of Risk-Based Regulation: Insights from the Environmental Policy Domain' (2006) 32 *Environment International* 1065.

98 Pidgeon and Butler, n 12 above; I. Lorenzoni, N. Pidgeon and R. O'Connor, 'Dangerous Climate Change: the Role for Risk Research' (2005) 25 *Risk Analysis* 1387; Morgan et al, n 34 above, 270; H. Bulkeley, n 84 above, 442–444; Rothstein, Huber and Gaskell, n 1 above, 91.

99 Mark Stallworthy comments that law-makers address new problems, including those posed by climate change, against a broader picture of regulatory evolution. He continues that this evolution 'has seen a developing emphasis on risk-based management. This can be characterised by features that include *ex ante* setting of clear objectives, across identified timelines, supported by transparent and participatory processes.' See Stallworthy, n 60 above, 418.

100 cf D. Kysar, 'Climate Change, Cultural Transformation and Comprehensive Rationality' (2004) 31 *Boston College Environmental Affairs Law Review* 555.

orchestration. A review of the current climate change package casts doubts on whether these messages have been fully absorbed. Regarding the need for rapid change, the EU undeniably promotes climate change mitigation through technological innovation, as evidenced in, for example, the Renewables and Ecodesign Directives.[101] However, once innovating products and technologies reach the market, they are likely to fall subject to the incremental, almost plodding process of risk decision-making that typifies EU product and technology regulation, thus robbing the innovation initiative of its momentum.[102] What is currently missing is a more systematic discussion of whether the relatively greater risk of inertia warrants a relaxation of the risk regulatory hurdles that scientific and technological innovations traditionally must pass. Particularly when it comes to the introduction of controversial energy sources and technologies such as nuclear energy and carbon capture and storage, there is a pressing need to address questions of risk-risk tradeoffs within the regulatory regime.[103]

Compartmentalisation, too, risks finding its way into climate change regulation, with unwelcome results. It would be disingenuous to accuse the EU of blindness to the need of orchestration; its championing of a multi-pronged approach combining overall capping, emissions trading, innovation facilitation and energy efficiency standard-setting confirms otherwise.Yet old habits die hard and, upon reviewing the climate change package, we encounter some surprisingly narrow framing. For instance, the 2009 Directive on the Geological Storage of Carbon Dioxide (CCS Directive)[104] approaches the environmental risks posed by CCS technology in a notably insular manner, highly reminiscent of the compartmentalisation that characterises EU risk regulation. Although the preamble asserts that CCS technology 'should not serve as an incentive to increase the share of fossil fuel power plants', nor 'lead to a reduction of efforts to support energy saving policies, renewable energies and other safe and sustainable low carbon technologies', the Directive's objectives are narrowly constructed and focus on ensuring that novel CCS technology is deployed in an environmentally safe way. The Directive addresses the risk of carbon leakage, but understands 'leakage' only as the involuntary escape of $CO_2$ from a storage complex;[105] not as the resurgence of fossil fuel industries, whether in the EU or outside of it, in the wake of the commercialisation of CCS technology.[106] Even though the acceptability of the environmental risks posed by CCS technology will at least partly depend on the success of alternative mitigation approaches, the Directive's framework for the risk assessment of storage sites does not offer any entry-points for contextual information to be introduced. At present, opportunities for inter-regulatory learning and review are not built into the CCS regulatory framework.

101 notes 56 and 57 above.

102 Art 12 of Reg 443/2009 (n 57 above) requires the adoption of Commission measures to regulate innovative technologies by 2010. No such measures have yet been issued.

103 cf K. Bickerstaff, I. Lorenzoni, N. Pidgeon, W. Poortinga and P. Simmons, 'Reframing Nuclear Power in the UK Energy Debate: Nuclear Power, Climate Change Mitigation and Radioactive Waste' (2008) 17 *Public Understanding of Science* 145.

104 n 59 above.

105 CCS Directive, Art 3(5) *ibid.*

106 cf M. Babiker, 'Climate Policy, Market Structure and Carbon Leakage' (2005) 65 *Journal of International Economics* 421.

Finally, the unanticipated complexities of regulatory interdependency are at the heart of a recent disagreement between Gunther Oettinger, EU Energy Commissioner, and Commissioner for Climate Change, Connie Hedegaard. Oettinger recently unveiled a new draft directive containing energy efficiency targets for business, including sectors covered under the ETD. Although contributing to the energy efficiency pillar of the climate change package, stringent efficiency standards risk destabilising the market for emission allowances. Hedegaard therefore opposes the initiative and advocates achieving energy efficiency through cutting the number of permits available instead.[107] The dispute eloquently illustrates the need for orchestration at the regulatory and institutional level, as well as the relative inexperience of the EU Commission in accomplishing either.

**The opportunities of comparative learning**

Beyond reducing the risk of regulatory failure, the development of a new paradigm for risk regulation would foster opportunities for mutual support and comparative learning, to the advantage of 'core' risk regulation, environmental regulation, and climate change regulation alike.

Firstly, failure to develop an effective climate change mitigation regime could undermine existing risk regulation by reducing the manageability of uncertainty. Rules on the planting of genetically modified crops and on co-existence, for instance, are developed on the assumption of these crops maturing under relatively stable ecological conditions that are predictable at the point of application for regulatory authorisation. Uncontrolled climate change could rapidly and drastically affect the ecosystem in which GMO crops grow, and hence obliterate the value of conducted risk assessments.[108] From this perspective, the development of a new paradigm for risk regulation, responsive to systemic life-style risks such as climate change would not threaten conventional risk regulation but rather help to guarantee its survival.

Furthermore, new-found awareness of different risk discourses, and of their impact on regulatory objectives and strategies, could spur renewed investigation into health and environmental challenges that thus far have been either insufficiently articulated or lumped together under the broad heading of risk regulation. One area that might considerably benefit from such exercise is biodiversity protection. Within the EU, biodiversity protection is characterised by regulatory strategies in the typical EU risk regulation tradition, displaying a high degree of compartmentalisation, dependence on scientific evidence, itemised decision-making and low awareness of control uncertainty. They are also notoriously ineffective at curbing biodiversity loss.[109] Recent Commission communications

107 F. Harvey, 'Barroso tries to defuse emissions trading row . . . by quoting the Kinks' *The Guardian* 18 June 2011.

108 M. Zinn, 'Adapting to Climate Change: Environmental Law in a Warmer World' (2007) 34 *Ecology Law Quarterly* 61, 64.

109 See Commission Communication on 'Options for an EU Vision and Target for Biodiversity Beyond 2010' COM(2010)4 final, 19 January 2010; A. Ross, 'Modern Interpretations of Sustainable Development' (2009) 36 *Journal of Law and Society* 32, 44.

confirm the need for change, but still seek to accomplish this goal mostly by extending and pursuing better implementation of existing regulatory approaches.[110] The example of climate change could potentially start a more considered debate on whether other risks, such as biodiversity loss, 'behave' like technological risks, climate change risks, or come with their own set of set of idiosyncrasies, thus warranting the development of self-standing and hopefully more effective regulatory responses.

Finally, the conventional risk regulation and new climate risk regulation paradigms could function as valuable counterpoints in the analysis of regime weaknesses. If subservience to scientific rationality is a notorious weak spot of conventional risk regulation, then the Achilles heel of climate change regulation may well be its dependence on continued political willingness to subscribe to the EU's ambitious mitigation and adaptation strategy in the face of overwhelming control uncertainty. Hence, whereas commentators have called for a re-politicising of EU risk regulation in order to balance its in-built tendencies towards formalisation, compartmentalisation, and rationalisation, the survival of the climate change regulatory package might on the contrary hinge on the extent to which it can develop an autonomous *raison d'être*, with some degree of independence from the political context in which the climate risk paradigm took shape.[111] In considering de- or re-politicising strategies, the experiences gained under the two respective regimes could offer invaluable input.

Climate change control as an EU regulatory project is in its infancy. As it matures into a fully-fledged regulatory complex, opportunities for cross-regime learning are sure to multiply. For instance, the fictions of certainty and necessity, already fragile within the EU risk regulation paradigm, are bound to shatter against the overwhelming uncertainties of climate change control. It defies the imagination that, in this area, the EU would be able to make any stronger claims than it is doing the best it can, learning as it goes along, adapting to rapidly changing internal and external circumstances, and correcting earlier mistakes. Moreover, the presence of an overall, quantified target against which the EU's regulatory success, or lack thereof, can be measured, should sour any appetite for Panglossian enthusiasm. The development of new legitimating strategies in the face of systemic control uncertainty will offer important lessons on the EU's ability (or lack thereof) to step out of its eudemonic rationale and justify itself without firm guarantees of regulatory superiority.

This experience could, in turn, prove wonderfully instructive for EU risk regulation, which displays a keen awareness of the stifling impact of eudemonia, but has thus far not been able to muster a credible response.[112]

As to instructive exchanges flowing in the opposite direction, the EU risk regulatory experience, and particularly its history of contestation, could serve as

110 Commission Communication on 'Our life insurance, our natural capital: an EU biodiversity strategy to 2020' n 90 above.

111 See 'British economist tears EU climate policy to pieces' *ENDS Europe Daily* 4 September 2009, reporting that 'Dieter Helm, a professor at Oxford University and chair of the UK environment ministry's academic panel, says the climate and energy package is profoundly flawed because its targets are entirely political and do not make economic sense.'

112 Chalmers, n 31 above.

a crucial source of inspiration for the climate risk regime. For instance, the EU regulatory regime governing food safety has faced formative internal and external legitimacy challenges[113] which have forced EU regulatory bodies and reviewing bodies alike to grapple with many of risk regulation's most intractable challenges, ranging from the role of local preferences in centralised decision-making to the reconciliation between competing expectations of timeliness, certainty, and inclusiveness of EU rule-making. For all their limitations, EU institutions have tried to respond to calls for better governance, greater responsiveness, and resilience of risk regulation. The political momentum in favour of action against climate change may thus far have supplied a degree of insulation against claims of illegality and illegitimacy, but the cracks are already appearing,[114] as the turmoil surrounding the adoption of the 2009 climate change package attests.[115] Once climate change regulation starts to bite at the local level, and particularly if adaptation policies are reeled into the sphere of EU governance, contestation will be all but inevitable. The EU risk regulatory experience of challenge and response, and of the opportunities and limitations created through response and reform, will be invaluable to the climate risk paradigm as it seeks out and defines its approach to governance.

## CONCLUSION

The pursuit of an ambitious climate change policy constitutes a regulatory challenge that is different in scale and scope from anything the European Union has faced before. This challenge cannot and should not be met through the adoption of conventional risk regulation strategies, which respond to a different conceptualisation of risk and espouse fundamentally different aspirations from those that drive climate change control. Within the universe of climate change, the risks of the old far outstrip those of the new, change is valued over stabilisation, and orchestration is more productive than compartmentalisation. Consequently, regulating the risks of climate change is a both a quantitatively and qualitatively different exercise from regulating risks such as pesticide use, industrial pollution, or genetic modification.

This does not mean, however, that there is no role for risk regulation scholarship in the field of climate change. This article shows that, at the very least, the risk regulation paradigm offers an instructive comparator against which to identify and analyse the distinctiveness of climate change as a regulatory project. Yet the article pleads for something more ambitious, to match the ambition of the EU's climate change package itself: the full articulation of a new paradigm for risk regulation, commensurate with the scale and complexity that characterises contemporary environmental risks, of which climate change is the prime example.

113 Lee, n 28 above, 239–267; D Chalmers, 'Risk, Anxiety and the European Mediation of the Politics of Life' (2005) 30 *European Law Review* 649.

114 'European Leaders Clash over Pledges on Global Warming' *The Guardian* 11 December 2008; 'Poland Blocks Adoption of Low Carbon Roadmap' *ENDS Europe Daily* 21 June 2011.

115 'EU Struggles Toward Climate Package Consensus' *ENDS Europe Daily* 4 December 2008.

Such articulation, it is argued, will be invaluable to the European Union as it expands its regulatory arsenal towards climate change mitigation and, conceivably, adaptation. Ultimately, the development of a new paradigm might also help us to look at some old risk and environmental regulatory problems through new lenses, and perhaps come up with new responses.




(2011) 74(6) MLR 817–844

[19]

*Journal of Environmental Law* **22**:2 
doi:10.1093/jel/eqq001 Advance Access published on 24 February 2010

# Analysis

# The Treaty of Lisbon and European Environmental Law and Policy

Hans Vedder*


## Abstract

This contribution analyses the effects of the entry into force of the Treaty of Lisbon for European environmental law and policy. The central conclusion is that, apart from the new numbering and some new names for procedures and institutions, this does not entail any major changes. The new Energy Title, it is submitted, does not go beyond confirming the status quo. One potentially interesting innovation is the special treaty infringement procedure for non-communication of implementing measures. Similarly, a new paragraph on standing to challenge the legality of European acts (Article 230 EC) may result in wider access to justice also in environmental matters.


Keywords: EU law, environmental policy, Treaty of Lisbon, institutional reform

## 1. Introduction

The Treaty of Lisbon marks the last step in the European integration as far as the constituent treaties are concerned. Together with the Treaty of Maastricht, this treaty stands out from all the other amending treaties[1] in that it results in a complete overhaul of the legal framework of the Treaties and the structure of the European Union. It also shares, with the Treaty of Maastricht, a rather

*Department of European and Economic Law and Member of the Groningen Centre for Energy Law University of Groningen (h.h.b.vedder@rug.nl)

1 These are the Single European Act (1987), the Treaty of Amsterdam (1997) and the Treaty of Nice (2000).

eventful ratification process. Eventually, the Treaty of Lisbon entered into force on 1 December 2009. As a result the European Union and European Community will merge into one European Union, with the EC Treaty being replaced by a Treaty on the Functioning of the European Union (hereafter TFEU).

In this analysis, the impact of the Treaty of Lisbon on European environmental law and policy is analysed. To do this, the Treaty of Lisbon is first analysed in the light of the failed Treaty Establishing a Constitution for Europe[2] and the European Convention[3] that partly prepared that Treaty. In connection with this, a general overview of the Treaty of Lisbon as well as a comparison with the Constitutional Treaty is also provided.

## 2. The Treaty of Lisbon as a Successor to the Constitutional Treaty

Given that the Treaty of Lisbon basically had to preserve as much as possible that had found its way into the Constitutional Treaty, it will hardly come as a surprise that the most profound changes are of an institutional and procedural nature. The Declaration of Laeken, which contains the mandate for the European Convention was overwhelmingly concerned with the institutional side of the European Union and European Integration.[4] The result of the European Convention was subjected to the 2004 IGC and resulted in the Constitutional Treaty. When that was rejected in French and Dutch referenda, a two-year period of reflection ended with the mandate to draw up a reform treaty.[5] This mandate meant that the constitutional elements had to disappear from the reform treaty, whilst maintaining many of the 'innovations resulting from the 2004 IGC'.[6] Indeed, the differences between the Constitutional Treaty and the Treaty of Lisbon appear primarily cosmetic, with, for example, the Charter of Fundamental Rights no longer being a part of the Treaty,[7] but having the same status as the Treaties.[8]

2 [2004] OJ C310/1, hereafter referred to as Constitutional Treaty.
3 The proceedings of this Convention are available online from: <http://european-convention.europa.eu/bienvenue.asp?lang=NL&Content=>
4 The text of the Declaration is available from: <http://european-convention.eu.int/pdf/LKNEN.pdf>. Central themes to be addressed by the Convention were: A better division and definition of competence in the European Union, simplification of the Union's instruments, more democracy, transparency and efficiency in the European Union and towards a Constitution for European citizens.
5 Presidency Conclusions of 21/22 June 2007, 11177/1/07 REV 1.
6 Para 1 and Annex I to the Presidency Conclusions of 21/22 June 2007, 11177/1/07 REV 1.
7 It was Part II of the Constitutional Treaty.
8 Art 6(1) TEU. Hereafter EU will be used to refer to the old EU Treaty whereas TEU will refer to the Treaty on European Union as amended by the Treaty of Lisbon. For this article the consolidated versions of the TEU and TFEU published in the [2008] OJ C115 have been used.

## 3. The Treaty of Lisbon and European Environmental Law

The Treaty of Lisbon will have important effects for the structure of the European Union. The European Community and the EC Treaty will disappear and be replaced with the European Union. The EC Treaty will be replaced with what was Part III of the Constitutional Treaty and is now entitled the Treaty on the Functioning of the European Union. The Treaty on European Union (TEU) has the same legal value as the Treaty on the Functioning of the European Union (TFEU).[9]

We find a changed definition of qualified majority voting that will be applied to more areas than before. Similarly, the co-decision procedure will be called the ordinary legislative procedure[10] and will also be applicable to more policy areas. On the institutional side, the Presidency of the European Council,[11] the role of the High Representative,[12] the slightly increased importance of the President of the European Commission[13] and the possibility of a reduced number of members of the European Commission[14] are some of the highlights. The Treaty of Lisbon also merges the third pillar (Police and Judicial Cooperation in Criminal Matters, Title VI EU) with the first pillar.

### *3.1 Objectives*

To start with the more political side of the matter, the preamble to the TEU maintains the reference to sustainable development in the same weak manner as the current EU Treaty does.[15] Given that sustainable development already involves taking into account other factors in economic development, taking sustainability into account hardly amounts to an unequivocal commitment to environmental protection as such or even to sustainability. On the upside of things, the objectives of the Union (Article 2 EU) have been extended to incorporate what are now the objectives of the EC. This means that Article 3 TEU now includes a third paragraph that contains a slightly differently worded version of what is now Article 2 EC combined with Article 2 EU. This basically reiterates the Union's commitment to sustainable development and a high

9 Art 1, third paragraph, TEU and art 1(2) TFEU.
10 Art 289 TFEU in connection with 294 TFEU.
11 Art 15(5) EU.
12 *Inter alia* as a liaison between the Commission and the Council, arts 17(4) and 18 EU.
13 Art 17(6) EU.
14 Art 17(5) EU.
15 The eighth recital of the preamble to the EU Treaty reads as follows 'DETERMINED to promote economic and social progress for their peoples, *taking into account the principle of sustainable development* and within the context of the accomplishment of the internal market and of reinforced cohesion and *environmental protection*, and to implement policies ensuring that advances in economic integration are accompanied by parallel progress in other fields [emphasis added]' and will become the ninth recital.

level of protection and improvement of the quality of the environment. Interestingly, Article 2 EC refers to the sustainable development of economic activities,[16] whereas Article 3 TEU states that the European Union 'shall work for the sustainable development of Europe'. This makes sustainable development an ever more cross-cutting or horizontal objective that is not just confined to economic development but may also relate to technological development. The objectives of the Union have also been updated to include the agenda for relations between the European Union and the world.[17] According to this agenda the European Union shall 'contribute to [. . .] the sustainable development of the earth,[. . .] free *and fair* trade' [emphasis added]. The latter is particularly important in view of the important role that developing countries may play in achieving sustainable development.

The international agenda for the European Union contains another reference to sustainable development in the Title containing General Provisions on the Union's External Action. According to Article 21 TEU, this action shall 'foster the sustainable economic, social and environmental development of developing countries, with the primary aim of eradicating poverty; [and] help develop international measures to preserve and improve the quality of the environment and the sustainable management of global natural resources, in order to ensure sustainable development'.[18] These objectives shall guide external action in general but also the common foreign and security policy of the European Union. This is reinforced by the inclusion of an integration clause in Article 21(3) TEU.

The conclusion must be that environmental protection and sustainable development continue to occupy a prominent place in the objectives of the European Union. An issue that remains unresolved is the exact weight to be given to the various objectives where they are at odds with each other. For example, many people would include animal welfare in the definition of sustainable development and indeed the Treaty of Lisbon is unique in that it is the first treaty to recognise animals as 'sentient beings'.[19] Moreover, the same group of people will not consider bull fights as very conducive to animal welfare whereas they are clearly a part of the 'cultural heritage' of certain member states, and thus will be respected and safeguarded by the European Union.[20] The Court's jurisprudence on the reconciliation of the objectives of the Common Agricultural Policy may provide a hint about a possible solution to this problem.[21] However, it is submitted that a true solution to this problem

16 The reference in art 2, first indent, EU also appears to be confined to economic development.
17 Art 2(5) TEU.
18 Art 21(2)(d) and (f) TEU.
19 Art 13 TFEU, see further below Section 2.3.
20 Art 3(3), fourth indent TEU.
21 Joined cases C-133/93, C-300/93 and C-362/93 *Crispoltoni* [1994] ECR I-4863, para 31.

that respects both objectives is simply impossible.[22] Other, less extreme, cases of conflicting principles may well be resolved using the integration principle.

### 3.2 The Integration Principle

As far as integration principles are concerned, the Treaty of Lisbon presents an interesting surprise in that it contains three environmental integration principles. This excludes the numerous references to sustainable development, which basically entail an integration exercise as well, and the integration principle in the EU Fundamental Rights Charter.[23]

The first environmental integration principle is to be found in Article 11 TFEU. This provision is a literal transposition of the current Article 6 EC. This is compounded by Article 13 TFEU which contains a second and specialised integration principle for animal welfare. Finally, Article 194(2) TFEU envisages another specialised environmental integration principle for the Union's energy policy.

Whereas in the current situation the environmental integration principle can be distinguished from all other integration principles because of its unique position in the general principles Title, the Treaty of Lisbon will change this because more integration principles are promoted to the status of 'provisions having general application'. In Articles 7–13 TFEU we now find a general integration principle, a sex equality integration principle, an employment and social integration principle, a non-discrimination integration principle and a consumer protection integration principle alongside the environmental and animal welfare integration principle. In a way this demotes the environmental integration principle to 'just another integration principle' and thus leads to a number of questions. The first one relates to the possible hierarchy between these principles. The special status of the current Article 6 EC, which is the most often referred to integration principle, has certainly diminished.[24] The increased equality of integration principles is confirmed by Article 7 TFEU. This provision can be called a super-integration clause in that it requires the Union to ensure consistency between all its policies and activities. The conclusion must therefore be that there is no hierarchy between the various integration principles mentioned in Title II TFEU. This may be

22 The absolute and imperative language of art 3(3), fourth indent TEU appears to indicate a priority for the cultural heritage to the detriment of the level of animal welfare. The fact that the animal welfare integration principle itself also contains this essential reservation confirms this view.

23 Art 37 Charter of Fundamental Rights of the European Union [2000] OJ C364/1.

24 See on this special status: NML Dhondt, *Integration of Environmental Protection into other EC Policies* (Europa Law Publishing, Groningen 2003) 100 ff and SA de Vries, *Tensions within the Internal Market* (Europa Law Publishing, Groningen 2006) 18 ff.

different for those integration principles that were not promoted. For example, the cultural integration clause,[25] the industrial policy integration clause[26] and the cohesion integration principle[27] remain where they are, tucked away in Part 3 of the TFEU. The reasons underlying this distinction between the integration principles that have general application and those other integration principles is unclear. Moreover, it does not relate to the category (shared[28], supportive or coordinating[29]) of competence applicable to the policy area.[30] Finally, grouping these principles together brings to the fore interesting differences in their formulation. Articles 8 and 9 (sex equality and employment and social protection) are explicitly addressed to the Union whereas Article 13 (animal welfare) is addressed to the Union as well as the member states. The environmental integration principle and the consumer protection integration principle are formulated without an addressee but only in reference to Union policies and activities. Does this mean that animal welfare considerations are to be taken into account by the member states whereas environmental concerns are irrelevant for member states enacting a Union policy?[31]

### 3.3 *The Environment Title*

It has already been said that, apart from the abovementioned minor institutional differences, the current Articles 174–176 EC have basically been copy-pasted to become Articles 191–193 TFEU. A purely cosmetic change concerns the inclusion of climate change as an example of a regional or worldwide environmental problem that falls within the ambit of EU environmental policy.[32] Of course, the European Union has a well-developed climate change policy and moreover plays an active role in the international climate change arena. It is therefore submitted that the Treaty of Lisbon does not go beyond confirming an existing reality.[33] At most, the inclusion of

25 Art 167(4) TFEU, currently art 151(4) EC.
26 Art 173(3) TFEU, currently art 173(3) EC.
27 Art 175 TFEU, currently art 159 EC.
28 See art 4 TFEU.
29 See art 6 TFEU.
30 Environmental protection and cohesion are both listed in art 4 TFEU as shared competences.
31 As a result of Regulation 1/2003 the national competition authorities must also apply arts 101 and 102 TFEU, see further: HHB Vedder, *Competition Law and Environmental Protection: Towards Sustainability?* (Europa Law Publishing, Groningen 2003) 192 ff.
32 Art 191(1), fourth indent, TFEU.
33 This has not kept a number of politicians from adopting widely differing views on this provision, see J-P Bonde, *From EU Constitution to Lisbon Treaty*, 66 ff <http://www.indemgroup.eu/fileadmin/user_upload/groupdocs/Research_publication/From_EU_Constitution_to_Lisbon_Treaty_april_2008.pdf> For the short overview of the Treaty given by Belgian Minister De Gucht in the Belgian Parliament, see <http://www.dekamer.be/doc/flwb/pdf/52/0955/52k0955002.pdf> at 7.

climate change can be seen as a political signal on the part of the European Union.[34]

### 3.4 *The Energy Title*

An interesting innovation is the introduction of a Title on Union energy policy (Title XXI). Again, this Title probably contains little more than a codification of the status quo. Before the entry into force of the Treaty of Lisbon energy law was implemented on the basis of the provisions on the internal market (Article 95 EC), the competition provisions (Articles 81–88 EC) and environmental protection (Article 175 EC). The new Article 194 TFEU reiterates the connection with the internal market as well as the environmental protection component of European energy policy. Concerning the latter the third indent of Article 194(1) TFEU states that EU energy policy shall aim, *inter alia*, to 'promote energy efficiency and energy saving and the development of new and renewable forms of energy'. The Energy Title contains a legal basis in the form of Article 194(2).

Interestingly, the Energy Title allows only for an EU energy policy 'in the context of the establishment and functioning of the internal market and with regard for the need to preserve and improve the environment'. This places EU energy policy clearly in an environmental perspective. At the same time it entails a significant restriction of the scope of this Title in that such policy appears to be constrained to the internal market. This market entails free movement of goods[35] and undistorted conditions of competition.[36] This may allow only for a European energy policy insofar as imports and exports of energy are concerned. An external energy environment policy will probably have to be conducted on the basis of Article 192 TFEU as it is outside the scope of the internal market. The inclusion of climate change as a regional or worldwide environmental problem that may be addressed in the European Union's environmental policy confirms this.

34 Cf D Benson and A Jordan, 'A Grand Bargain or an "Incomplete Contract"? European Union Environmental Policy after the Lisbon Treaty' (2008) EEELR 280–90, at 284. This is also evidenced by the leadership position the EU sees for itself with the Energy and Climate Package.

35 Art 26(2) TFEU, currently art 14 EC.

36 Protocol No 27 on the Internal Market and Competition.

### 3.5 Competences and Decision-making

One institutional innovation that may very well have an impact on environmental policy[37] is the citizens' initiative.[38] According to this provision no less than one million citizens of the European Union who are from a significant number of member states may invite the Commission to come up with a proposal. As the wording already makes clear, this initiative is only an invitation. Even if the Commission follows up on the invitation, it is still for the Council and the European Parliament to turn a proposal into legislation.[39]

Whether this is likely to happen depends on whether or not there is a competence for the European Union to act and the decision-making procedures laid down for the exercise of that competence. As far as competences are concerned the Treaty of Lisbon again contains some innovations that will not directly affect environmental policy. There may, however, be a number of more indirect effects on environmental policy-making.

As part of an answer to the anxiety in some member states concerning the emergence of a European Super State, three categories of competences are introduced in the EU Treaty and TFEU.[40] The Treaty of Lisbon confirms that the European Union has an exclusive competence for the conservation of marine biological resources under the common fisheries policy.[41] Similarly, the already existing thoughts about environmental competence as a shared competence find their way back in the TFEU.[42] An interesting innovation is the explicit shared competence for the European Union in the energy area.[43] Up to the entry into force of the Treaty of Lisbon European energy law has developed on the basis of the internal market, competition and environment provisions. Following Lisbon, the TFEU will, as noted above, contain an explicit energy competence in the form of Article 194(2).

The member states' wish to 'curtail Europe' can be seen in various instances, for example where the TEU explicitly states that competences that have not been conferred to the European Union remain the member states'.[44] Also, Protocol No 25 on the Exercise of Shared Competences and Declaration No 18 in Relation to the Delimitation of Competences breathe an atmosphere where member states are not too keen on transferring sovereignty to the European

37 The first-ever citizens' initiative in the Netherlands concerned animal welfare and the transition to organic animal husbandry.

38 Art 11(4) TEU.

39 Nevertheless, this provision does address some of the issues brought forward by the Avosetta Group, see JH Jans (ed.) *The European Convention and the Future of European Environmental Law* (Europa Law Publishing, Groningen 2003) 117 ff.

40 These are the exclusive (art 3 TFEU) and shared competence (art 4 TFEU) and areas where the EU may only support, coordinate or supplement the actions of the member states (art 6 TFEU) excluding harmonisation (art 2(5) TFEU).

41 Art 3(1)(d) TFEU, cf joined cases 3, 4 and 6/76 *Kramer* [1976] ECR 1279.

42 Art 4(2)(e) TFEU.

43 Art 4(2)(i) TFEU.

44 Art 4(1) in connection with 5(1)(2) TEU.

Union level. Even though these provisions will probably not have any particular effects on environmental policy, they may indicate a reduced willingness on the part of the member states also to exercise competences conferred on the European Union.[45]

The subsidiarity principle that has been brought to the forefront of the political dialogue between national parliaments and the European Union only strengthens this view. Here, the EU Treaty[46] and Protocol No 1 on the Role of National Parliaments in the European Union convey a similar image of a closer national check on the use of EU competences. Again, the practical impact on European environmental policy will probably be minimal. Most environmental problems will easily pass the subsidiarity hurdle in view of their transboundary nature. Proposals, however, such as the currently pending one for a soil framework directive, may meet with more opposition from the member states.[47]

Concerning decision-making procedures, the Treaty of Lisbon was supposed to make European decision-making easier, for example by the introduction of more qualified majority voting in the Council. Moreover, the European Union's democratisation exercise was supposed to involve the national parliaments as well as European Parliament. As far as European environmental policy is concerned, the Treaty of Lisbon is disappointing in that in the fields most likely to be relevant for environmental policy, the Treaty of Lisbon contains no changes at all. Article 175 EC has been copy pasted to become Article 192 TFEU and the current decision-making procedures including the double legal basis in Article 175(1) and (2) have been maintained. As a result standard environmental legislation following the entry into force of the Treaty of Lisbon will be enacted using the ordinary decision making procedure (the current co-decision procedure) with the Council acting by qualified majority. The definition of a qualified majority has become slightly more complicated, notably concerning the transitional provisions,[48] but remains more or less the same. Similarly, environmental measures that are of a primarily fiscal nature, that affect limited resources or significantly affect a member state's choice between energy sources and energy supply will remain subject to a special legislative procedure. This will entail the Council acting unanimously following consultation of the European Parliament. This special legislative procedure comes with a '*passerelle*' that enables the Council unanimously to decide that another decision-making procedure applies (Article 192(2), last paragraph TFEU). This *passerelle* is certainly a welcome improvement for the position of the European Parliament in that it allows for making the ordinary decision

45 JH Jans (ed.) *The European Convention and the Future of European Environmental Law* (Europa Law Publishing, Groningen 2003) 117 ff.

46 Art 5(3) TEU.

47 COM (2006)232, see IP/07/1988 for an overview of discussions in the Council.

48 Laid down in Protocol No 36 on Transitional Provisions, notably Title II.

legislative procedure applicable whereas the current *passerelle* (Article 175(2), last paragraph, EC) only allows for a switch to qualified majority voting in the Council without any improvement of the Parliament's involvement. In view of the relatively 'green character' of the European Parliament, this is likely to have a positive effect if and when it is applied.[49]

Current European energy policy has been codified in the Treaty of Lisbon. Following the entry into force, the TFEU will contain an energy title with an explicit competence to establish the measures necessary to achieve the objectives of an EU energy policy. As these objectives also include a policy to promote energy efficiency and energy saving and the development of new and renewable forms of energy, this legal basis may also be used to enact environmental energy legislation. However, anyone expecting that this provision could be used to bypass the special decision making procedure in Article 192(2) TFEU (currently Article 175(2) EC) will be disappointed. Eco-taxation in the field of energy law[50] and all measures significantly affecting a member state's choice of energy sources and energy supply structure[51] are still subject to the special decision-making procedure. This effectively rules out an effective European energy eco-tax[52] and legislation on, for example, the desirability of nuclear energy. In fact, even a Europe-wide definition of what constitutes renewable energy may be difficult to achieve in the current legal framework.

Concerning eco-taxation the Treaty of Lisbon contains an institutional oddity in that a European measure in this field based on Article 192(2) TFEU requires the consultation of the Economic and Social Committee and the Committee of the Regions, whereas neither of these Committees needs to be consulted when such a measure is introduced in the energy field. This begs the question what the correct legal basis will be for energy eco-taxation. Obviously, both the environment legal basis and the energy legal basis could be used for such measures. The *lex specialis* rule would argue in favour of using the energy legal basis, but this would exclude the two Committees from the decision-making procedure. Denying an institution the right to be consulted is a serious procedural infringement and will mean that prerogatives of the Committee of the Regions have been infringed.[53] This means that the Committee of the Regions will have standing to bring an action under Article

49 See: D Wilkinson, D Benson and A Jordan, 'Green Budgeting', in A Jordan and A Lenschow (eds), *Innovation in Environmental Policy? Integrating the Environment for Sustainability* (Edward Elgar, Cheltenham 2008) 81.

50 Art 194(3) TFEU.

51 Art 194(2), second subparagraph, TFEU.

52 It is widely accepted that Directive 2003/96 [2003] OJ L283/51, on the taxation of energy products and electricity is ineffective. In this regard it is interesting to notice that the Commission has recently published a proposal for strengthening this Directive, see: <http://www.euractiv.com/en/climate-change/eu-mulls-carbon-tax-curb-global-warming/article-185832>.

53 For example, on the consultation of the European Parliament, Case C-65/93 *European Parliament v. Council* [1995] ECR I-653.

263, third paragraph TFEU. If past experiences in the European Union are anything to go by, inter-institutional cases on the correct legal basis of legislation are all but a thing of the past.

On the upside of things, the ordinary legislative procedure will be applied to the areas where the Council used to reign supreme, hampered only by the consultation of the European Parliament and the exclusive right of initiative for the Commission. As a result, we can expect greater involvement of the European Parliament in the agricultural policy as well as the transport policy of the European Union.[54] This influence of the European Parliament is further increased because of the Parliament's greater influence on the EU Budget. Notably concerning what was previously known as compulsory expenditure, made up largely by the agriculture budget, the Parliament's powers have increased.[55]

As far as fisheries policy is concerned, the future for the European Parliament looks equally bright. However, the most important element of fisheries policy as far as environmental protection is concerned is the setting of fishing quota. This, however, remains the exclusive domain of the Council, without any formal involvement of the European Parliament.[56] As regards international fisheries agreements, this means that whatever greening influence the European Parliament has, it is limited to fisheries policies agreements and does not extend to fishing quotas.[57]

### 3.6 *The Judicial System*

The European Court of Justice, that is now called the Court of Justice of the European Union, CJEU), has consistently played an important role in European integration as well as the implementation of European environmental law.[58] Indeed, fundamental doctrines such as direct effect, state liability and the free movement of goods have been and continue to be predominantly shaped by the Court. Moreover, the Court's influence on European integration and the development of these doctrines may not always have been to the liking of the member states. The Treaty of Maastricht contains some indicators of the desire on the part of the member states to somehow minimise the

54 Concerning transport policy, the EC Treaty already used the codecision procedure, but provided for the consultation of the European Parliament and unanimity in the Council whenever a transport measure could affect the standard of living and level of employment in certain regions, and the operation of transport facilities (art 72(2) EC). Following the entry into force of the Treaty of Lisbon, such effects shall be taken into account, but do not rule out the applicability of the ordinary legislative procedure.

55 Art 314 TFEU.

56 Art 43(3) TFEU.

57 Art 218 TFEU requires the European Parliament's consent for the conclusion of such agreements.

58 For an overview see: JH Jans, 'Environmental Spill-Overs from the European Court of Justice' (2008) 31 Fordham Int'l LJ 1360.

influence of the Court. Providing explicitly for the absence of direct effect of framework decisions—the EU-equivalent of a Directive—in Article 34 EU is one attempt to keep the Court's nose out of these matters. However, *Pupino* shows that it is a failed attempt.[59] Perhaps the best way of constraining the Court is the policy that has also been consistently followed by the member states since 'Maastricht'. This policy consists of simply refusing to expand the Court of Justice. All attempts at changing the Treaty to allow for more judges have only resulted in the possibility of more than one judge per member state in the Court of First instance. This possibility, however, has not been used to this date. The General Court, as the Court of First Instance is now known, has also still not been enabled to hear preliminary references, a significant part of the Court's caseload. The Treaty of Lisbon does not change this and can therefore be seen as a continuation of the member states' attempts to reduce the Court's impact on European integration through an increase of the workload.

### *3.7 Implementation and Enforcement*

As was mentioned above, the Court of Justice of the European Union has played an important role in European integration and more specifically European environmental law. The fact that, for example, Article 228 EC has to this date only been used in an environmental context bears testimony to this. The Treaty of Lisbon has an interesting surprise in this regard because it simplifies the infringement procedure and may thus make enforcement of European (environmental) law more effective. Basically, the current Article 226 EC procedure has been transposed to become Article 258 TFEU. The innovation concerns Article 260 TFEU. This contains a shortened or streamlined version of the current Article 228 EC. The first paragraph contains the duty for member states to comply with judgments of the Court. This is compounded in the second paragraph with a procedure that enables the European Commission to bring a case before the Court after having given the member state in question the possibility to react. This means that the current procedure with a statement of objections and a reasoned opinion is reduced to just one exchange of views between the Commission and the member state. The remainder of the procedure is identical with the Commission asking for and the Court being able to impose a lump sum or penalty payment.

Furthermore, a specialised procedure is introduced for infringement proceedings concerning non-communication of implementing measures for directives. Article 260(3) TFEU allows the Commission to directly ask for the imposition of a lump sum or penalty payment. The Court may then impose a lump sum or penalty payment not exceeding the amount requested by the

59 Case C-105/03 *Pupino* [2005] ECR I-5285.

Commission. The latter requirement is not to be found in the procedure on the basis of Article 260(2) TFEU which leads to the question whether that procedure enables the Court to impose a lump sum or penalty payment that exceeds the amount requested by the Commission. In view of the Court's standard jurisprudence according to which it is not bound by the Commission's suggestion for a lump sum or penalty payment, this should indeed be possible.[60] The Court deduced this from the wording of Article 228(2) EC, and the Treaty of Lisbon did not change the wording of Article 228 EC in this regard.

A final innovation on the part of the Treaty of Lisbon to be noticed because of its effect in environmental matters is the change to what is currently the fourth paragraph of Article 230 EC. This provision has gained some notoriety in combination with the Court's refusal to open up standing for non-privileged applicants. In the environmental context *Greenpeace* is the judgment in point.[61] For environmental NGOs the Aarhus Regulation[62] may change matters, but it is at this moment unclear whether this suffices for the Court to reconsider its case law.[63] If this is not enough Article 263 TFEU more or less copies Article 230 EC, with the notable exception of the fourth paragraph. This now reads as follows:

> Any natural or legal person may, under the conditions laid down in the first and second paragraphs, institute proceedings against an act addressed to that person or which is of direct and individual concern to them, and against a regulatory act which is of direct concern to them and does not entail implementing measures.

The effect of this appears to be that the current requirement of direct and individual concern is replaced with a requirement of direct concern only for regulatory acts. In addition, the regulatory act must not entail implementing measures. The main problems concerning this provision relate to exactly these last two elements. The 'regulatory act' is nowhere specified in the TFEU, and what the absence of implementing measures entails is equally gnomic.

60 For example, Case C-387/97 *Commission v Greece* [2000] ECR I-5047, para 80, Case C-304/02 *Commission v France* [2005] 3 CMLR 13, para 85 (analysed (2006) 18 JEL 289) and Case C-121/07 *Commission v France*, judgment of 9 December 2008, nyr, para 61

61 Case C-321/95 P *Stichting Greenpeace Council (Greenpeace International) and Others v Commission* [1998] ECR I-1651

62 Regulation 1367/2006 [2006] OJ L264/13.

63 JH Jans and HHB Vedder, *European Environmental Law* (Europa Law Publishing, Groningen 2008) 214. The judgment of 15 October 2009 in Case C-263/08 *Djurgården-Lilla Värtans Miljöskyddsförening v Stockholms kommun genom dess marknämnd*, nyr, does, however, show that the Court is willing to adopt a rather extensive interpretation of the Aarhus Package insofar as it is addressed to the member states.

## 4. Greening the Treaties: Environmental Protection and the Internal Market

In the period leading up to the negotiations of the Treaties of Maastricht, Amsterdam and Nice several environmental campaigns were launched in order to 'green the Treaties'.[64] These attempts dealt with the role of environmental concerns after harmonisation[65] and as a justification of restrictions of the free movement of goods.[66] The idea underlying this appears to be that the European Union does not pay enough attention to environmental concerns when these are balanced with internal market considerations.

Compared to the making of the Constitutional Treaty, drafting the Treaty of Lisbon was a much less open and transparent procedure. The Convention process, whereby a convention consisting of representatives of the European institutions and national institutions deliberated in public hearings, provides an invaluable insight into the role played by the various interests and institutions. Even though the Treaty of Lisbon preserves the convention procedure, the Treaty itself was drafted in the traditional intergovernmental way with high level national representatives negotiating in relative obscurity. As a result, the impact of the environmental lobby is much more difficult to qualify and quantify.[67]

As has already been noted, the Treaty of Lisbon and the Constitutional Treaty are primarily concerned with the institutional side of the European Union and European integration. The more substantive side of the matter clearly figured less prominently on the negotiation agenda. As far as innovations in substantive EU law are concerned, the focus is on so-called services of general interest. The Treaty of Lisbon elaborates Article 16 EC with a legal basis, albeit without changing this provision's character of a political declaration.[68] This is topped off with another primarily political declaration in the form of the Protocol on Services of General Interest.[69] In view of *Sydhavnens*[70] and the increasing use of market based instruments to protect

64 For an overview see S Stetter, 'Maastricht, Amsterdam and Nice: The Environmental Lobby and Greening the Treaties' (2001) EELR 150–9.

65 This concerns the environmental guarantee in art 95(4)–(6) EC.

66 This would involve adding environmental protection to the list of grounds in art 30 EC. Moreover, see G Monti, 'Article 81 EC and Public Policy' (2002) 39 CML Rev 1057–99 for a proposal to include such concerns in art 81(3) EC.

67 S Stetter, 'Maastricht, Amsterdam and Nice: The Environmental Lobby and Greening the Treaties' (2001) EELR 150–9, contains an overview and impact analysis of the environmental lobby campaigns during previous treaty amendments.

68 Art 16 EC will become art 14 TFEU. The political character follows from the fact that importance of such services is underlined *without prejudice* to the (unamended) provisions of the TFEU that govern the relation between such services and internal market law.

69 Protocol No 26.

70 Case C-209/98 *Sydhavnens* [2000] ECR I-3743, notably para 75.

the environment,[71] this may mean a shift in the balance between environmental protection and the internal market. However, as *Sydhavnens* shows, EU law as it stands at the moment is quite capable of balancing environmental concerns with the internal market in a satisfactory manner.[72]

## 5. Conclusions

The tenor of this analysis has been that the impact of the Treaty of Lisbon on European environmental law is most likely to be minimal. Given the Treaty's primarily institutional focus this should not come as a surprise. On the institutional side of matters, the limited improvements of decision-making procedures represent a small step forward, as do the increased possibilities for enforcement of implementation. Whether these institutional improvements will actually improve environmental policy, let alone the level of environmental protection, is uncertain at best. In view of its 'green' track record, the increased role for the European Parliament could result in more environmental legislation or a greater role for the environment in other policy areas. Whilst the Treaty is hardly effective when it comes to really enabling European environmental law making (unanimity is still required for eco-taxation and environmental policies affecting energy sources), the uncertainties created, for example concerning standing of private parties, are even more problematic.

In this regard, the need for this Treaty can be questioned. The reality is that a Union of 27 Member States has managed to pass several high profile pieces of environmental legislation, despite the old decision-making procedures.[73] Another aspect of this reality is that the Commission continues to table (environmental) proposals and is still bringing infringement cases before the Court. Perhaps the Court is the main loser in the Treaty of Lisbon in that it is still (indeed, perhaps even more so than before) facing an increasing work load and with only two extra judges. From this perspective, the enlargement treaties may be more important as they will at least result in extra judicial capacity.

71 Green Paper on market-based instruments for environment and related policy purposes, COM (2007) 140.

72 Moreover, Case C-405/07 P *Netherlands v Commission* [2008] ECR I-8301 shows that the environmental guarantee in art 95 EC is quite adequate.

73 For example, Directive 2008/1 concerning integrated pollution prevention and control [2008] OJ L24/8 and Directive 2008/98 concerning waste [2008] OJ L312/3, Directive 2008/99 on environmental crime [2008] OJ L328/28. Furthermore, the Energy and Climate Package has been adopted [2009] OJ L140.

*Journal of Environmental Law* **22**:1 
doi:10.1093/jel/eqp032 Advance Access published on 3 December 2009

# The Climate is No Commodity: Taking Stock of the Emissions Trading System

Gerd Winter*

However beautiful the strategy, you should occasionally look at the results.

Winston Churchill[1]

## Abstract

'Cap and trade' is the nucleus of the so-called flexible mechanisms of climate protection: the maximum use of a resource (here, a particular quantity of greenhouse gas emissions) is determined; from this, individual emission allowances are derived and allocated. Emission allowances can be traded—in other words, they can be purchased and sold. They can also be acquired by investing abroad, if this leads to a reduction of emissions. As elegant and perfect 'cap and trade' might appear, we have to ask whether this instrument meets the expectations it has raised. This can, however, be questioned. The article sketches out the 'cap and trade' system (Section 1), illustrates 'cap and trade's' lack of success (Section 2) and explains its failure arguing that economic logic has supplanted ecological logic (Section 3). This argument is followed by a reflection on whether the approach should altogether be abandoned or reformed through putting it into a framework of the regulatory tradition (Section 4). The article takes Germany as a case where it is felt important to look at implementation at the national level.

*Research Center for European Environmental Law, University of Bremen. (gwinter@uni-bremen.de). I am grateful to Chris Hilson and the two anonymous referees for their valuable comments.

1 Cite taken from AB Pittock, *Climate Change* (2nd edn Earthscan, London 2009) 322.

Keywords: climate protection, emissions trading, cap and trade, flexible mechanisms

# 1. The Design of 'Cap and Trade'

## 1.1. The 'Cap' Element: Assigned Emission Amounts

In the Kyoto Protocol of 1997, a number of industrial nations committed themselves to reducing the annual average of their greenhouse gas emissions within the so-called 'first commitment period' from 2008 to 2012 to an amount that equals at most 95% of the overall total of 1990—the year which was set as base year.[2] Ninety-five percent signifies the average of the quotas of all individual states.[3] The EU's quota is 92%. This quota multiplied with the amount of released emissions in 1990 and the five years of the first commitment period results in the so-called assigned amount of permissible emissions.

In line with the so-called bubble—permissible according to Article 4(1) Kyoto Protocol—Council Decision 2002/358/EC[4] distributed the EC's overall quota among its Member States by allocating differentiated emission commitments. For instance, Germany received less (namely only 79%) in comparison with Spain with 115%. The contributions 'are differentiated to take account of expectations for economic growth, the energy mix and the industrial structure of the respective Member State'.[5]

The Member States are meant to achieve their emission targets primarily by measures of their own within their territory. However, they can also relieve their economies[6] by purchasing additional emission allowances from other states or by acquiring them through the Clean Development Mechanism

2 These are the so-called Annex I states, ie those countries listed in Annex I of the Framework Convention on Climate Change (FCCC), thereby agreeing to oblige to particular commitments. Cf Art 4(2) FCCC and Art 1(7) Kyoto Protocol. Art 3 of the Kyoto Protocol sets the 95% ceiling, while Annex B of the Kyoto Protocol specifies the quotas for individual states. For the sake of simplification, in the following, I will speak of Annex B states rather than Annex I states, where appropriate.

3 As the USA did not ratify the Protocol, its intended share of the reduction does not apply. This increases the overall proportion to 97.2% or reduces the reduction proportion to 2.8%. Cf Greenhouse gas projections and trends in Europe, EEA Report 5/2008, p 29. (Thanks to Dr Hans-Jochen Luhmann, Wuppertal Institute for Climate, Environment and Energy, for this suggestion.)

4 Council Decision (EC) 2002/358 concerning the approval, on behalf of the European Community, of the Kyoto Protocol to the UNFCCCand the joint fulfilment of commitments thereunder [2002] OJ L130/1–3.

5 Council Decision 2002/358/EC, recital 12.

6 Cf M Ehrmann, 'Das ProMechG: Verknüpfung des Europäischen Emissionshandels mit den Flexiblen Mechanismen des Kyoto-Protokolls' in M Oldiges (ed), *Immissionsschutz durch Emissionshandel— eine Zwischenbilanz* (Nomos, Baden-Baden 2007) 110.

(CDM) or Joint Implementation (JI).[7] This increases the assigned emission amount for the acquiring state.[8]

A part of the quotas of the Member States which concerns the emissions from commerce, private households and transport—is handled by dint of classical instruments; for those, a variety of mixtures of Community and national law applies, especially a mélange of regulatory law, subsidies and charges. The other part, concerning emissions from the energy sector and industry, is subject to the so-called flexible instruments[9], which I will focus on in the following. For these instruments, Directive 2003/87[10] provides a framework under Community law.

According to Articles 9–11 Directive 2003/87, for the two so-called allocation periods—2005–07 and 2008–12—national allocation plans have to be developed, which must follow certain criteria established in Annex III of the Directive. In Germany, this is handled in line with the key act of climate protection, the Greenhouse Gas and Emissions Trading Act (*Treibhausgas- und Emissionshandelsgesetzes*, TEHG).[11] For each allocation period, the so-called macroplans and microplans are developed and made mandatory by Allocation Acts (*Zuteilungsgesetze* 2007 and 2012, hitherto ZuG 2007 and ZuG 2012).

For the first allocation period (2005–07), ZuG 2007 and ZuG 2012 assigned the energy sector and industry 503 Mt/a $CO_2$[12] and 453.07 Mt/a $CO_2$ for the second period (2008–12).[13]

7 For more details, see Sections 2 and 3.

8 Art 3(10) and (12) Kyoto Protocol. The transfer through purchase or JI leads to the respective reduction of quotas assigned to the transfer state (Art 3(11) Kyoto Protocol). This is not the case for CDM projects, as the transfer states in this case are not among the Annex B states.

9 See Section 2.

10 Directive 2003/87 (EC) of the European Parliament and of the Council establishing a scheme for greenhouse gas emission allowance trading within the Community and amending Council Directive 96/61/EC (Text with EEA relevance) [2003] OJ L275/32–46. The directive was amended by a directive of 2004 tying CDM and JI into the system (Directive 2004/101 (EC) of the European Parliament and of the Council amending Directive 2003/87 (EC) establishing a scheme for greenhouse gas emission allowance trading within the Community, in respect of the Kyoto Protocol's project mechanisms with EEA relevance [2004] OJ L 338/18–23. A second amendment of 2008 extended the system from the industry and energy sectors to aviation (Directive 2008/101/EC of the European Parliament and of the Council amending Directive 2003/87/EC, so as to include aviation activities in the scheme for greenhouse gas [2008] OJ L8/3–21). The last amendment of 2009 prepares the system for the second commitment period that begins after 2012 (Directive 2009/29/EC of the European Parliament and of the Council amending Directive 2003/87/EC, so as to improve and extend the greenhouse gas emission allowance trading scheme of the Community [2009] OJ L140/63–87). In the following, if different versions of articles of the Directive are important, I will speak of Directive 2003/87 in its version of 2008 and 2009, respectively.

11 ss 7–12 TEHG.

12 s 4(2) ZuG 2007. The unit $CO_2$-eq (eq for equivalent) signifies a unit of $CO_2$ or an amount of another greenhouse gas that corresponds to a unit of $CO_2$. For the first two allocation periods only emissions from installations emitting $CO_2$ were subjected to the emissions trading scheme. See Directive 2003/87/EC Annex I. In the article, I will therefore simply speak of $CO_2$ if referring to the EC and its first two allocation periods but of $CO_2$-eq if other climate gases than $CO_2$ are included.

13 s 4(2) ZuG 2012; s 4(2) ZuG 2007 set 495 Mt/a for the second period, yet this was subject to alterations.

For these quotas, the *Zuteilungsgesetze* develop criteria for the allocation of allowances to individual operators, based on aforementioned microplans. The criteria are pre-structured under Community law but provide the Member States with some leeway.

In line with ZuG 2007, all emission allowances[14] were allocated free of charge. For existing installations, grandfathering was applied. This means that installations received emission allowances to the extent that they had produced emissions during a certain base period. In order to give an incentive for emission reduction, a so-called compliance factor of 3% was deduced from the allocated quantity. Older installations that had recently been modernised (such as the lignite-fired power plants in Eastern Germany) were rewarded by waiving the compliance factor. Installations with combined heat and power generation received a special allocation of emission allowances as a reward for their high energy efficiency. Installations built after the start of the first compliance period received emission allowances to the extent necessary for the implementation of best available technology (BAT). If an operator reduced the production in his installation after the emission allowances were allocated, he had to return the respective quantity. In Germany, banking was not allowed—in other words, there could be no transfer of unused emission allowances from the first to the second allocation period. The aim of this was to prevent the new overall emission target from being diminished for the second allocation period; the more so as there would have been an incentive for operators to purchase cheap emission allowances in the first allocation period and keep them for the second.

For the allocation period 2008–12, ZuG 2012 adheres to many of these criteria, but it also entails important changes. Of the allocated 453.07 million emission allowances, 40 million will be sold.[15] The remainder is allocated free of charge as in the past. Overall, one can notice a shift from grandfathering to the so-called 'benchmarking'. Only existing industrial installations remain subject to grandfathering, while the base period for the calculation of historical emissions is brought forward, allowing for more realistic calculations.[16] All energy plants and younger industrial installations are subject to benchmarking according to BAT, BAT being defined by more demanding criteria than before.[17]

14 An emission allowance is defined as the permission to emit one tonne of $CO_2$-eq within a certain period of time (s 3(4) TEHG).

15 s 19(1) ZuG 2012. At the moment, the sale takes place by successive offers at the market; from 2010 onwards, it will be via auction (s 21 ZuG 2012). According to Art 10 Directive 2003/87 in its version of 2009, from 2013 onwards, all emission permits shall be auctioned.

16 s 6 ZuG 2012.

17 ss 7–9 and Annex III ZuG 2012.

### 1.2. *The 'Trade' Elements: Flexible Mechanisms*

The flexible mechanisms consist of emissions trading, CDM and JI. They are meant to help states to achieve their permissible emission quota as cost-effectively as possible. States and operators shall have a choice between the reduction of emissions by investment and the purchase or other acquisition of emission allowances.

The FCCC mentions the flexible mechanisms only in general terms as an option for action. The Kyoto Protocol also does not stipulate them, but establishes certain structures for the case that contractual states want to use these mechanisms.[18] Part of them—the tradeability of emission allowances—was made mandatory on the EU level, while whether CDM and JI measures should be allowed was left to be decided by the Member States.[19]

#### 1.2.1 Emissions trading

The Kyoto Protocol enables emissions trading among states, among companies as well as between states and companies. In order to prevent states from refraining from genuine climate policy but relying largely on the purchase of emission allowances, the Protocol stipulates that emissions trading shall only be 'supplemental' to other domestic climate protection activities.[20]

The relevant EC secondary law does not harmonise the emissions trading among Member States or with third countries, rather it leaves it to bilateral agreements between participating states or between states and international institutions. However, Directive 2003/87 largely harmonised the rules of emissions trading between companies and other persons.[21] Member States have to keep an emissions trading registry following certain standards. This registry lists the issue, holding, transfer and cancellation of allowances. The registry is accessible to the public.[22] A so-called Central Administrator of the EC monitors transactions.[23]

National law further specifies the emissions trading regime. In Germany, the acquisition of emission allowances by the state itself is not envisaged; therefore, no legal basis was provided for such transactions. The law puts the transfer of allowances into legal forms (contract, act of transfer, recording of transfer in the emissions trading registry). Emission allowances issued by another Annex B state are put on a par with German emission allowances,

18 Arts 6, 12 and 17 Kyoto Protocol.
19 See Arts 12 and 11(a) Directive 2003/87.
20 Art 17 Kyoto Protocol.
21 In practice, it is almost solely operators that hold emission permits. Yet, other persons can also acquire these permits, such as NGOs, who want to raise prices by reducing supply.
22 Art 19 Directive 2003/87.
23 Art 20 Directive 2003/87.

once a German operator has purchased them; the same applies to emission allowances from Non-EU-countries listed in Annex B of the Kyoto Protocol, if the EC has concluded a respective agreement with them.[24]

In law, trading is regularly regarded as a bilateral transaction between the vendor and vendee of an emission allowance. In reality, many transactions are conducted via a stock exchange, the European Energy Exchange—Section Emission Allowances—in Leipzig, which undertakes fiducially the buying and selling for its customers.

### 1.2.2 JI

This mechanism comprises an investor[25] from an Annex B country who (co-)finances a project and is allocated those emissions saved by the project as so-called 'emission reduction units' (ERUs).

The Kyoto Protocol stipulates 'additionality', requiring that any such project 'provides a reduction in emissions by sources, or an enhancement of removals by sinks, that is additional to any that would otherwise occur'.[26] Moreover, 'supplementarity' applies to JI, as it does to emissions trading—that is to say, the investor country has to pursue an independent climate policy apart from JI measures.[27]

The Marrakesh Accords[28] flesh out these requirements, especially concerning the calculation of the baseline (in other words, the state of emissions without the project) in order to determine whether a project is 'additional'[29] and also regarding the involvement of independent entities in both the validation of the project design and the verification of the project results. The criterion of 'supplementarity' is by Decision 15/CP.7 No 1 extended to apply also to the country hosting the investment. The execution of administrative supervision is partly shifted to the international level: a Supervisory Committee is established, which at strategic points is involved in validation and verification procedures. The Committee especially accredits and monitors independent consultants, and it decides when there is doubt about whether project plans and project results are compatible with relevant regulations.[30]

24 See on the one hand, s 13(1) TEHG with Art 12(1)(a) Directive 2003/87 and, on the other hand, s 13(3) TEHG with Arts 12(1)(b) and 25(3) Directive 2003/87.
25 This can be a private investor or a state body.
26 Art 6(1)(b).
27 Art 6(1)(d).
28 These are resolutions of the Seventh Conference of Parties, which met in Marrakesh in 2001. The Eighth Conference of Parties confirmed these decisions, after the Kyoto Protocol came into force (FCCC/KP/CMP/2005/8/Add.1, 30 March 2006).
29 In Appendix B of the Annex to the Marrakesh Accords Decision 16/CP.7, it is said: 'The baseline for an Art 6 project is the scenario that reasonably represents the anthropogenic emissions by sources or anthropogenic removals by sinks of greenhouse gases that would occur in the absence of the proposed project.'
30 Annex to Marrakesh Accords Decision 16/CP.7, Nos 3, 35 and 39.

At the EC level, the stipulations of the Marrakesh Accords are incorporated by reference and further complemented, such as by the provision that ERUs acquired between 2005 and 2007 can be used in the first commitment period (2008–12), and that the overall emission target of a state has to be reduced by the quantity that has been transferred as ERU to an investor in another state.[31]

At Member State level, this system is further complemented. The Member States are also responsible for execution, though it should be noted that the Supervisory Committee is also involved, as already mentioned above. Germany adopted the Project Mechanisms Act (*Projektmechanismengesetz*, ProMechG), which regulates the approval by the German state as investor country of projects abroad and as a host country of domestic projects. The Act specifies the substantial requirements of projects, especially of 'additionality', and adds other requirements, such as the obligation to ensure that the project 'does not cause any severe adverse environmental impacts.'[32]

### 1.2.3. CDM

This mechanism involves an investor[33] from an Annex I state who (co-)finances a project within a non-Annex I state and who is allocated those emissions saved by the project as so-called 'certified emission reduction units' (CERs).

As in the case of JI, the Kyoto Protocol stipulates the 'additionality' of the project.[34] Here, further standards are required which are even stricter than in the JI system, namely 'real, measurable and long-term benefits related to the mitigation of climate change'.[35] Article 12 does not contain the requirement of 'supplementarity' but the Marrakesh Accords CP.7 Decision 15 No 1 introduced it to also apply to investor countries (but not host countries) of CDM projects.

The Marrakesh Accords further specify these requirements. In comparison to the JI regime, the density of regulatory and administrative intervention is somewhat higher. Regulations detail the requirement of 'additionality', especially the setting of the baseline as well as certain requirements to the administrative infrastructure of the country hosting the project. Similar to JI, an Executive Committee is established, which further details regulations, accredits operational entities and takes decisions on disputes about the validation, verification and certification of projects.[36] Independent expert bodies (called Operational Entities) are asked to validate projects and to verify their performance. Operational Entities are also responsible for the certification of

31 Arts 11(b)(3) and 4 Directive 2003/87.
32 ss 3 and 5 ProMechG.
33 Again, this can be a private actor or a state body.
34 Art 12(5)(c) Kyoto Protocol.
35 Art 12(5)(b) Kyoto Protocol.
36 Annex to the Marrakesh Accords Decision 17/CP.7, Nos 5, 41 and 65.

project results.[37] In some respect, this replaces the allocation of ERUs by the host countries in the JI regime—a responsibility that host countries of CDM project are apparently not thought to be able to exercise adequately.

At the EC level, the regulatory system of the Marrakesh Accords is incorporated by reference. Complementary regulations are added, such as the stipulation that CER acquired in projects from 2000 onwards can be used in the first commitment period (2008 12).[38]

At Member State level, the Marrakesh and EC system is incorporated and complemented further. In Germany, the ProMechG regulates the investor country's approval to CDM projects. Besides 'additionality', the Act, resounding Art 3 (14) Kyoto Protocol formulates a further requirement, namely that the project 'does not cause any serious adverse environmental impacts' and that it 'does not oppose the sustainable development of the host country in an economic, social or ecological respect, and in particular, does not contravene any existing national sustainability strategies'.[39] The Member States are also responsible for execution in individual cases, though it should be noted that the Executive Committee and the Operational Entities have relevant influence, as already mentioned.

While from a legal perspective, CDM projects are bilateral concepts, investors are also allowed to link up and create funds acting on their behalf. The Prototype Carbon Fund has in this respect been the most important entity, which was established by the World Bank as a private–public partnership between states and private actors. It has organised emission reduction projects and sink projects for its participants and obtained CERs for them. In addition, it has been active in JI projects and thereby obtained ERUs.[40]

## 2. Effects

In the following, it shall be investigated whether the flexible mechanisms have improved climate protection, or in more concrete terms, whether they have led to a reduction of $CO_2$ emissions. To prove the effects of legal regimes is methodologically a rather difficult undertaking, as cause and effect become blurred before the background of complex social reality. Effects that occur after a norm has entered into force can have other causes than the norm itself. In turn, the fact that conditions have not changed after a norm has come into effect does not prove that the norm has no or only

37 Annex to the Marrakesh Accords Decision 17/CP.7, Appendix A.
38 Arts 11(b)(3) and 4 Directive 2003/87.
39 s 8 ProMechG.
40 The fund runs 24 projects. Since 2007, new projects are not managed, but only given advice by the Carbon Finance Unit of the World Bank. <web.world-bank.org/WBSITE/EXTERNAL/TOPICS/ENVIRONMENT/EXTCARBONFINANCE> accessed 20 October 2009.

minor impact. It is possible that the potential effect of a norm was diverted by other factors.

Before assuming an agnostic position when faced with such difficulties, one should keep in mind that when politics considers certain instruments, it often operates with widely unfounded claims of effects. In view of this situation, a methodologically reflected attempt to tease out cause and effect still represents a contribution to improve our knowledge, even if it cannot produce waterproof results.

Accordingly, I confront the legal regime of flexible instruments, which is meant to reduce the emission of $CO_2$, with data about actual emissions. At first, I present data that concern all $CO_2$ emissions of EU Member States. They encompass all emission sources, those subject to the classical instruments and those subject to flexible instruments. Then, I present data about those sectors subject to flexible instruments.

The reduction targets promised in the Kyoto Protocol have thus far not been achieved.[41] It is true that this target is actually set for the commitment period 2008–12 and it might be possible that it will be met. Still, the instruments of the Kyoto complex—classical approaches as well as the flexible mechanisms—were meant to set the actors on a path to achieve their final commitment. However, hardly any effect linked to these instruments can be discerned. As far as an emission reduction can be identified among Annex B states, it is mainly caused by the industrial transformation in the transition countries.

This point is substantiated in Figure 1. It shows that since 1990 the transition countries' $CO_2$ emissions fell by 41.3% and later 37% under the level of this year, while the remaining Annex B states' emissions increased on average by 10.9% with a slightly falling tendency to 9.9%. Only totalling the bad balance of Western states with the good balance (not motivated by climate reasons) of transition countries allows one to conclude that all Annex B states taken together fell in 2000 to 6.9% and increased until 2006 to 4.7% of the level of 1990.

Summing up, these data suggest that the Kyoto regime has hitherto not achieved its aim. The annual emission rates of non-transition countries have increased, although they were meant to decrease; the rates of transition countries have significantly dropped, yet not due to the Kyoto instruments but due to the economic meltdown in the transition period.

However, one has to consider that the Kyoto regime could have weakened an existing and even stronger growth trend in the annual emission rates of non-transition countries. This can be investigated by comparing states that have adopted Kyoto instruments with states that have not.

41 Although the reduction target shrunk to 2.8% after the USA dropped out, those Annex B states that ratified the Kyoto Protocol are obliged to honour the agreed quotas.

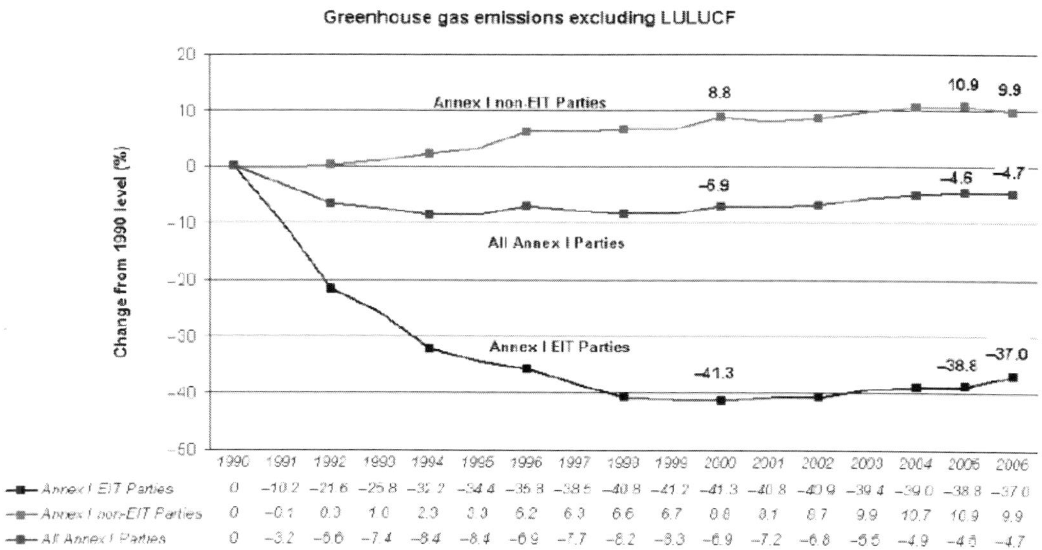


| | 1990 | 1991 | 1992 | 1993 | 1994 | 1995 | 1996 | 1997 | 1998 | 1999 | 2000 | 2001 | 2002 | 2003 | 2004 | 2005 | 2006 |
|---|---|---|---|---|---|---|---|---|---|---|---|---|---|---|---|---|---|
| Annex I EIT Parties | 0 | −10.2 | −21.6 | −25.8 | −32.2 | −34.4 | −35.8 | −38.5 | −40.8 | −41.2 | −41.3 | −40.8 | −40.9 | −39.4 | −39.0 | −38.8 | −37.0 |
| Annex I non-EIT Parties | 0 | −0.1 | 0.3 | 1.0 | 2.3 | 3.3 | 6.2 | 6.3 | 6.6 | 6.7 | 8.8 | 8.1 | 8.7 | 9.9 | 10.7 | 10.9 | 9.9 |
| All Annex I Parties | 0 | −3.2 | −6.6 | −7.4 | −8.4 | −8.4 | −6.9 | −7.7 | −8.2 | −8.3 | −6.9 | −7.2 | −6.8 | −5.5 | −4.9 | −4.6 | −4.7 |

**Figure 1.** Green house gas emissions of Annex I states.[42]

42 FCCC Secretariat document.<http://unfccc.int/files/inc/graphics/image/gif/trends .excluding.2008.gif.> accessed 20 October 2009. EIT denotes economies in transition.

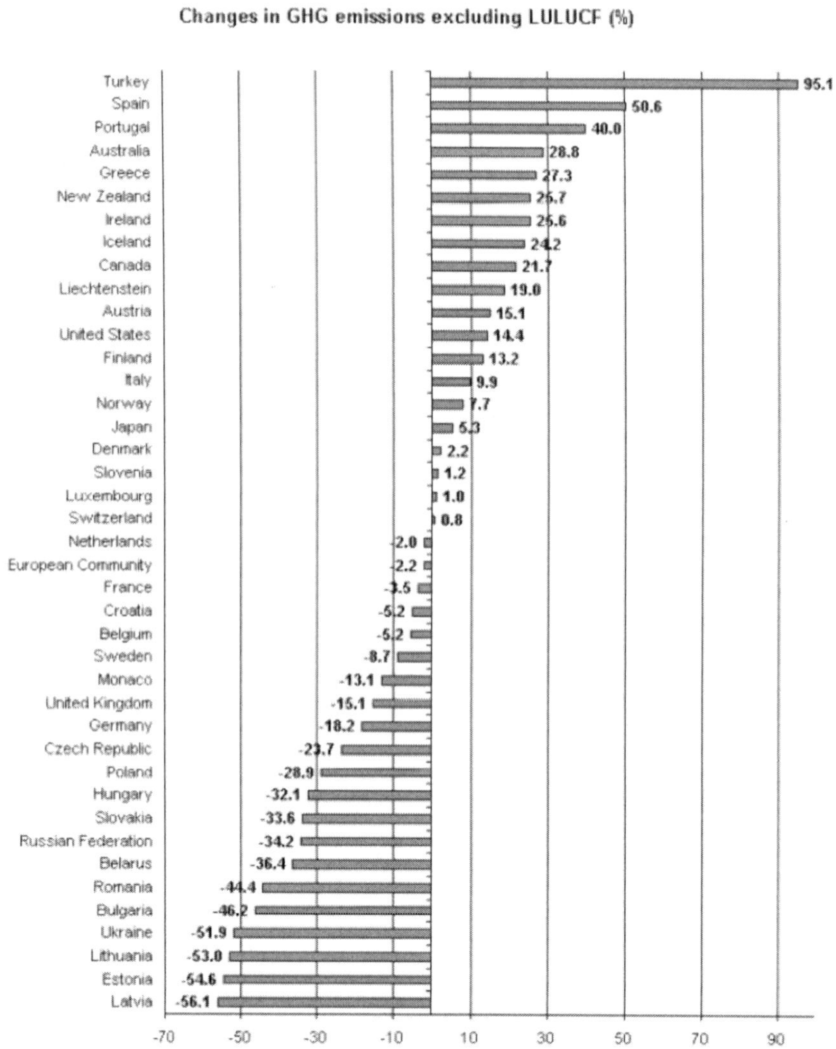


**Figure 2.** Changes of greenhouse gas emissions from 1990 to 2006.[43]

As illustrated by Figure 2, significant differences do indeed exist between the Annex B states, that is the states that have to employ the instruments of the Kyoto Protocol, and those states that have no such obligation, ie those

43 FCCC Secretariat document. <http://unfccc.int/files/inc/graphics/image/gif/total_excluding_2008.gif. LULUCF denotes land use, land use change and forestry.> accessed 20 October 2009.

Annex I states of the FCCC that are only subject to its more general obligations, namely the USA, Turkey and (until its ratification at the end of 2007) Australia.[44] The USA departs with 114.4% far from its initially signed but not ratified Kyoto rate of 93%. The deviation of Turkey is exorbitant with her 195.1% of the emissions of 1990. In the framework of the Kyoto Protocol, Australia agreed to an emission target of 108%, but significantly exceeds this margin with 128.8%.

As Figure 2 further shows, there are also significant differences between Annex B states. Within its 'bubble', the European Community is indeed allowed to balance out the different quotas of Member States, some receiving less and others more leeway. However, the enormous increases of some states such as Spain, Portugal, Greece, Ireland, Austria, Finland and Italy exceed by far the quotas they had accepted.[45]

Hence, we can record the fact that as compared with states not subject to the Kyoto obligations the Kyoto instruments have indeed slowed down the growth trend for the average of states they apply to. But in some of these states they had hardly any or no effect.

Figure 3 shows (for the EU-15) whether the slowdown where it is happening is sufficient or misses the Kyoto targets. On the one hand, a further increase assumed for a situation without climate protection measures (broken line) has been prevented. Emissions have more or less remained at the level of 1990. On the other hand, while a reduction is predicted from 2005 onwards (middle line), with the instruments of the first allocation period (2005–07) it will in no way realise the Kyoto target in 2010 (lower line with four target points). Therefore, the Commission acknowledged that stricter measures are required.[46]

If one now inquires into the specific effect of the flagship of climate protection law, the flexible mechanisms, it becomes apparent that they have exerted only very limited effect even on those states that have implemented the instruments most seriously, namely the EU Member States. I will discuss the EU-15 and Germany in turn. In order to exclude the effect of the industrial downturn of the 1990s especially in Eastern Germany, I suggest analysing the time period from 2003 to 2006/07[47] only. This is the time that the new

44 Kyoto Protocol, Status of Ratification of 12 October 2008. <http://unfccc.int/files/kyoto_protocol/status_of_ratification/application/pdf/kp_ratification.pdf.> accessed 20 October 2009.

45 In its 2007 report, the Commission predicted: 'By 2010, three Member States out of the EU-15, Germany, Sweden and the United Kingdom, are currently projected to be on track to achieve their targets using only existing domestic policies and measures. In addition, eight Member States are projected to reach their targets when the effect of the Kyoto mechanisms, carbon sinks and additional domestic policies and measures, that are already being discussed, are accounted for. According to this analysis, Denmark, Italy and Spain appear not to be able to achieve their Kyoto target.'

46 Cf Commission (EC), 'Progress towards achieving the Kyoto objectives' (Communication) COM (2007) 757, 27 November 2007, at 4.

47 For the EU-15, the only published data available is for the time until 2006, while data until 2007 are available for Germany.

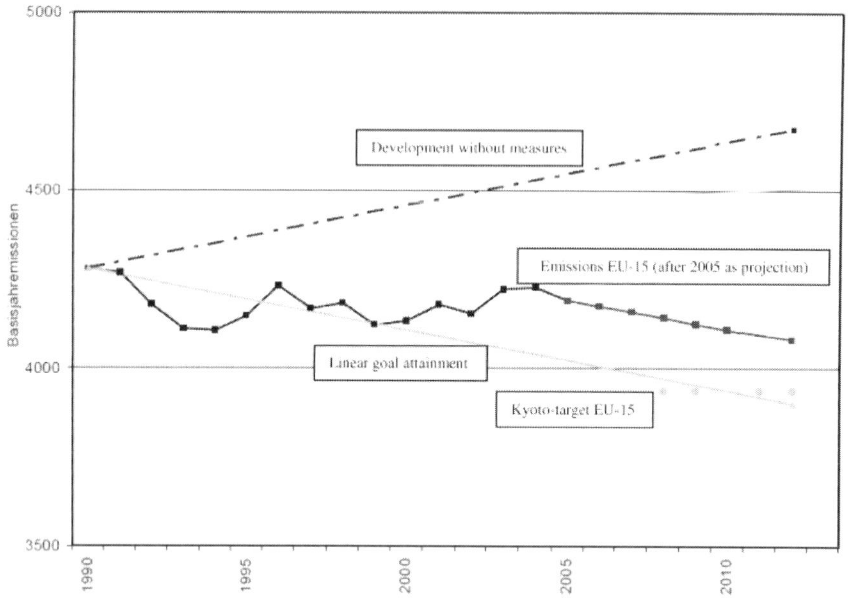


**Figure 3.** Actual and predicted emissions of the EU-15.[48]

instruments could have had an impact by anticipation (which has to be taken into account) or by subsequent effect. The economic sectors subject to the flexible mechanisms are energy and industry.

EU-15[49]: in the energy production sector, the overall emissions amounted in 2003 to 1,201 billion tonnes; in 2004 to 1,198 billion tonnes; in 2005 to 1,194 billion tonnes; and in 2006 to 1,194 billion tonnes; this means the effect of the flexible instruments resulted, from 2003 to 2006, in a comparably minimal reduction of 7 Mt or 0.6%. For the energy production in the manufacturing industry the following data apply: in 2003 544 Mt; in 2004 548 Mt; in 2005 543 Mt; and in 2006 537 Mt; this means a reduction of 7 Mt or 1.3% took place between 2003 and 2006. For the industrial processes sector the data are: in 2003 213 Mt; in 2004 219; in 2005 218; and in 2006 221; ie an increase of 8 Mt or 3.7 % between 2003 and 2006.

Germany: in the energy sector (comprising also energy producing industry) the $CO_2$-emissions amounted to 379 Mt (2005), 381 Mt (2006), 387 Mt (2007); this is an increase by 0.5 and 1.8%, respectively. For industrial processes the

48 Simplified version of a figure shown in Commission (EC), COM (2007) 757, 4.
49 All data taken from IPCC (International Panel on Climate Change), Greenhouse Gas Inventory Data. <http://unfccc.int/di/DetailedBy-Party/Event.do?event=go> accessed 20 October 2009.

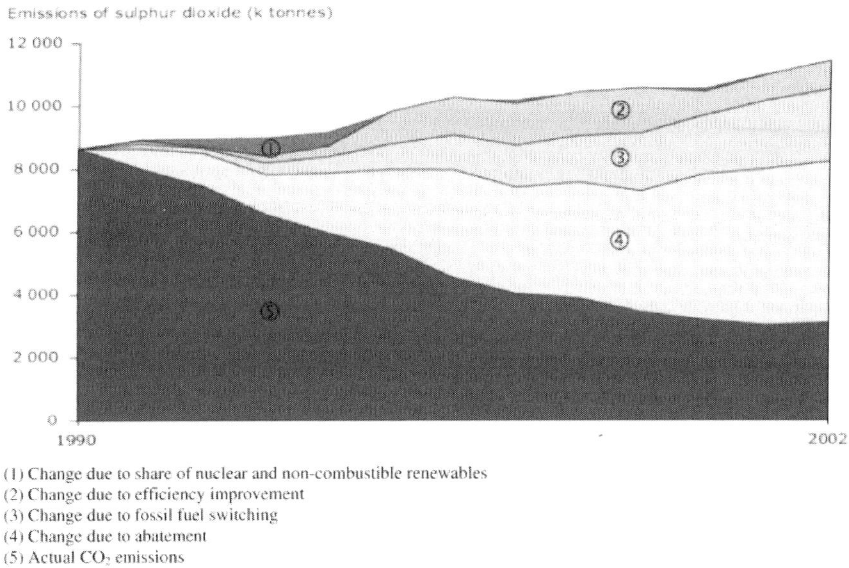


**Figure 4.** Reduction of $SO_2$ emissions of the EU-15 from 1990 to 2002.[50] (1) Change due to share of nuclear and non-combustible renewables; (2) change due to efficiency improvement; (3) change due to fossil fuel switching; (4) change due to abatement; and (5) actual $CO_2$ emissions.

figures are: 95 Mt (2005), 97 Mt (2006) and 100 Mt (2007); this is an increase by 1.9 and 2.9%, respectively.[51]

Overall, one can conclude that the flexible mechanisms have hardly induced any reduction of $CO_2$ emissions.

How disappointing this result is shows a comparison with a similar but much more successful regime, ie the regime for the reduction of sulphur dioxide and other gases, which acidify the soil and (among others) cause forest disease (*Waldsterben*). This regime has employed command and control instruments aiming at the phasing in of best available technologies. As shown in Figure 4, the regime has produced reductions of much higher proportion in a very short period of time. The emission of $SO_2$ was reduced by 70% in only 12 years. The figure also indicates the relative success of different technical measures of reorientation (renewable energies, efficiency

50 Adapted version of the figure shown in EEA Environment Outlook 2005, 95. <http://www.eea.europa.eu/publications/state_of_environment_report_2005_1/SOER2005_Part_A.pdf.> accessed 20 October 2009.

51 Arbeitsgruppe Emissionshandel zur Bekämpfung des Treibhauseffekts, 'Jahresbericht der Unterarbeitsgruppe 1, Querschnittsfragen' January 2009, 105. <http://www.bmu.de/files/pdfs/allgemein/application/pdf/jahresbericht_2008_uag1.pdf> accessed 5 July 2009.

improvement, switch to more environment-friendly fossil energy sources, technical emission avoidance).

In terms of legal instruments, both the international and national levels were quite productive. The key stages in the development of the regime were as follows. At the international level, the 1979 EC Convention on Long-Range Transboundary Air Pollution (LRTAP) established general obligations comparative to those of the FCCC. The 1985 Protocol of Helsinki fixed an overall reduction target of 30% of emissions in the baseline year of 1980 that was to be reached until 1993, ie within seven years (compare this with the 5% reduction goal of the Kyoto Protocol.) The target was further tightened by the 1994 Protocol of Oslo: while the quota were differentiated according to the technological and economic capacity of states, the average reduction target was set as high as 62% of 1980, to be reached until 2010. The hitherto last step was taken by the 1997 Protocol of Gothenburg that aims at a reduction of 75% until 2010, taking 1990 as a baseline, a year when much of the Helsinki target was already achieved. The targets were stepwise transformed into EC law by Directives which applied three regulatory strategies: one of technology forcing, phasing in BAT (EC Directives 84/830, 96/61, 2000/76 and 2001/80); the second setting environmental quality objectives (Directive 96/62 and daughter directives); and the third establishing overall national emission quantities for each Member State.

The comparative success of this regulatory regime appears as impressive, even if it is taken into account that the reduction of $CO_2$ emissions is technically more difficult and more dependent on consumer behaviour than in the case of $SO_2$.

## 3. Explanations

### *3.1. General Points*

In the following, I focus on explaining the failure of 'cap and trade'. To explain why hitherto the classical instruments (such as command and control, subsidies and taxes) have also failed in the climate protection area would require an analysis of its own. This would make it necessary to inquire, in particular, into the ineffectiveness of emissions policy concerning transportation, households and agriculture.

My argument is that, through the 'cap and trade' concept, a genuinely ecological problem has been translated all too radically into economic categories. All those involved are caught up in the logic of prices, sale, purchase, registration, transfer and return of emission allowances and have thereby lost sight of the ecological purpose of the overall enterprise.

It is true and must first be acknowledged that 'cap and trade' appears, judging from its core idea, highly elegant and efficient:[52] the community of states turns the climate from an environmental good, whose damage is reduced, into a resource, which is made scarce and allocated in portions.[53] States agree to a target, which is set reflecting ecological necessity. This target is meant to be reliably achieved but with the lowest possible cost—in other words in a cost-effective way. For that purpose, a parallel market for emission allowances is established, which helps to search for the cheapest avoider of social costs.[54]

In reality, however, the cap (the quota available to individual states) was the result of a political negotiation process in which what is ecologically necessary is relativised by different perceptions of climate development, by different calculations of costs, and potentially also of advantages of climate change, and by different opinions about the resilience of economies.[55]

This is normal political practice, which can only be acknowledged but hardly improved. It however becomes critical insofar as the quota is claimed to provide the rationale underlying the decision to allow for 'trade'. For 'trade' does ecologically only make sense, if the ecological rationality of 'cap' is assumed. Otherwise, 'trade' fails to have full ecological effect.[56] In the following, I argue that exactly this mismatch has occurred: by introducing economic logic, emissions trading assumes that the 'cap' is ecologically rational, which is however mistaken (Section 3.2). Moreover, the concept adds incentives that alienate the system from its ecological aim to an extent that compromises goal achievement (Section 3.3). In addition, it runs the risk of causing adverse side-effects (Section 3.4). Finally, it produces enormous transaction costs (Section 3.5).

### *3.2. Erroneous Premise*

Paradoxically, the system of emissions trading assumes the rationality of its aim, because it does not attempt to transcend the aim. If it recognised the

52 For its career, see J-P Voß, 'Innovation Processes in Governance: the Development of "Emissions Trading" as a New Policy Instrument'(2007) 34 Sci Pub Pol 329–43.

53 For such an allocation of scarce resources in environmental politics and its implications for distributive issues, see the seminal P Knoepfel, *Environmental Policy Analysis: Learning from the Past for the Future* (Springer, Berlin/Heidelberg 2007) 465 ff.

54 G Calabresi, *The Costs of Accidents: A Legal and Economic Analysis* (Yale UP, New Haven 1970); G Calabresi and P Bobbitt, *Tragic Choices: The Conflict Society Confronts in the Allocation of Tragically Scarce Resources* (WW Norton, New York 1978).

55 For the main arguments and strategies in the preparation of the Kyoto Protocol, see S Oberthür and H-E Ott, *The Kyoto Protocol: International Climate Policy for the 21st Century* (Springer, Berlin 1999).

56 For the relation of decisions at the first stage (determination of quotas) and second stage (choice of instruments) under scarce environmental resources, see in detail Knoepfel (n 53) 429ff, 455ff as well as under scarce general resources, see Calabresi and Bobbitt (n 54). The dependence of the second stage upon the rationale of the first stage is hardly touched upon in the literature.

insufficiency of the aim, it would introduce mechanisms that would encourage subsequent adjustments in the further course of events. This drawback distinguishes 'cap and trade' from quantified limit standards based on the rationale of regulatory law. Such standards provide a 'maximum' threshold. They are not meant to be exhausted but to be undercut for precautionary reasons, because it is understood that they are normally based on incomplete knowledge and might therefore erroneously be too liberal.[57] Instead, emissions trading redefines maximum ceilings as exploitable rights. The stock of emission allowances turns into an economic value, which is not meant to lie fallow: it is legitimately used to the very last piece, at the level of states and individual actors alike. An entrepreneur who does not use his allowances or does not sell them to others if he has no use for them would appear as economically irrational. A state which accumulates a reserve and preserves it for later extinction would appear as politically incompetent. According to German law, for instance, the reserve is meant to cover, besides administrative and litigation costs, the supplying of new facilities and the financing of additional purchases of emission allowances by the state.[58] Savings in order to take emission allowances out of use and thus reduce emissions are not intended.

### *3.3 Counter-productive Effects*

Some aspects even have an impact that prevents the utterly unambitious Kyoto aim (the reduction to 92% of 1990 levels in the average of the years 2008–12 in the EU) from being reached. The main reason is the current design of CDM projects. They make it possible to import emission allowances into the emissions trading system of the investor state and to increase its overall assigned amount of emissions without this being counted as an increase. While in the EU CER from CDM projects were not recognised in the first allocation period, they can be transferred to and generated during the second and will therefore have a definitive effect on the achievement of the climate goals for the first commitment period (2008/2012). The justification for CDM projects, it is true, is inherently reasonable: a tonne of greenhouse gas emissions can be avoided more cost-effectively in a developing country with antiquated technology

57 This was aptly expressed in a landmark judgment of the German Federal Administrative Court of 17 February 1984, BVerwGE 69, 37, at 43: 'The emission standards in force entail residual risks, which are, on the one hand, caused by the used measuring methods and, on the other hand, by the still incomplete knowledge of the harmfulness of certain emissions, their long-term effects as well as potential synergetic effects. Precaution [. . .] is then necessary when sufficient reason exists to assume that emissions *potentially* harm the environment and thence the suspicion of danger is given—even if the respective causal links have not yet been established in detail.' (Emphasis in the original.)

58 s 6(2) and (3) ZuG 2012. These earmarkings were not yet included in the ZuG 2007, but corresponded to practice.

than in a technologically advanced industrial country. It is therefore reasonable to provide incentives for private investment into climate protection in developing countries by allowing the CER, acquired through CDM, to be transferred into investor countries.

However, the amount of allowable CDM projects can be at odds with the principle of joint but differentiated responsibility, which requires that the industrialized states have a duty to enact climate policies at home.[59] The quantity of emissions that will enter the European system via the CDM is indeed remarkably large. CDM (plus JI) credits were estimated to amount to one-third of the overall reduction target of the EU.[60] With the 2009 amendment of Directive 2003/87, the allowable ceiling for CDM (plus JI) credits was set at as high as 50% of the reduction quota.[61] This quantity is even envisaged to further increase in the Kyoto II phase if the overall reduction quota is set at 30%.[62] At the end, it is imaginable that hardly any genuine reduction effort must be undertaken in the EU because almost all of the needed amounts of emission credits can be earned abroad.

CDM of the envisaged dimension is a failure not only in ecological but also in legal terms. Article 3(1) of the Kyoto Protocol commits Annex I states to reduce 'their' emissions. 'Their' is here commonly interpreted as signifying the territorial origin of emissions. With the shift to an economic logic, 'their' is now about to be turned into an economic balance term, which denotes the result of attributions.[63] It appears that this distorts the wording and original goal of the provision which is to induce industrialized states to bear most of the burden.

A particular effect is caused by the fact that CDM measures can, by increasing the permissible emission quantity of a country,[64] also affect those sectors that are meant to be subject to classical instruments of climate protection. A country can decide to transfer acquired CERs, and thus emission allowances, to the transport sector and to refrain from, for instance, restricting the

59 This principle was introduced by the FCCC, Art 3(1).

60 Ten Member States among the EU-15 will use Kyoto mechanisms, in order to achieve their Kyoto quota. They will annually acquire emission allowances for 107.5 Mt of $CO_2$. This will amount to not less than 31% of the entire reduction target of the EU-15, which equals 342 Mt. See Commission (EC), COM (2007) 757, 15 (n 46).

61 Art 11a (8) subpara 5 Directive 2003/87, as amended by Directive 2009/29/EC of the European Parliament and of the Council amending Directive 2003/87/EC so as to improve and extend the greenhouse gas emission allowance trading scheme of the Community [2009] OJ L140/63–87.

62 Commission (EC), 'Proposal for a Directive of the European Parliament and of the Council amending Directive 2003/87/EC so as to improve and extend the Greenhouse Gas Emission Allowance Trading System of the Community' COM (2008) 16, 23 January 2008, at 11.

63 H-J Luhmann and J Sterk, 'Klimaziele zu Hause Erreichen oder wo es am Billigsten Ist? Der Clean Development Mechanism als Klimaregime-interner Investitionsmittelgenerator' (2008) 2 Intl Pol Gesellschaft 111.

64 In a technical–legal sense, one should state more precisely that the quota assigned to a state remains unchanged; the acquired amounts are however not deducted from it.

emissions of motor vehicles or reducing individual transportation. This implies that the broad discretion on how to make use of acquired emission rights reduces the negotiation power of state agencies *vis-à-vis* powerful internal interests. In this way, the economic logic of the flexible instruments also infects regulatory law traditionally employed in other sectors than industry and energy.

Counter-productive effects appear also in the way how projects are conducted. The transfer of CER to the investor state can only be justified as 'additional' if the project is more climate-friendly than a reference project, which exists or would have been established without the transfer of the CER. In practice, reference projects with a bad climate balance are often chosen so that the superiority of the CDM project is not hard to prove.[65] In addition, it is not required that the sale of CER alone makes a project profitable; rather it is sufficient that the profit is increased.[66] Furthermore, the price for CER can be calculated arbitrarily as there exist no market prices for them. In practice, it is therefore often determined far below the market price for a tonne of $CO_2$.[67] Compared to emissions trading and JI, this reduces the costs for the purchase of CER in the club of Annex B countries, with the consequence that further incentives for investments in climate protection within the club are avoided.

### 3.4 *Adverse Side-effects*

Unintentional adverse side-effects can emerge at different points in the system. Such an effect can result from CDM measures in general[68] and in particular from land use, land use change and forestry (or LULUC) measures which count as CO2 sinks.[69] Applying the logic of exchanging forest creation for

65 A WWF study estimated that that by the end of 2007 additionality was unlikely or questionable for about 40% of the registered CDM projects and about 20% of all issued CERs. See L Schneider, 'Is the CDM Fulfilling its Environmental and Sustainable Development Objectives? An Evaluation of the CDM and Options for Improvement' <www.oekoinstitut.de/oekodoc/622/2007-162-en.pdf> accessed 20 October 2009.

66 Cf, for instance, the project description of the CGN Gansu Anxi Daliang 49.5 MW Wind Power Project in China, which compares the wind farm with coal-fired power stations and calculates an annual profit of 5.95%, which increases to 9.06% through CER sales. <http://cdm.unfccc.int/UserManagement/FileStorage/YN154LDIE7MOUTZHGOQAVBX68KWRP3> accessed 20 October 2009.

67 In the mentioned example, the price for a tonne of $CO_2$-eq is assumed to be eight euros.

68 Voigt, C., 'Responsibility for Environmental Integrity of the CDM: Judicial Review of EB Decisions', in: D. Freestone and Ch. Streck (eds.) *Legal Aspects of Carbon Trading: Kyoto, Copenhagen and Beyond*, OUP, Oxford (forthcoming), 272–279.

69 They are envisaged by Art 3(3) Kyoto Protocol. In the EU, it has hitherto not been possible to factor in such measures (Art 11a (3)(b) Directive 2003/87 before amendment of 2009). A Commission staff working document has advised continuation of the policy of excluding LULUCF activities from the trading system (Commission (EC), 'Accompanying document to the Proposal for a Directive of the European Parliament and of the Council amending Directive 2003/87/EC so as to improve and extend the EU greenhouse gas emission allowance trading system' SEC (2008) 52, 23 January 2008, at 59). Astonishingly, the exclusion of LULUCF measures was deleted in the 2009 version of Art 11a Directive 2003/87. This must be interpreted to mean that the issue falls back into the competence of the Member States.

money, it could then be profitable to replace existing biodiversity-rich forests or forests of local populations with fast-growing plantations.[70]

CDM projects can also de-motivate developing countries to pursue a genuine climate protection policy. Developing countries can simply remain passive until CDM projects begin to emerge. Such inaction is unfortunately accepted by the Kyoto regime, because while in the emissions trading and JI schemes the state selling emission rights or hosting the project is also subject to the supplementarity criterion, this is not required as a precondition for host states of CDM projects.[71]

A further side-effect of the CDM practice is that it directs the otherwise modest resources of development aid away from other social and ecological projects into climate protection. This could be avoided by only approving those CDM projects that are not supported by development aid. However, this thinking has not succeeded in practice. According to economical logic, it is regarded as desirable that investment takes place at all, irrespective of other policies being eroded.

### *3.5. Transaction Costs*

The expectation of economists proposing flexible mechanisms has been that the flexible mechanisms, due to their market similarity, cause lower transaction costs than traditional regulatory measures. This has proven to be wrong. The costs are not lower because the technical monitoring of emissions must be done at least as precisely as in such a regulatory system. They are even higher because the flexible instruments cause additional transaction costs to those in the regulatory system.

On the business level, the emission of greenhouse gases has, as before, to be operated and measured technically; in addition, emission allowances have to be managed, acquired and sold. At the administrative level, installations have to be monitored, similar to traditional regulatory law but with different objectives: while such regulatory law is concerned with preventing the violation of standards, the emissions trading regime is concerned with safeguarding transactions (since emissions are in any degree permissible as long as they are paid for). In addition to the technical monitoring, which accounts for the correct measurement of emissions, the economic transactions must be registered and supervised; these are costs that do not arise in standard regulatory law.

70 Commission (EC) SEC (2008) 52, 58 (n 68); Wissenschaftlicher Beirat Globale Umweltveränderungen, 'Über Kioto Hinaus Denken—Klimaschutzstrategien für das 21. Jahrhundert', Sondergutachten 2003, No 5.4.

71 For the obligation of the Annex I states see Marrakesh Accords Decision 15/CP7 No 1. For the CDM host states see Art 6 Kyoto Protocol.

Besides corporate bureaucracies and public administration, a level of supranational and international bureaucracy intervenes, which has to be paid for as well. Furthermore, new occupations are triggered by the system and have in fact emerged, such as the certified expert and the stockbroker. One also has to keep in mind the costs of numerous lawsuits provoked by the artificial market for emission allowances.

### 3.6. *Summary*

Overall, the failure of flexible mechanisms can be attributed to the overly radical economisation of an ecological problem. To take account of the economic consequences of ecological regulation has always been customary and helpful. But the parallel market for emission allowances, established as a means to cope with the externalities of the primary market (of the production and consumption of goods), has made absolute its own code and has tended to forget its genuine task, climate protection. 'Greenhouse gas emissions—a new commodity' announces the website of the FCCC confidently and adds: 'carbon is now tracked and traded like any other commodity'.[72] This way of thinking has been imported into the concept of Kyoto from the heartland of commodification, the USA; paradoxically, this country did not ratify the Protocol, as it perceived even the small requirements made as too expensive.[73] A hegemon can afford such behaviour. Others were more obedient, but perhaps followed bad advice.

## 4. Reform

If my diagnosis is accurate, namely that the economic rationale of the emissions trading system tends to forget its ecological objective and that thereby enormous costs for hardly any substantial improvements are caused, the question arises: what can be done? Should the flexible mechanisms be altogether abandoned?

This is indeed an option that should be considered more thoroughly than in the past. Pundits still focus on the attempt to understand the system inherently and to develop it further, yet they have run into losing sight of the overall picture. Doubts have to be raised as to whether the concept of 'cap and trade' is fundamentally flawed because it has an inherent dynamic towards over-differentiation thus distracting actors from goal attainment to

72 UNFCCC. <http://unfccc.int/kyoto.protocol/mechanisms/emissions.trading/ items/2731.php> accessed 20 October 2009.

73 For a defence of this position, see R Stewart and J Wiener, *Reconstructing Climate Policy: Beyond Kyoto* (The AEI Press, Washington DC 2003).

means perfection. Substantial and quick progress in climate protection is perhaps better achieved by more directly fostering new technologies and inducing behavioural change.[74] This can arguably be more effectively instrumented by a pragmatic mix of traditional regulatory law, subsidies, charges and voluntary agreements than by the fine world of flexible instruments. The European Commission has noticed this and is, as a result, propagating and enacting a broad array of measures promoting energy efficiency and renewable energy.[75] Hitherto, it has however not dared even to ponder the fundamental questioning of the flexible mechanisms.

On the other hand, a paradigm change from 'cap and trade' to a more complex tool set of technology forcing would perhaps come too early. After all, the flexible mechanisms were so new and unprobed that some time for experiments and learning was necessary. The Commission acknowledged that the system failed to reach its goals, and drawn consequences by proposing improvements of the system.[76] It is however doubtful if the reformatory measures go far enough.

All thought of reform should naturally start with demanding more ambitious targets, and this is indeed the subject of current negotiations of 'Kyoto II'. The Commission proposal goes for a reduction rate of 20% until 2020 (or 30% in case of agreement on a 20% average in the Kyoto II-round). Although a bold step forward, this is by far not enough in ecological terms given the 40–50% needed in order to set the system on a path towards the widely agreed final goal of 60–80% by 2050.[77] As stated before, it would however be illusionary to expect that those reduction targets accepted by states indeed reflect what is ecologically necessary.

The EU envisages a yearly reduction of allocated emission rights by 1.74% from 2010 onwards.[78] This is however only meant to ensure that the overall quota is reached, but not that the quota shall be overfulfilled.

The fact that targets have not been and will not be dictated by ecological reason but by political compromise should be mirrored in the design of the instruments employed to reach them. It is all too tempting to conceive them as 'assigned' amount, as formulated by the Kyoto Protocol, or emission allowance as denominated by the EU system: an environmental resource is then redefined as a disposable mass, which is, it is true, limited but, more importantly, also allowed to be used. That this is treacherous becomes clear if emission allowances are compared with emission restrictions defined by

74 See Pittock (n 1) 167–206.
75 For a recent overview of actual and planned measures, see Commission (EC) 'Second Strategic Energy Review. An EE Energy Security and Solidarity Action Plan' COM (2008) 781.
76 See Commission (EC), COM (2008) 18 (n 62).
77 Cf Pittock (n 1) 325.
78 Directive 2003/87 as amended 2009, Art 9(1).

classical environmental quality standards. The latter represent upper limits, which as well are the results of compromise. But in reaction to this very fact the understanding is that they should not be used to their full extent, if possible. This is a main concern of the precept of precaution, as stated, for instance, in the already cited judgment of the German Federal Administrative Court:

> the precept of precaution in § 5(2) Federal Emission Control Act [BImSchG] provides a kind of counterweight to the compromise represented by the safety thresholds in § 5(1) BImSchG and the associated limitations of risk; ... [measures of precaution] shall enforce a level of environmental quality, independent of harm limitations in effect, which seems realisable with regard to the existing potential of technology[79]

On closer inspection, the Kyoto Protocol can be harmonized with this approach. As its Article 3 links the assigned amount functionally with its aim of 'reducing their overall emissions of such gases by at least 5% below 1990 levels', the reduction target is here qualified as a minimum, not a maximum target. In the same direction points the precautionary approach which was adopted by the FCCC. It says in Article 3(3) that 'parties should take precautionary measures to anticipate, prevent or minimize the causes of climate change and mitigate its adverse effects'.

It is therefore essential that measures for an additional reduction of emissions are introduced into the concept of 'cap and trade'. They would add an element of the traditional regulatory style to the flexible mechanisms.

The first overall goal would be that states keep back and collect larger amounts of emission allowances until they lose their value at the end of the respective commitment periods. This can be achieved by four means:

(i) Annex B states should generally not be allowed to sell or buy emission allowances. They are political entities and as such in charge of good climate policy, they are not profit making actors on markets. Emissions trading should be the business of polluters, not of regulators.

(ii) The allocation of emission allowances should generally be shifted from grandfathering to BAT-benchmarking using an ambitious definition of the BAT. Instead, in the first allocation period (2005–07) existing installations received emission allowances following largely the grandfathering principle, minus 3% (the so-called compliance factor) which however only exerted a mild push towards emission reduction. BAT-benchmarking was only required for new and recently modernized installations, and BAT was rather unambitiously defined as the

79 BVerwG, 17 February 1984, BVerwGE 69, 37, 44.

"weighted average of emissions caused by energy production in modern power plants fueled with fossil fuels"[80], thus requiring average rather than best technologies and lacking pressure towards the use of renewables.[81] Commendably, for the second allocation period (2008–12) BAT-benchmarking is extended to all existing energy production facilities and defined in relation to products, not processes.[82]

(iii) The collection of non-used emission allowances should be readjusted from economic to ecological reason. Those who receive from the outset and for free more emission allowances than they need should not be allowed to keep them and use their market value as a cost factor in their tariff and price calculation. Likewise, a company which reduces its production cannot maintain the respective emission allowances. In pure economic terms the opposite would be logical, but in ecological terms it is absurd: the operator would receive a gift from the public and calculate its non-use as a cost factor. Compare this with cost calculation in a system of classical emission thresholds: no operator would calculate the undercutting of the ceiling (in other words, the foregone possibility to pollute more) as a cost factor. Of course, such allocation of unneeded emission allowances must be distinguished from the legitimate case where a company invests in improved efficiency, saves emission allowances and should thus be entitled to keep these for sale or as stock.[83]

(iv) Making operators pay for emission allowances is a potentially forceful tool towards undercutting the overall assigned emission amounts of a state, because operators may desist from buying when the price is high. At present, auctioning has been chosen as the best means of determining prices. As sketched out before, 10% will be auctioned already in the second allocation period (2008–12), and up to 100% later on.[84] However, auctioning does not prevent buying if the quantity on tender is large enough to satisfy all demand. Therefore, sales at fixed prices should be considered as an alternative. By determining

80 Reason for the bill of the Zuteilungsgesetz 2007 of 27 April 2004, BT-Drucks. 15/2966, 22.

81 See Sachverständigenrat für Umweltfragen, *Stellungnahme. Die nationale Umsetzung des europäischen Emissionshandels: Marktwirtschaftlicher Klimaschutz oder Fortsetzung der energiepolitischen Subventionspolitik mit anderen Mitteln?* (Berlin 2006) No 3.2.4.

82 Art 9 and Annex III ZuG2012. Unfortunately, the standard still significantly relies on fossil fuels. More push towards renewables and alternative production methods may be expected from harmonised benchmarking as announced in Art 10a (1) subpara 3 Directive 2003/87 as amended 2009.

83 Following economic reason, the Commission even requested the Member States to allow companies to keep emission allowances in case of a production cut. Fortunately, the European Court of First Instance called the Commission to its ecological task and quashed the decision. Still, the unused emission allowances when returned become part of the national reserve and are available for allocation to new installations. See Case T-374/04 *Germany v Commission* [2007] (CFI 7 November 2007) ECR II-4431.

84 Art 10 Directive 2003/87 as amended 2009.

> prices the states would have an additional tool of reducing sales in order to press for additional emission reductions.[85]

The second major goal would be concerned with the importation of emission credits from developing countries into industrial countries. The allowable quantity should be capped (at say 6–8% of the reduction quota, as was proposed in the earlier times of concept design[86]). States should be obliged to create a special and transparent fund for emission rights from CDM projects, thus laying how they perform in terms of joint but differentiated responsibility open. Furthermore, CDM projects should only be approved if they are in fact both 'additional' and 'supplementary'.

With these and other measures, the result could perhaps be achieved that the flexible instrument system is not an end in itself, but that it better serves the aim of climate protection. After all, the climate is not a commodity. It is a precondition of human life in the biosphere. Flexible instruments are helpful if used as a tool of ever more preservation of this precious good. They are destructive if catching minds and effort into a beautiful but ineffective and costly 'l'art pour l'art'.

85 In terms of a regulatory approach, if ambitious benchmarking is introduced, one can even envisage that part of the emission allowances needed could be allocated for free and only the remaining part sold.

86 J Levebre, 'Linking Emissions Trading Schemes: The EU ETS and the "Linking Directive"', in D Freestone and C Streck (eds), *Legal Aspects of Implementing the Kyoto Protocol Mechanisms: Making Kyoto Work* (OUP, Oxford 2005) 510–33, at 530.

# [21]

*Journal of Environmental Law* **21**:3 
doi:10.1093/jel/eqp019 Advance Access published on 2 July 2009

# Aspirations and Realities under the Water Framework Directive: Proceduralisation, Participation and Practicalities

William Howarth*

## Abstract

The European Community Water Framework Directive (2000/60/EC) adopts an innovative, holistic and target-orientated approach to the management of relevant waters, with the ambitious aim of achieving 'good status' for all relevant waters by 2015. At a 'half-way' stage towards full implementation, this article takes stock of practical implementation in England and Wales, and reflects more generally upon the challenges of implementation. On proceduralisation, the discussion suggests that substantive elements are seen to be greatly overshadowed by the breadth of national implementation discretion. Avoiding realisation of good status is allowed and broadly worded derogation provisions are interpreted to enable this. Incongruities between the ideals underlying public engagement and the realities of applying complex environmental legislation are evident. Issues for resolution shift from broad concerns about the desired state of the water environment to highly technical questions about operationalising methodologies (that are likely to exclude public engagement).

Keywords: Water Framework Directive, proceduralisation, participation, England and Wales

*University of Kent. (w.howarth@kent.ac.uk). An earlier version of this paper was presented at a workshop on Ocean and River Basin Governance, funded by the AHRC and held at the University of Dundee on 2 May 2008. The author is grateful to the organisers of, and participants in, the Workshop for many helpful observations. Further gratitude is due to Martin Hedemann-Robinson and Donald McGillivray of Kent Law School for commenting on a draft and to the Editor of this journal for helpful suggestions.

> ... EU environmental legislation has become more general in the last two decades, leaving more and more monitoring and implementation discretion to EU Member States. This has led to a situation that where a country or an administration ... does not have the determination to provide for an appropriate protection of the environment, environmental law is not sufficiently precise and stringent to ensure this protection.[1]

> 'In some instances, it may prove disproportionately costly or technically impractical to achieve in the short term the ambitious targets that are demanded. That is why some flexibility is built into the Water Framework Directive, but it is crucial that this flexibility is not abused.'[2]

## 1. The Water Framework Directive

The European Community Water Framework Directive[3] must be placed somewhere near the 'high water mark' of Community environmental legislation both in terms of its general ambitiousness and in respect of its innovative qualities. As has been stated, 'it is the most significant piece of European environmental legislation ever introduced'.[4] It adopts a holistic approach to the management of waters which takes account of the wider ecosystem and applies a hydrological management approach based upon river basin districts. The water management planning process is target-orientated insofar as it involves a sequence of actions directed towards the achievement of environmental objectives for all surface waters (including estuaries and coastal waters) and groundwaters within river basin district management plans. The environmental objectives set out in the Directive are to be achieved within specified deadlines by means of programmes of measures for their realisation. Centrally important, is the objective of good chemical and ecological status for all relevant waters by 2015, though account also needs to be taken of social and economic factors, and the general aim of securing sustainable development.

The achievement of the environmental objectives of the WFD is through a series of stages that are set out in the Directive. In outline, these involve the transposition of obligations into national law, identifying competent authorities, undertaking initial 'characterisations' of waters and compiling registers of protected areas, undertaking monitoring programmes, identifying

1 L Kramer, 'The Environment and the Ten Commandments' (2008) 20 JEL 6.

2 Foreword, House of Lords European Union Committee, 27th Report of Session 2006–07, *Wa. Framework Directive: Making it Work*, HL Paper 136 (2007).

3 Council Directive (EC) 2000/60 establishing a framework for Community action in the field of water policy, hereafter 'WFD'.

4 T Le Quesne and C Green, *Can We Afford Not To? The Costs and Benefits of a Partnership Approach to the Water Framework Directive* (WWF 2005) 4.

significant issues, producing draft and final river basin management plans and programmes of measures to realise the environmental objectives. All of these challenging water management planning tasks need to be undertaken in accordance with requirements to 'encourage' involvement of 'all interested parties' in the implementation processes. The Directive may be seen as a testing ground for a multi-level approach towards environmental governance which seeks to extend decision making as far downwards to individual citizens as is feasible.

The WFD is also set in a unique context of multi-level guidance that will have profound implications for the way it is implemented and the environmental benefits that will result. As it has been put, 'there is a need to shift away from a central policy-making process dominated by state action to a more complex, multi-level system of governance and a steady extension of environmental imperatives into previously 'non-environmental' sectors'.[5] Many aspects of the Directive are of considerable technicality and it is important that common understandings of these are reached between Member States. For that purpose, a Common Implementation Strategy has been established at European Community level, involving working groups of experts and stakeholders from Member States producing a series of documents on key aspects of implementation of the Directive.[6] These documents are expressly stated to be 'non-legally binding', but are important in establishing a coherent application of key elements of the Directive across the Member States. Within Member States further guidance has been provided on particular aspects of the Directive. In the case of the UK, work has been undertaken on establishing common standards and conditions across the different jurisdictions, by the UK Technical Advisory Group (UKTAG) on the Water Framework Directive. The UKTAG comprises representatives of agencies with responsibility for implementation of the WFD in different parts of the UK, bodies with responsibility for nature conservation and invited standing representatives on particular issues.[7] Although advisory in character, this guidance is important in securing a consistent approach to UK-wide implementation and in some respects is likely to provide the basis for statutory guidance on the national implementation of the Directive (discussed below).

The ambitious nature of the WFD, adopted in 2000, is recognised in the timescale that has been set for the implementation, with an initial deadline of 2015 for meeting the key environmental objectives under the Directive.

5 D Woods, 'Stakeholder Involvement and Public Participation: A Critique of Water Framework Directive Arrangements in the United Kingdom' (2008) Water Env J 258–9.

6 Commission (EC), 'Common Strategy on the Implementation of the Water Framework Directive 2001' <http://circa.europa.eu/Public/irc/env/wfd/library?l=/framework.directive/guidance.documents&vm=detailed&sb=TitleforfurtherCISguidancedocuments> accessed 10 June 2009.

7 UK Technical Advisory Group (UKTAG) for Water Framework Directive Implementation: Terms of Reference (2004) <http://www.wfduk.org> accessed 10 June 2009.

At the present, therefore, implementation is somewhere around the half-way stage along the timescale that has been set. Transposing legislation has been put in place, river basin districts and competent authorities identified, characterisation reports compiled, monitoring programmes implemented and consultation on significant issues and draft river basin management plans is underway.[8] The critical stages of finalising River Basin Management Plans and putting in place programmes of measures remain to be completed. At this 'half-way' stage it may be helpful to take stock of what has been done by way of practical implementation and to reflect upon what this shows about the challenges of implementing the Directive and its general approach. Are the original concerns about the enforceability of the Directive well founded? (those concerns being, that it is over ambitious in its objectives, insufficiently stringent in its legal formulation and too generous in the discretion that it gives to Member States in respect of implementation.)[9]

## 2. Themes for Discussion

The half-way stock taking exercise that is envisaged is capable of ranging far and wide into the multifarious topics raised by implementation of the WFD and, inevitably, some selectivity is needed.[10] Here developments in England and Wales are to be reviewed against two broader themes: proceduralisation and participation.

There is a general view that more recent EC environmental law is characterised by its greater dependence upon procedural, rather than substantive, regulatory approaches. Procedural approaches involve the use of mechanisms that require Member States to follow specified procedures, whilst not necessarily guaranteeing particular environmental quality outcomes. By contrast, earlier Community environmental legislation may be seen as emphatically substantive in requiring precisely specified standards for polluting emissions

8 Commission (EC), Towards Sustainable Water Management in the European Union: First Stage in the Implementation of the Water Framework Directive 2000/60/EC, COM (2007) 363; House of Lords European Union Committee, 27th Report of Session 2006–07, *Water Framework Directive: Making it Work*, HL Paper 136 (2007).

9 See, eg the issues raised by D Grimeaud, 'Reforming EU Water Law: Towards Sustainability' (2001) EELR 41–51, 88–97, 125–135.

10 For general academic literature on legal aspects of the Water Framework Directive see D Matthews, 'The Framework Directive on Community Water Policy: A New Approach for EC Environmental Law' (1997) YEL 191; W Howarth, 'Accommodation without Resolution? Emission Controls and Environmental Quality Objectives in the Proposed EC Water Framework Directive' (1999) Env L Rev 6; Grimeaud (n 9); A Farmer, 'The EC Water Framework Directive' (2001) Water L 40; G Kallis and D Butler, 'The EU Water Framework Directive: Measures and Implications' (2001) Water Pol 125; W Howarth and D McGillivray, *Water Pollution and Water Quality Law* (Shaw and Sons Ltd, Kent 2001) ch 5; and H Unnerstall, 'The Principle of Full Cost Recovery in the EU Water Framework Directive – Genesis and Content' (2007) 19 JEL 29.

and environmental quality to be met. Failure to secure environmental quality requirements of this kind would amount to a breach of Community law, and enforcement has been strict in not allowing defences in respect of circumstances within the control of a member state.[11] Procedural legislation is characterised by the absence of requirements of this kind. Provided that specified regulatory procedures are complied with, Community obligations are met, regardless of what level of environmental improvement or deterioration ensues as a result. The procedural approach is admirably consonant with the requirements of the EC Treaty for subsidiarity and for measures that do not go beyond what is required to achieve a desired objective,[12] but raises concerns as to whether it allows Member States too much flexibility in their approach to environmental protection, with the consequence that Community-wide minimum standards for environmental quality are not realised.

In respect of the WFD, the balance between substantive and procedural requirements needs to be considered in the context of the approach to national implementation that has been evident so far. Certainly, the Directive illustrates many instances of the application of procedural mechanisms in water management planning, but also it envisages that water planning should be conducted 'purposively'. That is, water management plans of the kind provided for under the Directive are to be established for the purpose of 'actually meeting' the environmental objectives of the Directive by the stated deadlines. To what extent is compliance secured simply by following stipulated procedures irrespective of environmental outcomes?

A second theme, which to some extent is interwoven with proceduralisation, is participation and the role of the public in the implementation of the WFD. Public participation is far from being the only example of proceduralism in the WFD, since the various planning, monitoring and reporting exercises that fall under the Directive are also strongly procedural in character. However, the role of public participation is especially significant. Notably, the Directive goes beyond previous Community measures in the obligation that it imposes upon Member States to 'encourage' participation of all interested parties in water planning matters. Although traditional forms of 'consultation' have been facilitative in enabling public representations to be made and taken

11 Illustrated by early cases before the European Court of Justice where the UK was found guilty of breaching water directives and circumstances within national control were not found to amount to a defence. Howarth and McGillivray (n 10) s4.15.

12 Art 5 EC Treaty provides that 'in areas that do not fall within its exclusive competence, the Community shall take action, in accordance with the principle of subsidiarity, only if and insofar as the objectives of the proposed action cannot be sufficiently achieved by the Member States and can therefore, by reason of the scale of effects of the proposed action, be better achieved by the Community. Any action by the Community shall not go beyond what is necessary to achieve the objectives of this Treaty.' For a general discussion of the implications of subsidiarity, see W Wils, 'Subsidiarity and EC Environmental Policy: Taking People's Concerns Seriously' (1994) 5 JEL 85.

into account in environmental decision making, 'encouragement' seems to envisage something beyond this. The procedural issue is about what this means in practice (what needs to be done to 'encourage' public engagement rather than merely 'enabling' it?). The associated substantive question is whether environmental decisions that are reached in this way are a means of securing genuinely better environmental outcomes, which are in the longer-term collective interest in realising sustainable development.

## 3. Proceduralisation

From the inception of the EEC, under the 1957 Treaty, to the present, environmental law has evolved remarkably in both content and style. Over an initial period of about 3 decades, up to the Single European Act of 1987, environmental legislation may be seen to have arisen largely as an offshoot of the need to realise a common market. Early legislation was justified because of the environmental impacts of trade-related activities and primarily sought to harmonise minimum requirements for pollution control on the basis that pollution does not respect national boundaries. Following the 1987 Act, competence in respect of environmental action found a new justification in the quality of life of European citizens. As a consequence, a plethora of measures was adopted spanning environmental issues extending well beyond the compass of the single market. However, the general style of these measures followed a traditional regulatory approach of prohibiting environmentally unacceptable practices and/or requiring specified quality objectives or standards to be secured. Increasing attention has been drawn to the limitations of prohibitive, sometimes dubbed 'command and control', approaches to environmental regulation. More recently, greater emphasis has been placed upon expanding the range of regulatory instruments that are in place to address environmental concerns. Numerous examples of regulatory prohibition of environmentally-unacceptable activities remain the mainstay of Community environmental law. Nonetheless, the contemporary approach involves the appreciation that environmental governance may be better realised through the greater application of more flexible mechanisms for protection of the environment.[13]

'Flexibility' in environmental governance is manifested in various forms which may involve education, information and economics, as alternatives to regulatory prohibition, in improving environmental quality. Another aspect of flexibility is to be seen in the increasing application of 'proceduralisation' in

13 See N Gunningham, 'Environmental Law, Regulation and Governance: Shifting Architectures' (2009) 21 JEL 179, forthcoming, for discussion of historical trends in the development in environmental law.

environmental legislation.[14] Although difficult to define precisely, 'proceduralisation' broadly involves the imposition of constraints upon those entrusted with environmental decision making. These constraints prescribe the basis upon which decisions are to be made or the environmental management actions that must be taken, the factors to be taken into account at various stages of the decision-making process and the monitoring of the impacts, 'without determining the final outcome of that process'. Hence, the setting of mandatory environmental standards at Community level, defined precisely for each environmental sector and activity, has been supplemented by regulatory mechanisms which set out the basis for action, but allow greater national and local flexibility and discretion in determining what particular substantive outcomes need to be realised.

A fairly longstanding illustration of a procedural approach is to be seen in the requirements for environmental impact assessment of development projects that are likely to have a significant impact upon the environment.[15] More recently, a comparable approach has been taken to the strategic environmental assessment of plans and programmes.[16] In each instance the object of Community legislation is that the relevant project or plan should be subject to scrutiny of its environmental implications before approval or adoption. Environmental assessment needs to be undertaken in accordance with procedures that allow for participation at all levels and for representations to be taken into account by the decision-making body. Most significantly, however, the need to adhere to specified environmental assessment procedures does not dictate the final decision. Providing that the procedures are correctly followed, there is nothing to prevent the approval of projects or plans that may result in significant environmental harm.[17]

Another illustration of proceduralisation can be seen in the Community Directive on Integrated Pollution Prevention and Control[18] which requires Member States to regulate industrial installations by applying the best available techniques to minimise the impacts of emissions upon the environment. Within the context of the Directive, 'best available techniques' is a profoundly

14 Generally see J Black, 'Proceduralizing Regulation' (2000) OJLS 597, and (2001) 21 OJLS 33; J Scott, 'Flexibility 'Proceduralization' and Environmental Governance in the EU' in J Scott and G De Burca (eds) *Constitutional Change in the European Union* (Hart, Oxford 2000); R Macrory and S Turner, 'Participatory Rights, Transboundary Environmental Governance and EC Law' (2002) CML Rev 489; M Lee, *EU Environmental Law* (Hart, Oxford 2005) ch 6; and CF Sabel and J Zetlin, 'Learning from Difference: The New Architecture of Experimentalist Governance in the EU' (2008) ELJ 271.

15 Council Directive (EEC) 85/337 Environmental Impact Assessment Directive as amended by Council Directive (EC) 97/11.

16 Council Directive (EC) 2001/42 Strategic Environmental Assessment Directive.

17 W Howarth, 'Substance and Procedure under the Strategic Environmental Assessment Directive and the Water Framework Directive' in J Holder and D McGillivray (eds), *Taking Stock of Environmental Assessment: Law, Policy and Practice* (Cavendish Publishers, London 2007) 149.

18 Council Directive (EC) 1996/61 concerning integrated pollution prevention and control [1996].

open-ended concept and the normative imprecision of this leaves Member States with a substantial freedom to interpret it as they see fit. In effect, this involves a decentralisation of responsibility for substantive environmental decision making, with Community legislation setting a procedural framework for the exercise of substantive discretion on environmental standards by the Member States.[19]

For some, proceduralisation might be seen as a regrettable retreat from the vital need to harmonise minimum environmental standards at Community level, given the unwillingness of Member States to take unilateral action for that purpose because it is regarded as undermining national competitiveness.[20] However, proceduralisation has attractions to others who are concerned about the effectiveness, efficiency and authoritarianism of past approaches to environmental legislation. Conventional regulatory approaches are seen as inappropriate to address persistent, complex or diffuse environmental problems and result in ever more intrusive, complex and inflexible rules.[21] In a climate of concern about the democratic legitimacy of the EC, the acknowledgement that environmental problems may be better addressed at a decentralised level has much political resonance.[22] Similarly, flexibility and proceduralisation may be seen as a sensible application of the need for subsidiarity in Community lawmaking in not going beyond what is needed to address particular concerns.

## 4. Public Participation in Environmental Decision Making

An aspect of flexibility and decentralisation which has gained increasing emphasis over recent years is the general consensus in favour of public participation in environmental decision making. Again, this may reflect the same concerns about democratic legitimacy and environmental authoritarianism that have been previously referred to. Nonetheless, the view that a more 'bottom-up' approach to environmental decision making is preferable has gained increasing ground in various legislative initiatives. A better approach towards Community environmental governance is seen as one which is less

19 J Scott, 'Flexibility 'Proceduralization' and Environmental Governance in the EU' in J Scott and G De Burca (eds) *Constitutional Change in the European Union* (Hart, Oxford 2000); B Lange, 'Searching for the Best Available Techniques – Open and Closed norms in the Implementation of the EU Directive on Integrated Pollution Prevention and Control' (2006) Int J L Context 67; and generally see J Holder and M Lee, *Environmental Protection, Law and Policy* (2nd edn Cambridge, CUP 2007) ch 9.

20 See, eg the quote from L Kramer in preface to this paper.

21 Lee (n 14) 165.

22 M Lee, 'Public Participation, Procedure and Democratic Deficit in EC Environmental Law' (2003) 3 Eur Env L Ybk 193.

hierarchical and involves greater sharing of environmental responsibility between the Community and its citizens.[23]

There are two key justifications for public participation in environmental decision making. The first is that it is more democratic and the second is that it will result in better decisions.[24] On the first point, the remoteness and technocratic character of the Community legislative process, and the limited capacity of environmental groups or individuals to influence this, has long been recognised.[25] A more inclusive legislative approach, which is more in tune with the idea of subsidiarity, is one which allows individuals a greater say in the regulatory actions that impact upon them. Hence, legislation which provides greater flexibility in its implementation should be more responsive to local needs and individual concerns. In addition, it has been suggested that greater transparency in the establishment of legislative objectives will result in greater care being taken to implement regulatory measures in good faith.[26] Increasingly, the view is taken that public involvement is a means towards 'deliberative democracy' where opposing views about an environmental proposal are debated in a way that produces informed rational argument and reasons for a decision that are likely to be widely accepted.[27]

The view that public participation will lead to better decisions, is premised upon the argument that the technocratic arguments of a kind that are likely to be presented by 'experts' neglect relevant factors that may be provided by others with non-expert backgrounds. For example, local residents might be in a better position to present information about the local impacts of a decision.[28] Moreover, representations from a wide range of participants may provide an input of relevant opinions and values that would otherwise be overlooked.[29] More broadly, public engagement in environmental decision making might be

23 See, eg the emphasis placed upon participation in the Commission (EC), White Paper on European Governance, COM (2001) 428 and the European Parliament and Council Decision (EC) No.1600/2002 laying down the Sixth Environment Action Programme, Art 10 which requires environmental policy objectives to be pursued through extensive consultation and strengthened participation.

24 Generally see J Steele, 'Participation and Deliberation in Environmental Law: Exploring a Problem-solving Approach' (2001) OJLS 415; K Getliffe, 'Proceduralisation and the Aarhus Convention: Does Increased Participation in the Decision-making Process Lead to More Effective EU Environmental Law?' (2002) 4 ELR 104; and M Lee and C Abbot, 'The Usual Suspects? Public Participation under the Aarhus Convention' (2003) MLR 80.

25 L Kramer, 'The Elaboration of EC Environmental Legislation' in G Winter (ed) *European Environmental Law: A Comparative Perspective* (Dartmouth, Aldershot 1996) 302; S Mazey and J Richardson, 'Environmental Groups and the EC: Challenges and Opportunities' in A Jordan (ed) *Environmental Policy in the European Union: Actors, Institutions, and Processes* (Earthscan, London 2002) 150.

26 WWF, *WWF's preliminary comments on Public Participation in the context of the Water Framework Directive and Integrated River Basin Management* (2001) 2.

27 JS Dryzek, *The Politics of the Earth: Environmental Discourses* (2nd edn OUP, Oxford 2005).

28 R McCracken and G Jones, 'The Aarhus Convention' (2003) JPEL 803.

29 Steele (n 24).

seen as beneficial for reasons of environmental education, awareness raising and enhancement of 'environmental citizenship'.[30]

Against these claims for the merits of public participation there are counter arguments. In respect of the claim for enhancing environmental democracy, there is the concern that participation processes are capable of being hijacked by special interest groups which do not represent the 'general public' interest. For example, environmentally significant projects such as wind farms which are widely recognised to be of national and international environmental benefit may have adverse local impacts, and local objections may be more prominent in deliberations than national benefits of a project. Similarly, the greater willingness and capacity of local residents to engage in participation than those with more remote concerns, has the potential to localise the debate at the expense of overshadowing wider and longer-term environmental considerations. 'Sustainable development' is generally seen to involve recognition of the rights of future generations to a satisfactory environment,[31] whereas the more immediate desires of present-day participants in environmental decision making may fail to reflect this. Similarly, in relation to the argument that public participation results in 'better' decisions, the evaluation of this depends upon the sense of 'better' that is at issue.[32] What counts as a 'better' decision in terms of reducing local impacts may be seen as the opposite of this in respect of its national or international implications or consequences for future generations.

At best, the overall balance of cost and benefits of public participation in environmental decision making may be seen as ambivalent. It seems to presuppose that there is a 'general public interest' in the matter under decision and that a sufficient level of public engagement will allow this to emerge and be afforded prominence above the individual and group representations that may be advanced. The problem, of course, is the question of whether there is actually such a thing as the 'general public interest', as opposed to a range of individual and sectoral interests that may be presented to a decision-making body.

Setting aside these reservations, the general idea of 'public participation' is seriously ambiguous in relation to its practical implications. The form in which it is to be put into practice admits many possible degrees of involvement, from situations where the public are merely informed of the outcome of the decision-making process to situations where they are given the full practical

30 A Dobson, *Citizenship and the Environment* (OUP, New York 2003); and C Hilson, 'Greening Citizenship: Boundaries of Membership and the Environment' (2001) 13 JEL 335.

31 The widely cited definition from the World Commission on Environment and Development, *Our Common Future* (1987) at 43 characterises sustainable development as 'development which meets the needs of the present without compromising the ability of future generations to meet their own needs'.

32 See the review of literature on the benefits of active involvement in environmental decision-making in Le Quesne and Green (n 4) 11.

responsibility for taking that decision.[33] Somewhere between the two extremes lies the traditional practice of 'consultation' that has been adopted in the UK for many years. This involves information about proposals for action by governmental bodies being placed in the public domain and members of the public and interest groups being invited to make representations for or against the proposals.[34] This is a long-established model for facilitating public participation, but it is not the only model or necessarily the best one.[35] The recent preference for public participation as an aspect of the movement towards greater flexibility in European Community environmental legislation, including the WFD, can be seen as opening up a wide range of practical options. The implications of these options need to be carefully considered, particularly in the light of how they may operate in practice.

## 5. The International Context on Participation

In favouring public participation in environmental decision making the European Community may be seen as acting within, and being influenced by, a wider international context on this issue. The key global international basis for participation in environmental decision making is Principle 10 of the Declaration from the United Nations Conference on Environment and Development of 1992.

> Environmental issues are best handled with the participation of all concerned citizens, at the relevant level. At the national level, each individual shall have ... the opportunity to participate in decision-making processes. States shall facilitate and encourage public awareness and participation by making information widely available ...[36]

33 SR Arnstein, 'A Ladder of Citizen Participation' (1969) 36 J Am Plan Assoc 216; WWF, *WWF's preliminary comments on Public Participation in the context of the Water Framework Directive and Integrated River Basin Management* (2001) 3.

34 See, eg Environment Agency, *Working together: Your Role in Our Environmental Permitting Decision Making* (2007) on the consultation processes adopted by the Agency in relation to environmental permitting decisions.

35 Le Quesne and Green (n 4) 11. For discussion of the role of participation in water management contexts, see J Newig, C Pahl-Wostl and K Sigel, 'The Role of Public Participation in Managing Uncertainty in the Implementation of the Water Framework Directive' (2005) Euro Env 333; and N Videira and others, 'Public and Stakeholder Participation in European Water Policy: A Critical Review of Project Evaluation Processes' (2006) Euro Env 19.

36 Principle 10, Rio Declaration, United Nations Conference on Environment and Development (1992) <http://www.un.org/documents/ga/conf151/aconf15126-1annex1.htm> accessed 10 June 2009. This principle has been reaffirmed in Johannesburg Declaration on Sustainable Development (2002) which states that sustainable development requires 'broad-based participation in policy formulation, decision-making and implementation at all levels'. Johannesburg Declaration, Principle 26 <http://www.un.org/esa/sustdev/documents/WSSD_POI_PD/English/POI_PD.htm> accessed 10 June 2009.

At a regional international level, these issues have progressed furthest in The United Nations Economic Commission for Europe's 'Aarhus Convention'.[37] Although preliminary reference is made to the democratic or improved decision-making justifications outlined above,[38] the main emphasis of the Convention is upon a human rights rationale for matters relating to public participation. Hence, the objective of the Convention states:

> In order to contribute to the protection of the right of every person of present and future generations to live in an environment adequate to his or her health and well-being, each Party shall guarantee the rights of... public participation in decision making... in accordance with the provisions of this Convention.[39]

Most pertinently, in relation to public participation concerning plans, programmes and policies relating to the environment,[40] it is provided that:

> Each party shall make appropriate practical and/or other provisions for the public to participate during the preparation of plans and programmes relating to the environment, within a transparent and fair framework, having provided the necessary information to the public. Within this framework [requirements to allow reasonable time-frames to allow the public to participate effectively; at an early stage when all options are open; and ensuring that due account is taken of the outcome of public participation in the decision] shall be applied. The public which may participate shall be identified by the relevant public authority, taking into account the objectives of this Convention...[41]

'The public concerned' in relation to this obligation are defined to mean 'the public likely to be affected by, or having an interest in, the environmental decision making' and, for this purpose, environmental non-governmental

37 The United Nations Economic Commission for Europe Convention on Access to Information, Public Participation and Decision making and Access to Justice in Environmental Matters (1998). Adopted by European Environment Ministers meeting in Aarhus (Denmark) 25 June 1998, and entered into force 30 October 2001 <http://www.unece.org/env/pp/treatytext.htm> accessed 10 June 2009. See *The Aarhus Convention: An Implementation Guide* (2000) <http://www.unece.org/env/pp/acig.pdf> accessed 10 June 2009. For commentary see J Jendroska and S Stec, 'The Aarhus Convention: Towards a new Era in Environmental Democracy' (2001) Env Liability 140; and W Upton, 'The Human Factor: Public Participation, Third Party Rights and Aarhus' (2003) ELM 219.

38 A recital to the Aarhus Convention recognises that 'improved access to information and public participation in decision-making enhance the quality and the implementation of decisions, contribute to public awareness of environmental issues, give the public the opportunity to express its concerns and enable public authorities to take due account of such concerns'.

39 Aarhus Convention Art 1.

40 See also Art 6 Aarhus Convention on participation in decisions on specific activities and Art 8 on preparation of executive regulations and/or legally binding instruments, which may also have relevance to activities related to the implementation of the WFD.

41 Art 7 Aarhus Convention.

organisations are deemed to have an interest.[42] The extent to which this definition encompasses the 'general public' is not as clear as it might be,[43] though the Implementation Guide to the Aarhus Convention envisages a wide interpretation of the 'public' and a 'ladder' of involvement whereby different groups of stakeholders are identified depending upon their level of involvement, ranging from the right to information to direct decision making.[44] However, the extent of 'the public concerned' is left largely to the discretion of the relevant public authority in identifying who should count as 'participants' for these purposes.

## 6. Public Participation under the Water Framework Directive

In implementing the Aarhus Convention in EC law, it is notable that amendments of certain environmental directives were necessary to secure full compliance with the public participation obligations under the Convention.[45] However, no amendments of this kind were thought necessary to meet the Convention obligations under the WFD, which was regarded as compliant with the Aarhus obligations on public participation. This is reflected in a recital to the Directive which states:

> To ensure the participation of the general public including users of water in the establishment and updating of river basin management plans, it is necessary to provide proper information of planned measures and to report on progress with their implementation with a view to the involvement of the general public before final decisions on the necessary measures are adopted.[46]

If anything, the rather unqualified wording of this recital, which is couched in terms of 'ensuring' public participation rather than merely facilitating it,

42 Art 2(5) Aarhus Convention.

43 Lee and Abbot (n 24) 86, though it has been suggested that 'the public concerned' is a term that is wide enough to encompass not only those affected by a decision, but also those with an interest in it, which may be of a legal or factual kind, hence all members of the general public will probably come within the ambit of the 'concerned public', J Adshead, 'Public Participation, the Aarhus Convention and the Water Framework Directive' (2006) 17 J Water L 185, 190.

44 Economic Commission for Europe, *The Aarhus Convention: An Implementation Guide* (United Nations, New York 2000) 85–6.

45 Council Directive (EC) 2003/35 of the European Parliament and the Council providing for public participation in respect of the drawing up of certain plans and programmes relating to the environment and amending with the regard to access to justice Council Directive (EEC) 85/337 and Council Directive (EC) 96/61, amends provisions on public participation in the national permitting procedures on environmental impact assessment and integrated pollution prevention and control, and introduces requirements for access to justice.

46 Recital 46 WFD.

seems to go beyond the Aarhus obligations in this respect. A similar emphasis upon the importance of public engagement is reflected in another recital which states:

> The success of this Directive relies on close cooperation and coherent action at Community, Member State and local level as well as on information, consultation and the involvement of the public, including users.[47]

The same emphasis upon the importance of public engagement is found in the body of the WFD, where an obligation is placed upon Member States to 'encourage the active involvement of all interested parties' in the implementation of the Directive. This duty applies in relation to the production, review and updating of river basin management plans, which must be published and made available for comment to the public.[48] Public participation, therefore, is envisaged as an essential requirement at all stages in the production of plans and specified documents relating to this must be published, with background documents and other information to be made available on request. A period of 6 months is to be allowed for comment on the documents, for the specific purpose of 'allowing active involvement and consultation'.[49]

Given the essentially voluntary character of participation, it would be logically impossible to 'compel' members of the public to engage in 'participation' on water management planning matters arising under the WFD. Nonetheless, the wording of the Directive comes as close to mandating Member States to ensure that public participation takes place, insofar as is reasonably possible and certainly fulfils the Aarhus requirements in this respect.

The important questions are about how these obligations are translated into national law and how faithfully they are implemented in practice. The obligation to 'encourage' active involvement seems to suggest something beyond the ordinary elements of a consultation process, involving a 'potentially much deeper form of participation, although there is little compulsion here',[50] perhaps indicating a shift towards a model of 'active citizenship' in which power is shared between a wide range of stakeholders.[51] However, the obligation to encourage involvement falls short of a duty to ensure that this actually occurs and the WFD itself gives no further indication as to what kind of 'encouragement' is needed.

47 Recital 14 WFD.
48 Art 14(1) WFD.
49 Art 14(2) WFD.
50 Lee and Abbot (n 24) 100. Similarly, respondents to national consultation on WFD 'stressed that public involvement included, but did not stop at, providing information and consulting'. See Department for Environment Food and Rural Affairs, *Third Consultation Paper on the Implementation of the EC Water Framework Directive* (2000/60/EC) (2003) para 2.273.
51 Macrory and Turner (n 14) 505.

The Common Implementation Strategy Guidance on the WFD[52] affirms that 'participation' involves more than mere consultation, so that 'interested parties participate actively in the planning process by discussing issues and contributing to their solution'.[53] The guidance also notes that, beyond consultation, still higher levels of participation are provided by shared decision making and self-determination. 'Shared decision making' implies that interested parties not only participate actively in the planning process, but also become partly responsible for the outcome. 'Self-determination' implies that at least parts of water management are handed over to the interested parties. The view taken in the guidance is that encouraging a high level of participation in the development and implementation of plans should be considered the core requirement for active involvement. Although the latter two forms of participation are not specifically required by the Directive, they may often be considered as best practice.[54]

## 7. Participation in WFD Transposing Legislation

In relation to England and Wales, the main transposing legislation, The Water Environment (Water Framework Directive) (England and Wales) Regulations 2003,[55] provide fairly extensive requirements for public participation. In relation to activities relating to the establishment of environmental objects and programmes of measures for river basin management plans, the Environment Agency must 'take such steps as it thinks fit, or the appropriate authority may direct', to 'provide opportunities for the general public and those persons likely to be interested in or affected by its proposals to participate in discussion and the exchange of information or views in relation to the preparation of those proposals'. The Agency must also publicise its draft proposals and consult those persons on the proposals.[56]

Further provision is made in relation to public participation on river basin management plans, requiring public participation in the establishment of river basin management plans through publication of various matters relating to these plans 'in such manner as the Agency considers appropriate for the purpose of bringing it to the attention of persons likely to be affected by it'.

52 Commission (EC), Common Implementation Strategy for the Water Framework Directive (2000/60/EC), Guidance Document No.8, Public Participation in Relation to the Water Framework Directive (2003) para 2.2.
53 Ibid 10.
54 Ibid 11.
55 SI 2003/3242, hereafter referred to as 'Transposing Regs'. See also the Water Environment (Water Framework Directive) (Northumbria River Basin District) Regulations 2003 SI 2003/3245 and the Water Environment (Water Framework Directive) (Solway Tweed River Basin District) Regulations 2004 SI 2004/99.
56 Reg 10(2)(b) Transposing Regs.

Again it is to 'take such steps as it thinks fit, or the appropriate authority may direct, to provide opportunities for the general public and [listed statutory consultees] to participate in discussion and the exchange of information or views in relation to the preparation of the draft plan'.[57] Additional provision is made for the information that must be accessible to the public at the Agency's principal office.[58]

Although there are differences in wording (the 'public', 'the general public' and 'persons likely to be interested') and significant discretion is afforded to the Environment Agency, the overall impression is that the England and Wales transposing regulations successfully give effect to the requirements for public participation set out in the WFD.[59]

## 8. Participation in Practice

What the broad legal obligations on participation that have been recounted actually entail in practice is more difficult to interpret.[60] A general concern is that the practical challenges of engaging the wider general public may mean that a narrower 'stakeholder' or representative approach to participation is needed. Beyond that, many of the issues needing to be resolved in implementing the WFD are readily capable of being placed in complex scientific or technical methodological contexts, which will have the effect of marginalising participants from outside a narrow community of expert stakeholders. As the issues become more specific and specialised, the pool of potential participants becomes progressively smaller, though the importance of decisions does not diminish, where, as often, 'the devil is in the detail'. The upshot of this is that, widespread 'participation' can mask the real distribution of influence in decision making, where the most crucial decisions are eventually made by a handful of key players.[61] The danger of this is that meeting the formalities of

57 Reg 12(2) Transposing Regs.

58 Reg 18 Transposing Regs.

59 Adshead (n 43) 189.

60 See the written evidence from the Foundation for Water Research, which expresses some critical views on the effectiveness of public participation under the WFD and response from Baroness Young, Chief Executive of the Environment Agency, House of Lords European Union Committee, 27th Report of Session 2006–07, *Water Framework Directive: Making it Work*, HL Paper 136 (2007) 26 onwards. See Le Quesne and Green (n 4) 27, where it is maintained that that the model of stakeholder engagement proposed by the Environment Agency is inconsistent with government policy in other areas. See also Ph AK Rault and PJ Jeffrey, 'Deconstructing Public Participation in the Water Framework Directive: Implementation and Compliance with the Letter or with the Spirit of the Law?' (2008) Water Env J 241, stressing the need for public participation to be seen as a 'flexible, adaptive process' for which no blueprint exists.

61 W Maloney and J Richardson, *Managing Policy Change in Britain: The Politics of Water* (Edinburgh University Press, Edinburgh 1995) 170–1.

'public participation' in practice may be possible in a way that effectively defeats its purposes.

Discussion of how public engagement under the WFD is to be secured in practice is provided in the Environment Agency publication, *A Framework for Stakeholder Engagement* (2005).[62] This indicates the intention of the Agency to secure involvement of stakeholders at the different levels at which this needs to be undertaken. At a national level, a group of stakeholder organisations will be established to contribute to development of national programmes of measures and new regulatory mechanisms. At river basin district level, external input will be channelled through liaison panels, consisting of representatives of statutory bodies and other interest groups, co-operating on the preparation of district level river basin management plans. At catchment level, existing consultation arrangements are perceived to meet the need for engagement, with some flexibility to meet local circumstances. At a local scale, no formal arrangements are envisaged, though individuals and existing networks will be selectively engaged, where local issues arise. Alongside the proposals for engagement at national, district, catchment and local levels, the Agency will continue to draw on the expertise provided by statutory committees concerned with flood defence, environmental protection and fisheries, ecology and recreation.

These arrangements are broadly reaffirmed by the Department for Environment, Food and Rural Affairs (DEFRA) and Welsh Assembly Government, in *River Basin Planning Guidance* (2006). This suggests that the Agency 'should see itself as the chair or co-ordinator of a group of key decision makers and deliverers which is responsible for investigating a set of collective problems and devising and negotiating solutions to them'.[63] In effect, the Agency's role is to 'organise the process'.[64] In addition, the specific arrangements for engaging different groups of interested parties need to be put in place. As a minimum, this must comply with requirements for public consultation set out in WFD and transposing regulations and should involve establishing a liaison panel for each river basin district comprising representatives of key organisations likely to be affected. The essentially advisory role of the river basin district liaison panels should include discussion and negotiation about the content of the river basin management plan, scrutinising the

62 See also Environment Agency, *Water for Life and Livelihoods: A Framework for River Basin Planning in England and Wales* (Environment Agency 2006). For a discussion of contrasts between approaches to public participation in other parts of the UK, see D Woods (n 5). Comparisons may also be drawn with IG Bush and others, 'Public Participation – Drawing the Boundaries' (2005) Water Env J 181, concerned with public participation in the mapping of access land under the Countryside and Rights of Way Act 2000.

63 Department for Environment, Food and Rural Affairs (DEFRA) and Welsh Assembly Government, in *River Basin Planning Guidance* (2006) para 11.2 <http://www.defra.gov.uk/environment/water/wfd/pdf/riverbasinguidance.pdf> accessed 10 June 2009.

64 Ibid.

ongoing river basin planning process; and tracking and pursuing progress with the implementation and enforcement of the plan and programme of measures. Membership of liaison panels should be tailored to the river basin district, but should include representatives of three broad types of organisation: regulators who are responsible for enforcing WFD measures, those responsible for delivering WFD measures and organisations representing the sections of the public who will be affected by implementation. It is recognised that public consultation alone is unlikely to be sufficient and in addition, the Agency will need to ensure that there are appropriate arrangements in place which enable information about impacts, mechanisms and measures to be fed into river basin management plans from both the national and local levels.[65] Whilst the recognition of a need for something beyond public consultation is in accordance with the aim of 'encouraging' public engagement required by the WFD, subject to guidance, the challenging task of putting in place 'appropriate arrangements' to secure this seems to be left entirely to the Agency's discretion.

Some insights into the practical operation of participation at ground level may be drawn from the initial stages of the pilot project on the Ribble river basin conducted by the Environment Agency between 2003 and 2004. Member States have undertaken to conduct pilot projects in 15 nominated pilot river basins, selected for their landscape and social diversity, in order to harmonise approaches towards implementation and, amongst other things, to test the methods of engagement provided for in the Common Implementation Strategy. Reports on the pilot projects, including the Ribble project, have been submitted to the European Commission.[66]

The Ribble pilot project utilised diverse mechanisms to convey background information, facilitate consultation in the planning process and to encourage active involvement of interested parties in all aspects of local implementation of the WFD. Broadly, the project adopted a hierarchical approach to stakeholder engagement, comprising four levels of involvement: a project team, a stakeholder forum, local organisations and community groups and the general public, with the various kinds of engagement adopted at the different levels. The stakeholder forum, comprising representatives of some 50 local or regional organisations, was seen as providing a central means for communication between those with key involvements and as making a significant contribution to development of a local 'vision' for environmental protection and improvement. This was supplemented by expert meetings on small working groups

65 DEFRA and Welsh Assembly Government, *River Basin Planning Guidance* (DEFRA 2006) ch 11.

66 P Fox and others, *Public Participation and River Basin Planning – Early Experiences* (Environment Agency, 2004) and see the independent evaluation of this by M Davis and Y Rees, *Public Participation in the Ribble River Basin* (2004) (produced as part of Workpackage 5 of the HarmoniCOP ('Harmonising Collaborative Planning') Project) <http://www.harmonicop.uos.de> accessed 10 June 2009. See also the discussion of the Ribble Project in E Louka, *Water Law & Policy* (OUP, New York 2008) ch 15.

dealing with particular issues. Wider soundings were provided by diverse meetings with groups or individuals and presentations, to raise awareness and to identify and gather perceptions of the key issues from interested bodies. In order to gather more general public opinion, a telephone questionnaire survey of a cross-section of households was undertaken to identify the perceptions of individuals and to ascertain their willingness to become involved in river basin planning. Communication, at all levels, was facilitated by an electronic newsletter and a website, which were regarded as an economical and efficient means of conveying information about the project.

The summary conclusions drawn from the Ribble project stressed that public participation is vital in engaging, and gaining the confidence of, the public at an early stage in the river basin planning process. In respect of interpreting the obligation to encourage the involvement of 'all interested parties' it was noted that 14% of the general public expressed an interest in involvement, though the majority of these were from particular social groups. Those most likely to become involved were aged below 35, AB social grade, city dwellers and members or supporters of environmental organisations that were already represented as stakeholders. Social selectivity was also evident in the membership of the stakeholder forum, which was seen to be 'dominated by professional middle-aged people'.[67] More generally, it was noted that urban community groups from ethnic minority backgrounds were under-represented at specific events. This amounted to a considerable omission given the cultural diversity of the pilot area, incorporating major towns such as Preston, Blackburn and Wigan.[68]

Overall, the pilot study concluded that the experience of testing and developing public participation methods and tools for early river basin planning for the Ribble supported many of the principles of the Common Implementation Strategy. However, reaching this finding involved a significant cost in terms of resource commitments from a wide range of bodies and individuals. In addition, it is recognised that time constraints upon the project were a significant limiting factor and that increased marketing and advertising would have increased accessibility and involvement. Beyond that, the study recognised that there is a danger of 'raising expectations too high', and that participants need clearly to understand the process that they are engaged in and its limitations.[69]

67 Fox and others (n 66) 65.
68 Ibid.
69 Similarly, see the conclusions offered in Bush and others (n 62) concerned with public participation in the mapping of access land under the Countryside and Rights of Way Act 2000.

## 9. Substance and Procedure in the WFD

The arrangements for participation in the implementation of the WFD are entirely procedural in character, but may be seen as a component of an overall project that is more substantive in its environmental objectives. Returning to the first key theme of the paper, what can be learnt about the relative scope of substantive and procedural requirements of the Directive from the way in which implementation has been approached in practice? From the national perspective, what balance does it strike between 'soft' and 'hard' environmental requirements?

From the introductory observations on the scope of the WFD, it is clear that it contains a series of procedural regulatory and administrative tasks, relating to transposition and identifying competent bodies for river basin districts. Beyond that, the exercise of river basin management planning may be characterised as a series of procedural requirements needing to be met by specified deadlines. However, the language of the Directive suggests that these tasks are not ends in themselves, but rather that they are means towards meeting the environmental objectives of the Directive. The search for substance involves closer examination of these.

On first impressions, the environmental objectives of the WFD appear to have considerable substantive content.[70] A clear indication of this is in the environmental quality objective of the Directive that requires implementation by measures that prevent deterioration of the existing quality of surface and groundwaters.[71] 'Non-deterioration' in environmental quality is a clear example of a substantive environmental requirement insofar as a failure to achieve this would seem to provide a basis for infringement proceedings against a defaulting state.

Insofar as the WFD comprises a consolidation of previous Community water quality legislation, it has re-enacted important substantive water quality requirements deriving from those directives. The concern that adoption of the WFD might serve as a pretext for any weakening or removal of past water quality standards is met by an emphatic recital statement to the effect that 'the implementation of the Directive is to achieve a level of protection of waters at least equivalent to that provided in certain earlier acts . . .'.[72] The broad implication is that where an environmental quality standard has been provided for in a previous water directive, at least equally stringent requirements are imposed by the WFD. More specifically, where pre-existing legislation requires a quality objective or standard to be met, and this cannot be

70 See HFMW van Rijswick, *Moving Water and the Law: On the Distribution of Water Rights and Water Duties Within River Basins in European and Dutch Water Law* (Europa Law Publishing, Groningen 2008), particularly pp 24 and 30, arguing for a substantive interpretation of the obligations under the WFD.

71 Art 4(1)(a).i and Art 4(1)(b).i WFD.

72 Recital 51 WFD.

achieved by existing controls upon emissions, stricter conditions must be imposed to ensure the objective or standard is met.[73] In part, this has the consequence that environmental quality standards established pursuant to the Dangerous Substances Directive must be adhered to in implementing the WFD,[74] but the same approach applies to 'other' existing legislation setting relevant objectives or quality standards.[75] Beyond non-deterioration (below existing water quality standards) the WFD incorporates mechanisms for the adoption of further water quality standards for substances that have not been provided for under current legislation. Hence, the 'framework' character of the Directive envisages additional measures being adopted against pollution of water by individual pollutants or groups of pollutants presenting a significant risk to or via the aquatic environment.[76]

Although provision is made for the repeal of various directives,[77] where their coverage has been brought within the WFD, there is no suggestion that this involves any removal or reduction in stringency of water quality requirements. Indeed, the introduction of a 'combined approach' of requiring both emission limits and water quality objectives to be met[78] involves greater stringency as compared with the previous 'parallel approach' of allowing Member States to meet *either* emission limits *or* water quality objectives.

On first impression, the need for waters to achieve 'good status' within a specified timescale has a strongly substantive feel to it. However, on closer scrutiny, this requirement has some significant procedural aspects which deserve careful examination. In the first place, the obligation upon Member States is 'not' a simple unqualified obligation actually to achieve good status of all relevant waters by a specified date. Critically, the wording of the Directive requires various actions to be taken 'with the aim of achieving' good status by 2015.[79] If good status is an 'aim' rather than a 'requirement' of the Directive, then a member state would not be in breach if it failed to realise good status

73 Art 10(3) WFD, providing for a 'combined approach' to point and diffuse sources.

74 Council Directive (EEC) 76/464 on pollution caused by certain dangerous substances discharged into the aquatic environment of the Community. The five 'daughter' directives to the Dangerous Substances Directive, setting environmental quality standards for specific substances, are listed in WFD, Annex IV.

75 Although the WFD is not explicit as to what 'other' legislation is relevant here, it is possible that water quality standards provided for under the Agricultural Nitrates Council Directive (EEC) 91/676 and the Drinking Water Quality Council Directive (EEC) 80/778 as amended might be examples that fall within this category.

76 Art 16(1) WFD, on strategies against pollution of water. See Council Decision (EC) 2455/2001 establishing the list of priority substances in the field of water policy and amending Council Directive (EC) 200/60 and COM (2006) 397; COM (2006) 398 on proposals for a Daughter Directive on environmental quality standards for priority substances; and Council Directive (EC) 2008/105 on environmental quality standards in the field of water policy.

77 Art 22 WFD.

78 Art 10 WFD and Howarth (n 10).

79 Art 4 WFD uses this form of words in relation to various categories of waters. See also Commission (EC), Proposal for a Council Directive Establishing a Framework for Community

within the deadline, providing that it took the necessary actions.[80] Put bluntly, the timely achievement of good status is legally irrelevant. What is required is the taking of necessary actions, however ineffectual these may turn out to be. Arguably, if the 'necessary' actions are taken they should logically produce the desired result of achieving good status. That may be the practical reality in some instances, but there can be no 'guarantee' that the measures that are adopted will necessarily be effectual. The point remains that actual achievement of good status is not a substantive requirement. Putting in place measures is what is legally required and this is largely a procedural matter.

Another respect in which achieving good status seems to serve as an aspiration rather than a substantive obligation is because of the range of derogations, exceptions and defences which are allowed in relation to its realisation. These relate to artificial or heavily modified surface waters (which are only required to meet the lesser objective of 'good ecological potential'), phased achievement of objectives, less stringent environmental objectives, temporary deterioration of water status and new modifications of physical characteristics and sustainable development activities.[81] The cumulative effect of applying these exceptions may be that there are actually quite extensive bodies of water to which the good status requirement is not applicable. The extent to which this happens will depend significantly upon the exercise of discretion by the Member States.

## 10. National Interpretation of the Derogations, Exceptions and Defences

The extent of the national discretion that exists in interpreting and applying the environmental objectives of the WFD has only become apparent with the process of establishing formal guidance for implementing the Directive. National guidance of this kind for England and Wales is provided in the Department for Environment, Food and Rural Affairs and Welsh Assembly Government, *River Basin Planning Guidance* (2006).[82] This constitutes statutory guidance[83] from the Secretary of State and the Welsh Ministers to the

Action in the Field of Water Policy COM (97), 49, *Explanatory Memorandum* s3.3.3 which characterised 'good status' as a 'common level of ambition', suggesting that something less than a binding legal obligation was envisaged.

80 See Grimeaud (n 9).

81 Under Art 4 WFD.

82 See DEFRA and Welsh Assembly Government (n 65). For commentary see Anon, 'Government Formalises Delaying Tactics on Water Framework Targets' (2006) 380 *ENDS Report* 40.

83 Under Reg. 20(3) Water Environment (Water Framework Directive) (England and Wales) Regulations 2003; Reg. 5 Water Environment (Water Framework Directive) (Northumbria River Basin District) Regulations 2003 and Para16(2) of Schedule 1 to the Water Environment (Water Framework Directive) (Solway Tweed River Basin District) Regulations 2004.

Environment Agency as to the ways in which its powers should be exercised in implementing the Directive.

The guidance notes the need for achievement of good status of water bodies by 2015 and preventing the deterioration of waters, and terms these the 'default objectives' of the WFD. It also sets out the circumstances where Member States may deviate from achieving those default objectives and instead aim to achieve what are referred to as 'alternative objectives' (that is, the derogations, exceptions and defences referred to above). Significantly, the alternative objectives, and the defences for failing to achieve objectives, are seen as mechanisms for considering other environmental, social and economic priorities alongside water management priorities and prioritising action over successive river basin planning cycles.

When formulating river basin management plans, it is advised that the Environment Agency 'should make full use of the alternative objectives. They are an integral part of the WFD objectives and their use should be a normal part of river basin planning'.[84] There may be good reasons for this advice in view of the general concern that the Directive should be implemented cost-effectively.[85] Nonetheless, it seems capable of elevating what might have been thought to be exceptional derogations from the good status requirement into the norm. In effect, the Agency is being urged to avoid applying the good status requirement wherever it is possible to apply any of the alternatives. The practical effect of this is difficult to ascertain, but there is potential at least for what might have been regarded as the main objective of the Directive, achieving good status, to be sidelined in the effort to bring waters within the criteria needed to 'avoid' achieving good status.[86]

More recently, further indications have been provided as to the scope for derogation from the good status obligation in the DEFRA and Welsh Assembly Government *Consultation on River Basin Planning Guidance* and the subsequent guidance following from this.[87] It was acknowledged from the outset that the consultation document was written for a 'regulatory audience', rather than members of the public, and the strongly technical character of much of its content reflects this. Nonetheless, the aim was to provide further statutory

84 (n 65) paras 4.17–4.19 and 9.6–9.9.

85 Generally, see Cabinet Office Regulatory Impact Unit, *Better Policy Making: A Guide to Regulatory Impact Assessment* (2003) para 5.35, which states that it is Government policy not to 'gold-plate' directives by implementation that goes beyond the minimum necessary for compliance.

86 See Anon, 'Just 31% of Rivers Covered by Water Framework Directive' (2006) 379 ENDS Report 19.

87 DEFRA and Welsh Assembly Government, *Consultation on River Basin Planning Guidance Volume 2* (February 2008). The final version of this guidance is *River Basin Planning Guidance Volume 2* (DEFRA 2008) <http://www.defra.gov.uk/environment/water/wfd/pdf/riverbasinguidance-Vol2.pdf> accessed 10 June 2009. The final guidance omitted some of the introductory discussion on the consultation process contained in the consultation document and, for that reason, reference is made to both documents.

guidance to the Environment Agency as to the exercise of its powers in relation to the Directive. Although the exercise of these powers will affect a wide range of stakeholders, their representatives had been previously involved with the implementation of the WFD and, it was confidently asserted in the consultation, 'are familiar with the issues and their complexities'.[88] The consultation and evental guidance are also set in a context of various guidance documents formulated at European Community level, under the Common Implementation Strategy, and proposed guidance provided by the UKTAG and research studies undertaken at national level.

Key issues that are ranged over in the final guidance, *River Basin Planning Guidance Volume 2*, which will have significant implications for the application of the good status obligation in practice, concern standards (the adoption of classification guidance proposed by the UKTAG); objectives (the levels of certainty of these and the status of the preference for extending deadlines, rather than setting less stringent objectives); the incorporation of policy trends in river basin planning; Welsh issues; the meaning of 'technical infeasibility' as a basis for an alternative objective to good status; the account to be taken of distributional issues in assessing 'disproportionate cost' as a basis for alternative objectives and whether the impact assessment for the WFD presents a fair picture of the expected costs and benefits.

Although the issues covered are complex and far-ranging, a key focus is upon the consideration that needs to be given to the relationships between natural conditions, technical feasibility and costs and benefits when setting environmental objectives for particular waters. These considerations are seen as mechanisms for considering environmental, social and economic priorities alongside water management priorities, in accordance with the overall concern for sustainable development. Equally they raise critical issues about the extent to which good status will actually be realised in practice.

For example, the WFD requires Member States to 'make judgements about the most cost-effective combination of measures in respect of water uses to be included in the programme of measures'.[89] In response to this, Common Implementation Strategy guidance[90] has been provided and extensive national research has been undertaken on the principles to be applied in cost-effectiveness analysis under the WFD.[91] This methodology will be vitally important in determining the categorisation of waters and the justification for improvement measures. The upshot of the research on cost effectiveness

88 Ibid, para 1 of the Consultation document.

89 Annex II(b) WFD.

90 Common Implementation Strategy, Guidance Document No. 1, *Economics and the Environment: The Implementation Challenge of the Water Framework Directive* (WATECO, 2003).

91 RPA Consortium, *Development of a Methodology to Determine the Cost-Effectiveness of Measures and Combinations of Measures for the Water Framework Directive* (2005) and ICF International, *Preliminary Cost Effectiveness Analysis of the Water Framework Directive* Revised, After Stakeholder Review (December 2007) <http://www.wfdcrp.co.uk> accessed 10 June 2009.

methodology is that 'costs need to be phased significantly in order to achieve a proportionate implementation of the WFD, given the likely level of benefits' and 'a longer term adaptive approach to river basin planning will ultimately be more effective and cost-effective than a more ambitious initial approach given the current state of knowledge'.[92]

The WFD also provides for the good status objective not to be met for waters where this involves 'disproportionate cost' or where measures are 'disproportionately expensive'.[93] Again, this has been subject to research on the development of methodologies for determining 'disproportionality',[94] which has established guiding principles for disproportionate cost analysis. This rather technical guidance concerns matters such as the amount of evidence that is required in decision making and the relevant geographic scale of decisions. It also emphasises a general presumption against putting monetary values on certain types of benefits which are not well understood, such as non-use values.[95] In general, disproportionality is seen to arise where the negative consequences (such as compliance costs, impacts on non-water outcomes and distributional issues involving where costs will fall and whether they will be affordable) outweigh the positive consequences (such as water status improvements). The problem here, as in many other environmental contexts, is the difficulty of quantifying the positive consequences of an action with any precision, given the likelihood that these will concern non-monetary environmental benefits. It might be thought that this is an area in which public estimation of the importance of a good quality water environment might be helpful in assessing its non-use valuation. The concern is that technical methodological solutions to assessment of non-use valuation are capable of giving insufficient weight to this.

Taking a step back from the technicality and detail which lies behind formulation of the guidance, the critical question is about what it all means in terms of the realisation of good status for waters within the WFD. The obligation to achieve good status appears in a different light when viewed in the context of the guidance. It is an obligation that is heavily qualified by national interpretations of economic considerations such 'cost-effectiveness' and 'disproportionate' cost, and these are addressed in a technical way that is capable of excluding broader public discussion of whether they serve to give sufficient priority to environmental improvement.

This is not to suggest that implementation of the WFD should be achieved in an extravagant way, or that it should neglect the need to balance

92 DEFRA and Welsh Assembly Government (n 87) paras 138 and 139.

93 Art 4 WFD.

94 Jacobs, *Report on Guidance on Evidence required to Justify Disproportionate Cost Decisions Under the Water Framework Directive* (2007) <http://www.wfdcrp.co.uk> accessed 10 June 2009.

95 DEFRA and Welsh Assembly Government (n 88) *Consultation* para 148 and final *Guidance* para 10.6.

environmental priorities against social and economic facts, as required by sustainable development. However, it is to suggest that key aspects of the WFD are being implemented in a highly technocratic way that is not readily available to public participation or scrutiny. The statement, at the commencement of the consultation document, that it was prepared for a 'regulatory readership' is tantamount to an admission of this. The concern is that critical issues in the implementation of the Directive are being re-characterised and determined in a way that is likely to be the exclusive preserve of a relatively small number of technically expert stakeholders.

On the other hand, this may show something important about the limits of public participation. Public participation presupposes that the issues at stake are issues on which the general public are likely to have opinions on which they will be willing to express a view. There is no difficulty about this where debate surrounds fairly tangible local impacts, but where issues can only be addressed by those conversant with the language of the specialist disciplines that are involved, the likelihood of any productive public discussion is limited. The problem, for implementation of the WFD, is that its practical implications have been seen to be less dependent upon generalities and more upon particularities, the technicality of which places them outside the potential sphere of public participation. For those committed to the benefits and furtherance of public participation, this may be regarded as a matter of concern. For those initially sceptical about the value of public participation, or those practically engaged in ensuring that tasks under the WFD are achieved in a timely, practical and cost-effective manner, it may be a seen as a recognition of the inevitable.

## 11. Concluding Observations

In conclusion, the concerns about the enforceability of the WFD, raised earlier, must be returned to: that it is over ambitious in its objectives, insufficient stringent in its legal formulation and too generous in the discretion that it gives to Member States in respect of implementation. Clearly, the half-term stocktaking that has been undertaken, of implementation progress in England and Wales, is unlikely to produce a categorical conclusion about these concerns and any attempt to provide one would probably be premature. Nonetheless, the 'glass-half-full' view is that the WFD has prompted momentous initiatives in water management which should yield major benefits in the quality of the aquatic environment in due course. The 'glass-half-empty' view is that the national approaches to implementation that have been reviewed suggest that actual achievement of good status by 2015 is likely to be the exception rather than the norm. If that happens, it might be seen to be due to a combination of the three concerns.

On the more specific concerns of the discussion, with public participation and proceduralisation, the following concluding observations may be offered. On public participation, the discussion has illustrated some of the incongruities between measures for public engagement which rest upon high ideals (democratisation and improved decision making) and the realities of applying complex environmental legislation in a member state that is committed to doing the minimum needed to secure compliance with EC obligations. It is simply too easy for the issues to move from the general concerns about the state of the water environment, on which members of the public are likely to have an opinion, to highly technical questions about operationalising methodologies that are the preserve of a relatively small number of specialists. It may be that public input could have an influence upon minor aspects of implementation, but many of the big issues have been effectively placed outside public debate by the technicalities involved.

On proceduralisation, the WFD has elements of substantive content, but these are greatly overshadowed by the breadth of those areas where national discretion on implementation prevails. Realisation of the good status objective, which seemed to be a key purpose of the Directive, is capable of being subsumed in its importance to the need to 'avoid' applying good status to waters wherever this is possible. Conceivably, the excessive exercise of national discretion in this way might be subject to scrutiny by the European Commission[96] and perhaps proceedings before the Court of Justice,[97] but it is far from clear in what circumstances intervention would be justified. The overall picture is that the 'new' content of the WFD (as opposed to those respects where it largely re-enacts pre-existing requirements) is strongly procedural. The aspects of national implementation practice that have been reviewed indicate that the various derogations, exceptions and defences under the Directive are likely to be exploited to the full in minimising the cost of implementation, with commensurate limitations to environmental improvement.

96 For a European Commission review of initial implementation of the WFD see, *Towards Sustainable Water Management in the European Union – First Stage in the Implementation of the Water Framework Directive 2000/60/EC* COM(2007) 128 and SEC(2007) 362 and 363.

97 Initial decisions of the European Court of Justice under the WFD have established failures to transpose the WFD or to provide timely reports in *Commission v Greece* (C-264/07, failure to report under Art 5), *Commission v Italy* (C-85/07, failure to report under Art 5) and *Commission v Luxembourg* (C-32/05, failure to communicate transposition legislation under Art 24). The decision concerning Luxembourg does contain some general observations on the character of the obligations under the WFD (see para 43, where it is noted that 'overall consideration of the directive shows that most of its provisions . . . require Member States to take the necessary measures to ensure that certain objectives . . . are attained, whilst leaving the Member States some discretion as to the nature of the measures to be taken). No case has yet come before the Court where the extent of the implementation discretion allowed to a member state has been directly scrutinised. On the review of implementation discretion more generally see C Hilson, 'Legality Review of Member State Discretion Under Directives' in T Tridimas and P Nebbia (eds) *European Law For the Twenty-first Centuary: Volume 1* (Hart, Oxford 2004).

# [22]

# REACH: Combining Harmonization and Dynamism in the Regulation of Chemicals

*Joanne Scott**

## 1. Introduction

Europe has a new Chemicals Agency. Its establishment is inextricably tied to the emergence in Europe of an ambitious new framework for the regulation of chemicals. This framework is known by the acronym REACH, and it concerns the **R**egistration, **E**valuation, **A**uthorisation and **R**estriction of **Ch**emical Substances.[1] The establishment of a *European* Agency, and the European-level *harmonization* of chemicals policy seems to mark an important step in the direction of a centralization of regulatory power. However, it is the argument of this chapter that reality is more complex, more subtle, and certainly more promising. The European Agency does not stand on high at the apex of a hierarchically organized system for the regulation of chemicals. It forms part of a system of governance which is intensely fractured. Power is shared among a multiplicity of actors, operating at different levels of government, and in the private as well as the public spheres. No single actor has autonomous decision-making power. Rather, each is empowered, in different circumstances and in different ways, to play a role in maintaining the dynamic quality of regulation in the face of information deficits and uncertain risks. Different actors can play a role in seeking to ensure the continuous generation of new and better information about risk and about the mitigation of risk, and in seeking to prompt regulatory decisions which are appropriately responsive to this. This fracturing of power creates a governance framework which is complex. But it is also a framework which seeks to combine,

* Many thanks to John Applegate, Maria Lee, and Peter Oliver for very useful comments on an earlier draft. The students in the EUI Academy (2007) were outstanding in helping me get to grips with the intricacies of REACH. Many thanks to them also.

[1] Regulation 1907/2006. This both lays down the REACH framework and establishes the European Chemicals Agency.

in a novel way, harmonization with dynamism, and uniformity with structures for regulatory learning.

In the year 2000 the Lisbon European Council framed an ambitious goal for Europe; in short, to become the most competitive and dynamic knowledge-based economy in the world. The chemicals sector is one in which Europe has achieved considerable economic success. Nearly half of the world's leading chemicals companies are based in Europe, and Europe enjoys a healthy and growing trade surplus in chemicals.[2] Nonetheless, until recently at least, Europe's chemicals regulation was not worthy of this success, representing an impediment to innovation, and an insufficient basis for sustainable growth. The reasons for this were many. But the pernicious bottom line was the incentive structure generated by the regulatory framework. There had grown up a regulatory gap in the treatment of old and new chemicals.[3] The regulatory burden attaching to new chemicals entering the market was such that it was easier and less costly to continue to use old chemicals which were largely exempt. The impetus to innovation was dulled and industry convenience came to prevail over safety. The EU's new chemicals regime represents an ambitious attempt to alter the incentive structure between old *and* new chemicals, and to do so in a manner which achieves a high level of protection of human health and the environment.

The volume and complexity of the Regulation is such that a lengthy book would be required to offer a full exposition and analysis. Running to 141 articles, 17 annexes, and 10 appendices, the densely printed Official Journal text amounts to 280 pages. At the heart of these 280 pages is a system for the regulation of old and new chemicals which makes the generation and dissemination of information about chemicals a priority. This information is intended to ensure that sensible decisions can be taken about which substances to focus investigative attention on, about when and how to restrict the use of chemicals, and about when to ban them completely. It is also intended to ensure that market transparency will create conditions in which chemical users—commercial users as well as consumers—will not only be properly informed about safe use, but will be able to exercise choices in favour of safer alternatives. When it comes to high-risk categories of chemicals, the availability of suitable and safer alternatives, will be a reason for the regulator to ban them.

In keeping with the theme of this volume as a whole, this contribution focuses upon the governance approach embodied in the REACH regulation, and upon

[2] For facts and figures on the European chemical industry see <http://www.cefic.be/factsandfigures/level02/profile_index.html>.

[3] For this purpose old chemicals are known as existing chemicals and are those dating from before 1981. See Koch, L. and Ashford, N.A., 'Rethinking the role of information in chemicals policy: implications for TSCA and REACH', *Journal of Cleaner Production* 14 (2006) 31 at <http://web.mit.edu/ctpid/www/tl/docs/Koch&Ashford1.pdf> for a brief overview and critique of the EU's chemical regime. See also for an excellent outline of the main elements and legal issues arising, Molyneux, C.G., 'Chemicals' (2008), 8 *Yearbook of European Environmental Law* (2008).

certain key features ('core elements') which characterize this. The core elements pinpointed in this paper are industry responsibility, contestability, substitution, provisionality, and transparency. Three observations, flowing from the discussion which follows, may be usefully highlighted from the start.

First, and perhaps most important, REACH is concerned with product regulation, the regulation of chemical substances. Product regulation here, as elsewhere, bears heavily on trade, in both the EU and the WTO. This trade dimension comes to the fore in the regulation. It is exhaustive in the harmonization which it achieves. It takes Article 95 as its legal basis, and contains a clear free movement clause. Member State recourse to the treaty-based free movement exceptions will be pre-empted. By contrast to much recent environmental law in the EU, the regulation is about harmonization not diversity, and offers reduced flexibility to Member States. But this surface impression does not tell the whole story. This is because the harmonization which it achieves is provisional and contestable. A wide range of mechanisms are established to allow for the contours of the provisional harmonization bargain to be contested, including in the light of experience in the individual Member States. At every turn, whether it is in relation to which substances are to be evaluated, which are to require authorization or restriction, or in relation to labelling requirements, Member States (and the Commission) are empowered, on the basis of clearly defined procedures, to seek to use their local knowledge to persuade the European Union as a whole, of the need to revise applicable norms, in order to ensure effective fulfilment of the Regulation's framework goals (high level of protection of human health and environment in particular). By contrast to the more traditional Article 95 EC Treaty opt-out, these procedures for contestation are multi-level and multi-actor, and eschew an approach which places the Commission on high, supposedly omniscient in its capacities to make judgements about regulatory right and wrong. Because of this, REACH offers an important lesson in thinking about governance in EU environmental law. By making harmonization provisional and contestable, and by creating mechanisms for contestation and regulatory learning, the EU has begun to articulate a model for regulatory federalism which seeks to respond to the imperatives of free trade *and* those of environmental/health protection.

Second, although in the form of a regulation, the implementation phase is all-important under REACH.[4] This becomes starkly clear by looking at the list of substances requiring authorization; empty at the time of enactment! The governance arrangements for the adoption of implementing decisions are varied and

[4] As John Applegate points out, it was at the implementation stage that the US chemicals regime in the form of the Toxic Substances Control Act, met its most pronounced failures. Careful scrutiny of implementation practices and decisions will be essential to any long-term evaluation of REACH. See Applegate, J. S., 'Synthesizing TCSA and REACH: Practical Principles for Chemical Regulation Reform', *Ecology Law Quarterly* forthcoming.

complex. As is typical, comitology procedures play an important part.[5] But on the whole the overall framework for decision-making is more inclusive than in the past.[6] This is not only a result of the enhanced role *sometimes* played by the European Parliament as a result of the new regulatory committee with scrutiny procedure.[7] It is also because interested third parties are given significant opportunities to participate in decision-making processes, and to have their viewpoints taken into account. In the discussion of substitution below, it is suggested that these opportunities for participation create a mildly adversarial mechanism, somewhat reminiscent of the kind that Wendy Wagner has in mind in her elaboration of a competition-based approach to the regulation of chemicals.[8]

Third, REACH places considerable emphasis upon information as a regulatory tool. At its heart, it is intended to mitigate the overwhelming data deficit which exists in relation to older chemical substances. REACH is also concerned with the communication of information, up and down the supply chain, and to consumers and to the public at large. As it stands, however, there exists an important gap. Labelling requirements relate only to chemical substances and preparations (mixtures of chemical substances). Consumer articles, such as textiles or furniture for example, containing chemical substances are not covered. Even where an article contains a chemical substance of very high concern (for example a carcinogenic substance) consumers will not be alerted to this by the presence of a label. Thus, to the extent that REACH seeks to harness the power of the marketplace to encourage innovation in the development of less risky alternatives, its labelling rules would seem to fall short.

The discussion which follows is often technical and dense. This is unavoidable when examining a regulatory regime of this volume and complexity. This should not be allowed to disguise either the intrinsic importance of the subject under discussion for environment and human health protection,[9] or the fascination of the governance forms which this regulation embodies. It is in the minutiae of law's construction of decision-making procedures and conditions for action that the politics of risk regulation are played out.

[5] For background to the concept of comitology see Craig, P. and de Búrca, G., *EU Law: Text, Cases and Materials* (OUP, 2007), pp. 118–23.

[6] See on this theme LSE Working Paper 07–2008, Heyvaert, V., 'The EU's Chemicals Policy: Towards Inclusive Governance?' at <http://www.lse.ac.uk/collections/law/wps/WPS2008-07_Heyvaert.pdf>.

[7] See again Craig and de Búrca, supra n. 5. For further details of the new regulatory committee with scrutiny procedure, see Article 5a Council Decision 1999/468. By 'sometimes', it is simply meant that this new procedure applies to some decisions to be adopted under REACH, but by no means all. Further details on this will emerge in the sections which follow.

[8] Wagner, W., 'Using Competition-Based Regulation to Bridge the Toxics Data Gap' at <http://search.ssrn.com/sol3/papers.cfm?abstract_id=1090090>.

[9] See, for a brief overview, chapter 1 of the Royal Society for Environmental Pollutions chemicals study at <http://www.rcep.org.uk/chreport.htm>.

## 2. Core Element: Industry Responsibility

### A. Registration

#### *1. What does registration require?*

REACH imposes an informational burden on industry. It does so through the introduction of a default rule: 'no data, no market',[10] generating a strong incentive for the information to be provided. Chemical substances manufactured or imported at or above a one tonne threshold must be registered with the new Chemicals Agency.[11] The Regulation establishes detailed rules for identifying substances requiring registration.[12] These include substances on their own, or in preparations (such as a detergent).[13] Also included are substances in articles, where the one tonne threshold is met, and where the substance is intended to be released under normal or reasonably foreseeable conditions of use.[14] Even where there is no intention that the substance be released, the Agency may require registration of substances in articles where it has grounds for suspecting that the substance is released and that this presents a risk to human health or the environment.[15] A number of substances enjoy total or partial exemptions under the regulation.[16]

[10] Article 5.

[11] Article 6(1). The threshold is determined at the level of an individual manufacturer or importer, and calculated on an annual basis. Note that in some situations a notification obligation will apply even in the absence of a registration requirement. This implies a much reduced informational burden but an informational burden all the same. See especially Article 9(2) in relation to the R & D exemption. See also n. 14 below in relation to notification of substances in articles under Article 7(2). Note also that the reference to 'notified substances' in Article 24 refers to a different concept. Here, notification under the old regime is being treated as registration for the purpose of the new one. On the Agency see Articles 75–111 and: <http://echa.europa.eu/>.

[12] The general definitions are provided in Article 3 where the concept of a substance is defined as a chemical element and its compounds in the natural state or obtained by any manufacturing process, including any additive necessary to preserve its stability and any impurity deriving from the process used, but excluding any solvent which may be separated without affecting the stability of the substance or changing its composition.

[13] Article 6(1). A preparation is defined in Article 3(2) as a mixture or solution composed of two or more substances.

[14] An article is defined in Article 3(3) as an object which during production is given a special shape, surface, or design which determines its function to a greater degree than does its chemical composition. Note a reduced obligation to notify (as opposed to register) the Agency of substances of very high concern in articles, where it is present above a concentration of 0.1% w/w, even where it is not intended to be released. The concept of substances of very high concern will be raised in the discussion below on authorization. This lesser notification obligation can only be excluded where the producer or importer can exclude exposure to humans or to the environment during normal or reasonably foreseeable conditions of use. See Articles 7(2) and (3). Registration would thus seem to rest on a subjective test (intended to be released), whereas notification rests upon an objective test.

[15] Article 7(5). This is still subject to the one tonne threshold. The Agency's decision is not subject to appeal by the Agency Board of Appeal (see Article 91) but it is susceptible to review by the Court of First Instance (see Article 94).

[16] See in particular Articles 2 and Annexes IV and V. Included among other things in Annex V are substances occurring in nature if they are not chemically modified or dangerous.

Prominent among these are polymers,[17] and certain intermediaries.[18] Likewise, substances manufactured or imported for the purposes of product or process oriented research and development are automatically exempted for five years.[19] This may be extended, upon request, by the Agency for a further five-year period; ten years in the case of medicinal products for human or veterinary use.[20]

The registration requirement took effect for new substances on 1 June 2007. Existing substances, known as phase-in substances, are able to benefit from transitional arrangements.[21] For these substances registration will proceed in stages, beginning in 2010 for very high volume substances and for certain risky substances, and ending in 2018.[22] Pre-registration is required for phase-in substances seeking to benefit from these transitional arrangements.[23] Upon submission of a registration document, the Agency will perform a completeness check. Where a registrant receives no indication to the contrary from the Agency within a three-week period, it may begin or continue to manufacture or import the substance in question.[24]

The intensity of the informational burden imposed by REACH is variable. First, and critically, the basic requirement rests upon an open-ended standard, rather than a detailed rule. This requires that each registrant must submit a technical dossier, and this must include all physico-chemical, toxicological, and

[17] These are exempted from registration, although requirements may be extended in the future to polymers where a practicable and cost-effective way of identifying risky polymers is established. Polymers are large molecules consisting of repeated chemical units joined together. Plastics are polymers, for example.

[18] Intermediaries are chemicals used to make other chemical substances. On-site and transported isolated intermediaries are subject to limited registration requirements subject to the substance being rigorously contained during its whole life-cycle. Monomers used for this purpose do not fall within this. See Articles 17–19.

[19] Article 9.

[20] See Article 9(7) for the conditions which apply. Any decision taken by the Agency here will be subject to appeal.

[21] Article 23. See Article 3(2) for a confusing definition of the concept of phase-in substances. These include substances included in the European Inventory of Existing Chemical Substances (EINECS). Note that where an existing substance has been notified under the earlier regime under Directive 67/548, this will be regarded as a registration for the purpose of REACH. See Article 24. The aim of the regulation is to address the 'burden of the past' meaning substances not covered by the earlier regime.

[22] Very high volume means 1,000 tonnes or more here, and the risky substances to be registered by 2010 are those which are category 1 carcinogens, mutagens, or reproductive toxicants (CMRs) (no volume threshold) and those which are very toxic to the aquatic environment posing risks of long-term adverse effects (100 tonne threshold). See Article 23(1).

[23] Article 28. The relevance of this will become clear when talking about joint submission and data-sharing below.

[24] See Article 20(2) on the completeness check and Article 21(1) on timing. Note that the Agency has a three-month rather than a three-week period to respond in relation to phase-in substances registered within two months of the end of the transitional period. This is presumably due to concerns about the high number of last-minute registrations which will be submitted at this time, and reflects the fact that there are considerably more existing than new substances.

ecotoxicological information that is *relevant* and *available* to the registrant.[25] This standard is accompanied by more specific rules setting out the minimum information to be included. In the main, the nature of this minimum will be determined by reference to volume.[26] For registered substances, more information is demanded as production volume increases. For the lowest tonnage level (up to 10 tonnes) the standard requirements in Annex VII will apply.[27] Every time a new tonnage threshold is reached (10 tonnes, 100 tonnes, and 1,000 tonnes) an additional annex will bite, imposing additional informational demands. Information on the intrinsic properties of substances may be generated by means other than tests, provided that the conditions set out in Annex XI are met.[28] Indeed, wherever possible, information shall be generated by means other than vertebrate animal tests,[29] and all available *in vitro* data, *in vivo* data, historical human data, data from valid qualitative or quantitative structure-agency relationships ((Q) SAR), and from structurally related substances (read-across approach) is to be assessed first before new tests are carried out.[30] But as noted, such data will only be able to substitute for the results of the standard testing regime where they meet the requirements of Annex XI. These are expressed in open-ended, standard-based, terms; adequacy, reliability, and scientific validity for example. It will be for the Agency to evaluate registration documents to ensure that these requirements have been met.[31]

Two additional points may be usefully made in relation to the nature of the informational burden incurred by industry. First, Annex IX and X apply at the 100 tonne and 1,000 tonne marks respectively. In each case, the registration is to include testing proposals for the provision of the specified information, rather than the information itself; subject to the broad disclosure standard set out above.[32] It will be for the Agency to examine testing proposals, and to draft a decision accepting, rejecting, modifying, or supplementing the testing proposals.[33] Second, the 10 tonne volume threshold is of particular pertinence.

[25] Article 12(1). A guidance note on information requirements is set out in Annex VI, but does little to build upon this. It does make it clear that registrants have to be somewhat proactive in collating information by, for example, undertaking a literature search.

[26] There is one exception to this. More information has to be submitted for Annex III phase-in substances than non-Annex III phase-in substances. For the latter no toxicological or ecotoxicological information is required, but only physico-chemical information in accordance with s. 7 of Annex VII. Annex III substances include category 1 and 2 CMRs, as well as substances with dispersive or diffuse effects for which it is predicted that they are likely to meet the classification criteria for any human health or environmental effects endpoints under Directive 67/548.

[27] Subject to the previous footnote for non-Annex III phase-in substances.

[28] Article 13(1). [29] Ibid.

[30] Annex VII, penultimate Recital.

[31] It will do so in the course of dossier evaluation to be discussed below. See especially Article 41 (1)(b) and the rubric to Annex XI.

[32] See Article 12(d) and (e) and Annexes IX and X.

[33] Article 40(3). Where any Member State proposes an amendment to the Agency draft decision, and where the Member State committee is not unanimous in its support, the final decision will be adopted by the Commission on the basis of a regulatory committee procedure.

It is at this stage that the obligation to conduct a chemical safety assessment and to submit a chemical safety report (CSR) kicks in.[34] This will require human health, environment, and physico-chemical hazard assessments, as well as an assessment of whether the substance may be characterized as persistent, bioaccumulative and toxic, or very persistent and very bioacumulative (PBT/vPvB). For dangerous substances and those which are PBT/vPvB, an enhanced CSR will be required, to include an exposure assessment and risk characterization.[35]

## 2. *Industry accountability in registration*

It has been suggested that REACH creates perverse incentives for industry. '[P]roducers have an incentive to underestimate risk in order to avoid outside intervention into self-regulation. This seems to be a key governance problem of REACH.'[36] It is then essential to consider the range of mechanisms put in place in an attempt to keep industry honest and forthcoming in its provision of information. Two principal mechanisms are put in place; one premised upon hierarchical oversight, and the other upon peer review.

Hierarchical control is largely predicated upon the concept of dossier evaluation.[37] This involves two core elements, an examination of testing proposals and a compliance check of registrations.[38] Where, on the basis of compliance checking, the Agency concludes that the registration is not in line with the relevant information requirements, it may prepare a draft decision requiring the registrant to submit additional information.[39] For compliance checking, the Agency is required to examine at least 5% of registrations in each tonnage band.[40] It shall give priority, 'but not exclusively', to certain categories of registrations, namely those falling short in providing the standard Annex VII information, those concerning priority substances included on the Agency rolling action plan for substance evaluation, and those in respect of which specified information has

[34] See Article 14 and also Annex I containing general provisions for assessing substances and preparing chemical safety reports. Annex I, unlike the previously mentioned Annex IV, is not framed as a guidance note.

[35] Article 14(4) and Annex I, sections 5 and 6.

[36] Hey, C., Jacob, K., and Vokery, A., 'Better Regulation by New Governance Hybrids: Governance Models and the Reform of European Chemical Policy', Environmental Policy Research Centre paper at <http://papers.ssrn.com/sol3/papers.cfm?abstract_id=926980> p. 13.

[37] Title VI, chapter 1.

[38] Compliance checking should be contrasted to the previously mentioned concept of a completeness check under Article 20. By contrast to compliance checking, the completeness check 'shall not include an assessment of the quality or the adequacy of any data or justifications submitted', and is more a tick-box exercise about the categories of information received.

[39] Article 41(3). The procedure for the final adoption of this decision is laid down in Articles 50 and 51. In essence, the Agency enjoys autonomy unless it receives a Member State proposal for the amendment of its draft decision. In this event, the Agency can only decide if it enjoys the unanimous support of the Member State committee, otherwise the Commission will decide acting on the basis of a regulatory committee procedure.

[40] Article 41(5). This percentage may be varied on the basis of a regulatory committee with scrutiny procedure. See Article 41(7).

been submitted separately rather than jointly by manufacturers and/or importers.[41] Also of practical assistance in assisting the Agency in concentrating its compliance checking efforts, is the fact that any technical dossier submitted upon registration must indicate, for certain key categories of information, where this has been subject to review by an assessor prior to submission.[42] While there is no requirement that any such assessor be independent, it is stated that he or she must have appropriate experience. It may well be in the interests of companies to flag up the existence of internal procedures for review, in a bid to obviate the need for time-consuming and costly external review.

One of the stated grounds for prioritizing registrations for compliance checking hints at the nature of the second, non-hierarchical, mechanism for promoting industry accountability in the provision of information. The regulation establishes a binding, but non-absolute, requirement that key information, including physico-chemical, toxicological, and ecotoxicological information be jointly submitted by manufacturers and/or importers, with one registrant acting as lead registrant for this purpose.[43] A registrant may offer a reasoned justification for separate submission of this information on specified grounds only. These are disproportionate cost, substantial commercial detriment caused by the commercially sensitive nature of the information, and disagreement with the lead registrant on the selection of information.[44]

The mechanics of joint registration are different in the case of non phase-in (new) and phase-in (existing) substances. For non phase-in substances, potential registrants have a duty to inquire from the Agency whether a registration has already been submitted for the same substance.[45] If several potential registrants have made an inquiry for the same substance, the Agency shall inform each about the other, thus facilitating joint registration. For phase-in substances seeking to benefit from the transitional arrangements, there is a duty to pre-register, and to participate in a substance information exchange forum (SIEF).[46] Among other things, this SIEF will facilitate the exchange of key information including the physico-chemical, toxicological, and ecotoxicological information to be jointly submitted.

41 Article 41(5).

42 This relates to physico-chemical, toxicological, and ecotoxicological information under Annexes VII–XI, as well as chemical safety reports and information on manufacture, use, and classification and labelling of a substance.

43 See Article 11 referring to categories of information in Article 10. These categories of information are, in turn, spelt out in greater detail in Article 12. Certain additional categories of information *may* be jointly submitted at the discretion of the manufacturers/importers, including the chemical safety report, while others *must* be submitted separately, including specified information on manufacture, use, and exposure.

44 Article 11(3).

45 Article 26. This also applies to phase-in substances which are not making use of the Article 23 transitional arrangements.

46 Articles 28 and 29.

It is possible to speculate that the concept of joint registration might promote industry accountability in the provision of information, by inculcating an ethos of peer review. Where a manufacturer or importer disagrees with the information to be submitted, that manufacturer or importer may justify remaining outside of the registration consortium. Any attempt on the part of a registrant to manipulate data, or to be less than forthcoming in sharing relevant (unreliable) data, runs the risk of being signalled to the Agency by an absence of cooperation between industry actors in registration. As noted, departure from the default position of joint registration serves to increase the likelihood of hierarchical, Agency, compliance control; the fact of individual submission being one of the factors according to which the Agency will concentrate its efforts in compliance checking. Needless to say, the accountability reinforcing potential of joint submission is, even at best, less than absolute. It would do nothing to prevent industry consortia from collectively withholding or manipulating data.

Along with joint registration, data sharing also emerges as a key feature of REACH.[47] This is intended in large part to avoid and reduce vertebrate animal testing.[48] It is interesting to ask whether it might serve also to facilitate industry accountability in the provision of information.

For registered substances, information submitted as part of registration will become freely available after twelve years.[49] Even during this period, previous registrants have an obligation to share information with potential registrants in so far as this information involves testing on vertebrate animals.[50] Even where a substance has not been previously registered, all potential registrants participating in a SIEF are obliged to request and share data involving testing on vertebrate animals.[51] Again, subject to rules on cost-sharing, any holder of such a study will be precluded from proceeding to registration until he provides the study in question.[52] If a relevant study involving tests (all tests, and not merely tests on vertebrate animals) is not available, only one such study will be conducted per

[47] See Title III, Articles 25–30. This will be facilitated by initiatives not formally part of the REACH framework. See for example the launch by OECD of eChemPortal: The Global Portal to Information on Chemical Substances. This Internet gateway provides free access to information on intrinsic properties of chemicals as well as hazard and risk assessments. It allows for the simultaneous search of multiple databases.

[48] See Article 13 and Annex XI establishing the range of data sources which can be used to provide information on intrinsic properties on substances, and adumbrating the circumstances in which this can be used.

[49] See Articles 26(3) and 27(1).

[50] Article 27(1). Previous registrants may choose to share other categories of information. Article 27 lays down the procedure to be followed where there is no agreement between previous and potential registrants. Subject to rules on cost-sharing, ultimately the Agency will disclose the relevant information. The Agency's decision will be subject to appeal.

[51] Article 30.

[52] Article 30(3).

information requirement within the SIEF for the benefit of all members, and the resulting information duly shared.[53]

While in some respects the regulation does anticipate disagreements between registrants (actual and potential) on data sharing,[54] it does not contemplate circumstances in which one registrant remains dissatisfied with the content or methodology of a study conducted by another registrant. Not only does it not impose an obligation on a registrant to repeat the study in these circumstances, but neither does it expressly permit it to do so. Yet from the point of view of industry accountability it is critical that received wisdom be susceptible to challenge. In view of this, the underlying premise that testing on vertebrate animals be undertaken only as a last resort, and that the duplication of other tests should be limited, must be read as leaving room for additional testing where the reliability of existing data has been credibly questioned. The concept of data sharing is an important one. It has the potential to strengthen arrangements for peer review between industry actors by increasing transparency and mutual oversight. At the same time peer review cannot function in a meaningful manner if earlier tests, and the results emanating from them, are treated as anything more than presumptively valid.

## B. Applications for Authorization

Certain substances of 'very high concern' may not be placed on the market without authorization, even at very low volume, and below the one tonne threshold for registration.[55] These substances are to be listed in Annex XIV.[56] When seeking authorization, applicants must 'analyse the availability of alternatives and consider their risks, and the technical and economic feasibility of substitution'.[57] Applicants must likewise submit the specified information, including a chemical safety report where this has not been previously submitted as part of the registration process.[58]

Like registration, authorization imposes an informational burden on industry. But it does more than this. In most cases authorization will be granted where the risk to human health or the environment is adequately controlled. It will be for the applicant to document this in its CSR.[59] This will require the applicant to

[53] Article 30(2). The members of the SIEF shall take reasonable steps to reach agreement as to who is to carry out the test. If no agreement is reached, the Agency shall specify who is to perform it. Again, this is subject to cost-sharing requirements.

[54] See Articles 27(5)–(7) and 30(3).

[55] Article 55 for the terminology of very high concern. This applies to substances on their own, in preparations and incorporated into articles.

[56] We will look later, in the next section on contestability, at how the content of this list is to be determined. At the time of adoption of the regulation, the Annex was empty.

[57] Article 55 and Article 62(4)(e).

[58] See Article 62 specifying the information to be submitted, and especially Article 62(4)(d). Note Article 62(5)(a) leaving applicants the discretion as to whether to submit a socio-economic analysis.

[59] Article 60(2).

show that estimated exposure falls within the relevant exposure limits, and that the likelihood and severity of an event occurring due to the physico-chemical properties of the substance is negligible.[60] The relevant authorities will assess whether the applicant has made his case, taking expert advice, but it is plain that the burden of proof falls upon the applicant.[61]

There is perhaps more ambiguity about burden of proof for those substances made subject to different authorization conditions. For PBTs/vPvBs, and substances for which no exposure limits can be determined, authorization will only be granted 'if it is shown that socio-economic benefits outweigh the risk to human health or the environment', and where there are no suitable, less risky alternatives.[62] The regulation is not explicit in identifying who bears the burden of demonstrating this. While an analysis of alternatives must be submitted as part of the application package, it is up to the applicant to decide whether to submit a socio-economic analysis.[63] While the various information submitted by the applicant will represent an element to be considered in reaching a decision, ultimately the decision will take into account all available information on risk and on the availability of alternatives.[64] A positive authorization decision may in principle be reached on the basis of information not brought forward by the applicant. Still though, in essence, the role of the applicant will be to persuade the regulator that the conditions for authorization are met, and to refute available information which might suggest otherwise.

Authorization, like registration, places an information burden on industry. In the case of authorization, it does so by reference to substantive standards, such as that represented by the concept of adequate control. Information and arguments submitted by industry in the course of authorization will not be taken at face value. It will be evaluated by experts including, where they deem it appropriate, in the light of additional information submitted by third parties.[65] Equally though, the claims of the experts will not always go unchallenged, with applicants enjoying an opportunity to make further comments along the way.[66] For the

[60] Section 6.4, Annex I. The exposure limits are in the form of Derived No-Effect Levels for human health (the level of exposure to the substance above which humans should not be exposed. See sections 1.0.2 and 1.4 of Annex I); and Predicted No-Effect Concentrations for environmental effects (see sections 3.0.1 and 3.3.1, Annex I).

[61] Note that Article 61(1) provides that the applicant submit an updated CSR as part of the process for the review of authorizations '[i]f he can demonstrate that the risk is adequately controlled'. 'Demonstrate' clearly places the burden of proof on the applicant. It is suggested that 'document' does so also.

[62] Article 60(4). As we will see below, the suitability of alternatives implies an assessment of their technical and economic feasibility for the applicant.

[63] Recall Article 62(5).

[64] Article 60(4).

[65] The procedure for authorization will be considered more fully below. By experts what is meant here are the relevant committees on Risk Assessment and Socio-Economic Analysis. See generally Article 64, especially Article 64(3) and (4).

[66] Article 64(5) ensuring that the EU administrative law requirement of right to be heard is complied with.

substances concerned, the default position is one of prohibition. It is not for the regulator to justify this, but for the potential user to challenge it. It is only when the potential user succeeds in making a prima facie case that the conditions laid down are met, that the regulator will incur a burden of justification to justify a ban.

## 3. Core Element: Contestability

One of the most intriguing, and potentially important, aspects of REACH is the way in which it combines harmonization with provisionality and contestability. The now dominant model of environmental regulation in the EU, premised upon substantive flexibility and proceduralization, is not well suited to product regulation in areas where uniformity is required in order to ensure the proper functioning of the European internal market. This presents a dilemma. Harmonization may be anticipated to come at the price of sacrificing the benefits of a more flexible approach. There is an upside to flexibility in that it is tolerant of regulatory diversity, and hence creates opportunities for regulatory learning on the basis of diverse Member State experience in implementation. Harmonization, on the contrary, by definition demands a singular response and would seem to exclude a role for Member States as laboratories for regulatory experimentation and learning. REACH, though, takes an imaginative step towards addressing this dilemma, and does so by inculcating the regime with the overlapping values of provisionality and contestability.

REACH takes Article 95 as its legal basis, and takes the form of exhaustive harmonization. Substances which comply with the regulation can be traded freely in the EU.[67] Recourse to the treaty-based free movement exceptions will be pre-empted.[68] But still, the Member States are not silenced. The regulation, and to a lesser extent the Treaty, preserve spaces for Member State contestation of the trade/regulation bargain struck. The contours of that bargain are provisional, and Member States are empowered in multiple ways to seek to destabilize it. There remains space for local knowledge to be integrated in a bid to provoke regulatory change. This local knowledge having been presented, the burden then falls on the EU decision-maker to justify its decision in relation to it, including from the point of the regulation's broad objectives, and in a manner which is compatible

[67] Article 128.

[68] Article 129. But note that, consistent with the case law of the European Court, recourse to these exceptions will be precluded only to the extent that the issue is covered by the harmonizing measure. This is apparent from Case 5/94 *Hedley Lomas* and reinforced by Article 128(2). So, for example, if a Member State wanted to restrict a chemical substance more strictly, for reasons not covered by REACH, it would remain free to do so, subject to the demands of other legislation, and with complying with the conditions in the Treaty-based free movement exceptions.

with the precautionary principle which underpins the regulation as a whole.[69] To this end, five particular points of entry are established in the regulation, and a further point of entry exists in the treaty. Each will be discussed in turn.

## A. Substance Evaluation

It is for the European Chemicals Agency (the Agency) to draw up a list of priority substances for evaluation by Member States.[70] It will draw up a three-year rolling action plan of substances to be evaluated. Using risk-based criteria developed in cooperation with Member States,[71] and on the basis of an opinion from the Member State committee,[72] the Agency shall include substances in respect of which there are grounds for considering that they constitute a risk to human health or the environment. A Member State may notify the Agency at any time of a substance not on the list, whenever it is in possession of information that suggests that it is a priority for evaluation.[73] The Agency has the final word, and its decision is not subject to appeal before the Board of Appeal.[74] But still there is room for Member State contestation, placing a burden of justification on the Agency to explain why it has rejected the Member State's suggestion. The Agency *shall* include substances where there are grounds in any appropriate source of information, including presumably in a Member State petition, that it presents a risk, and hence a refusal to add a substance at the behest of a Member State would be subject to judicial review before the courts.

## B. Substances Requiring Authorization

REACH establishes a prior authorization requirement for substances of 'very high concern'.[75] Unlike the registration requirement, this bites regardless of production volume. The regulation establishes definitively that this will apply to certain categories of substance. These include those which are category 1 or 2 carcinogens, mutagens, or reproductive toxicants.[76] It also applies to PBTs and vPvBs in so far as they meet the criteria set out in Annex XIII.[77]

Beyond this, however, the concept of a substance of very high concern remains open-ended. Additional substances may be subjected to this prior authorization requirement when they meet certain criteria and when they are added to the Annex XIV list.[78] The applicable threshold is a high one. It captures substances in

[69] See Article 1(1) for a statement of these objectives, and Article 1(3) for the inclusion of the precautionary principle.

[70] See Articles 44–48.

[71] These criteria shall consider hazard information, exposure information, and tonnage. See Article 44(1).

[72] See Article 44(2).

[73] Article 45(5).

[74] Article 93.

[75] Article 55.

[76] Article 57(a–c).

[77] Article 57(d–e).

[78] Article 57(f).

respect of which there is scientific evidence of probable serious effects to human health or the environment and which give rise to a level of concern which is equivalent to those of the other substances specifically listed.[79]

The process for adding or removing substances to the Annex XIV authorization list is a complex one. It culminates in the adoption of a decision on the basis of the regulatory committee with scrutiny procedure, the new comitology procedure enhancing the powers of the European Parliament.[80] Along the way Member States are empowered to push in the direction of the inclusion of additional substances, by arguing in favour of their inclusion on a preliminary candidate list.[81] In particular any Member State may choose to submit a dossier for substances which it believes meet the various criteria laid down, to forward this to the Agency. Interested parties will be given an opportunity to comment on this. In the absence of any such comments from interested parties, or from the Agency itself, the substance in question will be added to the candidate list. Where comments are received the matter will go to the Member State committee. In the absence of unanimity in this committee, a decision to add the substance to the candidate list of substances requiring authorization will be taken on the basis of a regulatory committee procedure, namely the older procedure not involving the European Parliament to any significant degree.[82] Of course, inclusion on the candidate list at the behest of a Member State does not imply inevitable inclusion on the final list. What is less clear is whether inclusion on the candidate list is a prerequisite for inclusion on the final list. This is an important question given the different procedures which apply: regulatory committee for the candidate list and regulatory committee with scrutiny for the final list, reflecting a greater role for the European Parliament in respect of the adoption of the final list. The capacity of the European Parliament to use its veto powers to bargain for the inclusion of additional substances will be greatly curtailed if the final list may only include those previously included on the candidate list, in respect of the drawing up of

[79] Substances with endocrine disrupting properties, or PBTs and vPvBs not meeting the Annex XIII criteria are given by way of examples of the kind of substances which might meet this threshold.

[80] Article 58(1) and Article 58(8). This is the procedure referred to in Article 133(4) of the Regulation. It refers to Article 5a of Council Decision 1999/468, which was recently introduced by Council Decision 2006/512. A full discussion of the various comitology forms is outwith the scope of this chapter. Suffice it to note that under this new procedure the European Parliament, like the Council, can veto the Commission's draft decision, on the basis that it exceeds the implementing powers conferred by the basic instrument (REACH in this case), or that the draft decision is not compatible with the aim or content of that basic instrument, or does not respect the principles of subsidiarity and proportionality. This is an important constitutional development as it puts the Parliament on a more even footing with Council in the adoption of implementing (executive) acts, as is already the case in respect of legislative enactments in most areas under the EC Treaty.

[81] See Article 59 which lays down the opportunities and obligations of Member States in this respect, and the relevant decision-making procedure.

[82] That is to say that the candidate list will be adopted in this event by regulatory committee procedure, whereas the final list will be adopted on the basis of a regulatory committee with scrutiny procedure. The regulatory committee procedure is that referred to in Article 133(3) and this, in turn, refers to Article 5 of the comitology decision, supra n. 80.

which the European Parliament is not much involved. Also, in that the Member States' contestatory powers bite only in relation to the candidate list, the more preliminary authority enjoyed by this, the more influential their contestation may be anticipated to be.

To my mind it seems unlikely that the final list must draw exclusively from substances included on the candidate list.[83] Were this to be the case, priority substances included in an Agency recommendation for inclusion in the final list[84] would have to be ignored if that substance did not also appear on the candidate list for inclusion. It is notable in thinking about this, that the Agency does not enjoy an autonomous right of initiative in relation to the candidate list. Only the Member States and the Commission may set in train the process of seeking to have a substance included on this candidate list.[85]

## C. Restrictions

Annex XVII contains a list of restrictions concerning the manufacture, use or placing on the market of substances. This may be amended where there is an unacceptable risk to human health or the environment which needs to be addressed at Community level.[86] Member States may seek to contest the boundaries of Annex XVII by setting in train a procedure to consider its amendment, where it considers that the risk presented by a substance is not adequately controlled and needs to be addressed.[87] Where this demonstrates that action on a Community-wide basis is necessary, it shall submit this dossier to the Agency in order to initiate the restrictions process. The detail of the process for the adoption of new restrictions will be considered alongside the process for the adoption of authorization decisions below.

## D. Harmonized Classification and Labelling

The regulation provides for harmonized classification and labelling of certain substances, and specifically for CMR (categories 1–3) and for respiratory sensitizers.[88] These shall 'normally' be added to Annex I of Directive 67/548. Harmonized classification and labelling may also be provided for 'other effects' on a

[83] Although it is clear that this could be implied by the language of Article 59(1) which presents the role of the candidate list as being such as to identify which substances meet the Article 57 criteria.

[84] See Article 58(3) and (4).

[85] Article 59(2) and (3). When the Commission exercises its right to initiate this procedure, it will ask the Agency to prepare a dossier on its behalf. But the Agency cannot, independent of instructions from the Commission, move to the preparation of a dossier of this kind.

[86] Article 68(1).

[87] Also the Commission may request the Agency to prepare a dossier of this kind. The Agency will do so when it considers that there is a risk to human health or the environment which is not adequately controlled. See Article 69(1) and (2).

[88] Article 115.

case-by-case basis if justification is provided demonstrating a need for Community-level action. The competent authorities of Member States may submit proposals to the Agency to this effect.[89] The Agency committee for risk assessment will adopt an opinion on this proposal, giving the parties concerned the opportunity to comment, and the Agency shall forward the opinion and comments for the adoption of a decision under Article 4(1) of Directive 67/548.[90]

## E. Member State Safeguards

Article 129 establishes a Member State safeguard clause. This provides for the adoption of provisional (maximum 60 days) protective measures where a Member State has justifiable grounds for believing that urgent action is essential to protect human health or the environment. This is subject to an oversight procedure, whereby the Commission, acting on the basis of a regulatory committee procedure, will decide whether to authorize or approve the provisional measures. Where the provisional measure is approved, the Commission shall consider whether the regime as a whole needs to be adapted, and the Member State in question is required to initiate a Community-wide restrictions process as discussed above.

## F. Article 95 EC[91]

Whenever an EU legal act is based on Article 95 of the EC Treaty, certain 'opt-outs' are constitutionally guaranteed by Article 95(4) and 95(5). Though subject to a common procedure, the two sub-paragraphs differ in their scope. Article 95 (5) relates to the adoption by Member States of a new regulatory measure after the enactment at EU level of the harmonization measure in question. This is narrowly drawn, justifiable only on grounds relating to the protection of the environment or working environment, and even then only due to the emergence of new scientific evidence relating to a problem specific to that Member State. The Article 94(4) opt-out, by contrast, relates to the maintenance of national measures in place even before the enactment of the EU harmonizing act. The range of grounds on which Member States may rely is broader, including those specified in Article 30, as well as environment and working environment. Thus, for example, this would include public health.

[89] As with the candidate list for authorization and new restrictions proposals, the Member State shall submit an Annex XV dossier setting out the justification.

[90] Article 115(2). The formulation here in terms of participation is different, concerned as it is with 'parties concerned' rather than 'interested parties'.

[91] Note also Article 67(3) providing that Member States may maintain any existing and more stringent restrictions in force, relative to Annex XVII, until 1 June 2013, subject to their being notified according to the Treaty. The deadline for notification is not set out but it must be before 1 June 2009, as the Commission is required to publish an inventory of notified restrictions by this date. Many thanks to Peter Oliver for clarifying this point for me.

Under the Article 95 opt-outs, it is for the Commission to approve or reject the national provisions in question, usually within a six-month period. For this reason, Member States are obliged to notify their measures to the Commission. Any measure not so notified will be deprived of legal effects. In the course of reaching its decision, the Commission will scrutinize compliance with the various conditions, and verify also that the measure does not constitute a disproportionate obstacle to the functioning of the internal market.[92] As the recent Austrian case concerning genetically modified organisms shows, the Commission's decision will be susceptible to judicial review.[93] Where a Member State measure is authorized, it will be for the Commission to examine whether to propose an adaptation to the harmonizing measure in relation to which the Member State is opting out.[94]

The Article 95 opt-outs (or their predecessors) have been invoked nineteen times by Member States in relation to chemicals, with Member State measures receiving approval on thirteen occasions.[95]

Article 95 has something in common with the other channels for contestation in REACH; not least the fact that a successful Member State opt-out acts as a catalyst for the Commission to consider proposing an adaptation to the regulatory bargain for the Community as a whole. By contrast to the other mechanisms though, it is the Commission alone which is responsible for making a determination about whether to reject or approve the application in question. In this setting the Commission is unconstrained by either comitology or other consultation requirements.[96]

## G. Contestability: The Limitations

It is apparent from the above that the Member States enjoy multiple opportunities to contest the harmonized settlement represented by the regulation. They may do so by exploiting the opt-out possibilities established under Article 95 EC or by the safeguard clause in REACH. These possibilities are quite narrowly drawn. More particularly, and more unusually, Member States may also contest the boundaries of the regulatory settlement by setting in train a process of

[92] To preserve the useful effect of these opt-outs, the Commission read the 'no obstacle' requirement as meaning 'no disproportionate obstacle'.

[93] Joined Cases C-439/05 P and C-454/05 P *Land Oberösterreich and Austria v. Commission* (judgment of 13 September 2007).

[94] So, for example, in relation to the Dutch example above, the Commission had proposed an amendment to the EU framework governing creosote and creosote-treated wood.

[95] See the list at: <http://ec.europa.eu/enterprise/chemicals/legislation/derogations/index_en.htm>.

[96] For a recent discussion of the limits to even the applicant Member State's right to be heard, see Cases C-439/05 P and C-454/05 P Land *Oberösterreich and Republic of Austria v. Commission*. Here the ECJ places emphasis upon the importance of achieving a speedy resolution of such issues, without time-consuming information exchange (para. 41).

reflection, according to which there will be detailed and reasoned contemplation of the need for change. Member States are accountable in making recourse to these procedures, not least through the frequent requirement that their bid for change be accompanied by a dossier which lays down the reasons for this and the evidence on which the conclusion of that Member State is based. The contours of such dossiers are set out in Annex XV.

Like the Member States, the Commission too enjoys certain opportunities to launch such processes. This is most apparent when it comes to the drawing up of the candidate list of substances requiring authorization, and in relation to the restrictions process.[97] That said, the Commission's powers are more circumscribed, notably in respect of the restrictions procedure.[98] Here, the conclusion of the Commission that a substance poses a risk will be examined by the Agency. The Agency will not automatically draw up a dossier upon request by the Commission but will do so only where it shares the Commission's view that the substance poses a risk which is not adequately controlled, and that action on a Community-wide basis is necessary.[99]

Still, this leaves the question of which other actors enjoy these formal opportunities to destabilize the settlement, and to contest the boundaries of the regulation. Two observations are pertinent here.

First, the Agency's autonomous capacity to do so is limited. While it is a central actor in all of the decision-making processes, regardless of where the initiative to contest originates, its powers to contest directly the regime's existing boundaries are constrained. Of course it enjoys considerable autonomy in drawing up the rolling action plan of substances to be made subject to evaluation.[100] And it is empowered to recommend substances for inclusion on the final list of those requiring authorization.[101] Beyond this it is an agent of the Commission, being made responsible for the preparation of a dossier, at the Commission's request, in respect of the candidate list of substances and the restrictions process. It is particularly significant that the Agency enjoys no independent right of initiative in seeking to launch a restrictions process.

Second, although interested parties are offered multiple opportunities to make their views known in the course of adopting implementation decisions, including

[97] See Article 59(2) and Article 69(1).

[98] The Commission does not enjoy the same powers to contest in respect of substance evaluation, harmonized classification and labelling, or the safeguard clause. Though recall the discussion above about the emergency powers of the Commission in the context of review of authorization decisions.

[99] Article 69(1) and (2). This is in contrast to the Commission's contestatory role in respect of authorization, where a Commission request to the Agency to draw up a dossier to consider a substance for inclusion on the candidate list will not be second-guessed by the Agency but carried out without question. See Article 59(2). This probably reflects the Agency's own role in recommending substances for inclusion on the final list under Article 58(3). This provides the Agency with the opportunity to make its own views known.

[100] See again Articles 44–48.

[101] Article 58(3).

in the course of drawing up the candidate and final lists of substances requiring authorization, and in relation to the restrictions process, such interested parties are not empowered themselves to set in train the various reflection processes. Neither industry actors or NGO voices, nor academics or other experts, are given formal recognition as catalysts for revision in the light of new information or better understanding. As noted, the boundaries of the regime are porous. But the range of actors which can seek to alter them is noticeably confined. It is to be regretted that other persons or organizations do not enjoy the capacity to bring forth evidence-based dossiers to launch formal inquiries about the need for change. It would be reasonable to think that the Agency might serve as an intermediary in this event, to examine dossiers submitted, in order to ensure that frivolous claims do not progress. In much the same way as the Agency will examine the credibility of the Commission's claims in seeking to launch an inquiry into the need for new restrictions, so too it could serve as a gatekeeper for attempts at de-stabilization brought forth by civil society actors.

## H. A Note on Authorization and Restriction Procedures and Criteria

It has been illustrated above that Member States enjoy multiple opportunities to contest the boundaries of the regulation. They enjoy very limited authority to impose stricter standards than those laid down in REACH, but they may in various ways set in train a procedure to consider ratcheting those standards up. Ultimately, decisions will be taken in accordance with the procedures laid down. Important differences exist between these procedures. This may be most starkly illustrated by reference to the distinct procedures for the adoption of authorization and restrictions decisions.

### *1. Authorization*

#### (a) Procedure

The Agency committees shall issue draft opinions on an application for authorization.[102] The Committee for Socio-Economic Analysis shall take into account any information on alternative substances or technologies submitted by interested third parties.[103] Interested parties are not invited to comment more generally. However, the applicant is given an opportunity to comment, and the

[102] See Article 85 on the Committee for Risk Assessment and the Committee for Socio-Economic Analysis. These comprise members appointed by the Agency's Management Board from a list of nominees established by the Executive Director on the basis of Member State nominations. At least one nominee put forward by each Member State will be appointed, but not more than two. Members will be appointed for their role and experience in performing the Agency's task. The committees shall aim to have a broad range of relevant expertise, and to this end each committee may co-opt up to five additional members, chosen on the basis of their specific competence.

[103] Article 64(4)(b) and 64(2).

committees shall consider the comments, taking this argumentation into account when appropriate. It shall submit its opinions, with the written argumentation attached, to the Commission, the Member States, and the applicants.[104] The Commission shall adopt a draft decision and adopt its final decision on the basis of a regulatory committee procedure.[105]

(b) Criteria

The Article 60, para. 2 criteria apply to authorizations for Annex XIV substances except where these are PBTs or vPvBs, or where it is not possible to establish a DNEC or a PNEC. In this case, authorization will be granted if it is established that the risk to human health and the environment is adequately controlled in accordance with section 6.4 of Annex I.

For other authorization substances, Article 60, para. 4 will apply. For these substances, authorization will only be granted if it is shown that socio-economic benefits outweigh the risk to human health or the environment, and if there are no suitable alternative substances or technologies. In considering the availability of alternatives account will be taken of the overall risk profile of an alternative, and of its technical and economic feasibility for the applicants.[106]

*2. Restrictions*

**(a) Procedure**

When a Member State or the Agency prepares a restrictions dossier demonstrating the need for a Community-wide restriction, interested parties will be given an opportunity to submit comments and/or a socio-economic analysis.[107] The Agency Committee on Risk Assessment shall draw up an opinion taking into account these comments (but not the socio-economic analysis).[108] The Agency Committee for Socio-Economic Analysis shall formulate a draft opinion, taking into account any socio-economic analyses submitted by interested parties. It will invite interested parties to comment upon this. It will adopt its final opinion taking into account earlier socio-economic analyses submitted, and subsequent comments received.[109] These committee opinions will be submitted to the Commission.[110] If the conditions for imposing a restriction are satisfied (see below) the Commission shall prepare a draft amendment to Annex XVII, taking its final decision in accordance with a regulatory committee with scrutiny procedure. Where its draft amendment diverges from the original proposal (put forward by the Member State or Agency), or does not take the opinions of the

[104] Article 64(5).
[105] Article 64(8).
[106] Article 60(5)(b).
[107] Article 69(6).
[108] Article 70.
[109] Article 71(1) and (2).
[110] Article 72(1). In the absence of an opinion from either or both of the committees the Agency shall inform the Commission and state reasons for the absence.

committees into account, the Commission shall annex a detailed explanation of the reasons for the differences.[111]

**(b) Criteria**

Restrictions will be imposed when there is an unacceptable risk to human health or the environment, arising form the manufacture, use, or placing on the market of substances, which needs to be addressed on a Community-wide basis.[112]

### *3. Comparison of the authorization and restrictions procedure*

There are important differences in the procedures for the adoption of authorization and restriction decisions.

First, interested parties enjoy a broader right to submit comments under the restrictions procedure. Under the authorization procedure their right to intervene is restricted to the submission of information about alternative substances or technologies.

Second, authorization decisions are adopted by a regulatory committee procedure, whereas restriction decisions are adopted by regulatory committee with scrutiny. Thus the European Parliament is greatly empowered in the latter.

Third, an individual applicant enjoys a right to be heard under the authorization procedure.

Fourth, under the restrictions procedure the Commission is not obliged to take the Agency committee opinions into account. In this event it must offer a reasoned justification. While there is neither an obligation to take the committee opinions into account under the authorization procedure, nor any obligation to offer reasoned justification for departure, the case law of the European Court would seem to imply that both are necessary in any case. In each case the case law would suggest that departure from these expert opinions is circumscribed by an obligation to offer reasons and evidence for so doing. Where the committee offers scientific advice, departure is countenanced only where the Commission can offer scientific justification at a level which is commensurate with the committee opinion.

Taking the first two differences together, it is clear that there are opportunities for public participation, directly and indirectly through democratically elected representatives, enhanced in relation to the restrictions procedure, by comparison to the authorization procedure. Yet, particularly for the most risky substances requiring authorization under Article 60(4), the conditions for authorization are anything but purely scientific. Wide judgement is called for, in balancing costs and benefits, and in assessing the suitability of putative alternatives, including their economic feasibility for applicants.

[111] Article 71.

[112] Article 68(1) and Article 73.

Elsewhere, interested parties are given greater opportunities to comment, when the power of the European Parliament in comitology declines. Thus, in drawing up the candidate list for authorization, interested parties are allowed to comment, but the power of the European Parliament is diminished by recourse to the traditional regulatory committee procedure.[113] In drawing up the final list, by contrast, the European Parliament is involved by dint of the scrutiny procedure, but the individual right to comment is curtailed.[114] Both the restrictions and authorization procedures are unusual; the former by combining parliamentary involvement with direct public participation, and the latter by curtailing both.

## 4. Core Element: Substitution

One consequence of REACH is that it will narrow, and ultimately close, the regulatory gap between new and existing chemicals. In the past the additional regulatory burden attaching to new chemicals has created a perverse incentive, favouring the continued use of existing chemicals, even where these existing chemicals are risky, and even where safer alternatives exist or could readily be developed. REACH seeks to alter this incentive structure. It does so most obviously by requiring the phased registration of existing chemicals. And it does so expressly when it comes to the authorization and restriction of risky chemicals.

As noted in the previous section, certain very risky substances will require prior authorization. Those applying for authorization are obliged to analyse the availability of alternatives and to consider their risks, as well as the technical and economic feasibility of substitution.[115] All applications for authorization are to include this analysis. This procedural obligation is combined with a substantive requirement that, for many of the substances requiring authorization, approval will only be granted if there is no suitable alternative substance or technology.[116] Suitability will be determined having regard to overall risks, as well as to the technical and economic feasibility of alternatives for the applicants.[117] It will be determined within the framework of the authorization procedure set out earlier in this paper. It will be for the Agency Committee for Socio-Economic Analysis to assess alternatives. It will do so having provided an opportunity for interested

[113] See Article 59.

[114] Article 58(1). Individuals do have an opportunity to comment on the Agency recommendation identifying priority substances. See Article 58(4).

[115] Article 55.

[116] Article 60(4). This requirement applies when para. 4 rather than para. 2 of Article 60 is applicable. This is the case for PBTs and vPvBs, and for other high-risk chemicals included on the final authorization list where it is not possible to determine a level of exposure threshold above which humans should not be exposed, or an environmental concentration threshold below which adverse environmental effects are not expected to occur. See Annex I, 1.0.1. and 3.0.1.

[117] Article 60(5).

third parties to submit information on alternatives, and having given the applicant a further right to submit comments following the publication of a draft opinion.[118] While the Commission is not bound by the Agency opinion, it is obliged to justify departure from it, including in relation to the suitability of alternatives.[119]

There is something here which is resonant of Wendy Wagner's proposal for 'competition-based regulation' in relation to chemicals.[120] According to this, the role of a regulator should be to adjudicate upon claims of environmental superiority, by inviting competitor companies to petition for certification of their product as superior, and for the restriction or banning of inferior products.[121] Superiority determinations should take shape within the framework of an adversarial procedure which is robust in its ability to guard against over-blown claims or misstatements of fact.

It might be argued that REACH creates just such an inclusive forum for adjudication on the suitability of alternatives, and for the banning of substances where a 'superior' alternative is shown to exist. The process of adjudication is mildly adversarial. The Agency does not take the word of the applicant as gospel, but invites the submission of rival information on alternatives from 'interested parties', including on the part of competitors. In certain respects, REACH goes further than Wagner proposes. For example, even more expensive alternatives may be deemed suitable, so long as they remain within the realm of economic feasibility. In other respects, however, REACH falls short of the Wagner paradigm. It applies only to high-risk substances, and not even to all of them.[122] Also, while, as noted in the previous section, there is some fluidity in what is to count as a high-risk substance, the initiative to expand the list rests in the hands of the Commission and Member States (and to a lesser extent the Agency). Competitors are not empowered to petition for a substance to be included on this list, and hence are not able to play a role in galvanizing the superiority adjudication.

This emphasis upon substitution is further reflected in relation to the restrictions process. Restrictions may be imposed where a substance presents an unacceptable risk to human health or the environment. Consistent with Wagner's suggestion in relation to the US Toxic Substances Control Act (TCSA),[123] here what counts as an unacceptable (unreasonable under TCSA) risk will be determined taking into account the socio-economic impact of a

[118] Articles 64(2) and (5).

[119] This obligation is inherent in the administrative law of the EU. See Case T-11/99 *Pfizer*.

[120] Supra n. 8.

[121] What counts as superior is stated at p. 22: 'If a company establishes that their product is significantly safer to public health or the environment than a competitor product for an identified set of uses, and is available at roughly the same price per application, then the product could be certified as competitively superior for those uses.'

[122] Recall the discussion above about the different conditions for authorization under Article 60(2) as compared to Article 60(4).

[123] Wagner, supra n. 8, p. 20.

restriction, including in the light of the availability of alternatives.[124] Once again, it is for the Agency Committee on Socio-Economic Analysis to draft an opinion on the proposed restriction. In so doing, it is obliged to take into account the analyses or information submitted by interested parties, including presumably information on the availability of alternatives.[125] While once again it is not within the gift of a competitor to set a restrictions process in motion, this process having been launched by a Member State or by the European Commission, a competitor is able to play an important role in providing information and in contesting received wisdom, including in relation to the socio-economic impact of putative restrictions, in the light of their knowledge of available alternatives.

The capacity of REACH to re-calibrate incentive structures in chemicals regulation, in favour of the development of 'green(er)' alternatives, will depend in large part on the way in which the substitution dynamic in authorization and restrictions plays out in practice. It will depend upon the willingness of the various political actors to use the vague language (suitable or available alternatives) to sanction the existence of workable alternatives, and upon the willingness of independent scientists and particularly competitor companies to come forward to play a role in the quasi-adjudicative process for certifying the existence of alternatives. REACH asks much less of competitor companies than Wagner would like. It merely asks them to engage in a process the impetus for which comes from elsewhere. It does not ask them, or indeed allow them, to instigate this process themselves. For a competition-based approach to regulation to work, competitors must be willing to succumb to a strategy of 'divide and rule' on the part of the regulator, and to be willing to attest formally to the superiority of their product relative to that of an industry rival. In an admittedly attenuated form, REACH may provide a test case for this. It will provide an occasion to assess the willingness of industry to participate in authorization or restriction processes concerning a competitor's product, and the willingness of industry to adduce evidence about alternatives in a bid to provoke a negative authorization decision or the imposition of restrictions in relation to that competitor's product. Time will tell.

## 5. Core Element: Provisionality

### A. Review of Authorizations

As will be discussed in more detail below, substances of very high concern will be subject to an authorization requirement, even at very low volume.[126] Where

[124] Article 68(1). [125] Article 69(6)(b) and (71)(1) and (2).
[126] See Section B above.

authorizations are granted, these will be subject to a time limited review, and will normally be subject to conditions, including monitoring.[127] They will also be subject to the all-important proviso that the authorization holder will incur an absolute obligation to ensure that exposure is reduced to as low a level as is technically and practically possible.[128] This is somewhat reminiscent of the IPPC concept of best available techniques, a standard which gives rise to an evolving rather than an absolute obligation.[129] What is interesting here is that while socio-economic considerations will be directly relevant in the authorization process, and while the availability of substitutes will be subject to an economic feasibility test, this obligation to attain lowest exposure is not subject to any economic or cost-benefit balancing test. Admittedly it is only concerned with one element of the overall risk package—exposure as opposed to hazard—but even so it provides a strong instrument to the regulator in performing its review functions.

Authorization decisions will remain valid until they are amended or withdrawn subject to the obligation on the authorization holder to submit the review report discussed above, at least eighteen months before the expiry of the authorization time limit.[130] Review may be routine, associated with the time limit, or ad hoc. The Commission may conduct an ad hoc review at any time, if the circumstances of the original authorization have changed in such a way as to affect risk to humans or the environment, or if new information on possible substitutes becomes available.[131] Authorization may be withdrawn or amended, following a routine or ad hoc review, if under the changed circumstances it would not have been granted, or if suitable alternatives have since become available.[132] Where there is a serious and immediate risk for human health or the environment, authorization may be suspended pending the review.[133]

It is significant that review of authorization provides an opportunity to link REACH to other aspects of the EU's environmental programme. It is explicit in providing for the possibility of review in so far as IPPC environmental quality standards are not met or environmental objectives under the Water Framework Directive are not achieved.[134] In this way, REACH is somewhat parasitic for the attainment of its objectives, upon the monitoring regimes established by other instruments. The Water Framework Directive, in particular, lays down elaborate

[127] Article 60(8). The authorization will specify the time-limited review period and any monitoring arrangements.

[128] Article 60(10).

[129] Directive 96/61, Article 2(12).

[130] Article 61(1).

[131] Article 61(2).

[132] Article 61(3).

[133] Article 61(3). This is very much the Commission's equivalent to the Member State safeguard clause in Article 129 to be discussed below.

[134] Article 61(4) and 61(5). See also Article 61(6) which provides for the automatic withdrawal of authorization where the substance is subsequently prohibited or restricted under Regulation 850/2004 on persistent organic pollutants (POPs).

and detailed requirements on the monitoring of water status, and on the regular reporting by Member States of the results of this.[135]

## B. Reporting/Review/Revision

Along the way, in the lengthy course of the adoption of REACH, difficult and contested choices had to be made. It is striking, in the light of this, to note that the regulation is self-consciously provisional, in that it explicitly contemplates the circumstances for its own revision. It does so not merely in the abstract, or in general terms, but on the basis of carefully defined questions for inquiry, and in an institutional setting which confers specific review responsibilities on the Commission.[136] During the twelve-year period following the entry into force of the regulation, the Commission is charged at different points with reviewing specified elements of the regime, and with bringing forward proposals for reform. In keeping with Article 131, amendments to the regulation's multiple and extensive annexes may be achieved by the Commission acting on the basis of a regulatory committee with scrutiny procedure. For amendments to the main body of the text, the Commission will be compelled to bring forward proposals for the adoption of legislative acts.

The range of questions to be addressed by the Commission is extensive, with nine specific tasks set out. The Commission is required to review the scope of certain obligations, including some which were among the most controversial during the enactment phase. Thus, for example, the Commission is to consider whether in the future to require a chemical safety report for substances produced at relatively low volume, below the current 10 tonne threshold;[137] or whether to modify the Annex XIII criteria for identifying PBTs and vPvBs.[138] The Commission will consider whether to extend the more rigorous authorization procedure to endocrine disrupting substances;[139] and whether to extend the duty to

[135] Directive 2000, Annex V. This might go some way to addressing concerns raised that REACH is not sufficiently committed to environmental monitoring as part of its approach to identifying and regulating against risk. See McEldowney, S., 'EU Chemicals Regulation: A Foundation for Environmental Protection or a Missed Opportunity?' Vol. 4 *Yearbook of European Environmental Law* (OUP, 2005).

[136] See Article 138.

[137] Article 138(1) to be carried out by 1 June 2019, except in so far as it relates to CMR (categories 1 and 2) substances in which case it is to be completed more quickly, by 1 June 2014. Looking at the precise wording, this would seem to include a review of this requirement for substances not currently subject to registration because they are manufactured or imported in quantities of less than one tonne.

[138] This is to be carried out more expeditiously, within one year of entry into force, by 1 June 2008.

[139] This is to be carried out by 1 June 2013. It will be recalled that Article 60 establishes two procedures for authorization under para. 2 and para. 4. At present Article 57(f) substances are subject to para. 2 except in the circumstances laid down in Article 60(3). As such they may be authorized so long as the risks are adequately controlled, and without being subject to an alternatives assessment, or a balancing of socio-economic benefits against risk.

communicate information on substances in articles to dangerous substances not currently included on the prior authorization list.[140]

In all but one case, the Commission's review obligations are one-off, to be carried out by the date specified. In the odd case out, there would appear to be a regular, recurring, obligation on the Commission to review the information requirements for substances produced at a volume of 1–10 tonnes.[141] This review obligation is explicitly linked to the Commission's obligation to produce a five-yearly general report on the operation of the regulation.[142] This general report will be issued following the submission of implementation reports by both Member States and the Agency.[143]

This regular reporting cycle also provides an important opportunity for reflection and review. Member State reporting is an endemic feature of EU environmental law. In practice, the Commission shapes the submission of information by Member States by issuing a questionnaire.[144] This serves to facilitate transparent comparison of Member State approaches, and of their achievements to date by the Commission in its synthesis report. It is early days with REACH, and as yet no such reports have been issued. There is, however, experience in other areas which is illustrative of the potential inherent in reporting and review mechanisms of this kind. Over the years, the scope of the Environmental Impact Assessment Directive has been extended, and its obligations sharpened. Many of the most important amendments introduced have their origin in lessons learned on the basis of Member State and Commission reports.[145] Member States come to constitute laboratories for experimentation in the implementation of often open-ended obligations. Experiences are then

[140] Article 138(8). This is to be undertaken by 1 June 2019, taking into account practical experience in implementing the article.

[141] Article 138(3).

[142] Article 117(4).

[143] Article 117(1) and 117(2). Under Article 117(3) the Agency also incurs a three-yearly obligation to submit a report on the status of implementation and use of non-animal test methods and testing strategies. This information will assist the Commission in performing its review function under Article 138(3) discussed above. The existence of a reporting obligation of this kind acquired a legal significance in the recent *Mangold* case (Case C-144/04). This was a factor cited by the Court in justifying its decision to conclude that the German law in question should be set aside as contrary to an EU directive, even though the deadline for implementation has not passed. In so doing, it relied upon the *Inter-Environnement Wallonie* doctrine (Case C-129/96), concluding that the regular reporting obligation incurred by states invoking a time-limited extension, implied the existence of a standstill obligation, whereby Member States were precluded from adopting measures which would make it impossible to achieve compliance at the end of the time-limited period.

[144] The Agency Forum (see n. 146 below) is responsible for establishing an electronic information exchange procedure. As with the Water Framework Directive, it is likely that this will result in informally agreed templates for the submission of information in reports, which will make it easier for the Commission, and others, to spot gaps, and compare performance across Member States. On the Water Information System for Europe (WISE) see, <http://www.wise-rtd.info/>.

[145] For a fuller discussion see Scott, J. and Holder, J. 'Law and New Environmental Governance in the EU' in de Búrca, G. and Scott, J. (eds.), *Law and New Governance in the EU and the US* (Hart Publishing, 2006).

pooled, allowing examples of good and bad practice to inform the revision of the overall regime. The reporting and review cycle provides an institutional framework for the integration of on-the-ground experiences in implementation, and for the organized and transparent participation of Member States in shaping the revised framework binding on all Member States.

This remains important in the context of REACH, although it is in the form of a Regulation, and although, given its internal market focus, it promotes greater upfront harmonization across Member States than is frequently the case. Still, Member States enjoy sometimes substantial flexibility in implementation. This is notably the case when it comes to enforcement. Article 125 simply requires Member States to 'maintain a system of official controls and other activities as appropriate to the circumstances'. Article 126, in similarly enigmatic vein, provides that they 'shall lay down the provisions on penalties applicable for infringement... and shall take all measures necessary to ensure that they are implemented. The penalties provided for must be effective, proportionate and dissuasive.' It is then hardly surprising that it is stipulated that Member State reports shall include sections on evaluation and enforcement, including the results of official inspections, the monitoring carried out, the penalties provided for, and other measures taken during the reporting period.[146] In this way, the reports serve an accountability as well as a learning function, rendering transparent and comparable Member State performance in areas characterized by open-ended norms and flexibility in implementation.[147]

## 6. Core Element: Transparency

### A. Information in the Supply Chain

A key premise of REACH is that effective risk management requires effective communication across the entire supply chain for chemicals. Communication should be two-way: down-stream to ensure the provision of up-to-date information necessary to facilitate safe use; and up-stream to allow for new,

[146] See also Article 127. This also states that the common issues to be covered in the reports shall be agreed by the forum. This is to be established by Article 86, and will be a successor to CLEEN, a chemicals enforcement network which has been in effective operation for over ten years. It shall comprise individuals selected by each Member State, an Agency representative, as well as representatives of the Commission, with stakeholders being invited to attend as observers. The forum may also co-opt up to a maximum of five additional members in a bid to ensure a broad range of relevant expertise among members.

[147] The activities of the Forum are laid down in Article 77(4) and include proposing, coordinating, and evaluating harmonized enforcement projects and joint inspections, identifying enforcement practices in enforcement, developing working methods and tools of use to local inspectors, developing an electronic information exchange procedure, and examining proposals for restrictions with a view to advising on enforceability.

on-the-ground, experience based information on risk and risk management to be fed back to the manufacturer or importer.[148]

At the core of the REACH system is the concept of the Safety Data Sheet (SDS). The requirements of this are set out in the Annex II 'guide', in a bid to ensure consistency and accuracy in the presentation of data. It is to include information on the intrinsic properties of substances; known uses; handling, storage, and disposal information; first aid, fire-fighting and accidental release measures; and exposure limits and control measures. These are designed 'to enable users to take the necessary measures relating to protection of human health and safety at the workplace, and protection of the environment'.[149]

The provision of an SDS is mandatory in only a limited range of situations. These concern the supply of substances or preparations which are dangerous, substances which are PBTs/vPvBs (meeting Annex XIII criteria), and substances included on the Article 59(1) candidate list for authorization.[150] Recipients may also receive, upon request, an SDS for certain preparations which contain substances which though not dangerous, pose human health and environmental hazards or which are PBTs/vPvBs not meeting the Annex XIII criteria.[151]

Outside of these situations, suppliers of substances on their own or in preparations still incur a duty to communicate specified information down the supply chain. This includes information about restrictions and authorization, but also more generally available and relevant information about the substance that is necessary to enable appropriate risk management measures to be identified and applied.[152]

The above is concerned with disclosure of information on substances on their own or in preparations. For substances in articles, controversially, different requirements apply.[153] Here, there will never be an obligation to prepare an SDS. For the most hazardous substances, identified on the basis of their inclusion on the Article 59(1) candidate list for authorization, there is instead merely a general, and relatively weak, disclosure requirement. This takes the form of a standard rather than a rule. It requires the disclosure of sufficient information to allow safe use. But it is subject to a proviso. Subject to an absolute obligation to provide information on the name of the substance, only information *available* to the supplier need be supplied.[154] The concept of availability is not defined.

[148] The discussion will focus here on downstream provision of information, but see Article 34 on the duty to communicate up-stream.

[149] Annex II, Recital 2. Where the relevant actor has been required to prepare a CSR as part of the registration or authorization process, it shall include the relevant exposure scenarios in an annex to the SDS. See Article 31(7). These only form part of a CSR for dangerous or PBT/vPvB substances.

[150] Article 31(1). The reference in Article 31(1)(c) to points (a) and (b) in the context of Article 59 (1) is quite confusing. This refers back to (a) and (b) of Article 31(1) and not Article 59(1) and reflects the fact that some substances included on the candidate list will also be dangerous and/or PBTs etc.

[151] Article 31(3). This is subject to specified minimum concentration thresholds.

[152] Article 32(1). [153] Article 33.

[154] The concept of availability applies also under Article 32 concerning substances and preparations not requiring an SDS. But here the bottom-line disclosure requirement is more expansive, including information on authorization and restrictions.

More generally in thinking about the scope of obligations to supply SDS and other supply chain information requirements, it is important to contemplate the place of the final consumer. In thinking about this, it is crucial to be aware that information in the supply chain, including SDS, is to be supplied to recipients of substances on their own or in preparations. The definition of a recipient is given in Article 3(34) and is narrower than might otherwise be assumed. This means a down-stream user or distributor being supplied with a substance or a preparation. While it is plain that a consumer is not a distributor,[155] it transpires that neither does a consumer constitute a down-stream user for the purpose of the regulation. Only industrial or professional users are constituted as such.[156] Hence, when it comes to that part of the REACH package which is concerned with information in the supply chain (Title IV), consumer entitlement to receive information is somewhat lacking. Consumers are entitled to request such information as is necessary to allow for the safe use of an article containing a substance of very high concern, apart from information on the name of that substance, though this obligation is subject to the relevant information being 'available' to the supplier.[157]

It is then apparent that there are shortcomings or gaps in arrangements for the communication of information down the supply chain, and particularly in respect of consumers. These shortcomings are particularly pronounced in respect of substances in articles, where an SDS is never required. In view of these shortcomings, it is important to ask to what extent they are mitigated by other aspects of the REACH transparency package. To determine this, it is necessary to look at the rules laid down on harmonized classification and labelling on the one hand, and on public access to information on the other.

## B. Classification and Labelling of Substances

By contrast to information in the supply chain which is directed in the main at professional and industrial users, harmonization of classification and labelling of chemicals aims primarily at the protection of consumers and workers.[158] This is true both for the current EU system and for the Globally Harmonized System of

[155] See Article 3(14). A consumer does not store a substance and place it on the market for third parties.

[156] Article 3(13).

[157] See Article 33(2). This is also subject to a concentration requirement. See also Article 31(4) which may create an incentive to provide consumers with information. Where the ultimate user is a consumer and not a professional or industrial user, provision of this information to the consumer will mean that an SDS will only have to be supplied upon request. This is important as consumers will be able to receive, upon request, information on the presence of substances of very high concern in articles.

[158] But note Article 35 which provides that workers and their representatives shall be granted access by their employer to SDSs and other information on substances and preparations that they use or may be exposed to in the course of their work.

Classification and Labelling of Chemicals (GHS) which the EU is in the course of implementing.[159]

The core function of both the old and new system is to harmonize hazard classes for dangerous substances and preparations (so-called mixtures under GHS), to draw up a list of substances with harmonized classifications for specific hazard classes, and to regulate packaging,[160] and the provision of information to consumers and workers through labelling,[161] including hazard statements,[162] precautionary statements, and pictograms.[163] There are also rules on advertising, to avoid misleading customers. Where a substance or preparation is not subject to harmonized classification, it must be classified in accordance with established hazard classes by the supplier prior to it being placed on the market. The regime also provides for a publicly accessible classification and labelling inventory, containing the relevant information submitted to the Agency as part of the registration or notification process.[164]

A detailed evaluation of GHS is outside the scope of this paper. What is crucial for our purposes is that it provides a framework for the protection of consumers, in a way that the supply-chain information requirements do not. But equally it is plain that the scope of application of this framework is limited in that it applies only to substances on their own or in preparations (mixtures). With one exception, it does not apply to substances in articles, even where these are intended to be released or where it is reasonably forseeable that they might be in the course of normal use.[165] When it is recalled that SDS are never required for substances in articles, and that consumers may only receive available information on request, including at a minimum the name of the substance, there does still appear to be a significant gap in the protective regime constituted by the

[159] To this end, the provisions of Title XI of REACH on classification and labelling will be moved to the new classification and labelling regulation. See COM(2007) 355 final for the proposal for a regulation on classification, labelling, and packaging of substances and mixtures, which will implement in the EU the international criteria agreed by the UN Economic and Social Council.

[160] See, for example, Annex II, Part III which provides for child-proof fastenings and tactile warnings.

[161] See Annexes II–V of the proposed regulation setting out the information to be included. Note that this includes in Annex II supplemental labelling provisions derived from the existing EU regime and not yet provided for by GHS. Similarly, in Annex III, additional hazard statements are required for hazards not currently part of GHS. Annex VI runs to more than 900 pages, comprising the list of substances with harmonized classifications.

[162] See Annex III. These provide information on the hazardous properties of substances. For example 'Explosives, Unstable Explosives' or 'Flammable Gases' or, more extreme, 'Reproductive Toxicity', 'Acute Toxicity', or 'Carcinogencity, Hazard Category 1A, 1B'.

[163] See Annex V, reproducing the GHS hazard pictograms, such as flames, skull and crossbones, exclamation marks, a highlighted human chest, or fish in the environment.

[164] See Article 114 REACH, and Article 113 specifying the information to be included. At present the notification obligation under REACH applies both to the registered substances and preparations and to dangerous substances even when these are not subject to a registration obligation. Under the new proposal, registered substances will be treated as having been notified as the registration process already requires the submission of information on classification and labelling.

[165] The exception concerns flammable aerosols.

transparency requirements.[166] How significant depends in part upon how the ambiguous line separating articles from preparations will be drawn. Assistance should be provided in this regard by the REACH guidance document on substances in articles.[167]

Also, as has been seen, transparency is just one prong of a multi-faceted approach to the regulation of chemical substances. Restrictions may be imposed on the manufacture, placing on the market, or use of substances, including in articles. Already Annex XVIII includes restrictions designed to protect the general public, including through a range of prohibitions on sale to it. Requirements to provide information, including to consumers, do not appear to be a regular feature of the current restrictions laid down.

Moreover, substances of very high concern are subject to authorization, including for use in articles. Nonetheless, as outlined above, even for the most dangerous substances authorization may be granted where socio-economic benefit is deemed to outweigh risk, and where there is no suitable, technically and economically feasible, alternative. Thus even substances acknowledged to be of very high concern will remain on the marketplace, including for inclusion in consumer products. It is true that authorization may be made subject to conditions, and that there is no reason why the provision of consumer information could not form the basis of any such conditions. However, this remains an ad hoc, uncertain, case-by-case solution, to what seems to be a systemic weakness in the Regulation.

There are a number of reasons to think that REACH would be improved by incorporating more extensive requirements for the provision of information to consumers about substances in articles, especially substances of very high concern. This would enable consumers to make independent, informed, judgements about risk, in respect of substances over which there is uncertainty and disagreement among experts. It would also provide a push toward the substitution of dangerous chemicals by less risky alternatives, harnessing the power of the market to generate incentives for research and development, and for recourse to safer alternatives.[168]

[166] Recall though that when authorizing a substance, including for use in an article, conditions can be imposed and these could also take the form of consumer information requirements. Likewise, restrictions may limit the sale of articles containing hazardous substances to the general public. There are many examples of this in the existing Annex XVII.

[167] REACH Implementation Project (RIP) Working Group 3.8. For general information on RIP, and for the Guidance on the Requirements for Substances in Articles, see: <http://ecb.jrc.it/reach/rip/>. For the kind of debate this has stimulated see, for example, the submission by Edana (the International Association Serving the Nonwovens and Related Industries) concerning the status of impregnated tissue paper as an article rather than as a container with preparations. See <http://www.europeantissue.com/Files/070307-EDANA+%20ETS%20Paper%20on%20Articles%20under%20the%20REACH%20Regulation.pdf>.

[168] This argument gains strength when we look to experience in California in relation to 'Proposition 65'. See Applegate, supra n. 4, for an overview and further references. He observes that '[a]s California has found with its Proposition 65, pointed public information is a strong incentive to use only the safest chemicals'.

## C. Access to Information

The Chemicals Agency will be subject to the general EU law framework on access to information.[169] REACH, however, is proactive in indicating the accessibility of different categories of information. To this end, it establishes a traffic lights approach, laying down three lists which we call red, amber, and green.[170] Information included in the red list will not normally be accessible; it 'normally' being deemed to undermine the protection of commercial interests.[171] This includes details on the full composition of a preparation, the precise use of a substance or preparation, except in so far as this is required as part of the registration or authorization process, the precise tonnage of the substance or preparation, and information pertaining to links between a manufacturer or importer and his distributors or down-stream users. The Agency may, however, disclose this information where urgent action is essential to protect human health, safety, or the environment, including in emergency situations.[172] Information in the amber list will be available, except where a party submitting the information provides a justification at the time of registration as to why publication could be harmful to its or another party's commercial interests, and where this justification is accepted as valid by the Agency.[173] Information on the green list will be made publicly available.[174]

The categories of information listed on both the green and amber lists extend to information about substances on their own, as well as those included in preparations and in articles. On this basis, consumers will, invariably,[175] be able to obtain upon request to the Agency, information about the intrinsic properties of substances, including those in articles, details of human health and environmental thresholds (DNELs and PNECs), information about classification and labelling, and guidance on safe use. More often than not, and absent a justification to the contrary, they will also be able to receive summaries of tests and other activities undertaken to generate information for registration purposes, and information in the SDS.[176] All of this shall be made publicly available, free of charge, over the Internet.

Given the focus on substances in articles above, it is important to consider how much information the Agency will hold on these as a result of the other dimensions of REACH. First, it will hold information on substances in articles where these must be registered.[177] Second, the Agency will hold a more limited

[169] Article 118 explicitly provides that Regulation 1049/2001 applies to it.

[170] Articles 118–119. [171] Article 118(1).

[172] Article 118(2). [173] Article 119(2).

[174] Article 119. [175] Article 119(1).

[176] Article 119(2).

[177] Recall Article 7(1) and (5), namely when the one tonne threshold is met and the substance is intended to be released under normal or reasonably forseeable conditions of use, or the Agency suspects that it will be, thus presenting a risk to human health or the environment.

amount of information on substances in articles which are notified to it; namely substances of very high concern, included on the candidate list for authorization, where the volume and concentration threshold is met.[178] Third, the Agency will hold information on substances in articles, where these substances appear on the final Annex XIV list specifying substances requiring authorization.[179] Given the information to be supplied to the Agency under these various headings, it is apparent that the vigorous consumer would be able to ascertain which substances are used in articles, at least where the release condition is met or where the article appears on either the candidate or final list for authorization. For substances in articles requiring registration or authorization, copious other information on that substance will also be available. This is especially true of substances requiring authorization, which will entail the supply of a CSR and an analysis of alternatives. The availability of information on alternatives is of the utmost importance, as it will allow consumers and non-governmental actors to target their campaigns to situations in which substitution is feasible but economically costly.

Bringing these three sections on access to information together, especially in relation to information on substances in articles, there would seem to be a missing link. While the Agency will hold considerable information, and in the main give public access to this, neither the supply-chain information requirements, nor the labelling rules, are such as to alert consumers to the presence of substances in articles, even where these substances appear on the candidate or final list for authorization, and are thus acknowledged to be of very high concern. It would be an important step in the right direction, were the labelling rules to require the presence of such substances in articles to be highlighted on a label. Even if it were not required that the substances present be named individually on the label, it would be an important step to acknowledge the presence of such substances as a category and to provide details of where consumers might turn to receive further information.

## 7. Conclusion

The REACH package is complex and rich in its governance dimensions. Even in relation to these dimensions, this essay is far from being comprehensive. Other arrangements for collaboration between Member States in the implementation of REACH, including arrangements for networked norm elaboration through soft law, have not been examined here.[180] These arrangements, as well as the work of

[178] Article 7(2).

[179] Recall Article 62 identifying the categories of information to be submitted as part of the applications process.

[180] See supra n. 167. See Lee, M. and von Homeyer, I. in current volume for a discussion of the comparable process under the Water Framework Directive. Thus, for all the differences between REACH, with its emphasis on harmonization, and the Water Framework Directive, with its

the Agency Forum briefly touched upon above, require further investigation, to consider their contribution to effective and/or legitimate transnational governance in this area.

Even without these aspects though, the REACH package is interesting. It is about product market integration *and* environmental/health protection. While the former militates in the direction of harmonization, the latter militates against a complacent centre, convinced that it enjoys a monopoly on regulatory wisdom. In keeping with this, REACH is emphatic but tentative in the harmonization which it achieves. It is emphatic in that it leaves little room for unilateral Member State departure from it, as is exemplified by the free movement clause. At the same time, and in a manner which might seem contradictory but is not, REACH is tentative in the harmonization which it achieves. It constructs multiple channels which allow for the contestation of the regulatory bargain which it embodies. Far from being complacent, the EU centre actively institutes a multi-level and multi-actor dialogue about risk and about how best to respond to it.

emphasis upon appropriate flexibility, each of these has spawned a broadly similar process for norm elaboration. In the Water Framework Directive this is known as the Common Implementation Strategy, in relation to REACH (humorously or not) it goes by the acronym 'RIP', meaning the REACH Implementation Projects. See: <http://reach.jrc.it/> for an insight into the many activities being conducted under this rubric.

# [23]

Sieps
Swedish Institute for European Policy Studies

European Policy Analysis
JUNE · ISSUE 2012:6epa

Jill Wakefield*

# Common Fisheries Policy Reform and Sustainability

## Abstract
Despite rigorous rules of regulation, the European Union's Common Fisheries Policy has failed to deliver any of its stated objectives. The principles governing the operation of the policy are not sufficiently well-defined and have not been effective to deliver anticipated outcomes of economic, environmental and social sustainability. This article looks at how this concept of sustainability has been understood in the common fisheries policy with regard to the marine fish resource and how its meaning is to change under the proposed reform of the policy. While under the current policy, sustainability is an undefined concept concerned with meeting human needs, in the Proposed Regulation the concept presents a concrete target to guarantee the sustainability of the resource itself. Nevertheless, as with earlier fisheries reform, the Proposed Regulation focuses on the process of regulation rather than addressing the outcomes of its operation. It is submitted that the Proposed Regulation will do no more than ameliorate the current situation, so the EU needs to introduce a mechanism to impose a financial cost on industrial fishing activity which will ensure the sustainability of the resource. Market-based instruments, used to good effect to address other environmental problems within the EU, should be deployed to protect marine fisheries.

## 1 Introduction
The European Union's Common Fisheries Policy (CFP) established an equal access regime for the common fish resource, founded on principles of equality and relative stability. Regulation of the resource is to facilitate exploitation, albeit sustainable exploitation, and it is the promotion of economic activity that drives the policy. In implementation, the policy is to apply the precautionary approach to deliver outcomes of social as well as economic and environmental sustainability. In 2010, the European Commission summarised the actual outcome for this conflicted policy: 'Currently, most fish stocks are exploited at levels well in excess of their maximum sustainable yield, in other words the optimal volume of catches that can be taken each year without threatening the future reproductive capacity of a fish stock.'[1] The Commission described the current situation of overfishing, fleet overcapacity, heavy subsidises, low economic resilience and decline in the volume of fish caught by European fishermen in its Green Paper on the reform of the CFP and, with masterful understatement, concluded, 'the current CFP has not worked well enough

* Dr Jill Wakefield, Associate Professor, School of Law, University of Warwick, Coventry CV4 7AL, UK. E-mail: j.wakefield@warwick.ac.uk

** For a list of abbreviations used in this article, see page 13

1 European Commission, Facts and Figures on the Common Fisheries Policy, (Luxembourg: Publications Office of the European Union, 2010) 4

to prevent those problems'.[2] The CFP has never addressed the core issue characteristic of all common pool resources whereby those accessing the resource do not pay for it and, in consequence, exploit it to exhaustion.

In July 2011, the Commission published a Proposal for a Regulation (Proposed Regulation) that is intended to govern the operation of the CFP for the coming decade and overcome the problems inherent in the policy.[3] Although the proposed reforms will add to the already complex and labyrinthine system of regulation,[4] the measures mark a very significant shift in emphasis. Environmental sustainability is the immediate objective of the policy and the Commission goes further describing the conservation of marine biological resources as the fundamental pillar to achieve the objectives of the CFP.[5] Environmental sustainability of fish stocks is to be achieved through the restoration of fish stocks to maximum sustainable yield by 2015.[6] This is the first time a quantifiable target has been set for the policy, rather than simply anticipating sustainable outcomes.

However, the reforms proposed are not as radical as they might at first appear, for the target of maximum sustainable yield is not to be binding and the principles according to which the target is anticipated to be achieved are those underpinning the current regime. To date, these retained principles have operated to facilitate a system of exploitation leading to degradation. Although the Commission recommended that the most pernicious of these principles, relative stability, be eliminated it has become an entrenched value of the CFP and the Member States have refused to countenance its removal.[7] Moreover, no mechanism for transferring the true costs of resource exploitation onto the fishing industry is provided in the Proposed Regulation and this promises to be the most serious obstacle to achieving sustainability once the new fisheries regime is established. In promoting sustainability for other common resources, the EU has used market-based instruments to internalise user costs, as seen in the carbon trading scheme. Consideration must be given to extending market-based instruments to achieve a sustainable fish resource.

## 2 Current and Proposed Regulation

### 2.1 The current regulations

It was not until 1983 that the Member States were able to agree a common management system for marine fishing when the Regulation adopted set the objectives of the policy to include 'the conservation of the biological resources of the sea and their balanced exploitation on a lasting basis and in appropriate economic and social conditions'.[8] The provisions that have regulated the sector since 2002 are set out in the Fisheries Regulation for the management and conservation of the fish resource which has the general objective to 'ensure exploitation of living aquatic resources that provides sustainable economic, environmental and social conditions'.[9] Three outcomes are anticipated to be delivered: a commercially viable industry, sustainable environmental conditions and support for poor coastal communities dependent on fishing. These outcomes are to be delivered through an undefined 'sustainable exploitation' which is to function in accordance with the application of the precautionary approach.

Enormously complex rules have been devised to control fishing activity. Measures include: the setting of total allowable catches; quotas limiting the catch that may be landed; effort management limiting the amount of capacity and activity that may be put into catching fish; technical measures to aid conservation and limit the environmental impact of fishing which deal with such matters as fishing gear and closures of fishing areas. The 2002 reform introduced powers to establish recovery plans for stocks that have been fished beyond their biological sustainability,[10] and long-term (multi-annual) management plans to maintain single or multiple stocks,

[2] European Commission, Green Paper: Reform of the Common Fisheries Policy, COM(2009) 163 final, 4-5
[3] European Commission, Proposal for a Regulation of the European Parliament and of the Council on the Common Fisheries Policy, COM(2011) 425 final, (Proposed Regulation)
[4] See R. Churchill and D. Owen, The EC Common Fisheries Policy (Oxford, 2010) for a detailed account of the operation of the CFP.
[5] Proposed Regulation COM(2011) 425 final, Explanatory Memorandum, 7
[6] Ibid. Article 2(2)
[7] Ibid. Explanatory Memorandum, 4: 'Relative stability is generally seen as a central pillar of the CFP, especially by Member States.'
[8] Council Regulation 170/83 of 25 January 1983 establishing a Community system for the conservation and management of fishery resources, OJ 1983 L24/1, repealed
[9] Council Regulation 2371/2002 on the conservation and sustainable exploitation of fisheries resources under the Common Fisheries Policy, OJ 2002 L358/59 (Fisheries Regulation), Article 2(1)
[10] Ibid. Article 5

taking 'account of interactions between stocks and fisheries', within their biological limit for exploitation.[11] In addition, the Commission was given emergency powers to be exercised in the event of 'a serious threat to the conservation of living aquatic resources, or to the marine eco-system' because of fishing activity to impose restrictions for up to six months.[12]

The overriding importance of the sustainability of the fish resource was emphasised in the 2002 reform of the CFP when the ecosystem-based approach was formally adopted.[13] This coheres with the EU's Sixth Environmental Action Programme of 2002, expiring in 2012, which set out a thematic strategy for the protection and conservation of the marine environment seeking to promote the sustainable use of the seas and the conservation of marine ecosystems.[14] The Programme calls for greater focus on prevention and the implementation of the precautionary principle with regard to the protection of human health and the environment.[15] The instrument also observes that 'a prudent use of natural resources and the protection of the global eco-system together with economic prosperity and a balanced social development are a condition for sustainable development.'[16] The action programme is based particularly on the polluter-pays principle, the precautionary principle and preventive action, and the principle of rectification of pollution at source.[17] Marine environmental protection is to be pursued under integrated maritime policy (see below), including the implementation of the ecosystem approach endorsed by the European Council in December 2007.[18] An ecosystem approach to fisheries management is 'about ensuring goods and services from living aquatic resources for present and future generations within meaningful ecological boundaries.'[19] Meaningful ecological boundaries are to be maintained in accordance with FAO guidelines so that fisheries impacts keep populations within viable levels and maintain biological diversity.[20] Scientific advice is essential to these assessments.

Year on year, fishing operators must demonstrate compliance with increasing numbers of requirements, while the supervision and policing of the fisheries regime is onerous for the enforcement authorities both at European and Member State level. Despite all the efforts at effective regulation, this process-driven fisheries policy has not delivered the desired outcomes.

### 2.2 The proposed reforms: maximum sustainable yield as a concept of sustainability

A new fisheries regime is presented in the Proposed Regulation that is intended to govern the operation of the CFP from the start of 2013 until the end of 2022, focused on an ecosystem based approach with its central platform being to introduce a standard for extraction at maximum sustainable yield (MSY) to restore and maintain fish stocks. For the future, therefore, EU fisheries will be subject to a target, albeit non-binding, that, by 2015, 'exploitation of living marine biological resources restores and maintains populations of harvested species above levels which can produce the maximum sustainable yield'.[21]

The mid-twentieth century concept of MSY as exploitation in the greatest harvest that can be taken annually while maintaining the average size of the stock has gradually taken on a different meaning. Developments in environmental law and policy now link MSY with the wider marine ecosystem. The 1992 UN Conference on Environment and Development adopted Agenda 21 to promote sustainable development to protect the environment including the oceans and integrate this objective with those social, economic and development

[11] Ibid. Article 6
[12] Ibid. Article 7
[13] Ibid. Article 2(1)
[14] Council of the European Union and the European Parliament Decision 1600/2002/EC, laying down the Sixth Community Environment Action Programme, OJ 2002 L242/1
[15] Ibid. Recital 5
[16] Ibid. Recital 6
[17] Ibid. Article 1
[18] European Council, Conclusions on Maritime Policy in the meeting of 14 December 2007, available at: http://ec.europa.eu/maritimeaffairs/conclusions_20071214_en.html
European Council 'Council conclusions on integrated maritime policy, 2973rd General Affairs Council meeting, Brussels, 16 November 2009', available at: http://www.se2009.eu/polopoly_fs/1.23727!menu/standard/file/111184.pdf
[19] European Commission Communication, 'The role of the CFP in implementing an ecosystem approach to marine management' COM(2008) 187 final, 3
[20] Food and Agriculture Organisation of the United Nations, The Ecosystem Approach to Fisheries. FAO Technical Guidelines for Responsible Fisheries. No 4, Suppl. 2 (Rome, 2003, FAO)
[21] Proposed Regulation, Article 2(1)

objectives otherwise pursued by States.[22] At the same time, the UN Convention on Biological Diversity (CBD) was adopted, conceived as the mechanism that would translate the principles of Agenda 21 into firm commitments. At the World Summit on Sustainable Development in Johannesburg in 2002, States agreed MSY as the standard for fishing and adopted a 'Plan of Implementation' including the achievement of sustainable fisheries. The Plan recognises that attaining sustainable fisheries will require action at all levels to 'maintain or restore stocks to levels that can produce the maximum sustainable yield with the aim of achieving these goals for depleted stocks on an urgent basis and where possible not later than 2015',[23] and while this standard is not binding it is the agreed base objective for all fisheries.

Since 2006 the Commission has sought to implement the changed understanding of MSY within fisheries management to a concept of sustainability rather than exploitation,[24] explaining the extraction of fish should be at a level no greater than that which calculates the largest average long-term take from the stock of fish without depressing its ability to reproduce.[25] The Proposed Regulation is anticipated to meet the EU's international commitments on MSY with the restoration and maintenance of fish resources at levels which can produce the maximum sustainable yield, not later than 2015. Even where scientific information is wanting 'proxies' are to be applied to achieve maximum sustainable yield.[26] This coheres with the target set for fisheries in the Commission's 2011 communication on the EU's biodiversity strategy which set out the means of achieving the CBD targets adopted by the European Council in 2010[27]. MSY is to be reached by 2015 following which fisheries are to be treated as integral to their ecosystems with 'a population age and size distribution indicative of a healthy stock, through fisheries management with no significant adverse impacts on other stocks, species and ecosystems, in support of achieving Good Environmental Status by 2020, as required under the Marine Strategy Framework Directive'.[28]

Unfortunately, the Proposed Regulation does not impose an obligation the restore stocks to MSY but merely aims to ensure that this is done.[29] A weak definition of MSY is given in the Proposed Regulation as being 'the maximum catch that may be taken from a fish stock indefinitely'.[30] EU stocks have suffered from both recruitment overfishing, that is excessive fishing effort or catch so that the adult population (spawning biomass) is too small to replenish itself, and growth overfishing, fish caught at a smaller size than would produce the maximum yield per recruit. MSY has various meanings and can be measured in various ways. While the current state of a stock or the potential yield from a stock is readily estimated,[31] calculating the optimum biomass to deliver MSY is problematic because of uncertainties in the relationship between stock size and recruitment as well as variabilities in the marine environment. Following consideration of various options in the Impact Assessment,[32] the Commission is aiming for fishing mortality that delivers maximum yield per recruit (Fmsy) by 2015,[33] with the intention this should

22 The World Summit on Sustainable Development, Johannesburg 2002; The Convention on Biological Diversity approved by Council Decision 93/626/EEC, OJ 1993 L309

23 The Johannesburg Plan of Implementation, Article 30(a), accessed at: http://www.un.org/jsummit/html/documents/summit_docs/2309_planfinal.htm

24 Commission Communication, Implementing sustainability in EU fisheries through maximum sustainable yield, COM(2006) 360 final

25 Commission Memorandum/06/268 'Fishing at MSY levels means catching the maximum proportion of a fish stock, that can safely be removed from the stock while, at the same time, maintaining its capacity to produce maximum sustainable returns, in the long term.'

26 Proposed Regulation, Recital 5

27 European Council, Conclusions on Biodiversity in the meeting of 15 March 2010, available at: http://register.consilium.europa.eu/pdf/en/10/st07/st07536.en10.pdf

28 Commission Communication, 'Our life insurance, our natural capital: an EU Biodiversity Strategy to 2020', COM(2011)244, paragraph 3.4, Target 4

29 Proposed Regulation, Article 2(2)

30 Proposed Regulation, Article 5

31 J.R. Beddington and G.P. Kirkwood, 'The estimation of potential yield and stock status using life-history parameters', Philosophical Transactions of the Royal Society B:Biological Sciences 2005; 360:163–170, 163, 'The potential yield of a fish stock can be readily estimated from its demographic parameters and these in turn can be estimated using well-understood methods of sampling, experimentation and statistical estimation. The current state of a stock can be estimated in a variety of ways, both directly via research surveys and indirectly using information on catch levels, their age composition and the effort levels associated with taking those catches.'

32 European Commission, Impact Assessment SEC(2011) 891

33 Proposed Regulation, Explanatory Memorandum, 2; Proposed Regulation, Preamble 5, Article 2

be considered an upper limit rather than a management target reference point.[34]

The Proposed Regulation includes measures previously used to control fishing activity but these have now been reclassified as 'conservation measures'. There is a new requirement to land all catches, so that the discarding of fish caught outside quota is to be phased out.[35] Tools familiar from previous regulatory instruments include the adoption of multi-annual plans, setting targets for the sustainable exploitation of stocks and adapting capacity to fishing opportunity. There is a commitment, reiterating earlier legislation, to shift from single stock total allowable catch (TAC) systems for setting extraction rates to multi-stock management multi-annual plans that aim for the maintenance or restoration of fish stocks above levels capable of producing maximum sustainable yield.[36] While the TAC is deemed to have worked well when it was simply used to allocate fishing opportunities between Member States,[37] in practice, it has consistently been set at levels that exceed biological sustainability, and is ill-suited to respond to the serious conservation challenges facing the EU. Nevertheless, the TAC has been retained as the main management device pending the introduction of the multi-stock multi-annual plans.

Multi-annual plans are anticipated to deal with mixed fisheries, in which preference could be given either to the most valuable stocks or to the most sensitive stocks, a matter considered in the Impact Assessment but not specifically addressed in the Proposed Regulation. The multi-annual plans will be long-term, adopted as an absolute priority for stocks outside safe biological limits but also used for stocks at or within safe biological limits.[38] Management plans are to be based on sound scientific advice, so that emphasis is placed on the obligation of Member States to gather the data necessary for the preparation, implementation and enforcement phases of the policy.

Great attention has been paid in recent years to adjusting property rights to regulate the use of natural resources.[39] To eliminate overcapacity in the EU fishing fleet, access to the resource is to be controlled,[40] and the Proposed Regulation stipulates the adoption of individual transferable rights (ITRs) currently used by some Member States across the whole of the EU: '[A] mandatory system of [revocable] transferable fishing concessions (on fishing opportunities for regulated stocks) as from 2014 for all vessels with the exception of vessels under 12 meters with passive gear'.[41] ITRs are perceived as 'a major driver for fleet capacity adjustment'. The impact assessment has shown 'clear positive and significant contributions from such a system of transferable fishing concessions to eliminate overcapacity and to improve economic results of the fishing industry'.[42] While 'the implementation of an individual transferable quota management system could contribute to the conservation of fish stocks, reduce over-capacity and enhance profitability of the fishing industry',[43] there is evidence that the benefits promised by economic theory is not borne out in practice,[44] and while it may be conceded ITRs have their niche they are no panacea.[45]

As to external fisheries policy, the Sustainable Fisheries Agreements with third countries are to be continued.[46] It is recognised that both external policy and actions should be fully aligned with the principles and objectives of the CFP, and full participation should be maintained in international fora, including the regional fisheries

34 Commission Staff Working Paper, Summary of the Impact Assessment on the Proposal for a Regulation of the European Parliament and of the Council on the Common Fisheries Policy, SEC(2011) 892

35 Proposed Regulation, Article 7

36 Ibid. Article 9

37 European Commission, The Common Fisheries Policy: A User's Guide (Brussels, 2009) 15

38 Proposed Regulation, Preamble, paragraphs 16-17

39 For a comprehensive account, see, R. Barnes, Property Rights and Natural Resources, (Hart, Oxford and Portland, Oregon, 2009)

40 Proposed Regulation, Articles 27-33

41 Proposed Regulation, Explanatory Memorandum, 8, Preamble paragraph 29 and Articles 27-33

42 Proposed Regulation, Explanatory Memorandum, 7

43 M. Salomon, 'Marine environment protection for the North and Baltic Seas', Marine Pollution Bulletin 49 (2004) 1127–1128

44 E. Pinkerton and D.N. Edwards, 'The elephant in the room: The hidden costs of leasing individual transferable fishing quotas' Marine Policy 33 (2009) 707–713, challenge assumptions of economic theory used to promote the benefits of ITQs.

45 T. Tietenberg, 'The Tradable-permits Approach to Protecting the Commons', in D. Helm (ed.), Climate Change Policy, (Oxford University Press, Oxford, 2005), 167-193, 193

46 Proposed Regulation, Articles 41-42

management organisations, the UN and FAO to press for better management and conservation of international fish stocks.[47] However, the principles on which external fisheries policy is set do not correspond with those informing EU internal fisheries policy. Thus, although the CBD calls for MSY by 2015, in international fishing arrangements the EU may agree indefinite deferment.[48] Whilst the EU professes to act in accordance with a precautionary approach both internally and externally, in practice this may not be so. For example, the EU is party to the North East Atlantic Fisheries Commission (NEAFC).[49] Despite the International Council for the Exploration of the Sea (ICES) advising NEAFC to set a precautionary limit of 20 000 tons for deep-sea redfish catch in the Irminger Sea in 2009, 2010 and 2011,[50] following EU proposal, the catch for 2011 was set at 38 000 not reducing to the ICES recommendation until 2014.[51]

While the CFP is to remain outside the scope of the EU's maritime environmental protection programme, the terms of the Proposed Regulation attempt to harness the operation of the CFP to environmental protection provisions by requiring the integration of Union environmental legislation requirements.[52]

## 3 Fisheries and the Integrated Maritime Policy

An integrated approach was deemed necessary to give coherence to hitherto discrete marine policies including maritime transport, fisheries, energy, surveillance and policing of the seas, tourism, the marine environment, and marine research, which for too long had 'developed on separate tracks, at times leading to inefficiencies, incoherencies and conflicts of use.'[53] The Marine Strategy Framework Directive (MSFD) is the environmental pillar of the integrated maritime policy, designed to 'protect and preserve the marine environment, prevent its deterioration or, where practicable, restore marine ecosystems in areas where they have been adversely affected',[54] and aims to achieve 'good environmental status' for European seas by 2020.[55] The quality required is for healthy, productive seas which are sustained not just for current generations but for future generations. It is for each Member State to assess the state of their marine environment, according to eleven qualitative descriptors of the marine environment specified in the MSFD. This individual assessment, in concert with the assessments of other Member States in the area, will define 'good environmental status' at regional level so that clear environmental targets and monitoring programmes may be established.[56]

Although fisheries receive specific attention under the MSFD, fisheries are not subject to its direction and the MSFD notes that they will continue to be regulated exclusively through the CFP. However, as a result of the MFSD, some measures adopted under the Fisheries Regulation may be given wider application. Thus, conservation measures available under the CFP to be taken following scientific advice, such as the full closure of fisheries in the event of fish stock collapse, may be augmented so that closure may be ordered 'to enable the integrity, structure and functioning of ecosystems to be maintained or restored and, where appropriate, in order to safeguard, inter alia, spawning, nursery and feeding

47 Proposed Regulation, Explanatory Memorandum, 8, Articles 39-40
48 ICCAT Report 2010-2011 (II), 80. The current date for MSY for East Atlantic and Mediterranean tuna is 2022 but with only a 60% probability of achievement.
49 The North East Atlantic Fisheries Commission (NEAFC), established in 1981, began accepting scientific advice from the International Council for the Exploration of the Sea only in 2003-4. See Permanent Committee on Management and Science of the North-East Atlantic Commission 30 September – 1 October 2010, discussion on Irminger Sea redfish, 7
50 Morten Vinther, ICES Advice for 2011, Presentation to the 29th Annual Meeting of NEAFC, 9th November 2010, London
51 NEAFC, Multi-Annual Interim Conservation and Management Measure for Deep and Shallow Pelagic Redfish in the Irminger Sea and Adjacent Waters to apply from 2011 to 2014 in the NEAFC Convention Area, commencing 10 May 2012
52 Proposed Regulation, Article 2(4)
53 Ibid. 4
54 Directive 2008/56/EC establishing a framework for community action in the field of marine environmental policy (Marine Strategy Framework Directive), OJ, L164/19, Article 1(a)
55 Ibid. 'Good environmental status' is defined in Article 3(5) as meaning: 'the environmental status of marine waters where these provide ecologically diverse and dynamic oceans and seas which are clean, healthy and productive within their intrinsic conditions, and the use of the marine environment is at a level that is sustainable, thus safeguarding the potential for uses and activities by current and future generations'.
56 Commission Decision of 1 September 2010 on criteria and methodological standards on good environmental status of marine waters, OJ 2010 L232/14, Recital 6

grounds.' Beyond this, while future reforms of the CFP are to take account of the terms of the MSFD there is no further reference to the CFP.[57] Currently, when the marine strategy is applied in the context of the fisheries policy, it is the objectives and principles laid down in the Fisheries Regulation that determine policy.

In the Proposed Regulation the Commission has sought to devise a fisheries policy that will cohere with the broader integrated maritime project and its emphasis on long-term sustainability. Hence, the thrust of the Proposed Regulation is to effect a change in values so that the sustainability of the resource becomes accepted as the key to the sustainability of the economic activity. However, to make such a transition the existing principles of regulation would have to be recalibrated to direct the policy along its new path and, unfortunately, no such amendment is proposed.

## 4 Resource Sustainability and Sustainable Exploitation

Sustainable development is a principle of EU internal market policy.[58] By operation of Article 11 TFEU, 'environmental protection requirements' are to be integrated into defining policy and into its implementation particularly with a view to promoting sustainable development, so although mandatory such requirement may not override other policy considerations such as socio-economic imperatives.[59] Under the current CFP, exploitation of the resource is to be sustainable which is defined in the legislation as meaning, exploitation 'in such a way that the future exploitation of the stock will not be prejudiced' or adversely impact marine eco-systems.[60] Sustainable exploitation was anticipated through the application of the precautionary approach and, despite its failure, it is this mechanism the Proposed Regulation assumes will deliver the sustainability of the resource.

### 4.1 Precaution

Under the Proposed Regulation, while sustainable exploitation is no longer an objectives of the CFP,[61] it is retained in the recitals, underpinning and providing the unifying thread within the body of the Proposed measure. 'Sustainable exploitation of marine biological resources should be based on the precautionary approach, which is to be derived from the precautionary principle referred to in the first subparagraph of Article 191(2) of the Treaty.'[62] Although the precautionary approach is 'derived' from the precautionary principle it is a management approach particular to the CFP and does not apply the precautionary principle.

Article 15 of the Rio Declaration explained the precautionary principle, as agreed by the signatory states, to mean that lack of full scientific certainty of serious damage should not postpone cost-effective preventive measures, so that erring on the side of caution to exclude risk is justified according to the precautionary principle. The precautionary principle was incorporated into EU law in the environmental chapter of the Maastricht Treaty which at the same time stipulated that environmental protection requirements *must* be integrated into the definition and implementation of other Community policies.[63] The General Court has confirmed the comprehensive reach of the precautionary principle holding that 'it is intended to be applied in order to ensure a high level of protection of health, consumer safety and the environment in all the Community's spheres of activity.'[64] According to the Court

57 Marine Strategy Framework Directive, Recitals 39 and 40

58 Article 3 TEU: 'The Union shall establish an internal market. It shall work for the sustainable development of Europe based on balanced economic growth and price stability, a highly competitive social market economy, aiming at full employment and social progress, and a high level of protection and improvement of the quality of the environment. It shall promote scientific and technological advance.'

59 'Environmental protection requirements must be integrated into the definition and implementation of the Union policies and activities, in particular with a view to promoting sustainable development.'

60 Defined in Fisheries Regulation, Article 3

61 Proposed Regulation, Article 2

62 Ibid. Recital 7

63 Article 174(2) TEC, now Article 191(2) TFEU: 'Union policy on the environment shall aim at a high level of protection taking into account the diversity of situations in the various regions of the Union. It shall be based on the precautionary principle and on the principles that preventive action should be taken, that environmental damage should as a priority be rectified at source and that the polluter should pay.' Before the introduction of the environmental chapter into Single European Act of 1986, the EU's first environmental action programme provided that agricultural policy, which includes fisheries, was to take account of concern for the protection of the environment: European Commission, Programme of action of the EC on the Environment, OJ 1973 C112/1; Ex Article 6 TEC, now Article 11 TFEU

64 Joined Cases, T-74, 76, 83-85, 132, 137, 141/00, Artegodan GmbH and Others v Commission, [2002] ECR II-4945, paragraph 183

the precautionary principle is an autonomous 'general principle of Community law requiring the competent authorities to take appropriate measures to prevent specific potential risks to public health, safety and the environment, by giving precedence to the requirements related to the protection of those interests over economic interests.'[65]

The Court of Justice has never found it necessary to explain the difference between the precautionary approach and the precautionary principle but, where the precautionary principle has been invoked with regard to the CFP, the Court has been careful to substitute the terminology of legislation, observing that it is the 'precautionary approach' which is to be applied in the Fisheries Regulation 'in taking measures designed to protect and conserve living aquatic resources, to provide for their sustainable exploitation and to minimise the impact of fishing activities on marine ecosystems'.[66]

### 4.2 The precaution approach in management measures

If the precautionary approach were to apply the precautionary principle to give priority to environmental vulnerability in the context of scientific uncertainty, this should be evident the general management of the fisheries regime. Although there is a general requirement to apply the precautionary approach to all management decisions, the Fisheries Council has exceeded extraction levels advised by its scientific experts on a routine basis. A recent study analysed TACs for eleven stocks from 1987 to 2011 and found that in 68% of cases scientific recommendations on catch levels had been exceeded, and these politically-adjusted TACs averaged catches 33% above scientifically recommended levels. The authors modelled the effects of such politically-driven decision-making on stock sustainability and found that this failure to adhere to scientific advice dramatically increases the probability of a stock collapsing over the next forty years.[67] From this evidence, general management of fisheries does not apply the precautionary principle to promote the environmental sustainability of the fish resource over the competing social and economic aspects of fisheries. However, there are specific powers available to the institutions to adopt measures to displace fishing activity in favour of the protection of the resource available to the Commission in emergency measures and to the Fisheries Council in recovery plans.

### 4.3 The precautionary approach in emergency measures

Emergency measures may be adopted by the Commission on its own initiative or at the request of a Member State, first, if there is evidence of a serious threat to the conservation of living aquatic resources, or, secondly, if fishing activities have caused a threat to the marine eco-system, in either case requiring immediate action.[68] Even in the case of a serious threat, emergency measures are not mandatory and the length for which they can be imposed is restricted to a six month period renewable once. Sparse use has been made of these powers; emergency measures have been adopted to protect cold-water coral reefs from the effects of trawling off Scotland,[69] anchovy in the Bay of Biscay,[70] and, in 2003, Baltic Sea cod stocks.[71] More usually, emergency measures are deployed to control the import of fish from outside the EU on the ground that their import poses a potential threat to human health.[72]

---

65 Ibid. paragraph 184

66 Case C-453/08 Karanikolas and Others, ECR I-0000, Judgment of 2nd September 2010, Paragraph 45

67 B.C. O'Leary, J.C.R. Smart, F.C. Neale, J.P. Hawkins, S. Newman, A.C. Milman, C.M. Roberts, 'Fisheries Mismanagement', Marine Pollution Bulletin, 62(2011) 2642-2648

68 Fisheries Regulation, Article 7(1):

69 Commission Regulation (EC) No 1475/2003, OJ 2003 L 211/14

70 Commission Regulation (EC) No 1037/2005, OJ 2005 L 171/24

71 Commission Regulation (EC) 677/2003 establishing emergency measures for the recovery of the cod stock in the Baltic Sea, OJ 2003 L 97/31

72 Although emergency measures are used to control fishing, only one measure is in force to control fishing inside EU waters, Commission Regulation (EC) No 677/2003 establishing emergency measures for the recovery of the cod stock in the Baltic Sea OJ 2003 L 97/31. Emergency measures are more often used to control the import of fish, such as: Commission Decision of 12 November 2008 on emergency measures suspending imports from Peru of certain bivalve molluscs intended for human consumption, OJ 2008 L307/9; Commission Decision of 30 September 2009 on emergency measures applicable to crustaceans imported from India and intended for human consumption or animal feed, OJ 2009 L 258,31; Commission Decision of 12 July 2010 amending Decision 2008/630/EC on emergency measures applicable to crustaceans imported from Bangladesh and intended for human consumption, OJ 2010 L 178/312

In contrast with the current situation, the Proposed Regulation marks a substantive change with regard to emergency measures. Any serious environmental threat to marine biological resources or the marine ecosystem, whatever its cause and whichever element of the marine ecosystem is at risk of being affected, may be capable of displacing fishing activity. Moreover, these measures are not time-limited, the only stipulation being that they must be temporary rather than permanent.[73] However, it would appear there is little chance these temporary measures will apply the precautionary principle because the 'serious threat' triggering the adoption of these measures must be sufficiently certain as to require immediate action. Action by an administrative authority to prevent undertakings engaging in the lawful pursuit of economic activity for which they have been established and on which the livelihoods of their employees depend is a very serious matter and would have to be objectively justified; intervention on a lesser ground of scientific uncertainty would be unlikely to be justifiable.

## 5 Monitoring and Control

While the issue of illegal, unreported and unregulated fishing was addressed in legislation adopted in 2008,[74] the more complex problems of effective monitoring and control of the use of the fish resource by participants in the CFP were sought to be resolved in a new control system.[75] Subsequently, the Commission has continued to emphasise that the success of any reform to the fisheries regime is predicated on the effective control of fishing activity. In its Communication to the Council and European Parliament concerning the Proposed Regulation the Commission observed that achieving the sustainable resource objective 'depends greatly on a winning combination of *compliance* by operators and effective *enforcement* by public authorities'.[76]

In the Proposed Regulation the Commission has sought to introduce a principle of conditionality to the availability of certain financial and other resources for both Member States and individual operators.[77] Compliance with the CFP rules would be a precondition for accessing funding so that any breach would risk an interruption or suspension of payments. It is to be wondered that during over the thirty years of regulation the linking of funding and compliance has not be firmly established. Its omission has meant that no culture of compliance among operators has evolved. Now, the success of the proposed reforms are to depend on the belated establishment of effective, proportionate and dissuasive sanctions.[78] But the detail reveals that such sanctions as are adopted will be imposed only in the event of serious infringement and will be applied only for the year of the breach.[79] Whether such limited financial detriments will be sufficient to deter operators from circumventing the rules remains to be seen. What is certain is that any chance of success is dependent on the detection of infringements, requiring Member States to commit substantial sums to monitoring activities which they may or may not be inclined to do. Developing a culture of compliance requires time and time is not on the side of reform in fisheries.

## 6 Shifting Responsibility for Environmental Sustainability

In its 2007 Green Paper on the use of market-based instruments (MBIs) for environmental and related policy purposes the Commission suggested that, rather than relying on traditional civil liability mechanisms to protect the environment, an alternative solution could be found in MBIs operating within a clear regulatory framework.[80] These would provide flexibility but also offer a cost-effective way to achieve policy objectives in situations of market failure, in particular those sectors exploiting

---

73 Proposed Regulation, Art 13(1): 'On the basis of evidence of a serious threat to the conservation of marine biological resources, or to the marine eco-system and requiring immediate action, the Commission, upon a reasoned request of a Member State or on its own initiative, may decide on temporary measures to alleviate the threat.'

74 Council Regulation 1005/2008 of 29 September 2008 establishing a Community system to prevent, deter and eliminate illegal, unreported and unregulated fishing, OJ 2008 L 286/1

75 Council Regulation 1224/2009 establishing a Community control system for ensuring compliance with the rules of the common fisheries policy, OJ 2009 L 343/1

76 COM(2011) 417 final, 8, section 2.5

77 Proposed Regulation, Recital 52

78 Ibid. Article 46(2)(d) and (e)

79 Ibid. Articles 51 and 52

80 European Commission, Green Paper on market-based instruments for environment and related policy purposes, COM(2007) 140 final. One radical idea being pursued is using MBIs for habitat banking, see, Report for European Commission DG Environment, The Use of Market-Based Instruments for Biodiversity Protection – the Case of Habitat Banking, (February 2010), available at:
http://ec.europa.eu

environmental assets of a public nature which entirely lack any costs internalisation mechanism or which do not sufficiently account for the 'true' or social cost of economic activity.[81]

The OECD set out the polluter pays principle as an economic mechanism to allocate costs and encourage the rational use of scarce environmental resources and thereby rectify the negative externalities that arise from activities that damage environmental goods.[82] A user-pays principle is given definition by the UN: 'The user-pays principle is the variation of the polluter pays principle that calls upon the user of a natural resource to bear the cost of running down natural capital.'[83] From an economist's perspective both principles internalise costs and there is no distinction to be drawn between them.

### 6.1 EU market-based instruments to promote environmental sustainability

Despite its preference for regulation, MBIs have been adopted by the EU for a range of environmental problems. The EU's Environmental Liability Directive (ELD) institutes an insurance-based public law regime based on the polluter-pays principle for the prevention and remediation of environmental damage and reduction in the costs of such damage borne by society. A dual system of liability is established by the ELD imposing strict liability on operators in listed activities and fault-based liability for non-listed activities. The Environmental Liability Directive took cognisance of the change in commercial culture that large-scale polluter-pays liability created. It was a new situation for both operators and Member States, and Member States were advised to encourage operators to obtain appropriate insurance or other forms of financial security and if these were not available to ensure that such instruments were developed by the market.[84]

A user-pays based regime of liability has been established by the EU's Water Framework Directive (WFD) and the Directive makes no distinction between user-pays and polluter-pays principles, stating that water usage should be costed in accordance with the polluter-pays principle: 'the principle of recovery of the costs of water services, including environmental and resource costs associated with damage or negative impact on the aquatic environment should be taken into account in accordance with, in particular, the polluter-pays principle'.[85] The water resource is characterised as a particular common resource: 'Water is not a commercial product like any other but, rather, a heritage which must be protected, defended and treated as such.'[86]

The ability of the polluter-pays principle to transfer responsibility for environmental damage to those causing damage may lose efficacy where pollution is diffuse, caused by virtually all human activity as witnessed in greenhouse gas emissions into the sink of the global atmosphere. Indeed, as the Environmental Liability Directive observes, 'not all forms of environmental damage can be remedied by means of the liability mechanism' and particularly pollution of a widespread, diffuse character, where it is impossible to link the negative environmental effects with acts or failure to act of certain individual actors.[87] Market-based solutions, nonetheless, may be applied in such situations. Indeed, the EU has embraced a market solution for carbon emissions, establishing a trading scheme which came into force in 2005 and has become the largest carbon market in the world.[88] Emitters who wish to emit more than the allowable units they hold must buy additional allowances and these sale and purchase transactions produce a price per unit of pollution. Tradable fishing rights are to be made mandatory under the Proposed Regulation but, unlike the carbon trading scheme which imposes responsibility on the polluter for air quality, the trading in rights for fish extraction impose no responsibility on the user for fish restoration and maintenance.

---

81 European Commission, Green Paper on market-based instruments for environment and related policy purposes, COM(2007) 140 final, 3

82 OECD Council Recommendation on Guiding Principles concerning International Aspects of Environmental Policies, C(72) 128 final, OECD 1972, 11 ILM 1172 (1972), 6

83 United Nations Glossary of Environmental Statistics

84 Directive 2004/35/CE on environmental liability with regard to the prevention and remedying of environmental damage, OJ 2004 L143/56, Article 14

85 Directive 2000/60/EC of the European Parliament and of the Council of 23 October 2000 establishing a framework for Community action in the field of water policy, OJ 200 L 327/1, Recital 38

86 Ibid. Recital 1

87 Directive 2004/35/CE on environmental liability with regard to the prevention and remedying of environmental damage, OJ 2004 L143/56, Recital 13

88 Directive 2003/87/EC of the European Parliament and Council establishing a scheme for greenhouse gas emission allowance trading within the Community and amending Council Directive 96/61/EC, OJ 2003 L275/32, as amended

### 6.2 International market-based instruments to promote environmental protection

An insurance-backed liability mechanism has been adopted at international level to deal with vessel-source oil pollution and the incidence of serious oil pollution events covered by the regimes established under the Convention on Civil Liability for Oil Pollution Damage (CLC) 1969 and the Convention on the Establishment of an International Fund for Compensation for Oil Pollution Damage 1971 (Fund 71). Pollution incidents have steadily diminished, suggesting greater care in the industries concerned. As liability regimes, the primary objective of the Conventions is to compensate those individuals damaged, and monitoring of the scheme suggests that individuals suffering damage are being adequately compensated. Nevertheless, the CLC regime institutes polluter-pays responsibility for the clean-up of the spill in that the polluter is required to reimburse States affected for the cost of environmental clean-up. There is little responsibility for remediation written into these conventions and the signatory States have not shown themselves willing to increase the burden on a key industrial sector. States have preferred to bear the excess cost of clean-up themselves, taking on the mantle of final insurers in such pollution events. The scheme operates well for the purposes of compensation and remediation to baseline level and it is open to the signatory States to increase responsibility for remediation. The EU Member States rejected a more comprehensive coverage proposed by the Commission in 2003.[89]

The most important innovation of the CLC was the imposition of strict liability upon the shipowner: 'the owner of a ship at the time of an incident...shall be liable for any pollution damage caused by the ship as a result of the incident.'[90] All responsibility for a pollution event is ascribed to the shipowner, regardless of whether there was fault and regardless of whether the shipowner had acted diligently to prevent harm. Once harm has occurred though the oil spill from the vessel, the individual responsibility of the shipowner is engaged. Fund 71 introduced a general, collective responsibility for the oil receivers to cover any excess not met by the shipowner. This was novel in that responsibility for the effects of the oil spill were accepted by third parties uninvolved in the damaging act but benefiting from the transport of the resource. Subsequent instruments extended the types of damage that are compensatable beyond clean-up to include reasonable reinstatement of environmentally damaged areas as well as increasing the amount of compensation recoverable.[91]

### 6.3 Adopting an insurance-based system to secure sustainability for EU fisheries

The application of the polluter/user pays principle in the CLC and Fund model provides two exemplars of responsibility, individual and collective. The scheme presents a blueprint for a mechanism that would transfer responsibility for the sustainability of fisheries from the EU and Member State authorities onto the users of the resource. Following the CLC model, the EU should consider adopting an insurance-based system of responsibility to achieve the restoration and maintenance of fish stocks. Just as those exploiting the oil resource are made responsible for its damaging effects on the marine environment so the damaging effects of fishing on the fishing resource should be imposed on those operators who most benefit from its use, the industrial fishing sector and the fish receivers. However, if the industry is to be responsible for the maintenance or, indeed, the improvement in the state of fish stocks, there must be an objective and quantifiable basis against which its performance may be measured.

The findings of the consultation on the reform of the CFP show that there is support for results-based management from environmental NGOs, industry and the European Parliament, as well as some Member States, but this is qualified by the requirement for 'clear objectives and measurable targets'.[92] The objective of bringing all stocks

[89] European Commission, Proposal for a regulation of the European Parliament and of the Council on the establishment of a fund for the compensation of oil pollution damage in European waters and related measures, COM (2000) 802 final

[90] CLC 69, Article III(1)

[91] The International Convention on Civil Liability for Oil Pollution Damage 1992 (CLC 92) and the Convention on the Establishment of an International Fund for Compensation for Oil Pollution Damage Fund Convention 1992, Article 2(3). Subsequently, also, Protocol of 2003 to the International Convention on the Establishment of an International Fund for Compensation for Oil Pollution Damage, 1992, in force 2005, establishing the Supplementary Fund, providing a third higher tier of compensation, but to date only twenty seven States have signed up to this Protocol.

[92] European Commission, Staff Working Document, Synthesis of the Consultation on the Reform of the Common Fisheries Policy, SEC(2010)428 final, 7

up to MSY levels by 2015 imposes a positive obligation on operators. Moreover, there is no reason why this objective should not be achieved because, of those who responded in the CFP consultation process, 'most contributions share the objective to gradually reach exploitation rates matching with MSY in 2015.'[93] Responsibility for the state of a fishery at the end of a fishing cycle needs to be instituted. As the date for achieving MSY has been set at 2015, and the Proposed Regulation should be amended to make it legally-binding, the objective for the fishing industry is already in place. The licensing system needs to incorporate a term whereby those making use of the resource, whatever the nature of their property interest, are required to account for the resource in 2015 at MSY level. Beyond this, the industry must meet the further obligation that the MSY level achieved in 2015 is maintained at a level that will deliver good environmental status for European seas by 2020.

## 7 Conclusion

Over the years during which the CFP has been in operation, the understanding of environmental sustainability has changed and the protection of the environment and natural resources have come to be promoted internationally. The sustainability of the fish resource has always been a central concern of the Common Fisheries Policy but fish sustainability competes with economic and social priorities in the decision-making process. The management of fisheries according to the precautionary approach does not apply the precautionary principle and therefore does not defer to environmental vulnerability and scientific uncertainty. Consequently, fishing activity is constrained only in exceptional circumstances despite the clear evidence of an ever diminishing resource.

The Proposed Regulation marks a very significant development in that sustainability of the EU's fish resource is finally recognised as key to delivering economic viability for the industry and support for coastal fishing communities. Determining appropriate levels of fishing effort and catch is to be within the strictures of achieving MSY by 2015. However, the failure to define MSY or to make it legally-binding is likely to seriously undermine the impact of these reforms. Although the precautionary approach to the management of fisheries now has a target, it is non-binding and decision-makers will have no justification in preferring the protection of the resource over the protection of jobs or the exploitative activity of the fishing industry. In the current economic climate and the difficulties faced by all EU governments with regard to jobs and growth, the pressure to facilitate economic activity and the appropriation of the marine resource is bound to intensify rather than diminish. In such circumstances, there is a pressing need to transfer the responsibility for the sustainability of the fish resource to those who are using it and profiting from it. An insurance-based scheme would achieve this end and enable the industry to play a positive role in sustaining the resource on which it depends.

93 Ibid. 8

# Part V
# Regulation and Environmental Human Rights

# [24]

# The Human Right to Natural Resources

The poorest man hath as true a title and just a right to land as the richest man.
– Gerard Winstanley

## Introduction

This chapter examines and defends the environmental human right to ownership of natural resources. Ownership is 'the ideology of valid possession' (Sumner, 1979). The recognized system of ownership therefore legitimizes property rights (Sumner, 1979). For the purpose of this research, ownership rights to natural resources are defined as 'enforceable authority to undertake particular actions related to a specific domain' (Ostrom and Schlager, 1996). The claimed human right to natural resources is applicable to local environmental resources such as water, lakes, land, forests and sub soil resources. Ownership of industry, services or the global commons, such as the atmosphere and oceans lie outside of the focus in this chapter.

The chapter begins by establishing that ownership systems to natural resources are socially constructed. A choice therefore exists as to which system is to be adopted by a polity. Differentiating between six specific ownership systems will substantiate this claim. Two of these systems in particular; (i) private property rights and (ii) common property resources (CPRs) will be compared and contrasted from the perspective of basic human rights. The system of assigning rights to natural resources derived from the paradigm of economic rationality constructs property rights in terms that maximizes allocative efficiency and aggregate production. The focus on economic variables comes at the cost of dismissing claims of human rights to (i) cultural self-determination and (ii) freedom from hunger, as well as causing systematic environmental degradation. An alternative structuring of property rights based around CPRs is suggested to be more conducive to facilitating cultural diversity and the satisfaction of basic human needs, as will be exemplified through an analysis of global food provision. Juxtaposed to private property rights, CPRs are furthermore found to lessen the human impact on the environment.

Continuing the theme permeating previous chapters, the capitalist organization of the global economy is identified as the most important structural barrier for the recognition of the claimed environmental human right to natural resources. The characteristic ability of global markets to divert resources into supplying luxury goods for the opulent explains why essential resources are simultaneously denied to the impoverished.

By endorsing a subsistence based CPR economy, rather than the exchange based economy of capitalism, the environmental human right to natural resources links the human rights agenda to a less environmentally destructive economic system (*The*

*Ecologist*, 1993). Processes of environmental commodification and distanciation that characterize global capitalism will be examined as causing particular concern from the ecological perspective. Distanciation facilitates economic benefits to be acquired by an individual or institution in one location through a process that imposes the environmental and social costs on people living elsewhere in the world, thereby spatially separating the benefits of consumption from the environmental damage caused during the production process (Saurin, 1993).

Although the principle of CPRs is vindicated in this chapter as the ownership system most conducive to the realization of the claimed environmental human right to natural resources, this chapter does not address the practicalities of implementation. Such concerns relate, for example, to how specific resources can be equitably allocated between communities. These matters of implementation are best resolved in a case by case basis, taking all relevant local factors into account to ensure that all can meet basic needs (Costanza and Folke, 1996). Specifying a precise or universally applicable model for the implementation of this human right would also arbitrarily curtail, rather than facilitate cultural diversity (Hanna, Folke and Maler, 1996). Furthermore, discussion relating to the implementation of the claimed environmental human right is rather premature so long as the principle to the right remains unrecognized.

## The Social Construction of Property Rights

Sagoff reminds us that far from being universal or unchangeable, the nature, meaning and extent of property rights to environmental resources is a constructed function of the legal and economic regimes that define them through utilizing a political ideology (Sagoff, 1995). The validity of this claim establishes the possibility to choose between alternative systems of resource ownership rights. Systems of rights to natural resources can be differentiated into the following six broad categories.

### *[i] Open Access Resources*

An open access system of resource exploitation describes a situation that allows everyone unlimited access to environmental resources. This system has no mechanisms for limiting the ecological impact of human exploitation and has subsequently been correctly criticized for inexorably leading to overuse and environmental degradation (Vogler, 1995).

### *[ii] No Access*

No access systems deny all humans access to a given spatial area. The only notable example of a no access system is the Antarctic Wilderness Area that, under international agreement, has been designated as an area from which anthropogenic activity is to remain entirely absent (Vogler, 1995). The no access model effectively reverses the benefits and drawbacks of the open access system. The model is of great benefit to biodiversity and habitat preservation but prevents humans from using environmental resources to provide even for their own needs. This model could be applied to designated areas that are of particular importance to biodiversity but is unattainable on a global scale given the needs of the human populace who are also living parts of the eco-system.

*[iii] State Control*

This system of environmental resource ownership places property rights under the control of the state and has been severely criticized from a number of positions. Neo-liberal economists characteristically decry the notorious allocative inefficiencies of such a centralized system. Further strengthening the state is also problematic for the realization of human rights, given the nature of the state as an instrument of power as discussed in chapter four. From the ecological perspective, state ownership of natural resources has often preempted environmental degradation as environmental concerns are subordinated to considerations of power and economic growth. This is exemplified through the granting of logging concessions to the corporations responsible for widespread deforestation in East Asian states (World Rainforest Movement and Forests Monitor Ltd., 1998). In cases where the state does not allow corporate control over resources but reserves this right for local inhabitants, nationalized resources invariably degenerate into open access systems as non-compliance with complex or inappropriate bureaucratic regulations becomes established as the norm (Berkes, 1996).

*[iv] Public Goods Systems*

Public goods relate to global environmental commons such as the atmosphere, climate and oceans which, by their global nature, lie outside the sovereign jurisdiction of any particular state (Vogler, 1995). Strictly speaking, public goods systems therefore describe the global nature of important environmental categories rather than conceptualizing property rights over environmental resources. The notion of public goods is nonetheless significant to discussions over resource rights since this highlights how resource decisions made at the local level can impact at the national, international and global levels, for example in the case of climate change or the over-exploitation of fish stocks (Vogler, 1995).

*[v] Private Property Rights*

Under the capitalist system of assigning resource rights, legal recognition of individual claims to environmental resources is a function of market (exchange) transactions. Land and environmental resources are treated as commodities, since they are demarcated and separated from the surrounding land. Land is therefore commodified by virtue of being bought and sold by individuals or corporations at a price specified by the market. Decisions relating to land use, as well as the resulting incomes, are thereafter seen as the private concern of the property holder. Under capitalist conditions, land-use decisions are invariably made according to commercial criteria and considerations of private gain. The landowner is legally empowered to exclude the rest of the community from utilizing privately owned land.

The private property system of environmental resource rights is therefore an expression of economic rationality. This position is predicated upon the normative belief that market conditions ought to define resource rights. This belief is derived from the ideology that the general good of society is achieved by maximizing (i) allocative efficiency and (ii) aggregate wealth.[1] Proponents of economic rationality characteristically universalize or normalize private property rights as the only legitimate system of resource ownership (Johnston, 1995).

Although most liberal political theorists defend individual property rights to land, not all conclude that ownership titles should be decided by the market (Kramer, 1997). From the broad range of positions advocated by different liberal theorists, radicals have allocated land rights on an egalitarian basis, irrespective of individual wealth. Beitz for example concludes on the grounds of equality of opportunity that, 'each inhabitant of the world has an equal basic entitlement to natural resources' (Beitz, 1981). Similarly Locke had previously stated a right for each individual to claim a part of nature, as long as they leave 'enough and as good' for others (Wood, 1984). Locke's designation of property rights was clearly influenced by his political agenda to justify the ownership of American lands by individuals, rather than the crown. Still, the fact remains that capitalist property rights over land can be criticized on radical liberal grounds since the latter utilizes the language of human rights to impose limits on the unlimited ownership of natural resources by the wealthy (Kramer, 1997). This claim articulates the concern that, when denied control over land, individuals are restricted in the potential to shape their lives. The requirements of freedom requires a basic entitlement to natural resources. Under this radical liberal interpretation, unfettered agrarian capitalism becomes a repressive social system denying the impoverished the means to provide for their own subsistence requirements.

The radical liberal critique of capitalism is nowhere better exemplified than through Thomas Paine. In *Agrarian Justice*, Paine claimed that the introduction of the system of private land ownership had deprived the community of the right to make free use of the earth. Paine demanded either respect for egalitarian ownership rights to land, or else a system of compensation for the loss of this right (Paine, 1987). Under the latter option, each owner of land should pay rent to a collective fund corresponding to the size of their holding and that the proceeds of this fund should be distributed amongst all members of the population equitably (Paine, 1987).

An example of the implementation of the radical liberal right to land is evident in the case of the distribution of land in America during the second half of the nineteenth century following Lincoln's Homestead Act. This legislation distributed free land titles to millions of acres that had been forcibly taken from the native Americans (Greider, 1997). The right of English people to allotments also reflects a right of individuals to land. A differentiation between capitalism and radical liberalism on the question of resource ownership has been noted here since it raises a degree of ambiguity relating to the defense of a market-based system of land rights from the perspective of liberal political theory.

*[vi] Common Property Resources (CPR)*

Australian Aborigines and indigenous North Americans had no concept of private land ownership until the first Europeans made land claims (Baird, 1987). Referring to indigenous culture in the Malaysian state of Sarawak, a native elder rejected private property rights to land by insisting that 'the land belongs to the countless numbers of people who are dead, the few who are living, and the multitude of those yet to be born' (quoted in World Rainforest Movement and Forests Monitor Ltd., 1998). In many non-capitalist cultures, land is perceived not as a commodity to be exploited for private profit, but rather as a spiritual phenomena, central to cultural practices and accessible for all members of the community who are duty bound to protect the land for other individuals. Resource rights in non-capitalist cultures are typically based upon a variant of the CPR system.

CPRs can be defined as systems within which long term use rights for environmental resources, such as land, timber, water and sub soil resources, are controlled by identifiable groups (Agarwal and Sunita, 1992). CPR systems are consequently characterized by a construction of resource management rules to meet communal needs based on collective choice arrangements (Clay, 1994; *The Ecologist*, 1995). CPRs are controlled by local community groups, rather than by individuals or states, and provide livelihoods for the people directly managing them, rather than commodities for global markets (Chatterjee and Finger, 1994). The decentralized and diverse nature of CPR systems prevents a more specific definition of this type of ownership regime, since the specific form taken is derived from local environmental conditions and cultural traditions.

To operate effectively, CPRs require clearly defined rules of resource access for communities, households and individuals, enforceable by a system of monitoring and graduated sanctions to prevent over usage at any of these levels (Costanza and Folke, 1996). Numerous studies have documented the various norms, monitoring systems and sanctions against rule breakers that have been implemented to protect resources. These studies relate for example to CPRs in Africa (du Bois, 1994); the forests in Törbel (Ostrom, 1990); three million hectares of agricultural land in the Hirano, Nagaike and Yamanoka regions of Japan (Ostrom, 1990), and the Cofyal forest run by the Yanesha Indians in the Peruvian Amazon (Sachs, 1995). The Huerta irrigation system of the Valencia region of Spain has allocated water between villages for up to 1,000 years and has various levels of monitoring to ensure the enforcement of the correct distribution of scarce water to each farmer. The success of this system is reflected in an infraction rate of only 0.008 per cent, despite the compelling incentive to cheat since 'stealing water during a dry season ... might on occasion save an entire season's crop from certain destruction' (Ostrom, 1990).

Research conducted by Ostrom supports the claim that CPRs can be effective in enforcing rules that restrict resource usage by individual members (Ostrom, 1990). Ostrom's study into the social and environmental effectiveness of CPRs concluded that violations of the usage rules in CPR systems was exceptional, even when opportunities to break the rules were plentiful and the sanctions relatively light (Ostrom, 1990). This result was achieved because of clearly defined boundaries of resource usage, collective (participatory) choice arrangements, monitoring systems, graduated sanctions, conflict resolution mechanisms and relative autonomy from state structures (Ostrom, 1990). The enforcement of rules in CPR systems is typically achieved by allowing a portion of the fines extracted from rule breakers to be kept by the individual who monitored and caught the infractor (Ostrom, 1990). In the same way that citizens generally pay the correct amount of taxes, Ostrom concludes that individuals in the commons generally adhere to the rules or adopt a strategy of quasi-voluntary compliance when they have confidence that the other members of the community will similarly adhere to the rules (Ostrom, 1990).

As well as requiring mechanisms to resolve disputes between individuals within a commons system, neighboring CPR systems must also have procedures for deciding conflicts. In the Philippines, for example, competing claims to water rights among different communities have customarily been decided by inter-village councils composed of elders from the relevant communities (*The Ecologist*, 1995). Dispute resolution mechanisms between communities have been credited with successfully extending the applicability of CPR systems beyond fixed resources such as land, forests and lakes and to migrating fish stocks and other non-exclusivist natural resources (Costanza and Folke, 1996).

## Social Power as the Deciding Variable in Determining the System of Resource Rights

The political significance of deciding upon a system of ownership rights over environmental resources resides in the observation made by both Barry and Beitz that claims to natural resources stand logically prior to any claims to products which are subsequently produced from these resources (Goodin, 1985). Therefore, choosing a system of ownership rights to natural resources is a fundamental variable in questions of equity, of economic justice, of the distribution of power in society and of human rights. Identifying the criteria through which to establish ownership rights to natural resources therefore becomes a central question.

Goodin argues that unequal ownership of natural resources can be justified on the grounds that 'some people have done something to render those pre-existing resources useful to mankind, if only by discovering them' (Goodin, 1985). Yet Goodin presupposes here the very condition which is correctly problematized by Beitz and Barry, namely that of original ownership rights to natural resources. Whereas a petrochemical corporation for example locates and utilizes oil reserves in the Third World, this only occurs as a result of the legal and economic institutions that had previously been constructed to legitimize private property rights to natural resources (Wiwa, 1995). Constructing a legal basis to empower certain people and exclude others from making claims to natural resources is therefore in the first instance a social and political, rather than a jurisprudential or economic question, since a decision must be initially made as to whose claims to natural resources should be legitimized and protected.

The methodology that is employed here for understanding the legal institutionalization of one system of rights to natural resources over other possibilities is to focus on social power relations within which ownership rights are embedded (du Bois, 1994; Vogler, 1995; Taylor, 1998). Of the six categories of conceptualizing rights to environmental resources outlined above, this chapter now juxtaposes CPR to private property rights. Private property rights have been chosen for analysis since these represent the form of legal resource ownership rights in the capitalist global economy. CPRs have been chosen as the second system of resource ownership since this system offers a distinct and widespread alternative through which to compare and contrast the system of private property rights.

Private property rights institutionalize the power relations of capitalism by facilitating inequality in the allocation of environmental resources along the lines advocated by a focus on economic rationality. CPRs in contrast characteristically benefit the disempowered and marginalized since CPR systems tend to focus on self-reliance and on serving the basic needs of all members before resources are diverted into the production of luxury goods for profit, gain or income (Makhijani, 1992; *The Ecologist*, 1995).

## Land Rights as Human Rights

A number of theorists have interpreted existing human rights texts as legitimizing the communal right to natural resources (Haas, 1970; Vincent, 1986; Crawford, 1992; Wisner, 1995). Endorsing this claim, it will now be argued that organizing rights to environmental resources according to the logic of economic rationality violates the human rights to self-determination and to be free from hunger. In particular, the global mining and cash crop economies exemplify how capitalism diverts resources to supply market demands at the expense of considerations of basic human rights.

### *The Right to Cultural Self-Determination*

The stipulations of existing legal agreements on human rights assign environmental resource rights to groups rather than to individuals. Both the ICCPR and the ICESCR omit to even mention human rights to private property. Instead both covenants grant rights to natural resources to peoples, derived from the right to self-determination. The ICESCR, part 1, article 1 and the ICCPR part 1, article 1 stipulate the following in identical wording:

1 All peoples have the right of self-determination. By virtue of that right they freely determine their political status and freely pursue their economic, social and cultural development.
2 All peoples may, for their own ends, freely dispose of their natural wealth and resources without prejudice to any obligations arising out of international economic co-operation, based upon the principle of mutual benefit, and international law. In no case may a people be deprived of its own means of subsistence (Council of Europe, 1992, p. 18 and p. 32).

Of particular significance in this article is the derivation of a peoples distinct cultural development as an aspect of the right to self-determination.

Other articles in international human rights covenants that mention natural resource rights tend to reinforce this designation of group rights. ICCPR part 5, article 47 and ICESCR part 4, article 25 both state that; ‘nothing in the present

Covenant shall be interpreted as impairing the inherent right of all peoples to enjoy and utilize fully and freely their natural wealth and resources'. The legal right of peoples to sovereignty over natural resources is further supported by General Assembly Resolution 1803, article 1, that declares a 'right of peoples and nations to permanent sovereignty over their natural resources'.[2] In all of these cases, rights to natural resources are linguistically stipulated as a group right. In no human rights text is it explicitly stated that ownership rights over natural resources are assigned to individuals or corporations.

Both the right to self-determination and the derived right to natural resources have been traditionally interpreted as an individual, rather than as a communal right in formal international human rights discussions (Evans, 1996). This interpretation facilitates iniquitous resource ownership benefiting corporate agribusiness at the expense of local communities, reflecting a political interpretation of human rights that accommodates the distribution of power in the capitalist political economy.

The systematic violation of the right to cultural self-determination remains a salient feature of organizing the global economy according to private property rights over natural resources. The supreme cultural importance of traditional lands to indigenous cultures is evident from the response of indigenous communities faced with separation from their lands. To facilitate commercial exploitation of sub soil resources on indigenous peoples lands, members of the Macuxi, Kaiowa and Guarani tribes in Brazil have, for example, been relocated to reserves in a demonstration of contempt for their rights to cultural identity (*The Ecologist*, 1993). Traditional lands are revered by these tribes 'as irreplaceable and even to be defended at all costs' (*The Ecologist*, 1993). Dramatically illustrating how commercial operations can violate cultural self-determination, members of the Guarani tribe have been committing mass suicide, 'as loss of their land leaves them with no reason to go on living' (*Brazil Network Newsletter*, 1996b).

The US based Occidental corporation is currently in a dispute with indigenous people in Colombia who have similarly threatened to commit mass suicide if oil exploration proceeds as planned on their traditional tribal lands. In 1992, Occidental signed a contract with the Colombian government to explore a 200,000 hectare area in eastern Colombia that is also home to 4,000 U'wa people (Luxner, 1997; Wright, 1997). Chief Cobaira of the U'wa tribe has stated that:

> any kind of tampering with our land goes against the core of our traditions, but our cries seem to be falling on deaf ears ... . If the white man starts making holes and sucking the veins of our most revered Mother Earth we will have no choice but to bring our lives to an end (quoted in Gamini, 1996, p. 13).

The culture of the U'wa is threatened by the privatization of their lands through (i) the pollution of their sacred lands that oil exploration entails, (ii) the increased violence that the oil project will inevitably bring, or (iii) by the tribe committing mass suicide in response to the project (Project International, 1997). This case exemplifies the centrality of traditional lands to the customs, culture and existence of tribal communities and the culturally destructive results of commodifying and privatizing rights to land. Indigenous communities characteristically have a spiritual relationship to their land, perceiving the environment as an intricate part of their cultural personality rather than as an exploitable commodity (Nettheim, 1992). Such a cultural interpretation of the land is incommensurate to that of the capitalist model. Floriano Carique, founder of Mapuche,[3] states that:

> Indigenous thought does not distinguish the environment from the self. Kume Moignen, or harmony, is central to our lives. We must live well with ourselves, with the community, our physical environment and with the cosmos (*Multinational Monitor*, 1995b).

Stockton similarly remarks that in Australia the aborigines commonly state that 'I am the land' (quoted in *The New Internationalist*, 1987). It is the cosmological aspect of their cultural beliefs that Aborigines view rights to land as originating with the design and creation of the world rather than with alienable legal title. Aborigines look at land as being a part of the wider whole and therefore also as a part of themselves, and that they are a part of the land (Hill, 1995). Demonstrating both the incommensurability of capitalism with aboriginal culture, and the subtle cultural imperialism evident in modern politics, Hill remarks that the focus on a cultural definition of land is a feature that white Australians fail to comprehend, regardless of their level of sympathy for Aboriginal land rights (Hill, 1995). The key conclusion to be drawn from these examples is to establish the relativism of the capitalist commodification of land. As we have seen, many indigenous cultures do not commodify land and suggest alternative land use systems that are not predicated upon short-term resource exploitation. Human rights to self-determination and to a traditional cultural heritage are ignored when the incommensurate values and ontological categories of capitalist conceptualizations of land use are imposed on non-capitalist cultures. Yet this is precisely the logic of global capitalism, of commodifying natural resources and allowing the market to decide subsequent usage, regardless of the non-economic purpose of land for distinct cultural traditions (*The Ecologist*, 1993).

The irrelevance demonstrated by the actions of commercial actors for environmental values and the cultural rights of non-capitalist societies is a structural feature of capitalism (Gill, 1995), as can be exemplified through the recent history of petrochemical MNCs. In 1996, Occidental received military assistance to force the Siona and Secoya peoples of the Ecuadorian Amazon to give up their land to enable oil exploration (Project Underground, 1997c). Survival International has charged Mobil with risking the lives of remote indigenous people in the Peruvian Amazon since Mobil workers introduced whooping cough and pneumonia to the communities whilst conducting oil explorations (*Multinational Monitor*, 1996).

Chevron and FINA have both demonstrated an interest to drill for oil and gas in the sacred Badger Two-Medecine land,[4] that is central to the cultural and religious practices of the Blackfeet Nation.[5] In 1987 the Human Rights Committee ruled that oil and gas exploration was threatening the culture of the indigenous Lake Lubicon Band in Canada in violation of article 27 of the ICCPR that guarantees the rights of minorities to culture, religion and language (Cameron and MacKenzie, 1996).

The same process of neglect for the cultural rights of indigenous communities is also evident in the case of certain hydroelectric projects. Fighting the James Bay hydroelectric project in northern Quebec in 1992 that affects an area containing 10,000 Cree and 6,000 Inuit, the Cree Vice-Grand Chief Diom Saganash asserted that tribal peoples are threatened by hydroelectric projects all over the world. He argued that:

> our basic human rights, right to a livelihood and right to survival are threatened by these projects being forced upon us. They are killing our ways of life (quoted in Park, 1992, p. 15).

Mining corporations have similarly pursued private commercial interests at the expense of the human right to cultural self-determination. *The Ecologist* states that 'indigenous people are regularly dispossessed of their lands to make way for mines without compensation or any share of the profits' (*The Ecologist*, 1993). The US mining giant Peabody has been reported to be strip-mining coal on sacred Dineh and Hopi lands in Arizona (*Inter Press Service*, 1997). In 1985, mining corporations operating in Australia campaigned against political recognition of aboriginal land rights because of a concern over potential rising costs and denial of access to resources in the event of land being ceded to aboriginal communities (*The New Internationalist*, 1987). In 1992, US based Golden Star Resources began mining gold reserves in the interior of Suriname.[6] The firm's operations led to the forced eviction of thousands of indigenous people. In September 1995, conflict at mining sites exploded as police shot at Maroon people trying to access their traditional forests (Colchester, 1995). In all these cases, corporations benefit from the enforcement of private property rights to natural resources at the expense of indigenous communities losing control over their cultural lands.

Cultural rights to self-determination are routinely subordinated to accommodating mining operations when this contributes to economic growth. The same pattern is also evident in the case of logging operations. McMillan Bloedell and Interfor have been criticized for over-exploiting the temperate rain forests of the Nuu-Chah-Nulth and Nuxalk indigenous peoples of British Colombia, Canada (*Inter Press Service*, 1997). Mitsubishi's operations have polluted the lands of the Lubicon Cree of Alberta, Canada (*Inter Press Service*, 1997). Logging by Russian, Japanese, South Korean, and US MNCs has destroyed the resource base of the Udege indigenous people of Siberia and caused soil erosion and siltation of river systems upon which the indigenous community depended for its subsistence (Sachs, 1995; Worldwatch Institute, 1995). These cases exemplify how corporations violate the right to cultural self-determination and how the trend is legitimized through the system of private property rights to natural resources. For the right to cultural self-determination to mean anything other than subordination to the global capitalist economy, the resource base required for the subsistence and independence of non-capitalist cultures must first be secured (Hitchcock, 1997). Property and ownership rights to natural resources are required since there can be no cultural self-determination where non-capitalist communities suffer invasions of their lands at the behest of global markets. The granting of access or usufruct rather than ownership rights to natural resources would be insufficient conditions for the realization of the right to self-determination since ultimate ownership of lands would not be controlled by the communities themselves. The ability and readiness of corporations to disregard considerations of cultural diversity in favor of the search for profits means that non-capitalist societies require the conditions for independence and self sufficiency, of which the ownership of traditional lands is the most important prerequisite.

For the reasons given in chapter five in the case of the right to an environment free from toxic pollution, the legal recognition of the right to environmental resources is an insufficient requirement for the realization of this right. It is unlikely in the extreme that new laws by themselves will protect the cultural diversity of non-capitalist cultures from corporate interests, given that the efficacy of law depends on power relations in the political economy as explained in chapter four. For the human right to environmental resources to be realized, anti-systemic forces have to organize and campaign to challenge the power relations that presently legitimize the cultural imperialism of global capitalism. Recent political activism by indigenous communities in Latin America exemplifies how human rights claims to natural resources can garner popular support around an organic challenge to the global market system.

The Committee for the Defense of Human Rights in Honduras (CODEH) has campaigned for the rights to ownership of tribal lands on the grounds that this is 'inextricably linked' to human rights of free expression of tribal identity and lifestyle (Phillips, 1997). Claims to land rights from indigenous peoples were affirmed at the Legal Commission of the International NGO Conference on Indigenous Peoples and the Land.[7] Stressing the importance of land to cultural traditions of indigenous nations, the declaration produced at this venue stated an 'inseparable connection between land rights of Indigenous Peoples and the right of self-determination' (Nettheim, 1992). The 1986 Quito Declaration,[8] similarly challenged the capitalist political economy by demanding 'an end to assimilationist policies' and 'juridical recognition of territorial rights based on prior ownership including rights to the resources of the sub-soil and recognition of systems of self government' (Smith, 1992). Rights to natural resources are therefore claimed in this declaration as a means for achieving cultural and political independence from the forces of the capitalist economy (Smith, 1992).

Coinciding with the day that NAFTA took effect,[9] the Zapatista Army of National Liberation (EZLN) launched an armed revolt against the Mexican government. Based in the Chiapas region, the rebellion was composed largely by Mayans who challenged the loss of indigenous lands, or ejidos.[10] The right to ejidos, guaranteed under article 27 of the 1917 Mexican constitution, was abolished in 1992 as a part of pro-market reforms undertaken by President Carlos Salinas de Gortari (Stea, Elguea and Bustillo, 1997). A significant feature of the Zapatista uprising was the way in which the movement rejected the pro-market structural adjustments of the Salinas government and instead demanded land rights as a means of securing political and economic independence from the market (Pi-Sunyer and Thomas, 1997). The uprising was also characterized by indigenous opposition to the environmental degradation of the forests in Chiapas, especially in the Lacandon Biosphere Reserve, where the introduction of monoculture cash crops had degraded the ecological biodiversity of this region (Stea, Elguea and Bustillo, 1997). The Zapatista uprising therefore exemplifies a campaign for cultural independence and environmental protection based around demands for land rights.

The conclusion of this discussion is that private property rights to natural resources are unable to secure human rights to cultural self-determination since land use patterns are instead determined by market forces. Placing rights to natural resources in the hands of local communities would empower local groups with the means to achieve independence from the tyranny of the market. The foregoing analysis argued that such empowerment is a prerequisite for the human right to cultural self-determination to be prioritized over considerations of profit that are institutionalized in the capitalist system.

*The Right to be Free From Hunger*

The claimed human right to ownership of environmental resources is necessary to realize the right to be free from hunger as stipulated in the ICESCR.[11] Hunger is a necessary consequence of adopting a market based system of natural resource ownership rights and is largely avoidable through assigning rights over environmental resources to local communities.

Capitalist property rights to land ownership are excellent at supplying market demands but at the necessary expense of causing hunger for hundreds of millions of people who lack the funds to access the market mechanism (Goodman and Redclift, 1991). This situation presently applies to 1.3 billion people, approximately one fifth of the world's population (Flavin, 1997). Subsequently, 40,000 children die daily from the combination of malnutrition and poor sanitation (Galtung, 1994). More than 800 million people suffered from chronic under-nourishment during the period 1980–90 (Chanrasekhar, 1997).

These statistics result from individuals and groups lacking the sufficient land to provide for their own subsistence requirements. Refuting the claim that hunger results from a lack of overall land availability, the evidence demonstrates that hunger is the principal result of commodifying land and thereby redirecting use to serve market demands. This process is exemplified in the case of those living in the Dande Valley of northern Zimbabwe, who were deprived of access to wildlife, forests and fish after their traditional lands were sold off as by the state to raise revenue. The land is now used for cash crops and hunting by paying tourists. Traditional hunting practiced by the indigenous population has been criminalized as poaching and a formally self-sufficient community has become dependent for survival on food from NGOs and from the Zimbabwean state (Tandon, 1993).

The trend towards cash crop production exemplifies how environmental resources are skewed away from providing for basic needs and towards serving luxury markets when land rights are privatized. That starvation is a function of food entitlement rather than of overall availability explains why only sectors of the population who lack income starve and why, 'there has probably never been a famine in which every group has suffered' (Sen, 1983). The net weight of food exported from Ireland during the 1845–50 famine exceeded the weight of foods imported during the same period (Metress, 1996). Similarly, more food was exported from famine areas than was imported in the cases of the 1973 Ethiopian famine and of the 1974 Bangladeshi famine (Sen, 1983). Despite the threat of famine, Sudan sold 400,000 tons of sorghum to the EC in 1989 (*Third World Resurgence* editors, 1994). Further evidence for this trend is provided by Goodman and Redclift who conclude that the food crisis in developing states is caused primarily by a regressive distribution of income (Goodman and Redclift, 1991).

Therefore, hunger is a consequence of land use being diverted through the market mechanism to prioritize the fancies of opulent consumers who are disproportionately located in Western states (Smith, 1981).

The privatization of communal lands in Mexico has changed the use of agricultural lands from serving communal needs to serving luxury markets. Land has been diverted into producing luxury goods such as strawberries and feed grains for animals, foods that are priced beyond the means of most Mexicans (Goodman and Redclift, 1991). Honduras has the lowest level of per-person daily calorific consumption in the Western hemisphere. Governmental incentives for cash crops have ensured rapid expansion in this sector of the Honduran economy since 1965, whilst the availability of basic foods such as maize, beans and sorghum for the domestic population has consistently declined (Phillips, 1997).

This evidence refutes the contention that hunger is a consequence of overall scarcity, a theory typically advanced by corporate agribusiness. Monsanto's Chief Executive Officer (CEO), Robert Shapiro, writes for example in the introduction to the company's 1996 Environmental Review that the use of genetically engineered crops 'will help immensely in closing the gap between hungry people and adequate food supplies' (quoted in Bruno, 1997). In contrast to this claim, the evidence reviewed above suggests that hunger is a function of skewed production patterns in favor of luxury markets under conditions of capitalism. For example, 5 million hectares of land around the world are used to grow tobacco, illustrating how capitalism determines land use to serve frivolous market fads rather than in response to human needs (Brown, 1997). This conclusion is further supported by the fact that during the Ethiopian famine of 1983–4, while thousands died of hunger, fields bloomed with carnations destined for European markets (Sachs, 1995).

Mass starvation continues because under conditions of capitalism, those without the necessary money to buy food have no legally recognizable claim to food. In 1980 the world cereal harvest measured 1,556 million tons. Only 0.002 per cent of this would have been required to adequately feed the 15 million children who died that year from hunger and hunger related illnesses (George, 1984). The UNESCO summarizes that 'the overall availability of food in the world is not a problem. There is enough food to offer everyone in the world around 2,500 calories a day – 200 calories more than the basic minimum' (UNESCO, 1995).

Current patterns of starvation are a constructed function of the global market economy, of commodifying land in the hands of private individuals and corporations who thereafter use the land for cash crops to maximize profits. This fact is made most evident through analysis of the global meat industry. Rifkin observes that:

> 145 million tons of grain were fed to livestock in 1979. Of that, only 21 million tons were available to human beings, after the energy conversion, in the form of meat, poultry and eggs. The rest, 124 million tons of grain and soybeans became inaccessible to human consumption .... If world-wide agricultural production were shifted from livestock feed to grains for direct human consumption, more than a billion people on the planet could be fed (Rifkin, 1992, p. 13).

Energy conversion refers to the 90 per cent of calorific energy that is lost to humans when plants are fed to non-human animals that are subsequently consumed by humans (Regan, 1984). The Artist Hunger Network highlights the inverted logic of the argument of raising cattle to provide protein for humans in pointing out that 'it takes 10 pounds of protein in the form of grain to create 1 pound of protein in the form of flesh to be eaten'.[12] Sagoff reminds us that 'the world already produces enough cereals and oilseeds to feed 10 billion people a vegetarian diet adequate in protein and calories' (Sagoff, 1997).

The criticism that the right to be free from hunger is unattainable, meaning that it can be neither expected nor delivered due to an aggregate lack of resources, must therefore be recognized as an untenable claim. It has been argued here that hunger is a product not of an aggregate lack of resource, but rather a product of relying upon the market mechanism to decide between competing claims to resources. In 1998 the UNDP estimated that an additional $13 billion would have been required to achieve basic health and nutrition for all (Thomas, 1999). This compares with global military spending in the same year of $780 billion (Thomas, 1999). Violations of the right to be free from hunger are tolerated, normalized and reproduced by political choices designed to serve powerful groups benefiting from the capitalist political economy and can be effectively redressed by changing political priorities to focus on satisfying basic human needs.

One effective way through which the prioritization of basic needs can be institutionalized is by implementing a communal right to the ownership of natural resources. The dynamics of this process can be summarized as following from the tendency of community controlled lands to be used to provide for the basic needs of all members and to therefore cultivate food rather than cash crops. Food security theorists have convincingly demonstrated that hunger is most effectively avoided through ensuring that communities have the environmental resources required to meet their own subsistence needs (George, 1984). Through an analysis of the implementation of land reforms in Mexico, Bolivia and Kenya, Rehman concluded that distributing the ownership of natural resources to local communities, 'realizes equitable growth in the agricultural sector whilst arresting the growth of rural poverty' (Rehman, 1993). Further evidence in support of this claim is provided by the International Labor Organization (ILO) which found that, 'redistribution of land rights is the most direct and effective method of improving food entitlements of the poor' (quoted in Tomasevski, 1993). The communal right to natural resources would compliment and help realize the right to be free from hunger since local communities are thereby empowered with both the resources and opportunities to provide for their own subsistence requirements.

## Land Rights as a Function of Environmental Criteria

A pressing resource issue from the perspective of environmental politics is of how to construct human activity to ensure that the impact of human societies upon natural habitats is minimized. In the case of rights to environmental resources, CPR systems have been identified by a number of theorists as being advantageous from the perspective of environmental protection. It is important to state that this does nothing to validate claims to environmental resources made using the discourse of human rights, but environmental considerations nonetheless offer another set of criteria to inform political decisions relating to the design of resource rights.

*Private Property Land Rights Cause Environmental Degradation*

Exemplified by Garret Hardin, many neo-liberal economists maintain that CPR systems are, in environmental terms, inherently disaster prone (Hardin, 1968). Predicting the actions of each individual within a CPR system, Hardin concluded that over-exploitation would result from all members seeking to maximize their personal income from the common resource, leading inexorably to environmental degradation. Applying his theory to the case of a number of herdsmen sharing a single grazing field, Hardin argued that:

> the rational herdsman concludes that the only sensible course for him to pursue is to add another animal to his herd. And another … . Each man is locked into a system that compels him to increase his herd without limit, thereby leading to overuse and environmental degradation (Hardin, 1968, p. 1244).

As Vogler points out, the assumptions of this 'tragedy of the commons' scenario are, however, a product of capitalist theory, making the claim at best questionable when applied to diverse societies that are sustained by value systems typified by communitarian norms (Vogler, 1995). In particular, Hardin assumes that all individuals will make choices characterizing the logic of economic rationality. Yet these values are often absent from non-capitalist societies. Hanna and Jentoft have for example demonstrated that people naturally act collectively when there are positive incentives in their specific cultures to do so (Hanna and Jentoft, 1996). Human nature is largely defined by the structural incentives of the societies in which people have been conditioned. Hardin's research is therefore vulnerable to the charge of falsely universalizing the individualistic and materialistic values of economic rationality. Moreover, environmental degradation often occurs when natural resources are privatized because the anti-social assumption of individualism of the Hardin model becomes a self-fulfilling prophecy. Citing cases of fisheries in Norway and Canada, Hanna and Jentoft demonstrate that it is the removal of the individual interest from the collective interest that causes overuse of resources:

> Traditional resource management practices of many local subsistence exchange economies have been weakened or destroyed through interactions with external markets that have undermined the moral authority for resource management (Hanna and Jentoft, 1996, p. 48).

Thus, in extending the market mechanism in an attempt to prevent the tragedy of the commons, environmental damage is exacerbated rather than alleviated (Hanna and Jentoft, 1996). As *The Ecologist* editors point out, the tragedy of the commons is therefore more accurately described as a 'tragedy of enclosure', where traditional communal controls on resource use are destroyed by the wider structural incentives of profit concerns operating in a capitalist economy (*The Ecologist*, 1993).

In failing to differentiate between CPR and open access systems, Hardin also fails to appreciate how CPRs institutionalize community controls to prevent patterns of over-exploitation. Typifying confusion on this issue, Demsetz interpreted overhunting and the subsequent eradication of many fur-bearing animals in eastern Canada as being due to a lack of property rights (Gowdy, 1999). In fact, as Gowdy demonstrates, it was the introduction of the capitalist economy that caused the collapse in numbers of favored species as profit concerns replaced traditional customs in determining hunting patterns (Gowdy, 1999). Traditional customs that had previously prevented overuse related to environmental awareness, religious restrictions and a fear of reprisal from the spirit world. Indeed, indigenous cultures are typified by a characteristic underuse of resources, compared to the ecological potential (Gowdy, 1999). That native American hunters drove large numbers of bison off cliffs has been presented as evidence that indigenous cultures are unable to maintain ecological sustainability. Yet it was only with the arrival of the Europeans that numbers of bison in North America were decimated from 40 million to 500 animals (Gowdy, 1999).

Organizing land use according to economic criterion is mutually exclusive to the organization of use according to ecological principles. The capitalist system of natural resource rights leads inexorably to environmental degradation because the economically efficient use of resources requires the usage of pesticides, monocultures, cash crops, deforestation and habitat destruction. Monocultures are crops that are grown in isolation from other species to maximize yields, typically in combination with the use of pesticides and insecticides. From the ecological perspective, such an approach creates de facto deserts, devoid of any notable biodiversity, except for the single species of cultivated crop. Cash cropping also entails environmental damage since large numbers of landless or land-poor peasants deprived of the land turned over to cash crop production are forced onto steep hillsides, rain forests, and other environmentally sensitive or agriculturally marginal areas (Thomas, 1996). The clearing of land for cash crops in the Brazilian Amazon resulted in the destruction of 40,000 square miles of rain forest between 1966 and 1983 (Rifkin, 1992; Monbiot, 1996). Jose Lutzenberger, former Brazilian Minister of the Environment, testified that the iniquitous ownership of land in the state was creating land shortages and pushing peasants into the Amazonian rain forest (Human Rights Watch and the Natural Resources Defense Council, 1992).

Private property rights systems of land ownership also tend to cause environmental damage because of the feature of distanciation. Distanciation separates areas of environmental degradation caused in the manufacturing of a product from the place where the good is finally consumed. That is to say, distanciation 'increases the distance between those making the decision and experiencing the consequences' of environmental policies relating to land use (Johnston, 1995). The inevitable result is less environmental protection since the individuals making decisions are spatially and consequentially removed from the environmental impact of their decisions. By way of an example, the British based corporation Rio Tinto Zinc plans to mine ilmenite and titanium dioxide in 4,000 hectares of pristine Madagascan rainforest for use in toothpaste (Nuttall, 1995). Eventual consumers will almost certainly be unaware that the production of their toothpaste involved the destruction of rain forests and will neither suffer, nor pay for that environmental damage, since they will most likely live as far from the site of destruction as the employees who proposed the mining operation. In an increasingly deregulated global economic system, the possibilities available for guaranteeing meaningful environmental protection become increasingly circumscribed.

*CPR Protection of the Environment*

Communal ownership systems to natural resources are more environmentally benign than the market model because subsistence and long term environmental sustainability typically replace the profit motive in determining resource use. The decentralized nature of CPR systems as well as the pool of common knowledge about the local environment built into CPRs over the generations allow commons based systems to effectively respond to natural disturbances and reduce the chances of large scale ecological collapse (Costanza and Folke, 1996).

The right to ownership of natural resources could be implemented to minimize economic activity that degrades the environment over the long term. A decentralized economic system cannot eradicate the conflict between human interests and environmental protection, but evidence suggests that the CPR systems can help minimize the environmental effects of human activities. George Monbiot succinctly explains the predisposition of CPRs to conserve resources when he asserted that:

> I had seen environmental destruction following land alienation. When traditional landholders are dispossessed and either private businesses, large proprietors or state bureaucracies take over, habitats are destroyed. I came to see that rural communities are often constrained to look after their land well, as it is the only thing they have, and they need to protect a diversity of resources in order to meet their diverse needs (Monbiot, 1996).

Examples of the ways in which CPRs are conducive to environmental protection can be illustrated through specific cases. One such study describes how a 1988 National Forest Policy in India granted usufruct resource rights to local communities and subsequently reversed a policy of deforestation (Pye-Smith and Feyerabend, 1995). The Communal Areas Management Program for Indigenous Resources (CAMPFIRE) in Zimbabwe uses customary practices of group ownership to sustain the natural wildlife resource base, allocating resource usage rights around the criterion of ecological sustainability (Zimbabwe Trust, 1990; Derman, 1995).

Another example of an ecologically beneficial CPR system is that of forest management practiced by the Sherpas of Nepal. Traditionally, the 'shingo naua', or forest guards, have prevented deforestation by controlling which trees could be felled and by punishing transgressors (McNeely, 1991). The extractive reserves established by the rubber tappers of the Brazilian Amazon also exemplify an ecologically sustainable CPR. These reserves are co-operatives of rubber tappers and indigenous communities based around an economic system that preserves the forest eco-system whilst harvesting renewable forest products such as rubber, fish and nuts (Mendes, 1989; World Rainforest Movement and Forests Monitor Ltd, 1998). This system has protected biodiversity and the eco-system from quick profit uses and deforestation and is now practiced in 10 per cent of the land area in the

Brazilian province of Acre (McNeely, 1991). Refuting the assumptions underlying Hardin's critique of the commons, successful exclusion under CPR systems is the rule rather than the exception (Berkes, 1996). There was, for example, no widespread tragedy of the commons in England before the enclosure movement since rules such as 'stinting' limited the number of animals each owner could graze on the commons (Berkes, 1996). Because of the fusing of individual and public interests in CPR systems, members adhere to norms and social values since these are (i) identified with self interest, (ii) enforceable through sanctions and (iii) individuals are politically involved and ethically committed to the group (Hanna and Jentoft, 1996).

*Resource Rights and Global Capitalism*

CPR systems of resource use are a necessary, rather than a sufficient, condition for environmental protection (*The Ecologist*, 1995). The institutionalization of CPRs alone will be unlikely to prevent ongoing environmental degradation whilst global capitalism remains in place. Implementing CPRs without structural changes to global capitalism can be expected to change only the agents of environmental destruction. Chapters one and four detailed how the capitalist political economy structurally determines patterns of environmental degradation. When placed within a capitalist structure, traditional taboos on resource overuse in CPRs are broken down and, as numerous examples testify, individuals typically become over exploiters to gain short term profits (McNeely, 1991; Bodley, 1997).

The director of indigenous governance programs of the University of Victoria points out that there is no basis for rationalizing processes of environmental degradation within North American indigenous cultures and traditions.[13] When such degradation has occurred on indigenous lands, this has invariably been as a result of the structural commercial incentives operating in the global economy rather than because of the indigenous culture. In particular, the commodification of nature combined with market incentives dictate that it is more profitable for the present owners of resources to exploit, and thereby gain revenue from mineral and forest reserves, rather than to conserve them.

Exemplifying the limitations placed by global capitalism upon the possibilities for CPRs to protect the environment, the Kayapo Indians of the Brazilian Amazon negotiated contracts with loggers and miners for large-scale extraction of mahogany and gold on their lands after a successful and high profile land rights campaign led the Brazilian government to cede to the indigenous group a 65,000 square-kilometer reserve (Sachs, 1995). Several Kayapo chiefs have since used the income from the sale of the contracts to buy satellite dishes, cars and private jets, whilst most tribal members continue to suffer endemic poverty (Sachs, 1995). Transferring resource rights to communities in the absence of structural changes to the global economy will therefore dictate that these groups will most likely replace individuals, states or corporations as the agents of environmental degradation. An inquiry into alternative structural arrangements more conducive than capitalism to long term environmental protection lies largely outside the scope of this research, but the reader can be directed to the works of Herman Daly for some useful analysis (Daly, 1994; Daly and Cobb, 1995).

## Conclusions

Private property rights legitimize ownership of natural resource in the global capitalist economy. This system of ownership commodifies land and grants legal title to individuals or corporations who purchase the land. Under this system, land rights are therefore a function of private wealth. An alternative system of ownership rights provided by CPRs has been discussed in this chapter. CPR systems suggest an alternative to the choice between market and state that have both proved so disastrous for the environment in the past. CPR systems politicize the ownership of natural resources and thereby facilitate the use of land according to socially agreed criteria (Ostrom, 1990).

The conclusions of this chapter are threefold. Firstly, recognition of the human right to ownership of natural resources was argued to be required for the realization of human rights to (i) cultural self-determination and (ii) freedom from hunger. Secondly, the implementation of this right is required on a communal, rather than an individual, basis. Formal, politically motivated interpretations of international law notwithstanding, neither the ICCPR nor the ICESCR stipulate rights for individuals to own natural resources. Resource rights are instead reserved in both covenants for peoples, indicating a focus on basic needs and self-determination rather than global capital.

Although CPRs have historically prioritized social and environmental over economic criteria in determining patterns of resource usage, this feature has been largely corrupted by the expansion of global capitalism. The third conclusion of this chapter is therefore to reject the possibility of achieving ecological sustainability in the global capitalist economy. It has been argued that the characteristic ability of capitalism to provide a multitude of goods for the rich alongside insufficient goods for the impoverished makes the structure incapable of providing for universal basic needs. Exemplified through cash crops, the consumption of luxury consumer goods necessarily deprives the impoverished of entitlement to resources that are instead diverted by the market mechanism to satisfying frivolous desires of the opulent. Future generations will inherit a world impoverished through climate change, biodiversity impoverishment and resource depletion as a result of current economic decisions predicated upon the use of the environment as advocated by the logic of economic rationality. The human rights and environmental discourses have therefore separately and in tandem problematized the capitalist economic system.

## Notes

1 See chapters 1 and 5 for a detailed discussion of the role and significance of these concepts.
2 See 'Permanent Sovereignty Over Natural Resources', General Assembly Resolution 1803 (XVII), United Nations GAOR Supp. (Number 17) at 15, UN Doc A/5217 (1962); http://www.umn.edu/humanrts/ instree/c2psnr.htm.
3 Peoples Organization, Chile.
4 An area south of Glacier National Park in Montana, USA.

5 Response to research questionnaire received from Darrell Geist, president, Cold Mountain, Cold Rivers, 28 October 1998 and from Jamie Lennox, membership coordinator, Alliance for the Wild Rockies, 10 June 1998.
6 North East Latin America.
7 Held at Geneva in 1981.
8 A declaration from the indigenous people of Latin America.
9 1 January 1994.
10 The Zapatistas are composed primarily of the Tzotzil, Tzeltal, Chol, Tojolabal, Mam and Zoque Mayans.
11 Article 11 (para 2) stipulates 'the States Parties to the present Covenant, recognizing the fundamental right of everyone to be free from hunger, shall take, individually and through international co-operation, the measures, including specific programmes, which are needed ... taking into account the problems of both food-importing and food-exporting countries, to ensure an equitable distribution of world food supplies in relation to need'.
12 Response to research questionnaire received from Artist Hunger Network, 31 October 1998.
13 Interview with Dr Taiaiake Alfred at the University of Southampton, 29 April 1999.

## References


Agarwal, A. and Narain, S. (1992), *Towards a Green World*, Centre for Science and Environment, New Delhi.

Baird, V. (1987), 'Land Rights and Wrongs', *The New Internationalist*, No. 177, November, pp. 4–6.

Barry, B. (1995), *Justice as Impartiality*, Clarendon Press, Oxford.

Beitz, C. (1981), 'Economic Rights and Distributive Justice in Developing Societies', *World Politics*, Vol. 33(3), pp. 321–46.

Berkes, F. (1996) in S. Hanna, C. Folke and K. Maler (eds), *Rights to Nature: Ecological, Economic, Cultural and Political Principles of Institutions for the Environment*, Island Press, Washington DC, p. 87.

Bodley, S. (1997) in B.R. Johnston (ed.), *Human Rights and the Environment at the End of the Millennium*, Alta Mira, Walnut Creek.

Brazil Network (1996b), *Brazil Network Newsletter*, May/June.

Brown, T. (1997), 'Ideological Hegemony and Global Governance', *Journal of World-Systems Research*, Vol. 3(2), pp. 250–58.

Bruno, K. (1997), 'Corporate Watch Gives Winter Greenwash Award to Monsanto', *The Corporate Planet*, http://www.corpwatch.org/trac/greenwash/monsanto.html.

Cameron and MacKenzie (1996) in A.E. Boyle and M.R. Anderson (eds), *Human Rights Approaches to Environmental Protection*, Clarendon Press, Oxford.

Chanrasekhar, C.P. (1997), 'The Right to Food', *Third World Resurgence*, No. 79, March, pp. 35–6.

Chatterjee, P. and Finger, M. (1994), *The Earth Brokers: Power, Politics and World Development*, Routledge, London and New York.

Clay, J.W. (1994) in B.R. Johnston (ed.), *Who Pays the Price?*, Island Press, Washington DC.

Colchester, M. (1995), 'Asia Logs Surniname', *Multinational Monitor*, Vol. 16(11), November, http://www.essential.org/monitor/hyper/mm1195.05.html.

Costanza, R. and Folke, C. (1996) in S. Hanna, C. Folke and K.G. Maler (eds), *Rights to Nature: Econological, Economic, Cultural and Political Principles of Institutions for the Environment*, Island Press, Washington DC.

Council of Europe (1992), *Human Rights in International Law*, Council of Europe Press, Brussels.

Crawford, J. (1992) in J. Crawford (ed.), *The Rights of People*, Clarendon Press, Oxford.

Daly, H. (1995) in J. Kirkby, P. O'Keefe and L. Timberlake (eds), *The Earthscan Reader in Sustainable Development*, Earthscan, London.

Daly, H. and Cobb, J. (1994), *For the Common Good*, Beacon Press, Boston.

Derman, B. (1995), 'Environmental NGO's, Dispossession and the State: The Ideology and Praxis of African Nature and Development', *Human Ecology*, Vol. 23(2), pp. 199–215.

du Bois, F. (1994), 'Water Rights and the Limits of Environmental Law', *Journal of International Law*, Vol. 6(1), pp. 73–84.

*The Ecologist* (1993), *Whose Common Future? Reclaiming the Commons*, Earthscan, London.

*The Ecologist* (1995) in J. Kirkby, P. O'Keefe and L. Timberlake (eds), *The Earthscan*

*Reader in Sustainable Development*, Earthscan, London.
Evans, T. (1996), *US Hegemony and the Project of Universal Human Rights*, Macmillan, Basingstoke.
Flavin, C. (1997) in L. Brown *et al.*, *State of the World 1997*, WW Norton and Company, New York.
Galtung, J. (1994), *Human Rights in Another Key*, Polity Press, Cambridge.
Gamini, G. (1996), 'Andes Tribe Makes Suicide Threat to Halt Oil Drilling', *The Times*, 4 October, p. 13.
George, S. (1984), *Ill Fares the Land*, Institute for Policy Studies, Washington DC.
Gill, S. (1995), 'Globalisation, Market Civilisation and Disciplinary Neoliberalism', *Millennium*, Vol. 24(3), pp. 399–424.
Goodin, R.E. (1985), *Protecting the Vulnerable*, University of Chicago Press, Chicago.
Goodman, D. and Redclift, M. (1991), *Food, Ecology and Culture*, Routledge, London.
Gowdy, J. (1999), *Coevolutionary Economics: The Economy, Society and the Environment*, Kluwer, Boston.
Greider, W. (1997), *One World, Ready or Not: The Manic Logic of Global Capitalism*, Simon and Schuster, New York.
Haas, E.B. (1970), *The Web of Interdependence*, Prentice Hall, Englewood Cliffs, NJ.
Hanna, S. and Jentoft, S. (1996) in S. Hanna, C. Folke and K.G. Maler (eds), *Rights to Nature: Ecological, Economic, Cultural and Political Principles of Institutions for the Environment*, Island Press, Washington DC.
Hanna, S., Folke, C. and Maler, K.G. (1996) in S. Hanna, C. Folke and K.G. Maler (eds), *Rights to Nature: Ecological, Economic, Cultural and Political Principles of Institutions for the Environment*, Island Press, Washington DC.
Hardin, G. (1968), 'The Tragedy of the Commons', *Science*, Vol. 162, pp. 1243–8.
Hill, R.P. (1995), 'Blackfellas and Whitefellas: Aboriginal Land Rights, The Mabo Decision and the Meaning of Land', *Human Rights Quarterly*, Vol. 17(2), pp. 303–22.
Hitchcock, R.K. (1997) in B.R. Johnston (ed.), *Human Rights and the Environment at the End of the Millennium*, Alta Mira, Walnut Creek.
Human Rights Watch and the Natural Resources Defense Council (1992), *Defending the Earth: Abuses of Human Rights and the Environment*, Natural Resources Defense Council, Washington DC.
Inter Press Service (1997), 'G-7 Environment: Indigenous Tribunal to Try Sumiteers', 19 June, http://www.oneworld.org/ips2/.
Johnston, B.R. (1995), 'Human Rights and the Environment', *Human Ecology*, Vol. 23(2), pp. 111–23.
Kramer, M. (1997), *John Locke and the Origin of Private Property*, University of Cambridge Press, Cambridge.
Luxner, L. (1997), 'Business Bats for Colombia', *Multinational Monitor*, Vol. 18(5), May, http://www.essential.org/monitor/hyper/mm0597.12.html.
McNeely, J.A. (1991), 'Common Property Resource Management or Government Ownership?', *International Relations*, Vol. 10(3), May, pp. 211–26.
Makhijani, A. (1992), *From Global Capitalism to Economic Justice*, Apex Press, New York and London.

Mendes, C. (1989), *Fight for the Forest: Chico Mendes in his Own Words*, Latin American Bureau, London.

Metress, S. (1996), 'The Great Starvation and British Imperialism in Ireland', *The Irish People*, 10 January, http://www.vms.utexas.edu/~jdana/iplunger.html.

Monbiot, G. (1996), 'The Land is Ours', Schumacher Lecture, 19 October, Bristol, http://www.oneworld.org/schumachersoc/lectures96/monbiot.html.

*Multinational Monitor* (1995b) 'Mapuche Put Earth First', *Multinational Monitor*, Vol. 16(11), November 1995, http://www.essential.org/monitor/hyper/mm1195.09.html.

*Multinational Monitor* (1996), 'Behind the Lines', *Multinational Monitor*, Vol. 17(11), November, http://www.essential.org/monitor/hyper/mm1196.01.html.

Nettheim, G. (1992) in J. Crawford (ed.), *The Rights of People*, Clarendon Press, Oxford.

*New Internationalist, The* (1987), 'This Singing Land', *The New Internationalist*, No. 177, November, pp. 12–3.

Nuttall, N. (1995), 'Campaign Launched to Save Madagascan Forests From Mining', *The Times*, 19 January, p. 7.

Ostrom, E. (1990), *Governing the Commons*, Cambridge University Press, Cambridge.

Ostrom, E. and Schlager, E. (1996) in S. Hanna, C. Folke and K.G. Maler (eds), *Rights to Nature: Ecological, Economic, Cultural and Political Principles of Institutions for the Environment*, Island Press, Washington DC.

Paine, T. (1987), *Thomas Paine Reader*, Penguin, London.

Park, P, (1992), 'Canadian Cree Take Quebec's Hydro Scheme to Tribunal', *New Scientist*, Vol. 133(1806), 1 February, p. 15.

*Permanent Sovereignty Over Natural Resources* (1962), General Assembly Resolution 1803 (XVII), 17 United Nations GAOR Supp. at 15, UN Doc A/5217, http://www.umn.edu/humanrts/instree/c2psnr.htm.

Phillips, J. (1997) in B.R. Johnston (ed.), *Human Rights and the Environment at the End of the Millennium*, Alta Mira, Walnut Creek.

Pi-Sunyer, O. and Thomas, R.B. (1997) in B.R. Johnston (ed.), *Human Rights and the Environment at the End of the Millennium*, Alta Mira, Walnut Creek.

Project International (1997), 'Occidental and Shell Threaten U'wa of Colombia', 19 October, http://www.alphacdc.com/ien/uwa.html.

Project Underground (1997c), 'Occidental: Supporting Suicide', 27 October, http://www.moles.org/ProjectUnderground/drillbits/motherlode/oxy.html.

Pye-Smith, C. and Feyerabend, G.B. (1995) in J. Kirkby, P. O'Keefe and L. Timberlake (eds), *The Earthscan Reader in Sustainable Development*, Earthscan, London.

Regan, T. (1984), in T. Regan (ed.), *Earthbound: New Introductory Essays in Environmental Ethics*, Temple University Press, Philadelphia.

Rehman, S. (1993), *Agrarian Reform and Social Transformation*, Zed Books, London.

Rifkin, J. (1992), 'Bovine Burden', *Geographical Magazine*, July, pp. 12–6.

Sachs, A. (1995), *Eco-Justice: Linking Human Rights and the Environment*, Worldwatch Paper 127, Worldwatch Institute, Washington DC.

Sagoff, M. (1995) in A. Brennan (ed.), *The Ethics of the Environment*, Dartmouth, London.

Sagoff, M. (1997), 'Do We Consume Too Much?', *The Atlantic Monthly*, Vol. 279(6), June, pp. 80–96, http://www.theatlantic.com/atlantic/issues/97jun/consume.html.
Saurin, J. (1993) in C. Thomas (ed.), *Rio: Unravelling the Consequences*, Frank Cass, Ilford.
Sen, A. (1983) in A. Gauer (ed.) *South – South Strategy*, Third World Foundation, Penang.
Smith, D.M. (1981), *Where the Grass is Greener*, Penguin, Harmondsworth.
Smith, L. (1992), 'Indigenous Rights', *Race and Class*, Vol. 33(3), p. 104.
Stea, D., Elguea, S. and Bustillo, C.R. (1997) in B.R. Johnston (ed.), *Human Rights and the Environment at the End of the Millennium*, Alta Mira, Walnut Creek.
Sumner, C. (1979), *Reading Ideologies*, Academic Press, London.
Tandon, Y. (1993) in W. Sachs (ed.), *Global Ecology*, Zed Books, London.
Taylor, A. (1998), 'The Significance of Non-governmental Organisations in the Development of International Environmental Policy: The Case of Trade and Environment', PhD thesis, Southampton University, Southampton.
Third World Resurgence editors (1994) (untitled), *Third World Resurgence*, No. 50, October, p. 18.
Thomas, C. (1996), 'Unsustainable Development?', *New Political Economy*, Vol. 1(3), pp. 404–408.
Thomas, C. (1999), 'Where is the Third World Now?', *Review of International Studies*, December, Vol. 25, pp. 225–44.
Tomasevski, K. (1993), *Development Aid and Human Rights Revisited*, Pinter Publishers, London.
UNESCO (1995), 'Fact File', *United Nations Economic and Social Council Courier*, March, p. 30.
Vincent, R.J. (1986), *Human Rights and International Relations*, Cambridge University Press, Cambridge.
Vogler, J. (1995), *The Global Commons: A Regime Analysis*, John Wiley and Sons, Chichester.
Wisner, B. (1995), 'The Reconstructing of Environmental Rights in Urban South Afrida', *Human Ecology*, Vol. 23(2), June, pp. 259–84.
Wiwa, K.S. (1995), 'Nigeria in Crisis', *Review of African Political Economy*, Vol. 22(64), June, pp. 234–56.
Wood, N. (1984), *John Locke and Agrarian Capitalism*, University of California Press, Berkeley.
World Rainforest Movement and Forests Monitor Ltd. (1998), *High Stakes: The Need to Control Transnational Logging Companies*, World Forest Movement, Montevideo.
Worldwatch Institute (1995), 'Worldwide Repression of Peaceful Environmental Protestors Spurs new Coalitions with Human Rights Activists', 9 December, http://www.antenna.nl/news/women/180days/mn00161.html.
Wright, S. (1997), 'U'wa Indigenous Leader Beaten and Threatened', *Rainforest Action Network*, 20 October, http://www.alphacdc.com/ien/uwa.html.
Zimbabwe Trust, Department of National Parks and Wildlife Management and the CAMPFIRE Association (1990), *People, Wildlife and Natural Resources – The CAMPFIRE Approach to Rural Development in Zimbabwe*, Zimbabwe Trust, Harare.

doi 10.1350/enlr.2010.12.1.074

# Environmental Principles and Environmental Justice

Ole W. Pedersen*

**Keywords**: Environmental justice, precautionary principle, polluter pays principle, sustainable development.

**Abstract**: This article offers an analysis of the compatibility between the emerging concept of environmental justice and a number of more well established environmental principles. These include the precautionary principle, the polluter pays principle and sustainable development. The article argues that, for all three principles, a comparison with environmental justice gives rise to conflicts as well as conformity. The main reason for this is the ambiguity and inconsistency of environmental justice and the three principles.

## 1. INTRODUCTION

One characteristic of environmental law and policy is the central role that so-called environmental principles play in the shaping of decisions, formulation of policies and governance in general. These principles are often hard to define and their application frequently varies. Such principles include the precautionary principle, the principle of prevention, the polluter pays principle and sustainable development. These principles form part of both international and domestic environmental law and policy, albeit to varying degrees. For instance, some argue for a right to sustainable development and others assert that the principles of prevention and precaution form part of customary international law. Taken together, these principles have, over the last 30 years, become an essential part of the environmental lawyer's vocabulary. More recently, the concept of environmental justice has emerged as a basis for questioning established norms of environmental law and policy in general and, in some instances, the environmental principles in particular.

This paper aims to analyse the congruence between the well-established environmental law principles of precaution, prevention, polluter pays and sustainable development, and environmental justice. While much can be said (and much has been said) about the principles, the aim of this paper is not to provide a fully fledged analysis of the principles. Instead, this paper aims to start a debate on the role of environmental justice as a concept and its compatibility with the more well-established norms of environmental policy and law. The reason for this is two-fold. First, in light of the emergence of environmental justice as a concept in the UK and Europe, it is important to attempt to define the boundaries and meaning of the concept. Secondly, while environmental justice and its emphasis on fair distribution and processes on the face of it seems benign, it is important to subject the concept to critical scrutiny, given the possible implications of its claims of injustice. An additional point is that, given the pervasiveness of the well-established environmental

* Newcastle University Law School (ole.pedersen@newcastle.ac.uk). The author wishes to acknowledge the helpful comments received on earlier versions of this paper by Donald McGillivray, John Paterson, Aylwin Pillai, Chris Rodgers and Anne-Michelle Slater, as well as the two anonymous referees of *Environmental Law Review*. All mistakes and omissions remain those of the author.

principles, it equally becomes relevant to question these principles in the name of justice in an attempt to further debate about their longevity.

The outline of the paper is as follows. A brief introduction to the concept of environmental justice is provided in Part 2. In Part 3, the paper analyses the relationship between environmental justice and the precautionary principle. This is followed by an analysis of the compatibility between the principle of prevention and environmental justice in Part 4. In Part 5, similarities and differences between the polluter pays principle and environmental justice are considered. Part 6 assesses the relationship between sustainable development and environmental justice.

# 2. ENVIRONMENTAL JUSTICE

The foundations of environmental justice were laid following the civil rights struggles of the United States when African-American communities in the 1970s and 1980s came to perceive the siting of waste facilities and other environmental harms as unjust.[1] Early examples of environmental injustice include the siting, in 1979, of a waste facility in a predominantly African-American neighbourhood in Northwood Manor, Houston, only eight years after the siting in the same neighbourhood (when the area was predominantly white) had been rejected by local authorities.[2] Through local activism, grassroots networks and campaigning, an entire environmental justice movement gradually came about in the US, eventually succeeding in drawing national attention to local struggles. Throughout the 1980s and 1990s, impetus was added to the environmental justice argument when a series of studies, in one way or the other, all seemed to confirm the instinct of environment-harming facilities being sited in the 'path of least resistance'.[3] On the back of this evidence, campaigners set out to facilitate environmental justice, originally phrased under the heading of 'environmental racism', under a wide range of 'justice' definitions.[4]

- First, an equal distribution of environmental harms was sought through calls for *distributive justice*.[5] This distributive focus is what may be seen as the historical origin and underpinning of environmental justice. Since then, however, multiple layers have been added to the definition of environmental justice.
- Secondly, calls were made for *procedural justice*, emphasising issues of participation, access to information and justice for minority neighbourhoods, and for decisions to be made in accordance with the concept of 'free informed

1 See, in general, R. D. Bullard, *Dumping in Dixie: Race, Class, and Environmental Quality* (Westview Press: Boulder, Colorado, 2000) and L. W. Cole and S. Foster, *From the Ground Up: Environmental Racism and the Rise of the Environmental Justice Movement* (New York University Press: New York, 2001).

2 R. D. Bullard, 'Environmental Racism and "Invisible" Communities' (1994) 96 *W. Va. L. Rev.* 1037 at 1038. The reasons for refusing the 1971 application had, *inter alia*, been: (1) that the proposed landfill would be too close to a school; (2) it would lower the residents' property values; (3) it would create health hazards from rats, rodents and other vermin; and (4) it would increase truck traffic and endanger the lives of children walking to school.

3 A. Kaswan, 'Environmental Justice: Bridging the Gap between Environmental Laws and "Justice"' (1997) 47 Am UL Rev 221 (1997) and M. B. Gerrard, 'Reflections on Environmental Justice' (2001) 65 Alb L Rev 357.

4 See R. R. Kuehn, 'A Taxonomy of Environmental Justice' (2000) 30 *Environmental Law Reporter* 10681, and R. J. Lazarus, 'Pursuing "Environmental Justice": The Distributional Effect of Environmental Protection' (1993) 87 *Northwestern University Law Review* 787.

5 See, for instance, Principles of Environmental Justice, Principle 2, Bullard, above n. 1, calling for 'geographical equity' at 116 and Executive Order 12898 of 11 February 1994, 'Federal Actions to Address Environmental Justice in Minority Populations and Low-Income Populations'.

consent'.[6] This procedural approach is also recognised outside the civil rights origin of environmental justice. Thus, in Europe, the 1998 Aarhus Convention seeks to achieve 'access to justice' in environmental matters.[7]

- Thirdly, as portrayed in the influential work of David Schlosberg, environmental justice has been pursued under a heading of *'recognition'*.[8] This approach emphasises, in contrast to definitions dealing with distribution only, an explicit need for recognition of minority populations and underlying social conditions alongside the distributive and procedural approaches.
- Fourthly, environmental justice campaigners have called for a *substantive right for all individuals to be protected from environmental degradation*.[9] This approach emphasises the equal right of all people to be effectively protected from environmental harms and it echoes calls made in the human rights debates on environmental issues where it is occasionally argued that a substantive human right to a healthy environment is desirable.[10]
- Fifthly, although this was not a feature of the early environmental justice arguments, some environmental justice groups have started to cast their nets more widely, emphasising 'productive justice' which questions the prior reasons and decisions controlling the production of environmental burdens.[11] In other words, instead of focusing on the distribution of harm and anthropocentric exposure to such harm, certain environmental justice campaigners take a more holistic approach when challenging decisions that present a potential environmental risk before such decisions are implemented.
- Finally, and in line with the 'productive justice' approach, environmental justice calls are increasingly being applied outside anthropocentric social justice settings and to the non-human sphere of the environment and animals. This is done under the heading of 'ecological justice', borrowing from environmental ethics, where justice is taken to encompass obligations towards the environment.[12]

6 See, for instance, Bullard, above n. 1 at 116, calling for 'procedural equity'; Kaswan, above n. 3, calling for 'political justice' at 279; K. Shradder-Frechette, *Environmental Justice, Creating Equality, Reclaiming Democracy* (Oxford University Press: Oxford, 2002) 27; and L. A. Binder, 'Religion, Race and Rights: A Rhetorical Overview of Environmental Justice Disputes' (1999) 6 *Wisconsin Environmental Law Journal* 1 at 24–27.

7 Aarhus Convention on Access to Information, Public Participation in Decision-making and Access to Justice in Environmental Matters (1999) 38 ILM 517.

8 D. Schlosberg, *Environmental Justice and the New Pluralism: The Challenge of Diversity for Environmentalism* (Oxford University Press: Oxford, 1999); D. Schlosberg, 'Reconceiving Environmental Justice: Global Movements and Political Theories' (2004) 13(3) *Environmental Politics* and D. Schlosberg, *Defining Environmental Justice: Theories, Movements, and Nature* (Oxford University Press: Oxford, 2007). See also S. Foster, 'Justice from the Ground Up' (1998) 86 Cal L Rev 775.

9 See Bullard, above n. 1 at 122; R. D. Bullard, *The Quest for Environmental Justice, Human Rights and the Politics of Pollution* (Sierra Club Books: San Francisco, 2005) 25; R. D. Bullard, 'Levelling the Playing Field through Environmental Justice' (1999) 23 *Vt L Rev* 453 at 454, and Bullard, above n. 2 at 1041.

10 See, most recently, S. J. Turner, *A Substantive Environmental Right: An Examination of the Legal Obligations of Decision-Makers towards the Environment* (Kluwer Law International: Austin, 2009).

11 See R. W. Lake, 'Volunteers, NIMBYs, and Environmental Justice: Dilemmas of Democratic Practice' (1996) *Antipode* 28:2 at 165, and D. Faber, 'The Struggle for Ecological Democracy and Environmental Justice' in D. Faber (ed.), *The Struggle for Ecological Democracy, Environmental Justice Movements in the United States* (Guildford Press: New York, 1998) 15.

12 See, most prominently, D. Schlosberg, *Defining Environmental Justice*, above n. 8.

In addition to these approaches, calls for environmental justice are increasingly being asserted in settings of space, history, gender, transport, energy, youth activism and housing.[13]

It is thus evident that environmental justice is a rather broad and wide-reaching concept emphasising multiple notions of justice. One rationale behind this is partly to be found in the original definition of the environment adopted by the environmental justice movement as being 'where we live, work and play', underlining the change of focus compared to conventional environmental groups emphasising nature conservation.[14] Coupled with this is the fact that 'justice' is hardly a static or easily identifiable concept. Hence, it makes little sense to talk of *one* definition of environmental justice. We are instead forced to accept that the concept of environmental justice is vague, nebulous and can mean many different things to different people. Perhaps that is partly why it has been so successful at the grassroots level. In spite of this success, it may be worth pondering whether this in-built ambiguity does not, at the same time, render the concept meaningless while perhaps depriving the concept of value? Whereas it is tempting to answer such questions in the affirmative, it must be borne in mind that, as the concept is making its way into the UK, ambiguity is to be expected as differences between the UK and the US in terms of demography, ethnography and social characteristics are obvious.[15]

Moreover, one central characteristic of environmental justice, and arguably the greatest advantage of the concept, is that, partly as a result of its many definitions, it has succeeded in facilitating debates on environmental issues, laws and decisions. In this light, the concept of environmental justice has, notwithstanding problems of definition, an important role to play. What is more, it is evident that environmental justice brings to the fore a series of questions and concerns making a comparison with established environmental norms relevant. It is to this comparison that we will now turn.

## 3. THE PRECAUTIONARY PRINCIPLE AND ENVIRONMENTAL JUSTICE

In layman's words, the precautionary principle can be taken to mean 'better safe than sorry' or 'prevention is better than cure'.[16] The principle thus assumes action prior to an activity being carried out and before its results are known.[17] Despite these simplifications of the principle's remits, its application is far from straightforward. This is underlined by

13 See, in general, J. Sze and J. K. London, 'Environmental Justice at the Crossroads' (2008) 2(4) *Sociology Compass* 1331; G. Walker, 'Beyond Distribution and Proximity: Exploring the Multiple Spatialities of Environmental Justice' (2009) 41(4) *Antipode* 614; K. Bickerstaff and J. Agyeman, 'Assembling Justice Spaces: The Scalar Politics of Environmental Justice in North-east England' (2009) 41(4) *Antipode* 781; S. Buckingham and R. Kulcur, 'Gendered Geographies of Environmental Justice' (2009) 41(4) *Antipode* 659; and G. Walker and H. Bulkeley, 'Geographies of Environmental Justice' (2006) 37 *Geoforum* 655.

14 C. Lee, 'Developing the Vision of Environmental Justice: A Paradigm for Achieving Healthy and Sustainable Communities' (1995) 14 *Virginia Environmental Law Journal* 571 at 571 and Di Chiro, 'Environmental Justice from the Grassroots: Reflecting on History, Gender, and Expertise' in Faber (ed.), above n. 11 at 105.

15 See A.-M. Slater and O. W. Pedersen, 'Environmental Justice: Lessons on Definition and Delivery from Scotland' (2009) 52(6) *Journal of Environmental Planning and Management* 797, discussing environmental justice in Scotland.

16 See J. Paterson, 'Sustainable Development, Sustainable Decisions and the Precautionary Principle' (2007) 42 *Natural Hazards* 515 at 517, and D. B. Resnik, 'Is the Precautionary Principle Unscientific?' (2003) 34 *Stud. Hist. Phil. Biol. & Biomed. Sci.* 329 at 329.

17 N. de Sadeleer, *Environmental Principles: From Political Slogans to Legal Rules* (Oxford University Press: Oxford, 2002) 91.

the fact that it has found application in a wide range of areas in varying circumstances.[18] The precautionary principle can be traced back to the 1970s to what was then the Federal Republic of Germany (FRG), where the principle of *vorsorge* emerged in clean air legislation before the Bundestag in an attempt to curb damage to the environment as a result of acid rain and smog.[19] On the international scene, the principle initially found application in law relating to the protection of the marine environment, particularly in a number of regional instruments and agreements. For instance, the parties within the North Sea Ministerial Conferences made references of a precautionary nature in their 1984 Bremen Ministerial Declaration and specific reference to the principle in the 1987 London Ministerial Declaration.[20] More recently, the principle has become a central part of European Union policy relating to the environment, finding its way into the Treaty on the Functioning of the European Union.[21]

Principle 15 of the Rio Declaration, which embodies the precautionary principle, states that 'where there are threats of serious or irreversible damage, lack of full scientific certainty shall not be used as a reason for postponing cost-effective measures to prevent environmental degradation'.[22] The main aim of the principle is thus to prevent harm to human health and the environment, where the full effects of a given action are not yet known. As Principle 15 implies, a central trait of the precautionary principle is whether a threat of harm exists. In examining whether a threat exists or not, the concept of risk is central.[23] This part of the precautionary principle is arguably the one part with the strongest environmental justice implications.[24] Very simplified, the concept of risk can be seen as falling in two parts: risk assessment and risk management.[25] Under risk assessment, the likely outcome and magnitude of a specific action is measured and considered – often based on scientific inquiry and data.[26] Risk management is the process by which a decision on how to deal with the outcome yielded in the risk assessment is made – often by politicians and governments.[27] These processes hold a number of environmental justice implications.

18 E. Fisher, J. Jones and R. V. Schomberg, 'Implementing the Precautionary Principle: Perspectives and Prospects' in E. Fisher, J. Jones and R. V. Schomberg (eds), *Implementing the Precautionary Principle* (Edward Elgar: Cheltenham, 2006), and E. Fisher, *Risk Regulation and Administrative Constitutionalism* (Hart: Oxford, 2007). See also C. Sunstein, *Laws of Fear: Beyond the Precautionary Principle* (Cambridge University Press: New York, 2005), noting at 120 that '[f]or every regulatory tool, there is a corresponding Precautionary Principle'.

19 See, in general, S. Boehmer-Christensen, 'The Precautionary Principle in Germany – Enabling Government' in T. O'Riordan and J. Cameron (eds), *Interpreting the Precautionary Principle* (Cameron May: London, 1994) 35–36.

20 See, in general, de Sadeleer, above n. 17 at 94–95 and M. MacGarvin, 'Precaution, Science and the Sin of Hubris' in T. O'Riordan and J. Cameron (eds), above n. 19.

21 TFEU Art. 191(2). For an application of the principle by the courts, see E. Fisher, 'Is the Precautionary Principle Justiciable?' (2001) 13(3) *Journal of Environmental Law* 315, *Ireland* v *United Kingdom* (2002) 41 ILM 405 for international application, and Case C-T-13/99 *Pfizer Animal Health SA* v *Council of the European Union* ECR II-3305 for a European application.

22 Rio Declaration on Environment and Development (1992) 31 ILM 874, Principle 15.

23 See, in general, F. Warner, 'What If? Versus If It Ain't Broke Don't Fix It' in T. O'Riordan and J. Cameron (eds), above n. 19.

24 See, for instance, B. Goldman, 'An Environmental Justice Paradigm for Risk Assessment' (2000) *Human and Ecological Risk Assessment* 6(6) 541, noting at 541 that '[I]n a way, environmental justice is a risk analyst's worst nightmare'.

25 D. T. Hornstein, 'Reclaiming Environmental Law: A Normative Critique of Comparative Risk Analysis' (1992) 92 *Columbia Law Review* 562 at 570. A third part is sometimes considered to be that of risk communication.

26 P. M. Kannan, 'The Precautionary Principle: More than a Cameo Appearance in United States Environmental Law?' (2007) 31 *William & Mary Environmental Law & Policy Review* (2007) at 410–411.

27 Ibid.

First and foremost, the process of risk assessment and its reliance on scientific methods is often seen by environmental justice campaigners as going against the central focus of environmental justice as these have claimed to rely on notions of ethics, equity and social justice.[28] Such differences partly lay behind the call for popular epidemiology raised by some environmental justice activists stressing the evidence and testimony given by local residents, rather than technological evidence from scientists and bureaucrats.[29] In this way, the critique of the use of risk assessment by environmental justice campaigners can be seen as following the well-trodden debates on risk and democracy which have tended to fall along instrumental lines.[30]

Similarly, environmental justice advocates criticise the statistical generalisations of environmental issues in the risk assessment process.[31] Environmental justice activists have, for example, pointed to the '70kg white male problem', which is seen as not taking into account the variability in human susceptibility to certain risks.[32] For instance, centrally calculated thresholds of contamination levels in, say, fish are sometimes based on an average consumption of a white male, which may not reflect the varied susceptibility that some minority populations face as a result of their diets being high in fish.[33] This situation does not, however, hold true for all environmental risks. In the UK, the Environment Agency has a policy of calculating the maximum level of allowable exposure to radioactive activity based on the level of exposure faced by the so-called 'critical group' – that is, the group which is at greatest risk of exposure.[34] Moreover, environmental justice campaigners have argued that risk assessment often does not consider the individual's specific situation, which may lead to a different susceptibility. For instance, variations in genetic and medical combinations as a result of race, lifestyles, and socio-demographic features are all factors that can change an individual's susceptibility to a particular risk, which

28 See E. Gauna, 'Federal Environmental Citizen Provisions: Obstacles and Incentives on the Road to Environmental Justice' (1995) 22 *Ecology Law Quarterly* 1. See, however, M. D. Adler, 'Risk Equity: A New Proposal' (2008) 32 *Harvard Environmental Law Review* 1, who criticises the environmental justice movement's criticism of risk assessment for being too simplistic in that it focuses only on differences in social status, thus neglecting differences between individuals of the same social status.

29 See, for instance, P. Novotny, 'Popular Epidemiology and the Struggle for Community Health in the Environmental Justice Movement' in D. Faber, above n. 11 at 141–148; D. N. Scott, 'Confronting Chronic Pollution: A Socio-Legal Analysis of Risk and Precaution' (2008) 46 *Osgoode Hall Law Journal*, discussing the use of so-called 'body burdens' and 'bucket brigades' both relying on local activities; F. Fischer, *Citizens, Experts and the Environment* (Duke University Press: Durham, 2000), citing Brown who notes that 'popular epidemiology' is 'a process in which lay persons gather statistics and other information and also direct and marshall the knowledge and resources of experts'; and B. Bryant, 'Pollution Prevention and Participatory Research as a Methodology for Environmental Justice' (1995) 14 *Virginia Environmental Law Journal* 589, arguing in favour of participatory research.

30 See Fisher, above n. 18. Here it could be argued that the criticism levelled against authorities and institutions in general by environmental justice campaigners accusing administrations of suffering from an indifference to difference (by e.g. not paying attention to the plight of minority communities and not employing minority employees) is, to some extent, aimed at addressing what Fisher characterises as questions of 'administrative constitutionalism'.

31 Hornstein, above n. 25 at 626.

32 See R. R. Kuehn, 'The Environmental Justice Implications of Quantitative Risk Assessment' (1996) U Ill L Rev 103 at 121.

33 See B. E. Hill and N. Targ, 'Protecting Natural Resources and the Issue of Environmental Justice' in Kathryn Mutz (ed.), *Environmental Justice and Natural Resources: Concepts, Strategies and Applications* (Island Press: Covelo, 2001) 290–293 and C. A. O'Neill, 'Variable Justice: Environmental Standards, Contaminated Fish, and "Acceptable" Risk to Native Peoples' (2000) 19 *Stanford Environmental Law Journal* 3.

34 See http://www.environment-agency.gov.uk/research/library/data/34345.aspx. See also T. W. Simon, 'In Defense of Risk Assessment: A Reply to the Environmental Justice Movement's Critique' (2000) *Human and Ecological Risk Assessment* 6(6) 555 at 558, arguing that claims of difference in susceptibility are overblown.

may not form part of the risk assessment because of the general nature of how that risk is assessed.[35]

Furthermore, environmental justice campaigners complain that traditional risk assessment rarely takes into account cumulative exposure to risk. That is, risk assessment will often, because of its relative complexity, only consider one particular risk and one particular outcome, and not a combination of a number of different risks and outcomes.[36] This is seen as striking at the centre of the environmental justice problem, as the main argument behind environmental justice is that certain minorities take upon them a disproportionate burden of harms as a result of a concentration of polluting facilities. This results in a situation where a community is subject to a number of different risks that individually would be acceptable, and thus perceived as fair, but because of the cumulative effect the community sees itself as unfairly treated.[37] This problem is further exacerbated by the fact that, although a risk assessor knows the effects of overexposure to one risk, few may know the effects of so-called pollution mixes. Again, problems like these are partly why environmental justice activists are rarely impressed with scientific and statistical generalisations and call for local epidemiology.[38]

Another environmental justice problem with the application of risk assessment is the forum in which such assessment is carried out. As the exercise of risk assessment is, to a large degree, based on scientific methods and empirical evidence, it sometimes remains closed to the communities facing the risk.[39] In spite of the complexities and difficulties entailing a risk assessment exercise, it is often argued that where the assessment is carried out in a purely scientific setting away from those facing the risk, such an assessment is detrimental to the concept of environmental justice.[40] This is highlighted where the risk assessment exercise is not necessarily perceived as objective. Although scientific methods are often portrayed as objective and unbiased, the risk assessment procedure is seen as being open to individual and subjective interpretation.[41] Such problems are intensified in situations where one party to an environmental justice conflict has better access to influence than the other party. This is, for instance, seen where the mere understanding of a risk assessment requires specific expertise and substantial resources – something often not available to communities pursuing an environmental justice claim.[42] In addition, where the risk assessment is carried out by a government agency, the capture theory (under which the agency and the regulated subject become intertwined and share a common ground) may add to the unfair balance.[43]

35 Kuehn, above n. 32 at 123–124.
36 Ibid. at 117–118.
37 Ibid.
38 See above n. 29.
39 See T. J. Lowi, 'Risks and Rights in the History of American Government' (1990) *Daedalus*, Fall 17, noting, at 18, that 'those speaking the loudest against risk-alleviating policies were among society's most risk-insulated persons'.
40 De Sadeleer argues that risk assessors need to become more aware of the 'social dimensions' of their exercise by creating more room for deliberation and that risk assessment must not be considered a purely scientific enterprise to which only experts have access, above n. 17 at 195. See also K. Sexton, 'Socioeconomic and Racial Disparities in Environmental Health: Is Risk Assessment Part of the Problem or Part of the Solution?' (2000) *Human and Ecological Risk Assessment* 6(6) 551 at 571, noting that 'Interpreting risk assessment to include only "hard" quantifiable (or quantified) factors, and disregarding or marginalizing "soft" non-quantifiable (or not quantified) variables, has tended historically to preclude considerations of pertinent issues, such as social class, ethnicity, race, and culture'.
41 Kuehn, above n. 32 at 134.
42 Ibid. at 130–131.
43 Ibid. at 133.

Similarly, recent work on the precautionary principle has, in light of the principal application of the principle in administrative settings, highlighted the need for administrative capacity, legitimacy and good risk governance when it comes to applying the precautionary principle and communicating the particular risk.[44] Equally, in the context of environmental justice in the US, where accusations of institutional indifference to the situations of minority populations were and are prevalent, questions of legitimacy and proper communication have played a central role.[45]

The problems of lack of openness and transparency in the risk assessment process can be remedied, however, through the process of risk management. Where risk assessment is based on scientific inquiry and methods, risk management has the potential to take place in the public domain and ought to be open to the public. Thus, what may be seen as the 'democratic' side of the precautionary principle may facilitate environmental justice objectives where the political responses to certain risks are openly debated through processes involving all interested parties.[46] This may be the case on both the domestic as well as the supra-national level; for instance, in its Communication on the precautionary principle the Commission notes that decision-making procedures should be transparent and involve all interested parties.[47] Accordingly, in order for the risk management decisions to be in line with environmental justice arguments, decisions ought to be taken as openly as possible.[48]

Finally, one problem with risk assessment is that it is often treated as a solution rather than a tool. Just as politicians are perhaps more likely to weigh short-term benefits over long-term ill effects, it can be argued that they are not very likely to dismiss the results of a risk assessment exercise because of public or community concern.[49] Under this scenario, the risk assessment becomes the end rather than a method to aid the decision-makers in the risk management situation.[50]

In spite of the discrepancies between the precautionary principle, its notion of risk, and environmental justice, some areas of compatibility do exist between the two. First, the precautionary principle is generally thought to hold a presumption in favour of protecting the environment and human health, which means that the principle generally places the burden of proof on those who carry out an activity that threatens the environment or human health.[51] Although the legal, administrative and judicial connotation of such presumptions is unclear and may vary significantly from context to context,[52] the question of the onus and burden of proof is often seen as central in environmental justice questions. Such a change in the burden of proof falls in line with calls made by environmental justice campaigners and is similar to the 'environmental justice framework' proposed by

44 E. Fisher and R. Harding, 'The Precautionary Principle and Administrative Constitutionalism: The Development of Frameworks for Applying the Precautionary Principle' in Fisher *et al.*, above n. 18.
45 L. Pulido, 'A Critical Review of the Methodology of Environmental Racism Research' (1996) *Antipode*, 28:2.
46 See L. Auberson-Huang, 'The Dialogue between Precaution and Risk', (2002) 20 *Nature Biotechnology* 1076–1078, terming this process 'risk-analysis', whereby risk assessment is integrated with policy concerns, social, cultural, political, and economic issues, considering this an 'analytic-deliberative process'.
47 Commission of the European Communities, 'Communication from the Commission on the Precautionary Principle', COM (2000) 1 at 4.
48 Ibid.
49 J. S. Freeman and R. D. Godsil, 'The Question of Risk: Incorporating Community Perceptions into Environmental Risk Assessments' (1994) 21 *Fordham Urban Law Journal* 547 at 567–568.
50 Kuehn, above n. 32 at 128–129.
51 De Sadeleer, above n. 17 at 203. See also Kannan, above n. 26 at 422–423.
52 Fisher, above n. 18 at 44, and J. Jones and S. Bronitt, 'The Burden and Standard of Proof in Environmental Regulation: The Precautionary Principle in an Australian Administrative Context' in Fisher *et al.*, above n. 18.

Robert D. Bullard in an attempt to abate environmental justice problems.[53] Furthermore, the principle's focus on avoiding harm to human beings and the environment has the potential to maintain natural ecosystems – without which less well off populations would be even worse off.[54]

Similarly, it can be argued that a 'strong' adherence to the precautionary principle, rather than the utilisation of risk assessment, will fall in line with environmental justice concerns.[55] Thus, at least on a theoretical level, where a threat of harm is identified, regardless of magnitude and likelihood, a 'strong' interpretation of the principle would mean that the activity causing the threat should cease, which would then result in no environmental injustices occurring. A reliance on such an interpretation would help to avoid future incidents of environmental injustice. However, such 'strong' interpretation of the precautionary principle is untenable and does cause serious problems.[56] First, it is highly questionable whether the principle can at all be said to be absolute.[57] Secondly, an absolute adherence to the principle prohibiting any form of activity entailing harm would be futile and put undue restraints on life in general.[58]

At the same time, it is worth bearing in mind that some of the above identified problems with the precautionary principle and its reliance on risk assessment and management are not *per se* due to a fault with the principle itself. Instead, many of the environmental justice problems identified as a result of risk assessment and management may be a result of the sometimes misunderstood application of these regimes.[59] As already noted, risk assessment is sometimes viewed as an end in itself rather than an instrument designed to help the decision-maker.[60] As noted by former head of the US EPA, William Ruckelshaus, '[W]e should remember that risk assessment data can be like a captured spy: if you torture it long enough, it will tell you anything you want to know'.[61]

Another problem is the fact that perceptions of risk often vary regardless of susceptibility and exposure. Although environmental justice activists claim to exercise intuition when relying on popular epidemiology, it is evident that, in some instances, serious differences exist in perceptions of what actually constitutes a risk. This includes, for instance, perception of risk associated with nuclear power plants, X-rays, flight safety and unhealthy diets.[62] However, the stark differences in risk perception between the public and risk assessors should not be dismissed; the challenge for the decision-maker is to strike a

53 See, for instance, Bullard, above n. 1 at 122.
54 R. Attfield, 'The Precautionary Principle and Moral Values' in T. O'Riordan and J. Cameron (eds), above n. 19 at 159.
55 See, for instance, N. Kibert, 'Green Justice: A Holistic Approach to Environmental Injustice' (2001) 17 *Journal of Land Use & Environmental Law* at 178.
56 This is most prominently highlighted in the work by Cass Sunstein. See C. Sunstein, *Laws of Fear: Beyond the Precautionary Principle* (Cambridge University Press: New York, 2005).
57 De Sadeleer describes the principle as a 'directing principle', being somewhat less binding than more prescriptive rules, above n. 17, Chapters 5 and 6. See also Attfield, above n. 54, arguing (at 160) that the principle is not fundamental or overriding.
58 See, in general, Sunstein, above n. 56. One way, however, to avoid this overly restrictive version of the principle would be to apply the version advocated by Resnik when he argues that one should apply the precautionary principle to take *reasonable measures* to avoid *plausible* and *serious* threats. See D. B. Resnik, 'The Precautionary Principle and Medical Decision Making' (2004) *Journal of Medicine and Philosophy* 29(3) 281, emphasis added.
59 Kuehn, above n. 32 at 128.
60 See also Sexton, above n. 40.
61 W. D. Ruckelshaus, 'Risk in a Free Society' (1984) 14 Envtl L Rep 10.190 at 10.191.
62 See, in general, P. Slovic, J. Flynn and M. Layman, 'Perceived Risk, Trust, and the Politics of Nuclear Waste' in P. Slovic (ed.), *The Perception of Risk* (Earthscan: London, 2000).

fair balance between the two.[63] Here, the precautionary principle does itself offer some guidance, as the principle is designed to deal with *uncertain* risks.[64] This is contrasted by purely hypothetical *residual* risks, which society is bound to live with, and *certain* risks, which are governed by the principle of prevention.[65]

It is thus clear that discrepancy, as well as compatibility, exists between the precautionary principle and the concept of environmental justice. The principal cause for discrepancy between the two is the role that risk assessment and risk management play within the precautionary principle. These two parts do, in some instances, lead to confrontation with ideas of public participation, emphasis on social justice, and popular epidemiology – all ideas that are central to environmental justice. On the other hand, the part of the precautionary principle that emphasises a change in the burden of proof, notwithstanding the legal ambiguity of such assertions, can form part of the environmental justice advocate's toolkit.

# 4. THE PRINCIPLE OF PREVENTION AND ENVIRONMENTAL JUSTICE

Closely linked to the precautionary principle is the principle of prevention. From the outset, however, it is evident that the principle of prevention is not easy to define.[66] Indeed, it could be argued that there is not *one* principle of prevention – rather, the principle manifests itself through a wide array of different procedures, mechanisms and instruments. In spite of this, the principle has been labelled a 'beacon of environmental law' and 'a sort of golden rule'.[67] On the international level, the principle of prevention is closely tied to the obligation of states not to cause harm to the environment of other states, as this has been established by the *Trail Smelter* decision and elaborated in Principle 21 of the Stockholm Declaration and Principle 2 of the Rio Declaration.[68] The principle of prevention has since found application in numerous international agreements including Article 3 of the UN Framework Convention on Climate Change (UNFCCC),[69] Article 2 of the OSPAR Convention,[70] Article 4(2) of the Basel Convention,[71] and Article 14 of the Convention on Biological Diversity.[72] Likewise, Article 191(2) of the Treaty on the Functioning of the EU gives emphasis to preventive action just as secondary EU environmental law relies on the principle.[73] In particular, the reference to the principle in Article 191(2) has added impetus to the principle, as Member States are thus obliged to take the principle into account

63 See Hornstein, above n. 25, arguing (at 615) that the public's varying concerns 'are hardly inconsequential values that should clearly be ignored in any rational calculation of a risk's social utility'.
64 De Sadeleer, above n. 17 at 156–161.
65 Ibid. at 160. De Sadeleer argues that the risk should be considered scientifically likely as opposed to speculation and hypothesis. See also Resnik, above n. 58 at 336, noting that the threats addressed by the precautionary principle must be credible threats.
66 De Sadeleer, above n. 17 at 60.
67 Ibid. at 89.
68 *Trail Smelter Arbitration Tribunal* (1939) 33 AJIL 182; Declaration of the United Nations Conference on the Human Environment (1972) 11 ILM 1416, and Rio Declaration, above n. 19.
69 United Nations Framework Convention on Climate Change (1992) ILM 849, Art. 3.
70 Convention for the Protection of the Marine Environment of the North-East Atlantic (1993) 32 ILM 1069, Art. 2.
71 Basel Convention on the Control of Transboundary Movements of Hazardous Wastes and their Disposal (1989) 28 ILM 657, Art. 4(2).
72 Convention on Biological Diversity (1992) 31 ILM 818, Art. 14.
73 See nn. 76–77 below.

when transposing EU law based on Article 192.[74] However, in order to establish some tangible definition from the many references to the preventive principle and its compatibility with environmental justice, it is necessary to look closer at some of the ways in which the principle has been applied.

Under international law, the duty to prevent harm to the territories of other states manifests itself in a duty of due diligence that requires states to introduce policies, legislation and controls aimed at preventing harm and minimising the risk of transboundary harm.[75] Thus, in domestic as well as EU law, the extensive range of environmental law and statutes can all be seen as a way of 'implementing' the principle of prevention.[76] One such example is seen in the latest EC Directive on waste, which in Article 1 has as its aim to prevent the production of waste while it places prevention at the top of the waste hierarchy, just as Article 29 of the Directive imposes waste prevention programme obligations on Member States.[77]

The principle of prevention is arguably the principle that has the greatest potential to address environmental injustices. In his environmental justice 'framework', Bullard places an emphasis on the prevention of pollution before harm occurs. It is argued that instead of having to 'wait until causation or conclusive "proof" is established', authorities ought to take action based on prevention.[78] As an example of where preventive action is required, Bullard refers to the exposure to lead from leaded paint, which many African-American children have faced as a result of poor standards of housing despite the well known ill effects associated with high blood lead levels.[79] On the face of it, the emphasis on prevention seems appropriate and, from a regulatory standpoint, rather uncontroversial. However, from a judicial point of view, the approach away from causality and proof may cause difficulties as an 'environmental justice framework' that neglects issues of causality may have a hard time convincing the judiciary that an injustice has taken place.[80]

At the same time, other problems persist. With reference to the issue of waste, the principle of rectification at source, which is also recognised in Article 191(2) TFEU, can be seen as being closely linked to prevention. Rectification at source has clear environmental justice implications if some of the early environmental injustice examples from both the US and the UK are recalled. One such example, from the early 1980s in the US, was the dumping of PCB contaminated soil in Warren County, North Carolina. To the dismay of the predominantly African-American community, it was chosen as a burial ground for contaminated soil which had been salvaged from across the state.[81] In the UK, one example which is often seen as a case of environmental injustice is the plight of the com-

74 See A. Doyle and T. Carney, 'Precaution and Prevention: Giving Effect to Article 130r without Direct Effect' (1999) 8(2) *European Environmental Law Review* 44.

75 P. Birnie, A. Boyle and C. Redgewell, *International Law and the Environment* (Oxford University Press: Oxford, 2009) 147–149, and de Sadeleer, above n. 17 at 72.

76 See de Sadeleer, above n. 17 at 70–72, listing a number of domestic examples.

77 Directive of the European Parliament and of the Council on waste repealing Directive 2008/98/EC, Arts. 1 and 4.

78 See, in general, R. D. Bullard (ed.), *Confronting Environmental Racism, Voices from the Grassroots* (South End Press: Boston, MA, 1993) 203–206; R. D. Bullard (ed.), *Unequal Protection: Environmental Justice and Communities of Color* (Sierra Club Books: San Francisco, 1994) 7–12; Bullard, above n. 1 at 121–125.

79 Ibid.

80 The problems that environmental justice plaintiffs have faced in US courts can be seen as an example of this.

81 R. D. Bullard, 'Race and Environmental Justice in the United States' (1993) 18 Yale J Int'l L 319 at 328, and D. Taylor, 'Environmentalism and the Politics of Inclusion' in Bullard (ed.), above n. 78.

munity of Greengairs in Lanarkshire, Scotland.[82] As in Warren County, Greengairs found itself on the receiving end of PCB contaminated soil collected from across the UK, which was the result of unresolved issues with the operator's licence. The community started a campaign, supported by Friends of the Earth Scotland, in the name of environmental justice. Environmental justice proponents could feasibly argue that a strict adherence to the principle of rectification at source would avoid perceived injustices like those in Warren County and Greengairs – had the waste been dealt with *in situ* it would not have had to be transported to these communities. On the other hand, where, for instance, certain types of waste are of such a precarious and dangerous nature that they will need special treatment and expertise, and such facilities are located in low-income neighbourhoods, environmental and health considerations point towards transporting such waste to the relevant facilities, although this may be far away from the source.

When the principle of prevention is partly 'implemented' through a portfolio of domestic environmental laws, other issues of relevance to environmental justice arise. For instance, the principle carries with it a reliance on cost–benefit analysis.[83] This is witnessed where the principle is qualified, as it often is, by reference to a particular harm being either 'serious' or 'significant' before action is taken.[84] In such cases, the authority deciding whether preventive action is needed will have to weigh the probability of damage against the possible environmental, health and socio-economic benefits and costs.[85] Often such use of cost–benefit analysis, and its reliance on willingness to pay principles, is considered to be at odds with environmental justice arguments.[86] Such arguments should come as no surprise given the often heated debates taking place in environmental discussion on the role of cost–benefit analysis.[87] As noted by Hsu:

> What worries environmental justice advocates about cost–benefit analysis and the economic way of thinking is that it seems to give license to the tyrannization of minorities, as long as there is an increase in wealth. Thus, cost–benefit analysis and other economic instruments seem to open the door to the oppression of poor minorities (both in the ethnic and the political sense) for the benefit of the rich.[88]

82 K. Dunion, *Troublemakers: The Struggle for Environmental Justice in Scotland* (Edinburgh University Press: Edinburgh, 2003).

83 It is worth noting at this point that cost–benefit analysis is not merely relevant to the principle of prevention but equally plays a role under the precautionary principle; see, for instance, Commission of the European Communities, above n. 47, and Sunstein, above n. 56 at 130. Likewise, it can be argued that cost–benefit analysis raises environmental justice concerns in its own right independent of both the precautionary principle and the principle of prevention. However, due to space constraints, cost–benefit analysis is here dealt with as part of the principle of prevention.

84 The principle can in some instances be applied as an absolute norm – for example, where certain substances are outlawed entirely based on the harm they cause.

85 De Sadeleer, above n. 17 at 80–81.

86 See P. Wenz, 'Just Garbage' in L. Westra, and P. Wenz (eds), *Faces of Environmental Racism: Confronting Issues of Global Justice* (Rowman & Littlefield: Lanham, Md, 1995); P. Wenz, 'Does Environmentalism Promote Injustice for the Poor?' in R. Sandler and P. C. Pezzullo (eds), *Environmental Justice and Environmentalism: The Social Justice Challenge to the Environmental Movement* (MIT Press: Cambridge, Mass., 2007); E. Gauna, 'An Essay on Environmental Justice: The Past, the Present, and Back to the Future' (2002) 42 *Natural Resources Journal* 701 at 710–712; C. Rechtschaffen, 'Advancing Environmental Justice Norms' (2003) 37 *University of California Davis Law Review* 95 at 104; and T. Yang, 'Balancing Interests and Maximizing Rights in Environmental Justice' (1999) 23 *Vermont Law Review* 529 at 542.

87 See, in general, M. Sagoff, *The Economy of the Earth: Philosophy, Law and the Environment* (Cambridge University Press: Cambridge, 2008).

88 S. Hsu, 'On the Role of Cost-benefit Analysis in Environmental Law: A Book Review of Frank Ackerman and Lisa Heinzerling's *Priceless: On Knowing the Price of Everything and the Value of Nothing*' (2005) 35 Envtl L 135 at 171.

Often, however, the reality is less clear-cut and less simple and discussions on and criticism of the use of cost–benefit analysis are often somewhat entrenched and partisan.[89] Here it is worth recalling, as was the case with the precautionary principle, that cost–benefit analysis, and its reliance on monetisation and ranking, is a process tool, or a metric, not a final resolution.[90] Moreover, it is important to bear in mind that what cost–benefit analysis ranks is not necessarily harm itself but *risk* of harm, many environmental justice studies assume an uncritical causal link between risk and harm.[91] Of course, here environmental justice advocates may equally assert that one problem is the fact that the risk to a small minority group is ranked lower than the risk facing a larger group (what may be termed the 'scale problem').[92] Indeed, where such assumptions are deemed to be unfair and/or inappropriate, it may even be possible to address these through cost–benefit analysis. Cass Sunstein has, for instance, argued that it is possible to adjust any cost–benefit analysis so that it takes into account distributive problems.[93] Thus, it could very well be that cost–benefit analysis can actually work in favour of an environmental justice argument. Where environmental decision-making includes information on who and which social group benefits and/or receives the burden, such cost–benefit analysis can, through deliberation, lead to increased transparency and actually facilitate more informed decisions.[94] In this way, cost–benefit analysis could possibly facilitate environmental justice.

Another point worth making in relation to cost–benefit analysis and environmental justice is that the use of such weighing of benefits and costs is likely to play an increasingly prominent role in policy-making in light of scarce resources.[95] Thus, critics of cost–benefit analysis are arguably better off trying to address the shortfalls of cost–benefit analysis instead of seeking its eradication.[96] One such argument could, for instance, be the usage of 'number per life saved' numbers instead of willingness to pay.[97] Or, as noted above, pursue the inclusion of distributive impacts as part of the cost–benefit equation.[98]

Thus, like the precautionary principle, the principle of prevention can be seen as giving raise to both conflict and conformity with a concept of environmental justice. Again, this is perhaps not surprising given the multiple ways in which both the principle of prevention and environmental justice manifest themselves.

89 F. Ackerman and L. Heinzerling, *Priceless: On Knowing the Price of Everything and the Value of Nothing* (The New Press: New York, 2004).
90 Hsu, above n. 88 at 144.
91 Ibid. at 157–158.
92 Ibid. at 160.
93 C. Sunstein, 'Lives, Life-years, and Willingness to Pay' (2004) 104 *Columbia Law Review* 205 at 213, 'The Arithmetic of Arsenic' (2002) 90 Geo LJ 2225 at 2260, 'Selective Fatalism' (1998) 27 J Legal Stud 799 at 812, and R. H. Pildes and C. Sunstein, 'Reinventing the Regulatory State' (1995) 62 U Chi L Rev 1 at 46–47.
94 C. Sunstein, 'Cognition and Cost–benefit' (2000) 29 J Legal Stud 1059 at 1092–1093, and Hsu, above n. 88 at 171–172.
95 See C. Sunstein, *The Cost–Benefit State: The Future of Regulatory Protection* (American Bar Association: Chicago, 2002). This book, however, deals only with the use of cost–benefit analysis in the US. See also O. W. Pedersen, 'Benefits and Costs of the Environment: Copenhagen Consensus 2008' (2008) *Journal of Environmental Law* 20(3).
96 See, in general, R. I. Revesz and M. A. Livermore, *Retaking Rationality: How Cost–Benefit Analysis Can Better Protect the Environment and Our Health* (Oxford University Press: New York, 2008).
97 Sunstein, above n. 95 at 9.
98 See, for instance, Executive Order 12866 Regulatory Planning and Review of 30 September 1993, 58 Fed. Reg. No. 190 735, directing agencies to take into account 'cost of enforcement and compliance (to the government, regulated entities, and the public), flexibility, distributive impacts and equity' at 5. See also M. D. Adler and E. A. Posner, *New Foundations of Cost–Benefit Analysis* (Harvard University Press: Cambridge, Mass., 2006) 131.

# 5. THE POLLUTER PAYS PRINCIPLE AND ENVIRONMENTAL JUSTICE

Whereas the precautionary principle grew out of national law, the polluter pays principle emanates from the international sphere. The polluter pays principle saw light in 1972 when the Organisation for Economic Co-operation and Development (OECD) issued a number of recommendations on international economic aspects of environmental policies.[99] In its recommendations, the OECD argued, '[P]ublic measures are thus necessary to reduce pollution and to reach a better allocation of resources by ensuring that prices of goods depending on the quality and/or quantity of environmental resources reflect more closely their relative scarcity and economic agents concerned react accordingly'.[100] The Recommendation further noted that the polluter pays principle is to be used for the 'allocating [of] costs of pollution prevention and control measures to encourage rational use of scarce environmental resources' as well as to 'avoid distortions in international trade and investment'.[101] Thus, the polluter pays principle started out as a principle of economic thinking aimed at avoiding economically irrational distortions of the market, rather than a principle aimed at curbing environmental harm for the sake of the environment. This is further underlined by the OECD Recommendation, which notes that any measures under the principle should not be accompanied by subsidies that would create significant distortions in international trade and investment.[102]

Following the OECD Recommendation, the principle gained prominence in other international settings. In 1973, the polluter pays principle made it into the First Environmental Action Programme of the EC and has since reappeared in all of its following programmes.[103] The principle also appeared in Recommendation 75/436/Euratom, ECSC, EEC of March 1975, specifying the application of the principle in order to 'avoid distortions in trade and competition incompatible with the proper functioning of the common market'.[104] The polluter pays principle has since then found application in a number of EC directives and Article 191(2) TFEU.[105] On the international level, the polluter pays principle has, *inter alia*, found application in Principle 16 of the Rio Declaration,[106] the OSPAR Convention[107] and the Baltic Sea Convention.[108]

In addition to being a principle of cost allocation, the polluter pays principle has been used as a principle of rectification and liability, in line with principles of tort and delict.

99 OECD, 'Environment and Economics Guiding Principles Concerning International Economic Aspects of Environmental Policies', Recommendation of May 1972, C(72) 128.
100 OECD Recommendation, above n. 99 at A(a) 2.
101 Ibid., A(a) 4.
102 Ibid.
103 De Sadeleer, above n. 17 at 29.
104 75/436/Euratom, ECSC, EEC: Council Recommendation of 3 March 1975 regarding cost allocation and action by public authorities on environmental matters. The Recommendation lists two exceptions where the application of the principle may be limited: (a) where its immediate application is likely to lead to serious economic disturbances or may give rise to greater social costs, and (b) where, in the context of other policies, investment affecting the environment benefits from aid intended to solve certain problems. Similarly, the 1972 OECD Recommendation notes that the principle should be the objective of all Member States but that 'there may be exceptions or special arrangements' allowing for a less strict adherence to the principle.
105 TFEU Art. 191(2).
106 Rio Declaration, above n. 22.
107 OSPAR Convention, above n. 70, Art. 2(2).
108 Baltic Sea Convention, Art. 3(4). De Sadeleer, above n. 17 at 23, argues that a distinction should be made between those international agreements that refer to the principle in their preambular provisions and those that refer to the principle in their substantive provisions.

This is, for instance, seen in a 1989 Recommendation adopted by the OECD Council on the application of the polluter pays principle.[109] The Recommendation notes that '[I]n matters of accidental pollution risks, the Polluter-Pays Principle implies that the operator of a hazardous installation should bear the cost'.[110] Similarly, and more recently, Directive 2004/35 on environmental liability draws on the polluter pays principle.[111]

However, a number of general problems with the interpretation of the polluter pays principle exist. Some of these problems may, at the same time, lead to difficulties in relation to a concept of environmental justice. First, a general problem with the polluter pays principle is to identify who the polluter actually is. Although this might seem obvious, this question is also relevant to environmental justice and the norms of ethics and social justice inherent in the concept of environmental justice.[112] The polluter pays principle arguably works most effectively where the costs of pollution prevention associated with certain goods are passed on to the consumer in order to create market-driven incentives to change shopping patterns which harm the environment.[113] Ideally this would then lead to those products and goods that pollute the environment becoming more expensive and pollution-free products becoming more price-competitive in the long run. However, such ideals are not necessarily reflected in real life and it remains the situation that most environmentally-friendly products are more expensive to produce, and thus more expensive to buy, which in turn puts them out of reach for some financially less well off social groups, leaving them unable to get out of the shopping and consumption patterns that harm their environments and arguably raising environmental justice concerns.[114]

Similarly, ways of implementing the polluter pays principle can lead to confrontation with environmental justice. De Sadeleer argues that the principle can be implemented either through regulatory standards prohibiting or limiting the damage associated with the activity, or through taxation reflecting the economic value gained through the polluting activity.[115] Whereas the use of regulatory standards is, in an environmental justice setting, relatively harmless, the use of taxation might not be. Although a tax on activities harming the environment can be designed to work progressively and is aimed at changing behaviour, thus making itself superfluous with time, taxes often hit the least well off the hardest.[116] An example could be a carbon tax imposed equally on all households, rich as well as poor, aimed at taxing household energy use (without necessarily compensating poor households), which would work regressively as poor households already pay significantly more per unit of energy than do rich households.[117] Again, this would seem to be at odds with concerns of environmental justice, holding that the least well off already take upon themselves an unfair burden of problems associated with the environment.

109 Recommendation of the Council concerning the Application of the Polluter-Pays Principle to Accidental Pollution, C (89) 88 of 7 July 1989.
110 Ibid. at 4.
111 Directive 2004/35/CE of the European Parliament and of the Council of 21 April 2004 on environmental liability with regard to the prevention and remedying of environmental damage, Art. 1.
112 See above n. 28.
113 S. E. Gaines, 'The Polluter Pays Principle: From Economic Equity to Environmental Ethos' (1991) 26 *Texas International Law Journal* 463 at 472–473.
114 See E. Fisher, 'Sustainable Development and Environmental Justice: Same Planet, Different Worlds?' (2003) 26 *SPG Environs Envtl. L. & Pol'y J.* 201 for a similar argument.
115 De Sadeleer, above n. 17 at 21.
116 See H. C. Bugge, 'The Polluter Pays Principle: Dilemmas of Justice in National and International Contexts' in J. Ebbesson and P. Okowa (eds), *Environmental Law and Justice in Context* (Cambridge University Press: Cambridge, 2009).
117 See, for instance, P. Ekins and S. Dresner, 'Green Taxes and Charges: Reducing their Impact on Low-Income Households' (Joseph Rowntree Foundation, 2004).

Another problem of defining the scope of the polluter pays principle is to do with the cost that the polluter, once he has been identified, has to pay. Here it might be appropriate to distinguish between the principle defined in a strict sense and the principle defined in a wider sense.[118] In the former, the principle is designed only to bring the pollution to a level accepted by authorities and is thus limited to partial internalisation; in the latter, the principle is designed also to allocate social damages associated with the pollution.[119] This distinction runs, to some extent, parallel with the one made between the principle's economic and legal interpretation.[120] Whereas the original aim of the principle was to avoid distortion of international trade and investment, which would argue in favour of limited or narrow internalisation, it can be argued that the principle's shift in focus now also to include issues of liability argues in favour of a broader and complete internalisation of costs associated with a polluting activity.[121] From an environmental justice point of view, the latter argument of complete internalisation would be the preferable option, as this would seem to include social costs resulting from the polluting activity rather than just the strictly monetary costs of pollution prevention and control.

Additionally, an environmental justice problem with the polluter pays principle is the principle's original focus on trade and investment and thus its 'free market spirit'. First and foremost, environmental justice activists attack the spirit of the free market, which is to some extent seen as leading to the problems of the environmental injustice communities.[122] This is, for instance, seen in the stance taken by environmental justice campaigners against what they call the 'path of least resistance'.[123] Furthermore, in order to tackle environmental justice problems, government action is often seen as not only necessary but vital – something that does not necessarily go down well with the historical free-market ideals in the polluter pays principle. Secondly, the principle's opposition to subsidies and aid can be seen as being at odds with environmental justice. This is mainly in the situation where environmental justice arguments are applied to the international setting. Here, mechanisms of transfer of aid, technology and assistance – transfers that can be justified on environmental justice grounds – can be seen as being in violation of the polluter pays principle, as the principle ostensibly opposes government aid and subsidies.[124]

Similarly, notions of differentiated responsibility, as developed under international environmental law, represent a prima facie violation of the polluter pays principle.[125] It may be argued that this infringement of the polluter pays principle would take place where the principle is interpreted as an absolute principle. Such absolute assertions, however, would appear to be unfounded.[126] The recommendations produced by, for instance, the OECD and the EU do allow for exceptions. This underlines the argument that the principle is not absolute and deviations from the principle on social, economic or environmental grounds

118 De Sadeleer, above n. 17 at 42.
119 Ibid. See also J. Pezzey, 'Market Mechanisms of Pollution Control: "Polluter Pays", Economic and Practical Aspects' in R. Kerry Tuner (ed.), *Sustainable Environmental Management: Principles and Practice* (Belhaven Press: Boulder Co., 1988), who calls this 'standard PPP' and 'extended PPP'.
120 Gaines, above n. 113 at 470.
121 See, in general, de Sadeleer, above n. 17 at 42–43.
122 See, in general, D. Faber, 'The Political Ecology of American Capitalism: New Challenges for the Environmental Justice Movement' in Faber (ed.), above n. 11. See also Kuehn, above n. 32 at 207.
123 See above n. 3.
124 See, however, U. Kettlewell, 'The Answer to Global Pollution? A Critical Examination of Problems and Potential of the Polluter-Pays Principle' (1992) 3 *Colo. J. Int'l Envtl. & Pol'y* 429 at 477, asserting that the polluter pays principle does not operate very well in the international setting and is mainly a principle applicable in closed systems of domestic law and policy.
125 See below, Part 6.
126 See Gaines, above n. 113 at 477.

are justifiable.[127] Thus, the prima facie violation of the polluter pays principle through transfer of aid, technology and assistance turns out to be permissible just the same.

However, in spite of the discrepancies between the polluter pays principle and environmental justice, some common ground does exist. This is most obvious where the polluter pays principle is utilised as a principle of liability. Here, the principle can be seen as an answer to the calls made by environmental justice campaigners for a more equitable distribution of the harms and burdens associated with polluting activities. This function of the principle can be termed the distributive side of the principle, which is considered to be a cornerstone of environmental justice.[128] This is particularly the case where the costs that the polluter has to bear are taken to encompass social costs rather than just the costs of pollution prevention.

Thus, the polluter pays principle, like the precautionary and preventive principles, gives rise to confrontation as well as reconciliation with a concept of environmental justice. The main problems with the polluter pays principle, from an environmental justice point of view, are the principle's focus on free-market ideals, which on an ideological level goes against certain aspects of environmental justice, and the ways in which the principle is best implemented – through taxes which have the potential to hit the already hard-done-by populations the hardest. However, at the same time, the principle can be utilised to achieve central environmental justice goals – mainly of a fairer distribution of harms and costs from polluting activities, where it operates as a rule of liability.

## 6. SUSTAINABLE DEVELOPMENT AND ENVIRONMENTAL JUSTICE

The most influential principle and most recognised concept of environmental regulation and policy-making is without doubt that of sustainable development. Although the wide use and recognition of sustainable development would imply that the concept is easily defined, it is clear that, for sustainable development, with recognition comes ambiguity.[129] Sustainable development was referred to in the 1985 ASEAN Agreement on the Conservation of Nature and Natural Resources.[130] Prior to that, the World Conservation Strategy gave credence to the term 'sustainable development' when it was published in 1980.[131] However, it was not until the publishing of *Our Common Future*, by the World Commission on Environment and Development (WCED) in 1987, that the term 'sustainable development' gained full recognition outside the area of conservation.[132] More prominently, the principle is now found in Article 11 TFEU under which the Union must 'promote

127 Ibid.

128 See de Sadeleer, above n. 17 at 29.

129 R. E. Saunier and R. A. Meganck note that 'there are literally hundreds of definitions of sustainable development' in their *Dictionary and Introduction to Global Environmental Governance* (Earthscan: London, 2007) 242.

130 ASEAN Agreement on the Conservation of Nature and Natural Resources, Preamble.

131 International Union for Conservation of Nature and Natural Resources (IUCN) with advice from UNEP and WWF, 1980.

132 The World Commission on Environment and Development, *Our Common Future* (Oxford University Press: New York, 1987). Sustainable development is defined by the WCED (at 43) as: 'Development that meets the needs of the present without compromising the ability of future generations to meet their own needs. It contains two key concepts:
- the concept of "needs", in particular the essential needs of the world's poor, to which overriding priority should be given; and
- the idea of limitations imposed by the state of technology and social organization on the environment's ability to meet present and future needs.'

sustainable development'.[133] Broadly speaking, the debate on the compatibility between environmental justice and sustainable development is divided into two camps: one arguing that a nexus and similarities exist between the two concepts; the other arguing that the two concepts are incompatible. As a general observation, it can be argued that the camp arguing against compatibility is mainly grounded in theoretical thinking, whereas the camp supporting an argument of co-existence partly rests on more pragmatic arguments.

Andrew Dobson emerges as the most credible advocate for the argument against compatibility between sustainable development and environmental justice. Dobson argues that, on the theoretical level, the two concepts are incompatible and notes that while the two concepts 'will cross at important points, they by no means always travel the same road, and they may not even always head in the same normative direction as far as distributive issues are concerned'.[134] This assumption rests on an interpretation of sustainable development that emphasises environmental sustainability rather than development.[135] Dobson sees sustainable development as merely one conception of the broader environmental sustainability, while criticising the WCED definition for being too eclectic and vague.[136] When emphasising environmental values and sustainability over concerns for human development and well-being, it is perhaps not surprising that Dobson reaches the conclusion that the two concepts are incompatible. Thus, Dobson's argument of incompatibility is best interpreted in light of his dismissal of the definition of sustainable development developed by the WCED. It is by now well established that this definition is widely considered to encompass three main strands. These are: (i) economic development; (ii) environmental protection and conservation; and (iii) human equity.[137] Therefore, where such a definition is partly insufficient to environmental justice activists, as it places equity concerns on an equal footing with the environment and economic development, it is equally unacceptable to Dobson, who would like to see the environmental concerns gaining the upper hand. Such differences are perhaps more stark where sustainable development is interpreted as emphasising ecological sustainability. Bosselmann, for instance, sees the social equity side of sustainable development as being secondary to ecological 'sustainability'.[138] Such approaches seem difficult to align with a concept of environmental justice focusing on equality. But, on the other hand, an environmental justice definition which entails notions of eco-justice, as noted above, arguably accommodates such differences.

Apart from the differences between environmental justice and sustainable development in the weight attached to equity, the two concepts also differ in geographical scope. Whereas environmental justice started out by focusing on local issues and struggles, sustainable development emerged from the setting of international diplomacy.[139] In addition, environmental justice came about mainly thanks to a bottom-up approach, unlike sustain-

133 Art. 11 TFEU.
134 A. Dobson, *Justice and the Environment Conceptions of Environmental Sustainability and Dimensions of Social Justice* (Oxford University Press: Oxford, 1998) 26.
135 Ibid. at 58–61.
136 Ibid.
137 J. B. Ruhl, 'The Co-Evolution of Sustainable Development and Environmental Justice: Cooperation, then Competition, then Conflict' (1998) 9 *Duke Envtl. L. & Pol'y F.* 161 at 180.
138 K. Bosselmann, *The Principle of Sustainability: Transforming Law and Governance* (Ashgate: Aldershot, 2008). See also A. Ross, 'Modern Interpretations of Sustainable Development' (2009) 36(1) *Journal of Law and Society*, both relying on the Earth Charter.
139 See Dobson, above n. 134 at 16.

able development, which was largely developed through a top-down structure.[140] This difference is highlighted by the fact that sustainable development often varies from the local to the international setting, which in itself may have environmental justice implications. For instance, international or regional agreements deciding on the allocation of natural resources, based on assumptions of sustainable development, can easily have serious distributive effects at the local level, which could make it a matter of environmental justice.[141] Similarly, where strong local opposition to certain facilities, a trademark of environmental justice, simply leads to the disputed facility being sited in another neighbourhood, the local opposition appears to have done little for the cause of sustainable development and its long-term focus. However, the opposite situation may easily occur – for instance, where local knowledge, know-how and work are utilised to preserve habitats or animals in a sustainable manner.[142]

Although the two concepts can be said to vary in geographical scope, there are indications that this is starting to change. In this light, it may be asserted that sustainable development is the broader of the two concepts.[143] This assertion has led some to argue that, in the long run, sustainable development will 'get the better of' environmental justice as sustainable development is more adaptive and less ideological.[144] Not only has sustainable development found application at national as well as regional and local levels, but environmental justice is increasingly being applied to the international scene. This is particularly clear in the area of climate change, where arguments of 'climate justice' play a role in the debate as to which countries ought to shoulder responsibilities.[145]

Finally, as with the precautionary and polluter pays principles, it is possible that a strong adherence to sustainable products and solutions may lead to results that conflict with ideas of environmental justice. It has been argued that the broad focus on environmentally friendly solutions in the name of sustainable development – for instance, in the production of housing and commodities – will lead to situations where sustainability only reinforces already existing patterns of social inconsistencies.[146] This is seen where sustainable commodities or housing are too expensive for the less well off social groups, who in turn become caught in an environmentally damaging pattern of consumption.

On the other hand, and in spite of the various theoretical incompatibilities and differences in scope, some obvious areas of consensus do exist between environmental justice and sustainable development. First, it might be argued that they depend on each other to the degree that one is not possible without the other. This assumption rests on the notion that sustainable development is, generally speaking, the overarching policy of which environmental justice might be seen as being a part. This is, for example, seen in the campaigning for environmental justice in the UK, where Friends of the Earth Scotland (FoES) argue that sustainable development is not attainable without environmental

140 See also J. Agyeman, R. D. Bullard and B. Evans, 'Exploring the Nexus: Bringing Together Sustainability, Environmental Justice and Equity' (2002) 6(1) *Space & Polity* 77 at 88.

141 See, for example, Donald T. Hornstein, 'Environmental Sustainability and Environmental Justice at the International Level: Traces of Tension and Traces of Synergy' (1998) 9 *Duke Envtl. L. & Pol'y F.* 291 at 297–298.

142 Ibid.

143 Ruhl, above n. 137 at 163 and 171.

144 Ibid. at 165–166. Ruhl argues that in that process sustainable development will have adopted some of the key issues from environmental justice.

145 See below n. 182.

146 Fisher, above n. 114 at 202–203.

justice.[147] This assertion is to some extent backed by the emergence of the concept of 'just sustainability'.[148] 'Just sustainability' rests on a definition of sustainable development which is different from the one put forward by WCED, as sustainable development is defined as 'the need to ensure a better quality of life for all, now and into the future, in a just and equitable manner, whilst living within the limits of supporting ecosystems', without being seen as a rigid and absolute paradigm.[149] Thus, 'just sustainability' emphasises the interdependence of social justice, economic well-being and environmental stewardship, while focusing on the creation of sustainable communities able to facilitate global changes.[150] A central focus of the concept is on proactive agendas that aim to address environmental questions early on rather than, as in the case of some of the early environmental justice struggles, focusing only on reactive questions of siting.[151] Under the heading 'just sustainability' it is argued that the approach taken by, *inter alia*, FoES is evidence of the compatibility between environmental justice and sustainable development.[152]

While caution should be exercised when emphasising the importance of a campaign slogan of an NGO, it is evident that Agyeman, Bullard and Evans have a good point when they argue that 'there are encouraging signs that this constructive dialogue is emerging [between the two camps of environmental justice and sustainable development], and it is our contention that this is both essential and overdue'.[153] Likewise, although such approaches are non-legal and taken in a social science context, they have strong merit in discussions on the compatibility between sustainable development and environmental justice, given the interdisciplinary and exceptionally broad nature of both concepts.

When sustainable development is interpreted in the way it is by Agyeman *et al.* – that is, with a focus on improving social living conditions – the room for co-existence between sustainable development and environmental justice becomes evident.[154] This interpretation, however, may not be all that far away from the 'original' definition developed by the WCED in 1987. For instance, it has been argued that the many subsequent interpretations of sustainable development have overemphasised the meaning of economic growth and in that process left behind other central aspects of the WCED Report.[155] Langhelle argues that, although the economic message in WCED is important, it is not the only message in the Report.[156] He convincingly argues that the definition of sustainable development developed in WCED is in fact one leaning towards a socio-economic ideal, with the concept of 'needs' at its core. The striving to fulfil the needs of *all* mankind's development is the overarching goal, only restricted by the (rather large) caveat that the development has

147 See E. Scandrett, K. Dunion and G. McBride, 'The Campaign for Environmental Justice in Scotland' (2000) *Local Environment* 5(4) 467–474. However, the correctness of such assertions is at best doubtful as it is difficult to see, at least on a theoretical level, why sustainable development should not be possible without social justice. Again, this depends on the interpretation of sustainable development, but where it is taken to mean environmental sustainability it can be argued that, for instance, dictators and despots can pursue, and have throughout history pursued, aims of environmental preservation without adhering to norms of social justice. See Dobson, above n. 134 at 5.

148 See J. Agyeman and B. Evans, '"Just Sustainability": The Emerging Discourse of Environmental Justice in Britain' (2004) 170(2) *The Geographical Journal* 155.

149 J. Agyeman, *Sustainable Communities and the Challenge of Environmental Justice* (New York University Press: New York, 2005) 6.

150 Ibid. at 89.

151 Ibid. at 3.

152 See also Agyeman, Bullard and Evans, above n. 140 at 77.

153 Ibid. at 88.

154 Ibid. at 80–81.

155 See O. Langhelle, 'Sustainable Development: Exploring the Ethics of Our Common Future' (1999) 20 *International Political Science Review* 129.

156 Ibid. at 130.

to be sustainable.[157] Thus, a notion of social justice is seen as 'built-in' to the definition of sustainable development.[158] Obviously such interpretations of sustainable development can be criticised for being too anthropocentric and for not taking account of the environment.[159] However, to this it might be argued that the WCED definition of sustainable development calls for conservation of development, not for the conservation of the environment, meaning that environmental considerations are in place, but they are not the overarching aims of sustainable development.[160]

Alongside these arguments of common ground, it is worth also noting the more practical similarities between sustainable development and environmental justice. From the outset, environmental justice has been shown to be about procedural aspects as well as distributive ideas. These procedural aspects include public participation, access to information and access to justice, and are familiar aspects of sustainable development. For instance, Agenda 21, the action plan for the national implementation of sustainable development, holds specific recommendations on these measures.[161] Agenda 21 declares that states should promote public participation,[162] access to environmental information,[163] and secure access to redress procedures for environmental decisions.[164] In addition, Agenda 21 holds specific chapters on the importance of the inclusion of women, indigenous groups and communities, and NGOs,[165] as well as the promotion of local Agenda 21 as a strategy for sustainable development at the local level.[166] These chapters all encapsulate aspects that are equally important to environmental justice. Similarly, the Johannesburg Declaration on Sustainable Development touches upon some of the common themes between sustainable development and environmental justice when it recognises the need for an 'equitable ... society' while 'reinforcing ... social development and environmental protection – at the local, national, regional and global levels'.[167]

In addition, support for the importance of these procedural mechanisms can be found in the discussion on the legal status of sustainable development in international law. Although it is doubtful whether states are under any obligations under international law to adhere to a principle of sustainable development when carrying out development, it has been argued that certain procedural obligations curbing various aspects of development do arise.[168] These mainly relate to carrying out environmental impact assessments

157 Ibid. at 132–133.
158 Ibid. at 139. See also O. Langhelle, 'Sustainable Development and Social Justice: Expanding the Rawlsian Framework of Global Justice' (2000) 9 *Environmental Values* 295.
159 See, for example, A. Ross, 'Is the Environment Getting Squeezed out of Sustainable Development?' (2003) *Public Law* 249 (with reference to the UK); and D. Wirth, 'The Rio Declaration on Environment and Development: Two Steps Forward and One Back, or Vice Versa' (1995) 29 *Georgia Law Review* 599 (in general).
160 Langhelle, above n. 155 at 134.
161 The UN Programme for Action from Rio, 'Agenda 21: Programme of Action for Sustainable Development' (1992). The principle of public participation was also reaffirmed as part of sustainable development in the 'New Delhi Declaration of Principles of International Law Relating to Sustainable Development' by the International Law Association in April 2002, Resolution 3/2002, and in the 'Johannesburg Principles on the Role of Law and Sustainable Development' by the Global Judges Symposium on Sustainable Development and the Role of Law in August 2002; see (2003) 15 *Journal of Environmental Law* 107.
162 Agenda 21, above n. 161, para. 7.3.
163 Ibid., para. 8.4.
164 Ibid., para. 8.7.
165 Ibid., Chapters 24, 26 and 27.
166 Ibid., para. 28.3.
167 Johannesburg Principles, above n. 161.
168 See A. Boyle and D. Freestone, 'Introduction' in A. Boyle and D. Freestone (eds), *International Law and Sustainable Development, Past Achievements and Future Challenges* (Oxford University Press: Oxford, 1999) 16–17.

(EIAs) and to facilitate public participation in relation to decisions harming the environment. In particular, the latter procedure of public participation is integral to environmental justice, which further supports an argument of common ground between sustainable development and environmental justice.

Another more practical argument supporting the co-existence between environmental justice and sustainable development is the fact that, at policy level, evidence of the merging of the two concepts is starting to develop. This trend is taking place in the UK, where the UK Government and the devolved administrations combine policy objectives of sustainable development and environmental justice and thus, to some extent, fall in line with the approach taken by, for instance, FoES.[169] This combination is seen in the strategies for sustainable development at the central level, where the UK Government recognises the problem of environmental inequalities,[170] and at the devolved level, where the Welsh strategy for sustainable development notes that it is based on social justice.[171] The Northern Irish strategy notes that sustainable development in Northern Ireland must support environmental justice.[172] In Scotland, the Scottish Executive (now the Scottish Government), under the previous administration, dedicated an entire chapter to environmental justice within its sustainable development strategy (although the change in regime at Holyrood has since largely rendered this approach and strategy extraneous).[173] Although political initiatives like these are perhaps not necessarily definite confirmation that the two concepts share a common ground, it is a clear indication that, at least on a political level, the two concepts are seen as intertwined.

The links between sustainable development and environmental justice are perhaps best highlighted through the concept of common but differentiated responsibility (CBDR) – a concept strongly linked to sustainable development. CBDR rests on the assumption that the application of equivalent environmental standards between developing and developed countries is inappropriate because of differences in the level of development and capacities to deal with environmental problems. CBDR played an important role in, *inter alia*, the making of the 1992 UNFCCC[174] and its 1997 Kyoto Protocol.[175] Article 3 of the UNFCCC states that parties should protect the climate system on 'the basis of equity and in accordance with their common but differentiated responsibilities'.[176] In this process, the developed countries are to take the lead, and the 'special needs and circumstances of developing countries' and those that are 'particularly vulnerable' should be given special consideration.[177] In addition, the Convention is rich in provisions laying down rules for the transfer of technical and financial assistance from developed to developing countries.[178] Most importantly, the Kyoto Protocol does not explicitly create any new obliga-

169 See also J. Agyeman and T. Evans, 'Toward Just Sustainability in Urban Communities: Building Equity Rights with Sustainable Solutions' (2003) 590 *ANNALS; AAPSS*, November 35, referring to similar trends at community level in the US.
170 HM Government, 'Securing the Future – Delivering UK Sustainable Development Strategy' (2005) 134.
171 Welsh Assembly Government, 'Sustainable Development Action Plan' (2004) 49.
172 Northern Ireland Government, 'First Steps Towards Sustainability' (2006) 6, and S. Turner, 'Laying the Foundations for a Sustainable Northern Ireland: The Review of Environmental Governance' (2007) 58(4) *Northern Ireland Legal Quarterly* 446–450.
173 Scottish Executive, 'Choosing Our Future' (2006) 40. See, however, Sustainable Development Commission Scotland, *Sustainable Development: A Review of Progress by the Scottish Government* (2008) 12.
174 United Nations Framework Convention on Climate Change, above n. 69.
175 Kyoto Protocol to the United Nations Framework Convention on Climate Change (1998) 37 ILM 32. See also L. Rajamani, *Differential Treatment in International Environmental Law* (Oxford University Press: Oxford, 2006) 179–191.
176 UNFCCC, above n. 69, Art. 3 and 3(b).
177 Ibid., Art. 3(b).
178 Ibid., Art. 4(3), 4(4), 4(5) and 4(8)–(10).

tions for developing countries and plainly excludes them from its core obligations.[179] The fact that the Protocol explicitly excludes developing countries from primary obligations is, in itself, a significant indication of the importance attached to the notion of differentiated responsibility.[180]

This strong emphasis throughout the Convention and Protocol on differential treatment of developed countries vis-à-vis developing countries implies noteworthy considerations of fairness and equity.[181] Whether this then amounts to a central notion of 'climate justice' is perhaps less certain; Brunnée argues that the notion of differentiated responsibility in the climate regime plays an important role in *framing* a debate about 'climate justice', but does not currently constitute a global principle of 'climate justice'.[182] The argument is, *inter alia*, based on the fact that, in order for an internationally shared principle of 'climate justice' to emerge, a common understanding of such a principle must exist.[183]

From the foregoing analysis it is thus clear that the two concepts of environmental justice and sustainable development differ in some areas, while at the same time sharing some common ground. Although this appears to be self-contradictory, the verdict on whether the concepts are conflicting or consistent greatly depends upon the interpretation chosen of the two principles, in particular that of sustainable development. Similarly, the great variety in interpretations is no doubt down to the broad acceptance that sustainable development has received, which arguably is attributable to the relative vagueness of the concept. In this light, it can be argued that the two concepts have to a great degree benefited from each other: environmental justice has benefited from the broad political acceptance that sustainable development has enjoyed and sustainable development has benefited from the relative intensity and force of the environmental justice argument.[184] Furthermore, it can be argued that where one reaches the conclusion that the two concepts can co-exist, they may supplement each other.

# 7. CONCLUSION

This paper has intended to analyse the compatibility between the concept of environmental justice and the influential environmental principles of the precaution, prevention, the polluter pays and sustainable development. The overall findings indicate that the four principles give rise to conflict as well as consensus. As for the precautionary principle, it was revealed that a reliance on risk assessment and risk management can lead to conflict with norms of public participation, involvement and popular epidemiology. On the other hand, the part of the precautionary principle that argues in favour of reversing the burden of proof (notwithstanding the uncertain legal significance this has) so that the polluter will have to show that the activities are not harmful strikes a chord with environmental justice arguments.

179 Ibid., Art. 10(1). See also D. French, '1997 Kyoto Protocol to the 1992 UN Framework Convention on Climate Change' (1998) 10(2) *Journal of Environmental Law* 229–231.
180 Rajamani, above n. 175 at 194.
181 T. M. Franck, *Fairness in International Law and Institutions* (Clarendon: Oxford, 1995) 380–386. See also D. Shelton, 'Equity' in D. Bodansky, J. Brunnée and E. Hey (eds), *The Oxford Handbook of International Environmental Law* (Oxford University Press: Oxford, 2007) 650, and K. Mickelson, 'Competing Narratives of Justice in North-South Environmental Relations: The Case of Ozone Layer Depletion' in Ebbesson and Okowa (eds), above n. 116, for wider discussions on CBDR.
182 J. Brunnée, 'Climate Change, Global Environmental Justice and International Law' in Ebbesson and Okowa (eds), above n. 116, emphasis added.
183 Ibid.
184 Ruhl, above n. 137 at 178.

Likewise, it was found that for the principle of prevention congruence and differences exist. These mainly related to the use of cost–benefit analysis by authorities when assessing the need for action. One point worth noting here, however, is that much of the environmental justice criticism levied at both risk assessment and cost–benefit analysis stems partly from the principles being applied inappropriately. Thus, such misunderstandings are easily addressed.

As for the polluter pays principle, it was argued that the principle's initial focus on a 'free market' approach could lead to ideological disputes with environmental justice activists. However, the part of the polluter pays principle that allows for full cost allocation of social costs as a way of establishing the polluter's liability, resonates well with environmental justice considerations.

As for the concept of sustainable development, it was argued that, on a theoretical level, the two concepts may not necessarily share a common basis. Although such arguments very much depend upon the approach taken to sustainable development, it was argued that the two concepts share numerous considerations. Both concepts emphasise procedural mechanisms as ways of achieving their respective goals. At the same time, an argument of consensus is supported by the fact that a linking of the two is already, and increasingly, taking place.

Thus, it is evident that, for the influential principles of environmental law and policy-making, the relationship with environmental justice is one of diversity and variation, as well as accordance and agreement. This conclusion is perhaps not surprising, as none of the principles or environmental justice can be said to be either absolute or supreme, just as it may be argued that to a great degree the principles seem to overlap one another. Most importantly, though, environmental justice as a concept provides a framework for the probing of established environmental law and policy norms and concepts. It is submitted that such a contribution is very welcome. On the other hand, the inherent vagueness of, and many different approaches to, environmental justice may lead to some questioning its utility and relevance. The same can be said for some of the environmental principles. Here, however, it is clear that ambiguity has far from eliminated neither the influence of environmental justice nor that of the environmental principles. One will only have to look to the US to witness the strong influence exercised by the environmental justice movement and to the pervasiveness of the principle of sustainable development to acknowledge their respective authority.

Although such vagueness is perhaps frustrating, it is inevitable in light of the interdisciplinary and broad nature of both environmental justice and, for instance, sustainable development. In light of this, one point remains to be made. As the concept of environmental justice is emerging in the UK and is starting to demand attention from policy-makers and lawyers alike, it is important to constantly and critically assess calls made for environmental justice. Unfortunately, with vagueness comes the possibility of abuse and exploitation and the otherwise worthy goal of environmental justice deserves better.

# Part VI
# Environmental Regulation and New Technologies

# [26]

# The age of regulatory governance and nanotechnologies

*Roger Brownsword*

## 4.1 INTRODUCTION

In their introductory overview, Graeme A. Hodge, Diana M. Bowman and Andrew D. Maynard (2010) have highlighted seven particular regulatory challenges that they expect to be presented by the development and application of nanotechnologies. If we are to rise to these multifarious challenges, we need the right kind of regulatory environment – an environment that incentivizes the scientific and technical communities to improve their understanding and handling of nanomaterials, an environment that is properly geared to assess and manage risk as well as to ensure that the benefits of nanotechnologies are shared, and perhaps above all an environment that engenders public trust and confidence (Brownsword and Somsen, 2009).

Hodge, Bowman and Maynard also flag the point that there is more to meeting a regulatory challenge than resorting to a hard law instrument – or, at any rate, to command and control forms of legal intervention. There is a sense in which regulation is broader than law. Yet, what exactly do we mean by 'the regulatory environment'? And, once we know a regulatory environment when we see one, what is it that makes it the 'right kind' of regulatory environment for the development and application of nanotechnologies? These are the two principal questions to be addressed in this chapter.

## 4.2 WHAT IS A 'REGULATORY ENVIRONMENT'?

The age in which we live has attracted many descriptions – from the risk society, to the surveillance society, building (or, so some claim) to the crime society (Beck, 1992; Lyon, 2001; Koops, 2009). It is supposedly an age of pluralism, post-modernism, and globalization. If it is also an age of regulatory governance, then what kind of an age is this? What do we mean by the 'regulatory environment', by 'regulation' and by 'governance'? And, in an age of regulatory governance, is there any role for 'law'? In an attempt to get our bearings, we can start by clarifying our terms.

**The Regulatory Environment**

When we say that emerging technologies – whether nanotechnologies, neurotechnologies, or biotechnologies – are situated in a particular regulatory environment, the essential idea is that, when we act, whether we act as developers and commercial exploiters, or as users and appliers, of particular technologies, we do so in a context that has a certain coding for action; a coding that signals whether various acts are permitted (even required) or prohibited, whether they will be viewed positively, negatively, or neutrally, whether they are incentivized or disincentivized, whether they are likely to be praised or criticized, even whether they are possible or impossible, and so on. In such a setting, actors are faced with a range of signals indicating whether it is right to act in a particular way, whether an act is prudent, and even whether an act is possible. This is not to say that we are always aware of the full extent of the relevant coding; we will probably be aware of some parts of it but, sometimes, we might find that our actions elicit code-related responses that come as a surprise, pleasant or otherwise. This is also not to imply that we always act in a way that involves a considered response to the coding of which we are aware – sometimes we simply follow our instincts rather than reflect on what we ought to do. However, if we are to act reflectively, the character of the regulatory environment will have a bearing on our actions.

So much for the general idea. To be more specific about the characteristics of a regulatory (or regulated) environment is not entirely straightforward because, while some environments are regulated in a top-down fashion (with regulators clearly distinguishable from regulatees), others are more bottom-up (in the sense that they are self-regulatory); and, while some are reasonably stable, others are unstable (and conflictual), and so on. However, by way of an initial attempt to specify the characteristics of a regulatory environment, we can highlight the following four matters:

1. the intentionality that underlies the regulatory environment (the purposive nature of the environment);
2. the bearing of the environment on the practical reason of regulatees;
3. the normative and non-normative coding elements; and
4. the variety of coding instrumentalities (or modalities).

First, a regulatory environment is not the product of unintentional design. To the contrary, an environment that is coded for action is only a regulatory environment in the relevant sense where regulators have self-consciously put in place a range of coding signals that are intended to direct or channel behaviour in a particular way. In other words, the regulatory environment is purposively produced. So, for example, if we find ourselves in a room that has just one door through which we can enter or exit, it does not follow that this is a regulatory environment: unless the room has been designed precisely in order to channel entrance and exit through the one and only door, it is not a regulatory environment – our options for entrance and exit might be limited but we are not, as such, regulated.[1] This is not to say that regulators should take no interest in architectural or design features that operate to channel behaviour in particular ways (even if this is not the intention of the architects or designers). If regulators wish to create an environment that is conducive, say, to health or to privacy, they can adopt regulatory measures that encourage architects and technologists to default to health-promoting or privacy-enhancing designs.

Secondly, the strategy of regulators – that is, the strategy of regulators in shaping the conduct of their regulatees – is to engage with the practical reason of regulatees. In such an environment, regulatees will experience the regulatory coding as a social fact that variously constrains or supports what they otherwise wish to do.

Thirdly, in such an environment, regulatees will find that their practical reason is engaged at one or more of the following three levels:

1. the coding signals that some act, x, categorically ought or ought not to be done relative to standards of right action – regulators thus signal to regulatees that x is, or is not, the right thing to do; or
2. the coding signals that some act, x, ought or ought not to be done relative to the prudential interests of regulatees – regulators thus signal to regulatees that x is, or is not, in their (regulatees') self-interest; or
3. the environment is designed in such a way that some act, x, simply cannot be done – in which case, regulatees reason, not that x ought not to be done, but that x cannot be done.

Finally, the modes of channelling that make up a particular regulatory environment can range from law through to architecture, from the law of trespass (prohibiting entry) to a locked door or a password-protected website. So long as the regulatory modality is intended to shape the conduct of regulatees by engaging some dimension of their practical reason, it is a relevant input.

So much for a regulatory environment in which one class (regulators) endeavours to direct the actions of another class (regulatees); an environment in which regulatees experience the regulatory signals as external and as bearing in, via their practical reason, on their actions; and an environment that is clearly distinguishable from other regulatory environments, having its own particular identity as the regulatory environment that it is. We might imagine, however, a variety of regulatory environments that do not correspond so closely to this characterization. For example, where a group self-regulates, where a single class initiates and then subjects itself to a regulatory code, the regulatory environment no longer involves a sharp division between those who are regulators and those who are regulatees; and the same applies when regulatees (such as netizens) resist the signals given by regulators (Murray, 2007). There is also the possibility that there might be some competition between rival classes of regulators – for example, between religious leaders and political leaders, or between civilian leaders and military leaders, or between professional and technical leaders and the political classes. Where this is the case, where one ostensible regulatory environment overlays or competes with another, there is little point in asking which is '*the* regulatory environment'; for, in such circumstances, the signals to regulatees are mixed and the environment is likely to be unstable.

**Regulators**

Who are the regulators? Who is it that is responsible for constructing a regulatory environment? In principle and in practice, the coding that makes up the regulatory environment will come from many sources, governmental and non-governmental, public and private, secular and non-secular, 'official' and 'unofficial', and it will be more or less formal. Accordingly, we might have a diversity of regulators seeking to instate their own particular regulatory environments for their target regulatees. In some cases, a particular regulatory environment will be in the background, in other cases it will be in the foreground; and in some cases, as we have said, regulators will be competing with one another, as a result of which regulatees will be confronted by overlapping and conflicting regulatory signals.

**Regulation**

When we talk about 'law', 'regulation', and 'governance', we are referring to a range of coding inputs that make up the regulatory environment. Law is distinctively a normative input and the regulatory environments with which lawyers are familiar are normative – but, by contrast, regulation can code both for what ought or ought not to be done, and for what can or cannot be done.

'Regulation' can be understood as the most generic of the terms, signifying:

> the sustained and focused attempt to alter the behaviour of others according to standards or goals with the intention of producing a broadly identified outcome

or outcomes, which may involve mechanisms of standard-setting, information-gathering and behaviour-modification (Black, 2005: 11).

Put simply, 'regulation' refers to any instrument (legal or non-legal in its character, governmental or non-governmental in its source, direct or indirect in its operation, and so on) that is designed to channel behaviour. Seminally, Lawrence Lessig (1999a, 1999b) has identified the following four regulatory modalities (or modes of regulation), namely, the law, social norms, the market, and architecture (or, code). So, for example:

> The government may want citizens to wear seatbelts more often. It could pass a law to require the wearing of seatbelts (law regulating behavior directly). Or it could fund public education campaigns to create a stigma against those who do not wear seatbelts (law regulating social norms as a means to regulating behavior). Or it could subsidize insurance companies to offer reduced rates to seatbelt wearers (law regulating the market as a way of regulating behavior). Finally, the law could mandate automatic seatbelts, or ignition-locking systems (changing the code of the automobile as a means of regulating belting behavior). Each action might be said to have some effect on seatbelt use; each has some cost. The question for the government is how to get the most seatbelt use for the least cost (Lessig, 1999a: 93–4).

We need to be careful when we treat architecture or code as part of the (normative) regulatory environment. Some technologies function in a normative way; others simply design out what would otherwise be an option. Hence, whether we are considering smart cars, smart homes, or smart regulatory styles, we need to be sensitive to the way in which the regulatory environment engages with regulatees, whether it directs normative signals at regulatees enjoining them to act in particular ways, or whether the technology of regulation simply imposes (non-normatively) a pattern of conduct upon regulatees whether or not they would otherwise choose to act in the prescribed way.

**Law**

The most formal contribution to the regulatory environment is made by the 'law'. By this term, we mean that set of posited instruments – treaties, constitutions, codes, legislation, and the like – as well as particular precedents laid down by courts that are conventionally taken to be the sources that are relevant to the determination of the 'legal' position. Admittedly, this suffers from some circularity; in effect, it says little more than that the term is being used in accordance with the positivist conventions that prevail in many places. Such a usage would not satisfy legal idealists who, in general, conceive of the law in a way that necessarily connects it to higher order moral standards – legal validity is to be understood as a species of moral validity, legal obligation as a species of moral obligation, legal reason as a species of moral reason, and so on. Nor would this usage satisfy legal pluralists who see law in many settings both below and beyond the high level institutions of the nation state. However, for our purposes, we can bracket off the difficult jurisprudential issues: for present purposes, it suffices to say that 'law' represents a particular class of normative signals that take their place in the larger regulatory array.

**Governance**

Finally, there is the term 'governance'. According to Lewis Kornhauser (2004: 381), we should treat legal systems as a particular kind of governance structure, from which it follows that disputes concerning the concept of law should be understood as disputes 'concerning the property or properties that distinguish legal systems from other types of governance structures'. Whatever we think that particular distinguishing property or properties might be, the clear implication is that governance is a more inclusive category than law. If governance is to be given a broad sweep, we might simply use the term as another word for regulation, or perhaps as referring to all forms of regulation that are not legal (as in the locution 'law and governance'). Arguably, however, what the lexicon of regulation most needs is a term that highlights those regulatory inputs that are non-governmental. For, beyond those regulatory activities that are carried out by, or on behalf of, government and its agents, there are the activities of those many non-governmental agencies (including religious and professional associations, technical standard-setting bodies, advisory bodies, and a host of others) that seek to impose a pattern of behaviour on their membership or who order group relationships. It is the normative signals transmitted by all of these important classes of agents that represent the distinctive sphere of 'governance'.

To summarize, when we put together the different strands of (governmental) law, (governmental) regulation, and (non-governmental regulatory) governance, we have the ingredients – ingredients that are still largely normative – that make up the particular 'regulatory environment'.

## 4.3 WHAT IS IT THAT MAKES A REGULATORY ENVIRONMENT THE 'RIGHT KIND' OF REGULATORY ENVIRONMENT?

In principle, we might assess any aspect of the regulatory environment, irrespective of whether government has responsibility for it. However, in practice, it is that stretch of regulatory coding for which government is responsible that is likely to attract the greatest public debate – and, of course, in the legal community, it is particularly those regulatory interventions that have been articulated in a legal form that will be the focus for critical assessment.

Essentially, an assessment of the regulatory environment, or some part of it, will check out the following five matters:

1. whether the purposes adopted by regulators (and the standards expressed) are legitimate – that is, whether regulators are trying to do the right kind of thing;
2. whether the position taken by regulators is prudent (and, in the case of nanotechnologies, sufficiently precautionary) relative to the community's interest;
3. whether the means by which regulatory objectives are set and pursued are legitimate – that is, whether regulators are going about their business in the right kind of way (in the case of nanotechnologies, particularly whether the public is appropriately engaged in the policy process);
4. whether the regulatory intervention is effective (relative to the background regulatory objectives) – that is, whether the regulation is fit for purpose; and
5. whether regulation is properly connected to its technological target.

In regimes of regional regulation, there is also a large question about whether cosmopolitan ideals are satisfied, that is, whether regulators are paying proper regard to fundamental values as well as legitimate local difference. Within the compass of this short chapter, however, it is not possible to explore this question.[2]

Some regulatory environments might be perfectly adequate in relation to some of these criteria but inadequate in relation to others – for example, a particular regulatory environment might be highly effective relative to the regulators' objectives but those objectives may lack legitimacy, or vice versa. To be comprehensively adequate, a regulatory environment would need to pass muster on all five counts.

Long chapters, indeed long books, could be written about each of these five criteria; but, for present purposes, it suffices to indicate some of the key aspects of each of these measures of adequacy.

## The Legitimacy of Regulatory Purposes and Standards

The first question that we should ask about any particular regulatory environment is whether it meets whatever standards of legitimacy we might apply. Regulators have to answer to many constituencies, each with their own criterion of right action, each with their own view of what regulators should be doing. For some, the regulatory imperative will be to do everything that can be done to smooth the way for technological innovation that holds out the promise of having beneficial applications. For others, regulators should be more cautious, being mindful that there is a concern, as Henk ten Have (2006: 6) has put it, 'that unbridled scientific progress is not always ethically acceptable'.

What, then, are the perceived ethical problems associated with nanotechnologies? In its *Opinion on the Ethical Aspects of Nanomedicine* (2007), the European Group on Ethics in Science and New Technologies (the EGE) highlights (at para 4.1) the following ethical questions relating to the development of nanomedicine:

> How should the dignity of people participating in nanomedicine research trials be respected? How can we protect the fundamental rights of citizens that may be exposed to free particles in the environment? How can we promote responsible use of nanomedicine which protects both human health and the environment? And what are the specific ethics issues, such as justice, solidarity and autonomy, that have to be considered in this scientific domain?

The ethical backcloth against which the EGE identifies these issues is a broad one, ranging from the *European Charter of Fundamental Rights* (the Nice Charter) through to the UNESCO *Universal Declaration on Bioethics and Human Rights 2005* (see ten Have and Jean, 2009; Yusuf, 2007). Although the latter is addressed specifically to 'ethical issues related to medicine, life sciences and associated technologies', it presents us with a starting point for thinking about the legitimacy not only of regulation directed at biotechnology but also of the regulation of neurotechnology and nanotechnology (at any rate, in its biomedical applications).

Elsewhere, I have suggested that, if we are to broaden and deepen our ethical reflections in relation to nanotechnologies in general or, as in the case of the EGE Opinion, nanomedicine in particular, we need to be more explicit about the ethical background (Brownsword, 2008b). The key features of that background are as follows.

First, there are three root ethical forms: goal-orientated (consequentialism), rights-based, and duty-based. This threesome constitutes, so to speak, the basic ethical matrix.

Second, the basic ethical matrix sets the pattern of ethical reflection no matter which technology is under consideration, no matter which techno-ethic is being articulated. Whether we are applying bioethics, cyberethics, or neuroethics, the pattern of ethical reflection is dictated by the matrix. And, this holds good when we turn to nanotechnologies and nanoethics.

Third, each of the root forms is open to a variety of substantive articulations. In modern bioethics, the leading articulations are: utilitarian (for goal orientation), human rights (for rights-based), and dignitarian (for duty-based). This articulation comprises a plurality that I have referred to elsewhere as 'the bioethical triangle' (see, for example, Brownsword, 2003, 2008a).

Fourth, within the bioethical triangle (and in the matrix more generally), although there can be cases of convergence and consensus, we can expect disputation and division as protagonists argue from rival ethical axioms. Crucially, because those who argue from dignitarian principles regard some actions and practices as categorically wrong – in the case of nanotechnologies, we can expect dignitarian rejection of any innovations that seem to involve the commodification of the human body (see Gordijn, 2006) – there is no room for compromise or accommodation with this corner of the triangle.

It is worth pausing over the dignitarian concern about commodification. Imagine that nanomedicine develops to the point where nanosensors in our bodies monitor our health; and, where problems are detected, nanometric drug release systems are activated. Such early warning systems and nano-responses seem to be good for our health, but they might have a downside when viewed through a dignitarian lens. Thus, as Bert Gordijn (2006: 729) has put it:

> [S]uch developments will contribute to a more technologically inspired image of the body as something very similar to a machine. The body will increasingly be regarded as a whole, made up of many different components that might be fixed, enhanced or replaced if necessary. Development, functions, and appearance of the body will seem less and less fixed by nature and less frequently accepted without change, and more frequently controllable by technology. Instead of being in charge of our own health we might increasingly trust technology to take over this responsibility. In the process however, the body will be treated almost like the inanimate material of a machine. Hence, the body might become increasingly de-hallowed and de-mystified.

To the extent that nanomedicine adopts or encourages the functional view that is already evident in human genetics and the new brain sciences, this will compound dignitarian concerns about commodification. The promise of in vivo nanosensors and drug release systems, like the promise of regenerative medicine, sounds fine until it is set alongside the disaggregation of humans into their component parts. Is there really no distinction between humans and, say, a motor car or a computer – just so many parts, so many functions, so many models? Moreover, if nanomedicine leads to a blurring of the boundary between man and machine and if this gives rise, in Gordijn's (2006: 731) words, to 'feelings of uneasiness, creeping disorientation and even existential panic', then the dignitarians will not be on their own in being anxious about such developments.

Fifth, to return to the ethical background, there are no ethically neutral pockets or platforms for regulators: what we make of such commonplace principles as that regulators should prohibit conduct only where it is 'harmful to others', or should ensure that actions proceed only on the basis of 'informed consent', depends entirely upon where we are coming from in the matrix or the triangle. The unarticulated interpretation of 'harm' shoots through debates about both risk and precaution; and, to leave nanomedicine to the governance of informed consent is to invite a multitude of regulatory approaches to the importance of consent as well as to the specification of what constitutes a 'free' and 'informed' choice.

This leaves many questions unanswered – for example, how ethics relates to morality, where virtue ethics fits into the matrix, and where feminist ethics belongs in the bioethical triangle, and so on. Above all, however, it leaves unanswered the question of how, in pluralist settings, regulators are to set standards that, by common consent, are legitimate.[3]

**The Prudence of the Regulatory Position**

Regulators routinely seek to defend their positions by appealing to the general interest. However, where there are concerns about the possibly hazardous and potentially risky nature of emerging technologies, there will be a question about whether regulators have been sufficiently precautionary in their approach. As with legitimacy, however, prudence qua precaution is far from straightforward.

In the case of nanotechnologies, it is the unknown properties of nanomaterials that present one of the principal difficulties for regulators:

> [M]ost countries require a new chemical to be assessed before it can be sold. But nanoparticles of an existing chemical may have properties so different from the bulk form that new nanoparticles should be treated as if they were new chemicals. Regulations may assume that the nanoscale version of a chemical behaves in the same way as it does in bulk which it may not. A carbon nanotube could be thought of as graphite, but it also has a structure that resembles asbestos. It is essential to find out whether these tubes behave like pencil lead or like a highly dangerous material (Standage, 2005: 328).

Hence, in one report after another, we find an emphasis on the importance of exercising precaution in the process of creating and developing products and therapies that make use of nanotechnology components (see, for example, Quebec Commission, 2006). Not surprisingly, the tone of the EGE opinion (2007) is not dissimilar. Adopting the precautionary principle as a general tool for risk management, the EGE (2007: para 5.4) recommends that, in the light of the principle,

> the uncertainties and knowledge gaps associated with new nanotechnology-based diagnostics, therapies and preventive measures should be identified. These uncertainties need to be characterised and measures have to be developed in order to reduce them as far as possible.

This is not to say that the precautionary principle should be applied disproportionately to create 'zero-risk' situations; rather, according to the EGE (2007: para 4.2.3), 'risk management actions should be aimed at identifying the "acceptable risk" threshold with regard to the values at stake – and respect for the human body is undoubtedly one of the values deserving the highest legal protection'.

Placing these reflections in the broader setting of risk-profiling, it is clear that regulators need to tailor their interventions to the perceived risk-profile presented by a particular technology. In principle, the elaboration of a risk-profile for a particular technology should draw on the following considerations:

- the *kind* of harm (physical, environmental, social, economic, moral, political, and so on) to which the risk pertains (compare Jasanoff, 1995);
- the *severity and scale* of the harm if the risk eventuates; and
- the *probability* of the risk materializing.

In practice, the judgments that we make depend on which of these considerations we take into account, how much weight we give to them, and which considerations we prioritize. With regard to nanotechnologies, there is a problem about getting the risk-profile to a meaningful first base. Quite simply, as the Quebec Commission (2006: ii) (like many others) puts it, the difficulty is that we cannot be confident about 'the probability that an event will occur and the nature and significance of damages resulting from the same event'.[4]

Nevertheless, whichever ethical perspective one adopts, there surely will be concern about the potential harm that nanomaterials, nanodevices, free nanoparticles and unembedded carbon nanotubes, and the like, might occasion (The Royal Society and Royal Academy of Engineering (RS-

RAE), 2004). Humans are vulnerable; the physical environment might be at risk; and, in general, care needs to be taken before nanoproducts are brought to market (Brownsword, 2009). On the other hand, the promise of nanomedical solutions will create a pressure for expedition, particularly if such nanoapplications are available in other countries and they are seemingly safe and effective. It is all very well enjoining regulators to set their sights on acceptable risk; but, under conditions of uncertainty, and with divided opinion in the community, regulators will find it extremely difficult to satisfy the conflicting demands that are made of them.

## The Legitimacy of Regulatory Means

The test of whether regulators are going about their business in the right kind of way covers many facets of the regulatory enterprise – from standard-setting, through monitoring, and correction (Yeung, 2004). Generally speaking, though, we can say that it is a test that bears on (i) the relationship between regulators and regulatees, and (ii) the instruments used by regulators.

### (i) Regulators and regulatees

Regulators, particularly governmental regulators, are expected to operate in ways that are transparent and accountable and that involve appropriate measures for stakeholder and public participation. Hence, where a legislative framework is agreed for the application of a new technology, this will usually be preceded by public consultation, media debate, parliamentary debate, and so on. However, it is not always the case that the operative rules regulating the use of a technology – especially a technology in its embryonic stage – have been publicly debated and transparently agreed in this way. Quite possibly, all that we have is informal codes or guidelines that are self-regulatory coupled with fall-back general legal provisions such as those found in the criminal law and the law of torts. This, however, might not be thought to be adequate.

Quite rightly, the EGE (2007: para 4.4.2.2) advises that every step should be taken to encourage public participation and debate (see, too, RS-RAE, 2004). Moreover, the EGE (2007: para 4.4.2.2) appreciates that there is more to this than an exercise in public relations:

> The participation of the public in all stages of the development of this innovative research sector is therefore important not only for the public acceptance of nanomedicine and nanotechnology, *but also for the adoption of a nanotechnology strategy where public concerns are approached and discussed from the beginning* (emphasis added).[5]

In other words, experts should advise on their best guess as to the nature and probability of the apprehended risks but the public should be fully engaged in characterizing which risks are material, which risks are acceptable and, where there are conflicting interests involved, which priorities should be set. Echoing such thinking, Ronald Sandler and W.D. Kay (2006: 679) argue:

> [S]cience and industry experts have an important role to play . . . They are well positioned to see what is possible, what is feasible, and what is required to achieve certain economic and technological ends. They thereby play a crucial informational role. But knowledge of what can and cannot be done, and of what is and is not required to do it, is quite different from knowledge of what ought and ought not to be done. What ends should be prioritised, how resources should be allocated in pursuit of those ends, and constraints on how those ends ought to be pursued are ethical and social questions to be addressed in the public sphere, not economic and technological ones to be worked out in boardrooms or laboratories . . . So while scientists and industry leaders may be 'elite' in their knowledge of the science and business of nanotechnology, this status does not imply that they are 'elite' with respect to the [social and ethical] issues associated with nanotechnology . . .

These sentiments resonate with the thinking in a report prepared for the Washington-based Project on Emerging Nanotechnologies (Davies, 2006) according to which the public needs to be involved in two capacities: first, as citizens, members of the public are stakeholders in assessing the larger social and ethical risks associated with nanotechnology; and, second, as potential consumers of nanotechnology products, members of the public need to be able to make informed choices. Bearing in mind the resistance to GM in some parts of Europe, this surely makes a lot of sense – and it does so whether one approaches the matter from a utilitarian perspective, where the issue is about retaining public confidence and trust, or from a human rights perspective, where the issue is about due process and enfranchisement.

**(ii) Regulatory means**

Much attention has been given to whether regulators select the optimal mix of regulatory instruments. The legitimacy test, however, is not about whether the selected instruments will be effective. The test is one of whether the instruments are legitimate in the eyes of citizens. So long as regulators are relying on law, peer pressure, market signals and the like, there is no real problem; the question of legitimacy arises where the regulatory instruments involve a technical fix of some kind. The question reflects a mix of concerns, some that are rather obvious concerns about privacy and the like, others that are more subtle and that relate to the corrosion of the conditions for practices that we value. Moreover, as Mark Rothstein and Meghan Talbott (2006: 160–161) have emphasized, we cannot afford to judge each technological instrument of regulation in isolation from the larger context of State surveillance and control:

> The prospect of expanded use of DNA forensics needs to be placed in context. In a world in which personal privacy is difficult to maintain against an onslaught of computer file sharing, surveillance cameras, biometric imaging, thermal imaging, and other technological 'advances', for many people, the last 'off limit' area for access to personal information is law enforcement . . .
>
> Assume that a hypothetical country routinely required all of its residents to submit the following items to the police: a DNA sample, a yearly photograph, handwriting exemplar, voiceprint, fingerprints, hair samples, retinal scans, bank statements, credit card information, health records, and other details of their personal life. Obviously, ready access to this information by police would help solve crimes. Nevertheless, such comprehensive information submission to law enforcement would be widely viewed as hallmarks of a repressive, totalitarian state . . .

With developments of this kind – where nanotechnologies become part of the apparatus of a profiling and surveillance society, where preventive detention or secured channelling is the order of the day – there is a radical change in the regulatory environment. This is a development that has deep implications for a community's liberal culture.

**Regulatory Effectiveness**

As Hodge, Bowman and Maynard (2010) rightly observe, a great deal of innovative legal scholarship has been applied to the question of regulatory effectiveness.

For the regulatory style to be 'smart' and 'responsive', it is essential that regulators become more imaginative, breaking the deadlock between those who advocate more regulation and those who advocate less, abandoning any idea that 'one regulatory size fits all', developing a sensitivity to the differing motivations and attitudes of regulatees, and recognizing the limits of single instrument approaches (Ayres and Braithwaite, 1992; Gunningham and Grabosky, 1998; Braithwaite, 2008).

However, the idea that regulation will be effective if only regulators are smarter in selecting and combining their instruments falls a long way short of what our regulatory intelligence already tells us. For example, in a recent paper, Robert Baldwin and Julia Black (2008: 94), conclude:

> Regulation is really responsive when it knows its regulatees and its institutional environments, when it is capable of deploying different and new regulatory

logics coherently, when it is performance sensitive and when it grasps what its shifting challenges are.

Hence, it would be more accurate to say that, *other things being equal*, a smart selection will deliver a more effective intervention than a single instrument approach. The problem is that there are many other factors to hold steady under the *ceteris paribus* clause.

If we stand back from the empirical and ethnographical detail provided by a myriad of quantitative and qualitative impact studies, we can see that there are three key sources of weakness that are liable to impact on the effectiveness of a regulatory intervention. Stated bluntly, where there is regulatory failure, the locus of the problem has to be (i) with the regulators themselves, or (ii) with the response (including the resistance) of regulatees, or (iii) with some disruptive factors external to the regulators and regulatees – and, quite possibly, the problem will be found to lie in more than one of these loci.

So, first, the locus of the problem might be with the regulators themselves, with their integrity and competence, as well as with the adequacy of their resources. Where regulators lack integrity, they are prey to corruption or capture. Granted, corruption or capture implies a lack of integrity, too, on the part of regulatees; but the root of the problem is with the weakness of regulators. Where regulators are not corrupt but simply incompetent, they might be unclear about their regulatory purposes; or the standards that they set (where this is their regulatory strategy) might fail to give workable guidance to regulatees. As Lon Fuller (1969) highlighted many years ago, a workable legal (regulatory) order implies that the rules are published and clearly articulated, that the provisions are not overcomplex, that the rules are not constantly subject to revision, and so on. In short, regulatees need to know where they stand. Where the resources available to regulators are inadequate, they might act on poor policy advice – for example, they might seriously miscalculate the consequences and indirect effects of their intervention (Radetzki et al., 2003); and their ability to monitor compliance and correct for noncompliance might be severely limited. Of course, where there is a strong culture of compliance among regulatees, detection and correction are less important regulatory activities; but there is no counting on such a culture being in place.

Second, it is critical for the effectiveness of a regulatory intervention that regulatees respond in the right way. It can hardly surprise regulators that some regulatees respond in exactly the wrong way, that they have to contend with professional and habitual criminal classes as well as occasional acts of criminality. However, an important part of our regulatory intelligence is to account for, and to anticipate, noncompliance in what we might assume to be generally law-abiding sections of the regulatee population. In some cases, it might simply be that regulators have failed to give regulatees clear guidance – in which event, the remedy lies with a more competent regulatory performance. In other cases, regulatees know precisely where they stand but they also know how to respond in a way that protects their self-interest. Again, regulators should not be surprised that regulatees (particularly regulatees with business interests) should think that a calculation of rational economic interest is the appropriate way to determine how to respond to a regulatory intervention. Similarly, regulators should not be surprised that those who are opposed to the particular regulatory position might actively pursue whatever avenues for challenge and review are lawfully available (and anticipate that, while such challenges are underway, this might operate as a chill factor). There are, however, cases where regulatees know where they stand and yet they defy the regulatory position, whether openly (as in the case, say, of peer-to-peer file sharing) or covertly (as might be the case with the use of cognition enhancers). So long as regulators are not pushing at an open door, they must either try to minimize resistance *ex ante* or have a strategy for dealing with it *ex post*.

Third, it is perfectly possible that the relationship between regulators and regulatees is aligned for effectiveness and yet a regulatory intervention fails. For example, a regulator might initiate a highly effective strategy that encourages investment in new nanotechnologies; but, then, there is a global economic crisis, funding for research and development dries up, employees in infant hi-tech businesses lose their jobs, and what was a highly successful intervention is now a failure. The locus of this failure, however, is neither the regulators nor the regulatees. Rather, the problem here is that of a disruptive externality – and, in a globalizing world, national regulators are particularly vulnerable to such disruptions.

**Regulatory Connection**

It has been frequently remarked that the development and application of technologies moves too quickly for the law, as a result of which we find legislative frameworks (such as that provided for by the *Human Fertilisation and Embryology Act 1990*) becoming rapidly disconnected from their particular technological targets (in the case of the 1990 Act, the target technologies being those associated with embryology). However, this is but one (and perhaps the most obvious) dimension of the challenge of regulatory connection. Stated comprehensively, this challenge relates to three phases of the regulatory cycle: first, there is the matter of getting regulation connected to the technology – a phase insightfully discussed by Gregory Mandel (2008, 2009) in relation to emerging nanotechnologies; second, there is the matter of keeping regulation connected; and third there is the matter of reconnection (where the regulation has become disconnected).

A helpful way of framing the issue of connection is to consider two variables: first, the extent and relevance of the regulatory array that is already in place when a connection issue arises; and, second, the particular stage of technological evolution that we are at (in other words, whether we are dealing with a technology that is novel and uncertain or reasonably familiar and well understood).

**(i) The regulatory array**

One of Mandel's suggestions is that there should be an early inquiry into the state of extant regulation (as well as the appropriateness of the extant configuration of regulatory agencies). In the case of emerging technologies that are either thought to be high-risk or that are surrounded by uncertainty about their risk profile, such an inquiry will tend to focus on the extant regulation concerning health, safety and the environment – as is the case, currently, in relation to developing nanotechnologies (Bowman and Hodge, 2007; Lin, 2007; Phelps, 2007; Guerra, 2008). Where the technology is thought to have an acceptable risk profile, the inquiry will focus on the regulation of liability. And, where the regulation is thought to be risk free, the focus will be on the adequacy of the relevant facilitative regulation – whether this is patent law or contract law (as was the case with the early debates about the regulation of e-commerce). Although there might be no part of the regulatory array that is specifically dedicated to the emerging technology, and although there might be gaps in the array, it will rarely be true to say that an emerging technology finds itself in a regulatory void.

If we conceive of the regulatory environment as being designed to minimize the negative effects of the technology and maximize the positive effects, the regulatory array is likely to comprise a broad range of provisions. To simplify, we might conceive of three key divisions within the regulatory array. In one division, the regulatory purpose is to regulate against negative effects. Here, the principal regulatory segments will be designed:

1. to assess the health, environmental and safety risks presented by an emerging technology;
2. to authorize the particular and specific applications of a technology once it has achieved general regulatory clearance under (1) – whether this is a bespoke authorization process or a general default principle such as that of informed consent;

3. to penalize dangerous and abusive acts related to the technology (through the criminal law); and
4. to provide for compensation in the event of injury or damage to an agent's protected interests (as is the case with tort, product liability, and data protection regimes, and the like).

In a second division, the principal regulatory segments will be designed:

5. to incentivize the development of beneficial technologies (as is the case with patent law);
6. to facilitate the circulation and exploitation of the technology (for example, by refining contract law); and
7. to ensure fair access (as with competition law and the law of taxation).

Finally, in a constitutive division, there will be overarching provisions (for example, concerning respect for human rights and human dignity) that will apply across the array to monitor compliance with the community's fundamental values.

**(ii) The stage of technological development**

Turning to the other variable, that of the stage of technological evolution, it seems undeniable that '[t]echnological revolutions do not arrive fully mature' (Moor, 2008: 27). Rather, they take time, unfolding in stages and gathering pace as knowledge, understanding, and use of the technology spreads. Indeed, this very point is highlighted by Mandel (2009) when he contrasts the relative maturity of green biotechnologies with the lesser maturity of nanotechnologies, and (especially) synthetic biology. The question, therefore, is whether, in James Moor's (2008) terminology, we are in the introduction, permeation, or power stage of the development, utilization, and penetration of a particular technology.

To frame the challenge, however, is not to answer it. With nanotechnologies likely to develop rapidly, it remains a formidable challenge to articulate sustainable regulation that is both effective and legitimate.

## 4.4 CONCLUSION

In an age of regulatory governance, just as we are learning about emerging nanotechnologies and the like, we are also learning about the technology of regulation itself. Whether we are dealing with the regulation of emerging technologies or with the emerging regulation by technologies, we face some complex questions (compare Brownsword and Yeung, 2008). To rise to the challenge of creating the right kind of regulatory environment, we need interventions that offer the right support and incentives for beneficial nanotechnological development while, at the same time, putting in place appropriate measures for the minimization of risk. We are learning more with every year; but, just as there is plenty waiting to be learned about nanotechnologies so, too, our regulatory intelligence – whether relating to legitimacy, effectiveness or connection, whether concerning precaution, proportionality, or participation (compare Beyleveld and Brownsword, 2009) – still has a long way to go.

## NOTES

1. Compare the debate about whether the design of Robert Moses' bridges on the New York parkways was intended to have the (racially discriminatory) effect of making it more difficult for the poor, mainly black, population to reach the beaches on Long Island (Manders-Huits and van den Hoven, 2009).
2. See further Brownsword (2008a: Ch 7).
3. In this light, para 4.1.16 of the European Commission's (2008) Recommendation (on a code of conduct for responsible nanosciences and nanotechnologies research), according to which: '[Nano] research organisations should not undertake research aiming for non-therapeutic enhancement of human beings leading to addiction or solely for the illicit enhancement of the performance of the human body.' Can we safely assume that the scope of 'illicit enhancement' is agreed?
4. In Andy Stirling's terms, this is a paradigmatic case of 'ignorance' (Stirling, 2008: 103).
5. See also the Council for Science and Technology (2007) and Einsiedel and Goldberg (2006).

## REFERENCES


Ayres, I. and J. Braithwaite (1992), *Responsive Regulation*, Oxford: Oxford University Press.

Baldwin, R. and J. Black (2008), 'Really responsive regulation', *Modern Law Review* **71**, 59–94.

Beck, U. (1992), *Risk Society: Towards a New Modernity*, London: Sage.

Beyleveld D. and R. Brownsword (2009), 'Complex technology, complex calculations: uses and abuses of precautionary reasoning in law', in Paul Sollie and Marcus Düwell (eds), *Evaluating New Technologies*, Dordrecht, Netherlands: Springer, pp. 175–90.

Black, J. (2005), 'What is regulatory innovation?' in Julia Black, Martin Lodge and Mark Thatcher (eds), *Regulatory Innovation*, Cheltenham, UK and Northampton, MA, USA: Edward Elgar, pp. 1–15.

Bowman, D.M. and G.A. Hodge (2007), 'Nanotechnology "down under": getting on top of regulatory matters', *Nanotechnology Law and Business*, **4**, 223–33.

Braithwaite, J. (2008), *Regulatory Capitalism*, Cheltenham, UK and Northampton, MA, USA: Edward Elgar.

Brownsword, R. (2003), 'Bioethics today, bioethics tomorrow: stem cell research and the "dignitarian alliance"', *University of Notre Dame Journal of Law, Ethics and Public Policy*, **17**, 15–51.

Brownsword, R. (2008a), *Rights, Regulation and the Technological Revolution*, Oxford: Oxford University Press.
Brownsword, R. (2008b), 'Regulating nanomedicine – the smallest of our concerns?' *NanoEthics*, **2**, 73–86.
Brownsword, R. (2009), 'Nanoethics: old wine, new bottles?,' *Journal of Consumer Policy*, accessed 16 June 2009 at www.springerlink.com.ezproxy.lib.monash.edu.au/content/f020211848hrk548/fulltext.pdf.
Brownsword, R. and H. Somsen (2009), 'Law, innovation and technology: before we fast forward – a forum for debate', *Law, Innovation and Technology*, **1**, 1–73.
Brownsword, R. and K. Yeung (eds) (2008), *Regulating Technologies*, Oxford: Hart.
Council for Science and Technology (2007), *Nanosciences and Nanotechnologies: A Review of Government's Progress on its Policy Commitments*, London: CST.
Davies, J.C. (2006), *Managing the Effects of Nanotechnology*, Washington, DC: Project on Emerging Technologies.
Einsiedel, E.F. and L. Goldberg (2006), 'Dwarfing the social? Nanotechnology lessons from the biotechnology front', in Geoffrey Hunt and Michael Mehta (eds), *Nanotechnology: Risk, Ethics and Law*, London: Earthscan, pp. 213–21.
European Commission (2008), *Recommendation (on a code of conduct for responsible nanosciences and nanotechnologies research) C(2008) 424 final,* Brussels: EC.
European Group on Ethics in Science and New Technologies (2007), *Opinion on the Ethical Aspects of Nanomedicine*, opinion no 21, Brussels: EGE.
Fuller, L.L. (1969), *The Morality of Law*, New Haven, CT: Yale University Press.
Gordijn, B. (2006), 'Converging NBIC technologies for improving human performance: a critical assessment of the novelty and prospects of the project', *Journal of Law, Medicine and Ethics*, **34**, 726–32.
Guerra, G. (2008), 'European regulatory issues in nanomedicine', *NanoEthics*, **2**, 87–97.
Gunningham, N. and P. Grabosky (1998), *Smart Regulation*, Oxford: Clarendon Press.
Hodge, G.A., D.M. Bowman and A.D. Maynard (2010), 'Introduction: the regulatory challenges for nanotechnologies' in Graeme A. Hodge, Diana M. Bowman and Andrew D. Maynard (eds), *International Handbook on Regulating Nanotechnologies*, Cheltenham, UK and Northampton, MA, USA: Edward Elgar, pp. 3–24.
Jasanoff, S. (1995), 'Product, process, or programme: three cultures and the regulation of biotechnology' in Martin Bauer (ed), *Resistance to New Technology*, Cambridge: Cambridge University Press, pp. 311–31.
Koops, B.-J. (2009), 'Technology and the crime society: rethinking legal protection', *Law, Innovation and Technology*, **1**, 93–124.
Kornhauser, L.A. (2004), 'Governance structures, legal systems and the concept of law', *University of Chicago-Kent Law Review*, **70**, 355–80.
Lessig, L. (1999a), *Code and Other Laws of Cyberspace*, New York: Basic Books.
Lessig, L. (1999b), 'The law of the horse: what cyberlaw might teach', *Harvard Law Review*, **113**, 501–46.
Lin, A.C. (2007), 'Size matters: regulating nanotechnology', *Harvard Environmental Law Review*, **31**, 349–408.
Lyon, D. (2001), *Surveillance Society: Monitoring Everyday Life*, Buckingham: Open University Press.
Mandel, G.N. (2008), 'Nanotechnology governance', *Alabama Law Review*, **59**, 1–62.
Mandel, G.N. (2009), 'Regulating emerging technologies', *Law, Innovation and Technology*, **1**, 75–92.
Manders-Huits, N. and J. van den Hoven (2009), 'The need for a value-sensitive design of communication infrastructures', in Paul Sollie and Marcus Düwell (eds), *Evaluating New Technologies*, Dordrecht, Netherlands: Springer, pp. 51–60.
Moor, J.H. (2008), 'Why we need better ethics for emerging technologies', in Jeroen van den Hoven and John Weckert (eds), *Information Technology and Moral Philosophy*, Cambridge: Cambridge University Press, pp. 26–39.
Murray, A.D. (2007), *The Regulation of Cyberspace*, Abingdon: Routledge-Cavendish.

Phelps, T.A. (2007), 'The European approach to nanoregulation', in Nigel M. de S. Cameron and M. Ellen Mitchell (eds), *Nanoscale*, Hoboken, NJ: Wiley, pp. 189–210.
Quebec Commission on the Ethics and Science of Technology (2006), *Ethics and Nanotechnologies: A Basis for Action*, Quebec: Commission de l'éthique de la science et de la technologie.
Radetzki, M., M. Radetzki and N. Juth (2003), *Genes and Insurance*, Cambridge: Cambridge University Press.
Rothstein, M.A. and M.K. Talbott (2006), 'The expanding use of DNA in law enforcement: what role for privacy?', *Journal of Law, Medicine and Ethics*, **34**, 153–64.
Royal Society and the Royal Academy of Engineering (2004), *Nanoscience and Nanotechnologies: Opportunities and Uncertainties*, London: RS-RAE.
Sandler, R. and W.D. Kay (2006), 'The National Nanotechnology Initiative and the social good,' *Journal of Law, Medicine and Ethics*, **34**, 675–81.
Standage, T. (ed) (2005), *The Future of Technology*, London: Profile Books.
Stirling, A. (2008), 'Science, precaution, and the politics of technological risk', *Annals of the New York Academy of Sciences*, **1128**, 95–110.
ten Have, H. (2006), 'UNESCO and ethics of science and technology', in UNESCO (ed), *Ethics of Science and Technology: Explorations of the Frontiers of Science and Ethics*, Paris: UNESCO, pp. 5–16.
ten Have, H.A.M.J. and M.S. Jean (eds) (2009), *The UNESCO Universal Declaration on Bioethics and Human Rights*, Paris: UNESCO Publishing.
Yeung, K. (2004), *Securing Compliance*, Oxford: Hart.
Yusuf, A.A. (2007), 'UNESCO standard-setting activities on bioethics: speak softly and carry a big stick', in Francesco Francioni (ed), *Biotechnologies and International Human Rights*, Oxford: Hart, pp. 85–96.

# [27]

# Rethinking regulatory governance for the age of biotechnology

**Colin Scott**

## 1 INTRODUCTION

The rapid development of biotechnology in the last 30 years, with applications to human health and reproduction, and to the agricultural, insurance and security sectors, has generated varied policy responses from governments in the OECD countries. Though often labelled 'biotechnology regulation' the vast bulk of the policy literature is concerned with the construction of only one element of a regulatory regime – the normative structure of principles, standards and rules. Biotechnology regulation, as a field of public policy, has not yet matured to the point where other elements of regulatory regimes – notably processes for monitoring and mechanisms of behavioural modification – are routinely considered or problematized.

This pattern of neglect of the machinery for implementation of regulatory policy is common to the emergence of earlier regulatory regimes – for example, occupational health and food safety (Paulus 1974). As with those earlier stories it creates risks that the norms, elaborated after much advice and discussion, may not be rendered effective in practice. On the other hand there is an opportunity to consider an array of mechanisms, going beyond traditional instruments of command and control, through which regulatory norms might be made effective. Such an analysis reveals not only variety in the mechanisms of regulatory implementation, but also highlights the possibility that norms agreed through state decision-making processes might be bypassed and even destabilized by alternative mechanisms for the generation and application of norms over biotechnology.

## 2 BIOTECHNOLOGY AND REGULATION

Biotechnology is not especially new. The fermentation of alcoholic drinks and the creation of cultures for making cheese and yoghurt are early applications that date back to antiquity. Similarly the selection of animals for breeding, and the development of new or better crops and flowering plants have occurred for many hundreds of years. Processes of genetic modification are extremely well established within human activities and accordingly might be thought to raise few entirely new ethical and political issues (Nuffield Council on Bioethics 1999).

Notwithstanding the long history of biotechnology there has been, in the last 20–30 years, a qualitative change in the policy debates, linked to concern and even panic about the potential application for new techniques for the engineering of plant and animal life, and in particular genetic modification (Ungar 2001). It is significant that the term biotechnology was coined as late as 1919.

This chapter provides an initial set of observations about the development of biotechnology regulation in response to these heightened policy concerns from the perspective of contemporary scholarship within the generic field of regulation. Within regulation scholarship there is a tendency to take policy objectives as given and to focus on the means by which they may be delivered – What types of rules? What types of regulatory institutions? How to monitor for compliance? What mechanisms of enforcement? (Baldwin and Cave 1999).

It seems to me that those embedded within the world of biotechnology policy have a nearly opposite set of preoccupations that focus on the development of the appropriate normative structures (an exception is provided by the regulatory analysis of Salter and Frewer 2003). Both approaches have weaknesses, of course. The latter risks neglecting how implementation of the policy might be made effective. The former tends to neglect the extent to which policy is made, implicitly or explicitly, through processes of implementation. Both approaches exhibit a bias towards privileging state norms and institutions – with an implicit assumption that governments can be and should be the main focus both for policy-making and implementation. An alternative perspective on regulation starts with the observations that in many and perhaps most regulatory domains the resources relevant to the capacity to regulate are widely dispersed among state and non-state actors, and that control within regulatory settings is not restricted to the development and enforcement of legal rules (Scott 2004). So, for example, whilst governments have a monopoly over the power to legislate, biotechnology firms possess much of the information that makes regulation possible, retailers exert considerable contractual power over food producers and, in some instances, non-governmental organizations (NGOs) possess some of the capacity to make regulation legitimate and to enforce either official or unofficial norms, for example, through direct action. The chapter does not claim to provide an authoritative analysis of the state of biotechnology regulation. Rather it is intended to use knowledge developed in the generic field of regulation to stimulate thinking about biotechnology.

The policy issues surrounding contemporary applications of biotechnology to human health and food production are concerned with five main sets of issues. The array of issues are concerned with safety of new technological applications (in particular in respect of food), the protection of the environment from irreversible change (in particular in respect of crops), the protection of consumers' economic interests (largely focussed on issues of disclosure and labelling), the protection of intellectual property rights and the complex ethical issues concerned with such issues as genetic testing, cloning and therapeutic applications of recombinant DNA.

## 3 BIOTECHNOLOGY AND THE FIELD OF REGULATION

The striking thing about this regulatory field is that so much of the public policy discussion focusses on epistemological issues concerned with what we know about these technologies and how we know it (Black 1998). In contrast with other fields of regulation a remarkable proportion of attention is devoted to the development of institutional structures for advising on and making policies and remarkably little to the machinery for implementing or enforcing the policies (Levidow et al. 1999). Thus, much attention is devoted to the important question as to what biases should operate in developing protective norms (and in particular whether to adopt the precautionary principle) but little attention is devoted to asking to what extent the protective norms are actually protective or to problematizing the machinery through which the policies are delivered.

We might go so far as to suggest that biotechnology policy has not yet matured into a field of regulation at all. In particular it does not seem to have encountered the severe doubts experienced in so many domains about the capacity of the state to exert public interested control over social and economic actors (Baldwin 1997). These doubts are expressed in many different ways. An early and well-known form of critique, sometimes labelled the Economic Theory of Regulation, focussed on an apparent tendency (particularly in the United States) for regulatory agencies to serve the interests not of the public, but rather of powerful private interests (Peltzman 1976). Sociologists of law have developed analyses of regulatory governance that focus on the communication problems between the various differentiated social sub-systems. This analysis questions the very possibility of deploying law for instrumental regulatory purposes (Teubner [1987] 1998). My own perspective on this particular issue is shaped by empirical work in which we have noted how widely dispersed are the resources of authority, information, wealth, organization and capacity to bestow legitimacy that make regulation possible among a variety of state and non-state actors (Scott 2001).

Anxieties about the capacity of what we might call 'classical regulation' to exert effective control has generated much discussion about the development of 'new instruments' for regulation. A recent analysis of new instruments in the environmental domain deployed a continuum comparing the extent of constraint imposed on firms, ranging between the highly constraining stick approach of classical regulation with the less constraining carrot approach of economic instruments such as subsidies, tradeable permits and taxes, with the least constraining sermon approaches that promote the dissemination of information as means to promote or shape choices in the market (Jordan et al. 2003).The promotion by the state of voluntary agreements features somewhere in this spectrum.

Casual usage of the term regulation often makes us think of regulatory agencies exercising control by reference to legal rules. In the biotechnology area much formal legal authority remains with government departments, rather than with agencies. Law is used:

1. to impose bans: for example, on human cloning and on commercial planting of GM crops;
2. to permit activities only within agreed limits: for example, controls over the use of the results of genetic testing by insurance companies;
3. to permit activities only with a licence;
4. to permit marketing of products only subject to certain conditions: for example, labelling of GM products.

We can see that these various uses of law take in the full range of the continuum of 'old' and 'new' regulatory instruments. This highlights a weakness in both the classical and the new instruments approaches to regulation, which is a relatively narrow focus on the conduct of government departments and agencies and on the deployment of law as setting normative standards or incentivizing compliance with such standards.

Given the anxieties raised by the development and application of biotechnology it is surprising that more has not been said about the capacity of classical regulation to exert control. It is not as if the biotechnology sector is without its regulatory fiascos. An American *cause célèbre* is the StarLink case. StarLink is a patented variety of genetically modified maize given regulatory approval in the United States for animal feed, but not for human consumption. A pressure group detected strains of the proteins unique to StarLink in taco shells marketed in the fast food outlets of

Taco Bell in September 2000. The manufacturer withdrew the products and subsequently other manufacturers detected similar proteins in their products and recalled them (Bratspies 2003).

The StarLink case is interesting because it demonstrates the failure to consider appropriate techniques for checking that restrictions imposed on the product were applied. The emergence of the product in human foodstuffs was not detected by a regulatory agency, but by a pressure group that proved itself to be the effective monitor for violations. The internal procedures of the various manufacturing firms involved had apparently not detected the problem. The consequences in terms of costs of recalls and for public confidence in regulation and in food markets were severe and international sales of American corn slumped when the relevant proteins were detected in shipments to Japan (Bratspies 2003).

The StarLink crisis was permitted to occur by the establishment of a regime of standard setting and authorization without paying attention to the methods of monitoring and enforcement (Bratspies 2003, p. 631). This is not to say that vigorous agency monitoring and enforcement was the only appropriate mechanism for addressing the issue, but rather that some attention has to be paid to the processes for implementing regulatory norms once they have been agreed. It is clear here that the state does not have a monopoly of power – there are major firms and interest groups with capacities for control. It is also apparent that the mechanisms that might have affected behaviour in this story are not restricted to legal oversight and might also include concerns with protection of reputation, transmission of emergent community norms and the interplay of forces in the market.

Regulation is more than just a set of norms. Cybernetic approaches to regulation suggest that a viable control system must have some goal, norms, standards or rules; some mechanism for monitoring or feeding back information about the performance of the regulatory system against the goal, norms, standards or rules; some means by which to modify behaviour that deviates from the required goal, norms, standards or rules (Hood et al. 2001).

Law's role in the monitoring and behaviour modification components of regulation is not unimportant. Here law is deployed to empower government agencies to engage in monitoring and collection of information and to empower departments, agencies, or courts to impose penalties or provide rewards for certain types of behaviour. But law also underpins self-regulatory regimes where firms come together to create binding rules and processes for themselves within an associational regime. The next section of the chapter offers an analysis of the full range of potential forms of control that might apply to any particular regulatory domain.

## 4 VARIETY IN CONTROL

Once we open up regulation into its components of goals, feedback and behavioural modification it is clear that in addition to the limited legal controls the regulation of the biotechnology sectors is, to varying degrees, subject to control through the pressures of competition and society. So, for example, rivalry between firms might be as important a factor in explaining the take-up and development of new technologies as a governmental regulatory regime. Such rivalry might even be harnessed for public purposes, for example, through a tendering process to determine which firm should win the contract to supply new seeds to a particular region's farmers.

The variation in the development of social norms relating to the development of GM crops appears to be a major explanatory factor in understanding the contrasting behaviour of firms in the United States and Europe. A striking example is provided by recent events in respect of GM maize in the UK. The UK government has indicated it is prepared to license GM maize for commercial crops, but Bayer, the main supplier of the technology, has decided to withdraw from the UK market. European governments at both EU and national level have taken a cautious approach to permitting the development of commercial GM crops, making reference to the application of the precautionary principle (Bernauer and Meins 2003). American frustration at the evidence that European consumers are even more cautious is spilling over into international trade litigation in which the right of European governments not only to ban GM crops, but also to require labelling of GM products (and thus inform doubtful consumers of which products to avoid) is being questioned (Prakash and Kollman 2003). Again the commercial actors appear at least as responsive to societal pressures as to governmental regulatory facilitation, as with Monsanto's decision to abandon its investment in herbicide-resistant GM wheat globally (Stokstad 2004).

Any adequate understanding of regulation should be able to accommodate the pressures based in rivalry and the application of social norms, capable as they are of bypassing the state altogether. To put the point another way, the biotechnology sector is subject to regulation whether or not the state does the regulating. Indeed, extensive standard setting by state agencies risks crowding out the capacities of businesses and civil society organizations to participate in or determine standard setting processes, and risks missing opportunities to promote 'ownership' of regulatory norms.

Attention to the diverse modalities of control is not restricted to the level or norms but also on the feedback and modification machinery. It is the disaggregated behaviour of buyers and sellers or of users and objects of competitive information in wider social settings that make competitive forces work. With social norms monitoring tends to be implicit, with social sanctions such as ostracization forming central mechanisms of behavioural modification (though community-based regulation can be formalized and linked to non-state hierarchy within self-regulatory regimes also). Key examples are provided within the application of biotechnology to human health. The machinery of public regulation is highly dependent on professional norms and monitoring within the medical and research communities (Kerr and Cunningham-Burley 2000). Inspection functions of the kind carried out by the UK Human Fertilisation and Embryology Authority (HFEA) are in essence a form of meta-regulation over the community-based control exerted through the professions.

Additionally, and acting on the insight of Lawrence Lessig that control can be built into the 'architecture' of products such as software (Lessig 1999), the behaviour of users of biotech products can be regulated by design features. The potential for using design to control behaviour has long been recognized in settings as diverse as prisons and Disney World (Shearing and Stenning 1985). A key commercial application of control-through-technology in the biotechnology sector is provided by the 'trait protection system' or 'terminator technology', which prevents the replanting of GM seeds from year to year, thus requiring farmers to make fresh purchases each year. The use of technology provides an alternative mechanism to legal enforcement to protect intellectual property rights in new products (Pendleton 2004, pp. 1–10).

It would, no doubt, be possible to build technological controls into GM crops for other than commercial purposes. Consequently, as with design features built into software to control the way it is used, design has at least the potential to form a basis for control. Indeed, technology-based controls could be used to promote regulatory compliance. It appears theoretically possible to build into GM products such as the famous StarLink corn, discussed above, features that would inhibit its marketing for purposes for which it is not licensed. In the case of StarLink if we assume that when animals are given corn (authorized) it is raw but that when it is prepared for humans (unauthorized) it is always cooked, it is possible to imagine accompanying the licence for growing and marketing the product with a requirement that technology is built into it such that it discloses itself as genetically modified when cooked. For example, it might turn blue after exposure to heat.

Thus, following Lessig's analysis of modalities of control (Lessig 1999) with adaptations (Murray and Scott 2002) it is possible to suggest that the hierarchical mechanisms associated with state law are but one of four possible modalities of control, the others being competition, community and design (see Table 2.1 below).

*Table 2.1 Modalities of control in biotechnology regulation*

| Modality of Control | Regulatory Form | Biotechnology Examples |
| --- | --- | --- |
| Hierarchy | Prior approval | Licensing (e.g. pharmaceuticals, GM crop planting) – controlling access to market |
| | Compulsory disclosure | Mandatory labelling (e.g. GM crops) – controlling information distribution |
| Competition | Market rivalry | Generic production of genetically engineered drugs – effects on price |
| Community | Public opinion – represented in direct action, spending decisions, etc. | Determining acceptability of commercial GM crop planting – affecting viability |
| Design | Built-in controls on use of products | Terminator technology in GM crops – controlling farmers' capacity to replant |

These modalities are often not applied in pure form, but rather in combination. So, for example, hierarchical requirements relating to disclosure of information about GM foods are an important precondition to controls based both on competition and the application of community norms. The idea discussed above in respect of StarLink of designing technology-based controls into products so as to aid their regulation by hierarchical means is also a hybrid mode, combining hierarchy and design.

An objection to the analysis based in modalities of control might be to argue that relative to hierarchical control the other modalities are rather trivial. This may be true in some settings. But the field of biotechnology appears to be one in which the potential for control through community norms, through competitive pressures and through design does yield important examples. Hierarchical regulation may be rather more visible because it is formalized and institutionalized. This does not mean that it is always effective or that the explanation of how actors in a particular domain behave is explicable by reference to a regime of hierarchical regulation. The examples involving GM crops, discussed above, where governments have authorized commercial crops but firms have decided not to proceed, provide the clearest examples where, we might hypothesize, some other form of control is at play and is dominant in shaping the behavioural response. Indeed, in this case, some interplay between community norms and the market is undermining official government regulatory policy.

In some instances state regulation of one form or another underpins control based in competition or community or design. This is true in the case of licensing decisions underpinning competition through generic drugs and mandatory labelling underpinning consumer decisions on GM foods. But in other cases the application of modalities of control other than hierarchy appears to be spontaneous, in the sense that it was not initiated by the state for state purposes. In such instances it may or may not be right to refer to the mechanism of control as regulation, but it is surely impossible to wholly ignore such controls where they affect behaviour within regulatory regimes, in some instances enhancing the publicly set objectives and in other cases undermining them.

In addition to the descriptive objections to recognizing other modalities of control, there are also normative objections. It might be argued that if we subscribe to some version of the rule of law then it is wrong to permit other modalities of control to undermine public policy as it is set down in legal instruments. There are additionally moral objections to mechanisms of control that do not allow the subject control of choices as to their conduct (discussed in more detail in Roger Brownsword's contribution to this volume – Chapter 3). These objections apply most particularly to design-based control where the subject is physically inhibited from doing anything other than that permitted by the designer (Tien 2004). To a greater or lesser extent this objection, and the underlying argument that the subject is robbed of their responsibility for their actions by such mechanisms, applies also to control based in community or in competition, since participation in both markets and communities often requires us to accept their norms as a condition of participation, and non-participation may not be a viable option.

In the next section of this chapter we investigate the experience of hybrid forms of control in different regulatory settings and evidence as to the effects of such regimes. Central cases are likely to involve the combination of hierarchy with other modes of control. But equally interesting in the case of biotechnology regulation are instances where hierarchy is not present. We focus on experience of environmental regulation because of its proximity to some of the issues in biotechnology regulation.

## 5 EFFECTS AND EFFECTIVENESS

Stories of attempts by governments to exert control over social and economic activities are littered with accounts of counterproductive regulation (Grabosky 1995), fatal remedies (Sieber 1981) and catastrophes

(Moran 2001). Unintended effects are a pervasive consequence of human activity (Elster 1989). The focus in biotechnology regulation on the use of law to set norms, with the neglect both of other aspects of a viable regulatory regime, and of other modalities of regulation than law is liable to risk such unintended effects in these sectors too. The central questions addressed in this section are how to use the awareness of the potential of unintended effects and how to think about potential mixes of control types so as to maximize chances of producing intended effects.

Counterproductive effects in regulation are liable to result from a failure to anticipate how targets of regulation are likely to behave in the face of new regulatory requirements. The history of environmental regulation is full of such examples, for example, where rigorous new standards over vehicle emissions push up the cost of new cars to the extent that citizens retain older cars for longer, increasing rather than reducing total emissions. The development and marketing of GM foods provides an example of a product where the interplay of market behaviour and regulatory rules has led to effects within European markets that were not anticipated by governments.

Observations about variety in the availability of modalities of control alert us to the diffusion of both capacities and techniques by which regulatory effects are secured. Part of the problem of emphasizing state capacity and the use of legal rules in regulation is that it neglects or downplays not only the alternatives that might be available to do the job, but also the role that those alternatives will play in mediating whatever state regulation action is put forward in any case.

Putting the case positively, systems of control may emerge that are not wholly dependent on state action and legal rules, but which nevertheless effectively address the risks that policy-makers would want to address. In this section of the chapter I will make some observations about self-regulation in the biotechnology sectors and then consider regimes for environmental regulation that combine different modalities of control with apparent success. I have chosen regimes of environmental regulation to examine because they are longer established and better documented with empirical evidence than regimes for biotechnology regulation. But there are areas of overlap between biotechnology and environmental regulation and considerable potential for learning about the latter to inform regulatory policy in the former.

## 5.1 Self-regulation: The Case of Nuclear Power

Self-regulation is an important and long-established form of control, which draws on and develops norms within a community (for example, of professionals or businesses), often institutionalizing them and establishing mechanisms for monitoring and enforcement (Black 1996). A very well documented case involves self-regulation in the US nuclear power industry. Following the accident at Three Mile Island in 1979 there was global panic about the risks associated with the development of nuclear power as a key source for meeting future electricity needs. In many countries the cost and riskiness of nuclear energy, together with consideration of security issues, has led to the sector being established and retained within the public sector. In the United States, where the Three Mile Island accident occurred, there has been a long tradition of private ownership of electricity generation capacity including nuclear power. Though there have been public ownership experiments, notably in the Tennessee Valley Authority, private ownership has generally been the rule.

The characteristics of riskiness and moral panic attaching to the nuclear industry also affect some parts of the biotechnology sector. The industry response to Three Mile Island may be instructive. The circumstances of the industry response are beautifully captured in the title of Joseph Rees's book *Hostages of Each Other* (Rees 1994). The various firms within the US nuclear industry came to understand that the failure of any one of their number to act effectively on issues of nuclear safety would threaten the viability of the industry as a whole. Accordingly they developed the Institute of Nuclear Power Operations (INPO) as a system of self-regulatory standard setting and monitoring, which, in Rees's assessment, proved remarkably cohesive and effective. It was not an entirely freestanding self-regulatory system, since it depended for its enforceability on the actions of state regulatory agencies. Rees himself has referred to this aspect of the self-regulatory regime as 'the gorilla in the closet' (Rees 1997, p. 519).

So, the INPO story in the US is about the spontaneous response of an industry fearful of the consequences of inaction to the extent that the community of firms initiated tight controls that each was prepared to tolerate as the price for ensuring the future viability of the industry. The community-based controls were given added weight from the possibility of invoking the hierarchical capacity of state regulatory agencies. It is possible to argue that in some areas of the biotechnology industry the major market actors are similarly 'hostages of each other', in the sense that regulatory failures are liable to affect not just the firm responsible or whose products are directly affected, but the industry as a whole. The case is well illustrated by the StarLink affair, discussed above, where infractions of authorization (without any evidence of harm to human health) affected the whole international market for the supply of GM maize. The production of GM crops critically requires confidence in the standards of the market as a whole in a way that is not true of other potentially risky products such as cars. Put another way a major safety failure involving a Ford vehicle may have positive effects for the market position of General Motors and is unlikely to reduce the size of the car market overall. Major safety failures in the GM crops domain could kill off the entire market. Whilst the producers of GM crops will want to compete with each other, their viability is dependent on no safety scandal affecting any part of the industry. As with nuclear safety, cooperation and self-policing might be an attractive way to reduce the risks to the industry, though this will likely involve elements of governmental enforcement too. What about the possibility of a system of self-regulatory control that does not invoke the state's monopoly over legitimate force?

### 5.2 Combining Controls Based in Community and Competition: The Case of Forestry Standards

Environmental campaigners have long had concerns about the conduct of the logging industry in North America and elsewhere, and in particular with the problem of management of forestry and the environmental damage associated with excessive and inappropriate logging. The problems are global in scope, and it has proved very difficult to secure agreement on standards at the inter-governmental level.

An alternative response to national regulation or inter-governmental standard setting has come from the Forest Stewardship Council (FSC) established as a non-profit organization in 1993 (Meidinger 2003). The regime of control administered by the FSC extends to forestry in 60 countries and is a product of internationalization of environmental campaigning and linkages to the global marketplace. The FSC was established by NGOs, led by the WWF, as a mechanism for certifying good practice, but is recognized as legitimate by market actors (Cashore 2002, p. 507). The FSC regime combines interaction of the forestry industry and environmental campaigning movement in a hybrid form of control that draws on community- and competition-based forms of control – referred to by one commentator as non-state market-driven (NSMD) governance (Cashore 2002). The FSC rapidly spawned *industry-led* competitors in North America, which sought to develop recognition for alternative self-regulatory standards (Cashore 2002, pp. 508–9).

The normative structure of the regime derives from what are essentially community-based processes of interaction, institutionalized through the FSC, with market-based mechanisms. Indeed forest certification programmes 'recognize officially those companies and landowners who *voluntarily* operate "well-managed" or "sustainable" forestlands according to predefined criteria' (Cashore 2002, p. 505). The market element of the regime derives from the capacity of environmental groups to 'sell' the virtues of FSC certification to retailers as a positive symbol of retailer commitment to the environment and a mode of boosting sales. Retailers who accept the case are then able to use their economic power to contract only with suppliers who are FSC certified or at least to prefer such suppliers (Cashore 2002, pp. 509–10). At the supply end of the chain, firms that are seeking to maintain or extend market share and secure FSC certification are liable to apply the standards across all their activities, not just to the extent required to meet purchaser requirements in some countries. This rippling effect of the regime is an important feature and a product of globalization of markets.

### 5.3 Combining Hierarchy and Architecture with Community: The Case of Intentional Oil Pollution

An important question for the four-way analysis of controls and hybrid forms is to ask what does the design-based control add to the picture and to the potential for regulation. What is it that can be done through technological control that cannot be achieved through market, hierarchical or community-based controls? An important case that provides a partial answer to this question is provided by the history of attempts to prevent intentional pollution of the seas with oil. This is a domain in which there are many non-state actors with governance capacity, in addition to national governmental and inter-governmental organizations (Furger 1997).

The problem is that the operational practices of oil tankers involve the leaving of relatively small oil deposits after cargoes have been delivered. This 'clingage', representing 0.3–0.5 per cent of the original load, was routinely discharged to the sea before collecting the next cargo, either with sea water taken into the tanks to act as ballast for return voyages or as part of the process of cleaning tanks with high pressure sea water (Mitchell 1994, pp. 72–3). Intentional discharges accounted for a larger proportion of oil pollution to the sea than notorious accidental spills. The story of attempts to control intentional oil pollution at sea is one that demonstrates the weaknesses in depending on treaties made under public international law as mechanisms for promoting regulatory objectives. The key international treaty addressing this problem, the 1954 International Convention for the Prevention of Pollution of the Sea by Oil (OILPOL), was discredited by the 1970s because it proved very difficult to enforce discharge rules aimed at reducing pollution in the face of incentives by tanker operators to maintain their discharge practices. The weakness in the regime was identified as the human element – the requirement of a deliberate but virtually undetectable act of compliance (Mitchell 1994, p. 258).

Alive to the issues concerning intentional pollution the oil industry had developed two technologies geared towards its reduction. The first of these is to construct ships with segregated ballast tanks (SBTs) such that a separate ballast tank is created for sea water, which never carries oil, and does not require monitoring. Residues from loads ('slops') have to be retained separately on board and are subject to monitoring. Tank cleaning is addressed by a separate technology referred to as crude oil washing (COW), which uses oil to clean tanks, increasing the proportion of the load delivered (Mitchell 1994, pp. 78–9).The regulatory solution was for the International Convention for the Prevention of Pollution from Ships of 1973 and its 1978 protocol (MARPOL 73/78) to require the use of both technologies for new tankers with a reduction in the intentional pollution by four-fifths (Mitchell 1994, pp. 79, 258). For tankers already in service the convention required adoption of one or other of the technologies (Mitchell 1994, p. 258).

The MARPOL regime changed the point for regulatory enforcement from the moment at which a discharge is made to the point at which tankers were bought and put into service. As Mitchell points out, at this point compliance is dependent not only on the conduct of the tanker owner, but also the builder, a classification society (which certifies the quality of completed ships) and an insurance company (Mitchell 1994). In effect these other, non-state actors, become part of the regime for promoting compliance with the design standards. This non-state role is supported by the power of governments to detain tankers found to be in breach of pollution control standards. Thereafter the technology itself inhibits a substantial proportion of the targeted conduct. In any case, once the costly equipment is installed it is cost-effective to use it properly. Proof of the effectiveness of basing the regime on compliance with equipment standards rather than behavioural controls lies in data showing a very high degree of compliance with the SBT and COW requirements. By the mid-1980s nearly all tankers had both forms of technology on board. The critical difference between the two aspects of the regime was the way in which equipment standards were embedded within a configuration of actors capable of detecting violations and steering violators towards compliance and that compliance with the equipment standards then made non-polluting behaviour rational (Mitchell 1994, p. 292). Put another way the use of such equipment standards, through transparency and the involvement of many state and non-state actors, creates a system of 'redundant prevention' (Braithwaite and Drahos 2000, p. 288). Rules prohibiting discharge were targeting behaviour that tanker operators could engage in privately and with few opportunities for detection.

## 6 CONCLUSIONS

The field of biotechnology regulation does not yet seem to be troubled by the kind of anxieties affecting instrumental regulation in other policy domains. Yet there is already evidence in respect of GM crops in Europe that state regulation designed to promote confidence and thus create a viable market for the new technology has been undermined by a combination of direct action and the preferences of a doubtful public. Effective regulation of biotechnology applications in human health has not yet been so politicized.

It is difficult to avoid the thought that some policy fiasco or catastrophe is waiting to happen, and on a larger scale than the StarLink case. The domain has in common with the Enron case the necessity of a high degree of trust in core professionals and their capacity to develop and apply norms that support the public regulatory regime. This chapter is suggestive of a more holistic approach to biotechnology regulation in which the diverse capacities for control may be deployed to the benefit of the regime as a whole, rather than remain as neglected sources of vulnerability.

Thus where NGOs have an interest in setting standards, monitoring behaviour and realigning deviant behaviour they may become a central focus of a regulatory regime (as with the Forest Stewardship Council). Such NGO regimes of private regulation may be bolstered by the commitment of market players to use their contracting practices to recognize and give legitimacy to such regimes. This is particularly so where retailers and other big purchasers have higher brand recognition and greater public trust than suppliers. Market actors may also respond by establishing regimes in competition with NGOs, using purchaser choice as a mechanism for determining which regimes survive and develop by reference to which regime purchasers think will enhance their market positions.

Professional and other trade associations have also been demonstrably important in some environmental protection regimes, and clearly play key roles in some aspects of biotechnology, notably in medical applications. In some instances the concern for reputation of the industry as a whole may incentivize key actors to establish and develop regimes of standards, monitoring and enforcement that can effectively protect all players from the adverse consequences of a major regulatory failing or scandal.

None of this is to suggest that the state is not important. In some instances the mandating of technological controls is likely to be a governmental (or inter-governmental) function, as with controls of intentional oil pollution, which facilitates the operation of other modalities of control. In other instances, standard setting may occur through community mechanisms, but the capacity of the state to apply sanctions proves necessary to encourage compliance with those non-state standards, as with the US nuclear power story. Competition-based controls are liable to require some underpinning of the state, not just in competition policy in some instances, but also in the enforcement of contracts.

An intriguing question is whether we must envisage the state as always present in such regulatory settings, as a kind of meta-regulator over structures of control that have their own distinct orientation and mechanisms, but which the state can seek to fine tune to deliver public objectives. Alternatively is it likely that the incentives to operate controls over biotechnology regulation based in some combination of community, competition and design will leave the state with no necessary role, at least for some of the industries involved? This is one of the key issues for observers of regulation as the field of biotechnology evolves.

## REFERENCES


Baldwin, R. (1997), 'Regulation: After "Command and Control"', in Keith Hawkins (ed.), *The Human Face of Law*, Oxford: Oxford University Press.

Baldwin, Robert and Martin Cave (1999), *Understanding Regulation*, Oxford: Oxford University Press.

Bernauer, T. and E. Meins (2003), 'Technological Revolution Meets Policy and the Market: Explaining Cross-national Differences in Agricultural Biotechnology Regulation', *European Journal of Political Research*, **42**, 643–83.

Black, J. (1996), 'Constitutionalising Self-regulation', *Modern Law Review*, **59**, 24–56.

Black, J. (1998), 'Regulation as Facilitation: Negotiating the Genetic Revolution', *Modern Law Review*, **61**(5), 621–60.

Braithwaite, John and Peter Drahos (2000), *Global Business Regulation*, Cambridge: Cambridge University Press.

Bratspies, R.M. (2003), 'Myths of Voluntary Compliance: Lessons from the StarLink Corn Fiasco', *William and Mary Environmental Policy Law Review*, 593–649.

Cashore, B. (2002), 'Legitimacy and the Privatization of Environmental Governance: How Non-state Market-driven (NSMD) Governance Systems Gain Rule-making Authority', *Governance*, **15**, 503–29.

Elster, Jon (1989), *Nuts and Bolts for the Social Sciences*, Cambridge: Cambridge University Press.

Furger, F. (1997), 'Accountability and Systems of Self-governance: the Case of the Maritime Industry', *Law and Policy*, **19**, 445–76.

Grabosky, P. (1995), 'Counterproductive Regulation', *International Journal of the Sociology of Law*, **23**, 347–69.

Hood, Christopher, Henry Rothstein and Robert Baldwin (2001), *The Government of Risk*, Oxford: Oxford University Press.

Jordan, Andrew, Rudiger K.W. Wurzel and Anthony R. Zito (eds) (2003), *'New' Instruments of Environmental Governance*, London: Frank Cass.

Kerr, A. and S. Cunningham-Burley (2000), 'On Ambivalence and Risk: Reflexive Modernity and the New Human Genetics', *Sociology*, **34**, 283–304.

Lessig, Lawrence (1999), *Code: and Other Laws of Cyberspace*, New York: Basic Books.

Levidow, L., S. Carr and D. Wield (1999), 'Regulating Biotechnological Risk: Straining Britain's Consultative Style', *Journal of Risk Research*, **2**, 307–24.

Meidinger, Errol (2003), 'Forest Certification as a Global Civil Society Regulatory Institution', in Errol Meidinger, Chris Elliott and Gerhard Oesten (eds),

*Social and Political Dimensions of Forest Certification*, Regmagen-Oberwinter: www. forstbuch.de.
Mitchell, Ronald B. (1994), *Intentional Oil Pollution at Sea*, Cambridge, MA: MIT Press.
Moran, M. (2001), 'Not Steering but Drowning: Policy Catastrophes and the Regulatory State', *Political Quarterly*, **72**, 414–27.
Murray, A. and C. Scott (2002), 'Controlling the New Media: Hybrid Responses to New Forms of Power', *Modern Law Review*, **65**, 491–516.
Nuffield Council on Bioethics (1999), *Genetically Modified Crops: the Ethical and Social Issues*, London: Nuffield Foundation.
Paulus, Ingeborg (1974), *The Search for Pure Food*, London: Martin Robertson.
Peltzman, Sam (1976), 'Toward a More General Theory of Regulation', *Journal of Law and Economics*, **19**, 211–40.
Pendleton, C.N. (2004), 'The Peculiar Case of "Terminator" Technology: Agricultural Biotechnology and Intellectual Property Protection at the Crossroads of the Third Green Revolution', *Biotechnology Law Report*, **23**, 1–29.
Prakash, A. and K.L. Kollman (2003), 'Biopolitics in the EU and the US: A Race to the Bottom of Convergence to the Top?', *International Studies Quarterly*, **47**, 617–41.
Rees, Joseph (1994), *Hostages of Each Other: The Transformation of Nuclear Safety Since Three Mile Island*, Chicago: University of Chicago Press.
Rees, J. (1997), 'The Development of Communitarian Regulation in the Chemical Industry', *Law and Policy*, **19**, 477–528.
Salter, B. and L. Frewer (2003), 'The Changing Governance of Biotechnology: The Politics of Public Trust', *Applied Biotechnology, Food Science and Policy*, **1**, 199–211.
Scott, C. (2001), 'Analysing Regulatory Space: Fragmented Resources and Institutional Design', *Public Law*, Summer, 329–53.
Scott, Colin (2004), 'Regulation in the Age of Governance: The Rise of the Post-regulatory State', in Jacint Jordana and David Levi-Faur (eds), *The Politics of Regulation*, Cheltenham, UK and Northampton, MA, USA: Edward Elgar, pp. 145–74.
Shearing, Clifford D. and Philip C. Stenning (1985), 'From the Panopticon to Disney World: The Development of the Discipline', in Anthony N. Doob and Edward L. Greenspan (eds), *Perspectives in Criminal Law*, Toronto: Canada Law Book Inc.
Sieber, Sam D. (1981), *Fatal Remedies: The Ironies of Social Intervention*, New York: Plenum Books.
Stokstad, E. (2004), 'Monsanto Pulls the Plug on Genetically Modified Wheat', *Science*, **304**, 1088–9.
Teubner, Gunther (1987), 'Juridification: Concepts, Aspects, Limits, Solutions', in Robert Baldwin, Colin Scott and Christopher Hood (eds) (1998), *Socio-legal Reader on Regulation*, Oxford: Oxford University Press.
Tien, L. (2004), 'Architectural Regulation and the Evolution of Social Norms', *International Journal of Communications Law and Policy*, **9**; http://www.digital-law.net/IJCLP/.
Ungar, S. (2001), 'Moral Panics Versus the Risk Society: The Implications of the Changing Sites of Social Anxiety', *British Journal of Sociology*, **52**, 271–91.

# [28]

# GMOs in the EU: the scope of the debate

## INTRODUCTION

The law applying to GMOs is deeply embedded in its social context. The breadth as well as the depth of concerns about agricultural biotechnology, and the resulting ambiguity about what is at stake, create interesting challenges for law and for those charged with reaching decisions in particular cases. This chapter explores in some detail the scope of the debate on GMOs, beginning with an outline of some of the main arguments in favour of the technology as well as the main concerns, before turning to a discussion of the hegemony of risk as a basis for decisions. The innovative and extensive process of review and public participation carried out in the UK during the regulatory hiatus created by the EU moratorium provides a case study.[1]

A number of GM 'events' begin to provide a sense of the scope and the depth of concern about GMOs. In 1998 and 1999 a series of high-profile 'direct actions' took place against GMOs in the UK, as individuals and groups destroyed trial fields of GM crops, in front of both cameras and the police. Lord Melchett (the then executive director of Greenpeace) used the media attention to raise what he saw as the 'very serious threat to the environment' posed by GMOs, as well as Greenpeace's concern about both the institutions controlling the technology and the institutions controlling the decision making: 'the chemical industry think they have some sort of private right to plant this stuff and cause this pollution to the environment and this threat . . . the public have a right to protect the environment'.[2]

In France, similar protests have had an even higher profile. As recently as December 2007, José Bové and a number of other protestors used the opportunity of their sentencing for destruction of GM crops to announce a hunger

[1] See Chapters 1 and 3 for discussion of the moratorium. The UK did not support the EU moratorium, but entered into a voluntary moratorium by agreement with industry.

[2] BBC News website 29 July 1999, http://news.bbc.ca.uk/1/hi/uk/406191.stm (accessed December 2007).

strike in the cause of a one-year ban on GMOs in France.[3] As in the UK, the threats and uncertainties of GMOs and their control are highlighted in these protests. In addition, the French protests, spearheaded by the Confédération Paysanne, positioned GMOs firmly as a threat to the maintenance of local and culturally distinctive food, and firmly in the sights of the anti-globalisation movement.[4]

Also in 1998, the dispute over scientific evidence in the 'Pusztai' affair made headlines in the UK for weeks. Dr Arpad Pusztai announced on a *World in Action* television documentary that rats fed on GM potatoes suffered from stunted growth, suppressed immune systems and reduced body weight. He was suspended from his employment, to general media excitement, and his data were disputed (and have never been fully rehabilitated). The very public conflict brought to centre stage a range of credible concerns about the uncertainty of the impact of GMOs, and highlighted the sometimes controversial nature of scientific claims. Doubts about the safety of GM food have been raised persistently since. In 2007, for example, *Le Monde* published details of a claim that rats fed with Monsanto's MON863 corn suffered negative effects on the liver and kidneys. Highlighting the imbalance of knowledge and information between regulator and industry, these conclusions were based on a reinterpretation of the company's own data, which Greenpeace had obtained through a German court order.

A further prominent 'event' in the politics of genetic modification arose in famine threatened southern Africa in 2002.[5] Food aid provided by the US contained GMOs that had not been authorised by the recipients. A number of countries accepted the aid only on condition that the seeds were first milled. The US refused to mill it, claiming it was too expensive, but South Africa

---

3 A four-month prison term was commuted to a fine, Reuters, 10 December 2007, http://uk.reuters.com/article/environmentNews/idUKL1011368420071210 (accessed December 2007).

4 See http://www.confederationpaysanne.fr/ (accessed December 2007). José Bové has been imprisoned before for direct actions – and quite dramatically, with helicopters and a dawn raid to avoid his supporters. Crops have more recently been destroyed in at least France, the Netherlands and Germany; see European Commission, *Second Report on the Experience of Member States with GMOs placed on the Market under Directive 2001/18/EC on the Deliberate Release into the Environment of Genetically Modified Organisms* COM (2007) 81 final.

5 Institute for the Study of International Migration, *Genetically Modified Food in the Southern Africa Food Crisis of 2002–2003* (Georgetown University School of Foreign Service, 2004). This report illustrates that the situation is far from straightforward. See also Jennifer Clapp, 'The Political Economy of Food Aid in an Era of Agricultural Biotechnology' (2005) 11 *Global Governance* 467; Noah Zerbe, 'Feeding the Famine? American Food Aid and the GMO Debate in Southern Africa' (2004) 29 *Food Policy* 593.

stepped in. Whilst the countries demanding milling continued to state concern about the health impacts of GM maize consumption, the milling of the whole-kernel maize meant that no GM seeds could be planted, reducing the risk of crossing with local varieties. Zambia, however, would not accept the GM food aid at all, arguing that the population's high consumption of maize (which is a staple in southern Africa, so that comparison with US consumption is not necessarily helpful) could lead to unanticipated health impacts, and also that lack of resources would make it difficult to address any problems.[6] The US accused the EU, which was in the middle of its moratorium, of contributing to hunger – the countries of southern Africa had a strong interest in remaining GM-free in order to maintain exports to the EU. Others retaliated with accusations that the US's food aid policies were economically motivated, and that the US was trying to force GM agriculture into Africa. The mud-slinging, and at the very highest diplomatic levels, was extraordinary.[7] And it placed the African food shortage firmly in the context of EU/US disagreement over agricultural biotechnology. For current purposes, the moral outrage around this case highlights the distributional questions inherent in the export of agricultural biotechnology. This case also emphasises the impact of globalisation on local control of decision making, with the future of farming and food production decided very far from where the impact of those decisions will be felt.

Together, these episodes dramatise concerns about human health and the environment, which are underlined and massively complicated by profound scientific uncertainty. Governance issues about the authority or legitimacy of decision making are disputed, and concerns about the distribution of the costs and benefits of GMOs are compounded by the effects of globalisation. We are looking not just at questions of perception or fear, things that might be turned around by persuasion, education or reassurance. These issues are complex, substantive, nuanced and deep-rooted. Later chapters will examine the extent to which the legal frameworks applying to GMOs allow or enable the full range of concerns to resonate in regulatory decisions, particularly at the EU and World Trade Organization (WTO) levels. Finding a regulatory home for the deliberation of the full range of perspectives is far from easy, and a constant theme of this book.

---

[6] Addressing errors such as 'Starlink' in the US has cost millions of dollars; see below, p. 00.

[7] For a taste, see Institute for the Study of International Migration, above n. 5. Joseph Murphy and Les Levidow, *Governing the Transatlantic Conflict over Agricultural Biotechnology: Contending Coalitions, Trade and Standard Setting* (Routledge, 2006), quote letters published in the *Wall Street Journal* from European Commissioners and from US Trade Representative Robert Zoellick, pp. 156–57.

## THE GM DEBATE

Disagreement about the appropriate role of GMOs in agriculture and in food production is intense and sometimes bad-tempered. Those supporting GMOs paint those resisting as irresponsibly disregarding the greater public interest, and opponents characterise proponents similarly. There are many and powerful reasons for staying alive to the potential of GMOs, and relatively few of those resisting the technology are against it always and forever. The purpose of the technology, its governance and the control of its impact are all important factors.

Of the extensive range of concerns about GMOs, not all are readily accepted as legitimate, or as suitable subjects for regulation. The very identity of the problem that law and regulation has to solve is up for grabs.[8] Concerns about safety (broadly environmental and health issues), whilst challenging, can be incorporated into regulation in a way familiar from many other technological developments. More problematic is a less precise category of 'other' (political, ethical and socioeconomic) issues, which also requires the attention of regulators. The division is not as neat as that, and there are significant dangers in carving out the technical and the 'other'. Most obviously, the 'categories' overlap: environmental and health impacts raise ethical and political questions around the distribution of risks and benefits, for example. This is particularly so for long-term and unpredictable risks, and the inevitable uncertainty about the effects of GMOs underscores the burden of justification on those introducing the technology. Moreover, if presented as objective and inevitable fact, the scientific element of a decision can hide from view the value and ethical judgments pervading the decision itself, so that it looks as if only the protestors are making such judgments.[9] We might also note here that 'values' (or 'public values', also public goods[10] or collective goods) are perhaps overused terms, which will be used much more in this book. These terms are often used to distinguish 'public' perspectives on the world from private or individual interests, developed in the context of deliberation around

[8] Julia Black, 'Regulation as Facilitation: Negotiating the Genetic Revolution' (1998) 61 *Modern Law Review* 621.

[9] Brian Wynne, 'Creating Public Alienation: Expert Cultures of Risk and Ethics on GMOs' (2001) 10 *Science as Culture* 445; Joanna Goven, 'Processes of Inclusion, Cultures of Calculation, Structures of Power: Scientific Citizenship and the Royal Commission on Genetic Modification' (2006) 31 *Science, Technology and Human Values* 565.

[10] No term of art is implied here, but to economists public goods are goods that are non-excludable (withholding benefits from one means withholding from others) and non-rival (consumption by one does not reduce their availability).

the public interest, rather than preformed in a self interested context.[11] In this book, the intention is rather more simply to capture the full range of issues raised by GMOs. Environmental and human health protection are important values as is the pursuit of economic prosperity, but discussion of values goes beyond questions of risk, embracing also the 'other' issues discussed here. And again, it must not be thought that only protestors have 'values'. The purposes of GMOs, controlling the environment or growing the economy, are value based and should be equally subject to scrutiny.

### Why Push Ahead? The Danger of (Pre)caution

Most generally, the precedent set by abandoning or partially abandoning a technology would challenge deep-rooted and successful ideas about progress through science. And the economic promise of GMOs is substantial, not only in its own right, but also as part of the great post-industrial hope of the 'knowledge economy', as discussed in Chapter 1.

But equally importantly, the claimed and potential benefits of GM technology seem to be limited only by the imagination, and include advantages in respect of all the major risks identified by those who oppose agricultural biotechnology, that is, environmental, health and 'other' socioeconomic, political and ethical benefits. Biotechnology beyond the farm has myriad actual and potential applications,[12] but here the emphasis is on farming with GMOs. Policy makers are increasingly emphasising benefits as they come to terms with the continuing reluctance of the EU public to accept biotechnology in agriculture,[13] and it is probably true that demonstrable benefits would influence the willingness to accept risks and uncertainties, and other difficulties in this area. If the social benefits do not materialise, however (and so far, on the whole they have not) problems of credibility will multiply.

The hoped-for environmental benefits of GM technology could address many of the problems associated with contemporary farming. The development of plants that do not need fertilisers (perhaps because they fix nitrogen from the air), for example, would avoid the pollution of water sources by

---

[11] Mark Sagoff, *The Economy of the Earth: Philosophy, Law and the Environment* (Cambridge University Press, 1988), provides the classic exposition for environmental lawyers.

[12] See Eleni Zika et al., *Consequences, Opportunities and Challenges of Modern Biotechnology for Europe* (JRC, European Commission, 2007) for discussion.

[13] See for example European Commission, *Life Sciences and Biotechnology – A Strategy for Europe* COM (2002) 27 final (the *Life Sciences Strategy*), and European Commission, *Communication on the Mid-term Review of the Strategy on Life Sciences and Biotechnology* COM (2007) 175 final. For a positive, but reasonably sober, review of what is going on, see Zika et al., above n. 12.

fertilisers. The negative impacts of irrigation (soil salination, water shortages) could be avoided by GM drought-resistant plants. The modification of animals or their feed could lead to a reduction of the amount or noxiousness of effluent. Very closely targeted pest resistance could end the loss of biodiversity associated with chemical pesticides. And improved yields could mean that less land needs to be given over to agriculture, even as improved adaptability means that more marginal land could be farmed. The pragmatic appeal of these possibilities is immense, even if they are largely in the future, and even if individual 'technical fixes' fall short of addressing the fundamental nature of ecological harm.

Biotechnology could also respond to past environmental harms. One of the seminal 'patenting life' cases, *Diamond v Chakrabarty,* involved a bacterium engineered to break down crude oil.[14] Genetic modification of crops identified as useful biofuels could increase availability or efficiency and reduce reliance on fossil fuels. The ability to engineer plants to thrive in harsh environments (drought-resistant, salt-resistant wheat with strong short stalks to withstand storms) is on some accounts urgent as we face human-induced climate change. EU policy makers talk a lot about the potential for GM technology to buy our way out of climate change.[15] The ambiguity of progress is unavoidable – scientific and material advance has caused unintended increases in the level of greenhouse gases in the atmosphere, leading to potentially horrific climate change, but a new and equally transformative technology promises the possibility of life more or less as we know it. Again, the pragmatic appeal of the technical fix is enormous.

The modification of agricultural products to address the health problems of the wealthy world, for example by reducing the cholesterol content of dairy products or providing appetising child-friendly flavours for healthy vegetables, is another promise of agricultural biotechnology. GM non-food crops could also provide novel ways to manufacture pharmaceuticals, by synthesising drugs or hormones more cheaply or efficiently than is otherwise possible, or allowing drugs to be eaten rather than injected. This is perhaps a more compelling use of new technology than chocolate flavoured broccoli. More controversially, genetic engineering of animals could increase the supply of organs for transplant through xeno-transplantation, by reducing the chances that animal organs will be rejected by the human body. Non-food crops could contribute to cleaner or more efficient industrial manufacturing, as fields replace factories, producing plentiful and clean raw materials for industrial processes, such as biodegradable plastics. A turn to these alternative uses of

---

14 *Diamond v Chakrabarty* 447 US 303, 100 S Ct 2204, discussed in Chapter 5.
15 Above n. 13.

agricultural land diversifies the rural economy. Even in much of the developed world, agriculture is a troubled industry and diversification or improved production could just tip the balance for marginal employment.

The promise of a 21st-century 'green revolution', providing the poor with a means to feed themselves and to escape hunger and poverty, is difficult to ignore. Modifications of staple crops have the potential to provide improved yields (for example, through pest or disease resistance) or enhanced nutrition (by changing the nutritional content of staple food) and to make more marginal land available for growing food. The risk that such innovations will be lost is the darkest spectre faced by those who resist the development of GMOs. As the Nuffield Council on Bioethics puts it, '"More food for the hungry", unlike "tomatoes with longer shelf-life", is a strong ethical counterweight to set against the concerns of the opponents of GM crops.'[16]

However, the notorious food surpluses of the developed world over recent years raise questions about the possible contribution of GMOs to ending hunger: poverty, inequality, lack of access to land are as likely to be a cause of hunger as lack of food – lack of demand rather than lack of supply.[17] Many would be willing to accept that hunger is in part, in some times and places, a problem of underproduction. The current commercial reality of agricultural biotechnology, however, is that it focuses on two GM traits (herbicide tolerance and insect resistance) in a small number of commodity crops (mainly corn, soy, oilseed rape/canola and cotton). Almost by definition, these benefit farms with high chemical inputs, so more commercial, probably larger, farms. Most biotechnology research is not about feeding the poor or saving the environment, but is driven by the market and by economic objectives. This commercial imperative, a focus on 'wealth creation', can apply to government-funded as well as private sector research.[18] Even the most commonly cited example of the promise of GM, 'golden rice', suggests that the challenges are

---

16 Nuffield Council on Bioethics, *Genetically Modified Crops: the Ethical and Social Issues* (1999); see www.nuffieldbioethics.org/ (accessed December 2007).

17 See Amartya Sen, for example, *Poverty and Famines: An Essay on Entitlement and Deprivation* (Oxford University Press, 1981). For a provocative discussion of the potential of increased supply, see Mark Sagoff, 'Biotechnology and Agriculture: The Common Wisdom and its Critics' (2001) 9 *Indiana Journal of Global Legal Studies* 13.

18 Even in respect of public funding, the 'wealth creation' objective of scientific research can dominate, and can favour particular industrial sectors. In respect of the UK, see Agriculture and Environment Biotechnology Commission (AEBC), *What Shapes the Research Agenda? In Agricultural Biotechnology* (AEBC, 2005), especially para. 3.5.1. See also Tony Blair, 'Britain's Path to the Future – Lit by the Brilliant Light of Science', 3 November 2006, The King's Centre, Oxford, in which the then Prime Minister emphasised the commercial advantage that can be provided by science.

not simply technological, and even go beyond mistrust of the motives of those controlling the technology. Vitamin A deficiency contributes to childhood diseases and blindness in many children with diets heavily dependent on rice. Golden rice is modified (by the insertion of genes from the daffodil and bacteria) to contain higher levels of beta carotene, which converts into vitamin A. Critics claim however that the distribution of vitamin A pills could reduce vitamin A deficiency at much lower cost, or, better still, that diets should be improved through mixed farming, including local green vegetables that are less available when agriculture concentrates on commodity crops.[19]

The commercial imperative underlying research and development undermines the ethical argument from the proponents of agricultural biotechnology. Non-profit organisations (rich universities, or charities and developing nation governments[20]) could be pressured to fill this gap, and China and India seem also to be special cases, technologically advanced states facing many of the challenges of a developing country. And although the promise of agricultural biotechnology for the very poor remains largely unmet, and the continued absence of progress is likely only to increase cynicism, benefits for the very poor remain a real possibility.[21] Indeed, the possibility of feeding the world through GM is probably no less likely or imminent than mass redistribution of resources within and towards the developing world. It demands some humility. The same applies to the environmental potential of GMOs, currently somewhat hypothetical, but a possibility that merits consideration.

**Safety Concerns**

One dominant set of concerns about GMOs focuses on safety, primarily of the environment and of human and animal health.[22] The possible negative envi-

---

[19] See the discussion in Thomas Bernauer, *Genes, Trade, and Regulation: The Seeds of Conflict in Food Biotechnology* (Princeton University Press, 2003); Bill McKibben, *Enough: Genetic Engineering and the End of Human Nature* (Bloomsbury Publishing, 2003), pp. 141–4. The angry response provoked by Dick Taverne, 'The Real GM Food Scandal' *Prospect* November 2007, berating those objecting to GMOs for preventing the commercialisation of innovations like golden rice, can be followed at http://www.prospect-magazine.co.uk/list.php?category=171&issue=620 (accessed December 2007).

[20] Sagoff, above n. 17.

[21] The Nuffield Council reviews existing modifications that could benefit developing countries, above n. 16, para. 4.29. For a more pessimistic view, see Friends of the Earth International, *Who Benefits From GM Crops?* (FoE, 2006).

[22] An interesting place to look for a detailed examination of the main concerns is the UK Science Review: GM Science Panel, *GM Science Review: First Report: An Open Review of the Science Relevant to GM Crops and Food Based on the Interests and Concerns of the Public* (2003).

ronmental impacts of GMOs are disputed, but potentially serious. Some of the familiar environmental problems associated with conventional intensive farming could be intensified by GM technology. The two commercially dominant modifications involve herbicide-resistant and pesticidal crops.[23] So for example, adding a gene from the *Bacillus thuringienesis* (Bt) soil bacterium, which is toxic to certain pests, to a crop plant such as maize or cotton creates a plant with pesticidal properties. Other crops are modified to resist the application of certain herbicides (Monsanto's 'Roundup Ready' crops are best known), so that weed-killer can be applied at any stage of the growing cycle without killing the crop. Herbicide or pesticide tolerance is a serious problem in conventional farming, coming about as susceptible individuals die off and pests or weeds that survive breed resistance into their population. It requires farmers to turn to other pesticides and herbicides, leading to ever escalating chemical supplements, with ecological and economic impacts. It is a phenomenon that could be intensified by the widespread cultivation of crops modified to allow for constant exposure to pesticides or herbicides. Bt resistance is particularly worrying because Bt is one of the few pesticides allowed in extreme cases to organic farmers, so that widespread resistance could deprive organic farmers of a last-resort pesticide. Further, and again as with conventional pesticides, there are indications that crops modified to kill particular pests may be toxic to certain non-target species, most notoriously the discovery in laboratory tests that pollen from Bt corn can harm the larvae of the iconic (in the US) monarch butterfly.[24]

There are many other environmental concerns about GMOs. 'Clean' fields, free of weeds and pests, would have an obvious impact on farmland biodiversity: what are birds to eat in this promised land? There is also a downside to the potential to make ever more marginal land accessible to agriculture, since this could increase agricultural land take even further from current levels.[25] The spectre of 'superweeds' has also received a great deal of attention. The

[23] See the worrying discussion of Bt resistance measures in the US, Rebecca Bratspies, 'The Illusion of Care: Regulation, Uncertainty, and Genetically Modified Food Crops' (2002) 10 *New York University Environmental Law Journal* 297.

[24] John E. Losey, Linda S. Rayor and Maureen E. Carter, 'Transgenic Pollen Harms Monarch Larvae' (1999) 399 *Nature* 214. For a discussion of the initial report and subsequent criticisms of it, see Sheila Jasanoff, *Designs on Nature: Science and Democracy in Europe and the United States* (Princeton University Press, 2005) pp. 108–9. Whilst the effect of GM crops in the field is vigorously debated, it is accepted that pest-resistant crops can be harmful to non-target wildlife in the laboratory: GM Science Panel, *GM Science Review: First Report: An Open Review of the Science Relevant to GM Crops and Food Based on the Interests and Concerns of the Public*, para. 6.3.1, available at http://www.gmsciencedebate.org.uk (accessed December 2007).

[25] This should be placed alongside the promise that increased yields reduce the amount of land needed for agriculture, given growing populations.

concern is that a modified gene could enter the natural environment, by cross-pollination with wild relatives, or as a volunteer, that is a crop that self-seeds and persists outside the field environment. This new plant could be difficult to control, if the genetic modification is for herbicide tolerance, or it could out-compete native wild plants, if modified for traits such as tolerance of pests, frost and/or drought.

The existence and gravity of risks to human health from the cultivation or consumption of GMOs are, like the environmental risks, disputed, but potentially serious.[26] There is concern that a modified gene could enter cells in the human gut, leading to new and unthought-of diseases. Less dramatically, unanticipated nutritional differences between GM and non-GM food could lead to widespread but initially faintly perceptible effects on public health. And allergic reactions to a particular GM food (or to the pollen of GM crops) are certainly possible: the modification of soybeans by a gene from the Brazil nut to make them more nutritious (introducing methionine, a nutrient that soybeans lack) also transferred a major food allergen from nuts to soybeans.[27] And finally, the difference between non-food and food maize, for example, is not apparent to the human senses. If GM crops not suitable for human consumption enter the human food chain, there is a possibility of harm, and again there is a notorious example. Because of concerns about allergenicity, 'StarLink' maize was approved in the US only for use as animal feed, and explicitly not for human consumption. When StarLink maize was discovered in the human food chain, there was an outcry, mass withdrawals of products from the market and enormous associated costs, although it is claimed that there were no impacts on human health.[28] If 'biopharming', that is, modifying crops to grow the raw materials for industrial or pharmaceutical processes, becomes commercially viable and widespread, the risks from unwanted material in the human food chain are intensified.

[26] It is notoriously difficult to identify the long-term impact of food; see GM Science Panel, above n. 22, Chapter 5.

[27] Stephen Nottingham, *Eat Your Genes: How Genetically Modified Food is Entering Our Diet* (Zed Books, 1998), p. 92.

[28] See Rebecca Bratspies, 'Myths of Voluntary Compliance: Lessons from the StarLink Corn Fiasco' (2003) 27 *William and Mary Environmental Law and Policy Review* 591. StarLink corn was also found in food aid to Bolivia, but in this case the efforts to recall it were less dramatic; see Clapp, above n. 5. The EU legislation takes steps to avert any potential StarLink crisis, by requiring all authorised GMOs to meet the requirements for both food and feed: 'experience has shown that authorisation should not be granted for a single use, when a product is likely to be used for food and feed purposes; therefore such products should only be authorised when fulfilling authorisation criteria for both food and feed', Regulation 1829/2003/EC on Genetically Modified Food and Feed [2003] OJ L 268/1, Recital 10.

One final concrete controversy has arisen over the use of an antibiotic resistance gene as a 'marker' in GMOs.[29] The genetic modification of a plant can be carried out by inserting the desired gene into plant cells, which are then regenerated into a plant. A marker is used to identify successfully transformed cells, allowing breeders to preserve desirable strains. It is very common to use an antibiotic resistance gene as a marker. But concern has intensified in recent years about overuse of antibiotics and the development by bacteria of resistance to antibiotics, which would make the treatment of disease by that antibiotic ineffective. That general concern has become a part of opposition to GMOs. In particular, if bacteria living in the gut could pick up the resistance there could be a serious impact on human health.

Many of these safety issues involve side effects of industrial agriculture and food production that are vaguely familiar, and not even entirely unexpected. They are very difficult to regulate, but do not necessarily challenge our ordinary way of doing business. The most intractable issue around new technology is the nature of scientific uncertainty. Everything we know about GMOs lies in the shadow of ignorance, the prospect of harm that we have not even thought of. By definition we cannot test for these impacts, so the difficulty goes far beyond 'data gaps', problems that can be resolved through more or better science. This is as much a social as a scientific problem,[30] but our regulatory systems, as explored further below and in the next chapter, generally discount ignorance. The very good reason for this is that proof of safety is simply impossible, and our world would look rather poorer had we declined innovations because of that inability to prove safety. However, it is odd to resolve not even to contemplate the possibility of harms we have not thought of. We might hold those uncertainties in the account against the benefits of a new technology, particularly if those benefits are also uncertain. Understating or normalising uncertainty, as our regulatory systems often do, means also assuming the objectivity and inevitability of choices made on a scientific basis. This in turn diverts attention from the value assumptions and commitments of the regulatory framework.

A further limitation to our scientific knowledge arises from the release of GMOs into unpredictable and variable real-world social and ecological systems. Human behaviour is not predictable, and precautions will not always be taken. We have seen this in all areas of regulation, including GMOs. And knowledge of the operation of ecological systems is at best incomplete and fragmented. The cumulative impact of genetic modification is extraordinarily

[29] This is explicitly addressed in the EU regulation; see Chapter 3, pp. 00–00.

[30] Brian Wynne, 'Uncertainty and Environmental Learning: Reconceiving Science and Policy in the Preventive Paradigm' (1992) 2 *Global Environmental Change* 111.

complex, and every time a different modification is introduced, additional complexity is introduced. 'Gene stacking' could result from unsought crosses of GM varieties with each other or with conventional crops or wild relatives, with a complex range of 'advantages' (or disadvantages) for the resulting plant. The real-world conditions cannot be replicated in the laboratory, and so impacts are not readily 'tested' in advance.[31] This 'indeterminacy' of effects is a further and profound form of uncertainty that scientific risk assessment can barely begin to tackle.[32]

Brian Wynne consistently emphasises the importance of these different and profound types of uncertainty. He identifies a rejection of the confidence expressed in institutional predictions as a central part of the public response to GMOs.[33] Whilst 'risk' along identified parameters (pesticide resistance, allergic reactions, and so on) is complex and likely to be disputed for many years, it is a familiar debate, and fits reasonably readily into familiar political and legal frameworks. The same cannot be said of more profound types of scientific uncertainty.

## Other Concerns

As in respect of many new technologies (although in this case perhaps more visibly so), there are persistent concerns about agricultural biotechnology that are not directly related to the environmental/health risks discussed above. Public debate on GMOs in the UK revealed that 'the public do not view GM as purely a scientific, or environmental, or economic, or political or ethical issue. All of these aspects are important to them.'[34]

GMOs have become one of the focal points of the anti-globalisation movement. The challenges of new technologies, which by definition have the potential to bring with them unknown risks and unthought-of benefits, are compounded by the speed with which new technologies and new risks cross borders. Whilst the anti-globalisation movement has been derided as lacking clear objectives, it is hardly surprising that the very rapid increase in move-

---

31 The limitations of laboratory testing tend to be raised by environmental groups challenging the confidence of regulators and industry. We should note, though, industry reliance on this argument in response to the allegations about the impact of Bt corn on the larvae of the monarch butterfly (above n. 24); see Jasanoff, above n. 24, p. 109. This is picked up by the WTO *EC–Biotech* Panel; see Chapter 6, p. 00.

32 Again following Wynne, above n. 30.

33 Wynne, above n. 9.

34 *GM Nation? The Findings of a Public Debate* (AEBC, 2003), para. 42, emphasis omitted. The GM Nation website (www.gmnation.org.uk) is no longer available, but the report can be found on the AEBC website, http://www2.aebc.gov.uk/aebc/reports/gm_nation_report_final.pdf (accessed December 2007).

ment of goods, capital and technology around the world provokes political upheaval. Increased intensity of global interactions raises serious questions about the survival of democratic, culturally individual decision making, and about the distribution of power and resources. These questions are highly visible in the case of GMOs, especially with increasingly globalised scrutiny of domestic regulation through institutions like the EU and the World Trade Organization, discussed in Chapters 3 and 6.

Agricultural biotechnology is thought likely also to enhance corporate control over agriculture, in particular because the capital resources required for research and development seem to point towards large corporate dominance.[35] Historically, agricultural research and development has been the domain of the public sector, but from the late 1980s it moved into the private sector. This was consistent with an increased reliance on the private sector and the market to provide public goods at that time, and is also linked with the development of intellectual property protection, discussed in Chapter 5. Biotechnological innovation also allows greater control by a single supplier over different elements of agriculture, as, for example, the same company supplies the herbicide-resistant seed and the herbicide.

Intensive conventional agriculture has already taken us quite far from local relationships between consumers and producers, but further intensifying transnational corporate influence shifts control of farming further towards more remote, profit-driven, corporate agendas. Impacts are likely to be felt far from where decisions are made. This is particularly difficult for developing countries, but European farmers may also find themselves squeezed between powerful suppliers and a concentrated retail sector. Agricultural biotechnology raises questions about how the risks and benefits of new technology will be distributed between industry, farmers and consumers. A related point is that, because they are a capital-intensive form of agriculture, GMOs are thought likely to encourage agricultural intensification and an increase in monocultures. Single crop species are usually more vulnerable to pests and disease than mixed farming, raising food security issues as well as environmental problems. And as ever, the poor are most vulnerable to shocks. It is also possible that, rather than providing benefits for the poor, agricultural biotechnology

[35] On the question of corporate control as a central feature of concern, see Emma Hughes, 'Dissolving the Nation: Self-Deception and Symbolic Inversion in the GM Debate' (2007) 16 *Environmental Politics* 318, p. 325 and following. Joyce Tait and Joanna Chataway, 'The Governance of Corporations, Technological Change and Risk: Examining Industrial Perspectives on the Development of Genetically Modified Crops' (2007) 25 *Environment and Planning C* 21, discuss the long lead times and multinational corporation dominance of the 'innovation trajectory for the sector as a whole', p. 24.

will contribute to the undercutting of developing world agriculture by developed world agriculture, for example as tropical produce is modified to grow in cold climates.

A striking illustration of the ways in which farmers may be tied into an increasingly capital intensive system is in the development of 'terminator' gene technology (one form of 'genetic use restriction technology', or GURT).[36] A terminator gene renders harvested seed sterile, preventing the saving of seed for sowing in subsequent years, and similar technology could prevent breeding from GM animals. GURTs are familiar from the development of hybrids in the 20th century, which provide improved yields but are not suitable for breeding.[37] Farmers are prepared to purchase hybrid seeds every year for the benefits of the technology. By contrast, the terminator gene *in itself* provides no benefit for farmers. Although a terminator gene is likely to be marketable only if another genetic modification provides benefits worth the annual purchase, freedom of choice could be eroded by limited competition between seed companies, as well as by national government policies or international aid. Moreover, the gene itself benefits only the seller. The implications of terminator technology for poor or subsistence farmers in the developing world are potentially huge. Purchasing seed is a significant investment for poor farmers, and doing so every season increases the riskiness of farming. If marginal benefits of the GM crop turn out not to match the costs, poor farmers face devastating problems. Whilst the risks are less extreme, terminator technology could pose difficulties for farming in the developed world, especially small-scale farming. Terminator technology also has drawbacks for plant breeding, potentially further concentrating this industry, as well as ruling out small-scale improvements to seed by individual farmers and farming communities. And the spread of sterile seed into the natural environment or into a neighbouring crop could be catastrophic.

This particular technological advance clearly advantages the powerful, and binds farmers into a financial obligation to buy seed every year. On the other hand, terminator technology is said to have the potential to prevent gene spreading, averting a potentially significant negative environmental impact of GMOs. Environmental interest groups, however, reject this as a role for terminator technology, arguing that the technology is not sufficiently reliable to

---

[36] See the discussion in Graham Dutfield, 'Should We Regulate Technology through the Patent System? The Case of Terminator Technology' in Han Somsen (ed.), *The Regulatory Challenge of Biotechnology: Human Genetics, Food and Patents* (Edward Elgar, 2007).

[37] They are not necessarily sterile. Although they do not 'breed true', they can be used for breeding, and often are, perhaps being regenerated with newly purchased seeds every few years rather than every season.

prevent negative environmental impacts, even if it can work well enough to prevent seed-saving being economic. The potential negative impact of terminator technology is recognised in two decisions under the Convention on Biological Diversity, which call for more research on the environmental and socioeconomic impact of GURTs.[38]

The distributional impacts of GMOs cut both ways. Regulation in the EU has potentially profound impacts beyond its borders, and the US certainly alleges that the EU's position on GMOs contributed to hunger in southern Africa in 2002. Even more than environmental and health impacts, the socioeconomic impacts of GMOs are difficult to predict, escape experimental calculation, and are probably impossible to recall once they have happened. The intention here is not to choose between different views but to emphasise the importance of the debate. Urbanisation and changes to the rural economy have complex roots, and the costs and benefits of technological change in agriculture have obviously not been straightforwardly bad. But technological change in farming does seem to encourage urbanisation and the flight of small farmers, as capital replaces land and labour as the central factor in agriculture. The detailed effects of the last 'green revolution' remain controversial, but it at least benefited richer farmers earlier than others, and some locations still lag behind. And, unlike the last green revolution, this one is dominated by the private sector and subject to property rights. Given that the focus here is on EU regulation, the complex and disputed impacts of the genetic revolution on developing countries can only be touched on. It might be observed, however, that questions of global distribution should form a legitimate element of the regulatory debate in the EU.

Many of the fears about the socioeconomic impact of GM crops are tied to an underlying concern that, through unwanted contamination of non-GM seeds (by cross-pollination, spilling of seed, mixing in processing), or because the structure of the seed supply industry makes sourcing of non-GM seeds increasingly difficult, virtually all farmers will practise GM agriculture and be subject to the conditions of the owners of the technology. The Soil Association argues that, once commercial growing of GM crops was widespread, it very quickly became difficult to purchase non-GM maize, soy and oilseed rape on the United States market, and even more so in respect of rape in Canada.[39] The concern that opportunities to avoid GM agriculture, dominated by a powerful corporate agenda, may shrink quite rapidly is closely related to another overarching factor of socioeconomic concern, which focuses on distributional

[38] Conference of the Parties V, Decision V/5 (2000), and Conference of the Parties VIII, Decision VIII/23 (2006).

[39] Gundula Meziani and Hugh Warwick, *Seeds of Doubt* (Soil Association, 2002), Chapter 7.

values. Ulrich Beck highlighted some time ago the ways in which technology distributes risk and benefit, and in the picture he draws of the 'risk society' the distribution of bads (rather than goods) becomes the focus of political life.[40] At the moment, it seems as if the risks of this particular technology are likely to go to the more vulnerable (including developed-world publics and future generations, as well as poor farmers), and the benefits to the economically powerful producers. In these circumstances, the grand claims of those pushing the technology look weak, and the debate continues to be shaped by the question of what the technology is really *for*.

The pervasiveness of GMOs raises more specific questions, including consumer choice and difficulties for farmers who wish to market their produce as being free of GMOs, particularly organic farmers.[41] If organic farming is simply an economic choice, allowing profit to be made from romantic ideas of connection with nature, history is littered with industries that fail when faced with a new competitor. Even if this is all that is at stake, however, there should be the opportunity to debate whether the particular form of connection with nature provided by organic farming is worth the price of limitations on GMOs. But the issues are rather different in any event. First of all, the new industry does not simply out-compete the existing industry. By the pervasiveness of its product, GM farming makes it difficult for the existing industry (organic farming) to distinguish itself on the market, and hence to justify the price premium its survival requires: after all, why buy organic if it all contains GM material anyway? And secondly, organic agriculture is arguably *more* than a simple economic choice. Organic agriculture provides a range of social benefits: environmental benefits most obviously, but also social and rural development, animal welfare benefits and, most controversially, public health benefits.[42] In these circumstances, the ability of organic production to distinguish itself from conventional or GM agriculture is of social importance. Chapter 4 returns to this subject.

We should also explore here some of the more autonomous ethical objections to GM agriculture. This cannot be anything like a full analysis, but some discussion is necessary if we are to examine the considerability of ethical concerns in regulation. Safety questions of course raise ethical issues, for example the ethical acceptability of risk to the environment or the health of producers, or responsibilities to future generations. Whilst some would argue

---

40 Ulrich Beck, *Risk Society: Towards a New Modernity* (Sage Publications, 1992).

41 See further Chapters 4 and 5.

42 These are benefits discussed in European Commission, Staff Working Document, *European Action Plan for Organic Food and Farming* SEC (2004) 739; see section 1.4.

that these are the *only* meaningful ethical issues at stake in GM technology, it is clear that there are other public responses to GMOs that might usefully be categorised in this camp.

A range of perspectives come together in concerns about setting limits for human ingenuity. The 'biocentric' ethical position identifies the cause of our environmental crisis as lying in a misunderstanding of the human place in nature. The dualist understanding of the world, with people separate from nature, is understood to create an illusion that human beings can conquer nature, and that further technological development and control of nature will improve the world. Biotechnology is then just the latest and most extreme example of the desire to control and subjugate nature.[43] The fear has to be that we compound our problems, or at best for, anyone who believes in environmental limits, we simply delay the moment of reckoning. Similar concerns about the moral status of nature, although from a very different starting point, are expressed by the more common reference to misconceived attempts to 'play god' through technology.[44] This is apparent also in those parts of the popular press that have branded GM food 'Frankenfood'. Following his assertion that he is happy to eat GM food, and indeed that he gives it to his children, Tony Blair, the then UK Labour Prime Minister, was pictured on the front of the *Daily Mirror* (traditionally a Labour supporting newspaper) as a Frankenstein's monster, under the headline 'The Prime Monster'.[45] Whilst the 'Frankenfood' rhetoric has been widely dismissed as scare mongering and unhelpful,[46] the Frankenstein story may be a secular take on the 'playing god' idea, reflecting an instinctive anxiety about the consequences of human overreaching. When

---

43 Peter Bunyard and Fern Morgan-Grenville, *The Green Alternative* (Methuen, 1987), quoted in Andrew Dobson, 'Biocentrism and Genetic Engineering' (1995) 4 *Environmental Values* 3, pp. 231–6.

44 Georgiana Kirkham, '"Playing God" and "Vexing Nature": A Cultural Perspective' (2006) 15 *Environmental Values* 173.

45 *The Mirror* 16 February 1999. See the discussion in Alan Irwin, 'Constructing the Scientific Citizen: Science and Democracy in the Biosciences' (2001) 10 *Public Understanding of Science* 1. See John S. Applegate's discussion of the Frankenstein story, 'The Prometheus Principle: Using the Precautionary Principle to Harmonize the Regulation of Genetically Modified Organisms' (2001) 9 *Indiana Journal of Global Legal Studies* 207.

46 As recently as the end of 2006, the UK's Better Regulation Commission, *Risk, Responsibility and Regulation – Whose Risk is it Anyway?* (2006), approached the issue thus: 'the headline "Frankenstein foods" made it virtually impossible to have a balanced, evidence-based consideration of the advantages and disadvantages of genetically-modified crops in the UK. The headline stuck in people's minds and steered the debate in one direction only. A calmer consideration may have yielded a targeted regulatory option that could have dealt with the scientific uncertainties and public fears while retaining the possibility of commercial development for the UK', p. 17.

we put this alongside the high profile of ignorance and uncertainty in this area, concern about the consequences of institutional or scientific hubris has a substantive basis.

This book concentrates primarily on GM crops, but when we think about GM animals ethical issues may apply with extra force. This is not simply about degrees of animal welfare, complicated by the possibility of engineering animals with reduced capacity for suffering.[47] The 'intrinsic value' of a 'natural animal' makes concerns about transgressing boundaries much more visible when animals rather than plants are modified, for example in the creation of pigs that produce less noxious effluent, lower-fat meat, or organs for transplantation:

> What will it mean to come across a rabbit in the woods once genetically engineered 'rabbits' are widespread? Why would we have any more reverence or affection for such a rabbit than we would for a Coke bottle?[48]

While this leaves open all sorts of questions about our ability to develop these sorts of moral sensibilities, and indeed questions about existing reverence for rabbits and all they represent, it raises the possibility of meaningful losses. And, whilst at the moment we are moving only single or small groups of genes, the creation of a 'chimera' would exacerbate these issues still further. In the absence of imminent commercialisation, modification of animals has had a relatively low profile in comparison with the outrage about the actual modification of crops. Whilst the cloning of Dolly the sheep and her sisters had a high profile, this was probably at least as much because it made urgent the consideration of cloning of human beings. Whether and under what conditions society will be prepared to accept development of GM animals is still to be worked through.

From whichever direction we approach these ethical concerns, we arrive in the contentious area of the 'natural' versus the 'unnatural'.[49] It is difficult to make sense of a natural/unnatural distinction, and it should go without saying that all sorts of injustice have been the result of a distinction between natural and unnatural behaviour, or an assertion of limits set by god. Certain extreme

---

47 The distinction between animal rights and animal welfare becomes more urgent in the case of reduced sentience: 'And the animal welfare freaks won't be able to say a word, because this thing feels no pain' – of ChickieNobs, Margaret Atwood, *Oryx and Crake* (Virago, 2003), p. 238. Animal welfare is a factor in EU GMO regulation; see Chapter 3.

48 Bill McKibben, *The End of Nature: Humanity, Climate Change and the Natural World* (Bloomsbury, 2003), p. 230.

49 See the discussion of the Nuffield Council, above n. 16, especially paras 1.39–40.

forms of biocentrism can be uncomfortably misanthropic. Moreover, traditional farming involves the identification and manipulation of preferred traits in animals and plants, without any necessary regard for the integrity or value of the organism itself. And, although some natural limits that agricultural biotechnology can escape, particularly the ability of different species to breed, in the past had to be respected, the precise location of the boundary is elusive.

The ethical issues around proper limits to human ingenuity have been more closely examined with respect to *medical* biotechnology, for example human cloning or stem cell research. Perhaps the concerns are simply more compelling in respect of the application of technology to humans, but there are parallels with farming.[50] Just as some see human identity as at stake in questions of human biotechnology,[51] some see the natural world (and its identity) as fundamentally compromised by biotechnology. Bill McKibben (talking about human-induced climate change) argues that now that human beings have become so large in our numbers and impact that we affect everything, even the weather, we witness the end of nature as an autonomous entity.[52] The loss expressed here is compelling in its seriousness. Even if we find it difficult to empathise with McKibben's almost spiritual approach to the natural environment, or just find these emotions an unhelpful approach to policy, it does not seem appropriate (or even necessary) to dismiss this type of concern out of hand.

It is, however, an enormous challenge to come up with a way to take the various spiritual/religious concerns about biotechnology seriously. If the depth and complexity of intuitions about limits to technology are not acknowledged, we accept that any technological development is permissible – in effect, that what we can do we should do. But, at the other extreme, there is a danger in simply throwing up our hands and allowing the most morally conservative sections of society to dominate decision making, banning on those grounds the products of genetic modification. Andrew Dobson's approach is useful. He

---

50 See the interesting discussion of the 'bifurcation' of institutional consideration of agricultural and medical biotechnology in the US, Adam D. Sheingate, 'Promotion versus Precaution: the Evolution of Biotechnology Policy in the United States' (2006) 36 *British Journal of Political Science* 243. In the UK and EU as well, the medical and agricultural applications of biotechnology went down different regulatory routes, although in the EU in particular there is an effort at an integrated policy approach – perhaps in part to allow other approaches to biotechnology to 'borrow' the legitimacy of medical advances.

51 Jurgen Habermas, *The Future of Human Nature* (Polity, 2003); Francis Fukayama, *Our Posthuman Future: Consequences of the Biotechnology Revolution* (Profile Books, 2002); McKibben, above n. 19.

52 McKibben, above n. 48. The separateness of nature in this analysis takes us away from strict biocentrism.

canvasses the possibility that questions of biocentric value should be part of the assessment of an application of biotechnology, but without precluding the development of biotechnology:

> a case-by-case examination is appropriate in which the guideline questions would be *what* is being done to *whom* (or to what), and *why*. Biocentrics might merely demand in this context that the moral considerability of species . . . be taken into account as a further factor in the decision-making process.[53]

This is akin to Habermas' thoughts (in respect of human biotechnology) on 'keeping one's distance from religion, without closing one's mind to the perspective it offers'.[54] The saddening that results from living in an altered, 'unnatural' world may not be thought adequate, or indeed sufficiently distinct from what has gone before, to merit rejecting an entire technology. That does not mean that it should be unaddressed, irrelevant in decision making. Moreover, if addressed directly, it is likely that some ethical positions could be balanced by any real benefits to new applications of GM technology. Intuitive assessments of whether the cost is worthwhile can apply even if the cost is in our relationship with nature, or playing god (or Frankenstein). This is an ultimately anthropocentric approach, and will not satisfy the true biocentric, as it assumes that human wants and needs ultimately trump natural integrity. Nevertheless, it at least takes seriously the concern, shared with biocentrics, for the integrity of our relationship with nature, and brings into the open the question of what this technology means, and what it is for.

## Conclusions: the Purposes of GMOs

There is little real consensus on what the regulation of GMOs should be about. An enormous range of issues seek a voice in the regulatory process. Certainly, safety for the environment and human health are important values and should be and are an important part of the regulatory framework. But the regulatory framework needs to go beyond safety and risk and engage properly with a fuller range of questions. As we see throughout this book, this is to a significant degree accepted in the mainstream approach to decision making. But the mere articulation of different perspectives is not enough for them to be heard, and that is proving far more difficult. The radical uncertainties and ignorance around new technologies demand greater interrogation of the purposes of GMOs, individually and in general, so that those who bear the uncertainties know why.

53 Dobson, above n. 43. Note that Dobson does discuss in this article the controversy over the existence of 'species'.

54 Habermas, above n. 51, p. 113.

Official and supportive discourse on GMOs is grasping the importance of purpose. The front page of the Commission's biotechnology website is worth citing at length:

> There are currently over 6.4 billion people living on the planet, a figure which is increasing by 77 million each year . . . today over 1.2 billion people, mainly women and children, are living in extreme poverty. Coping with this future population increase will pose severe social and environment challenges for global leaders, not least of which will be providing enough food to go round.
>
> . . . New biotechnology techniques have the potential to deliver improved food quality and environmental benefits through agronomically enhanced crops. Enhanced food and feed quality may be linked to disease prevention, and may result in the reduced use of chemical pesticides, fertilisers and drugs, leading to more sustainable agricultural practices in both the developed and developing world. Advances in biotechnology can also result in major health care benefits, allowing for the production of cheaper, safer drugs in large quantities . . .[55]

This is an interesting acknowledgement that what a technology is *for* does matter, although it is also a fairly crude effort to change minds. These promises of agricultural biotechnology are presented as if they were straightforward scientific fact, rather than hope and expectation. The controllability of the world is assumed, and the potential of molecular biology makes it seem suddenly possible to rethink profound social problems as if they were technical or scientific problems: a technical solution to poverty, lost crops, environmental degradation, climate change. This is also profoundly uncertain and value laden, and tells us little about how we should respond to the current generation of commercially driven GMOs.

## THE HEGEMONY OF RISK?

Regulation (in the narrow sense of authorisation decisions) of GMOs concentrates (although not exclusively) on questions of 'risk', particularly risk to the environment and to human and animal health.[56] The discussion in the previous

[55] http://ec.europa.eu/environment/biotechnology/index_en.htm (accessed December 2007). The webpage goes on to mention 'the need for responsible policies at EU and international level to ensure . . . concerns are addressed and that the protection of the environment and human health remains a priority at all times'.

[56] The regulation is examined in Chapter 3. Elizabeth Fisher, 'Risk and Environmental Law: A Beginner's Guide' in Benjamin Richardson and Stepan Woods (eds), *Environmental Law for Sustainability* (Hart Publishing, 2006), discusses the way in which environmental regulation in particular turned into a question of 'risk' in the last two decades of the 20th century.

section should make clear the inadequacy of any regulatory framework that addressed only these questions. It should also be clear that, even in respect of health and the environment, scientific uncertainty massively complicates decision making on risk. There seems to be no end to the academic debate about the roles of and relationships between science and politics. Because, whilst science is not free of politics, and public views are not devoid of scientific underpinnings, there is a disjunction in the case of GMOs between public alarm and a mainly sanguine set of experts.

For many years, it was assumed by elites, governments and regulators that these sorts of disagreement rested on a combination of public ignorance of science and public irrationality when absolute safety cannot be assured. But a range of arguments and observations from the social sciences seem finally to have coalesced to convince decision makers, at least in principle, that non-experts have something positive to offer decision making. So, for example, longstanding observations that expertise arises in a particular historical, cultural and political context, and (sometimes imperceptibly and unconsciously) incorporates individual and collective value judgments, mean that the results of expertise are not the inevitable and objective 'sound science' that is promised.[57] In this context, alternative individual and collective value judgments should be heard. And increasing awareness of scientific uncertainty makes it much more difficult to use 'the facts' as the only rational basis for decisions. This is not to argue for relativity, or to dismiss the importance of expertise. But inevitable and inherent limitations to scientific analysis, such as the problems of ignorance and indeterminacy discussed above at pp. 00_00, are compounded by more banal errors, data gaps and necessary assumptions. An understanding of the fragility of the expert (scientific) view in the regulation of new technologies makes it difficult to dismiss out of hand competing public perspectives on risk. And those competing perspectives are not irrational, but are based on substance. For example, expert risk assessors may focus on numbers (lives lost/illness), whilst the public takes a multi-dimensional and qualitative approach, with particular hazards meaning different things to different people., depending on underlying values and the context of the risk.[58] So the broader concerns about agricultural biotechnology, including the distribution of risk and benefit or a view of the risk as externally imposed, will affect the level of risk perceived by the public, and most importantly the *acceptability* of that risk. As well as broadening the understanding

---

57 Sheila Jasanoff's work is an important example of this approach, above n. 24; also, for example, *The Fifth Branch: Science Advisers as Policymakers* (Harvard University Press, 1990).

58 See for example the work of Paul Slovic and his colleagues, such as Paul Slovic, *The Perception of Risk* (Earthscan, 2000).

of 'risk', these different approaches can challenge the very conceptualisation of the problem as one of risk. A complex social problem such as what to do about agricultural biotechnology is likely to be misconceived if regulated only in terms of risk.

There are still respectable arguments in favour of keeping important and expensive matters of risk regulation away from the public,[59] but critiques of a wholly technical approach to 'risk', and recognition of the complexity of good decision making, are now in principle part of the mainstream in the EU, and also the UK.[60] The new orthodoxy emphasises a more open approach to decision making, and accepts in principle the political, contextual and value-based nature of regulation. A great deal of political attention has been paid to uncertainty in the scientific process, to public perceptions of risks and to public values that fall outside traditional scientific assessments. The evolution of policy thinking on risk cannot be properly explained by reference to any one event, but some of the intellectual and institutional roots of change can be found in the BSE crisis discussed in Chapter 1, which led to inescapable political awareness of uncertainty in the EU and its Member States. Periodic crises over risk issues and scientific information have continued to draw public attention to the fallibility of administrative decision making, and underlined its political sensitivity. The relationship between expertise and the public, between technocratic and popular decision making, is a significant challenge in the regulation of agricultural biotechnology.

Whilst science clearly cannot provide all of the information and judgments needed to make decisions on agricultural biotechnology, equally clearly we need the information that only it can provide. Ensuring ultimate political responsibility (and public involvement), alongside adequate scientific and technical advice, has proven difficult, despite increasing recognition of its necessity. The institutionalisation of a clear division between the decision-

59 See for example Stephen Breyer, *Breaking the Vicious Circle: Toward Effective Risk Regulation* (Harvard University Press, 1993); Cass R. Sunstein, *Risk and Reason: Safety, Law and the Environment* (Cambridge University Press, 2002), 'celebrates technocracy', but does subject technocracy to 'deliberative democracy'.

60 Alan Irwin, 'The Politics of Talk: Coming to Terms with the "New" Scientific Governance' (2006) 36 *Social Studies of Science* 299. See the material associated with European Commission, *White Paper on European Governance* COM (2001) 428 final. In the UK, see especially House of Lords Select Committee on Science and Technology, Session 2000–01, 3rd Report, *Science and Society* (although the Better Regulation Commission, above n. 46, is far more ambivalent, and arguably suggests something of a backlash). Of course this is not new everywhere! Some Member States, for example Denmark and the Netherlands, have been operating in an open and discursive way for some years, and may even be retreating; see Irwin, ibid. Barry Commoner, *Science and Survival* (The Viking Press, 1963) is an early argument on the topic.

making responsibility of political institutions and the advisory role of experts has been a common response to this dilemma. The EU has taken this division seriously, and in a number of contexts, most prominently for current purposes food, formalises the division of 'risk analysis' into separate stages of 'risk assessment', a technical process, and 'risk management', the political process during which final decisions are made.[61] This approach is pursued in the regulation of GMOs, as discussed in Chapter 3.

The recognition, through space for political 'risk management', that decisions on GMOs are politically significant is welcome. The distinction between the technical and the political is not, though, as clear cut as the risk assessment/risk management dichotomy might suggest. The dichotomy is really an effort to add a new alertness to the political nature of decision making onto old ways of doing things, without fully thinking through the implications. In particular, the uncertainties and implicit value judgments of the science/risk assessment stage may be under-examined. And then in turn the political judgment may be overly constrained by the 'advice'. In his detailed and subtle examination of the decision-making process leading up to the nuclear bombing of Hiroshima and Nagasaki, Jonathon Glover provides a chilling example.[62] Certain crucial issues, for example whether a harmless demonstration of the bomb would bring about swift Japanese surrender, were misconceived as technical questions (as questions of capacity), and delegated to a technical committee. The committee did not take a fully rounded view of the decision it faced, concentrating on technical aspects of the use of nuclear power. The political decision makers in turn saw themselves as constrained by technical advice: 'To look closely at this, one of the central decisions of the twentieth century, is to become aware of a moral vacuum'.[63] The historical force of agricultural biotechnology remains to be seen. Even in the cases that are most obviously morally significant, however, the inappropriate conceptualisation of a decision as technologically determined, rather than value based, can impoverish decision making and allow for the evasion of responsibility.

The precautionary principle, which famously acknowledges the place of scientific uncertainties at the centre of decision making, is an important oppor-

[61] See European Commission, *Communication on the Precautionary Principle* COM (2000) 1 final; Regulation 178/2002 Laying Down the General Principles and Requirements of Food Law OJ 2002 L 31/1.

[62] Jonathon Glover, *Humanity: A Moral History of the Twentieth Century* (Pimlico, 2001), Chapter 12. Closer to home, Liz Fisher's discussion of the BSE crisis in the UK is interesting, raising the question of what the scientific advice was *for* – the providers of the advice and the recipients saw the advice very differently; see Elizabeth Fisher, *Risk: Regulation and Administrative Constitutionalism* (Hart Publishing, 2007), Chapter 2.

[63] Glover, above n. 62, p. 105.

tunity to open up space for broader perspectives on regulation. The precautionary principle provides, at its most basic, that scientific uncertainty does not in itself preclude regulatory action. Depending on the approach to the precautionary principle chosen, that regulatory action could be constrained by, for example, the severity or irreversibility of the risk, or by a cost–benefit analysis of regulatory action.[64] The precautionary principle is subject to vastly different interpretations and roles, and this is not really the place for a lengthy analysis of the competing philosophies of either risk or administration revealed by these debates. But the precautionary principle is an important principle of EU law, and hence also of the regulation of GMOs.

The precautionary principle applies broadly in the EU, to the regulation of environmental protection, human health and safety.[65] The European Court of Justice (ECJ) and the Court of First Instance (CFI) have both had a number of occasions on which to consider the precautionary principle, and the Commission has published an important Communication on the subject.[66] The precautionary principle is routinely taken to mean that 'where there is uncertainty as to the existence or extent of risks to [for example] human health, protective measures may be taken without having to wait until the reality and seriousness of those risks become fully apparent.'[67] The CFI has held that risk assessment is a necessary first step in the application of the precautionary principle, although by definition the risk assessment is not expected to provide certainty.[68] The Commission also characterises decision making in areas of

---

64 See for example *Rio Declaration on Environment and Development* (United Nations Conference on Environment and Development, 1992); European Commission, above n. 61.

65 Article 174EC applies the precautionary principle to the environmental title of the Treaty. Cases T-74/00, T-76/00 and T-141/00 *Artegodan and Others v Commission* [2002] ECR II-4945 provide one of the decisions explaining the broader application of the principle. See discussion in Veerle Heyvaert, 'Guidance Without Constraint: Assessing the Impact of the Precautionary Principle on the European Community's Chemicals Policy' (2006) 6 *Yearbook of European Environmental Law* 27; Nicholas de Sadeleer, 'The Precautionary Principle in EC Health and Environmental Law' (2006) 12 *European Law Journal* 139.

66 European Commission, above n. 61.

67 Case C-241/01 *National Farmers Union v Secretariat General du Gouvernement* [2002] ECR I-907; Case C-180/96 *UK v Commission* [1998] ECR I-3903; Case T-13/99 *Pfizer Animal Health SA v Council* [2002] ECR II-3305, para. 139. This is cited also in European Commission, above n. 61.

68 See especially *Pfizer*, above n. 67, and Case T-70/99 *Alpharma Inc v Council* [2002] ECR II-3495. These decisions were delivered on the same day. The decisions are almost identical, except that in *Alpharma* an expert committee had not been consulted, whilst in *Pfizer* the institutions had consulted the relevant committee but did not follow its advice.

environmental and public health protection as beginning with scientific risk assessment. The CFI distinguishes between a 'purely hypothetical' approach to risk and risk which is 'adequately backed up by the scientific data available at the time'.[69] The former may not be the subject of even precautionary regulation, but the latter is. This distinction is far from self-executing, illustrating clearly (in the words of Advocate General Mischo) 'the tension inherent in applying the precautionary principle: on the one hand, a measure cannot be based on a purely hypothetical risk, yet, on the other hand, one cannot wait until the risk has been established with certainty'.[70] Identifying a precise 'trigger point' for application of the precautionary principle is probably not possible, not least because this is context specific, depending on acceptability of risks in particular cases,[71] but it does not seem to have been set particularly high in the cases.[72] The language of 'plausible risk'[73] and 'reasonable scientific doubt'[74] are later efforts to find a way through this quagmire.

The precautionary principle can provide an important way to explain regulatory actions when uncertain science cannot. Inevitably, the precautionary principle does change the nature of the evidence required by the proponent of an activity, requiring at least a greater level of explanation than 'no evidence of risk'. The EU courts however seem also to go further and require the prioritisation of public over economic objectives: 'The protection of public health, which the contested regulation is intended to guarantee, must take precedence over economic considerations'.[75] This fits in with arguments that the precautionary principle, in the face of dominant economic explanations for policy, should be used to provide a connection with 'collective, democratic interests and the public domain'.[76] But the current operation of the precautionary principle seems not to be as absolute as this might suggest. The current batch of decisions are supportive of EU 'precautionary' action but, even though the

---

69 *Pfizer*, above n. 67, para. 144. European Commission, above n. 61, refers consistently to 'potential risk'.

70 Case C-192/01 *Commission v Denmark* [2003] ECR I-9693, para. 101.

71 Theofanis Christoforou, 'The Precautionary Principle and Democratizing Expertise: A European Legal Perspective' (2003) 30 *Science and Public Policy* 205.

72 Veerle Heyvaert, 'Facing the Consequences of the Precautionary Principle in European Community Law' (2006) 31 *European Law Review* 185.

73 *Denmark*, above n. 70, para. 102 (Advocate General's Opinion).

74 Case C-127/02 *Landelijke Vereniging tot Behoud van de Waddenzee v Staatssecretaris van Landbouw, Natuurbeheer en Visserij* [2004] ECR I-7405, para. 59.

75 *Pfizer*, above n. 67, para. 456.

76 Mike Feintuck, 'Precautionary Maybe, but What's the Principle? The Precautionary Principle, the Regulation of Risk, and the Public Domain' (2005) *Journal of Law and Society* 371, p. 372. Note that Feintuck rejects the process approach to the precautionary principle and argues strongly for a substantive content to the precautionary principle.

application of the precautionary principle is mandatory,[77] the broad discretion that the Courts grant the institutions makes it likely that the precautionary principle will rarely be successful in a challenge of an insufficiently precautionary decision.[78] Application in respect of Member State implementation of EU legislation might be more demanding. In a case about Member State obligations under EC nature conservation legislation, the ECJ has held that action at the point of 'reasonable scientific doubt' is mandatory.[79] The key to this will be in the application of 'reasonable' (although elsewhere in the decision the reference is simply to 'doubt'). This decision, moreover was taken in a specific legislative context, and in particular we should note that the national implementation of nature conservation legislation does not attract the same sort of internal market pressure as might products, including GMOs.[80] Internal market rules are discussed further in Chapter 3.

But more generally, the EU judiciary is unlikely to be intending a move towards a rather tricky interpretation of the precautionary principle, which posits that whenever there are threats to the environment or health the proponent of an activity must prove its safety, without reference to costs and benefits. Given that proof of 'no risk' is rarely if ever available, this 'absurdly strong'[81] approach to the precautionary principle could create equal and opposite risks to those created by the risky activity itself. As Cass Sunstein puts it, the problem with a strong approach to the precautionary principle is not that it 'leads in the wrong directions, but that it leads in no direction at all'.[82] Sunstein's argument is that the precautionary principle can only provide answers (of any description, right or wrong) because we fail to notice the risks of *not* developing a technology like genetic modification. This is an important observation, usefully placed alongside the normal and undoubted failure of regulators and developers to notice long-term, diffuse and uncertain risks, which the precautionary principle is supposed to address. The immediate benefits of certain technologies are easily visible, whilst the long-term and diffuse risks may be missed or under-emphasised.

---

77 *Artegodan*, above n. 65, para. 184.

78 Heyvaert, above n. 65. The Court considers whether there has been a 'manifest error or a misuse of powers or whether the Community institutions clearly exceeded the bounds of their discretion', for example *Pfizer*, above n. 68, para. 166.

79 *Waddenzee*, above n. 74

80 See de Sadeleer, above n. 65.

81 To borrow from the discussion of 'strong sustainability' in Herman E. Daly, 'On Wilfred Beckerman's Critique of Sustainable Development' (1995) 4 *Environmental Values* 49.

82 Cass R. Sunstein, 'Beyond the Precautionary Principle' (2003) 151 *University of Pennsylvania Law Review* 1003, p. 1054.

But the EU institutions, including the courts, do not fall into the trap identified by Sunstein. Not only is cost–benefit analysis emphasised in the application of the precautionary principle,[83] but the search for 'zero risk' (which seems to mean here proof of no risk) is explicitly rejected. In its rejection of a 'purely hypothetical approach to the risk',[84] the CFI in *Pfizer* approves the parties' agreement that 'a "zero risk" does not exist, since it is not possible to prove scientifically that there is no current or future risk associated with the [activity]'.[85] As discussed above (pp. 000–000), this makes sense to the extent that, if a failure to prove safety were necessarily to *preclude* a development, innovation would never be allowed. But the *Pfizer* approach rejects even the *possibility* of basing regulation on the inability to prove safety. Given that the benefits of the GMO in question may also be hypothetical or uncertain, this is a highly restrictive approach. The centrality of scientific evidence and risk assessment techniques means that the precautionary principle cannot be used to examine 'ignorance' – 'we don't know what we don't know'. Even in the application of the precautionary principle, law silences certain forms of uncertainty, on the assumption that uncertainty will be managed by science.

As noted above, the EU approach requires precautionary decisions to be 'adequately backed up by the scientific data available at the time'. However, scientific advisors are denied the final word because, whilst they are expert bodies, they have neither democratic legitimacy nor political responsibilities, and decisions on 'acceptable' risk are political. The Courts will, though, police the scientific credentials of the *political* decision. So a decision in which a political institution disregards the opinion of its scientific advisor must be accompanied by 'specific reasons for its findings', and the reasons provided by the decision maker 'must be of a scientific level at least commensurate with that of the opinion in question'.[86] Along similar lines, when EU institutions are

---

83 See for example *Pfizer*, above n. 67, paras 469 and following; European Commission, above n. 61, para. 6.3.1. Whilst cost–benefit analysis in this context is not necessarily a formal exercise of attributing values to different harms and benefits, the requirement that the pros and cons be weighed up reminds us that we cannot always assume a severe regulatory response in the face of the precautionary principle.

84 *Pfizer*, above n. 67, para. 143; Case T-392/02 *Solvay Pharmaceuticals BV v Council* [2003] ECR II-4555, para. 129.

85 *Pfizer*, above n. 67, para. 145; Commission, above n. 61. The phrase 'zero risk' is somewhat ambiguous – attempts to reduce the probability of an *identified* rather than hypothetical hazard to zero may be legitimate; see C-121/00 *Hahn* [2002] ECR I-9193 in respect of national measures; *Solvay*, above n. 84, in respect of Community measures. Alternatively, de Sadeleer, above n. 65, argues this just applies to the withdrawal of a product from the market, p. 163.

86 *Pfizer*, above n. 67, para. 199. Note the ECJ's rejection of a CFI decision for assuming that a scientific opinion should be followed, 'without explaining why the Commission was obliged to follow that opinion', especially given the existence of

required to assess complex facts of a technical or scientific nature, they can only adopt a preventive measure without consulting the relevant EU level scientific committee in 'exceptional situations', and where there are otherwise adequate guarantees of scientific objectivity.[87] Even if it is true that the way the CFI applies these conditions gives them little 'real bite', in terms of constraints on discretion,[88] they at the very least structure the form and the presentation of the decision, which must be scientific.

There are other interesting positions on the precautionary principle, which would take more seriously the many and profound manifestations of scientific uncertainty. If the precautionary principle implies a recognition that 'the facts' alone cannot be used to justify a decision, because the factual context is contingent, then alternative forms of legitimacy must be required.[89] Most commonly, the alternative legitimacy is sought in traditional forms of political legitimacy, which might include public participation in a decision. Alternative legitimacy is also sought in alternative forms of expertise. Below we will see how the incorporation of alternative fora of expertise, economic and ethical, have been used to bolster authority on GMOs in the UK.

The precautionary principle in the EU is impossible to pin down. It operates in a range of very different legal contexts – the two mentioned so far are scrutiny of EU measures and scrutiny of Member State implementation of EU law – and in different legislative frameworks. Moreover, the precautionary principle operates in the EU at the juncture (or perhaps maelstrom) of a number of legal and administrative contexts, embracing not only the 27 Member States but also the different bodies operating within the EU. And the application of the precautionary principle is highly context specific.[90]

We return to this case law in Chapter 3 (especially pp. 000–000). For now, though, we can say that the EU approach to the precautionary principle

other relevant scientific opinions, Case C-198/03 P *Commission v CEVA Santé Animale SA* [2005] ECR I-6357, para. 53.

87 *Alpharma*, above n. 68, para. 213.

88 Heyvaert, above n. 72. Note also Karl-Heinz Ladeur's observation of the degree of discretion left to administrative decision makers, 'The Introduction of the Precautionary Principle into EU Law: A Pyrrhic Victory for Environmental and Public Health Law? Decision Making under Conditions of Complexity in Multi-Level Political Systems' (2003) 30 *Common Market Law Review* 1455.

89 Elizabeth Fisher, 'Precaution, Precaution Everywhere: Developing a "Common Understanding" of the Precautionary Principle in the European Community' (2002) 9 *Maastricht Journal of International and Comparative Law* 7.

90 See Fisher, above n. 62, for discussion of the different contexts of the precautionary principle, and the importance of those contexts. In Chapter 3 below, the role of the internal market comes to the fore, and in Chapter 6 the impact of the World Trade Organization.

emphasises the continued centrality of scientific risk assessment in 'precaution'. The Commission and the Courts insist that the precautionary principle must not be used to justify arbitrary or irrational decision making, assessed by the normal tools such as cost–benefit analysis and proportionality. But the high profile of the precautionary principle in the EU suggests that the logic of the precautionary principle's critique of scientific uncertainty has been accepted, and the EU interest in 'democratising expertise' suggests that it has been taken seriously.[91] Demanding reference to what science and expertise is available is no bad thing, but, in the ultimate return to science as the only legitimate basis for the final regulatory decision, there is a failure to grasp the profound implications of the limitations of science.[92] The EU approach to the precautionary principle attempts to manage uncertainty with the tools of science. This fundamentally misunderstands the real nature of uncertainty, which cannot always be resolved by more or better science and is too narrowly understood if thought to rest only on scientific disagreement. The return to science also undermines the regulation of non-safety issues. Debate around, for example, the commercial trajectory of GMOs is less compelling if we are under the illusion that decision making is based on objective and inevitable facts.

The EU's understanding of the precautionary principle is not on its own an effective tool with which to address the breadth of debate on agricultural biotechnology. And we should expect those with power to make use of legally entrenched opportunities. So the potential for disruption to food security raised by those who oppose agricultural biotechnology is likely to be matched by the potential of agricultural biotechnology to contribute to solutions for hunger under the same (precautionary) rubric. In short, regulatory reassurance that GMOs are subject to the precautionary principle falls far short of addressing the extent of the debate. The challenge is no longer in forcing legislators and regulators to accept the complexity of scientific evidence or the relevance of concerns not subject to scientific evidence. It is in making that acceptance mean something. The next section begins to explore this.

---

[91] As part of the 'governance' project, above n. 60, see Report of the Working Group, 'Democratising Expertise and Establishing Scientific Reference Systems' (2001), and European Commission, *Communication on the Collection and Use of Expertise by the Commission: Principles and Guidelines 'Improving the Knowledge Base for Better Policies'* COM (2002) 713 final.

[92] Joanne Scott and Ellen Vos, 'The Juridification of Uncertainty: Observations on the Ambivalence of the Precautionary Principle within the EU and the WTO' in Christian Joerges and Renaud Dehousse (eds), *Good Governance in Europe's Integrated Market* (Oxford University Press, 2002), observe that the precautionary principle might conceal rather than resolve the tension between expert and popular government.

## DECISION MAKING ON GMOS: THE UK EXAMPLE

A purely scientific approach to risk assessment, indeed any sort of focus solely on questions of risk narrowly defined, would exclude a very wide range of concerns in the case of agricultural biotechnology. In the UK, science dominated the agenda on GMOs for many years and concern not based on scientific evidence of potential harm was dismissed as irrational, ignorant or at best irrelevant.[93] This narrow framework for decision making went along with a resistance to public involvement. The UK, however, known for its traditionally opaque approach to decision making in technical or scientific policy, was by 2005 described as 'the most active experiment station for the politics of biotechnology'.[94] UK agricultural biotechnology policy now recognises (at least in principle) the importance of public values and public participation, reflecting more general changes that both accept a more expansive approach to risk and move beyond a framing of GMOs solely in terms of risk. In 2003 the UK held an elaborate consultation on the commercialisation of GMOs, in response to public pressure, but more specifically to a proposal by a government advisory commission. The Agriculture and Environment Biotechnology Commission, an independent body set up precisely to provide strategic advice to government on the ethical and social issues associated with agricultural biotechnology, advocated a public debate that would 'expose, respect and embrace the differences of view which exist, rather than bury them'.[95] The public debate was filled out with two other strands: an economic study and a scientific review.

The government's Strategy Unit carried out a study into the overall costs and benefits of GM crops to the UK, resulting in a lengthy report, *Field Work: Weighing up the Costs and Benefits of GM Crops*.[96] Cost–benefit analysis is enormously controversial, along conceptual, ethical and practical lines. There is a danger that a concentration on economics in decision making can hide important uncertainties and value judgments behind a display of apparently inevitable numbers. Any attempt to simplify the complex issues surrounding GMOs behind a façade of objectivity would have been resisted and probably

---

93 See for example the discussion in Black, above n. 8; Matthew Kearnes et al., 'From Bio to Nano: Learning Lessons from the UK Agricultural Biotechnology Controversy' (2006) 15 *Science as Culture* 291.

94 Jasanoff, above n. 24, p. 9. For now we concentrate on the UK level, turning to the EU in the next chapter.

95 Agriculture and Environmental Biotechnology Commission, *Crops on Trial* (AEBC, 2001), para. 21. The AEBC was wound up in 2005.

96 Cabinet Office, *Field Work: Weighing up the Costs and Benefits of GM Crops*, available at http://www.cabinetoffice.gov.uk/strategy/publications.aspx (accessed December 2007).

counterproductive. And, in the context of the enormous uncertainty that we are dealing with here, there have to be questions about what can be achieved by attributing values to the various costs and benefits. The report is circumspect, emphasising the limited evidence and data on which it is based, and making 'no attempt to provide a single "net present value" of total costs and benefits'.[97] Instead, it paints a complex picture that emphasises the difficulty of the *political* judgments to be made, assessing the pros and cons of different regulatory approaches for the future of GM agriculture in the UK, including the possibility of 'shocks and surprises', and emphasising uncertainty.[98]

The Science Review was set up to consider the current state of the science behind GM issues, including clarifying the state of knowledge and areas of uncertainty. Its main novelty was in taking the questions for review from the public, examining the science on 'popular concerns and questions about GM crops and food'.[99] This reminds us how unhelpful it is to attempt to set up boundaries between science and politics, when it should be possible for them to inform each other. One of the important functions of the Science Review was to identify gaps in knowledge, looking more widely than case-by-case review under the regulatory provisions. There is clearly a danger that case-by-case review under the regulations (discussed in Chapter 3) will miss cumulative effects and unexpected interactions. The GM Science Review Panel published its final report in January 2004.[100] In respect of the many concerns identified, the Review asks whether there are 'gaps in our knowledge or scientific uncertainties' and whether these are significant. This is an important and innovative exercise, potentially responding directly to one of the major concerns about GMOs: uncertainty. But the answers provided to these questions are on the whole slightly disappointing. The Review identifies research necessary to fill gaps in knowledge. This is a useful first step, but one that addresses only a particular type of uncertainty, capable of being met by more or better research. Beyond this, the Review tries to reassure, focusing particularly on the existence of strong regulation. By way of example, in respect of the 'possible nutritional and toxicological differences in GM food', the Review closes with the following:

> wide-ranging regulations have evolved for GM crops over the last two decades and development will continue . . . in many respects there is far greater safety evaluation of GM crops and derived foods, which require extensive testing in comparison

---

97 Cabinet Office, above n. 96, para. 1.5.4.
98 Cabinet Office, above n. 96, Chapter 4.
99 GM Science Panel, above n. 22, p. 28.
100 GM Science Panel, *GM Science Review: Second Report: An Open Review of the Science Relevant to GM Crops and Food Based on Interests and Concerns of the Public,* available at http://www.gmsciencedebate.org.uk.

> with conventional crops, which often require no mandatory testing at all. As in all walks of life uncertainties exist but the benchmark for GM food is that it should be as safe as conventional food, which already has a history of safe use.[101]

The Report also repeatedly emphasises that uncertainty is the normal state of affairs. As well as the above, for example:

> Absolute certainty about lack of allergenicity cannot be achieved . . . in this or any other risk assessment. The likelihood that all regulatory and safety testing procedures fail is probably small but cannot be quantified at present as no data are available that allow us to do so. This, however, is not a unique situation in risk assessments. Absolute safety does not exist.[102]

Whilst the Science Review was innovative and progressive – an effort to move beyond some of the limitations of regulatory risk assessment in this area – the omnipresent and more complex issues of uncertainty were not really addressed. What to do about ignorance and indeterminacy is as much a social as a scientific problem, and so this is not wholly surprising in the work of scientists. But the Science Review repackages uncertainty as a manageable and routine risk. And the government response to the Review, if anything, emphasises this confident managerial approach to the problem of scientific uncertainty. Government considered the key conclusion of the Review to be that 'GM is not a single homogeneous technology', and so blanket judgments cannot be made.[103] In the words of the Secretary of State, the Review 'reported no verifiable ill-effects from extensive human and animal consumption of products from GM crops over 7 years, and it concluded too that current GM crops were very unlikely either to invade the countryside or to be toxic to wildlife.'[104] This is far from capturing the emphasis on uncertainty even in the Review itself, and reminds us of the possibility that politicians and scientists will expect too much from each other. And consistently with the Review, when looking at uncertainty, the government concentrates on the promise of new or recent research, as well as the existence of safety regulation.[105] So, for example, in respect of the uncertainty identified around the 'Impact of the use of broad spectrum herbicides that is associated with the cultivation of herbicide tolerant crops, including the implications throughout rotations and on higher

---

101 GM Science Panel, above n. 22, p. 78. There are many similar examples.

102 GM Science Panel, above n. 22, p. 89.

103 Department for Environment, Food and Rural Affairs, *The GM Dialogue: Government Response* (DEFRA, 2004).

104 Secretary of State Margaret Beckett's Statement on GM Policy, 9 March 2004.

105 DEFRA, above n. 103, annex 2.

trophic levels (e.g. farmland birds)', the government response is to refer to the 'Farm Scale Evaluations' (FSEs), which were scientific studies addressing the biodiversity impact of particular GM crops at the farm level.

Whilst not strictly part of the 2003 GM Dialogue, the results of the FSEs obviously met with interest. They were progressive in their assessment of the impact of the entire farm management regime associated with particular GM crops on biodiversity, rather than the GMO in isolation. The FSE results demonstrated that certain genetically modified herbicide-tolerant (GMHT) crops, with their associated herbicide regimes, resulted in lower levels of field biodiversity than was the case for their conventional counterparts managed conventionally. Another, by contrast, resulted in greater levels of field biodiversity than was the case for its conventional equivalent, conventionally managed.[106] Perhaps the most controversial element of the FSEs was the benchmark against which the GM crops were measured. Using conventional farming as the benchmark was described as 'unambitious'. And GMHT forage maize was compared with a conventional crop treated with a herbicide called atrazine, which was described in evidence to a parliamentary committee as a chemical that 'turns a maize field from what was once a diverse grass field . . . into a wildlife desert. It is really ground zero as far as wildlife is concerned.' The use of atrazine has now been phased out for environmental reasons, and this comparison was described by the parliamentary committee as 'invalid'.[107] GM agriculture is clearly going to look better in terms of biodiversity when judged against intensive farming than against, for example, organic farming.[108] The controversy over choice of comparator (conventional farming and atrazine) reminds us that the technical information provided to decision

106 See ACRE, *Advice on the Implications of the Farm-Scale Evaluations of Genetically Modified Herbicide Tolerant Crops*, 13 January 2004. The results are only applicable to particular management regimes and so are of less relevance if future management techniques (either for the GM crop, or for the conventional comparator) change. The Department for Environment, Food and Rural Affairs has stated that, when seeking renewal of authorisations, new evidence providing a comparison with conventional practice current at that time will be required: DEFRA, *Government Response to the Environmental Audit Committee Report: GM Foods – Evaluating the Farm Scale Trials*, Second Report, Session 2003–04.

107 Environmental Audit Committee, 2003–2004 Second Report, *GM Foods – Evaluating the Farm Scale Trials* HC 90-I, Conclusion, paras 1, 48 and 14.

108 This comparator was accepted (apparently with no inhibitions) by the GM Science Panel, above n. 22. We should also recall the commonplace observation that farming is generally less well environmentally regulated than point source industrial pollution (e.g. factories). The comparator need not be farming at all. This is particularly pertinent if farming really is going to replace factories for the production of certain materials – bio-pharming must not be allowed to shift pollution from heavily regulated and monitored factories to weakly regulated and monitored fields.

makers is framed by a value-laden decision. In many cases, these values could be hidden by their apparently technical nature. In this case, however, the wide and heated discussion of the FSEs illustrates how transparency of scientific assessment can bring judgments and alternatives into the open: science as an open and political endeavour.

Described by its organisers as an 'unprecedented event – a special public debate before a potentially far-reaching change in public policy',[109] the public debate strand of the GM dialogue went under the slightly sinister title of *GM Nation?*. It constituted a self-consciously deliberative and inclusive exercise.[110] Whilst there have been criticisms of the process, this has generally been in the context of an acknowledgement of the experimental nature of the process, and of the financial and time limitations.[111] The core activity of *GM Nation?* was a series of public meetings around the country, including a few high-profile regional events, together with a larger number of smaller local meetings, from which written feedback was provided to the Steering Committee. The *GM Nation?* public meetings tended on the whole not to follow the traditional approach to public meetings in the UK. Rather than revolving around platform addresses from experts, followed by questions from the floor, and in line with the deliberative ethos of *GM Nation?*, attendees were encouraged to listen and engage with other opinions, as well as put forward their own views. *GM Nation?* was an interesting and innovative approach to public participation, moving beyond (although including) simpler forms of written consultation, allowing or encouraging engagement between the participants. The *GM Nation?* process swept up the 'other' issues that provoke concern about GMOs, as well as allowing lay discussion of scientific and economic issues. There appeared to be no attempt to impose a framework of 'acceptable' ways of discussing the 'problem'. Instead, the public framed the issues for the debate through discussion workshops.[112]

The *GM Nation?* debate demonstrates what can be done in terms of public involvement in complex policy areas. It also illustrates some of the difficulties with moves to more extensive public participation, which should not be greeted uncritically. Not least, participation absorbs time and financial

---

109 *GM Nation? The Findings of a Public Debate* (2003).

110 Its record in both of those respects is mixed, Understanding Risk Team, (T. Horlick-Jones et al.), *A Deliberative Future? An Independent Evaluation of the* GM Nation? *Public Debate about the Possible Commercialisation of Transgenic Crops in Britain, 2003* Understanding Risk Working Paper 04-02.

111 Understanding Risk Team, above n. 110; Environment, Food and Rural Affairs Select Committee, Session 2002–2003 18th Report, *Conduct of the GM Public Debate*, HC 1220.

112 *GM Nation? The Findings of a Public Debate*, paras 14–18.

resources, and the design of an effective system is hugely difficult. The question of *who* participates is always controversial, as the rhetoric of inclusion that goes along with participation is matched by the real dilemma of exclusion. Those poor in time or other resources (just poor perhaps), the uneducated or the inarticulate are likely to be excluded. In this case, there were clearly difficulties reaching out beyond the 'usual suspects' with a pre-existing interest in agricultural biotechnology. And the purposes of *GM Nation?*, as is often the case with exercises in public participation, were unclear, even retrospectively.[113] Government had undertaken to respond to the results of the GM Dialogue, and, although there was 'widespread cynicism' about the impact of the debate on decision making,[114] the 'dialogue' was unique for the UK. At the very least its political riskiness suggested a desire to engage with public debate on this issue. There was clearly no commitment to seek or follow a majority view on GMOs, but there equally clearly was an effort to make all parties feel that they have sufficient say in decision making. *GM Nation?* sought to bring into the fold a range of information that would be difficult to locate in a single bureaucracy, including external information on the economics and the science, but more strikingly, information on public views.

Perhaps the most significant inherent difficulty with such a far-reaching public participation process, however, is quite what will be done with the results. In particular, there is a question as to how much freedom (legally, economically, politically) government has to respond to unwelcome views. Undeniably, the timing of the debate in this case was problematic, since considerable economic and organisational commitments were already in place. And such an ambitious programme was only possible at all because of the unanticipated regulatory hiatus prompted by the moratorium, itself the result of public pressure. Government made a joint response to the three strands of the dialogue. It claimed to 'take public concern very seriously' and to have 'weighed public opinion alongside the scientific evidence'.[115] It accepted that people are 'generally uneasy', and that there is 'little public support for early commercialisation'.[116] Indeed, the polarisation associated with GMOs was not particularly apparent. The government response acknowledged the 'complex range of issues and concerns' that shape peoples'

113 Understanding Risk Team, above n. 110.

114 Understanding Risk Team, above n. 110. The 'institutional body language' of government may have been problematic: a number of ministers had made clear their support of GM, and the Prime Minister had criticised anti-GM protestors before the debate got underway, p. 35.

115 DEFRA, above n. 103, Executive Summary, para. 1.

116 DEFRA, above n. 103, Executive Summary, para. 7.

views on biotechnology,[117] reinforcing its acknowledgement of the legitimacy of issues going beyond technical assessments of risk to health and the environment. The government claimed to have 'taken into account a range of different policy objectives: environmental protection, food safety, consumer choice, sustainable food and farming, thriving rural communities, science and innovation, industrial competitiveness, international development, and trade'. There was no suggestion that government had a purely technical or scientific decision to make. To borrow from Andrew Dobson in another context, we might be forgiven for thinking that government 'had fully grasped the normative dimension' of decision making on GMOs, 'and was determined to factor it into decision-making'.[118] The government response, however, turned very quickly to its commitment to 'evidence-based policy-making', for which we might read a far more familiar reliance on scientific evidence: 'the scientific evidence supports neither an outright ban nor a blanket acceptance of all GM crops'.[119]

As it went through 'each of the concerns raised in the public debate', the focus was on responding to those concerns through rigorous safety and approval processes. The concerns were listed as follows: (1) caution and precaution; (2) protecting human health; (3) protecting the environment; (4) providing choice for consumers; (5) providing information; (6) openness and transparency; (7) gaps in scientific knowledge; (8) developing countries; (9) no need for GM crops?; (10) ethical issues.[120] The response of government to the first six issues was basically to explain how both current regulatory practice and available scientific information, including that gained during the Dialogue, responded to these issues. So, for example, on concerns about human health, the government response was as follows:

> The science review concluded that there is no evidence to suggest that current GM foods pose a greater risk to human health than their conventional counterparts. All GM food and animal feed is strictly regulated in the EU and is subject to a comprehensive safety assessment. The EU approval process has recently been further strengthened and we believe that it is sufficiently rigorous to ensure that approved GM foods are as safe as their non-GM counterparts.[121]

Public concern was met primarily with reassurance, by reference to scientific evidence and its use by regulators. Scientific values were emphasised, and the possibility and desirability of controlling our environment was assumed. The

117 DEFRA, above n. 103, Chapter 3, para. 3.1.

118 Andrew Dobson, *Citizenship and the Environment* (Oxford University Press, 2003), p. 153.

119 DEFRA, above n. 103, para. 11 (Executive Summary), and para. 4.4.

120 DEFRA, above n. 103, Chapter 5 (numbering added).

121 DEFRA, above n. 103, para. 16.

last four criteria are potentially more challenging, not obviously susceptible to this type of reassurance. Nevertheless, the government response was not ambitious. As discussed above, when addressing concern about gaps in scientific knowledge, the government acknowledged uncertainty and promised further research. This faith in more or better science slightly misses the point. The most profound dilemmas around ignorance (we don't know what we don't know) and indeterminacy (the unpredictability of real-life ecological and human systems) were not addressed, and yet lack of knowledge was a key concern in *GM Nation?*. On the question of developing countries, government asserted the value of developing countries making their own decisions on GM crops. This is clearly true, but disingenuous in its silence on the influence of EU policy.

The public debate identified the 'need for GM crops' as a significant issue. This is an enormously important and complex question, feeding into the appropriateness of bearing uncertainty and the purpose and role of agricultural biotechnology. The government dealt with this very briefly, citing immediately the Economic Review to the effect that, whilst there is currently limited economic value to the UK in GM crops, they have the potential to offer greater benefits. This silences the circumspection of the Economic Review. And, rather than engaging with the underlying question of what the technology is really for, the government responded to this question from a wholly economic perspective, even to the extent of saying that 'ultimately the market will decide'.[122] Again, this rather misses the point of who benefits from GMOs and how, and is based on unacknowledged uncertainties, not to mention unstated values. And the final, and related, question of ethical issues was met by reference to the Nuffield Council on Bioethics, to the effect that 'there is an ethical obligation to explore [the] potential benefits [of agricultural biotechnology] responsibly, in order to contribute to the reduction of poverty, and to improve food security and profitable agriculture in developing countries.' The Nuffield Council on Bioethics is part of a charitable trust, with no formal authority but considerable informal influence. In the report cited by the government, it dismissed the notion that ethical concerns should limit development of biotechnology, beyond questions of safety (that is, the ethical implications of harming the environment or the health of farmers).[123] It took a utilitarian approach to weighing the costs and benefits of GMOs, and dismissed any attempt to distinguish between forms of agriculture on the basis of their 'naturalness'. This utilitarian approach assumes that we have a better understanding of the effects of GMOs than we do, shackling the ethical debate to the

[122] DEFRA, above n. 103, para. 5.7. See Chapter 4 for a discussion of labelling.
[123] Nuffield Council, above n. 16.

scientific evidence. The Nuffield Council addressed also the argument that 'industrialisation' of farming is 'culturally impoverishing', leading us to 'lose touch' with the 'sense of things', but determined that this provides 'little justification in banning GM crops . . . when the rest of society travels so substantially in [this] direction'.[124] The overlap between expertise and implicit values and assumptions is especially pronounced.

The appeal of 'expertise', when faced with the prospect of having to engage with competing perspectives on new technology, is very clear. The effort to sidestep or defer, or sometimes even resolve, political disagreement by delegation to experts is very familiar. And the experts relied on here are not just experts in science and technology. So the economic experts are presumed to have an authoritative view on the need for GMOs. Whilst economic information has a great deal to offer, this closes out alternative understandings of progress, and assumes that the dominance of commercial objectives in the pursuit of this technology is unproblematic. And ethical experts are deemed to provide a response to ethical dispute. Whilst, of course, there is much to learn from those practised in a particular form of discourse, there is a danger that the professionalisation of ethics could put ethics (like 'risk') beyond the reach of popular politics or ordinary political deliberation, disempowering the ordinary language of politics and further constraining political decision making. The approach of government minimises the value assumptions implicit in its own policy, whilst emphasising the values implicit in the perspectives of those outside the official discourse. Everyday intuitions on social and ethical impacts of GMOs may be rejected or may be wrong, but should not be silenced.

The government ostensibly accepted the wide range of issues that are at stake in the regulation of GMOs. However, the rhetorical responsiveness to a full range of considerations proved difficult to match with the actual practice of decision making, where government has tended to go back to expert advice and scientific information. Strides were taken in the provision of institutions for open decision making, for cooperative and communicative regulation. However, the weight of the different perspectives clearly varies, and certain voices continue to find a place in the debate more easily than others. This provides a useful case study of both the potential for progressive approaches to assessing biotechnology and the need to look behind what decision makers say they are doing. Later chapters examine some of the legal pressures that point towards the narrowing of the basis for decisions. There are also political pressures. Science remains a very powerful legitimising force, with an air of objectivity and inevitability that cannot be found in political judgments.

---

124 Nuffield Council, above n. 16, para. 1.43.

The far-reaching claims made for agricultural biotechnology remind us that scientific endeavour is not isolated from social and ethical expectation. Social scientists talk about the 'imaginaries', the projections and expectations, associated with new technologies,[125] the visions of social transformation through science that are bound up with basic research. Such imaginaries have considerable power, but neither their realism nor their desirability is subject to much discussion at the early stage of 'basic' research. And, at the later stage, there is a danger that the search for a technical solution to the problem identified is a fait acompli. So, for example, GMOs might be associated with increasing agricultural production of staple crops in parts of the world where hunger is a problem. At the early stages, there is no external questioning of the likely trajectory of actual research, nor whether this would be the best way to tackle poverty. A social, economic and political problem (extreme poverty) is hence reconceptualised as a technical problem.[126] This can obscure possible alternative solutions. But, in addition, the risks and feasibility of the technical solution become the central question, and it is natural to turn to the technical experts for an answer.[127] This is related to the very long and honourable tradition of progress through science and technology, to which profound concerns around biotechnology pose a genuine challenge. Where science cannot provide sufficient authority for a particular stance, alternative sources of authority are sought. Here, those alternative sources of authority are economic and ethical expertise, which share some of the air of objectivity and independence of science.

'Public opinion' should not of course be followed in all cases: there is rarely even a monolithic public opinion *to* follow, and in any event public opinion can be manipulated, difficult to identify, and discriminatory, ignorant or ill-informed. But, just as it is rhetorically accepted that the scientific information is not decisive, so religious or ethical inputs can be significant without being decisive. An open engagement with the underlying basis for public concern (however difficult and controversial the identification of that underlying basis inevitably is) would have a number of benefits, aside from the virtue of democratic responsiveness. It would put into practice the basic acceptance that policy on GMOs is not a wholly scientific question, but one resting

[125] See the discussion in Kearnes et al., above n. 93. See also the discussion of 'visions' of nanotechnology in Royal Society and Royal Academy of Engineering, *Nanoscience and Nanotechnologies: Opportunities and Uncertainties* (2004).

[126] See the discussion in Kearnes et al., above n. 93; see also Habermas, above n. 51.

[127] Sagoff, above n. 17, provides a nice illustration: 'How can Malthusians plausibly argue that genetic engineering cannot achieve these breakthroughs? Only those well versed in the technology itself can speak to its possibilities, and they are full of optimism', p. 16.

on fundamental values about how we wish to live. If nothing else, religion and spiritual environmentalism have a powerful language for the uneasiness that surrounds certain new technologies. Government could ultimately prefer a particular scientific view, but on the basis of an explanation that, for example, in this case the dangers of ignorance are worth running, as they have been with earlier technological developments. Neither science nor moral absolutes can spare decision makers from the decision. Equally importantly, engagement with the basis of public concern would allow the considerations on which a decision is based to be challenged by competing positions in a way that is not possible if a political decision is justified by a convenient scientific framework. This in turn provides a level of 'check' on the risk of succumbing to irrationality and prejudice.

## CONCLUSIONS

The promised commercialisation of GMOs has raised new and challenging dilemmas for law and regulation. Subsequent chapters explore the legal response to GMOs in a number of fora. The purpose of this chapter has been to study the nature of the debate on GMOs, to allow an examination later of how that debate resonates within the legal framework for decision making. Some see agricultural biotechnology as a simple next step in the progress of agriculture, no different in kind from all other technical advances. Others see it as a qualitative change, altering our relationship with nature in profound and unfamiliar ways. Supporters of agricultural biotechnology promise environmental benefits, food for the hungry, a way to live with climate change, improved health, cleaner manufacturing and prosperity. Opponents are angry at the lack of attention paid to the possibility of environmental disaster, unpredictable risks to human health, impoverishment of all but large corporate investors and an end to our relationship with nature as we know it.

The breadth of concern places this debate beyond its own context of what we should do about GMOs, and firmly in the context of the appropriate path of industrial development and the appropriate role of technology. In the early days, the only acceptable terms of debate were narrowly scientific, and focused on provable negative impacts on, primarily, human or animal health and the environment. There are really two concerns about the reliance on scientific expertise, partially contradictory, but fundamentally connected, and going to the heart of the transparency and accountability of decision making. First, it is possible that political decisions made to respond to public opinion will be 'dressed up' as decisions. Secondly, the depth and extent of public concern will not receive a full response. It is increasingly accepted that science does not have all of the answers and that 'risk' does not capture all of the story.

This goes along with an acceptance that values matter to regulation and that the public has something to contribute to decision making. But questions remain about the extent to which law is capable of recognising and accommodating this broader framework. Sheila Jasanoff's identification of the dual nature of 'representation' is telling: 'It refers both to the self-presentation *of* the public within and before governing institutions, and the presentation *by* the public to those bodies of matters that are seen to be of collective significance'.[128] It is the latter that seems to be most testing. Whilst there are many possible roles for 'public participation', an important one for current purposes is linked with the need to explore this massive scope of issues raised by GMOs.

The 'why' question is crucial in the regulation of GMOs, as is the question of who owns and who benefits from this technology. We should also acknowledge that the unknowns go far beyond the scientific questions. Uncertainties extend to, for example, the impact of biotechnology on small farmers and its impact on the corporate role in the food sector. There are some powerful arguments for pushing ahead with GMOs in farming. Regret for the path not taken is always likely, and we should not think that there are easy answers. How these questions resonate in the regulatory framework applying to GMOs is a topic to which we return throughout this book.

128 Jasanoff, above n. 24, p. 281.

# Part VII
# Environmental Regulation and Economic Development

# [29]

# Environment and development – the missing link

**Philippe Cullet***

## 1. INTRODUCTION

International environmental law has grown at a rapid pace over the past few decades and now covers a range of issues of relevance to developed and developing countries (see generally Birnie et al., 2008). Further, a number of environmental problems addressed in environmental treaties are of global relevance; in other words, not amenable to solution at the national or regional level.

There are at least three ways to approach the link between environmental law and development at the international level. First, international environmental law has developed in the space of relatively few years into an area of law that is now fundamentally based on attempting to put conservation and economic development side by side and, ideally, reconcile the two objectives. The legally unclear umbrella notion of sustainable development provides the general framework within which all environmental issues are conceived today.

Second, the link between environment and development in international law is in large part underpinned by considerations of equity that have come to dominate the engagement of the South in a variety of environmental regimes. This is reflected in legal terms in the concept of differential treatment that provides, in its most evolved form, a new basis for commitments that are not based on reciprocity of obligations. This manifestation of equity or justice concerns in international environmental law is premised for the most part on different levels of economic development in the North and South. It is also the reflection of a political compromise and, thus, not entirely a principle-based response to the moral concerns raised by current environmental challenges. Indeed, differential treatment constitutes the middle ground where the North and South meet: between devel-

* Professor of International and Environmental Law, School of Law, School of Oriental and African Studies, London, UK.

oping countries having sought 'preferential' treatment since independence, and developed countries seeking the engagement of the South in tackling global environmental problems caused mostly by the North, as in the case of global warming and the ozone layer depletion.

Third, international environmental law has had an ambiguous relationship with the growth of environmental law in developing countries. It has, without doubt, contributed to the transmission of what are now basic principles of environmental law in many countries of the world and in this way may have sped up certain aspects of environmental protection in certain countries.[1] At the same time, the priorities set at the international level, which have not necessarily been dictated by developing countries, have often de facto become core concerns of environmental law and policy at the national level, regardless of the actual environmental situation of particular countries.

The relationship between environmental law and development needs to be understood through its varied and partly contradictory trends. This chapter highlights some of the main issues that define this relationship. The following section considers the link between environment and development through the lens of the notion of sustainable development, examining the general issues that arise in this regard. The third section considers some of the difficulties that have arisen in the development of international environmental law with regard to developing countries; in particular, the impact of economic development issues on environmental law. The fourth section then examines the notion of differential treatment, one of the ways in which the concerns of developing countries have been taken into account in recent environmental law. Finally, the fifth section considers ways in which economic globalization has affected international environmental law.

## 2. SUSTAINABLE DEVELOPMENT: ENVIRONMENTAL LAW'S CONCEPTUAL FRAMEWORK FOR THE 21st CENTURY

International environmental law has developed remarkably fast since its formal beginning in the early 1970s (see, for example, UNGA, 1972). Apart from the great number of legal instruments adopted, environmental law is also noteworthy for the development of a corpus of notions and principles

---

1 See, for example, the integration of the precautionary principle by the Indian Supreme Court in *Vellore Citizens' Welfare Forum v. Union of India*.

that have come to define not only the way in which environmental issues are addressed but also how they have impacted other areas of law.

One of the most remarkable developments that have taken place over the past few decades is the changing premises on which environmental regulation is conceived. Indeed, while an understanding of the links between environmental protection and development issues is already clearly articulated in the Stockholm Declaration,[2] early environmental treaties tended to be influenced more by a conservationist perspective (see, for example, Okereke, 2008: 14). This changed significantly over time and since the publication of the World Commission on Environment and Development (WCED) report in 1987, environmental issues have in principle not been considered in international law in isolation from their development component (World Commission on Environment and Development, 1987). Thus the 1992 Rio Conference was tasked by the UN General Assembly to address 'environmental issues in the developmental context'.[3]

The link between the use and conservation of the environment provided the bedrock for the changes that have led environmental law to be an area of international law that covers a huge spectrum: it includes not only environmental issues strictly speaking, but many other issues related to the core environmental issues addressed, such as human rights, health, trade, economic development, intellectual property protection and agriculture. The expansion of the scope of environmental law was due in large part to developing country concerns that conservation did not provide an appropriate angle to approach issues that were directly linked to livelihoods. In that sense, poverty has been an integral part of environmental law for the past couple of decades. Yet, at the same time as it was the poverty of developing countries that provided the trigger for broadening the scope of environmental law, the actual poverty of the majority of poor people in developing countries has not become the core concern of environmental law.

The acknowledgment of the intrinsic links between environmental issues and economic development from the local to the global levels has had a dramatic effect on the growth of environmental law. Indeed, if it was not for the fact that global warming is intrinsically linked to the basic economic development framework of most countries, it is doubtful that it would have acquired the prominence that it has been given over the past

[2] *Declaration of the United Nations Conference on the Human Environment*, Stockholm, 16 June 1972 (UNGA, 1972).

[3] *United Nations Conference on Environment and Development*, Resolution 44/228 (UNGA, 1989: para. 15).

few years. Even a key conservation treaty like the Biodiversity Convention owes its prominence at least as much to the links between conservation and use as to concerns for nature protection. These examples are symptomatic of a broader trend whereby most major environmental issues over the past couple of decades have become issues that are also major economic development concerns, from access to biological resources to trade in genetically modified organisms.

At a conceptual level, the notion of sustainable development encompasses the links between environment and development. Sustainable development is extremely useful as a catchphrase because it provided in the first place the background for understanding that environmental issues cannot be considered in isolation from their development impacts. While it is the economic dimension that still dominates the sustainable development discourse today, its relative flexibility has allowed social issues also to be considered a key component of sustainability. The open nature of the notion of sustainable development has also meant that it has progressively become one of the key defining elements of the international legal order. This is, for instance, illustrated by the fact that even an organisation like the World Trade Organization (WTO) that has no specific environmental mandate sees the fostering of 'the objective of sustainable development' as an overarching goal of the organisation.[4]

The widening acceptance of sustainable development as a key element of international law in general is a significant step forward because it provides a recognition that the links between, for example, trade and environmental protection cannot be ignored. Yet, at the same time, its widespread acceptability is also the cause of its irrelevance at a more specific level. There have been debates for a long time as to whether sustainable development can be deemed to be a principle of international (environmental) law. While there are strong arguments in favour of such recognition, this only shifts the tasks at hand. Indeed, the very reason why those involved in social movements, NGOs, the United Nations Environment Programme (UNEP), the WTO and the World Bank agree on the goal of sustainable development is because it is a malleable notion that can be given a multiplicity of definitions (on the different understandings of sustainable development, see Blewitt, 2008). Since the present international legal order does not provide a single specific definition, sustainable development remains at present an umbrella term that serves a useful purpose in drawing attention to the broad scope of the challenges at hand but does not point towards any specific policy direction.

4 See Preamble to the Agreement Establishing the World Trade Organization (GATT, 1994*a*).

One of the clearest cases in favour of recognising sustainable development as a binding principle of international law was made by Judge Weeramantry more than a decade ago. He argued that sustainable development 'offers an important principle for the resolution of tensions between two established rights. It reaffirms in the arena of international law that there must be both development and environmental protection, and that neither of these rights can be neglected' (*Gabčíkovo-Nagymaros Project*, 1997: 95). Judge Weeramantry sees sustainable development as the mechanism that provides an avenue to solve tensions between the two rights. To people who believe in the existence of a right to development and a right to a clean environment, this may be a simple extension of the right. This is not, however, the position of all states (see generally Bosselmann, 2008: ch. 2). While a majority of states have, in some way, integrated the right to a clean environment in their legal framework,[5] its recognition at the international level remains a distant prospect (see, for example, Shelton, 2007). With regard to the right to development, its explicit recognition in the 1986 Declaration has proved insufficient to build a consensus over its status and its content.[6] In other words, the definition that Judge Weeramantry proposed is a well-argued position, but one that would be disputed by a number of developed states.

This highlights the underlying North–South tension that can be found in a number of documents. Yet, the noteworthy aspect of 'sustainable development' is that it has transcended what could be seen as its original North–South context that sought to bridge the different perspectives of the North and South on environmental regulation. Sustainable development can today alternatively be conceived as the linchpin of an international organisation promoting free trade around the world like the WTO and an organisation seeking to foster stronger environmental regulation like UNEP. Similarly, it can provide the conceptual basis for an NGO advocating free flows of genetic resources across borders that may be used to develop genetically modified seeds, and for organic farmers seeking to protect their lands from the threat of genetically modified organism (GMO) contamination. This is what explains its wide appeal rather than its focus on the development concerns of developing countries or its focus on the situation of the most marginalised and the poorest.

The limitations of the umbrella notion of sustainable development –

[5] According to the list of constitutional provisions compiled by Earthjustice, 119 countries have a right to a clean environment (Earthjustice, 2008).

[6] *Declaration on the Right to Development*, 4 December 1986 (UNGA, 1986).

notwithstanding a number of legal principles that are well established – can be argued as constituting a more specific understanding of what sustainability implies. These include, for instance, the principle of integration of environment and development concerns; the prevention and precautionary principles; and participation, in particular that of women, and intra- and inter-generational equity.[7] The precautionary principle has, for instance, been integrated as a core element of the Biosafety Protocol.[8] This is significant for several reasons in the context of this chapter. First, the precautionary principle is one of the important novel conceptual developments that have taken place in international environmental law. Its inclusion in a treaty seeking to regulate a new technology where economic and commercial stakes are extremely high is a significant achievement. Second, given that the Protocol provides, in effect, safeguards for importing state parties, the use of the precautionary principle in this context provides a shield for developing countries that are in practice the main beneficiaries of the measures adopted. Third, while the Protocol is clearly an environmental law treaty, it is in no way a classical conservation treaty. In fact, the Biosafety Protocol is an instrument that regulates transboundary trade in GMOs. In other words, it is one of the environmental law treaties that focus on trade as the point of entry for introducing environmental safeguards. Overall, the Biosafety Protocol uses the precautionary principle to foster objectives that fall directly under the broader umbrella of sustainability in a context that is centred on conservation through the regulation of trade.

Sustainable development has on the whole become so important that it has come to define the relationship between environment and development. This is helpful in bringing out the links between the environment and the overall process of development. At the same time it can have unwanted side-effects insofar as it may affect the core environmental values of environmental law in favour of approaches that may eventually not be environmentally sound. Since there is no exact legal standard by which to judge 'sustainability', it pushes back the debate to the level of broader questions of environmental values. Thus, whereas it can be argued that the Clean Development Mechanism (CDM) fosters sustainability because it contributes to the global goal of climate change mitigation, the CDM can also be seen as a simple economic mechanism that redistributes the cost

---

7 *Rio Declaration on Environment and Development*, adopted at the UN Conference on Environment and Development, Rio de Janeiro, 14 June 1992 (UNGA 1992: Annex 1).

8 See the Cartagena Protocol on Biosafety to the Convention on Biological Diversity (Secretariat of the Convention on Biological Diversity, 2000).

of mitigation and uses up the cheapest emission reduction opportunities in developing countries that will not be able to benefit from them the day they have to cap or reduce their emissions (see Section 5 below).

## 3. ENVIRONMENTAL LAW AND DEVELOPING COUNTRIES: FOCUS AND PRIORITIES

The shift from what could be seen as a more conservationist agenda to the broader agenda of sustainable development is in principle a testimony to the fact that the position of the South has had an important influence on the development of environmental law. This also seems to be borne out by the fact that some of the basic principles of international environmental law directly refer to the development dimension of environmental regulation, such as the principle of integration of environment and development. Similarly, the rapid growth of differential treatment examined in the next section is a reflection of the importance of the South in shaping up environmental law.

Yet, international environmental law cannot be qualified as a developing-country-focused area of international law. In fact, there exist a number of areas of tension or conflict that have surfaced over time.

International environmental law has now addressed a number of issues, some of a relatively specific nature like wetland protection, some of an immense complexity like global warming. Yet, there is a lack of unity overall. This is due, in part, to the fact that there is no set of principles that apply by definition to all international environmental treaties. While it is hoped that a number of the Stockholm and Rio Declaration principles may have or will attain the status of customary law, this is only partly helpful because individual treaty regimes can have their own understanding of a given principle. The sort of unity that can be identified in contexts such as those of the WTO or the International Labour Organization (ILO) is largely absent in environmental law. Indeed, the 'cement' that binds environmental law are those soft law instruments, in particular the conference declarations, that provide the most evolved statements on the structure of international environmental law.

The fragmented nature of international environmental law is reinforced by the fact that UNEP has never had as strong a mandate as specialised agencies of the UN in their own fields or institutions like the WTO. Additionally, for a combination of reasons, the multiplicity of negotiating forums and the multiplicity of institutional setups – in particular, the different secretariats found in different regions of the world – have combined to ensure any progress in one area may have little impact in another area.

Further, while the setting up of UNEP as the only major UN programme in the South was a huge step forward, the last three decades have seen at least another three strong centres of environmental governance emerge in Europe and North America – Geneva, Bonn and Montreal – that have diluted the leadership role that Nairobi should have ideally played.

The absence of either a specialised agency dealing with environmental issues within which all environmental negotiations would take place and that would administer all treaties or an international covenant on environmental law has had negative impacts on the overall development of international environmental law from the point of view of the South and of the integration of the concerns and rights of the poorest and most marginalised.[9] Indeed, the development of international environmental law has taken place, in part, according to the priorities of the states identifying a new issue of concern and, in part, according to the availability of resources to implement new treaties. In both cases, the priority given to 'global environmental issues' is revealing in terms of the choice of issues addressed. The case of the ozone layer regime reflects, for instance, the push by developed countries having nearly exclusively contributed to an environmental problem with global consequences to develop a legal regime that would bind polluters and non-polluters alike (see, for example, Benedick, 1998). What is at stake is not the reality of the environmental issue but the fact that the same priority was not – and has not been – given to the impacts of economic development (in particular in the phase of economic globalization) on the poor (in particular the majority of the poor people in the South). The case of the ozone layer also reflects the importance of financial issues in the development of the environmental law regime since universal membership was only achieved after the cost of compliance for the South was made insignificant through implementation aid and technology transfer.[10]

The issue is not the extent to which developing countries were able to extract concessions in the negotiations of environmental treaties that did not constitute immediate priorities at the national level (such as in the case of the ozone regime or climate change) at the time of the adoption of the treaties. What matters is the way in which priorities were defined. A telling example is that of land degradation and desertification. In terms of the legal regime, its development only happened as an afterthought of

[9] On the debates concerning the need for an international environment organisation, see Biermann and Bauer (eds) (2005). With regard to the proposal for an international covenant, see IUCN (2004).

[10] See, for example, Gallagher (1992). The Montreal Protocol is the first international environmental treaty to have achieved universal participation in 2009.

the Rio process, with developing countries extracting the concession for their participation in the biodiversity and climate change negotiations (see Cullet, 2007). Even more difficult was the inclusion of land degradation as a 'focal area' in the Global Environment Facility. While this has nothing to do directly with environmental law priorities, the importance that implementation aid has acquired in making environmental treaties effective in individual countries implies that the sidelining of land degradation until 2002 reflected its lower priority for the global community of states despite its critical importance in a number of developing and least developed countries (see GEF, 2002).

The politics of the legal agenda is not an innocuous concern because addressing environmental issues cannot be separated from the development concerns of the majority of the South. There are thus two sets of issues that need to be addressed concurrently. First, international environmental law is tasked with addressing transboundary environmental issues. Most people would probably identify global warming as an issue that is intrinsically global in scope and perceive the need for cooperation on issues such as migratory species. The same level of agreement may not be apparent concerning an issue like biodiversity conservation or land degradation since most of the direct negative impacts are suffered within the country under whose jurisdiction the problem is taking place. Yet, today biodiversity conservation and land degradation are overwhelmingly understood as being issues that have important international aspects. In fact, there are a growing number of problems that may not be apparently transboundary but have an international dimension. Additionally, it is artificial to make a distinction between local air pollution and global warming since it is the same harmful emissions that are the subject matter of both. This, together with the fact that environmental law is concerned with the various links with related fields, makes it difficult to fix with precision the boundaries of the field.

Second, there is no institution which has been tasked with prioritising environmental issues at the international level. Given the multiplicity and variety of issues that qualify as international environmental issues, and given the absence of any framework treaty allocating priorities, this has happened largely in an ad hoc fashion. In practice, this has meant that law making is related to a specific policy proposal in one forum or another by a determined group of countries. The skewed priority list of international environmental law has arisen from this inchoate policy process that benefits countries taking the initiative. This would not necessarily be problematic if environmental issues had no links to the development process because this sectoral approach would simply imply that the international community is slowly covering issues one after the other. The links with development make the choice of issues more significant. Indeed, in the case of land degradation, not only was it a subsidiary priority at the time of the Rio Conference and a subsidiary issue for the GEF, but the Desertification Convention has remained a poor cousin of the other conventions addressing 'global' issues such as biodiversity and climate change.[11]

Further, the relative weakness of UNEP in the UN system cannot be ascribed only to its 'decentralised' location and the emergence of other centres of international environmental governance. Indeed, the power that has never been given to UNEP has not necessarily been left to an institutional vacuum. This is illustrated by the following two examples. First, while funding for the implementation of environmental treaties has played a key role in the success of environmental regimes, this funding has routinely been channelled through institutions that are, at least in principle, more responsive to donor concerns than UNEP. This is reflected even in the case of the GEF, which is credited with being more responsive to developing country concerns than its parent institution the World Bank. Second, the case of climate change illustrates the lack of commitment of the donor community to the global regime. On the one hand, attempts by developing countries to have adaptation given more importance led to the setting-up of the Adaptation Fund but its full operationalisation has proved to be difficult.[12] On the other hand, several special funding mechanisms have been established directly under the authority of the World Bank, from the early Prototype Carbon Fund to the recent Climate Investment Funds: the Clean Technology Fund and the Strategic Climate Fund. The latter include a sunset clause to avoid prejudicing ongoing climate change negotiations but at the same time propose that they may continue operation if the outcome of the negotiations so indicates (World Bank, 2008*c*: paras 53, 55, 2008*d*: paras 56, 58). There is thus an important degree of independence for these funds.

The policy preferences of developed countries, reflected in their push for certain regimes in preference to others, have resulted in a legal landscape that gives much more prominence to certain issues than others. Typically, over the past few years, climate change has become the environmental issue subsuming everything else. Interestingly, climate change was one of those global issues that bore no direct relationship to the environmental priorities of most developing countries when the United Nations Framework

[11] See Convention to Combat Desertification in Those Countries Experiencing Serious Drought and/or Desertification, Particularly in Africa, Paris, 17 June 1994.

[12] See, for example, Decision 1/CMP.4, Adaptation Fund (UNFCCC, 2009*b*).

Convention on Climate Change was being negotiated, with the obvious exception of countries facing, for instance, the threat of submergence. In the meantime, adaptation concerns have become widespread in most countries. Yet, while global warming is a major challenge for each and every country, an overwhelming majority of developing countries have much more pressing environmental and development concerns to address. This is not to say that developing countries are not concerned by global warming. There is, however, a significant difference in approach where the need to reduce air pollution at the local level for health and environmental reasons is addressed with a local rationale in mind from where it is done in the context of a global issue.

Another issue that significantly affects environmental law is the fact that it largely reflects the main concerns of states. As a result, while international environmental law fails to prioritise environmental concerns of the South, it is even less responsive to the concerns of the majority of the poor in the South. Thus, the only existing international treaty on water only addresses transboundary watercourse issues.[13] Similarly, when the first treaty specifically addressing food security was negotiated, and despite a specific mandate to define farmers' rights more precisely, negotiating states did everything apart from provide an effective farmers' rights regime.[14] These two examples are symptomatic because water and food are two of the most fundamental needs that are not fulfilled for hundreds of millions of people. There are good international law reasons explaining the failure of states to negotiate on issues that actually matter to people, such as sovereignty concerns with regard to water, yet the result is that international environmental law is not particularly responsive to the concerns of the poorest and most marginalised.

## 4. ADDRESSING THE NORTH–SOUTH GAP: THE DIFFERENTIAL TREATMENT ANSWER

As analysed in the previous section, international environmental law has, in certain respects, failed to respond to the development needs of the South. At the same time, international environmental law has been one of the most dynamic and responsive areas of international law in

13 Convention on the Law of the Non-navigational Uses of International Watercourses, Resolution 51/229, 21 May 1997 (UNGA, 1997).

14 International Treaty on Plant Genetic Resources for Food and Agriculture, approved by the Food and Agriculture Organization (FAO) Conference, 31st Session, Resolution 3/2001, 3 November 2001.

recent decades with regard to its engagement with the South. This can, for the most part, be explained by the fact that while law making has often been driven by concerns of the North, the issues addressed could only be solved with the active participation and engagement of the South. This pragmatic realisation that cooperation was required, and that the South had often no particular interest in collaborating, has led to the development of a series of new bases for international environmental law.[15]

At the broadest level, developed countries have appealed to the basic principle of solidarity to enlist the cooperation and participation of a majority of developing countries in legal regimes that did not necessarily reflect their own priorities (McDonald, 1996). This could be the case of climate change, where they had made only a minor contribution to the problem at hand and were not much affected at the time of the negotiations in the early 1990s; or GMOs, where one of the primary concerns was to avoid losing out on export markets for conventional or organic crops.

The principle of solidarity may be widely accepted, but it is not necessarily enough to make countries effectively engage on a specific issue. As a result, more specific mechanisms have been needed to ensure full and effective cooperation of all countries on issues that could not be solved by the actions of the North alone. The concept of differential treatment, which recognises that all international law measures need not be strictly based on the principle of formal legal equality, has been one of the main conceptual vehicles for ensuring developing country participation.

Differential treatment offers, in its most developed form, an avenue to adopt international measures that do not impose the same obligations on all states. This is, for instance, the case of the Kyoto Protocol.[16] A number of other mechanisms that are differently differential have also been introduced in environmental treaties. These include varying implementation time periods, where all states take on the same commitments but at different dates,[17] implementation aid, where certain states are only legally bound to implement their commitments upon receipt of financial

---

15 *Cf* Okereke (2008) arguing that 'from the perspective of North–South relations . . . distributive bargaining rather than environmental protection is the defining feature of international regime efforts'.

16 See Kyoto Protocol to the United Nations Framework Convention on Climate Change, Kyoto 10 December 1997 (UNFCCC, 1998*b*: 7).

17 Montreal Protocol on Substances that Deplete the Ozone Layer (Protocol to the Vienna Convention for the Protection of the Ozone Layer), Montreal, 16 September 1987.

or technological aid;[18] and legally less clear contextual provisions, where states are allowed to interpret the commitments they take according to their development situation.[19]

Differential treatment remains controversial and it has, for instance, been argued by a leading environmental lawyer that even if redistribution is necessary, it should not be undertaken by exempting the poor from 'efficient environmental and resource standards – giving them a "right to pollute" – rather than through a more straightforward step-up in aid and development assistance' (Stone, 2004: 294). Indeed, in international trade and economic law, a massive backlash against the granting of 'differential' or 'preferential' treatment has been visible since the 1980s. The pervasive inclusion of differentiation in international environmental treaties is thus doubly noteworthy.[20] First, differential treatment has been one of the most effective ways that states negotiating global environmental regimes have found to address the persistent inequalities among states forming the UN. Second, this has happened more or less at the same time as the scope for granting preferences in international trade law diminished to the point where the Uruguay Round was largely premised on returning to the principle of legal equality as a more effective basis for lifting developing countries out of poverty (*cf* Michalopoulos, 2000).

The concept of differentiation has several noteworthy features. Firstly, at a conceptual level it is a manifestation of equity. In fact, it constitutes an acknowledgment at the international law level of the principle that formal equality does not necessarily lead to substantive equality (see generally Cullet, 2003). While this should not have been a major discovery, because of the vast gap in economic development between the North and the South, it took more than three centuries and the process of decolonisation for the limits of formal legal equality to become obvious to most. More specifically, differential treatment is a reflection of a notion of distributive justice that was clarified a number of decades ago by Justice Tanaka, who asserted that '[t]o treat unequal matters differently according to their inequality is not only permitted but required'.[21] While this is not the conception of justice that is generally accepted today (for instance,

18 Convention on Biological Diversity, Rio de Janeiro, 5 June 1992: Art. 20(4).

19 See, for example, ibid: Art. 6.

20 More generally, Okereke (2008: 29) notes that almost all global environmental agreements since 1972 contain at least one reference to international justice and equity.

21 South West Africa (*Ethiopia v. South Africa*; *Liberia v. South Africa*) (1966: 306).

by the International Court of Justice), Justice Tanaka's statement reflects the fact that the need for a progressive evolution of the understanding of equality and equity has been felt at various levels in the decades following decolonisation.

Second, differential treatment turns out to be one of the legal mechanisms that provide a space to development concerns in international law. The fact that the most successful differential measures over the past couple of decades have been adopted in environmental law is, in some way, a reflection of the increasingly strong links between development and environmental concerns. This is reflected, for instance, in two principles of the Rio Declaration. Principle 6 first recognises, in general, the fact that there is a need for UN member states to give special attention to economic and environmental vulnerability, singling out the position of least developed countries. Principle 7 is more specific and addresses the different contributions that developed and developing countries have made to environmental degradation and their different capacity to address these problems. While this is not necessarily always linked to levels of economic development, in the case of some of the most important global problems such as global warming there is an intrinsic link between levels of economic development and contribution to the global problem. The acknowledgment of the link between the environment and development is thus direct, even though the legal consequences that flow from this statement are not made explicit.

Third, differential treatment offers results that can be compared with the 'preferential' treatment that was found earlier in international trade and economic law. Yet, the path is different. In the era of preferential treatment between the 1950s and 1970s, the driving force behind preferences was the attempt by newly decolonised countries to reorganise the structure of international law. As a result, in that era, developing countries were often pitted against developed countries. This yielded some results, in particular in political terms in the context of the call for a New International Economic Order; however, in strict legal terms, relatively little of substance was achieved.[22] As opposed to the relatively confrontationist path of the post-decolonisation years, international environmental law has developed in a much more consensual way. This is due to the fact that, while the relative power equations have not necessarily evolved significantly since the 1970s, negotiations around international environmental issues brought to the fore a new 'strength' of developing countries. The

[22] *Declaration on the Establishment of a New International Economic Order*, Resolution 3201 (S-VI), 1 May 1974 (UNGA, 1974).

necessity for the North to include them in the regimes negotiated implies that the South was in a much better position to extract concessions. These concessions can be analysed in conceptual terms as a manifestation of equity, but their genesis owes at least as much to hard practical realities as to lofty concepts.

The development of differential treatment in international environmental law reflects to a large extent the development concerns of developing countries. Yet, unlike in the era of preferential treatment, the South is not trying to engage the North in restructuring the international legal order. The South is here benefiting from the fact that environmental issues are so structured that its participation is often a precondition for addressing certain issues in an effective way. This has translated into 'different' commitments in several treaties, implementation aid has become a nearly necessary part of any treaty, and most treaties include a variety of contextual provisions which meet the concerns of countries that are unsure about their capacity to implement the commitments they take.

While the development of differential treatment is, on the whole, beneficial to the South, this is not necessarily the case in all its aspects. The case of capacity building under the Biosafety Protocol illustrates this point. From a differential treatment perspective, the biosafety regime provides procedural safeguards for an importing country and thus strengthens developing countries' position in negotiations with GMO exporters.[23] At the same time, one of the impacts of the Protocol is to ensure that all member states have a legal regime in place that regulates – but does not prohibit – the transboundary movement of GMOs. This restricts the options that developing countries have with regard to banning GMOs. In addition, significant capacity building was undertaken in the context of a relatively large UNEP/GEF project whose main intent was to ensure that developing countries that had ratified the Protocol had the actual capacity to deal with import requests (see, for example, GEF Council, 2000). In this case, capacity building ends up indirectly limiting the range of options that developing countries consider in adopting biosafety laws. This is, for instance, illustrated by the fact that while the African Model Law on Safety in Biotechnology had a strong liability and redress provision – something that is clearly positive for an importing country – some countries, like Cameroon, having drafted their laws in the context of the UNEP/GEF project, ended up with very weak liability and redress frame-

[23] See Articles 7–10 of the Cartagena Protocol on Biosafety to the Convention on Biological Diversity (Secretariat of the Convention on Biological Diversity, 2000).

works.[24] In other words, even an instrument that is very progressive from an environmental point of view – since it uses the precautionary principle as its main operative principle – and an instrument that, in substance, builds up procedural safeguards in favour of developing countries does not necessarily lead to results that are unequivocally positive for developing countries.

## 5. ENVIRONMENTAL LAW AND RECENT ECONOMIC REFORMS

Environmental law entered a phase of consolidation after a period of rapid development in the 1980s and 1990s. This is partly due to the realisation that the constant addition of new instruments was doing little to ensure their effective implementation and thus to improve environmental standards overall. It is in this context that implementation aid has become one of the key elements of most environmental regimes as technology and finance were identified as key stumbling blocks in the process of implementing international commitments in the South. The end of the 'growth' can also be ascribed to an increasing disenchantment with the way environmental policy had been conceived in the 1970s and 1980s, linked in large part to the changing economic policy environment. This section examines some of the main impacts of the neoliberal reforms on international environmental law.

### I. Economic Instruments and the Climate Change Regime

One of the important trends that can be noticed from the 1990s is the increased visibility of economic instruments in international environmental law. The Kyoto Protocol marks some sort of a watershed in this context. Indeed, the introduction of economic instruments became one of the key points that United States negotiators insisted upon in the Kyoto Protocol negotiations. This led to the inclusion of what we now know as flexibility. Flexibility refers to two new phenomena in international environmental law. The first is the flexibility which is given to countries with commitments to reduce their greenhouse gas emissions to implement part of their international obligations through projects in a different member

24 See Organisation of African Unity (2002: Art. 14); Law to Lay down Safety Regulations Governing Modern Biotechnology in Cameroon, Law No 2003/006, 21 April 2003: s. 11.

state. This is unprecedented because it provides a form of extra-territorial implementation of international commitments. The environmental justification for this new mechanism is linked to the global nature of the environmental issue that is addressed. Indeed, it matters neither where a given ton of greenhouse gas is emitted nor where emissions are reduced or avoided. As a result, where the frame of reference is the global environment good that is climate change mitigation, there is no need to differentiate between action taken in the United Kingdom or in Malawi.

Secondly, flexibility refers to the desire to ensure that environmental aims are reached in the most economically efficient way. This translates into the search for the cheapest emission reduction opportunities anywhere on the planet, regardless of the origin of the pollution. This has led to the development of what we now know as carbon markets. While this was not necessarily directly stated at the outset, one of the implications of the search for efficiency has been that the private sector plays an important and direct role in the implementation of the climate change regime. This is also novel in international environmental law.

Of the two different market mechanisms that have been set up under the Kyoto Protocol, the more important in a North–South context is the Clean Development Mechanism (CDM).[25] The CDM is, in effect, a project-based market mechanism that seeks to redistribute the cost of compliance with Kyoto commitments by providing a framework for undertaking emission reduction activities where they are cheaper than in the country with the commitment.[26] In other words, extra-territorial implementation of commitments is directly linked to an economic rationale – reducing the cost of compliance for countries with commitments – even though an environmental cloak has been put around the issue, as indicated in the previous paragraph. Additionally, the CDM includes a sustainable development veil that is meant to counterbalance the economic rationale for flexibility. In practice, however, while the international legal framework makes pious admonition for sustainability, where developing country governments fail to take action to ensure that benefits of the CDM are ploughed back into climate change mitigation or adaptation measures it turns into another commercial instrument for businesses in the North and the South.

The introduction of economic instruments was crucial for the participa-

---

[25] The CDM is defined in the Kyoto Protocol to the United Nations Framework Convention on Climate Change, Kyoto, 10 December 1997 (UNFCCC, 1998*b*: 11, Art. 12).

[26] See generally Decision 3/CMP.1 'Modalities and Procedures for a Clean Development Mechanism, as Defined in Article 12 of the Kyoto Protocol' (UNFCCC, 2006: 6).

tion of the United States in the Kyoto Protocol in the mid-1990s. In the meantime, economic instruments have been adopted by many countries as a key element of any climate change deal. In fact, they have come to play such a central role that they can be described as the linchpin of any global agreement on climate change mitigation. The CDM, joint implementation and emissions trading have thus turned out to be much more than a new supplemental way to implement an international treaty. They have led to a completely new outlook on the way international environmental treaties are shaped.

## II. Limited Overall Progress in Environmental Law

Since the 1992 Rio Conference, the conceptual development of international environmental law seems to have tapered off. The 2002 World Summit on Sustainable Development (WSSD) failed, for instance, to take international environmental law beyond what had been achieved in 1992 (see, for example, Galizzi, 2006). Further, it has been increasingly difficult to conclude negotiations on issues that could not be finalised at the time of the adoption of a particular treaty, as in the case of the liability and redress regime of the Biosafety Protocol.[27] Similarly, where liability and redress regimes have been adopted, states have been increasingly slow in ratifying these instruments.[28]

In international environmental law per se, there has been no significant weakening of standards adopted earlier. The same cannot be said, however, of the overall environmental dimension of international law. This is true, in particular, with regard to the international trade regime. In the context of a fast-evolving jurisprudence on trade and the environment, WTO panels have taken positions that at least indirectly affect environmental instruments. This is partly related to the way in which environmental treaties are considered by WTO panels, making them at best a relevant consideration in a decision that does not apply norms of international environmental law. It is also partly due to the often more specific nature of trade obligations, which may lead to an assessment of

[27] For the most recent version of the text under negotiation, see, for example, Group of the Friends of the Co-Chairs on Liability and Redress in the Context of the Cartagena Protocol on Biosafety (2009).

[28] This is, for instance, the case of the Basel Protocol on Liability and Compensation for Damage Resulting from Transboundary Movements of Hazardous Wastes and their Disposal, Fifth Conference of Parties, Basel, 10 December 1999, UNEP/CHW.5/29, Annex III, which has not yet entered into force.

norms that implicitly privileges trade rules over environmental norms with a frequent in-built potential for a broader interpretation.

Additionally, it is symptomatic that some of the most important environmental instruments, such as environmental impact assessments, are for all practical purposes not covered in international law as far as the South is concerned. This is due to the fact that the Espoo Convention remains, despite the opening-up of its membership to all states, a regional convention and one that was negotiated without the South.[29] Further, even if the Espoo Convention was widely ratified in the South, it would not cover some of the most important issues of relevance to the South, in particular aid and foreign investment.

The result is that one of the key impact assessment frameworks at the international level ends up being the World Bank's operational policy applicable to its lending activities. This is positive because it ensures that at least some projects get assessed. The major shortcoming is that this is not a framework that has ever been debated and negotiated in the form of an international treaty. Additionally, while it reflects the greening of the World Bank, this remains necessarily limited because protecting the environment is not, and maybe can never be, the core mandate of the Bank. There are also concerns that the Bank may be instrumental in certain cases in fostering the weakening of existing frameworks for impact assessment, as identified in the case of India by the independent people's tribunal on the World Bank (Independent People's Tribunal on the World Bank in India, 2007).

## III. Sustainable Development and Neoliberal Reforms

The progressive shift from 'environment' to 'environment and development' and eventually 'sustainable development' has had two different consequences. On the one hand, enshrining sustainable development at the heart of international law reinforces on a superficial level the idea that environment and development have effectively been integrated. On the other hand, the vagueness of the concept of sustainable development has had the unfortunate effect of making it easier for the language of neoliberal economic reforms to enter the domain of environmental law without necessarily being in open conflict with the basic tenets of the international-level orthodoxy. Thus, whereas environmental law was viewed for some time as a relatively new and innovative branch of international law that

---

[29] Convention on Environmental Impact Assessment in a Transboundary Context, Espoo, 25 February 1991.

had the potential to challenge some of the orthodoxy prevalent in other branches of international law, the past decade seems to indicate that this is not the case any more. This can be partly related to the linking of environment and development that has, over time, provided the basis for a weakening of the environmental part in favour of an economic development discourse. It can also be linked to the neoliberal discourse that is generally averse to governmental intervention.

The preceding remarks may appear out of place in a context where global warming has been given a central place in all areas of policy-making over the past couple of years. In fact, what seems to be progressively happening is that the environmental discourse is used as a tool to reconfigure economic policies under the guise of a broader environmental aim such as global warming mitigation. Thus, the shift in international environmental policy is, for instance, illustrated by the WSSD Plan of Action's frequent call for private sector participation and public–private partnerships in a variety of areas, including a reliance on the private sector to deliver integrated water management and water efficiency that 'give priority to the needs of the poor' (World Summit on Sustainable Development, 2002: 22, para. 26(g)). In other words, whether it is flexibility mechanisms that give the private sector what is probably its most direct role in the implementation of an international environmental treaty yet, or the reconfiguration of basic development goals such as access to drinking water as requiring the private sector for their fulfilment, the language of neoliberalism has increasingly infiltrated international environmental law.

## IV. Increasing Role of International Institutions in Shaping Environmental Law in the South

The link between environmental law and development is increasingly shaped by international actors. Thus, over the past decade, the World Bank has, for instance, taken a pro-active view of law making in the South. This is illustrated in the context of water in India where the Bank has, for instance, imposed on several Indian states the adoption of specific pieces of legislation as part of a water sector loan. The resurgence of conditionality in the context of economic globalization is in itself very important and a worrying development. More specifically, recent water-law-related conditionality reinforces the view that economic reforms prevail over the environment, as well as, for instance, the realisation of human rights. In the case of water, the main premise for law reform is that water must be seen as an economic good. The prescriptions of the Bank include the setting up of new 'independent water regulatory authorities' modelled on the framework used for electricity earlier.[30] The significance of the interventions of the Bank is manifold. In the context of this chapter, the following can be highlighted:

- First, the water law interventions of the Bank do not have a strong environmental component. This is surprising in general and more so in the Indian context where a general environmental perspective to water law is missing despite a piece of legislation focusing on water pollution.[31]
- Second, water is a multi-faceted issue that includes a major environmental dimension. This is sidelined by the focus on issues of 'management' in the water sector and on the conception of water as an economic good.
- Third, from a legal perspective, the single-minded focus on water as an economic good as a premise for law making in India is at best inappropriate. This is due to the fact that there is no basis in law to affirm that water is a tradable economic good.[32] On the contrary, various Supreme Court judgments affirm that there is a human right to water and that water is a public trust.[33]

## V. Deregulation in the Name of Stronger Regulation

Where international environmental law has been strengthened in recent years, the additional 'regulation' often comes in the form of indirect or hidden deregulation. This is, for instance, illustrated by the case of benefit sharing. Access and benefit sharing has become one of the main mechanisms to address the inequities of the international flow of genetic resources. This has been taken up in the context of several regimes but the only binding regime at present is that of the 2001 International Treaty on Plant Genetic Resources for Food and Agriculture. In furtherance of the Treaty provisions, the Governing Body adopted a standard material transfer agreement (SMTA) (see FAO, 2006*a*: app. G).

Benefit sharing, as conceived under the Treaty and the SMTA, is a form

---

30 See, for example, World Bank (2001*b*) and Uttar Pradesh Water Management and Regulatory Commission Act 2008.

31 India, Water (Prevention and Control of Pollution) Act 1974.

32 The main basis for affirming that water is an economic good in India is policy documents. While there has been a tendency to conflate water policies and water laws, this is inappropriate because the two are completely different instruments (see, for example, Cullet, 2009).

33 See, for example, *Subhash Kumar v. State of Bihar and others* (on the human right to water) and *MC Mehta v. Kamal Nath* (public trust).

of compensation that is conceived in the context of bilateral transactions. The recognition of the need for benefit sharing and the adoption of the SMTA constitute important additions to regulation since, in the absence of legal rights, farmers did not get any benefit when their varieties were used.

At the same time, the framing of access and benefit sharing in the form of a contract mechanism that involves only the two parties signing the contract reflects the absence of any public power in this context. This is particularly surprising and unwelcome in the context of benefit sharing because the actors signing the contract can, as a matter of principle, be – with exceptions – expected not to be on a level playing field. Problems arise, for instance, from the fact that it is in most cases the weaker party to the contract – such as a farmer or a group of farmers – that offers to transfer something under their control to another party – such as a university or private company – that will be largely free to use, modify and commercially exploit the seed and knowledge related thereto in any way they see fit. In other words, the party that benefits most from the contract – usually a legal entity – is also the one who most often proposes the transaction and has better resources to ensure that the contract fulfils all their interests. Some countries like South Africa have recognised the dangers posed by purely private transactions and propose at least a form of monitoring by a public authority.[34]

## VI. Unresolved Conflicts between the Economic and Environmental Regimes

Environmental law has also been indirectly and directly affected by the fact that potential or actual conflicts between the economic and environmental regimes are not given concrete solutions in the environmental law regime. This is damaging, for instance, in the context of any dispute that has a trade angle, as is the case of many issues that may arise at the international level. In a context where there is little by way of binding dispute settlement provisions in international environmental law, this leads to the dispute being brought nearly by default to the WTO, rather than, say, the International Court of Justice. This is not the place where a neutral resolution to any trade and environment conflict can be expected.

The identified problem in terms of dispute settlement is made worse by the fact that the international economic and trade law regime to a

34 See, for example, South Africa, National Environment Management: Biodiversity Act 2004: s. 82.

large extent does not even consider the possibility of a conflict with other international law regimes. There is thus very little to work from. This is illustrated, for instance, by the Agreement on Trade-Related Aspects of Intellectual Property Rights (TRIPS), whose single mention of the environment is in a narrowly construed exception to the principle that patents must be available in all fields of technology (GATT, 1994*b*: Art. 27(2)).

On the environmental law front, some attempts have been made to consider the links that exist and the problems that can arise. The primary link is in terms of technology transfer, which has been a key demand of the South in most international environmental law treaties since the 1970s. In most cases, the link between the fulfilment of environmental commitments and technology transfer is made but no specific mention is made of intellectual property rights as being of central importance to technology transfer. In a few cases, the link has been acknowledged.[35] This, however, only confirms that there is a link; it does not discuss the potential impediments to technology transfer that intellectual property rights foster (for instance, where importing countries cannot afford the royalty demanded). The most direct acknowledgment in a general provision that there is a potential conflict between the environment and intellectual property rights is found in Article 16(5) of the Biodiversity Convention.[36] Article 16(5) is an important provision because it does what no trade treaty does. It does not, however, provide a specific answer, because the broad commitments of the Biodiversity Convention do not lend themselves easily to identifying the point at which a conflict of norms would arise in a concrete situation.

Environmental treaties include other provisions confirming the presence of a conflict. This is, for instance, the case of the so-called 'savings clauses'. These clauses typically found in preambles tend to sidestep the real issue by emphasising the need for mutual supportiveness or harmonisation, then stating that the environmental law instrument does not affect other existing treaties and finally asserting that the present treaty is not subordinate to any other treaty.[37] The end result is that such clauses do not actually give any new guidance since they only restate things that are derived from existing principles of international law. Further, by empha-

35 See, for example, 'Decision VII/22, Review of the Financial Mechanism (Annex V, Action 21)' (Seventh Meeting of the Parties to the Montreal Protocol on Substances that Deplete the Ozone Layer, 1995).

36 See Convention on Biological Diversity, Rio de Janeiro, 5 June 1992: Art. 16(5).

37 See, for example, Preamble to Cartagena Protocol on Biosafety to the Convention on Biological Diversity (Secretariat of the Convention on Biological Diversity, 2000).

sising mutual supportiveness, as stated above, they tend to favour the trade/economic regime because environmental law provisions are usually more amenable to a broader array of different interpretations than trade/economic treaties.

Overall, existing international law tends to disregard the very possibility of a conflict between development law and environmental law (for instance, in the case of the TRIPS Agreement). Where links, overlaps and conflicts are acknowledged, no practical and specific solutions are proposed, as is the case in environmental law treaties. This is problematic because a treaty like the TRIPS Agreement has significant consequences for developing countries beyond the strict intellectual property rights regime. Thus, in the case of benefit sharing mentioned above, the TRIPS Agreement recognises neither farmer/healer knowledge nor what is now known in policy circles as traditional knowledge as forms of knowledge that can be protected by legal rights. This implies that all this knowledge is part of the public domain that can be freely used by any- and everyone because it is knowledge that does not meet the criteria for protection under existing intellectual property rights frameworks. Since intellectual property rights protect knowledge only in the context of its commercial exploitation, this leaves out all other rationales for protection, including any social, cultural, religious or environmental grounds for the protection of certain forms of knowledge. The end result is that in a context where knowledge can only be protected through what are recognised forms of intellectual property rights, all other knowledge is seen as hierarchically inferior, in practical and in legal terms.

## 6. CONCLUSION

Environment and development are today inseparable as far as international law and policy making is concerned. This is, for instance, reflected in the central role played by the notion of sustainable development. The understanding that the two are linked is most welcome and has, for instance, ensured that environmental law has evolved beyond a conservationist agenda and has started to consider a number of links going beyond the environment *stricto sensu*.

Yet, the central problem is that no specific legal meaning can be ascribed to sustainable development at the international level today. It can be used alternatively to justify neoliberal economic policies, welfare state measures and conservationist agendas. While some of the different perspectives can be reconciled, there exist also a number of areas of conflict. This is made more complex by the fact that, today, environmental law is much more than nature protection. Conversely, the environment is a major aspect of many other fields of international law. In a decentralised system there is thus no scope for imposing a definition of sustainable development that would apply in international environmental law as well as in all other fields. In fact, the only reason why people working on such diverse issues as the environment, human rights, economic development, trade and financial issues can agree on a single umbrella concept is because each can ascribe their own understanding of the term. As a result, the seemingly all-pervasive link between environment and development is in fact, at least in part, a front that lacks in depth.

This is not to say that the links between environment and development have not been made in various contexts. However, where the links are made, it has often been in a context which privileges an understanding of development as focusing on economic development. In other words, despite significant developments in conceptual terms over the past couple of decades, the practice of international law, as well as the practice of international institutions directly involved in 'development' (such as the World Bank), still indicates a significant bias in favour of growth and economic development as the core measure of development. This has in fact been reinforced over the past two decades with the sweeping neoliberal economic reforms that most countries of the world have witnessed.

Overall, much work remains to be done to ensure that the 'development' discourse does not use environmental arguments as a fig leaf to foster further economic development activities that are either environmentally unsustainable or socially regressive. At the international level, the development over the past two decades of the concept of differential treatment reflects a broad realisation of the need to take into account 'development' as a factor in environmental law making and implementation. Yet, much more needs to be done. Indeed, differential treatment per se does no more than address some of the basic inequalities that are in-built in the structure of international law. It does not necessarily lead to norms that intrinsically integrate environmental and human rights principles as core issues in environmental law and development. A much broader effort must be made to ensure that differential treatment is effectively coupled with a large-scale application of basic principles of environmental law such as the precautionary principle. It is only once such a broader framework is adopted that environmental protection will stop being in some cases an excuse for the promotion of certain economic agendas, as is the case with the development of carbon markets in the climate change regime.

# [30]



# THE HARMONIOUS SOCIETY, CORPORATE SOCIAL RESPONSIBILITY AND LEGAL RESPONSES TO ETHICAL NORMS IN CHINESE COMPANY LAW

JINGCHEN ZHAO*

*In 2005, President Hu instructed China's leading officials and party cadres to put "building a harmonious society" at the top of their agendas in order to build a society that placed people first. This vision shifts China's primary focus from GDP figures and economic growth towards a more balanced, people-oriented and sustainable model, maintaining growth but also addressing social and environmental concerns. From the corporations' perspective, actions taken by the government in response to the need for a more harmonious society have increased the level of corporate social responsibility (CSR) in China, making it a more relevant factor in the process of rapid economic development. It is suggested that the progressive and enlightened changes involved in adopting social elements in Chinese company law (CCL), with an associated emphasis on the rights of employees and creditors, will promote CSR in Chinese companies. The vision of a harmonious society will also encourage positive corporate decisions for the benefit of social welfare beyond mere compliance with regulatory norms. It is necessary to promote a beneficial relationship between corporate economic responsibility and social responsibility within the corporate law framework, in order to make a significant contribution to China's development towards a harmonious society. After the enforcement of CCL 2006, despite positive progress between 2006 and 2011 (reflected in the data regarding the performance of directors' duties towards stakeholders), the rapid development of the Chinese economy also raises many social problems which remain a concern. The enforcement of CSR-related legal requirements still depends on political interference, public awareness and business disclosure of social and environmental issues, all in the context of improvements in and support for a sound legal system in China.*

## A. Introduction

In 2005, Chinese President Hu Jintao instituted the "harmonious society" policy by establishing a new approach towards development in China. It was instructed by President Hu that the country's leading officials and party cadres

* Lecturer in Law, University of Salford. I would like to thanks the anonymous referee for his/her constructive comments and suggestions.

should place "building a harmonious society" at the top of their agendas, in order to build a society which puts people first. The programme is based on the goals of building a well-off society and creating a new socialist situation.[1] The purpose of building a harmonious society is to overcome the drawbacks of the immature and incomplete market within the Chinese socialist market economy, and to solve current and potential problems facing "rural areas, farmers and agriculture, the drainage of farmland, heavy pressure in the workplace and an incomplete social security system".[2] It is a policy to tackle a formidable challenge: managing 1.3 billion people with enormous diversity and across a massive territory.[3]

Over 1600 companies are listed on stock exchanges in China; most of these have been converted from state-owned enterprises (SOEs). With its recent rapid economic progress, China has now replaced Japan as the world's second largest economy.[4] Business evolution and development and corporate behaviours in China will certainly continue to capture the attention of many during the next decade. There is plenty of evidence which proves that the Chinese government is seeking to foster co-operation between business and society, with an expectation of positive responses from companies. Highly visible community partnership opportunities were created by the 2008 Olympic Games held in Beijing, and there was significant business participation in the massive relief efforts after the devastating Wenchuan earthquake in Sichuan province, when Wang Lao Ji, one of China's most well-known and highly esteemed herbal tea and soft drinks companies, donated 100 million RMB on 18 May 2008. A series of major safety scandals, where infant-milk products were found to be contaminated with melamine, spotlighted industry failure and the urgent need for regulatory reform. Furthermore, in response to protests in August 2011 the municipal committee of the Chinese Communist Party and the government of Dalian City ordered an immediate shutdown of the Fujia chemical plant, which produced the potentially toxic chemical paraxylene. Premier Wen Jiabao reaffirmed this decision by stating that "we must not any longer sacrifice the environment for the sake of rapid growth and reckless rollouts".

Corporate social responsibility (CSR) has become an integral part of business management strategy and practice in China. Current thinking about the scope of CSR in China is divided into two camps: the first interprets CSR in a broad sense, encompassing all corporate responsibilities including economic responsibilities, while the second delivers CSR more narrowly and relates it to corporate responsibilities excluding economic responsibilities, but

1 "Harmonious Society", *People's Daily*, 29 September 2007.

2 *Ibid.*

3 HC de Bettignies, "CSR 'Fatigue' and China's Performance" [January 2011] *The GRLI Partner Magazine* 31, 31.

4 At the end of 2010 China's economy was worth close to $5.8 trillion, while Japan's economy was worth $5.474 trillion.

including social, environmental, philanthropic and public services responsibilities, for example in relation to local communities.[5] It was suggested by Du that CSR can be divided into compulsory corporate social responsibilities and voluntary corporate social responsibilities, although it is widely accepted that CSR is normally defined as voluntary responsibilities beyond those required by legislation.[6] Du further suggested that compulsory corporate social responsibilities include measures against child labour, well-managed legal working hours and working environments, and fair treatment for employees without discrimination.[7] It is recognised that corporations will benefit from having a reputation as a company that "does good" by contributing to society in multiple ways; such a reputation might facilitate permission to open and operate business activities, foster a better business reputation, improve employee recruitment, morale and retention, influence consumer preference for products in terms of sales and switching, and bring cost savings from both suppliers and manufacturing.[8]

Questions naturally arise as to what, if any, linkage there might be between the harmonious society and CSR, and what possible contributions could the emphasis on a harmonious society offer to corporations in terms of their ethical improvement. This article explores whether the harmonious society will be relevant and influential in the upgraded and increased CSR engagement that has broadly been adopted in Chinese corporations. If actions drawn up and taken by the government in response to a more harmonious society increase the level of CSR in China and make the harmonious society a more relevant factor in economic development, might there be ways to accomplish this more efficiently through corporate law? It is recognised by the author that corporate

5 L Zhao, "The Transformation and Trend in Corporate Social Responsibility in China" (2005) 2 *Management Research* 7, 7–8.

6 Z Du, "Corporate Social Responsibility and Measures for Enforcement (Qiye de Shehui Zeren Jiqi Shixian Fangshi)" (2005) 4 *Journal of Renmin University of China (Zhongguo Renmin Daxue Xuebao)* 39, 42–44.

7 Du, *ibid*, 43.

8 KH Darigan and JE Post, "Corporate Citizenship in China: CSR Challenges in the 'Harmonious Society'" (2009) *Journal of Corporate Citizenship* 39, 42; for more discussions on the potential benefits for corporations which are socially responsible, see LW Lin, "Corporate Social Accountability Standards in the Global Supply Chain: Resistance, Reconsideration, and Resolution in China" (2007) 15 *Cardozo Journal of International Comparative Law* 321; AF Alkhafaji, *A Stakeholder Approach to Corporate Governance: Managing in A Dynamic Environment* (New York, Quorum Books, 1989); JW Anderson, *Corporate Social Responsibilities* (New York, Quorum Books, 1984); JJ Brummer, *Corporate Responsibility and Legitimacy: An Interdisciplinary Analysis* (New York, Greenwood Press, 1991); SN Brenner and EA Molander, "Is the Ethics of Business Changing" (1977) 58 *Harvard Business Review* 54; KE Goodpaster, "Business Ethics and Stakeholder Analysis" (1991) *Business Ethics Quarterly* 53; A Carroll, *Business and Society: Ethics and Stakeholder Management* (Cincinnati, South-Western Publishing, 1993); LS Munllia and MP Miles, "The Corporate Social Responsibility Continuum as a Component of Stakeholder Theory" (2005) 110 *Business and Society Review* 371; AL Friedman and S Miles, *Stakeholders: Theory and Practice* (Oxford University Press, 2006).

social responsibilities are voluntary corporate actions. However, many corporate actions are precursors to legal regulations, and many types of socially responsible corporate behaviours are also legally required. It is agreed that CSR is not a substitute for regulation to replace national and international legislations.[9] However, the enforcement of CSR will enhance the implementation of relevant statutory obligations, and will encourage positive corporate decisions for social welfare benefits beyond mere compliance with regulatory norms. It is argued that most corporate governance scholars have recognised the connection between "good behaviour towards stakeholders to whom no legal duty is owed and fulfilment of the shareholder primacy obligation required in corporate law and the role the courts have placed in guiding the way".[10]

This article is arranged as follows: Section B overviews the recent development of policy surrounding the harmonious society and notes the government's policy shift from aims related purely to profit and economic growth, towards a more balanced and sustainable framework. Section C examines CSR as a contemporary topic in China, and further discusses possible links with the theme of the harmonious society. It considers how the modern emphasis on the harmonious society fits with a theoretical analysis of CSR and the stakeholder approach, and in so doing highlights some possibilities in law which could act to regulate corporate behaviour in a socially responsible manner.

The article demonstrates that CSR has become institutionalised in China, and it also seems that the dominance of the harmonious society policy reaffirms and enhances the significance of ethical issues in Chinese companies.

[9] There are also arguments that CSR represents a step toward standards which will eventually be regulated, or which view CSR as an antidote to over-regulation; see IL Fannon, "The Corporate Social Responsibility Movement and Law's Empire: Is There a Conflict?" (2007) *Northern Ireland Legal Quarterly* 1, 4–9; see also S Learmount, *Corporate Governance, What Can Be Learned from Japan?* (Oxford University Press, 2002); I Hill, "How Finance Can Help Move CSR up the Agenda" (2006) 16 *The Cost and Management* 5; see also arguments from a common law perspective: *Evans v Brunner Mond Company Limited* [1921] 1 Ch 359; *AP Smith Manufacturing Co v Barlow* [1953] 13 N.J.145; *Shlensky v Wrigley* 237 NE 2d 776 (Ill App Ct 1968); *Green v Hamilton International* (1977) 437 F Supp 723, 729 New York; *R (on the Application of People and Planet) v HM Treasury* [2009] EWHC 3020 (Admin); *Re West Coast Capital (LIOS) Ltd* [2008] CSOH 72, 16 May 2008 (Outer House, Court of Sessions, Scotland, Lord Glennie), [21]; *Stone & Rolls Ltd (In Liquidation) v Moore Stephens (A Firm)* [2009] UKHL 39. For the interests of creditors (as a important external stakeholders) see: *Diplock in Lonrho Ltd v Shell Petroleum Co Ltd* [1980] 1WLR 627; *Lonrho Ltd v Shell Petroleum Co Ltd* [1980] 1 WLR 627; *Re Horsley & Weight Ltd* [1982] 3 All ER 1045; *Brady v Brady* [1988] 3 BCC 535; *Liquidator of West Mercia Safetywear Ltd v Dodd* (1988) 4 BCC 30; *Percival v Wright* [1902] 2 Ch 421; *Multinational Gas and Petrochemical Co. v Multinational Gas and Petrochemical Services Ltd* [1983] Ch 258; *Peskin v Anderson* [2000] BCC 1110; *Yukong Lines Ltd of Korea v Rendsburg Investments Corporation* [1998] BCC 870; *Spies v The Queen* [2000] 201 CLR 603, [2000] 173 ALR 529; *Kinsela v Russell Kinsela Pty Ltd* [1986] 4 NSWLR 722; *Re New World Alliance Pty Ltd; Sycotex Pty Ltd v Baseler* [1994] 51 FCR 425; *Grove v Flavel* [1986] 43 SASR 410; *Jeffree v National Companies and Securities Commission* [1989] 7 ACLC 556; *Re Trizec Corp* [1994] 10 WWR 127; *Re Saul D Harrison & Sons plc* [1995] 1 BCLC 14, *Re Welfab Engineers Ltd* [1990] BCLC 883.

[10] Fannon, *ibid*, 16.

Additionally, it shows links and overlapping aims between the target of establishing a harmonious society by 2020 and corporate objectives in a socially responsible corporation. The expectations of stakeholders are discussed in terms of their potential links with the proposed characteristics of corporations in a harmonious society. Section D analyses stakeholders' interests and changes in the Chinese legal system after recent shifts in government policy towards a more harmonious society. Special attention is given to Chinese company law (CCL) and to attempts to discover harmonious elements adopted in the New CCL 2006.

Enforcement of the law is also discussed in the context of an analysis of data concerning corporations' performance regarding stakeholders' interests from 2006 to 2011. Further suggestions for the future of legal enforcement of CSR-related laws are offered during an examination of three case studies, focusing on the three main stakeholders in building a harmonious society within a corporation—namely, the company's employees, customers and environment.

## B. The Harmonious Society and the Government's Policy Shift

The idea of building a harmonious society is not new for China. There is a variety of evidence of attempts to build a harmonious society in different dynasties in Chinese history. The concept is perfectly compatible with Chinese history and tradition.[11] It is described as a "scientific development concept",[12] which shifts China's primary focus from a model based purely on economic growth to a more balanced, Confucian-style approach aimed at maintaining growth while addressing daunting social concerns.[13] The modernised society policy was suggested by the Chinese government in the Chinese Communist Party's Sixteenth National Party Congress in November 2002. It was emphasised that building a harmonious socialist society is one of the six goals to create a well-off society.

[11] M Anthony, "The New China: Big Brother, Brave New World or Harmonious Society" (2007) 11 *Journal Of Future Studies* 15, 31.

[12] President Hu Jintao, "Scientific Outlook Development", lecture at Yale University, 24 April 2006; in the lecture, Hu clarified that

> "China will pursue a scientific outlook on development that makes economic and social development people-oriented, comprehensive, balanced and sustainable. We will work to strike a proper balance between urban and rural development, development among regions, economic and social development, development of man and nature, and domestic development and opening wider to the outside world; it is also rooted in the culture heritages of the Chinese nation."

[13] JP Gies and B Holt, "Harmonious Society: Rise of the New China" (2009) *Strategic Studies Quarterly* 75, 75.

The SARS crisis occurred in 2003 and the global financial crisis began in 2007, while concerns about social inequalities became a hot topic on the political agenda, thus foreshadowing the political project to develop a harmonious society.[14] Concerns about social inequalities and a perceived "justice gap" in reform policies were influenced by the intensifying and evolving nature of protests since the late 1990s,[15] and by the need, recognised by the Chinese leadership, to reach out to the common people.[16] The leadership of China responded to the unacceptable social costs and political risks of reforms implemented since the late 1970s by placing social justice at the centre of political attention. The harmonious society is seen as a departure from the model that emphasises socialist market reform and economic growth, towards one in which economic aims are balanced against the urgent need to tackle pressing societal and environmental[17] problems in China. It responds to the negative connotations of the pronouncement that "to get rich is glorious",[18] attributed to the former President Deng Xiaoping, who was the driving force behind the move to capitalism after Mao's death, and the focus on GDP and the economy in modern China.

In the party school, President Hu confirmed that the Chinese Communist Party and the central government had made building a harmonious society into a priority because "China is facing thorny domestic issues, as well as a complicated and volatile international situation".[19] Consequently, building a socialist harmonious society was officially noted as one of the five major capabilities of the Communist Party of China during the Fourth Plenum of the Sixteenth National Party Congress in September 2004. Recommendations made in the eleventh Five Year Plan were adopted by the National Party Congress during the Fifth Plenary Session of the Sixteenth National Party Congress in October 2005. In the Recommendations, more specific plans for the grand blueprint of a harmonious society were designed in order to promote social harmony and expand employment with the purpose of improving the social security system, regulating income distribution more rationally and ultimately enriching the spiritual and cultural life of the Chinese people.

[14] A de Haan, "The Financial Crisis and China's 'Harmonious Society'" (2010) *Journal of Current Chinese Affairs* 69, 82–83.

[15] D Kelly, "Guest Editor's Introduction" (2006) 38 *Contemporary Chinese Thought* 3; see also C Wong, "Rebuilding Government for the 21st Century: Can China Incrementally Reform the Public Sector?" (2009) *The China Quarterly* 929.

[16] J Yu, "Social Conflict in Rural China" (2007) 3 *China Security* 2.

[17] G See, "Harmonious Society and Chinese CSR: Is There Really a Link?" (2008) 89 *Journal of Business Ethics* 1, 1–2.

[18] For discussions on Deng's declaration and the Harmonious Society see also GK Sims, "The River Runs Black: The Environmental Challenge to China's Future" (2006) 65 *The Journal of Asian Studies* 403.

[19] "Building Harmonious Society Crucial for China's Progress: Hu", *People's Daily*, 27 June 2006.

The CPC Central Committee approved the "the Resolution on a number of major issues for CPC Central Committee regarding the building of a harmonious socialist society" in the Sixth Plenum of the Sixteenth National Party Congress in October 2006.[20] The Resolution clarifies the steps towards enforcing harmonious society decisions regarding ideology, objectives, tasks, principles and major deployments to build a socialist harmonious society by 2020. The Resolution highlights the

> "importance, guidelines, goals and principles of building a socialist harmonious society: coordinated development; social equity and justice; cultural harmony and the ideological and ethical foundations of social harmony; and the need to improve public administration to build a vigorous and orderly society."[21]

It is affirmed in the Resolution that the concept of a harmonious society will be regarded as an official policy of the Chinese Communist Party.

### C. Corporate Social Responsibilities in China and the Possible Link with the Harmonious Society

As a result of concerted efforts by the government, various Chinese corporations, including SOEs and privately owned companies, are producing sustainability and CSR reports. However, the concept of CSR in China is not new. In the centrally planned economic era after the inception of New China in 1949, corporations always performed good works to benefit society at large, and SOEs used to provide wider employee benefits, such as primary and secondary education for the children of their staff. In the field of human endeavour, three subdivisions can be distinguished: "economic, political and social activity—that is, business, government and society—in every civilization throughout time".[22] The interplay between businesses, society and government regulation creates an environment in which businesses can co-operate smoothly. On the other hand, socially responsible corporations, which act responsibly in relation to both the economic and the noneconomic environment, will also have tremendous impact on the creation of a harmonious society in China.

At first glance, a few possible links between CSR and the harmonious society can immediately be observed. First, the directors of corporations need to make

[20] Xinhua News Agency, "China Publishes Its Resolution on Building a Harmonious Society. State Council Information Office of the People's Republic of China", 15 February 2006, available at http://www.scio.gov.cn/zgxwybd/en/2006/22/200612/t103742.htm (all URLs last accessed on 23 February 2012).

[21] Xinhua News Agency, "China Publishes 'Harmonious Society' Resolution", available at http://www.china.org.cn/english/2006/Oct/184810.htm.

[22] JF Steiner and GA Steiner, *Business, Government, and Society: A Managerial Perspective, Text and Cases* (New York, McGraw-Hill, 13th edn, 2012), 4.

legitimate and fair decisions, and comply with rules regarding fair competition, social norms, business ethics and regulations against bribery. Secondly, corporations need to respect people's rights, especially in their strategic management policies. Thirdly, the philanthropic contributions of corporations to society at large also fit into the theme of a harmonious society, as does the protection of the environment, plants and animals.

Looking at the harmonious society from a theoretical standpoint, the term was defined by President Hu as a society "which gives full play to modern ideas like democracy, the rule of law, fairness, justice, vitality, stability, orderliness and harmonious co-existence between humankind and nature",[23] in a speech given during the event marking the sixtieth anniversary of the United Nations on 15 September 2005. It is viewed as a revolutionary change in mode for the development of China, and it has attracted growing interest from government and academics. Li regarded this policy change as a renewed focus on addressing social and environmental challenges, with a reduced priority given to economic growth where it conflicts with these non-economic objectives.[24] The concept combines aspects of traditional Chinese culture and metaphysics, including Confucian and Taoist thought, with the reality of a modernised and increasingly globalised China. Given the negative fact that greed and self-interest override the traditional Chinese concepts of harmony, family and working together as a group, the emphasis on the harmonious society is collectively a positive move.[25] It is a strong response to problems in China such as "income disparity, the urban and rural development imbalance, unemployment, an aging population and environmental pollution".[26] The idea of the harmonious society reaffirmed its corporate aspects by placing emphasis on corporate responsibility and accountability towards a wider group of constituencies than shareholders—namely, corporate stakeholders.

As for the future of the policy for the development of a harmonious society, a deadline was set in the Sixth Plenum of the Sixteenth Central Committee of the Communist Party to achieve the policy by 2020, overcoming a number of listed disharmonious elements, including:[27]

- widening of the gap between urban and rural development and development between different regions;
- people's rights and interests to be granted concrete respect and guarantees;
- unequal income distribution pattern;

[23] See "Harmonious Society Concept Draws World Attention", *People's Daily*, available at http://english.peopledaily.com.cn/200512/14/eng20051214_227940.html.

[24] P Li, "Scholar Explores Harmonious Society Concept", available at http://www.china.org.cn/english/2005/Mar/121746.htm.

[25] Anthony, *supra* n 11, 31.

[26] Li, *supra* n 24.

[27] See "Communiqué of the Sixth Plenum of the Sixteenth CPC Central Committee", *People's Daily*, available at http://english.peopledaily.com.cn/200610/12/eng20061012_310923.html.

- the employment rate is relatively high, but there is an absence of a social security system covering both urban and rural households;
- the basic public service system should be further improved;
- the efficiency in utilisation of resources needs to be enhanced;
- the need for improvement in environmental management; and
- the need to foster a sound moral atmosphere and harmonious interpersonal relationships.

Looking at the targets listed above, primary stakeholders,[28] including consumers, employees, local communities and the environment, will be regarded as parties whose interests should be taken into account in order to overcome disharmonious elements by 2020. It is also re-emphasised that the policy for a harmonious society is a person-centred governmental idea, placing people first and (from a corporation's point of view) focusing on stakeholders' interests in order to promote a more harmonised and supportive working environment and to create opportunities for sustainable development.

The policy was introduced in recognition of the social and environmental problems that arose as a result of rapid economic development in China.[29] Undeniably, many of these problems are closely related to the protection of stakeholders' interests by companies, which is a direct result of directors' duties stipulated and required under CCL 2006. Consistent with corporate objectives enshrined in Articles 1 and 5, the scope of fiduciary duties of fidelity and diligence to the company embedded in Article 148 have become broader, giving directors legitimacy in taking into account social morality and business ethics. The target also fits with the requirements of ISO 26000,[30] which is widely recognised by the government and corporations in China. It is reaffirmed by results from the questionnaires from the roundtable "Challenges and Opportunities for CSR Service Providers in China—Warming up for ISO

[28] For more discussions on stakeholders see RE Freeman, *Strategic Management: A Stakeholder Approach* (Boston, Pitman, 1984); B Mescher, "The Law, Stakeholders and Ethics: Their Role in Corporate Governance" (2011) 8 *Macquarie Journal of Business Law* 37; MBE Clarkson, MC Deck and NJ Shiner, "The Stakeholder Management Model in Practice" paper presented at the 1992 Annual Meeting of the Academy of Management, Las Vegas, NV; P Goldenberg, "IALS Company Lecture—Shareholder v Stakeholders: the Bogus Argument" (1998) *The Company Lawyer* 33; K Mitchell, BR Agle and DJ Wood, "Toward A Theory of Stakeholder Identification and Salience: Defining the Principle of Who and What Really Counts" (1997) 22 *Academy of Management Review* 853; M Evan and RE Freeman, "A Stakeholder Theory of the Modern Corporation" in M Snoeyenbos, R Almeder and J Humber (eds), *Business Ethics* (New York, Prometheus Books, 3rd edn, 2001).

[29] WT Woo, "Reframing China Policy: The Carnegie Debates; Debate 2: China's Economy—Arguing for the Motion" (Beijing, Carnegie Endowment for International Peace, Central University of Finance and Economics/Washington DC, Brookings Institution/University of California, Davis, 2006).

[30] For more discussions on the International Organisation for Standardization, see the website at http://www.iso.org/iso.

26000".[31] Chinese export-oriented companies and companies in coastal areas are most likely to apply ISO 26000. The guidance identified and set a few core subjects as priorities that a business organisation should address when integrating corporate social responsibilities in their corporate strategies; these include "organisational governance, human rights, labour practices, the environment, fair operating practices, consumer issues and community involvement and development"[32]. Therefore, the target and aims of a harmonious society will be consistent with the objectives of corporations as far as their social responsibilities are concerned. These are core subjects described in the guidelines that are closely related to corporate actions and stakeholders' expectations. However, it is also suggested in the guidelines that social responsibilities are dynamic issues that reflect the evolution of current and future social, environmental and economic concerns.[33]

"The turbulent state of the global economy threatens the financial stability, economic well-being and social contract between business, government and society."[34] In China, the emerging social structure seems to be at risk of succumbing to waves of financial hardship and change, although economic growth has been regarded as the theme of the past three decades. CSR and corporate citizenship created significant social capital, which assists communities in adjusting to the harsh realities of global change and enables businesses to interact with government and non-profit organisations to help people and build a more harmonious community relationship.[35] The corporations are clearly expected to deliver good products and excellent services; but they should also aim to "pursue values, not just value; and to help make the world a better place".[36] The "organic model" argues that a company should function as a social institution with an independent existence, rather than as the private property of its shareholders.[37] According to this model, "ownership", "control" and "public interests" should be separate from each other in the exercise of corporate power.[38] This gives the directors the rights to exercise some latitude to pursue other goals in their daily performance, particularly those which are

[31] For more information on the roundtable see the Sino-German Corporate Social Responsibility Project website at http://www.chinacsrproject.org/News_Show_EN.asp?ID=90.

[32] ISO 26000: Guidance on Social Responsibility (ISO, 2010), ch 6.

[33] *Ibid.*

[34] Darigan and Post, *supra* n 8, 39.

[35] *Ibid*, 40.

[36] J Bakan, *The Corporation: The Pathological Pursuit of Profit and Power* (London, Constable & Robinson, 2004), 31.

[37] J Dean, "Stakeholding and Company Law" (2001) 22 *Company Lawyer* 66, 66–67; see also M Stokes, "Company Law and Legal Theory" in W Twining (ed), *Legal Theory and Common Law* (Oxford, Blackwell, 1986), 155; D Millon, "Theories of the Corporation" (1990) 193 *Duke Law Journal* 20; M Horwitz, "Santa Clara Revisited: The Development of Corporate Theory" (1985) 88 *West Virginia Law Review* 173.

[38] JE Parkinson, *Corporate Power and Responsibility: Issues in the Theory of Company Law* (Oxford, Clarendon Press, 1993), 23.

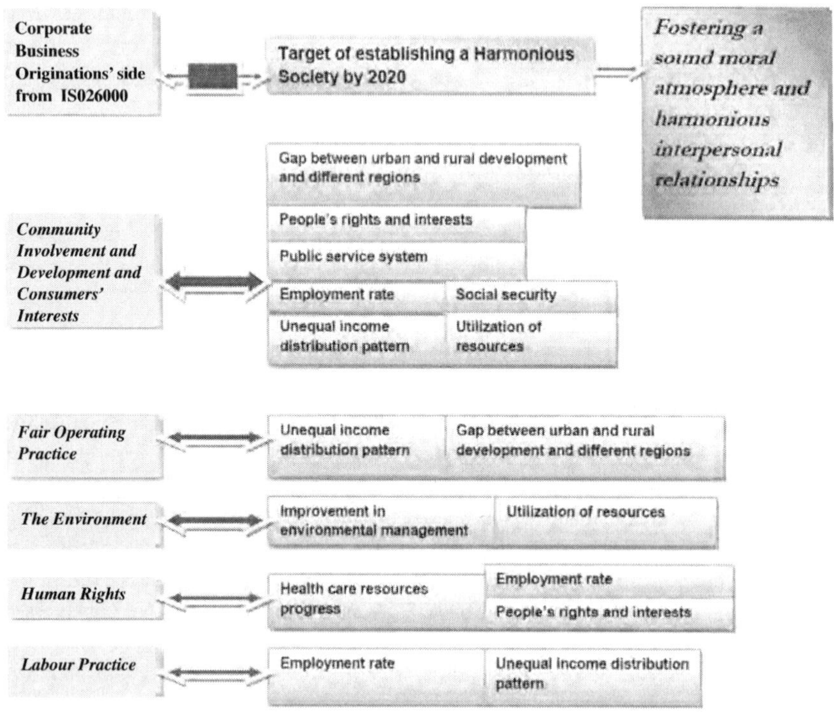


Fig 1 CSR and the Targets of Building a Harmonious Society

more socially responsible than the pure pursuit of shareholder wealth maximisation.

Applying the organic model in the case of China, the relationship between the targets of establishing a harmonious society by 2020 and the social and environmental aspects of corporate objectives can be explicitly demonstrated, as shown in Fig 1. It is obvious that the harmonious society policy and CSR are interrelated, with the core norm or value of corporate social responsibility lying in constructing a human-oriented harmonious society.[39] While the targets of establishing a harmonious society have a direct impact on a company's management strategy with regard to social responsibilities, raising the level of CSR, it is also the case that CSR can be used as a tool for creating a harmonious society in China,[40] by putting emphasis on the goal of common prosperity under the banner of serving the people to improve their quality of life.

[39] D Huang, Y Kong and Z Hua, "Symposium on China's Peaceful Development and International Law" (2006) *Chinese Journal of International Law* 261, 268.

[40] See D Karlsson, "Corporate Social Responsibility: A Tool for Creating a Harmonious Society in China" (Brussels, European Institute for Asian Studies, 2011); see also MH Jensen, "Serve

Responsible business is good business in the long term, having positive effects on customer relations and employee attitudes, and ultimately the share price and the cost of capital.[41] The adoption and application of the stakeholder theory will result in increased wealth for the whole of society, and when businesses correctly implement the strategy it has been likened to a win–win situation.[42] The instrumental power of stakeholder theory suggests that stakeholder management can be employed to achieve shareholder value, and a balance between the interests of the different stakeholder groups is essential in ensuring that an organisation continues to be viable and achieves other performance goals.[43] If the proposition is correct, namely that a link exists between CSR and the harmonious society, it is important to satisfy stakeholders' expectations in order to build a harmonious society at large. For a general commercial

**Table 1: Stakeholders' Expectations towards the Company**

| Stakeholder | Expectations of company | Nature of accountability by the company | Form of legitimacy relationship |
|---|---|---|---|
| Human resources (employees) | Remuneration and other conditions of employment; working conditions, opportunities for advancement and training | Company reports, employment news, bargaining information | Employment and contract law |
| Suppliers of fund (creditors) | Liquidity and solvency of company; value of security; cash generation; reliable repayment | Cover ratios, collateral, cash forecasts | Insolvency law, security regulations and (bank) lending regulations |
| Suppliers | Contractual payment of indebtedness and enduring relationship | Payment according to terms | Contract law, company law |
| Customers | Quality; service; safety; delivery; vfm{WHAT IS VFM?}; product development | Sales literature, advertising, servicing | Sale of Goods Act, contract law |
| General public and local community | Safety of operations; contribution to the community | Safety reports, press reports | Environmental law; company law and tax law |

Sources: DG Woodward, F Edwards and F Birkin, "Organizational Legitimacy and Stakeholder Information Provision" (1996) 7 *British Journal of Management* 340; S Turnbull, "Corporate Governance: Its Scope, Concerns and Theories" (1997) 5 *Corporate Governance* 180.

the People! Corporate Social Responsibility (CSR) in China" (Copenhagen, Asian Research Centre, Copenhagen Business School, 2006).

41 B Tricker, *Corporate Governance: Principles, Policies, and Practices* (Oxford University Press, 2009), 352.

42 S Cooper, *Corporate Social Performance: A Stakeholder Approach* (Aldershot, Ashgate, 2004), 13.

43 NA Shankman, "Reframing the Debate between Agency and Stakeholder Theories of the Firm" (1999) 19 *Journal of Business Ethics* 319.

company, stakeholders' expectations towards the company and the company's potential accountability to stakeholders can be analysed from data in Table 1.

Possible reform actions were also suggested in the Sixth Plenum to tackle these disharmonies, including the following measures:

- social equity and justice as a basic condition of social harmony;
- accelerated construction of a system to ensure social equity and justice, to guarantee people's rights and interests in political, economic, cultural and social fields, and to guide citizens to exercise their rights and fulfil their obligations according to the law;
- Institutional construction should be enhanced and social equality and justice should be safeguarded;
- development of cultural causes and cultural industries should be accelerated; and
- environmental protection and pollution control should be strengthened.

In addition, three logical approaches were suggested for the attainment of a harmonious society in China today:[44] first, the government should take steps to reduce inequalities by implementing a more balanced development strategy to ensure a more progressive redistribution of income through social welfare and services; secondly, the government should develop a fair and legitimate system to promote democracy and resolve social conflicts; and thirdly, it is also important to promote the idea of tolerance when addressing diversity in modern society, since people should learn to respect differences not just in religious beliefs and lifestyles, but also in the political dimension.[45]

The Chinese government responded positively in terms of encouraging more socially responsible corporations. The leaders of China and Chinese SOEs are becoming more conscious of the importance of improving awareness of CSR in the context of an increasingly complex relationship between the government, enterprises and civil society. Chinese leaders are fully aware that there are problems behind the shining statistical figures describing China's economic growth and expansion. China's impressive economic achievements in the past three decades have cost Chinese society many precious historical characteristics. In New York on 23 September 2008, Premier Wen Jiabao stated that "China will learn from the baby milk scandal and seize the opportunity to overhaul food safety control and promote better business ethics" at a luncheon held in his honour by the National Committee and the US–China Business Council.

[44] See the ideas and approaches suggested by Chen and Hu: K Chen, "The Importance of Building a Civilised Society in Building a Harmonious Society" (2006) 33 *Minjian* 1; A Hu, "China in 2020: Comprehensive Well-off and the Goal of A Socialist Harmonious Society" in J Zhou, A Hu and S Wang (eds), *Building a Harmonious Society: The Experiences of Europe and The Exploration of China* (Beijing, Tsinghau University Press, 2007), 165.

[45] KM Chan, "Harmonious Society" in HK Anheier and S Toepler, *International Encyclopedia of Civil Society* (New York, Springer, 2010), 821–23.

Premier Wen emphasised the importance of the enhancement of social morals, and suggested that "businessmen should run their business with the blood of morality".[46] He stated that China will adopt strong measures to ensure more responsible products. On a more generalised level, he also pointed out that "degradation of morality and lack of integrity has become a serious problem which would eventually hamper the rise of China".[47] In an online chat on 27 February 2010, Premier Wen reconfirmed that Chinese entrepreneurs must have "moral blood", and criticised those that cross the line for their own short-term interests because they hurt the interests of the whole of society.[48]

## D. An Effective Legal Environment to Promote a Harmonious Society

It is important to build a stakeholder-friendly legal environment so that managers are able to adopt socially responsible practices, assisting non-shareholder groups in their battles against corporate decisions that ignore stakeholders' interests. "Law's discourse has already signposted the way to consider and resolve corporate governance problems in the broader social responsibility context."[49] CSR is increasingly being appreciated as a crucial component of companies' "intangible assets", which are taking on greater significance in determining how investors view the present and future health of companies.[50] CSR is not designed to transfer the aim of profit maximisation to social purposes. Conversely, CSR supports a rationale that justifies profit maximisation. If company directors take social responsibilities into account, it is more sensible to define the ultimate purpose of directors' duties as the "maximisation of the total creation of wealth".[51] Company directors are required to consider the long-term view of social development in order to establish a healthy ecosystem

[46] See "Wen Jiabao Attends Welcoming Luncheon of American Friendly Organizations and Delivers Speech on China–US Relations", available at http://www.fmprc.gov.cn/eng/wjdt/zyjh/t514790.htm.

[47] See "Wen Jiabao Criticised Milk Clenbuterol: A Serious Moral Decline", available at http://www.cnkeyword.info/wen-jiabao-criticized-milk-clenbuterol-a-serious-moral-decline.

[48] Xinhua News Agency, "News Analysis: China Looks to Central SOEs to back Low-income Housing Project", 5 May 2011, available at http://news.xinhuanet.com/english2010/china/2011-05/05/c_13860819.htm; in particular, the Premier issued a moral sermon towards real estate developers, stating that "as members of society, real estate developers should have social responsibilities and moral blood". He reaffirmed that "within the body of every businessman should flow the blood of morality".

[49] Fannon, *supra* n 9, 3; see also O Hart, "Norms and the Theory of the Firm" (2001) *University of Pennsylvania Law Review* 1701.

[50] K Howell, "Introduction to DTI, Business and Society: Developing CSR in the UK" (DTI (now BIS), March 2001), 1. Around 50% of FTSE-100 companies published formal environmental reports in 2000, and this figure has increased steadily in recent years.

[51] For more discussion on the corporate objectives of social welfare and total wealth creation, see G Kelly and J Parkinson, "The Conceptual Foundation of the Company: A Pluralist Approach"

for their stakeholders and themselves, as well as a favourable natural and business environment for the survival of the company. It is argued that, from the start, voluntary CSR has been socially and economically driven.[52] Under the banner of CSR, it has to be realised that success and shareholder value cannot be achieved "solely through maximising short-term profit but instead through responsible behaviour", and attention to CSR must "bring about a change in business culture so that sustainable objectives become an integral part of corporate strategic planning and routine operational performance".[53]

## 1. Stakeholders' Interests: Key in Building a Harmonious Society from the Corporate Perspective

Like the idea of CSR itself, the role played by the law in CSR's form, implementation and communication has been a topic that has been discussed broadly.[54] It is recognised that CSR seems to work as an informal set of rules, but it also seems to be based on a set of fundamental principles in law. Specific instruments of international law, national law and standards all accommodate the main tenets of CSR.[55] Statutory laws are used by governments as instruments to make corporations undertake specific types of responsibilities, specifically by requiring corporations to report on CSR-related topics. Companies in the US and the UK are recruiting the services of CSR consultancies to produce CSR codes, write or verify CSR reports, train staff in CSR and market their CSR

in J Parkinson, A Gamble and G Kelly (eds), *The Political Economy of the Company* (Oxford, Hart Publishing, 2000), 113, 131.

52 D McBarnet, "Corporate Social Responsibility beyond Law, through Law, for Law: The New Corporate Accountability" in D McBarnet, A Voiculescu and T Campbell (eds), *The New Corporate Accountability: Corporate Social Responsibility and the Law* (Cambridge University Press, 2007), 9, 12.

53 F Martin, "Corporate Social Responsibility and Public Policy" in R Mullerate (ed), *Corporate Social Responsibility: The Corporate Governance of the 21st Century* (London, Kluwer Law International, 2005), 77, 78.

54 See JE Kerr, "The Creative Capitalism Spectrum: Evaluating Corporate Social Responsibility through a Legal Liens" (2008) *Temple Law Review* 831; JE Kerr, "A New Era of Responsibility: A Modern American Mandate For Corporate Social Responsibility" (2009) 78 *UMKC Law Review* 327; JE Kerr, "Sustainability Meet Profitability: The Convenient Truth of How the Business Judgment Rules Protect a Board's Decisions to Engage in Social Entrepreneurship" (2007) *Cardozo Law Review* 623; J Zhao, "Modernising Corporate Objective Debate towards a Hybrid Model" (2011) 62 *Northern Ireland Legal Quarterly* 361; J Zhao, "Promoting More Socially Responsible Corporations through UK Company Law after the 2008 Financial Crisis: The Turning of the Crisis Compass" (2011) *International Commercial and Company Law Review* 275; K Buhmann, "Corporate Social Responsibility" (2006) 6 *Corporate Governance* 188; B Choudhury, "Serving Two Masters: Incorporating Social Responsibility into the Corporate Paradigm" (2008) 11 *University of Pennsylvania Journal of Business Law* 631; C Parker, "Meta-regulation: Legal Accountability for Corporate Social Responsibility" in McBarnet *et al*, *supra* n 52; McBarnet, *supra* n 52, 9; B Horrigan, "21st Century Corporate Social Responsibility Trends—An Emerging Comparative Body of Law and Regulation on Corporate Responsibility, Governance, and Sustainability" (2007) 4 *Macquarie Journal of Business Law* 85.

55 Buhmann, *ibid*, 199.

credentials.[56] Legal requirements will play an increasingly important role in enforcing voluntary corporate policies. New legal developments are directly or indirectly fostering voluntary stakeholder policies and market pressure, to make what business previously perceived to be voluntary, or beyond the law, in fact legally enforceable.[57] Legal doctrines and processes are employed by corporations as part of their strategy, and market forces are stimulated and facilitated by legal measures.[58]

The legal environment consists of legislation, regulation and litigation. The general trend in the legal environment, with all three aspects on the increase, is towards the constraint of business behaviour.[59] With the growth of large and public corporations since the nineteenth century and an increase in the number and complexity of related laws and regulations, companies find themselves with continuously expanding duties to protect the rights of stakeholders, including employees, consumers, the public and even their competitors. Despite the fact that the requirements for ethical behaviour and CSR go beyond legal duties, "they are plucked from the voluntary realm and encoded into law".[60] Furthermore, corporations have always needed to anticipate expanding liabilities with necessary training for directors because of rapid technological change and the emergence of new laws and regulations.

When corporate directors are held responsible for their misbehaviour due to their lack of respect for human rights, labour rights and environmental protection, non-governmental organisations, investors, current or future employees, consumers, the local community, media and other stakeholders, it is necessary for the government to reassess the law, including its underlying principles.[61] While some progressive scholars and reformers have attempted to protect stakeholders by changing corporate law, others have looked to other legal regimes to regulate corporate behaviour. Directors will be required by laws outside of corporate law to consider the legal rights of various stakeholders. Corporate governance practices are typically influenced by an array of legal domains, such as securities regulation, accounting and auditing standards, tax law, contract law, employment law, environment law, consumer protection law and insolvency law.[62] All these decisions are made under the mandatory legal rules embodied by these legislative instruments. Those duties towards various stakeholders are the fiduciary duties of company directors, and are inseparable from corporate law and corporate governance. As a result, directors will, when

56 McBarnet, *supra* n 52, 9, 11.
57 *Ibid*, 31.
58 *Ibid*.
59 Steiner and Steiner, *supra* n 22, 42.
60 *Ibid*, 41.
61 Buhmann, *supra* n 54, 199.
62 OECD, "OECD Principles of Corporate Governance" (2004) available at http://www.oecd.org/dataoecd/32/18/31557724.pdf, 2.

they manage a corporation, find "their decision tree considerably trimmed and their discretion decidedly diminished by mandatory legal rules enacted in the name of protecting stakeholders".[63]

In China, the development of CSR continued when Liu Rui from Shanghai was relieved after he realised that it was illegal for his boss to refuse to sign a labour contract with him, and his rights were protected by the Labour Contract Law 2008.[64] Suan Xian from Beijing was pleased to be acknowledged in the government's proposals for drafting employment promotion regulation, which will prohibit discrimination against physically challenged and disabled people in the workplace. He is confident that he will be able to find a job after years of struggle. These incidences demonstrate that law and regulations have changed the daily life of Chinese people for the better, and illustrate the country's critical shift from regulating economic matters to resolving social problems.[65]

The changes in legal systems aimed at building a harmonious society come from various sources. These changes all focus on people's rights, and put people at the centre of society. The statutory changes that took place before and after the government's harmonious society policy were implemented are regarded as legislative evidence of building a people-centred society. It explicitly states in a constitutional amendment[66] that "the State respects and protects human rights".[67] The criminal law's requirements regarding the final verdict in all death sentences in the Supreme People's Court are also evidence of the Chinese government's commitment towards a harmonious society. It is stipulated in Chinese criminal law that

> "the death penalty shall only be applied to criminals who have committed extremely serious crimes. All death sentences except for those according to law should be decided by Supreme People's Court, [and] shall be submitted to the Supreme People's Court for verification and approval."[68]

Similarly, other evidence can be found in the Chinese Company Law 2006, the Labour Contract Law 2008, the Environmental Protection Law 2008, the Trade Union Law of China (amended in 2001), the Law on Consumer Interest Protection 1994, the Law on Air Pollution (amended in 2000), the Food Safety Law 2009, the Circular Economy Promotion Law 2009, the Renewable Energy Law 2006, the Law on Prevention and Control of Water Pollution (amended in 2008) and other secondary regulations, including the Regulations on Supervisors over Labour Rights and Security, the Rules on Minimum Wages, the CSR

[63] A Winkler, "Corporate Law or the Law of Business? Stakeholders and Corporate Governance at the End of History" (2004) 67 *Law & Contemporary Problems* 109, 111.
[64] See Labour Contract Law of China 2008, Art 14.
[65] Z Zhe, "Toward Harmonious Society through Rule of Law", *China Daily*, 10 March 2008.
[66] Approved by the Second Session of the Tenth National People's Congress.
[67] See Constitution of the People's Republic of China, Art 33.
[68] Chinese Criminal Law 1997, Art 48.

Guidelines for State Owned Enterprises by SASAC 2008 and the Regulations on Administrative Penalties for Damage to the Environment.

It is especially noticeable in the response to the financial crisis 2008 that one of the main purposes of government bodies in banking regulatory works was "to ensure the fulfilment of social responsibility by commercial banks".[69] This was stated in the "New Guidelines on Corporate Governance of Commercial Banks in China (Consultative Document), put forward in July 2011 and formulated in accordance with the Corporate Law of China 2006. In addition, in the same guidelines, the sound corporate governance of commercial banks was refined to include "a scientific development strategy, values and codes of conduct as well as social responsibilities".[70] Furthermore, in chapter 4 of the guidelines for "Development Strategies, Value Criteria and Social Responsibilities", the importance of CSR in commercial banks is once again reaffirmed through emphasis on considerations of the interests of depositors and other stakeholders within the bank.[71] It is significant to note that this legislative instrument has come a step further than previous documents by putting a "focus on the mid- to long-term development plans, strategic goals, business philosophies, market positioning, capital management and risk management and so on". Mid- to long-term development of strategic management goals in conjunction with valuable business philosophies are being carried out in parallel for the first time in Chinese legislative instruments aimed at prompting more social responsibility in commercial banks in China.

CSR and economic goals are related closely in both directions, since good CSR policies can also bring

> "the advisements of competitive advantage, better reaching market segments like ethical consumers and socially responsible investors, and enhanced opportunities for strategic alliance or other partnership as major business opportunities for corporations with external constituencies, and, from an internal point of view, enhancement of labour relations and employee commitment, and the achievement of overall better financial and strategic results."[72]

The approach adopted in legislation rests at the level of business organisation governance, since directors are required to interconnect various stakeholders' interests in the formation of their strategic management policy. The emphasis on CSR extends the reach of strategic planning towards people, and particularly bank employees, by adoptating harmonious society policies in the guidelines and putting people at the centre of society. Commercial banks are required to

[69] "Guidelines on Corporate Governance of Commercial Banks in China (Consultative Document)" (August 2011) Art 5.

[70] *Ibid*, Art 7.

[71] *Ibid*, Art 70.

[72] C Keinert, *Corporate Social Responsibility as an International Strategy*(Heidelberg, Physica-Verlag, 2008) 90.

"set up sound value criteria, corporate culture and business philosophies that highlight social responsibility so as to motivate employees to better fulfil their responsibility".[73] Apart from the internal stakeholders' interests, the interests of external stakeholders were also considered in the guidelines in relation to the public at large. Commercial banks are required to "fulfil their social responsibility in the economy, environment and social welfare", and have a disclosure requirement regarding their "social responsibility to report to the public on a regular basis".[74]

The legislative progress mentioned above demonstrates that the Chinese government also realises the importance of the long-term sustainable development of business. It is argued that recent developments in CSR theory have provided a socially responsible performance paradigm, establishing a solid foundation for stakeholder-oriented strategic management policies.[75] Recent developments in relation to CSR, such as corporate strategic policies, environmental stewardship and sustainability, may all be viewed as implementations of stakeholder theory.[76] Ignoring CSR in the post-crisis context would demonstrate a serious lack of understanding of the nature of business, since this ethical crisis is not unprecedented, even though its severity is.[77]

## 2. Enforcement of Corporate Law to Promote More Socially Responsible Corporations within a Harmonious Society

The theme and policy of "building a harmonious society" was implemented by the Chinese Communist Party in 2006 following President Hu's 2005 vision of introducing a harmonious society. Despite the fact that the vision and the policy do not explicitly refer to CSR, it is clear that CSR was initially, and still is, considered to be instrumental in achieving the socio-economic goals of this new policy.[78] A distinct body of comparative corporate law and regulations relating to CSR has become a key emergent trend in research on corporate governance and law in a number of jurisdictions.[79] International political

[73] "Guidelines on Corporate Governance of Commercial Banks in China (Consultative Document)", Art 77.

[74] *Ibid*, Art 80.

[75] J Zhao, "'Promoting More Socially Responsible Corporations through UK Company Law after the 2008 Financial Crisis: Turning of the Crisis Compass' (2011) 9 *International Commercial and Company Law Review* 275, 283–84.

[76] S Zambon and A Del Bello, "Towards a Stakeholder Responsible Approach: The Constructive Role of Reporting" (2005) 5 *Corporate Governance: The International Journal of Business in Society* 130.

[77] C Pedamon, "Corporate Social Responsibility: A New Approach to Promoting Integrity and Responsibility" (2010) *Company Lawyer* 172 at 172.

[78] CC Pinney, "Why China Will Define the Future Corporate Citizenship" (Centre For Corporate Citizenship, Boston College, Carroll School of Management, 2008), available at http://www.bcccc.net/index.cfm?fuseaction=Page.ViewPageandPageID=1905.

[79] B Horrigan, "21st Century Corporate Social Responsibility Trends—An Emerging Comparative Body of Law and Regulation on Corporate Responsibility, Governance, and Sustainability" (2007) 4 *Macquarie Journal of Business Law* 85, 85.

moves that draw attention to the impact of corporations on a triple bottom line (people, plant and people)[80] have produced a plethora of international regional agreements, encouraging governments to implement them through national legislations.[81] This is also the case in China. Chinese corporate law and regulation have reached new levels during the national engagement with CSR.[82] The move towards the adoption of CSR in the regulations is not an intentional result of rational individual or group decisions, but has occurred spontaneously since 2005 with rapid economic growth and the change to a market economy within the emerging framework of the harmonious society.[83] It is recognised by mainstream economic and legal scholars that the business world involves more than just corporate profit maximisation, free competition and enabling laws.[84] CSR concerns challenges to justice in the social, economic and environmental arenas, involving those who are affected by the behaviour of businesses. Local CSR initiatives in China are part of the global governance scheme, which not only creates a huge business space for corporations, but also helps national legislators to regulate more unusual areas.[85] The Chinese government has given increasing attention to CSR, while the Chinese regulatory and legislative authorities are suggesting that a commitment to CSR policy should adopted as a condition of approval for business licenses. Civil awareness campaigns on CSR are also aimed at building business compliance.[86]

After the enforcement of CCL 2006 and the financial crisis of 2008, it is interesting to note corporate responses to these legal requirements regarding CSR, as well as the impact of the global business climate on CSR in China. In the current hard times faced by the world, caused by the worst financial crisis in recent years, do people sincerely care about CSR? It might seem logical that attention should turn to profit-making and profit maximisation, in order to reduce the negative effects on the economy brought about by the financial crisis. But can China afford to profit at the expense of CSR? Environmentalists and other pluralists in the areas of corporate law and corporate governance are worried that sustainability and increased corporate responsibility towards social

80 See J Elkington, *Cannibals with Forks; The Triple Bottom Line of the 21st Century Business* (Stony Creek, CT, New Society Publishers, 1998).

81 C Nakajima, "The Importance of Legally Embedding Corporate Social Responsibility" (2011) *Company Lawyer* 257, 257.

82 X Huang, *Corporate Social Responsibility: Theory and Practice in China* (Bejing, Social Science Academic Press), 190–91; see also JH Liu, "Some Thinking about Strengthening CSR" in J Lou and P Gan, *Studies on Corporate Social Responsibility* (Beijing, Peking University Press, 2009), 199; J Shi and W Yang, "Legal Reanalysis of CSR" in Lou and Gan, *ibid*, 243.

83 M Feng, Z Chen and Z Wang, *Corporate Social Responsibility in China in a Harmonious Society* (Beijing, Economic Science Press, 2009), 46–48.

84 J Liu, *Corporate Social Responsibility* (Beijing, Law Press, 1999), 85–86.

85 LW Lin, "Corporate Social Responsibility in China: Window Dressing or Structural Change" (2010) *Berkeley Journal of International Law* 64, 67.

86 PB Potter, "Co-ordinating Corporate Governance and Corporate Social Responsibility" (2009) 39 *Hong Kong Law Journal* 675, 686.

and philanthropic concerns are being removed from the boardroom agenda as companies tighten their belts in the face of turbulent stockmarkets, the "credit crunch" and a looming economic slowdown.[87] Irresponsible corporate actions will eventually burst the risk balloon; the lesson to be learnt from the financial crisis of 2008 is to regulate risk management and act responsibly in line with public interests.[88] However, a question arises as to how effective the CCL has been in giving stakeholders in China "stakeholder legitimacy" through the business sector's impact on environmental and social issues.

*(a) Legislative Initiatives in Adopting CSR*

Compared with CCL 1994, which was mainly aimed at facilitating the profit-seeking motivation of SOEs, one of the most important initiatives in CCL 2006 is the adoption of CSR elements as part of the corporate objectives. With support from various sources, including the policy aimed at building a harmonious society, legislators finally decided to incorporate CSR into corporate law related legislation in China. Article 5 of CCL 2006 states that "a company must, when engaging in business activities, abide by the laws and administrative regulations, observe social morals and business ethics, be in integrity and good faith, accept regulation of the government and the public, and undertake social responsibilities". At the principle-based level, company directors are required to abide by the law and regulations while they focus on wealth and profit growth. "It is implied in Article 5 that apart from the interests of shareholders, employees and other stakeholders, the performance and activities of the company have a deep impact on market economic rules and public social interests."[89] Directors and supervisors are required by law to act in a socially responsible manner towards both internal and external stakeholders when pursuing shareholder wealth. Legitimacy is given to directors of corporations to observe social, moral and business ethics by undertaking social responsibilities.

The adoption of Article 5 of CCL 2006 is partly the result of the emphasis on the harmonious society as the current guiding ideology in China, but it also has a chain-reaction effect, calling for sustainable development and social welfare on the part of companies to combat the "disharmonious elements" in companies' decisions. The responsibilities and obligations prescribed by Article 5 are beyond the fundamental requirements and the bottom line for enterprises; they rest at "a higher level of responses from enterprise to social values and

87 See T Macalister, "A Change in the Climate: Credit Crunch Makes the Bottom Line the Top Issue", *The Guardian*, 6 March 2008; BF Souto, "Crisis and Corporate Social Responsibility: Threat or Opportunity?" (2009) 2 *International Journal of Economic and Applied Research* 36.

88 Xinhua News Agency, 'Social Responsibility Helps Business Fight Crisis', 9 April 2009, available at http://www.china.org.cn/china/opinion/2009-04/09/content_17578054.htm

89 J Zhao, "The Regulation and Steering of Corporate Social Responsibility in China: Stories after the Enforcement of Chinese Company Law" (2011) *International Commercial and Company Law Review* 400, 401.

expectations at ethical and moral levels".[90] In a more academic and systemic manner, Article 5 of CCL 2006 could be interpreted, based on the corporate responsibility pyramid,[91] as requiring companies to undertake corporate social responsibilities in the course of doing business. First, companies should comply with laws and administrative regulations (their legal responsibility); secondly, they should conform to social morality and business ethics, act in good faith, and subject themselves to government supervision (their ethical responsibility). The economic responsibility is enshrined in Article 1 by emphasising the interests of shareholders and the company as a whole.[92]

It is undeniable that there are many problems in the wording and the future implementation of Article 1. However, statutory interpretation is always regarded as a necessary path towards understanding, judging and solving problems in legislation, with necessary assistance from judgments on cases.[93] The scope and nature of Article 5 of CCL 2006 is still unclear both judicially and legislatively.[94] Regardless of difficulties concerning the enforcement of the legal requirements, Chinese legislators have taken an important step in realising the importance of ethical and social responsibilities at the primary stage of the development of a sound corporate governance system.

One of the "most problematic and controversial problems" in Chinese corporate governance and company law is the relationship between companies and their employees, particularly the ways in which workers are treated and managed.[95] The protection of the rights of employees dates back to the old company law, which did not explicitly refer to CSR but echoed some aspects of it. Employee participation in corporate governance, adopted in the old CCL 1994, "was more than a politically and economically path-dependent product".[96] More than a decade later, the new CCL 2006 further emphasises employees' rights in addition to Article 5, which gives directors legitimacy in considering stakeholders' interests.[97] Article 17 requires a company to "protect the lawful rights and interests of its employees, conclude employment contracts with the employees, buy social insurances, [and] strengthen labour protection

[90] L Zhou and Z He, "On Corporate Social Responsibility 'Beyond Law' in China" (2009) 4 *Frontiers of Law in China* 457, 460.

[91] AB Carroll, "The Pyramid of CSR: Toward the Moral Management of Organizational Stakeholders" (1991) 34 *Business Horizons* 39, 40–41.

[92] Zhao, *supra* n 89, 402.

[93] W Zhang, *Jurisprudence in China* (Beijing, Higher Education Press, 2007), 272; the formal interpretation to law in China can be divided into legislative or statutory interpretation, administrative interpretation and judicial interpretation; the most highly regarded interpretations will be the "Judicial Interpretations of the Supreme People's Court".

[94] J Lou, "A Literal Interpretation of Article 5, Clause 1 of China's Corporate Law and its Approach of Performance" in Lou and Gan, *supra* n 82, 224.

[95] L Miles, "Chinese Corporate Governance: but What about the Workers?" (2011) *Company Law Newsletter* 1, 2.

[96] Lin, *supra* n 85, 68; see CCL 1994, Arts 45, 52, 55, 56, 62, 121 and 122.

[97] CCL 2006, Art 17, 18, 52, 117, 118 and 126.

so as to realise safe production", as well as "reinforce the vocational education and in-service training of its employees so as to improve their personal quality". This extra provision may help to illustrate the intention of Article 5.[98] CCL 2006 also sets out a series of new stipulations regarding employees' participation. As far as limited liability companies are concerned, based on Article 45,

> "the members of the board of directors of a limited liability company invested in and established by two or more state-owned enterprises, or by two or more other state-owned investment entities, shall include representatives of the staff and workers of the company. Other limited liability companies can include representatives of the staff and workers of the company."[99]

Compared with the old company law, the new company law enlarges the scope of employees as internal directors in all forms of company. As far as joint stock limited companies are concerned, according to Article 109 of CCL 2006,

> "the members of the board of directors may include the representatives of the staff and workers of the company. The representatives of the staff and workers on the board of directors shall be democratically elected by the staff and workers of the company through the staff and workers' congress, workers' assembly or other forms."

This piece of legislation ensures that the voice of the employees will be heard and employees' interests will be considered at board meetings when decisions are made.

Labour unions also play an important role in promoting the interests of employees in the new Chinese corporate governance model. According to Article 18, a company's employees shall organise a labour union to carry out activities and safeguard the lawful rights and interests of the employees. The company shall provide necessary conditions for its labour union to carry out these activities.[100] "The labour union shall, on behalf of the employees, sign collective contracts with the company with respect to remuneration, working hours, welfare, insurance, work safety and sanitation, and other matters."[101] To make a decision on restructuring or any major issues concerning business operation or the formulation of important rules and regulations, a company shall solicit the opinions of its labour union, and solicit the opinions and suggestions of its staff and workers through the staff and workers' congress or in any other way.[102] This provision enhances employee participation in the governance of the company by enabling employees to enforce their democratic controlling rights over the company's decisions. It also affirms the improvement of Chinese

98 Zhao, *supra* n 89.
99 CCL, Art 45.
100 CCL 2006, Art 18.
101 *Ibid.*
102 *Ibid.*

government policy regarding CSR as far as employees' interests are concerned. However, Article 18 is only a primary principle-based provision, and focuses only on the "major issues" in corporate actions. Chinese corporate law still has a long way to go in order to reach a systematic and complete provision for employee participation in corporate governance.

Furthermore, according to CCL 2006,

> "a limited liability company shall have a supervisory board composed of no less than three members. Where a limited liability company has a small number of shareholders or is comparatively small in scale, it may have one or two supervisors instead of a supervisory board."[103]

The supervisory board shall supervise "the acts of the directors and senior executives performing their functions".[104] Additionally, they can "bring a lawsuit against the directors or senior executives in accordance with the provisions of Article 152 of Company Law 2006".[105] CCL 2006 provide that employees' representatives within the firm can act as supervisors[106] to secure the protection of workers within the firm by exerting pressure on directors to act as a mouthpiece for the workers.[107]

CCL 2006 allows non-state-owned enterprises to include representatives of their employees in their board of directors for the first time.[108] This progressive and enlightened approach corrects the misunderstanding that employees are the "hosts of the country" and are the only parties who are allowed to participate in corporate governance actions in SOEs. The new company law reconfirms the important position of employees as primary stakeholder groups in all forms of company in China.[109] However, regardless of whether the company could or should include representatives of its employees in the board of directors according to CCL 2006, there are no stipulations regarding the percentage or the exact number of employee directors on the board, which makes the employee director provision purely a cosmetic stipulation. Therefore, the percentage or the actual number of employees who can sit on the board of directors should be stipulated in detail, to ensure that these requirements are more than just hollow provisions which are difficult to implement.

103 CCL 2006, Art 52.
104 *Ibid*, Art 54(2).
105 *Ibid*, Art 54(6).
106 *Ibid.*
107 L Miles, "Chinese Corporate Governance: But What About the Workers?" (2011) *Company Law Newsletter* 1, 4; X Chao, "In Search of an Effective Monitoring Board Model: Board Reforms and the Political Economy of Corporate Law in China" (2006) 22 *Connecticut Journal of International Law* 1.
108 CCL 2006, Arts 45 and 109.
109 J Zhao and S Wen, "Promoting Stakeholders' Interests in the Unique Chinese Corporate Governance Model: More Socially Responsible Corporations?" (2010) *International Company and Commercial Law Review* 373, 380.

Moreover, it is stipulated in Article 1 of CCL 2006 that this legislation is enacted in order to "standardise the organisation and activities of companies, to protect the legitimate rights and interests of companies, shareholders and creditors, to maintain socio-economic order and to promote the development of the socialist market economy",[110] reaffirming the trend towards CSR as far as the legislative tenets are concerned. Furthermore, the interests of creditors, as primary external stakeholders, are explicitly mentioned in Article 1, along with the interests of the shareholders and the company itself.[111]

*(b) Common Regulation Elements between Establishing a Harmonious Society and Socially Responsible Concerns in Corporate Law*

Creating a harmonious society has been recognised as a driving force behind the growth of CSR. It is important to provide specific principles, laws, regulations and rules in order to place the development of a harmonious society in a prominent position. It is obvious that CCL 2006 adopts elements of the harmonious society policy in corporate legislation in order to promote stakeholders' interests in a more socially responsible manner. Apart from the link illuminated in Fig 1 (see above), there are also overlaps in the following areas: regulatory purposes, philosophy, environment and the controlling regulatory body. It is obvious that the related purposes of both CSR and the harmonious society rest on social and environmental concerns, shifting from the primacy of wealth maximisation and economic growth. Both aspects of government policy are a response from the Chinese government to the fact that its social and environmental burdens have outweighed its rapid economic growth in the last 25 years. The common ultimate purpose of both is to ensure the long-term interests of social welfare in a sustainable manner.

Part of the appeal of CSR is that it can lead to tremendous benefits for corporate identity and integrity when done in a sustainable manner. It is a win–win strategy for the mutual benefit of corporations and society.[112] As far as the regulatory philosophy is concerned, Chinese traditions and Chinese history, including Confucian thought, Taoism and *Guanxi* between people, the government and business institutions, all have a deep impacts on CSR and the

[110] CCL 2006, Art 1.

[111] For more discussions about stakeholders' interests and CSR in China see Zhao, "Modernising Corporate Objective Debate" *supra* n 54; Q Bu, "China's New Approach to CSR in Congo: Is the Leverage Turning to China" (2010) *International Business Law Journal* 485; for a discussion on corporate responsibility reports in China see AJ Sulkowski, SP Parashar and L Wei, "Corporate Responsibility Reporting in China, India, Japan and the West, Japan, and the West: One Mantra Does not Fit All" (2007 08) *New English Law Review* 787.

[112] Z Xu and N Liu, "Research on Win Win Management Control Mode of CSR Based on Society Harmony and Corporate Sustainable Development" in Proceedings of the 2008 International Conference on Management Science and Engineering, available at http://www.bmtfi.com/upload/product/200910/2008glhy02a19.pdf.

harmonious society, and make the social function of corporate law in China unique in the global field of corporate governance, especially when compared to classic market-oriented or network-oriented corporate governance models.

As for regulating the environment, both CSR and the harmonious society have become increasingly important since 2005, when the government realised the negative effects of over-emphasising GDP figures and economic growth, shifting focus instead to recognise the importance of establishing a more people-centred, unprejudiced and sustainable environment to make China a safe, reliable and attractive place to do business. The economic environment in modern China will not allow the Fortune 500 companies that existed 25 years ago to function today because they failed to adopt a strategy of sustainability.[113] Lastly, the Chinese Communist Party is the controlling regulatory body for both CSR and the harmonious society. Building a harmonious society is a central theme that will be implemented in law, regulation, social policy, management style and people's realisation and understanding across the whole of society.[114]

*(c) Enforcement of CSR-Related Law in China: Challenges and Opportunities for Building a Harmonious Society*

It is commonly accepted in China, as a reflection of Confucian philosophy,[115] that if an ideal man likes wealth, let him obtain and use it responsibly; this is claimed to be the origin of CSR in China.[116] In a harmonious society, the idea is that a responsible businessperson will carry out his or her business in a morally responsible manner. The Westernised concept of CSR was introduced to China back in the mid-1990s. CSR-related elements were accommodated in legislation in China as the result of an external push from multinational corporations, as well as internal driving factors from the modernised role of SOEs and the strong civil society with more demanding consumers, suppliers and local communities. With broader media coverage, more transparent information disclosure and better awareness of CSR, the leaders of government, legislators, civil society and consumers have begun to regard CSR as an important tool with which engage and challenge business. There has been development

[113] See W Valentino "Corporate Social Responsibility and Innovation", speech of at the 27th China Daily CEO Roundtable Luncheon, available at http://ceoroundtable.chinadaily.com.cn/cdrt/cdrt27/CSRBEGINS.html.

[114] There will of course be advantages and disadvantages to this approach, and the related arguments are worthy of future research; for a good discussion of the state-centric relational approach and society-centric governance, see S Bell and A Hindmoor, *Rethinking Governance: The Centrality of the State in Modern Society* (Cambridge University Press, 2009), 1–20.

[115] See Confucius (Kongzi), *The Confucian Analects*; it is argued that "Fu yu gui, shi ren zhi suo yu ye, bu yi qi dao de zhi, bu chu ye" ["Wealth and being rich is desired by everyone. However, ideal man should get it responsibly"].

[116] G Whelan, "Corporate Social Responsibility in Asia: A Confucian Context" in S May, G Cheney and J Roper (eds), *The Debate over Corporate Social* (Oxford University Press, 2007), 105.

in the regulatory environment and an evolution in civil society to act as both watchdog and partner to corporations in China.[117]

1. Improvements in Stakeholder Protection after the Enforcement of CCL 2006?

The use of the term "stakeholder" to refer to the various interests who participate in a business has been commonly accepted since the publication of Freeman's book *Strategic Management*[118] in 1984. The concept of stakeholders was defined as "those groups without whose support the organisation would cease to exist".[119] They have legitimate interests in or claims on the operations of the firm.[120] The groups which are most frequently seen as stakeholders are employees, customers, creditors, local communities, the environment, government, and society or the public at large. The stakeholder theory was defined by Clarkson, who stated that

> "the firm is a system of stakeholders operating within the larger system of the host society that provides the necessary legal and market infrastructure for the firm's activities. The purpose of the firm is to create wealth or value for its stakeholders by converting their stake into goods and services."[121]

The literature surrounding CSR and stakeholder theory has been widely embraced.[122] An important feature of the CSR approach is a move away from the traditional shareholder value principle to the stakeholder model, under which the directors are expected to owe responsibilities to wider society generally.[123] After the enforcement of CCL 2006, it is worthwhile to observe the directors' performance in engaging with various constituencies for a wider impact on society and the environment. Questions have been raised, such as: "Does the company clearly describe the roles of stakeholders, including clients,

117 L Zu, *Corporate Social Responsibility, Corporate Restructuring and Firm's Performance* (Berlin, Springer-Verlag, 2009), 45.

118 *Supra* n 28. For some examples demonstrating the acceptance of the term in major academic writings see Alkhafaji, *supra* n 8; JW Anderson, *Corporate Social Responsibilities* (New York, Quorum Books, 1984); Brummer, *supra* n 8; Brenner and Molander, *supra* n 8; Clarkson *et al*, *supra* n 28; Goodpaster, *supra* n 8.

119 Freeman, *supra* n 28, 31–32.

120 Carroll, *supra* n 8, 57; see also A Santana, "Three Elements of Stakeholder Legitimacy" (2012) 105 *Journal of Business Ethics* 257; R Phillips, "Stakeholder Legitimacy" (2003) 13 *Business Ethics Quarterly* 25.

121 M Clarkson, "A Risk Based Model of Stakeholder Theory" in *Proceedings of the Second Toronto Conference on Stakeholder Theory* (Toronto, Centre for Corporate Social Performance and Ethics, University of Toronto, 1994).

122 For more discussions on the collaborations see J Tsoi, "Stakeholder Perceptions and Future Scenarios to Improve Corporate Social Responsibility in Hong Kong and Mainland of China" (2010) 95 *Journal of Business Ethics* 391, 392–93.

123 I Carr and O Outhwaite, "Controlling Corruption through Corporate Social Responsibility and Corporate Governance: Theory and Practice" (2011) 11 *Journal of Corporate Law Studies* 299, 315.

suppliers, creditors, community and employees?"; "Is the company clear in the information disclosed to the public about environmental protection, the company's social responsibilities and charitable activities?"; and "Does the company provide an employee share scheme or other long-term employee incentive compensation plan relating to the creation of shareholder value?"

In a study carried out by the Centre for Corporate Governance, the Chinese Academy of Social Science and Protiviti Consulting,[124] a scoring system was used to evaluate various corporate governance aspects of the performance of 100 companies, based on the data gathered from official and/or publicly available sources, such as annual reports, articles of association, websites of the stock exchanges and the companies' websites as of 31 December 2010.[125] References were made to the OECD Principle of Corporate Governance, and the assessment was conducted under the six classic corporate governance categories,[126] including the "roles of stakeholders" in corporate governance. The combined average score for corporate governance for all the sample companies in 2011 was 63.6. Fig 2 shows that "roles of stakeholders" scored the third lowest, with an average of 58.6. However, this category showed the biggest improvement since 2006 compared with the other six categories.[127]

For the first time, the scores of the "roles of stakeholder" (which scored 34.2 in the 2009 assessment) exceeded the scores of the "responsibilities of supervisor" and "responsibility of board of directors". From the data, it is not hard to see that companies' performances in terms of both stakeholders' interests and "responsibility of board of directors" are below average. However, the trend towards improvement fits with the development of internationalised corporate governance. Chinese corporate governance is still at a compliance stage. Reform of the corporate governance framework in China, instigated by "active initiative of shareholders and co-management of stakeholders", is necessary.[128]

From the data analysis, adopting stakeholder theory in corporate management strategies is becoming more popular in Chinese corporations, and stakeholders

[124] "Corporate Governance Assessment Summary Report of the 100 Top Chinese Listed Companies for 2011", available at http://www.protiviti.com/zh-CN/Headlines/Documents/CN-2011-Corporate-Governance-Survey.pdf.

[125] *Ibid*, 2.

[126] These include "shareholders' rights", "fairness to shareholders", "role of stakeholders in corporate governance", "information disclosure and transparency", "responsibilities of board of directors" and "responsibilities of board of supervisors"; see OECD, *supra* n 62.

[127] From 21.0 in the 2006 assessment, 24.9 in the 2007 assessment, 27.3 in the 2008 assessment, 34.2 in the 2009 assessment and 55.6 in the 2010 assessment. The general improvement rate is 12.48%, with a 61.35% improvement for "shareholders' rights", 2.47% improvement for "fairness to shareholders", 179.05% improvement for "role of stakeholders in corporate governance", 4.46% deterioration for "information disclosure and transparency", 24.84% improvement for "responsibilities of board of directors" and 30.15% improvement for "responsibilities of board of supervisors".

[128] Centre for Corporate Governance, etc, *supra* n 124.

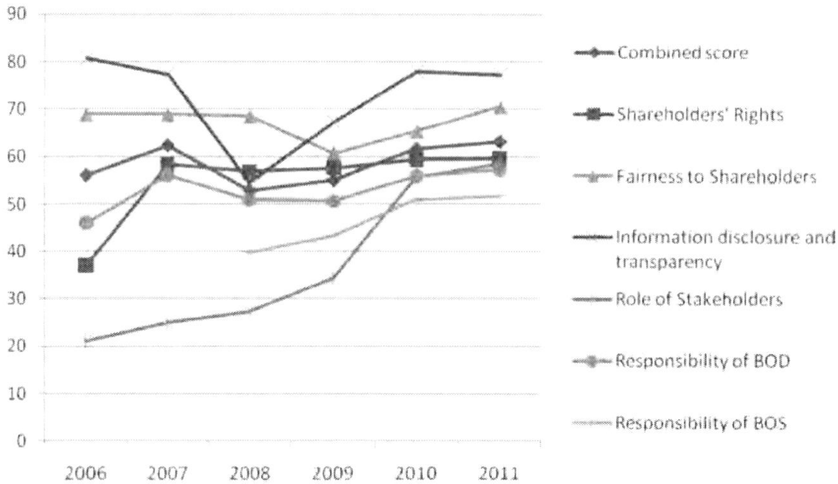


Fig 2 Distributions of Combined Sources and Individual Scores for the Six Corporate Governance Categories for the Six Years from 2006 to 2011. Based on the Centre for Corporate Governance, Chinese Academy of Social Science and Protiviti Consulting, "Corporate Governance Assessment Summary Report of the 100 Top Chinese Listed Companies for 2011", 3

are gaining a heightened profile in corporations. For those directors who are enthusiastic about balancing shareholder and stakeholder concerns, stakeholder theory offers them theoretical support and legitimacy (as adopted in Articles 1 and 5 of CCL 2006) to take stakeholders' interests into account by achieving a balance of risks and rewards.[129] Furthermore, from the perspective of obtaining more enforceable requirements for the consideration of stakeholders' interests, it will be a positive legislative step for China to include various stakeholders' interests in the directors' fiduciary duties, learning from the UK's legislative experience of the enlightened shareholder value principle.[130] It would be sensible to remind directors that, as well as the interests of shareholders, they also have to consider the interests of other constituents who are part of the company and have certain claims on the corporation's profits, no matter whether these claims are fixed or residual.[131] Systematic protections for stakeholders will mean that the directors must have a more thorough understanding of their duties. At the same time, the increasingly important role played by

[129] Dean, *supra* n 37, 69.

[130] See Section 172, Companies Act 2006; see also A Keay, *The Enlightened Shareholder Value Principle and Corporate Governance* (London, Routledge, 2012).

[131] Zhao, *supra* n 89, 403–04.

stakeholder engagement will force the establishment of a harmonious society to have regard to these issues.

2. Irresponsibility and Legal Responses in China after the Enforcement of the New Company Law: The Next Step Forward?

Despite the positive reflection from the performance data regarding companies' attitudes towards stakeholders, the rapid development of the Chinese economy also raises many social problems which remain a concern. Over the past few years, media reports have highlighted various incidents that demonstrate poor CSR practice in China. Although the general public seems to be gradually accepting the increasing number of high net worth individuals who have emerged, as well as their continually growing wealth, many people still cannot "rub off the deeply ingrained prejudice against wealth" because of their traditional beliefs that there is something inherently wrong with being rich.[132] This prejudice can also lead to crises of unfaithfulness, confidence and trust from the public towards corporations, which normally act to generate wealth and which are controlled and owned by the rich. This crisis of trust damages the stakeholders' moral reliance on corporations' socially responsible actions, and the public are starting to become suspicious about whether CSR is a means for more profit and wealth or an end in itself.

Employee suicides, faulty products for consumers, toxic emissions into the environment and overworked, underpaid or underage employees have all been major topics in the popular press. Attention to CSR is gradually being enhanced in the context of the current economic crisis, and corporations' socially responsible behaviours aimed at protecting their stakeholders from widespread "waves of layoff" are winning universal praise.[133] With a poor image of CSR in the globalised market, the willingness of individual companies to perform socially responsible actions will collectively improve the situation by building public trust and enhancing their competiveness in the long term. CSR is seen as a rewarding investment for the future, pointing companies towards a sustainable direction for development. The government and individual companies have adopted numerous environmental and social regulatory policy strategies, both mandatory and voluntary.[134] However, "with these regulations on the book, enforcement has been relatively lax".[135] It is argued that "incorporating CSR into law mires CSR in the problems of the Chinese legal system" due to ambiguity and unpredictability in Chinese legislations and deficiencies in implementation.[136] In the author's opinion, although it is too early to judge,

[132] H Li, "Don't Hate the Rich, Be One of Them", *People's Daily*, 2 April 2009.
[133] Xinhua News Agency, *supra* n 88.
[134] See Lin, *supra* n 85, 67–81; Zhao, *supra* n 89, 402–25.
[135] J Sarkis, N Li and Q Zhu, "Winds of Change: Corporate Social Responsibility in China" [2011 January–February] *Ivey Business Journal* 1, 1.
[136] Lin, *supra* n 85, 96.

incorporators can fundamentally change poor CSR records and practices in China; the data discussed in the previous subsection has already suggested an improvement since 2006.

However, there has been no shortage of controversy in China involving CSR-related issues when corporate actions seriously harm the rights of stakeholders, and the law seems very weak and inefficient in dealing with these cases. In the next section, the position and treatment of the main stakeholders in the process of building a people-centred harmonious society, including employees, the environment and consumers, will be discussed with the use of case studies to investigate the Chinese government's commitment to CSR. Regarding the interests of employees, as the important stakeholders built into CSR strategies with the aim of moving towards a harmonious society,[137] the enforcement of a Labour Contract Law in China in 2008 had a great impact on the treatment of employees, and also on how employees view their rights, in order to offer employees greater and more enforceable rights.

The requirements embedded in the law have also dramatically increased employers' costs, caused some companies to go out of business or to leave China for other jurisdictions, and caused many others to show reduced profits. It is argued that the Employment Contract Law 2008 is causing a major shakedown in the Pearl River and Pearl River Delta areas, where more than 8,000 companies went into insolvency or relocated their businesses. Conflict arises between the aim of CCL, to make China an attractive place for investments, and that of the Labour Contract Law, which has made China less attractive because of the duties imposed on employers. The Labour Contract Law is a big challenge for corporations in terms of their competitiveness and business ethics. It is not disputed that the promulgation and effect of this new labour law will have a long-term impact on the improvement of labour standards in China; however, its short-term impact is not so positive and cannot be overstated, since many articles, such as open-end contracts,[138] set overly high standards that cannot be reconciled with reality, and the new law has to rely heavily on the enhancement of government intervention for enforcement.[139]

Regarding the environment, the recent oil leak case at Bohai Bay has stimulated discussions about CSR in China in the context of public interest litigation. The State of Oceanic Administration estimated that the oil spill

[137] According to Art 1 of the Labour Contract Law of China 2008:

> "This Law has been formulated to improve and perfect the labour contract system, to make explicit the rights and obligations of both parties of the labour contract, to protect the lawful rights and interests of labourers and to build and develop harmonious and stable labour relationships".

[138] Chinese Labour Contract Law 2008, ss 12, 14 and 15.

[139] B Wu and Y Zheng, "A Long March to Improve Labour Standards in China: Chinese Debates on the New Labour Contract Law", The University of Nottingham China Policy Institute Briefing Series Issue 39, 8.

had polluted 5,500 square kilometres of Bohai Bay, making it the most serious marine ecological incident in China to date.[140] The spill and subsequent cover-up raised questions about corporate environmental transparency regarding public safety. Misleading statements about the spill, describing the damages caused, were issued by ConocoPhillips. Furthermore, there was a gap of 1 month between the report from ConocoPhillips to the State Ocean Administration and the release of the information to the public. Based on the Marine Environment Protection Law of China 1983, the State Administrative Department of Marine Affairs should file litigation on behalf of the nation against the polluters[141] for the discharging fee, the cost for eliminating the pollution and compensation for the loss sustained by the state.[142] The State Ocean Administration declared that it would sue ConocoPhillips China for ecological compensation. However, at the time of writing, nearly 5 months after the incident, no litigation has been filed.

According to Article 108(1) of the Chinese Civil Procedure Law, "the plaintiff must be a citizen, legal person, or an organisation having a direct interests with the case" in order to meet the conditions for filing a lawsuit. This requirement sets up a legal barrier which prevents non-governmental organisations from filing lawsuits in the interests of the public. The Bohai incident has led to discussion of a draft legal amendment that will enable relevant authorities and social groups to file public interest litigation in environmental pollution and food safety cases by including "relevant authorities" in the civil procedure law passed by the Standing Committee of the National People's Congress, the legislature in China, on 28 October 2011. In this case, pressure from the public played a determining role in law reform and CSR development.

It is obvious that the further development of CSR in China has to be achieved by informing the public, raising awareness of CSR-related issues.[143] Furthermore, the importance of environmental discourse should also be addressed, with the government's institutional mechanism for disclosure an important institutional underpinning for socialist democracy.[144] According to an official statement by Mr Pan Yue, Vice Minister of the State Environmental Protection Administration, environmental disclosure is a significant move to establishing a harmonious society, acting as a bridge for communication between the public

140 Xinhua News Agent, "CNOOC: Oil Leak in Bohai Bay Sealed", 25 October 2011.

141 Marine Environment Protection Law of China 1983, Art 5.

142 *Ibid*, Art 41.

143 Knowledge Wharton, "Corporate Social Responsibility in China: One Great Leap Forward, Many More Still Ahead", 29 April 2010.

144 Positively, the Shenzhen and Shanghai Stock Exchanges have taken environmental disclosure on board and released a "Guide to Listed Companies' Social Responsibility" by Shenzhen Stock Exchange, and a "Guide to Environmental Information Disclosure for Companies Listed on the Shanghai Stock Exchange".

and the government through which the public is able to exercise environmental rights to monitor development projects and polluting companies.[145]

With regard to faulty products and the health and safety of consumers, the Chinese baby milk scandal in 2008 gave China a timely reminder of bad practices in CSR. However, Zhao Lianhai, a Chinese activist who campaigned for better compensation for victims of the scandal and himself the father of a baby victim, was jailed for two-and-a-half years.[146] Zhao started a website called "home for kidney stone babies", enabling information exchange between the victims of the scandal. The website was later blocked and Zhao was sentenced to imprisonment on charge of "causing a serious disturbance".[147] As for the wrongdoers, the boss of the melamine workshop and his associate were given the death penalty, while the Sanlu dairy chief was sentenced to life imprisonment.[148] However, the sentences for government officials detailed after the scandal were never announced.[149]

This suggests that it is necessary to reconsider the reaction of the public and the government's responses to CSR. It is clear that inefficiency in the enforcement of CSR-related laws is not only a consequence of deficiencies in Chinese law enforcement. The problem is a collective one, with causes ranging from a poor information disclosure system, a disrespect of human rights records and unregulated political power to a high degree of political inference in the law, corporate governance and CSR.[150] This is worrying if the idea of a harmonious society is to help China in fostering a corporate business environment. This was noted by Liu Mengxiong, a member of the national committee of the Chinese People's Political Consultative Conference, who called for Zhao's release: "the government's decision to jail a man viewed favourably by the

[145] See Ministry of Environmental Protection of People's Republic of China, "Shoubu Huanjing Xinxi Gongkai Banfa Chutai Qiangzhi Huanbao Bumen he Wuran Qiye Gongkai Huanjing Xinxi: PanYue Huyu yi Gongzhong Shendu Canyu Tuidong Wuran Panjian" ["The Introduction of the First Regulation on Environmental Disclosure and Enforcement of Information Disclosure for Environmental Agencies and Heavy-Pollution Companies: Mr Yue Pan is appealing for In-depth Public Participation to Minimised Pollution and Emission"], 25 April 2008.

[146] "China Jails Tainted Milk Activist Zhao Lianhai", *BBC News Asia-Pacific*, 10 November 2010.

[147] Chinese Criminal Law 1997, s 293.

[148] "China to Execute Two over Poisoned Baby Milk Scandal", *The Guardian World News*, 22 January 2009.

[149] "China Court Jails Father of 'Tainted Milk Child", *The Guardian World News*, 22 January 2009.

[150] For more discussions on political interference and CSR, see PA Gourevitch and J Shinn, *Political Power and Corporate Control: The New Global Politics of Corporate Governance* (Princeton University Press), chs 4 and 6; W Li and R Zhang, "Corporate Social Responsibility, Ownership Structure, and Political Interference: Evidence from China" (2010) 96 *Journal of Business Ethics* 631; YL Cheung, W Tan and Z Zhang, "Does Corporate Social Responsibility Matter in Asia Emerging Market?" (2010) 92 *Journal of Business Ethics* 401; H Li, L Meng, Q Wang and L Zhou, "Political Connections, Financing and Firm Performance: Evidence from Chinese Private" (2008) 87 *Journal of Development Economics* 283.

public would only cast aspersions on the government and weaken public opinion on the justice system".[151]

From these three cases studies of corporate behaviours and their impacts, it is clear that Chinese CSR practices are unique, just like the Chinese control-based corporate governance model.[152] In the rapid process of Chinese economic development, social problems caused by profit-driven corporate decisions are hindering sustainability development in China. Radical restructuring and privatisation in an atmosphere of irresponsible corporate behaviour has brought severe social instability and a wide range of stakeholder reactions.[153] The enforcement of the law related to CSR in promoting stakeholders' interests depends heavily on political interference, public awareness, business disclosure of social and environmental issues, and the improvement and support of a sound legal system in China. The purpose of legal enforcement is to maintain a good corporate image, avoid unnecessary legal proceedings and consumer resistance, improve the efficiency of production and optimise the management of supply chains in a socially responsible manner. These aspects are key, from the point of view of the corporation, in supporting the enforcement of corporate objectives stipulated in CCL in terms of CSR and business ethics, in order to achieve the ultimate goal of establishing a genuine harmonious society.

The current enforcement of CSR-related law is still far from satisfactory. Enforcements are not clear, predictable or effective.[154] Enforcement is largely dependent on political power and government interference.[155] With the unique corporate governance system in China, the government could play an effective role in promoting CSR by adopting a relational approach suggested by Albareda *et al.*[156] Such a framework would apply to CSR public policies, permitting corporations and their stakeholders to analyse the vision and strategy of the government in promoting CSR by taking into account the new relation-

[151] China Decoded: Culture, News, and Stories from China, "Still Toxic: Father Protecting China Tainted Milk Scandal Jailed" (November 18 2010) available at http://www.chinadecoded.com/2010/11/18/still-toxic-father-protesting-china-tainted-milk-scandal-jailed/ (last accessed on 26 November 2011); see also H Xie and K Du, "Proposal for the case of Zhao Lianhai from National People's Congress and Chinese People's Political Consultative Conference", available at http://www.chinaelections.org/newsinfo.asp?newsid=207026 (last accessed on 26 November 2011).

[152] For the unique corporate governance model in China, see OK Tam, "Ethical Issues in the Evolution of Corporate Governance in China" (2002) *Journal of Business Ethics* 303; Zhao and Wen, *supra* n 109, 377–78; M Yan, "Obstacles in China's Corporate Governance" (2011) *Company Lawyer* 311.

[153] Zu, *supra* n 117, 301.

[154] X Wang, "Government Function on Cultivating CSR—A Thinking on Loss of Truck Fence" (2010) 5 *International Journal of Business and Management* 162, 164.

[155] For more discussion on CSR, corporate governance and political interference see C Shi, *The Political Determinants of Corporate Governance in China* (London, Routledge, 2012).

[156] L Albareda, JM Lozano, A Tencati, A Midttun and F Perrini, "The Changing Role of government in Corporate Social Responsibility: Drivers and Responses" (2008) 17 *Business Ethics: A European Review* 347, 359.

ships that the government is establishing with various social agents, including business and social organisations.

The study of three cases of CSR-related incidents and the government's application of law and regulations in each case shows how broad the scope of CSR-related law is. A common understanding and perception of the concept of CSR within the unique Chinese political framework and implementation strategies is vital for building a harmonious relationship between corporations, their stakeholders and the public at large. The application of CSR within the government's agenda in China is a domestic government-centred approach, with reference to international principles, norms and standards. A clearer blueprint of a CSR framework with Chinese characteristics is dependent on a clearer, broader and more globalised understanding of "increasing interdependent political, regulatory and commercial exchanges between sectors, and the perceptions and challenges different stakeholders".[157] This common understanding will speed up the construction of a system of mutual trust by providing a positive environment for companies to develop and implement CSR. At the same time, the government is obliged to set up regulations and opportunities to foster the development of CSR practice, and to extend the remit of CSR to ease the current crisis of trust in China

From an international perspective, along with the increasing influence of the "Made in China" brand and China's formal approval to join the World Trade Organization, many trade protections have already been implemented, such as anti-dumping, quality and technical barriers, and green barriers. From a domestic perspective, in the context of very rapid economic development, the conflict between social and economic benefits in Chinese corporations is becoming more significant. The government should play a leading role in responding to the urgent need for CSR. This role should be composed of a combination of: regulator, establishing and implementing relevant regulations and policies to improve CSR; promoter, raising awareness of social responsibility to promote the country's international and social image; and supervisor, strengthening the supervisions and punishing behaviours that are harmful to society and the environment at large.[158]

## E. Conclusions

The harmonious society, deeply rooted in Confucian tradition, has buttressed popular belief in the merits of respecting and caring towards the community

[157] *Ibid*, 360; see also DA Detomasi, "The Multinational Corporation and Global Governance: Modelling Global Public Policy Network" (2007) 71 *Journal of Business Ethics* 321; J Moon, "Business Social Responsibility and New Governance" (2002) 37 *Government and Opposition* 385.

[158] Wang, *supra* n 154, 164.

as part of an extended family. The application of the function of the family goes beyond the traditional limit of one's relatives, expanding to include the community, the country and society at large. According to the belief system based on these values, "duty to one's national family is morally espoused and an integral component to achieving the greatest possible good—a harmonious society".[159] The concept of the harmonious society is affirmed as an official policy of the Chinese Communist Party, which has a plan with clear targets to achieve the policy by 2020. This vision shifts China's primary focus towards a more balanced, people-centred and sustainable model aimed at maintaining growth but also addressing social and environmental concerns.

It can be concluded from the arguments in this article that history, politics and culture constitute the foundation for a comprehensive understanding of CSR in China. CSR is increasingly being appreciated as a crucial component of companies' "intangible assets", which are taking on greater significance in determining how investors view the present and future health of companies.[160] It can be concluded that a link does exist between CSR and the central tenets of a harmonious society. The harmonious society, under which people's rights are given the highest priority, will be reflected in corporations by an emphasis on stakeholders' interests in order to promote a more harmonised and co-operative working environment with sustainable development strategies for various stakeholders. The CSR movement has been a major factor in shifting corporate governance theory in a stakeholder-friendly direction, by demanding that companies go beyond the creation of short-term shareholder wealth in pursuit of broader objectives, such as sustainable growth, equitable employment practices, and long-term social and environmental well-being.[161] This is also the purpose of building a harmonious society from a corporate perspective, with an emphasis on "fostering a sound moral atmosphere and harmonious interpersonal relationships". This link also suggests that, conversely, the political and social environment has a marked effect on corporations by applying pressure on directors in the development of their strategic management policies.[162]

It has been found that the progressive and enlightened changes involved in adopting social elements in company law, as well as the emphasis on employees' rights, are beneficial in promoting CSR in Chinese companies, not only in SOEs but also in private companies, in order to achieve the target of establishing a harmonious society. Legitimacy has been given to the boards to act in

[159] Darigan and Post, *supra* n 8, 45; JM Burns, GR Goethals and G Sorenson (eds), *Encyclopedia of Leadership* (Minneapolis, Sage, 2004).

[160] Howell, *supra* n 50, 1; around 50% of FTSE-100 companies published formal environmental reports in 2000, and this figure has increased steadily in recent years.

[161] CA Williams and JM Conley, "An Emerging Third Way? The Erosion of the Anglo-American Shareholder Value Construct" (2005) 38 *Cornell International Law Journal* 493.

[162] J Cramer (ed), *Corporate Social Responsibility and Globalisation: An Action Plan for Business* (Sheffield, Greenleaf Publishing, 2006), 68–71.

a socially responsible manner by recognising the different tiers of responsibility defined in Article 5, going beyond mere compliance with regulatory norms for the benefit of the people in the corporation. The government plays a triple role in the enforcement of the law, promoting CSR as a regulator, a supervisor and a promoter. The constructive relationship between the harmonious society, CSR and progressive elements in CCL 2006 can be illustrated in Fig 3.

The regulation of morally oriented responsibility will remind and encourage corporate directors to promote their responsibility towards various stakeholders, and should ensure that people are always placed at the centre of corporate decisions. After the enforcement of CCL 2006, despite positive progress between 2006 and 2011, reflected in the data regarding the performance of directors' duties towards stakeholders, the rapid development of the Chinese

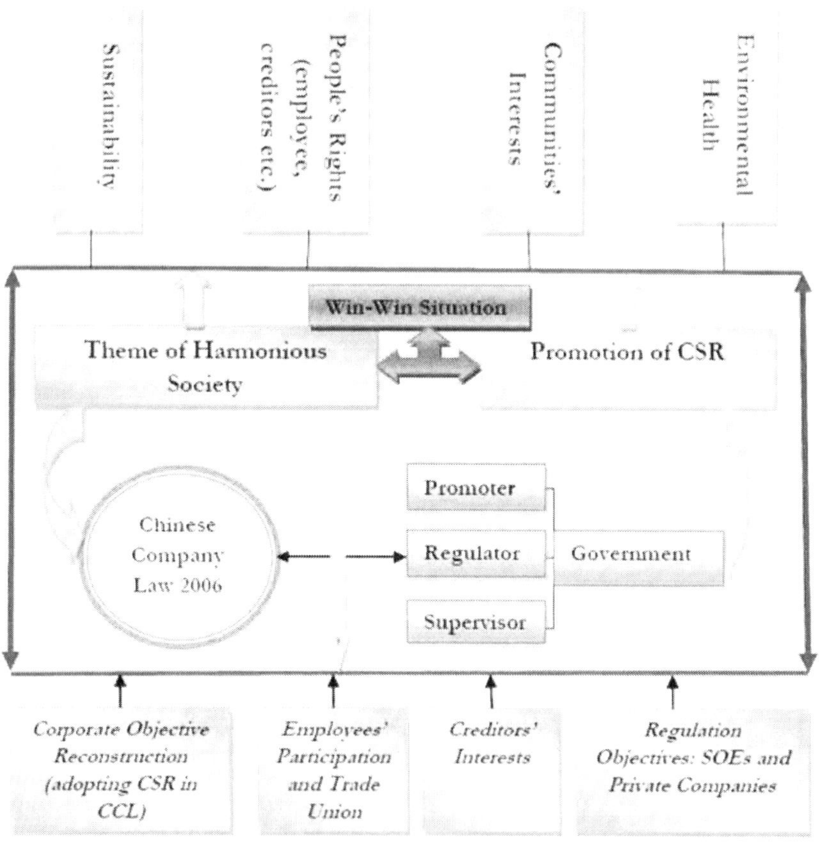


Fig 3 Connecting CSR, the Harmonious Society and Company Law

economy also raises many social problems which are still a cause for concern. The enforcement of CSR-related legal requirements still depends on political interference, public awareness, business disclosure of social and environmental issues, and the improvement and support of a sound legal system in China. After numerous CSR scandals in China, it is time to reconsider how to benefit society through commitment and trust between stakeholders and corporations, not only in China but also globally. The harmonious society is still only a start. It is a reminder for every Chinese person of the dangers of irresponsible behaviour, and it also helps Chinese people form a positive opinion about the future of their country.

# [31]

*Bulletin of the National Institute of Ecology* 15: 227-238, 2005
Gupta et al. (Editors): **Ecology and Environmental Management: Issues and Research Needs**


# Environmental Laws in India: Challenges for Enforcement

V.K. AGARWAL*
*Professor of Law, and Dean, Academic Affairs, Kurukshetra University, Kurukshetra 136119, India*

## ABSTRACT

There is no dearth of legislations on environmental protection in India but their enforcement has been far from satisfactory. There is need for the effective and efficient enforcement of the Constitutional mandate and other environmental legislations. The creative role of judiciary has been significant and laudable. Pursuant to the Constitutional provisions contained in Articles 48A and 51A(h), many Public Interest Litigations have been instituted in the Supreme Court of India against many industries for failing to provide adequate pollution control and also against Pollution Control Boards to direct them to take appropriate measures to ensure pollution control. For the purpose of efficient and effective enforcement of these lays, it is necessary to set up an Adjucatory Body which should consist of legal as well as technical experts. Caring for regulating and protecting the environment is essentially a desire to see that national development should proceed along the rational sustainable laws.

*Key Words*: Water Pollution, Air Pollution, Environmental Protection, Sustainable Development, Public Interest Litigation, Judiciary,

## INTRODUCTION

Today, the conservation, protection and improvement of human environment are major issues all over the world. Human environment consists of both physical environment and biological environment. Physical environment covers land, water and air. Biological environment includes plants, animals and other organisms. Both physical and biological environment are inter-dependent. Industrialisation, urbanisation, explosion of population, over-exploitation of resources, disruption of natural ecological balances, destruction of a multitude of animal and plant species for economic reasons are the factors which have contributed to environmental deterioration.[1] One country's degradation of environment degrades the global environment for all the

---

1 *Sachidanand Pandey v. State of West Benga'*, AIR 1987 SC 1109

countries.[2] The problem of environmental pollution has acquired international dimension and India is no exception to it.

In the present paper, an attempt has been made to briefly outline the Indian laws which are primarily and more relevant to protect and improve the environment. The enforcement of these laws has also been examined and evaluated.

## CONSTITUTIONAL AND LEGISLATIVE MEASURES

Stockholm Declaration of 1972 was perhaps the first major attempt to conserve and protect the human environment at the international level. As a consequence of this Declaration, the States were required to adopt legislative measures to protect and improve the environment. Accordingly, Indian Parliament inserted two Articles, i.e.,, 48A and 51A in the Constitution of India in 1976,[3] Article 48A of the Constitution rightly directs that the State shall endeavour to protect and improve the environment and safeguard forests and wildlife of the country.

Similarly, clause (g) of Article 51A imposes a duty on every citizen of India, to protect and improve the natural environment including forests, lakes, river, and wildlife and to have compassion for living creatures. The cumulative effect of Articles 48A and 51A (g) seems to be that the 'State' as well as the 'citizens' both are now under constitutional obligation to conserve, perceive, protect and improve the environment. Every generation owes a duty to all succeeding generations to develop and conserve the natural resources of the nation in the best possible way.[4] The phrase 'protect and improve' appearing in both the Articles 48A and 51A (g) seems to contemplate an affirmative government action to improve the quality of environment and not just to preserve the environment in its degraded form.

Apart from the constitutional mandate to protect and improve the environment, there are a plenty of legislations[5] on the subject but more relevant enactments for our purpose are the Water (Prevention and Control of Pollution) Act, 1974; the Water (Prevention and Control of Pollution) Cess Act, 1977; the Air (Prevention and Control of Pollution) Act, 1981; the Environment (Protection) Act, 1986; Public Liability Insurance Act, 1991; the National Environment Tribunal Act, 1995 and the National Environment Appellate Authority Act, 1997; the Wildlife (Protection) Act, 1972; the Forest (Conservation) Act, 1980.

The Water Act provides for the prevention and control of water pollution and the maintaining or resorting of the wholesomeness of water. The Act prohibits any poisonous, noxious or polluting matter from entering into any stream or well. The Act provides for the formation of Central Pollution Control Board and the State Pollution

---

2 See Armin Rosencranz, Shyam Divan and Martha L.Noble, *Environmental Law and Policy in India* (1991), p. 25

3 Inserted by the *Constitution (Forty-second Amendment) Act, 1976*

4 *State of Tamil Nadu* v. *Hind Store,* AIR 1981 SC 711; see also *Rural Litigation and Entitle Ji: at Kendra v. State ofUttar Pordesh,* AIR 1987 SC 359

5 E.g. Indian Forest Act, 1927; the Factories Act, 1948; the Atomic Energy Act, 1962; insecticide 1968.

Control Board. The new industries are required to obtain prior approval of such Boards before discharging any trade effluent, sewages into water bodies. No person, without the previous consent of the Boards shall bring into use new or altered outlet for the discharge of sewage or trade effluent into a stream or well or sewer or on land. The consent of the Boards shall also be required for continuing an existing discharge of sewage or trade effluent into a stream or well or sewer or land.

In the *Ganga Water Pollution* case[6], the owners of some tanneries near Kanpur were discharging their effluents from their factories in Ganga without setting up primary treatment plants. The Supreme Court held that the financial capacity of the tanneries should be considered as irrelevant while requiring them to establish primary treatment plants. The Court directed to stop the running of these tanneries and also not to let out trade effluents from the tanneries either directly or indirectly into the river *Ganga* without subjecting the trade effluents to a permanent process by setting up primary treatment plants as approved by the State Pollution Control Board.

The Water (Prevention and Control of Pollution) Cess Act, 1977 aims to provide levy and collection of a cess on water consumed by persons carrying certain industries and local authorities to augment the resources of the Central Board and the State Boards constituted for the prevention and control of water pollution. The object is to realise money from those whose activities lead to pollution and who must bear the expenses of the maintaining and running of such Boards. The industries may obtain a rebate as to the extent of 25%[7] if they set up treatment plant of sewage or trade effluent.

The Air Act has been designed to prevent, control and abatement of air pollution. The major sources of air pollution are industries, automobiles, domestic fires, etc. The air pollution adversely affects heart and lung and reacts with hemoglobin in the blood. According to Roggar Mustress, the American Scientist, air pollution causes mental tension which leads to increase in crimes in the society.

The Air Act defines an air pollutant as any 'solid, liquid or gaseous substance including noise present in the atmosphere in such concentration as may be or tend to be injurious to human beings or other living creatures or plants or property or environment.' The Act provides that no person shall without the previous consent of the State Board establish or operate any industrial plant in an air-pollution control area. The Central Pollution Control Board and the State Pollution Control Board constituted under the Water Act shall also perform the power and functions under the Air Act. The main function of the Boards under the Air Act is to improve the quality of air and to prevent, control and abate air pollution in the country.

The permission granted by the Board may be conditional one wherein stipulations are made in respect of raising of stack height and to provide various control equipments and monitoring equipments. It is expressly provided that persons carrying on industry shall not allow emission of air pollutant in excess of standards laid down by the Board.

---

[6] *M.C.Mehta v. Union of India*, AIR 1988 SC 1037. See also *Bhavani River v. Sakthi Sugar Limited* AIR 1998 SC 2059

[7] Substituted for '70%', w.e.f. 26.1.1992

In Delhi, the public transport system including buses and taxies are operating on a single fuel CNG mode on the directions given by the Supreme Court.[8] Initially, there was a lot of resistance from bus and taxi operators. But now they themselves realise that the use of CNG is not only environment friendly but also economical.

Noise has been taken as air pollutant within the meaning of Air Act. Sound becomes noise when it causes annoyance or irritates. There are many sources of noise pollution like factories, vehicles, reckless use of loudspeakers in marriages, religious ceremonies, religious places, etc. Use of crackers on festivals, winning of teams in the games, and other such occasions causes not only noise pollution but also air pollution. The Air Act prevents and controls both these pollutions.

The Environment (Protection) Act, 1986 was enacted to provide for the protection and improvement of the quality of environment and preventing, controlling and abating environmental pollution. The Act came into existence as a direct consequence of the *Bhopal Gas Tragedy*. The term 'environment' has been defined to include water, air and land, and the inter-relationship which exists among and between water, air and land and human beings, other living creatures, plants, micro-organism and property. The definition is wide enough to include within its purview all living creatures including plants and micro-organism and their relationship with water, air and land. The Act has given vast powers to the Central Government to take measures with respect of planning and execution of a nation-wide programme for prevention, control and abatement of environmental pollution. It empowers the Government to lay down standards for the quality of environment, emission or discharge of environmental pollutants; to regulate industrial locations; to prescribe procedure for managing hazardous substances, to establish safeguards for preventing accidents; and to collect and disseminate information regarding environmental pollution. Any contravention of the provisions of the Act, rules, orders or directions made there-under is punishable with imprisonment for a term which may extend to five years or with fine upto one lakh rupees or with both. The Act is an 'umbrella' legislation designed to provide a frame work for Central Government coordination of the activities of various Central and State authorities established under previous laws, such as the Water Act and the Air Act.[9]

The Parliament passed the Public Liability Insurance Act, 1991 to provide for public liability insurance for the purpose of providing immediate relief to the persons affected by accident occurring while handling any hazardous substance and for matters connected therewith. The Act provides for mandatory public liability insurance for installations handling any hazardous substance to provide minimum relief to the victims (other than workers) through the mechanism of collector's decision. Such an insurance will be based on the principle of 'no fault' liability as it is limited to only relief on a limited scale.[10] Such insurance apart from safeguarding the interests of the victims of accidents would also provide cover and enable the industry to discharge its liability to settle large claims arising out of major accidents. However, availability of

[8] *M.C. Mehta v. Union of India*, AIR 1998 SC 2963

[9] Supra note 2, p. 68

[10] See *Public Liability Insurance Act, 1991*, the Schedule

immediate relief under this law would not prevent the victims to go to Courts for claiming large compensation.

The National Environment Tribunal Act, 1995 was enacted to provide for strict liability for damages arising out of any accident occurring while handling any hazardous substance. The Act provides for establishment of a National Environment Tribunal for effective and expeditious disposal of cases arising from such accident. It imposes liability on the owner of an enterprise to pay compensation in case of death or .injury to any person; or damage to any property or environment resulted from an accident. The accident must have occurred while handling any hazardous substance. A claimant may also make an application before the Tribunal for such relief as is provided in the Public Liability Insurance Act, 1991.

The National Environment Appellate Authority Act, 1997 has been enacted to provide for the establishment of a National Environment Appellate Authority to hear appeals with respect to restriction of areas in which any industries, operations or processes shall not be carried out or shall be carried out subject to certain safeguard under the Environment (Protection) Act, 1986. After the establishment of the Authority, no Civil Court or other authority shall have jurisdiction to entertain an appeal on matters on which the Authority is so empowered under the Act. It is evident that this Act has been made with objective to provide speedy justice on environmental issues.

The Wild Life (Protection) Act, 1972 was enacted with a view to provide for the protection of wild animals, birds and plants. The Act prohibits hunting of animals and birds as specified in the schedules. The Act also prohibits picking, uprooting, damaging, destroying etc. any specified plant from any forest. The Act provides for State Wildlife Advisory Board to advise the State Government in formulation of the policy for protection and conservation of the wildlife and specified plants; and in selection of areas to be declared as Sanctuaries, National parks, etc. The Act is administered by a Director of Wildlife Preservation with Assistant Directors; and a Chief Wildlife Warden with other Wardens and their staff.

The Forest (Conservation) Act, 1986 was passed with a view to check deforestation of forests. The Act provides that no destruction of forests or use of forestland for non-forest purposes can be permitted without the previous approval of the Central Government. The conservation of forests includes not only preservation and protection of existing forests but also re-afforestation. Reafforestation should go on to replace the vanishing forests. It is a continuous and integrated process.[11] The Act is intended to save a laudable purpose and it must be enforced strictly for the benefit of the general public.

It is evidently clear that there is no dearth of legislations on environment protection in India. But the enforcement of these legislations has been far from satisfactory. What is needed is the effective and efficient enforcement of the constitutional mandate and the other environmental legislations.

[11] *Anupama Minerals V. Union of India & Others*, AIR 1986 A.P. 225

## ADMINISTRATIVE STRUCTURE

The Water Act and the Air Act are administered by the Central and State Governments and the Central Pollution Control Board and the Stale Pollution Control Board. The Boards have been vested with wide powers to issue any direction including the direction to order closure or stoppage of the supply of electricity, water or any other service to the polluting unit. It may be noted that similar powers are vested to the Central Government under the Environment (Protection) Act.

Further, under the Environment (Protection) Act, the Central Government has framed the Environment (Protection) Rules, 1986 laying down standards for the emission or discharge of environmental pollutants with respect to some major industries.[12] There are some other agencies also framing the standards, namely-Central Pollution Control Board, State Pollution Control Board, Bureau of Indian Standard and Local Authorities, i.e., Municipal Corporation. Apparently, there is multiplicity of pollution control standards for the same type of industries. However, under the Environment (Protection) Act, 1986, the power has been conferred upon the Central Government to lay down the standards of quality of air, water, soil, etc. It is hoped that this will ensure uniformity of standards through out the country. Further, many of the standards have not yet been laid down as stipulated under the respective Pollution Control Acts, may be due to non-availability of instrument to measure the parameters of pollution. This will adversely affect the process of enforcement of laws.

## JUDICIAL CONTRIBUTION

The right of a person to pollution free environment is a part of basic jurisprudence of the land. Article 21 of the Constitution of India guarantees a fundamental right to life and personal liberty. The Supreme Court has interpreted the right to life and personal liberty to include the right to wholesome environment.[13] The Court through its various judgements[14] has held that the mandate of right to life includes right to clean environment, drinking-water and pollution-free atmosphere.

### *Taj Mahal Case*

In *Taj Mahal's* case[15], the Supreme Court issued directions that coal and coke based industries in Taj Trapezium (TTZ) which were damaging Taj should either change over to natural gas or to be relocated outside TTZ. Again the Supreme Court directed to protect the plants planted around Taj by the Forest Department as under[16]:

[12] e.g., Caustic soda, cement, electroplating, man made fibers, oil-refinery, sugar industry, thermal power plants, cotton textile, stone crushing unit, composite woollen mills, etc.
[13] *Rural Litigation and Entitlement Kendra, Dehradun V. State of U.P.*, AIR 1988 SC 1037
[14] See for example, *Subhash Kumar* v. *State of Bihar*, AIR 1991 SC 420; *M.C. Mehta V. Union of India*. AIR 2000 SC 1997
[15] *M.C.Mehta* v. *Union of India*, AIR 1997 SC 734; see also *M.C.Mehta* v. *Union of India*, AIR 1999 S.C. 3192.
[16] *M.C.Mehta* v. *Union of India*, (2001), 9 SCC 520

The Divisional Forest Officer, Agra is directed to take immediate steps for seeing that water is supplied to the plants... The Union Government is directed to release the funds immediately without waiting for receipt of the proposal from the U.P. Government on the basis of the copy of the report. Funding may be subsequently settled with the U.P. Government, but in any set of circumstances for want of funds the officer is directed to see that plants do not wither away.

### *Dehradun Valley Case*

In that case[17], carrying haphazard and dangerous limestone quarrying in the Mussorie Hill range of the Himalaya, mines blasting out the hills with dynamite, extracting limestone from thousand of acres had upset the hydrological system of the valley. The Supreme Court ordered the closing of limestone quarrying in the hills and observed[18]:

> This would undoubtedly cause hardship to them, but it is a price that has to be paid for protecting and safeguarding the right of the people to live in healthy environment with minimal disturbance of ecological balance...

### *Smoking in Public Places*

In 2001, the Supreme Court of India imposed ban on smoking of tobacco in public places all over the country[19]. Smoking causes harm not only to the smokers but also to non-smokers who are forced to inhale the second hand smoke. More than 3 million people die every year in India as a result of smoking tobacco including bidis and cigarettes[20]. One lakh Indians get lung cancer every year because of smoking. Indeed, lung cancer kills 95% of its victims[21]. That is why the apex Court ruling has immense social value. But no one cares for the ban. As you know the cigarettes and bidis are openly sold in tobacco-free railway stations, bus stands, cinema houses, etc.

The statutory warning 'smoking is injurious to health' is printed in such small prints and colour that hardly it is readable. Even, if it is readable, it has not served any purpose. So it is the social awakening which can only help us to prevent smoking.

### *Pollution in Delhi*

In *Almitra H.Patel v. Union of India*[22], the Supreme Court reiterated the observations made in *Wadehra's* case[23]-Historic city of Delhi, the Capital of India, is one of the most polluted cities in the world. The authorities, responsible for pollution control and environment protection have not been able to provide clean and healthy environment

---

[17] *Rural Litigation & Entitlement Kendra* v. *Slate of U.P.*, AIR 1985 SC 652; see also AIR 1988 SC 2187

[18] *Id.*, at p. 654

[19] *Murli S.. Deora* v. *Union of India* (2001) 3 SCC 765

[20] See Hindustan Times, New Delhi, dated 5.11.2001, p. 10

[21] Ibid.

[22] AIR 2000 SC 1256

[23] *Dr. B.L Wadehra v. Union of India*, AIR 1996 SC 2969

to the residents of Delhi. The ambient air is so much polluted that it is difficult to breathe. More and more Delhites are suffering from respiratory diseases and throat infections. River Yamuna- the main source of drinking water supply- is the free dumping place for untreated sewcrage and industrial waste. Apart from air and water pollution, the city is virtually an open dustbin. Garbage strewn all over Delhi is a common sight. The Court directed the authorities to take immediate necessary steps to control pollution and protect the environment.

### *Sri Ram Food and Fertilizer Case*

In that case[24], a major leakage of Oileum Gas affected a large number of persons, both amongst the workmen and public. The Supreme Court held that where an enterprise is engaged in a hazardous or inherently dangerous activity and harm results to any one on account of an accident in the operation of such hazardous and inherently dangerous activity resulting in the escape of toxic gas the enterprise is strictly and absolutely liable to compensate all those who are affected by the accident and such a liability is not subject to any exception.

### *Public Health*

The Supreme Court has emphasised the importance of preservation of public health. In *Subba Rao* v. *State of Himachal Pradesh*[25], the Supreme Court ordered the closure of a bone factory which was polluting the environment by its pungent smell and making the life of the people miserable. No one can do business at the cost of public health.

With a view to preserve the environment and control pollution within the vicinity of tourist resorts of Badkhal and Suraj Kund, the Supreme Court directed the stoppage of mining activity within two Kilometers radius of these two tourist resorts[26].

In *Municipal Council, Ratlam* v. *Vardhichand & Others*[27], the Supreme Court held that the grievous failure of local authorities to provide the basic amenity of public conveniences drives the miserable slum-dwellers to ease in the streets, on the sly for a time, and openly thereafter, because under nature's pressure, bashfulness becomes a luxury and dignity a difficult art. A responsible Municipal Council constituted for the purpose of preserving public health cannot run away from its duty by pleading financial inability.

### *Public Park*

A place which is reserved for public park cannot be converted for use into a private nursing-home. In *Banglore Medical Trust* v. *B.S. Muddappa*[28], the Supreme Court set

---

[24] *M.C. Mehta v. Union of India*, AIR 1987 SC 1086
[25] AIR 1989 SC 171
[26] *M.C.Mehta* v. *Union of India* 1996 (4) SCC 351
[27] AIR 1980 SC 1622
[28] AIR 1991 SC 1902.

aside the decision of the Banglore Development Authority granting permission for converting the place reserved for public-park for the establishment of a nursing home and observed thus:

> The public interest on reservation and preservation of open spaces for parks and playgrounds cannot be sacrificed by leasing or selling such sites to private persons for conversion to some other use.

In another case[29], a park was in existence for many years. Because of the construction of underground shopping complex and parking, irreversible changes were made. The Supreme Court ordered for the demolition of the building on the site of the park and held that no authority has power to grant permission to change the land use of a site reserved for Public Park.

*Sustainable Development*

'Sustainable development' means development that meets the needs of the present without compromising the ability of the future generations to meet their own needs. The Supreme Court of India in *Vellore Citizens Welfare Forum* v. *Union of India*[30], elaborately discussed the concept of 'sustainable development' which has been accepted as part of the law of the land. The 'precautionary principle' and the 'polluter pays principle[1] are essential features of 'sustainable development'. The 'precautionary principle' makes it mandatory for the State Government to anticipate prevent and attack the causes of environment degradation[31]. The Supreme Court in *M.C. Melna* v. *Union of India*[32] observed thus:

> We have no hesitation holding that in order to protect the two lakes (Badhkal and Suraj Kund) from environmental degradation, it is necessary to limit the construction activity in the close vicinity of the lakes.

The 'polluter pays principle' demands that the financial costs of preventing or remedying damage caused by pollution should lie with the undertakings which cause pollution. The 'polluter pays principle' has been held to be a sound principle and as interpreted by the Supreme Court of India[33], it means that the absolute liability for harm to the environment extends not only to compensate the victims of pollution but also the cost of restoring the environment degradation. Remediation of the damaged environment is part of the process of 'sustainable development' and as such polluter is liable to pay the cost to the individual sufferers as well as the cost of reversing the damaged ecology.

The aforesaid study of cases clearly reveals that the Supreme Court of India has played a vital role for protection and improvement of environment. The jurisdiction of the Court has been expanded by way of Public Interest Litigation. The creative role of judiciary has been significant and laudable.

---

29 *M.I. Builders Pvt. Ltd v, Radhey Shyam Sahaoo*, (1999) 6 SCC 464.

30 AIR 1996 SC 2715

31 *M.C. Mehta v. Union of India*, (1997) 1 Camp L.J. 199 (SC)

32 Id., at 203

33 *Indian Council for Enviro-Legal Action* v. *Union of India*, AIR 1996 SC 1446; see also *Vellore-Citizens Welfare Forum* v. *Union of India*, AIR 1996 SC 2715; *M.C. Mehta* v. *Union of India* (1997) i Camp L.J. 199(SC)

## ENVIRONMENT COURT

We have noticed that in the past few years there is an increasing trend to the number of cases based on environmental pollution, ecological destruction and conflicts over natural resources coming up before the Courts. In most of these cases there is need for natural scientific expertise as an essential input to inform judicial decision-making. These cases require expertise at a high level of scientific and technical sophistication. The experience shows that the prosecution launched in ordinary Criminal Courts under the provisions of the Water Act, Air Act and the Environment (Protection) Act never reach their conclusion either because of the work load in these Courts or because there is no proper appreciation of the significance of the environment matters on the part of those in charge of conducting of those cases[34]. Moreover, any orders passed by the Authorities under Water Act, Air Act and Environment (Protection) Act are immediately questioned by the industries in Courts. Those proceedings take years and years to reach conclusion. Very often interim orders are granted meanwhile which effectively disable the authorities from ensuring the implementation of their orders[35]. It is, therefore, absolutely essential to set up a separate machinery to cut down the delays which are hindering the implementation of environmental laws. Further, the judicial officers alone may not be able to appreciate scientific and technical aspects. It is, therefore, submitted that the provisions be made for the establishment of the Environment Courts with one judge and two experts from the ecological and other sciences. To begin with, we may have a two-tier system one at the State level and the other at the National level which may later be extended even at the District level. Such Courts may be vested with the jurisdiction to decide both criminal prosecution cases under the various environmental laws and civil cases for compensation to victims of any activity leading to environmental damage or pollution. These Courts should be allowed to adopt summary proceedings for speedy disposal of the cases. The appeal from decision of the State Environment Courts may be preferred to the National Environment Court and appeal from the decision of the National Environment Court to the Supreme Court. The provisions should be confined to single appeal.

## CONCLUSION AND SUGGESTIONS

The aforesaid study leads us to the following conclusion and suggestions:

i) We have more than 200 Central and State legislations which deal with environmental issues. More legislation means more difficulties in enforcement. There is a need to have a comprehensive and an integrated law on environmental protection for meaningful enforcement.

---

[34] *Indian Council for Enviro-Legal Action* v. *Union of India & Others*, AIR 1996 SC 1446

[35] *Ibid.*

ii) It is not enough to enact the legislations. A positive attitude on the part of everyone in society is essential for effective and efficient enforcement of these legislations.

iii) The powers vested to the Pollution Control Boards are not enough to prevent pollution. The Boards do not have power to punish the violators but can launch prosecution against them in the Courts which ultimately defeat the purpose and object of the Environmental Laws due to long delays in deciding the cases. Thus, it is imperatively necessary to give more powers to the Boards.

iv) The Environment Protection Laws have failed to bring about the desired results. Consequently, for the purpose of efficient and effective enforcement of these laws, it is necessary to set up the Environment Courts; with one Judge and two technical experts from the field of Environmental Science and Ecology. These Courts should be allowed to adopt summary proceedings for speedy disposal of the cases. To begin with we may have such Courts at the State and National levels that may later be extended to district level on need-based principle. In order to discourage prolonged litigation, the provisions should be confined to single appeal.

v) There is a multiplicity of environment pollution control standards for the same type of industries. However, under the Environment (Protection) Act, 1986 now the power has been conferred upon the Central Government for laying down the standards for the quality of air, water and soil. It is hoped that this will ensure uniformity of standards through out the country.

vi) In order to enforce the environmental laws stringently, mere mis-description and technical flaws should be disregarded by the Courts. The creative role of judiciary has been significant and laudable. The jurisdiction of the Courts has been expanded by way of Public Interest Litigation. The Supreme Court of India has played a vital role in giving directions from time to time to the administrative authorities to take necessary steps for improving the environment.

vii) The Public Liability Insurance Act, 1991 which provides for mandatory public liability insurance for installation and handling hazardous substance to provide minimum relief to the victims, is a welcome step in the right direction. Such an insurance apart from safeguarding the interests of victims of accident will also provide cover and enable the enterprise to meet its liability.

viii) What we need is social awareness from below, not laws from the above. No law works out smoothly unless the interaction is voluntary. In order to educate people about the environmental issues, there should be exhibition of slides in the regional languages at cinema houses and television free of cost. Further, as directed by the Supreme Court of India[36], Environment studies shall be made a compulsory subject at

---

[36] *M.C. Mehta* v. *Union of India*, AIR 1992 SC 382

school and college levels in graded system so that there should be general growth of awareness.

ix) It needs to be appreciated that keeping in view the magnitude of finance required, a judicious mix of incentives, phasing and awareness creating, programmes about cost-effective technologies is essential as the first prong of the strategy to control environment degradation.

x) The traditional concept that development and ecology are opposed to each other, is no longer acceptable, since 'sustainable development' is the answer. The Supreme Court has accepted sustainable development as part of the laws of the land and has affirmed the 'precautionary principle' and the 'polluter pays principle' are essential features of sustainable development.

xi) The tapping of natural resources must be done with requisite attention and care so that ecology and environment may not be affected in any serious way. A long-term planning must be undertaken by the Central Government in consultation with the State Governments to protect and improve the environment and to keep up the national wealth.

xii) Finally, protection of the environment and keeping ecological balance unaffected is a task which not only the government but also every individual, association and corporation must undertake. It is a social obligation and fundamental duty enshrined in Article 51 A (g) of the Constitution of India.

[32]

VOLUME 1, ISSUE 1, OCTOBER 2011

# Global Responsibilities: India's Approach*

Rohan Mukherjee and David M. Malone**

*This article offers an examination of international developments central to globalisation in India and reviews India's approach to some prominent multilateral treaty systems such as the United Nations (UN), the World Trade Organisation (WTO), the international climate change regime, and the nuclear non-proliferation and test-ban regimes. It argues that, to be a responsible and true global player, India needs to move beyond its membership of narrowly based power caucuses within these regimes to constructively address the greater challenges that these treaties are focused on. Thus, India's engagement with the multilateral system needs to be one that serves the interests of the system rather than the national interests of India alone. Through a historical overview of India's multilateralism, the article probes India's variable contemporary performance in four substantive fields of foreign policy to assess India's multilateral stance during the post-Cold War period. It evaluates India's diplomatic approach to global challenges like climate change and the wider multilateral system to reiterate the need for India to engage further in multilateral diplomacy and address global challenges, going beyond narrow conceptions of the nation's bilateral partnerships. India's aspiration to be a great power will only materialise if it is prepared to balance its political and economic obligations, both nationally and internationally.*

## INTRODUCTION

India's voice carries significant weight today in multilateral forums largely

*To provide inputs for the research required for this article, both Pratap Bhanu Mehta and his colleagues at the Centre for Policy Research (CPR) and Rajiv Kumar and his colleagues at the Indian Council for Research on International Economic Relations (ICRIER) organised round-tables in February 2010. To all of them, the authors express heartfelt thanks.

**Rohan Mukherjee is a PhD student in the Department of Politics at Princeton University. He studies the international relations of emerging powers, especially India and China. His writings on Indian foreign policy have appeared in the journals Survival, International Affairs, International Journal and Global Governance.

David M. Malone is President of the International Development Research Centre (IDRC). A former Canadian Ambassador to the UN and High Commissioner to India, his book, Does the Elephant Dance? Contemporary Indian Foreign Policy was published by Oxford University Press in 2011. A scholar of the UN Security Council and related issues of war and peace, he teaches at the NYU Law School and is a Senior Fellow of Massey College in the University of Toronto.

due to its enhanced economic power, political stability, and nuclear capability. Although the assertion by a respected Indian editor that "the world concludes that India is a 'predictable player' with enduring national interest" may be optimistic or at least premature, there is certainly much greater willingness among major powers in the international system to engage India today – multilaterally as well as bilaterally – than there was sixty years ago.

Yet, as India's stature is growing, its stake in some forms of multilateralism is diminishing. In almost every international forum, India has explicitly engaged with smaller groups of powerful nations to affect outcomes at the expense of the more broad-based universalist approach it traditionally espoused (or claimed to) toward multilateralism. India has also significantly reduced its reliance on the multilateral treaty-based system as a whole, preferring instead bilateral relationships with major powers such as the United States, China, the EU, Japan, and Russia in almost every field of international cooperation from trade to nuclear technology. Even in organisations rooted originally in ideological or other forms of solidarity between members, such as the Non-Aligned Movement, and the Commonwealth (of which Kamalesh Sharma, an Indian, became Secretary-General in 2009) India of late has become somewhat detached.

This paper reviews India's approach to some prominent multilateral treaty systems such as the United Nations (UN), the World Trade Organisation (WTO), the international climate change regime, and the nuclear non-proliferation and test-ban regimes. India has over time gained prominence in each of these regimes and has been able to articulate and protect its national interests with a measure of success in each. However, we argue that to be considered a responsible global player, India will need to move beyond its membership of narrowly based power caucuses within these regimes to address constructively greater challenges that these treaties are focused on. India's engagement with the multilateral system therefore needs to be of the type that serves the interests of the system rather than the interests of India alone. By doing so, India can gain recognition as a true global player rather than a regional power whose interests are often at odds with the aims of the multilateral system.

The paper first provides a quick historical overview of India's multilateralism and then looks at India's variable contemporary performance in four substantive fields of foreign policy or forums of significance to India's multilateral stance during the post-Cold War period of wider multilateral transition and flux: the UN Security Council (UNSC); the World Trade Organisation (WTO) and its Doha Round negotiations culminating in 2008; international efforts to combat climate change through the Copenhagen UN conference of late 2009 and subsequently in Cancun in 2010; and the global nuclear non-proliferation and testing regime via the Nuclear Non-Proliferation Treaty (NPT) and the Comprehensive Nuclear Test Ban Treaty (CTBT). The concluding section elaborates challenges for India's approach to the multilateral system and reiterates the argument for a more comprehensive view of global challenges that goes beyond narrow conceptions of national interest.

## Historical Overview

Post-independence India was an enthusiastic supporter of the multilateral system, at that time comprised largely of the United Nations (UN) and its associated organisations. However, Delhi soon encountered a major setback at the UN on the issue of Kashmir, and since then India has been loath to allow any form of multilateral intervention not just in Kashmir but also in the South Asian region, much of which it regards as a sphere of influence more generally.[1] Delhi's aversion to any UN inclination to over-ride state sovereignty is evident even in its approach to peacekeeping – India's most celebrated contribution to the UN, through its generous provision of military and civilian staff – for which it emphasises the need for consent of the parties involved.

During the Cold War, India's non-aligned foreign policy and the desire to carry greater weight internationally than its frail domestic economy and military resources would permit led Delhi to continue its support for the multilateral system while trying at every turn to prevent either superpower bloc from usurping the mandate of the United Nations. India's stance toward various international issues – the 1950 Acheson Plan, the UN's role in the Korean War, the Indo-China conference of 1954, the Suez crisis – reflected this strategy. With the advent of the Non-Aligned Movement (NAM), India also began championing the cause of developing nations in UN forums in a more structured manner than before.

1 See C. Raja Mohan, "India and the New World Order," *Seminar*, August 29, 2003.

Following another setback with the UN over the Bangladesh War of 1971 and India's "peaceful nuclear explosion" of 1974, India's relationship with the multilateral system went into stasis, to be revived with the end of the Cold War and the re-emergence of the UN as a forum for multilateral cooperation on security issues.[2] The rest of the multilateral system also received a boost in the 1990s, with the unprecedented 1992 Rio Summit on climate change, the implementation of the Uruguay Round and establishment of the WTO from 1995 onward, the indefinite extension of the NPT in 1995, the adoption of the Comprehensive Test Ban Treaty (CTBT) in 1996, and the Kyoto Protocol on climate change in 1997. In all of these discussions and activities India was active and often played a leading role, but occasionally Delhi opted for a stance other than creative, positive diplomacy, as at the CTBT conference, where many saw it as a would-be "spoiler".[3]

As India's own economy grew after the domestic reforms of 1991, Third World leadership became only an intermittent and secondary goal of Indian foreign policy (indeed, the term Third World itself had lost its meaning). Afro-Asian solidarity had little meaning in WTO negotiations where African agricultural interests could be at odds with those of India.[4] India could no longer credibly claim to be "a spokesman of the Afro-Asians, the non-aligned, the under-developed and the small states" and use the UN to enhance its stature in this manner at a time when it had significant economic interests of its own to advance and defend.[5] Thus India's rising stature began to transform its approach to the multilateral system, as will be analysed in four issue areas below – UN Security Council reform, trade, climate change, and nuclear non-proliferation.

2 See David M. Malone (Ed.), *The UN Security Council, from Cold War to 21st Century*, Boulder, CO and London, UK: Lynne Rienner, 2004, particularly pp. 4-13, 617-649 and its chapter by Peter Wallensteen and Patrick Johansson, "Security Council Decisions in Perspective", pp. 17 -33.

3 Amitav Mallik, *Technology and Security in the 21st Century: A Demand-Side Perspective*, SIPRI Research Report No. 20 (Oxford University Press: 2004), p. 74.

4 See Amartya Sen's comments in P. S. Suryanarayana , "India will continue to grow, says Amartya Sen", *The Hindu*, 19 February 2009: "When the last Doha Round [of global trade talks] got busted, basically, the Chinese, the Indians, and the Brazilians didn't like what was being proposed … And, they wanted a bigger concession [on agriculture] … The Chinese, the Indians, and the Brazilians were right to demand it. On the other hand, the Europeans and Americans had put on the table some concessions which would have been very good for Africa. Now, when China, India, and Brazil busted the Doha Round, it served their interests quite well. It did not serve the interests of Africa."

5 Reddy, *India's Policy*, p. 45.

## India Rising: Reform of the UN Security Council

Prior to the 1990s, India's approach to the UN and the principles of international law enshrined in its charter had been cautious, aimed at safeguarding India's status and territorial integrity as a slowly emerging developing nation. Delhi often acted as an organiser of Third World interests that coincided largely with its own. Thus, the assertion by an Indian scholar that India has made "strenuous efforts to uphold (the) principle (of sovereign equality of states) for the benefit of developing countries."[6] Similarly, with Kashmir in mind, India had unambiguously held that the principle of self-determination could not be invoked to enable "the integral part of any country or sections of its population to secede" and that the principle only applied to nations as whole in the context of foreign domination or colonial exploitation.[7]

As its economy took off in the 1990s, India's stature and interests in relation to the UN system began to change. India's economic growth on the one hand cast it as a model for many other developing nations but also created a potential rift between it and the poorer nations of the world – for whom it had once routinely spoken – one that India did not take pains to address. With regard to the UN, India began a transition from 'rule taker' to tentative 'rule maker'. Delhi began suggesting reforms for the UN, especially in the composition of the UNSC. In 1992, Prime Minister Narasimha Rao argued for the latter on the grounds of maintaining the "political and moral effectiveness"[8] of the UNSC. The US responded in 1993 with the suggestion that UNSC expansion begin with Germany and Japan only, with indications that any new permanent members might not secure veto power.[9] The American response was a pointed reminder to India of its place in the international system at the time and of the cost its long history of anti-Americanism in multilateral institutions could still carry.

In 1991-92, India sat as an elected member in the UN Security Council during one of that body's busiest periods, with Iraq's invasion of Kuwait; Iraq's subsequent repression of its Kurds; the beginnings of the

6 Bimal N. Patel, "Introduction," in Bimal N. Patel (ed.), *India and International Law, Vol. 1* (Leiden; Boston: Martinus Nijh off, 2005), p. 1.

7 Pemmaraju Sreenivasa Rao, "General Principles of International Law and India," in Patel (ed.), *India and International Law, Vol. 1*, p. 52, quoting statements by Vijayalakshmi Pandit at the UN General Assembly on 30 Sep 1963 and M.C. Chagla at the UNSC on 5 Dec 1964.

8 Tad Daley, "Can the U.N. Stretch to Fit its Future?" *The Bulletin of the Atomic Scientists*, April 1992, p. 41.

9 J.N. Dixit, *India's Foreign Policy*, p. 273.

disintegration of Yugoslavia leading to a succession of wars in the ensuing years all featuring extensive UN involvement; the humanitarian plight of Somalis to which the UNSC responded with armed intervention; as well as ambitious UN peacekeeping operations in Cambodia, Mozambique, and El Salvador. India sought to temper the enthusiasm of Western powers and some others for armed intervention (as opposed to consent-based peacekeeping), its interventions in Council debates later seeming prophetic of the risks then being courted.[10]

In 1996, India, which had previously sat in the UN Security Council as a non-permanent member, ran again for an elected seat. It competed with Japan for the single Asian seat available and lost massively. Indian foreign service members spoke privately of the debilitating effects on their campaign of Japanese "checkbook diplomacy" in the developing world – and doubtless this factor played a role – but it seemed to occur to few in Delhi that the caustic performance of its delegation to the CTBT conference earlier that year might have alienated not a few of its NAM partners as well as many in the West.[11]

Despite its changing interests, India continued to demonstrate a lack of flexibility with regard to the international order that it wished to reform. The traditional unwillingness to trade off even small amounts of sovereignty for cooperative gains was evident in Delhi's approach, for example, to the International Criminal Court and the expanding role of the UNSC in the 1990s.[12] One of India's primary objections to the ICC was that it did not give full recognition to the primacy of national jurisdiction.[13] On other issues, India continued to make statements reminiscent of its unyielding positions from earlier decades. For example, as late as 2004, in a response to UNSC Resolution 1540 on proliferation of weapons of mass destruction, the government of India stated: "India will not accept externally prescribed norms or standards, whatever their source, on matters within the jurisdiction of its Parliament, including national legislation, regulations or arrangements which are not consistent with India's constitutional provisions and procedures, or are contrary to

10 For a discussion of the manner in which the UNSC widened its remit during this period, see Chinmaya R. Gharekhan, *The Horseshoe Table* (Delhi: Longman, 2006), p. 3

11 This was confirmed in extensive interviews of UN delegates in New York by David Malone in December 2006, and after the election.

12 Jerry Fowler, "The Rome Treaty for an International Criminal Court: A Framework of International Justice for Future Generations," *Human Rights Brief*, Vol. 6, Issue 1, Fall 1998.

13 Saumya Uma, *International Criminal Court and India: Responses to Queries Raised by Parliamentarians,* (Mumbai: Women's Research and Action Group, 2005).

India's national interests, or infringe on its sovereignty."[14]

Undoubtedly, Delhi was wary of the expanding scope of a UNSC in which India had no permanent membership. Fearing a more active UNSC with a wider remit, and feeling a sense of entitlement, India was increasingly committed after the 1996 election experience to reform of the Security Council. Later contention within the Council in 1999 over Kosovo, in 2002-2003 over Iraq and its decisive resolution supporting US self-defence after the events of 11 September 2001 were doubtless further elements leading India to wonder why it was not part of these systemically important conversations. Nonetheless, India's newfound status helped it cope better with the renewed interventionism of the United Nations. Delhi successfully prevented Secretary General Kofi Annan's post-1999 efforts to involve the UN in Kashmir and also rejected a UN resolution requiring India to curb its nuclear and missile programs.[15]

In the run-up to the 2005 UN Summit, India developed a comprehensive proposal for UN reform on the subjects of new permanent members in the UNSC, a more restrained and effective UNSC, greater balance between the principal organs of the UN, definite rules of procedure, and greater accountability of the UNSC to the General Assembly.[16] On UNSC membership, India banded with Brazil, Germany and Japan (together known as the G-4) in order to press for Council reform involving the creation of four new permanent seats for them (and another two for Africa, as well as four further elected seats). Speaking at a joint session of Congress after inking an important strategic partnership with the United States in July 2005, Manmohan Singh was unequivocal in his demand for the ultimate recognition of India's power. "There *must* be comprehensive reform of the United Nations to make it more effective and also more representative...In this context, you would agree that the voice of the world's largest democracy *surely cannot* be left unheard on the Security Council when the United Nations is being restructured."[17]

In spite of a determined push from all of the capitals involved, the effort failed. The G-4 had essentially argued their case on the basis of entitlement to the seats given their weight in international relations, their financial share

14 Rao, "General Principles," p. 44.

15 C. Raja Mohan, "India and the New World Order," *Seminar*, 29 August 2003.

16 Bimal N. Patel, "India and the UN Reforms," in Bimal N. Patel (ed.), *India and International Law, Vol. 2* (Leiden; Boston: Martinus Nijh off, 2005), p. 65.

17 Prime Minister Manmohan Singh's Address to the Joint Session of United States Congress, Washington DC, 19 July 2005, http://www.indianembassy.org/press_release/2005/July/23.htm. Emphasis added.

of the UN's bills, and their contributions to aspects of the UN's work such as peacekeeping. But this failed to address the concern of some member states more worried about the UNSC's effectiveness than the additional legitimacy a wider composition could impart, fearing that a much larger Council could become paralysed on key issues.

After an abortive attempt in 2006 to support an Indian candidate, UN Under-Secretary-General Shashi Tharoor, for the position of UN Secretary-General, India's ambitions for a greater role in the UNSC were left in limbo until President Obama's visit to Delhi in late 2010. In his speech to the Indian parliament, President Obama echoed the grounds on which India had advocated UNSC reform: "Indeed, the just and sustainable international order that America seeks includes a United Nations that is efficient, effective, credible and legitimate. That is why I can say today, in the years ahead, I look forward to a reformed United Nations Security Council that includes India as a permanent member."[18] This seemed an unequivocal endorsement of the Indian position, coming on the heels of India's election as a non-permanent member of the UNSC after a hiatus of 19 years. India's election was all the more convincing given that it received the support of 187 out of 192 countries (including Pakistan), compared to the 42 votes it received in 1996 when it lost to Japan.[19]

However, the initial enthusiasm generated by Obama's remarks were put to rest just a week after the President's visit, with US officials cautioning against undue optimism for what would no doubt be "a long-term and very complicated process."[20] While this did not surprise many observers, the President's speech remained an important signal from the United States for India to take on greater responsibility in the management of the multilateral system during its current tenure in the UNSC. As argued by one Indian newspaper, permanent membership for India was "an entirely different game, one subject to multiple pressures from the four corners of the world, including China and Pakistan, not usually well-disposed to India's enhancement on the world stage."[21] Nonetheless, some concluded that India's current non-permanent tenure on the UNSC could be "a useful tool in the quest for permanent membership."[22] In effect,

18 The White House, Office of the Press Secretary, "Remarks by the President to the Joint Session of the Indian Parliament in Delhi, India," November 08, 2010, available at: www.whitehouse.gov/the-press-office/2010/11/08/remarks-president-joint-session-indian-parliament-new-delhi-india.

19 *The Hindu*, "India in the Security Council," Oct 14, 2010.

20 *Indian Express*, "US throws water over Indian hopes for UNSC seat," 16 November 2010.

21 *The Asian Age*, "UNSC Win Is Also A Challenge For India," Oct 14, 2010.

22 Richard Gowan, "Indian Power and the United Nations," *World Politics Review*, 15 Nov 2010.

the burden of proof that it can be a responsible global player is now on India's shoulders, in what one Indian senior official has described as a "not a dress rehearsal"[23] for permanent member status, but might well be described as an audition before the likely still sceptical existing permanent five (whatever their publicly professed enthusiasm for India's candidacy for permanent status).

## From Universalism to Individualism: The WTO

Post-1991, India's approach to the multilateral trading regime received a major boost as its domestic program of economic liberalisation coincided rather happily with the Uruguay Round of trade negotiations. This not only prepared India domestically to deal with multilateral trade liberalisation, it also provided India a vital bargaining chip in multilateral negotiations.[24] In the words of a prominent Indian economist, "The gap between what the Uruguay Round required India to do and what India would have wanted to do of her own volition was reduced."[25] Although certain areas – intellectual property rights, services, agriculture, and quantitative restrictions – remained exceptions, India was far more comfortable with the multilateral trade regime after 1991 than it had ever been before.

Consequently, while it had remained largely a passive spectator in the GATT/WTO regime until the late 1990s, India spoke up at the 1999 Seattle meeting of the WTO against the inclusion of labour and environmental standards on the WTO agenda.[26] In the run up to the Doha Round of 2001, India challenged the efforts of developed nations to introduce the so-called "Singapore issues" – competition, investment, trade facilitation, and government procurement – into discussions, and emphasised the need for developed nations to fully implement their Uruguay Round commitments, especially in agricultural market access, textiles, and clothing. India also opposed the strict provisions of the Agreement on Trade-Related Aspects of Intellectual Property Rights (TRIPS) on compulsory licensing for the drug industry, an issue in which Indian pharmaceutical companies had an

23 Edith Lederer, "India Says Security Council Now More Credible'" Associated Press, 4 January 2011, available at http://www.msnbc.msn.com/id/40916795/ns/world_news-asia-pacific.

24 Veena Jha and Swapna Nair, "India and the WTO," in Samana Kelegana (ed.), *South Asia in the WTO* (Sage, Delhi: 2007), p. 61.

25 Bibek Debroy, "India's Economic Liberalisation and the WTO," in Suparna Karmakar, Rajiv Kumar, Bibek Debroy (eds.), *India's Liberalisation Experience: Hostage to the WTO?* (Indian Council for Research on International Economic Relations: 2007), pp. 40-41.

26 Sengupta et al, *Beyond the Transition*, p. 29.

important stake.[27] Ultimately, although India acquiesced in the launch of a new trade round at Doha in 2001, it walked away from that meeting satisfied with beneficial outcomes on labour standards, which were deflected to the ILO, a substantive discussion on agriculture, and an agreement on TRIPS and public health that would not require compulsory licensing for Indian-manufactured drugs in cases where public health concerns mandated cheaper drug access.[28]

India continued to benefit from its economic rise while maintaining developing country solidarity at the WTO. In 2003, Brazil and India formed the G-20 group of developing countries (which is distinct from the G-20 group of major economies that came together to tackle the global financial crisis) that effectively advocated their collective interests on a number of issues. In 2004, India was included in a small high-powered group at the WTO called the Five Interested Parties – along with the US, the EU, Brazil, and Australia – that superseded the traditional "Quad" of the US, the EU, Japan, and Canada. India's inclusion was a sign, beyond its economic significance, of the G-20's effectiveness as a negotiating bloc. It was also a sign of the US's acceptance of India as an important player in multilateral negotiations.

India was also in a better position to confront Western powers in the WTO since its trade portfolio no longer relied on them as much (gradually shifting toward China instead).[29] An important sign of India's multilateral transformation was the shift in its position on trade in services between the Uruguay and Doha rounds. Whereas in the past, India and Brazil, had opposed the inclusion of services in trade negotiations, India's services-led growth ensured that by 2004 – when services accounted for approximately 52 per cent of GDP, up from 28.5 per cent five decades earlier[30] – it was an ardent advocate of liberalisation in the modes of trade in services where it had significant interests.[31]

27 See Aaditya Mattoo and Arvind Subramaniam, "India and the Multilateral Trading System Post-Doha: Defensive or Proactive?" in Aaditya Mattoo and Robert M. Stern (eds.), *India and the WTO* (World Bank and OUP, Washington, D.C.: 2003), p. 328.

28 Sengupta et al, *Beyond the Transition*, p. 31.

29 Debashis Chakraborty and Amir Ullah Khan, *The WTO Deadlocked: Understanding the Dynamics of International Trade* (SAGE, Delhi: 2008), p. 2.

30 See Government of India, Economic Survey of India, 2008-09, Table A6: Gross Domestic Product at Factor Cost by Industry of Origin (in current prices). Services include trade, hotels, transport, communication, finance, insurance, real estate, business services, public administration, defence services and other services. Available at: indiabudget.nic.in/es2008-09/chapt2009/tab13b.pdf.

31 Chakraborty and Khan, *The WTO Deadlocked*, p. 5.

By 2004, India had proved itself an adept navigator of the international trade system. This was particularly true of the way in which Delhi had managed its interactions with the WTO dispute resolution mechanism. Although initially a flurry of cases – totalling thirteen – against India between 1995 and 1998 had forced reforms of the domestic market,[32] the subsequent period from 1998 to 2004 saw only an additional three cases, suggesting that India was able to quickly learn from its experiences and modify its domestic policies in line with WTO requirements.[33] Moreover, by 2004 India had itself filed 16 cases against other countries at the WTO's Dispute Settlement Body (DBS), of which it had won seven.[34] This suggested a measure of adaptability and learning in Delhi's approach to the new rules and procedures of the international trade regime.

Despite progress in other areas, intellectual property rights and patents remained a thorny issue for India (as did agriculture). During the Uruguay Round, India had argued for "the freedom of Member States to attune their intellectual property protection system to their own needs and conditions."[35] India's attempt to balance the IPR requirements of the WTO with its own developmental goals remained a constant theme throughout the subsequent rounds of negotiations. Particularly problematic were issues such as the transfer of technology, local working of patents to meet the reasonable requirements of the public, and the availability of medicines at affordable prices.[36] Despite objections, however, India has worked to modify domestic patent laws to conform to its international obligations under the TRIPS agreement. Needless to say, implementation of the new laws leaves much to be desired, as does the enforcement of TRIPS obligations by India's patent authorities. In the realm of pharmaceutical products, for example, a number of major drug companies that entered Indian markets following the change in domestic laws continue to face difficulties in having their patents upheld by domestic courts and India's patent office.[37]

32 Dipankar Sengupta, Debashis Chakraborty, Pritam Banerjee (eds.), *Beyond the Transition Phase of WTO* (Academic Foundation, Delhi: 2006), p. 28.

33 J. Chaisse and D. Chakraborty, "Dispute Resolution in the WTO: The Experience of India," in Sengupta et al (eds.), *Beyond the Transition Phase*,pp. 520-24.

34 *Ibid.*

35 V.G. Hegde, "India and the International Patent System," in Patel (ed.), *India and International Law, Vol. 1*, p. 106.

36 *Ibid*, pp. 116-117.

37 Geeta Anand, "Drug Makers Decry Indian Patent Law," *Wall Street Journal*, Feb 11, 2010.

In 2007-08, the Doha Round discussions proved a brass knuckles affair amidst a burgeoning global food security scare (with attendant inflation of basic produce prices in most countries). India and Brazil, speaking "for" the developing countries, confronted the United States on agriculture. While both Washington and Delhi were open to success of the talks, their political bottom lines collided in Geneva in July 2008. Rather damagingly for India's international image, in the final reel in Geneva, India was abandoned in its hard line by Brazil (which, like many African countries, on balance, wanted an agreement even at the price of greater compromise) and Indian Commerce Minister Kamal Nath stood out in his vehemence within the negotiations. "I reject everything" he was quoted as saying in response to a compromise paper others seemed to be prepared to swallow.[38] He was alone in seeming to claim credit for the talks' failure, with EU, US and Chinese negotiators, who had contributed considerably to the overall deadlock only too willing to deflect responsibility on to him.[39]

In India, Nath was largely portrayed in heroic terms.[40] However, in the Congress-led UPA coalition's second consecutive term following the 2009 election, Nath was shifted to the road transport and highways portfolio and replaced by Anand Sharma, known for his low-key style. India lost no time in calling over 30 leading trade ministers to Delhi for consultations, with the aim of advancing the Doha Round, perhaps in order to allow this change of personnel and style to sink in fully, and, in the words of one commentator, to cast India as a "pro-active participant in multi-lateral talks rather than a thorn in the flesh as the global media had suggested in 2008."[41]

Following the collapse of Doha round negotiations, however, Delhi mostly continued to eschew multilateral approaches, and, in parallel to the United States, favoured bilateral and regional trade agreements. By September 2009, India had conducted ten rounds of trade negotiations with Japan,

38 Blustein, *Misadventures*, p. 267.

39 Anthony Faiola and Rama Lakshmi, "Trade Talks Crumble in Feud Over Farm Aid", *Washington Post*, 30 July 2008.

40 One leading Indian economist noted during a confidential interview that if India's agricultural sector is such a "mess", then surely successive governments rather than the WTO have a great deal to do with this. Other experts note that India's interest in expanding internationally its services sector was barely mentioned in the WTO rows, suggesting that official decision-making is driven much more by political impulses than India's actual economic and social needs, even that it is "substantially data-free", often, perhaps unwittingly at times, setting up a conflict between "principles and outcomes." And, in spite of enthusiasm over Nath's theatrics in the short term, his performance today is assessed more critically even by a number of strong Indian nationalists as "too abrasive" (Conversations in Delhi, January and February 2010).

41 Rituparna Bhuyan, "WTO meet: Taking the Doha Round forward", *Indian Express*, 4 September 2009.

six rounds with the EU, and three rounds with the European Free Trade Association (EFTA).[42] In August 2009, India also concluded the ASEAN-India Free Trade Agreement (AIFTA), which had been in the works for a few years, and was a limited deal involving many opt-out options.[43]

## The Shape of Things to Come: Climate Change

India's approach to international environmental law has in some ways mirrored its approach to the international trade regime. In both cases, India has traditionally strived to balance the commitments of international law with the exigencies of domestic law and development. On the issue of environmental law, while India has taken steps to bring its domestic legislation in line with international requirements, it has also been vocal in articulating the consistent tension between developmental objectives and the requirements of international environmental law. Following the 1972 UN conference on the environment at Stockholm, India amended its constitution and domestic laws to accommodate international conceptions of environmental law. New laws such as the Air (Prevention and Control of Pollution) Act 1981 and the Environment (Protection) Act 1986 were passed. Following the Rio summit of 1992, India also legislated the National Environmental Tribunal Act 1995.[44] In the late 1980s and early 1990s, the Indian judiciary expanded the scope of the fundamental right to life and personal liberty guaranteed in Article 21 of the Indian Constitution to include environmental protection.[45] While making these changes, India has also consistently advocated financial assistance to developing nations by developed nations in order to achieve sustainable development, and the equitable sharing of benefits arising out of the utilisation of resources such as genetic resources.[46]

The tension between international environmental law and domestic priorities became most evident in the run up to the Copenhagen climate conference of 2009. Following the 2009 national elections, and a first term in which environmental matters received scant attention within the government, Prime Minister Singh appointed one of India's most talented

42 Patralekha Chatterjee, "Unhealthy effects of FTAs," *Asian Age*, 14 September 2009.
43 Data are not yet available to determine whether trade with India's new bilateral and regional trading partners has increased as a result of these agreements.
44 A. David Ambrose, "International Environmental Law and India" in Patel (ed.), *India and International Law, Vol. 1*.
45 *Ibid*, p. 255.
46 *Ibid*, pp. 256-257.

mediagenic younger politicians, Jairam Ramesh, to the environment portfolio. India's position had long been to stick closely to the terms of the Kyoto Protocol to the UN Framework Convention on Climate Change, under which industrialized countries committed to specific targets for emission reductions while developing countries were not required to do so under the "common but differentiated" responsibilities approach that had characterised UN discussions and agreements on the issue since the Rio Conference.

Ramesh began arguing within the government in favour of flexibility with regard to India's approach to climate change negotiations, in line with the reported determination of Prime Minister Singh that at Copenhagen, India should be "part of the solution to the problem."[47] Ramesh was quoted as having argued: "India must listen more and speak less in negotiations"as its stance is "disfavoured by the developed countries, small island states and vulnerable countries. It takes away from India's aspirations for permanent membership of the Security Council."[48] Ramesh was soon challenged by two of India's long-time negotiators, and reportedly also by the Prime Minister's Special Envoy on Climate Change, Shyam Saran, a former Foreign Secretary. Specifically, an offer articulated by Ramesh that India could offer to reduce India's carbon intensity by 20-25 per cent of 2005 levels by 2020 was questioned by the negotiators who queried the prudence of offering unilateral concessions without obtaining reciprocity from other countries.[49] Ramesh was quick to point out in Parliament that India's concession was not legally binding and would still permit economic growth; doubtless a useful tactic in parliament, but one that left India in somewhat of a negotiating quandary.[50]

Ramesh's arguments seemed to recognize on the one hand that India could not stand idly by as its own environment headed toward serious degradation, but also, implicitly, on the other that India needed to be in a position to offer something positive if non-binding – including a degree of international follow-up on its implementation of commitments at the negotiating table if it genuinely wanted to play – particularly in the big

47 See text of a conversation between Dr. Singh and Council on Foreign relations President Richard Haas, the transcript of which is dated 22 November 2009 to be found at: http://www.cfr.org/publication/20840/conversation_with_prime_minister_dr_manmohan_singh.html
48 Nitin Sethi, "Jairam for major shift at climate talks", *Times of India*, 19 October 2009.
49 Aarti Dhar, "Jairam irons out differences with negotiators," *The Hindu*, 7 December 2009.
50 For an analysis of India's negotiating quandary going into the Copenhagen conference, see Dhruva Jaishankar, "Taking the Heat: Where India stands on climate change", in *Pragati*, December 2009, pp. 3-5.

leagues. In the event, India offered [voluntary] emissions goals that would be subject to international "consultation and analysis" but not scrutiny or formal review.[51]

Following the Copenhagen talks, widely perceived as a fiasco, Prime Minister Singh mildly deplored their "very limited" progress.[52] But the outcome served India's diplomatic interests very well in allowing it to be "part of the solution," a last-minute truncated accord, offered by the four BASIC powers and the USA and acknowledged – however reluctantly and only by taking "note" of it – by the conference plenary, and also in underscoring that India was now an indispensable negotiating partner on key global challenges such as climate change. Unlike its posture in Geneva at the WTO in 2008, where China shielded itself behind an assertive India, at Copenhagen, India allowed China to take the heat for frustrating official and NGO activists campaigning for an ambitious outcome. Moreover, India, like the other major countries, submitted its implementation plan further to the Copenhagen accord by the deadline of 31 January 2010; it noted, however, that the plan would exclude the sensitive agriculture sector.[53]

The follow-up conference to Copenhagen at Cancun in late 2010 restored a modicum of faith in the multilateral process for most observers. India's participation in the conference was once again dexterous. While allowing China to bear much of the pressure on the BASIC group to accept legally binding emission cuts, the Indian negotiating team continued to lobby the developed nations for greater flexibility on technology transfers and funding of green initiatives in developing nations. The BASIC group itself faced some internal differences over the question of legally binding cuts, with China and India coming out against them and South Africa and Brazil in favour.[54] Nonetheless, Jairam Ramesh created significant confusion both in India and among the BASIC countries when a few days later he articulated the need for all countries to accept "binding commitments in some appropriate legal form."[55] While he was roundly criticized by the Parliamentary opposition in India for "selling out" the Indian position and

51 Evan A. Feigenbaum, "India's Rise, America's Interest," *Foreign Affairs*, Vol. 89, No. 2, March/April 2010, p. 90.

52 Praful Bidwai, "Fouling up the air," *Frontline*, 29 January 2010.

53 Express News Service, "India sends emission cut plan to the UN, leave out farm sector," *Indian Express*, 1 February 2010.

54 Betwa Sharma, "We are not for legally binding emission cuts: Jairam," *The Hindu*, Dec 10, 2010.

55 T. Jayaraman, "Taking stock of Cancun," *The Hindu*, Dec 13, 2010.

jeopardising a carefully crafted working relationship with China,[56] some perceptive analysts warned against reading too much into his statement,[57] which seemed designed to create greater negotiating flexibility for India than to lock India into any irreversible positions.

On balance, many at home perceived the results for India at Copenhagen and Cancun as positive rather than negative on the global climate conferences and their limited outcome.[58] In contrast to its positions at the WTO in 2008, India demonstrated agility in the run-up to both climate change conferences, and dexterity during the meetings, allowing it to emerge as one of the forgers of a compromise at Copenhagen and one of the nations willing to push negotiations forward productively at Cancun.

## Changing Winds: Nuclear Non-Proliferation And Testing

Perhaps the prickliest thorn in India's side as far as international treaties are concerned relates to the issue of nuclear weapons. India's position on issues of nuclear non-proliferation and testing has been marked by the consistent articulation of an alternative vision of global disarmament and non-proliferation, and its diplomacy in this realm has often resorted to "high-minded moral rhetoric."[59] Until the so-called nuclear deal concluded between the United States and India in 2007, endorsed by others in Vienna in 2008, India had suffered through diplomatic isolation on this issue for four decades.

India was one of the earliest advocates of nuclear disarmament when it called for the inclusion of the item "non-proliferation of nuclear weapons" on the UN's agenda in 1964.[60] India was also involved in the drafting of the Nuclear Non-Proliferation Treaty (NPT) in the early 1960s. However, it subsequently refused to sign the treaty itself in 1968 on grounds that it was discriminatory and divided the world into the nuclear 'haves' and 'have-nots'. India's 'peaceful nuclear explosion' of 1974 served to further

56 Priscilla Jebaraj, "Opposition slams Jairam's new climate formula," *The Hindu*, Dec 11, 2010.
57 T. Jayaraman, "Taking stock".
58 For editorial responses from two prominent Indian newspapers, see "Silver linings," *Indian Express*, 21 December 2010, and "Far from inspiring," *The Hindu*, 21 December 2009.
59 Amrita Narlikar, "Reforming Institutions, Unreformed India?" in Alan S. Alexandr off and Andrew F. Cooper (eds.), *Rising States, Rising Institutions: Challenges for Global Governance* (Brookings Institution Press, Washington, D.C., 2010), p. 120.
60 Chinmaya R. Gharekhan, "India and the United Nations," in Atish Sinha, Madhup Mohta (eds.), *Indian Foreign Policy: Challenges and Opportunities* (Foreign Service Institute, Delhi, 2007), p. 205.

isolate its position in international nuclear diplomacy, even though many of the principles India had promoted in the early 1960s – including the peaceful uses of nuclear energy and non-proliferation being a step toward universal disarmament and not an end in itself – had found their way into the NPT.[61]

India did not abandon its position even when the NPT came up for permanent extension in 1995. The following year, India doggedly opposed the Comprehensive Test Ban Treaty (CTBT) on grounds that the treaty did not preclude subcritical testing by nuclear weapons states. Thus India argued that the CTBT was merely a "threshold" ban and not a "comprehensive" ban.[62] This did not sit well with India's vision that the CTBT should really be a "Comprehensive Nuclear Disarmament Treaty."[63] Moreover, in the eyes of the world, India could not let itself be "captured" by the CTBT after opposing and avoiding the NPT for decades.[64] Although India did its best to prevent the CTBT from reaching the UN General Assembly for a vote, it was in the end predictably unsuccessful.

The events of 1995-96—combined with India's perceived security threat from Pakistan's covert nuclear weapons program (assisted by China)– precipitated India's second round of nuclear tests in 1998. Having refused to sign the original NPT, opposed its extension, and opposed the CTBT; India technically did not violate any international agreements. However, its actions did not endear it to supporters of the global non-proliferation regime. The 1998 tests were followed by American sanctions and condemnation from all corners of the international community. Nonetheless, in 2000, President Bill Clinton made a successful and highly publicized visit to India that initiated a longer process of US-India rapprochement. India, however, remained recalcitrant on the nuclear issue. In March 2004, then foreign minister in the BJP government, Yashwant Sinha, stated:

> *"It was the imposition of an imperfect non-proliferation order, evidence of which is all around us, that compelled us to make the transition from nuclear abstinence to that of a reluctant nuclear power. And, it*

61 Narlikar, "Reforming Institutions," p. 121.

62 Keith A. Hansen, *The Comprehensive Nuclear Test Ban Treaty: An Insider's Perspective* (Stanford Law and Politics, Stanford: 2006), p. 39.

63 Raju G.C. Thomas, "Should India Sign the NPT/CTBT?" in Raju G.C. Thomas (ed.), *The Nuclear Non-Proliferation Regime: Prospects for the 21st Century* (Macmillan, London: 1998), p. 285.

64 Hansen, *The CTBT*, p. 42.

> *was after we, as a nation, agonized over the issue for decades, that this Government finally took the plunge six years back.*"[65]

These words suggested a fundamental disconnect between India's vision and the reality of the global non-proliferation regime.

While a change of government in India in 2004 did not bring about a change in India's nuclear diplomacy, a shift in the second George W. Bush administration's priorities brought about a momentous development in India's relations with the international non-proliferation regime. In 2007, India concluded the '123 Agreement' with Washington that would produce an end to over three decades of nuclear isolation for India. Following intense lobbying by both the US and India, by October 2008 the deal had been approved by the International Atomic Energy Agency (IAEA), the Nuclear Suppliers Group (NSG), and the US Senate, achieving for President Bush his main positive foreign policy legacy. The agreement not only legitimised India's nuclear program and its non-proliferation record, it also opened the channels of nuclear commerce between India and other members of the NSG, most notably Russia and France.[66]

The India-US nuclear deal shook the global non-proliferation regime to its roots. Those in support of the deal saw it as a means of rewarding a de facto responsible nuclear power that had observed the letter and spirit of the NPT without actually signing it. India's obvious violations of the CTBT were less talked about. Supporters of the deal also argued that bringing India's civilian nuclear facilities under IAEA safeguards would be an effective way of injecting predictability into India's nuclear behaviour and locking India into the global non-proliferation regime.[67] Critics of the deal rightly worried about its impact on the regime itself. As one commentator observed, "it seems that India's exceptionalism and self-interest has paid off. But the more troubling issue is what happens to non-proliferation, and the long-term consequences of non-compliance in the international arena."[68] India's rhetorical use of the term "responsible nuclear state" was also viewed by some as a warning sign for the international regime: "What this means for international law is the recognition that the politically

65 Rao, "General Principles," p. 41.

66 BBC News, "India-Russia nuclear deal signed," 5 December 2009.

67 See Mario E. Carranza, "From nonproliferation to post-proliferation: Explaining the US-India nuclear deal," *Contemporary Security Policy*, 28, no. 3 (2007), pp. 464-93.

68 Priya Pillai, "India and the Nuclear Weapons Proliferation," in Patel (ed.), *India and International Law, Vol. 2*, p. 130.

savvy can and [do] affect international norms."[69] Although many in India disagreed, the world viewed the deal as a decisive victory for India and a dramatic transition from the status of nuclear pariah to recognised (and responsible) nuclear weapons state.

Events following the deal moved faster than the debates surrounding them. During President Obama's visit to Delhi in November 2010, the US became the first nuclear weapons state to endorse the idea of talks between the five nuclear weapons states (as per the NPT) and the three nuclear-armed states outside the NPT: India, Pakistan and Israel. As observed by an Indian journalist, "In doing so, India and the US have assembled the basic building blocks of a framework which has the potential to transcend the NPT, while remaining faithful to the twin goals of non-proliferation and the elimination of nuclear weapons."[70] An outcome of this nature would certainly help to bridge India's vision of non-proliferation with the rest of the world's, and also to diminish the controversies in India and abroad over India's opposition to the NPT and CTBT.

## Global Responsibilities: Is India Ready?

The close partnership between the US and India on the nuclear deal – essentially a bilateral agreement that has launched the transformation of a decades old multilateral regime – has created some concern over India's commitment to multilateralism. While a prominent writer in India expressed alarm at the "self-conscious revolt in India against multilateralism" that the US-India deal represented, he worried more about "how much like the US we [Indians] want to become unilateral, oriented towards hegemony more than stability of the world, and besotted with its own sense of power."[71] This sentiment points to a broader trend in India's approach to multilateral treaties, which is the tendency to eschew genuine multilateralism in favour of global governance by oligarchy. This approach not only tends to promote a very narrow conception of Indian interests, but also threatens to undermine the multilateral system as a whole.

Although reactions to some of India's actions and positions over time no doubt overstate the tilt against multilateralism in Indian foreign policy,

69 Fakiha Khan, "India and International Civilian Nuclear Energy Law," in Patel (ed.), *India and International Law, Vol. 2*, p. 156.

70 Siddharth Varadarajan, "In a first, India, US for dialogue of all nuclear weapon states," *The Hindu*, Nov 09, 2010.

71 Pratap Bhanu Mehta, "Five Balancing Acts," *Seminar*, January 1, 2007.

they do raise two important questions relevant today, as India emerges as a premier global interlocutor. First, what kind of power does India aspire to be, and how will it engage with others in years to come? Second, is the Indian foreign policy establishment attuned to engaging with the multilateral system not just on India's own terms but also on ones that actually will appeal to others and contribute to positive outcomes?

In 2003, in the run up to the American invasion of Iraq, Sonia Gandhi wrote: "Many in the United States are impatient with multilateralism, but in today's interdependent world there is simply no alternative to working in concert and collaboration with each other."[72] In 2004, Manmohan Singh outlined India's global philosophy, which he described as "cooperative pluralism" enshrined in the Sanskrit phrase and Hindu philosophy of *Vasudhaiva Kutumbakam* – the whole world is one family.[73] These statements, taken together, suggest a cooperative outlook ideally suited to multilateral institutions, the desire to transform them constructively, and a recognition that with greater power and influence comes responsibility in international affairs.

Nonetheless, there exists a gap between Prime Ministerial and other Indian aspirations for a more genuinely multilateral management of international relations on the one hand, and on the other India's negotiating position and style in a variety of forums and issue-by-issue. This gap is emphasised by a commentator on climate change: "In an ironic and to most Indians quite disturbing turn, India is increasingly portrayed as an obstructionist in the global climate negotiations. How did a country likely to be on the frontline of climate impacts – with a vast proportion of the world's poor and a reasonably good record of energy-related environmental policy and performance – reach this diplomatic *cul de sac*?"[74] The story is the same in trade – India holds up its economic liberalisation as a major achievement in facilitating the free flow of goods and services across borders, yet gets saddled with the blame for obstructing the Doha Round. Similarly on nuclear technology, India trumpets its record in non-proliferation and nuclear safety yet is excluded for three decades from multilateral access to nuclear technology and is consistently chided for refusing to sign up to the NPT and CTBT.

72 Sonia Gandhi, "Conflict and Coexistence in Our Age," *Seminar*, February 7, 2003.

73 Manmohan Singh, "India and the World," 5 November 2004.

74 Navroz K. Dubash, "Climate Politics in India: How Can the Industrialized World Bridge the Trust Deficit?" in David Michel and Amit Pandya (eds.), *Indian Climate Policy: Choices and Challenges*, (The Henry L. Stimson Center, Washington, DC: 2009), p. 49.

Domestic politics play a key role in determining India's positions on "hot button" international issues. And domestic politics in India have largely been geared toward constraining the positions of its negotiators, or pressuring them toward intransigent and dogmatic positions (or holding patterns) on key issues, for fear they may be seen as insufficiently sensitive to parochial national interests. Despite India's new membership of the multilateral power elite, the domestic chorus on multilateral challenges too often remains a resounding "No" – no increase in bound rate tariff triggers, no legally binding caps on emissions, no commitment to refrain from nuclear testing. Negotiators themselves, while they are often highly knowledgeable and sophisticated in the intricacies of multilateral agreements, are not equipped or mandated to pull domestic constituents along, at a time when India's domestic politics are getting more complex by the day.

While domestic politics constrain in one way, India's own ambitions and diplomatic strategies constrain in another. In every regime examined in this paper, India has either managed, or is trying, to become a member of the small group of great powers with agenda setting powers and the ability to influence decisions. Permanent membership of the UNSC, the Five Interested Parties at the WTO, the BASIC group of countries in climate change negotiations, and the India-US nuclear agreement all point to an Indian desire for a seat at the high table. However, without constructive negotiating positions or a focus on the underlying issues that a regime is trying to address, India remains ill equipped and unable to do its part at the high table. In most cases, India has focused less on the management of the multilateral system and more on very narrow conceptions of its national interest, often at the cost of the success of the regime in question (especially in trade and nuclear issues). As a result, despite its best intentions, India is not viewed as a fully responsible global player yet.

India therefore finds itself neither able to pull its domestic constituents along on multilateral diplomacy, nor able to demonstrate enough weight in the multilateral system to push its domestically determined agenda through without being labelled a spoiler or obstructionist. Delhi's growing drive to break free of the developing country mould and join the major powers in managing the multilateral system thus creates a tension and a degree of unpredictability in how India's positions are likely to evolve during international negotiations. Nitin Desai colourfully points out that the final Copenhagen agreement was achieved by the two "20% players" (the US and China in terms of carbon emissions) while India, which was among the "5% players" (with Japan and Russia) was only needed to provide some extra ballast on the Chinese side along with the two "2% players," Brazil and South Africa.[75] Given that the future of the international system is likely to be determined to a significant degree by Sino-US understandings and disagreements, India will likely continue to straddle as many multilateral divides as possible to keep its options open while its weight in international relations grows.

## Conclusion

Today, India's diplomacy is overwhelmingly bilateral in nature and generally quite successful in that realm. Multilaterally, it is organised more around smaller, plurilateral groupings of several meaningful states, or regional bodies.[76] This may be because as global challenges like climate change come to the fore, the responsibility to shoulder a part in their resolution, sometimes at real financial cost, is something other countries – including poorer developing countries – will expect India to take on. And India has not yet thought through the extent to which it is yet able and willing to take on such extensive and potentially expensive obligations. The voluntary, non-binding route in defining its commitments is more attractive for now, but as its economy and weight grows further, it will not find it easy to stick to this path. Balancing domestic politics with a desire for international status – both economic and political – will be India's challenge in the future.

75 Nitin Desai, "When two's company," *Times of India*, 4 January 2010.

76 G. Parasarathy points out, rightly that the West was very slow to notice this evolution of Indian foreign policy, in particular its growing engagement with ASEAN and other Asian actors. (Conversation, February 2010)

# Part VIII
# 21st Century Challenging Environmental Regulation

*Journal of Environmental Law* **21**:2 
doi:10.1093/jel/eqp012 Advance Access published on 13 May 2009

# Maturity and Methodology: Starting a Debate about Environmental Law Scholarship†

Elizabeth Fisher,* Bettina Lange,**
Eloise Scotford*** and Cinnamon Carlarne****

## Abstract

Many environmental law scholars perceive environmental law scholarship as immature. We discuss why this self-perception has arisen and argue that a common theme is methodology. We argue that the subject can only mature when we face its methodological challenges head on, and we identify four particular issues that have given rise to these challenges: the speed and scale of legal/regulatory change, the interdisciplinary nature of the subject, the heavy reliance in environmental law on a diverse range of governance arrangements and the multi-jurisdictional nature of the subject. We argue that there is a need for debate in the face of these challenges and identify some starting points for that debate.

Keywords: environmental law scholarship, methodology, interdisciplinarity, environmental governance

†We thank Chris Hilson, Judith Jones, Maria Lee, Jenny Steele, two anonymous reviewers and the participants at the Environmental Law Section of the 2008 SLS Conference for comments on previous drafts of this article. Any errors or omissions remain our own.
*Reader in Environmental Law, Corpus Christi College, University of Oxford, (liz.fisher@law.ox.ac.uk).
**University Lecturer in Law and Regulation, Centre for Socio Legal Studies, University of Oxford.
***Career Development Fellow in Environmental Law, Faculty of Law, University of Oxford.
****Assistant Professor, School of Law, University of South Carolina.

Let us be frank. According to environmental law scholars, environmental law as an academic discipline has spent the last 20 years coming of age.[1] The maturing of it as a scholarly enterprise has been eagerly awaited and predicted but adulthood has never arrived. Environmental law scholars still perceive that the best is yet to come.

The stubborn persistence of this perception of enduring immaturity signifies the need for environmental lawyers to take a harder look at, and talk more about, what they do, how they do it and why they do it. We see the need for an explicit and honest debate about the state of environmental law scholarship. To get that discussion going we put forward a very simple argument—environmental law scholarship can only come of age when scholars face the methodological challenges of environmental law research head on. This is because a lack of explicit and widespread discussion about methodology in environmental law scholarship has hampered the academic development of the subject and threatened the worth of environmental law as an intellectual discipline.

We can think of no better place to start a discussion about environmental law scholarship than in the *Journal of Environmental Law*. We know that what we have to say is controversial and provocative. As authors we are not arguing from any privileged position and we seek to avoid disciplinary imperialism.[2] We comprise a diverse group that includes an international environmental scholar, a socio-legal scholar, a regulatory/doctrinal scholar and a comparative/interdisciplinary scholar. In other words, we are, methodologically and intellectually, a profoundly divergent group of environmental law researchers. Yet, with that said, there is a striking convergence amongst our views as to the problems facing environmental law scholars.

The structure of this article is as follows. First, we briefly consider what is covered by the term 'environmental law scholarship'. Second, we examine why there has been an ongoing perception that environmental law scholarship is 'immature' as an academic discipline and how that perception reflects a questioning of the legitimacy of environmental law as an academic discipline. We identify four particular features of environmental law that have contributed to this state of affairs: its intellectual incoherence, the 'marginal' nature of the subject as an area of academic study, the poor quality of some

1 The language of imminent maturity pervades environmental law scholarship. See D Tarlock, 'Is There Any There There in Environmental Law?' (2004) 19 Journal of Land Use and Environmental Law 213; C Rose, 'Environmental Law Grows Up (More or Less) and What Science Can Do to Help' (2005) 9 Lewis and Clark Law Review 273; T Jewell and C Reid, 'Environmental Law' in D Hayton (ed) *Law's Future(s): British Legal Developments in the 21st Century* (Hart Publishing, Oxford 2000) 209; P Ryan, 'Did We? Should We? Revisiting the 70s' Environmental Law Challenge in NSW' (2001) 18 Environmental and Planning Law Journal 561; D Driesen, 'Thirty Years of International Environmental Law: A Retrospective and Plea for Reinvigoration' (2003) 30 Syracuse J Int L and Commerce 353.

2 D Rhode, 'Legal Scholarship' (2002) 115 Harvard L Rev 1327.

environmental law scholarship and the sheer difficulty of doing environmental law scholarship.

In the third section, we argue that discussions about immaturity are really discussions about the complex methodological challenges of the subject. A focus on these challenges provides a constructive starting point for a debate about environmental law scholarship. As catalysts for this debate, we identify four different overarching methodological challenges: dealing with the speed and scale of legal/regulatory change, engaging with the interdisciplinary nature of the subject, addressing the heavy reliance in environmental law on a diverse range of governance arrangements and tackling the multi-jurisdictional nature of the subject.

In the final section we identify five steps that environmental law scholars should consider taking in order to address these challenges: reflecting on the relationship between choice of method and research questions asked, mapping the subject, engaging with more general debates over legal methodology (including socio-legal methodology), getting to grips with interdisciplinarity and having a more explicit debate about how to assess the quality of environmental law scholarship. In identifying these steps we do not aim to provide a definitive 'how to' guide for environmental law scholarship; in fact, we seek to avoid being prescriptive, since there are no magic methodological formulas or solutions for environmental law scholars. Rather, we wish to initiate a widespread and critical discourse about how environmental law scholars can produce methodologically rigorous scholarship. Such a discourse is needed for environmental law scholarship to mature as a scholarly enterprise.

Three points should be made before starting. First, the starting point for this article is not how other legal and non-legal scholars perceive environmental law scholarship. Rather, our starting point is the harsh and critical way in which environmental law scholars perceive environmental law scholarship and themselves. Second, our general focus is upon UK/EU and international environmental law scholarship, although we also do refer to Commonwealth and US literature due to the fact that the boundaries between these bodies of scholarship are porous. Third, our focus on environmental law scholarship does not discount the fact that similar debates are going on in other sub-disciplines of law and law more generally. The issues discussed in this article are similarly difficult and confronting for legal scholars in other areas of legal scholarship.[3] The importance of these common challenges is illustrated in Section 4.3.

3 B Cheffins, 'The Trajectory of (Corporate Law) Scholarship' (2004) 63 CLJ 456; Rhode (n 2); Special Issue on Legal Scholarship, 63 University of Colorado Law Review 521–750 (1992); 'Special Issue - Legal Scholarship in the Modern World' 50 MLR 673–854 (1987); J Shaw, 'European Union Legal Studies in Crisis? Towards a New Dynamic' (1996) 16 OJLS 231.

## 1. Defining Environmental Law Scholarship

Before proceeding further it is important to define environmental law scholarship. Such an exercise is not semantic pedantry on our part. By defining the subject we want to make very clear what we are doing and not doing in writing this article.

Environmental law scholarship is a subset of legal scholarship. Legal scholarship is a pluralistic enterprise and there is a multitude of disciplinary approaches to the study of law.[4] Any definition of 'legal scholarship' or 'environmental law scholarship' that does not recognise this fact is fundamentally problematic. For this reason, a starting point for thinking about environmental law scholarship must be a broad definition of legal scholarship. Feldman has defined legal scholarship in the following terms:

> I define scholarship as *action* informed by a distinctive *attitude of mind*... *Legal* scholarship is a conception which results from the application of the concept of scholarship to the special kinds of problems that are discovered in the study of laws and legal systems.[5]

Those 'special kinds of problems' may vary with subject matter, research aim and disciplinary outlook. Those problems may not necessarily all be legal but the focus for analysis is the law, whether it is a focus on reasoning internal to the law or on law in context. In terms of research aim, scholarship may be undertaken for many different purposes, including addressing practical, policy and/or legal questions, informing law reform, classifying and systematising the law or undertaking an exercise in more open-ended intellectual exploration. For Feldman *all* of this scholarship amounts to scholarship if scholars working in a certain field are

> guided by certain ideals, which distinguishes scholarship both from the single-minded pursuit of an end and from dilettantism.
> The ideals include: (1) a commitment to employing methods of investigation and analysis best suited to satisfying that curiosity; (2) self-conscious and reflective open-mindedness, so that one does not assume the desired result and adopt procedures to verify it, or even pervert one's material to support a chosen conclusion; and (3) the desire to publish the work for the illumination of students, fellow scholars or the general public and enable others to evaluate and criticise it.[6]

4 D Feldman, 'The Nature of Legal Scholarship' (1989) 52 MLR 498; Rhode (n 3), 1329; M Dan-Cohen, 'Listeners and Eavesdroppers: Substantive Legal Theory and Its Audience' (1992) 63 Univ Colorado L Rev 569.

5 Feldman (n 4), 502.

6 Ibid 503.

Feldman's point is that the defining feature of legal 'scholarship' is that it is a product of scholars striving to realise certain 'ideals' in relation to intellectual endeavour.

*Environmental law* scholarship is scholarship predicated on the above ideals and addresses the 'special kinds of problems' that are discovered in the study of laws and legal systems that relate to the environment. Scholars have consistently highlighted the complex nature of those problems[7] and, as we shall see, those problems include methodological issues.

There are two important points to note from this definition. First, environmental law scholarship may take many forms. Thus, for example, it may be socio-legal, doctrinal or jurisprudential. The mark of good environmental law scholarship is not that it deploys a *particular* method but that it must deploy *some thought-out* method. Moreover, it must seek to avoid being a 'resolutely single-minded pursuit of an end' or mere 'dilettantism'.

Second, while environmental law scholarship is an aspect of environmental law as a subject, they are not equivalent concepts. The academic discipline of environmental law, and the scholarship that characterises it, is different from the identity of environmental law as a whole subject, which also includes the contributions of legislators, administrators and practitioners, amongst others. Thus, the success and quality of environmental law scholarship is not directly dependent on the success of environmental law as a body of law in achieving certain outcomes or promoting certain values.[8] These two issues are often conflated and, while we accept they are interrelated, the failure to differentiate has not helped in encouraging clear thinking about either environmental law scholarship or environmental law itself. In particular, it has meant that environmental law scholars have focused too much on the state of the environment and the law and too little on what they are doing. Rhode makes the point well in discussing legal scholarship more generally.

> We reflect endlessly on the deficiencies of other participants in the legal culture – judges, legislators, lawyers, and government officials – but rarely devote similar attention to our own inadequacies. On the relatively infrequent occasions like this one, when we are explicitly invited to discuss legal scholarship, we seldom focus on the structural sources of the problems that we identify.[9]

With regard to environmental law scholarship, this has meant that, while the discipline is understood to be in a problematic state, the focus has tended to

7 Jewell and Reid (n 1); Rose (n 1).

8 R Lazarus, 'Judging Environmental Law' (2004) 18 Tulane Envtl L J 201; D Wilkinson, 'Using Environmental Ethics to Create Ecological Law' in J Holder and D McGillivray (eds) *Locality and Identity: Environmental Issues in Law and Society* (Ashgate Dartmouth, Aldershot 1999).

9 Rhode (n 2), 1327.

be on the law and on other legal actors.[10] This article adopts a different focus by putting environmental law scholarship itself under scrutiny. We are looking at the 'structural sources' of our scholarly problems, and not legal solutions to environmental problems.

## 2. Why Environmental Law Scholarship Is Perceived as 'Immature'

It is an uncontroversial fact that most environmental law scholars wish to produce great legal scholarship. It is also the case that many environmental law scholars have produced great legal scholarship—evidenced by the prizes that environmental law scholarship has won, the pre-eminence of those who have published environmental law scholarship and the fact that environmental law scholars have posts in a diverse array of law faculties. Despite these successes, there still exists considerable intellectual self-doubt amongst environmental law scholars over the maturity—and, thus, perceived scholarly 'worthiness'—of environmental law scholarship.[11]

Indeed, there is a strongly held belief amongst environmental law scholars that the subject has not yet come of age as an area of legal scholarship and that the best is yet to come.[12] To put it bluntly—environmental law scholarship is characterised as immature.[13] Moreover, these perceptions have not shifted in over two decades.[14] Indeed, for environmental law scholars, environmental law scholarship seems to be like the Peter Pan of legal scholarship—'the discipline that never grew up'.

This lack of maturity may have its positive attributes (see Section 2.2 below), but for many scholars it means that the scholarly worth and legitimacy of environmental law scholarship is not yet fully established.[15] Since the subject

10 Lazarus (n 8); H Woolf, 'Are the Judiciary Environmentally Myopic?' (1992) 3 JEL 1; Ryan (n 1).

11 See, above n 1; L Kramer, 'The Environment and the Ten Commandments' (2008) 20 JEL 5.

12 C Hilson, 'Editor's Foreword' (2008) 20 JEL 1; R Macrory, 'Standards, Legitimacy and the Law – the New Environmental Agenda' (2001) 18 Environmental and Planning Law Journal 242; G Winter, 'Perspectives for Environmental Law – Struggling for Sustained Humanity' (2008) 20 JEL 11.

13 This idea of maturity is comparable to that of Lakatos' in relation to discussing the development of scientific disciplines: I Lakatos, 'Falsification and the Methodology of Scientific Research Programmes' in I Lakatos and A Musgrave (eds) *Criticism and the Growth of Science* (Cambridge University Press, Cambridge 1974).

14 W Howarth, 'Water Pollution: Improving the Legal Controls in Retrospect' (2008) 20 JEL 3; Kramer (n 11); O Lomas, 'Predicting the Unpredictable' (2008) 20 JEL 7; C Miller, 'Has Environmental Law Become Humdrum?' (2008) 20 JEL 8; Winter (n 12).

15 See, above n 1; Z Plater, 'Environmental Law and the Three Economies: Navigating a Sprawling Field of Study, Practice, and Societal Governance in Which Everything is Connected to Everything Else' (1999) 23 Harv Envtl L Rev 359; V Wagner and A Holbey, 'Environmental Law – A Global System of Law' (1999) 10 International Company and Commercial Law

has not come of age, the knowledge claims of environmental law scholarship are not fully recognised.

There are many different reasons why the immature image of environmental law scholarship persists. Four are particularly significant: the intellectual incoherence of environmental law as a subject, the perceived marginality of environmental law scholarship in the legal academy, the poor quality of some environmental law scholarship and the sheer difficulty of carrying out environmental law scholarship. An analysis of each of these reasons exposes what underlies the image of environmental law as immature.

### *2.1 Intellectual Incoherence of the Subject*

The first reason why environmental law scholars perceive their discipline to be immature is that environmental law, as a subject, is incoherent.[16] Incoherence here means that the subject has no single guiding logic, no overarching doctrinal framework or no 'constitutional' grounding. Thus, for example, Westbrook notes

> Despite being a burgeoning area of practice, environmental law is not a discipline, because it lacks the professional consensus on a coherent internal organization of materials a discipline requires. The field's intellectual incoherence makes teaching environmental law difficult, and gives rise to widespread frustration among professors and students. [17]

This view is echoed by others. Environmental law, as a subject, is ad hoc,[18] a conceptual hybrid,[19] straddling many fault lines,[20] and presumed to have no philosophical underpinnings.[21] It is a sprawl and that means environmental law courses tend to be superficial surveys.[22]

The reasons given by scholars for the subject's incoherence vary. For some scholars this incoherence is due to the narrow focus of practitioners—the

Review 239; A Philippopoulos-Mihalopoulos, *Absent Environments: Theorising Environmental Law and the City* (Routledge-Cavendish, Abingdon 2007) 25; C Reid, 'Environmental Law: Shifting Through the Rubbish' (1998) Juridicial Review 236–54.

16 D Tarlock, 'The Future of Environmental Law "Rule of Law" Litigation' (2002) 19 Pace Environmental Law Review 575; Plater (n 15), 359 and 374; R Macrory, 'Editor's Foreword' (2006) 18 JEL 1; Tarlock (n 1), 218.

17 D Westbrook, 'Liberal Environmental Jurisprudence' (1994) 27 UC Davis L Rev 619–21.

18 J McEldowney and S McEldowney, *Environmental Law and Regulation* (Blackstone Press, London 2001) 8–9.

19 M Stallworthy, *Understanding Environmental Law* (Sweet and Maxwell, London 2008) 4.

20 L Heinzerling, 'The Environment' in P Cane and M Tushnet (eds) *The Oxford Handbook of Legal Studies* (OUP, Oxford 2003) 703.

21 S Coyle and K Morrow, *The Philosophical Foundations of Environmental Law: Property, Rights and Nature* (Hart Publishing, Oxford 2004) 1.

22 Plater (n 15), 361.

practical anxieties of this group, and the speed of legal change undermine the development of intellectual coherence and thus hamper scholarly maturity.[23] For others, it is part of the historical reality of the subject[24] and, for others again, it is due to the failure of environmental law scholars to identify the conceptual basis of their subject.[25] Finally, some scholars find that the subject's incoherence stems from environmental law's operation in an 'unsustainable society' that is at odds with green legal theory.[26] The subject's incoherence as a body of law is thus viewed as the discipline's scholarly incoherence.

But many scholars have sought to address this incoherence, for instance by identifying an overarching intellectual paradigm for the subject.[27] The presumption is that once a paradigm is adopted, the subject will have 'grown up'. Such a paradigm often takes the form of a grand narrative, a set of common 'principles' or a single purpose for the subject.[28] The problem is that such efforts tend to deny both the complex reality of the subject and the importance of plurality of legal scholarship. Likewise, much ink has been spilled attempting to define the boundaries of the subject as if this exercise will bring with it intellectual coherence.[29] Despite the effort, no definitive definition of the subject has been forthcoming.[30]

As we will discuss below, we think that environmental law's incoherence is real but that it does not determine the immaturity of environmental law scholarship. However, many environmental law scholars do see it as a sign of the immaturity of their discipline and the fact that environmental law scholarship has not come of age. This perception arises not simply from self-doubt but from a conflation of the complexities of environmental law *as a subject* and the quality of the *scholarship* that environmental lawyers create in relation to their subject. The incoherence of environmental law is not something that must (or can) be tamed by the intellectual efforts of environmental law scholars; rather it is the acceptance of that incoherence, and its methodological treatment, that marks mature environmental law scholarship.

23 Ibid 364; Howarth (n 14), 3; Kramer (n 11), 5; D Farber, 'Foreword' (2005) 32 Ecol L Q 383–6.
24 Heinzerling (n 20), 703–4; McEldowney and McEldowney (n 18), 7–9; Woolf (n 10).
25 Philippopoulos-Mihalopoulos (n 15), 25; E Freyfogle, 'Five Paths of Environmental Scholarship' (2000) Univ Illinois L Rev 115; Coyle and Morrow (n 21).
26 M M'Gonigle and P Ramsay, 'Greening Environmental Law: From Sectoral Reform to Systemic Re-Formation' (2004) 14 Journal of Environmental Law and Practice 333–52; A Flournoy, 'In Search Of an Environmental Ethic' (2003) 28 Colum J Envtl L 63; Wilkinson (n 8).
27 Plater (n 15); Tarlock (n 1); Coyle and Morrow (n 21).
28 N de Sadeleer, *Environmental Principles: From Political Slogans to Legal Rules* (OUP, Oxford 2002); Freyfogle (n 25).
29 D Wilkinson, *Environment and the Law* (Routledge, London 2002) 40.
30 Stallworthy (n 19), ch 1.

## 2.2 *Perceived Marginality of Environmental Law Scholarship*

Second, environmental law is perceived to be immature by environmental law scholars in the sense that it is seen, as an academic discipline, as marginal to mainstream legal scholarship. This perceived marginality has four interrelated aspects that reflect both positively and negatively on the scholarly identity of environmental law. They are grounded in both pure perception and hard facts.

First, environmental law scholarship is perceived to be marginal in that it is a small area of academic study compared with other areas of legal scholarship. There is some evidence of this. Those who cite environmental law as a research interest in academic directories and on law faculty websites are fewer than those who cite interests in other 'applied' areas of legal research, such as family law, medical law, labour law and human rights.[31] Furthermore, environmental law has remained a relatively small option in UK law schools.[32] A low number of scholars working in an area does not mean that the area is marginal. In relation to environmental law scholarship, however, the small size of the scholarly community has promoted that assumption, particularly because of the second aspect of perceived marginality—the disconnection between mainstream legal and environmental law scholarship. This disconnection concerns the practical context in which environmental law scholars are operating. Within the UK at least, demand for environmental law teaching comes from a significant number of non-law students.[33] Likewise, environmental lawyers often find themselves writing simultaneously for lawyers and non-lawyers[34]—an activity which does not place them at the core of the scholarly legal academy. This disconnection of environmental law scholarship from mainstream scholarship is furthered by the fact that non-lawyers also write about environmental law.[35]

The third reason for perceived marginality can be related back to the radical roots of the subject in alternative politics and the new social movements.[36] Much early environmental law scholarship was grounded in radical challenges

31 A rough survey of the 2007/8 Society of Legal Scholars Directory shows that 111 Ordinary Members listed environmental law as a special interest compared with those listing interests in other representative 'applied' legal subjects; 121 listing labour law; 136 listing family law and 141 listing medical law. A slightly different picture emerges from a rough survey of declarations of academic interests in individual staff profiles from UK universities Websites. One hundred twenty-one academics listed environmental law as a special interest compared with 87 listing labour law; 123 listing family law and 133 listing medical law.

32 S Bell and others, *Teaching Environmental Law* (UK Centre for Legal Education, Coventry 2003) stating that 57% of environmental law courses had fewer than 25 students in them.

33 Ibid 8.

34 McEldowney and McEldowney (n 18); Wilkinson (n 29).

35 S Beder, *Environmental Principles and Policies: An Interdisciplinary Introduction* (Earthscan, London 2006).

36 T Bonyhady, *Places Worth Keeping: Conservationists, Politics and the Law* (Allen & Unwin, St Leonards 1993).

to mainstream legal and political ideas, which failed to encompass and/or recognise the issues of importance to environmental law scholars.[37] The 'marginality' of the subject was thus deliberate and marginality is thus a virtue of environmental law scholarship—the lack of maturity a sign that environmental law scholars have not narrowed their intellectual field of vision. Indeed, recognition by the mainstream brings with it the threat of assimilation and, thus, the loss of what is of intellectual value in environmental law scholarship.[38]

The fourth aspect of the perceived marginality of environmental law scholarship derives from the fact that, compared with other applied subjects, there seem to be relatively few articles of environmental law scholarship published in mainstream legal journals.[39] This lack of mainstream placement provides yet another sign for environmental law scholars of the marginality of their subject.

Table 1 illustrates that there are few environmental law articles published in some mainstream legal journals as compared with other applied legal subjects. The table compares the number of articles (excluding book reviews and short notes) published on environmental law (including associated areas of health risk regulation) with the number published in four other applied legal subjects in 11 mainstream English language journals published in the EU and UK between 2000 and 2007. As the boundaries of any legal subject are difficult to define, each applied subject has been defined broadly and these numbers should only be taken as rough guides.

Overall, there are fewer articles concerning environmental law than concerning other legal topics. In particular, it can be seen that there is relatively little environmental law scholarship published in law journals with a national or socio-legal focus. The latter is surprising considering that some of the ground breaking socio-legal work has been in the environmental area.[40] The situation is different, however, in journals with a European or international law focus. These journals publish a comparatively large body of environmental law scholarship relative to the other topics.

37 C Stone, 'Should Trees Have Standing?: Towards Legal Rights for Natural Objects' (1972) 45 South Calif L Rev 450.

38 Tarlock (n 1), 230; on a related point, T Jewell, 'Public Law and the Environment: The Prospects for Decision-Making' in T Jewell and J Steele (eds) *Law in Environmental Decision-Making: National, European and International Perspectives* (Clarendon Press, Oxford 1998) 79–80.

39 R Lazarus, 'Environmental Scholarship and the Harvard Difference' (1999) 23 Harv Envtl L Rev 327.

40 B Hutter, 'Socio-legal Perspectives on Environmental Law: An Overview' in B Hutter *(ed.) A Reader in Environmental Law* (OUP, Oxford 1999); K Hawkins, *Environment and Enforcement* (OUP, Oxford 1984); G Richardson, A Ogus and P Burrows, *Policing Pollution: A Study of Regulation and Enforcement* (Clarendon Press, Oxford 1982).

**Table 1.** Academic articles organised by topic published between 2000 and 2007

| Journal | Environmental law | Medical law | Family law | Labour law | Human rights |
|---|---|---|---|---|---|
| Generalist Academic Law Journals | | | | | |
| *Law Quarterly Review* | 4 | 11 | 17 | 10 | 32 |
| *Legal Studies* | 6 | 15 | 9 | 1 | 15 |
| *Oxford Journal of Legal Studies* | 5 | 8 | 2 | 3 | 8 |
| *Cambridge Law Journal* | 7 | 17 | 16 | 6 | 47 |
| *Modern Law Review* | 5 | 21 | 12 | 13 | 22 |
| *Journal of Law and Society* | 5 | 8 | 6 | 12 | 17 |
| *Social and Legal Studies* | 4 | 14 | 11 | 2 | 12 |
| Subtotal | 36 | 94 | 73 | 47 | 153 |
| International Law and Comparative Law Journals | | | | | |
| *European Law Journal* | 8 | 5 | 2 | 11 | 15 |
| *European Law Review* | 14 | 4 | 10 | 24 | 49 |
| *European Journal of International Law* | 14 | 0 | 0 | 4 | 33 |
| *International Comparative Law Quarterly* | 16 | 1 | 9 | 1 | 31 |
| Subtotal | 52 | 10 | 21 | 40 | 128 |
| Overall total | 88 | 104 | 94 | 87 | 281 |

While this table crudely reflects the marginality of environmental law scholarship, it does not explain why few environmental law articles are being published in mainstream UK legal journals. It is not simply that these figures do not reveal how many environmental law articles were submitted to these journals, how many were rejected, the basis of rejection or the ratio of submissions to rejections in other applied fields. More importantly, these figures also do not reveal the thought processes of environmental law scholars in deciding whether to submit articles to particular journals and even why they chose to write on particular topics. Indeed, the variability in the number of articles being published in different journals on these applied legal subject areas is a strong indication that the reasons for this state of affairs are institutionally and intellectually complex.

### *2.3 Poor Quality of Some Environmental Law Scholarship*

The third reason for the persistent image of environmental law scholarship as immature is the quality of some of this scholarship. To be very blunt, there is some truly woeful environmental law scholarship out there. It may be in the minority but we should not pretend that it does not exist. And we need to acknowledge that we as scholars may have had something to do with its existence, whether through writing it, reviewing it or supervising it.

There are a number of reasons for the existence of poor scholarship. Some of it is poor simply because it is mislabelled as scholarship. In this category we place purely descriptive environmental law commentary aimed at practitioners. More problematically, there is a body of environmental law scholarship that exhibits the two problems highlighted in Feldman's quotation above—'resolutely single-minded pursuit of an end' and 'dilettantism'. With regard to the former, there are many examples of commentary that is polemic at the expense of careful academic analysis. This type of work is often justified by a looming environmental crisis or by the need to promote a certain ideology. A common feature of this scholarship is a complete failure of the scholar to engage with the actual legal or socio-legal issues facing a court, legislature or decision-maker. Law is simply an instrument and the researcher applies no critical framework for understanding it.

With regard to 'dilettantism', there is a tendency for some scholars to be 'bower birds',[41] dragging everything into their scholarship that is adorned by a certain label such as 'environmental' or 'sustainable development' with very little critical awareness that these concepts cannot be taken out of context and may mean different things in different contexts. 'Precaution-spotting' is one example of this tendency to presume the same label means the same thing across jurisdictions.[42] Another example can be seen between disciplines with scholars happily picking and mixing social science disciplines. The literature on 'risk' is a case in point: scholars see the word 'risk' and presume it means the same thing in different disciplines and different bodies of social science thought.[43]

All disciplines suffer from the blight of poor scholarship. But poor scholarship directly contributes to the perception of the immaturity of environmental law scholarship in a way that poor scholarship in other disciplines does not. This is partly because of the combined effect of the existence of such scholarship with the marginal image of the subject. Because of this, marginality begins to look less like a sophisticated intellectual choice and more like an illustration of the inferiority and immaturity of the subject. More importantly, however, as environmental law scholars we lack consistent criteria for judging the quality of research. There is little within environmental law scholarship to assist in critiquing and ranking the quality of that scholarship. We know dreadful environmental law scholarship when we see it, but environmental law scholars have developed little discourse to define such scholarship. Much of this has to do with the fact that environmental law scholars recognise the value of diversity and wish to foster it—they eschew

41 The male of the Australian satin bowerbird (*Ptilinorhynchus violaceus*) collects anything blue (both natural and manmade) to adorn his bower as a means of attracting numerous female birds. This can result in a bower full of flowers, plastic straws and clothes pegs.

42 E Fisher, 'Precaution, Precaution Everywhere: Developing a "Common Understanding" of the Precautionary Principle in the European Community' (2002) 9 Maast J Eur and Comp L 7.

43 E Fisher, 'Risk and Environmental Law: A Beginner's Guide' in B Richardson and S Wood (eds) *Environmental Law for Sustainability* (Hart Publishing, Oxford 2006).

disciplinary imperialism. Moreover, the radical roots of the subject have made environmental law scholars appreciative of the need for new scholarly approaches and hesitant to be hypercritical of experimentation. The problem is that the line between dilettantism and innovative interdisciplinary research is a very fine one, as is the line between a 'single-minded pursuit of an end' and recognising that the law may have a particular normative or ideological basis which is being be promoted.

### 2.4 *Difficulties of Environmental Law Scholarship*

The final and most significant reason why environmental law scholars perceive environmental law scholarship to be less grown up than other disciplines has less to do with the *quality* of scholars and scholarship and more to do with the *problems* of scholarship. The perception of immaturity is a product of the fact that environmental law scholars are painfully aware of just how difficult an academic study of the subject is.[44]

The difficulty arises because environmental law regimes tend to be complicated mixtures of established legal concepts, *sui generis* reforms, non-legal regulatory ideals, policy and legal norms from a range of different jurisdictions. In studying any area of environmental law, there is an acute awareness of the limitations of particular methodologies,[45] a difficulty with knowing what the scope of analysis should be[46] and a tension between wanting to treat environmental law issues as part of a distinct subject as well as seeing them as examples of more generic legal problems.[47] Environmental law as an object of scholarship and research does not yield easily to a single paradigm, methodology or explanation.

In light of these difficulties, environmental law scholars have become plagued with professional self-doubt. They ponder whether their subject is too insular,[48] whether the subject fails to take into account particular regulatory or governance techniques,[49] whether environmental law scholars need to be equipped with skills they do not yet possess[50] and what is the appropriate

44 Hilson (n 12); T Jewell and J Steele, 'Law in Environmental Decision-Making' in T Jewell and J Steele (eds) *Law in Environmental Decision-Making: National, European and International Perspectives* (OUP, Oxford 1998).

45 Heinzerling (n 20); J Freeman and D Farber, 'Modular Environmental Legislation' (2005) 54 Duke L J 795.

46 Jewell and Reid (n 1); B Richardson and S Wood, 'Environmental Law for Sustainability' in B Richardson and S Wood (eds) *Environmental Law for Sustainability* (Hart Publishing, Oxford 2006).

47 P Cane, 'Are Environmental Harms Special?' (2001) 13 JEL 3; Jewell (n 38).

48 Hilson (n 12).

49 Rose (n 1); Freeman and Farber (n 45); Jewell and Reid (n 1).

50 Rose (n 1).

role for normative values in their scholarship.[51] What such self-doubt highlights is that the relationship between the maturity of the subject and the legitimacy of the subject is a very real one. The intellectual challenges of the subject make the validity of any knowledge claims difficult to justify.

## 3. The Need to Focus on Methodology and Methodological Challenges

The discussion above may appear overly ponderous. Who wants to reflect deeply on the discontents of environmental law scholarship when focusing on solutions would seem a far more productive enterprise. We, however, support such reflection because to understand why the 'coming of age' narrative has persisted in environmental law scholarship is to lay the foundation for a real debate about the state of the subject. In particular, two things are clear from the above discussion.

First, the perception of environmental law scholarship as immature is a profoundly complex one, replete with both positive and negative reflections of the subject and multiple intellectual strands. Immaturity, simultaneously, signifies the incoherence of environmental law as a subject, and the quality and marginality of, and difficulties inherent in generating environmental law scholarship. Getting to grips with this multi-dimensionality is part of getting to grips with environmental law as a body of scholarship.

Second, we see that a common theme in these multifaceted debates over immaturity is that of methodology, in particular how environmental lawyers address, and are faced with, methodological issues. There are many different understandings of methodology; but, taking a dictionary definition, it is the 'branch of knowledge' concerned with method, where method is defined as

> A special form of procedure or characteristic set of procedures employed (more or less systematically) in an intellectual discipline or field of study as a mode of investigation and inquiry, or of teaching and exposition.[52]

Methodologies may take many different forms, but generally speaking a methodology amounts to a systematic procedure that a scholar applies as part of an intellectual enterprise.

In our discussion above, the theme of methodology is ever-present, albeit in different ways. The marginality of environmental law scholarship is partly due to the fact that environmental law scholars have to, or choose to, deploy different methodologies from mainstream scholars. The poor quality of

51 D Kysar and J Salzman, 'Environmental Tribalism' (2003) 87 Minnesota L Rev 1099; Howarth (n 14), 3.

52 *Oxford English Dictionary*.

environmental law scholarship is nearly always related to the poor quality of scholarly methodology. The intellectual incoherence of environmental law as a subject is seen by some in the fact that there is no singular methodological approach to environmental law scholarship. The difficulties and challenges of environmental law scholarship are really methodological difficulties and challenges. Moreover, methodology is a concept inherent in the notion of legal scholarship. Feldman identified that producing good scholarship requires a focus on methodology, critical reflection and communication.[53] The greatness of legal scholarship is defined by a commitment to a belief in the importance of methodologies as part of the intellectual exercise of scholarship. A focus on methodology thus provides a way of simultaneously reflecting on the concerns of environmental scholars and the concept of great legal scholarship. This provides a valuable way forward for environmental law scholars to think about their subject.

In thinking about methodology, it is important to restate a point we made in Section 1. A commitment to the value of methodology is not a commitment to a particular methodology,[54] but is a commitment to developing methodologies that are 'best suited' to the type of questions being asked. Not only is a 'best suited' methodology an ideal in itself but it is also the focus for both critical reflection and communication, and so methodological rigour is critical to ensuring that all three 'ideals' of environmental law scholarship are adhered to. Methodologies are not formulas to be adhered to. As Feldman notes, scholarship requires self-reflection and a slavish reliance on rigid method is inconsistent with such critical analysis. As we will argue in Section 4.1, the first step towards methodological rigour is to recognise the reflexive relationship between methodology and the research questions we ask.

Despite the fact that anxieties about methodology underpin anxieties about immaturity, there has been little attention given to methodological issues beyond simple commands that environmental law scholars should read more widely,[55] should be more interdisciplinary,[56] should take into account different ways of governing[57] and should analyse a range of jurisdictions.[58] Environmental law scholars are told to do lots of things but there is little

53 Feldman (n 4), 503.

54 Ibid.

55 J Wexler, 'The (Non)Uniqueness of Environmental Law' (2006) 74 George Washington L Rev 260; Richardson and Wood (n 46).

56 Heinzerling (n 20); Macrory (n 12); Hilson (n 12).

57 J Scott and J Holder, 'Law and New Environmental Governance in the EU' in G de Búrca and J Scott (eds) *Law and Governance in the EU and US* (Hart Publishing, Oxford 2006); E Fisher, 'Unpacking the Toolbox: Or Why the Public/Private Divide Is Important in EC Environmental Law' in M Freedland and J -B Auby (eds) *The Public Law/Private Law Divide: Une Entente Assez Cordiale?* (Hart Publishing, Oxford 2006).

58 de Sadeleer (n 28); Richardson and Wood (n 46).

critical analysis of how they should do them and the challenges and choices they may face in doing all these different things.[59]

This dearth of critical analysis is largely due to the fact that it is very difficult to talk about methodology without careful consideration of the methodological challenges facing environmental law scholars. Or to put it another way—we need a discussion about why environmental law scholarship is so darn difficult as an intellectual enterprise. A challenge in starting such a discussion is that there are many different methodological challenges and issues that one could discuss. We pick four: the speed and scale of legal/regulatory change, the interdisciplinary nature of the subject, the heavy reliance in environmental law on a diverse range of governance arrangements and the multi-jurisdictional nature of the subject. We do not pretend that these four issues exhaust all the methodological challenges of the subject but we consider them a good starting point because, as will be seen, they reflect many of the reasons why the subject is perceived to be immature. We briefly examine them each below and the particular methodological challenges they raise.

### 3.1 *Speed and Scale of Legal or Regulatory Change*

The first challenge that environmental law scholars face is coping with the speed and scope of legal development in the environmental law field.[60] While this feature of environmental law development is well recognised, it is rarely analysed.[61] There are at least four important general features of legal development in relation to environmental law that give rise to significant methodological challenges.

The first is that most of this development has occurred in the last 35 years, which in legal terms is very short. Not only that but many areas of environmental law have been subject to a series of dramatic reforms which overhaul earlier reforms.[62] Legal development has often involved regulatory experiments rather than a linear progression towards a better model of regulation.[63] This means that scholars have been dealing with regimes, institutions and

59 See B Lange, 'Researching Discourse and Behaviour as Elements of Law in Action' in R Banakar and M Travers (eds) *Theory and Method in Socio-Legal Research* (Hart Publishing, Oxford 2005).

60 Reid (n 15); Heinzerling (n 20); Plater (n 15).

61 Cf. E Scotford, 'The New Waste Directive – Trying to Do It All . . .' (2009) 11(2) Environmental Law Review (forthcoming).

62 Such as the regime of Integrated Pollution Control in the UK: Royal Commission on Environmental Pollution, *Air Pollution Control: An Integrated Approach, Fifth Report* (Cmnd 6371, HMSO, London 1976); Part I, Environmental Protection Act 1990; Pollution Prevention and Control Act 1999.

63 E Fisher, *Risk Regulation and Administrative Constitutionalism* (Hart Publishing, Oxford 2007) 66–9.

laws with little history by which to assess or understand them. The case law is often thin and patchy, as is scholarly discourse. History is seen to be important but different historical foundations for the subject are identified in, inter alia, property law, pollution law, tort law and planning law.[64]

Second, much of the development in environmental law has been largely reactive, in that the catalysts for reform have been continuing shifts in governmental policy[65] and developments in scientific understanding and consensus. Contrast this 'reactive' identity with other legal subjects such as contract or property that are essentially concerned with establishing predictable rules by which society lives.[66] This reactive nature has meant that, while to understand any law requires appreciation of its wider socio-political context, there is a danger that that law is understood in purely instrumental terms.[67] Moreover, while environmental law may have developed reactively, it does also have a role in establishing the ground rules for consumption, production and the use of property.[68] This role is reflected somewhat crudely in the relatively recent shift in international environmental law, as well as in the EC Treaty, to the general prescription of environmental policy and laws, for example on the basis of ideas of precaution and intergenerational equity, in a way that is to be 'integrated' into all other areas of economic and social policy.[69]

Third, legislative and policy reform is often excruciatingly detailed and is not straightforward to understand. For a scholar to make sense of a regime there is a need to master a large amount of material that is often in novel forms and derived from diverse sources.[70] This requires a considerable commitment of research capital. Moreover, even when an area is mastered, much can depend on how a regime will be applied in the future and how it interacts with other regimes.[71] This is a particular problem for scholars in the UK where regulatory regimes are dominated by administrative and prosecutorial discretion.[72]

64 Cf R Cocks, 'Victorian Foundations' in J Lowry and R Edmunds (eds) *Environmental Protection and the Common Law* (Hart Publishing, Oxford 2000); Coyle and Morrow (n 21).

65 C Reid, 'Regulation in a Changing World: Review and Revision of Environmental Permits' (2008) 67 CLJ 126.

66 F Lawson and B Rudden, *The Law of Property* (Clarendon Press, Oxford 2002).

67 B Lange, *Implementing EU Pollution Control* (Cambridge University Press, Cambridge 2008); Kysar and Salzman (n 51); Jewell and Reid (n 1).

68 Coyle and Morrow (n 21).

69 UN Conference on Environment and Development, *Rio Declaration on Environment and Development* (1992), Principles 4, 15; Treaty of Rome, as amended, Arts 6, 174(2). See n 113 and accompanying text below.

70 L Etherington, 'Mandatory Guidance for Dealing with Contaminated Land: Paradox or Pragmatism?' (2002) 23 Statute L Rev 203; Lange (n 67), ch 5.

71 B Pontin and C Willmore, 'Displacing Remedies from Environmental to Planning Law: The Enforcement of Contaminated Land Legislation in Britain' (2006) 6 Ybk Eur Envtl L 97.

72 K Hawkins, *Law as Last Resort: Prosecution Decision-Making in a Regulatory Agency* (OUP, Oxford 2002).

Fourth, the development of environmental legal regimes stretches across traditional legal disciplines in English law, across jurisdictions (see Section 3.4), and across legal disciplinary boundaries within other jurisdictions. The scale of change in such regimes thus spans a broad array of legal areas, each with their own conceptual and jurisprudential boundaries and histories, and concomitant (often implicit) methodological traditions. Environmental law scholars must not only be general interdisciplinarians (see Section 3.2) but also be *legal* interdisciplinarians in that they must engage carefully with legal concepts and academic debates within other legal sub-disciplines.[73] Environmental law scholars must thus be administrative law, tort law, property law, criminal law and intellectual property law scholars. Moreover, developments in environmental law often borrow from these other areas of law in crude and surprising ways.[74] Many environmental regimes developed are also non-legal or have significant non-legal aspects.[75] All this means that environmental law scholars have a lot on their plate when it comes to grasping, analysing and reflecting critically on 'environmental law'.

This state of affairs results in environmental law scholars facing particular methodological challenges arising from the speed and scale of regulatory change. First, they rarely have the luxury of critical reflection but rather find themselves hastily responding to each new set of legal and regulatory changes. Scholarship thus often describes law reform but scholars rarely get a chance to reflect on change; just as one new set of changes is made sense of, another wave of reform comes along. This means that the line between scholarship and commentary becomes blurred since even to comment on the law, in all its frustrating detail, becomes a significant task. Moreover, commentary is important because the succinct description of rapid environmental law development by specialists is of considerable value. With that said, by itself, it is not scholarship.

Second, the sprawl of the subject means that most environmental lawyers can only focus on selected aspects of it. The temptation for environmental legal scholars is to pick one identifiable ('favourite') environmental area and stick to it. Thus we see clusters of scholarship around certain areas and themes. Where there are more overarching academic approaches, such as around environmental principles or the concept of integration, scholars tend not to engage in the detail of particular regulatory areas.[76] The same is true

73 We are grateful to Maria Lee for highlighting this. See M Lee, *EU Regulation of GMOs: Law and Decision Making for a New Technology* (Edward Elgar Publishing, Cheltenham 2008).

74 Royal Commission on Environmental Pollution, *Managing Waste: The Duty of Care* (Eleventh Report, Cmnd 9675, 1985); Fisher (n 63), ch 3.

75 Lange (n 67); Scott and Holder (n 57).

76 M Doherty, 'Hard Cases and Environmental Principles: An Aid to Interpretation?' (2003) 3 Yearbook of European Environmental Law 57; A Lenschow, 'New Regulatory Approaches in "Greening" EU Policies' (2002) 8 Eur L J 19.

of teaching; few courses attempt an exhaustive analysis of the subject.[77] The end result is that environmental law scholars resemble something akin to a group of international diplomats without a translation service. Important conversations are being had amongst clever and informed people, who are all at the right convention, but there is a limit to what they can achieve by simply being in the same room together. Some academics have argued that the problem is with the fragmentation of environmental law itself, looking to 'environmental principles' to unify and rationalise the subject.[78] But this ignores the fact that the subject *is* fragmented and sprawling. Despite this, identifying means of communication for, and thereby connections within, the subject is important. This is discussed further in Section 3.4.

Third, environmental law scholars are constantly in danger of using unsuitable frames of reference, particularly when studying new legal phenomena. Or to put the problem another way, there is a crisis of methodology because it is difficult to determine what questions to ask and what methods to use in asking such questions about new legal ideas. Thus, for example, the traditional demarcation between policy and law that a doctrinal common lawyer feels comfortable preserving and respecting is not so clear in the environmental law context: to preserve this distinction is to ignore the fact that law and policy are playing more nuanced roles in environmental law than those identified in mainstream legal scholarship.[79] Yet, at the same time, this does not mean that these conventional legal concepts are not relevant and scholars ignore the fundamental legal features of such concepts at their peril.[80] The same scholarly danger exists in analysing new environmental regulatory regimes and novel administrative practices, many of which involve conventional legal concepts—this issue is discussed further in Section 3.3.

### 3.2 *Interdisciplinarity*

The second often-cited methodological challenge in environmental law scholarship concerns interdisciplinarity, whether interdisciplinarity is understood in terms of the subject matter of environmental law itself being interdisciplinary[81] and/or scholars being expected to be interdisciplinary.[82] In other words, interdisciplinarity is perceived as both a reality and a methodological expectation of environmental law scholarship. Despite this being the case, there has been little analytical reflection on the nature of

77 Bell and others (n 32), 10–2; Plater (n 15).
78 de Sadeleer (n 28).
79 E Scotford, 'Mapping the Article 174(2) EC Case Law: A First Step to Analysing Community Environmental Law Principles' (2008) 8 Ybk Eur Envtl L 1.
80 Ibid.
81 Heinzerling (n 20), 702; Bell and others (n 32), 10.
82 Hilson (n 12).

interdisciplinarity in the subject and the label 'interdisciplinary' is often used to refer to very different aspects of environmental law scholarship. Indeed, references to interdisciplinarity are often references to at least four different features of environmental law scholarship. These four types of interdisciplinary enterprise are distinct from the need for 'legal interdisciplinarity' identified in Section 3.1. Each of these different forms of interdisciplinarity have their own inherent methodological challenges.

First, a reference to interdisciplinarity often highlights the fact that environmental law scholars need to understand environmental problems.[83] Understanding the problems that law applies to is a feature of all legal scholarship. But it is particularly pertinent in relation to environmental problems since those problems are often highly technical and points of disagreement in understanding environmental problems exist between different areas of specialisation, or are embedded within areas of specialisation. Disagreements over risk assessment methodology, regulatory impact assessment and the role of environmental models are just three examples among many.[84] This need for legal scholars to understand and keep pace with these technical debates is not in fact a challenge of interdisciplinarity, rather it is recognition of the fact that environmental law scholars (and environmental law practitioners for that matter) need to develop two different types of expertise.[85] First, they need to develop contributory expertise—that is, expertise that contributes to the development of legal scholarship.[86] It is this expertise with which this article is concerned. Second, scholars need to develop interactional expertise with other disciplines (both scientific and social scientific) so that their legal scholarship is based on a sound understanding of environmental problems.[87] Such expertise is interactional expertise because, while environmental law scholars must understand other disciplines' insights into environmental problems, environmental law scholars are not contributing to those disciplines directly.[88] It should also be recognised that interactional expertise needs to be dynamic and scholars thus particularly agile; such expertise will need

83 Rose (n 1); Heinzerling (n 20); C Cranor, *Toxic Torts: Science, Law and the Possibility of Justice* (CUP, Cambridge 2006).

84 Committee to Review the OMB Risk Assessment Bulletin – National Research Council, *Scientific Review of the Proposed Risk Assessment Bulletin from the Office of Management and Budget* (National Academy of Sciences, Washington, DC 2007); L Heinzerling, 'Regulatory Costs of Mythic Proportions' (1998) 107 Yale L J 1981; T McGarity and W Wagner, 'Legal Aspects of the Regulatory Use of Environmental Modeling' (2003) 33 Envtl Law Rep 10751.

85 H Collins and R Evans, *Rethinking Expertise* (University of Chicago Press, Chicago 2007). See also E Fisher, 'The Role of Environmental Courts in Developing Environmental Law: The Administrative Law Dimension' (2008) Brodies Lectures in Environmental Law <http://www.law.ed.ac.uk/blogsandpodcasts/podcasts.aspx> accessed 30 April 2009.

86 Collins and Evans (n 85), 24–7.

87 Ibid 28–40.

88 By 'directly', we mean contributing to the core of another discipline.

continual redevelopment in light of the pace of technological and scientific change. This sets a high bar for environmental law scholars.

The second type of interdisciplinary scholarship in which an environmental law scholar engages involves studying regulatory concepts that have a significant non-legal aspect and which are often derived from other disciplines.[89] The most obvious example of this is scholarship relating to governance and regulation. [90] This scholarship is discussed in detail in Section 3.3, but it is also relevant here as a distinct form of interdisciplinary enterprise. This is because the expertise of environmental law scholars in relation to these issues is more than interactional. Legal scholars are contributing to the development of expert knowledge about these concepts.[91] Examples of such regulatory concepts include emissions trading schemes[92] and regimes in which negotiation has a significant role to play.[93] It should be noted that dealing with these types of regimes is not only a challenge for environmental law scholarship but is also a feature of administrative law scholarship and socio-legal scholarship, where legal pluralism and other means of legal and non-legal ordering are major foci of research.[94]

The third reason why environmental law is often understood to be interdisciplinary is that environmental law scholarship and teaching often occur outside law faculties and in the context of other disciplines and problem-focused research. Much of that problem-focused research is undertaken in the wake of public controversy where there is an urgent search for answers.[95] While there are some exceptions, in these contexts law is understood not so much as a complex cultural phenomenon but rather as a 'plug and play' instrument that is expected to deliver certain results. Take, for example, a recent interdisciplinary reader on the environment that includes a selection of extracts from law articles on a wide range of topics and from judgments with little discussion about the important legal differences between these extracts.[96]

89 Scott and Holder (n 57).
90 J Scott and D Trubek, 'Mind the Gap: Law and New Approaches to Governance in the European Union' (2002) 8 Eur L J 1.
91 C Joerges and R Dehousse (eds) *Good Governance in Europe's Integrated Market* (OUP, Oxford 2002); G de Búrca and J Scott (eds) *Law and New Governance in the EU and the US* (Hart Publishing, Oxford 2006).
92 Committee on the Human Dimensions of Climate Change – National Research Council (ed) *The Drama of the Commons* (National Academies Press, Washington, DC 2002).
93 J Freeman and L Langbein, 'Regulatory Negotiation and the Legitimacy Benefit' (2000) 9 New York Univ Envtl L J 60; Scott and Holder (n 57); J Steele, 'Participation and Deliberation in Environmental Law: A Problem Solving Approach' (2001) 21 OJLS 415.
94 H Arthurs, *'Without the Law': Administrative Justice and Legal Pluralism in Nineteenth Century England* (University of Toronto Press, Toronto 1985).
95 M Strathern, *Commons and Borderlands: Working Papers on Interdisciplinarity, Accountability and the Flow of Knowledge* (Sean Kingston Publishing, Wantage 2004) 3.
96 G Edelson et al. (eds) *Environment: An Interdisciplinary Anthology* (Yale University Press, New Haven 2008) ch 22.

The concept that an extract of a judgment can have scholarly authority with little reference to the legal point being argued and the wider legal context seems absurd to a legal scholar but is not obvious to a non-lawyer. For many non-legal scholars, law is nearly always part of the solution but there is often very little appreciation of the complexity of legal institutions, ideas and processes involved.[97] When there is such an appreciation, it is rarely matched by a willingness to engage with such complexity. Rather, there is often frustration and boredom with a legal scholar's preoccupations with such issues—academic lawyers are described in less than flattering terms with their academic outlooks cast as 'unexciting and uncreative, comprising a series of intellectual puzzles scattered among large areas of description'.[98] The development of any discourse about environmental law methodology in such a context is profoundly difficult and consistently downplayed as less important than the functioning and responsiveness of the laws themselves.

The fourth reference to interdisciplinarity in environmental law scholarship is really a reference to the need to develop a new discipline to deal with environmental problems. Such a new discipline transcends traditional disciplinary boundaries, which are barriers to effectively addressing environmental problems.[99] This is often described as a need for 'transdisciplinarity', in which there is the development of a 'transcendent language, a meta-language, in which the terms of all the participants' languages are, or can be, expressed'.[100] This type of interdisciplinarity does not concern urgent problem solving but more the development of a new ambitious intellectual paradigm of environmental studies. The challenges and time required to create such an overarching paradigm are considerable.[101]

Identifying these types of interdisciplinarity is not about decreeing certain forms of interdisciplinary scholarship as illegitimate or wrong-headed. With that said, some interdisciplinary research does veer towards the 'single-minded pursuit of an end' and 'dilettantism'. Rather, identifying different forms of interdisciplinarity clarifies that interdisciplinarity, by being both a fact

97 Fisher (n 63), 14–6.

98 Cownie as quoted by McCrudden in C McCrudden, 'Legal Research and the Social Sciences' (2006) 122 LQR 632–7.

99 E Fisher and R Harding, 'The Precautionary Principle: Towards a Deliberative, Transdisciplinary, Problem-Solving Process' in R Harding and E Fisher (eds) *Perspectives on the Precautionary Principle* (Federation Press, Sydney 1999); H Nowotny, 'The Potential of Transdisciplinarity', (Seminar, Interdisciplines Website 2003) <http://www.interdisciplines.org/interdisciplinarity> accessed 1 April 2009).

100 G McDonell, 'Disciplines as Cultures: Towards Reflection and Understanding' in M Somerville and D Rapport (eds) *Transdisciplinarity: Recreating Integrated Knowledge* (EOLSS Publishers Ltd, Oxford 2000) 27.

101 J Thompson Klein, *Interdisciplinarity: History, Theory and Practice* (Wayne State University Press, Detroit 1990) ch 8.

and aspiration of environmental law scholarship, creates a range of different methodological challenges that scholars must engage with and reflect upon.

### *3.3 Governance*

The third issue in thinking about legal, particularly socio-legal, methodology in environmental law is that the creation of both—sometimes hybrid—public and private governance regimes in often novel and sometimes non-legal ways has been central to environmental law reform in the last decade.[102] This has been noted in relation to the two challenges above but is also a methodological challenge in its own right. This is because the phrase 'governance' is a 'catch-all' for 'any strategy, tactic, process, procedure, or programme for controlling, regulating, shaping, mastering or exercising authority over others in a nation, organisation or locality'.[103] Problems of governance can also be understood as problems of legal pluralism in that implicit in governance regimes are often novel forms of authority, legal and otherwise.[104]

The methodological challenge raised by governance regimes is that such regimes require scholars to take a 'more diverse view of state authority and its exercise'[105] but, in doing so, it is not clear what form such a 'diverse view' should take and how it differs from existing scholarly approaches. Indeed, the concept of governance is much admired and referred to in worshipful tones but rarely scrutinised and deconstructed by environmental law scholars.[106] Methodological difficulties tend to be overlooked.

Scrutiny and deconstruction, however, are not easy. These governance regimes, in departing from traditional, hierarchical modes of regulation, do so in *sui generis* and disparate ways. Thus, sometimes, legal rules provide a basic framework while the substance of legal decision-making is steered by policy. UK town planning and the contaminated land regime are examples of this governance approach.[107] By contrast, the EC Water Framework Directive[108] creates a complex regime of soft and hard law. This regime specifies general

102 D Fiorino, *The New Environmental Regulation* (MIT Press, Cambridge 2006); R Stewart, 'A New Generation of Environmental Regulation?' (2001) 29 Cap Univ L Rev 21; N Gunningham, 'Environmental Law, Regulation, Governance: Shifting Architectures' (this issue).

103 N Rose, *Powers of Freedom: Reframing Political Thought* (CUP, Cambridge 1999) 15.

104 Arthurs (n 94).

105 R Rhodes, 'What Is New About Governance and Why Does It Matter?' in J Hayward and A Menon (eds) *Governing Europe* (OUP, Oxford 2003) 66.

106 D Esty, 'The Case for a Global Environmental Organisation' in P Kenen (ed) *Managing the World Economy: Fifty Years After Bretton Woods* (Institute for International Economics, Washington, DC 1994); P Harris, 'The European Union and Environmental Change: Sharing the Burdens of Global Warming' (2006) 17 Colorado J Intl Envtl L Policy 309.

107 Town and Country Planning Act 1990 and Part IIA Environmental Protection Act 1990.

108 Directive 2000/60/EC Establishing a Framework for Community Action in the Field of Water Policy [2000] OJ L327/1.

legal duties through a complicated system of networked actors who develop legal and non-legal frameworks of water quality regulation for particular EC regions.[109] In contrast again are environmental governance regimes that involve self-regulation and rely on non-legal techniques, such as environmental management or rule systems, customary practices and environmental ethics internal to a particular private-regulated organisation.[110] Then there are schemes such as the new EC chemicals law, REACH, which reconfigures the conditions of market access for chemical manufacturers in the EC.[111] Thus, the environmental scholar ends up with a long list of regulatory examples that do not necessarily bear any relationship to each other—governance does not replace traditional frameworks with a single new paradigm of how the regulatory state does and should operate. Moreover, these reforms have not been limited to regulatory activities within the traditional boundaries of environmental law—rather such reforms have required scholars to think across existing areas of law and to analyse how environmental concerns are integrated into other areas of decision-making.[112] The most obvious examples of this are the types of governance arrangements provoked by the scope and operation of the integration principle in Article 6 EC and the closely related principle of sustainable development.[113]

There are no overarching methodological solutions for legal scholars dealing with the emergence of these environmental governance regimes. Rather, there are three significant challenges. The first challenge concerns determining whether there is any role for law at all and, if so, what that role is.[114] For a scholar to focus on law may be a misleading exercise in that more important features of a regime might be overlooked, such as institutional and local culture.[115] Yet, there is also a danger that ignoring the legal aspects of these regimes involves ignoring fundamental features—if not the backbone—of them.[116] While law comprises only a single component of the architecture

109 Scott and Holder (n 57); C Knill and A Lenschow, 'Compliance, Communication and Competition: Patterns of EU Policy Making and their Impact on Policy Convergence' (2005) 15 European Environment 114.

110 H Schepel, *The Constitution of Private Governance* (Hart Publishing, Oxford 2005); S Wood, 'Voluntary Environmental Codes and Sustainability' in B Richardson and S Wood (eds) *Environmental Law for Sustainability* (Hart Publishing, Oxford 2006).

111 Regulation (EC) No. 1907/2006 concerning the Registration, Evaluation, Authorisation and Restriction of Chemicals (REACH) [2006] OJ L396/1. See E Fisher, 'The "Perfect Storm" of REACH: Charting Regulatory Controversy in the Age of Information, Sustainable Development, and Globalization' (2008) 11 J Risk Res 541.

112 Jewell (n 38), 79–81.

113 Lenschow (n 76).

114 C Carlarne, 'Good Climate Governance: Only a Fragmented System of International Law Away?' (2008) 30 Law and Policy 4.

115 J Holder, *Environmental Assessment: The Regulation of Decision-Making* (OUP, Oxford 2005).

116 E Fisher, 'Administrative Law, Pluralism and the Legal Construction of Merits Review in Australian Environmental Courts and Tribunals' in L Pearson and C Harlow (eds) *Administrative Law in a Changing State: Essays in Honour of Mark Aronson* (Hart Publishing, Oxford 2008).

of some environmental governance regimes, it may be a vital component, the absence or inadequacy of which could render the entire regime ineffectual.[117] This tension reflects a more general 'dilemma' within legal scholarship of 'not taking law seriously or taking it too seriously'.[118] Moreover, it is not always clear what body of law is relevant. Thus, for example, should international and multi-level environmental protection governance regimes be understood in terms of administrative law or public international law or on some other basis?[119] Is focusing on the role of courts being too legally centralist or not?[120]

The second methodological challenge is that, in light of the sprawling, multi-dimensional and novel nature of these regimes, there is a potential oversupply of relevant legal and social science concepts, unresolved questions about new interactions between legal concepts, as well as the need to engage with sociological, economic and political science perspectives in order to understand how law contributes to these regimes. A scholar is thus faced with an embarrassment of riches when it comes to scholarly methodologies. Thus, for example, a range of categories has been developed in order to analyse various environmental governance regimes, such as 'command and control', 'economic incentive', 'self-regulation', 'co-regulation', as well as 'post-regulatory', 'procedural', 'expressive' and 'reflexive' environmental law.[121] While these phrases reflect a reality—the fragmentation of environmental law into a number of different types of regulation—they also raise the methodological challenge that a whole range of existing and novel legal concepts are potentially relevant for understanding environmental governance regimes. This is particularly the case with respect to governance regimes that mobilise different aspects of law, economics and social ordering. Thus, for example, to understand adequately emissions trading schemes, there is a need to understand property law, regulatory theory, Coase's theory and other economic ideas about the market, as well as theories of distributive justice. What is the 'best suited' methodology is by no means clear in such circumstances,[122]

117 E Fisher and P Schmidt, 'Seeing the Blindspots in Administrative Law: Theory, Practice, and Rulemaking Settlements in the United States' (2001) 30 Common Law World Rev 272.

118 D Galligan, *Law in Modern Society* (Clarendon Press, Oxford 2007) 4.

119 B Kingsbury, 'Global Environmental Governance as Administration: Implications for International Law' in D Bodansky, J Brunnee and E Hey (eds) *Oxford Handbook of International Environmental Law* (OUP, Oxford 2007).

120 J Scott and S Sturm, 'Courts as Catalysts: Rethinking the Judicial Role in New Governance' (2007) 13 Columbia Journal of European Law 565; Arthurs (n 94).

121 C Scott, 'Analysing Regulatory Space: Fragmented Resources and Institutional Design' (1995) PL 329; E Orts, 'Reflexive Environmental Law' (1995) 89 Northwestern University Law Review 1227; I Ayres and J Braithwaite, *Responsive Regulation – Transcending the Deregulation Debate* (OUP, New York 1992); N Gunningham and P Grabosky, *Smart Regulation* (Clarendon Press, Oxford 1998); G Teubner, L Farmer and D Murphy (eds) *Environmental Law and Ecological Responsibility: The Concept and Practice of Ecological Self Organisation* (John Wiley & Sons, Chichester 1994).

122 For a recent attempt to model scholarship relating to emissions trading, see S Bogojevic, 'Ending the Honeymoon: Deconstructing Emissions Trading Discourses' JEL (forthcoming).

nor is it when studying more straightforward regimes such as the use of regulatory contracts or negotiated rulemaking.[123] Even more mainstream regulatory frameworks are ambiguous. For example, should environmental impact assessment be understood and studied as radical reflexive environmental law or as a minor adjustment to normal administrative law principles?[124] In some cases the methodological choice will not matter, but in others it will lead to scholars asking themselves very different questions, having very different priorities and relying on different sources. In other words, fragmentation in environmental law is also created by methodological choices of scholars. Thus, for example, while traditional legal techniques privilege normative questions concerned with assessing environmental governance for compliance with standards of fairness, efficiency or specific legal principles, political science, sociology and economic analysis often start first of all from 'how' questions, seeking to understand governance regimes through an examination of the sociological, economic and political dynamics which underpin environmental governance.[125] Likewise, the concept of 'governance' is itself a methodological construct that emphasises some aspects of a regime as opposed to others—the same is true of 'constitutionalism'.[126]

Third, as scholars we need to be aware that such diverse environmental governance regimes play an important role in constructing our understanding of regulatory problems.[127] For example, traditional pollution regulation tended to be based on linear understandings of cause and effect between a particular pollutant and pollution with little regard paid to the surrounding environment.[128] More recent 'holistic' and 'integrated' regimes, such as the EC Water Framework and IPPC Directives,[129] focus on broader concepts of ecological quality that recognise that ecosystems draw for their existence on all three interconnected environmental media: air, water and land.[130] This shift in approach is not just a shift in regulatory technique but also in what is understood as the 'environment' and how to 'protect' it. In part this presents a

123 D Dana, 'The New Contractarian Paradigm in Environmental Regulation' (2000) University of Illinois Law Review 35; C Coglianese, 'Assessing Consensus: The Promise and Performance of Negotiated Rulemaking' (1997) 46 Duke L J 1255.

124 Holder (n 115); J Sax, 'The (Unhappy) Truth about NEPA' (1973) 26 Oklahoma L Rev 239.

125 McCrudden (n 98).

126 E Fisher, 'The European Union in the Age of Accountability' (2004) 24 OJLS 498–9; J Weiler, *The Constitution of Europe: Do the New Clothes Have an Emperor?* (CUP, Cambridge 1999) 223.

127 S Jasanoff, *Designs on Nature: Science and Democracy in Europe and the United States* (Princeton University Press, Princeton 2005); Fisher (n 63).

128 W Howarth, 'The Progression Towards Ecological Quality Standards' (2006) 18 JEL 3.

129 See n 108, above; Directive 2008/1/EC Concerning Integrated Pollution Prevention and Control [1996] OJ L257/26.

130 Howarth (n 128).

challenge of how scientific knowledge is integrated and utilised within these regimes.[131] However, it also presents a challenge in understanding how these regimes construct different understandings of the environment and environmental problems.[132] Thus, as a further example, in the UK the land contamination regime largely conceptualises land contamination as a problem of land use planning, while in the United States it is understood as a major public health issue.[133] The 'problem' of biotechnology is also framed differently in relation to different governance regimes.[134]

### 3.4 *Multi-Jurisdictional Nature of Environmental Law Regimes*

The final set of methodological issues and challenges for environmental law scholars derives from the fact that environmental law tends to operate in multi-jurisdictional frameworks. Legal and regulatory initiatives in one jurisdiction are often directly and indirectly related to legal and regulatory initiatives in another.[135] Nearly every environmental law scholar knows that environmental problems are often transboundary and that, therefore, environmental responses need to be transboundary as well. Beyond that, however, scholarly discussion becomes patchy. International environmental lawyers are more aware of the problems created by the multi-jurisdictional nature of environmental law regimes than are national environmental lawyers—the latter group are often blind to how a particular national law is embedded in a multi-level system. However, once identified, jurisdictional plurality provides an analytical challenge for almost every environmental law scholar. Environmental regimes not only sprawl across jurisdictions but also are often, as noted in Section 3.3, both legal and non-legal in nature and often have opaque institutional structures.[136] Again, what it means to be methodologically rigorous in studying such regimes is by no means obvious. In particular, there are three challenges that arise out of this complex feature of environmental law regimes.

The first methodological challenge was touched on in Section 3.1 and that is how to face the problem of issue fragmentation in environmental law, which

131 Lange (n 67), ch 6.

132 D Winickoff and others, 'Adjudicating the GM Food Wars: Science, Risk and Democracy in World Trade Law' (2005) 30 Yale J Intl L 81.

133 J Hird, *Superfund: The Political Economy of Environmental Risk* (Johns Hopkins University Press, Baltimore 1994); Pontin and Willmore (n 71).

134 Jasanoff (n 127).

135 G Winter (ed) *Multilevel Governance of Global Environmental Change: Perspectives from Science, Sociology and the Law* (CUP, Cambridge 2006).

136 E Vos, *Institutional Frameworks of Community Health and Safety Legislation: Committees, Agencies and Private Bodies* (Hart Publishing, Oxford 1999); C Joerges, 'Law, Science and the Management of Risks to Health at the National, European and International Level – Stories of Baby Dummies, Mad Cows and Hormones in Beef' (2001) 7 Colum J Eur L 1.

is highlighted and compounded in a multi-jurisdictional setting. Indeed, issue fragmentation has particularly characterised international environmental law and international law scholarship from the outset. Since the 1970s, each new international environmental treaty negotiated in public international law has created a set of issue-specific institutions, rules and procedures.[137] This problem-specific approach, often accompanied by the creation of multi-lateral environmental agreements and associated institutions, has enabled the negotiation of numerous laws and treaties to tackle complex environmental problems that otherwise would have gone unaddressed.[138] Single-issue legal development has created a field that can point to numerous success stories, such as reductions in ozone-depleting substances and control of trade in endangered species. It has also created a body of scholarship in which scholarly expertise is often limited to a particular subject matter. As Bodansky, Brunée and Hey note

> [A]n expert on the law of marine environmental protection might find it difficult to navigate an air pollution agreement. Similarly, an expert on the rules governing carbon sinks may have trouble communicating with an expert on international emissions trading, notwithstanding the fact that both issues fall under the Kyoto Protocol on climate change.[139]

The failure of scholars to address this balkanisation of scholarly expertise has meant that too much academic analysis is based on the descriptive study of regimes in isolation—often understood as one-off successes and failures—without a broader analytical perspective being taken.

Moreover, in international environmental law scholarship, overlaps and gaps are all too common, and scholars have, thus far, failed to develop effective mechanisms for facilitating coordination between distinct areas of international environmental law.[140] Indeed, by creating a field that encourages scholars to develop expertise in issue-specific as well as jurisdiction-specific environmental laws, the gaps and inter-linkages in and between environmental problems, between these specialist regimes and general public international law, and between international environmental law and other areas of law, are frequently left unaddressed in scholarship. This creates intellectual blind spots and a lack of co-ordinated analysis about the nature of international

137 Driesen (n 1), 356.

138 R Churchill and G Ulfstein, 'Autonomous Institutional Arrangements in Multilateral Environmental Agreements: A Little Noticed Phenomenon in International Law' (2000) 94 AJIL 623.

139 D Bodansky, J Brunnee and E Hey, 'International Environmental Law: Mapping the Field' in D Bodansky, J Brunnee and E Hey (eds) *Oxford Handbook of International Environmental Law* (OUP, Oxford 2007) 4.

140 G Palmer, 'New Ways to Make International Environmental Law' (1992) 86 AJIL 259–63.

environmental law.[141] Questions challenging the parameters of, and methodological approaches to, international environmental law include analysing the complex interaction between trade/development and environmental regimes, reconciling human rights and environmental protection, negotiating the boundaries between land law and environmental law, examining together international cultural heritage and national heritage and landscape laws, and conceptualising the relationship between international environmental law and public international law. These issues are dealt with in some scholarship,[142] but not in a connected way or not in a way which recognises that such issues are 'some of the most challenging questions with which any international lawyer will have to deal'.[143] Moreover, as in relation to governance, there needs to be an acute awareness that there are different ways to characterise these relationships and interfaces.[144]

All of this represents a methodological challenge because a failure to deal with this problem of issue fragmentation leads to a failure to identify common legal themes and legal problems. It is not so much that issue fragmentation is a problem because it gets in the way of a grand theory of international environmental law—as already stated we doubt the existence of such a theory—rather issue fragmentation results in a failure of scholars to focus on the legal interrelationships and commonalities that exist in environmental law. Or to put the matter another way—there is too much focus on identifying particular species of tree and not enough on analysing how particular identified species interact with the rest of the 'legal' ecosystem.

The second methodological challenge is the need to develop rigorous techniques for analysing the interrelationship between local, national, regional and international environmental laws. This interrelationship remains underexplored and scholarly debate on the proper methodology for undertaking

141 The development of 'soft' international environmental law is one example. See D Bodansky, 'Customary (and Not So Customary) International Environmental Law' (1995) 3 Ind J Global Legal Studies 105; C Chinkin, 'Normative Development in the International Legal System' in D Shelton (ed) *Commitment and Compliance: The Role of Non-Binding Norms in the International Legal System* (OUP, Oxford 2000).

142 O Perez, *Ecological Sensitivity and Global Legal Pluralism* (Hart Publishing, Oxford 2004); C Carlarne, 'The Kyoto Protocol and the World Trade Organization: Reconciling Tensions Between Free Trade and Environmental Objectives' (2006) 17 Colorado J Intl Envtl L Policy 45; S Baughen, *International Trade and the Protection of the Environment* (Routledge-Cavendish, London 2007).

143 A Boyle, 'Relationship Between International Environmental Law and Other Branches of International Law' in D Bodansky, J Brunnee and E Hey (eds) *Oxford Handbook of International Environmental Law* (OUP, Oxford 2007) 145.

144 E Scotford, 'Book Review: International Trade and the Protection of the Environment' [2009] Lloyds Maritime Commercial L Q 145; E Fisher, 'Beyond the Science/Democracy Dichotomy: The World Trade Organisation Sanitary and Phytosanitary Agreement and Administrative Constitutionalism' in C Joerges and E -U Petersmann (eds) *Transnational Trade Governance and Social Regulation: Tensions and Interdependencies* (Hart Publishing, Oxford 2006).

such analyses remains virtually non-existent.[145] This is despite the practical importance of this interrelationship becoming more obvious in case law and legislation.[146] Scholars tend to work in one jurisdiction with only occasional and rather crude inroads into another, often with a single-minded purpose in mind. Where there are attempts to provide a more overarching approach, they tend to suffer from being overly simplistic and from a lack of appreciation of the significance of legal culture.[147]

There are many instances of the need to study the importance of jurisdictional interrelationships and to understand the complexity of both national and international legal cultures. There is, for example, an urgent need to recognise that national climate change and nature conservation policies are closely related to international and other national regulatory initiatives.[148] Beyond describing this state of affairs, however, it is not clear how to develop a deeper legal understanding of these relationships, particularly when much of what going on is 'not law' and/or is at the very boundaries of international law and national law. While more scholars are beginning to look at cross-issue linkages,[149] the disciplines of domestic and international environmental law continue to inhabit relatively distinct scholarly domains. Add to this parallel existence the growing field of regional environmental law (such as European Community environmental law) and the situation grows even more complicated. The end result is that there is no obvious way to negotiate the national/international legal relationship, but it must be negotiated to make sense of these regimes.

This challenge relates to the third methodological challenge in thinking about the multi-jurisdictional nature of environmental law—the need to expand comparative legal analysis in environmental law. In particular, where and how to use comparative legal methodologies in environmental law must be addressed. This is becoming more important due to the increased transplantation and borrowing of regulatory and legal concepts between jurisdictions.[150] Environmental principles are a case in point.[151] Yet, environmental law

145 C Redgwell, 'National Implementation' in D Bodansky, J Brunnee and E Hey (eds) *Oxford Handbook of International Environmental Law* (OUP, Oxford 2007) 923.

146 Case C-459/03 *Commission v Ireland* [2006] ECR I-4635; Case C-188/07 *Commune de Mesquer v Total France SA*, Decision of the ECJ (Grand Chamber), 24 June 2008.

147 Fisher (n 63), ch 5.

148 C Carlarne, 'Climate Change Policies an Ocean Apart: United States and European Union Climate Change Policies Compared' (2006) 14 Pennsylvania State Envtl L Rev 435.

149 A Boyle, 'Globalising Environmental Liability: The Interplay of National and International Law' (2005) 17 JEL 3.

150 J Wiener, 'Something Borrowed For Something Blue: Legal Transplants and the Evolution of Global Environmental Law' (2001) 27 Ecol L Q 1295; P Busch, H Jorgens and K Tews, 'The Global Diffusion of Regulatory Instruments: The Making of a New International Environmental Regime' (2005) Ann Am Acad Polit Sci 146.

151 de Sadeleer (n 28); A Trouwborst, *Evolution and Status of the Precautionary Principle in International Law* (Kluwer International, The Hague 2002).

scholarship fails adequately to explore, or to provide methodologies for exploring, environmental laws across jurisdictions. In particular, there is little reference to important debates within mainstream legal methodology about how to carry out comparative legal analysis.[152] This is not to say that good comparative environmental law scholarship does not exist—it does—but comparative environmental law remains at best a marginal sub-field and there is little discussion of its methodology.

Moreover, the narrowness of current comparative analysis magnifies many of the problems already discussed. This is because states do frequently borrow legal tools from one another, and because local, state and regional environmental laws interact in complex and significant ways such that the relationships between domestic and international environmental law are subtle and multifaceted. The nuances of these cross-jurisdictional relationships impact the shape of environmental law at every level yet receive scant scholarly attention.

## 4. Developing a Critical Discourse: Five Issues for the Agenda

Our list of methodological challenges is alarmingly long. But this is entirely our point—environmental law scholars face a multitude of methodological challenges which occur in a variety of ways, for a range of reasons, and which highlight the rich and multi-layered nature of our discipline. These challenges are not easily met. There are no simple formulas, checklists or methodologies for scholars to adhere to. Nor are there deep foundations or a grand narrative of the subject waiting to be discovered.

The only realistic way these challenges can be met is through a widespread and honest discussion among environmental law scholars about these methodological challenges, and how they present in particular scholarly endeavours. Thus what the subject needs is not codification, unifying principles or an overarching theory, but rather an extensive, inclusive and critical discourse about how environmental law scholars can strive towards producing scholarship in the light of the methodological challenges of environmental law research. Pointing to the need for such a discourse may appear to be a cop-out but our point is that maturity and great scholarship does not come through arrogance, ignorance or over-simplification. It comes from careful self-reflective thought and discussion. This will take time, as well as the focusing of careful scholarly attention on individual projects, case by case.

152 See Section 4.3 below.

As we see it, for such a self-reflective discussion to develop, there needs to be focus on five substantive issues by environmental law scholars (and we are very much including ourselves in this group of scholars encouraged to respond to this agenda for action). These five issues flow from our discussion above; we identify them because we see that exploring these issues is a way for legal scholars to move beyond discussions about immaturity to *thinking more critically* about what it is environmental law scholars do and how we can do it better. We do not see these five issues as exhaustive but they provide an important and useful agenda for discussion. As with the various methodological issues and challenges identified above, we recognise them as overlapping but identify them as distinct since each is an important issue in its own right.

### 4.1 *Reflecting on Methodological Choices*

The first issue that environmental law scholars need to address more explicitly is the reflexive relationship between methodology and the research questions we ask. As already noted, methods should be appropriate to answer our research questions. But our implicit or explicit methodological perspectives also steer us towards particular types of research questions. There is a two-way, reflexive relationship between methodology, on the one side, and the questions we ask about environmental law, on the other. Recognising and scrutinising this relationship is an important first step to methodological and scholarly rigour.

As environmental law scholars, we cannot aim towards a unified method, but we need to be upfront and honest about this so as to put our methodological choices under the kind of self- and peer-scrutiny that legitimises our endeavours and demonstrates the challenging scholarly choices that we confront and make. In thinking through those choices, we need not only to broaden our frame of analytical possibilities but also to think about what we are trying to achieve. The importance of doing this can be seen most obviously in relation to the study of governance regimes where, as highlighted in Section 3.3, a range of methodological concepts can be used to study a particular regime. Thus, for example, methodologies that focus on actual social practices, such as 'communicative interactions',[153] have value in that they can be empirically studied, allow a more critical approach to be taken to law, focus on relationships ignored in conventional legal analysis and

153 D Nelken (ed) *Law as Communication* (Dartmouth, Aldershot 1996); G Teubner, 'After Legal Instrumentalism? – Strategic Models of Postregulatory Law, in: Dilemmas of Law in the Welfare State' in G Teubner (ed) *Dilemmas of Law in the Welfare State* (Walter de Gruyter, Berlin 1986); R Lofstedt, 'How Can We Make Risk Communication Better: Where Are We and Where Are We Going?' (2006) 9 J Risk Res 869.

also aid in the understanding of law. A study through the lens of theories of 'network governance'[154] is also valuable and yields different results. At the same time, however, social theory can be particularly illuminating in studying the ambiguous relationship between law and economic activity.[155] Moreover, associated scholarly areas such as legal geography provide a powerful prism through which to study how law constructs an understanding of the environment.[156] In each case, there are methodological choices to be made and those choices have scholarly consequences—methodology should never be taken as a given and methodological choice should always be either explicit or at least carefully considered and defensible.

It should also be stressed that this is not just an issue with respect to governance regimes; it is relevant to more traditional doctrinal analysis as well. Thus, for example, in the study of environmental principles there has often been a reliance on jurisprudential theories of 'legal principles' with little consideration of whether this is the appropriate analytical frame.[157] There are also methodological choices to be made in the study of the interaction between national and international environmental law. By making those choices more considered and explicit and by increasing scholarly dialogue about alternative approaches, there is a far greater chance that better choices will be made and better scholarship will result.

### 4.2 *Mapping the Subject*

The second step environmental law scholars should take is to recognise the importance of mapping environmental law as a methodological instrument and scholarly exercise. Mapping provides a means for developing a more spatial and temporal geography of the subject, which is an important step in analysing areas of environmental law more critically. It also is a tool for locating scholarship within the complex domain of environmental law and within law more generally. In other words, exercises in mapping go some way to addressing the various problems of issue and jurisdictional fragmentation discussed in Sections 3.1 and 3.4 above. As well, they aid scholars in their response to rapid developments in environmental law in so far as they provide

154 M Warning, 'Transnational Bureaucracy Networks: A Resource of Global Environmental Governance? The Case of Chemical Safety' in G Winter (ed) *Multilevel Governance of Global Environmental Change* (CUP, Cambridge 2006); M Castells, *End of Millenium* (2nd edn, Blackwell Publishers, Oxford 2000).

155 Hutter (n 40); see also U Beck, *Risk Society: Towards a New Modernity* (Sage Publications, London 1992).

156 N Blomley, D Delaney and R Thompson Ford (eds), *Legal Geographies Reader: Law, Power and Space* (Blackwell, Oxford 2001); W Taylor (ed) *The Geography of Law: Landscape, Identity and Regulation* (Hart Publishing, Oxford 2006).

157 See Scotford (n 79)—arguing strongly against this approach.

a wide frame for critical reference. Maps can become the translation service the subject so badly needs.

With that said, mapping must be done with an awareness that maps, like all models and going back to the discussion in Section 3.1, frame the world in a particularly chosen way and that they can serve a range of purposes.[158] Different scholars will map for different reasons and with different scholarly concerns in mind. The map of a doctrinal scholar will be different from the map of a social theorist, which will be different again from that of the legal theorist wishing to propose a theory of post-modern law.[159] These differences are not a reason to abandon mapping, however, but rather a reason to engage with these complexities. Indeed, it is this critical awareness of the contextual and constructed nature of the mapping exercise that distinguishes it from mere commentary.

There is of course a need to map in multiple dimensions to take into account the array of actors, institutions, norms, jurisdictions and regimes encompassed by the subject. The point of mapping is not that we might generate a single map of environmental law; rather, the hope is that we might assemble an atlas that reflects the broad terrain of environmental law in a variety of cartographical representations, which all contribute with their unique legends and keys to building a deeper understanding of the special world under scrutiny.

### 4.3 *Engaging with Legal Methodology Discourses*

The third step that should be taken by environmental law scholars is that they need to develop a greater appreciation of the debates about methodology that are being carried out by legal scholars. This of course includes socio-legal scholars.[160] The generally held perception of environmental law as existing at the fringes of the legal academy has meant that there has often been an unspoken presumption that general discourses about legal scholarship are not directly relevant to environmental law scholarship.

The discussion above makes clear that such a presumption is a fallacy. Environmental law scholars have much to gain from a more critical engagement with mainstream legal methodology debates. Moreover, we should not pretend that environmental law is the only subject undergoing a crisis

158 M Hesse, *Models and Analogies in Science* (University of Notre Dame Press, Notre Dame 1966).
159 Cf Scotford (n 79); Philippopoulos-Mihalopoulos (n 15); de Sadeleer (n 28).
160 H Genn, M Partington and S Wheeler, *Law in the Real World: Improving Our Understanding of How Law Works – Final Report and Recommendations* (Nuffield Inquiry of Empirical Legal Research, London 2006).

of maturity, and similar developments can be seen in other areas of law.[161] Environmental law scholars have much to learn from those debates as well.

Indeed, there is an irony in the fact that environmental law scholars have often been quicker to argue for the need for interdisciplinarity than for the need to engage with legal methodology debates. Yet within legal scholarship there is a rich and pluralistic discourse about law and its relationship to the rest of the society, particularly in the realm of socio legal studies.[162] One of the most striking features of the statistics in Table 1 above is how little environmental law scholarship has been published in socio-legal journals.[163] The same is true for comparative law methodology where little of the sophistication of debates about comparative legal analysis has found its way into environmental law scholarship.[164] Likewise, debates about issue fragmentation are actively being carried on in the more general international law context.[165]

It is also worth noting that engaging with debates about legal methodology is important for interdisciplinary research. To be interdisciplinary, one must have an appreciation of one's own discipline. This may seem counter-intuitive, but to contribute to broader discourses about environmental problems, environmental law scholars need to have a nuanced understanding of what they are contributing.[166] Yet we suspect that environmental law scholars often strive to have a more subtle appreciation of the methodologies of other disciplines than of their own.[167]

### 4.4 *Engaging with Discourses About Interdisciplinarity*

This relates directly to the fourth step that should be taken: environmental law scholars need to understand what it actually means to be interdisciplinary.

161 Cheffins (n 3); R Thomas, 'Deprofessionalisation and the Postmodern State of Administrative Law Pedagogy' (1992) 42 J Legal Educ 75; A Fischer-Lescano and G Teubner, 'Regime Collisions: The Vain Search for Legal Unity in the Fragmentation of Global Law' (2004) 25 Michigan J Intl L 999.

162 Galligan (n 118).

163 Three recent exceptions are J Holder and T Flessas, 'Special Issue: Emerging Commons' (2008) 17 Social and Legal Studies, 299–405; 'Special Issue: Global Warming, Governance and the Law' (2008) 30 Law and Policy 385–529; R Lee and E Stokes, 'Special Issue: Economic Globalization and Ecological Localization: Socio-Legal Perspectives' (2009) 36 J L Soc 1–166.

164 E Orucu and D Nelken (eds) *Comparative Law: A Handbook* (Hart Publishing, Oxford 2007); M Reimann and R Zimmermann (eds) *Oxford Handbook of Comparative Law* (OUP, Oxford 2006).

165 M Prost and P Clark, 'Unity, Diversity and the Fragmentation of International Law: How Much Does the Multiplication of International Organizations Really Matter?' (2006) 5 Chinese J Intl L 341; Fischer-Lescano and Teubner (n 161).

166 Cranor (n 83).

167 D Tarlock, 'Joseph Sax: Visionary Lawyer' (2008) 14 Hastings West-Northwest J Envtl L and Policy 17.

Above, we identified four different ways in which an environmental law scholar can be interdisciplinary—in regard to each of these there needs to be critical reflection. Thus, the challenges of interactional expertise should not be underestimated—such expertise is not just acquired by reading a couple of science textbooks.[168] Moreover, scholars also need to be more critical about the 'empirical and theoretical claims from other disciplines'.[169] Interactional expertise is not just accepting what another discipline has to say about the world as an unquestionable truth. Likewise, truly transdisciplinary research takes time and effort—a reality at odds with the fact that interdisciplinarity often taken places in projects that are rushed responses to crises.[170]

The real point is that very little interdisciplinary literature has found its way into environmental law scholarship. For many environmental law scholars the discussion in Section 3.2 will be new, even though much of it is typical of interdisciplinary scholarship. There is little general awareness that there are different types of interdisciplinary discourse and/or that environmental law scholars are interacting with a range of different disciplines in many different ways. Moreover, as already noted, environmental law scholars have not taken the lead in these interdisciplinary enterprises and often play a supporting role in another discipline's pursuit of its own intellectual agenda.

Environmental law scholars need to be more assertive—about what a study of law can contribute to environmental studies that is not contributed by other disciplines and about why exploring the nuances of environmental law within the field and at its disciplinary borders is more than mere academic self-indulgence.[171] Valuable interdisciplinary communication no doubt involves lawyers navigating the complexities of other disciplines, but such communication can only develop if environmental law scholars have confident methodological insights into their own work to share with those working in other disciplines.

### 4.5 *Developing a Discourse About the Quality of Environmental Law Scholarship*

The final step that should be taken in the development of a more critical scholarly discourse among environmental lawyers is the most difficult—it is the need to develop a more explicit discourse about how we as scholars can judge the quality of environmental law scholarship. Such a discourse is inherently about methodology and we see the development of this discourse

168 Collins and Evans (n 85), chs 3 and 4.
169 Heinzerling (n 20).
170 J Thompson Klein (n 101).
171 McCrudden (n 98), 646–9.

as being central to promoting rigorous environmental law methodology and thus scholarship.

First, the perception of environmental law scholarship as marginalised, young, but worthy, has arguably meant that scholars have often been less faultfinding and more encouraging than in other legal areas. As noted in Section 2.2, environmental law scholars value scholarly diversity and are wary of disciplinary imperialism. These are valid considerations but, at the same time, it cannot be the case that 'anything goes'.[172] We cannot ignore the fact that we need a more explicit discourse about what is, and what is not, great environmental law scholarship. Such a discourse should naturally grow out of discussions about methodology.

Second, and following on from this, it should be clear from the discussion so far that any standard of quality cannot be based on a single methodological approach. This challenge is not new to legal scholars; the pluralism of legal scholarship generally means that a relatively open-textured approach has been taken by legal scholars in judging the quality of scholarship, including interdisciplinary scholarship by legal scholars.[173] Yet no such discourse has developed in relation to environmental law scholarship and it is a discourse that is likely to be controversial in light of the many challenges we have highlighted above.

In particular, there is a challenge in reconciling the assessment of the quality of legal scholarship within the legal academy with quality assessment from the perspectives of other disciplines.[174] Within different disciplines there are different criteria for judging scholarship, which are products both of the scholarship itself as well as institutional cultures. We cannot ignore these differences. With that said, a good starting point for establishing a quality standard for environmental law scholarship is Feldman's definition of scholarship, set out in Section 1, in particular, the importance he places on critical reflection.

## 5. Conclusion

In this article we have been proactively candid. Our arguments may make uncomfortable reading, just as they were uncomfortable to write. We, like nearly all environmental law scholars, have been guilty of failing to get to grips with the methodological challenges of the subject. The discussion above is thus based on our experiences, frustrations and mistakes. Our overall

172 P Feyerabend, *Against Method: Outline of an Anarchistic Theory of Knowledge* (3rd edn, Verso, London 1993).

173 The operation of the Law Panel in the Research Assessment Exercise in the UK is an example of this.

174 See the discussion on accountability in interdisciplinary research in Strathern (n 95), 68–86.

conclusion is not to privilege one methodology, one disciplinary lens or one area of environmental law scholarship. Rather, environmental law scholars need to mobilise as a group to talk more frankly and honestly about these issues.

We realise that this is not easy. Maturity is sobering. But, for environmental law scholarship to come of age, scholars need to reflect critically on their research methodology. This is particularly necessary in relation to the speed and scope of regulatory change, interdisciplinarity, diverse governance regimes and the multi-jurisdictional nature of the subject. We have suggested five steps to aid in this process of critical reflection which cut across these four challenging issues: taking a reflexive approach to methodology choices, mapping the subject, engaging with debates about legal (including socio-legal) methodology, understanding more carefully the concept of interdisciplinarity and finally having an explicit debate about the quality of environmental law scholarship. The end result is likely to be messy, time-consuming and intellectually demanding. As Rose has noted about the subject more generally, 'a mature environmental law is not pretty',[175] but the worth of environmental law scholarship is more likely to be recognised if this demanding challenge is embraced.

175 Rose (n 1), 292.

# [34]

THE MODERN LAW REVIEW

# Paradoxes and Failures: 'New Governance' Techniques and the Financial Crisis

Julia Black*

This article examines the performance of four 'new governance' techniques of regulation in the period leading up to the financial crisis: principles based regulation, risk based regulation, meta-regulation and enrolment. These techniques have been advocated on the basis that they are responsive, flexible, and in enrolling others in the regulatory project thereby expand its capacity, and even its legitimacy. However, experience in the crisis revealed that in their implementation they can be out of touch or indulgent, focus heavily on auditable systems and processes, and that in enrolling others they can increase vulnerabilities and the potential for negative endogenous effects. The argument is not that there should be a return to adversarial 'command and control' regulation, rather that experience of these strategies in the crisis suggests a need to understand in greater depth the refractive effects of the organisational, technical/functional and cognitive dimensions of regulatory governance, if we are to understand and adapt its performance in different contexts.

## INTRODUCTION

The 2007–9 financial crisis had a complex cocktail of causes, and there is a significant literature by both regulators and commentators analysing just what went wrong. Indeed, in a recent review, Howard Davies identified thirty nine different causes from the prevailing literature,[1] ranging from the macro to the micro, from global imbalances and loose monetary policy to the practices of US mortgage brokers, credit rating agencies and testosterone-fuelled bankers, though the story that is told as to the causes of the crisis can vary with the position of the narrator.[2] Regulation was not the sole cause of the crisis, but it certainly had a significant role to play. Failings were made both by state and non-state regulators and by market actors at the global, EU and national level, ranging from transnational regulatory committees to financial institutions and their internal corporate governance structures, and an accepted narrative quickly emerged, at least amongst the regulatory elites, as to just what the main regulatory failures were.[3]

*Professor of Law and Research Associate, Centre for the Analysis of Risk and Regulation, London School of Economics and Political Science. Earlier versions of this paper were presented at conferences in Warwick (September 2011) and Oxford (January 2012) and I thank participants for their comments. I also thank Rob Baldwin, Cristie Ford, Martin Lodge and Niamh Moloney for reading and commenting on an earlier draft. The usual responsibilities remain my own.

1 H. Davies, *The Financial Crisis – Who is to Blame?* (Cambridge: Polity Press, 2010).

2 See J. Froud, A. Nilsson, M. Moran and K. Williams, 'Stories and Interests in Finance: Agendas of Governance Before and After the Financial Crisis' (2012) 25 *Governance* 35.

3 See eg Financial Stability Forum (FSF), *Report of the Financial Stability Forum on Enhancing Market and Institutional Resilience* (Basel: FSF, 2008); Financial Stability Board (FSB), *Improving Financial Regulation – Report of the FSB to G20 Leaders* (Basel: FSB, 2009); Financial Services Authority (FSA), *The Turner Review: A regulatory response to the global banking crisis* (London: FSA, 2009); FSB, *Senior Supervisors Group Report on Risk Management Lessons from the Global Banking Crisis of 2008*

 

Published by Blackwell Publishing, 9600 Garsington Road, Oxford OX4 2DQ, UK and 350 Main Street, Malden, MA 02148, USA

There are endless ways in which the crisis story can be told, and as many different ways of analysing it as there are possible combinations of social science schools of thought, from rationalist, interest group analyses through the various forms of institutionalism to interpretivist and constructivist approaches, and in many combinations. Moreover, the crisis moved financial regulation from the pages of academic journals to the front pages of the newspapers, with the result that everyone has their own interpretation of what went wrong, and each reader wants to hear the story that fits with their own preoccupations. So it is important to set out what this discussion is aiming to do, and what it is not. The focus here is primarily on the functional, operational side of regulatory governance. This is clearly not the only perspective that could be taken on analysing the crisis, but it is a valid one: regulation is a functional task and much mainstream regulatory literature is highly functionalist in its orientation. However, unlike most of that literature this article does not have a prescriptive agenda – it is not proposing a new strategy which can resolve all the problems identified. Nor is it adopting a political economy approach: it is not primarily concerned to examine in detail why these strategies were adopted in the first place (though it does not assume that in making that choice regulators or policy makers have a free rein), though does reflect on assumptions underlying their operation. Nor does it analyse how regulators responded to the crisis: this is not an exploration of the dynamics of the crisis-response or the construction of a post-crisis agenda.

Instead, this article explores a particular puzzle: why and how did so many of the 'new governance' regulatory strategies, which have been lauded in the last two decades as superior in many ways to traditional 'command and control' (CAC) regulation, fail? In exploring this question, it looks at the way that four of these strategies operated in practice, at least in the UK: principles based regulation; meta-regulation; enrolment; and risk based regulation, each of which is explained below. It illustrates how their operation both created and revealed internal contradictions and tensions which led to failure or paradoxical outcomes. It does not argue that command and control regulation is therefore superior. Rather, the conditions of complexity, uncertainty, fragmentation, ungovernability and dynamism which cause CAC regulation to fail, and to which new governance techniques are meant to offer a superior response, all remain. However, what it does argue is that the highly functionalist, toolbox approach, which focuses on fashioning and prescribing the appropriate regulatory tools in order to achieve desired outcomes (and in which many of us, including this author, have engaged), is necessary but insufficient to that approach's own ends, which are reformist and prescriptive. Regulation is a complex and multi-dimensional activity. Failures in any of these dimensions can create points of vulnerability, such that the carefully fashioned tool will simply not function as intended. Instead it is transformed in the very process of its performance, resulting in a number of paradoxes.

(Basel: FSB, 2009); de Larosière Group, *Report of the High-Level Group on Financial Supervision in the EU of 25 February 2009* (Luxembourg: Office for Official Publications of the European Communities, 2009); LSE Report, *The Future of Finance* (London: LSE, 2010).

The article first notes some of the paradoxes of regulation noted in other sectors, resulting from a wide range of different types of 'tools'. It then focuses on each new governance strategy in turn, drawing out some of the tensions and ambiguities which it argues are inherent in them and some of the paradoxes in their performance. It then goes on to argue that focusing on the organisational, cognitive and functional dimensions of regulation, in particular, can facilitate an understanding of why regulation fails, creates paradoxical effects, or otherwise does not perform as broadly intended.[4]

## REGULATORY PARADOXES AND FAILURES: SOME EXAMPLES

Paradoxes abound in the performance of regulation, leading to failures in that regulation not only fails to change behaviour, manage risks or achieve any other stated goals, but actually produces the opposite effects from those intended.[5] This is so regardless of the regulatory techniques adopted. For example regulation to reduce risks can inadvertently lead to greater risks, for example safety regulation can create moral hazard, increasing risk-taking activity. Clean-ups can lead to greater environmental harm. Regulation to enhance disclosure can inhibit it.[6] Warnings or bans on activities can produce the very conditions that they are designed to prevent: warnings about dangerous sports can make them more attractive to risk-seekers; conversely warnings that a particular bank is likely to fail can create a run on the bank, so precipitating its failure.[7] Rules can produce perverse incentives and prompt creative adaptation and the emergence of 'avoidance entrepreneurs'.[8] Regulation creates opportunity costs and can lead to negative spillover effects.[9] It can displace non-compliance to other areas within or beyond a regulatory jurisdiction or political domain, or to areas which are otherwise difficult to regulate.[10] Furthermore, it can lead to over-deterrence and

4 Whilst noting that those goals may not have been public interest goals but could have been the result of a form of 'capture', either the interest group capture familiar from the public choice literature, or I would suggest, 'cognitive capture', which is an explanation fitting more with institutionalist theories.

5 See eg P. Grabosky, 'Counterproductive Regulation' (1995) 23 *International Journal of the Sociology of Law* 347; R. Morgan and R. Clarke, 'Legislation and Unintended Consequences for Crime' (2007) 12 *European Journal on Criminal Policy and Research* 189; J. DiNardo and T. Lemieux, 'Alcohol, Marijuana and American Youth: The Unintended Consequences of Government Regulation' (2001) 20 *Journal of Health Economics* 991. F. Haines, *The Paradox of Regulation: What Regulation Can Achieve and What It Cannot.* (Cheltenham: Edward Elgar, 2011).

6 G. Narayanamoorthy, A. Arya, J. Glover and B. Mittendorf, 'Unintended consequences of regulating disclosures: The case of Regulation Fair Disclosure' (2005) 24 *Journal of Accounting & Public Policy* 243;.

7 Scheltema Commission, *Onderzoek DSB Bank* (The Hague: Commissie DSB Bank, 2010).

8 Morgan and Clarke, n 5 above, 189; D. McBarnet and C. Whelan, 'The Elusive Spirit of the Law: Formalism and the Struggle for Legal Control' (1991) 54 MLR 848.

9 G. Rauser, S. Hamilton, M. Kovach and R. Stifter, 'Unintended consequences: The spillover effects of common property regulations' (2009) 33 *Marine Policy* 24.

10 J. Hoek, 'Tobacco Promotion Restrictions: Ironies and Unintended Consequences' (2004) 57 *Journal of Business Research* 1250.

fear-generation and create deviance, for example through labelling otherwise compliant firms as potential deviants.[11]

Many of these effects, and more, were in evidence in the financial crisis. Risks were displaced as many of the riskier products and activities were shifted to the 'shadow banking' sector, which is not as closely regulated as banks. Firms engaged in 'rule entrepreneurship' and creative compliance, for example by using special purpose vehicles as ways of reducing their apparent risk exposure and therefore their capital requirements. Risk weightings of assets created, and continue to create, perverse incentives, for example with respect to securitisation and sovereign risk.[12]

The crisis also illustrated the potential for regulation to create endogenous risk and negative feedback loops, amplifying the very risks it is meant to be controlling, with near catastrophic results. Endogenous risk can arise either from the internal operation of the regime itself or from its interaction with other contiguous regulatory regimes. In attempting to become more sensitive to the relative risks of different assets, the capital rules introduced in Basle II inevitably introduced a set of pro-cyclical effects: as risks to the bank of loss went down (due to improved asset values or the credit-worthiness of its counterparties, for example, which are characteristic of an upturn in the macro-economic cycle), the amount of capital that banks needed to hold against them decreased. As risks to the banks of loss increased (eg due to decline in asset values or increased risk of default by counterparties, characteristic of a downturn in the cycle), the amount of capital required increased. This makes sense from the perspective of a banking supervisor, but not for macro-economists. For at the very time in the economic cycle that macro-economic policy makers want banks to increase lending and put money into the economy, financial regulators are requiring them to withhold it.[13] The regime also created incentive effects for banks by altering the amount of capital that banks needed to set aside for different activities, notably lowering it for mortgages and securitised instruments and not requiring additional weights for concentration risk, thus playing a significant role in the expansion of activity in these areas.[14]

The bail-outs also created a significant degree of moral hazard for the industry – though in a further working out of this paradox, banks are now finding that the effects can work in reverse: in the midst of the US and EU sovereign debt crisis, where markets do not think that their governments will be able to rescue them,

11 I. Ayres and J. Braithwaite, *Responsive Regulation: Transcending the Deregulation Debate* (Oxford: OUP, 1992).

12 BCBS (Basel Committee on Banking Supervision), *Report on Special Purpose Entities* (Basel: Bank for International Settlements, 2009).

13 See J. Danielsson, P. Embrechts, C. Goodhart et al, *An Academic Response to Basel II* (London: Economic & Social Research Council, 2001); C. Goodhart, 'Financial Regulation, Credit Risk and Financial Stability' (2005) 192 *National Institute Economic Review* 118; C. Goodhart, B. Hofmann and M. Segoviano, 'Bank Regulation and Macroeconomic Fluctuations' (2005) 20 *Oxford Review of Economic Policy* 591.

14 See BCBS, *Core Principles of Effective Banking Supervision* (Basel: Bank for International Settlements, 2006); A. Blundell-Wignall and P. Atkinson, 'The Sub-Prime Crisis: Causal Distortions and Regulatory Reform' (OECD Regulatory Policy Papers) 55–102 at www.oecd.org/dataoecd/33/6/42031344.pdf (last visited 30 January 2012).

banks' share prices are falling rapidly. There were also negative spillovers: deep-rooted failures of national financial regulation (of mortgage brokers in the US; banks in Iceland) were transmitted to other countries by global financial systems. Thus did the Florida dream turn into a global nightmare. But there were externalities from the crisis management strategies adopted too: for example, the Irish government's 100 per cent deposit guarantee, introduced in October 2008, caused a rapid exodus of cash from UK banks to Ireland, and the repatriation of assets by Western European banks to bolster their balance sheets had significant implications for the availability of bank financing in the peripheral European countries.

## NEW GOVERNANCE REGULATORY TECHNIQUES – HOW DID THEY FARE?

As this brief account illustrates, the list of regulatory paradoxes and failures in the financial context is long, and is not confined to the strategies discussed here. However these strategies are selected for attention as they are part of the new governance techniques which have been fashionable in academic and policy circles for some time, in contrast to the oft-derided 'command and control' (CAC) strategy of using detailed legal rules backed by criminal sanctions overseen by a government agency.[15]

The death of CAC regulation, to paraphrase Mark Twain, has been much exaggerated. CAC is still strongly prevalent in financial regulation in many places, notably the US. But, at least in the UK and at the global level, financial regulation contains a number of examples of 'new governance' regulatory techniques so favoured in the recent literature.[16] Notable amongst these are principles based regulation, meta-regulation, risk based regulation, and strategies of enrolment – both of gatekeepers and other regulatory regimes, state and non-state based.[17] So how did these fare in the crisis? The answer is that not only did each suffer

15 See *Recommendation of the Council of the OECD on Improving the Quality of Government Regulation* (Paris: OECD, 1995); OECD, *OECD Guiding Principles for Regulatory Quality and Performance.* (Paris: OECD, 2005); N. Gunningham and P. Grabosky, *Smart Regulation: Designing Environmental Policy* (Oxford: Clarendon Press, 1998); Better Regulation Task Force, *Alternatives to State Regulation* (London: Cabinet Office Publications & Publicity Team, 2000); Mandelkern Group on Better Regulation, *Better Regulation Final Report* (Brussels: European Commission, 2002); R. Baldwin 'Better Regulation: The Search and the Struggle' in R. Baldwin, M. Cave and M. Lodge (eds), *Oxford Handbook on Regulation.* (Oxford: OUP, 2010).

16 See J. Braithwaite, 'The New Regulatory State and the Transformation of Criminology' (2000) 40 *British Journal of Criminology* 222; J. Black, 'Decentring Regulation. Understanding the Role of Regulation and Self Regulation in a "Post-Regulatory" World' (2002) 54 *Current Legal Problems* 103; C. Scott, 'Regulation in the Age of Governance: The Rise of the Post Regulatory State' in J. Jordana and D. Levi-Faur (eds), *The Politics of Regulation: Institutions and Regulatory Reforms for the Age of Governance* (Cheltenham: Edward Elgar, 2004); C. Ford, 'New Governance, Compliance and Principles-Based Securities Regulation' (2008) 45 *American Business Law Journal* 1.

17 Ford 2008, *ibid*; J. Black, 'Enrolling Actors in Regulatory Processes: Examples from UK Financial Services Regulation' (2003) PL 62; J. Black, 'Mapping the Contours of Contemporary Financial Services Regulation' (2002) 2 *Journal of Corporate Law Studies* 253; J. Gray and J. Hamilton. *Implementing Financial Regulation: Theory and Practice.* (Chichester: John Wiley & Sons Ltd, 2006).

significant blows, but that the crisis revealed a number of tensions and internal contradictions within the strategies themselves. The rest of this section considers each of these in turn.

**Principles based regulation**

In the UK, principles-based regulation (PBR), so lauded by the FSA and the UK government just before the crisis,[18] was seen in the immediate aftermath to have suffered a fatal blow. In the words of Hector Sants,[19] then chief executive of the FSA, '[a] principles-based approach does not work with people who have no principles'. The FSA[20] instead announced that it was moving to 'outcomes-focused' regulation, though the difference between the two is arguably more apparent than real. Many of aspects of PBR, notably the focus on risks and outcomes, have a strong affinity with outcomes-focused or outcomes-based approaches to regulation which a number of UK regulators are currently adopting.[21] So the spirit of PBR remains, even though the branding has altered. Indeed, within financial regulation, the narrative of regulatory failure has shifted under the Coalition Government. Their diagnosis is that it was a failure of detailed rules and tick-box regulation which was the system's downfall, not principles based regulation at all. Indeed, in the Treasury (and Bank of England's) view what is needed (at least for banks) is fewer detailed rules and more 'judgement based' regulation.[22]

The debate surrounding PBR both before and after the crisis illustrates the impact of rhetoric on the perceptions and practice of regulation. The story currently being told by the Treasury and the Bank of how the FSA was regulating prior to the crisis is part of a clear political dynamic,[23] and in particular of the strategic distribution of blame in order to justify a change agenda: the need to deride the old regulatory structure in order to justify the change to the new.

But it also highlights the malleability of the strategy: the fact that two mutually opposing stories can be told of what the FSA was doing when it was acting as a 'principles-based' regulator illustrates the ambiguous nature of the strategy itself. PBR can easily be used as a marketing label to conjure up a regulatory Utopia – as it was by politicians in the pre-crisis battle for market share. Conversely, it can be a derogatory label used to conjure up regulatory ineffectiveness – as it has been

18 FSA, *Principles Based Regulation: Focusing on the outcomes that matter* (London: FSA, 2007).
19 H. Sants, 'Delivering Intensive Supervision and Credible Deterrence' speech presented at Reuters Newsmakers Event, London, March 2009.
20 FSA 2009, n 3 above.
21 See Financial Reporting Council (FRC), *Strategic Framework* (London: FRC, 2007); Care Quality Commission, *CQC Strategy 2010–2015* (London: Care Quality Commission, 2010); Tenant Services Authority, *The Regulatory framework for social housing in England from April 2010* (London: Tenant Services Authority, 2010); Local Better Regulation Office, *Promoting Regulatory Outcomes: Consultation Paper* (Birmingham: Local Better Regulation Office, 2011).
22 Her Majesty's Treasury (HM Treasury), *A new approach to financial regulation: the blueprint for reform* (London: Stationery Office, 2011).
23 See Froud et al, n 2 above.

(but not universally) post-crisis to explain what went wrong. As Cunningham has argued, it is indeed time to retire the rhetoric of PBR.[24]

Looking more analytically, briefly, PBR can take one or both of two forms: rule book PBR, which is how the rule book or code of conduct are written, and operational PBR, which is how the regulator performs its regulatory tasks.[25] Rule book PBR involves formulating rules which are broad, general and purposive and which may or may not be elaborated in further rules or guidance, for example, 'you shall act with integrity', or 'firms shall act in the best interests of their clients'. A contrast is often drawn with 'bright line rules', which contain specific, often quantitative provisions, and detailed, often prescriptive rules, which contain a number of preconditions or exceptions though, as many have noted, the relationship between them is more complex than might be assumed.[26] In PBR regimes, the principle forms the 'backstop' to those more detailed provisions, and acts as a guide to their interpretation and application in particular instances. Neither principles nor rules usually function particularly successfully without the other.[27] The FSA's own rulebook runs to several thousand pages.

Substantive PBR regimes have one or more of five key characteristics. It should be stressed that these are elements of an 'ideal type'. Given the variety of regimes that are styled, or style themselves, as PBR regimes, the construction of an ideal type necessarily means that some regimes will accord more strongly with certain features than others. But they have one or more of the following features: a purposive approach to interpretation of regulatory norms; a reliance on the internal management of firms; a focus on ensuring regulatees attain the purposes or outcomes of the regulation rather than technical compliance with detailed rules; a targeted approach to enforcement, and a re-distribution of responsibilities within the regulatory regime for ensuring and demonstrating compliance.[28]

What can we take from the mixed experience of the FSA's version of PBR? First, as noted, that it is important to disentangle the rhetoric from the reality. PBR has been equated with 'light touch' regulation and as such has been a lightning rod for political opprobrium, providing the rhetorical cover for the abolition of the FSA. It also has settled into academic accounts of how the FSA was regulating pre-crisis.[29] But it is important to stress that PBR need not equate

24 L. Cunningham, 'A Prescription to Retire the Rhetoric of Principles Based Systems in Corporate Law, Securities Regulation and Accounting' (2007) *Vanderbilt Law Review* 1411–1493.

25 J. Black, 'Forms and Paradoxes of Principles Based Regulation' (2008) 3 *Capital Markets Law Journal* 425; J. Black, 'The Rise, Fall and Fate of Principles Based Regulation' in K. Alexander and N. Moloney (eds), *Law Reform and Financial Markets* (Cheltenham: Edward Elgar, 2011).

26 C. S. Diver, 'The Optimal Precision of Administrative Rules' (1983) 93 *Yale Law Journal* 65; R. Baldwin 'Why Rules Don't Work' (1990) 53 MLR 321; R. Korobkin, 'Behavioral Analysis and Legal Form: Rules vs. Principles Revisited' (2000) 79 *Oregon Law Review* 23; J. Braithwaite 'Rules and Principles: A Theory of Legal Certainty' (2002) 27 *Australian Journal of Legal Philosophy* 47; F. Schauer, 'The Convergence of Rules and Standards' (2003) *New Zealand Law Review* 303; F. Schauer, 'The Tyranny of Choice and the Rulification of Standards' (2005) 14 *Journal of Contemporary Legal Issues* 803; Cunningham, n 24 above; FSA, n 18 above; Black 2008, *ibid*; Ford, n 16 above.

27 Braithwaite, *ibid*; Cunningham, n 24 above.

28 Black 2008, n 24 above.

29 See eg Froud et al, n 2 above.

to 'light touch' regulation.[30] The strategy that the FSA held up as exemplifying PBR when it first started extolling its move to being a 'principles-based regulator' was its 'Treating Customers Fairly' (TCF) initiative with respect to the retail markets, where it was far from 'light touch',[31] and arguably was starting to have a positive effect. But the FSA itself was responsible for over-selling the PBR approach, in fact using the label to cover two distinct strategies of regulation, one playing out in the retail markets, the other in the wholesale markets. The ambiguity of PBR enabled these two contrasting sets of regulatory strategy to be adopted under the same banner. Incidentally, it has also allowed the narrative of failure to shift course as the 'blame game' plays out,[32] as noted above.

Second, although there is a lively debate in the legal journals as to the effectiveness of different rule types as regulatory instruments,[33] there is no evidence that regulation through detailed rules fared any better. The US Securities and Exchange Commission (SEC), for example, which regulates mainly through prescriptive and detailed rules and with an aggressive approach to enforcement, notoriously failed to detect the Madoff fraud, sixteen years from the first warning signs.[34] There can be as many detailed rules as lawyers want to write, but if those responsible for enforcing them do not understand the activity that they are regulating, nor the rules that are in place, then it does not matter what form the rules take, they will be un-enforced. Detailed rules can also be quickly outdated, leaving regulators with nothing to enforce against even if they were willing and able to do so. They can also be easily gamed: for example, capital had to be set aside to cover one year loans to associated companies, so banks extended 364 days loans to associated SPVs (special purpose vehicles) instead, thus avoiding the rule.[35]

Third, it shows that PBR is a complex and paradoxical technique in a number of respects.[36] Not only can principles be implemented in such a way that they have the same effects as if they were written as detailed requirements, but the substantive practice of PBR can involve several other regulatory strategies which can be applied at varying levels of intensity. As the experience of TCF suggests, PBR need not equate to 'light touch' regulation, but equally it can, as it did in the case of the FSA's prudential regulation of banks. PBR is in practice a collation of strategies which can be applied with varying degrees of intensity. In the case of

30 Black 2008, n 25 above; C. Ford, 'Principles Based Regulation in the Wake of the Securities Crisis' (2010) 55 *McGill Law Journal* 257–307.

31 FSA, *Treating customers fairly – progress and next steps* (London: FSA, 2004); FSA, *Treating customers fairly – building on progress* (London: FSA, 2005); FSA, *Treating customers fairly – towards fair outcomes for consumers* (London: FSA, 2006); Black 2011, n 25 above; S. Gilad, 'Institutionalizing Fairness in Financial Markets: Mission Impossible' (2011) 5 *Regulation and Governance* 309.

32 C. Hood, *The Blame Game. Spin, Bureaucracy and Self-Preservation in Government* (Princeton NJ: Princeton UP, 2011).

33 Diver 1983, n 26 above; F. Schauer, *Playing by the Rules: A Philosophical Examination of Rule-Based Decision-Making in Law and Life* (Oxford: Clarendon Law, 1993).

34 US Securities and Exchange Commission (SEC), *Investigation of Failure of the SEC to Uncover Bernard Madoff's Ponzi Scheme – Public Version* (Washington, DC: US Government Printing Office, 2009) 41.

35 See Blundell-Wignall and Atkinson, n 14 above.

36 See Black 2008, n 25 above.

TCF, it involved a more intensive degree of supervision. Furthermore, across all sectors the FSA increasingly pursued a strategy of taking enforcement actions on the basis of breach of a Principle alone. However, with respect to prudential supervision (often of the same financial institutions) then supervision was less intense, with fewer regulatory resources dedicated to it, more dependent on firms' internal systems and controls, and in short, more trusting. Indeed one of the key reasons for regulatory failure (leaving aside the technical aspects of the rules regulating banks' capital requirements) was that regulators placed too much trust in financial institutions: witness the 'regulatory dividend' afforded to RBS prior to its bail-out.[37]

PBR is thus a complicated strategy in practice, capable of a range of different manifestations, as the contrast between the FSA's approach to supervising activities in the retail market as opposed to its supervision of (the same institution's) capital adequacy illustrates. It also makes considerable demands on the capacity of the regulator, including the ability of its staff to make judgements and to be robust in their dealings with banks if they lack detailed rules to fall back on and from which they can derive their authority, and indeed on the capacity of regulated institutions themselves. It is also critically linked to the next strategy examined here, that of meta- or management-based regulation: regulation of firms' internal systems and controls, and thus imports the strengths and weaknesses of that particular strategy, discussed below.

### Meta-regulation

A second, related, technique which was widely used is variously described in the literature as 'management-based' regulation, 'meta-regulation', 'enforced self-regulation', or the regulation of firms' own self-regulation. Under this strategy, regulators do not prescribe how regulatees should comply, but require them to develop their own systems for compliance and to demonstrate that compliance to the regulator. The equivalent in health and safety legislation is the 'safety case' that firms have to develop and which the regulator approves to manage their occupational health and safety risks. The arguments in support of the technique are that it gives firms greater flexibility, enables them to design systems and processes which are better suited to ensuring compliance within their own organisations than could be done by generic, prescriptive rules, and that it places the onus and responsibility on firms themselves to demonstrate compliance, rather than placing the onus on regulators to demonstrate non-compliance.[38] It has also been

37 The FSA's approach shifted rapidly in the wake of the crisis to one of 'intrusive supervision' and 'credible deterrence'. However, the Bank of England is currently proposing that the Prudential Regulation Authority (a subsidiary of the Bank of England which is due to take over prudential supervision of banks from the FSA with the enactment of the Financial Services Bill 2011) will be a 'judgement-led' supervisor, which is not so far from the description given of PBR before the crisis. See FSA, *Prudential Regulation Authority: The Future Approach to Banking Supervision* (London: FSA, 2011).

38 See eg C. Parker, *The Open Corporation: Effective Self-regulation and Democracy* (Cambridge: CUP, 2002); C. Coglianese and D. Lazer, 'Management-Based Regulation: Prescribing Private Management to Achieve Public Goals' (2003) 37 *Law and Society Review* 691; J. Braithwaite, *Regulatory*

advocated as a way of enhancing and giving legitimacy to market or community based governance, in a re-articulation of a strategy often termed co-regulation.[39]

In fact, regulators are always reliant on firms' internal systems to ensure compliance: meta-regulation simply raises this practical necessity to a conscious regulatory strategy. Although in principle the strategy has much to commend it, as has been well articulated elsewhere, its fundamental weakness is that firms' systems and processes are designed to achieve their own goals, not necessarily those of the regulator. Compliance systems may therefore end up running parallel to the organisations' core operations, rather than being integral to them, as is well noted in the business response and compliance literature.[40] As a result, meta-regulation is fundamentally reliant on the simultaneous presence of four elements: on firms having the appropriate culture to support the compliance systems which are put in place, on having the right incentives to pursue public objectives as well as private profits, and on regulators possessing sufficient skills and industry experience to evaluate firms, and having sufficient courage and political support to challenge them.

In the financial sector, meta-regulation was also adopted as a specific regulatory technique under the capital adequacy rules, where firms were allowed to use their own internal risk models to provide the basis for setting their capital requirements. The key regulatory instrument, referred to globally as Basle II, defined the parameters of the models they were to use, which then had to be approved by the regulators.[41] Their introduction was controversial,[42] and they were demonstrated to have significantly under-estimated the risks to which banks were exposed, and moreover to introduce an unsustainable element of pro-cyclicality into the system (in good economic times, banks had to hold little capital; in recessions, banks have to hold more capital, which can restrict their ability to lend and so to help reinvigorate the macro-economy).[43] Nonetheless, they still have a central role in the global capital regulatory regime, albeit now reinforced by greater capital requirements, some counter-cyclical correction and a leverage ratio under Basle III.[44]

Meta-regulation was also adopted as a broader regulatory philosophy, though not with this moniker, by regulators in the UK, and reliance on senior management was a key part of the substantive dimension of PBR as it operated

*Capitalism: How it Works, Ideas for Making it Work Better* (Cheltenham: Edward Elgar, 2008); C. Coglianese and E. Mendelson, 'Meta-Regulation and Self-Regulation' in R. Baldwin, M. Cave and M. Lodge (eds), *Oxford Handbook of Regulation* (Oxford: OUP, 2010).

39 C. Scott, C. 'Reflexive Governance, Regulation and Meta-Regulation: Control or Learning?' in O. De Schutter and J. Lenoble (eds), *Reflexive Governance: Redefining the Public Interest in a Pluralistic World*. (Oxford: Hart Publishing, 2010).

40 See eg C. Parker, C. and V. Nielsen (eds), *Explaining Compliance: Business Responses to Regulation* (Cheltenham: Edward Elgar, 2011).

41 Basel Committee on Banking Supervision (BIS), *International Convergence of Capital Measurement and Capital Standards: A Revised Framework* (Basel: Bank for International Settlements, 2006); BIS, *Core Principles of Effective Banking Supervision*. (Basel: Bank for International Settlements, 2006).

42 See eg D. Tarullo, *Banking on Basel: The Future of International Financial Regulation* (Washington DC: Petersen Institute for International Economics, 2008).

43 FSB 2009; LSE Report, n 3 above.

44 BIS, 'Overview of Basel II impact studies' (Basel: Bank for International Settlements, 2010) at http://www.bis.org/bcbs/qis/overview.htm (last visited 24 October 2011).

with respect to prudential supervision, noted above. In part this was due to the statutory requirement that the FSA take into consideration the responsibilities of firms' senior management, which it interpreted as meaning that it could not challenge the business decisions of the firm.[45] So whilst the Australian Prudential Regulation Authority (APRA) and Office of the Superintendent of Financial Institutions (OSFI) would challenge, and prevent, financial institutions from offering 125 per cent loan to value mortgages, for example, the FSA felt that it had no statutory basis for doing so.[46] This was a business decision for the firm; it was not the appropriate place of the regulator to determine business strategy.

It was also based on the assumption, which the FSA was not alone in holding, that as it was in the firms' interests to manage its risks well, the regulators could rely on banks' own internal management to ensure this, overseen by effective boards and monitored by shareholders.[47]

These assumptions were arguably based on cognitive capture and possibly even regulatory 'rapture'[48] rather than straightforward interest group capture. However they arose, the crisis has shown that these assumptions were deeply flawed. Regulators, not only in the UK, have now recognised that firms are not as competent in managing themselves as either regulators or the firms themselves had assumed, and that their incentives are clearly not well aligned with those of the regulators.[49]

Moreover, the crisis demonstrated that regulators were not relying on firms' internal systems and controls as such, but on skillful representations of those systems and controls constructed by those responsible for managing relations with the regulatory bodies. Management-based regulation was shown to have been myth-based regulation. This is not a new phenomenon.[50] For example, on asking banks to perform stress tests at the height of the crisis, the regulators found that banks did not have the systems, models and information to do so. Although regulators had asked banks to perform stress tests in the past, it became clear that banks had constructed largely fictional models purely for the benefit of the regulators. These really were the 'fantasy documents' that Clarke argues all

45 FSA, *A New Regulator for a New Millennium* (London: FSA, 2000); FSA 2009, n 3 above; Treasury Select Committee, *Banking Crisis: – regulation and supervision: Oral Evidence* (HC 144-I) (London: Stationery Office, 2009).

46 The DNB (the Dutch banking supervisor) felt similarly restricted, according to findings of the De Wit Commission (2010), cited in J. Kremers and D. Schoenmaker, *Twin Peaks: Experience in the Netherlands* (London: London School of Economics and Political Science, 2010). See also FSA 2009, n 3 above; FSA 2011, n 37 above.

47 FSB, *Senior Supervisors Group Report* n 3 above; OECD, *Corporate Governance and the Financial Crisis: Key Findings and Main Messages* (Paris: OECD, 2009).

48 J. Anderson, 'The Public Utility Commission of Texas: A Case of Capture or Rapture?' (1982) 1 *Review of Policy Research* 484.

49 FSA, *Observations on Risk Management Practices during the Recent Market Turbulence* (London: FSA, 2008); FSB, *FSF Principles for Sound Compensation Practices* (Basel: FSB, 2009); FSB 2009, n 3 above; Walker Review, *A Review Of Corporate Governance in UK Banks and other Financial Industry Entities* (London: Stationery Office, 2009); OECD, *Corporate Governance and the Financial Crisis: Key Findings and Main Messages* (Paris: OECD, 2009).

50 See eg W. Laufer, 'Corporate Liability, Risk Shifting, and the Paradox of Compliance' (1999) 54 *Vanderbilt Law Review* 1343.

disaster-management manuals to be.[51] Stress tests had been a way for banks to manage regulators, not to manage themselves.[52] In a further example, the Board report into the FSA's supervision of Royal Bank of Scotland (RBS) concluded that RBS earned its 'regulatory dividend' on the basis not of the robustness of its internal controls, but on the co-operative stance of its compliance personnel.[53] This is a supervisory strategy which accords strongly with 'responsive' regulation,[54] but proved in this case to be indulgent regulation.

What can we take from the FSA's experience in using meta-regulation in the period leading up to the crisis? First, to reiterate, that although the strategy may have weaknesses, reliance on firms' internal management to further the regulatory project is an inevitable element of regulation. Regulatory governance is in significant part a process of an organisation acting on a much larger set of other organisations, all varying widely in their regulatory capacity and organisational complexity. As with risk based regulation (discussed below), but for different reasons, there is no option to abandon 'meta-regulation' as a regulatory strategy – the fundamental inter-dependence of regulator and regulatee means that reliance is always present, if only implicitly. Regulators cannot be present at all times and in all places – even under CAC regimes they have to rely on firms complying with regulation continually, not just when the inspector calls. Meta-regulation does not create this reliance; rather it recognises and converts it from an inevitable fact of regulatory life into a conscious regulatory strategy.

Second, that meta-regulation also has a critical point of weakness. In this case, its fundamental weakness is paradoxically the element which is also its potential source of strength: that it relies on firms' processes, systems, controls and internal cultures to work, messy, fragmented and contested though they may be. This is a necessary reliance, but that which is a potential source of strength can also be its Achilles heel.

**Enrolment – gatekeepers and standards**

The third strategy is enrolment. The financial regulatory system is characterised by different patterns of enrolment, in which different organisations – transnational or national, public or private, have differential regulatory capacities and can enhance that capacity by enrolling others to perform different functions.[55] One strategy which has been shown to be successful in other contexts is to enrol gatekeepers. 'Gatekeepers' are those who are not directly the subject of regulation, but who have a strategic position over those who are. That position may either be conferred by legal rules (for example the requirements that all accounts

51 L. Clarke, *Mission Improbable: Using Fantasy Documents to Tame Disaster* (Chicago: University of Chicago Press, 1999).

52 A. Haldane, 'Why Banks Failed the Stress Test' (speech presented at Marcus-Evans Conference on Stress-Testing, London, 2009).

53 FSA, *The failure of the Royal Bank of Scotland: Financial Services Authority Board Report* (London: FSA, 2011).

54 See Ayres and Braithwaite, n 11 above.

55 Black 2003, n 17 above.

are audited, or that those performing certain activities are insured) or by market position (for example retailers (tobacco, alcohol), airlines (visas)).

The benefits of using gatekeepers are that regulators can leverage off the control that such actors have over the regulatees, and that the gatekeeper actors themselves have no particular incentives not to comply with the regulatory requirements as they would not benefit directly from non-compliance.[56] However, the incentive structures of gatekeepers may not always be so neutral. The retailer selling cigarettes to under 18 year olds does not benefit from non-compliance in that he or she gets to smoke, but they do benefit from the revenue from the sale. Auditors who sign off false accounts do not benefit from the increase in share price than may ensue, but they do benefit from continued business with the firm. As the corporate accounting scandals of Enron, World-com, Parmalat and their ilk demonstrated, those relied upon to act as gatekeepers can be less than reliable, and need not necessarily perform the role that regulators assume they will play. In the corporate sector, the failings arose from lawyers and accountants.[57] In financial markets, the most significant failure was that of the credit rating agencies (CRAs). The experience of enrolling CRAs illustrated that although gatekeeper regulation is a potentially useful regulatory strategy, whether the strategy is successful depends on the motivation, regulatory capacity, and most importantly, the broader market context, culture and incentives of those being relied upon to act as gatekeepers. Unless these are aligned with the goals of the regulatory regime, regulators will find that their reliance is dangerously misplaced.

Credit rating agencies normally rate the credit worthiness of corporations and have a long history, particularly in the US.[58] Their growth is due to a combination of market and regulatory factors: notably through the structure of US regulation, the industry is dominated by an oligarchy of three agencies, and through the structure of global capital regulation, their ratings have a privileged position, which creates incentives for issuers to acquire ratings.[59] Their role in the crisis is now well known. The banks which were creating asset-backed securities and products based on them paid ratings agencies to rate the securitised products in order to improve their marketability to investors. Ratings agencies did not directly benefit from whether the rating they gave was high or low. However, they did benefit from the revenue stream that came from giving ratings; revenue streams that were directly linked to the level of rating they gave.[60] In order to secure business, agencies rated products without really understanding what they were rating and caring even less, and often with the involvement of the bank

56 R. Kraakman, 'Gatekeepers: The Anatomy of a Third-Party Enforcement Strategy' (1986) 2 *Journal of Law, Economics, & Organization* 53.

57 J. Coffee, *Gatekeepers: The Role of the Professions in Corporate Governance* (Oxford: OUP, 2006).

58 T. Sinclair, *The New Masters of Capital: American Bond Rating Agencies and the Politics of Creditworthiness* (Ithaca: Cornell University Press, 2005); F. Partnoy, 'The Siskel and Ebert Of Financial Markets?: Two Thumbs Down for the Credit Rating Agencies' (1999) 77 Washington University LR 620.

59 Partnoy, *ibid*.

60 SEC, *Summary Report of Issues Identified in the Commission Staff's Examinations of Select Credit Rating Agencies* (Washington, DC: US Government Printing Office, 2008).

structuring the product. In the infamous words of one official at Standard and Poors, one of the leading CRAs, 'it could be structured by a cow and we would rate it'.[61]

Much attention has, often quite rightly, been given to the fact that investors placed undue reliance on ratings without performing their own due diligence. These were not products that were available to retail investors, but to professionals – those who should have enough expertise to evaluate them or enough money to pay others to do so on their behalf. However, of relevance here, the regulatory system has been just as negligent. Regulators enrolled not only ratings agencies but the models they employed to devise their ratings. As in the case of reliance on banks' internal risk models to calculate risk exposures and capital requirements, regulators embedded the agencies' proprietary models within their own regulatory codes, knowing too little about them and expecting too much.[62] In significant areas of regulation, and notably with respect to capital requirements, credit ratings are hardwired into the regulatory regime. In the Basle II regime, external ratings can be used to determine the risk weightings of exposures to sovereign debt, banks and corporations, and to differentiate the risk weights of securitisation tranches.[63] Central banks have also relied on credit ratings to determine what they will accept as collateral.[64] Changes in ratings act as triggers for regulatory action, and can create potential 'cliff effects' as the implications of a change in ratings sweep through the financial regulatory system.[65] The incorporation of ratings into the very core of financial regulation was introduced despite considerable misgivings on the part of regulators involved, and the ratings agencies themselves, for a range of reasons, not least that because outside the US, many large corporations were not rated, neither were very few small or medium-sized corporations, either in the US or elsewhere.[66] The consequences have been significant, not least because their introduction into the Basle II framework meant that fundamental inaccuracies in external ratings of securitised products were injected straight into the heart of its operation.

The regulators did not only enroll actors and risk models, they enrolled standards too. Relying on rules or standards made by other bodies is a common feature of polycentric regulation, resulting in the construction of significant rule complexes. In the area of financial regulation, a key example is the reliance of

61 CNBC, 'S&P Officials: We'd Do a Deal "Structured by Cows"' (2008) (online video) at http://www.cnbc.com/id/27321998/S_P_Officials_We_d_Do_a_Deal_Structured_by_Cows (last visited 24 October 2011).

62 E. Gerding, 'Code, Crash and Open Source: The Outsourcing of Financial Regulation to Risk Models and the Global Financial Crisis' (2009) 84 Washington & Lee LR 128.

63 BIS, n 41 above.

64 For example the European Central Bank only accepted A-rated products; however as the Greek crisis has demonstrated, in times of crisis this strict stance may have to be adjusted, and the ECB has had to say it will accept Greek bonds regardless of their rating.

65 FSB, *FSB Report on Principles for Reducing Reliance on CRA Ratings* (Basel: FSB, 2010); P. Van Roy, *Credit Ratings and the Standardised Approach to Credit Ratings in Basle II* (Frankfurt: European Central Bank, 2005); FSI (Financial Stability Institute), *2008 FSI Survey on the Implementation of the new capital adequacy framework in non-Basel Committee member countries* (Basel: Bank for International Settlements, 2008).

66 Tarullo, n 42 above.

banking regulators on the global accounting rules, notably those of the International Accounting Standards Board (IASB), and in the US, the Financial Reporting Council. The IASB rules are legally binding within the EU. There is significant controversy between the banking supervisors, articulated through the global committee, the Basle Committee on Banking Supervision, and the IASB as to the appropriate way to account for financial instruments In particular, for loan loss provisioning, which under IASB rules at the time was based on incurred losses, and the application of 'fair value' accounting for financial instruments (the 'mark to market' requirement). In particular, mark to market accounting requirements have been shown to have profoundly procyclical effects.[67] As market valuations fell, banks' capital requirements rose. To meet them, they needed to sell assets, further depressing prices. Private sector risk management techniques had the same impact, enhancing the links between valuation techniques, leverage and asset prices. As markets fell, requirements to put up margins rose. In order to meet those margin calls, firms had to sell assets, causing market prices to fall. Triggers in debt or over the counter (OTC) derivative contracts and haircuts on financing transactions based on market valuations or credit ratings added liquidity during the boom but drained it out when conditions were stressed, exacerbating deleveraging and asset sales in a vicious downward spiral.[68] Thus the interaction of rules emanating from different regulatory regimes, including private risk management practices, can create significant unintended consequences and negative endogenous effects.

Enrolment can confer benefits, extending regulatory capacity.[69] However, as the role of credit ratings in the crisis has demonstrated, it also creates significant dependencies and vulnerabilities.[70] It can also create opportunities for gaming the regulatory rules: for example, banks guaranteed the liabilities of their SPVs, which gained high credit ratings as a consequence. Banks then bought the commercial paper of their SPVs, relying on the high credit rating to reduce their capital requirements.[71] The role of credit-rating agencies as gatekeepers is being significantly re-evaluated.[72] Credit rating agencies are now to be regulated within the EU (Regulation No 1060/2009), and regulators and central banks are withdrawing their reliance on them for regulatory purposes.[73]

67 FSF, *Report of the FSF Working Group on Provisioning* (Basel: FSB, 2009); FSB, *Joint FSF-CGFS Working Group – The role of valuation and leverage in procyclicality* (Basel: FSB, 2009); FSB, *Joint FSF-BCBS Working Group – Reducing procyclicality arising from the bank capital framework* (Basel: FSB, 2009); de Larosière Group, n 3 above.

68 FSB 2009 *ibid*; BIS, *The Joint Forum Credit Risk Transfer: Developments from 2005–2007* (Basel: Bank for International Settlements, 2008).

69 J. Braithwaite and P. Drahos, *Global Business Regulation* (New York. Cambridge UP, 2000); Black 2002 and 2003, n 17 above.

70 Indeed, the crisis and its aftermath have demonstrated the fundamental reliance of monetary authorities on banks to act as sluice gates to push money out into the economy; when banks refuse to do so, monetary authorities are almost paralysed.

71 The revised rules now introduce a ban on banks recognising ratings gained through such guarantees. See BIS, *Enhancements to the Basel II framework*. (Basel: Bank for International Settlements, 2009).

72 FSB, n 65 above.

73 BIS, n 71 above; US *Dodd-Frank Wall Street Reform and Consumer Protection (Dodd-Frank) Act* Pub. L. No. 111-203, 124 Stat. 1376 (2010).

Enrolment can also lead to the situation in which, functionally, the 'proper' performance of one regime (accounting rules) can cause distortions in another (macro and micro prudential regulation) and, as the crisis illustrated, ultimately negative endogenous effects. In contrast to the exorcism of credit ratings from regulatory rules, however, in the case of the enrolment of accounting standards, the institutional structure of global financial regulation (and as a result national regulation) makes the relationship between the two regimes more complicated, and it is less easy to 'dis-enroll'. Significant adopters and users of the IASB's standards, in this case governments and global standard setting bodies, notably the (BCBS) and the Financial Stability Board, are exerting pressure on the IASB to amend its standards, but despite difficult negotiations with the European Commission none has withdrawn from them. Building rule-complexes through reliance and inter-referencing is a frequent feature of contemporary governance regimes, but can bring complex institutional dynamics into play, creating interdependencies between the enroller and the enrolled which can be complicated to manage, and difficult to undo.

**Risk based regulation**

The final technique to be considered here which was, and still is, used by many banking supervisors, is risk-based regulation. In a system of risk-based regulation, regulators identify the different risks to their objectives and focus resources and 'regulatory effort' on addressing those which they see as most critical.

Risk based regulation is not unique to financial regulation: over the last ten to fifteen years it has been increasingly adopted by regulators in areas as diverse as the environment, food safety, health and safety, legal services and financial regulation, and by a wide number of OECD countries.[74] Risk based regulation has immediate appeal for those seeking to organise and prioritise regulatory action, holding out the promise that regulators can 'manage uncertainty', to adapt Michael Power's characterisation of organisational risk management.[75] However, it should be emphasised that regulators, particularly those with a significant inspection/supervisory mandate, make these decisions every day, regardless of whether the regulator has formally adopted a 'risk based' approach. The differences in 'risk based' systems are that these decisions are (or should be) made at the top of the organisation as a key issue of regulatory strategy not at the field

74 B. Hutter, *The Attractions of Risk-based Regulation: accounting for the emergence of risk ideas in regulation* (London: Centre for analysis of risk and regulation, 2005); J. Black, 'The Emergence of Risk-based Regulation and the New Public Risk Management in the UK' (2005) PL 512; H. Rothstein, M. Huber and G. Gaskell, 'A theory of risk colonisation: the spiralling regulatory logics of societal and institutional risk' (2006) 35 *Economy and Society* 91; B. Hutter and S. Lloyd Bostock, 'Reforming Regulation of the Medical Profession: The Risks of Risk-based Approaches' (2008) 10 *Health, Risk and Society* 69; J. Gray, 'What Next for Risk-based Financial Regulation?' in I. MacNeil and J. O'Brien (eds), *The Future of Financial Regulation.* (Oxford: Hart Publishing, 2010); J. Black, 'Risk Based Regulation: Choices, Practices and Lessons Learnt' in *Risk and Regulatory Policy: Improving the Governance of Risk* (Paris: Organization of Economic Co-Operation and Development, 2010); J. Black and R. Baldwin, 'Really Responsive Risk Based Regulation' (2010) 32 *Law and Policy* 181.

75 M. Power, *Organized Uncertainty: Designing and World of Risk Management* (Oxford: OUP, 2007).




(2012) 75(6) MLR 1037–1063

officer/supervisor level as a matter of daily workload management; that they are systematic rather than idiosyncratic and ad hoc; and that they are explicit and transparent to all those within the organisation and to the firms that they regulate, rather than tacit and buried in the 'nouse' of experienced supervisors. So whilst risk based regulation (like meta-regulation) is inevitable, risk based *frameworks* can be useful for a regulator in providing a clear, well-articulated set of priorities which the regulator can use to manage its internal practices.

However, risk based regulation is Janus-headed. It faces inside the organisation, providing a systematic way of managing resources, decisions and personnel. It also faces outside the regulatory organisation, providing a structured system of decision making which the regulators can present to various legitimacy constituencies or audiences as justification for a legitimacy claim to be rational, ordered, and in control – all the hallmarks required for the legitimation of a regulator and the maintenance of its reputation in accordance with the modernist logic of regulation.[76]

As such, risk based regulation is an inherently complex and potentially self-contradictory strategy. Critically, risk based regulation in practice entails the management of three 'R's': risk, resources and reputation. Managing each of these elements is complex in itself. Managing them all successfully simultaneously can be impossible, as they can each pull in different directions.

Taking each in turn, with respect to the management of risks, the use of the term 'risk' is often a misnomer. Regulators and firms frequently operate in an unpredictable and uncertain world, where many risks are unknown and/or immeasurable, particularly in the context of financial regulation. What is described as 'risk' is often better described as uncertainty. 'Risk based regulation' is in these contexts a series of 'best guesses' as to what the future will hold and how resilient a firm's operations or the regulatory system as a whole will prove to be should those risks crystallise.

Risk based regulation is also (and in some cases primarily) a strategy for managing limited resources. As such, it means *not* focusing on things that regulators previously focused on. Risk based regulation is thus in large measure resource based regulation. In principle, resources should follow risks; but risks are often contested, leaving current resource allocation decisions open to challenge on the basis of differences in perceptions of risk and social or political priorities. Also, by their nature, risks can crystallise at unexpected moments – leaving past resource decisions open to challenge on the basis of hindsight.

Finally, risk based regulation is frequently adopted as a strategy to protect or enhance the regulator's reputation and legitimacy.[77] However, this is always going

76 J.W. Meyer, J. Boli and G. M. Thomas, 'Ontology and Rationalization in the Western Cultural Account' in W. R. Scott, J.W. Meyer, and Associates, *Institutional Environments and Organizations: Structural Complexity and Individualism* (Thousand Oaks, Calif: Sage, 1994); J. W. Meyer and B. Rowan, 'Institutionalized Organizations: Formal Structure as Myth and Ceremony' (1977) 83 *American Journal of Sociology* 340; Power, *ibid*; D. Carpenter, *Reputation and Power* (Princeton NJ: Princeton UP, 2010).

77 Black 2005, n 74 above, J. Black, 'The Development of Risk Based Regulation in Financial Services: Just "Modelling Through"?' in J. Black, M. Lodge and M. Thatcher (eds), *Regulatory Innovation: A Comparative Analysis* (Cheltenham: Edward Elgar, 2005); Black 2010, n 74 above.

to be a difficult 'R' to manage, as risk based regulation's logic of rationalisation and prioritisation does not fit well with public and political expectations for universal protection. Reducing regulatory intensity for some risks can therefore be a difficult thing for risk-averse officials to do, and for the public and politicians to accept. Resources may therefore go not to those risks which the regulator assesses in a more or less 'objective' or technical way to be the greatest, but those where failure would make it reputationally most vulnerable.

In the context of financial regulation, the risk based models of the Canadian and Australian banking supervisors, as well as that of the FSA, have a number of elements in common and have provided the springboard for the development of risk based approaches by supervisors in a number of different countries.[78] There is no clear correlation between the adoption of a risk based system of supervision per se, and the presence or absence of regulatory failure before or during the crisis. Although their models have much in common, as practised by the FSA and the Dutch central bank, risk based regulation failed.[79] In contrast, as practiced in Australia and Canada, it was apparently more resilient. Indeed, the Prudential Regulation Authority, which will take over the FSA's functions of prudential supervision, has announced an enhanced and revised risk based approach which has clearly taken inspiration from OSFI's and APRA's models in developing its new 'proactive intervention framework'.[80] However, the extent to which supervisory practices in both Australia and Canada were the reason for their banks' relative resilience, as opposed to other factors such as banks' high deposit base, non-reliance on wholesale funding, strong local lending, and restrictions on the mortgage market, is debatable.[81]

However, as noted above, risk based regulation has its own internal contradictions, weaknesses and pathologies. It is also equally prey to implementation failures as any other strategy. In the case of Northern Rock, the main problem lay in lack of control by senior management or by the risk division over its own internal operations: the risk based model simply was not followed, but no one outside of the immediate circle of officials responsible for Northern Rock was aware of this deviation. The power of the relationship manager was too great; the internal risk division too weak, and FSA senior management insufficiently engaged.[82]

It is the FSA's supervision of RBS which highlights the inherent tensions most clearly, however. The supervision of RBS, and by extension other large banks, demonstrated that the model itself had flaws. These flaws were linked to the wider

78 Black 2005, *ibid.*

79 FSA, 'The supervision of Northern Rock: a lessons learned review' (London: FSA, 2008); De Nederlandsche Bank (DNB), *Annual Report 2009* (Amsterdam: DNB, 2010) 138; DNB, *Supervisory Strategy 2010–2014 and Themes 2010* (Amsterdam: DNB, 2010) 83; DNB, *Annual Report 2010* (Amsterdam: DNB, 2011).

80 See FSA, n 37 above.

81 B. Hunt and D. Rozhkov, *Australian Banks: Selected Issues* (Washington, DC: International Monetary Fund, 2008); A. Beltratti and R. Stulz, *Why Did Some Banks Perform Better during the Credit Crisis? A Cross-Country Study of the Impact of Governance and Regulation* (Brussels: European Corporate Governance Institute, 2009); L. Ratnovski and R. Huang, *Why are Canadian Banks More Resilient?* (Washington, DC: International Monetary Fund, 2009).

82 See FSA, n 79 above.

assumptions relating to the FSA's construction of its role relative to the responsibilities of senior management, discussed below, and to the FSA's own prioritisation of resources, where more focus was placed on regulation of the retail markets than on supervision of the banking and shadow banking system.[83] They also lay in the broader framework of the Basle II capital rules, under which the FSA had reduced Northern Rock's capital requirements in June 2007, just weeks before it needed rescuing.[84] In addition, as with Northern Rock, operational and supervisory practices did not match up to the glossy presentations. Insufficient skills to supervise financial institutions' complex operations effectively and frequent turnover of staff at all levels led to poor supervisory practices, there was inadequate internal control over the implementation of its risk based approach, and where issues were identified, supervisors had insufficient resolve to challenge senior management.[85] A similar reticence was found with respect to the Dutch banking supervisors.[86]

The FSA's experience illustrates some of the internal contradictions and key points of vulnerability in the design and operationalisation of risk based systems. In designing the model, the selection and prioritisation of risks can be based on incorrect assumptions; the wrong indicators can be used and the right ones omitted. Equally, those outside the organisation may contest its risk prioritisation, though usually after the risk has crystallised. In its implementation, those higher up the regulatory organisation can lose sight and control of those lower down. Too much time can be spent analysing the risks and too little on acting in response to them. As with PBR or management based regulation, if regulators are too reticent to challenge senior management, have insufficient skills to analyse firms, are not sufficiently proactive to identify emerging risks and too slow to act when they do, then any risk based system will fail. In a review of supervisory practices, an IMF report suggested that all these failures characterised banking supervision in a number of countries, not just the UK.[87] The broader market and political context in which the regulator operates is also significant. The FSA has said on several occasions that they would not have had political support to impose tougher regulation on banks in the boom years preceding the crisis,[88] and they are probably right.

The crisis thus illustrated the fundamental tensions at the centre of risk based regulation, between the demands of simultaneously trying to manage

83 FSA *ibid*; FSA 2009, n 3 above; Gray, n 74 above; FSA, n 53 above.

84 In June 2007 Northern Rock had total assets of £113 billion and shareholders equity of £2.2 billion. Their risk weighted assets (RWA) under Basel II was £19 billion (16.7 per cent of total assets), compared to £34 billion under Basel I (30 per cent of assets), largely because of the reduced risk weight for residential mortgages. Under Basel II they had Tier 1 capital of 11.3 per cent of RWA, but only two per cent of total assets. This enabled them to increase their interim dividend by 30.3 per cent. Just prior to their rescue their regulatory capital was less than 10 per cent of the £23 billion that the authorities used to support it (Treasury Select Committee, *The Run on the Rock. 5th Report 2007–8* HC 56-1 (London: The Stationary Office, 2008); Blundell-Wignall and Atkinson, n 14 above).

85 FSA, n 79 above; FSA 2009, n 3 above; FSA, n 53 above.

86 Scheltema Commission, n 7 above.

87 J. Viñals, J. Fiechter et al, *The Making of Good Supervision: Learning to Say 'No'* (Washington, DC: International Monetary Fund, 2010).

88 See eg FSA 2009, n 3 above; FSA 2011, n 53 above.

risks, resources and reputation. Regulators need a political licence to operate, irrespective of their formal legal powers. Risk based regulation frequently operates in a political context that requires that the regulator lives a contradiction: the reality may be one of imperfect resource allocation, selection and prioritisation in the face of unknown and often unknowable risks with a built-in acceptance that some degree of regulatory failure is not only predictable but acceptable. However, the image a regulator has to convey is one of control, rationality and equal protection for all, rooted in the modernist logic of governability. The fate of the FSA illustrates the penalty a regulator can pay if it is judged (later) to have got its risk prioritisation wrong, even if that prioritisation was widely supported by the political establishment at the time.[89] Risk based regulation is thus an inherently contradictory strategy that can never, politically, speak its true name.

## UNDERSTANDING 'NEW GOVERNANCE' PARADOXES AND FAILURES

It is a trite, but no less true, observation that regulation is a complex and multi-dimensional activity. This makes the study of it endlessly fascinating; it also makes the performance of it endlessly unpredictable. This complexity creates multiple points of vulnerability, such that the carefully fashioned tool will simply not function as intended. Instead it is transformed in the very process of its performance.

The outcomes can be paradoxical, as others have suggested[90] and the above review has illustrated. Moreover, the crisis highlighted that each of the new governance techniques reviewed here has internal ambiguities and tensions. Principles-based regulation is a complex and ambiguous technique which can quickly turn either into 'light touch' or highly intensive regulation.[91] The regulation of a firm's internal systems and controls can simply be the regulation of a false representation of those processes, constructed for the regulators' benefit: its source of strength contains the seeds of its weakness. Enrolment can expand capacity but simultaneously introduce critical vulnerabilities and distortions. Risk-based regulation is at once managing the conflicting demands of risks, resources and reputation, but outwardly it has to maintain a different face.

To be clear, the argument being made is not that regulators should return to CAC regulation. The conditions of uncertainty, complexity, fragmentation, dynamism and fundamental ungovernability that led to the advocating of the responsive regulatory strategies propounded under the 'new governance' banner still remain.[92] It is rather that recognising and analysing the internal tensions,

89 FSA 2011, *ibid.*

90 See eg Haines, n 5 above.

91 Black 2008, n 25 above; C. Ford, 'New Governance in the Teeth of Human Frailty: Lessons from Financial Regulation' (2010) Wisconsin LR 441.

92 Black, n 16 above; Scott, n 16 above; Ford, n 30 above.

ambiguities and contradictions in each of these new governance techniques is important in understanding their character and operation.

The analysis also illustrates the limits of adopting a tools-based approach to resolve regulatory problems. It is a legacy of the 'diagnosis-prescription-cure' model of welfare economics, refined under 'smart' regulation and refined further in the new governance literature. As has been emphasised here, the characteristics of the tools or 'technologies' of regulation are important, but equally are broader contextual factors which interact with them.

Ford has argued that one of the critical vulnerabilities common to all regulatory techniques is the behaviour both of regulators and regulated.[93] I would agree. However I would argue that the performance of these strategies also emphasises the importance of three further dimensions of regulation, distinct but related. These are worth drawing out, at least briefly, as they provide a broader analytical framework in which to place the discrete analysis of each individual strategy, and to understand their interaction when used simultaneously, as all of these strategies were. These are the organisational dimension, the functional dimension and the cognitive dimension.[94] The dynamics of all the dimensions of regulatory governance are relevant to understanding its performance in any one instance.[95] However, for reasons of space, it is the dynamics of these three dimensions on which attention is focused here.

**Organisational dimension**

Much of regulatory governance consists of one organisation or set of organisations attempting to act on another, much larger set of organisations in order to attain a particular set of goals, for example to manage risk, correct markets, or pursue ethical ends. Understanding the organisational dimension to regulation is therefore critical to understanding the system as a whole. The organisational dimension, as constructed here, consists primarily of the formal and informal powers of and within organisations (including regulators), their regulatory capacity and their internal dynamics. It also includes broader patterns of power and control over organisations, notably the regulator, including the political, economic and social structures in which it is situated, its position within a network of regulators or system of multi-level governance, and who has powers, formal and informal, to veto its decisions or substantively shape its agenda (which others might separate out as the political dimension, but which are included here as it is argued that it is how these patterns of power are refracted through the different organisations involved in regulation which is significant to its performance).

93 Ford, n 91 above.

94 I argue elsewhere that there are three further dimensions, the behavioural dimension, the normative dimension (which includes legitimation) and the communicative/discursive dimension, but do not explore these here (J. Black, *The Nature of Regulatory Governance* (Cambridge: CUP, forthcoming)).

95 R. Baldwin, and J. Black, 'Really Responsive Regulation' (2008) 71 MLR 59; Black and Baldwin, n 74 above.

We know from the significant body of institutionalist work on organisations[96] and the literature on business responses to regulation[97] that any analysis of organisational behaviours has to be multi-level, and that behaviour, including responses to regulation, are shaped by the complex interplay of factors at the individual level (incentive structures and interests of key individuals); the level of internal organisational systems, processes and cultures; and at the macro-level: not only the organisation's immediate field but also the deeper normative and cognitive environment.

At the micro-level of actors, it was clear from the crisis that the incentives of key actors: regulators, banks, credit-rating agencies, and indeed investors, were fundamentally misaligned. At the level of organisational infrastructure, it became clear that internal systems, processes and cultures were inadequate and/or inappropriate, and that there were significant weaknesses in the regulatory capacity of both regulators and firms. I have argued elsewhere that regulatory capacity is a composite notion comprising both resources and disposition. The resources are information, expertise, legitimacy and authority, strategic position and organisational capacity. Disposition is the willingness and ability to use these resources to pursue regulatory goals.[98] Firms did not have the regulatory capacity required for management-based regulation to be robust. The financial crisis demonstrated that the FSA also lacked regulatory capacity, despite being a comparatively well-resourced regulator, contributing to failings in RBR, PBR and meta-regulation in particular. It did not have adequate information nor did it have adequate means of making sense of what it had. Bringing together relevant knowledge from different parts of the organisation, critically on macro and micro-level risks, was organisationally cumbersome.[99] Front line supervisors had insufficient skills and experience to evaluate the extent to which firms were managing risks, and insufficient resolve to challenge them when doubts arose. Their strategic position over banks was relatively weak, given the political context, notwithstanding the FSA's formal legal powers. Internally, the strategic position of those who should have been in control of the implementation of risk based regulation within the FSA was also too weak, mirroring the fate of risk managers in the banks themselves, notwithstanding the formal distribution of powers in either case. Furthermore the governing boards of both financial institutions and the FSA were distracted by other issues.[100]

96 See eg W. R. Scott, *Institutions and Organisations* (Thousand Oaks, Calif: Sage Publications, 2nd ed, 2001) especially 195–197; C. Oliver, 'Strategic Responses to Organizational Processes' (1991) 16 *Academy of Management Review* 145.

97 See eg V. Braithwaite (ed), *Taxing Democracy: Understanding Tax Avoidance and Evasion* (Aldershot: Ashgate, 2003); N. Gunningham, R. Kagan and D. Thornton, 'Social License and Environmental Protection: Why Businesses Go Beyond Compliance' (2004) 29 *Law and Social Inquiry* 307; B. Cashore, 'Legitimacy and the Privatization of Environmental Governance: How Non-State Market Driven (NSDM) Governance Systems Gain Rule Making Authority' (2002) 15 *Governance* 503; Parker and Nielsen, n 40 above.

98 There are slightly different views on what constitutes regulatory capacity: those identified here are expanded in Black 2003; an alternative is Hood's NATO: 'nodality, authority, treasure and organization', developed to describe tools of government. See Black, n 17 above; C. Hood, *The Tools of Government* (London: Macmillan, 1983); C. Hood and H. Margetts, *The Tools of Government in the Digital Age* (London: Palgrave Macmillan, 2007).

99 FSA, n 53 above.

100 FSF, n 3 above; FSA 2009, n 3 above; FSA 2011, n 37 and n 53 above; UBS, *Shareholder Report on UBS's Write-Downs. Report to Swiss Federal Banking Commission* (Geneva: UBS, 2008).

The broader 'environmental' level focuses on how an organisation responds to its environment or field, both the immediate political and market context, as well as deeper normative goals and values, and cognitive frameworks. In the case of the FSA, for example, the political context had a significant role to play in creating the conditions which led to the failure of PBR, RBR and meta-regulation in particular. In the wake of the crisis, the FSA complained of being given a contradictory political remit. On the one hand, it had a statutory duty to regulate financial institutions. On the other hand, the government had made it clear that it was not to regulate in a way that would damage London's position as an international financial centre. It simply did not have the political licence to challenge banks' business decisions.[101] Furthermore, cognitively, it operated on the assumptions, common to others in its organisational environment, that firms would manage their own risks (discussed further below) and that the global regulatory regime for banks' capital requirements, which as a member of the BCBS it was instrumental in writing, was adequate.

Given the primacy of both the regulators' and firms' organisational dynamics and the political context for the success of regulation, understanding the organisational dynamics of those involved, both regulators and regulated, is central to understanding how regulation is likely to operate. Critical failings occurred at the interface of the regulatory organisation with the organisations that it is meant to be regulating, or rather, that it is relying on to perform that regulation. To re-emphasise, that reliance is always there, even in CAC regimes. However, many of the new governance techniques raise this reliance to the level of conscious strategy and deliberately use the firm's internal systems and controls as a resource for their own regulatory projects.[102] As noted above, the crisis demonstrated that these internal organisational dynamics are at once a potential source of strength and a potential Achilles heel.

### Functional

The second dimension is the functional or 'technological' dimension. This comprises the strategies or technologies of regulation that are being used and their logics: the assumptions on which they are based and the particular pathologies that each technology has. Whilst the argument here is that we need to look beyond tools, it is not that they are unimportant. But regulatory strategies extend beyond those on the usual lists of new governance scholars. They include technologies of management and control such as financial models, which are the critical building blocks on which risk management strategies are built, both of firms and regulators. There is a wealth of critical literature on the role of those models in the crisis, and indeed in risk management more broadly, which

101 Treasury Select Committee, n 45 above. It is worth noting that the House of Lords Select Committee report on economic regulators had also praised principles-based approaches regulation stating that they 'hold out an important opportunity for the regulation, certainly of larger companies, to be significantly less restrictive.' HL, *Review of Economic Regulators* 2007–8 Session, para 428, though noting it could make regulation more unpredictable.

102 Power, n 75 above.

illustrates the significance of the representations of the world that the models create for the selection, assessment and management of risk, and indeed the discourse through which what is unknowable is translated into something which is manageable.[103]

Of the regulatory strategies reviewed here, risk based regulation provides a good illustration of 'model' failure. In the case of risk-based regulation, the experience of the FSA showed that the assumptions underlying ARROW II, its risk based model, were wrong in several critical respects.[104] But it also illustrated the importance of the logic of the strategy itself, and in this case the tensions that lie within the technique itself, between the management of risks, resources and reputation, all of which may require different responses to the same activity or state of affairs.

The above review also illustrates the need to consider the practical dynamics of strategies of enrolment. Both this crisis and the accounting scandals a decade ago clearly illustrate that the same attention has to be paid to any strategy of enrolment, whether of market actors or of the rules of other regulatory organisations, for whilst they can expand the capacity of the enroller, they can also introduce critical vulnerabilities and pathologies.

Related to that, it also emphasises the need to recognise the nature and consequences of the interaction of the logics of regulatory strategies which, though separate, operate on an organisation or situation simultaneously, either through deliberate enrolment or simply due to the simultaneous impact of parallel regimes. Most regulators use a wide variety of control tools and strategies but these often have divergent logics: they are based on different understandings of the nature of the system being regulated and of cause-effect relationships; or they embody different regulator to regulatee relationships and assume different ways of interacting.[105] The example above of the interaction of capital rules and 'mark to market' accounting rules illustrates that in certain conditions their interaction can create negative endogenous effects. Paying more attention to this dimension of regulation emphasises the need to analyse how regulatory regimes interact on the ground, due to the actions of regulatees (rather than conscious attempts by regulators to create such interactions). It also illustrates the need for, and yet the difficulty in attaining, a strong degree of coherence of policy assumptions and responses across different regulatory regimes to ensure that they do not impose conflicting requirements on regulatees, or indeed regulators,[106] or create unwanted endogenous effects.

**Cognitive**

Finally, the experience with the new governance techniques reviewed above illustrates the importance of the cognitive dimension in understanding how a

103 D. Mackenzie, *An Engine, Not a Camera: How Financial Models Shape Markets*. (Harvard: MIT Press, 2008); N. Taleb, *The Black Swan: The Impact of the Highly Improbable* (London: Random House, 2007); Power, *ibid*.

104 FSA, n 37 and n 53 above; Gray, n 74 above; Black and Baldwin, n 74 above.

105 Gunningham and Grabosky, n 15 above; Black, n 16 above; Black and Baldwin, *ibid*.

106 V. Waller, 'The Challenge of Institutional Integrity in Responsive Regulation: Field Inspections By the Australian Tax Officers' (2007) 29 *Law and Policy* 67.

regulatory governance regime operates or is likely to operate. Many of the failings of regulation had their roots in fundamental failures of understanding on the part of regulators as to how the markets were operating, and by firms as to the risks to which they were exposed, as discussed above. In the financial context, the cognitive failures ran deep, and continue to do so: markets did not behave as firms and regulators thought they would; and firms did not behave as regulators presumed. As senior economists advised the Queen, the crisis was caused by a 'collective failure of imagination'.[107]

These cognitive failings were fundamentally linked to the failures of key regulatory technologies. Of relevance here, cognitive assumptions which led regulators to rely on firms internal self regulation lay in a deeper philosophy, rooted in neo-liberalism, which was that markets were efficient, that individuals behaved rationally, and that therefore each firm had the appropriate incentives to ensure that it would manage its risks appropriately. The assumption had been that as both shared an interest in ensuring the financial institution survived, the regulators could rely on banks' own internal management to ensure this. Firms would manage their risks appropriately, boards would oversee them, and shareholders would act as monitors.[108] Similarly, assumptions as to the incentive structures and reliability of ratings produced by credit rating agencies underlay strategies of their enrolment. More broadly, it was the cognitive assumptions embedded in risk models used widely by banks and regulators alike that led each to believe that the risks both at the micro level of individual institutions, and at the macro-systemic level, were far less, and of a different nature, than they turned out to be.[109] If you do not understand how the system works, it is very hard to build in mechanisms either for managing risk or for ensuring the system's resilience when those risks crystallise. The crisis has prompted fundamental cognitive shifts in understandings of how the financial system operates, and the manageability of high impact but low probability events. However, regulators and others know that they fundamentally misunderstood the system, but they are struggling to create a new cognitive framework in which to develop policy responses.

## CONCLUSIONS AND REFLECTIONS

Any regulatory strategy can fail, and many can succeed. This is true for regulation by state and non-state regulators alike. The regulatory toolkit familiar to 'smart

107 On a visit to the LSE in November 2008 the Queen asked, 'Why did no one see this coming?' The British Academy forum of economists convened to answer the Queen's question wrote to her concluding that 'the failure to foresee the timing, extent and severity of the crisis and to head it off, while it had many causes, was principally a failure of the collective imagination of many bright people, both in this country and internationally, to understand the risks to the system as a whole'. Letter dated 22 July 2009. See FSA, n 3 above.

108 US HOUSE, Committee on Oversight and Government Reform, *The Financial Crisis and the Role of Federal Regulator* Hearing (Washington DC: Government Printing Office, 23 October 2010); FSA, *The Turner Review: A regulatory response to the global banking crisis* (London: FSA, 2009); Walker Review, n 49 above.

109 Taleb, n 103 above.

regulation' policy makers, or even 'new governance' or 'post-regulatory' scholars, can be beguilingly attractive, suggesting that regulatory success should be simply a matter of selecting the right tool. The toolkit approach is a useful starting point, but it can never be more than that, for regulation is a complex and multi-dimensional activity in which policy makers' edicts are inevitably transformed in the process of their performance. Understanding the dynamics of its different dimensions is critical to understanding the dynamics of this transformation, and thus how a regulatory governance system as a whole is operating.

The new governance strategies do have strengths in that they can potentially respond to the conditions of uncertainty, complexity, fragmentation and ungovernability that pervade any regulatory governance regime. But what can be underplayed are their own vulnerabilities, internal tensions and paradoxes.[110] The central claims of proponents of the new governance techniques to functional superiority over CAC regulation are that they are responsive, flexible, and in enrolling others in the regulatory project, they thereby expand its capacity and enhance its effectiveness and can even add to its legitimacy. However, their experience in the crisis revealed that in practice they can be either out of touch or indulgent, that they can be implemented in ways which focus heavily on auditable systems and processes, and that in enrolling others they can increase vulnerabilities and the potential for negative endogenous effects.

The final insight that we can take from the experience of the new governance techniques in the financial crisis is no less complex. It is that regulators need to observe and adapt, to engage in self-critical learning (in a 'double loop' way, of course, ie modifying actions and decisions in the light of what is learnt);[111] in short, to be reflexive. Again this is a fashionable prescription to make.[112] But although necessary, observation, learning and adaptation are fraught, conceptually and operationally.[113] Leaving aside the reputational difficulties of saying one has made a mistake,[114] regulators need to be able to actually recognise and evaluate unintended and counterproductive consequences and side effects of the regulatory regime when they arise. To do that properly is impossible: regulators do not have a crystal ball, nor do they have an all-seeing eye. However, no matter how complicated learning is, the experience of the crisis is that conventional measures of performance evaluation will not be enough.

If the financial crisis has a broader lesson for regulators elsewhere it is this: it is not enough to ask regulators or others to engage in self-critical learning, to assess whether they are performing their tasks well. It has to be asked whether they are performing the right tasks at all. Whilst observation and learning are important, those observing and learning may only see what they expect to see, and when they do see it will be through the refractive filters of their own

110 Ford, n 91 above.

111 C. Argyris, 'Single-Loop and Double-Loop Models in Research on Decision Making' (1976) 21 Admin Sci Quarterly 363; C. Argyris, 'Double Loop Learning in Organizations' (1977) (Sept–Oct) *Harvard Business Review* 115.

112 eg O. De Schutter and J. Lenoble, *Reflexive Governance: Redefining the Public Interest in a Pluralistic World* (Oxford: Hart Publishing, 2010).

113 K. Weick, *Sensemaking in Organizations* (Thousand Oaks, Calif: Sage Publications Inc, 1995).

114 Carpenter, n 76 above.

cognitive frames. Designers and regulators do need to build in structures for cognitive challenge and experimentation.[115] But such prescriptions can ignore the potential for challenges to go unheeded, either through plays of interest group power (because they are recognised but ignored by the powerful, in this case the banks), or because of cognitive constraints: they are simply not recognised as valid or relevant. The period leading up to the financial crisis had its Cassandras too.[116]

So things will always go wrong. This is not a message that fits well with the legitimacy claims that regulators make based on Weberian ideals of bureaucratic rationality and expertise, nor with the modernist logic of regulation, which has at its very core the claim to governability, and thus to success.[117] Nor is it a message which politicians or the public, or even academics, can find easy to accept. Getting it wrong, as the FSA has found out, can be fatal to the organisation's survival, no matter how much it has learned from the experience. However as we move towards the brave new world of regulatory reform, our new governance toolkit in hand, we have to remember that not only does each of these tools have internal ambiguities and tensions, but that unintended consequences and regulatory failures, by their nature, will always occur. Unless these complexities, both of the strategies themselves and of the contexts in which they are performed, are recognised at the outset, regulatory reform is bound to over-promise and under-deliver.

115 C. F. Sabel and W. Simon, *Minimalism and Experimentalism in the Administrative State* (New York: Columbia University Law School, 2011).
116 They included the Basle Committee on Banking Supervision itself, which was warning of liquidity risk as early as 2004.
117 Meyer, Boli and Thomas, n 76 above.